MW00804917

Gallipoli

New Perspectives on the Mediterranean Expeditionary Force, 1915-16

Edited by Rhys Crawley & Michael LoCicero

Helion & Company

In loving memory of Florence May Crawley
R.C.

For my parents Salvatore and Eileen
M.S.L.

Helion & Company Limited
Unit 8 Amherst Business Centre
Budbrooke Road
Warwick
CV34 5WE
England
Tel. 01926 499 619
Fax 0121 711 4075
Email: info@helion.co.uk
Website: www.helion.co.uk
Twitter: @helionbooks
Visit our blog http://blog.helion.co.uk/

Published by Helion & Company 2018
Designed and typeset by Mach 3 Solutions (www.mach3solutions.co.uk)
Cover designed by Paul Hewitt, Battlefield Design (www.battlefield-design.co.uk)
Printed by Gutenberg Press Ltd, Tarxien, Malta

Back cover: "The crusaders of Gallipoli". (*Kladderadatsch*, 16 January 1916)
Images obtained from open sources unless credited
Maps as individually credited

ISBN 978-1-911512-18-9

British Library Cataloguing-in-Publication Data
A catalogue record for this book is available from the British Library.

For details of other military history titles published by Helion & Company Limited contact the above address or visit our website: http://www.helion.co.uk.

We always welcome receipt of book proposals from prospective authors.

Contents

List of Illustrations

List of Maps

In colour section

Maps in colour section drawn by George Anderson © Helion & Company 2018.

In text

Abbreviations and Acronyms

A&SH	Argyll and Sutherland Highlanders
AAG	Assistant Adjutant General
AANS	Australian Army Nursing Service
AA&QMG	Assistant Adjutant and Quartermaster General
ADB	*Australian Dictionary of Biography*
ADC	Aide-de-camp
ADM	Admiralty records
ADMS	Assistant Director Medical Services
AG	Adjutant General
AHB	Air Historical Branch
AHQ	Army Headquarters
AIF	Australian Imperial Force
AIFO	*Australian Imperial Force Orders*
AIR	Air Ministry records
ALH	Australian Light Horse
ANZ	Archive New Zealand
ANZAC	Australian and New Zealand Army Corps
AOH	*The History of Australia in the War of 1914-1918* (Australian Official History)
AQMG	Assistant Quartermaster General
AWM	Australian War Memorial, Canberra
Bde	Brigade
BEF	British Expeditionary Force
BGGS	Brigadier-General, General Staff
BGRA	Brigadier-General, Royal Artillery
BGRE	Brigadier-General, Royal Engineers
BL	British Library, London
BM	Brigade Major
Bn	Battalion
C-in-C	Commander-in-Chief
CAB	Cabinet records
CAC	Churchill Archives Centre, Cambridge
CB	Companion of the Order of the Bath
CCS	Casualty Clearing Station
CDA	Commander Divisional Artillery
CEO	*Corps Expéditionnaire d'Orient*

CGS	Chief of the General Staff
CID	Committee of Imperial Defence
CIGS	Chief of the Imperial General Staff, War Office
CMG	Companion of the Order of St Michael and St George
CO	Commanding Officer
Col	Colonel
Coy	Company
CQMS	Company Quartermaster Sergeant
CRA	Commander Royal Artillery
CRE	Commander Royal Engineers
CUP	Committee of Union and Progress (Ottoman Empire)
CVO	Commander of the Royal Victorian Order
DA&QMG	Deputy Adjutant and Quartermaster General
DAAG	Deputy Assistant Adjutant General
DAG	Deputy Adjutant General
DAQMG	Deputy Assistant Quartermaster General
DCM	Distinguished Conduct Medal
DMO	Director of Military Operations
DQMG	Deputy Quartermaster General
DRL-A	Defence Regional Library, Adelaide
DSO	Distinguished Service Order
EMS	Eastern Mediterranean Squadron
FCNZ	Field Company New Zealand Engineers
FSR	*Field Service Regulations*
GBAD	Ground-based air defences
GHQ	General Headquarters
GOC	General Officer Commanding
GS	General Staff
GSO	General Staff Officer
HE	High explosive
HLI	Highland Light Infantry
HMAT	His Majesty's Australian Transport
HMHS	His Majesty's Hospital Ship
HMS	His Majesty's Ship
HMT	His Majesty's Troopship
HQ	Headquarters
IGC	Inspector-General of Communications
INV	Irish National Volunteers
IoW	Isle of Wight County Records Office
IWM	Imperial War Museum, London
KCB	Knight Commander of the Order of the Bath
KCVO	Knight Commander of the Royal Victorian Order
KOSB	The King's Own Scottish Borderers
L-of-C	Lines-of-communication
LH	Light Horse

LHCMA	Liddell Hart Centre for Military Archives, London
MC	Military Cross
MEF	Mediterranean Expeditionary Force
MGGS	Major-General, General Staff
NAA	National Archives of Australia, Canberra
NCO	Non-commissioned officer
NSW	New South Wales (Australia)
NZ&A	New Zealand and Australian Division
NZE	New Zealand Engineers
NZEF	New Zealand Expeditionary Force
NZFA	New Zealand Field Artillery
NZMR	New Zealand Mounted Rifles
NZPS	New Zealand Permanent Staff
NZSC	New Zealand Staff Corps
OC	Officer Commanding
PC	Privy Councilor
PMLO	Principal Military Landing Officer
POW	Prisoner of war
PRO	Public Records Office records
QAIMNS	Queen Alexandra's Imperial Military Nursing Service
QARNNS	Queen Alexandra's Royal Naval Nursing Service
QF	Quick-firing
QMG	Quartermaster General
RA	Royal Archives, Windsor Castle
RAF	Royal Air Force
RAFM	Royal Air Force Museum, London
RAMC	Royal Army Medical Corps
RE	Royal Engineers
Revd	Reverend
RFA	Royal Field Artillery
RFC	Royal Flying Corps
RGA	Royal Garrison Artillery
RM	Royal Marines
RMA	Royal Marine Artillery
RMF	Royal Munster Fusiliers
RML	Rifled Muzzle Loader
RMLI	Royal Marine Light Infantry
RMS	Royal Mail Ship
RN	Royal Navy
RNAS	Royal Naval Air Service
RND	Royal Naval Division
RNR	Royal Naval Reserve
RNVR	Royal Naval Volunteer Reserve
RSF	Royal Scots Fusiliers
RWF	Royal Welch Fusiliers

SAA	Small Arms Ammunition
SMS	*Seiner Majestat Schiff* (eg SMS *Emden*)
SPD	Socialist Party (Germany)
TBD	Torpedo Boat Destroyer
TF	Territorial Force
TNA	The National Archives, Kew
UK	United Kingdom
UVF	Ulster Volunteer Force
VAD	Voluntary Aid Detachment
VC	Victoria Cross
WD	War diary
WO	War Office records

Notes on Contributors

Dr Phylomena Badsey MA was awarded her PhD from Kingston University in 2005. Her thesis topic 'The Political Thought of Vera Brittain' was the culmination of many years research into women and the Great War. In December 2010 she was awarded from University of Birmingham MA in War Studies (with Merit). Phylomena specialises in nursing during the First World War. She also maintains a broad interest in women and warfare, occupation and social change.

Dr J.M. Bourne taught History at Birmingham University for 30 years before his retirement in September 2009. He founded the Centre for First World War Studies, of which he was Director from 2002-09, as well as the MA in British First World War Studies. He has written widely on the British experience of the Great War, including *Britain and the Great War* (1989; 1994), *Who's Who in the First World War* (2001), and (with Gary Sheffield), *Douglas Haig: War Diaries and Letters 1914-1918* (2005). John is currently editing the letters and diaries of General Sir Henry Rawlinson, again with Gary Sheffield, and is Hon. Professor of First World War Studies at the University of Wolverhampton.

Stephen Chambers is a battlefield guide, author and researcher with a passion for British military history. He is trustee and also the military historian of The Gallipoli Association, and author of several books on the campaign. His first book in the Pen & Sword *Battleground Europe* series, *Gallipoli: Gully Ravine* (2003), was highly acclaimed, along with his follow-on volumes; *Anzac: The Landing, Suvla* (2008), *August Offensive* (2011) and *Anzac: Sari Bair* (2014). His knowledge of British and Commonwealth military kit led to the publication of *Uniforms & Equipment of the British Army in World War One* (2004), the first serious work on the subject. His latest volume, co-authored with Richard van Emden, is *Gallipoli: The Dardanelles Disaster in Soldiers' Words and Photographs* (2015) which was published for the centenary. When not writing, Stephen is roaming battlefields, continuing with on-going research and guiding tours.

Jeff Cleverly is a retired British Army infantry officer. He has served on operations in Northern Ireland and Bosnia, and in combat in Afghanistan, where he was seriously wounded in action against the Taliban. He is a graduate of the United Kingdom Joint Services Command and Staff College and holds a Master's Degree in Defence Studies from King's College London. Jeff is currently undertaking PhD research on command during the Gallipoli campaign at the Australian National University. He lives in Canberra, Australia, with his wife and three young sons.

Brian Curragh graduated with distinction in 2012 from the University of Birmingham's Centre for War Studies' MA in British First World War Studies programme. His dissertation was entitled 'The Queen's Own Oxfordshire Hussars – "agricultural cavalry" or an elite unit?' He was also awarded the Max Rosen Prize for his essay 'How important were Tanks to British Military Success in the Hundred Days?' He has contributed chapters on Field Marshal Sir Henry Wilson in Spencer Jones (ed), *Stemming the Tide: Officers and Leadership in the British Expeditionary Force 1914* (2014) and the planning lessons learned from the Battle of Loos in Spencer Jones (ed), *Courage Without Glory: The British Army on the Western Front 1915* (2015). Brian is a member of the British Commission for Military History and, when not researching the relationship between Ulster and the Great War, is the Group Finance Director of a property development company in Hertfordshire.

John Dixon is a professional geologist with over thirty years experience in large-scale civil engineering and mining projects across five continents. During this time he authored a number of scientific and technical papers and articles. He has been an active member of the Western Front Association for over thirty years and has been leader for small-scale battlefield tours in France, Belgium and Gallipoli. John has a wide-ranging interest in the First World War and has travelled widely to research various aspects of the conflict, often connecting his professional positions to his interests in the conflict. He has written several books and numerous articles on different topics of the conflict. John currently resides in South Wales with his wife Francesca where he continues his research on a more or less full-time basis.

Peter Doyle specialises in the understanding of military terrain, with special reference to the two world wars. He is also an author specialising in the British experience of war, and the material culture of war. A member of the British Commission of Military History, and secretary of the Parliamentary All Party War Graves and Battlefield Heritage Group, he is the author of numerous military history and material culture of warfare publications. A regular speaker at conferences and in invited lectures, he has given numerous specialist battlefield talks and battlefield tours. Peter Doyle is an occasional visiting lecturer at the US Military Academy, West Point (2007, 2014).

Dr Meleah Hampton is an historian in the Military History Section of the Australian War Memorial. Her primary interest is in the operational conduct of the Great War on the Western Front, with a particular interest in the process of learning, applying and transmitting lessons learned on the battlefield. She is a graduate of the University of Adelaide and completed her PhD with a thesis on the 1916 battles for Pozières and Mouquet Farm under the guidance of Professors Robin Prior and Gary Sheffield. In 2009, Meleah was a Summer Scholar at the Australian War Memorial, completing a research paper on the relationship between Australians and Americans during the First World War. Following on from this she was a speaker at the 2008 International Conference on 1918 at the Australian Memorial. She has published a chapter on the American contribution during the First World War in its subsequent proceedings, Ashley Elkins (ed.) *1918: Year of Victory* (2010). Meleah is a member of the editorial staff of the Australian War Memorial's magazine, *Wartime*, and continues to research and write biographies for the Last Post Ceremony project. A keen "battlefield sniffer", having visited the Western Front many times, she currently resides in Canberra with her husband and three children.

Peter Hart was raised in Stanhope and Barton-under-Needwood and attended school in Chesterfield (1967–73) and Liverpool University (1973–76). He then did a post-graduate teaching course at Crewe & Alsager College (1976–77), and lastly a post-graduate librarianship at Liverpool Polytechnic (1979–80). He has been an oral historian at the Sound Archive of Imperial War Museum since 1981. Peter's previous books include *Passchendaele* (2000), *Jutland 1916* (2003), *The Somme* (2005), *Bloody April* (2005), *Aces Falling 1918* (2007), *A Very British Victory* (2008), *Gallipoli* (2011) and *The Last Battle* (2018).

Dr Simon J. House is an independent military historian and author. His first book, *Lost Opportunity: The Battle of the Ardennes, 22 August 1914* (Helion & Company 2017) is based on the research done for his doctoral thesis at King's College London and relies heavily on the author's linguistic ability in both French and German. Simon specialises in the history of the French army in the early phase of the First World War – in the Ardennes, Alsace, Lorraine and of course Gallipoli. Despite a life-long passion for military history, he came to the profession late in life, having previously been employed for 32 years as an accountant and senior executive at British Telecom before retirement in 2001. Simon is 66-years-old, married with three sons, six grandchildren and (thus far) two great-grandchildren. He lives in Southampton, England, and is currently researching his second book, this time on the subject of 'tipping points' during the Second World War.

Dr Gavin Hughes hails from Magherally, outside Banbridge in County Down, Northern Ireland. He was educated at the Royal Belfast Academical Institution and Saint David's University College, Profysgol Cymru/University of Wales, Lampeter. He specializes in the application of military historical methodology and narratives with archaeological theory and practice; the Roman Army during the Early Imperial Period (specifically the Agricola campaigns in Wales and Scotland); warfare in the British Isles from late Antiquity to the high medieval (specifically the early Norse and Hastings campaigns and 1st to 3rd Crusades); Fourteenth and Fifteenth Century warfare (including practical chivalry, arms and armour); The English Civil War and Thirty Years War; the Glorious Revolution (specifically Boyne and Aughrim campaigns); the Napoleonic Wars (specifically 1798 Irish Rebellion and Waterloo campaign); the Crimean War (specifically the Alma and Balaklava campaigns); Victorian Campaigns in Indian and Africa (specifically the Indian Mutiny, North-West Frontier and Zulu/Boer Wars) and the Great War (specifically Ulster/Irish Regiments).

Dr James Hurst is the author of *Game to the Last: The 11th Australian Infantry Battalion at Gallipoli* (Oxford University Press, 2005), now in its third printing by Big Sky Publishing. He earned his Bachelor of Science degree, majoring in Biochemistry and Microbiology, from the University of Western Australia, and was awarded his PhD from the Australian National University, Canberra, for his examination of the landing at Anzac, Gallipoli, on 25 April 1915. He has written historical articles for a range of journals and newspapers, presented papers and lectures in Australia, Canada and Turkey and is currently writing a book on the Life Guards during the 1815 campaign against Napoleon Bonaparte.

Dr Ross Mahoney is an independent historian specialising in air power and the history of air warfare. Between 2013 and 2017, he was the resident Historian at the Royal Air Force

Museum. A graduate of the University of Birmingham (MPhil and PhD) and the University of Wolverhampton (BA (Hons) and PGCE), to date he has published several chapters and articles, edited two books, and delivered research papers on three continents. Ross is a member of the Royal Historical Society and an Assistant Director of the Second World War Research Group.

Dr Linda Parker is an independent scholar and author. Her main writing focus is on army chaplaincy in the 20th century and has written several books on the subject for Helion & Company, the first, *The Whole Amour of God: Anglican Army Chaplains in the Great War* (2009) and the latest, *A Fool for thy Feast: The Life and Times of Tubby Clayton* (2015). Her other historical interests include the history of Polar exploration, and 20th century military history. Linda is a member of the Western Front Association and the Royal Historical Society.

Dr Simon Peaple recently retired as Head of History and Politics at Princethorpe College. He originally graduated in History at Bristol University and subsequently published an essay on Edward Gladstone and the working class with his tutor Professor John Vincent. After a career in marketing, he entered teaching and became a PhD candidate at Birmingham University where his tutor was Dr J.M. Bourne; the thesis was subsequently published as *Mud, Blood and Determination* (Helion & Company 2015) and was judged runner-up in the Army Historical Research Society's awards for best first book. Simon has also written a textbook, *European Diplomacy 1870-1939*. Simon is currently serving a fifth four-year term as a Labour councillor in Tamworth and was Mayor of his adopted home town from 1997-98.

David Raw was educated at Bradford Grammar School and London University where he graduated in History and Education. He is a retired Head Teacher now living in East Lothian, Scotland. He recently completed a Masters degree in First World War Studies at the University of Wolverhampton where his tutor was Professor Gary Sheffield. David's thesis was a study of Major-General Granville Egerton's command at Gallipoli. He is the author of "*It's Only Me*": *A Biography of Rev. T.B. Hardy VC DSO MC* (1988), the most decorated non-combatant in the First World War, and *The Bradford Pals* (2006) in the Pen & Sword *Pals* series. His forthcoming *The Egerton Diaries* will be published by Helion & Company in 2018.

Brigadier (Retired) Chris Roberts AM, CSC is a former infantryman with combat experience in South Vietnam, and subsequent command appointments at the regimental and operational levels. A graduate of the University of Western Australia, he is currently an Adjunct Lecturer at the University of New South Wales (Canberra), author of the seminal and highly acclaimed *The Landing at Anzac 1915*, (2013), several articles on the Gallipoli campaign, and co-author of *Anzacs on the Western Front* (2012). He is presently co-authoring a book on artillery at Anzac.

Dr Robert Stevenson is a former Australian Regular Army officer and now professional historian. He holds a Master of Arts from the University of New South Wales (UNSW) for which he was awarded the Defence Studies Prize for the most outstanding academic record of a student completing the Master of Arts specialising in Defence Studies, and a D. Phil, also from UNSW, for which he was awarded the Army History Unit's 2011 C.E.W. Bean Prize for the best postgraduate thesis on Australian Army history. A revised version of his thesis was published under the title *To Win the Battle: The 1st Australian Division in the Great War 1914-1918* (Cambridge,

2013). His most recent major publication is *The War With Germany* (Oxford, 2015), which was published as a volume of the Centenary History of Australia and the Great War series and was shortlisted for the Australian History Prize in the Prime Minister's Literary Awards for 2016. He is also an Adjunct Lecturer at UNSW (Canberra) and a contributor to the *Australian Dictionary of Biography*.

Katherine Swinfen Eady has a BA (Hons) in drawing and painting from Edinburgh and is a well-established Scottish colourist painter specialising in landscapes. An enduring interest in the First World War led her to complete an MA in The History of Britain and the First World War at the University of Wolverhampton. She has recently finished cataloguing the military papers of her Great-Grandfather, Colonel Harold Mynors Farmar, and has been commissioned by Helion & Company to publish a biography based on his military career.

Tom Williams is a retired Biomedical Scientist who completed a Master's degree in First World War Studies at Birmingham University. An interest in the Territorial Force led to a dissertation, under the supervision of Dr Michael LoCicero, on the training of the Territorial Force infantry 1908-14. This was followed by a contributory chapter, 'The Death of a Battalion: The 5th King's Own Royal Lancaster Regiment at the Second Battle of Ypres' in Spencer Jones (ed.) *Courage Without Glory: The British Army on the Western Front 1915* (2015). Tom still retains an ongoing interest in the training and performance of the Territorials before and after the formation of the Kitchener Armies.

Dr Ritchie Wood spent over forty years working abroad including lengthy spells as a mechanical engineer in the Malaysian tin mining industry, gold and coal mining in South Africa and lecturing at a steelworks college in Libya. On retirement Ritchie devoted himself to the academic study of the mining operations of the British Tunnelling Companies during the Great War. Awarded, at 74-years of age, a Doctorate at Swansea University in September 2012, his thesis subject concerned South Wales Miners contributions to First World War Tunnelling Companies. His recently published book *Miners at War* (2017) expands the story. He now enjoys lecturing around the country on events from 1900 including both the First and Second World Wars. Ritchie currently resides in Thornhill, Cardiff with his wife Marilyn and three adult children living nearby.

Acknowledgements

The origin of this mammoth volume lies with the popularity of the Spencer Jones edited series of volumes, *Stemming the Tide: Officers and Leadership in the British Expeditionary Force 1914* (2014), *Courage Without Glory: The British Army on the Western Front 1915* (2015) and *At All Costs: The British Army on the Western Front 1916* (2018). Inspired by readership desire for an equivalent Gallipoli campaign collection, *Gallipoli: New Perspectives on the Mediterranean Expeditionary Force, 1915-16* has benefitted from a great deal of earnest enthusiasm and support for which the editors are extremely grateful.

As with any compendium work, first and foremost acknowledgements must go to the excellent array of contributors for their scholarship, patience and willingness to comply with fixed deadlines. Their individual and collective goodwill ensured the editorial task was less onerous than first contemplated. Special mention must also be made of Helion & Company proprietor Duncan Rogers whose unstinting sponsorship and sound advice saw the complex project through from genesis to publication.

In addition to the chapter authors, a number of individuals and institutions unhesitatingly provided valuable time and unsparing assistance. Thus we are particularly grateful to the late Dr Bob Bushaway, Dr Spencer Jones, Professor Robin Prior, Professor Gary Sheffield, Professor Peter Simkins, Professor Peter Stanley, Professor Mesut Uyar, Dr Daniel Whittingham, Dr Christopher Wyatt, cartographer George Anderson, typesetter/designer Kim McSweeney and the helpful staffs of The National Archives (Kew), Imperial War Museum, National Army Museum, Royal Air Force Museum, Liddell Hart Centre for Military Archives at King's College London, Australian War Memorial, along with a host of other museums and archival repositories in the United Kingdom, Ireland, Australia and New Zealand that feature in the chapter footnote citations. "What thanks we owe to worth like thine! What praise shall we bestow? To thee the foremost honours are decreed ..."[1]

1 Homer, *The Iliad*, Book IV, Lines 292-94.

Introduction

From differences of opinion on whether the Mediterranean Expeditionary Force (MEF) could ever have succeeded, to debates on tactical questions and the assessment of individual performances, the Gallipoli campaign still arouses heated controversy. Fascination with its many facets continues to feed the voluminous literature. Books abound, but – as we hope this compendium shows – there is still much to explore and fresh perspectives to present. By drawing on original research from an impressive array of established and up-and-coming scholars, *Gallipoli: New Perspectives on the Mediterranean Expeditionary Force, 1915-16* explores a wide variety of aspects of the Allied military effort to force a passage through the Dardanelles and knock the Ottoman Empire out of the war.

This book has its origins in the success of the Spencer Jones series of volumes commencing with *Stemming the Tide* in 2013. The detailed examination of warfare a century earlier found in these compendium works resulted in Helion reader demands for a similar book focusing exclusively on Gallipoli. In part, this book is also a reaction to British readers, and therefore represents an attempt by a British press, to reclaim some of the Gallipoli story from what has largely been an Australian owned narrative (and to a lesser extent, New Zealand). As our many authors show in this compendium, context is everything in historical studies: the reality is that while Gallipoli continues to hold an important place in Australian and New Zealand history, it was a British-led coalition operation. Its challenges, and its ultimate failure, were shared by many. Lastly, we hoped that this book might combat some of the dross that has been published in recent years by authors for whom detailed archival research is an anomaly. Gallipoli is a complex set of multiple stories: to get close to understanding its complexities requires time spent in the archives.

We are conscious that our book's focus on the MEF excludes other important parts of the story: not least the crucial role performed by the Eastern Mediterranean Squadron, or the victorious Ottoman forces that absorbed the initial landings on their shores, and then fought back with such determination that the British Government eventually saw no other option but to cut its losses and run. While these factors are covered in passing throughout various chapters, there are no dedicated chapters on them. These omissions were a deliberate choice on our part.

First, our reasoning was that recent books on these topics do an excellent job examining their subjects, and we felt that those books do it better than we could. For the Ottoman story, we recommend readers consult Ed Erickson's *Gallipoli: The Ottoman Campaign* and Mesut Uyar's *The Ottoman Defence Against the Anzac Landing*. For the role of the British and French naval forces, we recommend Victor Rudenno's *Gallipoli: Attack from the Sea*, and the many conference proceedings published by the Royal Australian Navy and available online at http://www.navy.gov.au/spc/. The role performed by Indian infantry, artillery and logistic units was expertly covered in Peter Stanley's *Die in Battle, Do Not Despair: The Indians on Gallipoli, 1915* published by Helion in 2015, and hence does not receive a similar chapter here.

The second reason for our focus on the MEF was that we wanted the compendium to allow for a detailed examination of the force's many component parts, from General Headquarters down to battalion level, and across nations: hence we have chapters on a French corps, an Australian division, a New Zealand brigade, and a British battalion, amongst others. We also wanted to make sure that the book covered off on the major shifts in the campaign's history, but also to move away from a focus on the fighting alone and look at the "enablers", that is, those elements that ran in the background to support the forces on the ground.

We also saw the book as an opportunity to showcase some of the new and exciting research still being done on the First World War and the Gallipoli campaign. Thus we have a mixture of noted historians of the Gallipoli campaign utilising their expertise to look at the campaign, or aspects of it, in a new light. Then we have experts in other aspects of warfare, who have turned their minds from other wars, other theatres, other armies, other themes, and other times, to the study of Gallipoli. In so doing, they bring new perspectives and new methodological approaches, and indeed often unused archival sources, to the study of something long written about. We were delighted to be able to call on such a mixture of accomplished and promising historians – many of whom were invigorated by the interest in the centenary of the 1915 Gallipoli landings and the desire to correct the inaccuracies aired in public around that time – to contribute to this project.

The book is broken into three sections. Part I, "The MEF in Battle", consists of six chapters which chart the evolution of the campaign from its political and strategic beginnings through to the evacuation of allied forces in December 1915 and January 1916. For those unfamiliar with the key military events of the campaign, Part I provides the structural and contextual underpinnings for Parts II and III. In his chapter, Simon Peaple embraces the *longue durée* of history, examining the state of, and changes to, the relations between the British and Ottoman empires dating back to 1853. Combining the deep political and diplomatic historical awareness that is a feature of many of his other works, Peaple contextualises the road to the Dardanelles campaign, critiques the decisions of key decision-makers, looks at alliances, and in the process, provides a new perspective – one dealing more with geopolitics and politicians than military strategy and officers – that challenges other views of the disastrous campaign's birth.

Three Australian historians, James Hurst, Meleah Hampton, and Jeff Cleverly, then take us from the opening stages of the campaign through to the largest and last major offensive action, the August offensive: respectively, they deal with the landing of the Australian and New Zealand Army Corps (ANZAC) in April; the Second Battle of Krithia in May; and the new landings at Suvla Bay in August. Cleverly's chapter, which addresses the staff work surrounding the plans for the August offensive, should also be read by those interested in the command and control elements discussed in Part II. Michael LoCicero then turns his meticulous research and detailed analysis from the "last act" of the Third Battle of Ypres in December 1917 to the last actions at Krithia Nullah in November and December 1915 and shows us the importance – and inherent challenges – of maintaining the fight at Cape Helles when, in the Anzac and Suvla sectors, the focus was on evacuating. Alexandra Churchill closes out Part I in her fresh look at the MEF's evacuation using previously unseen archival material from the Royal Archives.

The 12 chapters of Part II, "Command and Control", examine those who ran the Gallipoli campaign, how they did it, and why they approached the challenge in a particular way. Between them, these chapters discuss themes such as command and staff work, and tell a story of the Gallipoli campaign at the operational and tactical levels of war, across each sector, from General Headquarters (GHQ) to battalions. While they can be read as individual case studies, the chapters have also been arranged hierarchically and chronologically, so that readers – if approaching them in order – can get a sense of how the campaign unfolded across time, and how the war was viewed differently depending on the level at which one commanded or fought.

Rhys Crawley's chapter on GHQ, and its personalities, provides the first in-depth insight into how GHQ functioned – or failed to function properly – throughout the campaign. In one of the very few English-language studies of the *Corps Expéditionnaire d'Orient*, Simon House's chapter reminds us of the centrality of the French contribution to the Gallipoli campaign. Similarly, Peter Hart, adopting the historical approach for which he is best known, takes us through the story of the Royal Naval Division using the words of its own personnel: the result is a gripping insight into the stresses and realities of war, and an understanding of that unique division's war. Katherine Swinfen Eady's chapter on Captain Harold Farmar, a staff officer in the 29th Division, reminds us of the important role performed by staff officers, shows us how they were often required to do other jobs at short notice, and gives us a glimpse of life in a headquarters at Cape Helles.

Our chapters then shift their attention north to the Anzac sector, where Robert Stevenson takes us through the 1st Australian Division's war from its raising in 1914, its composition and preparation, and its performance during the battles of the landing in April. One major theme throughout is the challenge of divisional command. Chris Roberts' chapter on brigade command at Anzac then analyses the responsibilities and performance of the next rung in the command chain. An expert on the Gallipoli campaign, and a former brigadier himself, Roberts's findings show both a theoretical and practical understanding of what such a command role entails. Noted historian, Christopher Pugsley, then firmly reminds us that the NZ in ANZAC is not without meaning: New Zealand were a core component within that antipodean army corps, and their story – which was largely a successful one at the tactical level – offers some important insights into coalition warfare and the reality of trench warfare to those who experienced it.

As the campaign progressed, and London released more resources for what it hoped would be a successful outcome, new divisions arrived to swell the MEF's numbers. This expansion brought with it new challenges: from preparing units for the fight, to personality clashes between commanders. The remaining chapters of Part II examine some of these challenges. Using previously underutilised primary sources, David Raw examines the health and related performance of Major-General Granville Egerton and his relationships with his corps commander, Lieutenant-General Aylmer Hunter-Weston, and the MEF's commander, General Sir Ian Hamilton. Tom Williams moves forward in time to cover the campaign as experienced by the 53rd and 54th Territorial Force Divisions at Suvla Bay. Brian Curragh's chapter on the 10th Division deals with many of the same experiences and activities, but he also writes the role of its commander into the historical record. Gavin Hughes similarly looks at the campaign as experienced through the eyes of Irish units. Lastly, J.M. Bourne – an academic mentor to many of this book's contributors – shows us what the campaign was like for a battalion in his case study of the 7th Battalion, The Prince of Wales's (North Staffordshire Regiment).

Part III, "Support, Enablers and Constraints", is made up of seven chapters detailing many of those elements of the Gallipoli campaign that have traditionally been given scant attention in the literature. These elements, however, provide an insight into how the campaign was fought, who supported it, and some of those things that hindered the MEF.

Ross Mahoney's chapter looks at the role of airpower throughout the campaign and puts it into the context of similar advances in using this new technology on the Western Front. Key to his work is the personalities of senior air officers and the factors that influenced their approach to airpower. Medical aspects of the campaign have been covered in much of the existing literature, but the work of naval nurses, and the roles they performed on the official and unofficial hospital ships – caring for those sick and wounded from the peninsula – will be new to many: Phylomena Badsey helps fill that gap with her chapter. Caring for soldiers' well-being was also a role performed by chaplains. Linda Parker explains how chaplains were recruited, trained, and the services they provided throughout the campaign's various stages.

Artillery, by definition in British doctrine, was seen as a supporting element: its purpose was to pave the way for the infantry to attack. Rob Langham shows us the important role they performed every day of the campaign, whether it be supporting troops in attack or providing counter-battery fire to protect them while in defence. Underneath the trenches waged another battle as both sides sank mines in an attempt to get under the other and blow them up. Ritchie Wood and John Dixon's overview of mining at Gallipoli reaffirms the difficulty of working in such conditions, and discusses some of the MEF's successes and failures in the underground war. Peter Doyle, who has published much on the Gallipoli campaign, treats us to an analysis of the importance of terrain, and how it featured during the Gallipoli landings. Our final chapter by Stephen Chambers examines the experiences of captivity for those taken prisoner by the Ottomans: we see what was said during their interrogations, we understand how – sometimes quickly – they learned and adapted to local customs, and we get an appreciation of their time as a prisoner from the moment of capture to the point of repatriation.

Collectively, we hope that these chapters give readers a detailed picture of the MEF's war and encourage readers to pursue further answers through further reading.

Rhys Crawley & Michael LoCicero

Part I

The MEF in Battle

1

Geopolitics and the Dardanelles: Poor Collective Decision-making

Simon Peaple

On reading John Terraine's insightful book, *The Road to Passchendaele* (1977), I remember being greatly impressed at the way in which he had taken the controversial campaign and stripped back the elements to chart the way it had come to pass. In writing this chapter, I have attempted to explain how Britain and its Allies came to fight the campaign known to many as either the Dardanelles or Gallipoli. The general background involves consideration of British foreign policy over a 60-year period prior to the Great War as well as the more immediate issues arising from the outbreak of the war itself. In recent years, it has ceased to be unfashionable to recognise the role of individual decision makers in history. This chapter, therefore, traces the story of the origins of the campaign from the geopolitical study of British international relations into the responses made by key individuals who held particular offices of state at the relevant point. Beginning its assessment in the calm waters afforded by Pax Britannica, the story reaches its denouement in a world where those who had made a decision to take Britain into a European war were floundering as to how to control the beast they had unshackled from the depths of Hades.

To say this is not simply to lay Gallipoli at the door of the politicians; on both sides, the pre-war certainties had turned to ashes in the mouths of the military. Helmuth von Moltke (the Younger) had stepped aside and his successor as Chief of the German General Staff, Erich von Falkenhayn had admitted Germany could not win.[1] Field Marshal Sir John French, Commander-in-Chief of the British Expeditionary Force, was a marked man and the French Commander-in-Chief, General Joseph Joffre, though deservedly acclaimed for the Marne, was causing growing concern to France's leaders as the scale of the casualties left French society in shock. France had responded well to the crisis but the reality of the battlefield could not be hidden from the Chamber where many conscripted deputies could report first hand, albeit "skewed" by their own experience of combat. The Hapsburgs and Romanovs, whose tottering regimes the war was designed to reinvigorate, had proved as incompetent in war as in peace. The Hohenzollerns had fulfilled their familial destiny to act as warlords but the Schlieffen Plan

1 Roger Chickering, *Imperial Germany and the Great War, 1914-18* (Cambridge: Cambridge University Press, 1998), p. 52.

had gone awry and the German General Staff insisted upon retaining Belgium which prevented a possible non-annexationist peace brokered by Britain. The foundation of the new German Empire by Otto von Bismarck and Helmuth von Moltke (the Elder), using extra-legal means to finance the army – which then forged the unification of the state assisted by Bismarck's diplomacy – created an army with a state rather than a state with an army. With the failure of the Schlieffen Plan in 1914, Germany was confronted with the very two front war Schlieffen had sought to avoid, but no politician had the authority to force the General Staff to meet Germany's political needs: in this lay the seeds of her ultimate defeat.

Why was Great Britain at war with its former ally Turkey?

During the 19th Century, Russia had invaded the Ottoman Empire and contributed to its decline as a European Great Power. Russia's invasion of the Danubian Provinces in 1853 had helped to bring Britain and France into war with Russia on Turkey's side in 1854 but the 60 years that separated these two events had seen a diplomatic revolution. The desire to block Russian expansion was expressed by the British Prime Minister, Benjamin Disraeli, on 5 October 1876: "Nothing can be more critical or more interesting than the position. [Prince Alexander] Gortchakoff [Chancellor of the Russian Empire] ... has made a false move, and his proposal for Russia to occupy Bulgaria, the very heart and most precious portion of European Turkey, with Constantinople almost in sight of the contemplated frontier, has roused and alarmed John Bull."[2] Liberal Party leader (and former Prime Minister) William Gladstone's attack on the Turks over the 1876 "Bulgarian Atrocities" had created huge difficulties for Disraeli in swinging British public opinion against Russian aggression but he was still able to assert British power in order to bring the Turkish Government in line. The superior attitude of Disraeli's Government towards Turkey was evident in the Prime Minister's letter to his confidant, Lady Bradford, on 12 October: "We had taken a decided step – many thought a rash one. Elliot was to tell the Porte that the recommendation of the armistice by England was England's last step; that, if refused, she should attempt no longer to arrest the destruction of the Turkish Empire, but leave her to her fate; and that our ambassador would leave Constantinople."[3]

The British had subsequently defended the Ottoman Empire from further Russian aggression in 1878 (which included the presence of the Fleet off Constantinople) when they helped force Russia to give back some of its gains under the Treaty of San Stefano. However, Disraeli was already contemplating a different policy. As he wrote on 17 October: "What if we could negotiate a treaty with Germany to maintain the present status quo generally? ...This would make us easy about Constantinople and relieve Bismarck of his real bugbear, the eventual alliance of England and France."[4] Britain also gained Cyprus from Turkey as a further buffer in case of future Russian pressure.

Despite their success in winning honours and public acclaim, for their part in these negotiations, Disraeli and his Foreign Secretary, Lord Salisbury, seemed to have returned from the

2 William F. Moneypenny & George E. Buckle, *The Life of Benjamin Disraeli*, Vol. II (London: John Murray, 1929), p. 951.
3 Ibid., p. 952.
4 Ibid., p. 953.

1878 Conference in Berlin with a diminished view of the Ottoman Empire. Andrew Roberts asserts that Salisbury intended to set up a system of informal control over the Ottoman Empire by infiltrating Englishmen into the Ottoman bureaucracy but that this was successfully resisted by the Pasha class.[5] The legacy of this attempt would hardly have assisted attempts by Britain to enlist Turkish support in 1914 and reduces the issue of the German battlecruiser SMS *Goeben* and light cruiser SMS *Breslau* – German ships that were handed over to the Ottoman Empire and said to have brought the Ottomans into the war with the Central Powers – to a more appropriate final act in a long running drama. Given the historical approach taken by Britain, Turkey's eventual decision to join the Central Powers looks less ungrateful than it might otherwise seem if we look only to the events of 1914.

The issue of finance, or more particularly the lack of it, also came to influence Anglo-Turkish relations. Salisbury, by now Prime Minister, had envisaged two grand projects being undertaken; the trans-Asian telegraph and the Scanderoon–Baghdad railway. The latter was to be financed by an £8 million loan to Turkey repayable at 3 percent over 30 years. However, the idea collapsed when Her Majesty's Treasury refused to help underwrite the loan.[6] Russia was opposed to the development because she wanted to develop a railway line through Persia. In 1907, Russian and British interests in the Persian Gulf clashed sufficiently for the Gulf to be omitted from the 1907 Convention between the two countries which otherwise arranged for a general settlement of all the outstanding issues between them.[7] Given the emphasis later placed upon the German negotiations relating to the Berlin–Baghdad railway this earlier British involvement adds to our understanding of Turkey's drift away from Britain.

The Turkish distrust of the British was well placed in that Salisbury subsequently tried to reach an agreement with Russia. In September 1896, Tsar Nicholas II accepted an invitation to visit Queen Victoria at Balmoral to mark the occasion of her becoming the then longest reigning monarch. Salisbury was keen to establish a *modus vivendi* with Russia and had already assured his Chancellor of the Exchequer, Sir Michael Hicks Beach, that the 53 year lease of the revenues from Cyprus was not an issue because the Ottoman Empire would no longer exist by then.[8] In the discussions that followed, Salisbury offered the Tsar a vision of a general settlement of the "Eastern Question" involving the dismemberment of the Ottoman Empire through an agreement of all the Great Powers which would then give Russia the control of the Straits. However, the Emperor subsequently backed away from this idea as too dangerous, involving as it would Christian powers overthrowing the world's leading Muslim ruler. Salisbury saw himself as leading Britain away from the mistakes of Lord Palmerston who, as Prime Minister, had allied Britain to other liberal powers such as France.[9] Salisbury, like Bismarck, was advocating a policy of *realpolitik*.

Britain's relations with Turkey were also affected at this time by the continuing negotiations over the Persian Gulf. Beginning in 1911, delayed by the war in 1912, they reopened in February 1913. Much of the negotiations centred upon the status of Kuwait which was to be granted

5 Andrew Roberts, *Salisbury: Victorian Titan* (London: Phoenix, 2000), p. 230.
6 Ibid.
7 Briton C. Busch, *Britain and the Persian Gulf 1894–1914* (Berkley, California: University of California Press, 1967), pp. 364-66.
8 Roberts, *Salisbury*, p. 643.
9 Ibid., p. 645.

autonomy with permission to use a variant of the Turkish flag. The final convention signed on 29 July 1913 covered a whole range of issues including the steamers on the Tigris–Euphrates and the rates for customs and rules for extradition as well as gains for Britain in securing the recognition of clients such as Kuwait and Bahrain. Although these areas had been settled by agreement, the negotiations had confirmed Britain's position as a power which was undermining that of Turkey.[10] To the nationalistic Young Turks – who felt Britain was undermining Turkey, as it had done with its occupation of Egypt, an Ottoman territory, in 1882 – it was easier to envisage an alliance with Germany who had no territorial claims upon Turkish territory.

Events within the Ottoman Empire then conspired to change the dynamics of Britain's relationship with Turkey. Amongst the opponents of Sultan Abdul Hamid II's increasingly autocratic rule was the Committee of Union and Progress (CUP) – generally referred to as the Young Turks – which had been founded in the early 1900s. Due to repression the group was strongest in the Balkan lands of the Empire but in June 1908 the Sultan's spies were able to uncover a CUP cell in the Ottoman Third Army. The cell's leader, Adjutant Major Ahmed Niyazi, decided to lead a revolt which triggered a revolution across Macedonia's cities. The Sultan's power, and his empire, soon started to unravel: Bulgaria declared independence, Austria-Hungary seized Bosnia and Herzegovina and Crete declared itself re-united with Greece.[11] The Sultan's attempt to regain control led to a counter-revolution and to splits within the army which may have caused the Western powers to underestimate the Turkish army's capabilities. Yet, by 24 April 1909, Third Army had taken control of Constantinople and the revolution was complete. Abdul Hamid II was deposed and succeeded by his brother, Mehmed V.[12] A further complicating factor in the relationship between the Entente powers and Turkey was the decision by Italy to invade the provinces of Benghazi and Tripoli in 1911. This meant that attempts to woo Italy to join the Entente would have to include leaving her in possession of the tenuous gains she had made despite a long, drawn-out guerrilla war, which made it difficult to offer Turkey an incentive to join the Entente.

The difficulties were highlighted by the Turkish decision in August 1911 to place an order for two dreadnoughts with the British company Vickers and Armstrong. The ships were more than the Ottoman Government could afford and so much of the money was raised by public subscriptions.[13] However, as the ships neared completion in early 1914 they also posed a major threat to Russian naval forces in the Black Sea, and the Greek Navy. The Russian Navy was increasing expenditure rapidly under the politically astute leadership of Admiral Ivan Grigorovich, who had been Naval Minister since 1911. Following the Young Turk revolution, and the Ottoman Empire's order for two dreadnoughts, the Russians ordered three dreadnoughts. Thus in 1914 the Turks were due to take delivery of two dreadnoughts a year ahead of Russia's new ships arriving.[14] It could therefore be argued that in the face of such popular fundraising and

10 Busch, *Britain and the Persian Gulf*, pp. 336-40.

11 Eugene Rogan, *The Fall of the Ottomans: The Great War in the Middle East, 1914-1920* (London: Penguin, 2015), pp. 4-8.

12 Ibid., p. 9.

13 Ibid., p. 31.

14 David Stevenson, *Armaments and the Coming of War: Europe 1904-1914* (Oxford: Oxford University Press, 2000), p. 149.

the strategic situation, the subsequent British decision to keep the Turkish ships pushed the Ottoman Empire into the arms of Germany.

This situation was then further complicated by the Balkan Wars of 1912–13 which increased the pressure on the Young Turks due to the initial defeats. The wars also drew the European powers into a region where there were deep political and religious differences which meant it was difficult to form an alliance with one country without alienating another. Although Turkish trade with Germany was expanding, it only accounted for 0.7 percent of Germany's overseas trade in 1909. During the Balkan Wars, the British played a key role by hosting the peace conference in London. This was made possible by the appointment of Alfred von Kiderlen-Waechter as German Secretary of State in 1910; he had spent considerable time as German ambassador in Bucharest and recognised that it was important to get on with Britain as disagreements there on minor issues would only add to the tensions that already existed. This was very important when it came to the Balkan Wars as Kiderlen-Waechter assured the other powers that Germany would support a non-intervention agreement; this gave France and Russia the encouragement they needed.[15] The mutual restraint exercised by Britain and Germany resolved key issues during the peace negotiations in April and May 1913, for example, over Scutari.

The growing tension between Greece and Turkey moved the emphasis on to areas directly relating to Britain's own interests, thereby ending the local entente with Germany. Britain's Secretary of State for Foreign Affairs, Edward Grey, wanted the Greeks to have the southern Sporades and knew that Turkey would have to be coerced into accepting this, so Britain's relations with Turkey were already deteriorating. Furthermore, Kiderlen-Waechter suffered a stroke on 30 December 1912 and his successor, Gottlieb von Jagow, had previously served as Ambassador in Rome. Jagow had been Kaiser Wilhelm II's fraternity brother at the Bonn Borussen and although Wilhelm was not initially enthusiastic about the appointment he soon told his naval secretary: "He's becoming admirably seasoned. The little man says he would be the first to recommend war to His Majesty if any one tried to dispute Germany's rights in Asia Minor."[16] As 1914 approached there was a more aggressive stance in Berlin and a deepening rift between the interests of Britain and Turkey which the Germans could exploit.

One of the key pressures for war in Germany was the rise of the Socialist Party (SPD) as the largest single political party in Germany. Fearing the pacifist tendencies of the Third International, of which the German SPD was a part, the Kaiser had been relieved by the decision of the parties in Germany to unite in the *Bruderbund* but peace short of victory would undermine further the credibility of a regime the Kaiser had already diminished through the notorious Eulenberg Affair and his foreign policy *faux pas* such as the *Daily Telegraph* interview in which he claimed to have masterminded Britain's victory in South Africa. The reality was that Germany must fight on. Even before the Schlieffen Plan failed she was forging an alliance with Turkey which replaced the unfaithful Italy as a Mediterranean partner for the Austro-German core of the Triple Alliance. German Staff visits in 1912–1913 had already convinced the German commanders that Italy was unlikely to fulfil its commitments to the Triple Alliance

15 R. J. Crampton, *The Hollow Détente: Anglo-German Relations in the Balkans, 1911-1914* (London: George Prior, 1979), pp. 28-9, 59.

16 Lamar Cecil, *The German Diplomatic Service, 1871-1914* (Princeton: Princeton University Press, 1976), p. 319.

which is why they were so keen to respond to the suggestion of sending a military mission to Turkey and prepared to accept the inevitable negative reaction from the Entente powers.

Meanwhile, in May 1913, the newly re-formed Young Turks government was concentrating upon military recovery from the Balkans. The Army, mainly equipped with German weapons, had suffered significant defeats at the hands of those like the Serbs who had largely bought equipment from the French.[17] The German military mission that was subsequently led by General Otto Liman von Sanders was therefore designed to ensure that Turkey did not break its links with German armaments suppliers and therefore move into the Entente camp. Kaiser Wilhelm continued to reassure Russia but papers from the German Foreign Office confirm that Wilhelm was actually trying to lure Britain away from supporting Russia: "It is about our prestige in the world which is severely attacked from all sides."[18] On 2 August 1914 – the day after Germany declared war on Russia – the Ottoman Empire, not yet at war, signed a treaty with Germany. This treaty was directed at assisting Turkey against its traditional enemy, Russia.[19] This confirmed the direction of policy indicated in the German Foreign Office papers and did not alter Britain's support of Russia. Throughout the 19th Century Britain had regarded the control of the Straits as a vital object of foreign policy and had supported Turkey to keep Russia at bay but from around 1885 that policy had altered towards accepting some kind of accommodation with Russia. There was no way that Grey would accept Germany becoming the dominant power in the Straits and therefore a possible assault on the Straits became a key issue.

Next day, 3 August 1914, Britain informed the Ottoman Government that it had decided to take over the two dreadnoughts nearing completion in British yards. This was a real blow to Turkish pride which had been badly damaged by the Balkan Wars. It is therefore important to understand the arrival of the *Goeben* and *Breslau* off Constantinople on 10 August in the context of this feeling that Britain had treated Turkey as an inconsequential power. Lord Grey's explanation for the decision seems to reinforce the view that the Turks were treated with Olympian disdain. He recorded: "This was quite legal. All ships of war built for foreign countries in British yards were subject to the right of the British Government to take them in an emergency. If the ships were for a neutral country, full money compensation would of course be paid for them. But the Turks were very sore."[20] There is no sense here of the devastating impact upon Turkish pride linked to the public drive to raise the money. It was probably the single decision most likely to strengthen the Germanophile wing of the Young Turks, particularly the Minister for War, Enver Pasha, and therefore make it inevitable that Turkey took the final steps towards war with the Entente powers.

According to Basil Liddell Hart, Britain's decision to keep the dreadnoughts was followed by a crucial conversation between Enver and Lieutenant-Colonel Friedrich Kress von Kressenstein, a member of the German military mission, which saw permission given for German ships to pass through the Dardanelles and orders to fire on any British ships which might attempt to follow them.[21] German Ambassador to the Ottoman Empire, Hans von Wangenheim's success

17 Stevenson, *Armaments*, p. 343.
18 Giles MacDonogh, *The Last Kaiser: William the Impetuous* (London: Weidenfeld and Nicolson, 2000), p. 347.
19 Basil H. Liddell Hart, *History of the First World War* (London: Pan, 1972), p. 157.
20 Viscount Grey of Fallodon, *Twenty-Five Years*, Vol. II (London: Hodder & Stoughton, 1925), p. 166.
21 Liddell Hart, *History of the First World War*, p. 158.

German military mission to Constantinople, December 1913. General Liman von Sanders, in visor cap, is fifth from the left.

in getting a treaty signed did not guarantee that Turkey would ally with Germany. Nonetheless, the Kaiser encouraged his officers to stay put: "I consider your duties there at the present critical period to be equivalent to any services you could render me here, if you carry out your difficult task in Turkey ... which is of such importance to us here."[22] The importance was underlined by contact between Berlin and Rear Admiral Wilhelm Souchon whose ships – *Breslau* and *Goeben* – were attempting to reach Constantinople. Berlin requested that Souchon reach Constantinople as soon as possible. He expected to arrive by 5:00 p.m. on 10 August.[23]

According to German officer Hans Kannengiesser – who places Enver and Kress at the centre of events – his regular meeting with Enver was interrupted by Kress with the news that the *Goeben* and *Breslau* had reached the Dardanelles and that Fort Chanak Kale needed to know whether to admit them. Enver's reaction was to say that he needed to consult the Grand Vizier but after pressed by Kress, stated: "They are to allow them to enter". He also directed that the English were to be fired on. "In taking such a step on his own initiative," Kannengiesser wrote, "Enver Pasha had naturally assumed a grave personal responsibility, and for him everything now depended on whether and how his ministerial colleagues would share this responsibility with him."[24]

The lack of value attached by Britain to a potential alliance with Turkey is summed up in Grey's statement: "Apart from this everything was done to make it easy and even profitable for Turkey to remain neutral." This was expanded upon in his letter to the British Ambassador in Constantinople, on 22 August 1914:

22 Hans Kannengiesser, *The Campaign in Gallipoli* (London: Hutchinson, 1927), pp. 24-25.
23 Dan van der Vat, *The Ship that Changed the World: The Escape of the Goeben to the Dardanelles in 1914*, (London: Collins, 1986), p. 144.
24 Kannengiesser, *The Campaign in Gallipoli*, pp. 25-27.

> We do not wish to repel Turkish desire for discussion, but the demands made are excessive. You may, however, when your French and Russian colleagues are similarly instructed say: The Three Allied powers will jointly give a guarantee in writing that they will respect the independence and integrity of Turkey, and will engage that no conditions in the terms of peace at the end of this war shall prejudice this independence and integrity. They will also secure for Turkey economic advantages such as the cession to Turkey of the German railway and other concessions.[25]

Enver Pasha.

Given the delay between the decision to take over the dreadnoughts and this letter to the ambassador with the additional injunction upon him to await his fellow ambassadors receiving instructions; it is no wonder that the Turks turned to Germany as an ally. On 24 November 1914, Sultan Mehmed V proclaimed a jihad against the British and French Empires but the overall response from Muslims in the two empires was very limited. Nevertheless, it was an added reason to look for an option that would knock Turkey out of the war.

The drift towards Turkey becoming an ally of Germany was not accelerated because, as Grey recorded, Britain did not declare war despite Turkey not fulfilling British demands for Turkey to follow international norms as a neutral power in relation to the *Goeben*, *Breslau* and their crews. At home, the view of Turkey as a weak nation was reflected in the *Hull Daily Mail* which stated that Turkey was about to make unreasonable demands and that opposing the Entente would lead to the destruction of Turkey.[26] The attack of Turkish and German vessels on Russian ships on 28 October 1914 finally ended the ambiguity.[27]

Why was the Asquith Government feeling insecure?

In Britain, King George V and his Government were trying to deal with the situation that had arisen. Henry Asquith had been Prime Minister since 1908. Bright and middle class, Asquith had excelled at Oxford University and risen high in politics assisted by a fortuitous second marriage. With a general election due in 1915, and given discord over many issues, Asquith was acutely aware that the Opposition were strong and a coalition could be on the cards. Should that eventuate, he wished to be in a position of strength.

25 Grey, *Twenty-Five Years*, Vol. II, pp. 166-67.
26 *Hull Daily Mail*, 1 October 1914, p. 1.
27 Grey, *Twenty-Five Years*, Vol. II, p. 168.

Prime Minister Henry Asquith.

Amongst his many problems – in addition to Home Rule in Ireland – were women and the working class. These were tied to the coalition issue; indeed, one of the reasons he rejected the demands of both the suffragists and suffragettes was that enfranchising propertied women would give additional votes to the Tories and leave him completely dependent upon his parliamentary allies for the opportunity to form a coalition government. But the resulting escalation in suffragette activity only served to highlight the political tensions in Western Europe's oldest democracy. The working class, through trade unions, were increasingly opposed to their employers and bitter struggles ensued. The Taff Vale Judgement by the House of Lords had made unions liable for the cost of strikes and so the unions had decided to form the Labour Party to represent the interests of their members. This in turn created problems for Asquith as the Labour Party was likely to win Liberal seats or to divide the non-Conservative vote under the First Past the Post system which had been introduced under the 1884-5 electoral reforms.

Why was the British War Council not prepared to sanction an offensive on the Western Front?

On 30 October 1914 the *Manchester Evening News* reported the bombardment of Odessa and the jubilant reaction in Russia to war with Turkey.[28] The next day, in a letter to Venetia Stanley, Asquith wrote: "Few things would give me greater pleasure than to see the Turkish Empire finally disappear from Europe, & Constantinople either become Russian (which I think is its proper destiny) or if that is impossible neutralised and made a free port."[29] It is easy to see why seizing the Dardanelles with Greek help – as had been discussed – would not be considered appropriate.

The Royal Navy – in what were the first shots of what would become the Dardanelles (or Gallipoli) campaign – carried out a long-range bombardment of the Turkish forts at the Dardanelles on 3 November 1914. First Lord of the Admiralty, Winston Churchill, later admitted that it gave him and the Royal Navy a false impression of the effectiveness of such fire.[30] It probably also alerted the Turks to the form in which a potential attack might be mounted.

28 *Manchester Evening News*, 30 October 1914, p. 5.
29 Michael Brock & Eleanor Brock (eds.), *H.H. Asquith Letters to Venetia Stanley* (Oxford: Oxford University Press, 1982), p. 300.
30 Ibid., p. 309.

Great Britain had entered the war in August 1914, at least officially, to protect Belgium. In reality, Britain declared war because of the growing commercial and naval rivalry with Germany and Britain's subsequent "entente" (understanding) with France which practically committed Britain to support France in a war against Germany. France expected the British on their left flank. Although the British Expeditionary Force (BEF) was an independent force, it rapidly became clear that the command of such a small military, initially 84,000 men, had to be set against the needs of the French who had mobilised over a million men. From the commencement of hostilities to the end of November, the BEF suffered nearly 90,000 casualties (86,237 other ranks and 3,627 officers).[31] The old army was finished.[32] Such losses exceeded 25 percent of its overall trained strength of 389,000 and it is important to bear this in mind when considering why Britain would look for answers beyond the Western Front.[33]

Equally important is the domestic context. The news was full of reports of casualties. The *Coventry Evening Telegraph*, for example, devoted a full column on 1 October 1914 to the casualty list and the wide range of regiments involved. No one could be in doubt regarding the bitter consequences of the intense fighting.[34] This concern for casualties and the return on the investment of such manpower was central to the paper that Asquith received from Churchill on 30 December 1914: "The losses involved in the trench jumping operations now going on on both sides are enormous & out of all proportion to the ground gained." Churchill concluded that the New Armies, when ready, should not be sent "to chew barbed wire" in Flanders or be wasted in frontal attacks.[35] A better answer lay elsewhere.

It is important not to read backwards from 1918 to see the discussion of alternatives as the first mistake by those opposed to Haig's focus on the Western Front where the decisive victory was ultimately obtained. Given the enormous shock of the appallingly high casualty rate in the early months of the war, it would be quite surprising if no other ideas had been suggested. Indeed, a number of alternatives were being mooted at the time.

In late November 1914, Asquith had established a War Council comprised of eight men.[36] It was expanded to 11 in January 1915.[37] Before it was a proposal from Sir John French, Commander-in-Chief of the BEF, asking for 50 new divisions to advance into Belgium focusing on the coast. The Secretary of State for War, Lord Kitchener, who was then planning a massive expansion of the BEF with a view to a decisive battle in France, was against the idea. The divisions within British military circles, however, meant that non-Western Front options started to present.

31 James Edmonds, *Military Operations in France and Belgium 1914,* Vol. 2 (Nashville, Battery, 1985), p. 467.
32 Spencer Jones (ed.), *Stemming the Tide: Officers and Leadership in the British Expeditionary Force 1914* (Solihull: Helion, 2013), p. 18.
33 Stevenson, *Armaments and the Coming of War*, p. 60.
34 *Coventry Evening Telegraph*, 1 October 1914, p. 1.
35 Brock & Brock (eds.), *H.H. Asquith*, p. 345.
36 Consisting of Asquith, Grey, Churchill, Kitchener, Lloyd George, Balfour, Admiral Fisher and Lieutenant-General Wolfe-Murray.
37 By adding Crewe, Haldane and Admiral Wilson.

Why did the British War Council decide to sanction a naval assault on the Dardanelles?

Lieutenant-Colonel Maurice Hankey's paper summarising the situation on the Western Front and expounding the idea of attacking Germany through Turkey, dated 29 December 1914, had been circulated by Asquith to the War Council. Hankey, who was Secretary of the Committee of Imperial Defence, envisaged an alliance with Greece and Bulgaria which would seize the Straits and open a route for Russian wheat to reach her allies along with 350,000 tonnes of shipping.[38] The Tsarist Ukraine produced one-third of all Russia's wheat, 80 percent of its sugar, and was responsible for the majority of Russia's grain export.[39] Freeing up trade through the Dardanelles would not only aid Russia's war effort but would also help ease Britain's sugar shortage. (Shipping rates had escalated to 300 percent of 1913 levels by 1915 so the opening up of the Russian sugar trade in its own vessels would have solved a number of problems facing the British Government).[40] German protests that trading through Sweden and Norway would breach neutrality meant that a more direct route to Russia was desperately needed.[41]

In parallel with (yet separate to) Hankey's memorandum, Asquith received a similar proposal from Lloyd George (which surprised Hankey given its similarity to his recommendations). Like Hankey, Lloyd George argued that victory on the Western Front would come at an intolerable cost. He criticised the military for a lack of forethought, and criticised the time it had taken Kitchener to respond to his suggestion that they find out what Russia's situation was. He regretted that this meant that they had not been able to resupply Russia whilst Archangel was open.[42] In this last remark he seemed to betray an ignorance of how difficult Britain was finding it to supply her own much more modestly sized force in Flanders without diverting ammunition to Russia. Lloyd George's main idea involved withdrawing 200,000 men from Flanders for operations in the Mediterranean. One element of this force would be part of massive offensive against the Austrians with 1.4 million men being mobilised for this assault by the Serbs and the other Balkan countries. The other element would be used to attack Turkey.

Field Marshal Lord Kitchener.

Then, on 2 January 1915, Grand Duke Nicholas, in overall command of the Russian armies, asked Britain for help. The situation in the East was desperate and he felt Britain was the power most interested in Turkey. According to Churchill, on 3

38 Liddell Hart, *History of the First World War*, p. 161.
39 Dominic Lieven, *Towards the Flame: Empire, War and the End of Tsarist Russia* (London: Penguin, 2015), p. 52.
40 Peter Dewey, *War and Progress: Britain 1914-1945* (London: Longman, 1997), pp. 36, 43.
41 *The Scotsman*, 1 December 1914, p. 3.
42 John Grigg, *Lloyd-George: From Peace to War 1912-1916* (London: Penguin, 2002), pp. 192-3.

January, Fisher told him that a naval bombardment would not achieve anything and that instead an expedition to invade Turkey should be despatched from Marseille under the command of Sir William Robertson. Admiral Fisher suggested this expeditionary force should comprise 75,000 men withdrawn from the BEF plus the Indian Corps, with the BEF reinforced by moving the territorial divisions out to France. Fisher's suggested landing place was Besika Bay. Greek troops would simultaneously attack Gallipoli while troops from Egypt would attack Haifa and Alexandretta.

Presciently, Fisher wrote that the meeting of the War Council would be like a game of nine pins with everyone's plan being bowled to knock out the others. Fisher also referred to the War Council as "Our Aulic Council" which was the name of one of two councils which ran the Holy Roman Empire and was therefore hardly a compliment as it suggests overlapping jurisdictions and a membership representing disparate groups. Churchill argues that Fisher's plan was impossible to achieve in its entirety as Robertson himself would have opposed it. But he recognised that Fisher's idea of using old battleships to force the Straits was the genesis of the idea for the eventual naval attack. This contradicts the idea that Churchill had a long-standing commitment to a naval assault on the Dardanelles.[43]

Faced with these proposals, Asquith called a series of meetings of the War Council. Churchill, reflecting Fisher's thoughts, contacted Vice-Admiral Sackville Carden, commander of the British squadron in the Mediterranean, and asked if the Dardanelles could be forced by ships alone. Carden, on 5 January 1915, replied that they could not be rushed but might be forced by extended operations.[44] The timing of this reply seems to fit with Sir George Arthur's belief that by the 7 or 8 January 1915, Churchill had decided to no longer support the idea of seizing Zeebrugge – one option he had been considering – and preferred to focus on the Dardanelles. The War Council appears to have seized – in the absence of a better alternative – upon Churchill's proposal (which was put forward on 9 January).[45] To the "navalists" it was a way of using seapower to assert Britain's will in the tradition of Nelson's destruction of the Danish fleet at Copenhagen; and Churchill and Fisher had, albeit at different times, considered attacking Schleswig-Holstein in order to destroy the German fleet at Kiel. To the Westerners it settled upon an idea that did not involve withdrawing army units from the Western Front.

Popular history has Churchill as the driving force. The assertion that Churchill had long been an advocate of the Dardanelles operation only partially fits with the detailed narrative of events in the days leading up to his 9 January proposal for a naval assault on Gallipoli. Elizabeth Greenhalgh accepts Churchill's line that the specific proposal to attack the Dardanelles was Churchill's, despite Hankey's contribution, whilst recognising that Lloyd George also came up with possible ideas in response to Kitchener's threat to not send any further troops to the Western Front.[46] Churchill's own account says that he wrote to the Prime Minister on 2 January 1915 and quotes his own letter saying that he had wanted to attack the Straits as soon as war had been declared.[47] This helps to explain why he was so willing to push the idea forward once the offensive on the Belgian coast had been abandoned. Kitchener, at this stage, was clear that

43 Winston Churchill, *The World Crisis 1911-1918* (London: Penguin, 2007), pp. 320-1.
44 Charles E. Callwell, *Field Marshal Sir Henry Wilson: His Life and Diaries* (London: Cassell, 1927), p. 201.
45 Ibid., pp. 198-9.
46 Elizabeth Greenhalgh, *The French Army and the First World War* (Cambridge: Cambridge University Press, 2014), p.100.
47 Churchill, *The World Crisis*, p. 318.

no troops were available and even informed the Russians that the British effort was unlikely to divert Turkish forces from where they were engaged against the Russians. Given this assessment it is hard to understand why the British and French carried out the operation at all.

Why did the British War Council decline the assistance of Greece?

The adherence of Turkey to the Alliance was potentially countered by the offer by the Greek Prime Minister, Eleftherios Venizelos, to put Greece's armed forces at the disposal of the Entente on 18 August 1914. Grey commented that Greece's offer of alliance was embarrassing whilst negotiations with Turkey continued, and especially so after the Turks declared war, given Russia's sensitivity regarding Constantinople.[48] Therefore, as Asquith recorded:

> We had a rather long Cabinet this morning ... The main question was as to what answer we should give to Venizelos's offer of a Greek alliance, not only against Turkey, but possibly also against Bulgaria if she should attack Servia [sic]. I am all against interfering in the Balkans among these small States: on the other hand, one does not want to snub Greece; & it took some time to hammer out a cordial yet not too committal reply.[49]

Venizelos was a staunch supporter of the Entente but there were other forces in Greece with which he had to contend. He faced considerable resistance from King Constantine – the Kaiser's brother-in-law – who responded cautiously to a request from Russia to join in seizing the Dardanelles by saying that any such combined operation must be subject to Bulgaria remaining neutral. Grey also wondered whether an Anglo–Greek expedition could have seized the Dardanelles by land and sea. He argued that such an attack might have succeeded but that such a view assumes that the Germans, Turks and Bulgarians would not have guessed at such a possibility. Further, he believed that the Greek proposal – that is, King Constantine leading a Greek army into Constantinople – could have led Russia to leave the war. Grey therefore concluded:

> we were wise enough to decline that offer too. Solidarity with Russia in the first two years of the war was essential to avoid defeat in France and the occupation of Constantinople by British ships and a Greek army would have been no compensation for a German breakthrough in the West and the capture of Paris or the channel ports of France.[50]

Such a view leaves the impression that Grey would have feared success at Gallipoli and he added that even the operations that were launched caused problems with Russia because they believed that Britain was trying to pursue its traditional policy of denying Russia access to the Mediterranean by taking control of Constantinople during the war. This point is reinforced by Grey's comment that the entry of Turkey into the war cleared the way for Greece to help in any way that did not involve taking Constantinople.[51]

48 Grey, *Twenty-Five Years*, p. 172.
49 Brock & Brock (eds.), *H.H. Asquith*, p. 182.
50 Grey, *Twenty-Five Years*, p. 190.
51 Ibid., p. 183.

Subsequently, Constantine was able to withdraw the support on the grounds that Bulgaria had now allied itself with Germany.[52] In fact, the Bulgarians did not irrevocably commit themselves to the Central Powers until the renewed offensive against Serbia on 11 October 1915 though the declaration of armed neutrality on 21 September 1915 pointed towards a decision.[53]

Despite his long-serving role as the Secretary to the Committee of Imperial Defence (CID), Hankey's (previously discussed) proposal can be seen as flawed in a number of aspects. Fundamentally, it ignored the practical impossibility of getting Greece and Bulgaria to work together. They had been allied during the First Balkan War when both had seen the benefits of attacking Turkey in concert with other former-Ottoman states in order to reduce Turkey's ability to fend them off and avoid the intervention of a great power (which action by one Balkan state alone might trigger). In February 1912, Bulgaria and Serbia signed an agreement to divide Macedonia when conquered. The Bulgarians hoped to see it remain an autonomous region of Turkey so that, as had been the case in Eastern Rumelia, they could subsequently absorb it into Bulgaria. The Serbs insisted that it should be partitioned; Bulgaria agreed but the fate of Skopje, and the region around it, was left undecided. The Greek Government was concerned not to lose its claims to parts of Macedonia, from whence Alexander the Great had come, and so it joined the Serbo–Bulgarian alliance to form the Balkan League, but inserted no clauses on the division of future territory. Here lay the seeds of future conflicts as one of the Bulgarian army's objectives was to advance down the Struma Valley to gain Salonika before the Greeks were able to.[54] These points alone should have made Hankey question his proposal to ally with both countries.

What makes Hankey's proposal even more strange is that after the initial successes of the Balkan Alliance against Turkey in 1912 the peace negotiations were chaired by Lord Grey in London. During these negotiations, fighting broke out again when Bulgaria attacked Adrianople which surrendered after six weeks on 26 March. Success in the First Balkan War and the unresolved elements in the pre-conflict agreements, made Bulgaria the target of an alliance between Greece and Serbia which led to the Second Balkan War from June to July 1913. Bulgaria's defeat in this second phase of the conflict led to her having to compensate Romania, by ceding the southern Dobrudja up to a line from Balchick to Silistra.[55] Bulgaria was also forced to give Greece control over areas of Thrace which was a further pertinent obstacle to Hankey's scheme.[56] Hankey should have been aware too that Grey had sent a letter to Sir Henry Bax-Ironside, Britain's ambassador in Sofia, on 13 November 1914 that specifically referred to Grey's understanding of the difficulties that lay before any attempt to reform the Balkan Bloc.[57]

In addition, Russia, one of Britain's allies, had declared war on Austria-Hungary in support of Serbia, in August 1914. Bulgaria's territorial ambitions lay in Macedonia and Thrace, the former of which was also coverted by Serbia as had been seen in the Second Balkan War. Russia backed Serbia's refusal to concede any territory in Macedonia to Bulgaria which limited the ability of the Entente to entice Bulgaria into an alliance. Germany, however, was able to promise Bulgaria the whole of Macedonia as well as more of Thrace and to persuade Turkey to

52 Ibid., p. 160.
53 R. J. Crampton, *A Concise History of Bulgaria* (Cambridge: Cambridge University Press, 1997), p. 141.
54 Ibid., p. 136.
55 Ibid., p. 137.
56 Simon Peaple, *European Diplomacy 1870-1939* (London: Heinemann, 2002), p. 25.
57 Grey, *Twenty-Five Years*, Vol. 2, p. 185.

allow Bulgarian control over the railway as far as Dedeagach.[58] Hankey's projected alliance with Bulgaria would founder on the twin rocks of national sentiment and *realpolitik*.

This legacy of bitterness was further reinforced by Germany's financial support for Bulgaria after the Second Balkan War. The Radoslavov Government in Sofia secured a loan of 500,000,000 leva from a consortium of German banks. Whilst no agreement between the two countries was signed it is clear that this moved Bulgaria closer to the Triple Alliance than the Entente.[59] Historian David Stevenson argues that the Germans and Austro-Hungarians initially failed to co-ordinate their efforts to win over Bulgaria.[60]

That Britain was heavily committed to Russia is reflected in the £586,000,000 loaned to her despite Britain herself having to finance a more considerable war effort than ever before.[61] The British focus on money was also reflected in an attempt by the Secret Intelligence Service, MI6, to bribe Turkey out of the war. The plan stemmed from an idea put forward by Hankey, and involved offering £4,000,000 to Turkey.[62] This operation sounds farfetched in its conception and came to nothing as the agents, Whittall and Eady, tentatively opened negotiations on the day that the Royal Navy carried out the initial bombardment of the Dardanelles.

Why was the French Government prepared to consider naval action in the Near East?

The rise of working class industrial discontent expressed through strikes was paralleled in France where the government took the extraordinary step of threatening to call up the railway workers in order to subject them to military discipline. The French Government also faced the strongest pacifist leader in Europe, Jean Jaurès. He remained unconvinced of the need for war right up to the eve of mobilisation when he was murdered by an assassin who believed he was striking a blow for France. Therefore, although France had rallied to the flag in 1914, it had suffered severely and large parts of North Eastern France were soon occupied by the Germans. Neither side succeeded in turning their opponent's flank.

Joffre shared concerns about the strategic impact of Turkey entering the conflict. He felt that the new enemy was not the strong military and financial power that it had once been but that, armed and directed by the Germans, Turkish soldiers would fight bravely. Joffre was also conscious of the threat to trade routes which went via the Suez Canal and to the complications that would arise in the Balkans. He recognised the difficulties Britain and France would have in confronting a Muslim power when they ruled so many Muslims in their own colonies.[63]

Joffre, like the British, was considering the impact of the losses France had already sustained in the war. Not long after Hankey's memorandum had been circulated Joffre was confronted with a proposal to send an army to fight against the Austrians. According to the French historian François Roth, Joffre was, by this time, facing discrete opposition from his president,

58 Crampton, *A Concise History of Bulgaria*, p. 141.
59 Ibid., p. 141.
60 Stevenson, *Armaments*, p. 352.
61 A.J.P. Taylor, *English History 1914-45* (Oxford: Oxford University Press, 1963), p. 42.
62 Keith Jeffery, *MI6: The History of the Secret Intelligence Service 1909-1949* (London: Bloomsbury, 2010), p. 121.
63 Joseph Joffre, *Memoires Du Marechal Joffre, tome premier* (Paris: Librarie Plon, 1932), p. 484.

Raymond Poincaré, who blamed Joffre for the dip in his popularity due to the temporary move of the government to Bordeaux. Their once close relationship was never re-established.[64] Joffre described the proposal as seductive but wrong in principle and impractical. One reason was a lack of sufficient troops. In January 1915 he wrote: "In less than 5 months of war, the permanent losses for the active and reserve armies (killed, prisoners and wounded so severely not to be available in future) is 420,000 men. If the war continues for another 10 months the permanent losses will be 840,000 men."[65]

Other issues that he felt relevant included the reality that there were only enough formations to hold the 600 kilometres of front currently held. To reduce the number of army corps available would prohibit any offensives in the future and would introduce vulnerabilities to the French Army's line. He also argued – the classic "westerner" argument – that it was important to focus on the principal theatre of operations. They needed to defeat the Germans, not the Austrians.

Joffre also saw impracticalities in intervening in the Balkans. He disparaged the value of Salonika as a logistic base. As a trained engineer, Joffre appreciated logistical issues and argued that the Serbian Army of 100,000 had only been kept supplied with great difficulty and therefore that the Salonika–Uskub railway would not be sufficient to supply 100,000 Serbs and 300,000 French troops. A landing in the Adriatic would be even more difficult.[66]

Despite Joffre's objection, historian Elizabeth Greenhalgh argues that Poincaré was receptive in the context of the stalemate that had been reached and that in the Chamber there would be support from the colonial bloc which was always keen to see France's influence extended.[67] French imperialist deputies were not a formal group but their common interests could influence opinion and votes. The initial reaction to the declaration of war by Turkey was regret on the part of the *Comite de l'Asie Francaise* because French had been growing to become the second language of the Ottoman Empire and they believed that in a partitioned Turkish Empire, Britain's share would be at least half and therefore no more than half of the empire would be open to French culture.[68]

On a military level, Françios Georges-Picot's proposal to send a force of up to 2,000 men to seize Lebanon suggests that recent defeats in the Balkans was leading to an under-estimation of Turkish fighting capability. On 3 August 1914, Victor Augagneur – who had been elected president of the *Comite d'Action Republicaine aux Colonies* the previous year – was made Minister for the Navy. Therefore, it was on his desk that Churchill's proposal landed on 18 January 1915 (though he may have had wind of the plan as early as 7 January 1915).[69]

Augagneur was concerned that the British would affect a landing at Alexandretta in order to help protect the Suez Canal. Alexandretta was a key entry point for Syria and therefore central to French colonial ambitions. It was also a long way from the Suez Canal and further aroused French suspicions regarding Britain's motives. This may explain why, on 26 January 1915, when Augagneur met Churchill in London that he agreed to Churchill's proposal for a British led

64 Francois Roth, *Raymond Poincare* (Paris: Fayard, 2000), p. 304.
65 Joffre, *Memoires*, p. 484.
66 Ibid., p. 485.
67 Greenhalgh, *The French Army*, p. 100.
68 Christopher M. Andrew & A.S. Kanya-Forstner, *France Overseas: The Great War and the Climax of French Imperial Expansion* (London: Thames & Hudson, 1981), p. 65.
69 Ibid., p. 71.

naval expedition – despite France having previously been assigned command of joint naval operations in the Mediterranean – for one involving British command but excluding Alexandretta. Churchill suggested to the French Ambassador that Paris keep a tight rein on who they told. The French Prime Minister decided against informing Alexandre Millerand, the Minister for War, to avoid annoying Joffre.[70] The French commander in chief in the Mediterranean, Vice-Admiral Augustin Boué de Lapeyrère, whose reputation had been damaged by the success of the *Goeben* and *Breslau* reaching Turkey, was similarly left in the dark. It was only on 13 February 1915, six days before the naval bombardment of the Dardanelles began, that Augagneur informed the rest of the French Cabinet of the plan.[71]

Winston Churchill.

Like France, there were also debates in Britain. Indeed, there was opposition to Churchill's plan from within the Admiralty. On 31 January 1915, for example, Admiral Fisher, the First Sea Lord, wrote to the Conservative leader Andrew Bonar Law, enclosing a paper which attacked the idea of naval bombardment of coastal defences. Whilst Fisher's opposition was not yet as firm as it was to be in May 1915 (when Fisher resigned), it was clear to Bonar Law that the apparently unanimous advice of the Admiralty was deceptive.[72]

Churchill sent these contested plans to the French Admiralty on 2 February 1915. A week later, Augagneur agreed to the plan against the advice of the naval staff. Joffre agreed to the plan as long as it was a naval operation only. Meanwhile, London realised that the operations, due to start on 15 February, would have to be postponed due to delays in assembling the relevant number of minesweepers. Nonetheless, Asquith saw the forthcoming bombardment as the "all important preliminary to our demarche in the Balkans."[73]

Subsequently, on 16 February the British decided they would need a force to carry out a potential landing. Asquith credits Hankey with having come to him with this advice. "I have for some time been coming to the same opinion, and I think we ought to be able without denuding [General Sir John] French to scrape together from Egypt, Malta and elsewhere a sufficiently large contingent." "If only these heart-breaking Balkan states could be bribed or goaded into action", he added. Such a statement ignores the fact that Asquith was actively against Greece occupying Constantinople which is so obviously the bribe they "needed". However, Asquith then finishes

70 Greenhalgh, *The French Army*, p. 101.
71 Andrew & Kanya-Forstner, *France Overseas*, p. 71.
72 Robert Blake, *The Unknown Prime Minister: The Life and Times of Andrew Bonar Law 1858-1923* (London: Faber & Faber, 1955), pp. 236-7.
73 Brock & Brock (eds.), *H.H. Asquith*, p. 426.

upon a note which so fits the fictional Sir Humphrey's dismissal of politicians: "It is of much importance that in the course of the next month we should carry through a *decisive* operation somewhere, and this one would do admirably for the purpose."[74] After six months of warfare, the government was in need of a victory. The French Cabinet agreed to send two divisions.[75]

The fragility of Asquith's hopes is evident when on 17 February he wrote that the bombardment, due to start on 19 February, "is an absolutely novel experiment, & I am curious & rather anxious to see how it develops".[76] The War Council, however, was still discussing whether to send military forces. Kitchener was opposed to sending out the 29th Division on the grounds that he wanted reserves in case the Germans defeated Russia; thus freeing forces for the West. Asquith, in contrast, was "strongly of opinion that the chance of forcing the Dardanelles and cutting Turkey in half, and arousing on our side the whole Balkan peninsula presents such a unique opportunity that we ought to hazard a lot elsewhere rather than forgo it."[77] In considering the possibility of rousing the whole Balkans "on one side" Asquith seems to have forgotten the issues that had divided the Balkan states in two recent wars.

Why did the British War Council not involve Greece even when it was clear the naval assault alone was not achieving the desired objectives?

The diplomatic impasse with Russia over the fate of Constantinople came to the fore again as it became clear that the naval bombardment was struggling to achieve its objectives. Venizelos's offer to supply three Greek divisions was received on 1 March 1915. Asquith recalled to Venetia Stanley: "I long to talk it all over with you, my dearest and wisest;"[78] it is unlikely his senior civilian and military advisors would have appreciated such sentiments. Asquith's sense that the government needed a victory might have been further increased by the Cabinet meeting on 4 March 1915, during these protracted negotiations over Constantinople, when Lloyd George, Churchill and Kitchener proposed imprisoning workmen who would not work. In an acidic series of comments in her diary, Margot Asquith recorded her view that this was the height of folly and that Churchill was a Tory who did not understand British workmen who were "a very good fellow, nearly always mismanaged and overworked."[79] With strikes on Clydeside and Cabinet colleagues losing touch with reality it is little wonder Asquith yearned for a decisive action and hoped it would come at Gallipoli.

By 6 March 1915, predictably, since both Grey and Asquith so clearly favoured this outcome, Asquith told Venetia that Russia was opposed to Greek participation because it was determined to incorporate Constantinople into the Russian Empire after the war.[80] Therefore, at a time when Russia was herself incapable of assisting her allies, she vetoed a possible option that might

74 Ibid., p. 429.
75 Greenhalgh, *The French Army,* p. 102.
76 Brock & Brock (eds.), *H.H. Asquith,* p. 434.
77 Ibid., pp. 445-6.
78 Ibid., p. 456.
79 Michael Brock & Eleanor Brock, *Margot Asquith's Great War Diary: The View from Downing Street* (Oxford: Oxford University Press, 2014), p. 87.
80 Brock & Brock (eds.), *H.H. Asquith,* p. 461.

allow the allies to free up access to one of her major exporting regions. As has been detailed above, the potential economic benefits for this for Russia were enormous but under pressure from Sazanov the Tsar preferred to preserve Constantinople for a future victorious Russia than help that victory forward through Greek intervention. The Russians then put forward specific proposals for the area they would control around Constantinople (on both the European and Asiatic shores) and this proposal was accepted by France on 8 March 1915 and the British on 12 March 1915. For the British there was the added sweetener that she would receive the zone in Persia previously designated as neutral under the 1907 agreement.[81] Once again, the potential for operational success at Gallipoli was hampered by geopolitical constraints.

Despite Bonar Law's agreement at the War Council that Constantinople would go to Russia in the event of victory, relations between he and Churchill remained mutually mistrustful. This was partly because Bonar Law was receiving views from Lieutenant-General Henry Wilson (principal liaison officer with the French), that the Dardanelles operation, and by implication Churchill as its proponent, were a mistake. On 17 March 1915, Wilson told Bonar Law that if the BEF was given sufficient men and ammunition, the Germans would be defeated on the Western Front. In Wilson's view, the operations at Gallipoli would be a distraction at such a vital point. He argued that the Entente would have to occupy both the Asiatic and European shores of the Dardanelles and therefore they would need to send enough troops to defeat the Turkish Army in European Turkey. For a man with a strong strategic brain, it is surprising that Wilson seems to have completely omitted any assessment of the significance of keeping Russia supplied. Wilson was, however, on sounder ground when emphasising that the supply of ammunition on the Western Front was already too low and that therefore any diversion of resources away from the Western Front was ridiculous. By rejecting Greek assistance, Grey was opting not to use additional resources and instead creating the need to divert army resources away from France and Flanders.

The decision regarding Russia clearly reflects Grey's concerns to keep Russia in the war at a time when she was suffering significant military reverses. Wilson recorded in his diary on 7 April 1915 that operations at the Dardanelles were not succeeding and "Winston ought to be, and must be, *degomme* over this." By 9 April 1915, Bonar Law's doubts about the Gallipoli expedition were serious and he expressed them to Wilson in this manner: "as far as I can gather, your views as to the seriousness of the operations are being amply justified. As I wrote you before, I was satisfied that the Government had jumped into all this without at all counting the cost."[82] That Churchill and Fisher were now busy preparing for an operation to attack Rotterdam can only have increased the belief that even Churchill no longer believed that Gallipoli would be a success.[83] It is also clear that Churchill's political opponents, with some support from within the military, were determined to oust him and were ready to make Gallipoli the public reason for doing so. The fact that Gallipoli went badly just made Churchill all the more vulnerable.

81 Hugh Seton-Watson, *The Russian Empire 1801-1917* (Oxford: Oxford University Press, 1967), p. 707.
82 Blake, *The Unknown Prime Minister*, pp. 240-1.
83 Callwell, *Sir Henry Wilson*, p. 222

Conclusion

Britain went to war with the Ottoman Empire because of a fundamental re-orientation of British foreign policy during the sixty years after the successful conclusion of the Crimean War. The Straits Convention of 1856 confirmed that the Sultan would not allow ships of war to enter the Straits, Bosphorous or Dardanelles "so long as the Porte is at peace."[84] It was this key agreement that Enver broke when he authorised the Turkish forts to admit the *Goeben* and *Breslau* and to fire on any pursuing British ships. Britain had guaranteed Ottoman integrity in 1856 but by 1914 Britain had come to see the Straits as lying within Russia's natural Empire (the 1907 Convention between Britain and Russia had defused much of the tension between the two countries and therefore gave effect to the Triple Entente).

Britain had also increasingly sided with Greece over their demands towards Turkey. The decision to buy the two Turkish dreadnoughts in 1914 denied Turkey the opportunity to establish naval superiority in the Black Sea. It was therefore bound to upset Constantinople. That the agreement with Germany was signed the day before the fate of the warships was officially communicated does not remove this decision from the chain of causation since the official outcome followed weeks of public consideration by the British Government. The arrival of the *Goeben* and *Breslau* led to a crystallisation of the issues and a phoney war until the end of October when Russia was attacked. The early retaliation, in the form of a naval bombardment of the Dardanelles, was a pointer to an idea but by no means conclusive in leading to the subsequent campaign.

The first of the conclusions reached by the Dardanelles Commission argued that the whole operation was not properly planned:

> We think that, when it was decided to undertake an important military expedition to the Gallipoli Peninsula, sufficient consideration was not given to the measures necessary to carry out such an expedition with success ... we think that the conditions of a military attack on the Peninsula should have been studied and a general plan prepared by the Chief of the Imperial General Staff ... special attention being paid to the probable effect of naval gun fire in support of the troops; and that it was the duty of the Secretary of State for War to ensure that this was done.[85]

Kitchener was therefore singled out as responsible for the failures at the planning stage but the commission did not address the central issue of whether it was the wrong project to undertake. The reference to the potential impact of naval gun fire was supported by the doubts originally expressed by Vice-Admiral Carden and by the naval staffs in both London and Paris. Nonetheless it ignores the evidence from Asquith and Grey that the alternative of a direct attack by land on Constantinople was ruled out entirely on non-military grounds despite the resources to carry it out being offered by Greece.

The Russian request for assistance in diverting Turkish, and possibly Austro-Hungarian, forces away from a struggling Russia was therefore a critical factor in persuading the Western Powers to look at the Dardanelles. That the Russian request effectively was rescinded in late

84 Michael Hurst (ed.), *Key Treaties of the Great Powers 1814-1914*, Vol.1 (Newton Abbot: David & Charles, 1972), p. 330.

85 The National Archives (TNA) CAB 19/1: Dardanelles Commission Report.

Die Götter über den Trojanischen Gefilden
Vater Zeus: „Scheußlich, liebe Athene: Damals wurde wenigstens um die schöne Helena hier gerauft und heute — um die schmierigen Kontobücher John Bulls!“

Contemporary German cartoon commentary on the Gallipoli campaign and perceived links to Great Britain's global financial dominance: Father Zeus: "It's shabby my dear Athena. At least once the beautiful Helen was fought for – today there is only the complexities of John Bull's account books!" (*Kladderadatsch*: 2 May 1915)

March ignores the fact that by this time plans were already in train. However, the Allies were, arguably inevitably, trying to assess their position in a war which had popularly been going to be over by the Christmas which had already passed.

Joffre's assessment was clear, the Western Front was the decisive theatre and therefore only naval forces could be spared for the Dardanelles. In Britain, the initial debate related to expanding the forces on the Western Front and utilising the Royal Navy to attack Zeebrugge. Whilst it is inevitably debatable whether the British Army in 1915 was capable of such an offensive, the use of naval gun fire support would suggest it was at least plausible (though the supply of ammunition to the BEF was already causing considerable concern and would have been worsened by a rapid expansion of the BEF). However, the military were divided and therefore opposed the "Belgian offensive" idea. Faced with obstruction, Churchill then moved his support to the idea of a naval assault on the Dardanelles which found common ground with Kitchener in that they now both agreed on what they did not want. In consequence, and very much given the lack of an alternative, the War Council adopted the proposal to undertake operations to seize the Dardanelles.

2

Into the Firing Line: A Reappraisal of the Battle at Anzac, 25 April 1915

James Hurst

An … appreciation … is … a logical process of reasoning by which a commander considers all the circumstances affecting the military situation and arrives at a decision as to the course of actions to be taken in order to accomplish his mission.

A Guide to the Tactical Appreciation, Junior Staff Course,
Land Warfare Centre, Junior Staff Wing

"He's a cheery old card", grunted Harry to Jack …
But he did for them both by his plan of attack.
Siegfried Sassoon, *The General* (1918)

Many times have the reasons for the failure of the Anzac landings on 25 April 1915 been discussed, in print and elsewhere. Whether the troops were put ashore at the right or wrong place, the reasons this may have happened, the role of terrain, over-running of objectives, the inspirational intervention of Lieutenant-Colonel Mustapha Kemal, insufficient numbers of Australian and New Zealand troops, and many other issues, have been conclusively and inconclusively argued. This paper will investigate another possible cause – the manner in which the battle was fought, particularly by the opposing commanders.

My 2013 doctoral thesis was a reconstruction of the experience of the 11th Battalion, Australian Imperial Force (AIF) on 25 April. This battalion was scattered from Fisherman's Hut in the battlefield's north to Second Ridge in its centre, from Battleship Hill on the heights to Third Ridge inland; a study of their experience is consequently a study of much of the battle that day. This article will fill a gap in this work by examining the fighting on the right, principally on 400 Plateau.[1] The Australian Official Historian Charles Bean described this as "the most costly struggle of the day … which … involved within a few hours nearly half of the 1st Australian Division … In this fighting there was lost half the flower" of that division.[2]

1 As relatively few members of the 11th Battalion fought at 400 Plateau and Bolton's Ridge, my thesis concentrated on the fighting from Second and Third ridges northwards.

2 C.E.W. Bean, *The Official History of Australia in the War of 1914-1918*, Vol. I (Sydney: Angus & Robertson, 1921), hereafter *The Story of Anzac*, p. 370.

This chapter will primarily consist of a comparison between Turkish regimental commander Lieutenant-Colonel Şefik Aker's account, supplemented by select Ottoman sources, and the Australian *Official History*. The reliance on Bean's work is a consequence of several factors, the main one being that his *Official History of Australia in the War, The Story of Anzac,* Vol. I, is the starting point for research on the Anzac landing and is often considered the "definitive" and accepted story of the battle. Yet many were the times I had stood on Plugge's Plateau or at other points at Gallipoli, tried to place myself in the shoes of Australian commanders of the day, pondered their decisions, as evidenced by the movements of their troops inland from the beach, and asked myself "why?" This in turn led to another "why" – why was it that I could read the *Official History* and many other works, and not be able to answer such basic questions? Consequently, this chapter provided an opportunity to examine the *Official History* more closely, and, as this source raises nearly as many questions as answers, when the latter are sought, to attempt to read between the lines, look behind the narrative and examine why the battle developed as it did.[3]

This examination is essentially in three parts. First, I will look at some of the early, important decisions made by the Australian commanders, and attempt to gain an insight into the latter's decision making. Second, I will compare this to their Turkish opponents' approach to the battle. Third, I will then examine some of the events on the battlefield to gain insights into how the battle was fought by Australian troops.

Diversion to the right

One decision central to recent debate about the Anzac landing is that made by the commander of the covering force, the 3rd Brigade's Colonel E.G. Sinclair-MacLagan. At some time that morning, MacLagan decided to divert the 1st Australian Division's 2nd Brigade from its planned objective of seizing the high ground on the left of the landing, to a defensive battle on the right. The 1st Division commander, Major-General W.T. Bridges,[4] wrote in his after-action report, that this change of plan was a response to the first Turkish counter-attack, which drove in the advanced elements of the covering force between 6 and 7 a.m.[5] Depending "on whether MacLagan's decision is considered to be wrong or right," he is considered pessimistic or pragmatic, and as either losing the Australian and New Zealand Army Corps (ANZAC) the initiative very early in the battle, never to be regained, or saving it from possible disaster from aggressive Turkish counter-attacks.[6] Thus it is remarkable that, a century after the event, conclusions about what occurred in that much documented battle can remain so polarising.

3 In addition, most of the unit war diaries for units who fought on 25 April 1915 at this time are very brief, or missing.
4 Major-General William Throsby Bridges (1861-1915), b. Greencock, Scotland 1861.
5 Australian War Memorial (AWM): AWM4 1/42/3 Part 2: Headquarters report, April 1915, and report by 'Headquarters, 1st Australian Division', 7 May 1915.
6 J.P. Hurst, 'Dissecting a Legend, Reconstructing the Landing at Anzac, Gallipoli, 25 April 1915, utilising the experience of the 11th Battalion, Australian Imperial Force', thesis (2013), p. 113. Since published as *The Landing in the Dawn: Dissecting a Legend – The Landing at Anzac, Gallipoli, 25 April 1915* (Solihull: Helion & Company, 2018).

The Plan

The aim of the operation was for Sir Ian Hamilton's Mediterranean Expeditionary Force to gain control of the Dardanelles by landing on the Gallipoli Peninsula and knocking out the Ottoman guns dominating the straits. The British 29th Division would undertake the main landing, at Cape Helles in the south, and the ANZAC would land further north, between Gaba Tepe and Fisherman's Hut. The Australians and New Zealanders were to push inland to a feature known as Mal Tepe and effectively cut the peninsula in half, thereby preventing Ottoman reinforcements from the north interfering with the Helles landings.

Bean described the plan thus: "The formal operation orders, of which the wording was perfect … informed" Lieutenant-General W.R. Birdwood, the ANZAC commander, that his covering force, was to land "between Gaba Tepe and … Fisherman's Hut … to seize and hold … the lower crests and southern spurs of Hill 971." The "main body of the corps" would seize "the inland spur of Hill 971" and the hill of "Mal Tepe," near the village of Boghali.[7]

Hamilton, Bean continues, "suggested" Birdwood "at least" occupy the "arrowhead of ridges" around Chunuk Bair, Battleship Hill "and their spurs running to the sea on either flank," creating "a strong covering position, and Hamilton left it to Birdwood's discretion whether" or not to seize "the actual summit of 971;" this reference to seizing 971 presumably referred to corps rather than the covering force. Birdwood thought "storming Mal Tepe" may be "difficult" and decided "that his first task" was to seize "971 and its seaward spurs," in other words the high ground.

Birdwood was concerned by the perceived presence of three Turkish field batteries, two inland and one apparently behind Gaba Tepe, and felt that the first troops ashore should rush them. He therefore "instructed General Bridges that the covering brigade should seize and occupy the ridge from Gaba Tepe towards Chunuk Bair. The rest of the Australian Division … would secure the main ridge to the north … and attend to the left flank." In other words, the covering force was to seize a ridge, Third Ridge, whose left (viewed from the direction of the Australian advance) was on the high ground, and whose right was near the promontory of Gaba Tepe, as well as points on Battleship Hill and short of the crest of Chunuk Bair. This did not include the crest of the range, which was to be taken by the 2nd Brigade.

Bridges, the divisional commander, then issued orders for the "main part" of the covering force, "to push inland, rushing the batteries" and taking Third Ridge. "The northern parties of the 3rd Brigade were to reach and hold Battleship Hill," while the remainder were to seize "knolls on" Third Ridge, "from Scrubby Knoll to Gaba Tepe."[8] Two companies of the 9th Battalion were to independently rush the battery behind Gaba Tepe.[9]

Covering Force landing

The covering force was the 1st Australian Division's 3rd Brigade, supported by the 1st Field Company Engineers. The fighting portion of this brigade was the 9th, 10th, 11th and 12th

7 Bean, *The Story of Anzac*, Vol. I., pp. 220-221.
8 Ibid., pp. 225-226.
9 Ibid., Vol. I, p. 226.

battalions.[10] Their first wave of roughly 1500 troops would disembark from battleships into pinnace-drawn rowing boats, and would then row themselves to shore; the second wave, of roughly 2500, would follow and land from destroyers which could approach the beach more closely.

The covering force landed under fire at about 4:30 a.m. and pushed rapidly inland. They had landed further north than expected and were concentrated on a narrower front. Many of the first wave assaulted Plugge's Plateau, before moving inland; numbers of the second, landing from the destroyers, moved inland from Anzac Cove in order to climb Second Ridge and head for their objectives on Third Ridge or behind Gaba Tepe.

At about 6:15 a.m., the 3rd Brigade's Brigade Major, Major C.H. Brand, who had been sent to 400 Plateau by MacLagan, ordered the 10th Battalion's Lieutenant J.L. Haig, not to "go too far forward. Don't go up that hill,"[11] apparently referring to Third Ridge. Bean explains that these were "the first definite orders for new tactics on the part of the covering force," and reached the first troops of the battleship tows of the 9th and 10th battalions as they arrived on 400 Plateau. The orders had come from MacLagan, apparently on Brand's advice.[12] MacLagan had landed with the destroyer tows and climbed Plugge's Plateau and had ordered that "instead of immediately advancing to the Third Ridge," the leading troops "should dig in and reorganise where they were – on the Second ridge."[13] Thus within two hours of landing, the advance was being ordered to stop short of the objectives on the centre and right. With little explanation in the *Official History*, this development is left in the air.

The portion of the force that had landed further north than anticipated had an extra ridge represented by Plugge's Plateau, between them and their objectives on Third Ridge. The troops were then ordered, for what reason we do not know, to dig on the Second Ridge. Those members of the 9th and 10th battalions who had landed in Anzac Cove, could by-pass Plugge's Plateau. They were confronted by Second Ridge, but as the 10th Battalion's first objective was on Second Ridge, this should not have been a hurdle in getting to their second objective, which was on Third Ridge; but they did not proceed. Bean's chronology of these developments also seems awry: the troops of the first wave had left Plugge's before MacLagan arrived there, so should have been well ahead of him, and those from the destroyer tows had landed near 400 Plateau and had headed straight there. After landing, MacLagan back-tracked to Plugge's and held an officer's conference before moving forward. In other words, something must have stopped the advance before "first definite orders"[14] reached the advanced troops an hour and a half after the landing.

The Victorian 2nd Brigade began landing soon after the 3rd. Their objectives were on the high ground on the left. As the companies came ashore, MacLagan advised their leaders that the plan had changed, and they were to proceed to the right flank – the first officers apparently heard this between 5:30 and 5:50 a.m.[15] This dramatic change of plan, to divert an entire brigade from advancing on the left to defence of the right, represents a major change from the planned

10 AWM: AWM4 1/42/3 Part 2: 1st Division Unit War Diary, Appendix 1, 18/19 April 1915.
11 AWM: AWM38, 3DRL 606, item 25.
12 Bean, *The Story of Anzac*, Vol. I., p. 344.
13 Ibid., pp. 343-344.
14 Ibid., p. 343.
15 Ibid., p. 363.

Australians disembarking and heading for shore, 25 April 1915.

strategy and objectives for the division as a whole. It is the divergence from the plan generally focussed on by historians.

A number of earlier developments indicate that MacLagan had been thinking defensively for some time before orders reached the 9th and 10th battalions on 400 Plateau and before he diverted the 2nd Brigade. Bean told us that earlier, "when MacLagan reached" Plugge's, soon after landing, he saw "the lump of the 400 Plateau" to his right front; this should have been his centre. The 9th and 10th had already left and "their companies were working towards the right front, apparently trying to carry out the original plan. If it was to be achieved, that was the sector in which a commander was needed."[16] This is all a little vague, but from Plugge's Plateau the 9th and 10th battalion's covering positions were indeed to the "right front" on Third Ridge, but other brigade objectives were on the high ground to the left. By stating "that was the sector in which a commander was needed", Bean implies, though does not state or justify, that within perhaps thirty minutes of coming ashore, MacLagan was seeing his main goal or priority to be the right flank, and possibly on Second, rather than Third Ridge.

Another significant but generally overlooked incident occurred earlier still. Major Miles Beevor, 10th Battalion, met MacLagan immediately after landing and before either left the beach. Beevor found the brigadier "most naturally very disturbed" that "we've landed in the wrong place!" "I know that, Sir," replied Beevor, "saw it from the Ship."[17] MacLagan instructed Beevor to take his company up the heights in front and "move southward," "select a defensive position facing inland, and dig in."[18] In other words, straight after coming ashore, Beevor had been ordered to dig in on Second Ridge. It would seem the decision had already been made to defend rather than advance – at least initially. Moreover, Beevor would have been aware of his orders before landing; the fact that MacLagan intervened, rather than just suggesting that he "carry on," also implies a change in thinking by MacLagan.

In addition, from Plugge's Plateau, MacLagan had directed two companies of the 11th Battalion to proceed to Second Ridge, instead of to their objectives on the high ground to its left; once again, the reasons for this are not given in the *Official History*. This might be partly explained by the fact that, had the covering force landed in its "correct" place, the 11th Battalion would at the time have been advancing along Second Ridge to its objectives on the left; despatching them to Second Ridge from Plugge's could therefore be perceived as an attempt to re-connect with the original plan. But in the plans, it was not intended to occupy Second Ridge but to use it as a route of march to the high ground. From Plugge's, the high ground was on the left; to reach it, proceeding to Second Ridge, to the front, was an apparently pointless, time-consuming deviation. The despatch of these companies and the battalion's machine gun section to Second Ridge, thereby diverting them away from their objectives on the left, also suggests concerns about the right.

Bean describes the logic thus: "MacLagan ... had decided that the whole plan of the landing must be changed." Briefings had warned commanders to expect a "heavy counter-attack" from forces inland of Gaba Tepe. "As the 3rd Brigade had been landed a mile too far to the north,

16 Ibid., p. 275.
17 Defence Regional Library, Adelaide (DRL-A), 940.481MYL: M.F. Beevor, 'My Landing at Gallipoli', pp. 11-12.
18 Ibid., p. 12.

there would be no force on the right adequate to meet this counter-attack.[19] Moreover, all chance of carrying out any semblance of the plans of the day had vanished, unless reinforcements were brought in on the right. The obvious solution was that the troops of the 2nd Brigade, now landing, should come in on the south instead of the north and take over the right flank from the 3rd."[20] If the reader is having trouble understanding the logic of this, join the club. The only way this explanation can make sense is if MacLagan believed the counter attack from the right was imminent, and that his brigade, being landed further to the left than planned, would not reach Third Ridge before the enemy; but if this was so, the 2nd Brigade, landing later, would not have made it in time either.[21] Moreover, MacLagan had, according to the *Official History*, already temporarily suspended the advance to Third Ridge.

Bean's explanation is a head-spinner. Some of the destroyer tows carrying the second instalments of the 9th and 10th battalions, the battalions detailed for the right, supported by elements of the 12th Battalion, had landed within the planned area, within striking distance of most of their objectives. From Plugge's Plateau, which was further away, troops had already been sent to the right, including elements of the 11th Battalion, who were supposed to be heading to the left. In other words, before the 2nd Brigade was diverted, there were already more troops heading for the right than intended in the plans. Surely the 3rd Brigade's reserve, the remaining portion of the 12th Battalion, could have been thrown in on the right if it was felt the line needed strengthening? The role of the reserve was to support the other battalions in achieving their objectives – reinforcing where required, filling gaps, taking advantage of opportunities. Did MacLagan believe the wrath of the Ottomans was so imminent, about to sweep away his brigade as they belatedly advanced to Third Ridge, that he needed to rush all available troops to Second Ridge and prepare to defend it? If so, what evidence did he have to believe this? Maclagan has frequently taken the blame for this decision and his actions have been robustly debated and criticised. Chris Roberts, for example, laid the blame firmly at MacLagan's feet and contends that this failure to advance spelled defeat for the ANZAC landing.[22] Yet there is a part of the equation missing from these arguments.

Deterioration of the Plan

Bean's overview reveals, though does not state, that the plans had been altered, or at least their emphasis had been changed, at each level of command until the 3rd Brigade's role became vaguely split into two mutually exclusive parts. This in turn appears to have been due to increasing concerns about a Turkish counter-attack on the right flank.[23] Historian Robin Prior's interpretation of the evolution of these orders was that Birdwood: [C]oncerned about being attacked

19 Bean, *The Story of Anzac*, Vol. I., p. 364.
20 Ibid.
21 Unless MacLagan's concern was Turks moving around his right from the south, but this appears unlikely as the guns of the Royal Navy could have prevented this and the 2nd Brigade was diverted to Second Ridge, not Gaba Tepe.
22 For example, see C.A.M. Roberts, 'The Landing at Anzac: A Reassessment', *Journal of the Australian War Memorial*, No. 22 (April 1993), pp. 25-34.
23 Bean, *The Story of Anzac*, Vol. I, p. 364.

from "both north and south," changed the plan, ordering that Gun (Third) Ridge "be taken as a first priority for the covering force. Only when Gun Ridge was secure should his force turn its attention to the heights of Sari Bair to the north."[24] This interpretation is based on Birdwood's instructions of 18 April, the day after his Operation Order No. 1,[25] in which the preceding paragraph reiterates the importance of the original objectives.[26]

This changed the priority of objectives from left to right. Peter Williams had also previously "noted a deterioration of orders at successive levels of command," interpreting it as "a progression in aim from attack to defence."[27]

The result may well have been confusion about the role of the covering force. Where now lay its primary aim: securing the arrow-head shaped covering position on the high ground on the left, for later exploitation by the remainder of the division, or the ridge from Gabe Tepe to Chunuk Bair, with a focus on defending against a counter-attack on the right? Or both? Unfortunately, it appears the latter. The line, and the magnitude of the task, had been expanded quite dramatically; as Prior put it, Birdwood had "extended the objective by some 1500 yards."[28] Of more concern was the priority: where did it now lie – Battleship Hill and Chunuk Bair on the left of the ridge, or the vicinity of Scrubby Knoll on the right? Attack or defence? In other words, if MacLagan had to fine tune his brigade's actions once ashore, for whatever reason, such as being put ashore further north than expected, on what basis was he to do so?

Specifically, in his "Instructions to G.O.C. 1st Australian Division" on 18 April, Birdwood had stated that "In view of the reported presence of guns" south-east of Gaba Tepe, "and of troops and guns in the Peren Ovassi valley," east of Gaba Tepe, the covering force would occupy the line noted above, namely, Third Ridge. The "rest" of the 1st Division should secure this line, "and the Northern Flank in the direction of Fisherman's Hut ... When this line has been secured, you will be guided by the situation as to whether to make a further advance, or consolidate your position."[29] It appears that Birdwood had thereby authorised, or given the impression he had, diversion of other units – the "rest" of the division – to reinforce the covering position, possibly explaining why MacLagan felt he could act as he did. Certainly the objective for the plan was Third Ridge, but it would seem that, once the mis-placed landing inserted an extra ridge between him and his enemy, MacLagan decided on a different covering position – Second Ridge. Either way, despite 100 years and many hundreds of books on the Gallipoli campaign, we are still scrambling for answers and trying to read between the official historian's lines.

24 R. Prior, *Gallipoli, The End of the Myth* (Sydney: University of New South Wales Press, 2009), pp. 110-111. Based on 'General Birdwood's Instructions to G.O.C. 1st Australian Division', 18/4/15, and C.F. Aspinall-Oglander, *Military Operations Gallipoli, Vol. I Maps and Appendices* (London: Heinemann, 1929), Appendix 15.
25 Birdwood, 'Operation Order No 1', 17 April 1915, *Military Operations Gallipoli, Vol. I Maps and Appendices*, Appendix 14.
26 P.D. Williams, *The Battle of Anzac Ridge, 25 April 1915* (Loftus: Australian Military History Publications, 2007), p. 38 quoted in James Hurst, 'Dissecting a Legend'.
27 Ibid., p. 38.
28 Prior, *Gallipoli, The End of the Myth*, pp. 110-111.
29 Birdwood, 'General Birdwood's Instructions to G.O.C. 1st Australian Division', 18/4/15, Aspinall-Oglander, *Military Operations Gallipoli, Vol. I Maps and Appendices*, Appendix 15.

Writers have recently focused on comments in Bean's notes, and to a lesser degree the *Official History*, that MacLagan was pessimistic about his brigade's role,[30] and even that he was "a naturally pessimistic man."[31] Perhaps these claims are reasonable – Bean noted that both Bridges and Birdwood thought MacLagan pessimistic about the operation, though no evidence is provided for the claim that he was "naturally pessimistic." Perhaps the officer tasked with covering the corps landing was being pragmatic more than pessimistic. In addition to the vague orders and untried nature of his brigade – and the Australian Imperial Force (AIF) as a whole – the changed orders had lengthened MacLagan's front and warned him to expect an attack from the right, yet he had been provided no additional resources to meet the expanded role. His three battalions, the 9th, 10th, 11th and 12th being brigade reserve, were responsible for capturing Gaba Tepe, taking and holding objectives on Third Ridge, capturing the heights on the left, and defending a front of 5000 yards or so. The terrain was extremely difficult and to a certain extent unknown, and, significantly, it was not known how reliable was the intelligence on enemy dispositions. Perhaps, rather than being "pessimistic," MacLagan, who had seen active service in India and the Boer War, keenly felt the responsibility of his role in establishing a covering position to protect the landing, and that his superiors were not being as realistic as they might have been. Perhaps this explains his comment to Bridges before the landing: "if we find the Turks holding those ridges in any strength, I honestly don't think you'll see the 3rd Brigade again."[32] MacLagan later told Bean that he "saw that if he lost only 50% of his men in the attack he would only have 2000 to hold 5000 yards."[33]

Third Ridge is the obvious place to establish a defensive line to thwart an attack from the directions expected: the south east, from Eski Keui; the east, from Peren Ovasi and Koja Dere; and to a lesser extent, the north-east, from Biyuk Anafarta. But the orders also make a priority of defence. This is why understanding the priority of the various objectives in the changed and vague orders becomes significant – what if the covering force commander didn't have sufficient resources to take and hold all the objectives on his map? How then should he prioritise? Was it more important to take the high ground or Third Ridge, or establish a safe covering position? Was the priority the taking of Third Ridge, or defence of the right flank? Third Ridge was the obvious ridge to hold, but the covering force would have been spread very thin.

Landing of the 2nd Brigade

From there the story immediately becomes muddier.

When the 2nd Brigade's commander, Colonel J.W. McCay came ashore, he met MacLagan and Major D.J. Glasfurd, of the 1st Division staff, descending Plugge's Plateau. "I want you to take your whole brigade in on my right," MacLagan said. By one account, MacLagan's wording was along the lines of: "Well McCay, the position is this, I've gone to the left following the

30 Bean, *The Story of Anzac*, Vol. I., p. 222; AWM: AWM38, 3DRL606 item 25.
31 C. Roberts, *The Landing at Anzac: 1915* (Newport: Big Sky Publishing, 2013), p. 95.
32 W.C. Belford, *Legs Eleven: Being the Story of the 11th Battalion (AIF) in the Great War of 1914-1918*, (Perth: Imperial Printing Co., 1940), p. 63.
33 AWM: AWM38, 3DRL 606 item 25.

enemy instead of to the right. If you can change your plans and go to the right, then it will settle the difficulty and things will be all right."[34] For his part, McCay was naturally unimpressed that he was being asked to "disobey orders," and suggested that he should go forward and see the position for himself, but received the response "There isn't time … I assure you my right will be turned if you do not do this." McCay then asked MacLagan if he could also assure "him that the left, where the 2nd Brigade should have been, was secure. MacLagan gave him the assurance, and M'Cay then agreed to throw his whole brigade in on the right."[35]

This is another bewildering exchange. The 2nd Brigade's objective on the left had not even been approached, let alone made "secure." MacLagan had not "gone to the left" chasing Turks – more than two companies, who should have been advancing on the left, had been diverted to Second Ridge.[36] Most of the 9th and 10th battalions were heading more or less in the direction of their objectives as per the original plans, although most would be ordered to stop before they got there.

As noted, Bean's explanation was that, as the 3rd Brigade had landed too far north, there "would be no force on the right" to meet the expected counter-attack, that "all chance of carrying out … the plans … had vanished, unless reinforcements were brought in on the right," and that the "obvious solution was that … the 2nd Brigade … should … take over the right flank from the 3rd."[37] This does not make sense; unless the two brigades swapped roles, and the 3rd Brigade headed to the left and took the high ground in place of the 2nd Brigade. Perhaps it had been decided to send the 1st Brigade to take over the 2nd Brigade's role, though this seems to be a major, disruptive and unwarranted change to the plans; it is unclear why it was believed that "all chance of carrying out" the original plans had "vanished."

Another great question mark over these deliberations is: to what threat did MacLagan think he was responding?

According to Bean's "overview of these decisions … MacLagan intended the 3rd Brigade's advance to continue when the 2nd Brigade arrived. After crossing Shrapnel Gully he saw 2,000-3,000 Turks on Third Ridge and decided that 'the 3rd Brigade should dig in temporarily' on Second Ridge or 400 Plateau."[38] This comes from Bean's notes of interview, which state that MacLagan "saw the enemy thick upon Gun Ridge and decided that the best thing was to dig in where he was until reinforcements came up. He put McCay in on his right. He meant to push on as soon as reinforcements came."[39] With the 2nd Brigade diverted from the high ground, "pushing on" presumably meant to Third Ridge.

As with much of the narrative on the landing, this explanation appears logical and reasonable until examined, at which point the connections between its constituent parts begin to disintegrate. The main Turkish force which Bean describes clashing with the Australians is Mustapha Kemal's *57th Regiment*, who he thought reached the battlefield on the Australians' left, not right, at about 10 a.m. And the quoted passage is preceded by the comment that when

34 Roberts, 'The Landing at Anzac: A Reassessment', pp. 25-34, Major W.H. Cass (Brigade Major, 2nd Brigade) quote. Cass, the brigade-major of the 2nd Brigade.
35 Bean, *The Story of Anzac*, Vol. I., pp. 364-365.
36 Hurst, 'Dissecting a Legend', pp. 114, 123.
37 Bean, *The Story of Anzac*, Vol. I., p. 364.
38 Hurst, 'Dissecting a Legend', p. 221.
39 AWM: AWM38 3DRL 606, item 25, E.G. Sinclair MacLagan, J.H.Peck, A.M. Ross.

Eyewitness artist's impression of the Anzac landing. (*Illustrated London News*, 3 July 1915)

MacLagan "got to the second HQ near top of Owen's Gully and began to get the strings in his hands – really excellent reports were coming in he says."[40] So what was the threat on the right, and what time did it make its presence felt?

Bean's chronology of these events and decisions is clearly all over the place; or at least, it is full of gaps which may or may not be visible to the reader. Bean's chronology of these events and decisions contain gaps which may or may not be discernible to the reader. In summary, the version of the story generally accepted since 1921, and only questioned in recent years, is that it was the presence of 2,000-3,000 Turks on Third Ridge that forced Brand's and MacLagan's hands, yet the Turkish counter attack described in the *Official History* was in a different direction and some hours off.

Herein lies one problem with judging MacLagan too summarily: Bean's chronology – based on information he had compiled from witnesses and reconstructed to the best of his ability – is awry. One of the problems is that quoted times on 25 April are often accepted as fact, but examination reveals them to be notoriously unreliable. One way to test quoted times is to reconstruct the events of that morning from primary sources and create alternative chronologies which often present a different picture to that accepted since publication of the *Official History* in 1921.[41]

40 Ibid.
41 Hurst, 'Dissecting a Legend'.

Threat from the right

A significant difficulty for any battlefield commander is determining what the enemy are doing – where are they and what are their intentions? Were those Turks seen moving through the scrub a small, relatively harmless party, a reconnaissance patrol from a large enemy force, or the spear-point of a major counter-attack? Comparison of the Australian history with 1935's "The Dardanelles: The Ari Burnu Battles and 27th Regiment,"[42] by *27th Regiment*'s commander, Lieutenant-Colonel Şefik, suggests the allied commanders repeatedly assumed the latter, when the reality may have been the former.

27th Regiment roughly equated to an Australian brigade, though it was numerically smaller. This was the regiment responsible for defending the coast around Ari Burnu, and it was their 4th Company, 2nd Battalion, who had been driven back by the 3rd Brigade. The regiment's 1st and 3rd battalions were at that time camped on the opposite side of the peninsula, near Maidos.

Şefik had graduated from the Imperial Military Academy in Constantinople and had seen extensive active service overseas.[43] This morning he had been woken by gunfire from an unfamiliar direction – the western coast, rather than the Straits, suggesting that the long-anticipated landings had begun. Şefik rushed to the telephone, discovered troops were being landed at Ari Burnu and issued orders for his regiment to assemble. The 1st and 3rd battalions, machine gun company and transport were soon ready to move,[44] but had not been given permission to do so: higher command was concerned that the Ari Burnu landing was a feint. The ominous sounds of small arms fire drifted over the intervening farmland, as elements of the regiment's 2nd Battalion fought along the coast. "Sometimes minutes seem like years,"[45] Şefik later wrote.

At 5:45 a.m., about an hour after Şefik had heard the first shots, his regiment "finally" received its movement orders: they were to "halt the enemy landing … between Ari Burnu and Gaba Tepe" and throw them "into the sea."[46] Rather than wait the half hour it would take his allocated mountain battery to join him, Şefik despatched some mounted troops to gather intelligence from the front,[47] and then hurried to the battle area. The spotters of the Royal Navy somehow missed seeing the marching columns, and a great opportunity to destroy the counter-attack before it reached the battlefield.

Şefik then marched northwards along the eastern side of Third Ridge, intending the ridge to shield his columns from allied eyes, and deployed a screen of small pickets along the crest to observe the enemy. Despite these precautions his column was watched by a party of the 9th Battalion under Captain J.M. Dougall from the slopes opposite.[48] The former Cameron Highlander "was greatly impressed" by the "orderly and excellent" deployment and presumed these to be "well-trained and regular troops."[49] Information on the invaders' whereabouts was gained from a wounded member of 4th Company, *2/27th Regiment*, and at Anderson Knoll

42 Private Collection: Şefik Aker, 'The Dardanelles: The Ari Burnu Battles and 27th Regiment' (1935).
43 M. Uyar, *The Ottoman Defence Against the ANZAC Landing, 25 April 1915* (Sydney: Big Sky Publishing, 2015), p. 63.
44 Şefik, 'The Ari Burnu Battles and 27th Regiment', para. 52.
45 Ibid.
46 Ibid., para. 53.
47 Ibid., para. 57.
48 Bean, *The Story of Anzac*, Vol. I., p. 356.
49 Ibid., p. 357.

[Kavak Tepe] Şefik stopped to survey the battlefield. Enemy troops were seen on Baby 700 and 400 Plateau. The veteran soldier counted 26 transports[50] offshore, multiplied this figure by 1,000 to gain a rough estimate of the enemy's possible fighting strength and scanned the scrub ahead to locate their flank. He deduced this to be the southern edge of 400 Plateau and began making plans to attack it.[51]

Şefik later wrote that his strategy was based on theoretical principles, namely of attacking "the enemy before he attacks you" and striking at his flank. Once this had been decided, he began identifying the risks and obstacles. Firstly, Kanlisirt [Lone Pine] was occupied by the enemy and dominated the valley across which his troops would have to advance. A second problem was possible naval gunfire on his left flank. A third was that, as he was outnumbered, an attack on the Australian right flank might provoke an advance by their centre, resulting in the loss of Third Ridge and ultimately, by attack from flank or rear, his regiment.[52] To counter these last two concerns he decided to select a better position from which to attack. He marched his troops further north, and on reaching the southern crest of Scrubby Knoll [Kemal yeri[53] or Hill 165], decided he had found the right spot.[54] From here, by attacking nearer the enemy's centre and on a sufficiently broad front, he could, for a short time at least, prevent the enemy counter attacking and getting around his flanks. In addition, Second Ridge and 400 Plateau would make it more difficult for the Royal Navy to shell his advancing troops. He ordered his battalions to assemble out of sight of the enemy while he and his officers surveyed the ground ahead, looking and listening, gathering information.[55]

"Observation, intelligence" and patrols,[56] confirmed that the Australians' left flank rested on Baby 700 and their right flank on 400 Plateau. Şefik believed the "front line" currently lay to the east of Baby 700 and Legge Valley.[57] He and his officers also tried to determine the enemy's goal, and presumed it to be the capture of the ridge line from Chunuk Bair to Gaba Tepe.[58] Thus shortly after arriving on the battlefield, *27th Regiment*'s command had identified the location and probable objectives of the advanced elements of the covering force and made a rough estimate of the potential size of the landing force. They had chosen the ground that best suited their plans and were now ready to execute their orders: "We set about the task of throwing the enemy into the sea."[59]

As noted above, one possible reason western historians have for many decades misunderstood this battle, is that chronologies have been unreliable. Bean did not have access to *27th Regiment*'s story, and the events described to him by Australians and witnessed by *57th Regiment*'s Zeki Bey, were all that he could contribute. This not only meant that Bean was "flying blind" when trying to interpret the eye-witness testimony – such as sightings of Turkish troops in the direction of

50 Şefik, 'The Ari Burnu Battles and 27th Regiment', para. 62.
51 Ibid., para. 62, 64.
52 Ibid., para. 64.
53 "Kemalyere", "Kemal yere", "Kemal Yere", "Kemalyeri" and possibly other forms of address have been utilised in western sources. "Kemal yeri" will be employed in this chapter unless quoted otherwise
54 Şefik, 'The Ari Burnu Battles and 27th Regiment', para. 65.
55 Ibid.
56 Ibid., para. 70.
57 Ibid.
58 Ibid.
59 Ibid., para. 71.

Third Ridge – but that *27th Regiment*'s story is all but invisible in the Australian *Official History*. Even today many sources still show Kemal's *57th Regiment* halting the Australian advance,[60] the version of the story that has been unquestioned for nearly a century.

Şefik thought he reached Hill 165 at "0740 hours."[61] By 7:55 a.m. he had sent to Divisional HQ a report on his decision to attack,[62] and soon "after 0800 hours" the tail of his column arrived and were "given 15 minutes rest."[63] These times precede those in secondary western sources by one to two hours.[64] Which times are more reliable? Extensive examination and cross-referencing reveal correlations between much of Şefik's chronology and Australian primary sources,[65] and allow his account to be "anchored" to other significant battlefield events. Linking the Ottoman and Australian primary source chronologies in this way reveals an unseen side of the battle.

Şefik contacted the commander of GOC *9th Division* via telephone to report that he thought it essential he engage the enemy on a wide front. He knew he was outnumbered and requested that *19th Division* "be sent quickly to" attack the enemy's left flank, while he attacked their right and centre.[66] In other words, Şefik intended to attack the enemy to stop their advance and knock them off balance, but knew more troops were required to halt such a large force. He later discovered Lieutenant-Colonel Mustafa Kemal and his *57th Regiment* had left camp and begun their march to Sari Bair ten minutes before he had telephoned his report.[67]

Şefik then explained the details of the attack to his officers, exhorting them "to rush headlong at the enemy on a broad front, throw him into confusion, and hurl him back";[68] and to avoid "heavy losses due to carelessness, insecure actions or lack of liaison."[69] The machine gun company, under Şefik's "orders and supervision" was to cover the attack, as was the artillery battery, when it arrived. Arrangements were made for positioning the first aid post and dumping ammunition, thus freeing the transport to bring more.[70]

"The Ari Burnu Battles and 27th Regiment" was written twenty years after the event, with all the benefits of hindsight and the opportunity to write the history as the author chose. I have not subjected this account to the strenuous examination I have inflicted on Bean's work. For example, Şefik describes his men as being the type "who cannot bear to be defeated by their enemies, are not afraid of the harshness and cruelty of war, are loyal to the national character and to their beloved country and are bold, zealous and sincerely devoted to their duties."[71] He also commented on the "zealous defiance" of the company that defended the coast, which probably

60 For example, L. Carlyon, *Gallipoli*, (Sydney: Pan MacMillan, 2001); *Gallipoli* (Endemol: Nine Network, 2014).
61 Şefik, 'The Ari Burnu Battles and 27th Regiment', para. 66.
62 Ibid., para. 68.
63 Ibid.
64 C.F. Aspinall-Oglander, *Military Operations Gallipoli*, Vol. I (London: Heinemann, 1929), p. 185.
65 Hurst, 'Dissecting a Legend', p. 149, among others.
66 Şefik, 'The Ari Burnu Battles and 27th Regiment', para. 71.
67 Ibid., para. 72
68 Ibid., para. 74.
69 Ibid.
70 Ibid.
71 Ibid., para. 49.

"confused the aggressors so they hesitated to advance quickly to carry out their main task."[72] In contrast to the high morale and standard of military efficiency described by Şefik, three of his men who "surrendered willingly" on 25 April, stated that: "They were called up 3 months ago … They are tired of war having been fed only twice daily on wheat porridge and beans. They have had no pay. They were unarmed as telephonists. The telephone has broken down …"[73] It is wise to remember that all was not as rosy as Şefik portrayed. Despite this, his account, when approached with caution and corroborated against other sources whenever possible, provides an invaluable contribution to the history.

These reservations aside, Şefik's account presents an image of a trained and disciplined regiment deploying for battle. Moreover, Şefik is not suggesting his response to the enemy was inspired by his talents or genius, but by application of theoretical principles, in other words, tactical or strategic training and thinking: he gathered as much information as he could on the enemy's strength, location and probable goals, then planned how he would carry out his orders and accomplish his goal. The image presented is of sound military principles being implemented by a leader with faith in his decisions, officers and men.

Comparison of Şefik's and western sources and triangulation of detail, reveals gaps, omissions and assumptions in western histories. Certainly, at some point the Australians did see 2000 Turks lining Third Ridge; but when MacLagan and Brand made their decisions to stall the advance to Third Ridge, between 4:45 a.m. and 6:30 a.m., the Turks were not there. Or, more correctly, the Turkish main body and counter-attack were not there.

Sometime before 6:00 a.m., according to Şefik, the commander of the Turkish 2nd Battalion, *27th Regiment*, who was at Gaba Tepe, sent a platoon "north east to make contact with the embattled 4th Company. This platoon, under Second Lieutenant Mustafa," continued on to Artillery Range [Third Ridge] and ended up fighting "north of Kemalyeri" [Scrubby Knoll].[74]

The chronology established in my 2013 doctoral thesis[75] makes it clear that the decision to halt and dig on Second Ridge and 400 Plateau could not have been forced by the appearance of *27th Regiment* "thick upon Gun Ridge,"[76] as the regiment had not yet reached the field. If Turks were visible on Third Ridge when these early decisions were made, they were probably small parties from the coastal garrison or "small formed bodies" moving "through the area."[77]

In other words, the 3rd Brigade's advance may not have been stopped "by 2,000 soldiers of … 27th Regiment … but by the sight of some other body of Turks", perhaps the single platoon from Gaba Tepe under Mustafa mentioned in the previous paragraph, "who happened to be marching through the area." The fighting withdrawal of the small Turkish outposts and movements of small bodies through the area may have so effectively "masked the true situation from the Australian commanders,"[78] that the latter misinterpreted a platoon moving across their

72 Ibid., para. 46.
73 AWM: AWM4 1/42/3 Part 2: Report, 'Prisoners of war taken near Kaba Tepe, Sunday, 25.4.15', 1st Division War Diary.
74 Şefik, 'The Ari Burnu Battles and 27th Regiment', para. 44.
75 Hurst, 'Dissecting a Legend'.
76 AWM: AWM38, 3DRL 606 Item 25: E.G. Sinclair MacLagan, J.H.Peck, A.M. Ross.
77 Hurst, 'Dissecting a Legend', p. 225.
78 Ibid., p. 225.

front as the Turkish counter-attack. The advance of the 1st Australian Division may have been stopped by the sight of an Ottoman platoon.

One of the aims of the preceding arguments and examination of detail is to gain an insight into the decision-making of the opposing commanders on that morning of battle, more than a century ago. Despite the fact that we have to make informed guesses about much of the thinking of the Australian commanders, and accept that Şefik's account was written with hindsight, it appears that the latter gathered information about the enemy, the ground and any other factors that could affect the battle, then planned his strategy. In other words, he conducted a form of "tactical appreciation" to assess the enemy's strength and goals and used this information to devise a plan to carry out his orders.

By contrast, the Australian commanders appear to have subjugated their offensive role and objectives to those of the enemy, probably before the enemy even reached the field. A deterioration in the clarity of the planning appears to have been followed by a deterioration of resolve. The Australian commanders' decisions appear to have been motivated less by a studied evaluation of the enemy and his movements, than by what they imagined the enemy to be doing.

One factor overlooked by historians, but which may have had a major impact on MacLagan's decision making, is the fragmentation of his force. A detailed study of one of the covering force battalions reveals its disorganisation to have been far greater than previously realised. This may have eroded the 3rd Brigade's fighting strength and MacLagan's confidence in his ability to control it. This degree of fragmentation has not been visible to western writers, and indeed, for the brigade, has not yet been determined. For example, Bean tells us the 11th Battalion's B Company was despatched to Second Ridge. In fact, neither the company second-in-command nor any of the platoon commanders was with the company. If the platoons were with their officers, the B Company OC would have been on Second Ridge alone; in fact, he must have had some of his men with him, but if so, they were not with their officers. Such facts should drastically change the way we view the battle: books and other accounts that claim that so many companies or so many men went to a certain point, unintentionally misrepresent the true situation. Sending a company commander with no officers and an undisclosed number of men to Second Ridge, is far different to sending over two hundred men under command of their officers. The brigade reserve, distributed over seven destroyers, was also spread over the length of the covering force's front.

Fighting on the right

The 2nd Brigade, consisting of the 5th, 6th, 7th and 8th battalions, began landing after the 3rd Brigade. Their objectives were on the high ground of the main range on the left of the landing. The first troops of the 2nd Brigade to be diverted to the right were of the 7th Battalion. Such was the perceived urgency that they were despatched before their brigade commander, McCay, had even made it ashore. The first of the brigade's senior officers to land, the 7th Battalion's Lieutenant-Colonel H.E. "Pompey" Elliott, was told by MacLagan that "the original plan could not be carried out, the 3rd Brigade having been landed a mile too far to the north."[79]

79 Bean, *The Story of Anzac*, Vol. I., p. 363. Elsewhere it is stated that Elliott was under the impression that some of the original plan was still to be carried out, and presumed his battalion would be leading the brigade's advance to Hill 971.

McCay landed soon after, spoke to MacLagan, and then ordered Elliott to fill a gap in the line, between the 9th and 10th battalions, on 400 Plateau.[80] One 10th Battalion NCO, Corporal George Mitchell, had landed with the first wave of the covering force. On reaching the plateau he asked Major Beevor the whereabouts of his company and received the reply "Some of them are ahead there, but you must stay here. We're entrenching."[81] It will be noted that the order given to Elliott appears to contradict Bean's earlier comments that MacLagan intended to push on once reinforcements arrived – filling a gap in the 3rd Brigade's line, which was digging in, suggests neither party was intending to advance.

Troops continued to be despatched to 400 Plateau as they arrived, at least in the short term, on shore. Most had vague orders to "reinforce a 'firing line' which was" generally "understood to exist ahead." "In some cases," wrote Bean, "whole companies found themselves pushed forward in this manner without any instructions whatever..." Thus did company after company of the 2nd Brigade advance, with great urgency, "into the fight, mostly with no definite order except to reinforce the 3rd."[82] This piecemeal despatching of troops onto 400 Plateau without any clear idea of what they were to do, nor even whether they or the force was to advance or defend, would continue throughout the morning.

When Major-General Bridges came ashore, at about 7:30 a.m.,[83] roughly three hours after the first troops had landed, he moved inland with Lieutenant-Colonel C.B.B. White. He somehow missed McCay and his HQ and saw 8th Battalion men "stationary" on Bolton's Ridge. White felt "that the precious hour in which an advance might still be made was being allowed to slip." Bean continues that "there seemed nothing to prevent an advance on the right," but "Bridges doubted whether all was going well with the left."[84] This is another of those comments that jars the logic – firstly, there was as yet no Turkish counter-attack on the left, and the troops due to head that way had been diverted right, on the basis that that was where the real threat lay. The 2nd Brigade had been diverted under great pressure to oppose an attack on the right, yet there was so little activity on the right that not only was there no attack to defend against, but it seemed even an advance was possible. Moreover, the Australian advance was supposedly stopped because of the Turkish counter-attack between 6:00 and 7:00 a.m.,[85] yet when Bridges went inland some time later, there was little happening. Aware that he did not understand the "whole situation," Bridges ordered the line on Bolton's to "hold fast" until he had visited Johnston's Jolly and walked along Second Ridge.[86] This again presents a confused picture. For what reason did Bridges agree to the halting of his covering force, who had landed hours earlier and should have been on Third Ridge, and of his 2nd Brigade, who should have been advancing towards the high ground on the left?

80 Ibid., p. 372.
81 AWM: 2DRL928: Mitchell papers, G.D. Mitchell.
82 Bean, *The Story of Anzac*, Vol. I., p. 369.
83 AWM: AWM4 1/42/3 Part 2: 1st Division War Diary, April 1915, Part 2, report by 'Headquarters, 1st Australian Division', 7 May 1915, p. 3.
84 Bean, *The Story of Anzac*, Vol. I., pp. 366-367.
85 AWM: AWM4 1/42/3 Part 2: 1st Division War Diary, April 1915, Part 2, report by 'Headquarters, 1st Australian Division', 7 May 1915, p. 3.
86 Bean, *The Story of Anzac*, Vol. I., p. 367.

As the Battalion's commanding officer, Lieutenant-Colonel McNicoll,[87] made his way from the beach, he passed MacLagan, who asked him "to extend the right flank of the 3rd Brigade." When the 5th Battalion splashed ashore they were confronted by "the tall form of General Bridges … running down the hill above. He was returning, flushed with haste, from his reconnaissance of the right … and, waving his cane, called to Colonel Wanliss: 'Wanliss, I want you to get your men together and reinforce the firing line with all available tools'," implying defence, "and ammunition. Don't wait for the rest of your battalion to get into formation – but push on."[88] Soon after, as they moved inland to do battle, some of the officers "realised with a shock that, except for the vague directions" Bridges had given Wanliss, "they had no instructions at all."[89]

Reading between Bean's lines, it appears that Bridges was not basing his decision to "hold fast" on what he had seen, namely, unopposed troops stationary on Bolton's Ridge wasting an opportunity to advance, but what he hadn't – what might have been happening elsewhere. This would appear to be confirmed by Bridges' biographer, Chris Coulthard-Clark, who wrote that Bridges was searching for McCay, to "find out how the anticipated opposition from the southern flank was being dealt with … he was alarmed that the troops holding" Bolton's Ridge "were not pressing on to the next objective," as all seemed relatively quiet. "He was satisfied however that the ridge provided the 2nd Brigade with a firm anchor for the right flank, and he therefore ordered the troops then stationary on the ridge to remain where they were."[90]

Bridges then attempted to attend to the left flank. The enemy fire sweeping down Shrapnel Gully had given him concerns that "there were Turks in the rear of MacLagan's troops on the left." He climbed Ari Burnu, as scaling "the steep ridge overlooking the beach" was "too difficult," and convinced himself that this was not the case. Bridges "could not spare any more time for reconnoitring. He had gained an overall impression of how matters stood," apparently from his visits to McCay's Hill and Ari Burnu, "and he knew the most savage fighting was taking place on the left." The hill on that flank, Baby 700, "was clearly the key to the left flank, and in fact to the whole bridgehead."[91] Once again, such passages, although providing possibly the only information the author could offer, give rise to more questions than answers. If the divisional commander realised the crisis would be on the left, why had the brigade assigned to capture the left been sent right?

Baby 700 would prove to be key, bitterly contested ground; but by secondary source accounts, the "savage fighting" there was still some hours away. Or, to put it another way, secondary sources have Kemal's counter-attack arriving on the high ground on the left some time around or after 10 a.m.; but the Australian commanders were reacting to perceived Turkish pressure there several hours beforehand, at the same time as they were fussing about the right.

87 W.R. McNicoll, 37, headmaster, of Geelong, born South Melbourne. McNicoll had sailed from Australia with the 7th Battalion, but the 6th Battalion's CO, Lieutenant-Colonel J.M. Semmens, had been returned to Australia from Egypt due to illness.

88 Bean, *The Story of Anzac*, Vol. I., pp. 381-382.

89 Ibid., p. 383.

90 C.D. Coulthard-Clark, *A Heritage of Spirit: A Biography of Major-General Sir William Throsby Bridges K.CB., C.M.G.* (Melbourne: Melbourne University Press, 1979), p. 154. Perhaps *27th Regiment* had by then been seen, but this seems unlikely as they are not mentioned, resistance is described as "anticipated" and the situation as "quiet".

91 Ibid., pp. 155-156.

Bridges then situated his HQ in a gully near the beach. As phone communications had been established, i.e. with MacLagan and McCay. [92] Bridges stayed by the phone. Divisional Headquarters took over control of the operation.[93]

Such narratives as these, probably accurate reflections of what happened, defy understanding. This is partly because of incorrect chronologies, with events from different times being thrown up as justifications for decisions made earlier. At the times significant decisions were made, perceptions of hard fighting or threats on either right or left could not have been correct. According to Bean, when Bridges was making decisions about the threat from the left, Kemal's regiment had not yet arrived, and Captain E.W. Tulloch was advancing against little opposition towards Battleship Hill; he would not be pushed back to Baby 700 for some hours. McCay was senior to MacLagan yet was acting on the latter's instruction. Bridges was superior to both, but also went along with MacLagan's decision making.

According to a range of secondary sources, MacLagan's intention was to push on once Second Ridge was consolidated, but despite being sent the 2nd Brigade, he did not do so. Bean tells us that MacLagan's aim was to push reinforcements forward and strike for Third Ridge once the nearer ridge had been consolidated. If so, would it not have been preferable for this advance to have been made by an organised and intact force from behind the ridgelines, then to send the troops forward into the open in dribs and drabs, with poor or non-existent orders? By rushing their troops piecemeal to 400 Plateau and elsewhere, the Australian commanders were dismantling their battalions as fighting units; they were disorganising their own force. Such hasty and inadequate orders and actions appear less conducive to establishing command and control than creating chaos and confusion.

Colonel (later Brigadier-General) E.G. Sinclair-MacLagan.

One of the disappointing aspects of this stage of the battle is that diversion of more of the 3rd Brigade to the right than planned, then following them with the first of the 2nd Brigade battalions, and leaving troops on Bolton's to anchor the right, did not relieve the anxieties of the commanders about that flank: rather than accepting that the right was now secure and focussing on the remainder of the battle, more and more troops were deployed to the centre and right. Perhaps keeping cooler heads and their units intact would have removed or alleviated commanders' concerns: if intact units had been sent forward under leaders with specific goals and objectives, the brigadiers and others would surely have had more confidence about the security of that flank and been able to turn their focus elsewhere. Blindly thrusting fragments of units into the scrub seemed to provide them no such assurance. Bridges, meanwhile, remained

92 Bean, *The Story of Anzac*, Vol. I., p. 367.
93 AWM: AWM4 1/42/3 Part 2: 1st Division Unit War Diary, April 1915, report, p. 3.

at his HQ near the beach, "apportioning out the reinforcements" as requests came in from the firing line.[94]

By about 9:00 a.m., ten of the sixteen companies of the reserve brigade, MacLaurin's 1st Brigade, consisting of the 1st, 2nd, 3rd and 4th battalions "had been committed to MacLagan," many of them being sent to defend Second Ridge. The remaining six companies had not yet landed.[95] Bean continues that all "the infantry of the division which had been landed had been absorbed into the battle," mostly to defend against an attack coming from the south east, yet "the inevitable counter-attack had hardly yet begun."[96] The 1st Division War Diary recorded at 9 a.m. that there were no enemy visible on Bolton's Ridge or between it and Gaba Tepe.[97]

A reserve may be viewed as the means by which a commander retains the initiative in battle. Premature depletion of one's reserve may lead to loss of the initiative and the ability to influence the course of the battle. A leader in battle should therefore be in a position to decide when and where to commit his reserves. Yet in this case, 1st Division command, in response to requests from the front, appears to have chosen – or agreed – to deplete his reserves as they came ashore; he was concerned about the left, but allowing his reserve to be sent right. The force had not yet attempted to reach its objectives but was already frittering away its reserve.

The 1st Division's after-action report does nothing to allay concerns about the command's grasp of the battle that morning. He lists the times various units came ashore, and to where they were despatched and described a Turkish attack between 6:00 and 7:00 a.m., which drove in the advanced parties of the 3rd Brigade but was "repulsed" between 7:00 and 8:15 a.m.[98] At or soon after 9:00 a.m. the 3rd Brigade "was being heavily shelled and was gradually giving way" from the forward slope of 400 Plateau;[99] at "10:35 a.m. the 3rd Infantry Brigade reported" that a hill, in the area of Russell's Top, "was seriously threatened and asked for support." Between "11:00 a.m. and 3:00 p.m. the left of the 2nd Infantry Brigade and the whole front of the 3rd Infantry Brigade was steadily attacked,"[100] and between "3:00 and 4:00 p.m. the enemy made a second counter-attack against the 3rd Infantry Brigade and left of the 2nd Infantry Brigade. This counter-attack was repulsed with the assistance of gun fire from His Majesty's Ships and the 26th Mountain Battery."[101] "Between 5:00 and 6:30 p.m. the enemy made a third and determined counter-attack" against 3rd Brigade. "No ground was lost by us on any part of our line."[102] His report gives the impression of a headquarters reacting to, rather than controlling, the battle, nor does its author appear to have grasped the key elements of the struggle. For

94 Coulthard-Clark, *A Heritage of Spirit*, p. 156.
95 The brigade had commenced landing before the last of the 2nd Brigade were ashore. The 1st Battalion was sent to 400 Plateau. Bean, *The Story of Anzac* Vol. I., p. 386. The 1st Division War Diary, stated that these two "Brigades had disembarked by 12:50 p.m. See AWM: AWM4 1/42/3 Part 1: 1st Division War Diary, April 1915.
96 Coulthard-Clark, *A Heritage of Spirit*, p. 156.
97 AWM4 1/42/3 Part 1: 1st Division War Diary, April 1915.
98 Ibid., pp. 3-4.
99 The map reference also covers the ridge to the plateau's north, though whether this is intentional or not is unclear.
100 AWM4 1/42/3 Part 2: 1st Division War Diary, April 1915, report by 'Headquarters, 1st Australian Division', 7 May 1915, pp. 4, 5.
101 Ibid., p. 5.
102 Ibid.

example, he seems oblivious of the loss of Baby 700 in the late afternoon, which crowned *57th Regiment*'s main counter attack and pushed the Australians and New Zealanders from the high ground, which they would not reoccupy during the campaign.

From the little information left to us, it is easy to gain the impression that, by despatching reinforcements in packets to the firing lines, 1st Division Headquarters was allowing the brigadiers at the front to control the course of the battle and was itself performing more of a support role. We are left to wonder how allocation of the reinforcements was prioritised: to what plan was headquarters working, or was it simply a matter of rationing the resources as they became available, to meet the requests of subordinate officers on the ridges?

One documented influence on Bridges was the sight of "parties of wounded limping back down to the beach, and the groups of soldiers who had been separated from their units and had returned to the beach because they did not know where else to go. He knew too that the brigades involved in the fighting in the ranges beyond the beach had virtually disintegrated."[103] The disintegration of the 1st and 2nd Brigades had in fact begun soon after they landed, as they were sent forward in fragments under orders of their Australian commanders.

The front lines

The troops despatched to 400 Plateau pressed on to a crest swept by shrapnel, rifle and machine gun fire, tearing through the dense scrub, killing and wounding troops advancing or prone, and littering the plateau with dead and wounded. At least, this is the picture throughout the day. The difficult part is working out when this heavy enemy fire began; it could not have been before the first troops of the 3rd Brigade reached the plateau and began to dig.

One 3rd Brigade officer who lived to tell the tale was the 9th Battalion's Major A. G. Salisbury. The first order he received after reaching 400 Plateau[104] was from MacLagan, telling him "to dig in" on the plateau; the second was to advance "to meet an imminent counterattack;" and the third was that "the advanced parties should be withdrawn, and the line again established on the 400 Plateau. But the third order largely failed because there was now no organised line to carry it out."[105]

Meanwhile, other parties had pushed further forward. 9th Battalion's Lieutenants A.J. Boase and G. Thomas had been ordered to cover Salisbury's line as it dug in and had reached the inland slope of Lone Pine. "Presently," wrote Bean, "Turkish reinforcements from the southern end" of Third Ridge "began to pass along the skyline" of Third Ridge, "first a line of pack mules, then a battalion of men." The "Australians sniped at them, but the range was long, and it was impossible to see the flick of the bullets in the scrub. Messages were sent back ... informing the main body of this movement."[106] These Turks were the two battalions of *27th Regiment*'s counter-attack; the resistance up to this time had been light and from but a few scattered parties. This surely represents a missed opportunity – the covering force had been ashore for over three hours, most or all of the 2nd Brigade was ashore, yet the enemy were being allowed to simply

103 Coulthard-Clark, *A Heritage of Spirit*, p. 155.
104 Bean, *The Story of Anzac*, Vol. I., p. 352.
105 Ibid., pp. 370-371.
106 Ibid., p. 376.

march in column onto the Australians' objectives and deploy. Each Australian battalion had 1000 rifles and two medium machine guns, and the force was backed by the guns of the Royal Navy, yet an enemy regiment was marching in full view – Boase and Thomas were not the only ones to have seen the movement – molested only by a little long-range sniping. The news should also have been of great value to the Australian commanders – they finally had definite information on the location and strength of the enemy counter attack; unfortunately, by that time, they had been deploying to meet the counter attack for hours. Shortly thereafter, Turkish fire began to fall on 400 Plateau. Later, their advance on Thomas and Boase's flanks forced the Australians to withdraw.[107]

As "section after section of Salisbury's companies" advanced over the 400 Plateau, they were fired upon by "many hundreds of ... rifles and several machine-guns ... But it was seldom that so much as a single Turkish infantryman could be seen ... the enemy simply lay in the scrub" and shot down the advancing Australians. In general, the Turks seemed far better at using cover and concealment on 25 April than the Australians, with many Australians complaining they could not see the Turks at all, other than in small parties moving in the distance. The "density of the scrub and the whirlwind of fire" tore "to shreds any organisation which such an advance ... permitted."[108] Once again this raises questions of lost opportunities – there had been many hours for an advance before the fire began sweeping the plateau. This also reflects one of the problems with the chronology in secondary sources: descriptions of enemy fire obliterating Australian efforts on the plateau are unwittingly linked to events earlier in the day. Salisbury, for example, was told to dig on 400 Plateau and when he subsequently tried to get forward, he was confronted by heavy fire. These events must have stretched over some hours, but merge together in the *Official History* and other sources. This repeated "blurring" of chronology and merging of events has drawn a veil over parts of the battle for 100 years; many decisions by the allied commanders were made long before the "whirlwind" of fire reached 400 Plateau.

Due to confusion about whether they should be advancing or digging, some parties advanced and others dug. The heavy fire that soon swept[109] the plateau meant that messengers were frequently hit and their messages not delivered, and the tall, dense scrub made it difficult to locate intended recipients or to use hand or flag signals. Parties of troops consequently acted in accordance with whichever version of the orders made it through to them. In the firing lines themselves, "no organisation or even communication along the line was possible."[110]

9th Battalion's Lieutenant C. Fortescue, had been ordered to hold a particular spot while Salisbury dug in, and selected a gully to avoid a line of fire that was hitting his men. Soon after, a "captain of the 8th Battalion", with orders "to reinforce the firing line," "sharply" asked "Fortescue what he was doing there. Fortescue's explanation ... did not satisfy him. The officer had seen no line of any sort. He told Fortescue to get on with his men into the firing line."[111] Fortescue appears to have been doing the intelligent thing – selecting a position from which he could fulfil his orders while providing cover for his troops. The anonymous officer appears to have been acting on vague orders and ignorance of the situation, and accordingly sent more of

107 Ibid., p. 377.
108 Ibid., p. 374.
109 Ibid.
110 Ibid., p. 378.
111 Ibid., pp. 378- 379.

Fortescue's men to their deaths. Perhaps a line existed somewhere in the scrub ahead, perhaps it had already been destroyed. Either way, many officers this day appear to have been imbued with little more notion than to push men blindly into the scrub and to form firing lines. The intended role of such firing lines is unclear. Before long Fortescue's party was reduced to seven men.

A comment by Bean gives some insight into the reason for this thinking. Salisbury continued to take "forward men of the 2nd Brigade," despite enemy fire "almost beyond endurance" and most of his officers becoming casualties. He was convinced "that the wisest course would be to withdraw" the line "into the shelter of the reverse slope. But the doctrine of the day was that a line should be in advance of the crest, and Colonel McNicoll of 6th Battalion ... was anxious to get his men forward. Salisbury led" out "several parties. His own men had mostly fallen."[112] Ensuring a good field of fire by occupying a forward slope might make good sense, but dead men could not provide effective fire. Perhaps the reason some officers persisted in pushing men into firing lines and using human flesh to fill gaps and occupy ground, was because it was what those officers knew how to do, and what the troops had been trained to do. It may not have been what the situation required.

Another problem for the advanced troops was lack of support, as the men behind, ordered to defend rather than advance, did not come up. This was compounded by friendly fire from the rear. Lieutenant R.C.G. Prisk's party, 6th Battalion, were forward on Pine Ridge, expecting to support the advance on Third Ridge. They were soon fired on by Australians on the ridges behind, but messages sent back stating that there were Australians in front did not stop the fire. Bean advises that "officers and men had been lectured upon 'ruses' employed by the Germans in France, and they were very slow to believe anyone who, coming from the enemy's direction, shouted that he was an Australian. The fire upon Prisk's party ... continued."[113] It therefore appears that the troops had been warned before battle of the enemy "ruse," but had not been provided with a means of dealing with it, by, for example, authenticating the message. The unlikely threat of an enemy ruse had therefore been allowed to derail battlefield communications and negate the training of officers and men, who had been taught to pass back messages and advise those behind of the progress of the battle. This must have played havoc with the flow of information to commanders. Unless a solution to the problem had been provided with the pre-battle warning, being forewarned did not equate to being forearmed. An enemy intelligence operative could not have hoped to achieve such a breakdown of communications had they actually used such a ruse. Prisk's situation was not unique.

Bean informs us that "In the early part of the morning ... it was uncertain whether the troops seen on Pine Ridge were Australian or Turkish; and ... Bridges and M'Cay, anxious to make certain of the southern flank, had ordered whatever troops were then on Bolton's Ridge to dig in."[114] This raises the alarming possibility that some of the concerns about defence of the right flank may have been motivated, or reinforced, by the sight of Australian troops ahead – in other words, some of the men digging in on Bolton's may have been doing so to defend against, rather than advance to support, their comrades.

In Prisk's case, "friendly fire" and lack of support had another consequence. From his position on the right flank he watched the commencement of the Turkish attack against Second Ridge

112 Ibid., p. 381.
113 Ibid., pp. 410-411.
114 Ibid., p. 413.

to his left. Being a Duntroon graduate he immediately considered the advantages and possibilities of launching an attack into the flank of the advancing Turks – exactly as was the Turkish commander's concern. But defence was his superiors' greater concern, and opportunities like Prisk's were not supported. Without the numbers to launch an attack, and with his own side shooting at him from behind, a counter-attack by Prisk's party was out of the question. There appears to be no record of Prisk's superiors, the battalion, brigade and divisional commanders, considering such a move – could not the battalions or companies diverted to the right be used to outflank the enemy's counter-attack, particularly as the navy was more likely to be able to support that flank? Perhaps the thorn in the Australian commanders' side – the Turkish observers at Gaba Tepe and the Turkish artillery – prevented this, but we have no record of any such out-flanking being considered. Turkish artillery was very weak at this early stage of the landing, but its influence in the minds of the Australian commanders appears great. One way of reducing the impact of enemy artillery would have been to close with their infantry, but the force had probably already been too fragmented for such an advance. Once again, it appears that while Şefik made efforts to establish what was actually going on, the Australian commanders may have been reacting to "what might have been" happening.

When Prisk later returned to his own lines, he was ordered to dig in on a clear patch, soon to be known as the Wheatfield, on the forward slope of Bolton's Ridge. Training, experience or common sense might have suggested that a clear patch of land on a forward slope within sight of the enemy was exactly the place to be avoided, and so it proved: Prisk's men immediately came under fire from a Turkish battery. The Wheatfield "made an easy mark" to Turkish artillery observers on Third Ridge, and "salvo after salvo burst about" the Australians. The clearing also highlighted any troop movement on or across it, which throughout the day attracted shell fire.[115] Veterans would probably have known to avoid such a spot. Earlier, on Russell's Top, the 12th Battalion's Lieutenant-Colonel Lancelot Clarke, his batman and Major C. H. Elliott[116] had fallen in rapid succession to Turkish rifle fire. A South African war veteran, Private L.E. Moggridge, observed that the well-worn track was an obvious target for a rifleman and warned everyone to stay clear of it.[117]

Prisk's experience highlights yet another problem. The Turkish battery shelling the Wheatfield was visible to Australians on the inland slope of Lone Pine. Lieutenant S. Grills, 7th Battalion, "could clearly discern two guns … and the burst of every shell on the Wheatfield."[118] Grills sent back reports at 11 a.m., noon, and 1 p.m., hoping each time to see the battery disappear in the smoke and debris of bursting naval shells, but "no British shell came that way." Major G.A. Bennett, 6th Battalion, also reported these guns, but as one of the map references distorted in transit, no counter-battery fire resulted, and the guns continued to fire.[119] There is no evidence in battalion, brigade or divisional unit diaries of signallers formally practising ship to shore communications before the landings. A wireless station was at some point established on the

115 Ibid., p. 414.
116 C.H. Elliott, 30, cashier, of Hobart.
117 L.M. Newton, *The Story of the Twelfth: A Record of the 12th Battalion, A.I.F. during the Great War of 1914-1918* (Hobart: J. Walch & Sons, 1925), p. 68.
118 Bean, *The Story of Anzac*, Vol. I., p. 414.
119 Ibid.

beach, but, Bean continues, "Communication with the ships was slow ... messages were eventually transmitted almost entirely by hand signalling."[120]

Grills eventually pulled his men back across the fire swept Lone Pine to deliver the message himself. He discovered remnants of firing lines, that the 7th battalion appeared to no longer exist, and later stumbled upon some signallers. His message was finally sent, but it took several more hours for anything to happen. The battery was not shelled until about 5 p.m., when it was almost immediately silenced.[121]

Inexperience had other consequences. Bean describes the Turkish battery "ploughing the Wheatfield, and to a lesser degree the rest of Bolton's Ridge,"[122] and to Grills it appeared that these guns were "working havoc upon troops" there.[123] But as it transpired, the shells "were not so deadly as they appeared. The Turks were bursting them too low, and the majority plunged into the soft soil of the field," doing but "small damage. In an hour only two of the party were hit."[124] Thus an impression of artillery-induced havoc was not supported by the reality of the situation; the artillery was, at least in this case, far less effective than perceived.

The experience of the 5th Battalion's Lieutenant A.P. Derham is but one of many similar accounts of local commanders attempting to make sense of the battle, of intelligently responding to the best of their abilities, but being outranked. After being told by Bridges to head inland with whatever troops were available, Major E.F.D. Fethers,[125] Captain R.P. Flockart[126] and Derham "pushed on."[127] Near the top they stopped while Fethers sent scouts to find the colonel and the firing line; beyond that, except for the "vague directions" Bridges had given Wanliss, "they had no specific instructions."[128] Derham realised the folly of advancing blindly into the scrub and enemy fire, halted his men below the crest, resisted impatient instructions from behind to push on, and conducted a reconnaissance.[129] A battle was apparently in progress, but he could see nothing of it. His company commander, Major R. Saker, ordered an advance. The men were "in column of fours," and Saker "gave the signal to extend. The men strung out into a long line in the scrub," and "began to advance ... Then the storm burst." For a few moments this parade ground deployment must have been the most dramatic spectacle on the battlefield, and the Turkish gunners didn't waste the opportunity.[130]

The survivors continued the advance by short rushes. By the time they reached the forward edge of the "Daisy Patch," a small, relatively clear open space, very few remained. There "were no orders and no firing line."[131] Derham could not even find the enemy, until, through his glasses, he eventually saw the "enemy's guns" just south of Scrubby Knoll. More sinister was the sight of Turkish infantry advancing towards him "in rough skirmishing formation." The Australians opened fire, the Turks broke into a run. Derham's party stood their ground, but

120 Ibid., pp. 392-393. Perhaps this also explains why Bennett's co-ordinates were distorted in transit.
121 Ibid., p. 415.
122 Ibid.
123 Ibid., p. 414.
124 Ibid., p. 416.
125 E.F.D. Fethers, 27 at embarkation, Church of England, bank accountant, of Malvern, Victoria.
126 R.P. Flockart, 27 at embarkation, Methodist, clerk, of West Brunswick, Victoria.
127 Bean, *The Story of Anzac*, Vol. I., pp. 381-382.
128 Ibid., p. 383.
129 Ibid., p. 384.
130 Ibid., p. 385.
131 Ibid.

one by one, were hit. Attempts at contacting his superiors failed, and despite being wounded, Derham eventually found "twenty men of his own company,"[132] who he led forward into the dense scrub of Lone Pine. They finally found the remains of a firing line – "All that remained", wrote Bean, of a previous advance, still holding out in the scrub. Among the "scattered debris" were a few unwounded men alongside wounded, dead and dying.[133]

One cannot help but wonder – to what end were young officers like Derham taking men forward into what would, by later parlance, amount to a killing ground? If neither men nor officers knew their role, how were they to make decisions, choose ground, think tactically? Throughout the day men were sent out onto ground that favoured an enemy who took advantage of cover, and the killing power of artillery and small arms fire.[134] When gaps appeared in the lines, reinforcements were called for to fill them, more men were sent forward, and the cycle repeated. Playing to the enemy's strengths became a self-fulfilling prophecy – the commanders decided places such as the 400 Plateau had to be held; men were sent onto its exposed crest where they were pounded by shrapnel and bullets; casualties meant that replacements had to be repeatedly despatched. Men were then diverted from roles which may have been of strategic value to places where they could do little but fall victim to enemy fire.

Also unclear is what their commanders thought they were achieving by pouring living men in to plug the holes left by dead and wounded. Bean wrote that "Probably neither MacLagan nor M'Cay, the two brigadiers responsible for this part of the line, had any conception of the heroic but useless advances which swept … over the plateau … or of the even more costly retirements."[135] It was a story common to Second Ridge and Baby 700.

I am loath to criticise anyone who was on the battlefield that day, but at least one of those fighting on 400 Plateau saw the folly of this approach. George Mitchell was well forward, surrounded by dead and dying, and the "sickening thud" of bullets tearing "through flesh bone and sinew." A message was passed along: "From the Brigadier – reinforcements coming up." "Fool," thought Mitchell. "Why doesn't he keep them alive behind the hill until their [the enemy's] charge hits us?"[136] Indeed.

The compulsion to form continuous firing lines probably originated in doctrine and training. In his report on the Landing, Bridges wrote that:

> [T]he operations consequent upon an opposed landing naturally led to continuous calls for reinforcements and it became necessary to throw in units as they became available. This led to a great admixture of units which was added to by the broken nature of the country. In the circumstances it must, I think, be regarded as satisfactory that a continuous line was established, and touch maintained between various units.[137]

132 Ibid., p. 386.
133 Ibid.
134 Unlike the bare plateau we know today, on 25 April Lone Pine was covered by tall scrub. There is however a difference between cover and concealment – the scrub provided little protection from bullets and shrapnel.
135 Bean, *The Story of Anzac*, Vol. I., p. 370.
136 AWM, 2DRL 928: G.D. Mitchell.
137 AWM4 1/42/3 Part 2: 1st Division War Diary, April 1915, p. 6, para 7.

This is even more surprising when the objectives prescribed in the plans for the covering force consisted of a series of disconnected posts.

The observations of one battlefield commander, New Zealander Lieutenant-Colonel W.G. Malone, appear to confirm these findings. On 27 April, Malone's battalion were ordered to respond to "a roar for reinforcements coming" to them from the ridge above. Brigadier-General H.B. Walker ordered Malone to send forward one of his companies, who would be told what they were to do when they reached the top. Immediately there was another cry for reinforcements, and Malone was told to send another company. Thus "450 of the best soldier men in the world" were sent to "chaos, and slaughter, nay murder." Malone responded to the next call for reinforcements by going forward himself to investigate. He found Lieutenant-Colonel G.F. Braund "who said he was in command ... He ... knew nothing. Had no defensive position, no plan, nothing but a murderous notion that the only thing to do was to plunge troops out of the neck of the ridge into the jungle beyond. There Turks, of whom very few were seen by my officers, were lying down shooting down all the bits of track ... and dropping our men wholesale."[138] This in many ways reflects the fighting on 25 April.

Lieutenant-Colonel W.G. Malone.

The observations of Corporal T.S. Louch, 11th Battalion, spill a little light on the thinking of the time. Louch survived to be commissioned and to command the 2/11th Battalion on the outbreak of the next world war. Before Gallipoli, he wrote: the "only weapons" the troops had been taught to fight with were "rifles and bayonets ... Battle training" had been "confined to advancing in short rushes and flopping down on the whistle blast."[139] In Egypt, field training was based upon:

> [F]rontal attacks on an imaginary enemy ... From afar we approached in company column until we got within the supposed range of the enemy guns, when we broke down into platoons and then into sections. When told that we were within rifle range, short rushes were made until about one hundred yards from our objective. We then fixed bayonets and lay down, firing lustily while reinforcements came from behind to thicken the attack ... someone ... would cry "Charge" and all would thereupon dash forward ... until the enemy position was overrun.[140]

138 J. Crawford (ed.), *No Better Death: The Great War Diaries and Letters of William G. Malone* (Titirangi, Auckland: Reed Publishing, 2005), pp. 164-165.
139 T.S. Louch, memoir, author's collection.
140 Louch, memoir, p. 11.

Although this may appear a little tongue-in-cheek, it matches the tactics used in many places on 25 April. Louch concluded that "The sad part of it was that all this was no sort of preparation for the kind of warfare we were to engage in at Gallipoli, or later in France."[141] "We had not been taught," he continued, "that a section was a tactical unit ... and that the job of a section commander was to lead. Looking back on it now, I can think of all the things that I might or should have done."[142] Perhaps, with hindsight and the benefit of later experience, other Australian commanders, at least those who were prepared to learn, would have felt the same. Perhaps 25 April was a tragic "weeding out" process for the AIF, with experience gained at the cost of men's lives.

Doctrine

Events at Z Beach on 25 April are all the more surprising considering British Army doctrine of the previous decade. Field Marshal Lord Roberts, Commander-in-Chief, had written in his Preface to *Infantry Training 1902* that:

> Modern fighting makes heavy demands on every individual engaged ... Not only must the superior officer possess the tactical skill conferred by practice and professional zeal; but the subordinate leader must be so accustomed to responsibility as to be capable, when necessary, of using his own judgement to further the general plan ... such development is impossible unless free play is given to individual intelligence and initiative.[143]

Chris Pugsley[144] described the adoption of the subsequent *Field Service Regulations* in 1905 as the "true revolution in the British Army ... The war in South Africa (1899-1902) caused a major re-examination of tactical doctrine"[145] and a change to "the use of extended infantry linear formations and the advance under fire by section rushes." Roberts emphasised "the need for concentration of fire and speed in manoeuvre ... by the local initiative of commanders ... the practical knowledge of these principles and rules can only be instilled by intelligent instruction and constantly diversified exercises on broken ground." Modern warfare renders:

> [D]ecentralisation of command in action an absolute necessity, no good results are to be expected unless the subordinate leaders have been trained to use their wits, and unless they have been given ample opportunities of acting on their own judgement ... and have constantly, in peace practices, been called upon to consider the necessity of departing from their original orders.[146]

141 Ibid., p. 11.
142 Ibid., p. 16.
143 C. Pugsley, *"We Have Been Here Before": The Evolution of the Doctrine of Decentralised Command in the British Army 1905-1989, Sandhurst Occasional Papers No. 9* (Central Library, Royal Military Academy Sandhurst), p. 3.
144 Ibid., p. 7.
145 Ibid.
146 Ibid., pp. 7-8.

Lower ranking officers like Derham appear to have demonstrated the intent of these instructions but seem to have often been overruled by superiors.

The first chapter of *Field Service Regulations Part 1 Combined Training 1905* described the issue of orders and the principle of "centralised intent and decentralisation of execution" in order to achieve "mobility and speed of execution through swift and efficient command." A comment which appeared in *Infantry Training (4-Company Organization) 1914*, is of significance to this study: "a commander in battle" should influence "the course of any action by the quality of his initial orders and once battle was joined by the employment of his reserve."[147]

These principles appear to be precisely what was often missing at Z Beach on 25 April. Orders were vague, superior officers appeared not to control the battle by quality of orders nor retention or deployment of reserves, and it is difficult to gauge the level of "tactical skill ... and professional zeal" of many leaders; concentration "of fire and speed in manoeuvre" were poorly executed, if not overlooked entirely. Decentralised command appears to have consisted of the divisional commander distributing reserves from the beach, while subordinate brigadiers made decisions. Battalion commanders acted with little battlefield awareness or a clear idea of their goals, and indeed, often without their battalions, which had been split into companies, often as they landed. The part of the equation that appears to have worked better was at the level of some of the lower ranking officers: Captain E.W. Tulloch, Lieutenant N.M. Loutit and others, acting on their own initiative, made it to, or near to, their objectives, but this counted for little as they were not supported by their superiors.

In 1914 the British Army "was the best equipped and best trained ... that Britain had ever mobilised," the product of a continuous cycle of training "to a common doctrine and with an organisational structure designed to put that doctrine into effect."[148] The new Australian nation could not boast the same: the AIF did not begin re-training with *Infantry Training (4-Company Organization) 1914* until it had been in Egypt for some weeks. This change in the structure of the infantry battalions to four companies of four platoons was necessary to implement the doctrine developed after the South African War. Brigadier-General Ivor Maxse considered these structural changes to be "vital if one was to give full effect to the command and control of fire and movement" and "enshrined the philosophy of decentralisation at the tactical level within units." Pugsley continues that it "was only through training that individuals and units could achieve the level of skills that gave them the pragmatism and flexibility to deal confidently with the situations they would face in battle."[149] For the AIF, the re-structuring and re-training could not begin until January 1915, and the 3rd Brigade left Egypt at the end of February.

Conclusion

"You make mistakes in your first battle".[150] This article was not inspired by a desire to criticise but to penetrate the fog and attempt to understand what happened to the Australian force on 25 April. Firstly, I will present three disclaimers to my conclusions: There is so little information

147 Ibid., p. 12.
148 Ibid., p. 13.
149 Ibid., pp. 11-12.
150 H.B.S. Gullett, *Not as a Duty Only: An Infantryman's War* (Carlton: Melbourne University Press, 1976), p. 21.

about the thinking behind the decisions made by the Australian commanders that I am loathe to make absolute judgements; there is much that we do not know; I have relied heavily on Şefik's account, but I am well aware that it is written with the many benefits of hindsight and it is easier to criticise than to "do" – the commanders on the day did not have the information we do, nor the opportunity to take time to study the events of this morning, without the pressures, responsibilities and risks of battlefield command.

It is also important to note that this chapter is not intended to be anti-Australian: the latter were organised and trained along British lines, and one quarter to one third of their rank and file were British-born, as were many of their commanders – including Bridges, MacLagan, Glasfurd[151] and Walker. On no level does this study intend to demean or belittle the courage or achievements of those who fought at Gallipoli in 1915: regardless of the factors thrown at the men in the ranks, once the commanders had made their decisions, it was probably the stoicism and grit of the men that prevented a disaster. Captain John Peck, adjutant to the 11th Battalion and permanent army officer, described the "conduct of the lads" this day as "splendid … cool, brave, and wonderfully intelligent considering their short period of training."[152] Peck would be described by Bean as "one of the best officers in the AIF" and by Newton Wanliss as "the ablest man who commanded a battalion of the AIF in France."[153]

That said, the decisions made on this day led to an extraordinarily costly campaign, which had a great impact on a small and young nation. Deficiencies in operational planning and tactical training may have been compensated for by initiative or experience, but in the main MEF infantry commanders had not yet acquired the experience to confront such a complex battle.

It appears that the Turks outfought the landing force on 25 April. This is not to suggest that their fighting men, their agricultural workers come soldiers, were necessarily better than their opposite numbers, but because of a range of factors. The Australian commanders, apparently more concerned about the Turks' response to their plans than achieving them, initially allowed themselves to be halted by an enemy who was not there. The commander of an enemy force of two thousand then seized the initiative from a force nearly three times that size.[154] His enemy in fact appear to have surrendered the initiative to him before he reached the field.

In recent years, MacLagan has borne the brunt of responsibility for this. Perhaps this is fair, perhaps not – he appears to have understood his primary responsibility to be to establish a covering position to defend the main force against the inevitable enemy counter-attack. He had been briefed to expect this from the east or south east but may have felt he did not have sufficient troops to cover the somewhat contradictory goals he had been set. In addition, his force had landed further north than intended, and landing on an enemy coast in the dark, he may have seen this as a major setback, requiring a significant response. Fault also lies with other commanders, particularly of the division, who subjugated their roles and objectives to helping MacLagan achieve his new ones. Given the limited evidence, this is all shaky ground, but it is likely neither MacLagan nor anybody else in the force had the experience or training necessary to command that most difficult of operations – a combined forces landing on a defended enemy coast. This in part may be due to

151 Although Indian-born, Glasfurd was residing in Great Britain at the outbreak of war.
152 J.H. Peck, Letter to wife (n.d.), Unidentified newspaper article dated 13 July 1915. Army Museum of Western Australia.
153 I. Grant, *Jacka, VC: Australia's Finest Fighting Soldier* (South Melbourne, Macmillan, 1990), p. 93.
154 Including the remainder of Şefik's coastal battalion, who were at Gabe Tepe or deployed nearby.

the limited time available to learn the new doctrine after arriving in Egypt. Further study on the training undergone by the AIF in January and February 1915 would no doubt deliver more.

This work is not complete, and that presented here is, I hope, a step in the process of stripping down and examining developments on 25 April. A study of messages received might present a partial idea of the sort of information on which the commanders were forming their image of the battle, but this would provide only a skeleton as not all messages have survived and would not include verbal messages. It may simply be that the failure of the Landing at Z Beach is less due to the misplaced landing and other factors debated over the last century, than the fact that officers and men were inadequately prepared for the task. The commanders "on the ground" appear to have neither gained an accurate tactical picture of the battle, nor to have acted strategically, other than to prepare to defend against a possible attack against their right flank.

Those allowed to survive and able to learn would earn a reputation as great fighting men. A comparison with their actions in 1917 shows how much and how rapidly they had learned. Significantly, Şefik appears to have applied learned principles with the confidence of experience, knowledge of the terrain and of fighting on familiar, home ground; he had been preparing for this day for many months. He applied what would today be called an appreciations process to the problem at hand: assessing the factors that might have an impact on achieving his goal, and then planning his strategy to achieve that goal. Kemal also used the word "appreciation" to describe his first moments on the battlefield. The Australian commanders may have been working to two main influences: their plan, and what they had been briefed to expect about the enemy. They appear to have been reacting to what they feared rather than what they saw, or of interpreting the latter in light of the former. Had they applied a similar process to their opposing commanders, they may have realised their initial problems were not as great as they perceived them to be.

I was once privileged to meet David Sabben, who as a young lieutenant had commanded a platoon during the hard-fought Vietnam battle of Long Tan. He suggested, on the basis of infantry training that had benefited from decades of development since MacLagan's time, that on 25 April the Australian commanders should have "thrown out the old plan and developed a new plan," or words to that effect.

Since working on this paper, I have interpreted his comments as follows. The force had not landed as planned and things were not perfect, but in battle, they could seldom be expected to be. It rapidly became necessary for the Australian command to adapt the pre-determined plan to their current situation to achieve their objectives, unless there was some significant reason to consider the objectives unattainable. At the time, it appears that the Australian commanders perceived that concerns about the enemy counter-attack provided that significant reason: instead of fine tuning the plan to enable them to attain their objectives, they appear to have changed the priority of the objectives and therefore the plan.[155] Conversely, given the vague and evolving planning process outlined above, perhaps they believed they were still working towards the intent of the original plan.[156]

155 As previously noted, Bean's explanation was that MacLagan believed his force to be too far to the left to defend the right.

156 French Emperor Napoleon Bonaparte went so far as to declare that "war was a series of accidents from which it was a commander's duty to extract maximum profit." A. Forrest, *Waterloo* (Oxford: Oxford University Press, 2015), p. 13.

Without accurate information about what was occurring on the battlefield, the commanders appear to have unnecessarily given up the objective of Third Ridge: there was at that time no enemy counter-attack. Indeed, when the first decisions were being made, the enemy counter-attack had not yet reached the battlefield. The Australian commanders appear to have been jumping at shadows. A "tactical appreciation" may have enabled them to see the situation more clearly and to alter their planning without abandoning their goals.

In his after-action report, Bridges concluded that breaking up his battalions as they came ashore in order to establish a "continuous line" was justified.[157] It may be unfair to judge on a single comment such as this, but Bridges' conclusion seems to support the battlefield events described earlier in this paper: the forming of firing lines seems to have been the *modus operandi* of the 1st Division's commanders. Less obvious are evidence of tactical leadership in the field and a determination to take control of a battle. Britain's *Infantry Training, Part VIII*, printed nearly 30 years later, when lessons had been learned and much progress made, stated "Battle drill must be our servant and NOT our master."[158] Firing lines were the means to an end, not the end itself. This manual also teaches the importance of conducting "appreciations",[159] as "Battle drills do not give you the answer to every problem; they do not absolve the commander from thinking." The point made is that drills, as exemplified by the forming of firing lines, are only part of the solution; "Appreciations ... have still to be made."[160]

On the other side of the battlefield, although the Ottomans reacted with tactical thought, confidence and aggression, Şefik and Kemal technically didn't achieve their goal either: they did not succeed in throwing the landing forces "back into the sea." One curious observation: from Plugge's Plateau, MacLagan's concerns can be appreciated; he was gazing at Second Ridge and 400 Plateau, with no idea what was happening beyond and no indication of the proximity of the Turkish regiments he believed were about to descend upon his force. However, MacLagan had landed near the toe of 400 Plateau; what if he had simply moved inland to 400 Plateau and Second Ridge, instead of back-tracking to Plugge's? The 9th Battalion troops from his destroyer, *Colne*, had done this, and he had ordered Beevor of the 10th to do the same. If he had done so, would he have seen, by perhaps between 5:00 and 5:30 a.m. or so, that Third Ridge was lying unoccupied in the gathering light, a prize for the taking, without an enemy counter-attack in sight? Could this have calmed his concerns about "the right" and changed those first significant decisions? What impact might this simple decision have had on the course of the battle, the campaign and many thousands of lives?

157 AWM4 1/42/3 Part 2: 1st Division War Diary, April 1915, p. 6, para 7.
158 War Office, *Infantry Training, Part VIII: Fieldcraft, Battle Drill, Section and Platoon Tactics, 1944* (London: War Office, 1944), p. 47.
159 Ibid., pp. 48-49.
160 Ibid., p. 48.

3

The Lowest Point: The 2nd Australian Brigade and the Second Battle of Krithia, 6-8 May 1915

Meleah Hampton

There is little choice but to determine the Second Battle of Krithia as a failure. Little ground was gained, and the British and the French suffered thousands of casualties in the process, even though the attacking forces did not come in contact with the main body of the enemy. The attempt to take the small village near the bottom of the peninsula, and press on to the heights of Achi Baba beyond, carried out a hurriedly planned attack which produced little success on the first day. The plan was repeated on successive days with little to no modification and increasingly miserable results. By the time the 2nd Australian Brigade was committed from its place in reserve, the battle was, more or less, at its lowest ebb; battalions were being committed to advances that showed no development over previous attacks and were extremely costly in lives and materiel for little to no gain. Their experience has been called "one of the most misconceived episodes in a misconceived battle",[1] and would be one of the worst among active operations on the Gallipoli peninsula.

The Gallipoli landings on 25 April 1915 gave the allies little more than a tentative toehold in enemy territory without any real progress towards the overall objective of the campaign. Nevertheless, British command believed that the landings and subsequent fighting had depleted the Turkish force on the peninsula, and at this point they should strike while the iron was hot. Lord Kitchener wrote to Sir Ian Hamilton to this effect, saying, "I hope the 5th [May 1915] will see you sufficiently reinforced to push on to Achi Baba at least, as time will enable [the] Turks to bring reinforcements and make unpleasant preparations for you."[2] Hamilton was further pressured to succeed by General Sir John Maxwell (GOC Egypt), who wrote in early May, "I see no reason for anxiety at present but any failure on Hamilton's part will make critical situation all over Moslem world, therefore we should take legitimate risks to avoid this."[3] It was made quite clear that the potential consequences of failure could be dire, and progress should be made as soon as possible. Fixing the situation on the Gallipoli peninsula by affecting an advance from Cape Helles towards the Turkish forts on the straits became the main priority of the campaign.

1 Robin Prior, *Gallipoli: The End of a Myth* (Sydney: University of New South Wales Press, 2010), p. 144.
2 AWM: AWM45/2/7: Kitchener to Hamilton, 11:30 a.m., 4 May 1915.
3 Ibid.

Even before the correspondence from Kitchener and Maxwell, Hamilton had been making moves to renew the offensive at Cape Helles. The main British force at Helles was the 29th Division, which had been consolidating its position at the tip of the peninsula since the failed First Battle of Krithia some days earlier. The division, like most if not all of the units on Gallipoli at the time, was exhausted by a hard-fought landing and difficult consolidation, worsened by the first attempt on Krithia. Reinforcements, although trickling in, were precious and hard come by. At the time much of the French force was still disembarking, which did not deter Hamilton from writing to General d'Amade, commanding officer of the French *Corps Expeditionnaire d'Orient*, "to request that you will continue to consolidate and strengthen your position and to make all preparations for the advance on Achi Baba, which I hope it will soon be possible to undertake."[4] To compound the problem of depleted manpower, they had little idea of the enemy force or its position on the peninsula. We now know that at least three divisions of Turkish infantry stood in front of Krithia, with at least another two divisions available to assist in defence of the area. But at the time, reconnaissance parties could only give a very partial picture of the Turkish defences and their garrison.[5] None of this blunted Hamilton's resolve to exploit a perceived weakness in Ottoman numbers and to press the advantage the British felt they held, by capturing the Achi Baba heights.

In many ways the plan for the second attempt to seize Krithia was determined by the landscape. The terrain at Cape Helles is deceptively flat and featureless. Small bits of scrub provided some cover, but for the most part the heights of Achi Baba to the north of the village of Krithia afforded a clear view of attacking forces. The only true cover came from four streams running in small gullies from north to south. They were generally known by the Turkish term for them, "dere", but also frequently referred to by the Indian term "nullah". The four most important streams, from left to right across the battlefield, were Gully Ravine, Krithia Nullah, Kanli Dere and Kereves Dere. This last stream emptied into the sea between the established French line above S Beach and their first objective. Between each stream lay the higher flat ground of a series of spurs: Ravine Spur on the left, then Krithia Spur between Gully Ravine and Krithia Nullah, Central Spur between Krithia Nullah and Kanli Dere, and Kereves Spur. The nullahs were quite wide in parts, up to 700 yards, but were only suitable for entry into and exit out of the battlefield rather than 'jumping-off' positions, standing as they did at right angles to the objective. With no established jumping-off trench, the infantry would have to filter forward and fan out to capture their objective from one of these shallow gullies.

The lack of knowledge of the Turkish position made the situation worse. At this time, the Turks were working feverishly to establish a continuous line of defence across the peninsula. They had dug in several strong points but relied heavily on snipers and machine gunners hidden in the scrub forward of their main line of defence. There were at least six or seven batteries of Turkish field guns and one battery of howitzers on or around Achi Baba and good observation of the entire battlefield. Any infantry attack was in danger of being dispersed by this firepower. The attacking force had little, if any, advantage in this situation.

The plan for the second operation against Krithia, largely formulated by the general officer commanding the British 29th Division, Major-General Sir Aylmer Hunter-Weston, was

4 AWM: AWM45/3/3: Hamilton to Monsieur le General de Division d'Amade, 1 May 1915.
5 AWM: AWM45/3/3: GOC, French Expeditionary Force to GOC Division, 1 May 1915.

Based on an officer's contemporary sketch: Second Krithia battlefield panorama as depicted from the ramparts of Sedd-el-Bahr fortress. Achi Baba is in the centre background with Krithia village on the immediate left. (*Illustrated London News*, 19 June 1915).

ambitious and complex. It was to take place in three phases. The first involved a general advance across the peninsula to almost a mile from the village of Krithia. From there the second phase would begin with the British 29th Division on the left advancing up Fir Tree and Gully spurs to a point beyond the village, before turning to the right to capture Achi Baba and surrounding high ground. On the right the French would advance to a similar line across the Kereves Spur in the first phase, but from then their advances would be much smaller and more easterly. Between the two, no attack was to take place on Central Spur. Instead, a temporary formation known as the "Composite Division" would facilitate the pivot here, advancing enough on the left to keep touch with the 29th Division's right flank, while keeping its right far enough behind to join the French.[6] Central Spur was a little more susceptible to fire from other slightly higher pieces of land, which made it a clear choice for a pivot position.[7] Overall, this was a complicated and detailed plan. The three distinct movements described in the orders were not timed. Instead, each new phase was to begin once the previous one had ended. So once the village of Krithia was captured, for example, the French force would be free to make its second advance.[8] There seems to have been little mechanism in place for signifying the end or the beginning of any particular phase, however. The complicated nature of the orders, and the rather loose connection between phases, had the dangerous potential to pull the attack apart, or to drive forces together should they make it to the heights.[9]

6 AWM: AWM45/3/3: 'Force Order No. 5', General Headquarters, 5 May 1915.
7 C.E.W. Bean, *The Story of Anzac*, Vol. II (Queensland: University of Queensland Press 1981 reprint of 1921 edition), p. 11.
8 AWM: AWM45/3/3: 'Force Order No. 5', General Headquarters, 5 May 1915.
9 Prior, *Gallipoli*, p. 140.

Artillery support for this operation would be light. Not only was there a relatively low number of guns, there was a strict rationing of ammunition. With five antipodean field artillery batteries sent south from Anzac on 3 May,[10] there were a little over 100 guns ashore – mostly lighter field guns. But labour was also in short supply, so many of the guns ashore languished in back lines with nobody to pull them forward and dig them in.[11] But although fewer guns than were available were used in the attack, no records indicate how many were in action for the operation itself. There would be additional firepower from the Royal Navy, but ammunition for that source was carefully rationed.

To further complicate matters, the Turks undertook a series of counter-attacks as British battle plans were being advanced. About 10:00 p.m. on 1 May, the Turkish artillery began to shell British-held trenches roughly in the centre of the line. This fire was on target as a result, it was supposed, of the Turks using their desultory fire over the previous two days to accurately register their guns. After around half an hour's fire, the Turks launched a determined infantry assault all along the line. In places they were able to penetrate as far as the reserve trenches but were eventually repulsed by fierce hand-to-hand fighting. The attack lasted through the night, and it was not until daylight that it became clear that the Turks would not get a foothold in Allied trenches. The result of this counter-attack was a further depletion of manpower both through casualties and the need to shore up the line. Reserves had quickly been drawn in, including the Anson Battalion from the Royal Naval Division that was dispatched to reinforce the French. The *Corps Expeditionnaire d'Orient* would not return the battalion for another two days.[12]

At 9:30 p.m. the following day the Turks again attacked the British and French line. The 29th Division reported that this "attack was easily repulsed and at no time during [the] night was [the] front of [the] 29th Division seriously threatened."[13] On the French front, however, General d'Amade requested two or three battalions in support as the counter-attack in his sector was "very vigorous".[14] His request was denied. The 29th Division only had its cyclist company and the Indian brigade left in reserve at this point, and Hamilton was "anxious to keep [them] intact for vigorous action in the coming offensive."[15] Despite the ongoing shortage of manpower, both in numbers and quality, and the precarious toe hold of his force on the Gallipoli peninsula, the upcoming offensive was still foremost in Hamilton's thoughts, despite the fact that every hour these counter-attacks reduced his capacity to launch it.

On the right the French continued to borrow heavily from British brigades. They were somewhat slow to return the borrowed battalions, reluctantly doing so before the Krithia operation was launched. The night before the attack began, the Turks attacked the French again. While their line did not break, the French were forced out of their positions in some parts. French field guns opened in response to requests for assistance. The English guns had also been requested,

10 AWM: AWM38 3DRL 8042/14: 'Extracts from ANZAC and 1st AUST DIV G.S. Diaries, May 1915: Transferring of two ANZAC Brigades and five batteries of FA to Cape Helles'.
11 Prior, *Gallipoli*, p. 140.
12 AWM: AWM38 3DRL 8042/14: '29th Division at Helles. Attacks in May 1915', Extracts from war diary, 29th Division, May 1915.
13 Ibid.
14 Ibid.
15 Ibid.

but a serious shortage of ammunition meant that careful checks were made to ensure that the use of precious stores of ordnance was warranted. As the attack seemed to be only on the French line, the English artillery refused to participate. All this upheaval and discord among the Allies further eroded preparations to launch the major attack on Krithia effectively.

Despite these difficulties, the Second Battle of Krithia began as scheduled with a preliminary bombardment of enemy positions at 10:30 a.m. on 6 May 1915. The British infantry were able to launch their attack on time at 11:00 a.m., while the French commenced their part of the operation 40 minutes late. Unfortunately, both infantry attacks floundered quickly in the face of withering Turkish machine gun fire. On Ravine Spur, the Lancashire Territorials were stopped after advancing several hundred yards by hidden enemy machine guns, the same fire that also stopped the 88th Brigade advancing along Krithia Spur. The French met with yet another Turkish counter-attack as they reached an enemy redoubt and were forced back. The artillery had failed either to destroy enemy machine gun positions, or to mitigate the fire from them by forcing gunners to take cover. Although some ground was taken, both the British and the French fell well short of their first-phase objective.

Undeterred by results from the previous day, the following morning the same plan was carried out again. That is, after a 30-minute bombardment of Turkish positions, the infantry advanced without additional artillery cover.[16] It was hoped that the preliminary bombardment would destroy the machine guns that had caused problems the previous day, but without having the guns accurately located on a map, and without the capacity to fire accurately enough to destroy them, this plan was little more than wishful thinking. Many battalions had been mixed together following the previous day's attempt on the line, but they were obliged to advance at 10:00 a.m. whether they had reorganised or otherwise.[17] Once again the artillery bombardment proved of very limited assistance. The Lancashire Fusilier Brigade were almost immediately pushed back by machine gun fire, and although reports were received that the 88th and 5th Royal Scots were able to carry Fir Tree Wood "well supported by artillery fire",[18] it appears that the 29th Division had overstated its advance. The left flank of the 88th Brigade was constantly exposed to enemy machine gun fire, putting it in danger. No advance anywhere took more than a few yards of ground, and no part of the line came into direct contact with the main body of Turkish troops. The enemy were proving perfectly capable of stopping any advance using shrapnel and machine gun fire from a distance. Nevertheless, Hamilton reported to Kitchener that "during a long day's fighting [we] failed to get the Turks properly on the run or to make good Achi Baba. But we have improved our position on the right where the French have captured trenches and, on the left, where just before sunset General Marshall with [the] 87th Brigade relieved the Lancs."[19] There was no mention of the exhausted state of his troops, the high casualty rate, or the desperate need for reinforcement, much less the superior defensive capability of the Turks.

Reinforcements for this battle had been allocated during the planning phase. However, due to the hurried nature of the operation, most were still in the process of being moved to Cape

16 AWM: AWM38 3DRL 8042/14: 'The Second Australian Infantry Brigade (Victorian) in the Advance on Achi Baba 6-8th May', 8 July 1915.

17 AWM: AWM38 3DRL 8042/14: '29th Division at Helles. Attacks in May 1915', Extracts from war diary, 29th Division, 7:40 a.m., 7 May 1915.

18 Ibid.

19 AWM: 45/2/7: Hamilton to Kitchener, 10:48 p.m., 7 May 1915.

Helles even as the battle began. Around the start of May some brigades of the East Lancashire Territorial Division, some of the French 2nd Division, and the 29th Indian Infantry Brigade were either arriving or their arrival was imminent.[20] To further bolster the force attacking Krithia, on the morning of 3 May Birdwood was ordered to "detail two brigades and two bearer sub-divisions of a field ambulance to embark tonight for Cape Helles, where they are required to take part in the attack on the Achi Baba Position tomorrow."[21] These two additional brigades were to come bearing 200 round of small arms ammunition and two iron rations each, and had to be ready to go on arrival. They were to be preceded by their commanding officers "to see [the] country and have task explained."[22] Fortunately for the ANZAC commander, delays at Cape Helles gave more time for selection, extraction and transportation of the brigades south. Birdwood conducted investigations as to which two brigades would be best to send, eventually deciding on the 2nd Australian Brigade and the New Zealand Brigade.[23] They were numerically stronger than others available, although they were still depleted and awaiting reinforcement as a result of recent operations.[24] Birdwood was reluctant to see them go, writing, "I of course realised [the] vital importance of [the] operation you explained to me for which I am sending my two best brigades, but till their return will be a little anxious."[25] He should perhaps have been concerned about the state in which they would return.

The New Zealand Brigade disembarked at Cape Helles between 3:00 and 5:00 a.m. on 6 May and by 9:00 a.m. were in bivouac after a straightforward transfer from Anzac.[26] The New Zealand Brigade was the first of the Anzac reinforcements to be called into action. At some point in the morning or early afternoon the following day the New Zealanders were ordered to make a quick reconnoitre of the approach to the battlefield, and at 2:30 p.m. on 7 May they were ordered to advance at once.[27] They had been in bivouac at Helles for a little over 29 hours. The New Zealand Brigade advanced using the most covered approach, but the bulk of the force stopped early and entrenched in order to defend against an enemy counter-attack. In the end the four battalions were relatively thinly stretched across the front, largely in support of the 87th and 88th Brigades. Most of the battalions were tired, men of the Wellington Battalion in particular, as they had been used to form carrying parties for ammunition for much of their time on the peninsula. The Wellingtons' war diary notes that "our pack animals could be used here to advantage on this level country, but they were on the transport at sea. The work knocks a lot of men up and they are not fit for work the next day."[28] Nevertheless, the Wellington Battalion was among the first sent into action. They had very little idea of what they had been detailed to do, having received orders that contained little more than the time to attack and a vague objective. The New Zealanders did as ordered with reports later recounting that "it was a splendid sight to see each co[mpan]y throw out lines of skirmishers and advance steadily under shellfire

20 Bean, *The Story of Anzac*, Vol. II, p. 7.
21 AWM: AWM38 3DRL 8042/14: Braithwaite to GOC, Anzac, 3 May 1915.
22 AWM: AWM38 3DRL 8042/14: GHQ to Anzac, received 12:15 p.m., 3 May 1915, 'Messages and Signals'.
23 AWM: AWM38 3DRL 8042/14: Anzac to GHQ, 1:35 p.m., 3 May 1915, 'Messages and Signals'.
24 AWM: AWM38 3DRL 8042/14: 'Messages and Signals'.
25 AWM: AWM38 3DRL 8042/14: Anzac to GHQ, 1:35 p.m., 4 May 1915, 'Messages and Signals'.
26 AWM: AWM45/3/3: 'Report from O/C New Zealand Infantry Brigade', 6 May 1915.
27 AWM: AWM45/3/3: 'Report from O/C New Zealand Infantry Brigade'.
28 AWM: AWM38 3DRL 8042/14: 'Extracts from war diary Wellington Battalion, May 1915'.

Australians landing at Cape Helles.

on the 7th. No man faltered or stopped although casualties were occurring at every stage of the advance."[29] The men advanced until company commanders decided it was a waste of life to go any further, at which point they dug in, having gained almost nothing. But it was quite clear that there would be no respite – Hamilton ordered that the attack would "be resumed tomorrow at 10:30 a.m. and will be pressed with the utmost vigour."[30]

The 2nd Australian Brigade, however, had had a much more difficult time in departing Anzac on the night of 5/6 May. The seven fleet sweepers designated to be their transport to Cape Helles did not arrive on time. The brigade had successfully withdrawn from its front-line position in the early evening, congregated on the beach, and had even loaded the first of the infantry into lighters ready to head out to the fleet sweepers, but was then forced to spend hours on the beach. Cold, fireless and overlooked, some twenty men were killed or wounded during the wait as a result of stray bullets from the front line.[31] When the fleet sweepers finally arrived at 2:30 a.m., and embarkation began nearly an hour and a half later, some of the smaller loading craft were found to be missing, and the carefully laid plans for which troops were to board which craft quickly evaporated. The brigade became muddled and units became gradually more mixed as the rest were loaded on board.[32] The benefit of the darkness was lost as the 2nd Brigade arrived at Helles at 6:00 a.m. The men were forced to disembark at Sedd-el-Bahr in daylight under heavy shellfire from the Asiatic shore.[33]

29 Ibid.
30 AWM: AWM45/3/3: 'Force Order No. 6', General Headquarters, 7 May 1915.
31 AWM: AWM38 3DRL 8042/14: 'The Second Australian Infantry Brigade (Victorian) in the Advance on Achi Baba 6-8th May', 8 July 1915.
32 AWM: AWM38 3DRL 8042/14: 'Embarkation of 5/6th May 1915'.
33 AWM: AWM38 3DRL 8042/14: 'The Second Australian Infantry Brigade (Victorian) in the Advance on Achi Baba 6-8th May', 8 July 1915.

The 2nd Division made bivouac about a mile from where they landed at Sedd-el-Bahr on the road to Krithia. It was described as "an open sandy plain covered with grass and beautiful flowers and a very fine grove of trees."[34] But as the writer of this report archly points out, although the surroundings were "beautiful [they were] not bullet proof", and the men were in full view of the heights of Achi Baba beyond Krithia. Any hole deeper than eighteen inches quickly filled with water, meaning the men had to build up breastworks to afford as much protection as possible from the desultory fire from Achi Baba.[35] As they did so, they could hear the battle.

From this position the brigade staff and commanding officers went forward to get an idea of the layout of the peninsula. From a low rise they could see Achi Baba and the heads of Kereves and Kanli Deres, as well as the village of Krithia. The group watched the battle of 6 May as it was launched around 11:00 a.m. and were impressed by the artillery fire that preceded the infantry advance. It was described as "a very lively bombardment of the whole of the Turkish position" during which the field gun batteries ashore "appeared to concentrate their fire on the hills overlooking Kereves Dere ... and the valleys which probably contained Turkish supports."[36] And, according to the observer, "their shooting was good."[37] But as the infantry advanced, the Australian officers could not fail to notice that "on the infantry advance being resumed the familiar tap tap was very soon heard again, apparently in increased volume."[38] The Australians noted that the enemy machine guns were not at all bothered by the artillery fire, and in fact enemy fire increased as the attack wore on. However, overall the observing Australians were left with a positive impression of the battle that day, reporting that the line had advanced hundreds of yards without any more than a few casualties. When the attack resumed the following day, the Australian brigade officers again had a clear view of proceedings. The brigade's commanding officer, Colonel J. W. McKay, spent most of the day forward, studying the ground over which his men would be attacking, as observing the British and the integration of artillery fire into the infantry attack.[39] Their observation did little to prepare them for what lay ahead.

By 8 May the Australian party recognised the familiar pattern of preliminary bombardment followed by an infantry attack. By midday it was clear that their turn would come soon as Major-General A. Paris, commanding officer of the Composite Division to which the 2nd Brigade was attached, ordered them forward to be prepared to act as support to the left centre. Reports indicate that within an hour of receiving the order, the brigade had moved along the Kanli Dere and turned left to its position only a short distance from the front line.[40] It was more likely three or four hours before the brigade was in position some 600 yards behind the front line.[41] This put the brigade in the middle of Central Spur, spread along Kanli Dere. Although the brigade expected to come under enemy fire, the Turkish guns failed to range on their positions, and they reached their bivouac without being fired upon. In this position they made camp, and, not expecting to be called to action before the morning, began cooking dinner.

34 Ibid.
35 Ibid.
36 Ibid.
37 Ibid.
38 Ibid.
39 Ibid.
40 Ibid.
41 Bean, *The Story of Anzac*, Vol. II, p. 21.

By this time, it was clear that there could be no further advance from Cape Helles without more men. But with the French struggling to maintain an advance on the right, it was considered imperative to continue to push the British attack on, if only to encourage the French. And so after nearly three full days' fighting for only negligible gains, Hamilton ordered a fourth attack along the entire line.[42] The last of the reserves, the 2nd Australian Brigade, was called into action. At 4:55 p.m. on 8 May a message was received by brigade command:

> [Y]ou will be required to attack at 5:30 p.m. precisely between the valley you are now in and the valley just S[outh] E[ast] of Krithia – Sedd El Bahr road. Move forward at once until you are in line with NZ Bde on your left and your right on the valley SE of Krithia Road.[43]

The Australian Official Historian, Charles Bean, later drily observed, "this message, received at such short notice that it was doubtful whether it was humanly possible to comply with it, flung an infantry brigade of the A.I.F. for the first and only time in the earlier years of the war into an ordered attack across open country."[44] The brigade major of 2nd Brigade, Major Cass, later recalled that General Paris, the commanding officer of the Composite Division, called Cass's headquarters shortly after this order was received. Cass recorded that Paris was an "old fool who wanted to know if we had bands and colours with us."[45] It seems that at least part of the plan was "to move forward with colours waving, and bands playing, and bayonets fixed, in order to drive the Turks from their position. As much use of the Bayonet as was possible was to be made in order to fully impress on the Turks that they had to go."[46] The appropriate musical equipment was not available to fulfil Paris' plan, and the infantry would have to advance in an ordinary fashion, with an emphasis on having bayonets fixed.

The 2nd Brigade had been training for precisely this kind of ordered attack in Egypt, but with such nebulous objectives and no chance to prepare, they were facing a difficult task indeed. The objective was described as "the ridge beyond Krithia with our left further forward than our right, which latter will link up with the French or the 2nd Naval Brigade at present on the French left." No map coordinates, trench system or any other means of identifying the objective was given. Other than an appeal that "every opportunity is to be taken to use the bayonet", there was no further specific information as to the manner or method of attack.[47] This order filtered its way down to battalions at around 5:20 p.m. – no more than 10 minutes before the attack was to begin. Perhaps the most telling source for the result of this hurried order on the 2nd Brigade comes in the form of a small annotation in the war diary. In a thin folder a note reads, "all the Brigade staff are casualties and there is no War Diary or any other documents available."[48]

42 Prior, *Gallipoli*, p. 144.
43 AWM: AWM4, 23/2/3: 'Report of Operations of 2nd Aust. Inf. Bde at Cape Helles from May 6th 1915 to ...'
44 Bean, *The Story of Anzac*, Vol. II, p. 22.
45 AWM: AWM38 3DRL 8042/14: Cass to Bean, 2 December 1921.
46 AWM: AWM38 3DRL 8042/14: 'The Second Australian Infantry Brigade (Victorian) in the Advance on Achi Baba 6-8th May', 8 July 1915.
47 AWM: AWM4, 23/2/3: 'Order by Col. J.W. McKay in 'Report of Operations of 2nd Aust. Inf. Bde at Cape Helles from May 6th 1915 to ...'
48 AWM: AWM4, 23/2/3: 'Report of Operations of 2nd Aust. Inf. Bde at Cape Helles from May 6th 1915 to ...'

The few documents that remain report that the brigade was able to start the attack on time (5:30 p.m.), although this seems unlikely with such short notice. Battalion commanders could only give "brief, indefinite details to their subordinates" before they left.[49] The 2nd Brigade deployed with the 6th Battalion on the left in contact with the New Zealanders, who had also been called out of reserve, and the 7th on the right running along the edge of the valley. Very quickly the battalions became muddled together, both those spearheading the attack, the 6th and 7th, and more particularly those in close support, the 5th and 8th, due to the simple fact that their officers were unsure which battalion they were acting in support of, and where that battalion was supposed to be.[50] Thanks to their training in Egypt, the two foremost battalions were able to put together at least a somewhat structured advance. The front line consisted of (from left to right) D and C Companies of the 6th Battalion and A and B Companies of the 7th. Each company advanced in a shallow column on a frontage of about 250 yards per company.[51] They were followed in close support by A and B Companies of the 6th Battalion and C and D Companies of the 7th. Using the dere as cover, the companies advanced in artillery formation until they reached the "Composite Division" trench, taking heavy casualties all the while. Dug across the Central Spur by the 1st Lancashire Fusiliers and the Drake Battalion two days earlier, this trench was always known to the Australians as "Tommies' Trench." Although the brigadier and some of his staff were aware of the existence of this trench, it came as a complete surprise to most of the uninformed infantry but was the first position where they could stop for a brief respite from the enemy fire before going forward to attempt to meet the enemy.[52]

Colonel (later Major-General) J.W. McCay.

Colonel McCay led the charge forward and, seeing his men resting in the trench, said to a nearby observer, "Now I must play the bloody fool act" before jumping over the parapet and crying out "Come on, Australia!" He strode along the parapet yelling at the first line of men to get out of the trench and advance, later recalling that "they came; Lord, but they're good boys. Each line of my men, three in all, naturally halted in the same way, but I was walking about, calling them and they came. Oh, but I'm proud of them."[53] He remained there, seeking out new groups arriving in the trench and urging them forward with all

49 AWM: AWM4, 23/2/3: 'Report of exactly what took place in 6th Battn ...', Major H.G. Bennett, CO 6th Battalion, 27 May 1915.
50 AWM: AWM4, 23/2/3: Bolton to GOC Composite Division.
51 AWM: AWM4, 23/2/3: 'Supplementary Account of Operations of 2nd Inf. Brigade on May 8th, 1915', Lieut.-Col. D.L. Wanliss.
52 Bean, *The Story of Anzac*, Vol. II, p. 27.
53 AWM: AWM38 3DRL 8042/14: McCay to Bean, 1 January 1922.

haste in order to push on the advance. The men, exhausted by the run into the trench while fully laden and under heavy fire, were only granted the briefest respite before moving on, but it seems that McCay's example was the inspiration they needed, and most groups moved on quickly. In the event they were not quick enough; at least one Australian officer reported that McCay threatened them with a revolver.[54] Speed was of the essence in this operation. Turkish machine guns picked off the attackers from the moment they left cover.

The advance was at least in part supported by artillery, which had been firing at Turkish positions before the attack. It was later reported that "it was found that the Turks were not in the position being shelled, they were much nearer."[55] Even so, the Australian infantry found "nothing to shoot at", and reportedly advanced without firing a shot.[56] Although there was no visible target for the infantry to focus on, enemy machine gun and shrapnel fire continued unabated. Each advancing wave lost men with regular monotony to the strangely disembodied enemy fire. In the 6th Battalion's position on the left, Major J. Gordon Bennett was in command of the supporting companies. He later recalled that before the men even reached Tommies Trench, "shrapnel started pouring into our position in the creek."[57] Stray bullets were flying overhead, although this fire had yet to cause many casualties. As the reserve line of the 6th Battalion waited to advance, the brigade staff captain, Lieutenant Hastie, came along and told them to "get on as quickly as you can. The Brigadier has personally led the firing line right up to the trench."[58] In the absence of any further information, the men of the 6th Battalion thought that this meant that at least part of the line had engaged with the enemy, and that McCay's "fool act" of inspiring his men was working; they were keen to get on and do the same. However, the men of the 6th Battalion were mistaken, and what Hastie actually meant was that the first line had reached a trench another 200 yards further on that was already held by British troops. Those who reached it were given no time to rest. Bennett almost immediately came across McCay, who said "Don't stop here. The 8th Battalion will get there before you… go on, push on. You need not run, walk."[59] Bennett could not stop to reorganise his line; instead he got out of the trench and walked forward with as many men as he came across along the way. He advanced his small force until he met,

> [A] very thin line in front of my left about 50 yards in front of our trenches, and none on my immediate front. I filled this gap, and seeing it was useless to push on further ordered the men to hang on and not go forward. To go forward from this position meant unnecessary loss and it also meant we might have lost the ground we had already won.[60]

Despite having only gained some 50 yards, and having no touch with anyone on the left, Bennett ordered his men to dig in where they were. As reinforcements arrived they began to crowd the

54 AWM: AWM38 3DRL 8042/14: Bennett to Bean, 2 December 1921.
55 AWM: AWM38 3DRL 8042/14: 'The Second Australian Infantry Brigade (Victorian) in the Advance on Achi Baba 6-8th May', 8 July 1915.
56 Ibid.
57 AWM: AWM4, 23/2/3: 'Report of exactly what took place in 6th Battn…', Major H.G. Bennett, CO 6th Battalion, 27 May 1915.
58 Ibid.
59 Ibid.
60 Ibid.

centre of the line, so they were sent to the left, where gradually the line was extended. The advance was discontinued.

On the other side of the line, the Captain Weddell, commanding A Company of the 7th Battalion (also in support), was given two minutes to move. He later reported, "after having formed up the company, I was told to get a move on, and when I asked what was expected of me, was informed that we were about to attack the enemy that I was to take charge of the firing line... and get into touch with the 6th Battalion on my left."[61] This is all the information Weddell received. His first question was to ask in which direction the attack would go. He was told to "go in a north easterly direction until I came to a road where I must change direction left [Krithia Road]. This I did."[62] From this point on, Weddell received no further orders. His men, too, reached the Tommies' Trench. At this stage he was with Major Cass, Brigade Major of the 2nd Brigade, who had more or less taken command of the 7th Battalion's forward advance. On arriving at Tommies' Trench, Weddell ordered the men to extend and, after two or three minutes' rest under heavy fire, Cass gave the order to advance. On this front the artillery were firing on a line only a few hundred yards in advance of the British line, and in parts were proving helpful in keeping enemy fire down.[63] Under Cass's orders, the men dashed forward 50 yards before being forced down, but they were then able to get up and make successive rushes under covering fire. They took heavy casualties, however, one being Major Cass. His last message was for Captain Weddell to take charge of the right of the firing line before he was left behind. Weddell put a great deal of effort into ensuring the 6th Battalion were able to advance as far as the 7th, noticing when they fell 300 yards behind and stopping his men to provide covering fire until they caught up.[64] As daylight began to fade, with only a few hundred yards gained, if that, the surviving members of the 2nd Brigade were left in pairs to scrape potholes in the ground for cover, one digging and one shooting until they had established cover. They had not met a Turk to fight, and they advanced no further.

The toll from this short advance was enormous. The infantry were advancing headlong into unstoppable machine gun fire with no protection. Colonel McCay, having somehow survived hours on the parapet urging his men forward, was wounded around 8:00 p.m. Major Cass was wounded leading the 7th Battalion, sending a last message to put Captain Weddell in charge of the right of the firing line before he was evacuated.[65] All the officers of A Company would be wounded or killed except Weddell, and only one officer remained in B Company.[66] The battalion's own commanding officer, Lieutenant-Colonel Robert Gartside, was killed in action while organising his men behind the forward advance. In the 6th Battalion, Bennett inherited command by default; he estimated that of the 20 officers in the battalion, only seven walked away from the battlefield.[67] The 2nd Australian Brigade began the battle with 2,900 members. At the end more than 1,000 of those were casualties – more than a third.[68]

61 AWM: AWM4, 23/2/3: Appendix A, Report by Captain R.W. Weddell, CO 7th Battalion, 27 May 1915.
62 Ibid.
63 Ibid., Weddell reported that "our own artillery ... materially assisted the advance."
64 Ibid.
65 Ibid.
66 Ibid.
67 AWM: AWM38 3DRL 8042/14: Bennett to Bean, 2 December 1921.
68 Bean, *The Story of Anzac*, Vol. II, p. 41.

Australian dead, 8 May 1915.

'D' Company, 7th Battalion AIF survivors.

The Second Battle of Krithia was a series of infantry assaults. The primary method of capturing ground was to send the infantry across no man's land to attack the enemy – preferably with the bayonet – and win the day. Artillery ammunition was strictly rationed, and its use was secondary to the main event. Nevertheless, the manner in which the limited store of ammunition was used to support the infantry at Krithia was expected to be significant. A half hour's bombardment on supposed Turkish positions was deemed enough to disrupt the enemy in such a manner that a show of banners and bands would cause the enemy line to fall away. There were many positive comments made later about the impressive sight the bombardments on the peninsula made. Lieutenant Heron of the 7th Australian Battalion wrote "we… experienced a most extraordinary example of excellent concentrated shrapnel shooting. It was literally hailing & the ground appeared to be in constant movement."[69] Major Bennet also recorded that "we had good artillery support, the guns raking the Turkish trenches during the attack." But his next observation was even more important: "but this did not stop the machine gun fire."[70] Impressive as it may have been to the uninitiated 2nd Brigade, the artillery fire did not do what it was supposed to do.

69 AWM: AWM38 3DRL 8042/14: Heron to Bean, 9 March 1922.
70 AWM: AWM38 3DRL 8042/14: Bennett to Bean, 2 December 1921.

Heron learned this through his time on the Western Front, writing that "after seeing some of the shooting in France I would venture the opinion that there was a good deal of ammunition wasted that day and that little damage was done. The artillery did not keep the heads of the riflemen and machine gunners down and did not assist us."[71] In most places the bombardment was simply too far off target. Cass later recalled that "in my opinion the shells were going as I judged at the time 1,000 yards or more too far and passing over the Turks who were shooting into us… I know that I felt that I should like to tell them [the artillery officers] how they were wasting ammunition for our fellows were close to the Turks and the shells were going far beyond."[72] This left the infantry out in the open, faced with heavy enemy machine gun, shrapnel and rifle fire, and without any form of defence. There is little wonder that casualties were so high for so little gain.

But the inadequate artillery cover was not the worst part of these operations. The simple fact that they were continued one after the other, with little if any modification, was responsible for the extremely high casualty rate and ultimately the failure of the operation. If insanity may be described as doing the same thing over and over again and expecting different results, the second Battle of Krithia is the definition of irrationality. Over three days, four operations were conducted on basically the same lines – a weak artillery barrage followed by an infantry attack in the face of undiminished enemy machine gun fire. Each of these resulted in heavy casualties for little territorial gain, but no tactical reassessment or development followed. Instead, another hurried attack was forced through, in every case so quickly that the infantry had little more than a vague idea of its objective. Not even the first operation started in ideal conditions, but instead was rushed through in the face of repeated Turkish counter-attacks and the resulting confusion in British lines. The fourth operation was perhaps the least excusable. After having had a clear demonstration of the futility of this haphazard approach over three days, the only change to this operation was the fact that the artillery barrage was a little weaker, and that it was conducted in the afternoon.

The Second Battle of Krithia should have given some very clear examples of approaches to battle to avoid in the future. Rushed operations with little warning for the infantry, no clear instructions, and inadequate artillery barrages were clearly responsible for the extremely high casualty rate. The lack of knowledge of the strength or location of the enemy compounded the problem. But this would not be the last time some or all of these mistakes would be repeated on the Gallipoli peninsula. In fact, it would not be the last time attacks on Krithia failed dismally. The lives lost in the pursuit of a swift and easy victory were lost in vain.

71 AWM: AWM38 3DRL 8042/14: Heron to Bean, 9 March 1922.
72 AWM: AWM38 3DRL 8042/14: Cass to Bean, 2 December 1921.

4

A Failure Inevitable? Command and Staff Work in Planning for the August Offensive and the landing of IX Corps at Suvla Bay

Jeff Cleverly

The Gallipoli August offensive was the doomed attempt by General Sir Ian Hamilton (C-in-C MEF) to overcome the tactical stalemate that had existed on the peninsula since the failure of the April landings. Its purpose was to sever Ottoman lines of communication about the mid-section of the Gallipoli Peninsula and set the conditions for a renewed naval thrust through the Dardanelles. Launched on 6 August, the offensive consisted of several feint attacks before a major breakout attempt by the reinforced Australian and New Zealand Army Corps (ANZAC). Under its GOC Lieutenant-General Sir William Birdwood, this reinforced formation sought to turn the Ottoman defences to the north. Simultaneously, a separate amphibious landing was to be made by British IX Corps (GOC Lieutenant-General Sir Frederick Stopford) at Suvla Bay, five miles north of Anzac Cove.[1] Subsequent operations did not achieve any of the major objectives and the offensive became yet another failure in the tragic Gallipoli campaign. Whilst popular accounts extolling the achievements of the ANZAC abound, relatively little has been written about the similarly unsuccessful operations of IX Corps.

Coinciding with Birdwood's attack, the first of the two British New Army divisions that formed the bulk of Stopford's IX Corps began to disembark at Suvla after nightfall on 6 August. The 11th (Northern) Division, which spearheaded the assault, managed to secure the beach-heads and vicinity shortly after dawn on 7 August. Throughout the remainder of that day two brigades of the 10th (Irish) Division also successfully disembarked, and later that night the heavily outnumbered Ottoman outposts were forced back onto prepared positions approximately three miles inland. Yet by 8 August, inertia beset IX Corps with little forward progress being made. A general advance by the New Army Divisions and elements of 53rd (Welsh) Division, a Territorial Force (TF) formation, was launched on 9 August, but this was stalled by an Ottoman counter-attack. The 53rd Division attempted a second advance on 10 August, but this also failed. On 12 August, a brigade of the 54th (East Anglian) Division (TF) attempted a similarly unsuccessful assault to clear the enemy from the eastern foothills. Thereafter, the

1 The acronym ANZAC will be used when referring to Birdwood's corps. The more general term "Anzac" will be used when referring to the geographical area of the Gallipoli Peninsula occupied by Birdwood's corps.

Lieutenant-General Frederick Stopford (GOC IX Corps) right.

opposing forces began to consolidate two to three miles inland. Yet, despite further attacks by the reinforced IX Corps on 15 and 21 August, the Ottoman lines could not be breached. The result was stalemate on the Suvla front. The collective failure led to Stopford's removal and ultimately contributed to Hamilton's dismissal.

Poor British performance at Suvla Bay has been regarded as the nadir of the Gallipoli campaign and, up until recently, Stopford held up as the primary scapegoat for the complete failure of August offensive. Whilst a more reasoned assessment of the GOC IX Corps' responsibility exists, questions concerning Hamilton's expectations and why the offensive failed to achieve even the most limited tactical objectives are in need of serious reappraisal.[2] Thus this chapter will examine the command and staff-work throughout the operational planning stages of the August offensive in general, and the IX Corps landings in particular. It will challenge the currently accepted view that the Suvla landings were practically irrelevant – a "sideline to a sideshow" as one recent historian has observed – and demonstrate that Hamilton held higher expectations for Suvla than the plan actually delivered.[3] Furthermore, it will also reveal how it was the manner in which planning was conducted, as much as the actual plans that ensured there was little chance of achieving even the most limited tasks assigned, let alone the more ambitious intentions harboured.

2 See: Robin Prior, *Gallipoli: The End of the Myth* (Sydney: University of New South Wales Press, 2010); Tim Travers, *Gallipoli 1915* (Stroud: Tempus, 2001); Rhys Crawley, *Climax at Gallipoli: The Failure of the August Offensive* (Norman, Oklahoma: University of Oklahoma Press, 2014) and Edward Erickson, *Gallipoli: Command Under Fire* (Oxford: Osprey Publishing, 2015).
3 Prior, *Gallipoli*, p. 209.

Background

By mid-May 1915, the strategic situation facing the British government was critical. On the Western Front, Sir John French's offensives at Neuve Chapelle and Aubers Ridge had failed with heavy cost; the murderous Second Battle of Ypres and the first successful use of poison gas by the Germans was an ominous sign of things to come. At Gallipoli, the inability of the navy to force a passage of the Dardanelles had spawned the 25 April landings at Cape Helles and Anzac. The overall strategic purpose was the capture of the Kilid Bahr Plateau, which dominated the Ottoman defences and was considered to be the "key to the opening of the Dardanelles."[4]

The Anzac landing failed to achieve either its preliminary objective, the capture of the Sari Bair range, or the ultimate object, which was to secure a position across the peninsula mid-section as a means of severing Ottoman communications to the Kilid Bahr Plateau and south to Helles.[5] As a result, ANZAC was imprisoned within a tenuous bridgehead centred on Anzac Cove. At Cape Helles, where the main landings had taken place, the British 29th Division also failed to secure its initial objective, the southern-most Kilid Bahr bastion known as Achi Baba.[6] By mid-May, following a number of increasingly costly advances at Helles, the MEF established approximately three miles from Achi Baba. Kilid Bahr remained a distant prospect inasmuch as the MEF was experiencing serious manpower and ammunition shortages.

On 13 May, Birdwood proposed a turning movement north of Anzac to capture the Sari Bair range, a relatively minor operation that would provide his corps with improved security and much needed elbow room.[7] Encouraged by Hamilton, Birdwood expanded this idea over the next fortnight into a more elaborate scheme, one that could be mounted from within the confines of Anzac and required the reinforcement of four additional brigades only. The initial plan, submitted to Hamilton on 30 May, involved the turning of the Ottoman right flank north of Anzac followed by the capture of the Sari Bair range. Following this, a short advance would be made from the southeast of the original Anzac position onto what was known locally as the "Third" or "Gun Ridge." If successful, the offensive would not only place ANZAC in a more favourable tactical position, but would also provide the MEF with a suitable starting point from which to launch further offensives.[8]

In London, Prime Minister Herbert Asquith's Liberal Government had been dissolved in the wake of the shell scandal. The succeeding Coalition Government, also under Asquith, formed the Dardanelles Committee as a substitute for the original War Council.[9] The general

4 Isle of Wight County Records Office (IoW): Aspinall Papers: Memorandum, Aspinall to Braithwaite, 23 March 1915; GHQ Force Order No. 1, 13 April 1915, in Historical Section Committee of Imperial Defence, *Military Operations: Gallipoli, Vol I, Maps & Appendices* (London: Heinemann, 1929), p. 7.

5 The National Archives (TNA): WO 95/4280: GHQ Instructions to GOC A & NZ Army Corps, 13 April 1915.

6 TNA WO 95/4280: GHQ Force Order No 2, 'Instructions for the Helles Covering Force', 19 April 1915.

7 TNA WO 95/4281: Letter, Birdwood to Hamilton, 13 May 1915.

8 TNA WO 95/4281: Letter, Birdwood to Hamilton, 16 May 1915; Letter, Birdwood to Braithwaite, 30 May 1915.

9 For more on the strategic problems confronting the British Government at the time, see David French, *British Strategy and War Aims 1914-1916* (London: Allen & Unwin, 1986).

public, encouraged by controversial war correspondent Ellis Ashmead Bartlett's vivid Gallipoli despatches, continued to demonstrate a keen interest in the Dardanelles, an interest matched by growing public support in the Australian and New Zealand dominions. Thus the new government, in addition to considering vital strategic issues, could not ignore popular support for a successful conclusion to the Gallipoli campaign. In parliament and in public, former First Lord of the Admiralty Winston Churchill also actively promoted the strategic possibilities of victory, "the only prize, which lies within reach this year.'[10] At the first Dardanelles Committee meeting (7 June 1915), it was agreed that Hamilton should be reinforced by the three remaining (10th, 11th, 13th) divisions of Kitchener's First New Army (later grouped as IX Corps under Stopford), "with a view to an assault in the second week of July", an aspiration subsequently delayed by one month owing to transport shortages.[11] Secretary of State for War, Lord Kitchener, informed Hamilton of this that same day thus setting the stage for the August push to come.

Diverging Expectations: GHQ Planning

Back at MEF GHQ, now established on Imbros, Hamilton set to work immediately. On 8 June he discussed the new situation with Vice Admiral John de Robeck (commander Eastern Mediterranean Squadron) and Commodore Roger Keyes, de Robeck's Chief of Staff. According to Hamilton they "worked off [sic] the broad general scheme in the course of an hour and a half."[12] At Anzac, Birdwood's staff had updated the 30 May scheme based on the strengthened Ottoman defences north of Anzac. They concluded that a second reinforced division (the aforementioned four supplementary brigades inclusive) ought to be kept "handy" as a safety margin. The scheme, however, went further with the suggestion that additional reinforcements, organised into "tactical formations", should also be made readily available in order to "turn success into decisive victory."[13] Birdwood's expanding plan introduced the possibility of advancing the ANZAC right flank beyond Gun Ridge and across the peninsula's mid-section towards Maidos, a movement that would sever Ottoman lines of communication to the south. This would achieve the original purpose of the April ANZAC landing.

The prospect of restoring operational level movement to the campaign also revealed Hamilton and Birdwood's mutual optimism. Whilst each acknowledged that possession of the Kilid Bahr Plateau was the MEF's primary aim, their language began to assume a more hopeful tone that suggested the enemy resistance would crumble in the vicinity of Sari Bair.[14] For example, Hamilton informed Birdwood how he envisaged the "main push and decisive movement" would originate from Anzac, and that he anticipated the seizure of Sari Bair "may prove to be the fulcrum for the lever which will topple over Germany and the pride

10 Winston Churchill, *The World Crisis 1915* (London: Thornton Butterworth, 1923), p. 408; Robert Rhodes James, *Gallipoli* (London: Papermac, 1965), p. 216.
11 TNA CAB 22/2: Conclusions of a meeting of the Dardanelles Committee, 7 June 1915.
12 Ian Hamilton, *Gallipoli Diary*, Vol I. (London: Edward Arnold, 1920), pp. 283-284.
13 TNA WO 95/4281: 'Notes on Further Operations by Australian and New Zealand Army Corps', untitled manuscript, Appendix IX (n.d.).
14 TNA CAB 19/31: Telegram, Hamilton to Kitchener, No. MF300, 7 June 1915; WO 95/4281: Letter, Birdwood to Hamilton, 7 June 1915.

of the Germans."[15] On 9 June, Hamilton and his chief of the general staff (CGS) Major-General Walter Braithwaite, discussed the emerging ANZAC plan with Birdwood and the other MEF corps commanders.[16] Hamilton later expressed his satisfaction at the outcome of this conference, remarking how the "whole scheme hinges on these crests of Sari Bair", which he believed was the "keep" to the Narrows beyond.[17] For his part, a enthusiastic Birdwood added weight to Hamilton's hopes by stating that the capture of Sari Bair might "compel the Turks either to come out and fight us to a finish, or capitulate."[18] Hamilton's propensity for effusive language cautions against drawing the conclusion that he had lost sight of Kilid Bahr as the MEF's primary objective; however, such optimism suggests there was a growing belief amongst Hamilton, Birdwood and their respective headquarters that the Sari Bair range was, as opposed to Kilid Bahr, the key to unhinging the Ottoman defence.

Hamilton's operations staff, however, was less sanguine about the prospect of swift victory. Led by Lieutenant-Colonel Cecil Faber Aspinall – subsequent official historian of the campaign – it examined a range of alternatives for the employment of the New Army reinforcements.[19] Aspinall, assisted by Major Guy Dawnay (GSO 2), addressed four options: new landings at Bulair or the Asiatic shore; Birdwood's Anzac scheme; and a continuance of the offensive at Cape Helles. The Bulair and Asiatic options were quickly dismissed due to consequent dispersal of naval and military forces *vis-à-vis* the submarine threat. It was also recognised that the Helles option, despite the opportunity to capture Achi Baba, would be a costly affair similar to the three previous offensives there. This left Birdwood's Anzac scheme as offering the most effective means by which enemy communications could be disrupted. Unlike Hamilton and Birdwood, who were starting to entertain the possibility of a direct link between the capture of Sari Bair and Ottoman defeat, Aspinall and Dawnay considered seizure of Sari Bair as a means to conduct further operations to deny the enemy on Kilid Bahr of men and materiel. This guarded conclusion, wholly consistent with the original strategic objective set for the campaign, held that a decision could only be achieved once Kilid Bahr was in British hands. Moreover, significant reinforcements in hand, this process would take considerable time before fruition.[20] Notwithstanding the prevailing differences between Hamilton and his operations staff, the decision was made to launch the next offensive from Anzac: "I only await the promised reinforcements", Hamilton cabled the War Office on 13 June, "to enable me to take the next step in the prosecution of my main plan from ANZAC."[21]

15 Liddell Hart Centre for Military Archives (LHCMA): Hamilton Papers, 7/1/6: Letter, Hamilton to Birdwood, 18 May 1915.
16 TNA WO 95/4264: GHQ General Staff War Diary, June 1915.
17 Hamilton, *Gallipoli Diary*, Vol 1, pp. 283-84, 288.
18 TNA Kitchener Papers, PRO 30/57/62: Letter, Birdwood to Fitzgerald, 20 June 1915.
19 C.F. Aspinall-Oglander, *Military Operations Gallipoli*, Vol II (London: Heinemann, 1929), p. 67. Aspinall changed his surname to Aspinall-Oglander prior to an inter-war marriage. His original surname will be utilised throughout this chapter.
20 TNA CAB 19/31: Telegrams, Hamilton to Kitchener, No. MF300 and MF 304, 7 and 8 June 1915. Guy Dawnay wrote these two telegrams, which were released in Hamilton's name. See Imperial War Museum (IWM): Williams Papers, 69/78/1: Diary 3 March-21 August 1915, 5 June 1915 for comments concerning the writing of GHQ telegrams at the time.
21 TNA CAB 19/31: Telegram, Hamilton to War Office, No. MF 328, 13 June 1915.

By mid-June GHQ plans were beginning to take shape. It was decided to employ, in addition to the three New Army divisions, the 52nd (Lowland) Division (TF) and the 29th Indian Brigade, previously deployed at Helles, to Anzac. Two of the New Army divisions and the Indian brigade were attached to ANZAC as the turning movement force. This left the remaining divisions (one New Army and 52nd Division) available to disembark at Anzac "as more room became available."[22] Hamilton did not specifically state how he planned to employ the remaining two formations; however, in a telegram to the War Office on 13 June, he speculated that an "advance of little more than 2 miles in a south-eastern direction" would enable the MEF to dominate land communications southwards down the peninsula.[23] This meant that GHQ was considering deploying the remaining New Army division and 52nd Division to extend Birdwood's proposed advance beyond Gun Ridge. Hamilton's 13 June telegram also claimed that such a move would enable ANZAC artillery to interdict the Turkish sea communications through the Straits.[24] Although still at the embryonic stage, it was apparent that the MEF's offensive plans would be based on the capture of Sari Bair, the subsequent breakout to be astride the peninsula mid-section from the right of the existing Anzac position. Kitchener concurred, remarking that it "would have the most excellent effect."[25]

On learning of the arrival dates of the New Army divisions, Aspinall submitted a memorandum to Hamilton on 23 June. Its purpose was "to decide where these divisions are to be employed."[26] This submission, a repetition of the original appreciation undertaken by the GHQ Operations section, was significant for several reasons. First, that it had been compiled at all highlighted the dysfunctional nature of the GHQ decision-making process. Unsurprisingly, Aspinall's second appreciation reflected his earlier recommendation to launch the next offensive at Anzac, a concept that Hamilton had already approved and Kitchener had granted sanction.[27] Yet, according to Guy Dawnay, the decision of where to employ the divisions was still in the balance, and was dependent on the outcome of the memorandum.[28] The primary cause of this puzzling series of circumstances was Braithwaite's staunch conviction that the offensive should be launched from Cape Helles instead. The doctrinaire and strong-willed Braithwaite, Birdwood observed, "obsessed with the idea of Achi Baba." Moreover, his considerable influence over Hamilton meant that the decision to employ the New Army reinforcements at Anzac was apparently no longer *fait accompli*.[29] Aspinall and Dawnay shared Birdwood's frustration with Hamilton's stubborn CGS. "Unfortunately", Guy Dawnay confided to GHQ cipher officer Orlo Williams, "the CGS [Braithwaite] is not convinced of the feasibility of his [Birdwood's ANZAC] plan: he rather inclines to landing near [Cape] Helles and turning the flank of the Achi Baba trenches."[30] Dawnay also intimated that Braithwaite was not inclined to "wholeheartedly" support a decision to attack at Anzac. As Hamilton's CGS and principal adviser, Braithwaite was the sole conduit between the C-in-C MEF and his junior operations staff.

22 Aspinall-Oglander, *Military Operations*, Vol II, pp. 67-71.
23 TNA CAB 19/31: Hamilton to War Office, No. MF 328, 13 June 1915.
24 Ibid.
25 LHCMA: Hamilton Papers, 7/4/16: Letter, Fitzgerald to Braithwaite, 19 June 1915.
26 IoW: Aspinall Papers, OG/AO/G/4: Memorandum, Aspinall to Hamilton, 23 June 1915.
27 LHCMA: Hamilton Papers, 7/4/16: Letter, Fitzgerald to Braithwaite, 19 June 1915.
28 IWM: Williams Papers, 69/78/1: Diary 3 March-21 August 1915, 23 June 1915.
29 Australian War Memorial (AWM): Bean Papers, AWM38 3DRL 8042/24: Birdwood to Bean (n.d.).
30 IWM: Williams Papers, 69/78/1: Diary 3 March-21 August 1915, 23 June 1915.

Braithwaite's ambivalence towards the Anzac scheme and his interposition between Hamilton and staff can only have increased the growing divergence between the C-in-C and Aspinall's Operations section, which by then was responsible for detailed planning of the August offensive. In addition, this incident also indicated Hamilton's reluctance to impose his will upon GHQ's planning, the full implications of which would become apparent as it progressed.

The second significant aspect of Aspinall's 23 June memorandum was the reiteration of Aspinall and Dawnay's speculation that the coming offensive would bring the campaign to a swift conclusion. Thus the document made clear that the capture of Sari Bair and consequent severing of Ottoman lines of communication were unlikely to provide the opportunity for decisive battle and Ottoman surrender. This assessment was distinctly at odds with Hamilton and Birdwood's optimism. "Such a success" Aspinall observed, "might not, and probably would not, be decisive, as the Germans would naturally endeavour to make the Turks [sic] retreat south to Kilid Bahr where they could still be supplied with food and ammunition across the Narrows."[31] Thus Aspinall and Dawnay still anticipated a lengthy campaign, one which would extend beyond the initial Anzac assault on Sari Bair. Subsequent operations would require the MEF to fight its way across the peninsula as far as the Kilid Bahr upland.

The identification of Suvla Bay as an alternative advanced base to Anzac also emerged from the Aspinall memorandum. Further to this, he expressed concern about Anzac's limited capacity to sustain protracted operations, and the difficulties of landing stores due to anticipated inclement weather during the succeeding autumn.[32] This concern would have been further justified after the announcement that two TF divisions might also be available for the forthcoming offensive. Consequently, Aspinall introduced the idea of utilising Suvla Bay as a supply base in the wake of Sari Bair's capture: Suvla Bay "could be made into a useful advanced base in the case of a successful advance into the [Maidos] plain from the existing Anzac position."[33] Aspinall also observed that a tramway could "eventually" be constructed from Suvla as a means of expediting supply.[34] Hamilton subsequently approved the memorandum on 25 June, so the original decision to launch the next offensive at Anzac was finally confirmed. However, this time the scheme had been expanded to include the Suvla Bay landings.[35]

An apparent absence of enemy forces in the Suvla area was another important factor to emerge during planning. Aspinall and Dawnay presumed that the weakly held sector would more than likely fall to the MEF once the ANZAC attack secured the Sari Bair range. This assumption was significant because the Royal Navy lacked the small landing craft at the time.[36] Captain Edgar Anstey, one of Aspinall's subordinates, also noted that landing on a hostile shore was not under consideration at the time.[37] This meant that the Suvla landings were considered to be primarily administrative in scope as opposed to offensive. Although the navy subsequently provided suitable landing craft and plans were adjusted to reflect the need to overcome Ottoman opposition, the initial staff conception remained administrative rather

31 IoW: Aspinall Papers, OG/AO/G/4: Memorandum, Aspinall to Hamilton, 23 June 1915.
32 Ibid.
33 Ibid.
34 Ibid.
35 TNA CAB 45/241: Letter, Anstey to Aspinall, 6 June 1928.
36 IoW: Aspinall Papers, OG/AO/G/4: Memorandum, Aspinall to Hamilton, 23 June 1915.
37 TNA CAB 45/241: Letter, Anstey to Aspinall, 6 June 1928.

than operational. This conception conformed to the limited/defensive perspectives maintained by Aspinall and Dawnay. Both conceived the Suvla landing as a separate and discreet operation to the ANZAC offensive; its importance was considered in relation to the supply of extended operations following the seizure of Sari Bair and not a component part of the initial Anzac attack upon it. The navy, desirous for a secure anchorage from submarines and mines, also shared this view.[38] Dawnay subsequently observed: "Suvla stood out as the more or less obvious place"; it would also, he added, provide the MEF with a good harbour "for the winter in case we want it."[39]

By late June, having approved Aspinall's memorandum and accepted inclusion of the Suvla landing as part of the August plan, Hamilton must have understood his staff's protracted view of the campaign was at odds with his inherent optimism. Yet neither he nor Braithwaite appear to have arrested this growing divergence of expectations. One possible explanation for this lack of reconciliation may have been Whitehall's increasing expectation of a swift and decisive conclusion. Indeed, Hamilton had just been informed that Kitchener and the Coalition Government, having determined Gallipoli to be the only theatre where a victory could be achieved in 1915, "were most anxious to get through the Dardanelles this autumn."[40] Governmental pressure rose dramatically over the next fortnight, Kitchener informing Hamilton that he must achieve success "somehow or the other."[41] In response, Hamilton requested "offensive ammunition" for no more than two months, which suggests he anticipated a result before winter, a view inconsistent with that held by Aspinall and Dawnay.[42] Another explanation as to why Hamilton appears to have overlooked the unresolved dissonance within his staff was a general view that the Ottoman *Fifth Army* was in crisis following the series of offensives at Helles. In characteristic grandiloquent rhetoric, Hamilton afterwards wrote how, by early July, that "there is a feeling in the air – thrilling through the ranks – that at last the upper hand is ours. Now is the moment to fall on with might and main – to press unrelentingly and without break or pause until we wrest victory from fortune."[43] Whilst the tendency remained at GHQ to underestimate the enemy at this stage of the campaign, the C-in-C's imagination and overreaching optimism arguably led him, in contrast to his prosaically inclined staff, to draw dramatic conclusions with regard to Ottoman military capacity.

Meanwhile, the decision to include the Suvla landing as a component part of the forthcoming offensive meant that GHQ's earlier aspiration to employ all reinforcements at Anzac was in need of amendments. Two of IX Corps' New Army divisions and the Indian brigade were thus earmarked for Anzac whilst the third division and 52nd Division were to land at Suvla. Despite the absence of a comprehensive GHQ offensive order, by late June the operational concept can

38 Aspinall-Oglander, *Military Operations*, Vol II, p. 131; Sir Roger Keyes, *Naval Memoirs: The Narrow Seas to the Dardanelles 1910-1915* (London: Thornton Butterworth, 1934), pp. 376-377.

39 IoW: Aspinall-Oglander Papers, OG/AO/G/38: Letter, Dawnay to Aspinall, 6 March 1929; IWM: Dawnay Papers, 69/2/1: Letter, Dawnay to Cis, 9 August 1915.

40 LHCMA: Hamilton Papers, 7/4/16: Letter, Fitzgerald to Braithwaite, 19 June 1915; TNA CAB 19/28: Letter, Fitzgerald to Braithwaite, 25 June 1915.

41 TNA CAB 19/28: Letter, Fitzgerald to Braithwaite, 17 July 1915.

42 TNA CAB 19/28: Letter, Braithwaite to Fitzgerald, 7 July 1915; CAB 19/31: Telegram, Hamilton to Kitchener, No. MF 444, 13 July 1915.

43 Hamilton, *Gallipoli Diary*, Vol I, p. 340.

loosely be described in terms of three distinct phases.[44] The first was the turning movement north of Anzac and simultaneous landing at Suvla. The second consisted of a push to secure Gun Ridge from the centre and right of the existing ANZAC position. Expectations at the end of this phase was the capture of an intermittent line extending north of Suvla through Sari Bair southwards astride Gun Ridge as far as Gaba Tepe. In the final phase, 52nd Division, having disembarked on the morning after commencement of the offensive, would exploit the limited breakout from the right by advancing across the peninsula to Maidos. At this point, the MEF would have interdicted vital Ottoman sea and land communications. Retaining the two remaining Territorial divisions as a reserve, Hamilton intended to employ these formations as a means of final exploitation or deployment in subsequent operations elsewhere.[45]

From the outset, Hamilton's hopes for a conclusive result in the early stages of the offensive led him to place greater emphasis on the Suvla landing's close association with the initial ANZAC attack on Sari Bair. On 29 June, he informed Kitchener that he would "turn the enemy's right at Anzac" with the three New Army divisions. This suggests that the Suvla landing shared the same objective as the New Army divisions committed to Anzac.[46] On 4 July, Hamilton reinforced this correlation when he informed Vice-Admiral de Robeck that the Suvla formations were to "act in concert with the troops from ANZAC" and much would depend on the "celerity" with which the navy could land them.[47] Although the C-in-C's language remained somewhat vague, it appears that, rather than establishing a base from which to mount subsequent operations, he considered the Suvla operation to be closely related to the combined assault on Sari Bair.

At this stage, Birdwood submitted two important updates to his original Anzac offensive proposal that would further influence Hamilton's continued belief in the close relationship between the Anzac and Suvla landings. On 1 July Birdwood, still unaware of Hamilton's decision to include Suvla in the August scheme, recommended a brigade sized landing at Suvla to seize Chocolate Hill and the W Hills in order to secure the left flank of the Sari Bair assault. Moreover, if allocated additional divisions, he also proposed the simultaneous capture of Tekke Tepe Ridge, situated approximately four to five miles due east of Suvla Bay. Both tactical features in hand, the MEF would dominate the Anafarta Gap and the Ottoman land lines of communication beyond. To this end, Birdwood proposed sending "a strong striking force" through the gap prior to unhinging the Sari Bair defences. Thus Suvla Bay was the logical place from which such a thrust could be launched. At that stage, however, Birdwood lacked the resources to form a "striking force", so this part of the plan remained little more than an aspiration.[48]

The following day, 2 July, Birdwood discussed this proposal with Hamilton in what would be their last face-to-face meeting before the impending offensive. Informed of the intention to land IX Corps at Suvla, Birdwood, Hamilton observed, need only concentrate on the attack upon

44 MEF GHQ did issue one overarching order; however, it only provided a very broad overview of the proposed offensive. See TNA WO 95/4276: GHQ MEF Force Order No. 25, 2 August 1915. The interpretation here builds upon the work conducted by Rhys Crawley in his PhD thesis: 'Our Second Great [Mis]adventure': A Critical Re-evaluation of the August Offensive, Gallipoli 1915', which was subsequently published as *Climax at Gallipoli.*
45 TNA CAB 19/31: Telegram, Hamilton to Kitchener, No. MF 381, 29 June 1915.
46 Ibid.
47 TNA WO 158/889: Letter, Hamilton to de Robeck, 4 July 1915.
48 TNA WO 95/4281: Memorandum, Birdwood to GHQ, 1 July 1915.

Lieutenant-General Sir William Birdwood (GOC ANZAC).

Sari Bair. Nevertheless, Birdwood must have understood that GHQ would ensure close coordination of both corps when he recollected how Hamilton "looked at Suvla and Anzac combined as his main operation."[49] On learning about the availability of two Territorial divisions on 10 July, Birdwood provided GHQ with a second update to the first proposal whereby he recommended that a two division force be "shoved through [the Anafarta Gap] as quickly as possible behind, and in direct conjunction" with the ANZAC attack on Sari Bair and the occupation of Tekke Tepe. Hamilton also implied that anticipated heavy casualties during the main ANZAC attack and the reinforced Ottoman defences to the south of the Anzac position meant that a northward thrust through the less heavily defended Anafarta Gap might be the decisive act.[50] In a subsequent letter to the War Office, Birdwood stressed that such a thrust could get the "Turks [sic] on the run", in which case it was "possible that Stopford and I may be able to manage this between us."[51]

Birdwood's 10 July proposal was not taken further by GHQ. The primary reason for this may have been that the additional divisions required for the "striking force" were not due to arrive before the opening of the offensive. Furthermore, Hamilton, whose trademark optimism had been further fuelled by a perception that the MEF held a "moral ascendancy" over the enemy, was confident of success without the extra formations.[52] Notwithstanding its failure to gain traction at GHQ, the Anafarta Gap proposal was especially significant because it provided Hamilton with an alternative option for achieving victory should the capture of Sari Bair fail to bring about the Ottoman capitulation he hoped for. In any case, previous staff assessments of an extended campaign were the far more realistic proposition. It should also be recalled that

49 AWM: Birdwood Papers, 3DRL/3376 1/1: Diary 1 January 1915-2 January 1916; TNA CAB 19/33: Birdwood, evidence before the Dardanelles Commission, Q 21403.
50 TNA WO 95/4281: Memorandum, Birdwood to GHQ, 10 July 1915.
51 AWM: Birdwood Papers, 3 DRL/3376/11/16: Letter, Birdwood to Callwell, 27 July 1915.
52 TNA CAB 19/28: Letter, Braithwaite to Fitzgerald, 1 July 1915; CAB 19/29: Letter, Hamilton to Grimwood Mears, 6 November 1916; CAB 19/28: Letter, Braithwaite to Fitzgerald, 4 August 1915.

an element of Aspinall and Dawnay's original plan had been the deployment of follow on forces passing from Suvla southwards through the confined Anzac beachhead prior to breaking out to the south-east. GHQ's view of the recommended direction was at odds with Birdwood, whose increasing concern about strengthened Ottoman defences south of Anzac was the *raison d'être* of the Anafarta proposal.[53]

By identifying the possibility of switching the breakout flank from the south to north, Birdwood reinforced Hamilton's perception of the close relationship between the Suvla and Anzac operations. For his part, Hamilton was evidently interested in the northern alternative, writing to Vice-Admiral de Robeck on 14 July to request aerial reconnaissance of the proposed route through Anafarta Gap.[54] Birdwood, who did not meet with Hamilton again after 2 July, was convinced that the northern route into the Ottoman lines of communication is what Hamilton "hoped for as a result of the Suvla landing."[55] In fact, just three days after receipt of Birdwood's last proposal (13 July), Hamilton made very clear his perceived direct connection between the Suvla landing and success. "If the *landing operation* [my emphasis] is successful to the degree for which I hope, it will be the turn of the Navy to undertake the operation which is the primary reason of its presence here."[56]

By mid-July therefore, Hamilton had linked the Suvla landing with a successful conclusion of the Gallipoli campaign in two ways: first, a combined Anzac–Suvla attack upon Sari Bair range would achieve rapid and decisive success in what he later described as "one big rush."[57] Second, in the event the offensive failed to deliver immediate results, Hamilton had at his disposal an alternative option to deploy follow on forces through the Anafarta Gap, thus avoiding the need to pass them through Anzac in accordance with the original staff plan. In either case, Hamilton envisaged the Suvla landing to be bound closely within the offensive concept. Conversely, his operations staff, still contemplating a protracted campaign, considered the Suvla gambit to be an entirely separate and subsidiary operation. For example, Dawnay considered the Anzac and Suvla operations to be "quite distinct from the other" and, in stark contrast to Hamilton's irrepressible optimism, was quite pessimistic about the prospects for a decisive result.[58] Indeed, as Orlo Williams remarked on 21 July, "Dawnay is not very optimistic even about the result of success in our next big push. Seems to think the best one could hope for would be to get a strong position across the Peninsula and build up a safe base at Suvla Bay."[59] The divergence of opinion between Hamilton and his operations staff demonstrated that each harboured separate definitions of operational success.

Hamilton, fully aware that the MEF might have to fight all the way across the peninsula and onto Kilid Bahr, remained undaunted with regard to Ottoman ability to resist. Birdwood's forthright enthusiasm and increased strategic pressure from Whitehall also encouraged Hamilton's belief in Ottoman capitulation once the MEF appeared behind the Sari Bair range. At variance

53 AWM: AWM4 1/25/4: HQ ANZAC GS War Diary, July 1915: Appreciation of the Situation at Anzac, 9 July 1915; TNA WO 95/4281: Memorandum, Birdwood to GHQ, 1 July 1915; Memorandum, Birdwood to GHQ, 10 July 1915; AWM: General Staff War Diary, 1st Australian Division, August 1915: 'Note on proposed attack by 1st Australian Division', undated.
54 TNA WO 158/576: Letter, Hamilton to de Robeck, 14 July 1915.
55 TNA CAB 19/33: Birdwood, evidence before the Dardanelles Commission, Q 21266.
56 TNA CAB 19/31: Telegram, Hamilton to War Office, 13 July 1915.
57 LHCMA: Hamilton Papers, 7/1/9: Letter, Hamilton to Clive Wigram, 10 August 1915.
58 IWM: Dawnay Papers, 69/2/1: Letter, Dawnay to Cis, 9 August 1915.
59 IWM: Williams Papers, 69/78/1: Diary 3 March-21 August 1915, 21 July 1915.

with this, his more pragmatic operations staff retained a measured view of subsequent progress, which envisaged the capture of Sari Bair as the start of a long drawn out struggle for Kilid Bahr Plateau. This conceptual divergence between C-in-C and operations staff spawned a distorted understanding of Hamilton's intentions at Suvla.

Distortion: GHQ's Suvla Plan

The deployment of the bulk of 52nd Division (the TF formation chosen to complete the Anzac breakout) in an unsuccessful and costly Helles attack on 12/13 July meant that by the middle of that month, Hamilton had only the three New Army divisions and the Indian brigade immediately available for the coming offensive. As a result, Birdwood was allocated the 13th (Western) Division, a brigade of the 10th (Irish) Division and the Indian brigade from Cape Helles. Thus Stopford would have the 11th (Northern) Division and the remaining two brigades of the 10th Division for the Suvla operation. Hamilton would retain the 53rd and 54th divisions, scheduled to arrive after the opening of the offensive, as a general reserve.

While Birdwood was left to develop the Anzac scheme, Hamilton's rigid insistence on secrecy meant that Aspinall and the Operations section undertook the detailed planning for Suvla in isolation from the remainder of GHQ staff and IX Corps HQ, the latter only then arriving in theatre from Great Britain. Indeed, Hamilton had been so disturbed by the poor operational security during the initial April landings that he determined secrecy with regard to the Suvla landing as "ultra-vital", the planning thereof to be kept "within a tiny circle" of a trusted operations staff led by Aspinall.[60] In addition, the operations staff was also responsible for overseeing existing operations at Helles and Anzac whilst simultaneously organising the disembarkation, accommodation and sustainment of ANZAC reinforcements, which were to be secretly disembarked at Anzac Cove in the days prior to the offensive began.[61] Dawnay's letters to his wife during this period reflect the enormous pressure the Operations section was under at the time, which can only have been compounded by Hamilton's penchant for secrecy.[62] The direct effects of this excessive workload are difficult to quantify; however, when considered within the context of GHQ's ad hoc decision making process, it is possible to appreciate how much Aspinall and Dawnay – already out of step with Hamilton's thinking – may not have fully appreciated the MEF C-in-C's perceptions with regard to the August offensive as a determinate for final victory.

Aspinall and Dawnay's failure to fully appreciate Hamilton's aspirations are evident in several crucial decisions made at GHQ during this period. The first concerned command and control arrangements for Suvla and Anzac. Hamilton's first inclination was to personally command ANZAC and IX Corps from a small tactical headquarters situated at the Suvla beachhead.[63] With the Anzac and Suvla operations "combined as the main operation", the degree of coordination would maintain the unity of effort required.[64] Hamilton, as Aspinall subsequently

60 Hamilton, *Gallipoli Diary*, Vol. I, p. 328.
61 Aspinall-Oglander, *Military Operations*, Vol. II, pp 134-136.
62 IWM: Dawnay Papers, 69/2/1: Letters, Dawnay to wife, 1,15 and 22 July 1915.
63 TNA CAB 19/28: Aspinall, Statement to the Dardanelles Commission.
64 TNA CAB 19/33: Birdwood, evidence before the Dardanelles Commission, Q 21266.

observed, was "over-persuaded by the staff" to remain some 18 miles distant from operations.[65] This advice, which significantly reduced the C-in-C's ability to coordinate ANZAC and IX Corps, also reflected staff perceptions of the August offensive as two distinct operations.

The second decision was allocation of forces for the Suvla landing. At first, Hamilton wanted to employ the seasoned British 29th Division because of its status as a Regular Army formation, which had performed so valiantly at the Helles landings in April, a desire that was consistent with his aggressive view of the Suvla operation.[66] By this stage, the C-in-C MEF had refined earlier vague notions of IX Corps' deployment. The hope was that the first division ashore would advance rapidly inland to gain "possession of the line Anafarta Sagir – Ejelmer Bay [Tekke Tepe Ridge] before next morning [7 August]."[67] The speed of this thrust was crucial in order to ensure Suvla Bay was sufficiently secure for the second division to come ashore before pressing on "through the Anafartas to the east of Sari Bair", where it would join forces with ANZAC in an attack to "smash the mainspring of the Turkish [sic] opposition."[68] Hamilton's operations staff, however, convinced him that obtaining the splendid, yet battle-weary 29th Division was asking too much, so the task was allocated to the untried 11th Division.[69] Aspinall retrospectively conceded that Hamilton's instinct was right, but "other counsels prevailed."[70] This questionable advice was based on Aspinall and Dawnay's view that the IX Corps landing was not critical to the all-important Sari Bair assault. Braithwaite subsequently recalled that on confirmation of IX Corps' landing, the GHQ operations staff expressed relief that "the thing is done", which not only reinforces the limited expectations, but also suggests his own confusion regarding operational intentions.[71]

This limited perspective is also apparent in a 16 July correspondence between Aspinall and MEF GHQ Deputy Quartermaster General (DQMG) Brigadier-General S.H. Winter, which contained a series of movement tables detailing anticipated rates of advance at Suvla. Examination thereof makes it clear that 11th Division was expected to advance between two to three miles. This would place it in the region of the Chocolate and W Hills or nearly two miles short of Tekke Tepe Ridge, which Hamilton hoped would be captured within the first 24 hours. What is more, said movement tables indicated that 11th Division's advance to Tekke Tepe Ridge would not occur until 48 hours after coming ashore.[72] Aspinall subsequently claimed that he had stressed the importance of Tekke Tepe's swift capture. This is belied by staff which did not reflect the operational "celerity" Hamilton desired.[73] Further, the same movement tables denoted ANZAC seizure of the Sari Bair range within the first 24 hours of the IX Corps

65 TNA CAB 19/33: Aspinall, evidence before Dardanelles Commission, Q13934; Aspinall-Oglander, *Military Operations*, Vol II, p. 141.
66 Aspinall-Oglander, p. 139 and TNA CAB 19/33: Hamilton, evidence before Dardanelles Commission, Q25290-91.
67 LHCMA: Hamilton Papers, 7/1/15: Letter, Hamilton to Maxwell, 10 August 1915.
68 General Sir Ian Hamilton, *Ian Hamilton's Final Despatch* (London: George Dewnes, 1916), p. 80.
69 Aspinall-Oglander, *Military Operations*, Vol II, p. 139; TNA CAB 19/33: Hamilton, evidence before Dardanelles Commission, Q25290-91.
70 Aspinall-Oglander, *Military Operations*, Vol II, p. 139.
71 TNA CAB 19/33: Braithwaite, evidence before the Dardanelles Commission, Q13567.
72 TNA WO 95/4266: Aspinall, 'Memorandum on Impending Landing Operations', 16 July 1915.
73 TNA CAB/28: Statement to the Dardanelles Commission by Lieutenant-Colonel C.F. Aspinall; WO 158/889: Letter, Hamilton to de Robeck, 4 July 1915.

landing. Stopford's second formation ashore (10th Division), which Hamilton expected to combine with the ANZAC attack, was not expected to be in a position until the second day or anything up to 24 hours *after* Sari Bair was in MEF hands. Thus Aspinall did not plan for 10th Division's expected role in the assault. Furthermore, his 16 July correspondence makes clear that the movements of both corps were not synchronised to achieve anything like the decisive effect Hamilton sought. The consequences of this lack of coordination would be further compounded by the ill-fated decision to leave the C-in-C isolated on Imbros.[74]

This misleading impression of Hamilton's Suvla intentions was apparent in GHQ's initial instructions issued to Stopford on 22 July. Composed by Aspinall and signed by Braithwaite, the document articulated a general plan to deal the enemy "a crushing blow" from Anzac before driving "remnants south towards Kilid Bahr."[75] Moreover, the success of the overall offensive was dependent on the seizure of Sari Bair and the "capture and retention of Suvla Bay as a base of operations for the northern army."[76] The first of these tasks was to be carried out by ANZAC whilst IX Corps secured Suvla Bay. For its part, 11th Division was to land on a long stretch of coastline known as "New Beach", after dark on the evening of 6 August. The landing was timed to commence on ANZAC debouching to the north of their existing sector. The 11th Division's first task was to secure the immediate landing by clearing the enemy outposts guarding each side of the bay, before proceeding to capture the Chocolate and W Hills, which lay two miles inland. The capture of these hills by *coup de main* before daylight on 7 August was of "first importance" to prevent Ottoman artillery from interfering with the ANZAC assault on Sari Bair. There was a strong suggestion that an assault on these hills ought to have been made from the north, so as to avoid the strong defences believed to be oriented west and south west. The instructions went on to stress the need to "send a small force" to secure Tekke Tepe, which dominated the entire area east of Suvla Bay. There was no indication of the time this would take place. There was also no mention of 10th Division, IX Corps' second division ashore, beyond a vague inference of "hope" that it might afterwards assist the attack on Sari Bair.[77]

Suvla's relevance in these initial instructions was highlighted in relation to the supply of subsequent stages of the offensive only, and not about Hamilton's "crushing blow" upon Sari Bair, which was to be separately executed by ANZAC. IX Corps' support for the former was only implied at and even then, the instructions suggest this would not be required unless ANZAC ran into trouble. Maurice Hankey, the well-respected Secretary to the Committee of Imperial Defence and soon to be the British government's eyewitness to GHQ's conduct of the August offensive, subsequently observed that there were two opposing conceptions of the Suvla landing. Hamilton's desire for combined Anzac–Suvla operations against the Sari Bair range were offensive conceptions in design, but it was the security of Suvla Bay – a defensive conception – that "exercised on the whole a baneful influence on the operations."[78]

The "baneful influence" of the defensive conception was clearly apparent when Hamilton and Aspinall issued final instructions to Stopford on 22 July. The former subsequently observed the he "had a long and interesting talk" with Stopford, who Hamilton felt was in general agreement with

74 TNA WO 158/889: Letter, Hamilton to de Robeck, 4 July 1915.
75 TNA WO 158/576: Memorandum, Braithwaite to Stopford, 22 July 1915 (my italics).
76 Ibid.
77 Ibid.
78 TNA CAB 19/29: Hankey to Asquith, 12 August 1915.

the scheme.[79] Yet this version of events does not correspond with Aspinall's: he was "sent over to Helles[80] by the CGS [Braithwaite] to see General Stopford and unfold to him the plan of operations to be undertaken at Suvla and Anzac."[81] On arrival, "we got the maps out and I told him Sir Ian Hamilton's whole plan."[82] Thus it appears that the meeting was proposed by Braithwaite instead of Hamilton, who afterwards failed to recall presenting Stopford with the instructions at all.[83] Hamilton's inability to recollect the event was symptomatic of his reluctance to engage with planning detail, a trait subsequently confirmed when he sought reassurance from Braithwaite as to the locations of the Suvla landing beaches.[84] As a result of this command detachment, Hamilton more than likely utilised his "long and interesting talk" with Stopford to ensure that the IX Corps commander was "fully seized with his ideas" by emphasizing the offensive conception. In contrast, Aspinall's separate discussion with Stopford may have reflected written instructions that emphasized the defensive conception of the landing.

Aspinall sailed from Cape Helles under the impression that Stopford was satisfied with the plan. Stopford strongly disputed this, which suggests some confusion in his mind following the meeting with Hamilton and Aspinall.[85] Following a consultation with Brigadier-General Hamilton Reed VC (IX Corps' principal staff officer) and Birdwood, his confusion appears to have developed into serious doubts about his command's ability to secure Suvla Bay as a base (GHQ defensive conception) and the provision of support for the ANZAC assault (Hamilton's offensive conception) on Sari Bair.[86]

On 26 July Stopford and Reed visited GHQ to discuss these concerns with Hamilton. Unfortunately, the latter was not inclined to further discourse, seemingly because Braithwaite was absent at the time. The GOC IX Corps later recalled how Hamilton:

> [T]old me that I should in due course receive his operation orders, and that he would take an opportunity of riding over some day with his CGS [Braithwaite] to speak about them. He never did so, nor asked me to see him, and I never had another word with him on the subject before the operations began.[87]

In reply, Hamilton stressed that he would have been delighted to see Stopford at any time, recounting previous harmonious service together before the war.[88] Yet the next time he discussed

79 LHCMA: Hamilton Papers, 8/2/22: 'Statement read before the Commission on 9th January 1917'; Hamilton, *Gallipoli Diary*, Vol II, p. 5.
80 Stopford was in temporary command of VIII Corps during 17-24 July 1915.
81 TNA CAB 19/28: Aspinall, Statement to the Dardanelles Commission.
82 TNA CAB 19/33: Aspinall, evidence before the Dardanelles Commission, Q 13938.
83 LHCMA: Hamilton Papers, 8/1/13: Letter, Hamilton to Braithwaite, 10 February 1917.
84 IoW: Aspinall Papers, OG/AO/G/38: Letter, Hamilton to Aspinall, 24 December 1929; LHCMA: Hamilton Papers, 8/1/13: Letters, Hamilton to Braithwaite, 12 July and 17 August 1916.
85 TNA CAB 19/28: Aspinall, Statement to the Dardanelles Commission; CAB 19/33: Stopford, evidence before Dardanelles Commission, Q28110.
86 William Birdwood, *Khaki and Gown* (London: Ward, Lock & Co., 1941), p. 269.
87 TNA CAB 19/31: 'Statement by Lieut. General the Hon Sir F. Stopford Respecting the Operations of the 9th Army Corps at Suvla Bay, August 6th to 15th, 1915'; CAB 19/33: Stopford, evidence before the Dardanelles Commission, Q9990; LHCMA: Hamilton Papers, 7/4/9: Hamilton Staff Diary 20 July-9 August 1915.
88 LHCMA: Hamilton Papers, 8/2/22: Statement read before the Commission on 9th January 1917'.

operations with Stopford occurred on the evening of 8 August, nearly 48 hours after the landings had begun. Hamilton's detachment had been a feature of their relationship ever since their first meeting on 11 July, when he consciously chose not to divulge important information about IX Corps due to maintenance of secrecy concerns.[89] This aloofness resulted in Stopford seeking further clarification (26 July) from the GHQ operations staff instead. He queried Aspinall as to which objective – Suvla Bay security or support for the ANZAC assault – should have priority. This further highlights the prevailing scheme divergence between Hamilton and subordinate staff had caused the GOC IX Corps' operational uncertainty. "It is the wish of the GOC in C", Aspinall stated emphatically, "that the security of the harbour should be the first consideration and that that security is not to be forfeited by going to Biyuk Anafarta [in support of ANZAC]."[90] Edgar Anstey, the junior operations staff officer assisting Aspinall and Dawnay, reinforced this point: [The] "main object of securing Suvla as a base is looming larger in the plans as I always thought it should."[91] The 26 July conversation between Stopford and Aspinall was resolved in favour of staff requirements to prepare protracted operations well beyond the capture of Sari Bair. This defensive conception prevailed over all subsequent planning.

In contrast, Hamilton stressed the connection between the IX Corps' landing and the combined Anzac-Suvla offensive he hoped would bring the campaign to an end. On 27 July, Braithwaite expressed Hamilton's desire for an expeditious outcome clear in a letter to Kitchener's private secretary: "The necessity of carrying out prospective operations before the autumn gales is fully realized … and we are straining every effort to do so."[92] Hankey, in his capacity as the government's observer at MEF GHQ, also caught the optimistic mood. In language redolent of that of Hamilton and Birdwood, Hankey wrote to the British Prime Minister that the capture of Sari Bair "should bring about the surrender of the Turks."[93] Moreover, Hamilton also confirmed how the Suvla landing was intimately bound with the decisive ANZAC attack. In formal instructions issued to the commander of the French *Corps Expeditionnaire d'Orient*, the C-in-C MEF, a fluent French speaker, observed that his decision to concentrate forces "against the enemy's northern wing" and that of the "Australian and New Zealand Army Corps *and* the IX Army Corps will carry out the main attack."[94] This was one of six official directives issued to subordinate formations. However, it was the only one in which the Anzac and Suvla operations were described as a combination in relation to the Anzac offensive. Significantly, this was also the only formal directive that Hamilton personally signed and in which he was referred to in the first person. This suggests that if not actually composed by Hamilton, he had a far greater hand in the compilation than the other directives, none of which contained explicit linkage between the two component parts of the impending offensive.[95]

89 LHCMA: Hamilton Papers, 7/4/9: Hamilton Staff Diary 20 July-9 August 1915; Hamilton Papers, 7/1/16: Letter, Hamilton to Birdwood, 11 July 1915; TNA CAB 19/33: Stopford, evidence before Dardanelles Commission, Q9578-9581.
90 TNA CAB 19/33: Stopford, evidence before the Dardanelles Commission, Q9993.
91 TNA CAB 45/241: Quoted in letter, Anstey to Aspinall, 6 June 1928.
92 TNA CAB 19/28: Letter, Braithwaite to Fitzgerald, 27 July 1915.
93 TNA CAB 19/29: Letter, Hankey to Asquith (n.d.).
94 TNA WO 158/576: Memorandum, Hamilton to GOC Corps Expeditionnaire, 2 August 1915; my italics.
95 In addition, GHQ issued an overall "Force Order" for the offensive, two separate sets of instructions to IX Corps and one each to ANZAC and VIII Corps.

This gulf in operational intentions is evident in GHQ's final instructions (29 July) to Stopford. As in all correspondence (except Hamilton's directive to the French), they were composed by Aspinall and signed by Braithwaite. Largely because of the 26 July meeting, Aspinall revised certain aspects of the original instructions issued to Stopford on 22 July. Final instructions informed Stopford that his "primary objective" was to "secure Suvla Bay as a base for all the forces operating in the northern zone."[96] Hamilton's intention for a combined Anzac–Suvla assault on Sari Bair were then further distorted by the admission that the task of securing the bay might "require the use of the whole of the troops at [Stopford's] disposal", and that IX Corps need only endeavour to assist the ANZAC attack if this proved unnecessary.[97] Whereas the initial GHQ instructions vaguely implied "hope" that the second division ashore might assist the Sari Bair assault, its nebulous content was consistent with Hamilton's operational intentions and went a long way to alleviate the GOC IX Corp's expressed concerns.[98] Not only did GHQ's final instructions reinforce the MEF staff's defensive conception, it also put paid to the possibility that IX Corps might assist the ANZAC effort to gain Sari Bair.

Aspinall's 26 July conversation with Stopford and GHQ's final instructions effectively sanctioned XI Corps to employ its entire force to secure Suvla Bay and nothing more. Nevertheless, in directly addressing Stopford's concerns, these final instructions went further in removing key tasks originally designed to ensure security of the bay. Unlike the initial GHQ instructions, which stressed the need for IX Corps to secure Chocolate Hill and the W Hills by dawn on 7 August followed by an advance to "secure a footing" astride Tekke Tepe Ridge, the final instructions omitted these vital objectives. There was still time to rectify this error. However, permanent damage to Hamilton's intentions would prove fatal to the success of the offensive. While suggested provisions of support to ANZAC offensive efforts are discernable within the final instructions, they bore little in common with Hamilton's desire for IX Corps to "act in concert."[99]

Hamilton's inability to reconcile differing expectations for the impending August offensive distorted subordinate understanding of operational intentions, and allowed them to percolate into GHQ's final instructions to Stopford. His detachment from the planning process during this period ensured it was GHQ staff's defensive approach to the Suvla landing that was ascendant. As a result, any chance of IX Corps combining with ANZAC in the manner Hamilton hoped for had vanished.

Dilution

It will be recalled how Stopford's concerns with regard to IX Corps' ability to both secure Suvla Bay and support the ANZAC assault caused him to seek clarification from GHQ on 26 July. Thus the defensive priority of the operation was impressed by Aspinall in the ensuing conversation.[100] Reassured, Stopford remained uneasy about Suvla, which he considered to be an "ideal

96 TNA WO 361/4264: GHQ Final Instructions to IX Corps, 29 July 1915.
97 Ibid.
98 TNA WO 158/576: Memorandum, Braithwaite to Stopford, 22 July 1915.
99 TNA WO 158/889: Letter, Hamilton to de Robeck, 4 July 1915.
100 TNA CAB 19/33: Stopford, evidence before the Dardanelles Commission, Q9993.

place for defence."[101] His concerns were based on the inexperience of his troops in night work and the lack of available artillery.[102] This personal disquiet continued despite encouragement from Birdwood, who advised Stopford to trust in the element of surprise which, combined with sound comprehension of assigned objectives, would assist in overcoming the inherent difficulties associated with night operations.[103]

A significant factor influencing Stopford's anxiety was Brigadier-General Reed, the GOC IX Corps' irascible and domineering chief staff officer. Celebrated author Compton Mackenzie, a junior staff officer at GHQ, was seated next to Stopford during a headquarters luncheon. His recollections were highly prescient in his description of Stopford as a man of "great kindliness and charm … completely without hope of victory at Suvla."[104] The reason for this, Mackenzie believed, was Reed, who sat directly opposite Stopford: "[H]olding forth almost truculently about the folly of the plan of operations drawn up by the General Staff." For his part, the GOC IX Corps made no effort to "rebuke his disagreeable and discouraging junior" instead reassuring him in a "fatherly way."[105] Stopford, Mackenzie lamented, "was deprecating, courteous, fatherly, anything except the Commander of an Army Corps which had been entrusted with a major operation."[106]

Reed held powerful sway over his immediate superior and had arguably been the driving force behind the request to amend IX Corps' original instructions. From his first exposure to the plan, Reed had consistently maintained that the capture of Tekke Tepe was "too big a job" for IX Corps.[107] As an artillery officer, Reed's recent experience on the Western Front and previous service with the Ottomans during the Balkan Wars had convinced him that more guns were needed to drive the enemy, whom he considered to be "splendid infantry in trenches", from their fixed Suvla defences.[108] Moreover, he had little faith in GHQ's intelligence, which suggested – correctly, as it transpired – that there were relatively few defenders at Suvla and even fewer trenches. Reed was well qualified to present these concerns regardless of their validity. However, the significance of his contributions lay in the unnerving influence he had on Stopford's confidence.

Stopford held his first corps conference at Imbros on 27 July, the day after Aspinall had confirmed IX Corps' defensive role and five days after receipt of GHQ's initial instructions. Hamilton's insistence on secrecy meant Stopford was unwilling to divulge important operational details to his staff, the only instructions being that IX Corps was "going to have to

101 Ibid., Q28110-28112; TNA CAB 19/31: 'Statement by Lieut General the Hon Sir F Stopford Respecting the Operations of the 9th Army Corps at Suvla Bay, August 6th to 15th, 1915'.
102 TNA CAB 19/33: Stopford, evidence before Dardanelles Commission, Q9719; Aspinall-Oglander, *Military Operations*, Vol II, p. 150.
103 AWM: Birdwood Papers, 3DRL/3376/11/16, Letter, Birdwood to General Sir John Maxwell, 9 August 1915; AWM: AWM38 3DRL 8042/24: Bean Papers, 'Historical Notes, Gallipoli: Suvla Bay August 1915'.
104 Compton MacKenzie, *Gallipoli Memories* (London: Cassell, 1929), pp. 352-353. Mackenzie did not mention Reed specifically by name, but it is obvious to whom he was referring.
105 Ibid.
106 Ibid.
107 TNA CAB 19/33: Reed, evidence before Dardanelles Commission, Q20230.
108 Ibid., Q20115.

make a landing" and that they "must consider everything you can think of as regarding that landing."[109] Stopford, however, did discuss first instructions with Lieutenant-General Sir Bryan Mahon (GOC 10th Division) and Major-General Frederick Hammersley (GOC 11th Division).[110] At a subsequent meeting with both, the GOC IX Corps remarked that the primary task was to "seize the landing at Suvla Bay and secure it as a base of supply", after which IX Corps was sanctioned to support the ANZAC offensive.[111]

Major-General Frederick Hammersley (GOC 11th Division).

Stopford's emphasis on bay security led him to question whether or not GHQ had given sufficient attention to the capture of the Tekke Tepe Ridge in the initial instructions, which had mentioned a "small force" to picket the ridge. He considered this force insufficient and, according to his version of the 27 July conference, stressed to Mahon and Hammersley the "absolute necessity" of securing Tekke Tepe, the retention of which was essential to achieving the desired security of Suvla Bay.[112] Stopford also considered that the base would not be completely secure whilst the enemy remained in possession of Kiretch Tepe Ridge.[113] Thus 11th Division, having secured the landing beaches and detached a single battalion to Kiretch Tepe Ridge, would deploy its remaining two brigades "on the right" to capture Tekke Tepe by way of Chocolate Hill and the W Hills. The 10th Division, on subsequent disembarkation, would be deployed "on the left" to relieve Hammersley's battalion on Kiretch Tepe prior to an eastward advance along the length of the ridge to complete a pincer movement and "join hands" with 11th Division on Tekke Tepe.[114] At face value, the scheme was a clear and relatively simple concept predicated on both formations seizing vital ground. Had the planning that followed the divisional commanders' meeting conformed to this concept, IX Corps' chance of achieving the defensive task set for it by GHQ would have been that much greater, however, both Mahon and Hammersley appear to have left the first meeting without a clear understanding of operational intentions. For example, Mahon's recollection suggest that his discussion with Stopford solely focused on the difficulties confronting the ANZAC advance; 10th Division's assigned role was not apparent at that time.[115] Hammersley also recalled the conference differently with a more limited interpretation

109 TNA CAB 19/33: Stopford, evidence before Dardanelles Commission, Q22206.
110 Ibid., Q22195.
111 TNA CAB 19/31: 'Statement by Lieut. General the Hon. Sir F Stopford respecting the Operations of the 9th Army Corps at Suvla Bay, August 6th to 15th, 1915'; CAB 19/29: 'Statement to the Dardanelles Commission by Major-General F Hammersley'.
112 TNA CAB 19/33: Stopford, evidence before Dardanelles Commission, Q9909, Q10177.
113 TNA CAB 19/31: 'Statement by Lieut. General the Hon. Sir F. Stopford respecting the Operations of the 9th [sic] Army Corps at Suvla Bay, August 6th to 15th, 1915'.
114 TNA CAB 19/33: Stopford, evidence before Dardanelles Commission, Q27881, Q10001.
115 TNA CAB 19/33: Mahon, evidence before the Dardanelles Commission, Q11332-11336; CAB 19/30: Statement by General Sir B. Mahon.

of 11th Division's assigned role the topic of discussion. Stopford's uncertainty of mind, amplified by Reed's pernicious influence, suggests he was less lucid during this meeting than subsequent recollections reveal. Nevertheless, whatever clarity of thought he may have entertained dissipated as further planning details were discussed.

Stopford's initial scheme to secure Suvla Bay meant that the first challenge to the scheme prior to the 27 July conference had passed without action. In an effort to make 11th Division's line of advance against Chocolate Hill and the W Hills as simple and direct as possible, Hammersley requested, as a substitute for landing his entire division south and outside of Suvla Bay as originally planned, that two component brigades be put ashore inside the bay itself. This, he argued, would allow for capture of first objectives followed by a direct advance on Tekke Tepe, an approach that GHQ intelligence had assessed to be lightly defended as opposed to an advance from the south.[116] Stopford accepted this proposal prior to recommending it to GHQ despite the fact that the alteration would disperse 11th Division over some two miles of coastline. Nonetheless, GHQ accepted landing inside Suvla Bay in principle, however, Royal Navy concerns about unchartered shoals meant compromise between services. Thus it was agreed that only one of brigade would disembark inside the bay in an effort to minimise risk. Meanwhile, the two remaining brigades would land south of Suvla Bay as originally planned.[117] Paradoxically, in an effort to make the night advance on Chocolate Hill and the W Hills as simple as possible, the two inexperienced 11th Division brigades would land on widely separated beaches and conduct a complicated rendezvous across un-reconnoitered terrain prior to execution of an attack. This ill-fated amendment, which ultimately resulted in awful confusion on the landing night, was confirmed by GHQ final instructions issued to IX Corps on the morning of 30 July.[118]

As previously indicated, the major revision to final instructions encouraged Stopford to forego any genuine effort to support the ANZAC offensive. As he was not seriously contemplating an offensive role by this stage, it was the changes affecting IX Corps' defensive aim that Stopford now turned his attention. His primary concern *vis-à-vis* bay security related to operational requirements to secure Chocolate Hill, the W Hills and gain a footing on Tekke Tepe by dawn on 7 August. After once more emphasising the importance of the Tekke Tepe and Kiretch Tepe ridges to his divisional commanders at a second corps conference later on 30 July, the GOC IX Corps composed a lengthy memorandum to GHQ in which he outlined his plan of operations and attempted to address carefully considered flaws in its final issue instructions.[119] This document, submitted with corps landing orders to GHQ the following day, was particularly significant because the author, regardless of previous imprecise language expressed to his divisional commanders, confirmed his thoughts on the task ahead. In the absence of any other direct communication between Stopford and Hamilton prior to the landing, this memorandum

116 TNA WO 138/40: Memorandum, Stopford to GHQ, 31 July 1915; CAB 19/33: Stopford, evidence before Dardanelles Commission, Q 9681-9690.
117 TNA CAB 19/29: Statement by Acting Captain L. Lambard, 5 May 1917, Documents and Statements from Naval Officers submitted to Commission by Rear Admiral Keyes; Sir Julian Corbett, *Official History of the War: Naval Operations*, Vol. III (Uckfield: Naval & Military Press 2003 reprint of 1923 edition), p. 87.
118 TNA WO 95/4297: Neil Malcolm, 'The 11th Division at Suvla Bay'; WO 95/4276; HQ IX Corps General Staff War Diary, June-July 1915.
119 TNA CAB 19/29: 'Statement to the Dardanelles Commission by Major-General F. Hammersley'; WO 138/40: Memorandum, Stopford to GHQ, 31 July 1915.

was the only means by which the C-in-C understood Stopford's operational intent. Indeed, he advised Hamilton of the "proposed plan of operations for the capture and retention of Suvla Bay as a base of operations for the Northern Army."[120] The only mention of support for ANZAC operations was relegated to the last paragraph, which reiterated the advice offered by Aspinall some days earlier: "I fear that the attainment of the security of Suvla Bay will so absorb the force under my command as to render it improbable that I shall be able to give direct assistance to GOC ANZAC in his attack [on Sari Bair]."[121] Unfortunately, it appears Hamilton failed to read the document before the landing. Thus having delegated examination/interpretation thereof to subordinate staff, he remained unaware to what extent his operational intentions had been distorted.

Stopford's memorandum made it clear that his overriding concern was the security of Suvla Bay as a base inasmuch as it concentrated almost exclusively on 11th Division as the asset to secure Tekke Tepe: "I am convinced that in order to secure the reasonable immunity of Suvla Bay from shell fire, it is essential that we should be in possession of the high ground." [122] The GOC IX Corps also indicated a preferred seizure of the ridge "as quickly as possible", but the perceived threat to bay security and the ANZAC advance by the enemy defenders situated about Chocolate Hill and the W Hills meant that outlying terrain features were designated for capture beforehand. In an apparent *volte-face* over earlier concerns about night operations, Stopford explained how the capture of Chocolate Hill and the W Hills by nocturnal *coup de main* "would have such far reaching effects" as to make the assault worthy of effort. [123] He did not explain how this was so. Nonetheless, the imperative had been re-instated in IX Corps' operational design.

By dwelling upon the intermediate objective of Chocolate Hill and the W Hills, Stopford's original emphasis on Tekke Tepe became obscured. Indeed, IX Corps actually lacked the troops to achieve capture of the latter, in which case Stopford considered it "essential" that 11th Division should focus on the northernmost portion of Kiretch Tepe instead.[124] As a result of this change in tactical priorities, he indicated that the limit of 11th Division's advance should lie along the foot of the Tekke Tepe Ridge, at which point a pause would occur whilst "bold reconnaissance" would be conducted to ascertain a "correct appreciation" of the situation.[125] Only after this was done did Stopford suggest the establishment of "strong tactical points" along Tekke Tepe, although he did not identify any troops for this task.[126] The GOC IX Corps had, therefore, sanctioned 11th Division's halt at the base of Tekke Tepe as opposed to its tactically important crest line. Thus the chance of securing this vital piece of terrain was dwindling fast.

In Stopford's defence, it has been suggested that IX Corps lacked the resources to seize Tekke Tepe and achieve bay security.[127] This view certainly holds some merit, especially when the fact that Stopford's memorandum and the subsequent IX Corps order allocated tasks to 11th

120 TNA WO 138/40: Memorandum, Stopford to GHQ, 31 July 1915.
121 Ibid.
122 Ibid.
123 Ibid.
124 TNA CAB 19/33: Stopford, evidence before Dardanelles Commission, Q27881, Q10001.
125 TNA WO 138/40: Memorandum, Stopford to GHQ, 31 July 1915.
126 Ibid.
127 See Robin Prior, 'The Suvla Bay Tea Party', *Journal of the Australian War Memorial*, 1985 (7).

Division only is considered. Nevertheless, it will be recalled that on receipt of GHQ's blessing, he had been working on the assumption that both of his divisions could be deployed to complete the capture of Suvla Bay, whereas Hamilton hoped that the second division would be available to combine with ANZAC in order to "smash the mainspring" of Ottoman defences on Sari Bair.[128]

Neither Stopford's memorandum nor IX Corps' order allocated the seizure of Tekke Tepe to 10th Division. This is puzzling when one considers that the GOC IX Corps had previously indicated it would be used to push along Kiretch Tepe to Tekke Tepe as a left hook of the pincer movement.[129] Stopford subsequently explained how he purposely did not allocate 10th Division any tasks because he was unaware of what the situation would be, which suggests he changed his mind about his original intentions to deploy it on the left. Stopford's desire to retain an uncommitted division as a reserve is understandable, however, his original imperative to secure the Tekke Tepe Ridge suggests failure to assign an occupation force was a significant oversight, one that can be attributed primarily to a befuddled state of mind: "He [Stopford] had got into that sort of state", Hamilton later observed, "when he could not make up his mind whether he would sit down or stand up, or go into his tent or get out of it."[130] As the capture of Tekke Tepe was the means by which Stopford intended to secure Suvla Bay, his ultimate neglect of this suggests that he had lost sight of the operational objective.

Unfortunately, the IX Corps draft order attached to Stopford's memorandum further compounded the issue. Composed by Reed, it failed to assign units for the capture of Tekke Tepe, nor did allocate tasks to 10th Division.[131] In yet another retrograde step and in stark contrast to Stopford's memorandum, which, it will be recalled, had reinstated the need to capture the intervening Chocolate Hill and the W Hills by *coup de main* before dawn on 7 August, Reed's document merely indicated that 11th Division was to "occupy" both elevations without indicating a particular timetable. Reed afterwards admitted to writing the orders without specific knowledge of Stopford's memorandum. This by now familiar dichotomy of thought between commander and staff, in addition to Reed's aversion to an advance without extensive artillery preparation, more than likely explains why his order did not specify Stopford's reinstated time imperative. As a result, Reed's order only contributed to further dilution of IX Corps' defensive remit by dispensing with a sense of operational urgency with regard to seizure of assigned objectives.[132]

Despite distortion of Hamilton's intentions for a combined Anzac–Suvla offensive and dilution of IX Corps defensive purpose, Stopford was informed that his orders "met with the entire approval of the GOC in C." They were subsequently issued to 10th Division and 11th Division on 3 August.[133] Yet Hamilton, then 70 miles distant inspecting elements of 10th Division, did not read Stopford's orders prior to the landing, so his sanction would have been based on staff

128 Hamilton, Final Despatch, p. 80.
129 TNA CAB 19/33: Stopford, evidence before Dardanelles Commission, Q27881, Q10001.
130 LHCMA: Hamilton Papers, 7/1/6: Letter, Hamilton to Kitchener, 19 August 1915.
131 TNA WO 95/4276: HQ IX Corps Operation Order No 1, 3 August 1915.
132 TNA CAB 19/33: Reed, evidence before Dardanelles Commission, Q20104; CAB 19/31: 'Statement by Lieut General the Hon. Sir F. Stopford Respecting the Operations of the 9th Army Corps at Suvla Bay, August 6th to 15th, 1915', Appendix A.
133 TNA CAB 19/31: Stopford, Statement to the Dardanelles Commission.

The Bystander, September 15, 1915 367

Yorkshire's Roll of Honour

OFFICER CASUALTIES AMONG THE YORKSHIRE REGIMENTS IN GALLIPOLI

LIEUT. O. L. MARTIN
6th York and Lancaster Regt.
wounded

2nd LIEUT. M. Y. SIMPSON
6th (Prince of Wales's Own)
Yorkshire Regiment, wounded

LIEUT. E. M. WORSLEY
6th (Prince of Wales's Own)
Yorkshire Regiment, wounded

LT. N. MATTHEWS, R.A.M.C.
Attached 9th (P. of Wales's Own)
(West Yorks Regt.), wounded

2nd LT. L. K. GIFFORD-WOOD
6th (Prince of Wales's Own) Yorkshire Regiment, wounded

2nd LT. C. E. WHITWORTH
6th (Prince of Wales's Own) Yorkshire Regiment, wounded

LIEUT. R. O. GIRLING
9th (Prince of Wales's Own) West Yorkshire Regiment, wounded

CAPT. A. C. T. WHITE
6th (Prince of Wales's Own) Yorkshire Regiment, wounded

MAJOR M. D. WOOD
9th (P. of Wales's Own) West Yorkshire Regiment, wounded

CAPT. R. LUPTON
9th (Prince of Wales's Own)
West Yorkshire Regt., killed

CAPT. B. A. T. DUTTON
9th (Prince of Wales's Own)
West Yorkshire Regt., wounded

MAJOR M. G. COWPER
6th East Yorkshire Regt., wounded

LIEUT. J. C. BANKS
6th East Yorkshire Regt., wounded

LIEUT. R. A. RAWSTORNE
6th East Yorkshire Regt., missing

CAPTAIN H. L. WILLATS
6th East Yorkshire Regt., wounded

2nd. LIEUT. T. B. COULTAS
6th East Yorkshire Regt., wounded

Officer casualties, killed, wounded and missing, sustained by Yorkshire regiments of 11th Division during the Suvla operations. (*The Bystander*, 15 September 1915) assurance that the orders were satisfactory.[134] "[S]o long as I had good cause to believe that Stopford himself was fully cognisant of my plan and believed in it," Hamilton wrote afterwards to Aspinall, "I was not called upon to examine his divisional orders."[135] In all of his previous experience of command, the MEF C-in-C had "never known a Commander in Chief examine my orders to my troops." An advocate of delegation of command, he believed that it was the responsibility of the General Staff to "keep their own chief acquainted with Corps and Divisional orders."[136] It was this remote command style that ensured Hamilton was beholden to his staff's defensive conception and, consequently, to Stopford's reduced operational aspirations. Moreover, Hamilton's own staff also failed to identify the dilution of limited purpose within IX Corps' planning, something which Aspinall subsequently attributed to overconfidence and a belief held by GHQ that, once ashore, Stopford would overcome his nervousness and push on to secure the high ground.[137] It should, therefore, come as no surprise that dilution of operational purpose continued within subordinate planning. Indeed, orders issued to 11th Division on 5 August only directed the capture of Chocolate Hill, but not at any particular time. In a bitterly ironic twist of Hamilton's original intentions, the same order implied that the purpose of the ANZAC attack was to support IX Corps' landing.[138] Furthermore, 10th Division HQ did not issue landing orders, one of its brigade commanders only learning of the objective whilst in transit to Suvla Bay on the morning of 7 August.[139]

Conclusion

Hamilton's intentions for IX Corps to play an active role in a combined Anzac–Suvla attack were dashed well before the inexperienced troops of IX Corps set foot at Suvla Bay. Instead, the August offensive would be launched as two discreet tactical operations, which was consistent with his staff's expectation of a protracted campaign. Having failed to impose his will upon the planning process, Hamilton would turn to his alternative Suvla scheme in the days following the failure to seize Sari Bair. This option, it will be recalled, envisaged IX Corps securing the Anafarta Gap to facilitate the northern passage of reserves onto Ottoman lines of communication beyond Sari Bair. By this stage of the offensive, however, Stopford's indecision and the ambiguity compromised IX Corps' ability to secure Suvla as a defensive base, let alone provide it as the platform from which to launch further offensive operations. Whilst subsequent poor performance no doubt contributed to the IX Corps failure, it was flawed exercise of command and poor staff work at GHQ and corps level that ensured defeat.[140]

134 LHCMA: Hamilton Papers, 7/4/9: Hamilton Staff Diary 20 July-9 August 1915.
135 IoW: Aspinall Papers, OG/AO/G/38: Letter, Hamilton to Aspinall, 24 December 1929.
136 Ibid.
137 Aspinall-Oglander, *Military Operations*, Vol II, p. 150.
138 TNA WO 95/4297: 11th Division Operation Order No.1, 5 August 1915.
139 TNA CAB 45/242: Letter, Colonel H.T. Goodland to Aspinall-Oglander, 26 March 1931.
140 Combined IX Corps and ANZAC casualties sustained during the crucial 6-10 August 1915 period of operations, amounted to approximately 21,500 officers and men killed, wounded and missing. See Crawley, *Climax at Gallipoli*, p. 213.

5

The Last Offensive: Krithia Nullah, November–December 1915

Michael LoCicero

I know how to stand and fight to the finish. Twist and lunge in the War god's deadly dance.[1]

With the failure of the August offensive, pressing developments on the Western Front and a deteriorating Balkans situation, the Gallipoli campaign was, pending further high-level decision-making, considered by Whitehall to be strategically moribund.[2] The subsequent political-military wrangling that led to abandonment of the peninsula with the high-risk, but almost bloodless evacuations of Suvla Bay, Anzac Cove and Cape Helles have been the primary focus of the plethora of official government reports, participant and post-participant campaign narratives, whilst the concurrent fighting during September 1915–January 1916 is, more often than not, almost wholly ignored by these documents/works.[3] The enquiring general reader is thus left to explore relevant published formation/unit histories and personal memoirs for details of the myriad post-August operations that were indicative of a relapse into theatre-wide stalemate and resultant trench warfare.

Launched during this period, the series of small-scale operations, culminating in the officially designated action of "Krithia Nullahs" (29 December 1915),[4] were part of a dual scheme to improve the local tactical situation at Helles whilst simultaneously menacing important tactical objectives and diverting Ottoman attention away from the imminent evacuations of Suvla and Anzac. Ultimately successful in accomplishing its part in these strategic/operational intentions, the now veteran 52nd (Lowland) Division was the formation chosen to carry out the respective assaults.[5]

1 Homer, *The Iliad*, Book VII, Line 281.
2 See Edward J. Erickson, *Gallipoli: Command Under Fire* (Oxford: Osprey, 2015), pp. 219-28.
3 See Jenny Macleod, *Reconsidering Gallipoli* (Manchester: Manchester University Press, 2004).
4 The three attacks (November-December 1915) were ignored in the only Gallipoli despatch (6 March 1916) submitted for public consumption by C-in-C Eastern Mediterranean General Sir Charles Monro. Interestingly, official battle nomenclature for the Krithia Nullah operations (the above mentioned "Krithia Nullahs") relates to the 29 December attack only. See John Grehan & Martin Mace (eds.), *Despatches from the Front: Gallipoli and the Dardanelles 1915-1916* (Barnsley: Pen & Sword, 2014), Part 7 and Major A.F. Becke, *Order of Battle of Divisions Part 2A. The Territorial Force Mounted Divisions and the 1st-Line Territorial Force Divisions (42 – 56)* (London: HMSO, 1936), p. 114.
5 The 1/2nd (Lowland) Division (re-designated 52nd Division in May 1915) was formed with the establishment of the Territorial Force (TF) in 1908. Its component infantry primarily consisted of

The 52nd Division's introduction to combat on the Helles front as a much-anticipated reinforcement six months earlier was somewhat rushed and, given the relatively untrained state of the newly-arrived component infantry, extremely costly in available manpower. Disembarkation on to the peninsula began in early June 1915, after which the 156th Brigade was thrown into a "deliberately planned and meticulous" attack within weeks of arrival with unfortunate consequences.[6] Indeed, author Compton Mackenzie, an intelligence officer attached to MEF Headquarters, was "much struck" when, after the war, veteran and novelist George Blake[7] "indignantly" queried him as to why the division "was sent almost straight into action after landing, without a month's preliminary training ..."[8] The 52nd Division's first major action, "Achi Baba Nullah" (12-13 July 1915), was equally barren and costly.[9] Such was the subsequent animosity engendered over what was deemed by Blake, amongst many others, to be criminal ill-use of a relatively neophyte force that Major-General Granville Egerton[10] (GOC 52nd Division) harboured life-long personal vendettas against General Sir Ian Hamilton (GOC MEF) and Lieutenant-General Sir Aylmer Hunter-Weston (GOC VIII Corps up to 17 July 1915), both of whom he held most responsible for perceived mishandling of his command.[11] Egerton's time on the peninsula proved stressful and short-lived. Temporarily relieved of command during the Achi Baba Nullah action, he was replaced due to "nervous exhaustion" on 17 September 1915.[12] Major-General Hon. Herbert Alexander Lawrence assumed command of 52nd Division that same day.[13]

battalions (Royal Scots, Royal Scots Fusiliers, Argyll & Sutherland Highlanders, Scottish Rifles, King's Own Scottish Borderers and Highland Light Infantry) associated with the Scottish Lowlands. See Mike Chappell, *Scottish Units in the World Wars* (London: Osprey, 1994), pp. 13-18.

6 For the 'Battle of Gully Ravine' (28 June-5 July 1915), see Lieutenant-Colonel R.R. Thompson MC, *The Fifty-Second Lowland Division 1914-1918* (Glasgow: MacLehose, Jackson & Co., 1923), pp. 42-75; C.F. Aspinall-Oglander, *Military Operations Gallipoli*, Vol. II (London: Heinemann, 1932), pp. 83-96 and Erickson, *Gallipoli: Command Under Fire*, pp. 164-66.

7 George Blake (1893-1961). Writer who's most celebrated works are novels concerning Clydeside shipbuilders. His realistic depiction of their day-to-day lives is associated with a deliberate tendency to overcome perceived sentimentality in Caledonian literature.

8 Compton Mackenzie, *Gallipoli Memories* (London: Cassell, 1929), p. 204.

9 The promise of five more divisions by the War Office and Hamilton's desire to maintain "pressure on the enemy" appears to have been the *raison d'être* for 52nd Division's peremptory deployment. See Thompson, *The Fifty-Second Lowland Division 1914-1918*, pp. 76-128; Aspinall-Oglander, *Military Operations Gallipoli*, Vol. II, pp. 97-112; Tim Travers, *Gallipoli 1915* (Stroud: Tempus, 2001), pp. 108-10 and Erickson, *Gallipoli: Command Under Fire*, pp. 170-74.

10 Major-General Granville George Algernon Egerton (1859-1951). Commissioned Gordon Highlanders 1879; Afghanistan 1879-80; Egypt 1882; ADC Malta 1894-95; Sudan 1898; Commandant Hythe School of Musketry 1907-09; GOC Infantry Brigade Malta 1909-13; GOC 1/2nd Lowland/52nd (Lowland) Division TF March 1914-September 1915; Base Commandant September-December 1915. Note: Officers are described by the rank they held during winter 1915-16.

11 See David Raw's chapter in this volume.

12 See LHCMA: General Sir Ian Hamilton Papers, File 7/2/5, King's College, London and Elaine MacFarland, *'A Slashing Man of Action': The Life of Lieutenant-General Sir Aylmer Hunter-Weston MP* (Oxford: Peter Laing, 2014), pp. 205-08.

13 Major-General Herbert Alexander Lawrence (1861-1943). Commissioned 17th Lancers 1882; Staff College 1894; War Office Intelligence 1897-99; South Africa 1899-1900; DAAG and DAQMG 1901-02; resigned commission 1904; GSO I, GOC 127th Brigade, T/Deputy Inspector General of Communications 1914-15; GOC 52nd Division September 1915.

"A gigantic morgue and open latrine"

The repulse of the 6 August diversionary assault by 29th and 42nd divisions, launched in support of the Anzac and Suvla offensives, signalled the last significant offensive activity at Helles. Mining and bombing were the "chief developments" during the succeeding autumn and winter of 1915-16.[14] Extending west to east, from Fusilier Bluff to the Kereves Dere,[15] across the peninsula for approximately three miles (4.83 kilometres), the frontline was, from September to the evacuation, normally defended by three (two British and one French) divisions. Unable to break the deadlock, VIII Corps settled into routine trench warfare almost identical to that of the Western Front, the primary difference being the cramped, teeming rear area – overlooked by the forbidding Achi Baba feature and under regular shellfire from enemy batteries situated on and about that height and across the Dardanelles Straits on the Asiatic shore – that offered little in the way of shelter beyond ramshackle dugouts, shabby tented camps and beachfront shanties. The post-war history of 1/5th Highland Light Infantry (HLI) observed: "The ships which were lying off Cape Helles occasionally carried out minor bombardments. It was very interesting to watch the effect of their shells bursting when they got a direct hit on the Turkish lines, as of course we had no land guns of such heavy calibre. The ships were perfectly safe from any reply the Turkish artillery cared to make and we in the front line had to suffer for the navy's demonstration. No one really objected to this, although there was a lot of 'grousing', because we were glad to feel that we had the support of these big guns, which must have harassed the enemy tremendously."[16]

Four watercourse ravines ran towards the front. Known as Achi Baba Nullah, Small Nullah, Krithia Nullah, Gully Ravine/Saghir Dere, these natural conduits offered vital protective arteries for a tenuous supply chain, maintained by horse-drawn General Service wagons, mule transport and infantry carrying parties, extending, ship to shore, from beachheads to the forward area. A 52nd Division chaplain recalled:

> Thickets of brushwood and bramble cling to the banks of the nullah. In the sides, at intervals, are dug the little caves which form the cooking, sleeping and living rooms of the men posted here, protecting them from everything but a direct hit from a shell. The brook that meanders through the reeds in the bottom furnishes water for the horses but cannot be used with safety for anything but washing by the soldiers. Drinking and cooking water has to be brought at some risk from the springs, of which, fortunately, there are a few in the neighbourhood. Once in the nullah, or little gully, you cannot see over the edges, and there is safety in keeping your head down.[17]

14 "Krithia Vineyard" (6-13 August 1915). See Aspinall-Oglander, *Military Operations Gallipoli*, Vol. II, pp. 168-77, 389 and Erickson, *Gallipoli: Command Under Fire*, p. 190.
15 Dere: Gully.
16 Colonel F.L. Morrison, *The Fifth Battalion Highland Light Infantry in the War 1914-1918* (Glasgow: Macelhose, Jackson & Co., 1921), Chapter IV.
17 William Ewing, *From Gallipoli to Baghdad* (London: Hodder & Stoughton, 1917), pp. 134-35.

German cartoon with classic of Middle Eastern literature as a pointed reference to the lack of Anglo-French progress at Gallipoli: "One thousand and one nights in a trench and we have to produce our own fairy tales." (*Kladderadatsch*, 31 October 1915)

A 2-foot gauge tramway, extending inland from W Beach to "South Quarry" and divisional depots, supplemented the existing logistical support organisation.[18]

September and October 1915 were periods of unceasing labour as VIII Corps, now commanded by Lieutenant-General Sir J.F. Davies,[19] prepared for a winter campaign on the peninsula. The inevitability thereof meant the amassing of stores and equipment on the six (S, V, W, X, Gully and Y) Helles beachheads before consequent rough seas interrupted the off-loading of supplies on a regular basis. Reduced to less than half of its original 10,900 complement, 52nd Division carried on with a myriad of duties whilst defending the central Achi Baba – Krithia Nullah sector. A similar manpower situation prevailed within the other divisions attached to VIII Corps, Lieutenant-General Davies' command mustering just 15,212 effectives at the

18 TNA WO 95/4356: 117th Railway Company War Diary, August-December 1915.

19 Lieutenant-General Sir John Francis Davies (1864-1948). Commissioned Worcestershire Militia 1881; transferred Grenadier Guards 1884; Adjutant General Cape of Good Hope 1897; South Africa 1899-1902; DAQG War Office 1902-04; ADMO 1904; AQMG Western Command 1907; GOC 1st Guards Brigade 1909; Director of Staff Duties War Office 1913; GOC 8th Division 1914-15; GOC VIII Corps August 1915-January 1916.

close of September. The overall complement was further reduced with the early October evacuation of several regiments attached to the French *Corps Expeditionnaire d'Orient*.[20]

Patrols, sniping, bombing, carrying parties, trench improvements and salvage was carried out day and night by units worn down by casualties and disease. Periods in the trenches could last for weeks on end, 157th Brigade spending 52 days in the line "continually on working parties in addition to the usual trench duties" until relieved by 155th Brigade in early October. Temporary relief was obtained in so-called "rest camps" that were, given the limited space available for such rudimentary establishments, targeted by Ottoman gunners as a matter of course.[21]

Lieutenant-General J.F. Davies, (GOC VIII Corps).

Aptly described by one battalion medical officer as "a gigantic morgue and open latrine", Cape Helles had been transformed into a fly-blown plague-pit of typhoid, cholera and dysentery. Corpses in various stages of decomposition, buried beneath trench floors or revetted into sandbagged walls, were regularly unearthed by working parties, whilst piles of dead mown down during previous assaults and out of reach to both sides for months on end, rotted between opposing lines that were normally just 100 yards distant. "On one occasion a heap of the bodies which had been lying out in No Man's Land near East Krithia Nullah, probably since the beginning of June, and so were completely dried up, caught fire from a bomb explosion. Lest the blaze should attract Turkish shellfire, some of the Argylls who were in the line crept out and threw earth on the fire until it was out."[22] The extreme Mediterranean summer/autumn climate, prevailing filth and squalor, dearth of available water, monotonous diet of bully beef, tinned jam and biscuits, in addition to casualties sustained during the subsequent period of active trench warfare, took a steady toll of killed, sick and wounded, the total effective strength of 157th Brigade diminishing to 60 officers and 1,872 men by 30 September.[23] This figure included personnel detached for other duties, so the actual rifle strength per battalion was much less. Nevertheless, this was the strongest brigade within 52nd Division at the time. War Office prioritisation of reinforcements for the New Army ensured Territorial Force (TF) formations like

20 See Aspinall-Oglander, *Military Operations Gallipoli*, Vol. II, p. 391 and Simon House's chapter in this volume.
21 See TNA WO 95/4317: 52nd Division War Diary, Thompson, *The Fifty-Second Lowland Division 1914-1918*, pp. 129-51.
22 Ibid.
23 Helles illness evacuations, chiefly dysentery, during October averaged some 200 men per day during October. See Aspinall-Oglander, *Military Operations Gallipoli*, Vol. II, p. 389.

52nd Division were almost starved of drafts required to bring skeleton units up to strength.[24] The paltry numbers of disembarked reinforcements and consequent reliance on untrained junior officers as replacements for losses amongst experienced company and platoon commanders only retarded the rate at which the MEF was dwindling. Its combined strength, at or en route to the peninsula, by 10 October, numbered 114,087; "it should have mustered 200,540." Thus it was obvious, the British official historian later observed, "that the Expeditionary Force lacked the numbers, organisation and physical fitness essential to the success of any considerable offensive operations."[25] Available firepower, offshore naval gun support exclusive, hardly made up for this deficiency in numbers.[26] According to Robin Prior, "At Suvla there were just 20 heavy guns, at Anzac 35 and at Helles 22. The entire force therefore had 77 heavy guns, far fewer than a single assault division would have had on the Western Front."[27] Small-scale offensive operations to improve the local tactical situation were all the MEF was capable of by autumn 1915.

Threatening Krithia and Achi Baba

The November operation to seize Ottoman trenches at Krithia Nullah appears to have originated with 52nd Division Headquarters, VIII Corps Headquarters lauding such offensive initiatives by subordinate formations:

> The corps commander said that the offensive spirit seems to be growing healthily and producing effect in the schemes which divisions are undertaking for getting a footing in the enemy's trenches and extending it. Efforts must not be relaxed in this direction to raise the morale of our men and lower that of the Turks.[28]

Maintenance of troop morale and discipline was indeed a serious concern, as an unfortunate incident involving 90 men of 1/6th HLI the previous August appeared to demonstrate. Tasked with assaulting an enemy trench opposite the Vineyard sector, the ill-conceived night operation quickly broke down due to lack of artillery support and timing confusion. Appalled by the failure, VIII Corps Headquarters ordered a court of enquiry, the determinations thereof resulting in harsh words from Davies.[29] Like their Western Front counterparts, MEF commanders relied on aggression as a nostrum to perceived passivity inherent to the tedium of routine trench occupation. Accompanying this predictable institutional response was a developing professionalism in the practice of position warfare bolstered by quantities of the latest military technology (Verey

24 TNA WO 95/4317: 52nd Division War Diary and Thompson, *The Fifty-Second Lowland Division 1914-1918*, pp. 129-51.
25 Aspinall-Oglander, *Military Operations Gallipoli*, Vol. II, pp. 391-92.
26 The Helles sector always had a destroyer on duty off the left flank. Additional naval gunfire support could be summoned upon request. Ibid., p. 394.
27 Robin Prior, *Gallipoli: The End of a Myth* (New Haven, Connecticut: Yale University Press, 2009), p. 223.
28 TNA WO 95/4274: 'MINUTES OF CORPS COMMANDER'S CONFERENCE', 11 November 1915, VIII Corps War Diary.
29 See Prior, *Gallipoli*, pp. 221-23.

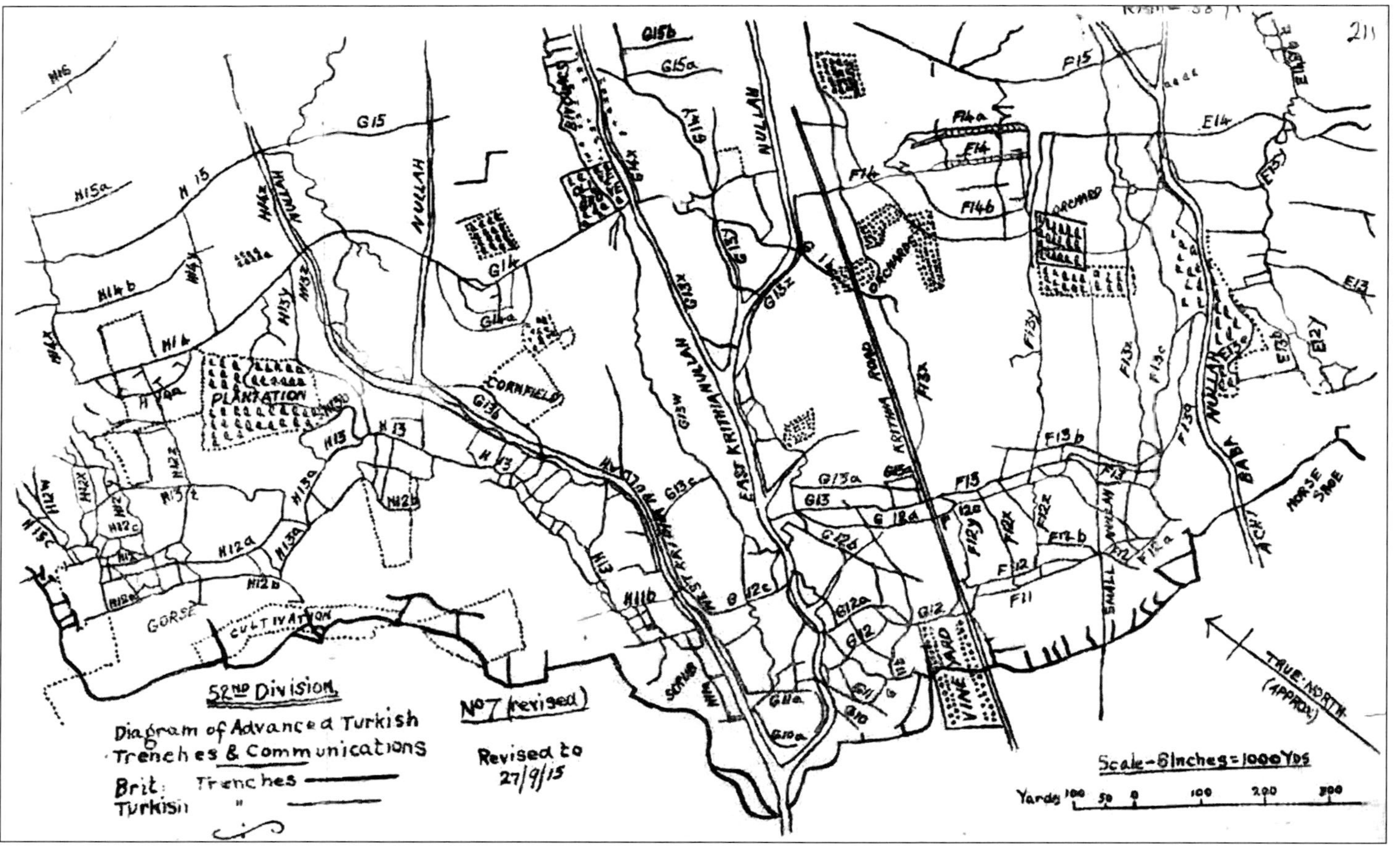

Map 5.1 52nd Division sector map, September 1915. (TNA WO 95/4317)

lights, trench mortars, new pattern bombs, periscope rifle frames, etc.)[30] that was in such short supply during the strategic phase of the Gallipoli campaign.[31] If the abortive Vineyard assault was indicative of the declining "state of the army and its leadership" at the time, the subsequent post-strategic phase demonstrated, as we shall see, that the MEF was making some important organisational, operational, tactical and technological strides prior to the evacuation.[32]

The tactical importance of the junction of East and West Krithia Nullahs was succinctly stated in the post-war 52nd Division history:

> This was the Turkish centre, and because of the utility of these nullahs as communication trenches, its capture would constitute a direct threat against Krithia and Achi Baba.[33]

The aforementioned desire to maintain morale and discipline through minor operations aside, that the hitherto unobtainable Krithia village and Achi Baba eminence could still be considered viable objectives during the post-strategic phase is curious when one considers that many British generals had, by early November, come to the conclusion that retention of Helles "by itself would be a costly and worthless undertaking." However, the primary reason for the retention of Achi Baba as a campaign aim appears to have been influenced by the Royal Navy's desire to maintain its blockade of the Straits entrance.[34] Meantime, the Asquith Government dithered over whether to sanction a risky withdrawal from the peninsula.

Defended by a labyrinth of trenches to the south, east and west, the Ottoman salient encompassing the Y-shaped confluence of East and West Krithia Nullahs – the two northern branches of the Kirte Dere – was immensely strong by Gallipoli standards:

30 For example, see TNA WO 95/4265: 'GSR 154', 12 November 1915 and lengthy treatise 'B' 29, November 1915, MEF War Diary for the 10 patterns of available bombs, bombing tactics and bombing organisation respectively,

31 One week after assuming command at Helles (14 August 1915), Lieutenant-General Davies requested special stores and material for a winter campaign. "Among his chief demands were hutments and road material." See Aspinall-Oglander, *Military Operations Gallipoli*, Vol. II, p. 394. For the impact of Western Front lessons and technology on the Gallipoli peninsula and other British theatre of operations, see Aimée Fox-Godden, 'Putting Knowledge in Power: Learning and Innovation in the British Army of the First World War' (PhD Thesis. Birmingham: University of Birmingham, 2016).

32 Aspinall-Oglander, pp. 462-63 and Prior, *Gallipoli*, p. 221.

33 Thompson, *The Fifty-Second Lowland Division 1914-1918*, p. 162. The divisional history further elaborated (p. 178) on the importance of nullahs as a means of overland communication: "The amount of ground which could be captured and held on Cape Helles was limited by means of communications between the new front line and the old one. If water, ammunition and rations could not be brought up, the ground could not be held. This need could usually be supplied only by digging trenches forward, a laborious and costly process; but where a nullah of any depth was available, forming a ready-made communication trench, the possibilities of being able to hold a larger area of captured ground were much increased. For these reasons the Turks probably regarded the forthcoming operations against the junction of East and West Krithia Nullahs as a prelude to further attacks on Krithia, and finally on Achi Baba."

34 Prior, *Gallipoli*, p. 226. Further designs against Achi Baba appear to have finally been abandoned by MEF Headquarters in mid-December. See AWM (Australian War Memorial): AWM4, 1/4/9 Part 2: 'Despd.2125', 18 December 1915 and Aspinall-Oglander, *Military Operations Gallipoli*, Vol. II, pp. 462-63.

> The Krithia Nullah near the Vineyard splits into two courses, known respectively as East and West Krithia Nullahs. The western bank of the latter stands about 40 feet above the level of the bed, but the ground on the east of the former slopes down more gradually to the floor of the watercourse. Just at the bifurcation the wedge of land between the two branches runs up the ridge in a gentle slope. The Turkish trench system was skilfully sited on the cliffs overlooking the West Krithia Nullah, then crossing the tongue of land, cut the slope on the east bank of the East Krithia Nullah and moved on to the trenches in the Vineyard. Since the nullahs formed the most tempting approaches up the hill – they had the irresistible appeal of the obvious – the Turks took care to construct their strongest works in their vicinity.[35]

Thus these formidable positions became the focus of a series of methodical siege warfare approaches (sapping and mining)[36] and infantry assaults to secure the forked watercourse junction and its immediate environs:

> The work of pushing forward various bombing saps at night was carried out several times in October and with complete success. From this time we may date the commencement of the systematic operations which finally drove the Turks out of a trench marked on the British maps as G.11a, and accordingly out of the main fork of Krithia Nullah.[37]

Executed by 52nd Division during the period 9-30 October, the first of these small-scale enterprises occurred on the 9 October when 1/5th King's Own Scottish Borderers (KOSB) extended a bomb sap east of Krithia Nullah. On the night of the 12/13 October 1/4th KOSB pushed the "Northeast Bombing Station" a further fifteen yards. "This brought it within fifteen yards of the Turks, and the first intimation of the change to the latter was a salvo of bombs at daybreak." The night of the 18/19 October saw 1/5th HLI advance the "Northwest Bombing Station from the Vineyard to very close quarters with the Turkish trench guarding East Krithia Nullah." An offensive scheme to storm a trench (a section of H.11a) that extended along the west side of West Krithia Nullah, drawn up by 1/7th Royal Scots, was passed on to 1/7th HLI following relief of the former. Launched under bright moonlight on 20 October, a small party of HLI "stole across" no man's land to discover the objective unoccupied. "Before the Turks realised what happened", the attackers had established a bomb stop barricade and dug a communication trench back to the British frontline without loss. "The portion captured ran directly across the cliffs of West Krithia Nullah, directly overlooking and almost enfilading the Turkish trench

35 Major John Ewing MC, *The Royal Scots 1914-1919* (Edinburgh: Oliver & Boyd, 1925), p. 212.

36 See Michael LoCicero, 'A Coda to the Second Battle of Ypres: International Trench, 6-10 July 1915' in Spencer Jones (ed.), *Courage Without Glory: The British Army on the Western Front 1915* (Solihull: Helion & Company, 2015), p. 322.

37 Thompson, *The Fifty-Second Lowland Division 1914-1918*, p. 160. According to the British official history, from the earliest days on the peninsula "the VIII Corps adopted a convenient method of naming the Turkish trenches. These were numbered serially, with a distinctive alphabetical prefix [G.11a, H.11a, etc., etc.] to denote the area to which they belonged. But no similar system was used for the British line, and the student who is accustomed to any of the orderly systems eventually evolved in France is bound to be somewhat confused by the names on the Gallipoli trench diagrams." See Aspinall-Oglander, *Military Operations Gallipoli*, Vol. II, p. 170, fn. 2.

G.11a, which ran across the more low-lying tongue dividing the two watercourses." Alert to the consequences, the Ottoman defenders "showed their appreciation of this very clever theft … of a valuable trench" with a fierce but unsuccessful bombing counter-attack the following night.[38] Debouching from G.11a, succeeding counter-attacks against the previously established barricade were repulsed with heavy loss on 22 October:

> All of this made the Turks very nervous, and they became extremely active making overhead cover, putting out wire and otherwise strengthening their lines. They also tried to destroy our bombing stations by bombing and shelling, but without success. Frameworks covered with wire netting and fixed at the end of bomb-saps, made it much more difficult for the Turks to throw grenades into the British T-heads [saps], and they copied this means of defence.[39]

The final operation for the month occurred on 30 October when 1/5th Royal Scots Fusiliers (RSF) pushed the H.11a barricade forward a few yards along the cliff of West Krithia Nullah. This minute advance made it possible for RSF bombers to reach G.11a with hand grenades. Concurrent with these bellicose activities, 52nd Division ran out T-head saps and excavated new fire trenches, "so that it steadily ate into no man's land about East Krithia Nullah."[40] Remaining vigilant to further British incursions, the Ottoman *13th Division* (commanded by German Colonel Albert Heuck) of *Mirliva* (Major-General) Fevzi (Çakmak) Pasha's *V Corps*,[41] continued to bolster the threatened Krithia Nullah defences whilst carrying on with what *Fifth Army* staff officer Major Erich Prigge described as an army-wide "low-intensity warfare" stance of nocturnal trench raids and offensive/defensive mining.[42]

15 November Assault: Plans and preparations

Operation orders for a comparatively larger assault were issued by 52nd Division Headquarters on 11 November 1915. The 156th Brigade (1/4th Royal Scots, 1/7th Royal Scots, 1/7th Scottish Rifles, 1/8th Scottish Rifles) was tasked with seizing Ottoman trenches G.11b and G.11 situated due east of East Krithia Nullah.[43] Having reviewed the divisional orders following receipt,

38 Thompson, p. 161.
39 Ibid.
40 Ibid., p. 162.
41 The Ottoman *V Corps* consisted of the *13th* and *14th* divisions. The *13th Division* (*4th*, *46th* and *60th* regiments) was, taking into account sector overlap by the neighbouring *10th Division* (*XIV Corps*) and *14th Division* to north and south respectively, opposite 52nd Division during November-December 1915. See Erickson, *Gallipoli: The Ottoman Campaign*, Appendix D for 'Order of Battle, Cape Helles Positional Battles, September 1915-9 January 1916'. Special thanks to Dr Mesut Uyar, University of New South Wales for identifying the relevant Ottoman formation and subordinate infantry units.
42 See Major Erich R. Prigge, *The Struggle for the Dardanelles: The Memoirs of a German Staff Officer in Ottoman Service … Translated with Introduction and Notes by Philip Rance* (Barnsley: Pen & Sword, 2017), pp. 291-93.
43 TNA WO 95/4317: '52nd (LOWLAND) DIVISION) ORDER NO. 18', 11 November 1915, 52nd Division War Diary.

156th Brigade composed and issued its own attack orders on 12 November. The objectives were, following capture, to be "consolidated and barricades erected in G.11b and G.11 and in the communication trench between the two, leading to G.12." In British hands, the enemy trenches were to be "joined at once" to the east end of the 'Northwest Bomb Station' and "as quickly as possible to G.10 at its west end and to the sap being dug forward from HOPE STREET in the centre." Thus secured, the "present barricades in G.11 will be removed" and communications opened through that trench. In concert on the left, the 'A' Bomb Station would be pushed forward far enough opposite the Ottoman bomb station in H.11a to allow for its occupation. New barricades would "then be erected in the trenches north and east of this point and it will be at once joined with the new saps now under construction from 'B' Bomb Station" and from the British firing line. As a signal for the infantry to advance, two underground mines to be detonated in sequence by VIII Corps Mining Company,[44] the first beneath G.11b "at junction with trench to be captured."[45] In addition, a third mine would be detonated below the Ottoman bomb station in H.11a in a separate operation. "As soon as this goes up", the order continued, "the infantry in H.11a will rush forward and from 'A' Bomb Station against their objective." On the advance of the infantry, the supporting artillery, having dispensed with a usual preliminary barrage as a tactical ruse to achieve surprise, would immediately cooperate by "opening a heavy fire on the support and communication trenches" behind the objective to render all "impassable" until captured trenches were secured and consolidated. As a supporting diversion, the component brigades of 52nd Division and Royal Naval Division were to draw enemy attention with rifle and machine-gun fire throughout the same period of seizure and consolidation.[46]

The Scottish Rifles battalions (CO Lieutenant-Colonel B.G. Bridge)[47] of 156th Brigade, with attached elements of Lanarkshire Yeomanry, were tasked with seizing the G.11b and G.11 objectives on the right. The Royal Scots battalions (CO Lieutenant-Colonel W.C. Peebles)[48] of the same brigade, with attached elements of Ayrshire Yeomanry, were to capture the Ottoman bomb station situated in H.11a on the left.[49] In order to expedite overland communications, the

44 VIII Corps Mining Company was formed from ad hoc mining squads by Captain H.W. Laws, a Royal Naval Division officer with considerable mine engineering experience, during the early summer of 1915. See Captain W. Grant Grieve & Bernard Newman, *Tunnellers: The Story of the Royal Engineer Tunnelling Companies During the Great War* (London: Herbert Jenkins, 1936), p. 79 and Richard Wood and John Dixon's chapter in this volume.

45 On completion of an underground defensive system in the Vineyard sector, five offensive galleries were run out towards the Ottoman lines. Paragraph three of 'Order No. 18' (see below), originally called for a second mine to be detonated under the enemy barbed wire obstacles, but this was cancelled in a subsequent "AFTER ORDER" dated 14 November. See Grieve & Newman, *Tunnellers*, p. 83.

46 TNA WO 95/4317: '156th Inf. Bde. Order No. 14', 12 November 1915, 52nd Division War Diary.

47 Biographical data for Lieutenant-Colonel Bridge could not be found despite an extensive search in the relevant *Army List*, *London Gazette*, etc. volumes.

48 Lieutenant-Colonel William Carmichael Peebles (b. 1871). Edinburgh-based electrical engineer; commissioned 5th Volunteer Battalion RSF 1894; CO 1/7th RSF 1910; survivor Quintinshill rail disaster, 22 May 1915. See Adrian Searle & Jack Anthony Richards, *The Quintinshill Conspiracy: The Shocking True Story Behind Britain's Worst Rail Disaster* (Barnsley: Pen & Sword, 2015).

49 The Scottish Rifles and Royal Scots battalions had, for all practical purposes, been amalgamated due to heavy losses. Thus "Every possible man was gathered to swell the very thin ranks of the 156th Brigade. Fourteen of its men in the Divisional Band returned to their units on the day previous to the attack." Thompson, *The Fifty-Second Lowland Division 1914-1918*, p. 179.

Ayrshire Yeomanry prior to embarkation for Gallipoli. (Private collection)

number of runners would be increased to four per battalion, two assigned to each commanding officer; the remainder attached to brigade headquarters. As a foil to possible Ottoman mining activity in the area, two small parties consisting of one NCO and three men of 2/1st Lowland Field Company Royal Engineers (RE) would also accompany the attackers. Their "special duty" was to "search for and cut all wires which may be leading to mines and to destroy any mines that may be found." Immediate reserves, in the form of a subsection of Lanarkshire Yeomanry, would be situated in the Redoubt Line under orders to be prepared to move forward at a "moment's notice."[50]

Assault force commanding officers were to make certain that scaling ladders were in position after sally ports and fire steps had been prepared for rapid egress from frontline and support trenches.[51] They were also to ensure that "sufficient empty sandbags, spare tools, water, bombs, etc., are all at hand and close to each communication trench being made to join up the captured

50 TNA WO 95/4317: '156th Inf. Bde. Order No. 14', 12 November 1915; 'Issued with 156th Bde. Order. No. 14 dated 12/11/15: Instructions for the Scottish Rifle Battn'; 'Issued with 156th Bde. Order. No. 14 dated 12/11/15: Instructions for Royal Scots Battn'; 'Issued with 156th Bde. Order. No. 14 dated 12/11/15: Instructions for a/BMGO [acting Brigade Machine Gun Officer] 156th Inf. Bde.', 52nd Division War Diary and Thompson, pp. 178-79. Sixteen officers and 921 men (Ayrshire Yeomanry and Lanarkshire Yeomanry) of the Lowland Mounted Brigade reinforced the manpower-depleted 52nd Division on 11 October 1915. See Becke, *Order of Battle of Divisions Part 2A,* p. 111.

51 Barbed wire obstacles situated in front of the British line were re-positioned "obliquely" to the line of advance "in order to admit of the passage of the assaulting troops." See TNA WO 95/4317: '156th Inf. Bde. Order No. 14', 12 November 1915, 52nd Division War Diary.

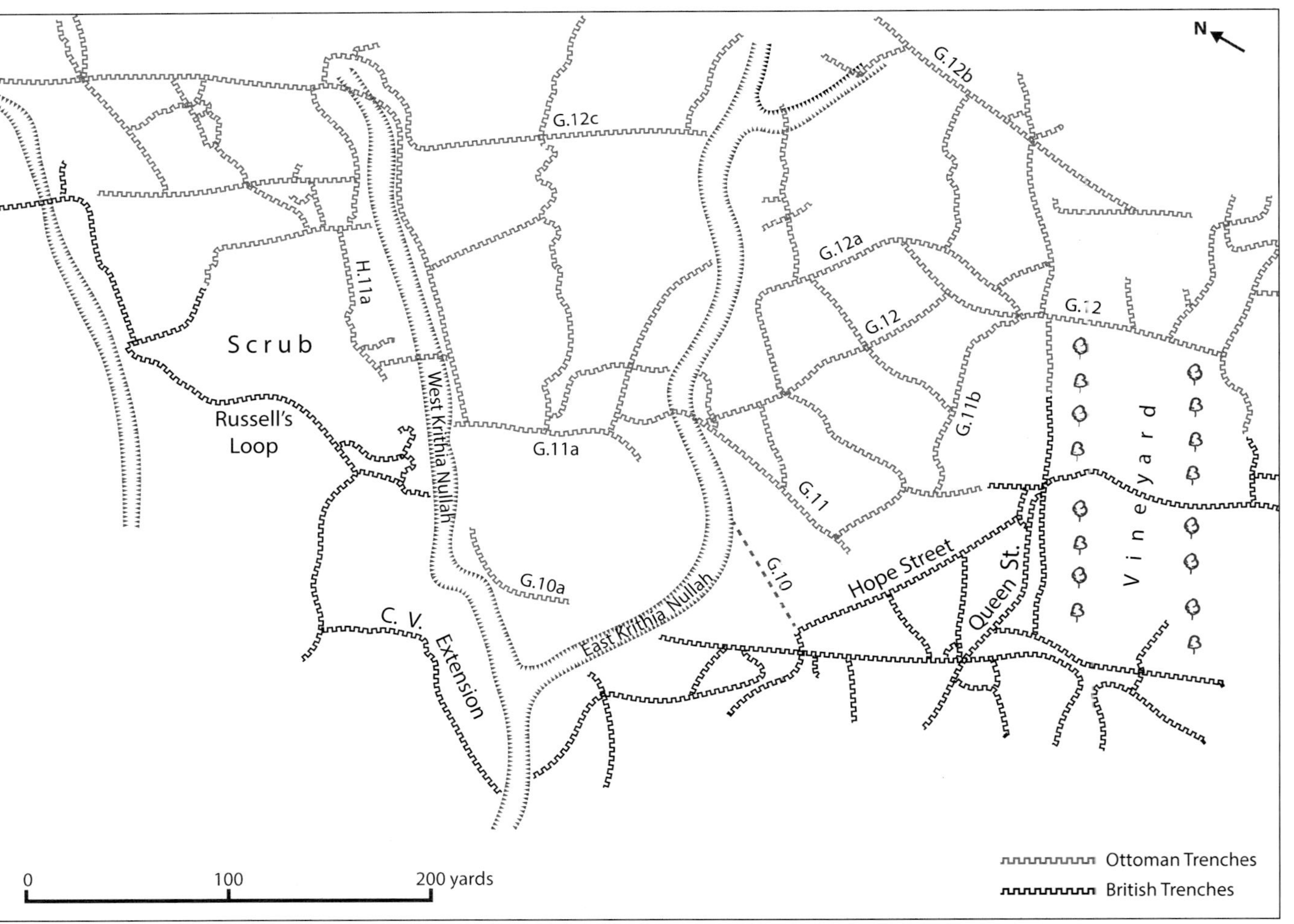

Map 5.2 Krithia Nullah and vicinity, 5 November 1915. (Map drawn by George Anderson © Helion & Company 2018)

trench." Prisoners taken during the assault were to be "placed under guard in the captured trench until it is joined up; they will then be marched down" to brigade headquarters by escorts detached from the reserve of Lanarkshire Yeomanry. "Any papers, plans, maps, or enemy material such as machine-guns or trench mortars etc." were to be passed on to brigade headquarters at the earliest opportunity. For his part, 156th Brigade's senior medical officer was to arrange for the evacuation of the wounded. Plans and preparations thus articulated, commanding officers were also tasked with making certain that officers knew "the exact point to which they are to lead their men and that every man knows exactly what he has to do, and that accurate information is rapidly forwarded" to brigade. For security purposes, "no orders, maps, letters, etc." would be "taken into action by any officer, NCO or man." All of these possessions were to be stored at brigade headquarters for safe keeping until after the operation had been carried out.[52] A final divisional "AFTER ORDER", issued on 14 November, related that the designated zero hour would be communicated by the divisional signal company on 15 November at 1:30 p.m., after which "all watches will be set." In addition to cancelling the mine detonation underneath the enemy barbed wire, the order also stipulated that two NCOs and 10 men of the designated Lanarkshire Yeomanry reserve were to act as prisoner escorts and defined up and down traffic routes for both East and West Krithia Nullahs. Meticulous orders spelled-out on reams of cyclostyled or handwritten foolscap, objective maps carefully rendered and issued, the Royal Scots post-war history subsequently observed that the projected assault, as planned, was actually two "self-contained enterprises since our attacking forces were separated by the tongue of land between the two nullahs ..."[53]

A "brilliant success"

Dispatched to the Mediterranean by the Cabinet war committee to form an "appreciation" of the Dardanelles campaign's future, Secretary of State for War Lord Kitchener convened conferences with local commanders and toured the peninsula during 9-20 November.[54] The onset of winter dispelled the maddening plague of flies and, with the corollary drop in temperature, improved the overall health of the MEF. Stormy weather throughout October and early November temporarily interrupted ship to shore traffic, damaged piers and washed away tramlines at Suvla, Anzac and Helles. In the latter sector, the trench raiding, bombing and mining operations conducted during October continued without pause into the next month as 156th Brigade prepared to assault the Ottoman salient. Zero hour was set for 3:00 p.m. on 15 November.[55] Able Seaman Joseph Murray (Hood Battalion, Royal Naval Division), attached to the tunnellers, recorded final efforts to prepare three offensive mines before Zero:

52 Ibid.
53 TNA WO 95/4317: '156th Inf. Order No. 14', 14 November 1915, 52nd Division War Diary and Ewing, *The Royal Scots 1914-1919*, p. 212.
54 See Aspinall-Oglander, *Military Operations Gallipoli*, Vol. II, pp. 413-26 and Erickson, *Gallipoli: Command Under Fire*, p. 226.
55 Aspinall-Oglander, pp. 424-25.

> The advance was timed for 3:00 p.m. tomorrow. We had thirty-one hours to dig thirty feet, prepare the recesses for three mines, lay them, tamp them and make sure they went off at the appointed second. One man dug for all he was worth for five seconds. The second man cleared away the hard clay, the third man filling the sandbags and the fourth taking over the digging. At each changeover each man took over the position behind him so that the man that had been digging had a short rest before taking over with the pick.[56]

Massed and ready in "parts of the line where three or four bombing saps ran down old trenches towards Turkish bombing saps" prior to the pre-determined jumping-off time, the attackers were armed and equipped as follows: "Rifle with fixed sword/bayonet, magazines charged, [magazine] cut-offs closed,[57] 250 rounds S.A.A., entrenching implements but no tools, 4 empty sandbags through waist-belt, iron rations, water bottle (filled)" and "gas helmet slung over shoulder."[58] Consolidating parties, to follow on the heels of the assault parties, would be equipped in the same way as their predecessors, but also carry "picks and shovels in such proportion as the C.O. considers desirable." Dashing forward at the same moment as the main assault parties, designated bombing parties, on entering the hostile entrenchments, were to proceed from "traverse to traverse" in order to "clear a portion of trench before rushing it", after which they would be employed to resist the inevitable enemy counter-attacks. As a means to determining rate of advance, each bombing party was to "carry a blue signal flag which will be held above the parapet from time to time to show the progress of the party and so enable out machine-guns to sweep the trench in front of them with fire."[59] In command of one of the parties tasked with joining the British frontline to the captured Ottoman trenches was Lieutenant Patrick Maitland Campbell of the Ayrshire Yeomanry:

> My orders were, as soon as the attack was launched, and the Turkish line captured, to start my first relief of six men digging like the Devil from A to B. The attacking force were to start digging as soon as possible from B to meet me. The attack was timed at 3 p.m. and was to be entirely surprise, no artillery preparation, the signal being the explosion of a mine ... Of course the object of my job was to get a trench made by which bombs, ammunition,

56 Joseph Murray, *Gallipoli 1915* (London: New English Library, 1977), p. 171.
57 The magazine cut-off was a fixed design feature found in pre-1916 manufactured Lee Enfield service rifles of various patterns. It allowed the soldier to "cut off" the magazine for single shot/safety purposes while conserving the remaining rounds as an ammunition reserve.
58 Poison gas was never deployed during the Gallipoli campaign. As a precaution, Hypo pattern gas helmets were issued to the MEF during late summer 1915. "Fortunately, however, the prevailing winds at Cape Helles, in which a gas attack was possible, blew towards the Turkish lines." Nevertheless, a possible enemy gas usage warning alert was distributed to all VIII Corps divisions on 11 November 1915. See TNA WO 95/4274: 'G/2992', 11 November 1915, VIII Corps War Diary; WO 95/4317: 'Operation Orders by Lt. Col. B.C. Bridges, Comdg. Scottish Rifles Battalion', n.d.; '156th INF. BDE. Report on Operations', 16 November 1915, 52nd Division War Diary and Thompson, *The Fifty-Second Lowland Division 1914-1918*, p. 138.
59 Thompson, p. 179 and TNA WO 95/4317: 'G.R. 42/10', 28 September 1915, '52nd (LOWLAND) DIVISION) ORDER NO. 18', 11 November 1915; '156th Inf. Bde. Order No. 14', 12 November 1915; 'Issued with 156th Bde. Order. No. 14 dated 12/11/15'; 'Instructions for the Scottish Rifle Battn, Issued with 156th Bde. Order. No. 14 dated 12/11/15' and 'Instructions for Royal Scots Battn', n.d., 52nd Division War Diary.

> rations, etc., could be supplied to the new line, and wounded, etc. taken from it – altogether an important one – and I had at all costs to be through by dawn of 16th. I had 35 or 45 yards to go through, very hard ground, almost rock, and working with one picker at each end was all that was possible. Even at that it seemed simple and safe enough; however, we were all to have our hands more than full for 24 hours.[60]

At 3:00 p.m. precisely, the underground mines were detonated "with mighty explosions that shook the whole ground in the vicinity, and immense brown and black columns of dust, earth and smoke were flung into the air, in form like a row of gigantic elm trees." Lieutenant Campbell, in the Scottish Rifles sector, observed: "Punctual to the moment, up went the mine with its bit of trench and bit of Turks …" Simultaneous with the three eruptions, the varied armaments of the protected cruiser HMS *Edgar*,[61] in conjunction with two monitors mounting 14-inch guns,[62] subjected the Ottoman support and reserves trenches to a shrieking deluge of off-shore shellfire. British guns (eight 18-pdr, four 15-pdr, three 12-pdr and four howitzer batteries), trench mortars (3.7 and Cairo Citadel manufactured "Garland" pattern tubes) and French guns "also joined in, and between the explosions could be heard the continuous chatter and rattle of machine-guns", the latter (22 Vickers/Maxim guns) to "assist the Eastern and Western operations and to check any attempted counter-attack." Ottoman batteries "replied heavily, but very erratically and did little damage", whilst hostile garrisons in neighbouring positions "who fired heavily" in response, "were caught by machine-gun fire and bombs and suffered considerably their fire becoming very wild."[63]

As the "dust from the explosion of the mines and shells clouded the sky" with a "sickening stench", Scottish Rifles and Royal Scots assault parties rushed forward to enter the Ottoman trenches.[64] One mine had obliterated the hostile bombing station in H.11a, the remaining two levelling G.11 and its attendant garrison. Isolated by the east and west assaults, the surviving defenders were observed "running backwards and forwards in a communication trench on the

60 P. M. Campbell, *Letters from Gallipoli* (Edinburgh: T & A Constable, 1916), p. 50. Special thanks to Jim Grundy for bringing this privately published source to my attention.

61 HMS *Edgar*: Class and type – *Edgar* class protected cruiser (nine vessels 1890-92); launched 1890; displacement 7,350 tons; length 3.875 ft. (1.18 m); beam 60 ft (18 m); armament 2 × BL 9.2-inch (233.7 mm) Mk VI guns, 10 × QF 6-inch (152.4 mm) guns and 12 × 6-pdr guns.

62 Four of eight Royal Navy monitors (HMS *Abercrombie*, HMS *Havelock*, HMS *Raglan*, HMS *Roberts*) serving at Gallipoli had 14-inch guns. See Ian Buxton, *Big Gun Monitors: Design, Construction and Operations 1914-1945* (Barnsley: Seaforth, 2012) and Jim Crossley, *Monitors of the Royal Navy: How the Fleet Brought the Big Guns to Bear* (Barnsley: Pen & Sword, 2016).

63 Thompson, *The Fifty-Second Lowland Division 1914-1918*, pp. 181-82; Aspinall-Oglander, *Military Operations Gallipoli*, Vol. II, p. 425; Campbell, *Letters from Gallipoli*, p. 50; TNA WO 95/4625: 'SITUATION. From 0600 15th November to 0600 16th November 1915'; 'ISSUED WITH 156th INF. BDE. Order No. 14 dated 12/11/15'; 'Instructions for a/B.G.M.O. [Brigade Machine-gun Officer] 156th Inf. Bde.'; 'ISSUED WITH 156th INF. BDE. Order No. 14 dated 12/11/15'; 'Instructions for O.C. Divisional Trench Mortars'; 'REPORT ON ACTION ON MACHINE GUNS 156th INF. BDE. AND FOUR MACHINE GUNS ATTACHED FROM 157th INF. BDE. during the operations on 15th and 16th Nov. 1915', n.d.; 'REPORT ON ACTION OF DIVISIONAL TRENCH MORTARS DURING OPERATIONS 15-11-15', n.d. and 'M.F. 836', 17 November 1915, MEF War Diary. The divisional history contains the most detailed published account of 52nd Division's operations from 15 November-29 December 1915.

64 Murray, *Gallipoli 1915*, p. 174.

HMS *Edgar*.

tongue of land, discharging their rifles in the air." Taking advantage of the achieved surprise, prevailing chaos and resultant enemy confusion, "160 yards of trench on East of Nullah and 120 yards on its west", were seized, "consolidated grenade stations being established in all communication trenches leading towards the Turkish trenches" by 3:17 p.m.[65]

The Scottish Rifles assault – first and second waves consisting of two officers and 45 men each – against the east branch of Krithia Nullah encountered little resistance, the stormers rapidly occupying both mine craters and the smoking shambles of G.11. Over the top, Lieutenant Campbell recollected, "went the infantry and the bombers, to the accompaniment of the most terrific artillery bombardment of the Turkish second line and communication trenches by all our guns. The scene and sound was glorious, and to us watchers it was a relief to see that the Turks had been caught off their guard and practically all our entire force were safely into the Turkish trenches." Following this, their primary task amounted to rebuilding G.11, "but this had been provided for, filled and empty sandbags were ready, despite enemy snipers the work was pressed on."[66] For his part, Campbell waited for 10 minutes after zero hour, but there was "no sign of anyone digging to meet us … so I took six of my men over and got them started; of course it was

65 Thompson, p. 180; TNA WO 95/4625: 'M.F. 836', 17 November 1915, MEF War Diary; WO 95/4317: 'Operation Orders by Lt. Col. B.C. Bridges, Comdg. Scottish Rifles Battalion', n.d.; '156th INF. BDE. Report on Operations', 16 November 1915; 'G.R. 34/3. OPERATIONS REPORT – NOVEMBER 1915', 2 December 1915 and 'REPORT ON ACTION BY BDE. MACHINE GUNS 156th INF. BDE. AND 4 MACHINE GUNS ATTACHED FROM 157th INF. BDE. during the operations on 15th and 16th November 1915', n.d., 52nd Division War Diary.

66 TNA WO 95/4317: 'Operation Orders by Lt. Col. B.C. Bridges, Comdg. Scottish Rifles Battalion', n.d.; '156th INF. BDE. Report on Operations',16 November 1915, 52nd Division War Diary; Campbell, *Letters from Gallipoli*, p. 52 and Thompson, *The Fifty-Second Lowland Division 1914-1918*, p. 180.

a risky rush, but none of them got hit. When I reached the captured trenches, I found everybody there had more than they could do getting these prepared for counter-attack."[67]

Two companies of 1/7th Royal Scots, supported by two companies of 1/4th Royal Scots, debouched from cliff-top jumping-off positions at Zero to secure the enemy's West Krithia Nullah defences. Advanced bombing parties "tore through a gap that had been prepared under the advanced barricades" to rush the northern extremity of H.11a. Exiting brick and timber-lined dugouts constructed just below the trench parados, the nonplussed Ottoman garrison, in a concerted attempt to ascertain what was happening, were either shot down or taken prisoner. H.11a having now been secured after some "brisk fighting", supporting bombers mistakenly pressed beyond the assigned objective as far as an adjacent cross-trench. Encountering a pocket of Ottoman infantry sheltering with fixed bayonets in excavated niches, a brief mêlée with bomb and bayonet ensued before a general withdrawal some yards back where a "stout barricade" was hurriedly constructed across a section of captured trench. Ottoman machine-gunners and snipers being very active, "much digging was necessary to clear a passage" through the accumulated mine explosion spoil. Shortly afterwards, Ottoman artillery enfiladed the newly-captured H.11a with shrapnel.[68] It was during this consolidation period that previously unsuspected enemy mine entrances were uncovered:

> The discovery in the captured area of two mining shafts, both of which led under our lines, suggested that we had forestalled a Turkish attack. One was practically completed; the other which ran under the bombing station from which our attack had been launched, was not quite in such an advanced stage of preparation … The entrances to both shafts were destroyed and barricades were placed in front of them.[69]

Repair and reconstruction efforts continued apace throughout a subsequent evening thunderstorm, some 10,000 sandbags utilised by 1/7th Royal Scots alone. Successive forays to seize the trench barricade by small parties of determined Ottoman infantry were driven off with rifle and bomb before sunrise put a temporary end to these precipitate counter-attacks.[70]

Consolidation continued under hostile rifle, machine-gun and shellfire throughout 16 November. "Owing to the heavy rain and mud, great difficulty was experienced owing to the jamming of rifle bolts throughout the night."[71] Ottoman efforts to seize the barricade during at

67 Campbell, p. 52.
68 Ewing, *The Royal Scots 1914-1919*, pp. 215-16.
69 Ibid., pp. 215-16. "As a possible way to break the deadlock, the Ottoman general staff organised the 254th Tunnelling Company and sent it to the peninsula." The 52nd Division history subsequently observed: "During the 17th the Royal Scots heard a voice in Turkish come from the ground in their mine crater, and rescued a very hungry Turk who had been imprisoned for two days in the Turkish mineshaft leading from it. Calls were heard on the 19th from the other mineshaft, which was in front of the barricade, and the Royal Scots out up a white flag, intending to save these imprisoned Turks. No response was made from the Turkish lines, and these men had to be left to their fate." See Erickson, *Gallipoli: The Ottoman Campaign*, p. 178 and Thompson, *The Fifty-Second Lowland Division 1914-1918*, p. 183.
70 TNA WO 95/4317: '156th INF. BDE. Report on Operations, II. Western Operation', 16 November 1915; 52nd Division War Diary; Thompson, pp. 180-81 and Ewing, *The Royal Scots 1914-1919*, pp. 212-13.
71 TNA WO 95/4317: '156th INF. BDE., Report on Operations', 16 November 1915, 52nd Division War Diary.

least five sorties from dusk the previous day to dawn on 17 November were repelled by the Royal Scots and Ayrshire Yeomanry. "An immediate counter-attack, however, drove the Turks back, and a new barricade was built close in rear of the ruins of the old one."[72] Lieutenant Campbell was in the thick of the fighting:

> I certainly shot two, and probably a good many more Turks to my own gun (one could only see them against the skyline), and my arm is still blue from the recoil of the rifle I used. I must say it was one of the most enjoyable mornings' sport I have had. One's whole idea was to bag as many as possible, and anxiety was never a recognisable element in the excitement. Needless to say, except for a few bombers, very few Turks got near us.

Four "half-hearted" counter-attacks were also turned back by the Scottish Rifles during the night of 16/17 November. "For a couple of days", the 52nd Division history later observed, "the Turks lay low. But they had been caught napping and were uneasy. They started digging hard in G.11a and the other trenches on the tongue of land."[73]

Brigadier-General L.C. Koe (GOC 156th Brigade)[74] effusively remarked: "The spirit of all ranks of the brigade and their devotion to duty was, both prior to, and during the operations, worthy of the highest praise". Lieutenant-General Sir William Birdwood (GOC MEF) expressed satisfaction with "the very successful attack on the Turkish trenches on the 15th instant for which careful preparations had been in progress for a considerable time."[75] Approximately 160 and 120 yards of Ottoman trenches situated about east and west Krithia Nullah respectively had been captured at a cost of 112 officers and men killed and wounded.[76] Booty seized during the eastern sector fighting amounted to 15 rifles, accompanying ammunition and a few bombs. One wounded prisoner and 18 rifles were captured during the western sector fighting, the injured captive claiming that a "large number of bombs and some Turks were buried by the explosion of the mines."[77] Ottoman casualties, based on body counts related in the post-war

72 TNA WO 95/4317: 'G.R. 34/3. OPERATIONS REPORT – NOVEMBER 1915', 2 December 1915, 52nd Division War Diary.

73 See TNA WO 95/4317: 52nd Division War Diary; WO 94/4321: 156th Brigade War Diary; WO 95/4321: 1/4th Royal Scots War Diary, 1/7th Royal Scots War Diary, Ayrshire Yeomanry War Diary, 1/6th Scottish Rifles War Diary; Campbell, *Letters from Gallipoli*, p. 53; Thompson, *The Fifty-Second Lowland Division 1914-1918*, p. 183 and Ewing, *The Royal Scots 1914-1919*, pp. 215-17.

74 Brigadier-General Lancelot Charles Koe (b. 1862). Commissioned Royal Irish Regiment 1882; Suakin Expedition 1885; Hazara Expedition 1888; Benin Expedition 1897; employed Ceylon Volunteers 1906; Commandant Peking Legation Guard 1911-15, GOC 156th Brigade August 1915.

75 TNA WO 95/4625: 'GENERAL REMARKS on Operations on 15-11-15 carried out by 156th Inf. Bde.', 19 November 1915 and 'M.F. 836', 17 November 1915, MEF War Diary.

76 Casualties sustained by 156th Brigade were as follows: Officers – three killed, two wounded; other ranks – 22 killed, 85 wounded. See TNA WO 95/4625: 'G.R. 141', 24 November 1915, MEF War Diary; WO 95/4317: 52nd Division War Diary; WO 94/4321: 156th Brigade War Diary; Thompson, *The Fifty-Second Lowland Division 1914-1918*, p. 183 and Aspinall-Oglander, *Military Operations Gallipoli*, Vol. II, p. 425.

77 Thompson, *The Fifty-Second Lowland Division 1914-1918*, pp. 185-86. The dearth of Ottoman prisoners taken during this operation is in keeping with the relatively low numbers obtained during the Gallipoli campaign, 10,022 captured/surrendered (3.1 percent) of the 315,500 estimated troops deployed. See Introduction in Metin Gürcan & Robert Johnson (eds.), *The Gallipoli Campaign: The Turkish Perspective* (London: Routledge, 2016), p. 9.

divisional history, amounted to an estimated 70 to 100 fatalities. "To these must be added the Turkish dead we did not see, and their wounded."[78]

Post-operational analysis, based on the usual series of after-action reports originating at formation/unit level,[79] commenced with an VIII Corps appreciation of the Royal Navy's contribution to the bombardment: "All who saw it agree to the accuracy and value of the monitors fire, but the chief point is that it has been established that co-operation in an attack has now become a practical reality and that a system has been established which, with further development, will prove a powerful factor both in attack and defence." As for the fire of supporting land batteries, "there is of course no record of the actual damage done, but the fact that the Turkish artillery, though they fired more ammunition than they have done since our big attacks some months ago, have never fired more wildly and their fire did practically no damage and did not hinder either the capture of the trenches or the consolidation of them afterwards, is sufficient evidence [of] success achieved."[80]

Compiled for the edification of division, corps and army headquarters by 156th Brigade, a general remarks overview document followed three days later. Brigadier-General Koe, after noting the assault had been "carried out without the slightest hitch occurring", observed that the "signal arrangements worked admirably" despite telephone lines severed by hostile shellfire. "All wires had been previously duplicated throughout", such breaks that did occur were repaired by signallers without delay. "The amount of stores, etc. consumed", he continued, "was considerable but every demand was met and showed that much thought and care had been devoted to detail." Careful attention to said details by the commanding officers concerned "reaped its own rewards. Every man was in his place and knew his work and every article required throughout the day was in hand when wanted." Indeed, "a large number of sandbags had been filled daily for some days prior to the operations, and this saved much time and labour during the actual consolidation as the bags were passed by chains of men at 2 yards interval." Medical preparations were, in Koe's estimation, equally good, "the arrangements for the evacuation of wounded which were made by the S.M.O. [Senior Medical Officer] of this Bde. were most satisfactory and there was no delay in their removal from the front line."[81]

As bombs and bombing were a primary technological/tactical feature of the 15 November assault and its immediate aftermath, a carefully considered after-action bombing methodology report based on recent combat experience was also distributed. "The success of the attack was due in a great measure to the speed with which it was made." Bombing tactics outlined in previous VIII Corps memorandums and employed by 52nd Division during the assault no doubt contributed to the fortuitous operational outcome. Nevertheless, it was essential, the document continued "that bombing parties should move down the enemy trenches as quickly as possible [,] the question of reducing the number of articles equipment to be carried" had thus arisen. In response to this perceived need for accoutrement limitation, a recommended bombing party

78 TNA WO 95/4317: '156th INF. BDE., Report on Operations', 16 November 1915, 52nd Division War Diary.
79 See LoCicero, 'A Coda to the Second Battle of Ypres: International Trench, 6-10 July 1915' in Jones (ed.), *Courage Without Glory*, pp. 357-58.
80 TNA WO 95/4625: '0/317', 16 November 1915, MEF War Diary.
81 TNA WO 95/4317: 'GENERAL REMARKS on Operations on 15-11-15 carried out by 156th Inf. Bde.', 19 November 1915.

equipment list followed. Moreover, the P08 field equipment small entrenching tool was found to be of little use for barricade construction, the "damper" of one bombing party carrying a shovel "which proved of great value." A suggested remedy was for small working parties of three shovel men to accompany designated bombing parties in order to assist with barricade construction. Bomb supply shortages were also encountered during the assault, the proposed solution being that designated bombers were to carry as many bombs as possible, and these, "without reducing speed [,] should be conveyed across the enemy trenches with the first rush." With regard to organisation, some "slight confusion was apparent" with adopted bombing party formations. "Several parties left their trenches in single file" causing "considerable delay, and men of parties lost touch with each other to some extent." To avoid this, future bombing parties were advised to debouch from trenches "in line in such order that a right or left turn, as the case may be, will place them, immediately on entering the captured trench, in such order as effectively to carry on bombing operations to the flank previously determined upon." Pressing on "a little in advance of the infantry", bombing party NCOs and men were to don "distinguishing armlets" by day and luminous armlets or tunic patches by night as a ready means of identification.[82] Having thus examined and disseminated organisational and tactical best practice obtained during the late operation, 52nd Division would shortly be tasked with further limited offensive efforts in the Krithia Nullah sector.

"Whip-hand of the Turks"

It was during late November and early December that the uncertain future of the Gallipoli campaign entered the dénouement phase. The recent collapse of Serbia in the face of a lightning Central Powers offensive ensured, with the opening of railway lines between Belgrade and Istanbul, that the Ottoman *Fifth Army*, at peak strength of 5,500 officers and 310,000 men the previous October, was reinforced with powerful Austrian 240mm mortars and 150mm howitzers. The first bombardment by these formidable weapons occurred at Suvla on 20 November, after which MEF morale plummeted. This unwelcome event, coupled with the arrival of German artillery, engineer and infantry specialists from the Western Front, signalled the end. "With winter fast approaching and the Turks still in possession of the high ground the opportunity to conclude the campaign successfully had passed." Kitchener's recent inspection tour was followed on 22 November by the Secretary of State for War's recommendation that Suvla and Anzac should be evacuated whilst Helles was retained in order to salvage a modicum of Imperial prestige. After some deliberation, the Asquith coalition government sanctioned the proposed withdrawals on 7 December.[83]

MEF meteorologists predicted that November would usher in "'glorious weather', and that though a few southerly storms might be expected, heavy gales and real winter weather need

82 TNA WO 95/4274: 'REPORT ON BOMBING METHODS ADOPTED BY 52nd DIVISION DURING THEIR OFFENSIVE ON THE 15th NOV. 1915', VIII Corps War Diary.

83 Erickson, *Gallipoli: The Ottoman Campaign*, pp. 178-79; Aspinall-Oglander, *Military Operations Gallipoli*, Vol. II, pp. 413-39; Robert Johnson, 'Contested Historiography: Allied Perspectives on the Gallipoli Campaign' in Gürcan & Johnson (eds.), *The Gallipoli Campaign*, pp. 35-37 and Alexandra Churchill's chapter in this volume.

not be feared till the latter end of January." Such hopes were dashed by successive gales during the first three weeks of the month which caused "considerable damage on all beaches, and on the 26th, Lieutenant-General Davies again reported that the evacuation of Helles was out of the question till his piers were repaired."[84] That same day the MEF experienced a powerful gale of "exceptional violence" which left it reeling after three days of icy torrential rain, hard frost and blinding blizzards which collapsed trench lines and prevented boats from approaching established beachheads. The consequent misery was worse at Suvla where flooding "proved an unbearable strain to men whose health had already been undermined by the hardships of the summer campaign." The Anzac and Helles garrisons suffered far less due to a surfeit of available caves and underground galleries in the former, and the fortunate circumstance that the majority of trenches were situated on sloping ground in the latter.[85]

The decision to retain Helles having been decided upon, VIII Corps Headquarters awaited the future with some anxiety, their primary concern being that the "landing of more troops, ammunition and stores, would be antagonistic to the preliminaries to a successful withdrawal." Another factor in this prevailing apprehension was "the knowledge that for regimental officers and men the uncertainty and grimness of their own outlook were utterly depressing." As a means of addressing personal misgivings relating to whether or not his sector would be abandoned, Lieutenant-General Davies determined that the only way to carry on with some success was "to keep the whip-hand of the Turks by constant offensive action. Emphatic orders were, therefore, issued to his divisions for the offensive to be maintained on all occasions and at every practicable point in the line." To this end, the Ottoman defenders were "to be driven from their trenches by trench mortars, catapults and grenades and the British line pushed forward by sapping, by mining and by the seizure and consolidation of important points." This aggressive forward policy, in addition to addressing plummeting morale, would soon play an important part in the pending evacuations of Suvla and Anzac.[86]

"A most successful diversion"

On 52nd Division's front, 157th Brigade (1/5th HLI, 1/6th HLI, 1/7th HLI and 1/5th Argyll & Sutherland Highlanders (A&SH)) relieved 156th Brigade on either side of Krithia Nullah by the afternoon of 21 November, after which a half-hearted Ottoman counter-attack, despite the observed exhortation of enemy officers, to reclaim the lost territory was halted before it could start by artillery, machine-gun and rifle fire. Hostile shellfire, intelligence sources later observed, "was heavier than has been known for some months." Almost continuous harassment of newly established bombing posts occurred over the next week before the Ottoman defenders conceded British gains. Routine trench warfare returned thereafter. Subsequent privations experienced throughout the great winter storm, during which 157th Brigade suffered only one frostbite case, were somewhat alleviated by effective corps/divisional response and, in comparison to conditions at Suvla, providential natural drainage. By this time rumours of

84 For Davies' earlier perspectives (20 November) on a mooted Helles evacuation, see Aspinall-Oglander, *Military Operations Gallipoli*, Vol. II, pp. 420, fn. 1 and 432.

85 Ibid., pp. 432-34.

86 Ibid., pp. 463-64.

possible evacuation had spread throughout the manpower reduced divisions of VIII Corps in which units such as the previously amalgamated 7/8th Scottish Rifles were down to an available rifle strength of just 120 men. The impending permanent withdrawal of the French contingent and return of less than half of the evacuated sick and wounded ensured that formations would remain under strength well into the New Year.[87]

The final evacuation of Suvla and Anzac scheduled for the night of the 19/20 December, Lieutenant-General Birdwood, now in command of the recently-designated "Dardanelles Army",[88] issued orders for VIII Corps to "undertake some small offensive action on the afternoon of the 19th" as a means of drawing Ottoman attention away from the northern sectors.[89] Davies duly composed outline plans for his immediate superior on 16 December:

> In accordance with the wishes of the Army Commander I am undertaking a small operation on the 19th instant. The preparations for the capture of some of the enemy's trenches opposite our left flank are not yet fully complete and therefore action on this flank will be confined to blowing some mines under the enemy's trenches, and establishing, if possible, an advanced grenade station on the extreme left. In the centre [,] the 52nd Division propose to occupy the trench G.11a across the bit of ground between the two branches of the KRITHIA Nullah and push forward their grenade stations into G.12 on the eastern side.

Mines were to be detonated at "various other points in the line near these and other divisions and the artillery will bombard portions of the enemy's position with trench mortars, etc." The GOC VIII Corps also expressed his desire for the "cooperation of the ships to the S.O. 1st Squadron, and as I understand that the object is to impress the enemy with the fact that a serious operation is intended, I trust that the V.A. [Vice-Admiral Sir John de Robeck] may be asked to place the necessary ammunition at the disposal of this squadron ..."[90] Operational intent thus communicated to the Royal Navy and formations directly concerned, 42nd Division, charged with seizing Ottoman trenches at Fusilier Bluff, and 52nd Division commenced planning and preliminary arrangements for the prescribed diversionary attacks.

Since the 15 November assault, Ottoman trenches astride the Krithia Nullah tongue consisted of G.10a situated at its south-western extremity, and the 120-yards long G.11a that extended across the stream bed-isolated headland approximately 80 yards to the rear. Two additional fire trenches, the first extending along the south-eastern side of West Krithia Nullah and the

87 TNA WO 95/4265: 'SITUATION: From 0600 21st November to 0600 22 November 1915', MEF War Diary; Thompson, *The Fifty-Second Lowland Division 1914-1918*, pp. 184-92 and Aspinall-Oglander, *Military Operations Gallipoli*, Vol. II, pp. 461-62.

88 See Aspinall-Oglander, p. 422.

89 Curiously, Birdwood, in a despatch to the War Office telegraphed the day after the withdrawal from Anzac and Suvla, observed: "[T]he evacuation was conducted on the following plan ... I decided that a surprise was more likely to be secured if a feint was not made elsewhere with a view to distracting the attention of the Turks ... It seemed to me that by pursuing our normal attitude toward them without alteration [,] the chances were greater that we might get away unobserved ..." This statement may be in reference to previously contemplated diversionary assaults on the ANZAC and IX Corps fronts. See AWM: AWM4, 1/4/9 Part 2: 'Despd. 2215', 20 December 1915.

90 TNA WO 95/4274: 'O.377/2', 16 December 1915, VIII Corps War Diary and Aspinall-Oglander, *Military Operations Gallipoli*, Vol. II, pp. 455-56.

Men of 1/4th KOSB reloading machine-gun ammunition belts, December 1915. (Private collection)

second (G.11y) running "along the centre or crest-line of the tongue", extended north-east into the labyrinthine Ottoman defences from G.11a. Assigned to secure G.11a and, situated on the eastern bank of East Krithia Nullah, sections of the neighbouring G.12 and G.12a in two separate east-west operations, 157th Brigade received attack orders from 52nd Division headquarters on 16 December.[91] The 1/5th HLI (CO Lieutenant-Colonel Frederick Morrison),[92] supported by the remaining three battalions of 157th Brigade, was selected to carry out the assault:

> On the 15th December the C.O. was summoned to Brigade Headquarters and informed by General Casson[93] that the Battalion was probably to attack two small trenches held by the enemy known as G.11a and G.12. This attack was to be carried out on the 18th or 19th December and instructions were given to the Colonel that a reconnaissance was to be made and a report forwarded stating the best possible manner in which the attack could be successfully carried out. G.11a was a peculiar trench situated on a tongue of land between the two branches of the Krithia Nullah, some few hundred yards north of a point where the nullah divided. The ground on both sides of this trench stood about forty feet high and was

91 TNA WO 95/4274: '52ND (LOWLAND) DIVISION ORDER NO. 27', 16 December 1915, VIII Corps War Diary and Thompson, *The Fifty-Second Lowland Division*, p. 193.

92 Lieutenant-Colonel Frederick Lansdowne Morrison VD (b. 1863). MA University of Glasgow 1879-83; Major and Hon. Lieutenant-Colonel 1st Volunteer Battalion HLI 1906; CO 1/5th HLI 1914.

93 Brigadier-General Hugh Gilbert Casson (b. 1866). Commissioned South Wales Borderers 1886; South Africa 1899-1901; GOC 157th Brigade April 1915.

> held by us entirely on the west side and partly on the east side. Owing to our overlooking this trench the Turks did not occupy it during daylight, but it was decided that they sent a few men forward at night to garrison this trench. Several frontal attacks had been made earlier in the year on this trench but without success. It was accordingly decided that on this occasion attacks would be made from the flanks.[94]

As Able Seaman Murray succinctly observed, "an attack from the front was out of the question by virtue of the terrain and the impassable mass of barbed wire. The attack had to come behind the Turkish frontline."[95]

Numbers to be engaged would amount to 23 officers and 333 men of which 1/5th HLI was to contribute 18 officers and 271 men (that is the entire unit strength). Final objectives were outlined by 1/5th HLI Headquarters on the following lines:

> (a) The north-west portion of G.11a from West Krithia Nullah inclusive to junction inclusive of G11.a, with the main central communication trench leading north-east from G.11a to G.12c. If the remaining portion of G.11a was found to be either unoccupied or very lightly occupied that portion was also to be seized and held.
> (b) The portion of G.12 lying between the East Krithia Nullah and the junction of G.12 with the enemy communication trench leading south from G.12 to Grenade Station No. 2.
> (c) That portion of the communication trench referred to in (b) as leading south from junction with G.12 to Grenade Station No. 2.[96]

Large blue signal flags were to be "carried at the head of each party and waved over the trenches occasionally", as a means of denoting progress to supporting artillery and machine-guns.[97]

Taking into account tactical, organisational and supply lessons learned from the 15 November operation, the 1/6th HLI, 1/7th HLI and 1/5th A&SH were to commit bombing teams amounting to 19, 28 and 20 officers and men respectively. Two companies of 1/7th HLI were also to be situated in close proximity as an immediate reserve. The 155th and 156th brigades were tasked with providing fire support with rifle and machine-gun fire throughout the assault and consolidation period, the former to garrison the "present frontline".[98] Remarking on the strength of the designated assault force, the published divisional history later observed, "a tiny force with which to try to distract the attention of the Turkish general staff from Suvla and Anzac to Cape Helles, but a larger was not available, and the determination of the attack had to make up for its weaknesses in numbers."[99]

94 Morrison, *The Fifth Battalion Highland Light Infantry in the War 1914-1918*, Chapter V.
95 Murray, *Gallipoli 1915*, p. 202.
96 TNA WO 95/4274: '52ND (LOWLAND) DIVISION ORDER NO. 27', 16 December 1915, VIII Corps War Diary and Morrison, *The Fifth Battalion Highland Light Infantry in the War 1914-1918*, Chapter V.
97 TNA WO 95/4274: '52ND (LOWLAND) DIVISION ORDER NO. 27', 16 December 1915, VIII Corps War Diary.
98 Ibid.
99 Thompson, *The Fifty-Second Lowland Division 1914-1918*, p. 192 and Morrison, *The Fifth Battalion Highland Light Infantry in the War 1914-1918*, Chapter V.

Zero hour was finally scheduled for 2:15 p.m. on 19 December. There would be no preliminary bombardment except for a few rounds fired by offshore monitors between 2:00 and 2:15 p.m., after which ships, and land-based batteries were to open fire for an hour's duration.[100] Trench mortars, catapults, grenades and the like would also be employed to simultaneously divert Ottoman attention. The decision having been made to forgo a preparatory barrage, the offensive mines, now under the supervision of the newly-arrived British 254th Tunnelling Company,[101] would provide an important shock element. By 15 December, the "O.C. Mines" reported that all would be ready by 18 December: "On the KRITHIA NULLAHS the one near H.12c would be short but could in all probability be made to bury Turks junction and give cover. The two at G.12 junction would also be short, but lips of craters could be made to meet there." Moreover, there were two to three mines that "could be fired if necessary along the bank of the NULLAH parallel to H.11a ..."[102] To expedite west assault forming-up within bluff-top jumping-off positions, "the engineers had tunnelled a way through the cliff rising from West Krithia Nullah to a point which they calculated was directly opposite the western end of G.11a. They did not carry the tunnel right through at this time but left an outer shell which could be knocked away when the attack was to take place." Able Seaman Murray, having laboured on this gallery for weeks on end, remarked:

> If the Turks had observed this opening in the cliff side in between their lines our months of hard work would have immediately become useless. There was also the potential danger to our own lines. Someone had to take the blame. We should have stopped digging sooner even though our measurements told us we had several feet to spare. We should have sent for authority much earlier notwithstanding the fact that our gallery was the least of three similar ones. It was because of this backwardness in comparison with the other two that we had been given the job of bring it into line ready for the great day.[103]

In addition to providing the attacking infantry with overhead cover, this shallow depth underground passageway, "a great piece of engineering work", allowed 1/5th HLI officer patrols to carry out further pre-assault reconnaissance missions opposite G.11a.[104]

A final message from VIII Corps Headquarters disclosed intent and expectations as a means of bolstering the morale of 42nd and 52nd divisions:

100 TNA WO 95/4724: 'O/377/3', 16 December 1915, VIII Corps War Diary. Ignored by the Royal Navy prior to 1914, the monitor's intrinsic value as coastal assault vessel soon became evident. "Their shallow draught allowed them to operate close inshore, and they could be built with 'bulges' in the hull to offer protection against torpedoes and mines." See Christopher M. Bell, *Churchill and the Dardanelles* (Oxford: Oxford University Press, 2017), p. 37.

101 The disembarkation of 254th Tunnelling Company, consisting of 8 officers and 86 other ranks, "came as a great relief" to the VIII Corps Mining Company veterans, all of whom were subsequently absorbed into the former unit. See TNA WO 95/4724: 'G.S.R. 237', 11 December 1915, VIII Corps War Diary and Grieve & Newman, *Tunnellers*, pp. 84-85.

102 TNA WO 95/4724: 'O/66/28', 15 December 1915, VIII Corps War Diary. A series of 20 offensive mines were to be detonated along VIII Corps' front in support of the 42nd and 52nd division attacks on 19 December. See undated map '17' denoting 11 offensive mines situated within 52nd Division sector in TNA WO 95/4321: 157th Brigade War Diary and Grieve & Newman, p. 85.

103 Murray, *Gallipoli 1915*, p. 202.

104 Morrison, *The Fifth Battalion Highland Light Infantry in the War 1914–1918*, Chapter V.

> For important reasons it is essential that there shall be no giving up of any portions of, or positions near, the enemy's trenches which may be gained by our troops today. This should be made known to the troops taking part in the attack [,] and all arrangements made to provide the necessary reinforcements and resources to maintain such positions for at least 24 hours [,] and to so adjust the line behind them that the final result of the operations is to make our line still stronger and hold it against counter-attacks which may be made in the course of the next few days.[105]

Objective "successfully accomplished"

All units in position by 2:00 p.m. on 19 December, company and platoon commanders gazed at wristwatch faces as the final minutes before jumping-off ticked by. Zero hour (2:15 p.m.): Four mines erupted beneath the Ottoman trenches. "One was in the Turkish continuation of Rosebery Street [section of H.11a captured on 15 November],[106] and brought down portions of the cliffs of West Krithia Nullah disposing, it is believed, of several machine-guns, which might have played down the nullah." The remaining three mines were detonated in support of the eastern assault; two at a dividing junction of G.12 and, on the far right, one below the intersection of four trenches opposite No. 1 and North Vineyard bombing stations. The desired effect of these explosions was "to disorganise the enemy communications on the outer sides of the East and West Krithia Nullah." Moments thereafter, supporting artillery and naval gunfire added to the defenders' discomfiture. An observer situated on the left flank remarked: "I started to count the shells but soon they were pelting over from both sides like bullets."[107] It was later determined that "the Turks appeared to expect the attack, but a few rifles in the front trenches can make much noise. Possibly presence of monitors kept them awake." The divisional history speculated that the enemy had been placed on alert after overhearing British tunnelling activity.[108]

The eastern assault proceeded according to plan, 'B' Company 1/5th HLI, assisted by two bombing teams of 1/7th HLI, seized G.12 and the communication sap leading into it. Stunned and disoriented, a handful of defenders, among whom was an officer, were shot down in the vicinity of the smoking crater. Consolidation parties followed in the first wave's wake moments later, after which three trench barricades were hurriedly constructed. The attackers, having reached the Ottoman trench without loss, began to suffer casualties under sporadic rifle and sustained shell-fire. "The consolidating parties had a very stiff job to face, as these trenches had been bombarded for some months, with the result that there was a large amount of broken earth to be cleared away before reaching hard undersoil. It was like working in sand." The captured trench was constructed in a way that limited fields of fire at established barricades from eight

105 TNA WO 95/4274: 'C/377/4', 19 December 1915, VIII Corps War Diary.

106 Christened thus in honour of Archibald Philip Primrose, 5th Earl of Rosebery (1847-1929), a Liberal statesman who served as prime minister from 5 March 1894 to 22 June 1895. He was also honorary colonel of the 1/7th Royal Scots. See Ewing, *The Royal Scots 1914-1919*, p. 215.

107 Rodney Ashwood, *Duty Nobly Done: The South Wales Borderers at Gallipoli 1915* (Solihull: Helion & Company, 2017), pp. 232-33.

108 Thompson, *The Fifty-Second Lowland Division 1914-1918*, p. 195 and TNA WO 95/4274: 'NOTES FOR CORPS COMMANDERS CONFERENCE 21-12-15', VIII Corps War Diary.

to 15 yards. Taking advantage of the situation, intense duals ensued as the Ottoman defenders tossed bombs into the advanced outposts. "By 3 p.m. that is in less than an hour there were very few unwounded grenadiers left at the two barricades … and Lieuts. Davie and Strachan (7th HLI) had to draw on the reserves." Despite heavy losses, consolidation "proceeded satisfactorily" until 6:00 p.m. when an Ottoman catapult, slinging forth heavy bomb projectiles, forced the besieged 1/5th HLI and 1/7th HLI aggregate up the trench. "Intermittent bombing never ceased, Turks being able to creep close up before being shot down or bombed." Two Ottoman counter-attacks, launched at 9:00 p.m. and just before midnight, against barricades running forward from G.12, were subsequently repulsed by rifle and machine-gun fire with heavy losses. Two more pre-dawn attempts were thwarted before they could fully develop.[109]

Packed into the dark and fetid passageway of the West Krithia Nullah tunnel, 'C' Company 1/5th HLI, supported by bombing parties detached from the battalion's other companies, began to exit the mouth of the subterranean shelter on the 2:15 p.m. detonation of the mine due north of Rosebery Street. Situated at the tunnel head, Murray helped clear away the thin soil cover left in place to camouflage the opening: "The galleries were full of troops who were to lead the attack – the Highland Light Infantry of the 52nd Division. We broke through into the Gully simultaneously with the exploding of the nine mines and the troops rushed through whilst the earth was still showering."[110]

The objective (G.11a) was "known usually to be unoccupied by the enemy at least by day, but the main central communication trench running back from G.11a to G.12c was known to be held by the Turks at various points, and it appeared to be very much a question of time whether they or the attacking party could first reach the junction of this trench with G.11.a." Hampered by the need to access no man's land from the tunnel mouth, "entrance to which was difficult and from which it would be necessary to emerge into the Nullah man by man", crucial minutes would be lost during hasty assembly of assault parties outside the previously hidden crawl-way, whilst reliance on the forward movement of individuals could result in disorganisation, confusion and failure. Instructions were, therefore, issued that each party was, on entering the nullah, to assemble and advance as quickly as possible.[111]

First out into the nullah was a bombing party assigned the task of seizing the central communication trench. On clearing the tunnel, they promptly shook out into formation prior to rushing up the slope leading to the western parapet of G.11a. Followed close behind by two additional bombing parties, no man's land was traversed within five minutes of the mine explosion. Moving forward west of the objective, these vanguard attackers encountered intense hostile rifle fire that forced them to seek cover in the Ottoman trench:

> The overhead traverses, which were in a state of disrepair owing to the trench being unoccupied by the enemy, were low and made progress difficult and slow. Lieut. Aitken, who was leading the first grenade team, had rounded the bend in the trench with a bayonet man of his team when they came under fire from a few yards range from an erection at the junction of the main communication trench with G.11a. The bayonet man was killed,

109 TNA WO 95/4321: 157th Brigade War Diary, Thompson, pp. 196-97 and Morrison, *The Fifth Battalion Highland Light Infantry in the War 1914-1918,* Chapter V.
110 Murray, *Gallipoli 1915*, p. 202.
111 TNA WO 95/4321: 157th Brigade War Diary and Morrison, Chapter V.

> and Lieut. Aitken wounded in the arm and leg. By this time the enemy were beginning to throw grenades from their central communication trench and getting them into G.11a. Lieut. Milne, Lieut. McDougall and many of the men were wounded. The parties were crowded, there being about forty of all ranks in twelve yards of trench ...[112]

Communication with Major Neilson, the officer commanding the western assault, proving impossible, Lieutenant Leith, the only unwounded officer available, ordered the construction of a barricade at the farthest point reached. A haphazard composition of sandbags, timber and wire, the obstacle was in situ by 3:30 p.m., "and during its erection grenades were constantly thrown at the enemy communication trench but with little effect, as they had to be thrown uphill from the trench while the enemy's grenades frequently rolled down into it."[113]

Exiting the tunnel mouth in the wake of the bombing parties, the main assault party entered G.11a with fixed bayonets. The designated commander, Captain Frost, led from the front prior to being mortally wounded on the parapet. "Somewhat shaken" by the loss of their leader, the attackers hung back until spurred on by the company sergeant major who "was in the rear of the party and still in the tunnel ..." Arrayed in the tightly-packed shaft immediately behind the assault party, the consolidation party – each man heavily encumbered with pick and shovel as well as rifle – encountered frustrating delays due to the urgent demand for more bombs from those at sharp end of the assault. Their subsequent entry into the fighting (3:30 p.m.) was succeeded by heavy casualties amongst officers and NCOs, the party under Lieutenant Dow, tasked with removing one of the Ottoman barricades, losing their commander as he entered the captured trench. Lieutenant Kirbe, commander of the party detailed to construct the nullah barricade, was killed within moments of leaving the tunnel. Their officer down, an NCO took charge to ensure the obstacle was erected by 4:00 p.m. A third consolidation party, moving forward to establish an advanced dump of stores and ammunition, successfully carried out the assigned task despite the loss of Lieutenant Turner, the subaltern in charge, and Company Quartermaster Sergeant (CQMS) Stewart.[114]

Meantime, on the immediate left, a fourth bombing party entered the northern extremity of G.11a where an Ottoman barricade was encountered approximately 20 yards up the communication trench extending parallel with West Krithia Nullah. Resistance being rapidly overcome with bombs, resultant confusion caused by the majority of bombers becoming entangled with the main assault party, allowed the defenders to reoccupy the lost barrier. Thus checked, the subaltern in charge ordered the construction of a new barricade at the trench junction.[115]

All five officers of 'C' Company having become casualties, the officer commanding the reserve company was sent forward to take charge. Dusk was in progress by the time Captain Morrison entered G.11a. Immediately taking stock of the situation, he determined that no further progress could be made to secure the central communication trench junction with G.11a. The approaching hours of darkness would be utilised to consolidate gains. This proved difficult owing to prevailing trench congestion which was subsequently alleviated by withdrawal

112 Morrison, Chapter V.
113 Ibid.
114 TNA WO 95/4321: 157th Brigade War Diary, Thompson, *The Fifty-Second Lowland Division 1914-1918*, p. 199 and Morrison, Chapter V.
115 Ibid.

of 20 surplus personnel and evacuation of the wounded whilst the Ottoman defenders were kept at bay by bombers established in key bombing stations. "About forty officers and men, almost a third of those actually engaged in this attack, had been killed or wounded, and many of them were still lying about between the tunnel exit and the barricade in G.11a, a distance of forty yards. The difficulties of evacuating wounded up the tunnel while stores and men were coming down can hardly be imagined."[116]

Consolidation carried on without serious interruption until, announced with a "burst of grenade throwing", the onset of an Ottoman counter-attack at 8:00 p.m. Detonating with sharp reports within the established bombing stations, hostile grenades reduced 1/6th HLI's committed bombing team from 18 to five men within minutes of the opening of the enemy onslaught. With the southern bombing station near the central communication trench abandoned and the remaining stations barely holding out, the beleaguered garrison was reinforced by a 45-man bombing party of 1/5th A&SH. Close-quarter fighting raged around the barricades until the Ottoman assailants were driven back.[117] The captured positions secure for the time being, 1/7th HLI supplied a replacement garrison, "but the bombing teams of 5th HLI and 5th Argylls were left as they were. The situation was one in which the giving of explanations to new men had to be avoided." The southern barricade remaining in enemy hands, a second or inner barricade, assembled with sandbags passed forward by a human chain, was already in place within a few yards of the former before relative quiet displaced the noise of battle by 1:00 a.m.[118]

In the eastern sector, consolidation was "well in hand" by daybreak on 20 December, several hot meals being sent forward to the captured Ottoman positions by 155th Brigade, which was still responsible for the former frontline. The inner barricade complete in the western sector by 5:30 a.m., a general withdrawal from the outer barricade was covered by a lone sniper left in place to engage available targets from what was now an advanced trench outpost.[119] On the left flank, 42nd Division's assault miscarried when the majority of attackers, advancing under cover of two mine explosions – one of which failed to form a crater – found themselves exposed to sustained enemy fire before, notwithstanding permanent gains made on the immediate right, being compelled to retire.[120]

The evacuation of Anzac and Suvla on the night of 19/20 December was surprisingly successful, the Ottoman defenders remaining unaware of the complete withdrawal until 4:00 a.m. on the 20th.[121] How much of a distraction the Helles diversionary attacks were remains open to debate, although Birdwood had little doubt of their operational efficacy:

116 Thompson, *The Fifty-Second Lowland Division 1914-1918*, p. 200.
117 Pte. J. Greig (1/6th HLI) and Cpl. R. MacIntosh (1/5th A&SH) were awarded the DCM for their actions during this fighting.
118 TNA WO 95/4321: 1/5th A&SH War Diary and Thompson, *The Fifty-Second Lowland Division 1914-1918*, pp. 201-02.
119 TNA WO 95/4321: 1/5th A&SH War Diary; Thompson, pp. 197, 201-02 and Morrison, *The Fifth Battalion Highland Light Infantry in the War 1914-1918*, Chapter V.
120 See TNA WO 95/4265: '42nd (EAST LANCASHIRE) DIVISION. REPORT ON OPERATIONS', 20 December 1915, MEF War Diary and Frederick P. Gibbon, *The 42nd (East Lancashire) Division 1914-1918* (London: Country Life, 1920), Chapter III.
121 Erickson, *Gallipoli: The Ottoman Campaign*, p. 179 and Aspinall-Oglander, *Military Operations Gallipoli*, Vol. II, p. 456.

> Yesterday [19 December] afternoon, to take the attention off the Northern Zone, I made Davies organise a fairly big attack on the Turks' trenches at Helles, where we had a tremendous bombardment by the Navy, which I think created a most successful diversion for two or three monitors and two cruisers were down there, hammering in as hard as they were worth with their big guns, and attracting the whole attention of the peninsula to them.[122] The attacks made were quite successful, and we took two or three Turkish trenches ... The attack we did carry out on their position at Helles about eight hours before we commenced the withdrawal from the other areas, may perhaps have deceived them more than I thought probable, as we know that they at once reinforced down there when the attack began ... while the co-operation of Davies in the attack from Helles was as wholehearted as you would expect.[123]

VIII Corps Headquarters was complimentary about the results of the latest Krithia Nullah attack regardless of the inability to "gain the whole of G.11a in spite of repeated efforts owing to the presence of a bomb proof work in the centre of the trench." Congratulatory messages from brigade, division and corps soon followed. Post-operational analysis determined troop morale to be "admirable" based on the observation that "2 subsequent counter-attacks have been successfully coped with by troops on the spot without any request for assistance ..." Artillery and machine-gun support was also deemed effective, neighbouring French batteries and machine-guns of the Royal Naval Division providing "valuable assistance", whilst French manufactured "Dumezils" (*Mortier de 58mm Type 2*), trench mortars capable of vertically dropping melanite-filled projectiles at fairly short range, "did very good work." As for bombing parties and application of lessons learned from the 15 November assault, "success was largely due to the systematic training and organisation which obtains in all divisions."[124]

With G.12 in the east and 30 yards of G.11a in the west secured, subsequent battalion roll calls determined that 157th Brigade sustained a combined loss of 124 officers and men killed and wounded.[125] Ottoman casualties, 52nd Division's historian observed, could only be "guessed at, but twenty dead were seen and counted before the trenches captured on the right, and they must have suffered severe losses from the bombing about G.11a and the mine explosion."[126] Word of the evacuations reached the attack participants on the 20 December. Taking into account the

122 Birdwood's determination that the 19 December attack succeeded in its diversionary purpose is interesting when one considers that VIII Corps' two-division assault of 6-7 August 1915 was unsuccessful in diverting Ottoman reinforcements from the north. See Erickson, *Gallipoli: The Ottoman Campaign*, pp. 140-44.

123 Royal Archives: GEO V/Q/2521/II/46 20/12/1915 – Lieutenant-General Sir W.R. Birdwood to Lieutenant-Colonel Clive Wigram (1873-1960), Assistant Private Secretary and Equerry to King George V. Text reproduced by kind permission of Her Majesty Queen Elizabeth II; special thanks to Alexandra Churchill for bringing this document to my attention. See also Aspinall-Oglander, *Military Operations Gallipoli*, Vol. II, pp. 455-56.

124 TNA WO 95/4274: 'REPORT ON OPERATIONS – 8th CORPS FROM 1st to 20th December 1915', 24 December 1915, VIII Corps War Diary and Morrison, *The Fifth Battalion Highland Light Infantry in the War 1914-1918*, Chapter V.

125 Casualties sustained by 157th Brigade were as follows: Officers – four killed, six wounded; other ranks – 19 killed, 95 wounded. See TNA WO 95/4321: 157th Brigade War Diary and Thompson, *The Fifty-Second Lowland Division 1914-1918*, p. 202

126 Thompson, p. 202.

operation's role in the overall withdrawal scheme, the 1/5th HLI's post-war historian dolefully remarked, "it was apparent that the object had been successfully accomplished, and it was certainly gratifying to learn this, as the actual results of the attacks judged in yards of trenches gained did not seem to justify the number of splendid officers and men whom we had lost."[127]

Krithia Nullah Redux

Anzac and Suvla now abandoned to the defenders, Ottoman efforts shifted to Cape Helles. Batteries opposite the evacuated sectors were duly transported south to reinforce those already opposite VIII Corps' front or deployed across the Straits on the Asiatic shore. "Shellfire from this time onwards became more severe than at any time since the landing. 'Strafes' and 'Hates' as the heaviest bombardments were termed, followed … in rapid succession, and throughout the daylight, sniping by the enemy artillery at any moving object never ceased."[128]

The future of the Dardanelles Army's only remaining beachhead was finally decided upon on 23 December when the newly appointed Chief of the Imperial General Staff (CIGS), General Sir William Robertson,[129] informed GOC Eastern Mediterranean General Sir Charles Monro[130] that preparations for the Helles evacuation had been officially sanctioned by the War Office, "but not to do anything in case the government decided to retain the peninsula." Subsequent discussions between Birdwood and Davies on Christmas Day 1915 produced a workable withdrawal scheme, based on the recent Anzac and Suvla operations, "tailored and re-worked for conditions at Cape Helles."[131]

Determined to be one of the most reliable VIII Corps formations prior to the 19 December operation, 52nd Division, which had carried out "every important offensive at Cape Helles" since August, was ordered to have another go at the Krithia Nullah defences. Indeed, Birdwood, in a Christmas day report to Monro, observed that the "best troops now serving at CAPE HELLES (other than the 29th Division) are those composing the 52nd Division."[132] Despite this praise and confidence, the Lowland Division's commander had serious personal reservations about his formation's morale and defensive capabilities. As Birdwood observed:

127 Morrison, *The Fifth Battalion Highland Light Infantry in the War 1914-1918*, Chapter V.

128 Some of the heaviest Ottoman bombardments to date occurred on 24 and 25 December, the latter targeting the "trenches about and behind Krithia Nullah" with heavy (9-inch and above) guns. See Thompson, *The Fifty-Second Lowland Division 1914-1918*, pp. 205-07.

129 Robertson replaced General Sir Archibald Murray as CIGS on 23 December 1915.

130 Monro was transferred from MEF HQ to command of all Eastern Mediterranean forces, Gallipoli and Salonika inclusive, on 23 November 1915.

131 Erickson, *Gallipoli: Command Under Fire*, p. 228. See also Aspinall-Oglander, *Military Operations Gallipoli*, Vol. II, pp. 461-65. Government sanction to evacuate Helles was granted on 23 December 1915.

132 Although recognised as in need of rest, 52nd Division, "present effective strength" of approximately 5,000 rifles, was in a "far better fettle" than 42nd Division. Taking into account the manpower deficit of both formations, MEF Headquarters requested an amalgamation of the two First-Line Territorial divisions. This was subsequently refused by the War Office. See TNA WO 95/4724: 'G.S.R./Z/54', 14 December 1915; 'H.W. 1311', 24 December 1915; 'G.S.R. Z.54', 25 December 1915, VIII Corps War Diary and Thompson, *The Fifty-Second Lowland Division 1914-1918*, pp. 207-08.

> Major-General Lawrence, for whose judgment I have the most regard, feels that he can no longer trust his men to maintain their position in the event of determined attacks, more especially should the enemy meet with any considerable initial success. Capable as they still are of answering the calls made on them by trench warfare pursuing a normal course, it is doubtful whether they have sufficient offensive power remaining to take by counter-attack any considerable length of trench the Turks might capture by Coup de Main.[133]

The 52nd Division's offensive capabilities having been deemed sufficient for one more local push, the purpose of the proposed operation is difficult to identify beyond the rationale provided by the divisional history.[134] With evacuation more than likely imminent, Thompson observed, "the best defence is an attack and the boldest course the safest; and now the Division was ordered to carry out another offensive, maintaining that moral superiority over the enemy, which it had done so much to be established."[135] No doubt the MEF's apparent willingness to launch further attacks also convinced the Ottoman high command that VIII Corps could quite possibly remain at Cape Helles well into the first quarter of 1916.

Its operational task accomplished, 155th Brigade was relieved by 157th Brigade on 20 December 1915, the latter fending-off numerous Ottoman night attacks on G.11a until relief by 155th Brigade six days later. Throughout this period torrential rainfall, interspersed with welcome spells of fine daytime weather, flooded trenches or reduced positions to channels of almost impassable mud whilst collapsing parapets, parados, dugouts and funk-holes.[136] On-going concerns about VIII Corps' manpower strength led to the decision to temporarily attach a brigade of 29th Division as reinforcement for the weakened 52nd Division. Deployed to Helles since 1 October, 87th Brigade took over the left of the 157th Brigade line. The former's sector contained advanced bombing saps extending towards the Ottoman line. The defenders, wary of British offensive activity in the vulnerable Krithia Nullah sector, managed to temporarily seize the saps early one morning prior to expulsion by the combined efforts of 87th and 157th brigades. This failed attack, the 52nd Division history surmised, "was undoubtedly the first step in an attempt to drive the British back from their trenches on the cliffs, to cut-off G.11a, and to push them back from the fork of Krithia Nullah." Frustrated Thus "the Turks could be heard working hard to improve their covered work near G.11a, and the other trenches on the tongue of land in order to prevent the junction of the nullahs falling entirely into British hands."[137]

133 TNA WO 95/4724: 'G.S.R. Z.54', 25 December 1915, VIII Corps War Diary. Post-strategic phase "normal course" trench warfare as opposed to large-scale offensives which, as Rhys Crawley rightly points out, "was beyond the abilities of the MEF" before and during the August push. See Rhys Crawley, *Climax at Gallipoli: The Failure of the August Offensive* (Norman, Oklahoma: University of Oklahoma Press, 2014), p. 67.

134 The apparent absence of related corps/division-level documents (operational orders, after-action reports, etc., etc.) as opposed to pertinent unit war diaries, may have been due to the loss or deliberate destruction thereof prior to the evacuation 10 days later (night of 8/9 January 1916) or wartime/post-war vetting. For its part, the British official history confirms the operational purpose related in the division history. See Thompson, *The Fifty-Second Lowland Division 1914-1918*, pp. 207-08 and Aspinall-Oglander, *Military Operations Gallipoli*, Vol. II, p. 468.

135 Thompson, p. 207.

136 TNA WO 95/4317: 52nd Division War Diary and Thompson, pp. 204-05.

137 See Thompson, pp. 204-05 and Captain Stair Gillon, *The Story of the 29th Division: A Record of Gallant Deeds* (London: Thomas Nelson & Sons, 1925), pp. 60-61.

Assigned to 155th Brigade, what would be the final Krithia Nullah assault benefited from the organisational/tactical developments and technological advances employed during the two previous operations.[138] Scheduled for 29 December, the 1/5th RSF (CO Lieutenant-Colonel Archibald Leggett),[139] supported by four bombing parties from 1/4th RSF, 1/4th KOSB and 1/5th KOSB, were to seize the remainder of G.11a at 1:00 p.m. Surprise, as far as trench warfare conditions allowed for, would be achieved by dispensing with a preliminary bombardment, all batteries, trench mortars, catapults and French howitzers to open fire on East Krithia Nullah and communication trenches leading to it following the detonation of two mines constructed by 2/1st Lowland Field Company RE.[140] With tunnels extending from the British-held portion of G.11a, an enemy "machine-gun nest which the Turks held just west of the centre of the trench, and the other below their central communication trench (G.11y)" were to be obliterated by the blasts. Come zero hour, the remainder of 155th Brigade, ensconced in the frontline, were to cover the advance with periscope rifles projecting from loopholes.[141]

Returning to the firing line, 1/5th RSF relieved 1/5th HLI on 26 December, the former receiving (27 December) "intimation that the battalion was to attack G.11a on the 29th inst. – Preparations for the attack commenced … All preparations for attack completed by 10 a.m. [29 December] & assaulting parties in positions by 12:45 p.m. …" All was ready in the minutes leading up to Zero; "the assaulting troops were taking shelter in the [cliff] tunnel and below bridge traverses in G.11a in anticipation of the mine explosions, when at 12:45 p.m. the Turks started to shell with H.E. the trenches about the nullah fork." One machine-gun was destroyed whilst all telephonic communication was severed.[142]

At 1:00 p.m. the mines detonated with a thunderous report, after which "the men in the adjoining trenches broke into prolonged cheering." Able Seaman Murray recalled: "Everything was ready, and the troops were assembled. At the appointed moment the plunger was pushed down and the redoubt that had held up our advance across the gully on the nineteenth ceased to exist."[143] Ten seconds thereafter the attackers, led by Captain Rogers, Captain Wilkie, Lieutenant McIntosh and Lieutenant McNaughton[144] and accompanied by mine searching teams detached from the 2/1st Lowland Field Company, rushed the craters. As a measurable guide to attack progress, advanced parties were issued with large blue flags that were to be occasionally waved as a signal to the artillery. The Ottoman garrison seemingly surprised, the hostile 12:45 p.m.

138 155th Brigade's "effective strength" on 26 December 1915 was 1.473 officers and men. See TNA WO 95/4320: 'App. 73. Weekly Effective Strength 155th Infantry Brigade December 1915', 155th Brigade War Diary.

139 Lieutenant-Colonel Archibald Herbert Leggett (b. 1871). Commissioned RSF 1897; South Africa 1899-1902; Royal Military Academy 1903-07; British Embassy Tokyo 1909-10; Brigade Major, Hampshire Infantry Brigade 1911-13; retired 1913; CO 1/5th RSF September 1915.

140 The bombardment was delayed in order to allow time for the heavier mine debris to fall: "[I]t was to be made ten seconds after the explosion of the mines." See Thompson, *The Fifty-Second Lowland Division 1914-1918*, p. 208.

141 TNA WO 95/4317: 52nd Division War Diary and Thompson, p. 208.

142 TNA WO 95/4320: 'Operation and Progress Report. 0600 28th to 0600 29th 15', 155th Brigade War Diary, WO 95/4320: 1/5th RSF War Diary and Thompson, p. 208. Telephone lines were not restored until 4:00 p.m.

143 Murray, *Gallipoli As I Saw It*, p. 210.

144 Nineteen-year old Lieutenant William James McNaughton 1/5th RSF; died of wounds 31 December 1915.

bombardment belied previously speculated enemy foreknowledge of the assault. Struggling to organise in the immediate aftermath of the mine explosions, the rattled defenders "offered a stubborn resistance" until the objective was quickly overwhelmed and occupied by 1:20 p.m.[145] Murray subsequently observed:

> In a matter of minutes, the Royal Scots Fusiliers were firmly established across the gully. A communication trench that ran from the redoubt to the Turkish main line was barricaded and used as an advanced bombing sap. Between forty and fifty prisoners [sic] were taken. The usual firing went on all day and most of the night, but our men held on to their gains.[146]

The captured trenches "were the whole of G.11a, 40 yards of G.11y, 40 yards of G.11z and the whole of communications trench connecting G.11y + G.11z."[147] Some 20 Ottoman corpses were counted whilst 26 prisoners, "in addition to much material", were obtained and gathered in. RSF losses remained comparatively light up to this time. "As was the rule, casualties mounted up in the repelling of counter-attacks, and from sniping during consolidation, before our men had found out what points were exposed to enemy marksmen." By 4:00 p.m. signallers had successfully linked up telephone lines from East Krithia Nullah to G.11a. As predicted, Ottoman batteries "poured shells of all kinds into this hollow at the junction of the nullahs" before launching the first counter-thrust at 5:10 p.m. This and three succeeding efforts were repelled during the night. "By 9 p.m., consolidation was complete, and all the barricades erected."[148]

Dawn on 30 December was followed by intense hostile artillery fire that "turned this nullah junction together with the cliffs about it, into an inferno of bursting shrapnel and H.E., blowing down parapets and causing many casualties. The hollow that was receiving this deluge of fire was only about 150 yards across, and the bulk of it was directed on G.11a and Dalmeny Street." Bombardments remained the sole enemy activity until 7:40 p.m. when an Ottoman assault party demolished one of the newly-established bombing posts, killing or wounding all occupants with a dynamite charge before being driven off by counter-attacking RSF bombers. Finally conceding the lost territory, "no further attack was made, and all remained quiet."[149]

Casualties sustained by 155th Brigade during the period 29-31 December amounted to 143 officers and men killed, wounded and missing.[150] Consolidation complete, discarded war mate-

145 TNA WO 95/4320: 155th Brigade, 1/4th RSF, 1/5th RSF war diaries and Thompson, *The Fifty-Second Lowland Division 1914-1918,* pp. 208-09. Although 29th Division took no part in the November–December assaults, its post-war divisional history notes that "nothing could keep 'Bomb Kelly' (afterwards Lieutenant-Colonel John Kelly VC) and the officer commanding KOSB out of the scrap, and after the final capture of a trench called G.11a on 29th December, he and his bombers of 1st KOSB [87th Brigade] did yeoman service in helping the Royal Scots Fusiliers to retain their grip of the hard-won territory." See Gillon, *The Story of the 29th Division*, p. 61 and Gerald Gliddon, *VCs of the First World War: Cambrai 1917* (Thrupp-Stroud: Sutton, 2004), pp. 136-46.

146 Murray, *Gallipoli As I Saw It*, p. 210.

147 The 52nd Division history later claimed that the POWs were members of the "Constantinople Fire Brigade". See Thompson, *The Fifty-Second Lowland Division 1914-1918,* p. 209.

148 TNA WO 95/4320: 'Intelligence Report. 0600 29th.12.15 to 0600 30th. 12.15', 155th Brigade, 1/5th RSF war diaries and Thompson, p. 209.

149 TNA WO 95/4320: 155th Brigade, 1/4th RSF, 1/5th RSF war diaries and Thompson, pp. 209-11.

150 Casualties sustained by 155th Brigade were as follows: Officers – five killed, eight wounded; other ranks – 41 killed, 102 wounded. See TNA WO 95/4320: 'Intelligence Report. 0600 29th.12.15 to

rial salvage and the gruesome task of purging the contested area of desiccated human remains, the majority lying about since the August offensive, amongst the more recent dead was carried out whenever conditions allowed for.[151] So ended the final MEF offensive operation at Helles.[152] Its task achieved, the exhausted 155th Brigade was relieved by 29th Division's 88th Brigade, lately re-deployed to Helles as a much needed reinforcement, on 31 December.[153]

Conclusion

In reference to the Cape Helles divisions and their on-going Gethsemane following abandonment of the Anzac and Suvla sectors, the British official history observed:

> Throughout this trying ordeal, the VIII Corps continued to maintain by bombing, sniping and minor operations, the moral ascendency it had established over the enemy. On the 29th [December] the 52nd Division completed the capture of the G11 line by seizing all portions of that trench which still remained in Turkish hands and held them successfully in the face of counter-attacks.[154]

At the operational and tactical level, this authoritative reflection by the volume's former MEF GSO1 (O) author[155] thus confirms Birdwood and Lawrence's stated confidence in 52nd Division's capacity to pursue "normal course" trench warfare prior to the Helles evacuation; official approval for the latter communicated to Davies on 30 December.[156]

0600 30th. 12.15', 155th Brigade War Diary and Thompson, p. 210.

151 The 1/4th RSF diarist recorded that "the following bodies were found in the NULLAH near our new trench and burned …"These were No. 3242 Pte. J.G. Hill; No. 2261 Pte. B. Whiteley; No. 2535 Pte. A. Blakeley. All were from 1/7th Manchester Regiment (127th Brigade, 42nd Division) which assaulted the Krithia Nullah defences during the 6-7 August 1915 diversionary operation. Moreover, "the following identity discs were found [:] No. 2726 Pte. R.J. Claren [sic Pte. C.B. Clarence] 2/8th [sic 1/8th] Manchester Regiment [;] [No.] 2674 Pte. W. Moorhouse 1/6th Manchester Regiment", also of 127th Brigade. Additional remains were identified and cremated over the succeeding days. All are commemorated on the Helles Memorial to the Missing. See TNA WO 95/4320: 1/4th RSF War Diary, Aspinall-Oglander, *Military Operations Gallipoli*, Vol. II, pp. 175-76 and Commonwealth War Graves Commission <https://www.cwgc.org/>

152 In the chapter chronicling the Helles operation of 6-7 August 1915, the British official history observed: "For the rest of August – and indeed, as events subsequently shaped themselves, for the rest of the campaign – the British and French troops in the south were destined to make no further serious attacks. The Turks similarly remained on the defensive and, except that the 52nd Division succeeded in straightening out its line to the west of the Vineyard in November [and December], the opposing fronts at Helles remained virtually unchanged from the 8th August till the final evacuation exactly five months later." See Aspinall-Oglander, p. 177.

153 Thompson, *The Fifty-Second Lowland Division 1914-1918*, p. 210.

154 Aspinall-Oglander, *Military Operations Gallipoli*, Vol. II, p. 468.

155 MEF General Staff Officer (1st Grade) Operations Lieutenant-Colonel, later Brigadier-General, Cecil Faber Aspinall-Oglander (1878-1959) subsequently authored the two volume official history (published 1929 and 1932 respectively) of the Gallipoli campaign.

156 TNA WO 95/4724: 'G.S.R. Z.54', 25 December 1915, VIII Corps War Diary. See Aspinall-Oglander, *Military Operations Gallipoli*, Vol. II, pp. 461-78 and Alexandra Churchill's chapter in this

Major-General Hon. H.A. Lawrence (GOC 52nd (Lowland) Division). (Author)

According to Gary Sheffield, "By the end of the campaign, units were undoubtedly more militarily effective at prosecuting trench warfare, and individual soldiers had become veterans. However, there is much evidence that morale in at least some parts of the MEF had suffered quite seriously."[157] With regard to morale and the ability "to maintain their position in the event of determined attacks", 52nd Division certainly rose to the occasion when fending off enemy counter-thrusts throughout the Krithia Nullah operations of November – December 1915.[158] Whether or not the division could have, in its reduced manpower state, stood up against a major Ottoman offensive such as that launched against 13th (Western) Division at Gully Spur on 7 January 1916 is impossible to determine.[159] Given its progressive application of recent operational/tactical methodology and developments, practical utilisation of the latest trench warfare technology (new pattern bombs, rifle periscopes and trench mortars for example) and overall military effectiveness in minor operation attack and defence, one suspects a hard-pressed 52nd Division would have foiled all hostile efforts both great and small.[160]

Today the once contested Krithia Nullah fork and immediate vicinity is surrounded by arable farmland that yields a rich agricultural harvest of which wheat appears to be the predominant crop. With the divergent watercourse ravines concealed by spinneys and thick undergrowth, only the most dedicated battlefield explorer ventures about and within the hidden streambeds where chance encounters with the occasional rusted shell fragment, shrapnel ball, spent rifle cartridge, rum jar shard and other forgotten debris serve as a poignant reminder of Lowland Scottish fortitude and sacrifice during the final months of the Gallipoli campaign.[161]

volume.

157 Gary Sheffield, 'Shaping British and Anzac Soldiers' Experience of Gallipoli: Environmental and Medical Factors, and the Development of Trench Warfare', *British Journal for Military History*, Vol. 4, Issue No. 1 (November 2017).

158 TNA WO 95/4724: 'G.S.R. Z.54', 25 December 1915, VIII Corps War Diary.

159 See Aspinall-Oglander, *Military Operations Gallipoli*, Vol. II, pp. 472-73, Erickson, *Gallipoli: The Ottoman Campaign*, p. 180 and John Bourne's chapter in this volume.

160 Special thanks to Dr John Bourne, Dr Daniel Whittingham and Dr Christopher Wyatt for their valuable insights on the MEF high command's view of 52nd Division morale and military effectiveness.

161 It was during a September 2017 exploration of Krithia Nullah that Manchester Regiment historian Michael Crane uncovered human skeletal remains exposed by embankment erosion. An underground tunnel, running approximately 50 yards to the west of the point where 1/5th HLI's 19 December assault tunnel broke into the western nullah, was also uncovered at this time.

6

The Decision to Evacuate the Gallipoli Peninsula

Alexandra Churchill

By October 1915, attempts by the British to pursue any kind of offensive land strategy at Gallipoli were at an end. The mood on the peninsula was muted: "This enforced inactivity has been very trying," wrote the commander of the Mediterranean Expeditionary Force (MEF), General Sir Ian Hamilton, "but there is such a terrible amount of sickness, and our effectives are so much below strength, that there is not much scope left for anything in the nature of serious attack. If only the Turks would attack us!"[1] Such a remark would not have instilled confidence in the ranks or amongst his subordinate officers. Growing numbers of those present believed that the campaign had lost direction. In command of 13th Division, Sir Frederick 'Stanley' Maude had led his men at Anzac in August before they were moved to Suvla. He was an efficient, proactive commander and sitting still doing nothing was more than he could bear. He laid his frustration down in writing in September.

> Our inaction is almost comic after the speed with which we dashed out here, and meanwhile the Turks are digging hard everywhere in front of us and making themselves stronger. I suppose that shortage of reinforcements is the reason, but surely that is our fault for trying to take on more than we can do with our small army.[2]

Two weeks later he was in much the same frame of mind: "What a hopeless country we seem to be, always a policy of drift, and what that means when war is in the balance every soldier will appreciate. Why are we waiting here indefinitely without guns, ammunition and men…"[3]

A more pressing concern than how to continue the campaign was the fact that winter was fast approaching and adequate plans had not been made for the supply, health or accommodation of thousands of men originally outfitted for a warm weather operation. One officer commanding

1 Royal Archives (RA) GV/Q/832/183. All Royal Archives references throughout this chapter point to an individual document. Readers seeking additional documentation particulars should contact the Royal Archives, Windsor.
2 Charles Callwell, *The Life of Sir Stanley Maude* (London: Constable, 1920), p. 164.
3 Ibid., p. 165.

a Yeomanry unit at Suvla Bay was outraged, despite having only been on the peninsula for two weeks:

> The authorities have known for months when the rains would set in, what provision would be necessary, yet they have done nothing. I am assured that there is not the least chance of the corrugated iron arriving for a long time. There is also a terrible shortage of sand bags and no timber to support the roofs even if we had the iron. Officers and men have for the most part one waterproof sheet and that is all. Already it is as cold as late autumn at home, and in January and February we know that there are blizzards and sometimes six feet of snow. Is NOTHING then going to be done for us until after the necessity has arisen? I speak with feeling, not for myself but for thousands of good fellows who tonight are worse off than I am.[4]

Unsurprisingly, large numbers of troops began to fall ill because of the worsening conditions. Hamilton complained of the amount of men he was losing from his force: "Almost without exception these sick are suffering from enteritis, which very easily turns into dysentery. The men do not die of it, but they seem to take a very, very long time to get well, and I think the doctors are far too ready to send them all away to England whence they never seem to come back at all." He also lamented that a higher ratio of officers had been dispatched away from the peninsula than of those in the ranks and added: "If only the depleted ranks could be filled up by some fresh recruits."[5] But given the circumstances it was little wonder that both at home and abroad, the sense in continuing the campaign, as opposed to the need for more troops, was now being questioned. "Why cannot the policy be definitely adopted either to go on with this or give it up?", asked Maude. "There should be no half measures; it only means further sacrifices in blood and money, which are heavy enough."[6]

Some believed that there were more important causes to be fought in Eastern Europe than the capture of the Gallipoli Peninsula, and that the men there could be better utilised elsewhere. Shortly before Bulgaria entered the war on the side of the Central Powers, King George V was presented with one argument being made in the British Cabinet: "Mr Balfour is a strong supporter of our adopting a vigourous [sic] policy in the Balkans, holding that it would be deplorable were we to desert Serbia and allow her to be crushed by the combined forces of Germany, Austria, Bulgaria." "These are also the views of the French Government", the advice continued, "and M. Vivian [Prime Minister of France] stated yesterday that 150,000 troops were not sufficient, but more likely 400,000 would be required."[7]

The question was, obviously, where on earth the Allies could hope to find 400,000 men for such a purpose. The likelihood that the French Commander-in-Chief, General Joseph Joffre, would refuse to lose Frenchman from the Western Front made Britain's First Lord of the Admiralty, Arthur Balfour, think the nearly half a million men in question would end up being British:

4 RA GV/O/1177/16.
5 RA GV/Q/832/183.
6 Callwell, *Maude*, p. 165.
7 RA GV/Q/838/14.

> He said that these would come from the Western Front and if needs be from Gallipoli: that the eastern Mediterranean must be regarded as one theatre of war and in that reason, we could with justice transfer troops from Gallipoli to Salonika. Our position in the Dardanelles is causing considerable anxiety … If the enemy could obtain an unlimited supply of ammunition they might render the situation untenable, unless we were prepared for a very heavy loss of men and it might be expedient to try and defeat the enemy in south-east Europe rather than on the Gallipoli peninsula.[8]

Lord Kitchener's aide, Oswald Fitzgerald, queried one of the three corps commanders at Gallipoli, Lieutenant-General Sir Julian Byng (GOC IX Corps at Suvla Bay), informally to assess the situation based on a number of criteria being argued in favour of remaining; including the chances of making a success of the campaign and the potential damage that withdrawal might do to British prestige in the East. Byng provided a detailed response:

> You ask me to give you my impressions of the Dardanelles and this I am trying to do, but you must realise that we know nothing of the political or international state of affairs and consequentially anything I say has probably been foreseen and prepared for.
>
> … Look at this situation squarely in the face. A big offensive seems unlikely to have any measure of success to balance great sacrifice in life that it would entail – and even if it had a measure of success, it does not seem that we have got rather nearer our objective (Constantinople) or have rendered our beach more secure from shell or weather.
>
> Besides, the troops in this army corps, owing to their enormous losses in trained officers will not be fit for big operations for a considerable time. They are rather disheartened by their casualties, constant work in digging and unloading trawlers under shell fire and the prospect of a winter campaign under conditions which will certainly not improve. They will of course get better as time goes on and become more inured to this form of warfare, but in the meantime sickness is reducing our ranks a good deal and if it mounts up (as is predicted by the medical authorities) it is quite possible that my Corps alone will require 100,000 men in drafts to keep it going through the winter.
>
> The Turkish shelling, though continuous, is nothing like France, but if they can increase their howitzers our casualties (now about 100 a day) will treble and quadruple as there is no spot safe from it and as more of the low lying land between this and Lala Baba gets more under water, we shall have to pack closer.
>
> The question of our prestige in these parts is always being brought up before us, but it seems to me that the defeat and humbling of Germany by action at the decisive point (France) would establish a far greater prestige than any local defeat of a portion of the Turkish army.
>
> In addition to our requirements in men, our artillery is by no means sufficient to break down the Turkish defence if we land more batteries we have not positions to put them in and the supply of ammunition even for those we have seems hardly sufficient, and the ships guns with their low trajectory have not the power or the rounds to clear the rocks of their defenders.

8 Ibid.

The Turks seem disinclined for offensives at the present time, as they know that our losses from shell and sickness are greater than theirs, but they have made preparations for a very perfect defensive, and to attack them here in force seems only playing their game.

I haven't gone into the question of the difficulty we shall experience in supplying the force during the winter when the weather prevents the lighters working. You probably know all that as well, if not better than I do.[9]

Lieutenant General Sir William Birdwood, commanding the Australian and New Zealand Army Corps (ANZAC) always admitted that his judgement was clouded by having been on the peninsula since the onset of the campaign in April and because of his emotional attachment to the gains made, which had been costly in terms of his own men. His heart told him that to leave would be unthinkable, after the blood expended thus far, but he tried to give Kitchener as pragmatic a response as possible when the latter asked his long-time friend for suggestions as to future advances. Birdwood replied at length on 12 October and provided a grim assessment:

As regards possibility of advancing far enough to free our beaches from shellfire; of the three zones, Cape Helles has been repeatedly attempted and, for the present, advance abandoned, so further advance from there cannot now be expected. In the Anzac position the Turks hold positions practically on higher ground all round … which gives them a great advantage … Progress in this zone, therefore must be very costly, unless we have practically an unlimited supply of gun and howitzer ammunition, or unless mining – which is a very lengthy process – is resorted to on a very large scale.

The Suvla position seems to afford the best prospects of an advance on the Peninsula, and I think it would be possible to work our left forward … and gradually gain the whole of the high ground … For the commencement of this move, the troops at present on the peninsula, if brought up to war establishment, are I consider sufficient, but the ammunition it is not so; consequently no further advance is possible until we have in hand a very large increase. It must be remembered that the whole of the troops on the Peninsula have been very seriously affected in the matter of health, and that a few of them could now be regarded as really strong men capable of physical exertion.

It will be recognised, of course, that any advance must be costly, while it is not possible to replace casualties rapidly at this distance from home. Anything like a long and continued advance, therefore, in the face of much opposition is problematical. I am, therefore, of the opinion that to carry through the movement contemplated, the capture of the high ground north of Anafarta … two further complete divisions of really good troops are necessary.

The above, as far as I can see is the only action possible on the Peninsula.[10]

Unfortunately, the one individual who seemed incapable of balancing the reality of the situation with future prospects for the campaign was the commander of the MEF, Hamilton. In his weekly news update, written on 7 October, he lamented to Kitchener the perceived treachery of

9 The National Archives, Kew (TNA) PRO/30/57/65: Kitchener Papers, Excerpts from Secret telegrams.

10 RA/GV/Q/838/33.

the French *Corps Expéditionnaire d'Orient* – which was pressing for an offensive on the Asiatic shore of the Dardanelles – but explained that:

> the whole atmosphere at Suvla becomes brighter and clearer every time I visit it, and this notwithstanding the terrible sickness which is devastating our ranks ... I would make two or three dashes now if it were not that I simply can't afford to lose the men... Still, Byng is steadily making preparations for our next coup, and I believe he will bring it off all right. Yesterday I visited Helles and inspected the fire trenches of the 52nd (Lowland) Division. Here also I am glad to be able to give you a very cheerful account, excepting again for the sickness which, however, at Helles seems to be distinctly, if slightly, on the downgrade. Davies is very well and very happy. He can carry some important lines of Turkish trenches and gain perhaps four or five hundred yards over a front of about half a mile, but it would cost 2,000 men and we can't afford any losses at present. But he is full of plans and work for gaining ground by sap and mine, and no one is left idle I assure you..."[11]

There were whispers that Hamilton was out of touch. When challenged by Kitchener, Hamilton denied not being fit for the job and claimed that he walked 75 miles a week in making his way about the peninsula. But just a few days later Kitchener wired Hamilton asking what his estimation would be as to the losses he would entail if he was ordered to evacuate: "No decision has been arrived at yet on this question of evacuation but I feel that I ought to have your views." Kitchener was not interested in Hamilton's views about what danger an evacuation might post to the British Empire; he just wanted a number.[12] Hamilton's response came immediately and unsurprisingly, he made evacuation, which he was firmly against, look like a grim option:

> Our losses would depend on such uncertain factors: enemy's action or inaction, weather, [I] question whether we could rely on all troops covering embarkation to fight to the last... impossible to give you straight answer, especially until I have permission to consult [the] Admiral. Once, discussing the very problem with General Gouraud [the commander of the French forces at Gallipoli] we came to the conclusion that at Cape Helles we must sacrifice two divisions out of a total of six divisions and Cape Helles [is the] easiest of three places to get away from. My opinion now is that it would not be wise to reckon on getting out of Gallipoli. [Until the end we would lose] stores, railway plant and horses. Morale of those who got off would fall very low. One quarter would probably get off quite easily then the trouble would begin. We might be very lucky and lose considerably less than I have estimated – on the other hand with all these raw troops at Suvla and all these Senegalese at Cape Helles we might have a veritable catastrophe.[13]

Andrew Bonar Law, leader of the Conservative Party and, in Asquith's coalition government, Secretary of State for the Colonies, was one who scoffed at this prophecy: "You must however remember that it is quite impossible of Hamilton to examine such a question with an open mind," he scribbled in a note to Kitchener. "Suppose you had to carry out this operation yourself

11 TNA PRO/30/57/65: Kitchener Papers, Excerpts from Secret telegrams.
12 Ibid.
13 Ibid.

do you really think that you could not do it without incurring any such disaster as Hamilton contemplates?"[14] Thus at the same time that Hamilton referred to "cheerful" troops, promising plans for future progress, and somewhat played down the effect of sickness, other correspondents painted a very different view, which contrived to make Hamilton look out of touch with events on his front, however strong his denials.

Justified or not, the perception had become that Hamilton was incapable of approaching the issue of whether evacuation was the best way to proceed with a level head, and this was a major contributing factor when he was removed from his command just days later. Both men were closely associated with Kitchener, and therefore it was perhaps unsurprising that Hamilton kept his response measured in front of Birdwood, who predictably related his reaction to Lord Kitchener at the War Office on 14 October:

> I have just been sent for by Sir Ian and much surprised at his news… I must say I feel very sorry indeed for him and for myself too, as I have always found him such a very charming and thoughtful chief to serve under… Many men in such circumstances would be ranting and raving, casting blame on everyone else, saying they were only made scapegoats for faults at home or in the field. He has done nothing of the sort, merely saying he would much have liked to see the thing through but that he has not yet succeeded and must go and there is an end to it, and that he has no intention of chewing his mouth when he gets home. I think he rather feels that his downfall is perhaps due to some extent to a newspaper correspondent's action, which is certainly very galling – and to the Suvla failing, the detailed merits of which I am unable to judge.
>
> I think you would sympathise with him more now than you may have before just, as I say, by seeing the real manly way in which he has taken it, with nothing dramatic or high flown about it – Personally I will regret his departure much, and my men will I am sure be sorry as though he hasn't been able to see very much of each corps, yet when coming round he has always been bright and cheery with them.[15]

Hamilton left his headquarters at Imbros on 17 October and Birdwood assumed temporary command. Twelve days later Hamilton wrote to the King's Private Secretary, Lord Stamfordham: "I have now been six days at home and hardly yet know whether I stand on my head or my heels." He was keen to make it clear that he had not explicitly been at fault. In his account of his dismissal, Hamilton claimed that Kitchener had assured him that his military reputation was intact and had diplomatically explained his removal as being necessary as a substantial number of the War Council were in favour of evacuation. "When they sent me a cable asking my opinion as to our probable losses, my answer was a complete stumper to that party, in fact, in the face of such an opinion, no Government could possibly have entertained the idea of clearing out." Thus Hamilton argued why he believed that he could emerge from the campaign unscathed. He had simply been taken out of the equation to make things easier. "They did not think I could weigh the idea of chucking up the sponge impartially. They said they wanted a fresh opinion on it and it had to come from someone who had not been placed in a position where his own career rested

14 Ibid.
15 Ibid.

on the decision." A second letter smacked of more desperation to make his argument for staying on the peninsula sound, as he pointedly asked Stamfordham to tell the King how cheerful and keen to have a go at the Turk his men had been as he walked "miles and miles" daily to see them all.[16]

But it is safe to say that not all were sorry to see the back of Hamilton. One officer raged about every aspect of the campaign after less than a month at the front, including the landings, lack of reinforcements, Hamilton's distance from his force and his "dithering":

> Thank God that suave and invertebrate adventurer Ian Hamilton has gone. He received, they say, a telegram to leave at once and report at the war office. Just that and nothing more! He had the effrontery to send a message to the troops of theatrical farewell, such as befits a super-journalist masquerading as a General, whose pen was ever sharper than his sword... I know nothing of his successor, but we all breathe a sigh of relief...[17]

For his part, Hamilton believed that he had shown loyalty to Kitchener and nobody else, and that he expected to be looked after as a result, whether that be reassuming command at Gallipoli or another posting:

> When you suddenly disappeared from London, I expect it never occurred to you how entirely en l'air you had left me. As you know, all these seven months since I have been away I have avoided correspondence even with old friends and patrons in this country provided they were in positions of power. This was entirely because I wished to work with you and for you alone. Well, now I do not know what is going to happen to you, much less to myself. I see certain influences at work, both amongst soldiers and civilians, which make me think you may end by cutting yourself clear altogether from the War Office. If so I shall have no one to turn to.
>
> The general mass of the public here seem to imagine that if Munro's recommendation is not accepted, and if the Dardanelles policy goes back to one of non-evacuation, I would naturally revert to my command there. I do not disabuse their minds, although I can see obstacles.
>
> Anyway, you are on the spot now and I am perfectly confident that, from all you will see yourself, and from all that Birdwood and the other Corps Commanders will tell you will realise that we did all possible out there with the means at our disposal. Also that a phenomenal budget of lies has been disseminated at home about the whole of this Dardanelles business. Therefore, taking everything together, I shall still cling to the hope that in view of our long association you will help me out of my present ambiguous position. There may be some further splitting up of the troops in the near East. This would give you a chance. Or, if there should be any truth in these reports of your forming one of an Allied Directing General Staff, do please think of me. For I would loyally assist you; I talk both French and German, and you know I can use my pen.

16 RA GV/Q832/186.
17 RA GV/O/1177/16.

> Goodbye for the present. If you have not time to answer yourself, I hope you will ask Fitz. to send me a line of reassurance.[18]

Hamilton never held an active command again. To compound his hopeless situation, he would be furious when he found out that he had been replaced by a man who believed that the war would be won and lost in France and Flanders. General Sir Charles Monro had commanded, in succession, a division, a corps and then Third Army on the Western Front. He departed for Gallipoli a short time after Hamilton's removal with a mandate to inspect the situation, and to be quick about it. On 30 October he visited Suvla, Anzac and Helles in a single day and delivered a damning assessment to Kitchener:

> After an inspection of the Gallipoli Peninsula, I have arrived at the following conclusions:
>
> - The troops on the Peninsula with the exception of the Australians and New Zealand Corps are not equal to a sustained effort owing to inexperienced officers, the want of training of men [or] the depleted condition of many of the units. We merely hold the fringe of the shore and are confronted by the Turks in very formidable entrenchments with all the advantages of position and power of observation of our movements. The beaches are exposed to observed artillery fire and in the restricted area, all stores are equally exposed.
> - Action by surprise can no longer be counted upon.
> - Belief from sources that heavy guns and ammunition on way from Constantinople.
> - On purely military grounds, therefore, in consequence of the grave daily wastage of officers and men which occurs, and owing to lack of prospect of being able to draw the Turks from their entrenched positions, I recommend the evacuation of the Peninsula.
> - [Of] losses [as a result] ... So much would depend on the degree to which the Turks attacked us during the withdrawal, on how far the re-embarkment could be conducted unobserved, and on weather conditions which prevail at the time.[19]

Included were the summaries of the three corps commanders. Birdwood was still inclined to want to stay:

> I agree with General Monro regarding grave disadvantages of our position and extreme difficulty of making any progress. But I consider evacuation would be considered by Turks as complete victory... I am, therefore, opposed to evacuation ... Fear moral effect on our troops of withdrawal would be bad while Turkish morale would proportionately rise. Season being so late and bad weather at hand I think actual withdrawal fraught with difficulty and danger, as ample time and continuous fine weather essential.[20]

The other two were far more brief. Byng simply observed: "I consider evacuation advisable." Davies initially wrote, "I agree with General Monro's views," although later backtracked somewhat to be in favour of retaining allied forces at Cape Helles. Having sought the views of

18 TNA PRO/30/57/65: Kitchener Papers, Excerpts from secret telegrams.
19 RA GV/Q838/37.
20 RA GV/Q838/38.

his generals, Monro told London: "I hold very strongly that our course of military action must be governed by our military resources."[21]

General Sir Charles Monro.

Despite the almost unanimous opinion of military commanders, the question of withdrawal still held potential political pitfalls. Monro's assessment was not what everybody wanted to hear, whilst the question of what to do in Salonika also confused the issue. The situation was also clouded by the views of some naval officers who were assessing whether or not it was viable to attempt to storm the Straits with naval forces. It might well have been borne of good intentions, but Major-General Arthur Lynden-Bell, Monro's Chief of Staff, referred to this drawn-out nonsense as "The swan song of the lunatics." It would eventually be dismissed as a course of action, but in the meantime, it was resolved that Kitchener – still deeply concerned about what damage an evacuation may do to British prestige in the East – would journey across the Mediterranean to see the situation for himself.

Kitchener, keeping his options open, telegraphed ahead to Birdwood the night before his departure with some thoughts. With regards to the possibility of the navy forcing the Straits, still yet to be ruled out, he told his subordinate that in the event, the land force should do all it could to assist. He wanted to examine fully the best possible landing site near the marsh at the Gulf of Xeros. He was already contemplating how he might raise the numbers for any such new endeavour by reducing the number of men in the trenches, or perhaps by evacuating Suvla alone: "All the best fighting men that could be spared, including your boys from Anzac and everyone I can sweep up in Egypt, might be concentrated at Mudros ready for this enterprise. Please work out plans for this, or alternative plans as you may think best. We must do it right this time."[22] Birdwood replied the same night and outlined some of the issues that would present themselves by following any new offensive course of action. As well as the weather, he informed Kitchener that: "30,000 men would be made available by evacuating positions here, but operation of evacuation would in itself entail considerable loss including guns."[23] He underlined the doubtfulness of carrying off any such endeavour successfully: "Byng and Davies and all their Division generals have very little faith in present power of endurance of their troops, and reply with few exceptions none are at present capable of more than 24 hours of sustained effort. The same applies to most of Australians owing to amount of sickness." He also argued against potential action in the Gulf of Xeros.[24]

21 Ibid.
22 RA GV/Q/880a.
23 RA GV/Q/838/34.
24 RA GV/Q/838/35.

Better informed, Kitchener had almost settled the matter in his own mind before he left England. He told Birdwood: "I fear the Navy may not play up owing to risk … The more I look at the problem the less I see my way through, so you had better very quietly and secretly work out a scheme for getting the troops off the Peninsula."[25] Kitchener arrived a week later. Birdwood, whose sensible head was beginning to win out over his emotional attachment, gave an officer friend an insight into the discussions held, as well as the disgust and dismay that evacuation was being openly discussed in public:

> Lord K himself then came out here, when meetings were held with [General Sir John] Maxwell [GOC British Forces in Egypt], Monro, [Sir Henry] MacMahon [High Commissioner in Egypt], [Vice-Admiral Sir John] de Robeck [commanding the Eastern Mediterranean Squadron] and myself. The apparent determination of Germany and Turkey to make a really big and well thought out attack on the [Suez] Canal was prominently brought forward, and both Maxwell and MacMahon laid great stress on the enormous importance of defending Egypt with a really strong force. It was put to me that we might be contained here by a comparatively speaking small force, while a big move was being rapidly carried on round our flank to Egypt – or strongish German reinforcements might come here and keep pounding us like the devil, while the main force was still moving on Egypt. I was then asked if I considered we should be pulling our full weight in the boat by staying here, while Egypt was perhaps being attacked by a large force and with practically no other troops available but ourselves for its defence. I could not but agree that we should not be doing so.
>
> … In ways though, I hardly fear we are being given a fair, sporting chance – I mean by these politicians at home. The debate in the house absolutely appalled me, and when I was told that General Monro's recommendations for evacuation had been announced in the house, I absolutely refused to believe it. Within 24 hours of these debates, (I forget if it was that one or Carson's speech) Turkish patrols for the first time came boldly out at nights, smelling along our trenches to find out how strongly they were held. It so happened that it did not then matter, as they did not all return, but they will doubtless continue this, and when we are weak it may be most serious. I am only expecting to read now any day a telegram saying that the actual date and plans of our withdrawal have been published. That such a thing could have been done at home is really quite incomprehensible to us all here, and you can imagine how appalled we have all been by it.[26]

On his return home, after a three day stay on the peninsula, Kitchener told his Cabinet colleagues: "The Government may well ask themselves whether they are justified in continuing a campaign which makes so tremendous a toll on the country in human life and material resources … It is evident that every alternative must be examined before we are committed to so dangerous and speculative a campaign in the Gallipoli Peninsula."[27] To begin with, Kitchener was hugely concerned by the situation regarding communication and supply. The men he met,

25 RA GV/Q/880a.
26 RA GV/V/Q/2521/II/43.
27 RA GV/Q/838/31.

too, were depressed with their stagnated situation. He addressed a number of points separately. With regard to the navy forcing the Straits he surmised that:

> attractive though this bold proposition is, and capable and brave though its adherents have shown themselves to be, it must be admitted that the overwhelming majority of naval officers in the Eastern Mediterranean are intensely opposed to it.
>
> … [We] might be justified in sanctioning it, provided they felt satisfied that the possible loss of the whole force engaged would not unduly weaken our naval superiority… It would, however, be a mistake for the Government to order an attack of this kind except in the last resort, or in any way to urge the Vice Admiral to a course to which he is opposed.[28]

Kitchener was even less enthusiastic about the possibility of offensive action: "I consider that advances from our present positions are very difficult; particularly from Helles and Anzac. Suvla gives some opportunity for improving our positions, but it seems very doubtful whether this would enable us to push through."[29] He added that even if they did succeed in taking the Gallipoli Peninsula, the chances of getting anywhere near Constantinople were slim. If the Cabinet were determined to claw back some integrity, he had a far-fetched idea "to make a dash into Syria, to capture Damascus, cut the Hejaz railway and occupy Syria. The powers which had conquered both Baghdad and Damascus would hardly be without prestige in the east, even if they had failed to take Constantinople itself."[30]

Having considered some of the strategic implications of withdrawal, Kitchener turned his eye to whether withdrawal was tactically possible. He believed so, but recognised that it could only be carried out with "utmost difficulty," and commanders on the spot had told him that they would likely have to leave guns and the wounded behind. As for politics, he thought that although it would be perceived that Britain had been driven into the sea, it might be possible to save some face. In the meantime, "careful and secret" preparations were being made for the possible evacuation of the peninsula, and Kitchener thought, having seen positions for himself, that the number of losses quoted were too high, and that owing to the shortness of distance to the beach and the idea of contraction lines, they could be considerably lower.[31] Kitchener left his information with his Cabinet colleagues who, by 19 November, had ruled out any new schemes in the region. Asquith informed Kitchener of their decision and asked his advice on the next step:

> His Majesty's Government have decided against the proposed expedition to Ayas Bay… In your further consideration of the strategical position in the Near East, in Turkey in Asia and in Egypt, please, therefore regard the scheme as, under existing conditions, withdrawn. Upon this assumption are you now able to give us your considered opinion as to the evacuation of the Peninsula, in whole or in part.[32]

28 Ibid.
29 RA GV/Q/838/39.
30 RA GV/Q/838/31.
31 Ibid.
32 RA GV/Q/880a.

Lord Kitchener inspects Cape Helles (above) and Anzac Cove (below), November 1915.

To recap, as early as mid-October Birdwood had outlined the lack of prospects for continuing the campaign. Monro had sent a scathing appraisal of the campaign as it stood at the end of the month, backed up by Byng and Davies. Kitchener had assessed all of the options, but having ruled out further commitments in the region and being pointedly told of the limitations concerning further advance, the matter was not settled. Thanks to the intervention of politicians, it would be more than a month before a decision was made as to evacuating the peninsula.

For his part, the First Lord of the Admiralty, Arthur Balfour, thought the MEF should stay put:

> I am prepared to admit that neither the Army alone nor the Navy alone, nor the two in combination, can either drive the Turks from the Peninsula or compel them to surrender. The question before us is, therefore, reduced to this: Ought we to cling to Gallipoli until it becomes (if it ever does become) quite untenable, or ought we to leave it alone?
>
> Our position on the Peninsula resembles a beleaguered fortress; and I am as reluctant to abandon it as I should be to abandon any other fortress which was well garrisoned, well provisioned and had no practicable breach in its defences. By such an abandonment we should lose credit in our own eyes, in those of our enemies and in those of our friends. Quite apart from its effect upon our prestige in the east (about which much has been said in the Cabinet) we have a character to lose in the west to Russia the blow would be staggering. Even those who rate at the lowest our military organisation and training have never denied us the quality of tenacity and courage, what will they say when they see us deserting without a struggle a position so important and hardly won?[33]

Balfour questioned himself whether the Cabinet had any right to sacrifice soldiers' lives on a point of honour. In answer, he claimed that it was more than that. Remaining on the Gallipoli Peninsula meant diverting enemy resources away from other theatres, and it meant stopping a potential communication route that might prove beneficial to the enemy. He even went as far as to say that whilst maintaining this "threat" to Constantinople, the Turk would be dissuaded from making a significant attack against Britain in Egypt. Finally, he acknowledged that although there were arguments for evacuation, defending the desert against Ottoman forces may be more difficult than it was on the peninsula, itself "which has been gloriously captured, is gloriously held, and may, perhaps, never be dangerously threatened." Yet, Balfour's perception of the well supplied, well garrisoned force, did not get past the King's Private Secretary, who scrawled a question as to sickness of the troops across his copy of the paper.[34]

Correspondence coming the other way gave a very different view. Major-General Alexander Godley had also written to one of King George V's aides, describing events at Anzac on the very same day that Balfour presented his argument for remaining on the peninsula:

> We are now of course in a state of uncertainty as to the future, but hope that it may be cleared up soon... the weather has broken now I think, and it is becoming really much colder. The day before yesterday we had our first real gale from the south. It washed away

33 RA GV/Q/838/28.
34 Ibid.

> two out of our four piers, and either sunk or wrecked on the shore every single picket boat, barge or lighter, except a few of the bigger ones, which got away to shelter at Imbros. However we had a reserve, both of food and water, and are quite prepared to be cut off for a bit, if necessary... Never in the history of the world was there such an extraordinary situation, as that stores would be landed on an open beach within, at one place only about 300 yards from our trenches, and under not only shell, but also rifle fire.[35]

Even if the politicians could not, the War Office appreciated the need for a timely decision. The Chief of the Imperial General Staff, General Sir William Robertson, received a letter on 22 November clarifying that, "there can be no certainty as to the results either of withdrawing or remaining. But one course or the other must be decided on at once."[36] But in the Cabinet, Lord Curzon, largely influenced by his communications with Hamilton, had put much effort into an argument for remaining at Gallipoli. Ever with a flair for the dramatic (although Churchill once said of him that he was a master at putting this sort of paper together, but that it was a pity he never put the same effort into carrying a matter through) he painted a grim picture of the final stages of an evacuation:

> The evacuation and the final scenes will be enacted at night. Our guns will continue firing until the last moment, notably those on or near to the beaches, but the trenches will have been taken one by one, and a moment must come when [every man for himself] takes place, and when a disorganised crowd will press in despairing tumult on the shore and into the boats. Shells will be falling and bullets ploughing their way into the mass of retreating humanity, on the water, the motor lighters and launches and row boats will be coming to and fro, and doing what they can. Conceive the crowding into the boats of thousands of half-crazy men: the wounded, the hecatombs of the slain (and the mortality amongst the sailors is not forgotten either). It requires no imagination to create a scene that when it is told, will be burned into the heart and conscience of the British people for generations to come. What will they say of those who have brought about this supreme and hideous disaster?[37]

Curzon also argued that Britain was not in the habit of running from an "Asiatic enemy," especially when she had chosen the front herself and it would be done "in the full glare of publicity... and on one of the greatest historical stages of the world ... We seem to be wildly grasping in the dark," he complained, "running in here and running out there, without the semblance of a coordinated design." He warned the Cabinet to remember "that the decision which they are about to take will be one of the most momentous in British history, and that each one of us will have to justify himself to our countrymen and to posterity, for what may turn out to be an indelible blot upon the British name."[38]

While Curzon was imparting the product of his considerably dramatic imagination, Major-General Maude, on the peninsula, was making notes in his diary: "Went up to 39th Infantry

35 RA GV/Q/2521/IV/50.
36 TNA PRO/30/57/65: Kitchener Papers, Excerpts from Secret telegrams.
37 RA GV/Q/838/29.
38 Ibid.

Brigade … Nearly blown away getting there, and could hardly make way against the headwind… Went on to see the 40th and 38th Infantry Brigades… waist high in mud and water in some places. Sent up extra fuel and rum on pack animals."[39] Then, two days later:

Major-General (later General Sir) Stanley Maude (GOC 13th Division).

> Last night after four days the gale subsided. The violence of it added to the snow blizzard and the icy cold, have been indescribable, but the way in which the division have stuck it out has been magnificent… I think it would be difficult, unless you had seen it to realise what the men have had to go through; it has been terrible for them, especially as they are not yet fitted out with warm clothing fully, nor have they material to make good shelters. We have had 1,350 sick in my division in the last three days, and I am afraid that there will be still more, and fifteen deaths from exposure; and yet I fancy that our total is about the lowest in these parts.[40]

And yet days later, still confident that he was in possession of the most accurate information coming from Hamilton and others in the anti-evacuation camp, Curzon, claiming that he was not exaggerating, continued with his violent imagery of the potential catastrophic failure of abandoning the campaign:

> When the three lines at Helles have been successfully evacuated, and there remains the last half mile to the beaches, does anyone believe that the orders to retire in batches to the lighters will be obeyed? … The motor lighters… will be weighted with the rush of fugitives pouring into them, and will very likely be swamped and sunk. Men will be wading into the waves, scrambling onto the boats, swimming hither and thither and being drowned by the hundred – and all this amid a continuous shell and rifle fire, and very likely in contact, on the beaches, with merciless steel of the bayonet. Taken at the very best it must be a gruesome and horrible scene. I would sooner see our forces perish under sustained assault with their faces to the enemy… than I would see them overwhelmed in this welter of carnage and shame.[41]

Despite Curzon's hysteria and the arguments put forward by the likes of Balfour, finally at the beginning of December the message appeared to be getting through that whatever the political

39 Callwell, *Maude*, p. 170.
40 Ibid.
41 RA GV/Q/838/29.

questions at hand might be, the force at Gallipoli was ill-equipped for the winter and the chances of fashioning anything positive out of the campaign were negligible. On 2 December, Asquith sent a memo to Buckingham Palace that indicated that the Government was nearing a decision:

> We saw K[itchener] and Admiral de Robeck at the War Committee this morning, and afterwards had a Cabinet, at which the sole topic was the proposed evacuation of Gallipoli. The proposal now is to evacuate Suvla and Anzac but to retain the position at Helles, to which the soldiers and the sailors attach great importance.
>
> After a good deal of discussion it was resolved that the two staffs should consider this afternoon the practicality of using the troops which we hope to get free from Salonika to reinforce the position at Suvla, and to make a push thence onto stronger ground capable of being held against the new guns and ammunition which are on their way from Germany.[42]

This discussion was taking place in spite of the military assessments made by commanders on the spot. "My own impression," wrote the Prime Minister, "is that they will reject that ... But I do not know. The Cabinet was adjourned till tomorrow, when we ought to arrive at a decision."[43] The decision could not come soon enough for those on the peninsula, least of all Maude, who, while he wanted a chance to fight as much as the most enthusiastic of soldiers, he just wanted a decision to be made. No reinforcements were arriving, nor sufficient material for constructing winter accommodation, and, to a man of Maude's temperament and instinct for looking ahead, the situation was to the last degree, exasperating:

> We are truly a nation of muddlers. But surely the procrastination of the last few months and the scandal which must necessarily result must wake the Government up. First, the want of decision by which we did not arrange either to go on or to get out of her months ago. Secondly, the total lack of provision of winter clothes for the troops in adequate quantities, and the absence of material for making shelters. It is all too lamentable and has cost many valuable lives that might have been saved.[44]

Finally, after meetings with the French – which affirmed their opinion that they would happily withdraw from Gallipoli but categorically did not want to surrender Salonika – the matter was solved. On 7 December the Cabinet decided to evacuate the Gallipoli Peninsula. Owing to the wishes of the Royal Navy, it was agreed to retain Helles (for the time being), not least so that the former could try and control U-Boat activity in the Straits. "[I] hope they have at last made up their minds," Maude wrote the following day. "Of course I would rather have gone for the Turks and smashed them, and I think we could have; but if the Government will not let us do that the only alternative is to get out of this and we ought to have done so long ago."[45]

42 RA GV/Q/838/30.
43 RA GV/Q/838/46.
44 Callwell, *Maude*, p. 171.
45 Ibid.

Evacuation of Anzac and Suvla

As the man who had to plan and oversee the execution of the evacuation of the Anzac and Suvla sectors, Birdwood was pragmatic about the situation. But that did not mean that it did not hurt. He felt guilty that his men did not yet know what awaited them:

> Going round my trenches ... only two days ago, it almost made one cry to think we will have to give up what has been like a child to me. Officers and men, who have no idea yet that we are withdrawing, were [telling] me with the greatest pride how they have done their best to carry out my wishes to make ourselves impregnable...[46]

He admitted that their positions lacked depth "terribly," even if he found it hard to marry that with the emotional plea that he and his boys at Anzac were ready to take on anything. The fact that at Suvla, Byng was apprehensive about whether or not he could even hold his position over the winter without substantial reinforcements, and that intelligence pointed to the arrival of both Austrian and German heavy artillery opposite them, convinced Birdwood that he had to change his assessment of the situation and support the idea of evacuation. He was worried, however, that Hamilton might think him two-faced:

> With these conditions before me, the position, I am sure you will agree, assumes a very different aspect, and though from a local point of view I am perfectly ready to hold out, and as I said would rather leave my bones on the Peninsula than leave it for fear of being driven out, yet I felt I had to subscribe to the telegram Lord K sent home to the Ministry as to the advisability of withdrawal. I have just written these details home to Sir Ian, and I feel sure that you will agree with me that I have not been in any way inconsistent in my views, but I feel that to simply and obstinately have said we must hang on regardless of the bigger imperial issues would have been great stupidity.[47]

The final scheme for evacuation was devised by the staff at Anzac. As historian Peter Hart has observed:

> On the basis that the Turks were fully capable of causing huge casualties by bombarding the beaches and launching disruptive attacks, [the] plan prioritised deception to try and conceal the evacuation until the very last moment. It was a brilliant piece of work that combined rigorously detailed planning with a considerable imaginative effort to fool the Turks.
>
> In the week before the evacuation the units holding Anzac and Suvla would be thinned out to the bare minimum required to hold the front. Then, over two nights, the reserve and support units would be evacuated on the penultimate night, while on the last night they would thin out the remaining units in stages, before the final parties pulled back, covered by small rearguards.[48]

46 RA GV/Q/2521/II/43.
47 Ibid.
48 Peter Hart, *Gallipoli* (London: Profile Books, 2011), p. 414.

To clear Anzac and Suvla meant the removal of some 83,000 men and 186 guns as a priority, along with all of the stores and equipment possible; all while trying to conceal their actions from the Ottoman troops opposite. Birdwood had assessed certain factors beyond his control that consequently gave him sleepless nights:

> You will realise how much I feel having to arrange to carry out this withdrawal, which is a really big business, and I suppose if anything more difficult even than our landing… First and foremost is the weather and second is the provision of the necessary small craft by the Navy.
>
> There is a third factor; too, viz. the moon. This will be full on 21st, and if I could choose my time, this is the very phase I would avoid. It is impossible to get off earlier than I am doing, as it has taken us all this time to collect the necessary small craft which are scattered about, and to withdraw the guns etc. which we can and will save before the final stage. I am then faced with the option of getting off as quickly as I can, or delaying, say, for another ten days, so as to get dark nights. After fully thinking it out, I have come to the conclusion that it is essential to seize the opportunity and go as soon as ever I can get off, moon or no moon, while with the certainty of bad weather coming on, I might not be able to get away at all. At present the nights are all cloudy, and if these will only continue, I could wish for nothing better, as it gives is the necessary light for embarkation work, while it would not give away our movements to the enemy. I simply dare not wait. As it is, I hardly dare hope that our present weather will last out the week, while I feel quite sure there would be no chance of it lasting longer. You can imagine how very anxious all these possibilities make me at present.[49]

Providing that these factors played into his hands, however, Birdwood remained confident that he could pull the whole affair off:

> I have I think worked out all details, and have tried to think of every dodge possible to delude the enemy and retard a possible following up. If my plans come off as I hope, I trust to get away a very great deal of valuable material, and to withdraw my men with really very small loss. Out of my 200 guns ashore I fear, however, that I may have to sacrifice up to a maximum of 41, but these at the last moment will be so completely blown to pieces as not to be of any value even as trophies, while any stores etc. that I have to abandon will also be blown up or burnt. The loss of guns of course goes to my heart, but to save men's lives it must be done, for no amount of material can come up in value for the life of one of these magnificent fellows who have been fighting for us here. The difficult time will of course be the last day, and it is during that time that I must keep artillery ashore, every gun having to do the work of four or five as would ordinarily be the case, and it will be impossible to withdraw these during the last night when a really large number of men have to be taken away up to full naval resources. It will I think be rather a triumph if things come off as I hope, but if they do not you will know that we have done our best, and as I say, I do not fear failure except for the … reasons I have given.[50]

49 RA GEO V/Q/2521/II/43.
50 Ibid.

At Suvla, Maude was now in his element as an administrative mastermind. A decision had been made and he could now take action. He was devoting much attention to plans to cover the embarkation places, as the plan to thin out the troops to such an extent that a very few would be manning the lines directly before they stole away in the night to embark made him extremely nervous:

> This is of course an attractive scheme, and one which I originally suggested, but it has the elements of a gamble. If the Turks find out we are on the move they will attack, and arrive pell-mell with the troops at the ships where there will be no covering force. They may find it out by aeroplane reconnaissance noting our empty trenches during the day, by the noise of troops retiring (they are always noisy at night) or by noting the increased activity of shipping. On the other hand, if we withdraw only to some second line on first night it will decisively tell the Turks that we are off and we shall have a bit of fighting on the second night.[51]

Birdwood was impressed with Maude and the other generals at Suvla, confessing that their preparations for final departure were superior to those of his men at Anzac. He did point out that the transports could get close to the stores in their sector, and that they had more piers, but he also wryly noted that some insubordination had also occurred:

> I must confess that Suvla took a real flying start! You will remember that we had orders to commence evacuating, when both Corps started making preliminary arrangements – then came an idea of the possibility of our not going, when I had to tell both Corps to sit tight for a bit, and in fact to put in more supplies for themselves. I have a shrewd suspicion that Suvla did not take much notice of this, but went on getting rid of stuff, and as it happens this has turned out all right.[52]

Birdwood was sure that the Turks had not rumbled their scheme of escape. Until 18 December deserters continued to cross into the British lines, and he hardly thought that the weight of shell being dropped on his positions would have been expended if the enemy thought for one moment that there was nobody in the front-line trenches, as was the case by then. He could scarcely believe his luck:

> Our intentions, too, would have been obvious to them, looking down as they do from the hills around on practically all our movements. As you know, not a single lighter can leave our beaches without being seen, and though we of course confined movements to the night as much as possible, yet a certain amount of craft was made necessarily seen moving about in the daytime. Curiously enough, they seem all along to have anticipated that we were making arrangements for an attack, and not a retirement.[53]

He came to believe that the MEF was quitting the peninsula at the best moment:

51 Callwell, *Maude*, p. 172.
52 RA GV/Q/2521/II/46.
53 Ibid.

> It may be that we got away just about the right time, for when I was going round 'Anzac' yesterday, the Turks, suddenly opened on us with new, very big howitzers, firing some excellently made, clean cut, steel shells of about ten inches in diameter. It is quite possible that these were the Austrian howitzers which we had heard about, and that they were just registering our positions before starting a big bombardment. In the course of about an hour they put in fifty of these big shells along the trenches, and though I believe no one was hurt, yet they seemed to fall all round, and I got covered with mud from one that came a bit nearer than usual.[54]

Thanks to his somewhat obsessive nature, Maude's division had "nearly got rid of everything worth taking away," but he was particularly anxious that no artillery should have to be left behind and destroyed at the last moment. On this matter he had some difficulty in inducing his corps commander, Lieutenant-General Byng, to permit reducing the guns to a very low figure, with only ten pieces remaining on the last day.[55]

There was nothing left for Birdwood to do but wait and ponder what might happen:

> Having made all my arrangements, I now spend all the time I possibly can with my different corps in going round and seeing how they are all getting on, and I shall certainly spend the last day with my troops at Anzac, as having landed with them on 25th April I have every intention of leaving with them now. What you say about the point of view of officers who have been serving in France is of course quite right, and it is a great difficulty to contend against, as no man seems capable of being able to look through more than one pair of spectacles. Men like Monro, who came out here to give an opinion, seem only capable of saying "Every man in France is wanted in France to kill Germans." I, on the other hand, who have been through everything here, and am perhaps incapable of seeing beyond the Dardanelles, say "Here we are! For goodness sake let us do all we possibly can to get through!"[56]

Despite his sorrow at leaving, Birdwood was satisfied that his men had salvaged all that was possible:

> During the preliminary stage of about a week, we have dribbled off nearly everything of value we possessed, and the last day I went round, I could find practically no ordnance or engineer stores left, while we evacuated nearly the whole of our animals leaving I think only fifty at "Anzac" out of a total of some 6,000 between the two Corps. Guns had of course been dribbled off gradually, every battery being reduced, first to a section, and then to a single gun with lots of ammunition for it, and finally single guns were dribbled off. We had 200 guns originally, and of these Suvla got off the whole of their 90, while "Anzac" evacuated 100 of their total of 107, the seven remaining being completely blown to pieces.[57]

Birdwood's prayers were then answered when the time for evacuation finally arrived:

54 Ibid.
55 Callwell, *Maude*, p. 174.
56 RA GV/Q/2521/II/43.
57 Ibid.

Evacuation of Suvla: Burning stores viewed from the deck of HMS *Cornwallis*. (Private collection)

> The weather was absolutely perfect. Two perfectly quiet, calm nights, with no wind, and I am thankful to say a certain amount of cloud to dim the strong moon. This saved the Navy from all anxiety as regards their boats being knocked about, hence we were able to work with complete confidence of success.
>
> The first night of my final stage was of course no trouble, for though I got rid of 10,000 men in each Corps that night, it left me with 10,000 in each to hold the respective areas for the remaining twenty four hours. What I most feared was a big storm coming on when I was short of strength, so you can imagine how thankful I feel. I carried out exactly the programme I had always intended, spending the last day but one in making all final arrangements at Suvla – cruising up and down the coast that night in a destroyer.[58]

Birdwood spent his final day at his "beloved" Anzac as planned, getting a last look at the original trenches dug on arrival in April, before withdrawing to spend the night aboard HMS *Chatham*. Unlike Birdwood, there was no time for the ANZAC to grieve about leaving the peninsula:

> You can imagine how anxious we all were on the very last night. Things at Suvla were practically quiet throughout the night, but I was a little disturbed when there was a good deal

58 Ibid.

> of firing off and on at "Anzac", at one time almost threatening an attack, but I was thankful that there was very little shelling. The Naval arrangements I may mention were absolutely perfect, and without any hitch of any sort. Boats all came in at the appointed times at the proper places. The last big lot, holding the trenches all round from the right of "Anzac" to the left of Suvla, were divided into three sections, who gradually withdrew through each other in turn, until very small parties were left covering the actual piers, and they, too, got quickly down on board and left. At times, constant heavy firing kept breaking out round the "Anzac" front which naturally made me very anxious to the end, as it was impossible to tell how much of this was being opened from the Turks' trenches, or how much the Turks had found out and were following on.[59]

All manner of ruses and distractions were employed to conceal what was happening from the enemy:

> We wrapped up the mens' feet in old sacking and blankets, so that there was not a sound made as they left the trenches. In a few places most cunning devices had been made by fastening a rifle onto the parapet and firing it by a weight arranged with a tin full of water and a hole bored in it, which could be timed to drop and pull the trigger at any given number of minutes after the trenches had been vacated. Several other dodges of the same sort were devised, such as candles burning for an inch or so, and then reaching a firework which exploded with a loud report. The results of all of them were evidently satisfactory, for the Turks never seemed to discover that we were off.[60]

There were larger pyrotechnic displays still to come:

> You will probably remember that some months ago I started making several really big tunnels under the enemy's positions, with the idea of sapping forward and having some very big blow ups under more than one of their main trenches. I had caused a tunnel under the most important of these, viz. Russell's Top, to be pushed on rapidly during the last fortnight, and this we charged with several hundred pounds of ammonal in three separate mines, which I ordered to be exploded at intervals of two minutes. When the rear part were well away these were fired with complete success, a volcanic eruption being seen for miles around, and quite competing on a small scale with Vesuvius! The result was wonderful, in that the whole of the Turks, evidently anticipating a big attack, lined their trenches, and for about an hour continued to fire away as fast as they possibly could load, meanwhile our men were well down on their way to the beach in comfort.[61]

With Birdwood's elevation to commander of the Dardanelles Army, Godley had been placed in charge of ANZAC. Far from Lord Curzon's depressing vision of fire and brimstone, Godley was thrilled with the conduct of his men: "The men were splendid. They were very angry at having to go, but once they realised that it had to be done they all played up thoroughly, and

59 Ibid.
60 Ibid.
61 Ibid.

every man was a policeman. Officers on duty on the beach told me, and I saw it myself too that their silence and orderliness was quite remarkable, and from first to last there was no panic and no undue taste to get to the boats."[62] Indeed, as Godley explained, the only concern at Anzac was the bickering amongst the men as to who would be the last to go:

> The great difficulty was to select the men to form the rear parties, only a few hundred of the rearguard, who were to be absolutely the last to leave the trenches. When companies were asked to volunteer for it, they all volunteered to a man, and when the selection was made there was a great deal of heartburning amongst those who were not asked to stay. Some of the men demanded to see their officers to lodge a complaint, as they had been first to land, it was their right to be the last to go. On the other hand, those who had lately arrived said that the others had had their chance and that it was their turn.[63]

Major-General Maude recorded – as was his nature – exact details as to events at Suvla in his diary:

> From about 11:30 a.m. onwards, our front line of trenches was only held by 200 men, till 1:30 a.m. when they finally withdrew. From 11:30 a.m. onwards the Salt Lake lines were only held by 100 men and three machine guns, the Lala Baba defences being held by 250 men and six machine guns. As soon as the final party from the trenches had passed through the Salt Lake lines, we closed the gaps in the wire and withdrew everyone except the Lala Baba garrison, and embarked them, and finally we embarked the Lala Baba garrison and the six machine guns…
>
> … We got everything away and left the Turks, who seemed quite unaware of what was going on, practically nothing. At 4:00 a.m. we lit a huge bonfire on which we poured several thousand gallons of… petrol and had a magnificent blaze. It was wicked waste and could have been avoided had more sea transport been available. No guns left behind by me, and only a few rounds which we buried. Weather simply perfect throughout and almost a flat calm, not too cold.[64]

Maude's men had even destroyed surplus sandbags by ripping them with bayonets or clasp knives to render them useless. He took the fact that nothing happened on either night beyond the usual sniping and firing to mean that the Turks had no idea what was happening. Birdwood was much impressed with the initiative of Byng in destroying that which he could not save:

> Byng organised the destruction of the stores he left behind very well indeed, and it was a wonderful sight to see at the last moment, as if by a wave of a magician's wand, the whole of his surplus stores suddenly bursting into flame, and forming huge bonfires. At "Anzac", I am sorry to say this was not done, and the enemy must have got a certain amount of food, though nothing that would last them for more than a few days, and of course not of any great value.[65]

62 RA GV/Q/2521/IV/117.
63 Ibid.
64 Callwell, *Maude*, p. 176.
65 RA GV/Q/2521/II/46.

As the last of the troops from Suvla and Anzac floated away, Birdwood recalled how the Turks had begun to bombard the empty British lines: "At nine o'clock in the morning, they seemed to turn every gun they possessed on to the trenches, and it is at all events some satisfaction to know they have got through and wasted a great deal of ammunition."[66] Godley shared a similar sentiment: "Though we are very sad at leaving the place where we have been for eight months, and where so many gallant souls are buried, it is some consolation to think how utterly bamboozled the Turk was as regards this evacuation."[67] Birdwood could hardly comprehend just how successful the evacuation of both corps had been:

> When you come to think that in a great many places our trenches are not more than twenty five yards apart, it certainly is a wonderful credit to the men that they should have been able to slip away as they did and I think shows a very high state of discipline which is altogether praiseworthy … I should imagine the higher German officers on the spot will come in for some well-served abuse, when it is known that they have allowed us to slip away from such a difficult position through what one might call the narrowest possible of bottle necks, (viz. one or two temporary piers) without being able to do us any damage. It was extraordinary too, that they had not the enterprise to push forward at once to find out the situation themselves, instead of allowing the whole of their heavy and light artillery to carry out a continuous, organised bombardment as they did on our evacuated position.[68]

Birdwood could not "help chuckling with delight at the thought of the German officers" being "hoodwinked."[69] Events soon proved that his decision to evacuate as soon as possible was vindicated. As he told a member of the King's Household on 21 December, the day after the last of the troops left Anzac and Suvla:

> More than ever do I realise how entirely we have to thank Providence for evacuating successfully as we have done. A real south-westerly gale sprang up at about 1:00 a.m. today. Had this been 24 hours earlier, it would probably have caught us with some six to eight thousand men still ashore, when getting off would have been extremely difficult. I had given orders that once embarkation had actually started on the final night, it was to be continued whatever happened, the men if necessary having to wade out up to their necks to be hauled into boats, but this would of course have entailed not only considerable loss at the time, but so much delay that we could not possibly have got through everything before daylight, when we should have come in for a bad time of it … To emphasise this, I may mention that my original plans were to have had the final night of evacuation on 20th/21st and it was only about ten days ago that I found out the Navy could manage to guarantee the collection of the necessary small craft 24 hours earlier than we originally thought, when I put forward the date by one day, which as you see has been of such wonderful and unforeseen consequence.[70]

66 Ibid.
67 RA GV/Q/2521/IV/117.
68 RA GV/Q/2521/II/46.
69 RA GV/Q/2521/II/45.
70 RA GV/Q/2521/II/46.

For now, at least, the commander of the Dardanelles Army could breathe a sigh of relief:

> You can imagine what a weight seems to have rolled off one's shoulders, when I got back here early this morning, and realised the astoundingly good fortune we had had, when a piece of bad fortune might have resulted in terribly heavy losses ... Now I feel that the only thing I want at the present moment is a really long sleep, as I have not had more than an hour in the last 48.
>
> Before closing, I should just like to mention that the whole of the success of this operation [excepting the Navy] is due entirely to the Corps Commanders – Byng and Godley, and their staffs, who made all arrangements most excellently, and left me really little of nothing to do beyond perhaps a suggestion here or a word of encouragement there during my practically daily visits to their positions.[71]

With the British and French still at Cape Helles, however, Birdwood's attention soon shifted to that end of the peninsula.

Evacuation of Cape Helles

Birdwood was glad that Helles had been retained, "for this I sincerely trust will prevent a terrible blow to our prestige, which I feel sure wholesale evacuation would have done. Helles will undoubtedly be subjected to heavy attack, but it has depth there which our other fronts have not, and I naturally am going to strengthen the place as much as I can with more infantry and artillery."[72]

But it was not to be. On 23 December General Sir William Robertson, Chief of the Imperial General Staff, penned a memo arguing that there was no point in retaining a hold on the Gallipoli Peninsula. Some thought it should be kept for morale, to avoid disappointment on the part of Britain's Russian ally, or to keep the Turks occupied or even to assist in facilitating future naval operations blockading the Dardanelles to enemy submarines. Robertson accepted the Russian argument. Of keeping the Turks occupied, he said that morale was irrelevant, that "the complete failure of the Dardanelles operations has greatly discounted this already, and nobody of intelligence now imagines that there is any likelihood of our forcing the straits." Plus, Allied forces were already fighting the Turks in the Caucasus, Persia and Mesopotamia. With regards to the navy, Robertson argued that "it is equally obvious that the retention of 50,000 at Helles would put a bigger strain on the Royal Navy because they would need to fully supply them." This "must throw a far greater strain upon the Royal Navy than mere blocking of the Dardanelles can cause." The General Staff, whilst hesitating to opine on naval matters, therefore recommended "that Gallipoli should be entirely evacuated and with the least possible delay."[73]

71 Ibid.
72 RA GEO V/Q/2521/II/43.
73 RA GV/Q/2521/II/70.

Thus Birdwood found himself busily planning another evacuation:

> I am arranging at Helles to withdraw 17,000 men in one night. We have 20,000 men there at present, of whom we get 3,000 tonight, and leave the balance for another twenty-four hours, but it is of course quite possible that heavy weather may spring up at any moment, in which case we are strong enough there to hold our own for a week, and all arrangements are made, if heavy weather should come on, to stand fast until the first fine night, when all will be withdrawn.[74]

Indeed, he claimed in retrospect that the only "really disturbing" factor in his calculations was the unpredictability of the weather.[75] As before, he had to contemplate abandoning or destroying a substantial number of guns:

> We have still for about fifty guns ashore – French and English, and I am afraid that I must make up my mind to sacrifice between 20 and 30 of these, but they will of course all be blown up at the last moment. Though these may sound a largish number ... they are really negligible. Among the British guns that we are abandoning, only one is what you might call modern weapon, viz. a 6" gun. Of the remaining English guns, we have got off all modern weapons ... leaving behind only the old ... howitzers, which have been brought out here by Territorials, and for which I understand no more ammunition is being manufactured. With the French guns I am getting away all their beloved 75s, and leaving behind only four 9.2" and two naval guns. They tell me that all of these have fired about 5,000 rounds each, and are really of little value to them, so I think we can blow them up without regret.[76]

Weeks had passed since the successful evacuation of Anzac and Suvla, and Birdwood was keen to impart the necessity for getting away while it was possible: "I ... told everyone that I expected them to get off with practically no loss ... I ... told them that if a sudden storm got up at the very last moment, when we were definitely committed to complete evacuation, the last remaining men must be got off at all costs – that if necessary, they were to wade out up to their necks, and then be pulled on board boats by ropes."[77]

Finally, there was one aspect of evacuation that was new to him, but it caused him little trouble. This was cooperation with the French:

> I am delighted to say that I have found my relations with the French, since I have been in command here, have been excellent, and I am most grateful to little General Brulard [*Corps Expéditionnaire d'Orient* commander] for the way he has met me in every detail. Some little time ago, by the wish of the French Government, we evacuated their Senegalese (24 companies) and 1,500 Creoles, so as to get them out of the cold. As soon as I got definite orders for evacuation here, I at once withdrew the whole of the remaining French infantry – about 5,000 men, so as not to have any possibility of divided command in the final

74 RA GV/Q/2521/II/47.
75 RA GV/Q/2521/II/50.
76 RA GV/Q/2521/II/47.
77 RA GV/Q/2521/II/50.

Der letzte Engländer auf Gallipoli.

German cartoon lampooning the MEF evacuation: "The last English on Gallipoli." (*Kladderadatsch*, 23 January 1916)

> rearguard, but General Brulard at once agreed to leave me the whole of his artillery, to be withdrawn entirely at my discretion, gun by gun … their [artillery commander] … taking his orders direct from mine, and giving me an entirely free hand about abandoning any of his guns. I have of course explained to him that every possible French gun we can get away will be withdrawn, while he agreed it would be out of the question to get away his six big guns, which he assured me were of very little value to them. The little man has played the game most thoroughly, and I am extremely grateful to him.[78]

Lieutenant-General Birdwood was not the only senior officer to participate in both evacuations from the peninsula. Indeed, after it had left Suvla, Birdwood sent Maude's division to Helles to replace an exhausted division there. As before, Maude was determined to remove as much materiel as possible, but it was proving difficult:

> Each walk that I take up to the trenches makes me feel somewhat sad. My fellows have been working … to try and get things away, but the whole place is so littered with stuff that it is difficult to collect it and bring it down to places where it can be put on carts and wagons. We are doing our level best to carry out your instructions to clear the area, and yesterday, for instance, we evacuated over thirty tons weight; but this seems only a drop in the ocean, and I am afraid that the enemy will get a considerable amount of booty when we withdraw. Still, I am telling them to keep pegging along, and I impressed this point particularly on brigadiers and commanding officers when I saw them up in the trenches

78 RA GV/Q/2521/II/47.

> this afternoon, although it seems scarcely necessary to do so as they are as keen about clearing things as I am myself.[79]

Just before the final evacuation, Birdwood wrote to a friend:

> I wrote and told you what a very trying time of it I had over "Anzac" and Suvla, and I am now again in the throes of the whole thing over Helles, which I am sincerely hoping to see through successfully tomorrow night. It is of course a very different proposition, as the Turks are naturally thoroughly awake to what may happen, and the latest prisoners tell us that German officers are consistently going round their trenches at night, so they evidently mean to have at us if they can. They keep aeroplanes flying over our position day and night, while they have lately been keeping up a continuous bombardment throughout the twenty four hours on our trenches, mostly with big shells ... which makes work extremely difficult and dangerous. Two nights ago, a note was thrown across into one of our trenches in German – "When are you finally leaving here? We shall meet again on the Suez Canal!" So they have evidently made more than an intelligent anticipation of our own and their intentions. In spite of this, I am full of confidence and hope of being able to withdraw successfully, provided always (as before) that the weather is kind to us, and I have every faith that this will be the case.[80]

One particular headache was proving to be the transport animals, whose fate he lamented deeply.

> I am sorry to say that we will have to destroy a goodish number ... before going, which may possibly amount to eight or nine hundred. We have had real bad luck regarding them which has been unavoidable. The first night when we started evacuation, I sent over a horse ship, which would have brought away 500, when the French flagship proceeded – apparently without much reason, to ram and sink her as she left the harbour here, defeating me for that night. The following night a high wind got up, making work practically impossible, and a whole lighter load of mules, that was on the point of being shipped, was driven out to sea and was lost.
>
> If only we could rely upon fine weather, we would of course be able to get off all our animals, but I dare not gamble with them against men's lives, and I feel I must take advantage of the first fine night to get away, and just destroy the remaining animals; but I mean to get off all I possibly can between now and the time of going. It will be a real load off my shoulders, and, if we succeed, Government should indeed be grateful for the efforts made by this force to see them through a very uncomfortable position.[81]

His worries, however, were mitigated somewhat by the close support of the squadron:

79 Callwell, *Maude*, p. 180.
80 RA GV/Q/2521/II/47.
81 Ibid.

> I am delighted to have Admiral de Robeck back here, and he has kindly come up here and made his headquarters alongside of me; we see each other daily to arrange about all details, as was the case with [Vice-Admiral] Wemyss before the other withdrawals. Admiral Fremantle is also here with two of the ships of his lately arrived squadron '*Hibernia*' and '*Russell*,' both of which I think are delighted to be here in time to join in, and we have been having some very successful shooting recently by them on the Turkish batteries on the Asiatic coast with I hope good result.[82]

The enemy, however, was not about to let the last of the invading force escape unscathed:

> On the afternoon of the 7th [January], the Turks suddenly developed a big attack on our right. They started with a very heavy bombardment with I fancy all their guns, and real intensive fire for four or five hours, knocking our trenches about a good deal, and I am sorry to say causing a certain amount of casualties in the 13th Division. Then we saw whole trenches fill up with men with fixed bayonets, and officers going along them evidently trying to induce them to charge. The men, however, appeared reluctant to do this except in one or two places, where small bodies of them left their trenches to come at us; but these were all either killed or wounded and no other attack matured. in the meantime our guns had of course opened on them, while the 'Edgar' and 'Wolverine' – a cruiser and a destroyer, who always keep off our left flank, got into them really well, the latter in fact using up the whole of her ammunition. The effect of this in crowded trenches, of which the ships knew the exact range, (for they have been on those particular targets for several months) must, I think we may take it, have created very considerable losses to the Turks and possibly this had the best of results for us.[83]

It was Maude's division that was attacked. He recorded the event in his diary:

> At 11:30 a.m. the Turks began shelling heavily all along the front and continued till 5:00 p.m. Those who have been at Helles the whole time say that it was the heaviest shelling that they have seen here. From 3:00 p.m. to 4:00 p.m. the shelling was intense, and at 3:45 p.m. the Turks opened heavy rifle fire. At 4:00 p.m. they sprung two mines near Fusilier Bluff, and at 4:15 p.m. they attacked Fifth Avenue and Fusilier Bluff resolutely. The attack was handsomely repulsed by the North Staffords, who however lost Walker, their colonel, one of our best commanding officers. The Turks tried to attack all along our front, but the officers could not get their men forward elsewhere. The Turks suffered heavily and division did splendidly, all battalions holding well to their position in spite of the fact that in many places their trenches were blown to pieces. Army Commander and Corps Commander both sent congratulatory messages. In spite of the fighting, brigades did well in getting their stuff away, including the packs which we are sending to Mudros tonight.[84]

82 Ibid.
83 Ibid.
84 Callwell, *Maude*, p. 182. See also J.M. Bourne's chapter elsewhere in this volume.

On this occasion, the weather was far less convenient for the purpose of putting thousands of men in range of enemy guns to sea in the middle of the night, as Birdwood explained the following day:

> Everything being settled for last night, the wind rather to our dismay began to rise about 7 o'clock. I went on board the flagship 'Lord Nelson' to join de Robeck, and we then went off on 'Chatham' to cruise up and down the position all night. I had been over to Helles during the day just to see that all final arrangements there were all fixed up, and that everybody was quite happy.
>
> The Admiral was of opinion that the wind would probably go down, and that in any case it was not sufficiently strong to warrant our putting off the operations, which of course we would not have done unless it looked really very bad. Several times during the night, when heavy squalls came on, our hearts rather jumped into our mouths, but, as when we evacuated "Anzac" and Suvla, Providence again stood by us, and saw us through all our difficulties. The work of the Navy was quite beyond praise, and for them the anxieties were tremendous as the rising wind of course made all their evacuations extremely difficult, and it only wanted to have been a little stronger to have probably made them impossible.
>
> To add to our anxieties, at about 10 p.m. we got a message from the right flank to say that a submarine was apparently coming down the straits on the surface. The Admiral was doubtful whether this was really the case, when half an hour later, the 'Prince George' (an old man-o-war now being temporarily used as a trooper) sent up two rockets, and signalled that she thought a torpedo had been fired at her, and that she had been hit, but not damaged. We at once started off full steam in pursuit, and cruised all about the place for an hour, but saw nothing, and you can imagine our relief on consequence, as the 'Prince George' had at the time 2,600 troops on board – but it made our anxieties none the less as 'Mars' with an equal number of men, and of course a large number of other ships were about.[85]

Major-General Maude had set up his divisional headquarters at Gully Beach at 5:00 p.m. in order to oversee the evacuation of most of his division:

> [S]o as to send detachments of 100, 200 and 400 ... forward to their forming-up place at W Beach, as 400 was a lighter-load. All were well up to time and numbers very accurate, which was very creditable considering yesterday's fighting and the immense amount of work which brigades have had to do cleaning up, getting orders out, etc. Indeed the embarkation people told me afterwards that this was the best division of the lot in getting away, and we scored consequently as we got a ship practically to ourselves for a very large part of the division. As night began to fall, the wind, which was in the south, began to freshen, and it looked as though there might be difficulties as regards embarkation. However all went well up to the departure of the last party from W Beach, and all were embarked at 11:00 p.m.[86]

85 RA GV/Q/2521/II/47.
86 Callwell, *Maude*, p. 183.

From then on, with the last men still to leave Cape Helles, the weather deteriorated further and Maude had to think on his feet lest he, along with them, be stranded on the peninsula:

> By 1:15 a.m., all the last detachments from the trenches, consisting of 555 all ranks, including R.E. [Royal Engineers] for closing gaps, control officers from control stations, etc., were all in at Gully Beach, and then the fun began.
>
> First, the lighters, of which there were to be two, were half an hour late. Secondly, one, in coming alongside the pier, ran aground and had to be abandoned. Thirdly, the two steamers provided for myself and staff were late. I decided to put as many as possible on the one lighter, and we got about 500 on, leaving still 135 to embark, including headquarters, R.E., R.A.M.C. [Royal Army Medical Corps], etc. Of these I had two pickets, consisting of one officer and 10 other ranks, out covering the beach. The embarkation on the lighter was very slow, and just as it was completed at 2:30 a.m. the Naval Transport Officer came to me and said that no further lighters were coming, that the sea was getting up, that the steamers could not take myself and my staff off, and that the rest of the troops and my divisional headquarters must go to W Beach to embark.[87]

Gully Beach was some two miles from W Beach, time was running out, the wind was rising and Maude and the remaining men under his command were isolated. They would also need to find gaps in the lines to get to their destination. Maude recalled:

> I realised that it might be a rush against time, for I did not know how soon W Beach would be cleared of the last lighter and it was then after 2:30 a.m., so I pulled in my pickets covering the beach and sent off the last remaining 135 men with 2 staff officers, hot foot, for W Beach. This left Hildyard, the A.D.M.S. [Assistant Director Medical Services] and myself and 12 men of my headquarters to dispose of. We had all the kit of headquarters with us, for which we had provided two steamboats, but as the horses had been shot and the vehicles destroyed, it was somewhat of a problem to get it along. Luckily however the A.D.M.S. remembered that there were three or four vehicle-stretchers lying handy, and these we got and loaded up. We could not go by the beach route as it was too heavy going, so we started uphill onto the plateau, and very hard work it was. We all puffed and blew like grampuses, especially as we were all warmly clad. I then sent Hildyard by the beach route to try and notify W Beach that we were going, and the A.D.M.S. and I and party pursued our weary way across the top. All went well until we came to the inner defences (except for an occasional fall in the dark), but, once there, we found that the garrison had been withdrawn and had embarked, and that the wire had been hermetically closed. One of the party however produced some wire cutters, rather like a pair of nail scissors, and after much hacking we managed to carve an opening. The Turks now began to pitch some shell about us which accelerated our movements a bit, and then we were again brought up by the inner defence trenches. As we could not get the stretchers over the ditch we had to abandon them and the very heavy stuff, and the men carried as much as they could over. Finally we reached W Beach, where Hildyard had obtained the last "Beetle," in which we made our

87 Ibid., p. 184.

> way at a slow rate and through heavy sea to Imbros, taking four and a half hours over the journey … Altogether it was an experience that I would not have missed for anything.[88]

"As the troops left," explained Birdwood, "all the dumps of supplies were set on fire, and formed huge bonfires which went on for hours with occasional tremendous explosions."[89] Maude watched the flames as he and his party made their way to Imbros. "It was a fine display of fire-works and we had a splendid view of them."[90] On the deck of HMS *Chatham*, an anonymous officer along "with everyone else heaved a very deep sigh of relief when from the quarter-deck … we saw flames from the stores shoot up and knew the last man had left Helles … If we had many wounded I was going ashore next day with a flag of truce (as I was to have done at Anzac) to bring them off if possible. Fortunately my services were not required."[91]

All things considered, Birdwood was thrilled with the final withdrawal from the peninsula:

> In spite of the weather, the Navy were able to stick to their original programme… The troops all got off on time, even though we had to abandon the use of one beach owing to the heavy swell running into it, and the men ready there had to be marched round about three miles to one of the other beaches … I am glad to say that we were able to get off more guns than I had at one time hoped for. We had to leave the good 6" gun, as it was essential to keep one long range gun up to the very last, and it was then impossible to move a big one like that. We, however, got away the whole of the howitzers, and only left ten of the old 15 pdr which may really be regarded as obsolescent weapons and of no value … The French are I think most awfully pleased not having had to sacrifice a single 75 and not to have suffered a single casualty … Our own casualties were one man wounded only, and he only slightly! By getting a real good hustle on about the animals during the last 24 hours, I am glad to say we were able to do much better than I had dared to hope for, and at the last we only had to leave behind 400 animals altogether, though even those I abandoned with the very greatest regret, and of course they were destroyed before the troops embarked – a horrible thing to think of, but a far better fate for them than falling into the hands of the Turks, to whom they would of course have been of the greatest value … We got off practically the whole of our ammunition, and though it was impossible to get all the transport carts away, we got off about half of them, and got away the wheels of the greater part of the remaining half, while naturally all those left behind were broken up. A considerable quantity of supplies naturally had to be left and all our hospitals that were left standing in the open, but, after all these (except perhaps the tents) cannot be of any great value to them for any length of time, while for the next few days the Navy will be bombarding them hard, and getting into Turks wherever they see a chance … The wonderful way in which we got off last night was due to the real good work put in by de Robeck and the Navy (with a wind at times of 42 miles an hour) and that of Davies and the 8th Corps Staff, who ran their show excellently, leaving precious little for me to do… I never dared to hope that we should get away with the complete immunity we did, because I always feared that there must be at all events some

88 Ibid., p. 185.
89 RA GV/Q/2521/II/47.
90 Callwell, *Maude*, p. 185.
91 RA GV/P/2116/28.

> losses in the last boats to leave, and I never dared buoy up Lord K with hopes that might be falsified by the weather, while if it was generally supposed that casualties would be heavy, and they were very slight, all would be the more pleased. The more I think of it, the more I do believe that we owe our immunity at Helles a good deal to the fact of the heavy Turkish attack 24 hours previously … when they probably made up their minds that we were going so strong that we could not contemplate going for a considerable time – further, they probably thought we should not attempt to leave on a night when it was blowing as hard as it then was, but that we would wait for calm weather.[92]

Birdwood realised now that he had truly come to the end of the Gallipoli campaign and hoped that after two separate evacuations that it would never fall to him to carry out such operations again:

> Now that it is all over, I am glad to think that I am probably one of the few remaining here, who actually landed on the Peninsula on our first day – the 25th April, and was still on it on the last – 8th January [1916], having had the good fortune to keep my health, and not having had to go away for a day. A few individuals of the 29th Division are I think the only other ones who can have done the same, as they are the only troops left here who landed on 25th April. The Naval Division have had a good long spell of it too, and have improved very much … Now I fancy I shall be off to Egypt almost immediately, and am quite looking forward to getting my boys together again – especially the Australians, from whom I hate to be separated … I now again feel a free man with no anxieties – but just a little done up, though only for a day or so.[93]

92 RA GV/Q/2521/II/47.
93 Ibid.

Part II

Command and Control

7

Shaping Operations: General Headquarters and the Gallipoli Campaign

Rhys Crawley

"The day-to-day organisation of an army for modern war is neither glamourous nor exciting. It does not fit well with traditional representations of martial skill, or valour."[1] And so Dan Todman opened his study of the British Expeditionary Force's General Headquarters (GHQ) in the First World War. Todman was correct: organisational histories focusing on the role, structure and experiences of those who served in GHQ don't feature on the best-seller list. Nor do they necessarily make for riveting reading. But that doesn't mean they are unimportant. Indeed, for one to appreciate the many acts of valour of the First World War, it helps to understand the context surrounding them. Why did a particular operation occur? How did it relate to other operations? And how did all those component parts relate to the wider strategy? The task of finding answers to such questions and conundrums fell to the commander in chief. After all, as *Field Service Regulations* (1914) made clear, the commander in chief was responsible "for the execution" of the government's strategic plans.[2] That is, it was his job – and in turn that of his staff at GHQ and his subordinates in the field – to transform the ideas and concepts of politicians into successful military outcomes.

This chapter grew out of this compendium's title: it seemed appropriate that a book on the Mediterranean Expeditionary Force (MEF) would have a chapter on how that force was run and organised. In the historiography of the Gallipoli campaign the role of GHQ is barely recognisable in the every-day hustle and bustle of battles and casualties. So, how did GHQ work? By what methods – and what measure of success – did it attempt to shape the strategy it had been dealt into workable operational plans? What did its own personnel think of GHQ's performance – either how it was run or who ran it? These are the types of questions that this chapter focuses on in its own attempt to provide a new perspective of the Gallipoli campaign more than a century after it was fought and failed. As such, this chapter examines what GHQ looked like,

1 Dan Todman, 'The Grand Lamasery revisited: General Headquarters on the Western Front, 1914-1918' in Gary Sheffield & Dan Todman (eds.), *Command and Control on the Western Front: The British Army's experience 1914-18* (Gloucestershire: Spellmount, 2007), p. 39.

2 War Office, *Field Service Regulations*, Part 2: *Organization and Administration* (London: HMSO, 1914), p. 22. Hereafter *FSR2*.

who its people were, what its functions were, and how it performed. In essence, the chapter aims to do for Gallipoli what Todman did for our understanding of GHQ on the Western Front.

Origins

Symptomatic of most that would follow in this campaign, the origins and composition of the MEF was anything but organised or ordinary. To attack the Dardanelles with a joint naval and military force had been discussed and debated since the outbreak of war in 1914.[3] But it wasn't until 11 March 1915 – well after combined British and French naval forces had commenced offensive operations against the Ottoman coastal defences at the Dardanelles; and the day after Britain had decided to send a military formation, the 29th Division, to the Mediterranean in case it was needed to support this fleet – that Lord Kitchener, Britain's Secretary of State for War, ordered the establishment of the MEF and its GHQ.[4]

The next morning, Friday 12 March, General Sir Ian Hamilton – Commander-in-Chief of Central Force (later known as Home Forces)[5] and regarded by the Germans as the most experienced soldier in the world[6] – was summoned to the War Office from his headquarters at Horse Guards, Whitehall, to see Kitchener, his old chief from the Boer War.[7] Hamilton entered Kitchener's office, "bade him good morning" and, after a brief pause Kitchener "looked up and said in a matter-of-fact tone, 'We are sending a military force to support the Fleet now at the Dardanelles, and you are to have Command'."[8] Kitchener's advice was unambiguous. He warned Hamilton against landing any permanent forces on what he accurately predicted to be the well-defended Gallipoli Peninsula. Ideally, from Kitchener's perspective, the MEF – approximately 75,000 strong – would not be used until the ships of the Eastern Mediterranean Squadron (EMS) had forced their way through the Dardanelles defences; or if they failed. "The employment of military forces on any large scale for land operations at this junction is only contemplated in the event of the Fleet failing to get through [the Narrows] after a serious loss of ships," he instructed.[9] Kitchener's strategic intent was similarly clear. The goal was the Ottoman capital, Constantinople, and Hamilton should save his troops and employ them against the

3 For these early discussions see Cecil Aspinall-Oglander, *Military Operations Gallipoli*, Vol. I (Nashville, Tennessee: Battery Press 1992 reprint of 1928 edition), Chapter 3.

4 Ibid., pp. 86-88. It appears that Kitchener first toyed with the idea of calling it the Constantinople Expeditionary Force but settled on Mediterranean Expeditionary Force on 13 March. See Ian Hamilton, *Gallipoli Diary*, Vol. I (London: Edward Arnold, 1920), p. 15.

5 A.F. Becke, *Order of Battle of Divisions, Part 4: The Army Council, GHQs, Armies, and Corps 1914-1918* (Uckfield: Naval & Military Press reprint of 1945 edition), p. 7.

6 John Lee, 'Sir Ian Hamilton, Walter Braithwaite and the Dardanelles', *Journal of the Centre for First World War Studies*, 1:1 (July 2004), p. 41.

7 For more on Hamilton's background see: John Lee, *A Soldier's life: General Sir Ian Hamilton 1853-1947* (London: Pan Books, 2000).

8 Hamilton, *Gallipoli Diary*, Vol. 1, p. 2.

9 Liddell Hart Centre for Military Archives (LHCMA): Hamilton 7/4/3: Instructions, 12 March 1915. The wording was slightly different in the official instructions issued on 13 March, which, instead of "serious loss of ships" said "every effort has been exhausted." See The National Archives (TNA): CAB 17/123: 'Instructions for the General Officer Commanding-in-Chief the Mediterranean Expeditionary Force', 13 March 1915.

strategic prize: to "surround Constantinople and reduce the place to surrender by starvation."[10] It was imperative that the "force must not therefore be fritted away by land operations in the Gallipoli Peninsula merely to save the risk of ships being hit by the enemy's shell fire."[11] "The essential point," Kitchener stipulated, "is to avoid a check which will jeopardize our chances of strategical and political success."[12]

A topic that surfaced during their conversation was who would be appointed chief of the general staff (CGS): the officer responsible for leading the staff, and the chief's "responsible adviser on all matters affecting military operations."[13] Hamilton wanted his then chief of staff, Major-General Gerald Ellison, with whom he had "worked hand in glove for several years" to join him. But Kitchener could not spare him and instead appointed the War Office's Director of Staff Duties, Major-General Walter Braithwaite. Like Braithwaite, the rest of Hamilton's staff were selected for him, and most were unknown to him.[14] It was a ridiculous situation imposed by two realities: the best and most experienced staff officers were already on the Western Front; and the haste with which this new GHQ was expected to leave England for its new theatre. Hamilton was not the only one trying to come to terms with his new appointment and the task ahead. As he later reminisced:

> My Staff still bear the bewildered look of men who have hurriedly been snatched from desks to do some extraordinary turn on some unheard-of theatre. One or two of them put on uniform for the first time in their lives an hour ago. Leggings awry, spurs upside down, belts over shoulder straps! I haven't a notion of who they all are …[15]

One of those to whom he was referring was Orlando ("Orlo") Williams. A clerk in the House of Commons, Williams had plans to enlist in the Royal Naval Division. That changed when, at 8:00 p.m. on 11 March, it was suggested he join the MEF as a cipher officer. In the 28 hours between his appointment and GHQ's hurried departure from London, Williams visited the War Office, was appointed a temporary captain, purchased his uniform from Harrods, dined with his wife, packed his things, farewelled his mother and younger sisters and caught a cab to Charing Cross train station.[16] There, at 5:00 p.m. on 13 March, Williams – along with Hamilton and 12 other members of the staff (plus an assortment of servants and clerks) – were seen off by family members and officials.[17] Amongst the crowd were two prominent individuals:

10 Ibid.
11 LHCMA: Hamilton 7/4/3: Instructions, 12 March 1915.
12 TNA CAB 17/123: 'Instructions for the General Officer Commanding-in-Chief the Mediterranean Expeditionary Force', 13 March 1915.
13 *FSR2*, p. 38.
14 Hamilton, *Gallipoli Diary*, Vol. I, pp. 7, 19.
15 Ibid., p. 16.
16 Imperial War Museum (IWM): 69/78/1: Williams Papers, Diary, 13 March 1915.
17 GHQ staff accompanying Hamilton on HMS *Foresight* were: Major-General Walter Braithwaite, Lieutenant-Colonel Montagu Ward, Lieutenant-Colonel Weir de Lancey Williams, Major Cuthbert Fuller, Captain Cecil Aspinall, Major Henry Grant, Captain Guy Dawnay, Captain Charles Bolton, Captain Stephen Pollen, Lieutenant George St John Brodrick, Second Lieutenant Val Braithwaite, Major Jack Churchill, and Captain Orlo Williams. In addition to the thirteen staff there were six clerks, four privates and seven troopers, servants and batmen. See Australian War Memorial (AWM): AWM4, 1/4/1 part 1: General Staff GHQ War Diary, 13 March 1915. Three members of

The Earl of Midleton – a Conservative politician who had been Secretary of State for War during the Boer War and was now Leader of the Irish Unionists – whose son, George, was one of Hamilton's aides-de-camp; and Winston Churchill, First Lord of the Admiralty (and one of the main proponents for naval and military action at the Dardanelles) whose brother, "Jack" was the camp commandant.[18]

After arriving in Dover and a brief passage across the English Channel on HMS *Foresight*, the staff caught another train to Marseilles, where they boarded HMS *Phaeton* for the long journey to the Dardanelles. They arrived off the island of Tenedos, where the fleet was stationed, just after 3:00 p.m. on 17 March. Almost immediately, Hamilton went on board HMS *Queen Elizabeth* where the commander of the EMS, Vice-Admiral John de Robeck, impressed upon Hamilton his determination "to exhaust every effort before calling for military assistance." Such determination, as history attests, did not endure. The next day the fleet suffered a major defeat and de Robeck soon turned to Hamilton for help; just over a month later the MEF landed on the Gallipoli Peninsula.[19] Before we progress to what GHQ did in those intervening weeks and the months that followed, however, it's first necessary to explain GHQ's role, its structure, and introduce some of its people.

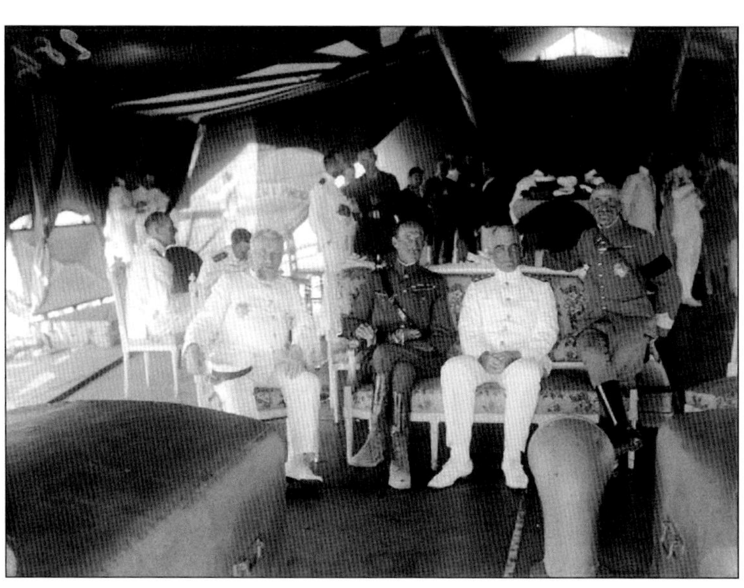

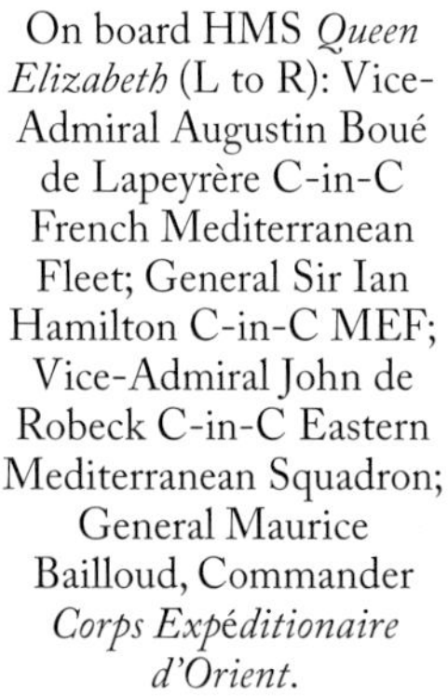

On board HMS *Queen Elizabeth* (L to R): Vice-Admiral Augustin Boué de Lapeyrère C-in-C French Mediterranean Fleet; General Sir Ian Hamilton C-in-C MEF; Vice-Admiral John de Robeck C-in-C Eastern Mediterranean Squadron; General Maurice Bailloud, Commander *Corps Expéditionaire d'Orient*.

the Intelligence section, Lieutenant-Colonel Charles Doughty-Wylie, Captain Wyndham Deedes and Captain Ian Smith joined GHQ on 18 March. See AWM: AWM4, 1/4/1 part 1: General Staff GHQ War Diary, 18 March 1915.

18 Hamilton, *Gallipoli Diary*, Vol. I, p. 16; IWM: 69/78/1: Williams Papers, Diary, 13 March 1915.

19 Rhys Crawley, 'The landing – plan and overview', in David Horner (ed.), *Gallipoli 100: Lest We Forget* (Sydney: Faircount Media, 2014), pp. 86-89.

Composition

The MEF was the third army-level GHQ established by Britain in the First World War.[20] GHQ's role, as in other theatres, was to manage the land war in that theatre.[21] British doctrine stipulated that GHQ's staff were to assist the commander in chief "in the supervision and control of the operations and requirements of the troops."[22] As the headquarters supporting the chief, GHQ was therefore charged with transforming their boss's visions into reality – to understand and "convey his will" to subordinates through plans and orders, to coordinate and administer the actions of lower formations and supporting elements, and to provide him with expert advice: their job, in essence, was to mirror his intent and shape and enable operations.[23]

Stipulated also in doctrine was the organisation of the staff, which was broken into three branches – the General Staff Branch (G); the Adjutant General's Branch (A); and the Quartermaster General's Branch (Q).[24] It is important to note that GHQ consisted of more than these three branches. In early April 1915, for example, MEF GHQ also had two technical experts attached to advise on artillery and engineer matters: Brigadier-Generals Richard Fuller (the Brigadier-General, Royal Artillery, or BGRA) and Alexander Roper (the Brigadier-General, Royal Engineers, or BGRE). There were 13 "special appointments" including a Royal Navy officer, two special service officers, two French liaison officers with the British and two British liaison officers with the French corps headquarters, three interpreters, the camp commandant, the censor and the provost marshal. GHQ also had two representatives of the administrative services and departments (the actual headquarters of administrative services and departments, which accounted for 24 officers – such as the Directors of Army Signals, Supplies and Transport, Ordnance Services, Works, Medical Services, Veterinary Services, and their supporting officers – supported but were not officially part of GHQ).[25] Then there were the "personal appointments", such as aides-de-camp, who sat outside the "staff" but were nonetheless part of GHQ.[26] Overall responsibility for coordinating the work of all three branches and other attached officers lay with the commander in chief, but this was generally – as was the case in the Dardanelles – delegated to the CGS.[27]

20 The British Expeditionary Force (BEF) and the British Forces in Egypt preceded it. By "army-level" we mean that it was the formation headquarters above corps-level. Edward J. Erickson, *Gallipoli: Command Under Fire* (Oxford: Osprey, 2015), p. 82.

21 For a discussion of the roles and responsibilities of a GHQ see 'The British General Headquarters of 1914-1918', *The Long, Long Trail* <www.1914-1918.net/ghq.htm> (Accessed, 12 February 2017). GHQ had no bearing on the naval campaign, which was the responsibility of the EMS and the Admiralty.

22 *FSR2*, p. 37.

23 Ibid., p. 25.

24 Ibid., p. 38.

25 LHCMA: Hamilton 7/4/17: 'Composition of the Headquarters of the Mediterranean Expeditionary Force', 6 April 1915. The details of GHQ staff (i.e. names and numbers) here and in the subsequent paragraphs of this section represent a snapshot of GHQ in the lead-up to the April landings. Personnel and GHQ's internal structures changed as the situation demanded, as people left, were promoted or, in some cases, were killed.

26 *FSR2*, pp. 42–43.

27 Ibid., p. 38.

MEF GHQ had most of the key positions as those in the BEF GHQ at the outbreak of war, although at Gallipoli roles were predominately at a rank one removed from those on the Western Front (the CGS in France, for example, was a lieutenant-general whereas he was a major-general in the MEF).[28] Hamilton's key staff officers were Braithwaite; the Deputy Adjutant General (DAG), Brigadier-General Edward Woodward, who ran the A staff; and the Deputy Quartermaster General (DQMG), Brigadier-General Samuel Winter, who was responsible for Q Branch.[29] Woodward had been Director of Mobilisation at the War Office when war broke out; Winter had worked as Hamilton's DQMG in Central Force for seven months before Hamilton's departure, during which time he "had displayed business acumen and business courage."[30] As with Braithwaite, the latter two were a rank lower than their equivalents on the Western Front (where, as major-generals, they were titled the Adjutant General and Quartermaster General).[31]

The General Staff Branch, which Braithwaite personally oversaw, consisted of the Intelligence and Operations sections plus attached officers. Its total strength in the lead-up to the April landings was 16.[32] The five-strong Intelligence section, under Lieutenant-Colonel Montagu Ward – an artillery officer who had spent his career in home defence and whose intelligence credentials were not clear to his staff – was responsible for understanding the enemy and the environment.[33] Its job was to inform the planning process with a deep and nuanced understanding of the enemy's whereabouts, intent and capabilities, and to do what they could to prevent the enemy learning about allied intent and capabilities.[34] The section was broken into four sub-sections, each staffed by one officer: I(a) "Information"; I(b) "Secret Service"; I(c) "Topography"; and I(d) "Censorship." Perhaps the only sub-section whose function is not clear from its name was I(b), which was responsible for conducting espionage and running networks of agents.[35] Ward's subordinate staff officers included Lieutenant-Colonel Charles Doughty-Wylie, Captain Wyndham Deedes, Captain Eden Powell, Lieutenant Tressilian Nicholas (a geologist who was attached for topography work), and Major Addis Delacombe, an Army Pay Department officer tasked with working the section's account.[36] In early April Lieutenant Eddie Keeling, a diplomatic secretary in the Cairo Residency was attached to G Branch as an additional cipher officer to work

28 For comparisons between the BEF and MEF GHQ structures see Becke, *Order of Battle*, pp. 7-9, 45-46.

29 Erickson, *Gallipoli*, p. 82.

30 TNA CAB 19/33: Evidence of Woodward to the Dardanelles Commission, 24 January 1917; evidence of Winter to the Dardanelles Commission, 4 January 1917. Hamilton's assessment of Winter is in LHCMA: Hamilton 8/1/46: Hamilton to Grimwood Mears, 24 May 1917.

31 Becke, *Order of Battle*, pp. 12, 45.

32 LHCMA: Hamilton 7/4/17: 'Composition of the Headquarters of the Mediterranean Expeditionary Force', 6 April 1915.

33 Compton Mackenzie, *Gallipoli Memories* (London: Cassell, 1929), p. 52.

34 For a short history of the role of intelligence at Gallipoli see Rhys Crawley, 'Most Secret', *Wartime*, 70 (Autumn 2015), pp. 18-22.

35 Jim Beach, *Haig's Intelligence: GHQ and the German Army 1916-1918* (Cambridge: Cambridge University Press, 2015), pp. 28-30; LHCMA: Hamilton 7/4/17: 'Composition of the Headquarters of the Mediterranean Expeditionary Force', 6 April 1915.

36 LHCMA: Hamilton 7/4/17: 'Composition of the Headquarters of the Mediterranean Expeditionary Force', 6 April 1915.

mainly with the Intelligence section. His counterpart, the previously mentioned Captain Orlo Williams, mainly worked with the Operations section.[37]

Operations section was commanded by Lieutenant-Colonel Weir de Lancey Williams who had spent most of his active life in India. Unless otherwise specially arranged, orders were drafted and distributed by this section (where, for example, Intelligence section required specific information, they asked Operations section who could then issue orders for special reconnaissance). Operations section was further broken into two sub-sections, O(a) and O(b). Generally speaking, officers in O(a) were responsible for drafting statements, orders, instructions and the like, which were then duplicated and distributed to branches and subordinate commands by O(b). Staff duties differed between jobs and each officer had their own defined tasks: some of those included keeping Williams appraised of information that may affect operations; managing information, such as messages received and orders circulated, so that it was at hand for planning purposes; advising Williams where appropriate; liaising with other branches and experts and incorporating their material into plans and orders; and, where required by Williams or his superiors, being sent out on "roving commissions" in the field.[38] His staff officers included Captain Cecil Aspinall, Captain Guy Dawnay, and Captain Charles Bolton all in O(a), and Major Cuthbert Fuller and Major Henry Grant in O(b).

The Adjutant General's and Quartermaster General's branches were smaller and, in a throwback to the lower priority afforded them since the Victorian era, were coordinated by the General Staff.[39] Functionally, the A staff dealt with personnel matters including appointments, promotions, discipline, unit organisation, medals and awards, pay, medical and chaplaincy. Q staff were responsible for logistics, including supply, transport, and equipment.[40] Supporting Woodward in A Branch were four staff officers: Lieutenant-Colonel Henry Beynon (Assistant Adjutant General), two Deputy Assistant Adjutant Generals (DAAG), Major Thomas Cox and Captain Arthur Egerton, and Captain Donald MacLeod (staff captain), and a 3rd Echelon headquarters of seven officers at Alexandria, which maintained the base personnel records.[41] Winter was supported by three officers in Q Branch: Lieutenant-Colonel Lancelot Beadon (Assistant Quartermaster-General, or AQMG), and two Deputy Assistant Quartermaster-Generals (DAQMGs), Major Ernest Gascoigne and Captain Frank Dunlop.[42] As discussed below, the lower status afforded the A and Q branches, their late arrival in theatre, and their physical separation from the G staff, affected GHQ's performance and the quality of its plans and preparations.

37 IWM: 69/78/1: Williams Papers, Diary, 26 March and 4 April 1915.
38 Isle of Wight Country Record Office (IoW): OG/AO/G/10: Aspinall-Oglander Papers, 'Duties of operations section, O (a)', n.d., pp. 1-2.
39 Tim Travers, 'Command and leadership styles in the British Army: The 1915 Gallipoli Model', *Journal of Contemporary History*, 29:3 (July 1994), pp. 411-12.
40 'Staff officers – Great War Forum' <http://1914-1918.invisionzone.com> (Accessed 26 September 2007); *FSR2*, pp. 44–48.
41 LHCMA: Hamilton 7/4/17: 'Composition of the Headquarters of the Mediterranean Expeditionary Force', 6 April 1915.
42 Ibid.

Performance

The resounding failure of the 18 March naval actions, which sunk or destroyed one third of de Robeck's warships, left the admiral convinced that he'd be sacked from a job that he was less than a week into. Over the next few days he concluded that the fleet could not succeed without military assistance.[43] Hamilton was having similar thoughts. After witnessing the naval fiasco, he told Kitchener: "I am being most reluctantly driven towards the conclusion that the Dardanelles are less likely to be forced by battleships than at one time seemed probable." At a conference in the flagship HMS *Queen Elizabeth* on the morning of 22 March both Hamilton and de Robeck agreed that the army was required to land and hold the peninsula. A new joint strategy was thus developed, and the Gallipoli land campaign was born.[44]

On 24 March, Hamilton and his staff sailed from Mudros Bay for Egypt, where the majority of the MEF's troops were then training. After spending a few days in Cairo, the staff moved to Alexandria, where they spent most of 29 March setting up GHQ. "It is an old house," wrote one officer, with no drainage, lights, or running water, and "the first day some of the staff visited the place they were severely assailed by fleas." The Operations section of G Branch, which was tasked with drawing up the plans for the forthcoming landing, established itself in a large room on the first floor; maps of Gallipoli were spread in the middle of the room. They worked from 9:00 a.m. until nearly 8:00 p.m. each day. These were the conditions under which Hamilton's skeleton staff tried to transform an unrealistic and over optimistic grand strategy into a workable military operation.[45]

The Operations staff got to work straight away and, as Orlo Williams attests, frictions were already beginning to show before the month was out:

> They have got a tremendously complicated and difficult piece of staff work before them to do very quickly. They have got to work out very carefully exactly how the force is to be embarked, how its supply etc. is to be managed, what special fittings and arrangements are necessary in view of the special problem of the Gallipoli peninsula. Also, there is the problem of the landing of the covering force, to be formed by the 29th Division. Capt. Mitchell, RN is attached to the staff to assist in naval matters and they are all deep in details of tugs, tows, lighters and horse boats. How many men each will hold, how long the round trip will take, how horses, bicycles, transport, guns and ammunition are to be landed and in what order. The plan is to land on the point of Cape Helles I believe. I rather gather that Aspinall and Co. find Col. Williams the GSO1 rather in the way.[46]

For his part, Lieutenant-Colonel Williams (no relation to Orlo) was clearly frustrated with the situation and the planning process. On 1 April he complained to his staff that "all possibility of surprise is gone." Much of the planning, he insisted, should have been undertaken in England.[47]

43 IWM: 69/61/2: Rayfield Papers, 'The decision to substitute a combined operation for the naval attack'.
44 Crawley, 'The landing – plan and overview', p. 87.
45 Ibid.
46 IWM: 69/78/1: Williams Papers, Diary, 30 March 1915.
47 Ibid., 1 April 1915.

One of the challenges GHQ faced in planning for the first amphibious operation of modern war was that there was not a full complement of staff on which to draw for input or expertise. Indeed, the speed with which the MEF was stood up had the undesirable outcome of splitting GHQ's branches. While most of the General Staff was ready to – and did – depart with Hamilton, the A and Q branches didn't. In fact, when he left London Hamilton still did not know who his senior logistician or senior medical officer would be.[48] As it happened, Brigadier-General Winter wasn't informed of his selection as Hamilton's Deputy Quartermaster General until the day his counterparts left London (despite the fact that he was already Hamilton's DQMG at Central Force, and that Hamilton had requested him for the job). He then had to select his subordinates and organise his branch which, along with the A Branch staff under Brigadier-General Woodward (who had similarly rounded up his team), the BGRE (Roper) and the BGRA (Fuller), left Paddington station for Avonmouth at 2:40 p.m. on 20 March. At 9:30 p.m. they boarded HMT *Arcadian* for their destination; they arrived at Alexandria, via Gibraltar and Malta, on the morning of 1 April. Some officers disembarked that afternoon, with the remainder going ashore the following morning.[49]

HMT *Arcadian*. (J. Serven)

By the time of their arrival the crux of the plan had already been determined. Rather than the three branches collaborating for the betterment of the plan, almost all details for the landing – including the administrative and logistics aspects – were calculated by the Operations staff. These officers were too busy to do a proper job, and, as Woodward – who was primarily responsible for medical arrangements – later said, they "have not sufficient knowledge of what to do."[50] Winter had expressed such concerns within days of his arrival, writing in the official war diary

48 Hamilton, *Gallipoli Diary*, Vol. I, p. 19.
49 TNA WO 95/4266: DQMG GHQ War Diary, 5 April 1915; AWM: AWM4, 1/4/1 part 1: General Staff GHQ War Diary, 1 April 1915; IWM: 69/78/1: Williams Papers, Diary, 1 April 1915.
50 TNA CAB 19/33: Evidence of Woodward to Dardanelles Committee, 24 January 1917.

that some of the administrative arrangements made by the General Staff were not as he or his staff would have done it. Although Winter managed to regain responsibility for some of these aspects, he nonetheless noted that: "It would have been advantageous if it could have been arranged for the Q and A officers to arrive here at the same time as the GS."[51] The British official historian, Cecil Aspinall-Oglander, himself a member of the General Staff, later concluded that "the separation of his [Hamilton's] Staff caused by this necessarily hurried departure was a misfortune from which the Expeditionary Force never quite recovered."[52]

Their staggered arrival was not the only problem. On disembarking in Alexandria Q Branch, for example, not only had to set up shop in a different location to the General Staff, but it had to split its own staff between the Hotel d'Angleterre and Hotel Metropole.[53] Even worse, however, was the fact that on 2 April – as the A and Q staff were unloading their gear – it was decided to establish GHQ on board HMT *Arcadian*, the very ship they had just left.[54] Adding insult to injury, Braithwaite instructed both branches to remain in Alexandria to help the French division get ready for its part in the landing.[55] On 7 April Hamilton, Braithwaite, the General Staff and the BGRA and BGRE boarded *Arcadian* for Mudros Harbour, where the force was assembling in preparation for the landing.[56] Separating the staff again "was a very great handicap", in the words of one Q Branch officer; his colleagues had only just started to "pick up the ropes" when their counterparts "went on to Mudros … and left us in Alexandria."[57]

Drawing upon a variety of intelligence sources – including aerial and sea-based reconnaissance, and the regional expertise of some of the Intelligence section personnel – the General Staff further developed their plans and prepared timetables for the landing. As before, A and Q branches were barely consulted. When they were, they couldn't read or respond to anything sensitive because all of the cipher officers, who could decode the encrypted telegrams, had sailed with GHQ. Lieutenant-General William Birdwood, commander of the Australian and New Zealand Army Corps (ANZAC), wrote that the decision to leave A and Q behind in Egypt was "unfortunate", as neither Hamilton nor Braithwaite "seem to have considered … the difficulties of supply, transport, etc." When A and Q and the rest of GHQ did eventually arrive in Mudros Harbour on 18 April, the orders for the landings, "minus dates and times", had already been issued to senior commanders.[58] Winter once again commented on the problem of splitting the branches for the second time:

> The experience of the past 10 days has shewn [sic] the advisability, if not necessity, for some member, at least, of the Q Staff remaining with GS and vice-versa, in the event of such a necessity unfortunately arising as the separation of the two Staffs, otherwise contradictory and duplicated instructions are bound to be issued, misapprehensions arise,

51 TNA WO 95/4266: DQMG GHQ War Diary, 5 April 1915.
52 Aspinall-Oglander, *Military Operations Gallipoli*, Vol. I, p. 89.
53 TNA WO 95/4266: DQMG GHQ War Diary, 17 March-4 April 1915.
54 Ibid.
55 Ibid., 7 April 1915. There is a conflicting account that Hamilton, not Braithwaite, ordered the DQMG and DAG to remain in Alexandria. See TNA CAB 19/33: Evidence of Woodward to Dardanelles Committee, 24 January 1917.
56 TNA WO 95/4266: DQMG GHQ War Diary, 7 April 1915.
57 TNA CAB 19/33: Evidence of Beadon to Dardanelles Committee, 26 January 1917.
58 Crawley, 'The landing – plan and overview', pp. 87-88.

and considerable delays are caused. Moreover, the close touch which should be maintained between the two Branches is broken temporarily and it is difficult to fill up the hiatus afterwards.[59]

The story of the landings, which occurred one week later – on 25 April 1915 – is told elsewhere in this book. What GHQ did during those operations, however, is less well known.

Unsurprisingly, given its track record, the staffs were again split. The General Staff, the BGRA, and assorted others joined Hamilton and de Robeck on HMS *Queen Elizabeth*; some went ashore (as discussed below); but the rest of GHQ, including A and Q, stayed on *Arcadian* where, because of restrictions placed on using her wireless, they remained largely out of touch while the landings unfolded (transport ships, of which *Arcadian* was one, were not permitted to use wireless during the operations. Flag signalling was therefore the only means of communicating between ships).[60] *Arcadian* remained alongside *Queen Elizabeth* until sundown on 25 April, when she returned alone to Tenedos Island. After a brief return to the Dardanelles the next morning *Arcadian* was again ordered back to Tenedos and, for all intents and purposes, remained separated from Hamilton and the General Staff until the evening of 27 April. Throughout that time, as Winter noted, both the A and Q staffs had "great difficulty in getting communication with the *Queen Elizabeth*."[61]

For those on *Queen Elizabeth* the landing was a period of intense activity. Progress reports came in from each of the sectors – Helles, Anzac and Kum Kale – and the staff did what they could to keep Hamilton appraised of the situation ashore, convey the general's desires to his commanders, while simultaneously informing London about their achievements and setbacks. Orlo Williams's diary records the trying and cramped conditions of working on board *Queen Elizabeth* while her 15-inch guns thundered above them. He was so busy deciphering and replying to telegrams during the first two days that the war diary, for which he was also responsible, was not filled until 27 April, when he and a colleague "worked for 6 hours in our shirtsleeves in the wireless man's cabins. The heat was sweltering and the 15" guns shook the whole place."[62]

Orlo's diary also records the feeling of some on the staff that actions ashore would have been better coordinated if an advanced GHQ had been established on the peninsula as soon as practicable. This, they argued, would have improved communications between GHQ and Hamilton's tactical commanders. As it stood, they believed, a floating GHQ both meant they were physically separated from the battle and entirely at the whim of the ships' commanders.[63] The reality of the situation, however, was that with troops established at numerous sectors on the peninsula, each separated by enemy-controlled terrain, *Queen Elizabeth* offered the only means by which Hamilton could confer with the admiral while simultaneously exercise control (or visibility, at the very least) of the entire land force; if he'd established GHQ ashore he would have lost contact with the other sectors.

59 TNA WO 95/4266: DQMG GHQ War Diary, 16 April 1915.
60 TNA CAB 19/33: Evidence of Woodward to Dardanelles Committee, 24 January 1917.
61 TNA WO 95/4266: DQMG GHQ War Diary, 24-27 April 1915.
62 IWM: 69/78/1: Williams Papers, Diary, 25-27 April 1915.
63 Ibid., 11 May 1915 and Orlando C. Williams, 'The Gallipoli Tragedy: Part One', *The Nineteenth Century and After*, No. 106 (July 1929), p. 89.

That is not to suggest that GHQ was disengaged. Indeed, GHQ officers were scattered across the landing beaches performing a range of roles. At V Beach – Cape Helles – for example, Brigadier-General Roper (the BGRE) served as the Principal Military Landing Officer (PMLO), in which capacity he was responsible for receiving and safe-guarding stores and supplies. Captain Frank Dunlop from Q Branch worked as his staff officer. Lieutenant-Colonel Williams and Captain Bolton, both from the Operations section, represented GHQ ashore and were tasked with marking forming up places, arranging for communications, keeping Braithwaite informed, and assisting the 29th Division where required; and Lieutenant-Colonel Doughty-Wylie and a junior officer went ashore to conduct intelligence studies. Captains Ian Smith and George Lloyd of the General Staff were similarly despatched to Z Beach – Gaba Tepe – for intelligence duties.[64] As Doughty-Wylie's case shows, these officers shared the same dangers as others on the peninsula. Having landed from the collier, SS *River Clyde*, he was killed while leading a series of attacks on 26 April; he was posthumously awarded the Victoria Cross for his actions on that day.[65]

By the end of the month GHQ was back together on the *Arcadian*.[66] Its existence as a floating headquarters, however, did not last much longer. Reports of the presence of German submarines caused GHQ to reconsider where and how it operated. Early discussions considered establishing a small GHQ at Cape Helles, but the dangers of this option, which would see Hamilton permanently within the range and sights of the enemy's guns, quickly ruled it out. Instead, at sunset on 12 May *Arcadian* left the coast of the Gallipoli Peninsula for Tenedos Island, where GHQ intended to set up camp on shore. At nightfall on 14 May, after most of the kit and stores had been unloaded and carried a mile inland, the staff was told that despite the work already underway, GHQ would instead move to Imbros Island. They steamed the next morning. Sitting on board ship in Kephalos Harbour again put GHQ largely out of touch, both with London and the front. Some of the staff managed to get ashore and have a look around the island on 17 May but had to go back to *Arcadian* at night. They dared not unpack their kit until things looked more certain; eventually a decision was made and the staff went ashore on the afternoon of 31 May.[67] Orlo Williams described his surroundings in his diary that evening:

> GHQ camp in a pleasant position on the low spit which curves round into Kephalo Point. Soil of the camp sandy covered with stubbly grass and here and there a few patches of corn. Officers' lines 4 rows of tents, and mens' lines run out at right angles. A few marques for office, and 3 marques as mess tents. The General has a little camp to himself by the one poor tree. The view of the hills of Imbros beyond the bay from here is very beautiful. On the southern side of the island sand dunes leading down to sandy beach made very nice bathing place.[68]

64 AWM: AWM4, 1/4/1 part 2: 'Allotment of General Headquarters for the operations', and 'Instructions for General Staff officers of General Headquarters landing on the 1st day of operations', 20 April 1915. Captain Lloyd (later Lord Lloyd of Dolobran), who was fluent in Turkish, joined GHQ as a special service officer and was placed in the Intelligence section. IWM: 69/78/1: Williams Papers, Diary, 26 March 1915. For an example of the messages these officers sent back to GHQ see Erickson, *Gallipoli*, pp. 126-28.

65 Peter Hart, *Gallipoli* (London: Profile Books, 2011), pp. 162-67.

66 IWM: 69/78/1: Williams Papers, Diary, 29 April 1915.

67 Ibid., 11-17, 28-31 May 1915.

68 Ibid., 31 May 1915.

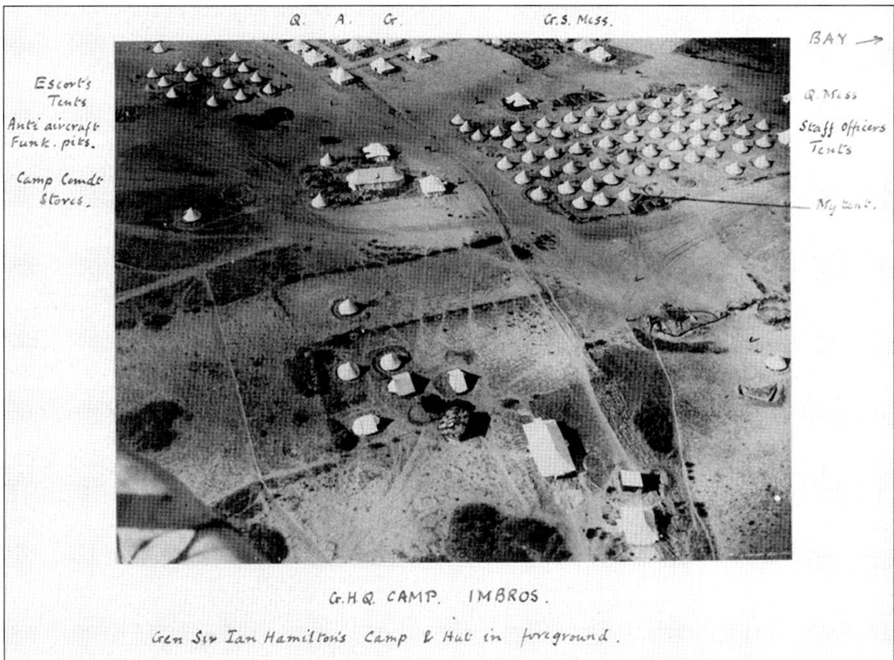

MEF headquarters, Imbros 1915: Hamilton's camp is visible in the foreground. The bell tents (top right) accommodated staff officers. (NAM 1965-10-209-22)

Within three weeks a casualty clearing station, field bakery, engineer base, and a camp for 4,000 men had sprung up where the cornfields were.[69] GHQ was thus established, but so too were many of its internal problems. It was also becoming clear to those GHQ personnel who spent time on the peninsula that officers and men were growing in their criticism of how GHQ was performing: they felt GHQ was failing to adequately support them with operational direction or the provision of basic necessities.[70]

Personalities

Undoubtedly underlying some of these problems were the stresses posed by the campaign's early failures, and the ever-present need to find an answer to the morass caused by staunch Ottoman defence. In the gripes shared between staff, however, the more common themes were structural deficiencies within GHQ itself, personality clashes, and the performance of their superiors.

Orlo Williams's diary, which has been referred to many times already in this chapter, provides the best insight into GHQ during this period. In mid-May, while pacing *Arcadian*'s deck, he and Eddie Keeling "compared notes" on GHQ's "internal politics." "Both of us, not being soldiers," Orlo wrote,

69 Ibid., 22 June 1915.
70 Ibid., 30 June 1915.

"are made recipients of the others' grievances, and there are a great many of them." GHQ gossip was recorded in his diary on a daily basis. Woodward, for example, was unhappy with Braithwaite who, Woodward felt, kept leaving him behind and failing to take him into his confidence; Winter was "worried to death" about camp infrastructure and logistic routes; and the Intelligence section of G Branch "quarrels all day with itself." Keeling, who did cypher work for the section, described to Orlo the "violent discussions" between the Intelligence staff, all of whom proclaimed to know the enemy better than each other.[71] Lieutenant-Colonel Ward, the head of the section, felt wronged by Braithwaite who he believed was breaking protocol by regularly calling for Ward's junior officer, Captain Deedes, over Ward.[72] Orlo understood why: Deedes was fluent in Turkish, was responsible for the hardest work, essentially ran the section, and would be Orlo's pick if there was ever a wager on who best knew the enemy.[73] For his part, Deedes "would have a good many people sacked if he could." Deedes was particularly concerned by Ward's "apathy" and his unwillingness to do anything about the "inertia" of his subordinates in the Intelligence section.[74] Others in the section were likewise dissatisfied with Ward's performance. Lloyd thought him "pigheaded", while Compton Mackenzie – who Hamilton had appointed to the staff in May based on the strength of his literary career – described Ward as "a methodical, lethargic, apparently slow-witted man … naturally inclined to scepticism", and therefore mistrusting of the intelligence that flowed into his office.[75]

There was also discord in the Operations section, although this was largely caused by personal politics and the jockeying for positions. The head of the section, Lieutenant-Colonel Williams, who went ashore during the landings, was transferred in late-April from his staff role to a field command.[76] There was a clear feeling in the section that it was a positive move, given their belief that Braithwaite had largely ignored Williams's advice during the planning phases.[77] Braithwaite replaced him temporarily with an artillery officer, Brigadier-General Hugh Simpson-Baikie, who Kitchener had sent out from the Western Front. Amongst the General Staff, Dawnay felt that Aspinall, who he described as "a very able fellow" with "just the right kind of training for this kind of job", should have been promoted GSO1 and given the job. Indeed, Aspinall reportedly took Simpson-Baikie's "intrusion very sorely." Orlo, on the other hand, felt that Simpson-Baikie might be the right man to work with Braithwaite, and "Aspinall does not really convince me on purely general grounds of out of the way ability."[78] Aspinall got his promotion in late-May when Simpson-Baikie was sent to Helles to command the 29th Divisional Artillery; Dawnay took Aspinall's old role.[79]

On the administrative side, there were few improvements for A and Q branches. In June, one external observer, the Director of Public Works in Sudan (and a Royal Engineers officer), Captain Macdougall Ralston Kennedy, felt obliged to report the state of affairs to Kitchener: "The AG's branch and the QMG's branch at GHQ here are really trying hard to do their best, but they are told nothing or practically nothing by the [Commander in Chief] … they are

71 Ibid., 'A word on internal politics'.
72 Ibid., 16 May 1915.
73 Ibid., 'A word on internal politics'.
74 Ibid., 30 June 1915.
75 Mackenzie, *Gallipoli Memories*, p. 52.
76 Aspinall-Oglander, *Military Operations Gallipoli*, Vol. I, p. 334.
77 IWM: 69/78/1: Williams Papers, 'A word on internal politics'.
78 Ibid., 10 May 1915.
79 LHCMA: Hamilton 8/1/4: Aspinall to Grimwood Mears, 10 December 1916.

General Hamilton (left) leads cheers for three French officers whom he had decorated with the Military Cross. Chief of Staff Major-General Braithwaite and Military Secretary Captain Pollen are also amongst the headquarters party. (AWM G00497)

therefore working in the dark, with, very often, chaotic results, and being only human they are disgusted and disloyal."[80] Kennedy expanded on his concerns in another letter to Kitchener in July where he painted a picture of hopeless logistics, administration, and a dysfunctional GHQ.[81] Woodward put these failures down to a lack of coordination and collaboration at GHQ. There were no daily conferences between branches, he later testified, until mid-July. He put the blame solely on Braithwaite who, he believed, "wanted to make it a one-man show."[82] Braithwaite later vehemently rejected the suggestion that he didn't take A or Q into his confidence, pointing out that they held meetings every Thursday until they were stopped on accord of Woodward's continual failure to show.[83] Winter agreed that communication between the staffs improved, while Aspinall refuted the notion that Braithwaite had tried to run the show by himself: "I was with him every day … and I know that his one aim and object during the whole time was that the most cordial relations with everyone should exist, he let everyone do his own work and he decentralised as much as he could. He was always trying to make everything run smoothly."[84]

The harshest criticisms of all were saved for Braithwaite and Hamilton. Orlo and Captain Guy Dawnay described the former as "a good fellow" but with "no brains".[85] Aspinall later confided that Braithwaite was a cipher – that he had no will of his own.[86] Captain Kennedy was scathing and described Braithwaite as "a fool, an obstinate fool, and a dangerous fool."[87] A

80 TNA PRO 30/57/62: Kitchener Papers: Kennedy to Kitchener, 9 June 1915.
81 Ibid., 3 July 1915.
82 TNA CAB 19/33: Evidence of Woodward to the Dardanelles Commission, 24 January 1917.
83 LHCMA: Hamilton 8/1/13: Braithwaite to Hamilton, 9 August 1917.
84 LHCMA: Hamilton 8/1/66: Winter to Hamilton, 17 August 1917; TNA CAB 19/33: Evidence of Aspinall to the Dardanelles Commission, 29 January 1917.
85 IWM: 69/78/1: Williams Papers, Diary, 10 May 1915.
86 LHCMA: Liddell 11/1930/2: Liddell Hart Papers, 'Talk with Brig-General Aspinall-Oglander', 14 January 1930.
87 TNA PRO 30/57/62: Kitchener Papers: Kennedy to Kitchener, 9 June 1915.

bigger concern was the extent to which the staff believed Hamilton out of his depth. Hamilton's own aide-de-camp, Captain Stephen Pollen, described his chief as "weak and too highly strung." Furthermore, he believed that Hamilton was afraid of Kitchener and therefore "never would run his own show in his own way."[88] Deedes and Dawnay similarly shared their opinion "that he really does nothing at all, never has a scheme, has a shallow, at times obstinate mind, no grasp of detail."[89] Captain William Godfrey, a Royal Marine officer on de Robeck's staff, characterised Hamilton as "a very charming man ... but he was no General."[90] He later expanded on this saying that both Hamilton and Braithwaite "were responsible for a lot of very bad work."[91] Vice-Admiral Rosslyn Wemyss, the most senior naval officer bar de Robeck, agreed. As he told his wife: "I cannot help saying that the General (Ian Hamilton) and his Staff seem to me to be callous, unsympathetic and tiresome – they certainly are not clever, nor do they make the best of what they have got."[92] He repeated his concerns the next week, describing the "ignorance and ... self-satisfaction" of Hamilton and GHQ as "something awful."[93] Whether or not these characterisations and critiques are accurate or fair is largely irrelevant: there clearly was discord within the staff and many officers had lost trust in their leaders.[94]

Expansion

Apart from the inevitable personnel changes that occurred as people moved in and out of jobs, GHQ also underwent an important structural expansion during this period with the creation of the position of Inspector-General of Communications (IGC).[95] The IGC's duties, as defined by *Field Service Regulations*, included "the selection, appropriation, and allotment of sites and buildings for depots of all kinds, quarters, offices, hospitals, plant and material of every description that may be required for the service of the L-of-C." The IGC was also "responsible for the disposition of all reinforcements, supplies, and stores on the L-of-C, and for sending up to within reach of field units ... Similarly, he arranges for the evacuation of all that is superfluous." In effect, the IGC coordinated all traffic on the lines of communication, and as such, needed to be an excellent administrator.[96]

Hamilton believed that an IGC would have been "superfluous" if sent out initially. His reasoning was that, with supply ships "able to come from the Base at Alexandria direct to the Peninsula", the work could be handled by the Base staff and Q Branch. At a conference on 24 May, however, Hamilton, Winter, and a naval adviser agreed that Q Branch could no longer

88 IWM: 69/78/1: Williams Papers, 'A word on internal politics'.
89 Ibid., 21 July 1915.
90 British Library (BL): 82385: Keyes Papers, Godfrey to Keyes, 6 June 1917.
91 BL: 82385: Keyes Papers, Godfrey to Keyes, 30 July 1917.
92 Churchill Archives Centre, Cambridge (CAC): WMYS 7/11/2: Wemyss Papers, Wemyss to wife, 12 August 1915.
93 CAC: WMYS 7/11/2: Wemyss Papers, Wemyss to wife, 19 August 1915.
94 Hamilton's biographer offers a stout defence of both men in John Lee, 'Sir Ian Hamilton', pp. 39–40.
95 It is not possible to chart every personnel change in GHQ's composition. Instead, the remainder of the chapter focuses on major changes that had an appreciable change in how GHQ functioned.
96 Rhys Crawley, *Climax at Gallipoli: The Failure of the August Offensive* (Norman, Oklahoma: University of Oklahoma Press, 2014), pp. 142-43.

handle the volume of work for three reasons: the large increase in the number of transports; the presence of submarines which had forced all supply ships from sitting off the peninsula to the safety of Mudros Harbour; and the "extra work" required to transfer stores and supplies from these ships at Mudros into smaller craft for a submarine-free voyage to the advanced bases at Anzac and Helles. The next day Hamilton asked London for an IGC.[97] The benefit of the role – which answered to Hamilton, but which took its instructions from Braithwaite – would, in Braithwaite's words, "take the burden of the executive work … off the shoulders of GHQ", especially the DQMG.[98]

Major-General Ellison, who had been Hamilton's preference for Braithwaite's job in March, was again his first pick for the new job.[99] Although London eventually agreed to release Ellison for duty in the Dardanelles (as the Deputy IGC), it did not agree that he was the best person for the IGC's job; Hamilton was "deeply disappointed", as he told Ellison.[100] Instead, and against Hamilton's advice, Kitchener "jammed" Major-General Alexander Wallace, a surplus officer in Egypt – and one without any experience with logistic chains or systems – into the role.[101] Wallace was, in Hamilton's words, "a round peg in a square hole"[102] and placed "into a position where he was out of his depth."[103] In hindsight, Winter agreed: "Wallace should never have been made IGC. He was a charming man with no knowledge of business."[104]

Wallace arrived on 7 June; his staff did not leave the UK until two days later.[105] Instead of collocating him at Imbros Island with the rest of GHQ, it was decided to establish his headquarters on HMT *Aragon* in Mudros Bay, an island some 55 miles distant. This was partly necessary, given that the naval transport officers – with whom the IGC had to work closely – were already there, and also because that was the location where supplies were transhipped into smaller craft before being ferried to the peninsula.[106] But it had the unfortunate consequence of keeping Wallace from GHQ, whom he also needed to work with. These challenges, mixed with Wallace's own competency, made for a shaky start. Before the month was out, Wallace was already clashing with his subordinates, was fighting against the reality that he did not have Hamilton's full confidence and was questioning his own ability to do the job. In a candid letter to Winter he wrote:

> I am writing so that you may be able to bring the contents of this to the notice of Sir Ian Hamilton. His telegraphic message received on Saturday evening discouraged me considerably. I shall always endeavour to meet his wishes, but I find it difficult to work with [Brigadier-General Gilbert] Elliot [Director of Works] and the result must be

97 LHCMA: Hamilton 8/1/46: Hamilton to Grimwood Mears, 24 May 1917.
98 National Army Museum: 8704/35/227: Ellison Papers, Braithwaite to Ellison, 13 August 1915.
99 LHCMA: Hamilton 7/1/17: Hamilton to Ellison, 7 April 1915.
100 LHCMA: Hamilton 7/4/25: Notes on meeting between Ellison and Kitchener, 11 July 1915; Hamilton 7/1/17: Hamilton to Ellison, 11 June 1915.
101 LHCMA: Hamilton 8/1/66: Hamilton to Winter, 23 September 1916; Crawley, *Climax at Gallipoli*, p. 143.
102 LHCMA: Hamilton 8/1/66: Hamilton to Winter, 10 October 1916.
103 Ibid., 23 September 1916.
104 Ibid., 12 October 1916.
105 Crawley, *Climax at Gallipoli*, p. 143.
106 LHCMA: Hamilton 8/1/46: Hamilton to Grimwood Mears, 24 May 1917.

> unsatisfactory. Having given my opinion of Elliot previously to you and also to Sir Ian I considered it fair to Elliot to inform him and have done so. General Elliot considers that I misjudge him and that is how the case stands.[107]

That was not the end of the matter. He continued, "I feel that the organisation of the Line of Communication and making it work is such a task that I sometimes doubt myself whether I am equal to it."[108] Winter's reply was hardly reassuring:

> I showed your letter to Sir Ian this morning and all he said at the moment was that many good men might well think to themselves that IGC of this vast Armada was too much for them. He is anxious … to give you every support and for your part he is sure you will try your best. If under such conditions the Communications run smoothly and well, he says you will feel you have rendered to the nation a very valuable service. [If] on the other hand experience should show that your strong points lie in other directions than those of running a great administrative machine then he is sure that by taking time and patience some solution may be found which will not harm your subsequent career.[109]

With the August offensive fast approaching, Hamilton could not afford a repeat of the dysfunctional logistic system that had disrupted preparations in April. On 6 July he wrote to Kitchener requesting a replacement for Wallace.[110] Elliot was also sent home for being "quarrelsome" – as he saw it – but returned in September to command an infantry brigade.[111]

Wallace's replacement, Lieutenant-General Edward Altham, came highly recommended "as one of the most able administrators we have in the Army."[112] That pleased Hamilton, who admitted that Altham "has now in front of him about the most tangled up job it has ever been the lot of a man to unravel."[113] As events proved, he was a perfect appointment.[114] Altham got straight to work, after his arrival on 22 July, on restructuring and improving the lines of communication. Within days he had approval to change how his headquarters interacted with the rest of GHQ – in effect bringing the two closer together by placing the administrative services and departments under his command, and transferring them from Imbros Island to his headquarters in Mudros Harbour – and had freed the DQMG and DAG from their work on the lines of communication, this allowing them to focus their efforts on administration in the field.[115] The noticeable improvement in the MEF's administrative efficiency was almost instantaneous.[116]

Other changes also occurred. In July, Winter became ill with severe dysentery. Hamilton put this down to how hard he worked. His symptoms included rapid weight and memory loss,

107 LHCMA: Hamilton 8/1/66: Wallace to Winter, 28 June 1915.
108 Ibid.
109 LHCMA: Hamilton 8/1/66: Winter to Wallace, 29 June 1915.
110 LHCMA: Hamilton 7/4/8: Hamilton to Kitchener, 6 July 1915.
111 LHCMA: Hamilton 8/1/66: Winter to Hamilton, 9 February 1917; TNA CAB 19/33: Evidence of Elliot to the Dardanelles Commission, 24 January 1917.
112 LHCMA: Hamilton 7/1/37: Smith-Dorrien to Hamilton, 28 July 1915.
113 Ibid., 10 August 1915.
114 TNA CAB 17/123: Hankey to Kitchener, 12 August 1915.
115 Crawley, *Climax at Gallipoli*, pp. 144-45.
116 TNA CAB 17/123: Hankey to Kitchener, 12 August 1915.

and he had to be replaced. "When General Winter came out with me", Hamilton wrote, "he was an energetic competent man fit to earn his living and enjoy life in whatever line of life fortune might direct his steps. When he left Mudros at the end of July he was a broken man and even now he is only a shadow of his former self. Even now [in 1917] he has not recovered his memory."[117] His breakdown came just before the August offensive; he went home on 6 August and was replaced as DQMG by Ellison.[118]

Climax

The August offensive was the largest and, as it happened, last major offensive operation of the Gallipoli campaign. Its story is told elsewhere, both in this volume and in other published works, but it is worth recounting what role GHQ played in its development and execution.

GHQ's composition in August was, apart from the new IGC position, similar to that in April. As we've seen, however, there had been some turnover of personnel and, in line with the dramatic increase in the size of the MEF – which grew by five divisions for the August operations – it also jumped in size from 52 in April to 75 by August. The largest increase was in "special appointments", which more than doubled in size to 27; other increases included an additional four officers in G Branch, two more personal staff to assist Hamilton, one officer each in A and Q Branch, one in the 3rd Echelon headquarters, and nine in the headquarters of administrative services and departments. The IGC's headquarters, which is not included in the above figure, included Altham and 12 others.[119] While all of these new people had jobs to do, it is important to recognise that much of the responsibility for planning the new offensive fell on the shoulders of two familiar characters: Aspinall and Dawnay.[120] The pressure on them was constant and intense, and is evident in a letter that Dawnay wrote to his wife on 9 August:

> I don't ever want to go through anything like the last four weeks again. I don't mind staying up till 2 a.m. or getting up at 6 – but the strain of grappling with the planning, preparing, arrangements of details, foreseeing etc etc – with all that there is hanging on it – well, the strain has been pretty severe. And, as for the last 48 hours, I can only say that waiting to hear the results of all this preparation is much worse than the preparation itself.[121]

Despite the consistency of Aspinall and Dawnay's involvement, the planning process for August was different than April. For one, the A and Q staff were more readily engaged, particularly on matters concerning casualty evacuation – which had failed dismally during the initial landings. Yet, the process wasn't perfect, nor was it consistent. Indeed, different planning approaches

117 LHCMA: Hamilton 8/1/46: Hamilton to Grimwood Mears, 24 May 1917; TNA CAB 19/33: Evidence of Winter to the Dardanelles Commission, 4 January 1917.
118 LHCMA: Hamilton 8/1/66: Winter to Hamilton, 9 February 1917; Crawley, *Climax at Gallipoli*, p. 145.
119 LHCMA: Hamilton 7/4/31: 'Composition of the Headquarters of the Mediterranean Expeditionary Force', August 1915.
120 IWM: 69/78/1: Williams Papers, Diary, 21 July 1915; IWM: 69/21/6: Dawnay Papers, Dawnay to wife, 24 July 1915.
121 IWM: 69/21/6: Dawnay Papers, Dawnay to wife, 9 August 1915.

were taken for the Anzac and Suvla Bay actions. On the former, for example, the ANZAC commander, Lieutenant-General Birdwood, and his staff were highly engaged and were largely left to their own devices to develop their plans. At Suvla, however, GHQ got involved in tactical details and, in contrast to Birdwood's experience, hardly involved IX Corps commander, Lieutenant-General Frederick Stopford, or his staff.[122] Another serious criticism levelled on GHQ is that it misinterpreted or misrepresented Hamilton's intent for Suvla Bay and, as such, watered down the objectives he wanted achieved there.[123] Such an eventuality speaks to the disunity and lack of adequate leadership in GHQ.

Between 6 and 10 August, as the offensive raged in the distance, GHQ eagerly awaited news from the front. Two of its own were sent to the Anzac sector to be GHQ's eyes and ears during the opening stages of battle. Captain Ian Smith, who had gone ashore at Anzac Cove in April, was to keep both GHQ and IX Corps informed of the progress at Anzac. Not able to get through to Stopford, he eventually walked along the shore until he reached 11th Division Headquarters at Lala Baba, whereupon he passed on Birdwood's impression of the situation.[124] Major Alexander (Sandy) Hore-Ruthven – who had earned a Victoria Cross in the Sudan in 1898 and was later the tenth Governor-General of Australia – was the second. Having arrived to serve with the MEF on 29 June, he was posted to Operations section where he assisted with military planning and acted as a liaison between GHQ and units in the field. After witnessing the charge at Lone Pine and the initial stages of the operations against the Sari Bair Ridge he returned to GHQ on the night of 7 August impressed by what he had seen, reported that "ultimate success appeared possible", but recognised that a deficiency in the quantity of lighters and small craft had led to congestion of the wounded ashore. Over the following weeks he was sent to-and-fro between GHQ and Suvla Bay to pass instructions to the commanders, survey the positions, and report back to GHQ.[125]

For those who remained at GHQ, it was a very different feel to their earlier cramped conditions on *Queen Elizabeth* and *Arcadian* during April. The first night of the new offensive "was a quaint night" at GHQ, wrote Orlo:

> Very different to that of the first landing. We kept the office open all night and I sat up till 4. Dawnay, Aspinall, [and others] … were up the same time. We were all prepared for a lot of work and very little turned up. Wires were few, and sometimes when a large one came it turned out to be an ordinary routine code wire. … We had cocoa and biscuits and chocolate and stood about … it was about as unlike the popular image of what goes on in a G[eneral] S[taff] during attacks which are vital as could be imagined.[126]

The pace of work was "only a trifle more electric" than normal conditions, Orlo explained. The "map in Aspinall's tent being spread out and stuck with flags to mark positions. Results

122 Crawley, *Climax at Gallipoli*, Chapter 1.
123 Jeff Cleverly, 'More than a sideshow? An analysis of GHQ decision making during the planning for the landings at Suvla Bay, Gallipoli, August 1915', *War in History*, 24:1 (2017), pp. 44-63. See also Cleverly's chapter in this volume.
124 AWM: AWM4, 1/4/5 part 3: Confidential report by Smith, August 1915.
125 LHCMA: Hamilton 8/1/56: Hore-Ruthven to Hamilton, 16 December 1916.
126 IWM: 69/78/1: Williams Papers, Diary, 6 August 1915.

of aeroplane reconnaissance coming in at intervals over telephone".[127] Hamilton himself spent time in the General Staff tent, and when business took him away, an aide-de-camp was left there to ferry any and all cables to the chief as soon as they came in.[128] Hamilton and his staff were hungry for information and were dismayed at the lack of it flowing in to GHQ, especially the "very scanty" information from IX Corps at Suvla Bay.[129] This hunger for updates, and the normalcy of their work tempo, meant that additional GHQ officers were able to be sent to the front to collect information and, as it turned out, urge the commanders to action.

On the morning of 8 August, for example, Braithwaite sent Aspinall to Suvla "to see how things were going" and, as had been the case many times throughout the campaign to that point, "collect reports" from the commanders.[130] He first visited the commander of the 11th Division, Major-General Frederick Hammersley, ashore before going to see Stopford at his floating headquarters in HMS *Jonquil*. What he saw caused him to wire Braithwaite: "Just been ashore and find all quiet. No shelling, no rifle fire, and apparently no Turks. Am confident that golden opportunities are being missed and look upon situation as most serious."[131] Meanwhile, Hamilton and his aide-de-camp, George Brodrick, had already left Imbros for Suvla.[132] When Hamilton arrived at HMS *Jonquil* that afternoon Aspinall handed him a copy of the wire. Hamilton then discussed the situation with Stopford before going ashore with Aspinall and the naval chief of staff, Commodore Roger Keyes, to order Hammersley to attack Tekke Tepe that night or early the next morning.[133] Hamilton remained on the peninsula for a short time before returning to HMS *Triad* for dinner.[134] Aspinall went back to GHQ that night with a view that chances were being wasted.[135]

The next morning Hamilton and Brodrick again went ashore and spoke with the 10th Division's commander, Major-General Bryan Mahon. Hamilton sent Guy Dawnay to deal with the 11th Division.[136] Dawnay recounted: "Finding General Stopford still at sea, I went ashore to the Eleventh Division HQ. There I failed to get access to General Hammersley but made vehement comment to his General Staff on their inaction. My comment was no less fruitless than vehement. I returned hot-foot to report to GHQ, at Imbros, only to gain the impression that I was looked on as unduly impatient."[137] It was clear to Orlo that all who returned from Suvla "did not seem very satisfied when they returned" to Imbros.[138]

The reality is that the failure of the August offensive on 10 August hit GHQ hard; the staff, who saw inertia at Suvla as the primary reason for its outcome, were "pretty down on the 9th Corps."[139] Orlo observed that his good friend, Dawnay, seemed "really down-hearted" by the

127 IWM: 69/78/1: Williams Papers, Diary, 7 August 1915.
128 Hamilton, *Gallipoli Diary*, Vol. 2, p. 55.
129 TNA CAB 19/33: Evidence of Aspinall to the Dardanelles Commission, 29 January 1917.
130 Ibid.
131 AWM: AWM4, 1/4/5 part 1: General Staff GHQ War Diary, 8 August 1915.
132 The saga of this journey is told in Crawley, *Climax at Gallipoli*, pp. 206-07.
133 TNA CAB 19/33: Evidence of Aspinall to the Dardanelles Commission, 29 January 1917.
134 LHCMA: Hamilton 7/2/49: Aspinall to Hamilton, 28 October 1915.
135 IWM: 69/78/1: Williams Papers, Diary, 8-9 August 1915
136 LHCMA: Hamilton 7/2/49: Aspinall to Hamilton, 28 October 1915.
137 IWM: 69/21/5: Dawnay Papers, Dawnay's comments on excerpt from Deedes diary, n.d..
138 IWM: 69/78/1: Williams Papers, Diary, 8-9 August 1915.
139 Ibid., 10-11 August 1915.

loss and was wracking his brain to come up with the next scheme, but was coming up empty. "He confessed he really didn't see what we could do or know what was going to happen." Dawnay told Orlo that the failure also "came very hard on Aspinall, who had done so well and saved the situation often." Orlo was inclined to agree: "He may have no large ideas and not much foresight, but in matters of organization and arrangement he has been extremely good – a first class staff officer."[140] Nonetheless, planning had to, and did, continue; both for coming operations to secure Suvla's perimeter, and to prepare the front for winter.

Reprise

The offensive's failure saw Stopford and some of his commanders sent home with their reputations in tatters.[141] The initial shakeup at GHQ was slight, although it added to the already-existing frictions amongst the staff. In late-August a new position, the Brigadier-General General Staff (BGGS), was created to supervise the Operations and Intelligence sections in G Branch, thus sitting immediately under Braithwaite and atop the existing branch structure. Braithwaite gave the job to his friend, Lieutenant-Colonel Reginald Taylor, who was then in theatre. Orlo recorded Aspinall's reaction at being overlooked for the role: "This puts Aspinall's nose quite out of joint and is hard luck on him. But as he is a jealous fellow I can't help being amused. I heard him being absolutely contemptible."[142] Another structural change saw the BGRE position upgraded to Engineer-in-Chief, responsible for providing advice, as before, but also coordinating all engineering services. Hamilton did not think Roper was a "big enough man" for the expanded responsibilities and instead promoted an officer his junior, Brigadier-General Godfrey Williams, into the position as a major-general.[143] When offered a promotion in rank to serve as the chief engineer of a corps – but which was actually a demotion in responsibility – Roper declined and asked to go home.[144] He vacated his position on 30 September and left the Dardanelles the next day.[145]

While all of this had been happening, Hamilton sent Dawnay home to report on the situation. Both Dawnay and Aspinall would've preferred Aspinall to go, but Dawnay, who was deemed the more sanguine of the two, and was close with the royal family and Prime Minister Asquith, was given the task. He left Imbros on 2 September with instructions "to answer all questions truthfully but in no way pessimistically." The importance of being honest with London's strategic card holders, "and doing something big for the nation's good" was not lost on Dawnay, but neither was the need to balance that with loyalty to Hamilton. Dawnay confided to Orlo that "a really strong man … would go home and get" Hamilton and Braithwaite "stellenbosched", to which Orlo replied that the national good was more important than their

140 Ibid., 17 August 1915.
141 Crawley, *Climax at Gallipoli*, pp. 210-12.
142 IWM: 69/78/1: Williams Papers, Diary, 25 August 1915.
143 LHCMA: Hamilton 7/2/33: War Office to Hamilton, 25 August 1915; GHQ to War Office, 27 August 1915; and War Office to GHQ, 27 September 1915.
144 For the offer and Roper's response see: LHCMA: Hamilton 7/2/33: Hamilton to Roper, 28 September 1915; and Roper to Hamilton, 28 September 1915.
145 TNA CAB 19/33: Evidence of Roper to the Dardanelles Commission, 23 January 1917.

chief's reputation.[146] Dawnay arrived in London on 10 September and spent most of the next three weeks meeting with the who's who of British political and military circles including King George V, Asquith and other senior politicians: Winston Churchill, Andrew Bonar Law, Edward Grey, David Lloyd George and Edward Carson; and leading military officials such as the Chief of the Imperial General Staff, the Director of Military Operations, and representatives of the Adjutant-General's Branch at the War Office. Much of his conversations focused on the failure of the August offensive and prospects for the future. His last meeting was with Kitchener, who said that he was not happy with the course of the operations and considered that the campaign had not been well managed. Dawnay arrived back at GHQ on 11 October, just in time for the next chapter in the MEF's war.[147]

On 16 October GHQ woke to news – contained in a private telegram the night before – that Hamilton and Braithwaite were being recalled.[148] Braithwaite was reportedly "dreadfully upset." Dawnay, who had earlier been critical of Braithwaite, now showed sympathy, writing home that it was Hamilton, not Braithwaite, who "was completely out of his element", explaining that the CGS "had never had one note of help or guidance or reasonable advice" from Hamilton "since the day we started out."[149] But it was too late. GHQ's top two officers and their aides-de-camp left for London the next day.[150] Thus of the senior GHQ officers who had been there in the beginning, only Woodward remained.[151]

Lieutenant-General Birdwood assumed temporary command of the MEF, with Ellison acting as CGS, until General Sir Charles Monro, who had been commanding Third Army in France, and the new CGS, Major-General Sir Arthur Lynden-Bell – who had worked in the same capacity for Monro in Third Army – arrived on 27 October.[152] Initial impressions amongst the staff were favourable. Monro already had a good reputation from his work as a divisional, corps, and army commander on the Western Front, and Lynden-Bell presented as a capable officer with a "lightening brain."[153] The new leadership team brought with them a DQMG, Major-General Walter Campbell, which meant that Ellison, who in three months had held four jobs, was given a fifth job commanding the expanding Base at Alexandria.[154]

In the intervening weeks, Kitchener had received Birdwood's assessment of the campaign's future, and London – under pressure from France following Bulgaria's declaration of war on Serbia – had all but committed to sending troops, which were being considered for Gallipoli, to

146 IWM: 69/78/1: Williams Papers, Diary, 2-3 September 1915; Robert Rhodes James, *Gallipoli* (Sydney: Angus & Robertson, 1965), pp. 315-317.
147 IWM: 69/21/6: Dawnay Papers, 'Secret 1915'.
148 TNA ADM 137/191: Kitchener to Hamilton, 15 October 1915.
149 IWM: 69/78/1: Williams Papers, Diary, 17 October 1915; IWM: 69/21/6: Dawnay Papers, Dawnay to wife, 19 October 1915.
150 IWM: 69/78/1: Williams Papers, Diary, 17 October 1915.
151 Brigadier-General Fuller, BGRA, went home ill in early October. He was replaced by Brigadier-General Sydenham Smith, previously the chief artillery officer in IX Corps (and commander of the NSW Artillery during the Boer War). IWM: 69/78/1: Williams Papers, Diary, 10 October 1915. Ward (GSO1 (I)) had also recently gone sick. He was replaced by another Royal Artillery officer, Lieutenant-Colonel Gerald Tyrrell, who had been a Military Attaché in Constantinople, 1909-13. TNA CAB 19/33: Evidence of Maxwell to the Dardanelles Commission, 22 February 1917.
152 IWM: 69/78/1: Williams Papers, Diary, 18, 27-28 October 1915.
153 Ibid., 28 October 1915.
154 Ibid., 27 October 1915.

General Hamilton's recall, a German cartoon perspective: Departure from the Dardanelles: "Farewell, you little sideshow." (*Kladderadatsch*, 7 November 1915)

Salonika instead. It was within this context of strategic and operational uncertainty that Monro arrived. His first task was to assess the situation and advise Kitchener on the best course of action. Specifically, Kitchener and his Cabinet colleagues wished to know whether they should hold on at Gallipoli or cut their losses and evacuate. In addition to Gallipoli, Monro was also to consider the broader impact of any decision on Egypt and Salonika. GHQ had anticipated this task and produced a memorandum canvassing the issues for Monro's consideration. Monro quickly reached a conclusion after seeing conditions first hand at Helles, Anzac and Suvla; on 31 October he "recommended the evacuation of the peninsula." He then set GHQ the task of developing a scheme for leaving Gallipoli.[155]

155 C.F. Aspinall-Oglander, *Military Operations Gallipoli*, Vol. II (London: Heinemann, 1932), pp. 388, 397-402.

His recommendation was met with mixed reviews. Kitchener reverted and asked whether Monro's corps commanders agreed with his assessment. Aspinall met with each and GHQ then forwarded their views to Kitchener; two supported evacuating while one, Birdwood, didn't on the grounds that he feared it could lead to Muslim uprisings.[156] Monro, in accordance with his directions to consider the broader region, then handed temporary command of the MEF back to Birdwood and left for Egypt to discuss the strategic impact of evacuation with Lieutenant-General John Maxwell, GOC Forces in Egypt.[157] Almost immediately, Kitchener, who couldn't accept Monro's position, sent a "most secret" telegram for Birdwood's eyes only: it said that Birdwood would be given command of the MEF, Monro would be sent to Salonika, and Kitchener would come out from London to assess the situation himself.[158] Dawnay, who had already formed "the very highest opinion of Monro", was "disheartened" that Kitchener would remove a commander in chief for expressing his opinion, especially when that opinion reflected the reality of the situation. Orlo predicted that it would "be very uncomfortable at GHQ; and Dawnay and Aspinall will hate it."[159] Birdwood, however, swore to secrecy those who knew of Kitchener's telegram and replied that it would be best if Monro retained his command.[160]

As is discussed elsewhere in this book, Kitchener arrived at Mudros on 9 November and spent the best part of two weeks touring the theatre, discussing the situation, and forming his own conclusions.[161] In the end, on 22 November, he accepted that nothing good could come from staying and recommended cutting their losses and leaving.[162]

Before he had reached that point, however, Kitchener decided that major structural changes were required. Given the additional forces destined for Salonika, he determined that rather than having two armies under independent commanders, it would be better to place both under Monro, who would command all forces in the Eastern Mediterranean. Birdwood would be given command of the Dardanelles Army, which would take responsibility for all forces on the Gallipoli Peninsula; another officer, who turned out to be Lieutenant-General Bryan Mahon, previously commander of the 10th Division under Stopford, would command the British force at Salonika. The new MEF GHQ, which would oversee the administration and operations of two armies – and coordinate their work – would relocate from Imbros Island to HMT *Aragon* in Mudros Harbour (leaving the existing camp at Mudros for Birdwood's headquarters, known as Army Headquarters – AHQ).[163] These changes took effect on 23 November.[164] That same day the Prime Minister told Kitchener – who was to leave for home the next day – that the War Council believed the whole peninsula should be evacuated.[165] As it stood, the on-again, off-again nature of the evacuation question delayed formal Cabinet approval until 8 December:

156 Ibid., pp. 406-07; IWM: 69/78/1: Williams Papers, Diary, 1 November 1915.
157 Aspinall-Oglander, *Military Operations Gallipoli*, Vol. II, p. 407.
158 AWM: AWM4, 1/4/8 part 2: Kitchener to Monro, 4 November 1915.
159 IWM: 69/78/1: Williams Papers, Diary, 5 November 1915.
160 Ibid., 9 November 1915.
161 See AWM: AWM4, 1/4/8 part 2: General Staff War Diary for details of these discussions.
162 Aspinall-Oglander, *Military Operations Gallipoli*, Vol. II, p. 421.
163 AWM: AWM4, 1/4/8 part 2: Kitchener to Asquith, 18 November 1915.
164 Aspinall-Oglander, *Military Operations Gallipoli*, Vol. II, p. 422.
165 AWM: AWM4, 1/4/8 Part 2: Asquith to Kitchener, 23 November 1915.

even then, permission to evacuate only extended to the Anzac and Suvla sectors; the Dardanelles Army was expected to hold its position at Cape Helles indefinitely.[166]

The majority of the senior positions from the old MEF GHQ went with Monro to form the new GHQ on HMT *Aragon*: Lynden-Bell (CGS), Woodward (DAG), Campbell (DQMG), Smith (BGRA), and Williams (Engineer-in-Chief). The directors of the administrative services and departments, who had shifted from Imbros to Mudros in August as part of Altham's shake up of the lines of communication, stayed where they were. Dawnay was promoted GSO1 and head of the Operations section at GHQ. Orlo went with him and traded his cypher role for a staff role in O(b).[167] They were joined by new staff who started arriving for duty almost as soon as the new GHQ was stood up.[168]

Some officers, however, remained at Imbros and continued their work in support of the Dardanelles Army and the Gallipoli campaign. Aspinall, for example, became BGGS Dardanelles Army (although initially as a lieutenant-colonel, not a brigadier-general, as the role was usually ranked) where – in concert with his counterpart at the new MEF GHQ, Brigadier-General Webb Gillman (also recently appointed) – he would eventually coordinate AHQ's planning for the evacuation.[169] Because it could call on MEF GHQ for assistance, Birdwood's AHQ was put on a reduced footing and not staffed to the same level as GHQ had been. The former roles of DAG and DQMG, for example, were combined into a Deputy Adjutant and Quartermaster-General (DA&QMG), Dardanelles Army; the job was given to Brigadier-General George MacMunn who had ably served in support of Altham since July. Brigadier-General Charles Cunliffe Owen, previously BGRA in the ANZAC, and Brigadier-General Alain Joly de Lotbinière, the MEF's Director of Works since July, were appointed Birdwood's BGRA and BGRE respectively.[170]

For all intents and purposes, the creation of the Dardanelles Army marked the end of MEF GHQ's intimate involvement with the Gallipoli campaign. Although it remained highly engaged on questions of strategy, and was in constant telegraphic contact with AHQ, the MEF's new role saw it act as a conduit between London and the new Army commands. Rather than directing how things would or should unfold at Gallipoli, it instead provided advice and focused on overseeing the combined actions at Gallipoli and Salonika. Detailed plans for the evacuation of Anzac and Suvla – and Helles when that was approved on 28 December – were left to Birdwood, Aspinall, their colleagues in AHQ, and the relevant corps commanders on the peninsula.[171] Unlike April and August, therefore, GHQ was only peripherally involved in the very successful evacuations that took place in December 1915 and January 1916.

That said, 23 November did not mark the end of GHQ's existence. It still had work to do. Despite the "discomfort" of again finding themselves confined to a ship, GHQ was nonetheless "very cheery". The main difference seemed to be the leadership provided by both Monro and Lynden-Bell. The latter, who Orlo described as "a regular bluff, loud voiced hearty soldier",

166 IWM: 69/78/1: Williams Papers, Diary, 8 December 1915.
167 Ibid., 26 November 1915.
168 Ibid., 23-24 November 1915.
169 There was no CGS in the Dardanelles Army, thus Aspinall became the senior staff officer in Birdwood's headquarters.
170 Becke, *Order of Battle*, p. 45.
171 AWM: AWM4, 1/4/8 part 2: Lynden-Bell to Birdwood, 25 November 1915.

set "a fearfully hearty tone" in GHQ. His BGGS, Gillman, was likewise popular.[172] The jovial atmosphere, however, would soon be severed. On 22 December, following the success of the Anzac and Suvla evacuations, Monro – who had achieved what he had been sent out to do – was ordered to proceed to Egypt, hand over command to General Sir Archibald Murray, and return home to take command of First Army in France. GHQ was to pick up and move with him to Egypt.[173] Lynden-Bell and Major-General Campbell were initially to go home with Monro, but the War Office reneged and ordered them to remain with GHQ. "CGS on hearing above sweated with rage. But it is a jolly good thing for us even if he only stays a short time," Orlo concluded.[174] After a night of festivities to welcome in the New Year, which involved a concoction of poker, rum and a piano, GHQ sailed for Alexandria at 8:00 a.m. on 1 January 1916.[175] They were to set up in the old Army Headquarters of Egypt, in Cairo, which was characterised as a "bare building" with no furniture or telephones. There was a feeling that their days as a GHQ were limited. Indeed, Dawnay was convinced, as Orlo put it, that MEF GHQ "is now a washout … Nobody wants us and we have no work to do, yet a new commander is about to arrive. The whole position is impossible and ridiculous. Salonica runs itself and Maxwell runs Egypt; and GHQ Medforce seems dying in rather undignified convulsions."[176]

The end was indeed nigh. The evacuation of allied forces from Cape Helles on 9 January 1916 marked the end of the Gallipoli campaign. The timing of the final operation was coincidentally impeccable: Murray arrived later that day and assumed command the next; "old Monro", as Orlo called him, "goes home with complete success in his pocket." The force was consolidated in Egypt and kept as a strategic reserve, ready to be deployed to Mesopotamia, India, France or elsewhere as required.[177] In late-January MEF GHQ moved to Ismailia, where it was co-located with the British Force in Egypt GHQ until 20 March 1916 when, under Murray, the two commands were merged into one, the Egyptian Expeditionary Force, that would over the next two years pursue Ottoman forces across the Sinai Peninsula and Palestine.[178]

Conclusion

No chapter on an institution such as this can ever convey the true sense of what it was like to work there. Our sources are limited, and words only express the sentiment and stresses of the environment so much. MEF GHQ was a busy, and at times dangerous place to be. It was, as Braithwaite later characterised it, an "overworked and understaffed" headquarters.[179] Its people, when they weren't visiting the peninsula, attended meetings, discussed ideas, planned operations, administered a multinational force of tens of thousands of troops in a far-flung expeditionary operation, and created, distributed and filed a mass of paperwork. They liaised with field

172 IWM: 69/78/1: Williams Papers, Diary, 4 December 1915.
173 Ibid., 22 December 1915.
174 Ibid., 23-25 December 1915.
175 Ibid., 31 December 1915-1 January 1916.
176 Ibid., 4-5 January 1916.
177 Ibid., 10 January 1916.
178 Becke, *Order of Battle*, p. 27.
179 Lee, 'Sir Ian Hamilton', p. 52.

commanders and maintained relationships with coalition partners and their naval colleagues. During the strain of operations, they sat anxiously waiting for information on how their plans were unfolding, they did their best to understand what was going on, attempted to bring some order and coordination to the situation, and all the while they recorded things for posterity and continued planning for subsequent actions. It was not an easy task, yet it was a largely thankless one. Some rose to the challenge and pulled their weight, others didn't. But most did their best.

These realities don't hide the fact that Hamilton's headquarters was dysfunctional. It is true that he didn't get to personally select his staff, as it is also true that some of GHQ's staff wouldn't have made the third-eleven. But there wasn't an abundance of suitably trained staff officers, either in numbers or expertise, across the entirety of Britain's forces to choose from – whether for Gallipoli or on the Western Front.[180] In any case, blaming the staff, or the field commanders for that matter, doesn't really cut it: many went on to prove their abilities time and again throughout the war. In the end, any and all failures of how MEF GHQ performed fall on the shoulders of Hamilton and his CGS, Braithwaite.

The failures of the campaign, however, rest not on these two but on those in London who conceived of the campaign and persisted to push for its continuation and expansion when all the signs pointed to its ultimate failure. Hamilton and GHQ were never given the tools or resources necessary to turn this strategic concept into a successful military operation. To bastardise Clausewitz, there was no relationship between ends, ways and means. Vice-Admiral John de Robeck, Hamilton's naval counterpart, summed up the strategic futility best: when considering the hypothetical of his fleet sitting off the Ottoman Empire's capital, he admitted: "it did not appear that the arrival of the British Fleet off Constantinople would have the desire effect, namely, of a revolution or of a refusal of further fighting which would force the Government to yield."[181] If one accepts that assessment – as I do – it leads to the conclusion that the Ottoman Empire could be defeated neither militarily or politically in 1915. That, however, is a discussion for another chapter.

180 For more on this see Simon Robbins, *British Generalship on the Western Front 1914–18: Defeat into victory* (London: Routledge, 2005), Ch. 3.

181 Quoted in Admiralty, *Report of the committee appointed to investigate the attacks delivered on and the enemy defences of the Dardanelles Straits* (London: Admiralty, 1919), p. 224.

8

The French Dardanelles Campaign 1915-16

Simon House

By the opening years of the Twentieth Century, the thousand-year-old Ottoman Empire was in the last stages of a terminal decline; it was however still a large and powerful political entity and, most importantly, its geographic position astride the Dardanelles made it a prize for other predatory nations. During the final decades of the 19th Century, "France had helped prop up the 'sick man of Europe' and prevented its collapse."[1] With the hope of converting friendship into political influence or more. Increasingly, however, Germany too had started to carve out a political position in the region, courting the Turkish government with economic and military aid. When war broke out between the Great Powers in August 1914, Turkey's stance was of considerable importance to both sides.

Analysing the relative strength of its own versus German influence at that moment in time, the French government perceived Turkey as a threat from the first days of the war.[2] Turkey had declared her neutrality but had also mobilised her armed forces, ostensibly to "protect" the Dardanelles Straits. The French government saw the mobilisation rather as a sign that sooner or later Turkey would join the Central Powers (Germany and Austro-Hungary) and as a cover for a probable attack on Greece.[3] Germany's presence in Turkey was strong; since 1913 General Liman von Sanders had led a military mission and was now de-facto head of the Turkish army. German Admiral Souchon, flying his flag from the battlecruiser *Goeben* that had entered Turkish waters on 10 August 1914 and had been purchased by Turkey and re-named *Yavuz Sultan Selim* – was on 13 September 1914 appointed commander of the Turkish navy. Gradually German pressure brought Turkey into the war on Germany's side, the final straw being an attack on 29 October 1914 by three Turkish torpedo boats on the Russian port of Odessa, an attack ordered by Admiral Souchon with the intention of forcing the Turkish government's hand. A French vessel, the *Portugal*, was in port at that time and was fired on by the Turks.

1 Robert A. Doughty, *Pyrrhic Victory: French Strategy and Operations in the Great War* (London: Harvard University Press, 2005), pp. 203-214.
2 *Les Armées Françaises dans La Grande Guerre, Tome VIII, Premier Volume* (hereafter AFGG VIII/1), (Paris: Ministère de la Guerre, État-Major de l'Armée, Service Historique; Imprimerie Nationale, 1923), pp. 3-17.
3 AFGG VIII/1, p. 3.

Within 48 hours French and British diplomats were withdrawn from Constantinople, and from 1 November 1914 a state of war was deemed to exist between the Triple Entente and Turkey. In response to the attack on Odessa, on 3 November 1914 an Anglo-French naval squadron made a token bombardment of the forts at Sedd-el-Bahr and Kum Kale on either side of the entrance to the Dardanelles. A more effective response to war with Turkey was made by the Russians, who mounted a major offensive through the Caucasus. Under pressure from the Germans on the Eastern Front and now facing a war on two fronts, the Russians appealed to Britain and France on 2 January 1915 to apply pressure on the Turks. Some French politicians (and a few military leaders especially from the Colonial Army) saw in Russia's appeal an opportunity for France to expand her Empire in the Middle East at the expense of the Ottomans. French eyes turned particularly to certain Ottoman provinces on the Eastern Mediterranean shore – Cilicia, the Bay of Adana, Alexandretta, and Syria. Note that in 1919 the Treaty of Versailles would give France a Mandate to "oversee" governance of those very territories. France's initial response to Russia's call for help against the Turks was therefore to authorise Millerand, the minister of war, to send a few troops to Syria to "fly the flag" and demonstrate French interest. Nothing, however, came of this idea, because on 7 January 1915 General Joffre signalled his implacable opposition to diluting his strength on the Western Front. Instead of action, there was more debate. The influential French leaders who favoured operations somewhere in the Mediterranean included Generals Franchet d'Espèrey, Gallieni and Castelnau, and they soon gained the political support of Aristide Briand who was to replace Viviani as premier on 29 October 1915. Franchet d'Espèrey and Castelnau favoured military operations in the Balkans; but Gallieni and Briand looked at the wider strategic issues, and the triangular relationship between Russia, Turkey and France: "It had long been an ambition of the tsars to complete their centuries of counter-offensive against the Ottomans by seizing Constantinople. The French were disinclined, the British even more so, to concede such a dramatic enlargement of Russian power in southern Europe".[4] France may have lacked trust in their Russian ally; but much of the subsequent French involvement in the Dardanelles stemmed from their equal distrust of their British allies, best summed up by a statement on 5 January 1915 by war minister Millerand to Delcassé: "[O]ur traditional interests in Asia Minor demand that the English not land there by themselves". The Balkan scenario gained early traction in French political circles, with Briand, Poincaré and Viviani discussing at a meeting on 1 January 1915 the possibility of sending half-a-million men to Salonika to strike through Serbia at Austria's rear. While the French debated, the British took action – a naval attack to force passage through the Dardanelles. France then hastened its involvement in the now inevitable Gallipoli campaign.

On 28 January 1915 Winston Churchill as First Lord of the Admiralty had obtained British Cabinet approval to the mounting of his proposed Dardanelles naval operation. France immediately offered a squadron from its own Mediterranean Fleet in order to make it a joint allied operation. Four armoured cruisers – *Bouvet*, *Gaulois*, *Charlemagne* and *Suffren* – were detached under Rear-Admiral Emile Guépratte from the fleet at Toulon and sent to the Greek island of Lemnos, which the British had chosen as their advanced base. The first attack took place on 19 February, in which Guépratte led one of three allied divisions under British Vice-Admiral Sackville Carden's overall command. A long-range bombardment of Turkish forts was

4 John Keegan, *The First World War* (London: Hutchinson, 1998), pp. 253-269.

ineffective, and bad weather caused the action to be broken off. It was resumed on 25 February, at closer range, with greater success. Turkish defences were destroyed by shell-fire, and British marines landed at Sedd-el-Bahr and Kum Kale with impunity and destroyed what was left of the forts. Turkish ground troops soon arrived, drove the allied landing parties back to their ships and used mobile field howitzers to force the warships back out of range. Turkish troops, albeit in small numbers but complete with machine guns and some field artillery, were left to protect the beaches on which the British marines had landed with such ease.

On 16 February 1915 the British War Council decided in principle to send troops to the region. Therefore, on 18 February the French government decided in principle to send a division as part of any joint expedition, and on 22 February 1915 French War Minister Millerand ordered the formation of a military expedition to the Dardanelles. Joffre grudgingly conceded to Millerand that a French contingent would have to accompany any British Expeditionary Force to the region; but true to his beliefs, he insisted that such a contingent would not be made up of troops withdrawn from his Western Front.[5] The troops for Gallipoli were therefore taken from the depots in France and North Africa; in other words miscellaneous smaller units, made up of native troops and older European conscripts, unattached to any existing division.[6] It was agreed that the French contingent would be about 18,000 men strong in all, roughly the size of a reinforced division. The commander would be General Albert d'Amade, a 58-year-old Colonial officer who had commanded the group of Territorial divisions that during the Battles of the Frontiers in August 1914 had covered the extreme left of the Western Front in the face of the strong German right wing heading for Paris; despite being a second tier general, he had acquitted himself reasonably well, and he was available.

On 28 February 1915 Millerand decided to mobilise the French contingent and concentrate the new units at the French North African naval base at Bizerte. On 1 March 1915 a new division staff was activated at Toulon and given the glorious title of *le Corps Expéditionnaire d'Orient* (the Eastern Expeditionary Corps). It consisted of a metropolitan brigade[7] with one Metropolitan and African regiment of infantry; a colonial brigade of two colonial regiments, each having two battalions of Senegalese infantry and one of European colonial troops; a cavalry regiment made up of units of the *Chasseurs d'Afrique*; and three groups of field artillery, two of 75mm field guns (12 guns in three batteries per group) and one of 65mm mountain guns (8 guns in two batteries). Logistical arrangements were put in place. Replacements for expected casualties were required to be sent from the depot that had supplied each original unit to a temporary expeditionary "holding" depot, initially at Bizerte. It was decided to send a strong advance guard into theatre. This advance guard, under *General de brigade* Masnou, consisted of the African regiment (*le régiment de marche d'Afrique*) from the Metropolitan Brigade, two squadrons of cavalry and the artillery group of 65mm mountain guns. On 4 March General Masnou left Toulon aboard the steamer *Armand-Béhic*, sailing directly to Mudros Bay and harbour, on the south coast of

5 AFGG VIII/1, pp. 18-19.
6 Ibid., pp. 18-30.
7 In the French Army of 1914 there were two distinct organisations, the Metropolitan Army – responsible for the defence of the Homeland – and the Colonial Army responsible for the defence of the Empire. The largest force and main organisational infrastructure of the Colonial Army was in French North Africa, with the "Senegalese" infantry coming from French West Africa – not just Senegal but Chad, Cameroon too.

Lemnos Island. His troops followed in a small convoy of merchantmen assembled at and sailing from Bizerte, arriving at Mudros on 11 March 1915. The main body of the division was shipped from Bizerte in convoys departing between 10 and 13 March; by 17 March the whole force was gathered, still aboard ship, offshore in the bay at Mudros. Finalising his command arrangements, General d'Amade decided on 16 March to give command of all the fighting elements of the division to General Masnou, retaining for himself the rather empty if prestigious role of Commander of the Eastern Expeditionary Corps; the kindest interpretation of this arrangement is that it freed d'Amade from day-to-day responsibility and allowed him to concentrate on operational and planning issues as well as liaison with his Allies. In parallel with this rapid French action, the British decided on 10 March to send the equivalent of four divisions under General Sir Ian Hamilton. When on 17 March General Hamilton arrived on Lemnos, d'Amade was able to join the discussions regarding planning and executing the landing. However, despite the timely arrival of most of the French division in theatre, the bulk of the British 29th Division would not arrive until early April, whilst the ANZAC was in Egypt undergoing basic training.

Whilst the generals prepared for a landing on the Gallipoli Peninsula, the Allied fleet made one final attempt to force the Straits by naval power alone, launched on 18 March 1915. The result was an overall fiasco when the warships ran into Turkish minefields, and the French ships suffered as badly as their British counterparts. *Bouvet* hit a mine and sank like a stone taking most of her crew with her, and *Gaulois* was seriously damaged by shellfire and had to withdraw for repair. At this point, it was realised that any residual element of strategic surprise had been lost. The opportunity to land proper ground forces unopposed, swiftly in the wake of a successful naval bombardment, had passed; any landings in the region would now be opposed. It was consequently decided to pause to draw breath, plan and organise the landing of the ground troops properly, and then re-launch the campaign. The lull, of course, gave the Turks and their German "advisors" more time to repair the damage to the Dardanelles forts and move fresh troops and artillery into the region, including Kum Kale on the Asiatic coast.

So, following the naval defeat in the Dardanelles on 18 March, Hamilton and d'Amade agreed to set up a joint expeditionary base in Egypt, using the well-organised facilities of the British forces there, rather than the primitive facilities then available on the Greek islands. On 23 March the order was given for the French Expeditionary Corps to join the British at Alexandria, leaving only *4 régiment mixte colonial*[8] as advance guard on Lemnos. Various support services – hospital, bakery, etc. – were gradually set up on the island, ready for the return of the French contingent, and another senior officer, General Baumann, arrived from France to command those rear echelon functions. Engineers were also left behind to construct a wharf for the exclusive use of d'Amade's force.

In Egypt, the French division set itself up in camp at Ramleh and commenced training. Because of Joffre's opposition to the use of experienced French troops from the Western Front, the men of the French contingent were an ad-hoc assembly of miscellaneous smaller units, made up of native troops and older conscripts from the depots, that would have to be formed into a new divisional structure, with new staff and a new commander.[9] On 5 April 1915, following a review by General Hamilton, General d'Amade conducted a solemn ceremony of presentation

8 The term *mixte* in the phrase *régiment mixte colonial,* refers to the two battalions of Senegalese and one European that comprised the regiments of the Expedition's colonial infantry brigade.

9 AFGG VIII/1, pp. 18-30.

Corps Expéditionnaire d'Orient review, Egypt, 5 April 1915. (*The Sphere*, 1 May 1915)

and consecration of new battle standards and flags to the new units under his command – units without a history, as the Official History puts it. Worse, d'Armade's soldiers were orphans, many being natives of West Africa, snatched from very different homes, grouped together and sent overseas to a strange land. Leaving aside the lack of training and experience of the individual soldiers, the lack of unit cohesion and the task of building morale posed formidable problems for d'Amade in his new command.

Meanwhile back in France, political and strategic issues developed in parallel with events in theatre. By the middle of May the minister of war had decided to send a group of heavy artillery, a squadron of aeroplanes, an extra logistics company and a hospital ship to fill out d'Amade's command. The heavy artillery group was made up of two batteries each of four big guns: one battery of de Bange 155L guns,[10] one of older 120L guns;[11] it was delivered direct to Lemnos in time for the start of the fighting. General d'Amade had also requested reinforcements in the shape of more mountain artillery and a brigade of Marines; this request was turned down with a vague promise of another ad-hoc division drawn from the depots in due course.[12]

On 15 April, the *Corps Expéditionnaire d'Orient* once more boarded their ships and sailed from Alexandria. General Baumann on the other hand was sent from Lemnos to Alexandria: for now French logistics would be run alongside those of the British at the expeditionary base in Egypt. By 21 April 1915 the French division was assembled on Lemnos and the nearby islands of Mitylène and Skyros and was ready for action. According to General Hamilton's plan, the French would provide a diversion for the main landings on the Gallipoli Peninsula by landing on the tip of the Asiatic (eastern) shore of the Dardanelles at Kum Kale.

The initial landing would be made by Colonel Ruef's Colonial Brigade, led by *6e régiment coloniale mixte* in the first wave supported by a battery of 75s and a detachment of engineers. The

10 At the start of the First World War, French heavy artillery had been neglected. There were, however, thousands of older heavy guns still in the depots and defending fortresses. The best of these was the *de Bange* 155mm long gun, introduced in 1877 and modified in 1914 to improve mobility. It was still considered an obsolete piece, but it was amongst the best that the French then possessed.

11 The *Canon de 120 Modele 1878* was a 120mm caliber gun dating from the mid-nineteenth century, pressed into service in 1914. It lacked a modern recoil system and had to be re-laid following each discharge.

12 AFGG VIII/1, p. 29.

first task was the assault and capture of the ruins of the ancient fort at Kum Kale, followed by the village behind. Once the position at Kum Kale was consolidated, Ruef would march on Yeni Shehr, the next village south down the Asiatic coast, with the objective of clearing the Turks out of the narrow neck of land between the sea and the Mendere river.

To get to Yeni Shehr, Ruef would have to capture and cross a low ridge (the Orkanie Ridge, named after a hamlet on its reverse slope). Here Ruef intended to set up his battery of four 75mm field guns, facing east across the river, where the main Turkish defences lay. The infantry would capture and fortify the village of Yeni Shehr where, under cover of the artillery, it could defend against expected counter-attacks. Such was the plan; Turkish resistance would alter both the timing and the extent of the advance.

At 07:00 a.m. on 25 April an Allied naval squadron commenced its bombardment of the proposed French landing site. French armoured cruisers *Jauréguiberry, Henri IV* and *Jeanne d'Arc* (reinforcements following earlier naval losses), supported by the British *Prince George* and the Russian cruiser *Askold*, all under French Admiral Guépratte, subjected Kum Kale fort and the shoreline to an intense bombardment. After two hours the small boats launched from the transports carried the first wave of troops to shore. They were greeted by gunfire from the fort; at least one machine gun had survived the naval bombardment. Despite casualties, the Senegalese

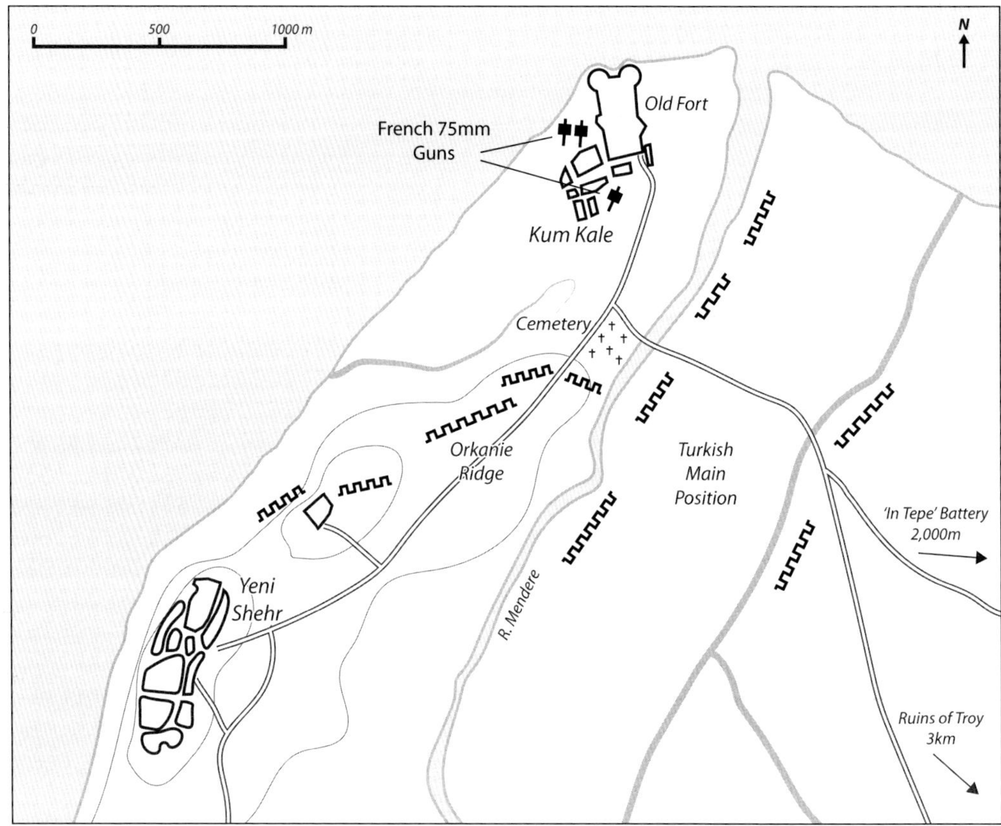

Map 8.1 French diversion at Kum Kale, 25 April 1915.
(Map drawn by George Anderson © Helion & Company 2018)

companies of *6e régiment coloniale mixte* captured the fort *à la baïonnette*, as the French historians say. By 11:00 a.m. the fort and village were in French hands. The next stage did not go so well. The advance out of the south side of the village was met with heavy fire from hidden trenches, both on the east side of the river where the main Turkish defences lay and on the flat sandy ground between the village and the Orkanie Ridge. A further set of trenches hidden in the cemetery covered the road to the only bridge over the river. After two brave but futile charges into the storm of machine gun fire, incurring heavy losses, it was decided to bring up a field gun to support the infantry. A third charge, however, failed to capture the cemetery despite artillery support, and Ruef wisely decided to call off the attempt that day. The infantry was ordered to dig in, barbed wire was brought up, and the positions gained consolidated.

The Turks counter-attacked furiously during the night, and four charges in succession were beaten off. Early in the morning of 26 April about 80 unarmed Turks gave themselves up. Several hundred more approached the French line as if to surrender, but still holding their weapons. In the confusion, with a translator trying to negotiate surrender terms, firing broke out, Turks slipped into nearby houses and were blasted out by cannon-fire. About 60 more prisoners were taken, the rest killed. The Turkish commander and eight of his men were then shot.[13]

The French attack resumed in the afternoon of 26 April. By then a fresh bombardment had been organised, with the cruiser *Savoie* sailing close inshore to add the weight of her guns to those of the battery of 75s on shore. The weight of shelling caused the Turks to abandon the Orkanie Ridge, and 500 prisoners were taken. The defending Turkish battalions seemed to be falling apart; at this point the French advance could have continued over the ridge and into Yeni Shehr. But orders had already arrived from General Hamilton that the diversion operation was at an end and re-embarkation would take place that night. A withdrawal from the ridge to the fort was methodically undertaken without any interference from the Turks. During the night of 26/27 April the evacuation was successfully executed, the only danger coming from Turkish heavy artillery at the "In Tepe" battery, whose heavy calibre shells caused considerable losses. When the count was made the next day, French losses were found to be 183 men and 13 officers killed, 575 men wounded, out of an approximate 3,000 involved (about 25 percent casualties). It was estimated that Turkish losses were of the order of several thousand, plus the 600 prisoners taken.

The French diversionary action at Kum Kale may be viewed as a complete success, given the prescribed mission; not so the British on the Gallipoli Peninsula. Major-General Hunter-Weston, leading the main landings at Cape Helles, had expected to land his troops against minimal opposition and advance three miles inland to occupy the high ground at Krithia and Achi Baba. He was stopped on the beaches, with tremendous casualties, by machine guns rather than numbers of defenders; where on his flanks subsidiary landings were made unopposed, he failed to reinforce success and consequently allowed the Turks time to recover and bring up reserves. The French viewed the British situation on the first night (25/26 April) as very serious if not critical. During the morning of 26 April, General Hamilton had to request that General d'Amade place two of his reserve battalions at the immediate disposal of the British 29th Division to replace British casualties; d'Amade was further requested to put a third battalion and an artillery battery on standby to land on the Gallipoli Peninsula in the near future. Given

13 AFGG VIII/1, p. 44.

that half of d'Amade's force was then still committed to the Asiatic shore, the requisition from reserve of one of d'Amade's two remaining regiments and all his remaining artillery testifies to the precarious situation in which the British found themselves.

During the night of 26/27 April, two battalions of *175e régiment d'infanterie* (175 RI, Lieutenant-Colonel Philippe) were put ashore on the British V Beach, and by dawn had taken over the right flank of 29th Division's line from the Old Fort down to the sea. Starting at about 3:30 p.m. on 27 April, *175 RI* under orders of Major-General Hunter-Weston took part in 29th Division's advance. The limited objective was to advance in order to link up with S Beach on the right, forming a continuous allied line from there across to X Beach on the Aegean coast. The French part of this minor operation was achieved against minimal resistance, because the Turks (as we now know) had withdrawn all but a few outposts to the higher ground in the north. By 5:30 p.m. Lieutenant-Colonel Philippe had linked up with Lieutenant-Colonel Casson of the South Wales Borderers at the so-called de Tott's Battery on the high ground at Hill 236 above S Beach.[14] Lieutenant-Colonel Philippe's two battalions dug in on the reverse slopes of Hill 236, facing north, with British troops on either flank. During the night of 27/28 April, the third battalion of *175 RI* was landed, and the French then took over the line on the right down to the sea, relieving the South Wales Borderers above S Beach.

Despite the failures of the first three days, General Hamilton's strategic plan remained unchanged: the capture and occupation of the high ground at Krithia and Achi Baba. But now instead of a swift advance from the beaches, there would have to be a formal assault on rapidly strengthening Turkish trenches. Major-General Hunter-Weston's plan for this assault, to be launched on 28 April, was to attack on his left with 29th Division in order to capture the high ground either side of the village of Krithia. Once that first objective had been gained, 29th Division's right-hand brigade would pivot to face east towards Achi Baba, lining the Sedd-el-Bahr to Krithia road. The French, leading once again with *175 RI*, would hold its right on the sea and advance its centre and left in echelon up the western side of the Kereves Dere Ravine (called the "Kereves Dere Spur" on British maps).

Once Krithia fell, Hunter-Weston believed that Achi Baba would be swiftly occupied. The assault that took place on 28 April would later be known as the First Battle of Krithia. It is interesting to note that all subsequent battles on the southern Cape Helles front of the Gallipoli campaign would never deviate from that original operational plan. What Hamilton, Hunter-Weston and d'Amade did not know, however, was that on the night of 26/27 April the Turks had started to organise a new defensive position, roughly on the 90 metre contour line (about 300 feet above sea level). That contour line runs from the northwest in front of Krithia down to the southeast on the Kereves Dere Spur. Consequently the French on the right would be assaulting the main Turkish position on 28 April, whilst the British on the left were initially only faced with outpost lines on slightly lower ground. If the French failed to advance and the British were caught in enfilade, it was in great part due to the command failure to appreciate where the Turkish strength lay.

During the night of 27/28 April General d'Amade sent the remainder of General Vandenberg's Metropolitan Brigade ashore to take part in the attack, supported by a battery of 75mm field

14 Ibid., pp. 44-49; and Brigadier-General C.F. Aspinall-Oglander, *Military Operations, Gallipoli*, Vol. I (London: Heinemann, 1929), pp. 277, 281-284.

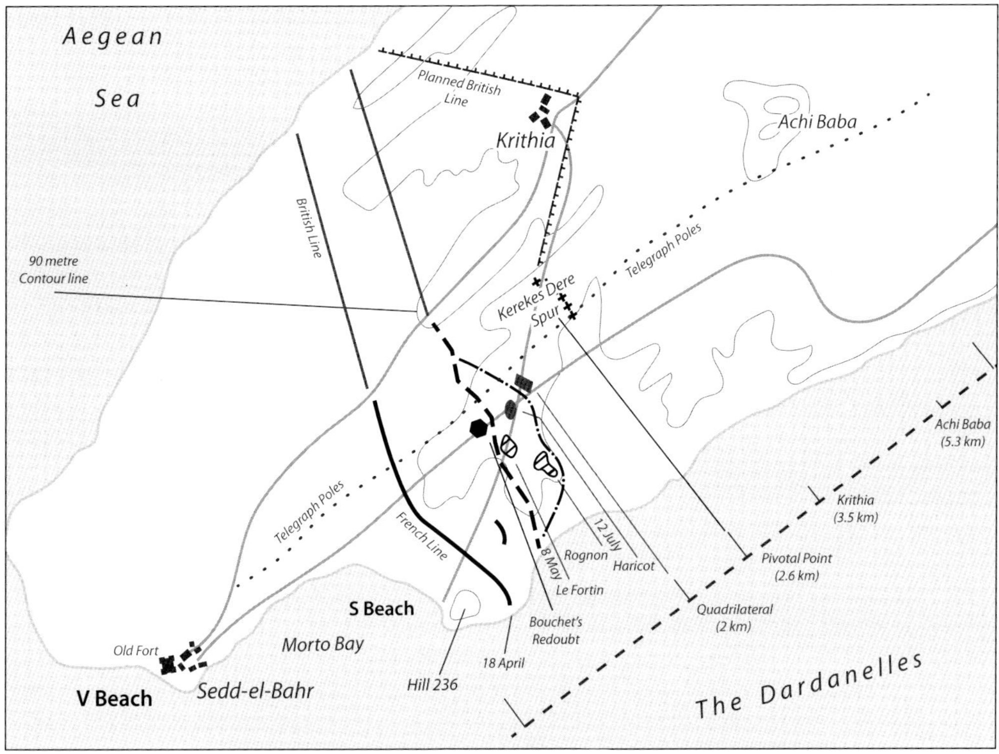

Map 8.2 French sector: Cape Helles front, April–July 1915.
(Map drawn by George Anderson © Helion & Company 2018)

guns. At 8:00 a.m. on the morning of 28 April, the brigade advanced with all three battalions of *175 RI* in the first line and *1 régiment de marche d'Afrique*, made up of a battalion of Zouaves and one of the Foreign Legion, in a second line. In an attempt to suppress Turkish enfilading fire, Vandenberg first sent a column of men out from de Tott's battery down into the mouth of the Kereves Dere Ravine and up onto the eastern (right-hand) spur. From there they could fire across the ravine in support of the main attack. The column gained the eastern spur but was driven off it by the intensity of the Turkish artillery bombardment – some of it coming from the Asiatic shore into their backs. Despite bringing the Zouaves up into the front line, Vandenberg was forced to dig in at the foot of the eastern spur in the mouth of the ravine. Indeed, at one point the Zouaves panicked and had to be rallied in order to hold the position. This was the beginning of a belief within the French command that "native" troops were unreliable in defence. It is noteworthy that the British Official History says that "all accounts agree that the gay French uniforms and white cork helmets were a severe handicap to their wearers, making them an easy mark for the enemy".[15] The main French attack, led by *175 RI* on the left

15 Aspinall-Oglander, *Military Operations*, Vol. I, p. 291.

and centre, followed the line of telegraph poles that led up the middle of the Kereves Dere Spur towards the plateau at the top of the ravine and (ultimately) Krithia.

Starting at 10:00 a.m., there was initial success, with the first series of slopes leading up to the Kereves Dere Spur being taken without serious resistance. After a short pause at midday, the advance was resumed but against stiffening resistance from trenches and strong points that were becoming more and more numerous. As the French climbed up towards the 90-metre contour line, they encountered the first trenches of the main Turkish position. Several local counter-attacks had to be beaten off. *175 RI* sought to match its pace of advance to that of the British on their left; but after advancing several hundred metres towards Hill 300[16] and suffering punishing levels of casualties, the troops went to ground some 400 metres short of a strong Turkish line of trenches liberally endowed with machine guns. Despite throwing in every company and every platoon, *175 RI* failed to get forward. It lost 75 percent of its officers and 25 percent of its men – a significant casualty level – and the surviving officers decided to await nightfall in order to regroup, reinforce and resupply. The Turks thought otherwise and launched a powerful counter-attack at about 5:30 p.m. aimed at the point where the French and British forces linked. The allies were forced to give ground; and as was so often the case in positional warfare, the French right wing withdrew as soon as it found its flank was "in the air", so that the Metropolitan Brigade found itself at the end of the day back in its starting positions. The French contribution to the First Battle of Krithia had achieved nothing, at a cost over two days of 27 officers (5 killed, the rest wounded) and 974 men (56 killed) out of a total of approximately 2,400 front line men (nearly 42 percent casualties). The French troops were exhausted and in need of time to recover while consolidating their positions. The Turks also had suffered heavily in their violent counter attacks and were from nightfall on 28 April relatively quiet. For the next three days, the allied line engaged in little more than minor skirmishing, whilst the generals took stock.

On the evening of 28 April, General d'Amade came ashore to take command of his division. He set up his headquarters in the ruins of the Old Fort on Hill 411 above Sedd-el-Bahr. Between 29 April and 1 May, he reorganised his forces. He brought Colonel Ruef's Colonial Brigade ashore, so that his whole division was on the peninsula. He then put both brigades in the line, each with one regiment up and one in reserve. On his left, in rugged terrain, he brought up the 65mm mountain gun battery to supplement the two batteries of 75s already in place. Finally, he ordered the armoured cruiser *Provence* to unship two 14cm (5.2 inch) naval guns and set them up in the fort. From there they could provide counter-battery fire against the big Turkish guns on the Asiatic shore, freeing up all the field artillery for the support of the infantry.

For the rest of the campaign, *le Corps Expéditionnaire d'Orient* would hold and fight on the right half of the Allied battle line at Cape Helles. And for the rest of the campaign, its operational objective would be the same: capture the Kereves Dere Spur, breaching the main Turkish position in doing so; line the Kereves Dere ravine from the sea up to the neck of the ravine; and thus provide the strong line on which the British would pivot in order to capture Achi Baba. From 28 April onwards, for the next eight months, only the tactics would change.

16 French official historians habitually identify terrain features in terms of their height above sea level. In this instance it seems that, taking British maps as their source, the French nominated "Hill 300" as approximately 300 feet above sea level. This corresponds to the 90 metre contour line, upon which the main Turkish defensive position was organised.

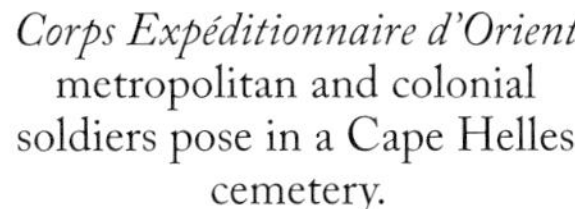

Corps Expéditionnaire d'Orient metropolitan and colonial soldiers pose in a Cape Helles cemetery.

By now it was obvious to the Allied high command that significant reinforcements would be required for the capture of Achi Baba. While Kitchener released a Territorial division from Egypt for duty in Gallipoli, the French War Minister decided on 30 April to send *156e Division d'Infanterie* (General Bailloud) urgently from the Western Front; once in theatre, it would be renamed *2e division du corps expéditionnaire d'Orient* (2 Eastern Division). The first elements sailed from France on 2 May 1915. Like the original (now 1 Eastern) Division, 2 Eastern Division had a colonial and a metropolitan brigade; the only difference was that the colonial regiments had two battalions of European troops instead of one, and one of Senegalese instead of two. This no doubt reflected reports of the unreliability of African troops in defence. The new division's colonial brigade (designated *4e brigade mixte coloniale*, General Simonin) was transported first, between 2 and 15 May. The first elements arrived in theatre on 6 May, after the next Allied attack had already started.

The Second Battle of Krithia took place between 6 and 8 May. Again. the French were asked to attack up the Kereves Dere Spur and establish what the British were now calling a "Pivotal Point" on the plateau at the top. The French *1 Eastern Division*'s attack started at 11:00 a.m. on 6 May. On the left, *2e brigade mixte coloniale*[17] made a direct assault towards the Pivotal Point in liaison with the British right wing. The *1e brigade métropolitaine*[18] on the right advanced in

17 AFGG X/2, pp. 859-864: Order of Battle of all French divisions: the original Colonial Brigade of the Eastern Division was renamed *2e Brigade mixte coloniale* on disembarkation of the second division.

18 Ibid., pp. 859-864. The original Metropolitan Brigade was designated with the numeral '1' on arrival of the second division.

support, attempting to drive the Turks off the spur and down into the ravine. By early afternoon the summit of the plateau was reached, and it looked as if the objective would be met. But before the final advance towards the Pivotal Point could be organised, a devastating Turkish counter-bombardment pinned the French down, and further forward movement became impossible. That evening the first two battalions of the *2nd Division* were placed at the disposal of General Masnou, who used them to back up his left flank. Digging in on the positions won halfway up the spur, the reinforced *1st Division* prepared to receive the inevitable counter-attacks, which came in during the night. Once again, the Turkish attacks failed with very heavy casualties.

During the night the disembarkation and deployment of General Simonin's *4e brigade mixte coloniale* was completed. Simonin was immediately charged with mounting a fresh attack on the Pivotal Point during the morning of 7 May. He led off with *8e régiment mixte coloniale* (three battalions), the attack being launched at 10:00 a.m. on 7 May. Despite very heavy casualties, and after eight hours of fighting, the lead regiment had fought its way to within 100 metres of the Pivotal Point; but it had neither the manpower nor the energy left to complete that final stretch. At nightfall, therefore, it was forced to withdraw to its start line. D'Amade had by then placed General Bailloud's *2nd Division* in reserve; but already one of its two brigades had been decimated on the very day of its arrival at Gallipoli.

General Hamilton was determined not to let up the pressure on the Turks and ordered a renewal of the attack on 8 May. This time the British bore the brunt of the attack, with no greater success than before; the French were content merely to bombard the enemy positions. It was by now abundantly clear to the French command that on the Kereves Dere Spur they were confronted by the main Turkish position and that Liman von Sanders was going to defend it at all costs and with plentiful reserves.[19] Not only was it able to use the dead ground within the ravine to resupply and reinforce its front line, but it had unrestricted and heavy artillery protection on its left flank from the batteries on the Asiatic shore, some of which (as has been pointed out before) were firing directly into the French rear. Remote from the front and ignorant of the strength of the Turkish Kereves Dere position, General Hamilton decided upon one last attack on 8 May, this time by all Allied forces all along the line. He ordered this fresh assault, with another 15-minute preliminary bombardment, to commence at "precisely" 5:30 p.m. And this time, General d'Amade gave up his protestations about the impregnability of the main Turkish position and gallantly ordered *1st Division*, reinforced by Simonin's brigade from *2nd Division*, to join in the general attack. D'Amade then went forward to the front line to inspire his men. His exhortations seem to have worked: the British official historian described the French attack thus:

> At 6 p.m. with drums beating and bugles sounding the whole French line surged forwards in a frenzy of enthusiasm. The red and blue uniforms of the French troops showed up with terrible clearness, and for a moment, to those watching in rear, it seemed as if the whole spur, including the "pivotal point" on the left flank, had at last been captured. But a minute later the Turks covered the ridge with high explosive shell. The trial was too severe. The left and centre recoiled ...[20]

19 Aspinall-Oglander, *Military Operations*, Vol. I, p. 344
20 Ibid., p. 347.

The French account of this action is more restrained. It describes how Simonin's troops came to within bayonet distance of the Pivotal Point on the left but could not make the last assault; how in the centre Ruef's 2 Colonial Brigade took a Turkish redoubt astride the road from Sedd-el-Bahr (later designated Bouchet's Redoubt); and how on the right Vandenberg's *1e brigade métropolitaine* secured a brief foothold on the very edge of the ravine before being dislodged by a Turkish counter-attack,[21] retreating right back to the foot of the spur. Crucially in the centre, however, they retained a foothold inside Bouchet's Redoubt that they would hold until the end of the campaign; and equally crucially, Bouchet's Redoubt was poised on the lip of the 90-metre contour line. Thus ended the Second Battle of Krithia. "Except on the French Front" wrote the British official historian, "the attack had been unable even to press back the enemy's advanced troops or locate his main line".[22]

After the battle the front stabilised, and a classic stalemated trench warfare scenario developed. The Turks held the high ground and had powerful artillery; and, thanks to the passive state of the Russians on the Caucasus and Black Sea fronts, together with the benevolent neutrality of Bulgaria, Enver Pasha had plenty of reserves available to pour into the Gallipoli Peninsula. On the Allied side, it was time for appraisal, and for change. British Major-General Hunter-Weston remained defiantly optimistic despite lack of progress and very heavy casualties. He was promoted. General d'Amade, by contrast, appeared weary, complaining, pessimistic and weighed down by the responsibility of commanding the Eastern Corps. Consequently, he was replaced on 15 May by General Henri Gouraud, who had made a reputation for himself on the Western Front. The appointment had been announced in advance; Gouraud sailed from France on 11 May, landing at Cape Helles on 14 May before taking up his post the next day.

The brief French occupation of front line Turkish trenches during the Second Battle of Krithia had delivered vital intelligence. Facing Gouraud on 15 May 1915 on the 90-metre contour line were four important strong-points that he would have to take if he was to clear the Kereves Dere Spur: from right to left, *Le Fortin "Le Gouez"* (named after the officer killed in its initial capture on 8 May); *Le Rognon* (kidney); *L'Haricot* (Bean); *Le Quadrilatère* (quadrilateral).

These would be the focus of the French attacks for the rest of campaign, as well of course as the lines of trenches that connected them. With Bouchet's Redoubt partially in their hands, the next nearest strong-point was *Le Fortin "Le Gouez"*, forward on the right. Behind it, poised on the lip of the ravine about 50-60 metres above sea level, the kidney-shaped redoubt *le Rognon* anchored the whole Turkish position. Five hundred metres inland, on the far side of a gap defended by four lines of trenches, *l'Haricot* was positioned on the high ground of the 90-metre contour, capable of enfilading the gap as well as blocking further progress from Bouchet's Redoubt. And 100 metres behind *l'Haricot* lay the most formidable of them all, *le Quadrilatère*. It was particularly important; it was furthest inland, it overlooked the British right wing on the route to Krithia; it had good artillery observation over the whole southern part of the peninsula; and it protected the main Turkish supply road for the Kereves Dere position. To reach the "Pivotal Point" *Le Quadrilatère* had to be taken, and to achieve that, *l'Haricot* and its maze of trenches had first to be conquered.

21 AFGG VIII/1, pp. 62-63.
22 Aspinall-Oglander, *Military Operations*, Vol. I, p. 347.

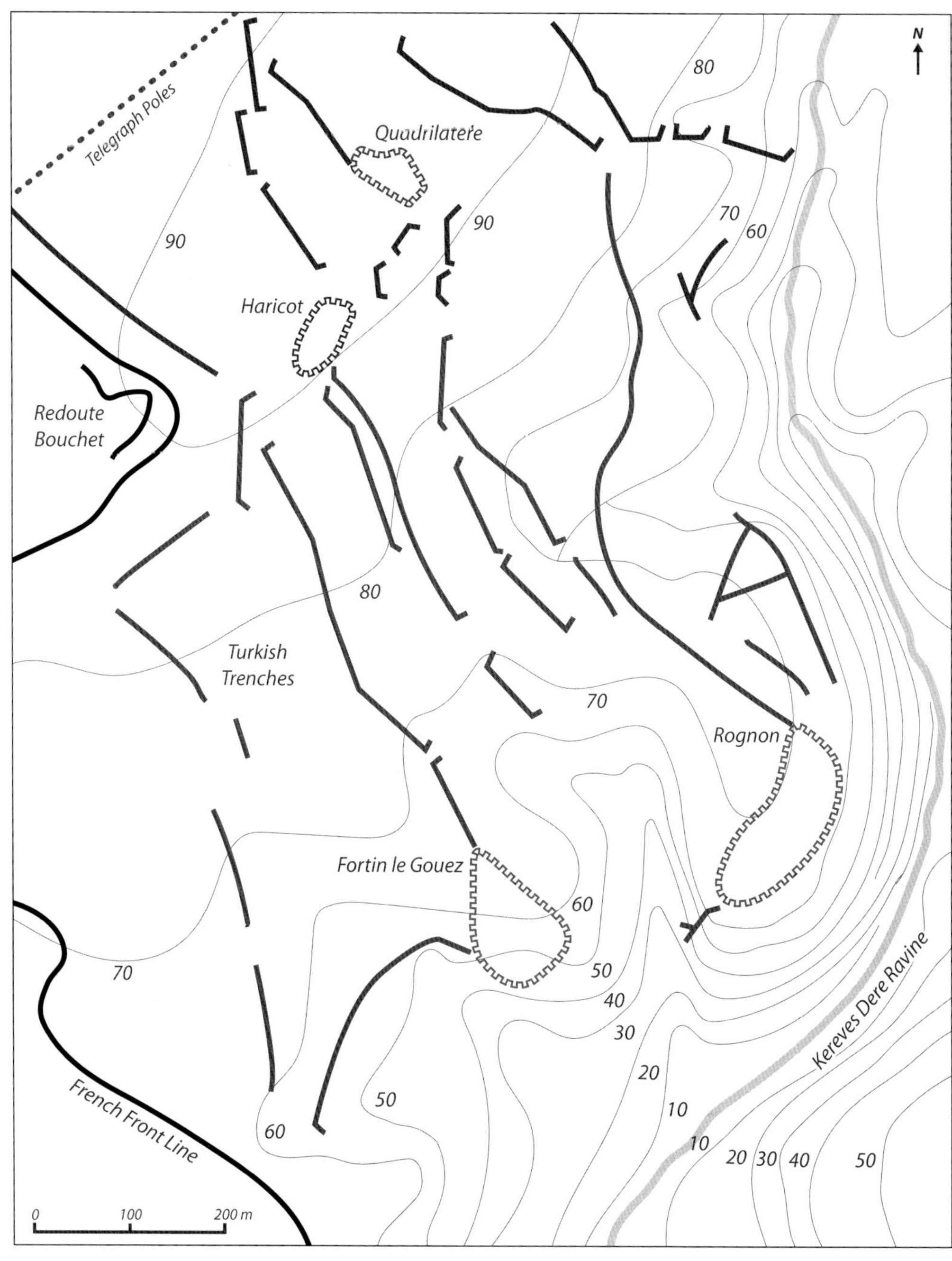

Map 8.3 Turkish redoubts situated on the 90-metre contour line.
(Map drawn by George Anderson © Helion & Company 2018)

Gouraud's impact was immediate. On his first day in command (having spent 24 hours observing) he issued a memorandum to his officers detailing what they were doing wrong and what he wanted corrected.[23] His observations included: poor placing of machine guns, trenches too wide, and too many men held in the front line. The lessons of the Western Front were now to be applied to Gallipoli. Gouraud also cabled the Ministry of War asking for, *inter alia*, more wire, grenades and heavy artillery. He was reiterating requests already made by d'Armade (for example for two batteries of 155mm howitzers, forty-eight 58mm "Dumézil" trench mortars and two 240mm super-howitzers with 250 shells each); but as the "new broom" he got an instant and positive reply detailing the name and departure date of each ship carrying his requirements.[24] He also demanded, and got, two squadrons of modern aeroplanes, one for bombing, the other of fighters to gain air superiority over the embryonic Turkish air force in the region.[25] On 18 May he sent his appreciation of the overall situation to General Hamilton. Whilst endorsing Hamilton's existing strategy of pushing forward from Cape Helles on the left, and identifying Achi Baba as the key to the campaign, Gouraud also laid out his operational ideas learned on the Western Front for a methodical approach to assaulting well-prepared field fortifications, emphasising mixed arm cooperation, especially between artillery and infantry but also including aeroplanes. For good measure, he suggested an alternative strategic approach of a landing on the Asiatic shore at Besika Bay and the capture of Chanak – but only if the British government could provide the required extra 100,000 men.[26] Gouraud presumably knew Joffre well enough to know that no such force would be forthcoming on the French side.

In addition to setting down operational and strategic appreciations and laying out demands for tactical improvement, Gouraud was not slow in issuing orders for fresh offensive action. On 18 May he sought support from the Royal Naval Division on his left in a small tactical advance of about 400 metres that he wanted to make along the line of the telegraph posts on his left flank. On 20 May he launched a surprise attack by Siminin's brigade at 4:00 a.m. on *l'Haricot* redoubt. Although the Senegalese took the redoubt, they retreated under a fierce counter-bombardment by heavy guns, suffering losses of about 250 men. A second attack on 22 May by Ganaval's *3e brigade métropolitaine* also failed: the Senegalese troops of *2e regiment de marche d'Afrique* hurled themselves forward and suffered serious losses (22 officers and 1,250 men of about 3,000) but could not break into the redoubt. It was after these abortive assaults on the redoubts, which were characterised by an initial success followed by failure to hold what had been gained, that the French command reorganised its mixed troops in a novel way. Recognising that the Senegalese (or *"troupes noires"* (black soldiers) in the blunt terminology of the day) were excellent in assault but weak in defence, each battalion was reformed with two companies of Senegalese and two of colonial Europeans; the implication being that the Senegalese would lead the assault and the Europeans consolidate the ground won.[27]

As well as the attacks on the redoubts, Gouraud undertook during May a series of small local actions to improve, straighten and strengthen his line. Chief amongst these were those that

23 AFGG VIII/1, Annex 197: *Old Castle, le 15 Mai 1915; Note de Service.*
24 Ibid., Annexes 196 and 198.
25 Ibid., p. 70.
26 Ibid., Annex 201: *Sedd-ul-Bahr, 18 Mai 1915; Gouraud à Hamilton; Note sur la Situation du corps expéditionnaire.*
27 Ibid., p. 78.

turned the Bouchet Redoubt from a small salient surrounded on three sides by the enemy into an integral strongpoint embedded within the French line. Then on 31 May a surprise assault on *Le Fortin Le Gouez* by the *légionnaires* of the third battalion of *1ere régiment de marche d'Afrique* carried the redoubt with very little loss; for the rest of the campaign the *Fortin* remained in French hands.

By this time both the French and British had been strongly reinforced with heavy artillery. For Gouraud, the first of the two batteries of new *Rimailho* 155mm howitzers had arrived at Lemnos on 26 May, with 100 rounds per piece and more to follow.[28] The guns were now in place on Gallipoli. Hamilton decided that it was time for another major attack on Krithia and Achi Baba, starting on 4 June 1915; the operational plan was unchanged. Gouraud's tactical plan for the French role in what would be known as the Third Battle of Krithia was this: with both divisions in line (1st on the right, 2nd on the left) to advance in two distinct phases, taking *l'Haricot* and *le Rognon* during phase one, culminating in an advance across the 500 metre gap between them to the edge of the ravine; and in phase two finally capturing *Le Quadrilatère* and advancing to occupy the "Pivotal Point". If possible and depending on events, at least two footholds would be won by crossing the ravine and ascending to the eastern spur. A small French naval squadron – light cruiser *Latouche-Tréville*, two torpedo boats and two armed sloops – would support the ground troops from positions offshore by firing up the ravine from the south at Turkish targets hidden from the French field artillery.[29]

At midday on 4 June after an hour-long bombardment by nine field, two mountain and two heavy batteries, the French infantry rose from their trenches and advanced towards the Turkish lines, in places a mere 100 metres away. Once again ferocious fire decimated their ranks and they were forced to retire, except on the right beyond *Le Fortin*, where a 250 metres length of Turkish trench fell into French hands. A second attack during the afternoon by fresh troops failed in similar fashion. Thirty-five officers and 1,997 men were killed or wounded for virtually no gain. Lest one think that such profligate waste was solely a French trait, it should be noted that on the French left the British 2nd Naval Brigade lost in this action over 1,000 of its 1,900 men: caught in enfilade by Turkish machine guns whilst advancing "as steady as if on parade" the whole Collingwood Battalion was virtually annihilated.[30] By 5:00 p.m. the whole Allied offensive had once again ground to a halt, with heavy losses for no appreciable gain.

It was clearly time for a strategic reappraisal of the whole Allied game-plan. In a telegram to the Minister of War dated 6 June 1915, Gouraud set out the impossibility of making frontal progress up the Gallipoli Peninsula. He advocated an indirect approach via a fresh landing on the Asiatic shore.

The planned reinforcements however were all British, and the British generals called the tune. A new landing at Sulva Bay and a swift advance across the top of the peninsula was decided upon. The French government was merely replacing Gouraud's casualties and the *Corps Expéditionnaire d'Orient's* role in the Gallipoli campaign was reduced to a supporting role on the Cape Helles front that was itself now secondary to a major offensive in the northwest.

MEF commanders, however, did not believe that the Cape Helles front should become entirely defensive; it could still perform a valuable role fixing and holding in the south major Turkish

28 Ibid., Annex 208.
29 Ibid., pp. 84-85.
30 Aspinall-Oglander, *Military Operations*, Vol. I, p. 48.

forces that could then be cut off by the new offensive in the northwest. So Gouraud continued to plan and execute small methodical actions designed to improve his position on the Kereves Dere Spur. And on 21 June Gouraud mounted a bigger attack. This time, he insisted on massed artillery preparation on a narrow front. His objective was to take out the Turkish positions on the high ground on either flank of the western spur, with an overall frontage of just 650 metres. On his left, Gouraud aimed once again to capture both *L'Haricot* and *Le Quadrilatère*; in the centre the assault would cross the 350 metres that separated them from the lip of the ravine. It was nothing new, there was nothing new to try, except by using more artillery more effectively. The bombardment started at 5:15 a.m. At 6:00 a.m. the guns increased their range and the infantry rose to the attack. Gouraud's preparation was by all accounts meticulous. Every man had been given a definite objective and a definite task. The French artillery was strong, and well-endowed with shells. But the French infantry still lacked skilled bombers and stocks of grenades for the bombers to throw. On the left *176 RI* was immediately successful thanks to the pulverising bombardment. *L'Haricot* was finally taken and held, the Turkish first and second lines of trenches were occupied, and positions were consolidated against the inevitable counter-attacks. Only *Le Quadrilatère* continued to defy the French. On the right *6e régiment mixte coloniale* achieved only limited success, in carrying the Turkish first line of trenches. They failed at the second line, which was heavily manned. There regimental commander Lieutenant-Colonel Noguès fell, badly wounded, and as was so often the case also on the Western Front, the loss of a charismatic officer was followed by a dramatic loss of morale. Shortly after Noguès was hit, at about 7:00 a.m., the troops fell back to their start line. The assault was renewed at midday but was again driven back with great loss. At 2:15 p.m. after a fresh bombardment a third attempt to get forward failed. At 3:00 p.m. General Gouraud issued draconian orders that the trenches must be taken before nightfall at all costs. Gouraud drafted into the attack the Senegalese companies of *1e regiment de marche d'Afrique*, whose élan took them back into the first Turkish trench; there the colonial companies of the regiment consolidated the position. At last a link was established with *176 RI* on their left. Whilst the Colonials were making hard and bloody work of their mission, *176 RI* had used the afternoon to get as far as a section of trench immediately in front of *Le Quadrilatère*; but they were done, they could not set foot in the redoubt itself.

From 23-25 June, there were minor French attacks, including another abortive attempt to get into *Le Quadrilatère*. Then on 30 June came an important French success. Judging that the Turks had been disorganised by the pounding attacks by the British on the western side of the peninsula, Gouraud launched a fresh unit – *7e régiment mixte coloniale* – at *Le Quadrilatère*, and at last succeeded in capturing not only the redoubt but several trenches beyond it. Although ground was then lost to counter-attacks, the French ended the day still in possession of at least part of the redoubt, thus denying the enemy its tactical potential and assisting the British to get forward. The action cost the French 15 officers and 865 men killed or wounded. And there was one final, dramatic, casualty. General Gouraud was seriously wounded by shrapnel whilst entering a field hospital on the beach to visit his troops. He was a victim of the Asiatic shore batteries, which had recommenced firing into the French rear as soon as the French naval squadron had withdrawn. The loss of Gouraud was a serious blow for the French expeditionary corps, and for the Allies as a whole. During his six weeks in command he had revitalised the French effort on Gallipoli, raising morale, improving technique, introducing new "western front" style tactics, and gaining significant success against the strong redoubts of the main Turkish position. Under his command the French had all but met the requirements of Hunter-Weston's operational plan. They had broken into the main Turkish position on the 90-metre contour line, capturing two of the four Turkish redoubts and nullifying the tactical value of the other two. Operational success, however, depended on reaching the "Pivotal Point" still some 600 metres away, and on the British reaching Krithia before pushing on to occupy Achi Baba; and that simply had not happened. Massive casualties weighed in the balance against minimal strategic return.

The commander of *2e Division*, General Bailloud, was temporarily promoted into Gouraud's place – he was the senior of the French general officers in theatre. Bailloud promptly resurrected the plan first mooted by Gouraud back in May for a landing on the Asiatic shore to eliminate the Turkish heavy batteries stationed there. At 7:35 a.m. on 12 July, General Bailloud launched his first attack as corps commander. More of the same: *2nd Division* on the left aimed to enlarge on its gains at *Le Quadrilatère* but failed dismally; *1st Division* on the right managed finally to capture *Le Rognon* and drive the Turkish defenders back to the very lip of the ravine. There, precariously crouching in a trench at the back of which was a sharp drop, the Turks somehow held on. To all intents and purposes at this point the French had finally cleared and occupied the Kereves Dere Spur. The British objectives, Krithia and Achi Baba, however, were as far away as ever.

Events in France catalysed what happened next to the French in Gallipoli. By June 1915 the French government was starting to lose confidence in General Joffre after a disastrous series of bloody offensives on the Western Front. The chief candidate to replace him was General Sarrail, a political general, ardent republican and favourite of many politicians. On 22 July, in an effort to shore up his position, Joffre sacked Sarrail from his post of commander of *Third Army* on the Western Front but was forced to appoint him to a fresh post; the Mediterranean seemed far enough away from Paris. But Sarrail insisted on getting an army not a corps, an attitude that gelled with the politicians who had long favoured increased commitment in the Mediterranean theatre. To cut an interesting story short, on 5 August 1915 General Sarrail was placed in command of a new Eastern army that the French government intended to place on the Asiatic shore of the Dardanelles in response to Bailloud's pressure and Gouraud's lobbying.[31] There would be a fresh landing at Kum Kale followed by an advance on Chanak; then a march along the Asiatic shore (See Map 8.4). Sarrail believed that six divisions would suffice for the job; intelligence reports showed just two Turkish formations (*2nd Division* and *8th Division*) spread thinly over the target area. Joffre did not agree with Sarrail. Whilst at last acknowledging that a new Mediterranean front was needed to restore mobility to a stalemated Western Front, Joffre was worried that Bulgaria was edging towards the Central Powers camp and threatening Serbia and possibly Greece; there was the possibility of an Italian intervention in the Balkan region; Salonika beckoned.

While the political strategic debate continued its slow and ponderous gestation in London and in Paris, Frenchmen continued to die on the Cape Helles front, more in the cause of pinning down substantial bodies of Turks than in a belief that the British might eventually capture Krithia and Achi Baba. On 7 August 1915 General Bouchard attacked alongside his allies once again. *2nd Division* on his left had the sole objective of clearing up possession of the Kereves Dere Spur; *1st Division* on his right even more modestly sought to take two specific Turkish trenches. Thousands of lives were traded for a few hundred metres of hilly terrain. Despite

31 AFGG VIII/1, pp. 100-114.

the commitment to Gouraud's methodical approach, French preparation was still insufficient – which means at the bottom line not enough artillery – and the attack foundered once again in the face of Turkish machine guns and saturating counter-bombardment. It did not help that fanatic resistance was maintained by numerous Turkish infantrymen despite massive casualties, and that copious Turkish reinforcements awaited their turn in the line. The French contribution to this latest diversion on the Cape Helles sector went ahead in parallel with the new British landing at Sulva Bay, which despite achieving complete surprise wallowed in inertia due to poor generalship and lost the golden opportunity to cut the neck of the peninsula in the north. When on 17 August General Hamilton decided to call off his Sulva offensive, the Gallipoli campaign was effectively over, even if it took many months for the fact to be recognised and acted upon.

In Paris, the political momentum to support General Sarrail's leadership of an Eastern Army continued unabated. Hence the scheme to land on the Asiatic shore still had legs, and still had some support in London. By now Salonika was being viewed as an addition to Gallipoli rather than an alternative. Sarrail would take Bailloud's corps from Gallipoli and the British agreed to take over the whole Cape Helles front. Joffre was then put under pressure to supply Sarrail with the rest of the new Eastern Army, from units then on the Western Front. But Joffre was in the process of finalising arrangements for his own autumn offensives in Champagne and Artois. He continued to argue forcibly against any dilution of his offensive capability in France and Belgium. A seminal Allied conference took place at Calais on 11 September 1915. Joffre wanted Sarrail to remain on the defensive at Gallipoli, it being agreed that to evacuate would entail too much loss of face. But Kitchener had already agreed with Millerand to send two British divisions from the Western Front to relieve Bailloud's corps for the putative Asiatic shore operation; at the Allied high command, things were getting complicated. On 15 September 1915 the Ministry of War asked Sarrail what he planned to do. Naturally he planned to use the four fresh divisions that the Ministry had promised to prise from Joffre, together with Bailloud's corps, to land again at Kum Kale and march up the eastern shore of the Hellespont. Equally naturally Sarrail demanded the complete infrastructure of a French field army: organising his six divisions into three army corps with appropriate support services, with seven groups of heavy artillery to prepare the attack and a brigade of cavalry for exploitation.[32] Sarrail planned to move north and take Chanak, destroying the heavy batteries there, before advancing further. With the French at Chanak, opposite Kilid Bahr and the narrowest part of the Narrows, it was expected that the passage through to the Sea of Marmara would be forced, the original strategic objective of the campaign.

At this point in the protracted three-month "negotiations" between Joffre, Sarrail and Millerand, fate intervened. Bulgaria finally decided to commit itself to the war, mobilising its army on the side of the Central Powers, a threat that the French government could not ignore. Orders were given to General Bailloud on 24 September 1915 to prepare his *2nd Division* for transfer to Salonika; on 5 October 1915 the first French troops landed there.

Back on the Gallipoli Peninsula, the remaining units of the corps – two mixed colonial brigades and two batteries of heavy artillery – were renamed the "Dardanelles Expeditionary Corps" and given to General Brulard. His command was barely of divisional strength, and the focus of Sarrail and his Army of the Orient was entirely on Salonika.

32 Ibid., p. 112.

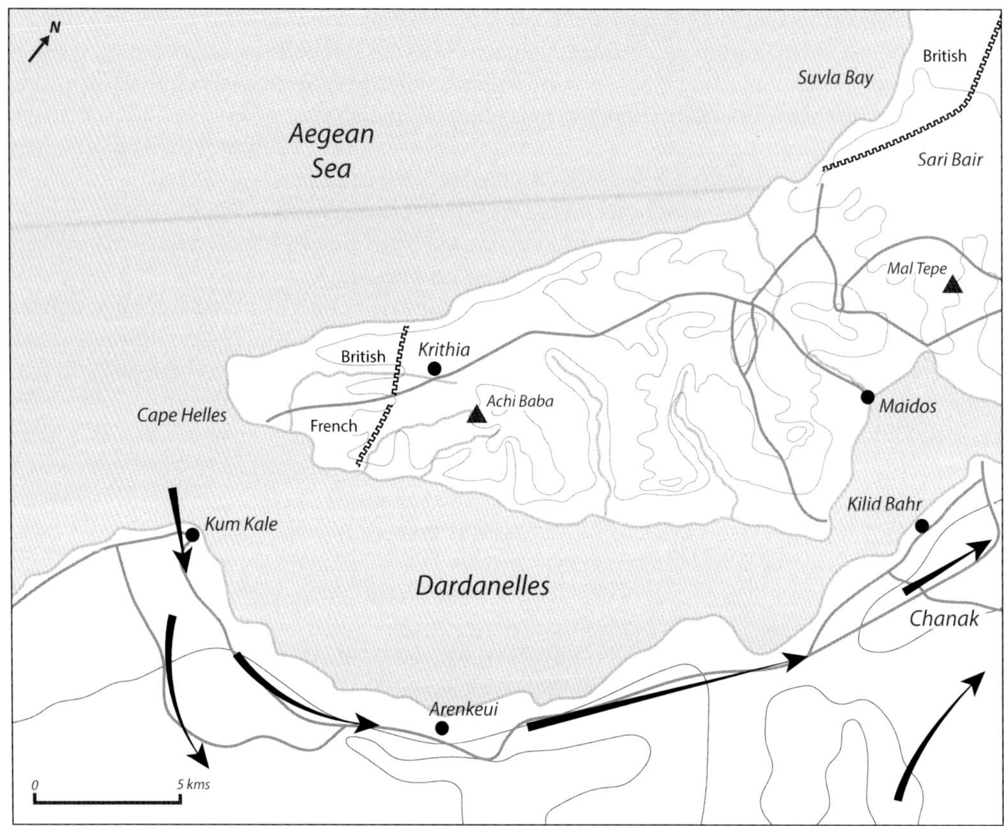

Map 8.4 Proposed French amphibious assault on the Asiatic shore, 5 August 1915. (Map drawn by George Anderson © Helion & Company 2018)

Left to its own devices, Brulard's command was still required to hold the original, two-division, front. Due to attrition and illness, Brulard was barely able to maintain 7,600 riflemen in the front line; the Turks deployed between three and four times as many. Furthermore, as the winter approached, cold wet weather increased the discomfort, illness and demoralisation of the Senegalese element of the residual unit. The winter of 1915/16 on Gallipoli was characterised by Turkish inaction and Anglo-French impotence. The French command worked on ways of safely withdrawing the Senegalese; but attempts to persuade the British to take back part of the front line proved unavailing, even though the French government offered the Senegalese as replacements for the release of British units then guarding Egypt.[33]

For France, the endgame at Gallipoli was driven by political not military principles. The final decision would rest with the British, whose campaign it had always been. General Hamilton, criticised for his poor leadership during the failed Sulva Bay operation, was recalled and General Sir Charles Monro sent out to replace him. Lord Kitchener made a personal visit and, shocked

33 Ibid., p. 118.

by his first sight of the terrain, recommended that Sulva Bay be evacuated. Evacuation, once begun, generated its own momentum. On 8 December 1915 at the Chantilly Conference the Allied high command agreed upon "the immediate and complete evacuation of the Gallipoli Peninsula".[34] On 23 December 1915 the French Cabinet issued orders to General Brulard to organise the evacuation of his remaining troops. Over two days, 3 and 4 January 1916, all French troops were evacuated successfully by the French fleet. Six French artillery pieces were left behind, disabled symbols of a dysfunctional campaign. The Dardanelles Expeditionary Corps was disbanded, its remaining troops either returned to France or sent to Salonika, where they made up the core of a new *17th Colonial Division*.

The French contribution to the Gallipoli campaign has been largely ignored by Anglophone historians. This chapter has set out to redress the balance. In the early period the "Cape Helles" sector was held by two divisions, one French and one British. Whereas the British never came close to their objective (the capture of Krithia and Achi Baba), the French had after eight weeks more or less achieved theirs, the clearing of the Kereves Dere Spur; and in doing so they had broken into and held significant sections of the main Turkish position. But to point this out is merely to assert "bragging rights" about who got furthest. In truth, Gallipoli was an exercise in futility; the ground gained by the French over eight months of battle was paltry, the butcher's bill staggering: overall 27,004 French casualties or 34 percent of those engaged for a territorial gain of no more than two thousand metres.

34 Ibid., p. 123.

9

A Strange Affair: The Royal Naval Division at Gallipoli

Peter Hart

This chapter does not intend to wrestle with the military progress or otherwise made by the Royal Naval Division (RND) at Gallipoli during 1915-16. Instead, I intend it as an impressionistic account to reflect on the unique nature of the RND. It will also examine how the men responded to the challenges as reflected in the personal accounts of officers and other ranks.

The RND was a strange anomaly created at the instigation of the First Lord of the Admiralty, Winston Churchill, on the outbreak of war in August 1914. Churchill had been made aware that there would be over 20,000 reservists for which no ships were then available, and he took the decision to form these men into a makeshift "division" for deployment ashore as a supplement to the six divisions of the Regular Army. A large body of naval recruits and reservists was thus put into training camps established around Deal, with a depot in the Crystal Palace exhibition grounds. Many of them had little or no experience, having only volunteered since the outbreak of war at the Royal Naval Volunteer Reserve depots, such as HMS *Calliope* at Newcastle upon Tyne. Overall there seemed to be a preponderance of recruits from the north-east of England, south Wales, Scotland and Northern Ireland. Recalled reservists had naval skills but were new to the exigencies of land operations. The RND officers and NCOs had mostly originated with the navy, although there were several officers detached from the Guards to instil some discipline into the troops. The ultimate intention was to create two new Naval Brigades, with a further Royal Marine Brigade attached to complete the division. However, only half of these marines were actually serving regulars. In military terms the RND was not a division *per se* as it lacked any artillery.

Little progress had been made beyond some basic foot drill in the first two months, so it was strange that the RND should already be considered a viable force by Churchill. In October 1914, he despatched the RND under the command of Major-General Sir Archibald Paris to reinforce the defence of Antwerp in an effort to prevent the Allied line being outflanked by the German thrust towards the Channel ports in the "Race to the Sea". Many of the untrained recruits of the 1st and 2nd Naval Brigades were filled with a self-confidence born of ignorance, but some wiser heads pondered on what might await them on departing for Belgium on 4 October:

> I felt very elderly and sombre and full of thoughts of how life was like a flash between darknesses, and that 'X' per cent of those who cheered would be blown into another world

Officers and men of the Royal Naval Division in training at Crystal Palace.

> within a few months; and they all seemed to me so innocent and patriotic and noble, and my eyes grew round and tear-stained.[1]
>
> Sub-Lieutenant Rupert Brooke, Anson Battalion, 2nd Naval Brigade

On disembarking at Antwerp, they were thrust into a line of shallow trenches amidst the inner ring of Belgian forts. It soon became apparent that they were almost useless. One incident summed it up perfectly:

> It was the first time most of us had ever fired a rifle, but we got some practice that night, I can assure you. The marksmanship was not brilliant! About the middle of the night someone noticed a white thing moving about half-way between us and the wood and the order was given for the Collingwoods to fire at it. We did so; there were about 1,000 of us and we fired about 200 shots apiece. Towards dawn the firing gradually died away and we saw our object, an old white cow, still calmly grazing away![2]
>
> Ordinary Seaman H. Mellanby, Collingwood Battalion, 1st Naval Brigade

Their inability to hit such a target speaks volumes for their lack of military inefficiency.

1 R. Brooke letter, 17/10/1914 quoted in G. Keynes (ed.), *The Letters of Rupert Brooke* (London: Faber & Faber, 1968), p. 622.
2 IWM DOCS: H. Mellanby transcript account.

It was evident that the arrival of the RND had not materially changed the situation and that Antwerp would still have to be abandoned. The retreat began on 8 October and proved a masterpiece of incompetence. Disorder spread through the marching columns. Although the Marine Brigade and 2nd Naval Brigade managed to reach the rendezvous and be entrained to safety, the 1st Naval Brigade was left behind due to a mixture of poor staff work and an inability to read a map. Commander Wilfred Henderson was faced with a terrible dilemma:

> When the men left the trenches at Antwerp they were not only hungry, but thirsty, and since then they marched about 30 miles. By the time the column got to St. Gilles-Waes, it was more like a mob on the verge of panic than like troops – the poor fellows were demoralised by utter fatigue. The few officers we had were as exhausted as the men and as they hardly knew their men and the men hardly knew them. But apart from exhaustion, demoralisation, lack of training, lack of officers, faulty and deficient equipment, no water bottles, no entrenching tools, our food and ammunition had been taken away to Ostend that morning. Under the conditions I have described, to have attempted to go forward, with troops in the last stages of exhaustion and whose morale I simply could not trust, without artillery support, with the certainty of having to fight a determined action against fresh regular troops, deliberately entrenched, was in my judgement senseless and a useless sacrifice of the lives for whom I was responsible. So I had to bow to the inevitable, and took the remains of my brigade into Holland.[3]
>
> Commander Wilfred Henderson, Headquarters, 1st Naval Brigade

The RND contribution to the defence of Antwerp had been negligible and yet they had suffered 2,613 casualties of which 60 were killed, 138 wounded, 1,479 interned and 936 taken prisoner.[4] Therefore 2,475 were lost for duration of the war – far more than had been lost in the Battle of Mons. The deployment had been driven by Churchill's restless arrogance coupled with his blindness as to the realities of war. On 10 October, the remains of the RND was evacuated back to Britain, where their ranks were replenished with fresh drafts and they resumed their training, moving during the winter to the new Blandford Camp. Slowly the RND reorganised and took shape as three brigade at various stages of training: the Royal Marine Brigade (Chatham, Deal, Plymouth and Portsmouth Battalions), the 1st Naval Brigade (Benbow, Collingwood, Drake and Hawke Battalions) and 2nd Naval Brigade (Anson, Hood, Howe and Nelson Battalions).

Other than its very existence, the most obvious eccentricity that marked out the RND was the nature of many of its relatively junior officers. They were a truly eclectic group, many of whom took great pleasure in being different and their eccentricities helped define the nature of the RND in these early days. A particularly colourful group had coalesced into the Hood Battalion and it is a strange accident of history that this rather unprepossessing battalion of raw naval recruits should have had such an amazing group of individuals acting as their officers – and for a while acting was probably the right term. The best known was the poet Rupert Brooke who had caught the zeitgeist of the age in his sombre poem, *The Soldier* written in 1914. But Brooke was far more than a mere scribbler. Wickedly funny, he was a good-looking,

3 W. Henderson quoted in L. Sellars (ed.), *RND: Antwerp, Gallipoli and the Western Front, 1914-1918*, Leigh-on-Sea, No. 4 (1998), pp. 273-275.

4 D. Jerrold, *The Royal Naval Division* (London: Hutchinson & Co, 1923), p. 89

somewhat *louche* character with an intriguing love-life, who threw himself into his military service with much of the enthusiasm he had previously given to his poetry. Then there was Frederick Kelly: a brilliant Australian musician who played the piano and composed classical pieces, but who also excelled at rowing to such an extent that he had an Olympic medal to his credit from the London Games of 1908. A driven man, he became a stern taskmaster to his men, whilst playing his own compositions and classical works to his fellow officers at every opportunity during the evenings in the mess. This may have been a mixed blessing for the less musically inclined. Another well-known intellectual figure was Patrick Shaw-Stewart, who was regarded by some as the "brightest of them all". Not as naturally good looking as Brooke, he seemed more often thwarted in love, but his poetic talents and overall brilliance were evident – although he had recently turned away from academia to become one of the youngest managing directors of Barings Bank. Denis Browne was a superb musician who excelled on both piano and organ, was a highly rated composer, a conductor and a music critic for several national newspapers. Less obviously gifted, but soon to be renowned in his own right, was an adventurous young New Zealander, Bernard Freyberg. The man required to bring order to this conglomeration of diverse talents was Lieutenant-Colonel Arnold Quilter, formerly of the Grenadier Guards. Although the Hood Battalion attracted most of the luminaries, the Hawke Battalion also had its share of characters including the writer Douglas Jerrold, Vere Harmsworth, the son of the newspaper proprietor Lord Northcliffe, and A. P. Herbert, a brilliant columnist in *Punch* magazine.

Patrick Shaw-Stewart as an Oxford undergraduate 1910.

The men these glitterati commanded were mainly working-class lads, with a fair proportion of old naval reservists recalled to the colours mixed with copious new recruits from the Royal Naval Volunteer Reserve recruiting centres at ports around the country:

> Bob Waldren was a huge miner and he used to go out and get solidly tight. I was in the second bed in the barrack room and when Bob came in drunk or semi-drunk he always insisted in kissing me goodnight. He said I looked like his son. I probably did but he used to say: "Goodnight Baker boy, I love you!" Of course, I had to put up with him – I didn't mind.[5]
>
> Private Harry Baker, Chatham Battalion, Royal Marine Brigade

5 IWM SOUND: T. H. Baker, SR 8721.

But sometimes things could get a little out of hand when drink had been taken to excess:

> One night, Peter came in very tight singing away just as it was lights out in the barrack room. Peter got in bed and somebody had fixed the bed strap on Peter's bed and pulled it right out and he went down with a terrific thump. Peter was flat on his back, well not exactly flat on his back but at an angle, "Holy Jesus", he said, "I'll shoot the bloody lot of you!" He got off the bed and loaded his rifle – we could hear him loading in the dark – and he fired five rounds, the whole lot, through the ceiling. Fortunately, they went through the floor of the upper deck and they didn't hit anyone in bed up there – they went out through the roof and knocked the tiles off. It was a wet night and it started to come pouring down through the top deck, through their beds and down through our deck. Within 5-minutes the guards collected Peter and took him off in his shirt and put him in the cooler. But he only had five days, so he got off very lightly!
>
> Private Harry Baker, Chatham Battalion, Royal Marine Brigade

At times communication between the officers and their men was rendered difficult by the very language that they theoretically shared:

> They were all Tynesiders, and most of them were miners. At first, I understood little of what they said, and they did not understand much of me: and there were two good fellows, from some Durham valley, whom nobody understood. They might have been foreigners.[6]
>
> Sub-Lieutenant A. P. Herbert, Hawke Battalion, 1st Naval Brigade

Collectively, the RND clung to its naval origins retaining naval ranks such as petty officers and commodores, and an ostentatious jargon with much reference to "port" and "starboard", instead of left and right, and "going ashore" instead of going on leave.

The RND had moved to a new camp constructed at Blandford by the end of January 1915. As a division it was still lacking in artillery and, at this stage of training, was perhaps comparable to one of the Kitchener Divisions which had also been raised since the outbreak of war. It had no experience whatsoever of acting as division in the field, or of the complex staff and logistical challenges thrown up by warfare. Yet Churchill considered that they were fit to take on the Ottomans (Turks) in support of his naval assault to try and take the Dardanelles Narrows and force the surrender of Constantinople. The original intent was that they would provide landing parties and a garrison for the captured Turkish forts on either side of the straits. First the Plymouth and Chatham Battalions, then the main body of the division would be sent out to the Eastern Mediterranean during February 1915.

Frederick Kelly.

6 A. P. Herbert, *A.P.H.: His Life and Times* (London: Heinemann, 1970), p. 40.

Even before they left, rumours began to circulate amongst the men that they were bound for the Dardanelles. It was thus ironic that when the Hood Battalion did leave Blandford on 28 February they did so in great secrecy:

> We had lots of friends in Blandford. But instead of going to Blandford Station, we were marched across the Downs. We missed all our people. All our friends who were waiting at Blandford to see the lads off. We didn't see anybody. You see it was a secret army – but we knew where we were going![7]
>
> Ordinary Seaman Joe Murray, Hood Battalion, 2nd Naval Brigade

The troop trains took them to Avonmouth, where they boarded their ships. Speculation was now rife and Rupert Brooke's letters were filled with a mélange of romantic imagery and a wicked sense of humour:

> I'm filled with confident and glorious hopes. I've been looking at the maps. Do you think perhaps the fort on the Asiatic corner will need quelling, and we'll land and come at it from behind, and they'll make a sortie and meet us on the plains of Troy? It seems to me strategically so possible. Will Hero's Tower crumble under the 15" guns? Shall I loot mosaics from St. Sophia and Turkish Delight and carpets? Should we be a turning point of history? Oh God! I've never been quite so happy in my life, I think. Not quite so pervasively happy; like a stream flowing entirely to one end. I suddenly realise that the ambition of my life has been – since I was two – to go on a military expedition against Constantinople. And when I thought I was hungry, or sleepy, or aching to write a poem – that was what I really, blindly wanted![8]
>
> Sub-Lieutenant Rupert Brooke, Hood Battalion, 2nd Naval Brigade

More prosaic thoughts filled the minds of many of the men of the Chatham Battalion on the SS *Cawdor Castle*:

> I should think that nearly everyone on the ship was seasick as we went across the Bay of Biscay. The old girl only tottered along at about six knots and it took a long time to cross the bay. It was the roughest crossing. Lots of the regular Royal Marines had served at sea, but we special service men had never been to sea before. We crossed the Bay hoping that the ship would sink at any moment because I for myself have never felt worse in my life. It was terrible. Even some of the crew were knocked out by this rough sea and said they'd never seen anything like it before. The food was terrible not fit for pigs in the main. Potatoes were served up in nets with shoots anything up to a foot long.
>
> Private Harry Baker, Chatham Battalion, Royal Marine Brigade

They sailed in convoy to Mudros harbour at the Greek island of Lemnos where they awaited deployment should the Royal Navy be successful in penetrating the Dardanelles. Utter failure of the attack on 18 March meant that serious land operations would have to be undertaken, so

7 IWM SOUND: J. Murray, AC 8201.
8 R. Brooke quoted by M. R. Brooke, *The Collected Poems of Rupert Brooke: With a Memoir* (London: Sidgwick & Jackson Ltd, 1929), pp. 138-139.

on 22 March the RND was despatched to Egypt to reorganise ready for the imminent landings. Whilst there, some ancillary elements joined. The Motor Machine Gun Detachment of the Royal Naval Air Service and the 1st Field Ambulance had sailed out with the infantry, but now the rest of the supply, engineer, medical and sanitary sections also joined – but still no artillery.

One officer who made his appearance was Sub-Lieutenant Charles Lister, whose insouciance could be said to define the outlook of the *glitterati* of the Hood Battalion. An intellectual with a light touch to life, he was son of the Liberal politician Lord Ribblesdale, but had rejoiced in socialist beliefs while at Eton. He took up a career with the Foreign Office and was attached to the British Embassy in Constantinople in 1914. He took a year's leave of absence to join the army and found his way to the Hood Battalion, attracted – as so many of them were – by the presence of Rupert Brooke. Lister defined the motives that had called this disparate group of young men to the colours, "The date of my birth determines that I should take active service."[9] His minimal experience in the yeomanry had not really prepared him for life in the RND:

> I had dysentery all the time at Port Said, so I missed the spectacle of Charles drilling stokers on yeomanry lines – an entrancing one, I have been told. There is one particularly circumstantial story of how he marched a body of men on to the parade-ground before the eyes of the Brigade, and in his resonant parade tone ordered them to halt in words more suited to the evolutions of quadrupeds.[10]
>
> Sub-Lieutenant Patrick Shaw-Stewart, Hood Battalion, 2nd Naval Brigade

Lister was an eccentric figure even amidst the officers of the Hood Battalion:

> Our party goes on happily. Charles Lister is a great gain even to those who don't understand him. He has the kindest heart imaginable, hasn't he? We laughed a good deal over the divisional notes on the character of the Turks, particularly at one which said they did not like night attacks because they hated the dark and invariably slept with a night light. Charles parodied them inimitably.[11]
>
> Lieutenant Denis Browne, Hood Battalion, 2nd Naval Brigade

While in Egypt, Rupert Brooke developed nagging health problems, suffering from an unpleasant combination of sunstroke and diarrhoea, yet he remained determined to stay with his men:

> While I shall be well, I think, for our first thrust into the fray, I shall be able to give my Turk, at the utmost, a kitten's tap. A diet of arrowroot doesn't build up violence. I am as weak as a pacifist.[12]
>
> Sub-Lieutenant Rupert Brooke, Hood Battalion, 2nd Naval Brigade

9 C. Lister quoted in Lord Ribblesdale, *Charles Lister: Letters and Recollections* (London: T. Fisher Unwin Ltd, 1917), p. 129.
10 P. Shaw-Stewart quoted in Ribblesdale, *Charles Lister*, pp. 156-157.
11 D. Browne quoted in Ribblesdale, p. 157.
12 D. Brooke quoted by Brooke, *The Collected Poems of Rupert Brooke*, pp. 138-139.

In April, the RND then began the move back to the Greek islands ready for the Gallipoli operations that were being planned by General Sir Ian Hamilton as commander of the Mediterranean Expeditionary Force. On 17 April they arrived off Skyros and carried out a series of landing exercises:

> My Company Commander Freyberg was a superb swimmer and we on several occasions did long distance swims in very cold water. I was defeated on one occasion of a 2-mile swim I had set myself in Freyberg's company and came into the boat after a mile and a half in bitterly cold water, deep and blue as a turquoise, but as yet unyielding to the sun's rays. It was the coldness of the water and the relative poorness of my circulation which beat me – not weariness of flesh or muscle.[13]
>
> Lieutenant Charles Lister, Hood Battalion, 2nd Naval Brigade

Within days Freyberg would put his swimming ability to good use. The rather dilettante attitude of many of the RND officers masked a determination to carry out their duty as encapsulated neatly by Lister:

> I am every day happier at having left the Staff, and the sight of one's own men lying down in line among the stones and scrub of these jolly hills warms the blood. I hope I shall be brave; I am sure they will.[14]
>
> Lieutenant Charles Lister, Hood Battalion, 2nd Naval Brigade

Unfortunately, Rupert Brooke was struck down with severe blood poisoning, apparently caused by an insect bite on his lip. As his temperature rocketed it became apparent that nothing could be done, and he died on Friday, 23 April. He was buried by his friends in an olive grove on Skyros. Many of the officers were deeply distraught by Brooke's untimely demise. Denis Browne wrote a reflective note when he later passed Skyros on 2 June:

> We passed Rupert's island at sunset. The sea and sky in the east were grey and misty, but it stood out in the west, black and immense, with a crimson glowing halo round it. Every colour had come into the sea and sky to do him honour, and it seemed that the island must ever be shining with this glory that we buried him there.[15]
>
> Sub-Lieutenant Denis Browne, Hood Battalion, 2nd Naval Brigade

Kelly was another who was particularly saddened by the death of Brooke and later, while in the Helles trenches, he managed to compose a short nine-minute orchestral *Elegy in Memoriam for Rupert Brooke* – a rather haunting piece which stands as a fitting memorial to both Brooke and Kelly.

The RND had only a peripheral involvement in the main landings at Helles on 25 April 1915, merely providing beach parties on V, W and X Beaches from Anson Battalion. Even so, Sub-Lieutenant Arthur Tisdall won a well-merited Victoria Cross for his heroic attempts to

13 IWM DOCS: C. Lister, Typescript account, pp. 52-53.
14 C. Lister quoted in Ribblesdale, p. 162.
15 D. Browne quoted in Brooke, *The Collected Poems of Rupert Brooke*, p. 159.

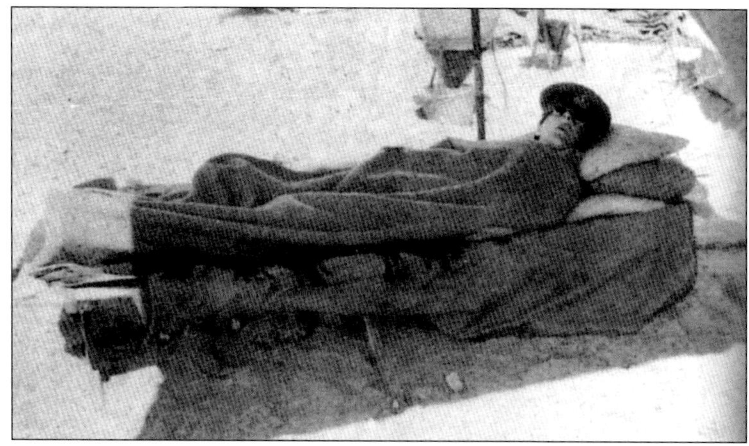

Rupert Brooke shortly before his death. (Private collection)

rescue the wounded stranded on V Beach. The Plymouth Battalion was, however, designated to land with the 1st King's Own Scottish Borderers at Y Beach on the northern coast of Helles, at the direct instigation of Hamilton, to act as a "thorn in the side" of the Turks, threatening communications between their reserve formations and the main landings. They were to attract the Turkish reserves and generally hold their ground before joining the general advance on Achi Baba by the end of the first day. Y Beach was actually little more than narrow strip of rocks, faced by scrub-covered cliffs rising some 150 feet and as such had been left undefended by the Turks. The troops landed around 4:15 a.m. and scrambled up to the top unopposed. Then the problems began, as they were beset by problems of command and control. There was confusion as to whether Lieutenant-Colonel Archibald Koe of the 1st KOSB, or Lieutenant-Colonel Godfrey Matthews of the Plymouths was in charge, but there was also no direction from Major-General Sir Aylmer Hunter-Weston commanding the 29th Division, whose attention was fully occupied with the main landings. The result was an uncomfortable stasis. Although isolated parties from the Plymouth Battalion explored towards and beyond the deep fissure of Gully Ravine that lay to the south of them, overall the landing force failed to either press forward, or to contact the troops landing at X Beach. Worse still, they failed to dig in properly.

Eventually as evening threatened and with no sign of the main body they pulled back and started to dig trenches above Y Beach. Soon the Turkish reserves began to make their presence felt:

> Shortly after the snipers made their appearance the order was passed along the line, "A large body of troops advancing over the skyline!" This message was followed by another, "A larger body of troops advancing over the skyline!" As our platoon had taken up a position about 10 yards from the top of the cliff it was not possible to see them advancing for some time after. They were 800 to 900 yards away, advancing in massed formation, shouting and waving their rifles above their heads. As soon as they came within a reasonable distance we opened fire upon them. They still rushed on, until the two cruisers who were supporting us HMS Goliath and HMS Dublin, each fired a broadside which completely scattered them. It was growing dark now and the Turks had taken possession of the trench 600 yards away.

> We had prepared ourselves for the worst. Shortly after dark they made their first charge, as we expected. They came up within 10 yards of our trench but by keeping up a rapid fire we held them back. They retired for a short time but there was a regular hail of bullets hitting the parapet of the trench and almost blinding us with dirt. The dirt was also getting into the mechanism of our rifles, which added to the difficulty of keeping up rapid fire The noise was awful: wounded groaning and calling for stretchers which never came; the incessant rattle of the machine guns and rifles; the wounded and dying Turks in front calling for Allah. To make matters more cheerful it began to rain.[16]
>
> Private John Vickers, Plymouth Battalion, Royal Marine Brigade

Their position was desperate with the precipitous cliffs immediately behind them. The Turkish attacks were pressed home all night. Panic began to set in. Although the Turkish counter-attacks were suspended in daylight, an evacuation was carried out on the morning of 26 April in a situation marked by considerable confusion. All told, the Y Beach landing was a fiasco. A lack of clear instructions, a divided and confused command chain, resulted in a complete lack of direction on the ground. After the initial landing, nothing was attempted, and nothing was achieved.

The other major RND involvement was a diversionary operation conducted in the Gulf of Saros during 25 April. This was intended to "pin" the divisions placed in the Bulair Isthmus of the Gallipoli Peninsula – always a major concern of the commander of the Turkish *Fifth Army*, General Otto Liman von Sanders. The operations can be best characterised as desultory. During a slow shore bombardment by the escort warships the eleven RND transports began disembarking into strings of rowing boats towed by steamers. But, as the boats went nowhere no one was fooled for long. In an attempt to introduce a more threatening element, a platoon of the Hood Battalion was ordered to make a small-scale landing on the beaches. Lieutenant-Commander Bernard Freyberg suggested that he could do this on his own to avoid unnecessary casualties:

> The boat was painted an angry black, flecked with grey spots, and a Maxim placed at the bows behind the sandbags. The scheme was that Freyberg should be towed out in this ship's boat, escorted by a destroyer to within two miles of the shore. He then should be dropped, swim to the beach and there light some lifeboat flares, while the Maxim on the ship's boat and the guns of the destroyer should make all the noise they could to attract the attention of the enemy. He started out about 9 o'clock and I shall never forget his toilet which consisted of the smearing of his whole person with a black oil-like substance to protect him against the cold of the sea.[17]
>
> Lieutenant Charles Lister, Hood Battalion, 2nd Naval Brigade

The platoon still went out in rowing boats setting off from the ship at 9:00 p.m. Freyberg started his solo swim from about two-miles out at 12:40 a.m. on 26 April:

16 J. Vickers quoted in S. M. Holloway, *From Trench and Turret: Royal Marines Letters and Diaries, 1914-1918* (Portsmouth: Royal Marines Museum, 1986), p. 40.
17 IWM DOCS: C. Lister, Typescript account, pp. 52-53.

> I started swimming to cover the remaining distance, towing a waterproof canvas bag containing three oil flares and five calcium lights, a knife, signalling light and a revolver. After an hour and a quarter's hard swimming in bitterly cold water, I reached the shore and lighted my first flare, and again took to the water and swam towards the east and landed about 300 yards away from my first flare where I lighted my second and hid among some bushes to await developments; nothing happened, so I crawled up a slope to where some trenches were located the morning before. I discovered they were only dummies, consisting of only a pile of earth about two feet high and 100 yards long, and looked to be quite newly made. I crawled in about 350 yards and listened for some time but could discover nothing.[18]
>
> Lieutenant Commander Bernard Freyberg, Hood Battalion, 2nd Naval Brigade

He set off another flare and then began his swim back. Ordinary Seaman Joe Murray was one of those left behind waiting in the rowing boats:

> All of a sudden there was such a flash, such a bloody flash – it was a destroyer setting off a salvo. We couldn't see the sea, but we could see the cliffs. As this flash went there was a panic really because it sort of shook us up. Well we hit something, whether it was driftwood I don't know. We sloped to starboard I know that, and I nearly fell out. I was trying to be a sailor – you can't hang on with both hands you have to do what they do. I went over, and my hand was in the water and – oh dear me – it was perishing cold. I don't know how Freyberg survived that swim.[19]
>
> Ordinary Seaman Joe Murray, Hood Battalion, 2nd Naval Brigade

There is no doubt that Freyberg was lucky to be picked up in the pitch dark:

> After swimming for a considerable distance, I was picked up by Lieutenant Nelson in our cutter sometime after 3 a.m. Our cutter, in company with the pinnace and the TBD *Kennet*, searched the shore with 12-pounders and Maxim fire, but could get no answer from the shore.[20]
>
> Lieutenant Commander Bernard Freyberg, Hood Battalion, 2nd Naval Brigade

Despite his courage, little was achieved – for as Charles Lister ruefully remarked, "The Turks had taken no notice of their antics."[21]

Following the main landings there was some confusion over the deployment of the RND, which found itself relegated to the status of reserve troops to be called upon as and when necessary, rather than deployed in strength as a division. The Drake Battalion was disembarked at Helles on 26 April, but the W Beach area was too congested to allow more units ashore and they remained on their transports. Then Birdwood requested help for his exhausted Australian and New Zealand Army Corps (ANZAC) who had made a heroic but failed landing at what would subsequently be called Anzac Cove. In response, four battalions from the Royal Marine Brigade

18 TNA WO 95/4290: B. Freyberg Report.
19 IWM SOUND: J. Murray, AC 8201.
20 TNA WO 95/4290: B. Freyberg Report.
21 IWM DOCS: C. Lister, Typescript account, pp. 52-53.

and 1st Naval Brigade would begin landing on 28 April. The Chatham Battalion moved inland to relieve the Australians on Second Ridge:

> Landing in horse boats on the open beach at dusk, we were led by an Australian guide up the bottom of a deep ravine. This was our first experience of being in enemy country. It was all rather eerie. In the darkness, the guide lost his way, which led to counter-marching and some confusion. He eventually brought us to a very steep slope, at the top of which the Australians were entrenched only a few yards from the edge of the ravine. We took over the trenches and they withdrew into rest.[22]
>
> Lieutenant Arthur Chater, Chatham Battalion, Royal Marine Brigade

This was an exacting introduction to modern warfare for many of the young marines:

> No one knew exactly where we were wanted or how to get there. It was a hard climb our hands were torn with the scrub. We arrived below the crest of the hill at 8 p.m. Orders came back to me that I was to remain where I was, the trenches were so full of dead and wounded that it would be difficult to move. I must have dozed off to be awakened but the voice of an Australian sergeant shouting, "Give them a good 3 feet!" I looked up and saw them dragging dead Australians over the crest and burying them close by where we were lying.[23]
>
> Private Bertram Wilson, Chatham Battalion, Royal Marine Brigade

The line was precarious in the extreme and the trenches were nowhere near deep enough:

> We took up these positions in the dark. We were along the top of this ridge and there was what you might call a ditch about 2-feet deep which the Australians had dug along the top and made a kind of trench. But there was very little protection there. Every few yards lay a dead man. So you had to crawl over him to take up your position. There were quite a number of dead men there. You could feel them and see them – that's not a very nice experience. Self-preservation was the main thing and you had to keep your head down as much as possible. The lower you could get, the better it was. I can assure you it was very steep, just like a railway embankment, all around, with scrub and bush and trees – not very big trees – but oddly enough quite a few that were like Scots firs. They hadn't managed to clean up all the snipers. There were still snipers in this bush behind the front line. They used to pick quite a number of men off before they got wiped [out] because they couldn't get out once they were behind the front line and we picked them off gradually. What you used to watch for in the dark was to see where the flash came from which betrayed where they were, and we picked up quite a number like that.[24]
>
> Private Harry Baker, Chatham Battalion, Royal Marine Brigade

22 IWM DOCS: A. R. Chater, Typescript account, p 5.

23 Brotherton Special Collections Library, Leeds University, Liddle Collection: B. I. Wilson, Diary, 29/4/1915.

24 IWM SOUND: T. H. Baker, SR 8721.

The Deal and Nelson Battalions landed next day and together the RND battalions took over responsibility for the northern half of the 1st Australian Division line.

However, the Turks had also been strongly reinforced and began a determined attempt to push the invaders back into the sea:

> The second day the Turks began to attack in the afternoon in huge numbers *en masse*. They came out of this scrub like rabbits towards you and – Oh my word! – we had a tough time repelling that. I'd got two men loading for me and I kept firing these rifles and they didn't get within 50 yards finally. I reckon if you missed one you'd probably have the next man. Mind you, you didn't get too much time to aim. You'd got to get on with the job. It was all over in minutes. They were heaped up wounded and dead.[25]
>
> Private Harry Baker, Chatham Battalion, Royal Marine Brigade

These Turkish attacks attained a crescendo at 4:00 a.m. on 1 May. Private Joseph Clements was manning his machine gun:

> There were flags flying, and bugles blowing, and they were coming over in droves. I'd got our gun fixed up and I sat there, and I was shooting, swinging it backwards and forwards, not taking aim but you couldn't miss. No more than 200-yards, there was so many, they weren't spread out because there wasn't the room for them to spread out owing to the rocky nature of the ground. There was a kind of an opening through which they were coming. We had this end and they were coming through the other end. I was firing, the No.2 he was seeing the belt ran and getting a belt out of the box ready. The others were taking a pot shot now and again with their rifles. You couldn't see the effects you were just firing into a kind of a big object. It didn't look like individual people.[26]
>
> Private Joseph Clements, Deal Battalion, Royal Marine Brigade

The Turkish frontal assault failed with heavy casualties.

Now it was the turn of the ANZAC to try and test the Turkish defences. On 2 May a night assault by two Australian and one New Zealand battalions on Baby 700 had failed, but on 3 May, the Chatham and Portsmouth Battalions were ordered forward up onto a hill via the head of Monash Valley:

> We fired away at all the Turks who kept advancing. They were then about one hundred and fifty yards away and they came up in almost mass formation, so we had very easy targets. An Australian came and lay next to me and on his right another man scaled this steep slope and it turned out to be Major Armstrong of the Portsmouth Royal Marines. Captain Richards was next to him and all the way to the right were men shoulder to shoulder lying on the ground. No cover at all, just lying on the ridge.[27]
>
> Private Harry Baker, Chatham Battalion, Royal Marine Brigade

25 IWM SOUND: T. H. Baker, SR 8721.
26 IWM SOUND J. Clements, AC 11268.
27 IWM SOUND: T. H. Baker, AC 8721.

The tangled terrain allowed a German machine gun in German Officers Trench, just north of Wire Gully, to get a clear shot into the rear of the men lying on the open ridge:

> Suddenly a machine gun crackled away at right angles to us, we were firing ahead and it was even behind us. This machine gun went along and that killed every man on the ridge except the Australian and me. We were the only two left. The Australian said, "The bastards can't kill me, they've had lots of tries, they can't kill me!" I looked again. The machine gun started barking again behind us. That came along it was knocking the sand up and that covered every man again. Every man, it came right along. I felt the bullets thud into the Aussie and he never spoke again. I felt as though I'd been hit by a donkey and I had a bullet through the right foot. When I saw those bullets coming along and I knew that it would be the end of me if they came along far enough. They say your past comes up, but I can say truthfully that I hadn't got much past at nineteen and all I thought of was ' Am I going to live', that's all I thought, that's what struck me, 'Am I going to be lucky', because I couldn't see how I could be with all these bullets coming along and I waited for it – it was inevitable.[28]
>
> Private Harry Baker, Chatham Battalion, Royal Marine Brigade

Baker had been fortunate, but then the Turks surged forward across what would soon be known as Dead Man's Ridge:

> I lay there, and I didn't know what to do. The Turks came and prodded various men with their bayonets, fortunately they didn't poke me, and I could hear them jabbering away and then they moved away again. "Well," I thought, "I must do something!" so I gave myself a push off and went bumpity – bumpity right down to the bottom of the ravine over dead men, rifles, bush, all kinds of things.[29]
>
> Private Harry Baker, Chatham Battalion, Royal Marine Brigade

He left behind the rotting corpses of his erstwhile comrades that would give the ridge its grim name. The Marines had done a sterling job of defending Anzac while the Australians and New Zealanders rested. Their reward was a harsh criticism, concentrating on their imagined physical frailty and lack of resolve in battle. The evidence shows that they did their job as best they could in the circumstances, and overall, they did it rather well.

Back at Helles, the 2nd Naval Brigade were put ashore on the night of 29 April and placed initially in reserve. The French *Corps Expéditionnaire d'Orient* (CEO), under the command of General Albert d'Amade, was on the right of the line when it was attacked throughout the night of 1 May. They lost some ground and next morning the Hood Battalion moved forward to advance alongside the French as they counter-attacked. The Hoods had no idea of what they were meant to be doing, or where they were, and were soon isolated, harassed by Turkish shrapnel fire. As they began to fall back Lieutenant Charles Lister was wounded:

28 Ibid.
29 Ibid.

> My company being in the second line retired last, and by the time we were moving the whole of our front was being searched with terrible effect. One of the shrapnel burst on the ground about thirty yards behind me and a pellet ricocheted the ground and struck me in the off-buttock. I thought it was a piece of stone at first. I had already been hit by several spent pellets without any effect. One went through coat and shirt and hardly marked my skin; another knocked in my water-bottle. However, this third one found its billet, and I was soon bleeding like a pig and walking indifferent well – I never fell down. It was an irritating moment, as I should have been there to rally our boys after the retirement. They did well, considering the trying circumstances and their relative rawness. I never saw a Turk within shooting distance. My return to the beach was easily accomplished for me on a stretcher, not so easily perhaps for the poor orderlies who had to carry me, and I had a feeling of great peace as I lay on my back and looked at the blue overhead. I should like to get back quick, because I have seen just enough to tantalize. It is rather like love-making in this.[30]
>
> Lieutenant Charles Lister, Hood Battalion, 2nd Naval Brigade

He had tried to continue but his wound was revealed by his blood-soaked trousers. One thing seemed apparent: Lister may have been a *dilettante*, but he had courage.

On 6 May, the Second Battle of Krithia began. It was fundamentally an advance to contact, for which purpose the 2nd Naval Brigade was attached to the CEO, moving forward in support of the French left flank as they attempted to press forward along the Kereves Spur. The men of the Hood Battalion found themselves advancing up the Achi Baba Nullah. The Turks may not have been visible, but their bullets seemed everywhere:

> It was a beautiful morning. We got to a farmhouse, what was left of them, knocked about but serviceable. We were lying alongside the corner of a vineyard, a bush hedge, 3 or 4 feet high a little ditch on the side. We started numbering. There must have been at least 50-60 men there. Then we were told to swing round behind the house and move forward. We found ourselves alongside another hedge of the vineyard. There was a big gap, about 12-feet wide, it looked like the roadway into the farm house. We lay there for a little then we were told to bear left, we were at the junction between the French and the British and we tried to keep connection with both flanks. We kept losing so many men we couldn't do it. We could never locate these snipers. There were no trenches; it was open fighting. We had to rush along the front of the house and go through this gap. Only four people got through, we had to climb over the dead and the wounded. We got about 10 yards in front, and down we went. The bullets were hitting the sand, spraying us; you were spitting it out of your mouth.[31]
>
> Ordinary Seaman Joe Murray, Hood Battalion, 2nd Naval Brigade

At the end of the day a rough line was established across the peninsula, with negligible gains. Two more days of fighting followed but little more was gained. During these first engagements,

30 C. Lister quoted in Ribblesdale, *Charles Lister*, pp. 168-169.
31 IWM SOUND: J. Murray, AC 8201, Reel 7.

Lieutenant-Colonel Arnold Quilter had been killed and the Hood Battalion had lost half its strength.

By this time trench warfare was beginning as both sides began to dig in for the duration. The character of the fighting changed to a trench warfare typical of the Western Front, but with a very limited battlefield of just a few square miles. The arrival of the Royal Marine Brigade from Anzac, coupled with advent of the bulk of the 1st Naval Brigade from Great Britain meant that by mid-May the RND was finally united under the command of Major-General Archibald Paris at Helles. Yet losses and the pernicious effects of dysentery had already reduced the strength of most of his actively involved battalions to around 500 men. The RND occupied the Achi Baba sector of the line with the French to its right and the 42nd Division on the left.

The next big battle was the Third Battle of Krithia on 4 June. By this time, they had few illusions as to what they were about to receive. The letters of Major Norman Burge, although clearly intended to be humorous, nevertheless illustrates the mood within the RND on the night before the attack:

> You always know when there's going to be a battle, because people come and tell you to get up, and bally well be smart about it too, at 2 a.m. So up you spring with a pleased smile and wring him warmly by the hand and put on everything you can find, prattling merrily all the time such as, "What a delightful morning! How nice you look, old dear!" Then someone strikes a match, 'cos he can't find his best girl's lock of hair to wear next his heart (messy habit I call it) and he is gently reproved by those in authority with a smiling, "Nay brother, nay, lest the light attract the attention of the enemy, so please blow out that light!" At least,

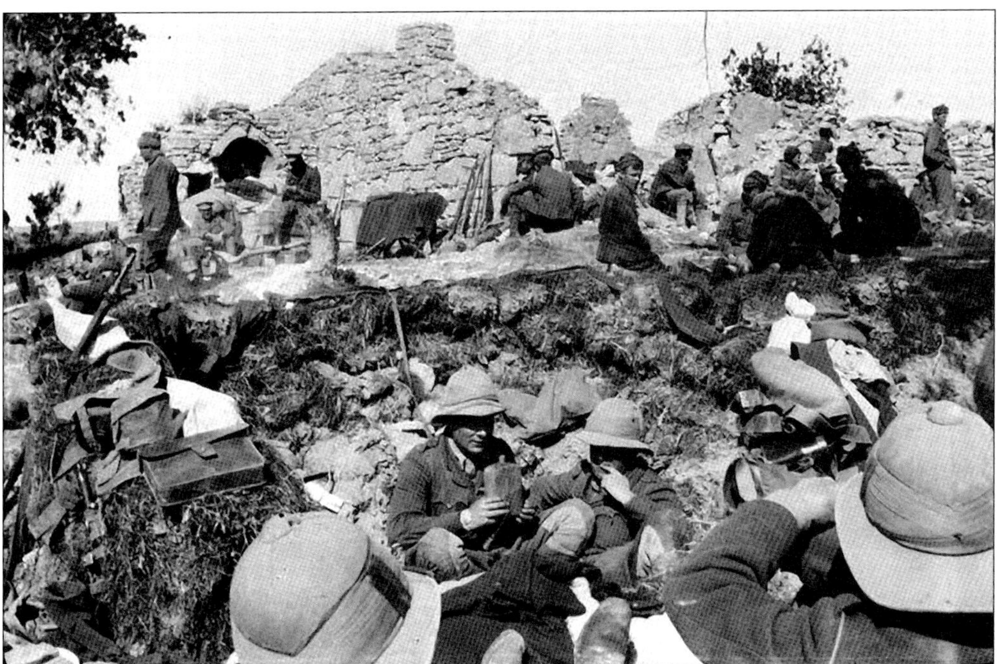

Cape Helles: Hood Battalion officers and men bivouac at the previously captured White House position.

> it's something like that, only generally longer and a little louder. And then the men fall in with a certain amount of scuffling. It appeared in the early stages that everyone desired to be an even number when they numbered off. This was because the odd numbers carried a pick or shovel as well as the ordinary gear. Now they know the value of these tools and the scuffle is to get them. Then everyone moves off and presently you get to a maze of trenches. When you get to the middle, you find a staff officer who says you're all wrong and you'd better go back. You argue with him, but more out of convention than anything else, 'cos he always wins. Well, you try to please him and go back, but you can't because another battalion is coming up and the trench is very narrow. Eventually a compromise is reached. One lot (the one who lost the toss) scrabble as close to the side of the trench as they can and the others squeeze pass, scraping grooves in the stomachs of the scrabblers with stray bits of equipment which may and do happen to stick out. As soon as the General has had two bits of bacon, the battle begins.[32]
>
> Major Norman Burge, RND Cyclist Company

The attack was meant to be preceded by a heavy bombardment commencing at 10:30, but this would be a disappointment to many of the men watching who knew their lives depended on the efficacy of the shelling:

> We were told that we were to have an intense bombardment. But when it got nearer to 12 o' clock, we said, "When are we going to have the intense bombardment?", and we were told we'd had that! Well now, whilst I don't know the numbers of shells fired I wouldn't have thought it was more than five or six thousand. Our general of artillery was affectionately known as 'Monsieur la general un coup par piece'.[33]
>
> Sub-Lieutenant Arthur Watts, Collingwood Battalion, 2nd Naval Brigade

For the soldiers of the Howe, Hood and Anson Battalions waiting in the trenches the period before going over the top was a living hell.

> In the firing line it was packed. We were standing there, couldn't sit down couldn't lie down, just standing there. The fellow next to me was messing about with his ammunition, fiddling about, cleaning his rifle, looking in the magazine. Another fellow was sort of staring. The blinking maggots from the dead bodies in the firing line were crawling round right under our noses. Every now and again if a bullet hit the parapet there was a 'Psssst'– wind – gas – it smelt like hell. The sun was boiling hot. The maggots, the flies – the stench was horrible.[34]
>
> Ordinary Seaman Joe Murray, Hood Battalion, 2nd Naval Brigade

For some it was all too much. Murray witnessed a case of a self-inflicted wound:

32 IWM DOCS, N. O. Burge, letter, 6/6/1915.
33 IWM SOUND: A. Watts, AC 8278.
34 IWM SOUND: J. Murray, AC 8201.

> Tubby was in an awful mess, he was only a youngster, eighteen and a half, well damn it all so was I. He was crying his eyes out, scared stiff, I said, "Come on Tubby, shake yourself up!" I didn't take any notice. He moved forward with his hands round his rifle, he actually put his hand on the trigger and bang. He's howling and jumping about like a cat on hot bricks, I said, "You bloody fool." I tried to bandage up his thumb which was on top of the muzzle. In the front of the tunic there's a little pocket where you have a field dressing, gauze and a bandage. I took it and start trying to bandage him up. The flies and the blood was squirting about all over the place. I put this gauze on, flies and all, I couldn't get rid of the flies, I tied it round the hand, I thought that'll do to get to the dressing station, no bother, but the damned thing fell off. I said, "Look Tubby, this bit's no good is it", he said, "No". So I got a hold of my knife and I start sawing away trying to cut this off. No, No, blood all over the place. So I put his thumb on the butt his rifle, put my knife on top and with a hefty blow I chopped the offending bit and the damned thumb fell on the floor. Now the bandaging was easy. He said, "You won't split on me?" I said, "Of course I won't split on you, it was an accident, as you were getting out of the trench and somebody behind us was firing and a bullet hit your hand on the rifle.[35]
>
> Ordinary Seaman Joe Murray, Hood Battalion, 2nd Naval Brigade

The bombardment stopped for 10 minutes at 11:20 a.m. to try and trick the Turks into thinking they were going over the top. The Turks unleashed with a torrent of fire and machine gun bullets smashing into the frontline parapet. There could be no illusions as to what awaited them when they went over the top for real at 12:00 p.m.:

> Honestly and truly the next half an hour was like an age. The bullets were hitting the parapet – Bang, Bang, Bang – actually coming through the parapet, disturbing the dead bodies, the stench – Ooooh dear me! It was horrible! I remember Lieutenant Commander Parsons standing on the ladder, he called out, "Five minutes to go men! Four minutes to go!" At that moment young Corbie – he'd be annoyed if I called him that – a young sub-lieutenant – only a youngster, he walked past me and said something to Parsons, so he missed number two or three. The next time, "One minute to go men! Now men!" He blew a whistle and off we go. The moment we started to leave this particular traverse where we were – it was 10 or 12 feet long – men were getting out by the ladders but falling back into the trench. I should imagine most of the men who attempted to attack on that particular order fell back either into the trench or onto the parapet. There was dead all over the place.[36]
>
> Ordinary Seaman Joe Murray, Hood Battalion, 2nd Naval Brigade

The survivors set off across No Man's Land:

> My Platoon Commander got through, I followed him up there. Parsons had already been killed. We got into dead ground. The Petty Officer said, "Well, come on, lad! C'mon!" We moved again and then lay down to get a breather. He was an old reservist, his bald

35 Ibid.
36 Ibid.

> head glittering in the sun – he'd lost his helmet. He was up on the trench with his rifle and bayonet, "C'mon! C'mon!" Around his head he'd got a white handkerchief and blood pouring down his face just like the pictures in the London Illustrated. He was bleeding dreadfully. I wanted to keep up with him, but he was now 20 yards ahead of me. I got to the trench and in I go – It was 10 feet deep! There was one or two dead, nobody alive.[37]
>
> Ordinary Seaman Joe Murray, Hood Battalion, 2nd Naval Brigade

The Turkish resistance seemed to melt away as they reached the Turkish trenches and the Hoods pushed through to take the second line albeit with severe casualties. It is estimated that they had lost about half their strength so unstained success would require rapid reinforcement.[38] Worse still, the French had been given an impossible task assaulting the redoubts at the head of the Kereves Spur. Once the French had been repulsed the Turks were able to direct a terrible enfilading fire into the right flank of the Collingwood Battalion as they came up in support at 12:15 p.m. The result was a massacre:

> I looked back and I could see the Collingwoods coming up in fairly good line. They hadn't reached our first line; they were coming up in reserve. They were lying down and getting up again and they would seem to be getting quiet a bashing. When they laid down, whether they were frightened, injured or killed I don't know but there didn't appear to be many getting up.[39]
>
> Ordinary Seaman Joe Murray, Hood Battalion, 2nd Naval Brigade

A party of Collingwoods was ordered to take some ammunition forward to the captured Turkish lines:

> I started off with a party of four chaps. None of those survived. We got hardly anywhere. The Turks spotted us immediately we went over the top. I was hit, and the leg went numb – I had no feeling in it at all. I had to scramble back into our trench. They were all 'standing to' wondering whether the Turks might counter-attack. What happened then I really don't know because the leg had made me groggy.[40]
>
> Sub-Lieutenant Arthur Watts, Collingwood Battalion, 2nd Naval Brigade

Watts would have his leg amputated. Few Collingwoods survived to reinforce the advanced positions and battalion casualties were such that the battalion was disbanded after the battle.

The Turks counter-attacked, feeling their way along the trenches into the right flank of the RND who had little chance to either consolidate, or dig the vital communication trenches back across No Man's Land. Soon a retreat was inevitable, although few of the men knew what was happening:

37 Ibid.
38 Jerrold, *The Royal Naval Division*, p. 188.
39 IWM SOUND: J. Murray, AC 8201.
40 IWM SOUND: A.C. Watts 8278.

> I remember seeing two officers away to my left – Denis Browne was one – taking about fifty men going forward. We went forward about half-a-dozen of us to a bit of a ditch – that was considered to be the third trench. All of a sudden, the right flank started retiring, the Anson Battalion. We were forced to retire, hopped back jumped over the second trench; then we scampered back to his first trench. I thought, "Well now if we can stop here we can hold them here!" I kept on turning round and firing, but there wasn't much opposition from the front, I couldn't understand why we were retiring, we weren't being pressed at all. We were almost near his first trench. I was out of puff, so tired and I thought, "One more trot and I shall be in the trench!" But when I got there it was full of Turks! So instead of stopping over the trench I leapt over the top and I was helped over by a bayonet stuck right in the posterior – right in the nick!!!!" I went falling right in front of the trench into a shell hole, lying flat in there.[41]
>
> Ordinary Seaman Joe Murray, Hood Battalion, 2nd Naval Brigade

Murray had to stay there all day with a Turk, oblivious to his presence, firing a rifle through a loophole just above his head. He only managed to get back to the British front line when night fell. Lieutenant Denis Browne had been badly wounded and was left behind in the pell-mell retreat. His body was never recovered but his pocket book was carried back containing a sad little note.

> I've gone now. Not too badly, I hope. I'm luckier than Rupert, because I've fought. Bit in the long run there's no-one to bury me as I buried him, so perhaps he's best off in the long run.[42]
>
> Lieutenant Denis Brown, Hood Battalion, 2nd Naval Brigade

Collectively, the RND ended up back in its jumping-off trenches and so the pressure shifted to the 42nd Division on their left. Any idea of a renewed attack that afternoon proved impossible, as the French and RND trenches were clogged with the dead, dying and wounded. After the battle the RND was reduced to a strength of just 7,349 men.[43]

The failure of the Third Battle of Krithia resulted in a change of tactics that, coincidentally or not, mirrored the "bite and hold" concept which had been under consideration since the Battle of Neuve Chapelle in March 1915. In accordance with these new approach, Lieutenant-General Sir Aylmer Hunter-Weston, (now commanding VIII Corps) and General Henri Gourard (CEO) had launched successful localised attacks on 21 June and 28 June to edge forward the right and left flanks.

By this time most of the men of the RND had far more mundane things on their minds. With the onset of high summer, they were sweltered in their dusty trenches. A diet which seemed to largely consist of tinned salted bully beef, Maconochies stew and pork and beans, dry biscuits, cheese, bacon and apricot jam was not designed to quench their thirst. Indeed, water supplies were a real problem and many of the wells had been polluted:

41 IWM SOUND: J. Murray, AC 8201.
42 D. Browne quoted in L. Sellers, *The Hood Battalion* (London: Leo Cooper, 1995), p. 105.
43 Jerrold, *The Royal Naval Division*, p. 148.

Royal Naval Division officers enjoying afternoon tea at Cape Helles. (Private collection)

> We had to go down with bottles. You took a puttee off, put a clove hitch round the handle of your canteen, gently lowered it down the well then filled your water bottles. But we always used to say there was a queer taste in that water. We'd been up the lines two or three times when the engineers finally put hooks down and up came a body. How it had got there no-one knew. How long it had been in we didn't know.[44]
>
> Ordinary Seaman Steve Moyle, Drake Battalion, 1st Naval Brigade

As ever Major Burge saw the lighter side:

> The sun is very hot and I'm very thirsty. That's the chief news. The only thing there is to drink is water that comes from a nasty well which tastes as if it had a dead mule in it (it probably has). However, we are given purifying tablets, which are very good and makes the water taste as if it had two dead mules in it![45]
>
> Major Norman Burge, RND Cyclist Company

Burge was a man who could hide the worst sufferings behind a humorous façade. The heat and the flies were enough to drive anyone mad, but he just laughed, at least in his letters home:

> My word it *is* baking hot today – the hottest we've had – no wind and 30 billion more flies than yesterday. I suppose there must be a maximum number allowed otherwise I don't know what will happen if each one is capable of laying so many thousand eggs per minute or whatever it is. They are getting so impertinent too – a reproving shake of the head is no

44 IWM SOUND: S. Moyle, SR 8257.
45 IWM DOCS: N.O. Burge, Letter, 6/6/1915.

> longer enough to dislodge one off your nose, but a slap is necessary and also in exasperation one sometimes slaps harder than was intended – which is more exasperating![46]
>
> Major Norman Burge, RND Cyclist Company

Disease was the main problem with the combination of rotting corpses, stinking latrines and millions of flies promoting an outbreak of virulent dysentery that gained rapid traction in July:

> There was a group of Turkish dead in front of my fire step, and I observed that in almost every case the head was thrown back and the mouth wide open. Into the gaping mouths the flies poured and out of the gaping mouths onto us they came.[47]
>
> Able Seaman Thomas Macmillan, Drake Battalion, 1st Naval Brigade

The latrines were primitive and soon became places of horror:

> The latrines were a trench roughly 6 feet deep and a yard wide. Roughly about 10 feet long. The seating was two posts driven into the ground at each end forming an 'X' and then a pole was lodged along on the cross piece. You sat on that in full view of everybody. Of course, it didn't matter a damn because there was nobody around, no women or anything like that. On one occasion I heard a terrific shout and the pole had snapped and the four men sitting on the pole fell into the muck. To get them out they had to put rifles down for them to hang onto. They came out like slimy rabbits. The sergeant who was near said, "Clear off down to the beach and get into the sea!" They had to because no-one wanted to get near them.[48]
>
> Private Harry Baker, Chatham Battalion, Royal Marine Brigade

Such calamities were not the real danger; the latrines were haunted by flies who bred there in their millions. The flies carried dysentery and spread it by landing on the food and buzzed around the very mouths of their victims. The results were devastating and soon hundreds of men were suffering agonies:

> With dysentery you keep on trying to discharge something but there's nothing to discharge, it's only slime, just slime, no solids at all. Then of course we didn't have any toilet paper and you had to wipe yourself with your hand, there's nothing else. Then you'd wipe your hand – originally on the grass, but grass was getting a bit short – rub your hands on the sand and your trousers.[49]
>
> Ordinary Seaman Joe Murray, Hood Battalion, 2nd Naval Brigade

And so the cycle of infection accelerated as the men were covered in germs. Able Seaman Thomas Macmillan saw one man so horribly afflicted by dysentery that not even a wound that ultimately proved fatal could distract him:

46 IWM DOCS: N.O. Burge, Letter, 22/6/1915.
47 IWM DOCS: T. Macmillan, Typescript account, pp. 59-60.
48 IWM SOUND: T. H. Baker, SR 8721.
49 IWM SOUND: J. Murray, SR 8201.

> I had discovered the stump of an old tree on the verge of the latrine, which accorded support for my back, shade from the sun and a certain amount of protection from shell fragments. There I used to sit and read. One day, when engrossed I heard a shell-burst ahead, followed by an ominous screeching which denoted that there was a nasty blow-back approaching. The latrine had its full complement of men in varying degrees of distress, and the blow-back got one of them in the armpit. The poor chap howled, "I'm hit, I'm hit," but continued under the spell of his dysentery attack, so commanding was the infernal scourge. On the cry being repeated one or two of us rushed to his assistance. We saw at once that he was badly wounded and hurried him off to the Field Dressing Station; but before we reached the place the wound had proved fatal.[50]
>
> Able Seaman Thomas Macmillan, Drake Battalion, 1st Naval Brigade

The soldiers were also plagued by para-typhoid, jaundice and – if their health degenerated too far – with "soldiers' heart", or disordered action of the heart. The shortage of soldiers was such that only those in the final stages of dysentery could be evacuated. The rest simply had to suffer. The strength of the RND battalions continued to dwindle. Yet they still received occasional drafts, and in the aftermath of the disaster of 4 June the officers' mess of the Hood Battalion was enlivened by the arrival of Sub-Lieutenant Ivan Heald, a noted humourist/journalist writing for the *Daily Express*. Heald was a man so devoid of natural military skills that at times he would drive his company commander – the forbidding Kelly – to despair. Yet his special skills did come in useful:

> Although he was cool and brave as a fighter, I think that Heald's greatest service to the battalion was during the months of July, August and September 1915, when hundreds were suffering from dysentery and fever. He did more by his cheeriness and sense of humour to keep everybody fit than all the medical comforts did. When things were at their worst, he was always at his best.[51]
>
> Lieutenant Commander Bernard Freyberg, Hood Battalion, 2nd Naval Brigade

The other main problem faced by the men of the RND was the lack of any safe rest areas. There was nowhere to go for safety. The Turkish shells could reach anywhere at Helles, indeed much of it was within rifle and machine gun range. The Turkish shortage of artillery and shells proved a boon and shelling was more of a theoretical threat than a real peril. Yet it was still a terrible experience for men caught close to a shell burst:

> You crouched as low down in the trench as you could, right flat down in the trench and as near to the parapet as you could because you hoped that any explosion would be behind. The ground used to rock and chunks of HE used to fly just like cats meowing. So long as you heard the explosion you were alright. If you didn't hear the explosion you were not there anymore![52]

50 IWM DOCS: T. Macmillan, Typescript account.
51 B. Freyberg, quoted in I. Heald, *Ivan Heald: Hero and Humorist* (London: C. Arthur Pearson Ltd, 1917), pp. 11-12
52 IWM SOUND: T. H. Baker, SR 8721.

Private Harry Baker, Chatham Battalion, Royal Marine Brigade

Some men got used to shell fire which meant that they could accurately judge the immediate danger. But the threat was always there:

> Most shell are gentleman. To begin with – the vast majority of 'em you hear coming and a very little practice enables you to tell the probable size of it (as if it mattered), its direction, (more important) and probable place of explosion (most important). So that newcomers duck and dive and assume most comic attitudes over noises which do not in the least disturb the equanimity of the cook.[53]
>
> Major Norman Burge, RND Cyclist Company

Sometimes though even the most experienced of warriors could be undone by a close shave:

> I've had a good many narrow squeaks – not any more than anybody else of course but somehow, they interest me more! The other night I'd just got back from the trenches – very hot and had got my head in a bucket of water. Therefore, I was the only one who didn't hear a shrapnel coming and bolt for cover – it burst just behind me and there was a deluge of bullets all round me. Then this morning I *did* hear one coming and couldn't bolt because I was literally caught with my trousers down. Didn't waste any time buttoning up though![54]
>
> Major Norman Burge, RND Cyclist Company

Sniping was also a major problem. The Turks soon proved themselves expert shots:

> One morning there was a Turk who they said was picking off our men and would I have a go at him. It was just 'stand to' and he was supposed to be on top of the trench. You could just see his head above the top of the trench. I lined up and fired. Just at that moment one whistled past my ear like that, 'Wheeee!' I reckon we both fired together, and we never had any more bother from him, but I reckon he missed by about that much. "Cor! That was close!"[55]
>
> Private Harry Baker, Chatham Battalion, Royal Marine Brigade

Around them was the constant reminder of their own mortality as the bodies left in No Man's Land from previous attacks. The whole peninsula reeked with a miasma of death:

> Well if you've ever smelt a dead mouse it was like that but hundreds and hundreds of times worse. It was a smell – the smell of death – you never got it out of your system. I've still got it; I can still remember exactly how it was.[56]
>
> Private Harry Baker, Chatham Battalion, Royal Marine Brigade

53 IWM DOCS: N. O. Burge, letter 22/6/1915
54 Ibid.
55 IWM SOUND: T. H. Baker, SR 8721.
56 Ibid.

The constant stress took a very real toll of their mental strength. Even the normally cherry Major Norman Burge momentarily revealed his emotions in a letter home:

> I've been rather trying to analyse one's feelings at different times and find it very difficult. Mostly, I think, one doesn't have any feelings to speak of and yet at other times you sort of look at things in a light you'd be rather ashamed of, that is if you didn't happen to know that all the other fellows are feeling just the same. I know they do, 'cos I asked them, and they said they did. So each of us was quite happy to find the others had nervousy moments. For instance, on a Monday – down here in the rest camp. You hear there's going to be a night advance of 100 yards on Tuesday. On Tuesday morning a sinister message all about stretchers and where the 'dressing station' will be at comes in etc and also what part of the line we'll be in and so on. I don't mind confessing that for a moment one feels as if you hadn't had your breakfast. Sudden flashes of awful horrors one can picture only too easily, intrude themselves on one's mind in a most insistent way. The uncomfortable feeling generally comes on when you know you've got to do something at a certain hour and you are just sitting down waiting for the clock to strike as it were. That feeling again stops with a click directly you begin doing it, whatever it may be, and from then on you cease thinking how absurdly inadequate Government pensions for widows are and mild wonders as to how the world can possibly get along without you – and all that sort of morbid nonsense.[57]
>
> Major Norman Burge, RND Cyclist Company

Day-by-day the RND was losing its manpower strength.

On 12 July, Hunter-Weston and Gourard's replacement commanding the CEO, General Maurice Baillourd, sought to advance in the centre of Helles. The RND was too debilitated for such an undertaking and the newly arrived 52nd Division had been moved into the Achi Baba sector for an attack designed to take place in two stages – in an attempt to allow the combined French and British artillery to deliver a meaningful bombardment.

Some success was achieved, but at great cost, and the Turkish trenches they had captured were vulnerable to any counter-attack. Despite their feeble situation, the Royal Marine Brigade was moved up to act as a reserve. In desperation, Hunter-Weston decided to fling them into the attack in a last attempt to increase the security of the new front line. In circumstances of great confusion, the Portsmouth and Nelson Battalions went into a doomed attack at 4:30 p.m. on 13 July:

> An order came down, to fix bayonets, and over the parapet, when the whistle blew, followed by another order, to go over two trenches, and hold on to the third at any cost. I turned to an old chum of mine and said, "It's come at last!" Shaking hands and wishing each other the best of good luck, over into the open we went. Many of the poor fellows only just got out the trench and before they had a chance to run were either killed or badly wounded. I cannot say how it was I missed such a fate, but I simply kept running, and I certainly was not in my right senses. I came to the first trench without getting hit and beheld a terrible sight. All I could see was dead bodies and I could hear the dying calling for water. But all

57 IWM DOCS: N. O. Burge, letter, 22/6/1915.

> I had in my head was to get over two trenches and hold the third at any cost. Still running, I came to the second trench, which I believe was a dummy trench, set with mines, so I jumped quite clear of that, and proceeded to the hoped-for position.[58]
>
> Able Seaman James Hart, Nelson Battalion, 1st Naval Brigade

The confusions were multiplying all around:

> The time I had been running made me begin to feel puffed out, and I began to think that if I went on much longer, at this rate I should soon be on Achi Baba, when all of a sudden, I came to a very deep slope in the ground, over which I had to jump. While jumping this little gulf I badly sprained my ankle, and when I got up to make another run for the desired trench I found I could only walk, running was quite out of the question. So, I started to walk on again, forgetting the dangers from the Turkish artillery, machine guns and rifles. An old chum of mine seemed to come out of the earth and walked with me. He was just about finished, but he asked me what I thought of it all, and I could hardly talk to him. All of a sudden, a bullet caught me, and it was a very funny sensation for it seemed to twist me round, and then I dropped flat to earth. It had hit me in the head, and I did not know where, for a minute. It felt as if it had hit me in the neck, but I found it had gone through my upper lip then into my tunic, at the top of my arm, just missing my arm. I was lying there in the open, feeling somewhat dazed wondering what to do next. I raised myself just a little and I saw that the advance trench was about 30 to 40 yards in front; also a few of my poor comrades lying dead near me. Then I thought that I would make a move towards the trench, but just as I was about to go I heard a rattle of bullets just over my head. I began to give myself up as finished, when I saw a large hole just beside me, made by one of the Turkish shells, which I thought would make good cover for me, but my second thoughts proved to save my life. I made up my mind to crawl forward and just as I did so another shell burst into the hole. This gave me a good shaking up, but at last I gained my desires – yet still they could not let me alone for the snipers were still trying hard for me. When I crawled over the parapet to my horror I saw lying dead at the bottom, the fellow who only a few minutes before had asked me what I thought of it all. His eyes just rolled over and closed, so I thought it was of no use to try and help him. He had been shot through the stomach.[59]
>
> Able Seaman James Hart, Nelson Battalion, 1st Naval Brigade

Eventually, the wounded Hart managed to get into the trench and take stock of their desperate situation:

> There were just a few running about in this trench and they seemed quite off their heads in excitement – there was one officer there to take charge of affairs. The first thing the fellows did was to make a parapet, of whatever they could get – and not being able to get enough sandbags they had to pile up the dead, in front of them for protection. I, with a good many others, was useless, so we had to lie in the bottom of the trench until night came. It was an

58 J.R.J. Hart, *My Part in the Great War at Home and Active Service* (Transcribed by R. Hart), Royal Naval Research Archive <http://www.royalnavyresearcharchive.org.uk>
59 Ibid.

> awful time to wait, and we were expecting all the time that the Turks would make a charge, to regain their trenches. But thank goodness they had had enough of it for one day – and so had we![60]
>
> Able Seaman James Hart, Nelson Battalion, 1st Naval Brigade

In a catalogue of disaster, they achieved nothing other than a modicum of reinforcement for the Scots in the old Turkish front line. Even amidst disaster one of the RND officers could still raise a smile:

> It was indescribable, just hundreds of men wandering about in the captured trench system in the burning sun, with corpses blackened and stinking lining the old Turkish firing steps, the sinister symmetry of their position being the only sign of any method at all. The redeeming feature of that occasion was A. P. Herbert's instruction to the sentries on his platoon frontage, "Remember, regard all Turks with the gravest suspicion!"[61]
>
> Lieutenant Douglas Jerrold, Hawke Battalion, 1st Naval Brigade

The men were soon suffering agonies of thirst. Dehydrated by their physical exertions, tormented by the cordite fumes and clouds of dust they were desperate for water. Behind them there were no communications trenches and the former No Man's Land still raked by Turkish fire:

> Our water bottles were now empty, and thirst increased with the increasing heat of the day; yet we had to carry on without water until the following day, when the Battalion Chief Petty Officer arrived with a large skin bag which looked for all the world like a diseased bagpipe minus the chanter. For a measure he carried a Wills tobacco tin, which normally contained two ounces of tobacco, and from this tin each man received two rations of water.[62]
>
> Able Seaman Thomas Macmillan, Drake Battalion, 1st Naval Brigade

This was the last real attack made by the RND at Gallipoli.

Yet there were still raids and small-scale attacks by both sides attempting to improve their localised tactical position in a battlefield where just a few feet could make all the difference. Lieutenant Charles Lister – who had re-joined the Hood Battalion – was involved in one such skirmish in late-July:

> The artillery shelled the advanced Turkish post for about 20 minutes while we massed, with a covering party of men with bombs and bayonets and a main body of men with sandbags, in the trench, ready to rush out up the old communication trench and push our sandbag barrier still farther forward. We realized the importance of rushing in immediately our shelling ceased. But as it turned out we were rather too close, for a shell fell among our people and buried six of them, who were, however, dug out unhurt or only

60 Ibid.
61 D. Jerrold, *Georgian Adventure: The Autobiography of Douglas Jerrold* (London: Right Book Club, 1938), p. 137.
62 IWM DOCS: T. Macmillan, Typescript account, p. 65.

> slightly wounded. The shell luckily did not burst. This was followed by a Turkish shell which fell right in the middle of us as we were all crouching for the rush, hit Freyberg in the stomach, killed another man, and covered me with small scratches, which bled profusely at the moment. We had by now got to our original barrier, so I got our covering party out and rushed them up the trench over quite a number of dead Turks. We stopped our men just short of the Turkish advanced post: threw bombs and at once started the new barrier – not a Turk in sight. The snipers, however, soon came back and made work at this point difficult, so we moved back and contented ourselves with a gain of about 40 to 50 yards on our old position. I have been hit in about six places, but all tiny little scratches.[63]
>
> Lieutenant Charles Lister, Hood Battalion, 2nd Naval Brigade

The RND was finished as a fighting force and on 1 August it was estimated there were only 129 officers and 5,038 men remaining.[64] Many of these were worn out, hollowed out by dysentery and stress. Not only this but General Paris was ordered to return some 300 stokers who were now required urgently for service with the fleet. Despite urgent pleas, there was a paucity of reinforcements or replacements and the division withered on the vine. The brigade organisation could not be maintained and one of the brigades ceased to exist in August. This left the 1st Naval Brigade (Drake, Nelson, Hawke and Hood Battalions) and the 2nd Naval Brigade (Portsmouth/Plymouth, Chatham/Deal, Anson and Howe battalions). Fortunately, the RND was not involved in the painful diversionary operations at Helles in an attempt to deflect attention from the main August offensives at Anzac and Suvla.

Charles Lister.

Charles Lister returned to Helles, but again did not last long. He was hit on 24 August and wrote to his father two days later:

> Just think, I have been wounded once more, the third time. We were in a trench, observing the Turkish trenches, when suddenly they fired some shells into our trenches. I went along to see what had happened, got my people back into a bit of a trench they had had to leave, then went down the trench, thinking the show was over, and then got it, being struck in the pelvis and my bladder being deranged, and slight injuries in the legs and calves. I have been operated on but am sketchy as to what has been done. I am on a hospital ship, comfy enough, but feeling the motion of it a good deal, and I have to be in bed and cannot change my position. The hours go slowly, as one does not feel very much up to reading. However, I got to sleep all right I feel this will be a longish job, and I don't know where I shall do my cure – perhaps Alexandria. My doctor is quite happy at the way things are going. The

63 Lister quoted in Ribblesdale, *Charles Lister*, pp. 211-212.
64 Jerrold, *The Royal Naval Division*, p. 148.

> shell that hit me killed one man and wounded the others. Forgive this scrawl, but it's not easy to write.[65]
>
> Lieutenant Charles Lister, Hood Battalion, 1st Naval Brigade

Cheerful as ever, but the next letter home came from Chaplain Mayne on the hospital ship *Gasconon* 29 August. It revealed that Lister had died from the effects of his wounds. The Chaplain responsible for his burial was none other than Ernest Raymond, the man who would subsequently become the high priest of Gallipolean romanticism with the publication of his much-acclaimed autobiographical novel *Tell England* in 1922.

The campaign then became merely a matter of survival. The resounding failure of the August offensive on the Anzac and Suvla front meant there was no hope left of success at Gallipoli. In these circumstances, one element of operations that took on an increased importance was underground mining. As there were insufficient Royal Engineers, numerous ex-miners from the RND were transferred to a newly formed VIII Corps Mining Company. Among them was Ordinary Seaman Joe Murray. They dug underground galleries to duplicate the lines above ground and when they heard Turkish counter-digging they would prepare a camouflet mine:

> We decided to make preparations for a blast. We had to make a recess in the side, a little bit to the left so that we didn't blow our own mineshaft. We had to stop him without stopping ourselves. Lieutenant Dean came up and he gave permission, the officer had to do that, and they came up with all their paraphernalia. There were three 10lb tins of ammonal. I put two detonators in one tin of ammonal, then I wrapped the cable round the tin and then round a sand bag so that when we pulled on the cable it wouldn't displace the detonator. Then we started tamping. All the sandbags were already filled and we packed them up to a barrier of about five feet, really tight. The point is that you have to make the place of least resistance upwards not along the tunnel or it would blow out your tunnel. The cable had to go right to the surface to the firing line. There the officer had the detonator box with batteries, two wires that he fixes and a plunger. The moment he pulls that plunger up he warns the officer in the line that, "Oh well, I'm going to do a bit of blasting, mind your heads." All the troops in the line stand to on the firing step with their rifle ready because we don't know what's going to happen. "Stand to, men". Down goes the plunger. As soon as the plunger goes down the lot goes up. I thought that's fine, thank the Lord for that. There was this terrific noise, mass of dust and great big chunks of clay falling everywhere.[66]
>
> Sapper Joe Murray, VIII Corps Mining Company

If they misjudged the moment, then the Turks could blow their workings up first – indeed Murray was once entombed and had to dig his way to the surface using only his seaman's knife.

By the middle of October, the RND was down to a strength of just 3,200 men.[67] For most of the men, routine line holding was the order of the day, with the deteriorating weather lending variety with a vicious rainstorm followed by a dreadful spell of freezing weather at the end of November. Still they endured and at least the flies disappeared as winter enfolded them.

65 C. Lister quoted in Ribblesdale, *Charles Lister*, pp. 226-227.
66 IWM SOUND: J. Murray, SR 8201.
67 Jerrold, *The Royal Naval Division*, p. 154.

Evacuation had been belatedly agreed by the wavering politicians back in London, the question was how. The garrisons of Suvla and Anzac showed how it could be done by a mixture of excellent staff work, deception and diversionary tactics to secure an almost casualty free evacuation on the night of 19/20 December. But this in itself added to the problems faced by the Helles garrison. A thorough reorganisation was set in train: the French were withdrawn and the 13th Division took the front line on the left, the 29th and 52nd Divisions were in the centre, and finally the RND was shuffled across to take over the Kereves Dere sector. Although the Kereves Dere, Kereves Spur and the Ravine du Mort had been a slaughterhouse in the early fighting the French had adopted a "live and let live" attitude once it was clear the campaign had no future. The French were nothing if not pragmatic:

> In many ways this was a rather weird sector. The lines ran right down to the water's edge at a point where a fair sized and very precipitous gulley, the Kereves Dere, opened out into the Straits. Here our lines were at the bottom of the gully with the Turks looking right down over us on the other side. A little further inland the positions were reversed, our lines being on the top of the hillside, whilst Johnny was at the bottom. In both, cases the communication trenches running steeply down the hillsides, were in full view of the chaps opposite, without any possibility of protection, short of head-cover. By all the rules of the game the locality ought to have been an exceptionally unhealthy one, and a happy hunting ground for snipers and whizz-bang merchants on both sides. Fortunately, however, our predecessors, jointly with Johnny, had devised a brilliant way out of the difficulty. On two trees between the lines, right down near the beach, wore two flags – one French; one Turkish. As long as nobody, from either side, ventured beyond those flags, there was to be no rifle fire during daylight hours in this particular region. The agreement was strictly adhered to with the result that this portion of the line was an absolute rest-cure. Wandering along the line, through an olive grove which it traversed, one found chaps placidly leaning over the parapet, or sitting on it. I succeeded in getting one or two photos of No Man's Land by the simple method of strolling out in front of the line near the aforementioned trees. I there and then formed the resolve that if ever I should have occasion to run a private war of my own, I would organize it on similar lines!
>
> Sapper Eric Wettern, No. 2 Field Company, Royal Engineers

In December the Turks had moved up their reserves and concentrated their artillery at Helles. Soon the shelling began to take a more threatening tone:

> On Christmas Eve the Turks put up the heaviest bombardment on our section that I had experienced and inflicted, despite the dug-outs, very severe casualties. The disadvantage of deep dug-outs is the extreme unpleasantness of leaving them. It is relatively easy to be conscientiously brave when you have no alternative, but excuses for remaining under cover where cover exists are damnably easy to find. Fortunately, I was robbed of mine because the telephone to the front line from battalion headquarters was seventy yards away from our Headquarters mess, and it had to be answered. I know nothing more unpleasant than walking along a trench which is being shelled by howitzers. The bullet which kills you is inaudible, so they say, but the howitzer which kills you is unmistakable. You can hear it coming down for some seconds and you know whether it is going to be close or not, and no

> parapet or trench can save you, so you just wait or walk on, feeling extremely curious as to what is going to happen. One's curiosity, I found, is strangely mundane. Curiosity about the next world is rare. And yet perhaps the most interesting thing of all is that no one has any sense of grievance against the enemy for trying to kill him, as he tried so very hard, on that unpleasant Christmas Eve, to kill us. And after it is all over, one has much the same feeling of exhilaration as after a cold bath.[68]
>
> Lieutenant Douglas Jerrold, Hawke Battalion, 1st Naval Brigade

Newly promoted Lieutenant-Colonel Norman Burge had returned from a period of convalescence in Egypt and had assumed command of the Nelson Battalion back in August. He was well aware that any evacuation of Helles would be a difficult military operation:

> At Anzac and Suvla the show was absolutely unexpected by the Turks – they got off all they could and left only the fighting men till the last two nights. Well, we are doing that too – but with this difference – that up there the fire trenches are not, I believe, more than 1500 yards from the beach. Here we are about 4-miles, and you have to stick to single file in communication trenches practically all the way – that delays things and wearies heavily laden men frightfully.[69]
>
> Lieutenant-Colonel Norman Burge, Nelson Battalion, 1st Naval Brigade

Gradually the garrison was reduced, with units leaving covertly at night. Every possible preparation was taken:

> I'm in charge of the divisional rendezvous and as these small scattered groups come in, I have to sort them out into their own particular units and pack them off to the beach. I don't quite know all details yet, but the idea seems to be that I've got to put the last man in on his right road, and once that's done, I can promise you that you won't see my heels for small pebbles! Of course, we hope that even if they do discover that we are retreating from our front lines pretty soon after we have commenced to go, that they won't come after us too quickly. In fact, we are discouraging little schemes of that kind by leaving large numbers of contact mines behind us and various other little booby traps, which should throw a considerable amount of cold water (otherwise melinite) on any thrusting and inquisitive spirits.[70]
>
> Lieutenant-Colonel Norman Burge, Nelson Battalion, 1st Naval Brigade

Yet Burge was most concerned by the threat posed by an awakened Turkish artillery:

> If they get into our first line trenches and find we've gone pretty soon after we've left – as I said before we don't mind their infantry – but every gun here and on the Asiatic side will at once be brought to bear on our communication trenches and the beaches. So it's a gamble.[71]
>
> Lieutenant-Colonel Norman Burge, Nelson Battalion, 1st Naval Brigade

68 D. Jerrold, *Georgian Adventure*, p. 153.
69 IWM DOCS: N.O. Burge, letter, 4-10/1/1916.
70 Ibid.
71 Ibid.

Gradually the Helles garrison melted away. Despite the tension, the officers of Hawke Battalion seem to have had a different set of priorities, as a jocular account of an exchange of signals reveals:

> The situation seemed to us most serious of all when an order came to destroy all stores of alcoholic liquor, coupled with a request for a telegraphic report to the effect that the order had been carried out. Within the appointed time the Hawke Battalion orderly room reported that "All surplus stores of alcoholic liquor has been destroyed", but it appeared this qualitative interpretation of the intentions of the staff was incorrect, and thirty-six hours later the mistake which had been made ... was pointed out in terms which were commendably explicit.[72]
>
> Lieutenant Douglas Jerrold, Hawke Battalion, 1st Naval Brigade

The staged evacuation was almost fatally interrupted by a Turkish attack launched on 7 January, fortunately, the much-reduced garrison assisted by ships of the Royal Navy managed to break up the assault and the Turks remained blissfully unaware their quarry was slipping away.

The final stage began on the night of 8/9 January. By then only 17,000 remained and their evacuation would take place in three waves. Lieutenant-Colonel Burge was in charge of the main control station for the RND as they fell back from the right-hand sector of Helles, where he was to remain until the last man had passed through at 2:30 a.m. Joe Murray had been recalled to the Hood Battalion. He recalled the precautions to ensure silence:

> All the gear that we had that jingled – water bottles, entrenching tools, even your bayonet scabbard – was taken away because it made a noise. We still had our sandbags on our feet and we were told: "Empty the breech and you've got to make your way to Krithia Road". We had a day's iron ration with us, a little bag with some small dog biscuits in to keep us going for a day and we had a bit of a bandage tied round our arm.[73]
>
> Ordinary Seaman Joe Murray, Hood Battalion, 1st Naval Brigade

The Turks still seemed totally unaware that anything else was happening:

> That all seemed normal to the Turk was proved by his periodicalrifle flashes from various fire positions; this is to show that his sentries were not sleeping. Little did he know that, at the moment, his rifle crackle and the rap-tap-tap of his machine guns were to us the sweetest music under Heaven. Had he remained silent how ominous it all would have seemed to the anxious watchers of the skeleton garrisons.[74]
>
> Able Seaman Thomas Macmillan, Drake Battalion, 1st Naval Brigade

For once Ivan Heald was taking the situation seriously:

72 D. Jerrold, *The Hawke Battalion: Some Personal Recollections of Four Years*, (London: Ernest Benn Ltd, 1925), pp. 108-109.
73 IWM SOUND: J. Murray, SR 8201.
74 IWM DOCS: T. Macmillan, Typescript account, p. 121.

> Never did man listen to sound so anxiously as I did, sitting alone in the old French dugout in the red glow of a charcoal brazier. I was fearful that any moment there might come clamouring in my ears the furious babbling splutter of rapid fire, which would mean an attack. But the hours wore on in a healthy sequence of occasional bombs and steady sniping, and half an hour before midnight I made a tour to the end of my line, where my commander, Freyberg, with Asquith and six men, were holding the chaos of mine craters and trenches which the French named La Ravine de la Mort. They both decided there was time to finish some biscuits they had left in a dug-out.[75]
>
> Sub-Lieutenant Ivan Heald, Hood Battalion, 1st Naval Brigade

The minutes seemed to last an eternity but at last the moment came they had been waiting for:

> A touch on the back of the last man and he climbed down from the firing step and touched the next man farther along, and quietly we filed out of the long firing line, and, as we stole away, I could hear the Turks coughing and talking in their trench 20 yards away. Two or three times, to hide the shuffle of the men's gear against the side of the trench, I jumped on the firing step and let my Webley-Scott bark at Achi Baba, and somewhere on the left someone fired a farewell Very light, which lit up the sandbags until the blackness came welling up out of the trench again as the rocket died away. So we shuffled past the telephone station at the top of the communication trench.[76]
>
> Sub-Lieutenant Ivan Heald, Hood Battalion, 1st Naval Brigade

Still to come was a small group of men under the command of Lieutenant Commander Bernard Freyberg who had with him Arthur Asquith and Frederick Kelly:

> We had the honour of being the very last company to leave the firing line on our sector and your humble was selected along with another two to hold a communication trench while the rest of the company retired. It was a big strain on our nerves as if the Turks tumbled and made a big attack there was only a thin line to keep them back. If the Turks made an attack, we had to hold it at all costs. 'Johnny' didn't tumble and after Mr Kelly had destroyed the telephone station I led the way as guide, Mr Kelly bringing up the rear. We couldn't help laughing as we could still hear Johnny sniping away as usual – stray bullets whizzing over our heads.[77]
>
> Private Thomas Goulden, Hood Battalion, 1st Naval Brigade

Ahead of them the troops that had left earlier were still trudging their way back to the beach:

> The Turk's own moon was in the sky, a perfect crescent with a star, and a wind rising dangerously from the north. Now and again a wistful sigh of a spent bullet, and ever wheeling behind us the shaft of the great Chanak searchlight. The men talked little among themselves, and I think we were all awed by the bigness of the thing and saddened by the

75 I. Heald, *Ivan Heald: Hero and Humorist* (London: C. Arthur Pearson, 1917), p. 176.
76 Ibid., pp. 176-177.
77 IWM DOCS: T. C. Goulden, Manuscript Letter, 16/1/1916.

> thoughts of the little crosses we were leaving behind us – the little wooden crosses that were creeping higher every day to meet the crescents on that great sullen hill.[78]
>
> Sub-Lieutenant Ivan Heald, Hood Battalion, 1st Naval Brigade

One by one the men were checked off by Burge and his team:

> At about 1:30 everyone was through and so even if we – the last 600 – had been collared the evacuation would have been a great success as we formed such a small proportion of the total numbers. But I don't think any of us last folks had any such high and uplifting thoughts. I hadn't anyway. At 1:45 the French blew up two 10" and two 4.7's which had to be left firing till then otherwise it would have given the show away. The flash and noise was just like the gun going off so the Turks didn't suspect.[79]
>
> Lieutenant-Colonel Norman Burge, Nelson Battalion, 1st Naval Brigade

When they were certain everyone had passed they too moved back to V Beach. In the event the beach was evacuated without trouble – despite the occasional harassing shell from Asiatic Annie. Joe Murray left an account that summed up the fears and discomfort of the men as they were packed into the lighters:

> We were so packed we couldn't move our hands up at all. I remember the chap in front of me was as sick as a dog. Half of them were asleep and leaning – we were packed up like sardines. It was dark, of course – no lights, no portholes. The damned thing started to rock. There must have been a shell dropped pretty close. You know we laughed at V Beach shelling – and there we were, no reason for laughing! Those that were asleep were half-awake and those that were sick were still being sick and it was stifling hot! I thought to myself, "Why the hell don't we get out of it?" We left there like a lot of cattle, dumped into a lighter and just pushed to sea, and nobody gave a tinker's cuss whether we lived or died.[80]
>
> Ordinary Seaman Joe Murray, Hood Battalion, 1st Naval Brigade

This was an understandable reaction, although not entirely fair given the diligent efforts of the staff and senior officers to ensure that they got away unscathed.

When the Turks finally realised what was happening their violent reaction showed Burge just how lucky he and his men had been to get away with it.

> What a hullabulloo! The Turks thought we were going at last and opened every gun they could on roads, communication trenches, beaches and anything else they could think of. Some of us had thought they wanted to let us get off – but this fire showed they had meant to make it as uncomfortable for us as possible.[81]
>
> Lieutenant-Colonel Norman Burge, Nelson Battalion, 1st Naval Brigade

78 Heald, *Ivan Heald*, pp. 177-178.
79 IWM DOCS: N. O. Burge, Letter, 10/1/1916.
80 IWM SOUND: J. Murray, SR 8201.
81 IWM DOCS: N. O. Burge, Letter, 10/1/1916.

Of 16,000 men serving with the RND at Gallipoli, over 13,000 had become casualties, or evacuated sick during the campaign. They left 2,491 of their dead behind them.[82]

The remnants of the RND was not a happy body of men during the weeks that followed, spent in their rest camps established on the offshore Aegean islands:

> General Paris was justly proud of his division, and whether it was his intention to visit all battalions in turn in order to express his appreciation, I know not. Suffice it to say that the `Hoods' were paraded for the General's inspection; and after saying some nice things, he announced his intention of giving the officers leave to England and the men, if they cared, leave to Malta. His speech was listened to in silence, but when the acting commander called for three cheers for the General the gallant `Hoods' gave him the `raspberry'. The General went pink and, in a fit of choler, cancelled all leave for the battalion and confined all ranks to camp for seven days.[83]
>
> Able Seaman Thomas Macmillan, Drake Battalion, 1st Naval Brigade

Their officers were less vociferous in expressing their opinions and Norman Burge had already turned his mind to a congenial future:

> Personally, I wouldn't mind a winter on the Suez Canal – with a mild engagement in which of course we rout the Turks with no loss to ourselves second and fourth Fridays![84]
>
> Lieutenant-Colonel Norman Burge, Nelson Battalion, 1st Naval Brigade

In fact, the RND were selected alongside the ANZAC and the 29th Division to serve on the Western Front. This was taken as a sign of respect for their fighting abilities, but on their arrival, they found that their ostentatious affectation of naval "habits" coupled with the somewhat lackadaisical attitude of some of their officers led to some scepticism as to its qualities amongst hard-bitten army commanders. As a result, they were held back until the Battle of the Ancre on 13 November at the tail-end of the Somme offensive. On that day "happy warrior" Norman Burge was killed in action.

82 C. Page, *Command in the Royal Naval Division* (Staplehurst: Spellmount, 1999), p. 66.
83 IWM DOCS: T. Macmillan, Typescript account, p. 128.
84 IWM DOCS: N. O. Burge, Letter, 10/1/1916.

10

Gallipoli Staff Officer: Captain Harold Mynors Farmar CMG DSO

Katherine Swinfen Eady

> *Future historians may say of us as Napier said of the Fusilier Brigade at Albuhera "Nothing could stop this astonishing Infantry".*[1]

These encouraging remarks can be found in the "Special Brigade Order" written by Brigadier-General Steuart Welwood Hare, GOC 86th Brigade, which was destined to land at Cape Helles on 25 April 1915. Collective memory and perception has surrounded the Gallipoli campaign in a sphere of myth and tragic mysticism. The association with classical mythology started in the campaign's immediate aftermath. Popular interwar novels and memoirs such as *Tell England* and *Gallipoli Memories* bound the campaign with heroic and historical references.[2] Even accounts of a more official nature such as *The Story of the 29th Division: A Record of Gallant Deeds* spoke of the campaign as being one of the "grand, heroic, Homeric episodes of the world's history."[3] At the core of much of the historiography was the belief that culpable failings within military high command combined with a doomed political strategy destroyed any real chance of success for the Mediterranean Expeditionary Force. This view was reinforced by Peter Weir's celebrated film *Gallipoli* (1981), where the narrative prevailed that incompetent British leadership squandered the lives of the decent individual soldiers. Recent scholarship has opened the debate, particularly surrounding the Anzac legend and performance of Dominion leadership.[4] However the overwhelming impression is still one in which lack of experience and training dominated the doomed campaign, particularly in relation to the command staff.

1 B. Smyth, *Lancashire Fusilier Annual 1914-15*, XXIV and XXV, 'Special Brigade Order for 86th Brigade by Brigadier-General S.W. Hare', p. 90.
2 See J. Macleod, 'The British Heroic-Romantic Myth of Gallipoli' in J. Macleod (ed.), *Gallipoli: Making History* (Abingdon: Frank Cass, 2012), pp. 73-85; E. Raymond, *Tell England* (New York: George Doran, 1922); I. Hamilton, *Gallipoli Diary*, Vols. 1 & 2 (New York: George Doran, 1920); C. Mackenzie, *Gallipoli Memories* (London: Cassell, 1929); J. Masefield, *Gallipoli* (London: William Heinemann, 1916).
3 S.A. Gillon, *The Story of the 29th Division: A Record of Gallant Deeds* (London: Thomas Nelson & Sons, 1925), p. vii.
4 See C. Pugsley, 'Stories of Anzac' in Macleod (ed.), *Gallipoli: Making History*, pp. 44-58.

This attitude towards the staff is not unique to the Gallipoli campaign. First World War historiography has not been kind to the staff at any level of the command hierarchy. The characterisation of "bristling, fierce scarlet Majors at the Base", portrayed by Siegfried Sassoon and others has not helped the staff's reputation.[5] The portrayal of incompetence started during the war – a quick glance at *The Wipers Times* is proof enough.[6] Peter Scott in his introduction to *Behind the Lines* by W.N. Nicholson, quotes a contemporaneous music hall joke, "If bread is the staff of life, what is the life of the staff? One big loaf."[7] This established perception that the staff kept themselves firmly behind the lines and away from any of the inconvenience or realities of war is as true of the interpretation of the campaigns in the mud of Flanders as on the Gallipoli Peninsula. First-hand accounts such as Reverend Creighton's *With the Twenty-Ninth Division in Gallipoli: A Chaplain's Experiences* (1916) strengthened the opinion that planning for the campaign was inadequate at best, incompetent at worst. He declared that "the whole thing has been bungled" and that "slaughter seems to be inevitable."[8] His prediction proved right, the losses amongst the officers, both staff and regimental, were very high. It is therefore more remarkable that the survivors were able to establish themselves at Helles.

The Gallipoli campaign has been assessed with reference to the strategic and political aspects; higher command performance has been evaluated but there remains a substantial lack of detailed research into the role of the junior staff officers who served on the peninsula. In fact, the role of junior staff during the First World War in general has received little academic scrutiny even though these positions were vital. The sentiment below could be expanded to include public perception in general:

> The uneducated, in a military sense – regimental officer, does not realize the immense amount of work, continuous responsible work, which falls to a Staff Officer and the amount of knowledge he must have to cope with it.[9]

By January 1915 the BEF had expanded from six infantry divisions and one cavalry to 11 infantry and five cavalry. This rapid growth during a period of intense combat impacted heavily on the established army organisation. As early as October 1914 the shortage of trained staff capable of supporting this increase was recognised:

> The Colonel thinks there will be many changes in this battalion when we get home, with officers. That they will now not leave so many senior men in one battalion, especially those with staff experience.[10]

5 W.N. Nicholson, *Behind the Lines: An Account of Administrative Staffwork in the British Army, 1914-1918* New Edition (Stevenage: Strong Oak Press, 1990), p. vii; See also S. Sassoon, *Base Details* (1918).
6 I. Hislop & M. Brown, *The Wipers Times, The Complete Series of the Famous Wartime Trench Newspaper* (London: Little Books Ltd., 2006).
7 Nicholson, *Behind the Lines*, p. vii.
8 Reverend O. Creighton, *With the Twenty-Ninth Division in Gallipoli* (London: Longmans, Green & Co., 1916), p. 42.
9 Private Papers of Colonel Harold Mynors Farmar CMG, DSO (1878-1961), collection of Mrs Sally Mclaren (Farmar Papers): Letter to his wife Violet Farmar, 18 June 1917.
10 Farmar Papers: FAR/LE/4, Letter from H.M. Farmar to Violet Farmar, 23-28 October 1914.

The 29th Division was the last Regular division available in early 1915 and was considered such an asset that it had been earmarked to go straight to France under Sir John French's command "enabling him to extend his lines and release French troops to assist General Joffre."[11] The division was unusual in that it was still largely comprised of Regular forces, experienced men honed by years of overseas service. However, the staff colleges at Quetta and Camberley had closed in late 1914 and the resultant shortfall of trained staff created "a situation for which no precedent existed."[12] It cannot therefore be assumed that brigades were staffed with trained and experienced men capable of accepting "orders and counter-orders as part of the daily ration."[13]

Recollecting in 1950, Brigadier-General Sir James Edmonds – British Official History (1922-48) compiler – remarked to fellow historian and author Brigadier C.N. Barclay that "In 1914 there were very few trained staff officers, that is men who had served on the staff of a command, a division, or a brigade with troops."[14] As the war progressed into 1915 this situation deteriorated further. Recent research by Douglas Delaney and Aimée Fox-Godden has shown that by April 1915 key placements within the Dominion forces staff were filled with Imperial officers. This placed added strain on remaining trained staff spread increasingly thin across the newly formed Kitchener armies, Dominion forces and existing divisions re-locating from across the British Empire.[15] The army acknowledged the shortage of trained junior staff officers but it was not until late 1916 that the establishment of a Junior Staff School in France formally addressed the problem.[16] This dearth of trained staff officers together with the limited forms of communications available to the combined force, heightened the inadequate planning and hindered liaison especially at brigade and divisional level. This became particularly relevant during the opening of the Gallipoli campaign.

In "The Transformation and Operational Performance of Brigade Staff", Fox-Godden notes that "The brigade was the smallest formation to have a formal staff structure", one in which "it was expected that the brigade major and Staff Captain would be capable of undertaking the

11 The National Archives (TNA) CAB 63/18: 'Memorandum by The Secretary, War Council', Dardanelles Committee, 30 June 1916, p. 10. See also TNA CAB 63/17: 'Memorandum by The Secretary, War Council', February 1915; TNA CAB 37/128/30: "The War, August 1914 to 31 May 1915", Note by Secretary of State for War.

12 J. Hussey, 'The Deaths of Qualified Staff Officers in the Great War: "A Generation Missing"?', *Journal of the Society for Army Historical Research,* 75, (1997), pp. 246-259, p. 254; cited in A. Fox-Godden, '"Hopeless Inefficiency"?, The Transformation and Operational Performance of Brigade Staff, 1916-1918' in M. LoCicero, R. Mahoney & S. Mitchell, (eds.), *A Military Transformed? Adaption and Innovation in The British Military, 1792-1945* (Solihull: Helion & Company, 2014), pp. 139-156, p. 143.

13 Nicholson, *Behind the Lines*, p. 65.

14 Liddell Hart Centre for Military Archives (LHCMA): 1/2B 5a: Edmonds Papers, Brigadier-General Sir James Edmonds to Brigadier C.N. Barclay, 7 April 1950, cited in S. Robbins, 'British Generalship of the Western Front in the First World War, 1914-1918', PhD thesis for King's College, University of London, p. 114.

15 For further details, see D. Delaney, 'Mentoring the Canadian Corps: Imperial Officers and the Canadian Expeditionary Force, 1914-1918', *The Journal of Military History*, 77 (July 2013), pp. 931-953. See also Fox-Godden, '"Hopeless Inefficiency"?: The Transformation and Operational Performance of Brigade Staff, 1916-1918', pp. 139-156.

16 See Fox-Godden, "Hopeless Inefficiency"?, pp. 139-156, p. 145. See also B. Bond, *Staff Officer, The Diaries of Lord Moyne, 1914-1918* (London: Leo Cooper, 1987), p. 131 for a description of the course at Hesdin.

other's duties in case of death, absence or promotion."[17] A role that was defined by the needs of the commander, the brigade major had to ensure the brigade understood its role and was supported in achieving the desired objectives. The brigade major had to be both operationally and tactically aware when "interpreting commands from higher headquarters, and transforming them into precise instructions and specific actions."[18] Given the level of historical criticism directed at staff during the Gallipoli campaign and the fact that the role of the brigade major under operational circumstances was pivotal, this chapter aims to throw light onto the role of Captain Harold Mynors Farmar, Lancashire Fusiliers, Staff Captain of 86th Brigade, the author's great-grandfather. As the senior surviving officer of the brigade headquarters, Farmar found himself in command of 86th Brigade from 8:30 a.m. till 7:00 p.m. on 25 April 1915. Had the established culture of the British military, personal training and experience, equipped this regular junior staff officer adequately for war?

Antebellum Military Experience and Training

The pre-1914 British Army is often represented as being slow to innovate, trapped in a hierarchal and cultural inflexibility, yet reformers such as Colonel G.F.R. Henderson had deliberately initiated an internal debate as early as the turn of the last century. His emphasis centered on the need for a shift in the command structure from centralised command to one based on individual initiative and bears particular relevance to the Gallipoli campaign:

> It may be observed that centralisation, the invariable refuge of administrative incompetency, exerted an evil influence both on the efficiency of the troops and on the character of the officers.[19]

The Second Anglo-Boer War (1899-1902) and observation of the Russo-Japanese War (1904-05) highlighted inadequacies with British Army training and tactics. Farmar's experience during the Boer War led him to make the following comment.

> Prior to the war with the Boer Republics, the training of the British Army was almost Crimean, and was not suitable to compete against the common-sense and natural aptitude of its Dutch opponents.[20]

The army responded by commissioning a series of reports that opened a substantial conversation within the military. The Esher Committee of 1904 and the Army Reforms of 1906-12 overseen by Lord Haldane resulted in a major re-thinking of traditional infantry tactics. Christopher Pugsley has argued in his "Doctrine Evolution" that *Infantry Training 1902* and *Combined*

17 Fox-Godden, "Hopeless Inefficiency"?, pp. 139-156, pp. 139-140.
18 Ibid., pp. 139-156, p. 140.
19 See G.F.R. Henderson, *A Collection of Essays and Lectures 1891-1903* (London: Longmans, 1910), p. 403.
20 H.M. Farmar, 'The Australians and New Zealanders', *Reveille* (Returned and Services League of Australia), 11: 8 (1 April 1938), p. 30.

Training 1905 led the way in establishing an inherent understanding of the necessity for both a combined arms approach and a "'centralised intent and decentralization of execution' based on the need to achieve mobility and speed of execution through swift and efficient command procedures."[21] According to *Field Service Regulations*:

> Decentralisation [sic] of command, and a full recognition of responsibilities of subordinates in action, are thus absolutely necessary; and leaders must train their subordinates not only to work intelligently and resolutely in accordance with brief and very general instructions, but also to take upon themselves, whenever it may be necessary, the responsibility of departing from, or from varying, the orders they may have received.[22]

This change in command philosophy defined how command may have to adapt to operational circumstances and still applies today. In his introduction to *Stemming the Tide*, Spencer Jones elaborates on the definition for command from Gary Sheffield, *Leadership & Command*, stating that "command is a managerial function that emphasizes direction, co-ordination and effective use of force at the commander's disposal."[23] Command has at its core authority, responsibility and accountability. It is different to Control. Jones also observed that "Tactical reform in the aftermath of the Anglo-Boer War had codified the British emphasis on leadership, *Combined Training* and its successor, *Field Service Regulations*, encouraged tactical flexibility and enshrined the authority of the man on the spot to make key decisions."[24] The nature of the Gallipoli campaign necessitated decentralised command particularly during the opening hours of the offensive and thus provides historians with a valuable opportunity to assess whether this relatively new ethos was understood and put into practice.

Deficiencies within the divisional staff was recognised by the official historian, Brigadier-General Cecil Aspinall-Oglander. He noted the "inadequate orders which Colonel Matthews originally received from divisional headquarters" and "the subsequent absence of that interest and attention which he had a right to expect from the Staff."[25] Tim Travers states that "the failure of Gallipoli can best be understood not as a series of individual command mistakes, but as a systems or structural failure."[26] He also blames many of the Helles landing difficulties on "Victorian and Edwardian army attitudes" and lack of flexibility.[27] Martin Samuels research is equally dismissive declaring that British staff officers had little "experience of command at

21 C. Pugsley, *"We Have Been Here Before": The Evolution of the Doctrine of Decentralised Command in the British Army 1905-1989, Sandhurst Occasional Papers No. 9*, p. 8; *Infantry Training 1902* (London: HMSO, 1902); *Field Services Regulations, Part 1*, Combined Training (London: HMSO, 1905).

22 *Field Services Regulations, Part 1*, p. 6; cited in Pugsley, *'We Have Been Here Before'*, p. 9.

23 S. Jones (ed.), *Stemming the Tide: Officers and Leadership in the British Expeditionary Force 1914* (Solihull: Helion & Company, 2013), p. 20; G.D. Sheffield (ed.), *Leadership & Command: The Anglo-American Military Experience Since 1861* (London: Brassey's, 1997), pp. 1-14.

24 Jones, *Stemming the Tide*, p. 22. See also Pugsley, *'We Have Been Here Before'*.

25 C.F. Aspinall-Oglander, *Military Operations Gallipoli*, Vol. I (Nashville, Tennessee: Battery Press reprint of 1929 edition), p. 215. Lt. Col. G.E. Matthews commanded the Plymouth Battalion, R.M.L.I. which landed at Y Beach on 25 April 1915.

26 T. Travers, 'Command and Leadership Styles in the British Army: The Gallipoli Model', *Journal of Contemporary History*, Vol. 29 (3), July 1994, pp. 403-442, p. 403.

27 Ibid., p. 411.

King George V inspects a battalion of 29th Division prior to embarkation for the Dardanelles, March 1915.

the operational level … Staff officers do not command. They rarely have to bear the responsibility of making an important decision quickly, with defeat the consequence of a mistake. On the contrary, staff officers merely request or suggest."[28] Travers and Samuels have assessed the British officer class as hierarchical and largely incapable of rising to the challenge of modern warfare.[29] Unquestionably the lack of adequate preparation for the entire campaign is evident and had serious ramifications.[30] However, it is an overly simplistic and generalist approach to link individual senior commanders' failure with a "structural failure."[31] The conditions faced by the invaders on 25 April and subsequent losses incurred required enormous flexibility and operational adaptability by surviving brigade and battalion officers.

The 29th Division had had very little time to prepare for the campaign. As late as 17 March 1915, Farmar informed his wife Violet, that "We have to learn now how to do combined naval and military landings, and to work out Staff arrangements."[32] Farmar was from a military family and, following his two elder brothers into the army, had been gazetted into the

28 M. Samuels, *Command and Control?: Command, Training and Tactics in the British German Armies 1888-1918* (London: Frank Cass, 1995), p. 60.
29 See T. Travers, *The Killing Ground: The British Army, The Western Front and the emergence of Modern Warfare, 1900-1918* (London: Allen & Unwin, 1987); T. Travers, 'A Particular Style of Command: Haig and GHQ, 1916-1918', *Journal of Strategic Studies,* 10 (1987), pp. 363-376.
30 See R.H. Beadon, *The Royal Army Service Corps: A History of Transport and Supply in The British Army,* Vol. II (Cambridge: Cambridge University Press, 1931), pp. 160-165.
31 Travers, 'Command and Leadership Styles in the British Army: The Gallipoli Model', p. 403.
32 Farmar Papers: FAR/LE/16, Letter from H.M. Farmar to V. Farmar, 17–23 March 1915, 17 March 1915.

Lancashire Fusiliers in May 1898 aged 20.[33] By July of that same year he was on active service in the Sudan for which he received the Khedive's Egyptian Medal with clasp.[34] He noted in his memoirs that the campaign had been "called a picnic. It was very hard. Food was atrocious. Drink was Nile water. Deep sand and great heat made marching a torture."[35] Aged just 20, Farmar fought with his regiment at the Battle of Omdurman. On 2 September 1898, as an infantry subaltern of just 4 months standing he was "doubled off to reinforce the front face – a trail of bullets falling amongst us as we did so. Major Blomfield was hit on my immediate right and Wolley Dod, Carter and myself, all got hit by spent bullets, rather like a good hard smack from a thrown stone."[36] He went straight from the Sudan to serve during the Crete Insurrection in October 1898. During the Boer War, Farmar served under General Sir Edward Hutton and saw action at Vet River, Zand River, Diamond Hill; in the Transvaal with 7th Dragoon Guards, as a subaltern of the Cavalry Transport Co and later with the 3rd Mounted Infantry, where he "spent a most happy year, brigaded with [the] New Zealand Mounted Rifles, Queensland Mounted Infantry, Queensland Bushmen and Canadian Royal Dragoons."[37] Farmar was Mentioned in Despatches (October 1901) by Lord Roberts. Within three years this young infantry subaltern had fought both in traditional infantry square formation and experienced mobile guerrilla warfare from horseback with a "ride of over more than 1100 miles."[38]

Farmar's academic capability was recognised by the military and fostered. Serving as Adjutant, 4th Lancashire Fusiliers from 1904-07, he was subsequently appointed to the Royal Military Academy Sandhurst staff during 1907-11:

> I had expected to serve under an old friend Sir Colin Mackenzie, but he was suddenly given command of the 1st Division, and I found myself reporting to a Commandant, who in private life was the kindest of men, but professionally was a driver with the energy of an untiring spirit. Under him Sandhurst was more efficient that ever it has been. To teach is an art which requires much understanding and unflagging work.[39]

Farmar states in his memoirs that his "work was a great interest" and that he "used to give lectures, and, having been trained for the Umpire Staff, to take practical exercises" and assess the students' performance.[40] After Sandhurst, he was appointed temporary staff captain to 7th Infantry Brigade (GOC Brigadier-General Laurence Drummond), 3rd Division (GOC Major-General Sir Henry Rawlinson). Farmar described this as "a delightful period in which I learnt

33 TNA WO 76/148: 'War Office, Records of Officers' Services', Preston Record Office, 20th Foot (Lancashire Fusiliers).
34 Ibid.
35 Farmar Papers: Autobiography of H.M. Farmar, p. 13.
36 Farmar Papers: FAR/10/96, 'Diary of events leading up to the Battle of Omdurman on 2 September 1898 and afterward on the journey via Crete to Malta, by Colonel H.M. Farmar C.M.G., D.S.O.'. See TNA WO 76/148: 'War Office, Records of Officers' Service', states Owen Cadogan Wolley Dod, without a hyphen, although much of the historiography has his name hyphenated.
37 Farmar Papers: Autobiography, pp. 21-22.
38 Ibid., p. 22.
39 Ibid., p. 40.
40 Ibid., p. 44.

a great deal from [Brigade Major] George Cory."[41] Having passed the Staff College exam in 1912 with high marks in military administration, Farmar hoped to be picked for the course but appendicitis put him out of reach of a nomination. He was, however, chosen to be one of the few officers to attend the London School of Economics short course on army administration (October 1912–March 1913) to receive a period of intensive staff training.[42]

There is little academic research into brigade-level administration and the prevailing viewpoint remains that the junior staff suffered from a lack of formal training. Nevertheless, Peter Grant's recent research into the LSE course cites Geoff Sloan, who acknowledged the course as a "radical experiment in British Military education."[43] Focused on the ranks of captain and major, the course aimed to instil detailed and clear administrative procedure at this crucial level of army administration. Grant's research concludes that the success of logistical administration during the First World War was "laid in the eight courses of 1907-14."[44] After the LSE, Farmar spent a brief time as a "lecturer on Military subjects for Infantry for the Inns of Court O.T.C.", prior to joining 1st Lancashire Fusiliers at Multan in the Punjab.[45] On the outbreak of war the battalion embarked for Aden in reserve for the Sheik Said Expedition where Farmar served on the staff of General Sir James Bell. During this time, he received the longed-for Staff College nomination but this time the war intervened, and he was posted to serve as staff captain to 86th Brigade.[46]

Cape Helles

The 86th Brigade "formed the covering force for the 29th Division landing on the Gallipoli Peninsula at Beaches, X, W and V" on 25 April 1915.[47] The objective was to secure the beaches and seize the high ground, north of the Achi Baba, "line points 141-138-114."[48]

41 Farmar Papers: Autobiography, p. 42; Captain George Cory, (Later General Sir George Cory), G.S.O. 3rd Division at the beginning of the War, he was moved to 51st Division a territorial division to enable newly formed divisions to gain experience from trained staff.

42 See 'Report of the Advisory Board, London School of Economics, on the seventh course at The London School of Economics, 3 October 1912, to 19 March 1913' (London: HMSO, 1913).

43 G. Sloan, "Haldane's Mackindergarten: A Radical Experiment in British Military education", *War in History*, 19:3 (2012), pp. 322-352, p. 351; cited in P. Grant, 'Learning to Manage the Army: Edward Ward, Halford Mackinder and the Army Administration Course at the London School of Economics, 1907-1914', in M. LoCicero, R. Mahoney & S. Mitchell (eds.), *A Military Transformed: Adaption and Innovation in The British Military, 1792-1945* (Solihull: Helion, 2014), pp. 97-109, p. 97.

44 Grant, 'Learning to Manage the Army', p. 108.

45 Farmar Papers: Autobiography, p. 42.

46 Ibid., p. 44. See also Farmar Papers: FAR/LE/7, Letter from H.M. Farmar to V. Farmar, 12-18 November 1914.

47 TNA WO 95/4310: War Diary, 86th Infantry Brigade, 25 April 191:, "attached to the Brigade were: One section London Field Company R.E., West Riding Field Company R.E. 1/2 Battalion Hampshire Regiment, the 2nd Battalion Royal Fusiliers landed on the beach known as X. The 1st Lancashire Fusiliers on Beach W; the remainder on Beach V from the Collier River Clyde." See also Gillon, *The Story of the 29th Division*; TNA WO 95/4356, 'Force Orders, includes Special Orders', April 1915-November 1915.

48 1st R. Dublin Fus.: Sedd-el-Bahr and Hill 141;1st R. Munster Fus.: village exclusive to Fort 2 (3) inclusive; 1st Lancashire Fus.: Trenches and redoubt on Hill 138; one company to assist 2nd Royal

"This high ground, the principal heights of which are Hills 114, 138, and 141, overlooks all the country between the western bluffs, the Achi Baba range and Morto Bay on the straits."[49] The brigade staff, Captain Farmar inclusive, was "ordered to land at Beach W. The ruined lighthouse was named as the spot where it would establish headquarters and to which reports would be sent."[50] The staff followed the Lancashire Fusiliers onto W Beach and witnessed the difficulties experienced by the first to land. The "losses incurred by the Lancashire Fusiliers far exceed the highest estimate of what the best-disciplined British infantry are expected to face."[51] Major-General Hunter-Weston had named Brigadier-General Hare "as the commander of the whole covering force" limited initially "to co-ordinating the action of the 86th Brigade."[52] The 88th Brigade was to secure V Beach and link up with 87th Brigade which was to land at Y and S Beach.

W Beach was considered to be a suitable landing place for the force necessary to support the invasion.[53] The navy had questioned the strength of the Turkish defences on 23 April, but this information "had not reached Brigadier-General Hare."[54] Lord Kitchener's instructions to MEF C-in-C General Sir Ian Hamilton clearly stated that "we must presume that the Gallipoli Peninsula is held in strength and the Kalid Bahr plateau has been fortified and armed for a determined resistance."[55] The Helles beaches were indeed heavily fortified and defended by capable, well-trained and equipped troops.[56] As the headquarters staff headed towards the shoreline in tows, "aimed fire began to strike."[57] Farmar was in the second tow. His brigade major, Major Thomas Frankland (Royal Dublin Fusiliers) was an experienced Regular officer who "had been in France since the beginning of the war, but had been recalled to help form the Division."[58] He was in the tow ahead and "had seen the first party of Lancashire Fusiliers, who had put ashore in the middle of the beach, suffer severely in the barbed wire entanglements near the water edge."[59] The Lancashire Fusiliers "were subjected to cross fire of machine guns and

Fus., with the capture of 114 and 2nd Royal Fus.: Hill 114, and to secure flank towards N.E. C.F. Aspinall-Oglander, *Military Operations Gallipoli*, Vol. I, Appendices (London: Heinemann, 1929) Appendix 19, p. 54 '86th Brigade Operation Order No. 1', 23 April 1915.

49 Gillon, *The Story of the 29th Division,* p. 14.

50 TNA WO 95/4310: 86th Infantry Brigade War Diary, January 1915-February 1916, digital image, p. 13.

51 Gillon, *The Story of the 29th Division*, p. 22.

52 Aspinall-Oglander, *Military Operations Gallipoli*, Vol. I, p. 217.

53 The Final Report of the Dardanelles Commission, Part II – Conduct of Operations (London: HMSO, 1917), p. 19.

54 Aspinall-Oglander, *Military Operations Gallipoli*, Vol. I, p. 228. fn. 2.

55 Aspinall-Oglander, *Military Operations Gallipoli*, Vol. I, Appendices, Appendix 1, 'Lord Kitchener's Instructions to Sir Ian Hamilton', 13 March 1915, p. 1.

56 For further understanding of the Turkish defences See E. Erickson, *Gallipoli: The Ottoman Campaign* (Barnsley: Pen & Sword, [2010] 2015).

57 Farmar Papers: FAR/10/94, Typescript with annotations in the hand of H.M. Farmar, 'The Landing of the 86th Infantry Brigade under Brigadier-General SW Hare on the Gallipoli Peninsula 25th April 1915, and its subsequent operations' by Major H.M. Farmar, p. 1.

58 Creighton, *With the Twenty-Ninth Division in Gallipoli*, p. 3.

59 Farmar Papers: FAR/10/94, 'The Landing of the 86th Infantry Brigade', p. 2; Thomas Hugh Colville Frankland, Royal Dublin Fusiliers was 35 when he died and is commemorated on the Helles Memorial. He was a brigade staff captain until September 1914, serving in France under General Haldane, then commanded the 2nd Battalion Royal Dublin Fusiliers before promotion to brigade major of 86th Brigade.

rifle fire."[60] The Turkish defenders' fire decimated the covering force. Hampered by weighty kit, they suffered terribly in the water and on the barbed wire obstacles:

> The survivors on the beach forced their way through and past the wire and pushed forward up the centre of the little valley leading from the shore, Captain Tallents and Lieut. Seckham displaying the utmost gallantry. Major Adams' Company had made for the cliff edge on the left of the beach, which they took, and ensconced themselves in some Turkish trenches. Major Frankland with the Brigadier, followed by a few men, went up the cliff still further to the left.[61]

Major Bishop, who had assumed command of the Lancashire Fusiliers five days earlier due to the ill health of Lieutenant-Colonel Ormond, remained with D Company together with Captain Bromley, the adjutant. Pinned down by overwhelming Turkish fire, the invaders were unable to co-ordinate an inland advance. The remaining survivors "had difficulty in getting up the very steep bits near the top" of the cliff.[62] Thus Hare, Frankland and half a dozen men found themselves isolated with the enemy only 20 to 30 yards distant:

> There were no Turks on the front edge of the cliff, so we were defiladed from the front, but were getting it pretty hot from the trenches on the East side of the mouth of the glen which formed the beach. When we got to the top we could see that the Lancs. Fusiliers were shoving on straight to their front up the glen but must have been losing frightfully from fire from the trenches on both sides. There was one trench just at the top of the cliff on the East side of the glen that was doing a lot of damage, but while we looked a shell from the Euryalus burst right in it and when the smoke cleared off no occupants could be seen, and some Fusiliers got up the cliff and into it before it could be reoccupied. When we got to the top of the cliff we found an empty trench at the very edge. The occupants must have been shot out of it by the bombardment. We collected about a dozen Fusiliers there and an officer, about all who had reached the top, and sent them off to charge a trench which was only about 50 yards off, not facing us but flanking the glen leading up from the beach.[63]

Crucially, Hare moved towards Hill 114 instead of Hill 138, the main objective:

> I could hear no firing coming from beach X and concluding that the Royal Fusiliers had landed without opposition I thought I would try and work round to meet them and bring them up to make a flank attack on the people who were opposing the Lancs. Fusiliers. The latter had made a certain amount of progress (it was wonderful that they made any) but I did not think they could possibly get far unsupported.[64]

60 Farmar Papers: FAR/10/94, 'The Landing of the 86th Infantry Brigade', p. 2.
61 Ibid., p. 2.
62 Ibid., p. 2.
63 Imperial War Museum (IWM): 18385: 09/86/1: Private Papers of Major-General Sir Steuart Hare, diary entry post 25 April 1915.
64 IWM: Hare Papers, 18385: 09/86/1, diary entry post 25 April 1915.

This point has been largely neglected in analysis of the campaign. Clearly, Hare changed his intended route to assist the Lancashire Fusiliers because "the main assault of the British in the centre was being held up and was in danger of failing altogether."[65] So it was that:

> Each separate party to land found itself with an individual task to perform and was at once closely engaged. At the moment when the troops were enduring the effects of a bewildering shock, they were given a course to pursue with confidence and cohesion. The Lancashire Fusiliers had the task on which depended the success of the troops landing on the beaches right and left of them. Had they failed the others must have been destroyed.[66]

The size of the landing beaches was determined too small to land the entire division, so the brigades had been divided amongst the disparate objectives. Because the beachheads were close, it was hoped that it would not be long before the brigades were able to join forces:

> No arrangements had been made for reinforcing the Lancashire Fusiliers at W, but it was expected that even if that battalion were held up by the Turkish defence, the garrison would quickly be "pinched out" by a successful advance from X and V.[67]

This dispersal of force necessitated a form of decentralised command and control. Hare could not exercise command effectively since no provision had been made for liaison staff and, as casualties increased, fewer staff was available to fill the roles necessary to reform and guide the attackers. Farmar subsequently observed that dividing the division created a situation where this "first attack on the Peninsula was made with a dispersal of force, which, when severe opposition was encountered, led to a lessening of confidence."[68] It was under these conditions that brigades needed to rely on individual initiative. Hare, understanding that his main covering force had been decimated, reacted to prevailing circumstances:

> I started with Frankland and two signallers and we were just above the top of the cliff not far from Cape Tekke when we found ourselves within about 100 yards of a trench full of Turks. We started to drop over the top of the cliff as they opened fire. I felt a tremendous blow on my calf and just got over the edge of the cliff when I sat down. Frankland and the signallers put on three field dressings without at all stopping the bleeding. If the Turks had had the enterprise to come out of their trench and look for us they could have bagged the lot.[69]

65 A. Moorehead, *Gallipoli* (London: Hamish Hamilton, 1958), p. 146.
66 Farmar Papers: FAR/10/94, 'The Landing of the 86th Infantry Brigade', p. 2.
67 Aspinall-Oglander, *Military Operations Gallipoli*, Vol. I, p. 219.
68 H.M. Farmar, 'The Gallipoli Campaign 1915: From the point of view of a Regimental Officer', *Journal of the Royal United Service Institution*, Vol. LXVIII (February –November, 1923), p. 641.
69 IWM: Hare Papers, 18385: 09/86/1, Diary Entry post 25 April 1915. See also TNA WO 95/4310: War Diary, 29th Division, Vol. I, 86 Infantry Brigade HQ, 9 January-15 September 1915, digital p. ref. 17, time given as 6:45 a.m.

Frankland (Brigade Major) administered basic medical assistance to Hare. The latter "told Frankland and the Signallers to carry on what they were doing" and "started to get back to the beach."[70] Farmar discovered the injured Hare, "alone where he had been bound up by Frankland. I gave him brandy and got help to take him to the beach, then met Frankland. The situation where we were on the left appeared to be progressing favourably",[71] so he hurried to the right:

> We met Haworth with his Company of Lancashire Fusiliers and got them forward. The men were a little dazed but did all they were told. There were only about 50 of our men left and all this day they confronted Turks, reported later when retiring, as numbering over 1000; this party were separated from any support by over a mile. Haworth led his men forward to the very foot of a Turkish Redoubt where he was stopped by a mass of wire entanglement. He and his men lay in some dead ground but any effort to cut the wire meant immediate destruction. Frankland and I went to see if we could get touch with the troops landing on our right but were fired at from close range. Probably snipers as there were only a few shots at a time. We got cover in a depression of ground and discussed the situation. Frankland said he wanted to see the ground on the right of Haworth with a view to getting round the redoubt and asked me to wait.[72]

Frankland was killed shortly afterwards. This left Farmar in command of the brigade. The latter stated that "there is no doubt that the action of the brigadier in landing with the foremost in this unprecedented enterprise, together with Major Frankland's mastery of the situation, were together largely responsible for success."[73] Historians have taken a different view, regarding the loss of the brigade commander as "a serious setback to the effective command of the landing at Helles."[74] The Official History observed that the GOC 86th Brigade and "his brigade major, with a small party of signallers, pushed forward on towards X Beach, to establish touch with the Royal Fusiliers. But this was no task for the commander of the covering force … the covering force was thus deprived of its leader at the very outset of the battle."[75] It also queries why both Hare and Frankland felt it necessary to land "with the first trip of tows at W Beach", stating that "this point was over-looked by the officer (Farmar) who wrote up the brigade war diary several days later, and not mentioned in the official despatch."[76] Robert Rhodes James goes further calling Hare's actions "reckless gallantry."[77] His decision to land in this first trip was done with the "somewhat unwilling permission of the divisional commander."[78] *Field Service Regulations* (1909) stated: "With a small force it may be possible to exercise personal supervision, but with very large forces the commander-in-chief should usually be well in rear, beyond the reach of distraction by local events, and in signal communication with his chief subordinates."[79] Hare

70 IWM: Hare Papers, 18385: 09/86/1, Diary Entry for 25 April 1915.
71 Farmar Papers: FAR/LE/32, Letter from H.M. Farmar to V. Farmar, 30 April 1915.
72 Ibid.
73 Farmar Papers: FAR/10/94, 'The Landing of the 86th Infantry Brigade', p. 2.
74 N. Steel & P. Hart, *Defeat at Gallipoli* (London: Macmillan, 1994), p. 90.
75 Aspinall-Oglander, *Military Operations Gallipoli*, Vol. I, p. 228.
76 Ibid., p. 223, fn.2.
77 R. Rhodes James, *Gallipoli* (London: Pimlico [1965] 1999), p. 119.
78 Aspinall-Oglander, *Military Operations Gallipoli*, Vol. I, p. 223.
79 *Field Service Regulations, Part I, Operations, 1909* (London: HMSO, 1909), p. 134.

had identified that force cohesion had been compromised having witnessed the heavy casualties sustained at W Beach, his intention was to manoeuvre available forces as a means of continuing the offensive:

> A message came through from the Royal Fusiliers that they had landed north of Cape Helles without much opposition. The attention of the Turks had been arrested by the Lancashire Fusiliers. It was arranged for the two battalions to fight for a junction and to secure themselves pending a further advance.[80]

With no available contingencies, it was entirely appropriate for Hare to adjust the plan to reflect the reality of the situation.[81] The Lancashire Fusiliers were meant to take the "Trenches and Redoubt on Hill 138, one Co to assist 2 RF in taking Hill 141."[82] Thus Hare re-directed the second wave of tows to secure a foothold on the left where it was safe to land. Having assessed the situation, he determined that the Lancashire Fusiliers would require support to achieve the stated objective, that is, the Royal Fusiliers would support the Lancashire Fusiliers, not the other way around.[83] The objective was a hill due north of the lighthouse. Regrettably, British maps had not denoted "a second and somewhat higher crest 400 yards to the south-east of Hill 138" also containing a redoubt.[84] This misunderstanding would further divide the Lancashire Fusiliers as they made "independent attacks on the two redoubts" without "making any further headway."[85]

Hare's reserve force consisted of 2nd Hampshire Regiment, but the battalion remained trapped aboard *River Clyde* off V Beach. Having witnessed the of heavy losses of the Lancashire Fusiliers, he attempted to contact the Royal Fusiliers at X Beach who, it was assumed, had encountered less opposition, to concentrate his troops and wheel the flank to reinforce the depleted Lancashire Fusiliers. "Hare was anxious as to the success of the X Beach landing, and for the co-operation of this battalion."[86] Nothing could be achieved until Hill 138 was secure, therefore it was entirely logical that Hare wanted to concentrate his remaining force to seize the objective. In a 1916 letter to Farmar, Hare observed that he "was hit while we were trying to work round to meet the R.F. not 'on our return.' By the bye did Frankland have time to tell you all that before he was killed because I don't know who else could?"[87] This letter was subsequently annotated *Yes. M.F.* (Harold Mynors Farmar). Farmar stated that following this,

80 Farmar Papers: FAR/10/94, 'The Landing of the 86th Infantry Brigade', p. 2.
81 See Aspinall-Oglander, *Military Operations Gallipoli*, Vol. I, Appendices, Appendix 13, Suggested Action in the event of the 29th Division, or the Australians failing to establish themselves ashore, p. 34.
82 TNA WO 95/4310: War Diary, 29th Division, 86th Infantry Brigade, 1 Battalion Lancashire Fusiliers, Appendix IX, 'Operation Order No 1 for landing, by Major H.O. Bishop Commanding 1 Ln. Fus.', 24 April 1915.
83 Aspinall-Oglander, *Military Operations Gallipoli*, Vol. I, Appendices, Appendix 19, 86th Brigade Operation Order No. 1, 23 April 1915, p. 54.
84 Aspinall-Oglander, *Military Operations Gallipoli*, Vol. I, p. 229: See also P. Doyle & M. Bennett, 'Military Geography: The influence of Terrain in the Outcome of the Gallipoli Campaign, 1915', *The Geographical Journal*, 165:1 (March 1999), pp. 12-36.
85 Aspinall-Oglander, *Military Operations Gallipoli*, Vol. I, p. 230.
86 Farmar, 'The Gallipoli Campaign, 1915, p. 644.
87 Farmar Papers: FAR/10/111, Typescript of letter from General Sir Steuart Hare, HQ 54th Division, to H.M. Farmar, 2 August 1916, p. 17.

Frankland "after satisfying himself that the ground gained was being consolidated, gave certain instructions, and went himself across the beach, giving the situation to those he passed, with the determination to establish the right flank. Which was in a most dangerous state."[88] Hare had placed paramount importance on tactical cohesion to ensure that Hill 138 would be secured, and the link could be made with the forces from S and Y beaches.

The landing at both S and Y beaches "had been regarded by GHQ as part of the 29th Division's covering force" under the GOC 86th Brigade's command, but it was "realised that it would be impossible for General Hare, who was himself landing at W, to exercise any adequate control over distant detachments. Consequently, his responsibilities were limited to the landings at X, W and V beaches whilst the local commanders at S and Y were subordinated to divisional headquarters."[89] Crucially, the Official History states that "The action to be taken by Colonel Matthews in the event of this advance from the south not materializing was not mentioned, and does not appear to have been considered."[90] The situation faced by Matthews can only be viewed in the context of communications between shore and divisional headquarters:

> Throughout the 29 hours' tenure of his position no word of any kind had reached him from divisional headquarters. Though Y Beach was only twenty minutes' distance in a destroyer from divisional headquarters, no officer of the divisional staff had been sent to gain a personal knowledge of his position. Not even a situation report had been dispatched to tell him what was happening at the southern end of the peninsula. To all intents and purposes, he had been forgotten.[91]

The Lancashire Fusiliers war diary states that survivors of the W Beach landing "were in possession of 114 hill and adjacent redoubts" by 9:00 a.m., with "Essex Regt. reinforced on our right."[92] They had asked "for information re R. Munster Fus. Landing, C. Coy, 1LF in redoubt North of Hill 114. D. Coy 1 LF just South of Hill 114."[93] Still aboard the *River Clyde*, the Royal Munster Fusiliers were, therefore, unable to link up with the Lancashire Fusiliers to capture Hill 138. Their commanding officer, Lieutenant-Colonel H.E. Tizard, observed:

> The plan of attack which had been altered just before embarkation on the vessel was that the unit under my command should attack the Hill 141 and the redoubt on the hill to the left of the bay in order to join up with the troops attacking from W beach and then to combine with them if necessary in an attack on Hill 138.[94]

88 Farmar, The Gallipoli Campaign 1915, p. 646.
89 Aspinall-Oglander, *Military Operations Gallipoli*, Vol. I, p. 202.
90 Ibid., p. 203.
91 Ibid., p. 211.
92 TNA WO 95/4310: War Diary, 29th Division, Vol. III, 86th Infantry Brigade, 1st Battalion Lancashire Fusiliers, digital image, p. 93.
93 Ibid. Time noted as 10:00 a.m., digital image, p. 93.
94 TNA WO 95/4310: War Diary, 29th Division, Vol. III, 86th Infantry Brigade: Report on the Landing from the Collier River Clyde at V Beach on April 25 1915 by Lt. Col. H. E. Tizard, digital image, p. 108.

I have found no evidence as to why or who changed the orders, but Tizard's account suggests that a signal for assistance to the Lancashire Fusiliers was received, this message conforming with Hare's view that the battalion was in need of reinforcements. Frankland was killed shortly after Hare was wounded. Farmar stated that:

> I then got the signal section at work and assumed command of the Brigade. With luck I got into touch with the troops on my right (who failed to land on the first day) they were stuck in a transport on the beach and lost heavily trying to get out of it. Also, I got into communication with the Royal Fusiliers two miles away on the left.[95]

Tizard, having been notified that Hare was wounded and Lieutenant-Colonel Carrington Smith had assumed command of 88th Brigade following the death of General Napier,[96] observed men attempting to disembark from the beached *River Clyde*: "In most cases the men were killed only about half the 2 companies I had sent out were left fit for work. [A]t this time", he decided, "that it was impossible to carry out the original scheme as to move out in any formation for the attack on to the objective given only meant certain death."[97] Moreover:

> He [Carrington Smith] agreed with me that it would be better to wait till dark and with that I went down to stop the men going out. The reason was that we had already lost a considerable number of men and that if I continued to send men over our force would probably not be strong enough to drive the enemy back.[98]

Carrington Smith was killed later that day. Brigade command then fell to Tizard.[99] The latter's account contradicts the Official History. It states that Carrington Smith was killed at about 10:20 a.m. Tizard then took over "the command and informed Major Hutchinson my next senior major to take over the battalion."[100]

Frankland had, just prior to his death, issued orders for 86th Brigade headquarters to be established at the lighthouse and instructed surviving troops to "endeavour to take the Turkish redoubts between our beach and Sedd-el-Bahr and to assist the Munster and Dublin Fusiliers landing there."[101] As Farmar later observed:

95 Farmar Papers: FAR/LE/32, Letter from H.M. Farmar to Violet Farmar, 30 April 1915.
96 Lt. Col. H. Carrington Smith was in command of the 2nd Hampshire Regiment (brigade reserve) and was the senior officer on board the *River Clyde*.
97 TNA WO 95/ 4310: War Diary, 29th Division, Vol. III, 86th Infantry Brigade, 'Report on the Landing from the Collier River Clyde at V Beach on April 25 1915 by Lt. Col. H. E. Tizard', pp. 110-111.
98 Ibid., p. 112.
99 See IWM: Hare Papers, 18385: 09/86/1, Letter from Captain H.M. Farmar to Major-General Sir Steuart Hare, 22 May 1915. The day's events took a heavy toll on Tizard. In a letter to General Hare written by H.M. Farmar on the 22 May 1915, Farmar stated that Tizard had come "up to the old Castle Ridge on the 26 April, but he was not up to the situation. The work was done by Doughty Wyllie and Williams. I think he was quite buzzed: willing to go anywhere and to fight any body, but incapable of commanding; Hutchinson took over command and has done very well."
100 TNA WO 95/4310: War Diary, 29th Division, Vol. III, 86th Infantry Brigade, Report on the Landing from the Collier River Clyde at V Beach on April 25 1915 by Lt. Col. HE Tizard, digital image pp. 113-114.
101 Farmar Papers: FAR/11/03, Letters from H.M. Farmar to V. Farmar, 5 and 6 June 1915.

> He wanted to get going on the right and to establish ourselves on Hill 138. Some 40 to 50 men, Lancashire Fusiliers, under Haworth, were given the order – and came up the cliff; until 4 p.m. they were the only troops on our extreme right; the nearest being a party of little more strength under Shaw, about 500 yards distant, and then there on the beach and inland from it.[102]

Captain Haworth was amongst the first to land with approximately 50 men remaining from his double Company; Captain Shaw had 12 men under command of Lieutenant Beaumont.[103] The majority of troops remained where they fell. Eyewitnesses speak of a long line of "still forms of many score."[104] Meanwhile:

> Shaw had moved his men onto the high ground to the right of the beach, which helped us. Haworth extended his men below the crest of the cliff, along a ledge, and then moved them towards the redoubt which one could see close behind a thick entanglement of wire. They got as far as the wire and then could get no further, there was a fold of ground in which they could lie without much risk. The Turks could not fire straight into it from their parapet. But any effort to cut the wire meant instant death. Cunliffe came up with a small party and took up a position between Shaw and Haworth. The ground rose to a ridge, on our right, which was at right angles to our line facing the redoubt; the ridge commanded both the ground we were on, and also, on the far side, the ground over Sedd el-Bahr. Beaumont, with 12 men, was sent to protect his flank; his advance was checked also by wire but he was able to prevent any Turks coming down on us. It is a mystery why we were not counter attacked.[105]

Cunliffe was accompanied by surviving machine gunners sans machine guns damaged or lost during the landing. Farmar recalled:

> We reached the lighthouse and pushed on until we got hung up by a redoubt protected by a maze of barbed wire. Fortunately, there was almost dead ground against the wire for a strip and in this most of the party lay until 4 p.m. from early morning. Twelve men were moved on to a ridge facing Sedd-el-Bahr, detached about 50 yards. The signal section were established under cover of the lighthouse, and they got communication with the Royal Fusiliers, the Euryalus and the River Clyde.[106]

This is an interesting point. Farmar clearly states that they "got communication" not that they merely sent signals and received none. From his training he would have understood that it was "of the first importance that information should be communicated with the least possible delay

102 IWM: Hare Papers, 18385: 09/86/1, Letter from Captain H.M. Farmar to Major-General Sir Steuart Hare, 22 May 1915.
103 See Farmar, FAR/10/94, 'The Landing of the 86th Infantry Brigade', p. 3.
104 *Lancashire Fusilier Annual*, p. 149.
105 Farmar Papers: FAR/11/03, Letters from H.M. Farmar to V. Farmar, 5-6 June 1915.
106 IWM: Hare Papers, 18385: 09/86/1, Letter from Captain H.M. Farmar to Major-General Sir Steuart Hare, 22 May 1915.

to the commanders for whose benefit it is intended."[107] However, the 29th Division war diary clearly states that the division did not fully appreciate the situation. At 7:30 a.m. the war diary observed: "Troops from collier appeared to be getting ashore well. Some shrapnel fire."[108] This was far from reality. Farmar later described the situation on V Beach:

> By running and then slipping over the edge of the cliff, we could see the *River Clyde* and get signallers to talk to her. By making way gingerly we could talk to some men who had landed from her, who had come as far as they could on the sea level but had reached a spot where they could not get further and could not climb up. There were very few of them and some of them were wounded. I reported to the Division that the two companies had landed from the Collier and the rest still appeared to be on board. I did not know that all those who appeared to have landed were dead. That beach on the first day proved impossible to live on. Every boat which was filled with men for landing had every soul in her killed before one got to shore. And only some thirty men, I believe, were able to get on dry land from the beached collier.[109]

By 8:00 a.m., 29th Division headquarters finally grasped that the collier was unable to land the men:

> Wire entanglements being removed on V beach, the troops who had suffered heavily crossing the pier and between it and the shore were unable to advance beyond the shelter of the steep sandy band which edged the beach.
>
> 9:00 a.m. Position on W Beach very much the same. ½ Company Lancashire Fusiliers on the right for to wire entanglements on Hill 138 but were unable to advance further, owing to rifle fire from the redoubt on top of the hill.[110]

This again confirms Hare's opinion that the Lancashire Fusiliers required support from the Royal Fusiliers to achieve their objectives. Following Hare's wounding, Frankland "sent word to tell Lieut-Colonel Newenham that he had assumed brigade command. Then, having assured himself that all was well on the left, he returned to the beach about 7:30 a.m. to organize the attack on Hill 138 and establish headquarters at the lighthouse."[111] Before Hill 138 could be taken, it was necessary to secure Hill 141. Lieutenant-Colonel Newenham (CO Royal Fusiliers) "could do nothing till that hill was captured. Shortly afterwards he too was badly wounded, before he could assume command of the brigade."[112]

The question of command succession is key here. Consulted archives do not reveal any succession plan. Newenham understood the situation on W beach and "had learned by signal that the

107 War Office, *Field Service Regulations, Part 1, Operations*, p. 124.

108 British Library (BL): MS 48356: Hunter-Weston Papers, Official War Diaries of the 29th Division and the 8th Army Corps, Vol. II, 'Gallipoli. January–July 1915'.

109 Farmar Papers: FAR/11/03, Letters from H.M. Farmar to V. Farmar, 5-6 June 1915.

110 BL: Hunter-Weston Papers, MS 48356, Official War Diaries of the 29th Division and the 8th Army Corps, Vol. II. 'Gallipoli. January–July 1915'.

111 Aspinall-Oglander, *Military Operations Gallipoli*, Vol. I, pp. 228-229.

112 Ibid., p. 228, fn.3.

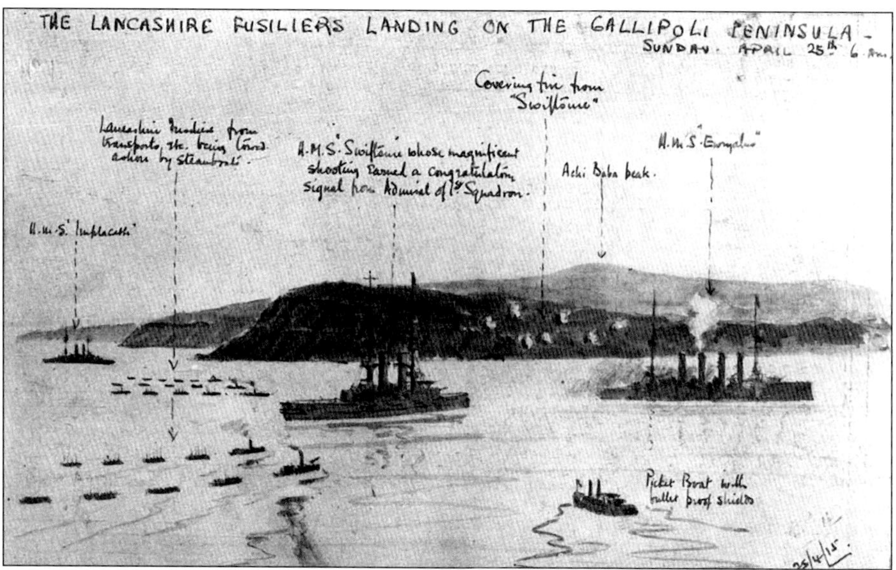

Eyewitness artist's rendering of the 1st Lancashire Fusiliers landing at W Beach. (*Illustrated London News*, 22 May 1915)

troops on Y Beach were hard beset, and could not join with his force on X, and that the landing on V was hung up. He had seen that the Lancashires were suffering terribly in even approaching their beach."[113] His orders were to join the Lancashire Fusiliers:

> I knew they had had a terrible time in the boats, as they were next to us going ashore. I collected all I could, after holding the left and front and leaving a reserve Company, to bring ammunition, water, etc., up the cliff, and moved to attack Tekke Hill; this we eventually captured on our side with the bayonet, losing heavily, at about noon. The *Implacable* was so close in that we heard her crew cheering us after the attack. I got signal communication with the brigade about 7:00 a.m; and with the K.O.S.B. at Y Beach later, to say they and the R.N.D. Battalion had landed but could not join up with us. I also learned that the landing on V Beach was rather hung up. It was therefore, most important to hang on to our bit.[114]

V Beach was indeed "rather hung up." Farmar, writing to Hare in May 1915, observed:

> We knew the Collier was in difficulties and Frankland left me in a fold of ground behind Haworth, asking me to wait there in case messages arrived, while he went to the ridge on our right to see if there was any way on there. Any attempt to cut the wire in front of us brought an impossible fire to live in. Some minutes elapsed before Kane came, asked where

113 H. C. O'Neill, *The Royal Fusiliers in The Great War* (London: Heinemann, 1922), p. 90.
114 Creighton, *With the Twenty-Ninth Division in Gallipoli*, pp. 56-57: Account related by Lieutenant-Colonel Newenham, CO 2nd Royal Fusiliers.

> Frankland was, and followed him; he came back and said he was killed. This about 8:45 a.m. He had stood up in order to see, and was shot through the heart, neck and head. We buried him two days afterwards.[115]

At this point Farmar assumed the role of brigade major: "[T]he ambition of being a Brigade Major to a regular brigade on active service had become a reality, but with great sadness. I had learnt to value Frankland."[116] Having landed at approximately 6:00 a.m., by 8:30 a.m. Hare had been seriously wounded and Frankland killed. This left the staff captain, Captain Farmar and Lieutenant Ronald Kane (Brigade Machine Gun Officer) from the headquarters staff to maintain order and instil confidence.[117] For his part, Farmar "withdrew under some shelter afforded by the walls, still standing, of the lighthouse and got our Brigade Signal Section at work. The Turks fired at us; I could not locate where from, but the signallers were excellent and established communication with our battalions on the left and with Division Headquarters; also, with the signallers on board the *River Clyde*, which had been beached below Sedd-el-Bahr."[118] At 9:00 a.m. Farmar dispatched a message to divisional headquarters:

> Redoubt East of Light House is holding up Lan Fus. We have half one company near this point. Two Companies in Collier of Mun Fus two ashore. One Co; Dublins ashore. Wire entanglements South of Forts, 1 & 2 stop us. Require machine guns.[119]

The Lancashire Fusiliers' situation was precarious. At 9:15 a.m. Captain Beaumont sent a handwritten note to the lighthouse where Farmar was ensconced: "Captain Haworth with 20 men still in front of barbed wire trying to land same time firing at rangers in front of from 168."[120] They had no hope of reinforcements from V Beach:

> A message received from Captain Farmar at the lighthouse at 9:30 spoke of troops at V being held up, but a study of existing records shows that for another hour and a half Divisional HQ did not realize that the hold-up was complete. During that time, they believed it was only our own shell-fire which was preventing the V Beach troops from moving left-handed to join up with the Lancashire Fusiliers.[121]

Brigadier-General H.E. Napier (GOC 88th Brigade) his brigade major, Captain Costeker, and "two platoons of the Worcestershire" and two companies of 2 Hampshire had attempted to

115 IWM: Hare Papers, 18385: 09/86/1, Letter from Captain H.M. Farmar to Major-General Sir Steuart Hare, 22 May 1915.
116 Farmar Papers: FAR/11/03, Letters from H.M. Farmar to V. Farmar, 5-6 June 1915.
117 TNA WO 95/4310, War Diary 29th Division, 86th Brigade, 7 February 1915.
118 Farmar Papers: FAR/11/03, Letters from H.M. Farmar to V. Farmar, 5-6 June 1915.
119 IWM: Hare Papers, 18385: 09/86/1, Brigade signal from Captain Farmar to Divisional Headquarters, 25 April 1915, 9:00 a.m.
120 IWM: Hare Papers, 18385: 09/86/1, Handwritten note from Captain Beaumont, Lancashire Fusiliers to Captain Farmar, Brigade Major 86th Brigade, 25 April 1915, 9:15 a.m.
121 Aspinall-Oglander, *Military Operations Gallipoli*, Vol. I, p. 239, fn.2.

land on V Beach between 9:30–10:00 a.m.[122] Napier, Costeker and many of their men were killed attempting to cross the hoppers to the shore. "Thus died the very man who by his rank, his nerve, and his knowledge, would have been of priceless value to the troops in the southern area during the rest of that vital day."[123] Tizard, on board the *River Clyde*, stated that Napier had come aboard with a staff officer after which he received "a message about this time from the 29th Division to say that the men must be pushed on … General Napier with his brigade major went down on to the lighter to try and get the men over not knowing what had happened."[124]

The landings on V, W and X beaches were "intended to be the main landings, those at S and Y merely intended 'to protect the flanks, to disseminate the forces of the enemy, and to interrupt the arrival of his reinforcements'."[125] Communication was therefore essential. The force (87th Brigade) landed at Y Beach – 1st King's Own Scottish Borderers (KOSB), one company of 2nd South Wales Borderers and the Plymouth Battalion (Royal Naval Division) had landed unopposed but were unaware of the difficulties encountered at other beaches. Their entire purpose "was to assist the main operations at Helles and Sedd-el-Bahr … to gain touch with the troops disembarking at X, and later in the day, when the main portion of the covering force drew level with this position, he was to join in the advance to the Achi Baba ridge."[126] Not only was there confusion between the Y Beach commanding officers as to who had overall command but Lieutenant-Colonel Matthews (CO Plymouth Battalion) was uncertain "whether actual contact was meant" or if only visual signalling communication was necessary with X Beach.[127] Neither was achieved, and at 11:45 a.m. he asked for guidance from divisional headquarters as to whether or not he should remain on the beach.[128] This signal remained answered and Farmar, as late as 2:30 p.m., signalled division headquarters that the KOSB was still awaiting orders.[129]

On W Beach the Lancashire Fusiliers held the pivotal brigade role. Hare's decision to deploy the Royal Fusiliers in support of the Lancashire Fusiliers meant that "the swift march upon and capture of Hill 114 turned the scale on W beach; and with the linking of the two beaches, a feasible, if precarious, foothold was established on the peninsula."[130] The Royal Fusiliers account states that "The first hours of the Lancashires' landing found them hardly able to do more than hang on."[131] The author, Herbert O'Neill, was palpably annoyed at the lack of attention his regiment received for their harrowing work, noting that Hamilton's despatch gave the "wrong

122 Aspinall-Oglander, *Military Operations Gallipoli*, Vol. I, pp. 239-240. See also TNA WO 95/4310: War Diary, 29th Division, Vol. III, 86th Infantry Brigade: 'Report on the Landing from the Collier River Clyde at V Beach on April 25 1915 by Lt. Col. H. E. Tizard,' digital image, p. 113.
123 Aspinall-Oglander, Vol. I, p. 240.
124 TNA WO 95/4310: War Diary, 29th Division, Vol. III, 86th Infantry Brigade, 'Report on the Landing from the Collier River Clyde at V Beach on April 25 1915 by Lt. Col. HE Tizard,' digital image, p. 113.
125 The Final Report of the Dardanelles Commission, P. 19.
126 Aspinall-Oglander, *Military Operations Gallipoli*, Vol. I, pp. 201-203.
127 Ibid., p. 203, fn. 3.
128 See IWM: Hare Papers, 18385: 09/86/1, Brigade Signal, to GOC 86th Brigade, from OC KOSB Blackwell, 25 April 1915, 11:45a.m., Marked received at 12:35 p.m.
129 See IWM: Hare Papers, 18385: 09/86/1, Brigade Signal, To GHQ from Captain Farmar, 25 April 1915, 2:30 p.m.
130 O'Neill, *The Royal Fusiliers in The Great War*, p. 93
131 Ibid., p. 93.

impression of the battalion's achievement",[132] thus it appeared that 87th Brigade had contributed to the success:

> The Royal Fusiliers not only carried the hill positions, but by 2 p.m. had also taken the entrenchments on the further side. Help from the 87th Brigade came at least two hours later, and to the weakened centre, not to the victorious right. The despatch, speaking of the Lancashires, also says that "a junction was effected on Hill 114 with the Royal Fusiliers," without any suggestion that, unless the 2nd Battalion had promptly marched upon and seized it, there would have been no possibility of effecting a junction.[133]

O'Neill further commented by quoting from H.W. Nevinson, *The Dardanelles Campaign* (1918): "No further advance could be made until 2 p.m., when, owing to the positions held by the two companies on the left, the landing had become fairly secure."[134]

The remaining units of 87th Brigade, commanded by Brigadier-General W.R. Marshall, landed on X Beach at approximately 9:00 a.m. with 1st Border Regiment and 1st Royal Inniskilling Fusiliers. Two additional battalions, previously under Marshall's command, had been split off to land was at Y and S beaches, so both units remained beyond his direct control. Moreover, Marshall was "hampered by lack of information" throughout the morning.[135] Wounded during mid-morning, he remained in command of the brigade:

> He [Marshall] knew, however, that the advance from W and V was held up, for from his position above X Beach he could see that Hill 141 and the two redoubts on Hill 138 were still in enemy occupation. But he had no knowledge of the strength of the enemy holding them. In these circumstances, remembering that his two battalions were the only divisional reserve, he decided that it would be wrong to commit them without orders.[136]

Aboard HMS *Euryalus,* Hunter-Weston and his staff were kept abreast of staff-level casualties with "depressing messages", but they failed to send replacements, respond to the KOSB signal, or keep Marshall or Matthews informed throughout the opening hours of the landing.[137] Farmar, from brigade headquarters at the lighthouse, attempted to coordinate the disorganised and depleted invasion force:

132 O'Neill, *The Royal Fusiliers in The Great War*, p. 93. See also 'Despatch from General Commanding the Mediterranean Expeditionary Force, Sir Ian Hamilton', General Headquarters, Mediterranean Expeditionary Force to The Secretary of State for War, War Office, London, 20 May 1915. See also Isle of Wight Records Office, (IOWRO) OG/AO/G/35, Letters and Notes commenting on Aspinall-Oglander's draft history of the Gallipoli Campaign, 1925-1928, marginal notes by Colonel C.A. Bolton on Gallipoli Chapters, p. 24 line 17: "Slowing advancing from X ... fighting their way. N.B. The R.F. are rather touchy about this phase. See their Reg. History. They think that despatches do not do them full credit." Subsequently annotated "Agree" by Bolton.
133 O'Neill, *The Royal Fusiliers in The Great War*, p. 93.
134 Ibid., p. 93.
135 Aspinall-Oglander, *Military Operations Gallipoli*, Vol. I, p. 245.
136 Ibid., p. 245. See also W. Marshall, *Memories of Four Fronts* (London: Hazel, Watson & Viney, 1929), pp. 58-59.
137 TNA CAB 45/259: Diary of Capt. C.A. Milward, Indian Army, Vol. II 1915, Dardanelles, p. 5.

> The Royal Fusiliers sent in precise and accurate reports, they got into communication with the 87th Brigade on their left, and I was able to get them to co-operate in the work of pushing back the enemy sufficiently far to give freedom in landing more troops.[138]

With no senior brigade staff available, Farmar was effectively in command of the 86th Brigade.[139] His task was to ensure that all component forces were not only in touch with brigade headquarters, but also understood the present situation.[140] The situation he faced was described as follows:

> I tried to find a senior officer to command the Brigade, but the Royal Fusiliers had lost all theirs. I could not get hold of Bishop or Pearson, [Lancashire Fusiliers] and the two battalions at Sedd-el-Bahr were cut off. So I had to control the situation to the best of my ability and continue to send messages and instructions as if the General were still on the spot.[141]

Hunter-Weston, still aboard HMS *Euryalus* "lying some 1,000 yards off W Beach" was an eyewitness to the Lancashire Fusilier landing.[142] The Official History states that encouraging news had reached him of the successes at Y, X and S.[143] Travers notes that "Hamilton was in better touch with the beaches than Hunter-Weston, who was actually in charge of the landings". Thus at 29th Division HQ, Hunter-Weston did not know what was happening to his own troops for some six hours."[144] Farmar's recollection contradicts this view, remarking in a post-war article that appeared in the *Lancashire Fusiliers Annual* that having assumed the role of brigade major following the death of Frankland at 8:30 a.m., he communicated directly with the division: "Divisional Headquarters remained on board HMS *Euryalus* where touch with all landings was obtained by wireless."[145] Farmar initially signalled to 29th Division HQ aboard *Euryalus* directly and, once the signal section at "GHQ W Beach" – not MEF GHQ – had been established, through that and on to divisional HQ.[146] This misunderstanding may explain Travers' assertion. Hunter-Weston's staff no doubt observed what was happening, Captain Milward 29th Division GSO3 confirming knowledge of the situation:

> And then we looked and all along the water's edge, below the wire entanglement, there was a row of dead men. We could see the splash of the bullets as the Turks fired at them. Presently out of this row of dead, some ten men sprang up and slowly and calmly proceeded to climb over the barbed wire. Two actually got across and lay down in the sand-hills beyond. The rest fell on the top of the barbed wire and lay there.[147]

138 Farmar Papers: FAR/11/03, Letter from H.M. Farmar to V. Farmar, 5 June 1915.
139 TNA WO 95/4310: War Diary, 29th Division, 86th Infantry Brigade, 1st Battalion Lancashire Fusiliers.
140 See IWM: Hare Papers, 18385: 09/86/1, 86th Brigade Signals, 25 April 1915.
141 Farmar Papers: FAR/11/03, Letter from H.M. Farmar to V. Farmar, 5 June 1915.
142 Aspinall-Oglander, *Military Operations Gallipoli*, Vol. I, p. 238.
143 Ibid., p. 238.
144 Travers, 'Command and Leadership Styles in the British Army: The Gallipoli Model', pp. 403-442, pp. 412-413.
145 Farmar, FAR/10/94, 'The Landing of the 86th Infantry Brigade', p. 5.
146 Aspinall-Oglander, *Military Operations Gallipoli*, Vol.1, Appendices, p. 55.
147 TNA CAB 45/259: Diary of Capt. C.A. Milward, Indian Army, Vol. II 1915, Dardanelles, p. 4.

According to General Staff documents, Hunter-Weston requested the dispatch of a hospital ship at 8:45 a.m., an action that implies he understood that losses were high.[148] In his signals, Farmar repeatedly suggested that the landing would meet less resistance at the lighthouse. Thus his attempts to have HQ redirect troops away from Turkish enfilade fire whilst simultaneously hoping to increase the attack force ratio. At 9:20 a.m. he sent a signal stating: "General Hare wounded Frankland killed. I am at Light House [sic]. Reinforcements can land safely under cliff North of W Beach. Munsters appear held up. Some still on-board collier. Others appear to [have] moved towards beach V."[149] Hunter-Weston "realizing that more infantry were required at W to confirm the success of the Lancashire Fusiliers" dispatched 1st Essex Regiment.[150] The battalion, having been diverted from V Beach, landed at 9:00 a.m. but it took a full hour to disembark:

> These suffered a good many casualties in their boats from long-range rifle fire; but once under cover of the cliffs they were able to wade ashore in safety, and a few minutes later were rushing up the W Beach gully to fill a gap between the right and left flanks of the Lancashire Fusiliers. Helped by this reinforcement the troops on the left were able to make better progress; by half-past eleven they had joined up with the Royal Fusiliers from X, and the whole of Hill 114 was at last in British hands. The remaining two companies of the Essex arrived about 10 a.m., and after some delay, due to no senior officer being left alive on shore to issue orders, tasks were eventually allotted to them by their own battalion commander, Lieut. Colonel O.G. Godfrey Faussett. One company was directed to the high ground south of the gully. The fourth company was sent right-handed towards Hill 138, and almost at once came under fire from the small redoubt which had brought the advance of Captain Shaw's party to a standstill earlier in the day.[151]

At 10:15 a.m. Farmar sent another signal requesting support for the Royal Fusiliers and Lancashire Fusiliers: "Hill 114. Our troops from Beach W are now engaged on this summit. Can you send support."[152] By 10:55 a.m., a staff officer on W Beach, Captain C.A. Bolton, signalled to the 86th Brigade: "Cannot Essex Regiment push forward. Advance should be pushed to Northern edge of ridge 138 to allow work of landing guns to progress on W Beach. Report situation."[153] Bolton, however, had not fully appreciated the situation. It was proving difficult to push forward. The 2nd Royal Fusiliers had suffered heavily in the intense fighting beyond X Beach. Lieutenant-Colonel Newenham and his second in command, Major Brandreth, were both wounded. "No company commander escaped, and the battalion was reduced to about half strength."[154] Bolton had landed in the second wave of W Beach tows. At 11:20 a.m. he signalled

148 TNA WO 106/704: Mediterranean Expeditionary Force, Dardanelles, General Staff (GHQ), Feb.-April 1915, HMS *Queen Elizabeth*, p. 86.
149 IWM: Hare Papers, 18385: 09/86/1, Brigade signal from Captain Farmar to GHQ, 25 April 1915, 9:20 a.m.
150 Aspinall-Oglander, *Military Operations Gallipoli*, Vol. I, p. 238.
151 Ibid., pp. 240-241.
152 IWM: Hare Papers, 18385: 09/86/1, Brigade Signal from Captain Farmar to GHQ, 25 April 1915, 10:15 a.m.
153 IWM: Hare Papers, 18385: 09/86/1, Signal to 86th Brigade from GSO GHQ W Beach, 25 April 1915, 10:55 a.m.
154 O'Neill, *The Royal Fusiliers in The Great War*, p. 92

to divisional HQ: "Send someone ashore to order advance. Essex Regiment hung up on a ridge North-East of W Beach. No brigade HQ here and no divisional staff."[155] In 1927, Bolton still maintained the view that Farmar had not established a brigade HQ, although it had been in the designated site since 9 a.m.[156]

> Frankly I must say that I have always criticised Farmar's actions on the 25th April. Undoubtedly, he behaved bravely in the firing line but he knew the Brigadier was wounded and the brigade major killed, and it was up to him in my opinion to form a brigade headquarter and get someone to function in Hare's place. I had not seen divisional orders so was not sufficiently au-fait with the divisional plan to take the place of the brigade staff and incidentally my instructions from C.G.S. were definitely against interfering.[157]

Lieutenant-Colonel L.R. Beadon, AQMG GHQ, disembarked at the same time as Bolton. In his capacity as a senior Army Service Corps officer, he did not assume command thus providing historians with a perceived lost opportunity. This may have been due to an assumption that another officer had already taken charge. Moreover, he may not have felt empowered within the prevailing military/cultural constraints to assume responsibility beyond sanctioned "Q" matters.[158] Beadon is not mentioned again in the Official History, so it must be assumed that 29th Division, still uncertain of the situation, preferred to land another staff officer. To this end, Colonel O.C. Wolley Dod (GSO1) was dispatched at 12:30 p.m. or thereabouts. Although there is a time discrepancy in Milward's account, he confirms the extraordinary fact that given the seriousness of the situation, Wolley Dod arrived with minimal staff support:

> With all our Brigadiers and two of the three brigade majors hit, someone was badly required ashore to run the show in this corner. About 11 o'clock, therefore, Colonel Wolley Dod, the GSO1, went ashore, but unfortunately for me, he decided to take one of the Administrative Staff with him, to look after water supplies and ammunition arrangements. A lull now ensued, and the General insisted on our going to lie down for an hour at a time.[159]

The administrative staff officer may have been Major Oscar Striedinger, Assistant DST (Director of Supplies and Transport), who landed at 12:45 p.m. Milward noted that "there were 83 corpses laid out on the beach when I got there."[160] Farmar sent a signal to GHQ W Beach at approximately

155 Aspinall-Oglander, *Military Operations Gallipoli*, Vol. I, p. 240, fn. 2.
156 See IWM: Hare Papers, 18385: 09/86/1, Brigade signal from Captain Farmar to Divisional Headquarters, 25 April 1915, 9:00 a.m.
157 See IOWRO, OG/AO/G/35, Letters and Notes commenting on Aspinall-Oglander's draft history of the Gallipoli Campaign, 1925-28; transcript of correspondence from Colonel C.A. Bolton C.B.E. to Aspinall, 15 August 1927.
158 See Nicholson, *Behind the Lines*, pp. ix-x, for a comprehensive explanation of staff functions; Q Branch "was responsible for all matters of supply, ordnance, transportation, permanent works, provision of material requirements."
159 TNA CAB 45/259: Diary of Capt. C.A. Milward, Indian Army, Vol. II 1915, Dardanelles, p. 6.
160 TNA WO 95/4304: War Diary of General staff, 29th Division, January–March 1915, 'Notes on Landing "W" Beach' by Major Striedinger, p. 5.

12:30 p.m. In it he reiterated that the most secure landing place was beneath lighthouse cliffs. He also requested naval fire support to engage the enemy's barbed wire obstacles:

> 200 have landed on V Beach. These cannot get forward. Connection between River Clyde and shore is very bad, and casualties occur as soon as men move from ship. Landing is possible near Light House. If company Lan. Fus. is withdrawn to edge of cliff our guns could break entanglements in square 162B and C. Landing is easy near Lighthouse and cliff accessible. If Redoubts 1 & 2 are taken it would facilitate capture of village.[161]

Success may have been achieved at this early stage, if Farmar's attempts to direct the battle at this time had been supported, which may have facilitated the early capture of the tactically vital Achi Baba eminence. The official historian (Aspinall) noted that Farmar had "sent by runner to W Beach a valuable message (see above) which he had already signalled to divisional headquarters on board the *Euryalus*."[162] Unfortunately, Wolley Dod did not receive the message untill 1:10 p.m., too late to direct the Worcestershire Regiment to disembark near the lighthouse instead of W Beach.[163] Aspinall also observed that Wolley Dod failed to grasp the situation on V Beach.[164] Aspinall clearly recognised the importance of Farmar's signal. The date is unclear, but sometime during the period 1924-26, Aspinall wrote to Farmar who was then serving in India as AQMG Southern Command:

> Herewith I am sending you my chapter on the events at Helles on 25th April and shall be very grateful to have your remarks on it. Since we met at the Club before you left for India I have found the original of your message to W Beach and am enclosing you a photograph of it for your information.[165]

The 29th Division war diary reveals that the division had been in possession of the correct information on V Beach for some time. Thus Wolley Dod should have been aware of the general situation:

> 11:30 a.m.: Troops W Beach gained ridge Hill 114. Troops on V beach still held up near beach. Queen Elizabeth shelling Sedd-el-Bahr and Hill 141. Troops on W beach held up by fire from Hill 138.
>
> S.O. GHQ asks for someone to take command on W beach and order advance Essex as nothing has arrived for 1 1/2 hours.
>
> 11:38 a.m.: 1 Coy Dublin Fusiliers as well as wounded at Camber unable to get on.[166]

161 IWM: Hare Papers, 18385: 09/86/1, Brigade Signal from Captain Farmar, Lighthouse to GHQ 'W' Beach, 25 April 1915, 12:25 p.m.
162 Aspinall-Oglander, *Military Operations Gallipoli*, Vol. I, p. 241.
163 Ibid., p. 241.
164 Ibid., p. 241.
165 Farmar Papers: FAR/10/112, Typescript of letter to Colonel H.M. Farmar, A&QMG Southern Command, Poona, India, from Brigadier-General C.F. Aspinall-Oglander, Historical Section (Military Branch) (n.d.).
166 BL: Hunter-Weston Papers, MS 48356, Official War Diaries of the 29th Division and the VIII Army Corps, Vol. II. 'Gallipoli, January-July 1915', 25 April 1915.

The divisional staff's lack of situational awareness was undoubtedly compounded by inadequate communications. The 29th Division artillery observation table, "Method of Signalling", stated that the signals would be "Visual at first, then Wireless."[167] In reality "Shore signalling stations were opened punctually, but too often they were unable to get into touch with anyone in authority on land who could give the fleet the information that it most required."[168] Signallers had access to signal lamps, heliographs and semaphore flags as well as wireless sets, all of which were subject to potential damage by sea water or loss. From his position at the lighthouse, Farmar observed that by "slipping over the edge of the cliff, a position could be reached from which the River Clyde could be seen, and visual communication was established."[169] This was done by heliograph and "shouting".[170] The battalions ashore had great difficulty contacting each other. Milward subsequently observed: "We could far better control the landings at the five different Beaches by signal from the ship … We could only signal to W and V Beaches directly", therefore how the division expected to establish centralised command and control is bewildering.[171] Hunter-Weston had no "anxiety about the Y Beach force," having had confirmation of a successful landing and in the afternoon of the 25 April, division headquarters received an "erroneous report that the troops at X and Y had joined hands."[172]

> 27 Turkish prisoners now on W Beach. KOS Borderers are established at Y and have stored SAA on top of cliff. They await orders at 11.45 a.m. RF hold position north east slopes of hill 114. They have joined up with LF on their right and one Co; Borderers on left 2 p.m. East attack on Hill 138 progressing rapidly.[173]

The Official History remarked as follows:

> [T]he word "Borderers" was a mistake. What the author of the message evidently meant was that the Royal Fusiliers on Hill 114 were in touch with the Border Regiment at X Beach. Unfortunately, the error was not discovered in time and for some hours it was believed that they were in touch with the KOSB and South Wales Borderers at Y.[174]

The author in question was Captain Farmar. The belief that he had composed an erroneous message is recounted in Hart and Steel's *Defeat at Gallipoli*: "[I]n writing out the signal, Farmar apparently made an easy mistake."[175] However, Farmar's signal message can be found in Hare's papers at the Imperial War Museum. Perusal thereof leads to the irrefutable determination that

167 Ibid., Table of Artillery Observation 'Method of Signalling', p. 68. See also IWM: 10048, Lieutenant-Colonel H.V. Gell, 'Signal Organization for Combined operations'; TNA WO 106/704, Signals Gallipoli, Account Furnished by Major H.C.B. Wemyss, Royal Signals.
168 Aspinall-Oglander, *Military Operations Gallipoli*, Vol. I, p. 206, fn. 2.
169 Farmar, FAR/10/94, 'The Landing of the 86th Infantry Brigade', p. 5.
170 Farmar Papers: FAR/10/103, Typescript of notes made by Margaret Paton of *The Times*, (n.d.).
171 TNA CAB 45/259: Diary of Capt. C.A. Milward, Indian Army, Vol. II 1915, Dardanelles, p. 2.
172 Aspinall-Oglander, *Military Operations Gallipoli*, Vol. I, p. 211.
173 IWM: Hare Papers, 18385: 09/86/1, Brigade Signal from Captain Farmar, Lighthouse, to GHQ, 25 April, 2:30 p.m.
174 Aspinall-Oglander, *Military Operations Gallipoli*, Vol. I, pp. 211-212, fn. 2.
175 Steel & Hart, *Defeat at Gallipoli*, p. 104.

he had indeed written "Borderers" in blue pencil prior to re-reading it and deliberately scoring "ers" out twice after which "'S' was added. Thus the word reads 'BorderS'."[176] Moreover, it is remiss of Hart and Steel not to state that Farmar had adjusted the error. In addition, it appears he fully understood the situation, had reminded his superiors that the KOSB awaited orders (and therefore had not moved), re-read the signal and corrected it prior to dispatch. Furthermore, the 29th Division war diary also notes that Captain Bolton forwarded a message at 3:10 p.m.:

> Situation as follows. KOSB established beach Y joined hands with Royal Fusiliers on Beach X who hold NE slopes of hill 114. They are in touch on right with Lancashire Fusiliers on Beach W.[177]

The same war diary also states in brackets that this report was subsequently found to be incorrect. Farmar signalled to Royal Fusiliers to "keep connection with force attacking 138."[178] He then signalled GHQ (W Beach):

> Have instructed RF intention to make good spur 200 square 168 to move with this object in view and to keep connection with force attacking 138. General and Brigade Major 88th Brigade Killed. Landing not yet effected from River Clyde. Attack on 138 progresses wire now being cut.[179]

At 4:35 p.m. he signalled that he had only two signallers with him and he could not reach the wounded or two maxim guns on the "shore just west of River Clyde."[180] Simultaneously, he signalled to Royal Fusiliers CO asking him to assume brigade command.[181] At some point during his time, Farmar visited the units seeking cover in a redoubt due east of the lighthouse to "get them on."[182] At 5:20 p.m. a signal was received from Captain Moore, stating he was Royal Fusiliers CO as "Col. Newenham, Major Guyon and Maj Brandreth wounded."[183] Ten minutes later, Farmar interviewed the Worcester and Essex colonels in order to explain "the situation and kept Headquarters of the Division informed throughout."[184] By this time, having established a telephone link with Wolley Dod at W Beach, he repeated the request for artillery support:

176 IWM: Hare Papers, 18385: 09/86/1, Brigade Signal, From Captain Farmar to GHQ, 25 April 1915, 2:30 p.m.
177 TNA WO 106/704: MEF, Dardanelles, General Staff (GHQ), Feb.-April 1915 – HMS Queen Elizabeth, p. 91.
178 IWM: Hare Papers, 18385: 09/86/1, Brigade Signal, From Captain Farmar to Royal Fusiliers, 25 April 1915, 2:45 p.m.
179 Ibid., Brigade Signal from Captain Farmar, Lighthouse 25 April 1915, 2:55 p.m.
180 Ibid., 4:35 p.m.
181 Ibid., Brigade Signal from Captain Farmar, Lighthouse to OC Royal Fusiliers, 25 April 1915, 4:35 p.m.
182 Ibid., Brigade Signal from Captain Farmar to GSO W Beach regarding hand-written Note from Major E. Leigh, Worcestershire Regiment, 25 April 1915, 4:30 p.m.
183 Ibid., Brigade Signal from Captain Moore CO RF to CMDG 86th Brigade, 25 April 1915, 5:20 p.m.
184 Farmar Papers: Letter from H.M. Farmar to V. Farmar, 5 June 1915.

Ruins of Cape Helles lighthouse.

> Hill 138 is in hands of Worcesters and I Co. Essex. I have seen Colonels Cayley and Godfrey Faussett. The latter is now about to push forward toward Hill 141.
> Artillery support on Hill 141 would be useful.[185]

At 6:00 p.m. Farmar sent a signal to the W Beach staff officer: "My only means of communication now is by cable to you. Lamps not yet on shore."[186]

The Lancashire Fusiliers war diary observes that it was not until 7:00 p.m. that "Wolley Dod, at Beach W assumed control, and called in Staff Captain, [Kane] 86th Brigade, to act as his Staff Officer."[187] This is confirmed by Farmar's earliest correspondence following the landing: "[F]or all yesterday, 8 a.m. to 7 p.m. I was alone commanding the brigade. At this hour I was sent for to assist Colonel Wolley-Dod, who was representing the Divisional General on shore."[188] Thus during the critical early hours of the offensive, Farmar became responsible for brigade cohesion and effectiveness. Together with Kane, he worked under intense strain with no senior staff support from 8:30 a.m. to 12:30 p.m., when Wolley Dod disembarked at W Beach.

185 IWM: Hare Papers, 18385: 09/86/1, Signal to GSO 'W' Beach from Captain Farmar, 'By Telephone' written in Pencil, 25 April 1915, 5:30 p.m.
186 IWM: Hare Papers, 18385: 09/86/1, Brigade Signal to GSO W Beach from Captain Farmar, Light House 25 April 1915, 6:00 p.m.
187 TNA WO 95/4310: War Diary, 29th Division, 86th Infantry Brigade, 1st Battalion Lancashire Fusiliers; Lieutenant Robert Kane took over the role of Staff Captain, previously Brigade Machine Gun Officer of 86th Brigade.
188 Farmar Papers: FAR/LE/30, Letter from H.M. Farmar to V. Farmar, 26 April 1915.

Farmar, relying on Kane to act in a liaison capacity from the morning of the 25 April, clearly thought very highly of the latter's capabilities.[189]

The high officer casualty rates sustained during the Cape Helles landings necessitated a devolved form of command capable of recognising and reacting to a chaotic and desperate situation. It is clear from this research that Brigadier-General Hare attempted to re-organise and adjust operations within the limited parameters available prior to his wounding. Brigadier-General Marshall received no messages from Division HQ that could have alerted him to the situation on W Beach. Therefore, he was unaware of the situation and offered no help. Brigadier-General Napier was dead.[190] Unable to pass on responsibility, Farmar assumed brigade command authority throughout the 25 April. All reports passed through his hand, after which he assessed the situation, kept division informed, issuing tactical orders while recommending revised assault plans to the division.[191] For their part, the 29th Division staff, although hampered by inadequate communications, failed to provide the necessary command and control oversight. Indeed, there appears to have been an inability to recognise prevailing operational circumstances and react accordingly. With no substantial command succession plan and a lack of suitable officers ashore, tactical decision-making devolved on surviving junior officers who relied on personal initiative. These serious command oversights are rather extraordinary given Major-General Hunter-Weston's oft-quoted belief that the amphibious landings were flawed and unworkable: "It may truly be called the achievement of the impossible," he nonetheless pressed ahead with the offensive, but without ensuring adequate staff cover.[192] Milward subsequently described the GOC 29th Division's four-phased scheme to seize Achi Baba as "over-sanguine."[193] This opinion was shared by Captain Harold Cawley, ADC to Major-General William Douglas (GOC 42nd (East Lancashire) Division):

> The first force that came here was ludicrously inadequate. The 29th division which affected the landing here was probably the finest force of its size that ever left England. The landing was a magnificent gain on the part of the officers and men though the planning of it and the naval cooperation was not anything to boast about.[194]

189 Ibid., letter from H. M. Farmar to V. Farmar, 10 October 1918: "I am so grieved that Kane is killed. He was a good soldier and a very brave man. He was commanding the only Battalion of the Munster Fusiliers left in the Field. I was very fond of him, and he is a great loss to his regiment as he understood and managed the men so well." Lieutenant-Colonel Robert Romney Godred Kane, DSO, Chevalier of the Legion of Honour, 1st Royal Munster Fusiliers (1888-1918).

190 Aspinall-Oglander, *Military Operations Gallipoli*, Vol. I, p. 245.

191 See IWM: Hare Papers, 18385: 09/86/1, Brigade Signal from Captain Farmar to GHQ W Beach, 25 April 1915, 12.25 p.m.: "If company Lan. Fus. is withdrawn to edge of cliff our guns could break entanglements in square 162B and C. Landing is easy near Lighthouse and cliff accessible. If Redoubts 1&2 are taken it would facilitate capture of village."

192 O'Neill, *The Royal Fusiliers in The Great War*, p. 86, citing Major-General Hunter-Weston, MP, *The Times*, 6 June 1921. See also BL: Hunter-Weston Papers, MS 48356, Official War Diaries of the 29th Division and the 8th Army Corps, Vol. II. 'Gallipoli, January July 1915', 'Copy of Appreciation of Situation at the Dardanelles, on 25 March 1915' by Major-General Aylmer Hunter-Weston, p. 358.

193 TNA CAB 45/259: Diary of Capt. C.A. Milward, Indian Army, Vol. II 1915, Dardanelles, p. 1.

194 LHMCA: GB0099: Letter from Captain HT Cawley to Frederick Cawley MP, August or September 1915.

Farmar was even more scathing: He "felt strongly that if the first Duke of Wellington had had to deal with such situations as happened in Gallipoli, he would have sensed the most crucial occasions and would have been on the spot with his staff. The fleeting opportunities would have been seized."[195]

Elaine McFarland's recent biography of Hunter-Weston contains remarkably little on the pivotal W Beach landing; Lancashire landing is described thus:

> There already appeared to be a row of dead men along the beach, but soon ten soldiers stood up and calmly climbed over the barbed wire; two got across and lay in the sand hills beyond, but the rest fell on top of the wire and remained there. Elsewhere, the "corpses" were only men's packs, and as the mist began to lift, Wemyss and Hunter-Weston could see that half of the force had in fact reached the base of the sandy cliffs at the back of the beach. By 7.30 a.m., the Lancashires had managed to establish a thin perimeter line and were moving northwards to link up with X beach, although their casualties were too severe to allow them to stretch out to V beach on the right.[196]

McFarland's view of Hunter-Weston as "a confused spectator at W Beach ... The two-way flow of information that he knew would be required in directing amphibious operations failed almost immediately, largely due to the high number of officer casualties ashore" is incorrect despite overwhelming losses.[197] Indeed, it can be determined from Captain Milward's diary that the divisional staff were kept abreast of casualties by the aformentioned "depressing messages."[198] Farmar's signals prove that he alerted the division to the situation, but that they failed to respond in a timely fashion. Moreover, within the Farmar papers is a letter from Commander J. Meriot, HMS *Euryalus* executive officer: "We feel for you all so in your grave losses as if you were of our own ship's company."[199] Given the armoured cruiser's crew appear to have collectively grasped the Lancashire Fusiliers' travails, how was it that, aboard the same vessel, the 29th Division staff did not? McFarland's somewhat sympathetic portrayal of Hunter-Weston is of a man confused by a dearth of adequate communications with the fighting troops:

> In response to a request to fill the command vacuum ashore, Hunter-Weston was forced to despatch Wolley Dod around noon, giving him authority to issue orders in his name. Shortly afterwards, the full extent of the crisis at V Beach became clear. A delayed signal from 86th Brigade arrived around 1 p.m., noting the plight of the pinned-down survivors and suggesting an alternative landing site, but it came too late to divert the reinforcements which had already been sent to W Beach.[200]

195 Farmar Papers: FAR/10/103, Margaret Paton typescript notes.
196 Elaine McFarland, *A Slashing Man of Action: The life of Lieutenant-General Sir Alymer Hunter-Weston MP* (Oxford: Peter Lang, 2014), pp. 147-148.
197 McFarland, *A Slashing Man of Action,* p. 148.
198 TNA CAB 45/259: Diary of Capt. C.A. Milward, Indian Army, Vol. II. 1915, Dardanelles, p. 5.
199 Farmar Papers: FAR/VIO/1-96, Letter from Commander J. Mariot, Executive Officer for HMS *Euryalus*, to Captain Bromley, Adjutant Lancashire Fusiliers, 3 May 1915; annotated thus: "Replied to by Captain Farmar", 3 May 1915.
200 McFarland, *A Slashing Man of Action*, p. 150.

This statement is very odd and confusing. The 29th Division's war diary states quite clearly that by 8 a.m. HQ was clear that the collier was unable to disembark its battalions:

> 8a.m. Position on West Beach much the same. No further advance. Wire entanglements being removed on V beach, the troops who had suffered heavily crossing the pier and between it and the shore were unable to advance beyond the shelter of the steep sandy band which edged the beach.
>
> 9:00 a.m. Position on W Beach very much the same. 1/2 Company Lancashire Fusiliers on the right for to wire entanglements on Hill 138 but were unable to advance further, owing to rifle fire from the redoubt on top of the hill.[201]

Farmar's message was received at Divisional HQ at 9:20 a.m.:

> Reinforcements can land safely under cliff N of W Beach where the larger portion of Lanc. Fusiliers made their way up the cliff. Also, that the Munster Fusiliers appeared to be held up and that some were still on board the collier while others appeared to have moved towards V beach. Major Frankland (Bde. Major) killed by the wire entanglement trying to get the men there to push on.[202]

This proves that divisional headquarters were aware that the safest place to land was beneath the W Beach north cliff, and that the Munster Fusiliers had not yet entered the fray. It is also clear from Milward's recollections that the divisional staff were well aware of the seriousness of the situation and recognised that there was a serious lack staff leadership on the peninsula.[203] To be fair, Hunter-Weston clearly expressed the desire to "lead the men to the attack" before being dissuaded by his staff.[204] Hunter-Weston, according to McFarland, had developed by 1914:

> An emotional commitment to offensive tactics, coupled with an unshakable faith in the role of personal leadership and individual morale. In other words, he fitted the template for the ideal officer in his own training manual – a modern professional who led from the front.[205]

Thus the GOC 29th Division, unable to lead from the front, failed to acknowledge the true situation. Could this have been the primary issue? Hunter-Weston certainly had no illusions about what had been achieved:

201 BL: Hunter-Weston Papers, MS 48356, Official War Diaries of the 29th Division and the VIII Army Corps, Vol. II. "Gallipoli. January – July 1915."
202 Ibid., 25 April 1915.
203 TNA CAB 45/259: Diary of Capt. C.A. Milward, Indian Army, Vol. II 1915, Dardanelles
204 Ibid., p. 7.
205 McFarland, *A Slashing Man of Action*, p. 78.

> We have managed it, we have achieved the impossible! We are established at the South End of the Gallipoli Peninsula. Wonderful gallantry on the part of regimental officers and men has done it.[206]

Post-Gallipoli Assessment

In October 1923 Farmar was asked to deliver a lecture on the Gallipoli campaign to the Royal United Services Institute (RUSI). In his opening remarks, he observed: "I believe the story of certain happenings may serve to accentuate the value of various principles laid down in our Training Manuals."[207] The nature of the Gallipoli landings relied on decentralised command, a structure that had been laid down in new doctrine taught primarily at divisional level.[208] Nevertheless, this also appears to have been understood at brigade level by both Hare and Farmar, but not supported at divisional level. Gallipoli was considered such a disaster that it was one of only two military campaigns, the other being Mesopotamia, that underwent official government assessment while the war was still in progress. Farmar was not called upon to testify to the Dardanelles Commission which understandably focused on political strategy and the inadequate naval/military response.[209] The opportunity was therefore lost for a systematic scrutiny of the campaign from the mid-level staff perspective, but then it was not in its remit to do so. Nevertheless, related command and control failures were of particular interest to General Sir Charles Harington who had served throughout the war in senior staff roles and was regarded by many as the "outstanding senior staff officer of his generation."[210] In his view, staff officers at division level and above "could have a critical influence upon lower formations and the troops themselves."[211] In 1920 Harington was fortuitously appointed Inter-Allied Commander-in-Chief Turkey. In need of a staff, he requested Farmar who accompanied his new chief on a Gallipoli veteran staff tour:

> Thirty-Nine Officers, Naval and Military, took part, working in syndicates of three each. All the information available from Turkish and German sources was at our disposal. The Collated results of the Tour were placed at the disposal of the Historical Section of the Cabinet.[212]

206 BL: Hunter-Weston Papers, Add MS 48364, Private War Diary, 29th Division and VIII Army Corps, Vol. X. "Dardanelles and Gallipoli, 13 March – 31 December", Letter of 27 April 1915.

207 Farmar, "The Gallipoli Campaign, 1915, From the point of view of a Regimental Officer", p. 641.

208 See Pugsley, *"We Have Been Here Before"*.

209 The Final Report of the Dardanelles Commission, Part II – Conduct of Operations, p. 20. For contemporary concerns See TNA CAB/24/1: Committee of Imperial Defence, 'Memorandum by General Sir Ian Hamilton on a Letter from Mr. K. A. Murdoch to the Prime Minister of Australia Commonwealth', November 25, 1915; E. Ashmead-Bartlett, *The Uncensored Dardanelles*, (London: Hutchinson, 1928).

210 P. M. Harris, 'The Men Who Planned the War: A Study of the Staff of the British Army on the Western Front, 1914-1918' (PhD Thesis. King's College London, 2014).

211 Ibid., p. 18.

212 Farmar Papers: FAR/10/100, 'Gallipoli, 1921', by H.M. Farmar.

Farmar's capacity to deliver objective commentary about his late Gallipoli experience is of great value in relation to devolved command. Following the peninsula staff ride excursion, he was asked to deliver the previously mentioned RUSI lecture with Field Marshal Lord Milne in the chair. Farmar observed that it would have been wise "to name Report Centres, in succession, up to each objective, for every Commander. He will not be tied personally, but, until another is reached, will leave someone to receive and re-direct messages."[213] Furthermore, "If Report Centres had been fixed it would have been easier to get and maintain touch. If *liaison* methodology had been adopted there would have been much greater cohesion, and, when darkness closed, a greater confidence felt."[214] Moreover, "quick re-organization and acceptance of responsibility was necessary. I believe", he continued, "in fully trusting subordinates with information, to help towards co-operation and teamwork."[215] Thus he clearly believed that it was necessary to arrange "for *liaison*, not only from subordinate to superior, but laterally between commanders and leaders of equal standing. Those employed need not be of particular rank, but individuals who are intelligent and in possession of the plans for their particular formation."[216] Farmar also stressed the importance of training, remarking that it was "very necessary in peace to practise exercises involving reorganization, allowing for casualties, bold personal reconnaissance by leaders, and quick exploitation: to encourage audacity even to exaggeration."[217] In addition, "Time is never wasted in making sound plans and in making these understood and having essential points written down. Two of the brigades lost their brigade commander and brigade major, and both units were depleted to the extent of over fifty percent by casualties."[218]

Colonel Harold Mynors Farmar at W Beach, 1921. (Mrs Sally McLaren)

Farmar concluded that it was necessary "to think of the psychology of leaders and men, and particularly in a dangerous situation not to be haphazard in the allocation of duties; second, to have no break in responsibility at what may be critical places."[219] In order to facilitate this:

213 Farmar, 'The Gallipoli Campaign 1915', p. 642.
214 Ibid., p. 646.
215 Ibid.
216 Ibid., p. 642.
217 Ibid., p. 649.
218 Ibid., p. 648.
219 Ibid., p. 650.

> Navigation lights placed to enable leaders to steer their desired course; search lights used to mark definite points at certain times, to enable bearings to be taken; definite localities marked at certain intervals by phosphoric or smoke shell; the principle of the life-saving line gun to be used by mountain artillery to give a line of direction for scouts to follow. Methods are now laid down for communication between Artillery and Infantry which help to solve the second problem. I have already touched on the subject of *liaison* and there remains the problem of methodical progression. First, I should like to urge the importance of giving ample time for every man to learn his role – in particular this gives confidence and leads to determination to succeed; of trusting subordinates and giving ample information. Second, an apparently complicated task becomes simple when split into its component parts: give each part as a separate task to a separate party of troops. In a night march prior to an attack I would suggest working it in stages and picqueting the route, marking the way between picquets with string – bundles of sticks and string are easily carried. Arrange Report Centres. If direction is temporarily lost it is simple to pick up the last position verified and to make good & good organization is the keynote of success.[220]

During the 1930s, the United States Marine Corps (USMC) studied the Gallipoli campaign, Farmar's assessment inclusive, with particular reference to combined operations, amphibious landings and command in order to formulate an institutional-wide doctrine.[221] Its conclusions "had a significant, and lasting, impact on subsequent USMC amphibious doctrine."[222] The campaign was also carefully studied prior to D-Day (6 June 1944) as a means of ensuring that 29th Division's failure to immediately advance beyond the beaches would not be repeated. Thus the proposed Normandy landings would successfully propel the invasion forces into a campaign centred on mobility as opposed to position warfare.[223] As for Farmar, he continued to fill staff appointments throughout the remainder of the war. His post-Gallipoli convalescence was followed by service as AA&QMG to 3rd Australian Division (GOC Major-General Sir John Monash) which saw action at Messines (7-14 June 1917). Farmar's overall competence was remarked upon at this time:

> I am not so sure that you do know how greatly I have prized your loyal help and co-operation, or your self-sacrificing labours for the benefit of myself and the whole Division – Having since the days of its first formation, taken so prominent a share in its organization and building up, it is impossible that any successor should be able entirely to fill your role, or replace you in its esteem and affection.[224]

220 Farmar, 'The Gallipoli Campaign 1915', pp. 650-651. For an example of the use of navigation lights in an offensive, see Australian War Memorial: 3DRL/2316, RCDIG0000615, Monash Papers, Personal Files Book 13, 16 August-30 September 1917, an action in which Farmar served on the staff of General Sir John Monash.

221 See K.L. Corbett, USMC, 'Marine Corps Amphibious Doctrine – The Gallipoli Connection', Citing the *Joint Overseas Expedition Manual* (US Joint Army-Navy Board, US Government Printing Office, 1933) <www.globalsecurity.org/military/library/report/1990/CKL.htm>

222 Corbett, USMC, 'Marine Corps Amphibious Doctrine'.

223 See also R. Parkin, 'A Capability of First Resort: Amphibious Operations and Australian Defence Policy, 1901-2201', *Land Warfare Studies, Working Paper No.117*, (May 2002).

224 Farmar Papers: FAR/10/111, Typescript of letter from General Sir John Monash to Lieutenant-Colonel H.M. Farmar, 12 September 1917.

Subsequent service as AA&QMG 35th (Bantam) Division (GOC Major-General George Franks) during the Third Battle of Ypres (31 July–20 November 1917) was followed by a brief spell as AQMG to General Sir Henry Rawlinson (GOC Fourth Army).[225] From September 1918 Farmar was AQMG "in the staff of the British Mission with General Pershing at American Headquarters", ending the war as AQMG IX Corps in the Army of Occupation.[226]

Conclusion

As early as 1902, Field Marshal Lord Roberts had recognised that:

> Staff officers cannot be improvised; nor can they learn their duties, like the rank and file, in a few weeks or months, for their duties are as varied as they are important. I am decidedly of opinion that we cannot have a first-rate army, unless we have a first-rate staff, well educated, constantly practised at manoeuvres, and with wide experience.[227]

During Farmar's first three months on the peninsula he served as brigade major for five different commanders. His endeavours rebuff the traditional misconception that British staff officers were hampered by amateurism. Far from being ignorant of the task, Farmar, through education, thorough training and experience, demonstrated professional competency and endurance under difficult circumstances. The overwhelming impression one gets from 25 April signals is the messenger's clear understanding of his role and attention to detail. The date, time and place are clearly denoted and all examples bearing his signature are clear, concise and demonstrate no measure of panic. It is only as the days wore on that his handwriting began to show signs of fatigue, but, crucially, they also demonstrate attempts to guide, inform and structure the ever-changing situation. Working closely with Hare and Frankland, available evidence demonstrates that Farmar understood his role as a staff officer was to support the men in every possible way as a means of achieving assigned objectives.[228] In 1920, Hunter-Weston acknowledged Farmar's military competence when the latter was nominated for Staff College a third time:

> I wish to add to this my support on the grounds that this officer proved himself during the operations under my Command at Cape Helles on the Gallipoli Peninsula in 1915. He temporarily was in control of the 86th Brigade of the 29th Division, after the Brigadier was wounded and the Brigade Major killed, and when matters were critical, at the original landing. On a later occasion too, he led the Brigade personally advancing when the enemy made a counter attack and the other troops in the line were either at a stand-still or in

225 Farmar Papers: Autobiography, p. 68.
226 Ibid., p. 73.
227 Cited in P. Simkins, 'John Terraine and the True Texture of the Somme: Some Personal Reflections', *The Western Front Association, Bulletin* 106, November 2016, pp. 25-35, p. 29, Field Marshal Lord Roberts, Minutes of Evidence taken before the Royal Commission on the War in South Africa, i, p. 441.
228 See TNA WO 32/4731: Publications, General (Code 24(A)), Staff Manual, Chapter II.

> retirement. He is an excellent officer whom I have had experience of both as a Commander of troops during trying fighting, and as a Staff Officer.[229]

Hare's subsequent assessment of his staff captain was rather more absolute:

> They never gave you half enough credit for what you did that day. You had the whole thing on your shoulders from the time Frankland was killed and I am sure if you had not taken the grip of affairs that you did our whole effort would have collapsed.[230]

In 1932, on the eve of his retirement, *Southern Newspapers* printed an article entitled CAREER OF COLONEL FARMAR:

> If the messages sent by him and received by the Divisional Headquarters at 9:30 a.m. and at noon, giving the general situation accurately and comprehensively, with local information, had been acted upon, an advance direct on Achi Baba could have been made there and then.[231]

Farmar's private papers demonstrate a personality centred on moral and physical courage. It is also clear that his military experience combined with extensive military training adequately prepared him for his role as staff captain.[232] His endeavours throughout 25 April helped ensure initial success during the Helles landings. Writing to Violet Farmar on 20 May 1915, 86th Brigade padre, the Reverend Creighton, wrote of her husband:

> I see him at intervals, but he is always being moved from job to job. He is such a valuable person that every Brigade Staff wants him. I hear nothing but golden opinions of him. His coolness and courage and unfailing courtesy through all the terrible experiences the 29th Division have had to face are remarked on by everyone.[233]

The reformation in traditional infantry training[234] set out by military thinkers such as Colonel Henderson is deserving of credit for producing a novel and progressive tactical programme:

229 Farmar Papers: Autobiography, p. 82, typescript copy of letter from Lieutenant-General Sir Aylmer Hunter-Weston, CO Army Corps to HQ Southern Command, Ref. WO Letter 43/Staff College/3112(SD1), 3 March 1920.

230 Farmar Papers: FAR/10/111, typescript copy of letter from General Sir Steuart Hare, HQ 54th Division, to H.M. Farmar, 2 August 1916.

231 Farmar Papers: 'Career of Colonel Farmar', *Southern Newspapers Ltd*, 31 October 1932. See also Aspinall-Oglander, *Military Operations Gallipoli*, Vol. I, p. 239, fn. 2.

232 See also P. Harris, "The Men Who Planned the War" & S. Bidwell and D. Graham, *Fire-Power, British Army Weapons and Theories of War, 1904-1905* (London: Allen & Unwin, 1982) for analysis of pre-war staff training and acknowledgement of effective adaptability.

233 Farmar Papers: FAR/10/111, typescript copy of a letter from Padre 86th Brigade, Rev. O Creighton, 20 May 1915.

234 See Henderson, *A Collection of Essays and Lectures 1891-1903*.

> The discipline of the mass is insufficient. The man must be animated by something more than the spirit of unthinking obedience. He must have been taught and taught so thoroughly that the idea has become an instinct, to depend on himself alone, to feel that his individual skill and individual endurance are the most important factors in the fight, and that when orders no longer reach him, he must be his own general.[235]

Indeed, Farmar, faced with these circumstances on W Beach, rose to the occasion:

> On 25 April 1915 Captain H.M. Farmar of the Lancashire Fusiliers landed on W Beach, Gallipoli Peninsula with the HQ 86th Brigade. After Landing, the Brigadier was wounded, and at about 8:30 a.m. the Brigade Major was killed. At this most critical time Captain Farmar assumed command of the brigade and managed to establish communication with the divisional commander on board HMS Euryalus with the S.S. River Clyde at V Beach, and with both the Royal and the Lancashire Fusiliers. The operation was successful.[236]

235 Ibid., p. 412. See also TNA WO 32/4731: 'Staff Manual 1912, Principle of Organization of Staff Duties', Chapter 2, p. 10.
236 Farmar Papers: FAR/11/05, transcript of Citation for Captain H.M. Farmar DSO.

11

Crisis in Command: Senior Leadership in the 1st Australian Division at the Gallipoli Landings

Robert Stevenson

It was a dark, overcast night on 25 April 1915 when, around midnight, the three senior commanders of the Australian and New Zealand Army Corps (ANZAC) huddled in conference at their improvised headquarters just above the stony beach soon to be christened Anzac Cove.[1] The first member of the trio was a tall, stooped man with a clipped moustache, who might easily have been mistaken for a college professor rather than Australia's senior military officer. Major-General William Throsby Bridges,[2] General Officer Commanding (GOC) 1st Australian Division, was the man primarily responsible for the defence of the narrow beachhead his troops seized early that day. The second figure was Major-General Alexander Godley,[3] the austere British commander of the New Zealand and Australian Division, whose troops had begun landing behind Bridges' men in the afternoon. The third was Lieutenant-General Sir William Birdwood,[4] the normally ebullient ANZAC commander.

Birdwood's task that day was part of the Anglo-French Gallipoli operation. The GOC ANZAC was charged by General Sir Ian Hamilton, commander of the Mediterranean Expeditionary Force (MEF), with seizing a beachhead half way along the peninsula, to allow an advance inland by ANZAC to the Mal Tepe plateau, thereby severing the Ottoman lines-of-communication. Success by the ANZAC would deny Ottoman reinforcement of their troops confronting the main landings by the British 29th Division at Cape Helles on the southern tip of the peninsula. Having pierced the enemy defences, the British forces were to advance, clearing the fortifications on the European shore of the Dardanelles that had foiled earlier attempts by the Anglo-French fleet to pass through the narrow waters and enter the Sea of Marmara to threaten the Ottoman capital of Constantinople (today Istanbul). Simultaneous

1 In this chapter "ANZAC" refers to the military formation; "Anzac" refers either to topographical features or to personnel belonging to the corps.

2 Chris Coulthard-Clarke, *A Heritage of Spirit: A Biography of Major-General Sir William Throsby Bridges KCB CMG* (Carlton: Melbourne University Press, 1979).

3 Sir Alexander Godley, *Life of an Irish Soldier: Reminiscences of General Sir Alexander Godley* (London: John Murray, 1939).

4 Field-Marshal Lord Birdwood, *Khaki and Gown: An Autobiography* (London: Ward Lock, 1941).

operations, including a demonstration by the Royal Naval Division against Bulair at the neck of the peninsula and a diversionary landing by the French 1st Colonial Division at Kum Kale on the Asian shore of the Dardanelles, were to distract the Ottomans and disguise the objectives of the principal landings.[5]

Unfortunately for the allies matters had not proceeded according to plan. The pre-dawn seaborne approach by the ANZAC covering force – the 3rd Australian Infantry Brigade – went awry in the dark as the boats carrying the lead troops landed in a congested huddle below the steep, coastal ridges of the Sari Bair Range rather than across a broad beach further south near the promontory of Gaba Tepe. Initial confusion was exacerbated by both a loss of control as the troops scrambled inland through a tangle of scrub covered ridges and a swift, determined enemy response which saw a day of confused fighting that see-sawed back and forth over the three ridges that ran like fingers south from the Sari Bair heights. Fears of an early counterattack on the vulnerable southern ANZAC flank caused the covering force commander, Colonel Ewan Sinclair-MacLagan,[6] to alter Bridges' plan so that the 2nd Australian Brigade, landing behind the lead troops, was redirected to the right flank rather than the left and securing Hill Q and Hill 917, the two highest and vital points on the range.[7] As Ottoman reinforcements arrived and pressure built, follow-on Australian and New Zealand units scrambled ashore to be thrown into the line wherever a crisis threatened. By late afternoon a ragged Anzac line clung to a toehold along the second ridge (also known as Anzac Ridge) rather than the original objective of the third (or Gun) ridge. Incessant Ottoman artillery fire severely tested the novice troops and as well as heavy casualties, by late afternoon there were an alarming number of stragglers choking the gullies behind the line or gathering on the beach.[8]

Just on nightfall, as active fighting died down, but nervous firing continued to ripple up and down the opposing lines, Sinclair-MacLagan made his way down from his command post to confer with Bridges. Sinclair-MacLagan and the commander of the 2nd Brigade, Colonel James Whiteside McCay,[9] held the centre and right of the thin line, while interspersed were scattered groups of Colonel Henry MacLaurin's 1st Brigade that had been doled out piecemeal during the afternoon.[10] To the north, more recently landed elements of the New Zealand Infantry Brigade, temporarily commanded by Brigadier-General Harold Walker, were intermingled with the Australians and clinging to the ground at the head of the valley (later titled Monash Valley) that ran between the first and second ridges and down to the beach.[11] When Sinclair-MacLagan arrived Bridges, recalling the colonel's dire pre-landing predictions of failure asked: "'Well, old pessimist,' he laughed – 'what have you got to say about it now?' MacLagan looked serious. 'I

5 Charles Edward Woodrow Bean, *The History of Australia in the War of 1914–1918. The Story of Anzac: From the Outbreak of war to the end of the First Phases of the Gallipoli Campaign, May 4, 1915*, 11th Edition (Sydney: Angus and Robertson, 1941), pp. 219–35 (hereafter *AOH*, Vol. I).

6 A.J. Hill, 'Sinclair-MacLagan, Ewen George (1868–1948)', *Australian Dictionary of Biography* (*ADB*), Vol. 11 (Carlton: Melbourne University Press, 1988), pp. 616–18.

7 Australian War Memorial (AWM) 4, 1/25/1 Part 7: ANZAC, 'Operation Order No. 1', 17 April 1915.

8 The narrative for this chapter draws on Bean and the two best recent accounts of the ANZAC landing: Chris Roberts, *The Landing at Anzac: 1915*, Second ed. (Sydney: Big Sky Publishing, 2015); Mesut Uyar, *The Ottoman Defence Against the Anzac Landing* (Sydney: Big Sky Publishing, 2015).

9 Geoffrey Serle, 'McCay, Sir James Whiteside (1864–1930)', *ADB*, Vol. 10, pp. 224–27.

10 Ann M. Mitchell, 'MacLaurin, Sir Henry Normand (1835–1914)', *ADB*, Vol. 10, pp. 327–29.

11 A.J. Sweeting, 'Walker, Sir Harold Bridgwood (1862–1934)', *ADB*, Vol. 12, p. 359.

don't know, sir,' he answered. 'It's touch and go. If the Turks come on in mass formation … on the left, I don't think anything can stop them'."[12]

Major-General William Bridges.

Earlier in the day, at about 3:00 p.m., Birdwood had gone ashore from the battleship HMS *Queen* to assess the situation. During the visit he was escorted to the top of the first ridge by Walker and there he surveyed the line from a position soon to be known as Plugge's Plateau.[13] Walker sketched the dangers of the exposed left flank but little could be seen on the distant scrub covered ridge and when Birdwood departed he did so without serious misgivings.[14] The corps war diary recorded after his return to *Queen* at about 8:00 p.m. that "the troops ashore were not secure but the situation was not such as to cause great alarm at that time."[15] Towards nightfall Godley also conferred with Walker and again the brigadier intimated that the situation remained "most serious."[16] Based on Walker's firsthand assessment, Godley decided to discuss matters with Bridges and the pair made their way to Headquarters (HQ) 1st Division, located in a gully above Anzac Cove. There Godley, Walker, Bridges and Colonel Cyril Brudenell White,[17] the General Staff Officer Grade One (GSOI) 1st Division, discussed the situation. It is not known precisely when or who first raised the possibility of a withdrawal, but the idea quickly took root with only Walker railing against the proposal.[18]

Despite Walker's vehement protests, the two divisional commanders feared the worse and they felt the need to present their case for evacuation to Birdwood. Around 9:15 p.m. the pair decided to send a message recalling the corps commander, who by that time was back aboard *Queen*. Bridges signaled at about 10:00 p.m., "General Godley and I both consider that you should come ashore at once."[19] Birdwood, clearly not expecting to be briefed on a plan to

12 Sinclair-MacLagan quoted in Bean, *AOH*, Vol. I, p. 454. Bean provides a slightly different version in C.E.W. Bean, *Two Men I Knew: William Bridges and Brudenell White, Founders of the AIF* (Sydney: Angus & Robertson, 1957), p. 62.
13 Birdwood claimed to have visited Walker's Top on the second ridge, which he called the "Sari Bair position" in a signal to Hamilton at 8:45 p.m., but Bean affirms that he only went to the top of Plugge's. Liddle Hart Centre for Military Archives (LHCMA): Edmonds Papers, GB0099, II/1/22: Birdwood to Sir James Edmonds, 10 March 1927; Birdwood, *Khaki and Gown*, p. 258; Bean, *AOH*, Vol. I, pp. ix, 455.
14 Bean, *AOH*, Vol. I, pp. viii–ix, 455.
15 AWM4, 1/25/1 Part 1: HQ ANZAC General Staff War Diary (GS WD), 25 April 1915.
16 Brigadier-General C.F. Aspinall-Oglander, *Military Operations Gallipoli*, Vol. I (London: HMSO, 1929), p. 267 (hereafter *BOH Gallipoli*, Vol. I).
17 Jeffrey Grey, 'White, Sir Cyril Brudenell Bingham (1876–1940)', *ADB*, Vol. 12, pp. 460–463.
18 Bean, *AOH*, Vol. I, p. 455.
19 Quoted in Bean, *AOH*, Vol. I, p. 456.

abandon the beachhead, made arrangements for the landing of the remaining infantry as well as further artillery and only then did he head back to the beach.[20]

Gathered to meet Birdwood were a number of key commanders and staff. The main figures were Bridges, Godley, Walker, Colonel Joly de Lotbiniere (Birdwood's Chief Royal Engineer), Brudenell White, Colonel Joseph Talbot Hobbs (Commander Divisional Artillery 1st Division),[21] and Colonel Neville Howse (Deputy Director Medical Services 1st Division). Importantly none of the Australian brigade commanders were in attendance. Bridges' dug-out was little more than a ledge cut into the gully-side, framed by a few sandbags, with a flap of canvas for a roof. It was too small to hold the whole group and so most gathered outside while the three senior officers conferred. Bridges and Godley lay before Birdwood their grave doubts as to whether their over-strained men could stand further shellfire and a heavy attack the next morning.[22]

Bridges was the chief instigator and his opinion carried more weight as it was his division that was bearing the weight of the defence, while Godley had yet to take formal command of his troops ashore. The dire assessment came as a shock to Birdwood who later claimed he was at first "horrified" at the suggestion and refused to accept it.[23] According to the corps war diary: "A long conference was held at which the necessity and possibility of re-embarkation were discussed. The GOC [Birdwood] decided that we must hold on – and he issued orders for the hastening of the disembarkation of more troops."[24] The war diary however, offers a rather truncated version of events that distorts what actually transpired.

Despite his initial reluctance, Birdwood was eventually persuaded "by the intense anxiety of his subordinates" and he agreed to pass a message to Hamilton.[25] Godley, making no reference to Walker's dissenting opinion, scribbled a signal by the light of a handful of guttering candles and Bridges' electric torch, which read:

> Both my Divisional Generals and Brigadiers have represented to me that they fear their men are thoroughly demoralised by shrapnel fire to which they have been subjected all day after exhaustion and gallant work in the morning. Numbers have dribbled back from firing line and cannot be collected in this difficult country. Even New Zealand Brigade which has only recently been engaged lost heavily and is to some extent demoralised. If troops are subjected to shell fire again tomorrow morning, there is likely to be a fiasco, as I have no fresh troops with which to replace those in firing line. I know my representation is most serious but if we are to re-embark it must be at once. Birdwood.[26]

20 The ANZAC war diary claims Birdwood landed around 8:00 p.m., Birdwood's autobiography gives no precise time nor does Godley's, while Bean states that the signal recalling Birdwood was not dispatched until 10:00 p.m. AWM4, 1/25/1 Part 1: HQ ANZAC GS WD, 25 April 1915; Birdwood, *Khaki and Gown*, p. 259; Godley, *Life of An Irish Soldier*, pp. 171–2; Bean, *AOH*, Vol. I, p. 456.

21 A.J. Hill, 'Hobbs, Sir Joseph John Talbot (1864–1938)', *ADB*, Vol. 9, pp. 315–17.

22 Bean, *AOH*, Vol. I, p. 457.

23 Birdwood, *Khaki and Gown*, p. 259.

24 AWM4, 1/25/1 Part 1: HQ ANZAC GS WD, 25 April 1915.

25 Bean, *AOH*, Vol. I, p. 458.

26 Sir Ian Hamilton, *Gallipoli Diary*, Vol. 1 (London: Edward Arnold, 1920), p. 143. Godley reproduced the same message but omitted his failure to address it. See Godley, *Life of An Irish Soldier*, p. 172.

Although Godley signed the message for Birdwood, he failed to address it to Hamilton, so when it was received offshore it was passed to the naval commander, Admiral Cecil Thursby aboard *Queen*. Lacking an addressee, Thursby assumed the message was for him and was about to head ashore to consult with Birdwood having signalled all ships off Gaba Tepe, "*Queen* to all transports. Lower all boats ready to send in to beach. Pass on."[27]

Fortuitously at about 12:50 a.m. HMS *Queen Elizabeth* arrived off Anzac with Hamilton aboard and Thursby was able to show the message to the MEF commander.[28] Thus only by accident did the crucial message reach its intended recipient. Hamilton consulted Thursby who advised that it was not possible to evacuate the troops that night and it would take at least three days.[29] After considering the advice of his senior staff, Hamilton issued his famous order which concluded, "You have got through the difficult business, now you have only to dig, dig, dig, until you are safe."[30] This message effectively ended the affair and the stage was set for the ill-fated eight month campaign.[31]

While historians have proffered many reasons for the failure of the ANZAC landing to achieve its initial objectives, none have suggested that it was primarily due to a failure of the 1st Australian Division's senior leadership. Despite this, it is clear that pressures of the moment precipitated a crisis in confidence that swept the division's senior officers as they feared their thin line might be overwhelmed and their men driven back into the sea and slaughtered. The loss of confidence Bridges suffered, in both himself and his command, and the dire state of the ANZAC line, all point to significant problems within 1st Australian Division's command structure. The aim of this chapter is to explore the background and makeup of the Australian command hierarchy on the day of the landings and offer some suggestions as to why Australia's premier division came so close to collapse in its combat debut. To do this we need to go back to the outbreak of war.

Raising the Australian Division

As the situation in Europe spiralled out of control in the summer of 1914, the Australian government offered to raise an Australian volunteer force of 20,000 troops to operate under British command even before war was declared. On 6 August, two days after the British declaration of war, the Secretary for State for the Colonies accepted Australia's offer and requested that the force be dispatched as soon as possible. Enquiries with the British government as to the desired

27 Bean, *AOH*, Vol. I, p. 460.
28 Ibid., pp. xv–xvi, 458; Hamilton, *Gallipoli Diary*, Vol. 1, p. 142.
29 The possibility of re-embarkation was considered in planning for the operation but not under the circumstances contemplated on 25 April. AWM4, 1/25/1 Part 8: Memorandum 1/33 'Re-embarkation', 24 April 1915.
30 Hamilton, *Gallipoli Diary*, Vol. 1, p. 142.
31 Although no conference notes were taken, references are made in both Australian and British official histories. The New Zealand history is more perfunctory, recording only that a withdrawal "was suggested, but a conference was held and the Generals decided to hold on", without mentioning Hamilton's intervention. Aspinall-Oglander, *Military Operations Gallipoli*, Vol. I, pp. 267–8; Bean, *AOH*, Vol. I, pp. 456–8; Major Fred Waite, *The New Zealanders at Gallipoli* (Auckland: Whitcombe & Tombs Ltd, 1921), p. 86.

makeup of force elicited the response "that a suitable composition of the expeditionary force would be two infantry brigades, one light horse brigade, and one field artillery brigade", which would only amount to about 12,000 troops.[32] Bridges, who on 5 August had been given the task of organising the force, objected fearing that the Australian contingent might be broken-up to serve within British formations. In a reply he drafted for the Defence Minister, the British government was advised that Australia expected the full offer of 20,000 troops to be accepted and as such had begun organising an infantry division, along with a light horse brigade. Britain accepted the proposal the following day.[33]

On 10 August the Commonwealth government announced that its offer of an expeditionary force had been accepted. The main body of what was to be titled the Australian Imperial Force (AIF) was the 1st Australian Division, although initially it was known simply as "The Australian Division" since it was not contemplated that any more divisions would be formed. The creation of such a body was outside the experience of all but a handful of officers in Australia at that time. Australia had never formed a permanent division and its largest peacetime military organisation was the brigade, comprising predominately infantry or light horse units, with supporting artillery, engineers and service support.[34] A division, on the other hand, was a much larger, diverse and complex organisation. In 1914 it consisted of 18,000 men and more than 5,000 horses, organised into some 20 different units ranging in strength from 500 up to about 1,000 men. Its main fighting elements were its 12 infantry battalions and its three brigades of field artillery, along with its own construction engineers and internal communications.[35] The division maintained an administrative tail of supply, ordnance, police, medical and veterinary support. These organisations watered, fed, clothed, armed, disciplined, paid and cared for all its personnel and animals. The commander and his staff were responsible for training the division, coordinating its arms and services and forging a team that could fight and win on the modern battlefield.[36] Little did Bridges know that he would be leading his division into battle in just eight months.

The first challenge Bridges faced was the geographical dispersion of Australia's population centres and the lack of a central mobilisation area where his force could be concentrated. This meant that the only practical solution was to decentralise the process so that each state-based military district was given a quota of troops to raise, roughly in proportion to its population base. In outline, an infantry brigade group was raised in each of the two most populous states – New South Wales (NSW) and Victoria – with the third brigade apportioned across the other four states.[37] Initiating the process, at 12:15 p.m. on 10 August, Army HQ in Melbourne dispatched

32 Bean, *AOH*, Vol. I, p 30.

33 A full-strength 1914 British division after mobilisation contained just over 18,000 men and the light horse brigade would add the other 2000 troops. General Staff, *Field Service Pocket Book (1914)*, (London: HMSO, 1914, revised 1916), p. 6; Bean, *AOH*, Vol. I, pp. 31–32.

34 Temporary divisions were occasionally formed for some of the annual training camps although these were more administrative than tactical. See Commonwealth Military Forces of Victoria, *Report of the Annual Continuous Training, 10th to 17th January 1910* (Melbourne: J. Kemp, 18 February 1910), p. 3.

35 Australian battalions were initially structured with eight companies, while the artillery brigades contained three batteries, each of four 18-pdr field guns. Robert Stevenson, *To Win the Battle: The 1st Australian Division in the Great War, 1914–18* (Melbourne: Cambridge University Press, 2013), pp. 35, 37-39.

36 Ibid., pp. 2–3.

37 AWM4, 1/1/1 Part 1: Chief of the General Staff, Diary of Events, 10 August 1914; Bean, *AOH*, Vol. I, pp. 37–38.

telegrams to the military district commandants directing them to publish a notice calling for volunteers and to begin arrangements for establishing camps. Later that day each district was advised of its quota. Although there were a number of minor adjustments made to the allocations, the broad allotments remained firm for this contingent and those formed later.[38]

Four days earlier, on 6 August, Bridges was appointed to command the 1st Division, which included the dual responsibility of administrative commander of the whole AIF. The choice of Bridges was not a foregone conclusion even though he was the most senior Australian officer and widely recognised as the first soldier of the Commonwealth. In fact Bridges originally suggested Lieutenant-General Sir Edward Hutton,[39] a retired British officer and former GOC of the Australian Military Forces, as the most suitable officer to command the Australian Division. Hutton's military credentials were impressive since he had already commanded a brigade, which included dominion troops, in the second Anglo-Boer War and had experience commanding the 3rd Division in Britain before his retirement in 1907. The Australian government rejected this sensible suggestion mostly likely because Hutton had maintained a contentious relationship with his political superiors during his tenure in Australia and the Commonwealth was determined to place one of its own in command.[40]

While Bridges was the government's selection he was not the ideal choice for such a complex and expansive mission. Scots-born, English educated, Canadian trained, Bridges had entered the Royal Military College, Kingston in 1877 but left without securing a commission and joined the NSW Permanent Forces in 1885. He rose steadily and was a protégé of Hutton during his tenure commanding the NSW colonial forces. The official historian, Charles Bean, who was an admirer of the man, provided a sketch of Bridges as:

> a slow but a deep thinker, his chief interest being in questions of an academic nature … A clever philosophical definition invariably gave him pleasure. He read widely, and his friends put him down as a typical professor. He had a tall bony, thin loose-limbed frame and the bent shoulders of a student. His manner was gauche and on occasions rude … His favourite form of answer was a grunt followed by a terse sentence. He was ruthless as to the feelings of others; he seemed to make no concessions to humanity; he expected none from it…Only those who watched him most closely knew that Bridges possessed one of those intensely shy natures which are sometimes combined with great strength. He had an abhorrence of the least show of sentiment, and would rather have gone to any extremity of rudeness than let a trace of it appear in his face, his voice, or his actions … He made men afraid of him, but he disliked them to show their fear.[41]

Aside from a psychological disposition which made him a difficult leader to follow, Bridges also lacked experience in command. He served briefly in South Africa as a major but aside from

38 *Australian Imperial Force Orders* (*AIFO*): No. 2, 26 August 1914; *AIFO*: No. 4, 29 August 1914; *AIFO*: No. 10, 5 September 1914; *AIFO*: No. 14, 10 September 1914; *AIFO*: No. 16, 14 September 1914; *AIFO*: No. 22, 21 September 1914 (bound set held by the AWM).

39 A.J. Hill, 'Hutton, Sir Edward Thomas Henry (1848–1923)', *ADB*, Vol. 9, pp. 415–8.

40 Craig Stockings, *Britannia's Shield: Lieutenant General Sir Edward Hutton and Late-Victorian Imperial Defence* (Port Melbourne: Cambridge University Press, 2015), pp. 47–58, 200–04, 224–48.

41 Bean, *AOH*, Vol. I, pp. 66–7.

service as head of the School of Gunnery and the founding Commandant of the Royal Military College, Duntroon, his reputation was made as a staff officer and administrator. Nor had he attended either of the British staff colleges. He was, neither by training nor experience, prepared for the challenge of leading a division into battle.[42]

Whatever misgivings he may have felt over his appointment Bridges submerged in a frantic schedule as he threw himself into the task of building Australia's first division. No matter his other limitations, Bridges was an excellent organiser and he began building the division from top down. The upper echelons of the command were drawn from the thin ranks of Australia's permanent soldiers, British officers on loan to Australia, and the larger body of Australia's home-defence, part-time militia, also known as the Citizens Forces. To command his three infantry brigades and brigaded artillery he selected three militiamen and a single British regular. At unit level the commanding officers (CO) and regimental officers were largely drawn from the militia. Hence, of the 631 original officers, only 24 had never served before. In all 68 were or had been officers of the Permanent Forces, while another 16 were regular officers of the British Army and a further 15 were retired British officers. An overwhelming 460 came either from the older militia forces or from the more recent compulsory service scheme. Only 104 had seen previous active service, mostly on the veldt in South Africa.[43]

Among the rank and file, experience was even thinner. While it was hoped that half of the volunteers would come from the ranks of the Citizens Forces, this expectation was not met. As matters transpired, only 2,263 volunteers were currently serving citizen soldiers, while another 1,555 were older ex-militiamen, and another 2,460 had at some time served in the Australian militia. Bolstering the local troops were some 1,308 former British regulars and another 1,009 former British Territorials. In the end, however, fewer than three in five had some prior military service and more than a third, some 6,098, had never served in uniform.[44]

To command this polymorphous group would require considerable skill and it demanded leaders of high calibre if the division was to be made ready and dispatched overseas within the prescribed four weeks. Instead of trying to centrally identify officers, Bridges decided upon the expedient of appointing his formation commanders and allowing them to select their unit COs. The COs were then given a free hand to choose their subordinates although they were guided by a committee established in each military district for the purpose of recommending candidates.[45] In this way the selection process was completed quickly, and units were given the maximum amount of time to form and train; but much depended on the initial selection of senior commanders and how good these men were at choosing the right subordinates.[46]

After appointing his key staff, Bridges selected commanders for his three infantry brigades and the artillery. It was these men who were to be the conduit of Bridges' plans and orders, turning them into reality. To command the NSW 1st Brigade, Bridges chose Colonel Henry Normand MacLaurin. A young Sydney barrister, MacLaurin was a serving militiaman who

42 Chris Clarke, 'Bridges, William Throsby (1861–1915)', *ADB*, Vol. 7, pp. 408–11.
43 Bean, *AOH*, Vol. I, p. 54.
44 AWM27, 352/19: 'Summary of – Personnel Statistics', attached to 1st Division Order No 43, 27 January 1915.
45 AWM27, 303/211: Memorandum 'To the Officer Commanding Q Battalion, 3rd Infantry Brigade, Australian Imperial Force (through the Commandant 1st Military District)', 14 August 1914.
46 Bean, *AOH*, Vol. I, pp. 48–52.

hailed from a socially-connected family. At 36 years of age he was younger than any of the original battalion commanders of the division as he relinquished command of the 26th Infantry to take up his new appointment.[47] To command his four battalions MacLaurin's selected militia officers mostly known to him from their pre-war service together or by reputation. Command of the 1st Battalion (AIF) went to Lieutenant-Colonel Leonard Dobbin, a British born, 46-year-old who at the time was in virtual military retirement having been placed in the officers' graveyard known as the Unallotted List.[48] Colonel George Braund, a 48-year-old British-born merchant and politician, came to the AIF from commanding the 13th Infantry. Dropping a rank, Braund took command of the 2nd Battalion, quickly earning a reputation as hard trainer although his strict abstinence from drinking, smoking and consuming meat made him something of an oddity to his men.[49] CO of the 3rd Battalion was Lieutenant-Colonel Robert Owen, a 52-year-old Australian who had served in the Sudan in 1885 before joining the British Army, only to retire as a major in 1902. He came out of retirement in 1914 and was affectionately nicknamed "Dad Owen" by his men.[50] Command of the 4th Battalion went to Lieutenant-Colonel Astley Onslow Thompson, who was born in Wales in 1865 and was a farmer and member of Australia's "squattocracy": In 1914 he too was on the Unallotted List.[51]

To command the Victorian 2nd Brigade, Bridges chose 49-year-old Colonel James McCay. Like MacLaurin, McCay was politically well connected and a long-serving citizen soldier. He had commanded a militia battalion back in 1900, served as Australian Minister for Defence in 1904–05 but in 1911 had declined the command of a militia brigade to command the Australian Intelligence Corps detachment in Victoria. By 1914 he was on the Unallotted List.[52] As with MacLaurin's choice of key subordinates, McCay favoured those officers with whom he had previously served. He selected Scots-born David Wanliss, a 50-year-old, British educated lawyer, currently commanding the 52nd Infantry, for command of the 5th Battalion.[53] For the 6th Battalion he chose an old comrade, James Semmens, a 46-year-old public servant who at the time was commanding the Victorian detachment of the Australian Intelligence Corps.[54] The 7th Battalion went to the mercurial Harold "Pompey" Elliott, a lawyer and serving CO 58th Infantry (Essendon Rifles). A talented militia officer, who had seen service in South Africa as a soldier where he was awarded the Distinguished Conduct Medal before being commissioned, Elliott was considerably younger than his peers, being only 36 years old at the time of his appointment. He was also the only one of the McCay's COs to have seen active service.[55] To

47 Bean, *AOH*, Vol. I, p. 51; Mitchell, 'MacLaurin, Sir Henry Normand (1835–1914)', pp. 327–29.
48 Bertie V. Stacy, Frederick J. Kindon, and H.V. Chedgey, *The History of the First Battalion AIF 1914–1919* (Sydney: First Battalion AIF Association, 1931), pp. 36–37.
49 Darryl McIntyre, 'Braund, George Frederick (1866–1915)', *ADB*, Vol. 7, 1979, pp. 392–93.
50 Ronald McNicoll, 'Owen, Robert Haylock (1862–1927)', *ADB*, Vol. 11, p. 112.
51 Ron Austin, *The Fighting Fourth: A History of Sydney's 4th Battalion 1914–19* (McCrae: Slouch Hat Publications, 2007), pp. 9–10.
52 Christopher Wray, *Sir James Whiteside McCay: A Turbulent Life* (South Melbourne: Oxford University Press, 2002), pp. 167, 85.
53 Bill Gammage, 'Wanliss, David Sydney (1864–1943)', *ADB*, Vol. 12, pp. 378–79.
54 Chris Coulthard-Clark, *The Citizen General Staff: the Australian Intelligence Corps 1907–1914* (Canberra: Military Historical Society of Australia, 1976), p. 85.
55 A.J. Hill, 'Elliott, Harold Edward (1878–1931), *ADB*, Vol. 8, pp. 428–31; Ross McMullin, *Pompey Elliott* (Melbourne: Scribe, 2008), pp. 70–72; Ron Austin, *Our Dear Old Battalion: The Story of the 7th Battalion AIF, 1914–1919* (McCrae: Slouch Hat Publications, 2004), pp. 8, 9.

command the 8th Battalion McCay chose William Bolton. A 52-year-old, English-born, public servant, Bolton was a well-known marksman and CO 70th Infantry.[56] He earned a reputation as "a soft-hearted commander very solicitous for his men."[57]

Command of the 3rd Brigade went to Colonel Ewen Sinclair-MacLagan who was on the staff at the Royal Military College, Duntroon. When war broke out, the 45-year-old British regular was on his second secondment to Australia having served with Bridges in NSW immediately following Federation and was later hand-picked by Bridges to serve as Director of Drill at Duntroon. Although Sinclair-MacLagan was a regular officer who had seen service in Waziristan on the North-West Frontier and in South Africa, where he was awarded the Distinguished Service Order, he had not commanded at either battalion or brigade level before.[58]

The four battalions of the 3rd Brigade were raised in the four outer states of Queensland, South Australia, Western Australia and Tasmania, with some battalions being drawn from multiple states. Command of the Queensland-raised 9th Battalion went to Lieutenant-Colonel Henry William Lee, a 46-year-old, English-born school teacher and commander of the 4th (Wide Bay) Infantry.[59] The 10th Battalion went to Colonel Stanley Weir, a 48-year-old South Australian public servant who was commanding the 19th Infantry Brigade. He proved to be Sinclair-MacLagan's most successful selection.[60] CO of Western Australia's 11th Battalion was Lieutenant-Colonel James Lyon Johnston, a 51-year-old Scotsman who was commanding the 84th Infantry (Goldfields Regiment). Command of the nominally Tasmanian 12th Battalion went to Lieutenant-Colonel Lancelot Fox Clarke, who at 56 years of age, was the oldest of the division's battalion commanders. Clarke received his first commission in 1884, had seen service in South Africa where he was awarded the Distinguished Service Order, and in 1914 was commanding the 91st Infantry.[61]

The unit commanders then selected their subordinates in consultation with their brigade commander. Again, the COs demonstrated a distinct preference for those with whom they had recently served. In the 6th Battalion Semmens took four members of the Victorian section of the Intelligence Corps with him.[62] This preferential treatment, while understandable in a small territorial army, did lead to some speculation on how fair the system was and undoubtedly there were cases of nepotism. Even Bean, a staunch protector of the AIF's reputation, noted that there were suspicions that initial officer selection was made more on the basis of social standing than on military ability. In this case Bean was specifically referring to the 1st Brigade where MacLaurin and his old second-in-command, Charles Macnaghten, worked closely together and strongly influenced the choice of officers. "Indeed, the notion began to spread that the selections

56 J.N.I. Dawes, 'Bolton, William Kinsey (1860–1941)', *ADB*, Vol. 7, pp. 337–38.
57 Bean, *AOH*, Vol. I, p. 133.
58 Hill, 'Sinclair-MacLagan, Ewen George (1868–1948)', pp. 616–18; J.E. Lee, *Duntroon: The Royal Military College of Australia 1911–1946* (Canberra: AWM, 1952), p. 13.
59 C.M. Wrench, *Campaigning with the Fighting 9th: In and out of the line with the Ninth Battalion AIF* (Brisbane: Boolarong Publications, 1985), pp. 508–10.
60 Neville Hicks & Judith Raftery, 'Weir, Stanley Price (1866–1944)', *ADB*, Vol. 12, p. 438; William Westerman, 'Soldiers and Gentlemen: Australian Battalion Commanders in the Great War 1914–1918', PhD thesis (Canberra: University of New South Wales, September 2014) p. 55.
61 National Archives Australia (NAA): series B2455, file CLARKE LF; 'Lieut.-Col. Clarke', *The Register* (Adelaide), 6 May 1915, p. 8.
62 Coulthard-Clark, *The Citizen General Staff*, p. 50.

were being made by a coterie of the Australian Club in Sydney", as Bean concluded.[63] Be that as it may, these commanders were expected to raise, train and lead their units into battle and so quite naturally they sought out subordinates with whom they knew they could work and trust. In reality no other system could have worked in the limited time available.

Once the command structure was established the units began filling out their ranks. Each of the formations and units were allotted recruiting areas from which to draw volunteers. While this territorial system was deliberately chosen by Bridges to stimulate a sense of community and cohesion within the units, maintaining the territorial integrity of units was difficult to achieve in practice.[64] Recruiting between units varied considerably depending on whether they were raised within a single military district or several, and depending on whether the unit was drawn from city or regional areas, or a combination of the two. The greatest challenge facing the COs however, was not finding soldiers, it was procuring suitable officers.

Most of Bridges' regimental officers were appointed from those who already held commissions in the militia. In the pre-1912 voluntary militia, officers were mostly drawn from the professional classes. Senior militiamen were most often businessmen, bank managers, senior public servants or pastoralists because they had the money, education and time to pursue their hobbies and philanthropic pursuits. Junior officers usually held relatively well-paid sedentary jobs in the public service, insurance or the law. With the introduction of universal service in 1912 little changed, and officers continued to be drawn from the 'white collar' middle-classes.[65]

An amateur ethos pervaded the Citizens Forces at that time, resulting in amateur capabilities. This was typified in the professional education and training of officers. Command training for junior officers was negligible and the manner in which officers were selected for promotion was reduced to theoretical examinations. One permanent officer observed in 1912, "the promotion of a young officer is not dependant on the zeal and ability which he shows in regimental work, but upon his success in examination. Yet, it will generally be admitted that the greater part of the subjects studied for examination [are] unassimilated and quickly forgotten and have little influence on the officer's mental equipment and habit of thought."[66]

Matters were little better in more senior ranks. Officers seeking promotion from major to lieutenant colonel were only required to pass the "Tactical Fitness for Command" examination. This two-part exam, half theoretical and half practical, was notoriously inadequate. In 1912 *The Advertiser* newspaper observed that "not many years ago…three hours, and sometimes less, was considered sufficient for an examination for lieutenant colonel."[67] Such a state may have been acceptable for long-service regular officers who had the opportunity to learn on-the-job under experienced seniors but for part-time officers, most of whom had no operational service, the situation was dire.

63 Bean, *AOH*, Vol. I, p. 54.
64 AWM38, 3DRL6673, 153: AIF112/2/10 to military district commandants, 11 August 1914.
65 David Denholm, *The Colonial Australians* (Ringwood: Penguin Books, 1979), pp. 172–73; Craig Wilcox, *For Hearths and Homes: Citizen Soldiering in Australia, 1854–1945* (St Leonards: Allen & Unwin, 1998), pp. 32, 65–66; 'Australia's Army', *The Argus* (Melbourne), 9 February 1914, p. 9.
66 E.H. Reynolds, 'Education and Instruction of Regimental Officers', *Commonwealth Military Journal*, January 1912, pp. 3–4.
67 'Defence Notes', *The Advertiser* (Adelaide), 26 October 1912, p. 8.

The combination of a command structure consisting of mostly amateur officers and a body of troops with a part-time mentality created a distinctive command culture and one markedly different from regulars. The style of command cultivated in the pre-war Australian army can trace its roots to the early volunteer forces that were the first local units. Although these veteran companies and volunteer forces served alongside the British regiments that provided the colonial garrison, their development owed little to the formidable and sometimes ferocious disciplinary regime of the British regular army and more to the various part-time volunteers who had long been part of Britain's military establishment.[68] Moreover it was largely a peace-time culture since under Australian law these units and their members could not serve outside Australia except as volunteers. It was for the most part the part-time, citizen-soldier that provided the norms of the early AIF.

Discipline in the old volunteer and militia units was generally easy and consensual because it was shaped by an environment of self-restraint and dignity. It was backed up by the volunteer's status as a citizen-soldier. Officers earned respect for their good judgement, social standing and ability to command men without talking down to them or falling back on punishments which were in any case usually impossible to enforce. Trouble most often began when officers coupled autocratic airs with a lack of ability to command.[69] The post-1912 compulsory Citizens Forces maintained a similar regime since it too was based on weekly drills and yearly encampments. Such a regime worked adequately for stay at home volunteers but with the expansion of the officer corps and the flood of compulsory enlistees from 1912 there were difficulties finding the right type of officer material as many of the newer officers proved incapable of controlling their men.[70] Similar problems occurred in the 1st Division notably after arrival in Egypt, culminating in the so-called Battle of the Wazier, although that was all in the future.

The Road to Gallipoli

Bridges formed his division in Australia between August and October and despite many difficulties, the various elements were readied and dispatched separately by ship to rendezvous at the port of Albany on the southwest corner of the continent. From there the convoy sailed on 1 November and the 1st Division was on its way to war. During the voyage the decision was made to divert the convoy to Egypt where the Australian and New Zealand contingents were disembarked, formed into the extemporised ANZAC and continued training.[71]

The training of the 1st Division's officers and soldiers before their departure from Australia was a planned if somewhat haphazard affair. From the outset the division's GSOI, Cyril Brudenell White, was responsible for developing the training programme, which he prepared at Bridges' direction. This programme divided training into three sequential stages: training to be undertaken before the division sailed, training on the voyage, and training after disembarkation.

68 On the influence of the British Army in colonial Australia see Craig Wilcox, *Redcoat Dreaming: How Colonial Australia Embraced the British Army* (Port Melbourne: Cambridge University Press, 2009).

69 Wilcox, *For Hearths and Homes*, pp. 33–34, 70–71.

70 'Easter Training', *The Argus*, (Melbourne) 29 March 1913, p. 19; Wilcox, *For Hearths and Homes*, pp. 71–2.

71 Stevenson, *To Win the Battle*, p. 31.

Although the programme was distributed to all formations and efforts were made to adhere to the plan, the mobilisation process meant that its application was at best uneven.[72]

While training began as soon as units were formed, efforts were plagued by chronic deficiencies. Equipment shortages, a dearth of qualified instructors and inadequate training facilities caused delays and interrupted unit plans. It was also a slow process as many of the recruits lacked prior military training. Initial efforts habitually began with foot drill, which in an era before the widespread motorisation of armies had a practical as well as a sociological purpose. Route marching was added for fitness and discipline.[73] During one of these activities CO 11th Battalion, Lyon Johnston, acquired his nickname "Tipperary" Johnston while the battalion was on the homeward leg of a five day route march when the battalion transport took a wrong turn and was temporarily lost. Lyon Johnston riding past a group of footsore soldiers tried to cheer them up by quipping: "Well, my lads! It's a long way to Tipperary, but we'll get there sometime."[74] It was during this foundation period that COs moulded the character and set the tone of their unit – for good or ill.

Training then progressed to musketry and some rudimentary tactical training. It is a commonly held misnomer that the AIF's soldiers had some natural ability with firearms as many were supposedly crack kangaroo shooters from the bush. These beliefs are not supported by the evidence and have been thoroughly debunked by the late Graham Wilson.[75] Members of the 1st Division were far more likely to be from the major urban centres of NSW and Victoria than they were from the back blocks of rural Australia. As for shooting, the 1st Battalion is typical when it recorded the results of its first range practice as "only moderate as [the] men were unacquainted with the Rifle."[76] Early musketry training was also limited by access to ranges and at the major mobilisation centres in Sydney and Melbourne there was considerable congestion as whole brigades attempted to qualify soldiers.[77]

Access to facilities improved in Egypt as new ranges were built but ammunition restrictions continued to hinder efforts. The initial allocation of 50 rounds per 18-pounder field gun, 2000 rounds for each machine-gun and 120 rounds per rifle for all training was progressively reduced to only 30 rounds per gun and 75 rounds for the other weapons, including the machine-guns.[78] This paltry allocation was barley sufficient for the majority of the division's soldiers to complete the musketry course and it meant that only about half of its soldiers were eventually classified as proficient shots.[79]

72 Bean, *AOH*, Vol. I, p. 99; Stevenson, *To Win the Battle*, p. 85.
73 For attitudes to early training and drill see Private G. Feist, letter, May 1915, quoted in Bill Gammage, *The Broken Years* (Ringwood: Penguin Books, 1975), p. 44; State Library of Victoria: MS11300, MSB401, Gunner Leo Gwyther, diary entry 18 December 1914.
74 Walter C. Belford, *Legs-Eleven: Being the Story of the 11th Battalion AIF in the Great War of 1914-1918* (Perth: Imperial Printing Company, 1940), p. 18.
75 Graham Wilson, *Bully Beef and Balderdash: Some Myths of the AIF Examined and Debunked* (Newport: Big Sky Publishing, 2012).
76 AWM4, 23/18/1: 1st Battalion (AIF), War Diary, 9 September 1914.
77 In Victoria it took a week for the 2nd Brigade's battalions to fire a single practice. Austin, *Our Dear Old Battalion*, p. 18.
78 AWM27, 352/19: 'Divisional Order No. 8', 14 December 1914; Divisional Order No 26, 8 January 1915; Divisional Order No 29, 12 January 1915.
79 In 1915 95 percent of the 1st Division had fired the musketry course but only 51 percent were classified as 1st, 2nd or 3rd Class shots or marksmen. AWM27, 352/19: 'Summary of – Personnel Statistics', attached to Divisional Order No. 43, 27 January 1915.

Egyptian interlude: 'D' Company, 1st Battalion AIF at Mena Camp, January 1915. (Private collection)

Aside from the soldiers, the division's leaders also needed training. Although the majority of the officers had some previous service, many were not currently active having come from the Unallotted List and these officers had to be brought up to date with changes in doctrine and uniform standards established.[80] In essence, the effect of the decentralised mobilisation process, delays and shortages in equipping the force, and the shortage of qualified instructors all retarded the best efforts of COs to train their units. Indeed, the effectiveness of training before the division sailed must be rated as marginal and it would be hard to reject Jeffrey Grey's conclusion that "the 1st Division was probably the worst-trained formation ever sent from Australian shores."[81]

In fairness to Bridges and his commanders it was always envisaged that the 1st Division would complete its training in Britain before going to France. So, when the convoy arrived in Egypt and the disparate elements of the division were finally assembled at Mena Camp, training began in earnest.[82] Uncertain of how long he would have to prepare his division, Bridges was keen to make a start. In the division's second order, issued on 10 December, commanders of the formations and direct command units were instructed to submit their training programmes to divisional headquarters within four days. Given that no decision had been made as to the immediate future of the 1st Division, an indicative time frame was provided: one month for sub-unit

80 For example, units introduced various 'Tactical Exercises Without Troops' which practised company commanders in planning and preparing orders. AWM27, 304/49: 'Scheme A1', 'Scheme A2', 'Scheme B', 'Scheme C', (n.d.).

81 Jeffrey Grey, *A Military History of Australia*, Third ed. (Port Melbourne: Cambridge University Press, 2008), p. 93.

82 AWM27, 352/19: 'Divisional Order No. 1', 9 December 1914.

(squadron, battery and company) training; ten days for unit (regiment and battalion) training; and ten days for formation (infantry brigades and divisional artillery) training; and this was to be followed by an undefined period for divisional work. Each formation was allocated an area around Mena and artillery and musketry ranges were established.[83] By any standard this was an ambitious programme.[84]

Four days after Birdwood arrived in Egypt to take command of the ANZAC he assessed his force. In a letter to Lord Kitchener he reported that the training of the corps was backward and that the troops had not been drilled in "bayonet fighting, no digging, very little musketry ... Their artillery too is very indifferent [but] the material is excellent."[85] The corps artillery commander would later recollect:

> The Australian artillery...was practically untrained. No one had ever worked with a bigger unit than a battery or battalion, and co-operation between units was unknown ... Two or three officers had done some artillery work, but the bulk were quite new. Except for a little training in Australia and Egypt, all the knowledge they had was from drill books and from what they had seen in Egypt ... Practice camps were started after I had got some ammunition, with some difficulty. Very few officers had ever shot a battery. The actual drill, and seeing where the shells burst, were good, but few knew what effective shrapnel ought to be.[86]

The training programme Bridges launched was by the standards of the day arduous and the soldiers in general threw themselves into it. Training lasted for at least eight hours a day (often more) every day except Sundays.[87] Company and battery training was supposed to last until January 1915 but on New Year's Day the infantry battalions, at Birdwood's insistence, adopted the newer British four-company organisation and on the following day began training anew. The battalions buckled down even if they were beginning from a very low point as one regular officer noted in mid-January: "Our infantry are our weakest point in the division."[88]

Unit and brigade collective training revolved around a series of deployments out into the desert followed by a tactical exercise that sometimes lasted several days. After one exercise involving the 2nd Brigade, a junior officer noted that it was the hardest 24 hours he had ever done: "Route march, attack, entrenching, outpost, return march."[89] By late March the same officer who had been so critical of the infantry just six weeks earlier would modify his opinion:

83 AWM27, 352/19: 'Divisional Order No. 2', 10 December 1914.

84 The New Army divisions were issued a training programme based on six months. From raising to landing on Gallipoli the 1st Division had a total of eight months, which included a month to mobilise, and a month at sea.

85 The National Archives (TNA): PRO 30/57/64 WL138: Kitchener Papers, Birdwood to Kitchener, 25 December 1915.

86 C. Cunliffe Owen, 'Artillery at Anzac in the Gallipoli Campaign, April to December 1915', *The Journal of the Royal Artillery*, 56:12 (1919–20), pp. 536–37.

87 Bean, *AOH*, Vol. I, p. 125.

88 Lieutenant William Dawkins, letter to brother, 11 January 1915, quoted in Judith Ingle, *From Duntroon to the Dardanelles: A Biography of Lieutenant William Dawkins* (Canberra: J. Ingle, 1995), p. 117.

89 AWM: 3DRL2632, 3/1: Morshead Papers, Captain Leslie Morshead, diary entry 9 February 1915.

> The training they have done here is absolutely strenuous as it could possibly be. The limit of what the men can do has been reached and under most adverse circumstances always marching in from 6" to 12" of sand and digging-in in difficult rocky country. The force physically is in the peak of condition and Australia never has, nor will turn out a fighting force to equal this 1st Division.[90]

Indeed, the units appeared to be making such progress that Bridges was encouraged to reduce working hours.[91]

Training culminated in a series of divisional schemes with Bridges manoeuvring his brigades in accordance with plans developed by HQ ANZAC. These training days were designed to practice the full range of divisional combat and service capabilities and the HQ reported favourably on the standard achieved. The GSOIII, Major Thomas Blamey, noted in the war diary: "Men worked very well – generally speaking an instructive day; work at Div HQ proceeded smoothly, 1st Inf Bde covering troops well disposed, attack well carried out."[92] As for the artillery, Birdwood still had concerns writing in early February, "I find that 80 percent of my Australian artillery and 50 percent of the NZ artillery have never yet seen a gun fired, so you can realise how far down one has had to begin with them."[93] Over the three months the gunners worked hard and progress was rapid although it remained at an elementary level.

While the ANZAC commanders were able to make their training hard in a physical sense, what they could not achieve, given the general shortage of material and especially ammunition, was the opportunity to make training realistic. Some form of battle inoculation could have introduced those non-veteran officers and soldiers to the confusion, noise and sights of battle. Certainly, some field firing was conducted but little attempt seems to have been made to run these activities under simulated combat conditions by day and night. It was simply peacetime training, only harder.[94]

By March, Bridges was aware that his division was to be committed to Gallipoli. This operation was to be an amphibious assault upon a defended shore – probably the most complex of all military operations. Today this type of operation is habitually allocated to permanently organised bodies of specialists who are trained and equipped just for such a task. This was not well appreciated in 1915 and in any case, Bridges just had to make do with what he had. Despite the short timeframe Bridges and his commanders did what they could to prepare for the landings. When the ships carrying the 1st Division arrived at Mudros, disembarkation and embarkation drills were practiced both by day and night. Unfortunately, poor weather precluded training on

90 Lieutenant William Dawkins to Mrs White (family friend), 24 March 1915, quoted in Ingle, *From Duntroon to the Dardanelles*, p. 140.

91 AWM: 3DRL1473, 93: Gellibrand Papers, '1st Australian Divisional Orders No. 47', 26 January 1915.

92 AWM4, 1/42/3 Part 1: GS HQ 1st Australian Division, War Diary, 1 April 1915.

93 Birdwood to Lieutenant-Colonel O. Fitzgerald (Secretary to Lord Kitchener), 2 February 1915, quoted in David Horner, *The Gunners: A History of Australian Artillery* (St Leonards: Allen & Unwin, 1995), p. 85.

94 Godley at least ensured that the leadership of his units had done some attacks with live ammunition and over a three-day period the officers and NCOs of the 4th Brigade (AIF), part of his New Zealand & Australia Division, carried out instructional attacks using blank ammunition and then ball ammunition. TNA: WO95/4280: ANZAC GS WD, 30 March–1 April 1914.

several days however, there were at least some attempts to conduct 'dress rehearsals' with the 3rd Brigade, which was selected as the corps' covering force.[95]

Much like the training in Egypt, however, preparations on Lemnos before the landings were limited and lacked realism. If the landing exercises were meant to be mission rehearsals, they only left many of the men understandably anxious. Most recognised the importance of this baptism of fire, even if most were fortunately too inexperienced to be truly daunted by the forthcoming operation. Private Tom Richards, a former rugby international noted "I don't feel the coming danger any more than I have felt anxious the night before an International football match."[96] Others looked forward to the challenge ahead even though they had no idea of what lay ahead for them. A 4th Battalion soldier recorded on the eve of the landings: "All the boys tonight are singing and are in great spirits, bayonets are sharpened and everything made ready for tomorrow."[97] Whatever the outward manifestations of bravado, it can be assumed that all felt the tension and the enormity of the task ahead and none perhaps more than the divisional commander. Even the normally stoic Bridges must have felt some apprehension on the dark night of 24 April as the transports sailed east and he and his raw division were about to face their first major test.

The 1st Division's orders for the landings were issued as "Operation Order No. 1" from the *Minnewaska*, the former passenger liner carrying HQ 1st Division, and were distributed one week before landings.[98] The passage of orders from Bridges down to the soldiers who had to execute the plan passed through five levels of command. In the first instance the GOC relied on his senior staff to draft the divisional orders. At brigade level the two lead brigades had independent tasks and for Sinclair-MacLagan he had to rely heavily on his unit commanders as each had widely separated objectives along the third ridge on a frontage of over five kilometres.[99] It was the same for McCay whose units were to seize two heights to the north covering nearly two kilometres.[100] Then at each succeeding level, command was devolved and unit and sub-unit commanders prepared their plans and orders. At each level the orders needed to be simple, clear and relevant; unfortunately, this was not usually the case and given the many variables most orders were necessarily broad, with much being left to the initiative of the COs responding to developments ashore.

At the bottom of the chain of command most junior leaders and soldiers felt that they were given precious little useful information. As an example of the quality of low-level orders, those for C Company 2nd Battalion contain an extensive list of identified enemy positions and outlines the brigades' first object, but it does not include a battalion mission or task and simply notes that there are "8 landing places between FISHERMAN's HUT and KABA [sic] TEPE."[101] Tom Richards went on to describe the brief given by his commander:

95 AWM25: 367/5: Captain C.G. Dix, '"Anzac": Impressions of the Landing and 14 weeks work on the Beach', p. 7.

96 Lance Corporal Tom Richards 24 April 1915 diary entry quoted in Greg Growden, *Gold, Mud 'N' Guts: The Incredible Tom Richards: Footballer, War Hero, Olympian* (Sydney: ABC Books, 2001), p. 7.

97 AWM: 1DRL/0240: Sergeant A.L. de Vine, diary entry, 24 April 1915.

98 AWM4: 1/42/3 Part 2: 1st Australian Division 'Operation Order No 1', 18 April 1915; 'Disembarkation Orders', 18 April 1915.

99 AWM4, 1/42/3 Part 2: 1st Australian Division 'Instructions to Officer Commanding Covering Force', 18 April 1915; AWM25, 367/175: 3rd Infantry Brigade 'Operation Order No 1', 21 April 1915.

100 AWM4, 1/25/1 Part 7: 2nd Infantry Brigade 'Operation Order No 5', 21 April 1915

101 AWM: 3DRL 2632, 3/1: Morshead Papers, 'Orders for Landing', 24 April 1915.

> He gave particulars of numbers and battalions landing and what was expected of them. His speech was full of fine humour, dealing chiefly with our funky condition and likely fear. It was hardly the kind of speech one would expect on the eve of big doings, as there was plenty of ridicule, nonsense, but no hard facts or detailed information. It seemed more as through we were preparing for a pantomime instead of grim warfare. Don't mean for one moment that he should have made us melancholy and miserable, but he could have given us something like an idea of what to expect.[102]

The reality is that this officer did not know himself and the lack of "hard" information was only a reflection of the inexperience of most commanders.

The Beachhead Battle and beyond

The initial landing by the Australian covering force in the predawn dark of 25 April was accomplished against light opposition and with slight loss. Just six Ottoman rifle platoons of the *2nd Battalion, 27th Regiment* covered nearly five kilometres of coastline in the vicinity of ANZAC landing area between Fisherman's Hut and Gaba Tepe and they did so without machine-gun support. Despite popular mythology, the landings did not occur on the wrong beach, as what became known as Anzac Cove was within the parameters set by the Royal Navy.[103] The bunching of the small boats during the final run-in to the beach did however, result in most of the first wave troops landings within the confines of the cove rather spread over a broader area to the south as anticipated. Despite this, Sinclair-MacLagan's troops brushed aside the light screen of Ottoman troops and advanced in a ragged line of small groups to the second ridge where the covering force commander halted them. By the time McCay landed, Sinclair-MacLagan had already changed Bridges' plan and with McCay's concurrence the 2nd Brigade was diverted to the southern sector of the second ridge instead of advancing to secure the vital ground on the Sari Bair range to the north. Bridges was forced to accept this change when he landed at about 9:00 a.m. The buildup of ANZAC forces continued and by 2:00 p.m. about 12,000 Australian troops were ashore, facing 5,000 Ottoman troops who were force marched to the area. Then in the afternoon disembarkation was halted for four hours as the transports were forced to move further offshore because of Ottoman artillery fire. By 6:00 p.m. about 15,000 ANZAC and Indian troops were ashore consisting of the three Australian infantry brigades of Bridges' division, half of the New Zealand Infantry Brigade, one Australian 18-pounder field gun, two Indian mountain batteries, a casualty clearing station, the bearer sub-divisions of the three Australian field ambulances and details of engineers and signallers. Despite the confusion of the initial landing, a comparatively favourable beachhead was secured. Although fragmented and fighting in small groups, with little overall coordination, the ANZAC was in occupation of most of the second ridge which, except at one point on the northern flank where a dangerous gap existed, was practical for defence. They had also succeeded in defeating a series of Ottoman counterattacks.[104]

102 Richards diary entry, quoted in Growden, *Gold, Mud 'N' Guts*, pp. 134–35.

103 Naval historian Tom Frame has effectively rebutted the long-held belief in an unpredicted offshore current and the misplacement of the landing. Tom Frame, *The Shores of Gallipoli: Naval Aspects of the Anzac Campaign* (Alexandria: Hale & Iremonger, Alexandria, 2000), pp. 183–210.

104 Stevenson, *To Win the Battle*, p. 115.

Anzac Cove: Unloading supplies shortly after the landing.

On the other hand, to the commanders on the spot, there appeared to be many disturbing signs. The 14 Australian and New Zealander infantry battalions had been unable to gain more than half the objectives which Hamilton had assigned to the four battalions of the corps' covering force. Owing to the broken ground and the thick scrub, every unit was widely scattered and tactical organisation fractured. Every available man had been thrust into the battle and for the moment, there were no reserves. The Ottoman defenders, in contrast, were correctly believed to have strong reinforcements in the immediate vicinity. So much small arms ammunition had been expended during the day that its replacement was causing anxiety and the lack of transport and the difficulties of sending water to the forward troops on the precipitous ridges presented the administrative staff with a seemingly insurmountable challenge. The number of ANZAC casualties could not yet be accurately estimated but were believed to be heavy. The arrival of these pessimistic assessments at Bridges' headquarters precipitated the conference at which withdrawal was proposed. This we now know was rejected by Hamilton, but it raises questions over the performance of Bridges and his subordinates.

The controversy surrounding Australian performance one the day of the landings was quietly shelved during the war due to the need for imperial solidarity. It was resurrected in the post-war period as Australia and Britain were preparing their respective official histories. Bean led the charge in 1921 with his hastily published first volume of the Australian history covering the raising of the AIF and the landings. While covering some controversial episodes, any criticism of Australian leaders or soldiers was muted. Five years later the Historical Section, which was responsible for the British Official History, sent copies of Cecil Aspinall's draft chapters about the Gallipoli landings to Australia for comment. According to Aspinall's account, the initial landing was relatively easy and successful but by the afternoon confusion among the Australians prevented any coordinated operations, which could have secured their objectives. Moreover, by late afternoon the "severe strain to young and untried troops in their first day of battle" was beginning to tell. "For many the breaking point had now been passed, and numbers of unwounded men were filtering back to the beach in an endless stream" so that "the gullies in the rear were choked with stragglers and men who had lost their way."[105]

When the draft chapters were circulated for comment in Australia they caused immediate concern. General Sir John Gellibrand, who was a divisional staff officer at the landings, felt that they offered "a cruel libel" although he had to confess that "There were criminal stragglers from Lieutenant-Colonel to Privates" but suggested "their number was negligible."[106] Thomas Blamey, who also served on the staff, offered various reasons for the confusion ashore none of which involved a breakdown of command and control.[107] Sir John Monash, who commanded the 4th Brigade in Godley's division, countered and was reported in the press as claiming that "Australian discipline under fire was the finest he had ever known."[108] Garnering this support Bean wrote to Aspinall laying out his case that the straggler problem was insignificant.[109]

At this point the story leaked to the press. Inaccurate newspaper reports claimed that the British official history had described the Australians as "a disorganised rabble" and that they were "ill-trained and ill-led."[110] These articles provoked a flurry of accusations, denials and counter criticisms from former Australian officers and a publishing bonanza for the popular press across the empire for nearly two months.[111] Bean moved quickly, writing to and castigating those papers that published the unsubstantiated and false reports but the damage was done and in their vitriolic rebuttals a number of senior Australian officers misguidedly attacked both Aspinall and the reputation of Britain's troops.[112] Aspinall replied to Bean's concerns, noting that he had in fact only cited Bean's own account and refuted any exaggeration of the straggling problem by referring to comments from others who were at the landings. He felt that, if anything, his account under-played the problem.[113]

Eventually the Australian government weighted into the debate demanding substantial amendments be made to the British volume, effectively eliminating any criticism.[114] Aspinall rightly felt slighted as a historian, acknowledging that he had found that particular chapter on the Anzac landings:

> [A] difficult one to write because the truth about the Australians has never yet been told and in its absence a myth has sprung up that the Anzac troops did magnificently against amazing odds... The draft, except in one quarter, met with entire approval. Sir Ian Hamilton, Sir W. Birdwood, General Sinclair MacLagan (who commanded the Covering

105 Aspinall quoted in Alistair Thomson, '"History and Betrayal": The Anzac Controversy', *History Today*, 43 (January 1993), p. 8.
106 AWM38, 3DRL 7953/27 Part 1: Gellibrand letter to Bean, 27 June 1927.
107 Ibid., Part 1: Blamey letter to Bean, 31 May 1927.
108 'Difficulties of the Landings', *The Advertiser* (Adelaide), 8 October 1927, p. 15.
109 AWM38, 3DRL 7953/27 Part 1: Bean letter to Aspinall, 9 June 1927.
110 'The Epic of Anzac', *The Australasian* (Melbourne), 15 October 1927, p. 42.
111 For the large body of articles see AWM38: 3DRL7953/29, Parts 1 and 2: Bean Papers.
112 AWM38: 3DRL7953/27 Part 1: Bean Papers, Bean letter to the editor, *The Daily Guardian* (Sydney), 7 October 1927.
113 AWM38: 3DRL7953/27 Part 1: Bean Papers, Aspinall letter to Bean, 27 July 1927.
114 AWM38: 3DRL7953/27 Part 1: Bean Papers, Acting Secretary Department of Defence, memo for Secretary Prime Minister's Department.

> Force), the War Office, the Admiralty, the New Zealand Govt. & War Office, all saw it & approved it without comment, and even General Edmonds himself pronounced it as 'excellent'. Col. Daniel [of the Foreign Office] also approved it. The one exception was the Australian Govt., who asked to have various amendments made. Some of these amendments were fair, others were at the expense of historical accuracy; but in the new draft every word that was objected to by the Australians has been expunged.[115]

When Aspinall's amended history was published in 1929 it was favourably received in Australia and Britain. The controversy of 1927 was quietly forgotten, and the Anzac legend remained untarnished.

Despite Australian claims there were firsthand observers who witnessed the confusion and straggling and they believed it was significant. Major Herbert Wallis, a British regular who was Staff Captain 2nd Brigade, saw for himself the conditions in the gullies and on the beach, describing 25 April was a "tragic day" of "chaos".[116] Sinclair-MacLagan offered his views soon after the landings on what he described the "general disintegration" of his infantry.[117] Talbot Hobbs, wrote after the war how he "could not help being depressed at the streams of wounded and the number of stragglers, making their way to the beach, already congested with wounded."[118] At one point McCay became infuriated with soldiers retreating to the beach, shouting that they were cowards and curs while driving them back towards the firing line with his drawn pistol.[119]

There was no suggestion by Aspinall that the majority of officers and soldiers shirked their duty. It cannot be denied however, that the straggler problem was serious, and it simply reflects the lack of experience of all. By nightfall divisional casualties were estimated at about 500 fatalities, 2,500 wounded and another 2,000 missing, amounting to about one third of the division's fighting strength.[120] In some cases in the absence of strong leadership, units simply disintegrated.[121] Exaggerated reports as to the seriousness of the situation arrived at various headquarters and most alarming was the disturbing number of leaderless men filtering back to the beach. These reports were made by Australian officers, notably McCay who reported to Bridges at about 5:20 p.m. that "a considerable number of unwounded men were leaving the firing line."[122] The heavy casualties among the senior and junior commanders had left many troops leaderless and there were probably up to 1,000 stragglers among the hundreds of wounded lying on the

115 Aspinall quoted in Thomson, 'History and Betrayal", p 10.
116 Ibid.
117 AWM4, 1/42/3 Part 2: 'Summary of Operations of 1st Australian Division from 25th April', 9 May 1915.
118 Sir Talbot Hobbs, 'A Gunner's Reflections: Gallipoli Campaign', *The Reveille*, 5:7 (31 March 1932), p. 29.
119 Wray, *Sir James Whiteside McCay*, pp. 13–22, 33.
120 Birdwood observed that there were about 2,000 ANZAC "missing", Bean thought that there were at least 1,000 men on the beach alone, Dawkins suggested somewhere between 600 and 1,000, while Williams suggests that another 1,000 were probably in the gullies behind the line. AWM: 3DRL3376/37: Birdwood Papers, Birdwood to GHQ MEF, 8 May 1915; Birdwood, *Khaki and Gown*, p. 259; C.E.W. Bean, *Gallipoli Mission*, (Canberra: AWM, 1948), p. 74; Ingle, *From Duntroon to the Dardanelles*, p. 156; Peter Williams, *The Battle of Anzac Ridge: 25 April 1915* (Loftus: Australian Military History Publications, 2007), p. 117.
121 Coulthard-Clark, *A Heritage of Spirit*, p. 155.
122 Bean, *AOH*, Vol. I, p. 454.

beach. Perhaps up to another 1,000 stragglers were also in the gullies behind the line. Some may have been avoiding the firing line, having become demoralised by Ottoman fire, while others may simply have lost their unit and were looking for someone to direct them. The collapse of command and control meant that many would not find their units for several days and it was not just the soldiers who were found wanting.

Although the achievement of the 1st Division in securing a toe-hold on the peninsula is worthy of acclamation, the fact remains that the division failed to achieve its mission of securing the heights of Sari Bair and the third ridge, and so it was unable to advance on Mal Tepe to cut the peninsula. The reasons for the failure have been catalogued in many publications, though Tim Travers provides a good summary of the commonly accepted issues including:

> [A] loss of surprise … the last-minute shift to the right flank orientation after the landing by Sinclair MacLagan; confusion in the difficult scrub country resulting in lack of cohesion, communication, discipline and direction; mediocre leadership in certain areas … failure to land field artillery, leaving Anzac troops under demoralizing and continuous shrapnel fire; a stern baptism of fire for mostly untried troops; relative failure of naval supporting fire; the lengthy four-hour halt in the landing troops in the afternoon of 25 April; a reasonably quick Turkish response; and very effective Turkish shrapnel and sniper fire.[123]

Whilst Travers acknowledges the problem of "mediocre [Australian] leadership in certain areas" he posits this as just one factor in a considerable list. However, many of his other reasons have their roots in the poor performance of Bridges and many of his subordinates. The shift to the right flank was a decision by Sinclair-MacLagan; the confusion and collapse of cohesion in the infantry was the direct result of the division's officers failing to keep their men in check and under control; the lack of artillery support was the result of the direct intervention of Bridges, his staff and Birdwood; and if the troops became demoralised, surely this reflects poorly on how the division was trained and prepared by its officers.

While many Australian commanders rose to the occasion and provided leadership, suffering a disproportionately high casualty rate in the process, others had their inexperience cruelly exposed and wilted under the chaotic conditions. While no one could doubt Bridges' personal courage, he was a difficult leader, and this led to some of his directions being badly executed and his support of the suggestion to abandon the landings smacks of panic.[124] If matters were deemed so dire in the evening, Bridges had an obligation to see for himself and not rely solely on the opinions of his brigade commanders. The evidence suggests that he made only one short reconnaissance on the morning of 25 April and thereafter spent his time with his headquarters staff near the beach.[125] A desperate situation required the personal presence of the commander and some inspirational leadership, Bridges offered his troops neither. One soldier later recalled:

> Bridges, Godley or White could have ascertained the condition of the troops by a 15-minute walk to the line at Steele's or Courtney's Posts – both pretty hot centres – where

123 Tim Travers, *Gallipoli 1915* (Stroud: Tempus, 2001), p. 82.
124 Coulthard-Clark, *A Heritage of Spirit*, p. 163; Bean, *Two Men I Knew*, pp. 67–68; Bean, *AOH*, Vol. I, p. 69.
125 Coulthard-Clarke, *A Heritage of Spirit*, pp. 154–55.

> demoralisation of the troops was completely non-existent. None did so. They permitted themselves to be dominated by the fears generated during the day's tension in the relative security of headquarters by the reports of returning wounded...if there was any demoralisation at ANZAC that night it was in their own headquarters.[126]

Nor was Bridges' physical lethargy his only failure. The commander knew when he landed at about 7:00 a.m. that matters had gone awry and while he could not rectify Sinclair-MacLagan's change of plan, he could have exercised better control over his reserves.[127] These he doled out throughout the day at every call of crisis. At the same time he appears to have made insufficient effort to collect the growing number of stragglers and either return them to the line or form an *ad hoc* reserve on the beach. Bean refers to certain staff officers collecting stray men and employing them as carrying parties or reinforcement groups but none of this work appears to have been preplanned despite Bridges and his key commanders having conducted an offshore reconnaissance to assess the ground.[128] Finally there is the matter of the use of the divisional artillery.

As the most technically qualified artillery officer in the Australian army Bridges might be expected to have employed his artillery to better effect but the evidence is that he thwarted every effort to bring his guns into action. Originally some 18-pounders were to have been landed by 9:00 a.m. but Bridges and Birdwood, without consulting Hobbs, agreed that no field artillery would be landed until later in the day. At about midday the Indian mountain guns were brought into action however by 2:30 p.m. these guns had been so badly pounded by the Ottoman artillery that they were unable to fire and were withdrawn to the beach leaving the infantry unsupported.[129] When the first 18-pounders were landed at about 3:25 p.m. an unnamed staff officer ordered that they be returned to their transport because no suitable positions could be found in the precipitous country despite Hobbs and his subordinates having identified some already. In this instance it appears that Birdwood ordered the guns returned, fearing their loss.[130]

The final charge that may be laid against Bridges is his lack of judgement in even suggesting the withdrawal. If an opposed beach landing is the hardest military operation to plan and conduct, a withdrawal at night in contact with the enemy is a close second. It is inconceivable that Bridges and Godley thought this could be actioned in the time they had and under the conditions they faced. Both commanders were aware that there were approximately 16,000 troops ashore. Pre-landing planning identified that the maximum capacity of the boats for ship-to-shore was about 2,000 even before the losses due to enemy fire during the day. They would also have been aware that the only practical evacuation routes ran down Monash and Shrapnel valleys between the second and first ridges. This route would be quickly dominated by the Ottomans if the firing line on the second ridge withdrew. With hindsight the sheer ludicrousness of the proposal led the three senior ANZAC commanders to distance themselves from it.

As soon as the situation settled down and it became clear that the ANZAC could hold on to their narrow position, the three senior ANZAC commanders all shifted the blame for

126 AWM: 3DRL3520: Bazley Papers, H.V. Howe letter to Arthur Bazley, 24 November 1963.
127 Coulthard-Clarke, *A Heritage of Spirit*, p. 156.
128 Bean, *AOH*, Vol. I, pp. 466–7.
129 David Coombes, *The Lionheart: A Life of Lieutenant-General Sir Talbot Hobbs* (Loftus: Australian Military History Publications, 2007), pp 42-45.
130 Horner, *The Gunners*, pp. 52, 91.

the suggestion to withdraw. Birdwood has already been quoted as claiming that he was only persuaded to signal Hamilton by the "intense anxiety of his subordinates."[131] After the war he wrote that he felt bound to report what his divisional commanders felt "if only because every report I had sent him [Hamilton] so far (and these reports had been largely based on what Bridges himself had told me) had been entirely optimistic."[132] Bridges claimed that the initial idea for withdrawal came from his brigade commanders, writing to his wife that they "thought they could not hold on for another day."[133] Godley in his autobiography also sheeted blame to his juniors writing that he was "delighted" to get Hamilton's message as this was passed "as far as possible to all brigadiers and commanding officers whose situation reports had necessitated the sending of Birdwood's message."[134] Bean backed the senior officer's stories.[135] While McCay did report considerable numbers of men were leaving the firing line and Sinclair-MacLagan expressed concerns over a renewed Ottoman counterattack, neither appears to have suggested a withdrawal nor were they present at the conference between Bridges, Godley and Birdwood. The decision to withdraw lay solely with the three seniors.

Then there is the matter of the performance of Bridges key subordinates who are also open to criticism. Of the infantry brigade commanders, Sinclair-MacLagan did well under trying conditions and his performance justifies Bridges confidence in him although there is the lingering belief that his realignment of the line in the morning undid the plan and squandered any chance for success. Bean is largely silent on MacLaurin who was killed soon after the landings. McCay appears to have been tactically adequate although Bean noted that his habit of threatening his men was "conformation of his excitability and foolish extravagance which robbed him of the respect of the men he led."[136] In Egypt Bridges had wanted to replace the commander of the 2nd Brigade because of his predilection to question every order and although he appears to have partially overcome his reputation as a difficult subordinate, McCay remained impulsive and was widely regarded by his men as a martinet who cared little for their welfare.[137] Talbot Hobbs tried his best with a bad situation, suffering constant disagreements with Birdwood and Bridges over the employment of the artillery but he too must also bear some of the responsibility for the failure to get his guns into action earlier on 25 April.[138] However Hobbs was not a party to the discussions over the withdrawal, recording in his diary that "General Birdwood, General Bridges & Staff [discussed] whether we should clear out or try & hang on, the position is extremely serious. I could not from where I was sitting keep hearing the discussion. I think they would decide to clear out but the navy can't do it…so they have decided to stay if we can hold on."[139]

Lower down the chain of command, the performance of the infantry COs was equally patchy. Once ashore the early fighting was largely a battalion and company commander's fight since the senior commanders lacked the means to coordinate their efforts. Here several COs proved poor

131 Bean, *AOH*, Vol. I, p. 458.
132 Birdwood, *Khaki and Gown*, p. 259.
133 Bridges to wife, 5 May 1915, quoted Coulthard-Clarke, *A Heritage of Spirit*, p. 162.
134 Godley, *Life of An Irish Soldier*, pp. 172–3.
135 Bean, *AOH*, Vol. I, p. 453.
136 AWM38: 3DRL 7953/27 Part 1: Bean letter to Aspinall, 8 September 1927.
137 Wray, *Sir James Whiteside McCay*, pp. 103, 105, 201.
138 Coombes, *The Lionheart*, pp. 42, 44, 66.
139 Hobbs diary, 25 April 1915, quoted in Coombes, p. 49.

choices. Bridges had already relieved James Semmens in Egypt due to chronic poor health and replaced him with Walter McNicoll, a school teacher and former part-time soldier, who had originally been appointed Second-in-Command 7th Battalion under Elliott.[140] Perhaps Bridges should have been more ruthless. Harry Lee went back to the beach soon after landing, leaving his men scattered and leaderless.[141] A similar inadequacy was observed in David Wanliss, while Leonard Dobbin is rarely mentioned in either official or unit histories, leaving the suspicion that his performance was also inadequate.[142]

Likewise, many of the junior leaders rose to the occasion while others proved indifferent or worse. A soldier in the 7th Battalion was probably closest to the truth when he lamented: "Our officers were too inexperienced, we had not enough training, and not enough information was given to the troops as to what was expected of them once they got ashore. There were no rallying points, and it was each man for himself for the first two or three days."[143] Popular accounts stress the strain on the soldiers during the landings, while they ignore the crisis among the division's senior leadership. For these officers the burden of command was particularly hard as the majority lacked operational experience, had only limited training and many were simply too old.[144]

In all fairness, 1st Division could probably never have won the landing battle, even with better leadership, given its technical, tactical and practical limitations: the limitations of the contemporary communications meant that Bridges struggled from the outset to control and coordinate his force in the fractured terrain, a lack of indirect fire support left the fighting largely to man and bayonet, and the inadequacy of its early training regime meant that many leaders and soldiers were not prepared for the shock of battle. At the end of that bloody day, it was the inadequacy of means to match ends that proved the 1st Division's undoing.

Epilogue

It was a dark, bitterly cold night on 18 December 1915 when in the early evening the first troops began leaving their trenches and making their way down towards Anzac Cove where lighters waited to carry then offshore to the waiting transports. Long columns of men marched in silence along deep trenches, their heavy tread deadened by sandbags laid along the trench floors and their way marked by trails of flour that stood out in the black night. At the beach the veterans quietly took their place in the boats. By 4:10 a.m. the next morning embarkation was complete, and the last man stepped off the pier. As the boat pulled away from the deserted shoreline, high above the beach on the brooding ridges an occasional rifle shot momentarily illuminated the old firing line, followed by the report of the shot as it echoed off the hill sides.

140 Ronald McNicoll, 'McNicoll, Sir Walter Ramsay (1877–1947)', *ADB*, Vol. 10, pp. 354–55.
141 State Library of New South Wales: MS2739: Rosenthal Papers, Rosenthal, diary entry 25 April 1915; Bean, *Two Men I Knew*, p. 56.
142 Bean, *AOH*, Vol. I, p. 387 and Vol. II, p. 88; Stacy, Kindon & Chedgey, *The History of the First Battalion AIF 1914–1919*, pp. 36–37, 40.
143 Private L. Pennefather, quoted in Austin, *Our Dear Old Battalion*, p. 72.
144 Bean, *AOH*, Vol. I, pp. 49–50.

Drip Rifle: Designed by Lance Corporal William Scurry (7th Battalion AIF), this self-firing device functioned by manipulated weight relief which resulted when two kerosene tins were positioned one above the other; the top tin full of water, the bottom tin empty with trigger string attached. To operate, two small holes would be punched into the upper tin, after which water would trickle into the lower tin thus discharging the rifle when sufficiently heavy.

The ingenious "drip rifles" would leave the impression that the empty frontline was still manned until long after the last man was long gone.

It was nearly eight months since the ANZAC landings on this fatal shore and finally the ANZACs were being spirited away just as their commanders had suggested on the night of the 25 April. The difference between the two situations however, was extreme. In April Bridges and Godley were panicked into their rash and ill-thought suggestion to abandon the beachhead and there was no plan and absolutely no chance of success. In contrast, the December withdrawal was a difficult but well-considered option to end a campaign that had clearly failed. The planning had taken a month and the staff work was mostly the product of Cyril Brudenell White, now a brigadier general and Birdwood's chief of staff. A thorough and professional plan brilliantly executed saw 35,000 men and most of their artillery thinned-out until the final night when the last 10,000 were whisked away under the very noses of the enemy. Not a soldier was lost. It was a triumph of meticulous planning rooted in hard won experience and executed by competent officers and disciplined men.[145]

The senior leadership of 1st Australian Division who executed this masterful operation were not the same officers who had led the division into battle in April. Bridges was dead, mortally wounded by an Ottoman sniper back on 15 May. Only one of the original formation commanders was present and that was Hobbs who still commanded the divisional artillery. MacLaurin was killed two days after the landings, McCay was wounded at Krithia on 8 May, and Sinclair-MacLagan was evacuated sick in May. Similarly, only a single original battalion

145 Bean, *AOH*, Vol. II, pp. 853–906; Stevenson, *To Win the Battle*, pp. 132–5.

commander was still with his unit. Onslow Thompson and Clarke had been killed on the day of the landings; Braund was accidentally shot by one of his men on 4 May; Owen was wounded in June and invalided home; Semmens' replacement McNicoll was severely wounded at Krithia; Bolton, broken and exhausted, relinquished command at own request in May; and Dobbin, Wanliss, Lee and Lyon Johnston were all evacuated sick. The indomitable "Pompey" Elliott, who was wounded at the landings, had returned and he was the only original infantry CO still commanding his battalion, while Stanley Weir was standing-in for Sinclair-MacLagan commanding the 3rd Brigade.[146]

The void created by the almost complete turnover of the division's senior hierarchy was filled by the next generation of Australia's combat leaders. After Bridges' death a succession of three officers commanded the 1st Division before Brigadier-General Harry Chauvel, an Australian Regular, assumed temporary command and oversaw the planning and conduct of the withdrawal. Commanding his three infantry brigades in December were: Brigadier-General Nevill Smyth, a British Regular who had commanded the 1st Brigade at Lone Pine during the August offensive and would go on to command the 2nd Australian Division on the Western Front; Brigadier-General John Forsyth, an Australian Regular, commanded the 2nd Brigade and would do so until October 1916; while tough old Weir temporarily commanded 3 Brigade. The replacement COs of the infantry battalions were, like their predecessors mostly former militia officers, although these men had come through the white heat of battle and proven their abilities on the Peninsula.[147]

While debate over the performance of the ANZAC on 25 April continues, little scrutiny has been given to Bridges and the role he and his brigade and battalion commanders played in the failure. It would be fair to suggest that most of the 1st Division officers at the Gallipoli landings lacked the prerequisite training, experience or both to execute their duties effectively in a difficult first action. Bridges was a superbly trained and technically competent artilleryman and intellectual staff officer, what he lacked was the right experience. Whatever his merits as an organiser and administrator, Bridges was a poor choice for a field command especially when his first opportunity was at the divisional level. For all his undoubted personal courage, which he amply demonstrated at the landings and the weeks following, on the night of 25 April he gave way to his fears under the intense psychological pressure and recommended a completely unworkable course of action that if implemented would most likely have resulted in the destruction of his division.

In fairness to Bridges he was placed in a very difficult position by his government. Hutton, for all of his personal foibles, would probably have been a better choice to raise and command the 1st Division, at least initially.[148] The Canadians were faced with a similar choice in 1914 and they chose Lieutenant-General Edwin Alderson, a British regular, to command their 1st Division. Alderson's prime competitor was Sir Sam Hughes, a Canadian-born militia officer and eccentric minister of militia who was temperamentally unsuited to high command. This fortuitous decision ensured that by the time Alderson was replaced in April 1916 he had shepherded the Canadian's through their training and first major action at Ypres in late April 1915

146 David Clare Holloway, *Combat Colonels of the AIF in the Great War* (Newport: Big Sky Publishing, 2014), pp. 29–34, 53–89, 275–76.
147 Ibid.
148 Hill, 'Hutton, Sir Edward Thomas Henry (1848–1923)', p. 418.

and his preparation of their early contingents stood them in good stead, allowing native-born officers to gain experience and eventually rise successively to division and corps command.[149] The New Zealanders chose Godley, who may have been an unsympathetic commander, but he too put the New Zealanders on a solid footing before Andrew Russell, a New Zealand-born former British regular, was promoted first to command the New Zealand and Australian Division in November 1915 and then to command the New Zealand Division in March 1916.[150] In Australia's case, nationalistic sentiment was allowed to trump military practicalities and with Hutton rejected, Bridges was thrust into a position he was not equipped to manage.

At brigade level, none of the three infantry commanders were trained or had commanded at that level before. Sinclair-MacLagan was the best of the group, having the advantage of regular training and previous operational experience but the disadvantage of limited command time; and his presumptuous decision to change the landing plan probably thwarted whatever slim chance there was for the division to capture its initial objectives on the first day. McCay's performance was more uneven and his impulsive nature quickly lost him the respect of his men so that he eventually became "the most disliked General with both men and officers throughout the AIF."[151] Following the debacle at Fromelles in July 1916, while commanding the 5th Australian Division, Birdwood quietly moved him to Britain to command the AIF training depots. MacLaurin's performance is the most difficult to assess since little is written of him although Bridges' decision to land his brigade last on 25 April indicates that he probably had less confidence in the young commander's abilities. His early death meant that he never had the opportunity to grow into a combat commander as others did – notably John Monash. Then there are the 12 battalion commanders who landed on that first day, most of whom were technically, mentally and physically not up to the demands of commanding an infantry battalion in modern combat for any extended period. Only Weir would survive the rigors of campaigning to take his battalion to France, while Elliott and NcNicoll would be promoted to command brigades.

The Anzac Cove landing is arguably Australia's national day of commemoration. Rightly or wrongly this event in the popular imagination is seen as the birth of the nation and the foundation of the Anzac legend and digger tradition. The firmly entrenched vision of gallant soldiers charging across a fire-swept beach to storm the perpendicular cliffs beyond is indelibly etched in the popular imagination. Thereafter the Anzacs clung tenaciously to their slim hold and there they remained for the next eight months. Thus a myth was born and one that usually ignores the role of command and leadership. Anzac mythology concedes little to Hamilton's fortunate appearance and the overriding of his subordinates' dire suggestion. As the humble private soldier – the digger – is the national hero of the Anzac landing legend, little scrutiny is directed at Australian middle and senior ranked officers, the only exception being Monash who has come to represent the archetypal citizen-soldier. In reality many of the first-generation officers – militia and regular – were of uneven quality and simply not up to the job.

149 Andrew Iarocci, *Shoestring soldiers: The 1st Canadian Division at War, 1914–15* (Toronto: University of Toronto, 2008), p. 17.

150 Colin Richardson, 'General Sir Alexander Godley: The Last Imperial Commander' and Glyn Harper, 'Major-General Sir Andrew Russell: Divisional Commander on the Western Front' in Glyn Harper & Joel Haywood (eds.), *Born to Lead?: Portraits of New Zealand Commanders* (Auckland: Exisle Publishing Toronto, 2008), pp. 39–53, 54–68.

151 AWM38, 3DRL606/116/1: Bean diary, 18 June 1918.

In the end, the nature of the pre-war Australian military forces, the rapid creation of the AIF and the swift commitment of the 1st Australian Division to battle, meant that there were few readily available officers who could have done a better job and there was simply too little time to adequately prepare those selected. Whatever the 1st Division became, and by 1918 it was one of the British Empire's best combat formations, the 1st Division at the Gallipoli landings was a brittle instrument wielded by unsteady hands. Under these circumstances the failure of the Australian Division on the first day was an inevitable tragedy.

12

Brigade Command: The ANZAC Experience

Chris Roberts

"I thought I could command men, I thought I could command men" Brigadier-General John Monash is reputed to have anguished amid the confusion surrounding his 4th Australian Infantry Brigade's situation, and failure to reach its objective on the morning of 7 August 1915.[1] Brigade command could be a tough and dangerous job, and in battle the commander was not always in charge of his formation's destiny – he was the conduit of turning a superior's plans and orders into practice, and while he could directly influence events he also relied on his own battalion or regimental commanders to carry his tasks through to fruition. In the historiography of the Great War, the place, role, and experiences of the brigade commander is rarely addressed; mostly a gap exists between studies of more senior commanders and those detailing the experiences of junior officers and soldiers.[2] For many of the ANZAC brigade commanders Gallipoli was their first real experience of command, and certainly under operational conditions. So who were these men, what was their background and experience for the responsibilities they carried out, what functions did they perform, what were the constraints they had to operate under, how did they perform, and did their role change as the campaign progressed?

Pre-War Notions of Brigade Command

In the hierarchy of British Army organisations the brigade was the smallest formation; consisting of units of the same type it was commanded by a brigadier-general, although Australian and New Zealand brigades were initially commanded by colonels. Whereas infantry brigades comprised a small headquarters, and four infantry battalions with a strength of 4,055 men, cavalry brigades with a headquarters, a signals troop, and three cavalry regiments numbered

1 Robert Rhodes James, *Gallipoli* (Sydney: Angus & Robertson Ltd, 1965), p. 272; Pedersen, P. A. *Monash as Military Commander.* (Melbourne: Melbourne University Press (MUP), 1985) p. 103

2 This gap has partially been filled by Simkins, Peter 'Building Blocks' in Gary Sheffield & Dan Todman (eds.), *Command and Control on the Western Front: The British Army's Experience 1914-18* (Staplehurst: Spellmount, 2004) pp. 141-171; and the very recent publication of Trevor Harvey's *An Army of Brigadiers: British Brigade Commanders at the Battle of Arras 1917* (Solihull: Helion, 2017).

1,718.[3] Artillery brigades, on the other hand, were the equivalent of a modern artillery regiment; being units rather than formations they fall outside the scope of this study. The primary role of the infantry brigade was to fight battles, while cavalry brigades were concerned with reconnaissance, screening larger formations, providing vedettes and advance, flank, and rear guards, and fighting either mounted employing shock action – the cavalry charge – or dismounted armed with the standard infantry rifle.[4] In Australia and New Zealand, however, the horsed arm was the mounted rifles, termed light horse in Australia, and often erroneously called mounted infantry. They performed all the functions of the cavalry except shock action and were issued only with the rifle and bayonet.[5]

Having no responsibility for the units that supported his brigade, such as artillery, engineers, medical, and transport, or the allocation and coordination of them in battle, pre-war the brigade commander's focus was on administering and supervising the training of his subordinate units, commanded by lieutenant-colonels, and was responsible for leading, directing, and controlling them on operations. He had two staff officers to assist him: the brigade major, for training and operational staff work, while the staff captain attended to administrative and logistic issues.[6] In battle he would be supported by artillery, but the brigade commander had little say in how the guns would be employed, except possibly when allotted a battery under his control. Responsibility for the tactical employment of the artillery lay with the divisional commander, and the Commander Royal Artillery (CRA) executed his orders as they related to the guns. The artillery would deploy and occupy positions under the direction of the CRA, although when tactical operations were not directly controlled by divisional headquarters, artillery and infantry would be "formed temporarily into groups under one commander" with artillery units placed at the disposal of the group commander.[7] Prevailing practice saw the infantry plan made separately, with the artillery then expected to support it.[8] Thus in terms of planning and execution, infantry brigade commanders and their supporting artillery operated independently of each other.

3 General Staff, War Office, *Infantry Training (4-Company Organisation) 1914* (London: HMSO, 1914) p. xiv; General Staff, War Office, *Field Service Pocket Book, 1914* (London: HMSO, 1914) p. 3, p. 7; Bruce Gudmundsen, *The British Expeditionary Force 1914-15* (Oxford: Osprey, 2005) pp. 51-53, p. 57.

4 Stephen Badsey, *Doctrine and Reform in the British Cavalry 1880-1918.* (Aldershot: Ashgate, 2008) Chapter 5; Spencer Jones, *From Boer War to World War: Tactical Reform of the British Army, 1902-1914.* (Norman: University of Oklahoma Press, 2012) Chapters 3 and 5.

5 Mounted infantry were just that: infantry units mounted on horses to provide them with mobility. Mounted rifles had wider roles. See Jean Bou, *Light Horse: A History of Australia's Mounted Arm.* (Cambridge: Cambridge University Press (CUP), 2010) p. 8, p. 28, pp. 68-70, p. 73.

6 *Field Service Pocket Book 1914,* p. 3, p. 7; Roger Lee, 'The Australian Staff: The Forgotten Men of the AIF.' in Peter Dennis & Jeffery Grey (eds.), *1918: Defining Victory,* (Canberra: Army History Unit, 1990) pp. 118-121; Simkins, 'Building Blocks.' pp. 146-147.

7 *Field Artillery Training (Provisional) 1912,* (London: HMSO, 1912), Sect. 151 p. 230; *Field Artillery Training 1914,* (London: HMSO, 1914), Sect. 151 p. 240; Marble, Sanders *The Infantry Cannot do with a Gun Less: The Place Of Artillery in The BEF 1914-1918* (New York: Columbia University Press, 2003), Chapter 2.

8 Shelford Bidwell & Dominick Graham, *Firepower: British Army Weapons and Theories of War 1904-1945* (London: George Allen & Unwin, 1982) p. 21.

In the decades prior to the Great War warfare was largely mobile involving the manoeuvring of formations and units on meeting the enemy. Battles were normally decided within the day they were fought, although a rare few were determined over periods of two or three days. Only in sieges were operations protracted, extending over weeks and months rather than days. It was a period of fluid warfare in which planning for battle was limited, decisions made quickly, orders were brief, and committal to battle was fast. In essence, most actions were what later became known as quick attacks. During the decisive campaign of the Franco-Prussian War, at Weissenburg, Worth, Spicheren, Mars-le-Tour, Gravelotte and Sedan the German armies had gone into action immediately on meeting the enemy with the outcome being decided by nightfall. Similarly in the South African War, the British mounted quick attacks at Elandslaagte, Stormberg and Diamond Hill. The set piece battle, or deliberate attack, with its lengthy, detailed planning, and comprehensive sets of orders were a thing of the future.

Brigadier-General (later Lieutenant-General) Sir John Monash.

Consequently, brigade commanders operated on the battlefield in the realm of the here and now, receiving orders at relatively short notice and executing them quickly. For the infantry, their objectives were largely determined for them by the divisional commander. The brigade commander then briefed his units, determined how they might best be deployed in battle, and was expected to get them to the right place at the right time in order to fight as part of a larger operation. In battle he moved with his units directing and manoeuvring them, making adjustments as events unfolded, and using his initiative in committing his reserve at a decisive moment or critical juncture.[9] Command in battle required leadership of a high order, with commanders exhibiting and instilling confidence in their men, exercising good judgement and decisiveness in meeting changing circumstances, and taking charge when things went wrong to ensure the mission was achieved. It was a difficult job, and even when the right decisions were taken disastrous consequences could occur or heavy casualties sustained against an enemy that strove to outfight and defeat them. Having no signals component for communications between him and his battalions, the infantry brigade commander operated close to his units on the battlefield, where he had visual observation and control over them – he fought alongside and shared the dangers of his troops. At the Gallipoli landings on 25 April 1915, for example, the leading brigade commanders went ashore immediately behind the first wave of assault troops – at Cape Helles two of the three British brigade commanders became casualties that morning, one being killed and the other seriously wounded,

9 Simkins, 'Building Blocks', p. 145.

while at Anzac on 27 April an Australian brigade commander was killed directing his men on the firing line.

British Command Philosophy

In conducting operations, commanders were given considerable latitude and expected to use their initiative to attain the objective set them. *Field Service Regulations, Part 1, Combined Training, 1905* outlined the British command philosophy:

> Decentralisation of command, and a full recognition of the responsibilities of subordinates in action, are thus absolutely necessary; and leaders must train their subordinates not only to work intelligently and resolutely in accordance with brief and very general instructions, but also to take upon themselves, whenever it may be necessary, the responsibility of departing from, or from varying, the orders they may have received.[10]

The same manual dictated that such departure was justified 'if the subordinate who assumes the responsibility is conscientiously satisfied that he is acting as a superior would order him to act if he were present.'[11] Its successor, *Field Service Regulations, Part 1, Operations, 1909* emphasised the decentralised approach:

> **An operation order should contain just what the recipient requires to know and nothing else.** It should tell him nothing which he can and should arrange for himself. The general principle is that the object to be attained, with such information as affects its attainment, should be briefly but clearly stated; while the method of attaining the object should be left to the utmost extant possible to the recipient, with due regard to his personal characteristics.[12]

Thus the British command philosophy was not that dissimilar to the oft-touted German *auftragstaktik* or directive control, and while a subordinate could alter his orders such a change had to be in accordance with achieving his commander's intent.[13]

ANZAC Brigades

Altogether twelve ANZAC brigades of the Australian Imperial Force (AIF) and the New Zealand Expeditionary Force (NZEF) fought at Gallipoli. Of these, ten were Australian (1st–7th Infantry and 1st–3rd Light Horse (LH)), the remaining two being the New Zealand (NZ)

10 Christopher Pugsley, *"We Have Been Here Before": The Evolution of the Doctrine of Decentralised Command in the British Army 1905-1989, Sandhurst Occasional Papers No. 9* (Sandhurst: Central Library Royal Military Academy, 2011) p. 9
11 Ibid.
12 General Staff, War Office, *Field Service Regulations, Part I, Operations, 1909* (Reprint 1914) (London: HMSO, 1914) p. 27. Emphasis in the original.
13 Ibid., p. 32.

Infantry Brigade and the NZ Mounted Rifles (NZMR) Brigade. 1st – 3rd Australian infantry brigades of the 1st Australian Division, and the NZ and 4th Australian infantry brigades of the understrength New Zealand and Australian (NZ&A) Division served throughout the campaign. To replace mounting casualties, the four mounted brigades arrived in mid-May, *sans* horses, and were attached to both divisions until the evacuation. In late August and early September, 5th–7th Australian infantry brigades (2nd Australian Division) arrived for the last three months of the campaign

Disregarding those who held temporary command for short periods, nineteen men from a range of backgrounds – professionally, socially and nationally – formally commanded these brigades during the campaign: fourteen Australians, two New Zealanders (one of whom was a British Regular Army officer), and three British. However, eight of them saw little action as brigade commanders. Henry MacLaurin (1st Australian Infantry Brigade) was killed two days after the initial landings, while Richard Linton died following the sinking of the *Southland* taking his 6th Australian Infantry Brigade to Gallipoli in September. Fifty-nine-year-old James Burston (7th Australian Infantry Brigade) was physically unable to handle the rigours of active service, being evacuated in October 1915 after one month on the peninsula. Charles Gwynn, who succeeded Linton, William Holmes (5th Australian Infantry Brigade) and John Paton, who succeeded Burston, all served during the defensive phase in the last three months of the campaign. Additionally, John Antill (3rd LH Brigade) and Gordon Bennett (3rd Australian Infantry Brigade) only assumed command towards the end of the campaign.[14] Their experience of brigade command on Gallipoli was too short to allow any objective discussion about them, although Paton was chosen to control the final hours of the withdrawal from Anzac. Of the remaining eleven men their military backgrounds varied, either being professional soldiers of the British Regular Army or the Australian Permanent Force (PF), or civilian part-timers who had come up through the indifferently trained Militia and Volunteers.

In an effort to improve military efficiency, both countries discarded the voluntary Militia and Volunteer Forces, and introduced part-time, compulsory training schemes: the New Zealand Territorial Force (TF) in 1910, and the Australian Citizen Force (CF) in 1911. Scattered regionally across each country, units were grouped into brigades but mostly trained independently; as Jean Bou notes the brigades "were, perhaps, still more theoretical than real."[15] Command of these brigades went to the part-time officers (the PF simply provided staff and instructors), and in reality the commanders spent much of the short time available to them on administrative issues, and directing the training of their scattered units, many of which were located across several sub-unit drill hills.

The opportunities to practice the art of command and controlling a brigade on manoeuvres were extremely limited, and often non-existent. Brigade level exercises if held, were on the last two or three days of an annual or biennial camp, and generally involved units being exercised under the brigade commander's supervision, rather than him being exercised. Nor were there

14 E.M. Andrews, 'Paton, John' in *The Australian Dictionary of Biography (ADB)*, Vol. 11, (Melbourne: MUP, 1988.); David Clare Holloway, *Combat Colonels of the AIF in the Great War.* (Newport: Big Sky, 2014) p. 31, p. 33, pp. 38-39, p. 41, pp 225-226; Roberts, Chris *The Landing at Anzac, 1915* (2nd Edition, Newport: Big Sky, 2015) pp. 137-140.

15 Jean Bou, 'An Aspirational Army: Australian Planning for a Citizen Forces Divisional Structure before 1920' in *Sabretache,* Vol XLIX, No 1, March 2008, p. 28.

any divisional headquarters to set, direct, and assess brigade level exercises. For Colonel John Monash of the CF 13th Infantry Brigade, two days were devoted to brigade manoeuvres on his first camp as commander in 1913. His post exercise critique, however, suggests his battalions were being exercised under his direction.[16] Moreover, these brigades would not serve in the Great War – the Defence Acts of both countries prohibited the employment of the TF and CF on overseas service. Consequently, when war broke out two new forces had to be raised from scratch – the NZEF and the AIF – and brigade commanders had to be found from those willing to volunteer for active service.

A Question of Experience

With the exception of two British Regulars, Brigadier-Generals Harold "Hooky" Walker and Neville Smyth VC, both of whom commanded the 1st Australian Infantry Brigade during the campaign and had held Regular Army unit commands prior to the war, the distinguishing feature of the remaining brigade commanders was their general lack of experience in command. The other two British Regulars, Ewan Sinclair-MacLagan and New Zealand born Francis Earl Johnston, had both seen active service, but had commanded nothing more than a rifle company. Seconded to the Australian Army in 1911 on promotion to temporary lieutenant-colonel, Sinclair-MacLagan was on the staff at the Royal Military College, Duntroon in 1914. Johnston was on leave in New Zealand in 1914 when he was promoted temporary lieutenant-colonel to command the Wellington Military District. On the outbreak of war both were promoted colonel and catapulted into command of the 3rd Australian and NZ infantry brigades respectively.[17]

New Zealand grazier Andrew Russell, like his countryman Johnston, had graduated first in his class from Sandhurst. After four years with the Border Regiment he resigned, returning to New Zealand where, in 1899, he formed a local militia mounted rifles unit, but did not serve in the South African War. A strong disciplinarian and advocate of hard training he was eventually appointed commander of the Wellington Mounted Rifles Brigade when the TF was formed, and of the NZMR Brigade when the NZEF was raised.[18]

The Australian PF and CF officers who held brigade command for much of the campaign had even less training or experience. Initially a Militia officer, Harry Chauvel transferred to the Queensland PF in 1896, and served in the South African War as a junior officer, which instilled in him the need for strong discipline and professionalism. On the federation of the colonies, he was absorbed into the Australian PF and served in a series of staff appointments, eventually being promoted colonel in 1913. As his biographer noted, however, he "could not be regarded

16 Pedersen, *Monash*, pp. 35-36.

17 War Office, *The Official Army List June 1914* (London: HMSO, 1914) p. 431, p. 489; *Who's Who 1916. Sixty-Eighth Year of Issue* (London: A&C Black 1916) p. 3024; A.J. Hill, 'Sinclair-MacLagan, Ewan George (1868-1948)', *ADB*, Vol 11 (Melbourne: MUP, 1988); Holloway, *Combat Colonels*, pp. 33-34, p. 39.

18 Christopher Pugsley, "Russell, Andrew Hamilton' in *The Dictionary of New Zealand Biography (NZDB)*, Vol. 3 (Wellington: Ministry of Culture,1996); Christopher Pugsley, *Gallipoli: The New Zealand Story*, (Auckland: Libro International, 2014) p. 55. Jock Vennell, *The Forgotten General: New Zealand's World War I Commander Major General Sir Andrew Russell* (Auckland: Allen & Unwin, 2014) pp. 14-20, pp. 40-43.

as a trained officer." On attachment to the British Army when war was declared Chauvel was appointed commander of the 1st LH Brigade, joining them in Egypt in December 1914.[19] Similarly, John Forsyth had served in the Militia before transferring to the Queensland PF in 1897, and later the Australian PF where he held junior staff appointments and undertook a year's exchange with a cavalry brigade in India. Promoted lieutenant-colonel in 1914, he enlisted in the AIF, raising the 4th LH Regiment and 1st LH Brigade, handing the latter over to Chauvel in Egypt. He assumed command of the 2nd Australian Infantry Brigade in July 1915.

The remainder had their military grounding in the Militia or Volunteers, of whom five had held brigade command prior to the war, including Holmes, Paton and Burston. Of the two who commanded for any length of time at Gallipoli, 57-year-old Melbourne land agent Frederic Hughes was initially a gunner before commanding the 11th LH Regiment from 1903, the 4th LH Brigade in 1907, followed by the CF 7th LH Brigade in 1911, and the AIF 3rd LH Brigade in November 1914.[20] He seems to have made little impression during his part-time career, as nothing is recorded about him other than his appointments. Civil engineer John Monash was a garrison artilleryman, and a keen student of military history who took his part-time soldiering seriously, establishing a high reputation for organisation, training, and meticulous staff work. Becoming Head of the Victorian Section of the Australian Intelligence Corps in 1908 he gained considerable exposure to brigade level tactics, both writing the narratives for and umpiring annual field exercises. Promoted to command the CF 13th Infantry Brigade in 1913 he trained his battalions rigorously and assumed command of the AIF 4th Infantry Brigade in September 1914.[21]

The remaining two had had regimental experience some years before the war. Victorian lawyer and politician James McCay had commanded a Militia infantry battalion from 1900 to 1908, before being appointed Head of the Australian Intelligence Corps. While running a successful law practice he entered Federal Parliament, where he was an energetic and effective Minister of Defence. Regarded as highly intelligent, he took command of the 2nd Australian Infantry Brigade in August 1914.[22] Blunt and tough, Granville Ryrie was a New South Wales grazier and politician noted for his horsemanship, humour and common sense. Commissioned in 1898, his rise was rapid, being promoted lieutenant colonel in 1904 to command the Militia 3rd LH Regiment, before going on the unattached list in 1911. He had served in the South

19 *Officer's List of the Australian Military Forces, 1 August 1914* (Melbourne: Government Printer, 1914) p. 230; *The Army List of the Australian Military Forces 31st March 1924* (Melbourne: Government Printer,1924), p. 240; A.J. Hill, *Chauvel of the Light Horse* (Melbourne: MUP, 1978), pp. 11-46.

20 *The Military Forces List of the Commonwealth of Australia, 1 January 1912.* (Melbourne: Government Printer, 1912) p. 230; *Officer's List of the Australian Military Forces, 1 August 1914* p. 230. Judith Smart, 'Hughes, Frederic Godfrey (1858-1944)' in *ADB*, Vol. 9, (Melbourne: MUP, 1983).

21 *Officer's List of the Australian Military Forces, 1 August 1914.* p. 230; Pedersen, *Monash.* pp. 18-37. Pedersen P. A. 'General Sir John Monash: Corps Commander on the Western Front' in David Horner (ed.), *The Commanders; Australian Military Leadership in the twentieth Century* (North Sydney: Allen and Unwin, 1984) pp. 89-92; Geoffrey Serle, 'Monash, Sir John (165-1931)' in *ADB* Vol. 10 (Melbourne, MUP, 1986).

22 *Officer's List of the Australian Military Forces, 1 August 1914*, p. 230; Christopher Wray, *Sir James Whiteside McCay: A Turbulent Life* (Oxford: Oxford University Press, 2002,) p. 2, pp. 16-17, pp. 55-72, p. 73.; Geoffrey Serle, 'McCay, Sir James Whiteside (1864-1930)' in *ADB*, Vol. 10.

African War, but whether he was active in developing his broader military knowledge is not easily discernible. In August 1914 he enlisted in the AIF, commanding the 2nd LH Brigade.[23]

At the outbreak of war only the British Regulars Walker and Smyth could be considered experienced enough to assume brigade command for active service. Of the remainder, their command experience was limited either to junior officers in the British Regular Army, part time service in the Militia, TF and CF, or as staff officers in the Australian PF. None could be considered trained or experienced for command on active service at brigade level. With the exception of Sinclair-MacLagan, Johnston and Russell they had no formal training, being largely self-taught and what little training there was focused on individual and unit requirements. All needed practice commanding and manoeuvring their brigades on exercises before they could be considered ready to do so in battle. They were not to get it.

Moreover, the forces they commanded were virtually untrained when the first of the brigades arrived in Egypt in December 1914. Their training began in earnest under Lieutenant-General Sir William Birdwood, GOC Australian and New Zealand Army Corps (ANZAC), but it was limited and disjointed, lacking the steady progression normally associated with military training. While brigade and divisional manoeuvres were conducted, they generally lasted from half a day to a day involving simple attacks against a defensive line. The NZ Brigade lost a month's training when it was deployed to defend the Suez Canal, and the 3rd Australian Infantry Brigade had its training curtailed at the end of February, when it was sent to Lemnos where training was limited and undertaken at unit level.[24]

Brigadier-General (later Major-General) Granville de Laune Ryrie.

When ANZAC departed Egypt at the beginning of April, the 1st and 2nd Australian infantry brigades had just under three and half months training. This included recruit training mixed with limited collective training of companies and battalions, brigade and divisional manoeuvres, route marches and ceremonial reviews. The NZ and 3rd Australian infantry brigades had even less – two and half months – whilst Monash's 4th Brigade, which arrived in late January 1915, managed to squeeze in two months. In essence, the initial ANZAC brigade commanders had little opportunity to master handling their formations under simulated battle conditions. Thus they lacked practice in dealing with the unexpected events, friction, and changing circumstances that inevitably occur on the battlefield, and the psychological pressures, stresses and decisions that go with them. In the coming operation Sinclair-MacLagan, McCay, MacLaurin,

23 *Officer's List of the Australian Military Forces, 1 August 1914.* p. 237; A.J. Hill, 'Ryrie, Sir Granville de Laune (1865-1937)' in *ADB,* Vol. 11.
24 Roberts, *The Landing at Anzac,* pp. 41-44.

Johnston and Monash were to experience the realities of brigade command in combat, and one of them would have a profound effect on the outcome of the initial operation.

The Anzac Landing

At the Gallipoli landings the 1st Australian Division's task was to seize the Sari Bair range in a two-phase operation. Landing immediately south of Anzac Cove, Sinclair-MacLagan was to seize a covering position along Third Ridge, from Chunuk Bair on the main range to the promontory at Gaba Tepe, providing a screen to cover the landing of the main body. Following behind, and echeloned slightly north to include Anzac Cove, McCay's job was to move up the main range, pass through the left hand corner of Sinclair-MacLagan's screen, and secure the highest features of Hill Q and Hill 971.[25] Contrary to some views, the planning for the operation was detailed, with the brigade and battalion commanders having clear instructions as to their tasks immediately on landing and their final objectives, with McCay detailing the routes each of his battalions were to take to reach them. Both brigade commanders had quite separate and ambitious tasks. Both would be relying heavily on their battalion commanders, with Sinclair-MacLagan's securing widely separated objectives on a frontage of over five kilometres, while McCay's battalions would have to seize two heights spread over nearly two kilometres.[26]

Not everyone was sanguine about the operation. Sinclair-MacLagan was pessimistic about the ANZAC landing, and was greatly concerned about the Ottoman defences at Gaba Tepe 1,300 metres south of the landing site. After reconnoitring the coast, he confided "if that place is strongly held it will be almost impregnable to my fellows."[27] On the eve of the landing his message to his troops stated "You may get orders to do something which appears in your positin [sic] as, [sic] to be the wrong thing to do and perhaps a mad enterprise. Do not cavil at it but carry it out wholeheartedly with the absolute faith in your leaders because we are after all only a very small piece on the board. Some pieces have to be sacrificed to win the game."[28] This was hardly an inspirational note and reflected a lack of the confidence so essential in exercising command in difficult circumstances. On leaving for the peninsula he lugubriously told

25 Australian War Memorial (AWM) AWM25 Item 367/156: ANZAC Operation Order No. 1 dated 17 April 1915; AWM4 1/25/1 Part 7: GOC ANZAC Instructions to GOC 1st Australian Division', ANZAC General Staff War Diary; AWM4 1/42/3 Part 2: '1st Australian Division Operation Order No. 1 dated 18 April 1915', 1st Australian Division General Staff War Diary.

26 AWM4 1/42/3 Part 2: 'GOC 1st Australian Division Instructions to Officer Commanding Covering Force dated 18th April 1915', 1st Australian Division General Staff War Diary; AWM25 Item 367/175: '3rd Infantry Brigade Operation Order No 1 dated 21 April 1915'; AWM4 1/25/1 Part 7: '2nd Infantry Brigade Operation Order No 5 dated 21 April 1915', ANZAC General Staff War Diary; AWM25, Item 367/17: '10th Battalion Operation Order No 1 dated 23 April 1915', 10th Battalion War Diary; AWM4 23/28/1: '11th Battalion Operation Order No 1 dated 24 April 1915', 11th Battalion War Diary.

27 Charles Bean, *Official History of Australia in the War of 1914-18,* Vol. I, *The Story of Anzac*, 6th ed. (Sydney: Angus & Robertson Ltd, 1937) p. 222.

28 AWM: AWM38 3DRL 8042/7: 'Message from Colonel E.G. Sinclair-MacLagan to the officers and men of the battalions of 3rd Aust Inf Bde prior to the landing.'

his divisional commander "if we find the Turks holding these ridges in strength, I honestly don't think you'll ever see the 3rd Brigade again."[29]

Unbeknown to him, across the proposed landing site were only two Ottoman rifle platoons, each of 81 men from the *2nd Battalion, 27th Infantry Regiment*, with another one in reserve and, contrary to most histories of the battle, they had no machine-guns with them.[30] All three were directly in the path of the assaulting troops – one on the heights above Anzac Cove, one in reserve 900 metres inland, and the third 1,200 metres south of the cove.[31] Landing slightly north than intended in the pre-dawn darkness, and not the one mile north so popularly quoted, the 3rd Brigade struck the single platoon above Anzac Cove, overwhelming it, and punching a gaping hole in the Ottoman screen. The 1st Australian Division's objectives lay directly ahead of them virtually undefended. Rather than exploiting this initial success, however, the offensive was curtailed, and the outcome of the battle was determined by the decisions of the leading brigade commander, rather than any action by the opposing Ottomans.

Coming ashore with his leading battalions, Sinclair-MacLagan directed his brigade major to go forward and take charge at the front, where on reaching Second Ridge the advancing troops were told to go no further. Meanwhile, Sinclair-MacLagan put the brakes on the advance, issuing orders for the brigade to halt and dig in on a line extending from Baby 700 and down Second Ridge to the 400 Plateau, some 1,600 metres short of his assigned objective.[32] Returning to the beach he intercepted the leading battalions of McCay's 2nd Brigade, diverting them to the lower ground on the right flank, rather than allowing them to proceed up the range to their objective on the heights. Intending to come ashore with his leading battalion, McCay was delayed when HMT *Novian* had trouble getting to her berth. When he finally arrived Sinclair-MacLagan confronted him, urging that he take his complete brigade to the right, advising "I've gone to the left following the enemy instead of to the right. If you can change your plans and go to the right, then it will settle the difficulty." When McCay remonstrated he was being asked to disobey his orders and suggested going forward to assess the situation for himself, Sinclair-MacLagan retorted "There isn't time. I assure you my right will be turned if you do not do this." Having been assured the left was secured, McCay agreed.[33]

Swapping the two brigades would not "settle the difficulty" and set things "right". The 3rd Brigade's mission was to provide a dispersed covering screen to delay and disorganise any enemy reinforcements approaching Third Ridge and Chunuk Bair. McCay's brigade was to pass

29 AWM38 3DRL 606/25/1: Charles Bean Diary No 25, pp. 45-46; Bean, Vol. I, p. 244.

30 Mesut Uyar, *The Ottoman Defence Against the Anzac Landing, 25 April 1915.* (Newport: Big Sky Publishing, 2015), p. 97; Aker Sefik, *The Dardanelles: The Ari Burnu Battles and the 27th Regiment*, translated copy in Imperial War Museum (IWM) 69/61/Bin 8 Rayfield Papers, para. 35, para. 47. Also in AWM MSS 1886; Roberts, *The Landing at Anzac*, Appendix 3 and Chris Roberts, 'Turkish machine-guns at the landing' in *Wartime*, No. 50, 2010, pp. 14-19 discuss why some Australians mistakenly believed there were Turkish machine guns facing them as they landed.

31 Mesut Uyar, *The Ottoman Defence Against the Anzac Landing, 25 April 1915.* (Newport: Big Sky Publishing, 2015), Map p. 95; Sefik, *The Dardanelles*, para. 34-35; Harvey Broadbent, *Gallipoli, The Turkish Defence – The Story from Turkish Documents* (Melbourne: Miegunyah Press, 2015), p. 31; Sefik, *The Dardanelles,* para. 34-35; Roberts, *The Landing at Anzac,* pp. 66-67.

32 Bean, Vol. I, p. 275, pp. 343-344, p. 347; AWM 38 3DRL 8042 Part 7, Major A. Salisbury statement.

33 AWM 3DRL 1722/2: 'Interview Bean and McCay'; AWM 3DRL 8042. Item 6: 'Early events of the 2nd Infantry Brigade at Anzac 25.4.14' by Major Cass. Cass was McCay's brigade major and witnessed the exchange.

through the northern corner of that screen and secure the vital ground. If these tasks were to be achieved, it was not simply a matter of reversing the missions with 3rd Brigade going to the left and 2nd Brigade to the right. They had two quite different roles. Tasks would have to be reallocated to battalions, and leaders briefed on the change if chaos and confusion were not to prevail. A reversal of roles, however, was never intended. 3rd Brigade had not gone to the left but had been ordered to dig in along Second Ridge reflecting a decision not to take either the covering position or the vital ground. In reality, Sinclair-MacLagan had misled McCay: he had not gone to the left, nor was he following the enemy – he was digging in short of his objective. In diverting the 2nd Brigade, Sinclair-MacLagan had usurped his divisional commander, and taken it upon himself to abort the 1st Division's mission.

These two decisions decided the fate of the battle within the first hour of the landing, changing the ANZAC operation from an offensive action to a purely defensive one, and handing the initiative to the outnumbered Ottomans. The ANZAC was now committed to defending a narrow, shallow beachhead with little room for manoeuvre on ground of no tactical value, which by early evening would be overlooked by the enemy. Moreover, these decisions were made without any evidence to justify taking them. The Ottoman platoon above the cove had scattered inland, the reserve platoon was making a fighting withdrawal up the main range, and the one south of the cove had withdrawn to Third Ridge.[34] The first Ottoman reserves, ten kilometres away near Maidos, (*1st* and *3rd battalions* and the machine gun company of the *27th Infantry Regiment)* began moving forward at 6:00 a.m., one and a half hours after the initial landing, to be followed by the *57th Infantry Regiment* at 8 a.m. It would not be until midday that a mere five Ottoman battalions (two of the *27th* and three of the *57th infantry regiments*) were in a position to launch a counter-attack against a defensive line which had sat on Second Ridge unmolested for almost six hours, and now numbered fourteen battalions ashore.[35] Sinclair-MacLagan's perceived threat to his right flank never materialised.

Why Sinclair-MacLagan acted as he did will never be known, but his lack of faith in the operation obviously played its part. He had complained the covering position was too long for a brigade to hold, and he would have been aware that his units were inadequately trained for such a role. With his inexperience of command at battalion and brigade level, and his battalion commanders and their units being raw, he might also have lacked confidence in his and their ability to control such an operation, and hence adopted the more easily conducted defence on a much shorter frontage, where he could maintain control over them. Sending his brigade major forward on reaching the beach, who instructed the leading troops to go no further, suggests he had determined this course of action either before or when he reached the shore.[36] In acquiescing to Sinclair-MacLagan's request, McCay possibly deferred to his greater experience as

34 Sefik, *The Dardanelles*, para. 36-38; Uyar, *The Ottoman Defence Against the Anzac Landing*, pp. 100-102, pp. 106-107, p. 109; Roberts, *The Landing at Anzac*, p. 110-113.

35 For a detailed analysis of the Anzac landing and the Ottoman response see Roberts, *The Landing at Anzac;* and Uyar, *The Ottoman Defence Against the Anzac Landing*. See also Sefik, *The Dardanelles*; and Broadbent, *Gallipoli, The Turkish Defence*, although Broadbent is sometimes contradictory, and at times misstates the category of units and guns; Chris Roberts, 'The landing at Anzac: A Reassessment' in *The Journal of the Australian War Memorial*, No 22, April 1993, pp. 25-34; Broadbent, Harvey, 'Gallipoli's first day' in *Wartime*, No 46, 2009, pp. 44-47 and Chris Roberts, 'An Australian Command Failure' in *Wartime*, No 70, 2015, pp. 24-29.

36 AWM 3DRL 1722, Item 2: Bean Extract Book; Bean, Vol. I, p. 275.

a Regular British officer, and with the latter having been ashore longer perhaps he believed Sinclair-MacLagan had a better grasp of the situation.

When Major-General William Bridges, an Australian PF officer and GOC 1st Australian Division, arrived he did nothing to take control or exert his influence on the ensuing battle; essentially control of the fighting was left to Sinclair-MacLagan and McCay throughout the day. The defensive position itself was unbalanced, with the bulk of the two brigades holding the lower end of the line, while the key terrain to the defence – Baby 700 on the main range – was thinly held by separate companies from different battalions. Although Sinclair-MacLagan recognised the importance of the feature, and asked for additional troops to be sent there, he failed to ensure they reached it. Nor did he visit the position to confirm his line was anchored on the high ground with a sufficiently strong force, or ensure a senior officer was placed in charge of its defence. This was a critical failure in the command and control of the overall defence. Remaining at his headquarters on MacLaurin's Hill, 1,200 metres away, he had no control of what would prove to be the critical fighting during the afternoon. The Ottoman counter-attack eventually drove the outnumbered defenders off Baby 700 and the upper reaches of Second Ridge. There they outflanked and overlooked the ANZAC main defensive line lower down the ridge and gained observation over the rear of the 3rd Brigade's left flank down Monash Valley, the principal route to the firing line.

Further south McCay had little control over his brigade. His verbal orders on the change of mission had been unclear, resulting in much of the 5th Battalion wandering into the 3rd Brigade's line on the 400 Plateau, and elements of the 6th and 8th battalions pushing out beyond the line McCay intended to hold, where they occupied scattered posts out of communication. MacLaurin's 1st Brigade was committed piecemeal by Bridges, leaving the former with no troops to command, and no thought was given to sending him to Baby 700 to take control of the fight for the key terrain.

Johnston, being sick, never came ashore, so Walker, ANZAC chief of staff, who had arrived at 8:00 a.m., took control of the NZ Infantry Brigade which was held in reserve, with two battalions being committed to reinforce the Australians. That evening, with ANZAC holding what was an untenable position, Bridges and Major-General Sir Alexander Godley, GOC NZ&A Division, supported by Sinclair-MacLagan, urged Birdwood to evacuate the whole force immediately. Only Walker, recognising such an action would be catastrophic, argued against the proposal.[37] Monash chose not to come ashore with his leading battalions that evening, instead arriving with the last one late on the morning 26 April, but whether he could have prevented the dispersal of his brigade is questionable. When the chaos of command was eventually sorted out, he was assigned to take charge of the defence from Pope's Hill to Courtney's Post inclusive.[38]

Altogether, the landing had been an uninspiring example of command and control at brigade and divisional level. While the plan had been ambitious for the inexperienced ANZAC, the Australians initially gained a striking success against a vastly outnumbered enemy, with their objectives lying virtually undefended directly ahead of them. Once ashore, however, the operation had been poorly executed and badly managed, surrendering the initiative to the enemy, losing control over the defence, and eventually being forced off the key terrain into an untenable

37 Bean, Vol. I, p. 455; Roberts, *The Landing at Anzac,* p. 169.
38 Pedersen, *Monash,* pp. 82-83.

position by a greatly outnumbered Ottoman force. In essence, the management and control of the battle reflected the inexperience and lack of training of the Australian formation commanders, and this was to be evident in the succeeding offensive actions over the next two weeks.

Attack on Baby 700

The next opportunity for offensive action occurred on 1 May when Birdwood sought to improve the inferior ANZAC position. Initially intended as a two divisional attack to retake Baby 700 and advance the line to the inland slope of Second Ridge, Walker, now commanding the 1st Australian Infantry Brigade following MacLaurin's death, argued against it citing the weakened state of the brigades, the divergence of the attack, and the ground over which it was to be made. His strenuous argument convinced Bridges to cancel the 1st Division's attack. Monash then followed suit, but his pleas fell on deaf ears. Godley insisted the NZ&A Division's attack would proceed, but in the event, it was postponed for 26 hours until the evening of 2 May.[39]

The details for executing the attack appear have been left to the brigade commanders, Monash and Johnston, which was in accordance with the command philosophy prevailing at the time. The latter's orders were brief in the extreme: at 7:15 p.m. the Otago Battalion would advance from the left of the 4th Australian Infantry Brigade to occupy Baby 700 to a point 440 yards NNW, after which the Canterbury Battalion would move onto Baby 700 prolonging the line to the left. The Auckland Battalion would be in reserve. There were no particulars as to where the Otagos would launch their attack from, or any other coordinating instructions, and although these were probably discussed face to face, the details appear to have been left to the battalion commanders.[40] Monash's order for the initial 1 May attack was more comprehensive, giving the objectives the brigade would capture, the timing by which the battalions were to be in position, where they would advance from and to, and the lines of advance they would take. The revised divisional plan for 2 May was issued at 3:00 p.m. on 1 May, but apparently Monash did not receive it until 2:15 p.m. the next day, five hours before Zero Hour. With limited time available he briefed his battalion commanders verbally to ensure they knew what was required of them. Johnston's written orders were not issued until 4:20 p.m.[41] There was no time for coordination between the two brigades, and the battalion commanders were left to execute the attack.

Launched out of the head of Monash Valley following a brief bombardment, the 16th Battalion planned to take the ground above Quinn's Post, while the Otago Battalion, emerging between Pope's Hill and Russell's Top, would seize Baby 700. Following this, the 13th Battalion would fill the gap between the two, and the Canterbury Battalion would cross over to Baby 700 and prolong the line to the coast. The attack was a complete failure, with the 16th and 13th

39 AWM4 1/25/1 Part 8: 'Army Corps Operation Order No. 5 dated 30/4/15.', NZ&A Division General Staff War Diary; AWM4 35/17/4: Appendix 9,'NZ NZ&A Division Operation Order No. 4 dated 30 April 1915', New Zealand Infantry Brigade War Diary; Bean, Vol. I, p. 583; Pedersen, *Monash*, pp. 70-72.

40 AWM4 35/17/4, Appendix 10: 'Operation Order No. 1 by Colonel F.E Johnston commanding NZ Infantry Brigade dated 2 May 1915', New Zealand Infantry Brigade War Diary.

41 AWM 3DRL/2316: 'Operation Order No. 3 by Col Monash Commanding Fourth Infantry Brigade dated 1-V-15.'; AWM4 35/17/4: NZ Infantry Brigade War Diary, 2 May 1915; Pugsley, *Gallipoli* pp. 180-190; Pedersen, *Monash* pp. 72-73.

battalions making limited gains before being driven to ground under heavy fire. The Otagos, delayed in moving up Monash Valley, attacked ninety minutes after the Australian attacks, suffering the same fate.[42]

Given an almost impossible task, Johnston and Monash were not entirely liable for the failure, and in the circumstances could have had little influence over events once their troops were committed. Yet their contribution to it was markedly different. Monash had protested about conducting the attack to no avail. Ordered to continue with it, he had reconnoitred the ground, planned as well as he could, issued detailed orders clearly defining what was to be undertaken, personally briefed his battalion commanders, ensured they knew their tasks, routes and objectives, and had urgently sought to get reinforcements up to support his hard-pressed battalions. Johnston, having recently resumed command of his brigade, had little knowledge of the ground, reconnaissance was lacking at both brigade and battalion level, and consequently insufficient time had been allocated for the Otagos to move from North Beach to the forming up place at the head of Monash Valley.[43] His orders had been issued very late and lacked any detail, although they may have been discussed verbally, and he seems to have exercised no control once the Otago's had been committed. Altogether, it had been a poorly planned and rushed operation that was reminiscent of the nature of battle prior to the Great War – brief orders, devolved execution to the brigade commanders, and quick action.

Second Battle of Krithia

Even less planning, briefer orders, and swifter action occurred during the 2nd Battle of Krithia. Having been shipped to Cape Helles on the night 5/6 May to participate in a renewed offensive, the NZ and 2nd Australian infantry brigades were thrown into the stalled battle at short notice.

The battlefield was open country, with the Ottomans having observation over the approaches comprising four gradually sloping spurs separated by gullies. From west to east they were Gully Spur, Fir Tree Spur, Krithia Spur (Charles Bean's Central Spur), and Kereves Spur.[44] Commencing on 6 May the British on Gully and Fir Tree Spurs, and the French on Kereves, had sought to take Achi Baba. On two successive days they had suffered heavily and were still well short of the Ottoman front line when the New Zealanders were committed on 8 May. It was reminiscent of the pre-war experience of quick attacks at short notice, and it was patently obvious that the senior commanders had yet to fully appreciate the deadly firepower of

42 AWM4 1/53/2 Part 3: 'Report on the Action on Night 2/3rd May 1915, Appendix 36, NZ & A Division General Staff War Diary; Bean, Vol. I, pp. 586-597; A.E. Byrne, *Official History of the Otago Regiment, N.Z.E.F. in the Great War* (Dunedin: J. Wilkie & Co Ltd, 1921), pp. 29-32; Captain C. Longmore, *The Old Sixteenth Being a Record of the 16th Battalion, AIF During the Great War 1914-1918.* (Perth, History Committee of the 16th Battalion Association, 1929) pp. 46-49; Pedersen, *Monash,* pp. 180-189; Pedersen, *The Anzacs: Gallipoli to The Western Front*, (Camberwell: Viking, 2007), pp. 66-68; Pugsley, *Gallipoli,* pp. 181-188. Pugsley incorrectly includes the 11th Battalion in Monash's brigade.

43 AWM4 35/17/3: NZ Infantry Brigade War Diary, 29 April 1915; Pugsley, *Gallipoli,* pp. 180-190.

44 These names are from the British designations of them. Oddly, Bean called Fir Tree Spur – Krithia Spur, and Krithia Spur – Central Spur, and Wray has followed suit.

magazine fed, breech loading rifles and automatic machine guns, despite the pre-war evidence and the experience of the previous week's fighting.

At 8:55 a.m. Johnston received the order to advance through the British 88th Infantry Brigade on Fir Tree Spur and attack Krithia. Brief in the extreme, it simply gave Krithia as his objective, his right flank as Krithia Nullah, and the advance to begin at 10:30 a.m. preceded by a 15-minute bombardment.[45] With little time to undertake reconnaissance, Johnston issued his brief written order at 10:10 a.m. – to attack Krithia and the trenches covering it. No references were given for each battalion's objective, although boundaries were laid down between them.[46] With his battalion commanders left to execute the attack, they and their battalions hurried across several hundred metres of open ground under fire to reach the British front line at Zero Hour, with no time to adequately brief their men, let alone reconnoiter the ground. Dashing forward at the appointed hour with little idea of their tasks, the New Zealanders were shot to pieces; the Wellington Battalion gained the most – perhaps 250 metres – the others were forced to ground after 90 metres or less.[47]

The fiasco was repeated that evening. At 4:30 p.m. Major-General Aylmer Hunter-Weston, GOC 29th Division, issued orders for the advance to be resumed an hour later, this time involving both Johnston's and McCay's brigades.[48] When Johnston received the order is unknown, but on passing it to his battalion commanders, they protested the brigade would be destroyed. Referring their views to Hunter-Weston, he was overruled. Following a 25-minute bombardment that had little effect, the New Zealanders attacked into a hail of fire with the same disastrous results, gaining little ground at great loss.

McCay received the order at 4:55 p.m. and ten minutes later issued his own: attack up the bare Krithia Spur with the 6th Battalion on the left, the 7th on the right and the 5th and 8th Battalions following in reserve. Located in Krithia Nullah, 450 metres behind the British front line (Tommies Trench), the brigade had to move to the flank of the New Zealanders by Zero Hour.[49] Receiving a telephone call from Hunter-Weston, McCay doubted it was possible to advance on time but was told it had to be done.[50] With insufficient time for the battalion commanders to disseminate orders to their companies, and with only a vague idea of where the objective lay, the brigade set off up the spur pelted by shrapnel with McCay and his head-quarters in the lead. Reaching Tommies Trench they sank into it under a galling fire. Climbing

45 AWM4 35/17/4, Appendix 13: 'Message to NZ Brigade from YB1 dated 8 May 1915', New Zealand Infantry Brigade War Dairy.

46 AWM4 35/17/4, Appendix 14: 'Operation Order No 4 by Colonel F.E Johnston commanding NZ Infantry Brigade dated 8 May 1915', New Zealand Infantry Brigade War Diary.

47 C.F. Aspinall-Oglander, *Military Operations Gallipoli*, Vol. I, *Inception of the Campaign to May 1915*, (London: William Heinemann Ltd), pp. 343-344; Pugsley, *Gallipoli*, pp. 201-203.

48 AWM4 35/17/4, Appendix 15: 'Message to New Zealand Brigade from 29th Division dated 4/30 p.m. 8 May 1915.', New Zealand Infantry Brigade War Diary.

49 AWM4 23/2/3: 'Report of Operations of 2nd Aust Inf Bde at Cape Helles from May 6th 1915 to [sic] dated 25/5/15.'. 2nd Australian Infantry Brigade War Diary; Bean, C.E.W. *Official History of Australia in the War of 1914 18*, Vol. II, *The Story of Anzac*, (Sydney, Angus & Robertson Ltd, 1924) p. 23; Wray, *Sir James Whitened McCay*, pp. 130-132.

50 Cass, McCay's brigade major, thought the call came from Major-General A. Paris, commanding the composite division, but McCay in a letter to Bean in 1922 insisted it was Hunter-Weston. Bean and others have related the call as coming from Paris, while Wray has stuck with McCay's version as the man who actually spoke on the phone. Bean, Vol. II, p. 23; Wray, *Sir James Whiteside McCay*, pp. 132.

onto the parapet, McCay turned to his men urging them on. They responded, while he directed the reserve battalions forward as they arrived, incurring their displeasure with his intemperate comments, damning some as cowards and threatening to shoot any laggards who would not advance.[51]

Pushing up the spur under increasingly heavy fire the Australians advanced another 500 metres, losing a third of the brigade before being driven to ground 400 metres short of the Ottoman front line with their flanks in the air. Chafing at his inability to control his brigade from Tommies Trench, McCay set off under a heavy fire with what was left of his headquarters, one sergeant and two signallers, and established it 70 metres behind the Australian front line, from whence he went forward alone to ascertain the situation. There he took control of the situation, before returning to Tommies Trench and bringing forward the officer commanding the 1st Lancashire Fusiliers, requesting his unit dig in behind the Australians as support. By midnight both flanks had been secured, and at 2:00 a.m., McCay returned to the rear to organise water, food and stretcher bearers to succour his men, when he was wounded and evacuated.[52]

The advances had been disastrous, but neither Johnston nor McCay could be held responsible. Given little time to respond, they had acted swiftly, and in the case of the second attack both had expressed concerns. However, two different styles of command were exhibited. Reflecting the pre-war notions of brigade command, McCay shared the danger with his men, exercised control over his battalions as best he could, moved forward to the front to ascertain the situation for himself, and organised for his flanks to be secured. Johnston, on the other hand, established his headquarters half a mile north east of Pink Farm,[53] well behind the front line, and appears to have had little control over his brigade, leaving the execution of the attack to his battalion commanders. Nonetheless, had he gone forward and exercised direct control as McCay had done, he and his headquarters most likely would have been rendered *hors de combat*, and it is highly unlikely he could have achieved anything useful during the brief and bloody assaults of his battalions. In reality, his approach was prescient of the way brigade command would be exercised as the war ground on.

Reflection

The first two weeks of combat had been disappointing. While hindsight makes it easy to criticise, the fighting had been reminiscent of offensives over the previous century, and the opening campaigns of 1914, reflecting the battlefield experience, training, and doctrine of the pre-war years. While the objectives had been set at divisional level, the execution and control of the tasks had been devolved to the brigade commanders. Success greeted ANZAC on 25 April, but the initiative had been thrown away by Sinclair-MacLagan's precipitous actions, and McCay's acquiescence in them. On 2 May and at Second Krithia the attacks were inadequately planned and rushed, and the brigade commanders had been given impossible tasks by their superiors. Monash had done all that could be expected of him, and while McCay failed to insist on extra

51 Wray, Sir *James Whitened McCay,* pp. 134-135, p. 141.
52 Bean, Vol. II, pp. 29-41; Wray, *Sir James Whiteside McCay*, pp. 133-140.
53 AWM4 35/17/4: 'Operation Order No 4 by Colonel F.E Johnston commanding NZ Infantry Brigade dated 8 May 1915', NZ Infantry Brigade War Diary.

time to launch his attack, he showed great gallantry in leading his men forward, took control where necessary, and ensured the ground won was retained. Conversely, in both actions Johnston was more hands off, devolving much of the planning and execution of the battle to his battalion commanders. Having seen the futility of the morning attack on 8 May, he failed to press his case that the evening assault would be hopeless, and thus sacrificed his men for little gain. Their performance, and that of Sinclair-MacLagan on 25 April, reflected their lack of training and experience at brigade level, and combat conditions quickly revealed the weaknesses and consequences inherent in that. Only Walker, the experienced British Regular, had performed well, including standing up to his superiors when he felt their proposals were poor, thereby avoiding fruitless attacks and unnecessary casualties.

Defence of Anzac

Having the moral courage to resist poorly conceived attacks was also the case with Russell. His NZMR and Chauvel's 1st LH brigades had arrived at Anzac on 12 May, where Russell took over the left flank of the defence, establishing his headquarters about 30 metres behind the front trenches on Russell's Top. Following the repulse of the massive Ottoman assaults on 19 May, Godley ordered an attack by 100 men against the enemy trenches at the Nek. On receiving protests from his commanding officers at the futility of the venture Russell backed them, advising Godley he would not order it. Despite Godley insisting it go ahead, Russell remained steadfast and the order was rescinded. At the same time Walker, temporarily commanding the 1st Australian Division after Bridge's death on the 15th, resisted Birdwood's proposal to launch a small and useless counter-attack across the series of spurs dropping off Lone Pine. When Ottoman troops established a position forward of No 2 Outpost on 27 May Russell immediately reacted, obtaining permission to capture and garrison it. When his troopers did so they found it untenable, being pinned down by the Turks on Table Top overlooking them. Although Godley ordered the new position be maintained, Russell insisted on withdrawing his men.[54] In all three cases, moral courage and commonsense prevailed. When they argued strongly enough, brigade commanders could influence their superiors against fruitless and costly ventures.

Brigadier-General (later Lieutenant-General) Henry George Chauvel.

As the campaign settled into the stalemate of entrenched warfare, the role of the brigade

54 AWM4 35/1/1: NZMR Brigade War Diary, 12-13 May, 28-30 May 1915; Bean, Vol. II, pp. 191-195; Pugsley, *Gallipoli*, pp. 225, 231-233, 247; Vennell, *The Forgotten General*, pp. 64, 66, 68-69.

commander began to change. Birdwood divided the defence into four sections, with the command of each assigned to a brigade commander. Chauvel's 1st LH Brigade shared the trenches in No 3 Section with the remnants of Monash's brigade, clinging to a precarious hold above the steep slopes at Pope's Hill, and Quinn's and Courtney's Posts. It was the most dangerous and vulnerable portion of the line, with Chauvel taking command on 13 May. He was soon to be tested in a critical situation.[55] Exploding a mine under the Australian trenches at Quinn's on 29 May, the Ottomans gained a foothold in them during the subsequent attack. Leaving his headquarters in Monash Valley Chauvel took personnel charge of the situation, organising reinforcements and directing action to clear the enemy from the captured trench. Disregarding the advice of his subordinate infantry commanders he ordered an attack across open ground to clear a small party of isolated Ottomans, which succeeded with minimal casualties largely because the Turks themselves launched an attack at the same time, masking any fire their countrymen could bring to bear on the Australians. A more prudent action would have been to clear them out by approaching along the trenches on either side, an option urged on Chauvel by junior officers. Nonetheless, at a critical time and under great pressure he went forward, took control of the situation, and demonstrated a cool and firm demeanour taking decisive action which retrieved the situation.[56]

The 2nd Australian Infantry Brigade returned to Anzac on 16 May, followed by Johnston's New Zealanders on the 20th, the same day Ryrie's 2nd and Hughes's 3rd LH brigades arrived from Egypt, bringing the total to nine ANZAC brigades on the peninsula. By now the nature of operations had changed as commanders and troops settled into the static defence of a wholly new form of fighting. The art of trench warfare had to be learnt, and brigade commanders had a widening range of functions imposed upon them. Entrenchments had to be properly developed, weapons, especially machine guns, sited to best advantage, effective trench routine and discipline established, reserves placed in locations to react quickly, the rotation of units in and out of the line had to be planned to provide relief and rest, and a greater level of coordination with flanking brigades was required. Raids and patrolling at the front and to the flanks were planned and organised. In all of this the brigade commander played an increasingly greater role. Moreover, they now had to work more closely with their supporting arms. Engineer field companies were now placed under the brigade commanders' direction, and supported them in building roads and gun positions, and pushing galleries under and forward of the front line, in which mines were placed under the enemy works or underground firing lines established.[57] On 25 May, instructions were issued regarding the artillery. While command remained at divisional level, control was delegated to the artillery brigades allotted to each defensive section, and direct communications were laid between the infantry brigade headquarters and their supporting artillery brigade. Thus infantry commanders could now make requests for fire direct

55 AWM4 35/1/1: NZMR Brigade War Diary, 12-13 May 1915; Pugsley, *Gallipoli,* p. 247; Vennell, *The Forgotten General*, p. 64; AWM4 10/1/9 Part 1: 1st Australian LH Brigade War Diary 12-14 May 1915; Hill, *Chauvel,* pp. 52-53; Pedersen, *Monash* pp. 86-87.

56 Hilll, *Chauvel*, pp. 55-57; Bean, Vol. II, pp. 218-220; Pedersen, *Monash,*, pp. 86-87.

57 AWM4 1/42/5 Part 2: '3rd Inf Bde Instructions to O.C 3rd Field Coy nd.'1st Australian Division General Staff War Diary; AWM4 1/42/5 Part 2, Appendix 2: '1st Australian Division Instruction dated 18 June 1915'; AWM4 1/42/5 Part 7, '1st Australian Division proposal dated 23 June 1916', 1st Australian Division General Staff War Diary.

to the artillery brigade supporting them, and determined which targets were to be engaged in support of their defence.[58]

Most brigade commanders located their headquarters immediately behind the firing line to control their defence sections. No. 1 Section headquarters was on Bolton's Ridge, No. 2 Section's was below MacLaurin's Hill, while No 3 Section's was in Monash Valley below Courtney's Post, and, as previously mentioned, Russell had established No. 4 Section's on Russell's Top.[59] They visited the firing line regularly, conversing with their junior officers and troops, and directing improvements to the line. Walker in particular was a frequent visitor, and Russell often took risks undertaking close reconnaissance; on at least one occasion venturing into no man's land at night, and almost getting himself shot by a vigilant sentry on his return.[60] Monash, on the other hand, controlled his brigade from further back and was criticised for not visiting the trenches except when accompanying senior officers, and for spending too much time in his dugout. He eschewed what he regarded as unnecessary risks and foolishly exposing one's self to fire, and while this led to criticism of his approach, several of his men thought highly of him.[61]

During June, the brigade commanders took greater control of the activities in their sectors, employing a more covert and less costly means to take ground, and carry the firing line forward using sapping and mining. Sinclair-MacLagan's 3rd Australian Infantry Brigade mined forward and established an underground firing line along Silt Spur. On the right flank during the last week of June his and Ryrie's 2nd LH Brigade extended the line on the upper end of Holly Spur, and south along Bolton's Ridge to Chatham's Post. Sending covering troops out at night, new positions were dug behind them while communication trenches linked up the old line with the forward diggings. From the Pimple at Lone Pine, and Steele's Post opposite German Officer's Trench, the 1st and 2nd Australian infantry brigades pushed tunnels forward, establishing an underground firing line halfway across no man's land in preparation for an attack on the enemy's works.[62]

Yet brigade commanders were still being directed to undertake pointless attacks at short notice, which some executed without protest. When the British VIII Corps mounted an offensive at Cape Helles on 28 June, that same day Sinclair-MacLagan and Ryrie were ordered to mount demonstrations to keep the Ottoman reserves at Anzac in place. Receiving the task at

58 AWM4 1/42/5 Part 8: 'Instructions for getting artillery fire on objectives quickly' dated 25/5/1915 in 1st Australian Division General Staff War Diary, May 1915. A forthcoming book by Chris Roberts and Paul Stevens on the artillery at Anzac describes the artillery changes, and the arrangements for the command and control of fire support.

59 AWM4 1/42/5 Part 4, Appendix No 9: Map dated 9/6/15, 1st Australian Division General Staff War Diary.

60 Vennell, *The Forgotten General*, pp. 64-65.

61 Vennell, *The Forgotten General*, pp. 64-65; Pedersen, *Monash*, pp. 82-83.

62 AWM4 1/42/5 Part 12: 1st Australian Division Summaries 19th to 27th June 1915, 1st Australian Division General Staff War Diary; AWM4 10/2/5: 2nd LH Brigade War Diary 19-21 June 1915; AWM4 10/2/5: 'Operation Memorandum No 1 by Colonel G. deL Ryrie, 2nd LH Brigade War Diary; AWM4 10/2/5 Appendix No. 2: Map of the Situation 1st Australian Division, 2nd LH Brigade War Diary; AWM4 1/42/5 Part 11: '2nd Field Company Memo dated 26/6/15.', 'HQ Ist Australian Division Memo dated 26/6/15.', 'Commander 1st Australian Divisional Engineers Memo dated 30/6/15.' and Map of the Situation. 1st Australian Division dated 30/6/15. 1st Australian Division General Staff War Diary; Bean, Vol. II, pp. 268-276, and Map No. 13 opposite p. 498.

10:30 a.m., Sinclair-MacLagan issued his order at 12:15 p.m. for an assault at 1:00 p.m. Two companies attacked at 1:05 p.m., neither entered the enemy works and were back in their own trenches by 3:30 p.m. For absolutely no gain, and without affecting the Ottomans one iota, it cost three battalions 28 killed, 108 wounded, and 35 missing. Ryrie's 2nd LH Brigade sent two troops out onto Holly Ridge at 12:50 p.m., while two squadrons attacked the Balkan Gun Pits south of Chatham's Post at 1:00 p.m. They were withdrawn to their own lines at 5:39 p.m. for the loss of 21 killed and 79 wounded.[63] The day's feints were a pointless exercise that achieved nothing other than adding to the casualty list. Neither brigade commander objected to the late notice, or the futility of the operation on such a small scale. But this was to change.

As part of the preliminaries for the August offensive, on 29 July Birdwood requested the 1st Australian Division conduct "some operation" that evening to give the impression the Corps was breaking out southwards – suggesting it be the one already under discussion to rectify the situation opposite Tasmania Post, where recent Ottoman trenches threatened the Australian line. Sinclair-MacLagan requested a delay for 24 hours, and the next day submitted a detailed proposal requesting a further delay until the night 31 July/1 August.[64] Organising suitable artillery support, mines to be exploded immediately in front of the Ottoman trench, and setting Zero Hour just before moonrise, Sinclair-MacLagan worked to give his assaulting infantry the best chance to take their objective with minimal casualties. It paid off. The trenches were captured and retained after hard fighting.

The August Offensive – Plans and Preparations

On the left flank Russell had been active controlling a patrol program into the rugged country north of Anzac. Pushing out through and beyond the Ottoman posts, it provided valuable information that the area was lightly held. From 13 May Birdwood had been considering means by which he could improve his position, and Russell's patrolling had shown the only practicable way lay in breaking out to the north. Preparations began for the August offensive, with detailed planning reverting to corps and divisional level, in which brigade commanders had little or no input. Considerable thought and discussion was undertaken with several appreciations being written on the various courses of action that could be undertaken.[65] Contrary to the previous attacks, extensive planning and preparations ensued, and the orders were detailed and prescriptive: not only were brigade commanders given their objectives as previously, but division now laid down the routes to be taken, timetables for each stage of the move, and when objectives were to be taken, together with other preparations. Artillery

63 AWM4 1/42/5 Part 10: 'Operation Order No 6 by Colonel E.G. Sinclair-MacLagan Commanding Northern No. 1 Section dated 28.6.15 Issued at 1215', 'Report on demonstration carried out by 3rd Infantry Brigade 28-6-15 KC 595'; 'Operation Memorandum No. 1 by Colonel G. de L Ryrie Commanding 2nd LH Bde dated 28 June Issued at 1209', and '2nd LH Brigade Report dated 29 June 1915', 1st Australian Division General Staff War Diary; Bean, Vol. II, pp. 292-305.

64 AWM4 1/42/7 Part 2: 'ANZAC Ga 493 dated 29/7/15', '1st Australian Division signal dated 29/7/15', 'Proposal KC374 from Sinclair-MacLagan dated 1400 30/7/15', 1st Australian Division General Staff War Diary.

65 See for examples of the appreciations see AWM4 1/42/7 Part 5: 1st Australian Division General Staff War Diary.

planning and control reverted to corps and divisional level. Brigade commanders were given little scope in how they should execute their tasks, other than local issues.[66] They now worked within detailed instructions of how their task was to be achieved. It was reminiscent of the detailed planning and coordination associated with the deliberate attack that was emerging on the Western Front.

In outline Smyth's 1st Australian Infantry Brigade would conduct a feint at Lone Pine on the evening of 6 August to draw in the Ottoman reserves. Later that night the 6th Battalion of Forsyth's 2nd Australian Infantry Brigade would attack German Officer's Trench. After nightfall the NZ&A Division, supported by British and Indian infantry brigades, would break out of the Anzac beachhead to the north, swing right and claw their way up steep, twisting and tangled spurs and gullies to seize the Sari Bair heights behind the Ottoman line.

At Lone Pine a lengthy bombardment designed to cut the wire, destroy trenches and neutralise the enemy on the left flank would precede the assault, followed by fire in depth and on both flanks once the attack began. Tunnels previously pushed halfway across no man's land led to the underground trench from which the first line of infantry would assault simultaneously with those at the Pimple, and the sections of the enemy trenches to be captured were specified. Further north, Forsyth determined to fire three mines in front of German Officer's Trench over a period of 40 minutes, making the enemy wary of filling his trenches with troops. After the third mine had been exploded the Australians would pass through the tunnels to the underground firing line in no man's land and assault from there. A complete rehearsal was undertaken beforehand, passing the attacking troops through the tunnels and occupying the assault line, and calculating the time it would take to do so.[67] These preparations were a far cry from the earlier quick attacks with brief orders and limited time to prepare.

For the breakout, Russell's NZMR Brigade would secure several Ottoman posts on the lower slopes of the spurs leading to Chunuk Bair; two battalions of the British 40th Infantry Brigade would then pass by and capture features either side of the mouth of the Aghyl Dere, which led up to Hill Q. The Right Assault Column, Johnston's brigade, would move through the NZMR and, advancing up the valleys either side of Rhododendron Ridge, seize Chunuk Bair. Commanded by Brigadier-General Herbert Cox, the Left Assault Column – Monash's 4th Australian and Cox's 29th Indian infantry brigades – would swing wider, pass through the 40th Brigade and move up the Aghyl Dere before splitting – Cox taking Hill Q and Monash Hill 971. All was to be completed before dawn, by which time Johnston's New Zealanders would be sweeping down the range and attacking Battleship Hill from the rear, while Chauvel's and

66 AWM4 1/42/7 Part 6: 'Memorandums, Orders and Instructions, 1st Australian Division War Diary; AWM4 1/42/7 Part 7: 'Operation Order No 9 By Brigadier-General H.B. Walker DSO Commanding 1st Australian Division dated 4th August, 1915, 1st Australian Division War Dairy; AWM4 1/53/5 Part 1: 'NZ&A Division Operation Order No 11 dated 5 August 1915, NZ&A Division General Staff War Diary; AWM4 23/4/1 Part 2: 'Operation Order No 5 by Brigadier-General J. Monash VD, Commanding Fourth (Australian) Infantry Brigade dated August 6th, 1915, 4th Australian Infantry Brigade War Diary; AWM4 35/1/4 Part 1: 'Operation Order No1 by Brigd-Gen A.N. Russell NZMR Bgde dated 5 August 1915, NZMR War Diary; AWM4 10/3/7: 'Consideration of Attack on Baby 700.', 3rd LH Brigade War Diary.

67 AWM4 23/1/8 Part 2: 'No 3 Operation Order by Colonel N.M. Smyth VC Commanding 1st Inf Bde. dated 5.8.1915', 1st Australian Infantry Brigade War Dairy; Bean, Vol. II, p. 600.

Hughes's LH brigades would assault the upper end of Second Ridge and Baby 700, catching the defenders in a pincer movement.[68]

It was an ambitious plan, and for those breaking out to the north it involved a highly optimistic timetable. Not only was the terrain brutal, but the New Zealanders, Australians and Indians had been fighting on the peninsula since late April without respite, with many of the men weakened and wracked by dysentery, and the recent ANZAC reinforcements were poorly trained. The tortuous valleys by which the brigades would advance were riven with gullies and spurs running off them, making navigation in the dark difficult. The Left Assault Column had a particularly difficult task. Pushing up the Aghyl Dere 29th Indian Brigade had to find the correct spur running up to Hill Q. Monash, after some distance, had to swing left into an offshoot valley, pass over Damakjelik Bair, drop down into Asma Dere, climb onto Abdul Rahman Bair, and then turn right to advance on Hill 971. In the dark this required navigational skills of an exceptional nature, firm leadership and control, and to meet the tight timetable – an unopposed advance.

Brigadier-General Francis Earl Johnston.

Briefings to subordinate commanders were thorough and timely. Taking his commanders forward to look over the ground Russell pointed out their objectives, and briefings were undertaken to ensure everyone knew their tasks.[69] Monash thrashed out every detail of his brigade's operation in a long conference with his battalion commanders on 5 August, and the next day briefed all leaders down to lance corporal.[70]

Execution – 6/7 August 1915

At Lone Pine, Smyth established his headquarters immediately behind the front line. The assault was successful, with the Australians gaining the Ottoman trenches with minimal casualties. However, three days of vicious trench fighting followed as the Turks sought desperately to recapture the lost ground. Smyth exercised firm control of the battle, maintaining close contact with his subordinates, calmly receiving reports, organising reinforcements and reliefs,

68 AWM4 10/1/13: 'Operation Order No. 1 by Brigadier-General H.G. Chauvel CMG Commanding No 3 Section ANZAC dated 6/8/1915' and attached memo, 1st LH War Dairy; AWM4 10/3/7: 'Operation Order No 1 by B Gen F.G Hughes dated August 5th 1915', 3rd LH Brigade War Dairy.
69 AWM4 35/1/4 Part 1: NZMR Brigade War Diary, 6 August 1915; Pugsley, *Gallipoli*, pp. 272, 275.
70 AWM 3DRL/2316: Item 20: Monash notes.

and venturing into the newly won trenches, where on one occasion he assisted in repulsing an Ottoman force advancing up Sasse's Sap.[71]

Things did not go well for Forsyth at German Officer's Trench. Following the Lone Pine attack, the Ottoman's shelled Steele's Post wrecking trenches, which delayed the attackers, and a blocked tunnel further held up the assault. It was not launched until an hour after the last mine exploded with disastrous consequences. As they emerged the Australians were immediately shot down. When Forsyth reported the failure, Walker, now commanding the 1st Australian Division, uncharacteristically ordered another attempt. Mounted two hours later it met the same fate. Although a third assault was ordered, Walker cancelled it accepting that failure was obvious. In the circumstances, Forsyth had been unable to exercise much control over events once the attack was launched, other than to carry out Walker's orders and report the disastrous results.

Russell established his headquarters at No 2 Outpost immediately opposite his first objective, the Ottoman held Old No 3 Outpost, from which a final reconnaissance and briefings were conducted.[72] Aided by a ruse his troopers captured their various objectives, albeit two hours behind schedule. Russell was not required to exert any control over the attacks; his contribution to the success lay in his careful preparation and frontline briefings to his regiments.

Johnston's infantry set out for the heights well behind schedule – his leading battalion didn't reach the Apex, a hollow at the head of the Chailak Dere some 500 metres short of Chunuk Bair, until after dawn, by which time Ottoman troops were defending the feature.[73] Johnston joined them around 6:00 a.m. and now had a crucial decision to make. His orders were to seize Chunuk Bair – a task expected to be accomplished before dawn. To achieve it the New Zealanders now had to cross the last 500 metres along the narrow Rhododendron Ridge in broad daylight with their front and right flank exposed to enemy on the main range. On the advice of Major Arthur Temperley, his brigade major, Johnston decided to pause until supported by the Left Assault Column, despite Birdwood emphasising that regardless of any delays by either column, the other must press on and seize their objectives. On hearing of the halt, however, Godley ordered Johnston to attack forthwith.[74]

Brushing aside Temperley's protests Johnston readily complied, giving the task to the Aucklanders whose commanding officer strongly recommended postponing the attack until nightfall. Faced with Godley's order and the certainty Chunuk Bair would be further reinforced, he rejected the advice. Wallingford, his brigade machine-gun officer, urged delaying Zero Hour by twenty minutes until he could bring sufficient machine-guns up to the Apex to cover the attack, but Johnston refused to consider any further postponement. At 11:00 a.m. the Aucklanders went forward, and suffering heavy casualties barely made 100 metres before taking shelter at the Pinnacle, a knoll 400 metres from the crest of Chunuk Bair. Johnston then ordered the Wellington Battalion to attack, but Lieutenant-Colonel William Malone refused

71 AWM4 23/1/2 Part 1: 1st Australian Infantry Brigade War Dairy, 6-9 August 1915; Bean, Vol. II, p. 519, p. 553, p. 559.
72 Ibid., NZMR Brigade War Diary, 6 August 1915.
73 Edward J. Erickson, *Gallipoli: Command Under Fire*, (Oxford: Osprey, 2015), p. 195; Edward J. Erickson *Gallipoli: The Ottoman Campaign* (Barnsley: Pen & Sword, 2010), p. 191; Broadbent, *Gallipoli, The Turkish Defence*, pp. 277-280; notes provided by Professor Mesut Uyar.
74 AWM4 35/27/7: New Zealand Infantry Brigade War Diary, 7 August 1915.

to send his men forward in daylight, saying they would do so that night. Faced with this blunt and firm refusal, Johnston finally acquiesced and advised Godley the height could not be taken in daylight.[75]

With Monash's brigade in the lead, the Left Assault Column was also behind schedule. In an effort to make up time, on the advice of a local Greek guide the column took a short cut through Taylor's Gap, between Bauchop's Hill and Walden Point. While well intentioned it delayed the advance a further three hours. The narrowness of the trail reduced the advance to single file, while Turks who had eluded the New Zealanders sniped at the column as it struggled through. Reaching the Dere, the head of the column halted as the leading officers tried to determine the safest route to take. Located in the centre of his brigade, and frustrated at the delay, Monash pushed forward and immediately took control of the situation, insisting they must adhere to the planned route and move on.[76]

Closely questioning the guide Monash sought to ascertain just where in the valley they were, then directed his 13th and 14th battalions to secure Damakjelik Bair on the eastern side of Aghyl Dere, as had been planned, before sending the 15th and 16th up the valley. It was then the Australians encountered stubborn resistance, and by dawn 4th Brigade was still nearly three kilometres from its objective arranged in an arc along Damakjelik Bair, with 29th Indian Brigade similarly deployed further up Aghyl Dere. Establishing his headquarters within the arc, Monash advised Cox that his men, weakened with dysentery, were too exhausted to continue. After a heated discussion, Cox reluctantly allowed Monash to entrench where they remained throughout 7 August.[77] The delay proved fatal; Ottoman reinforcements rushed forward occupying the ground ahead of the Australians.

Contrasting views of Monash at this time have been proffered. In an account written in 1936, Allanson of the 6th Gurkha Rifles thought Monash had lost his head "running about saying "I thought I could command men, I thought I could command men." However, in an interview on Gallipoli in 1915 he never mentioned it, instead relating, "Sleepy old John Monash – cautious if ever a man was – is one of the worst sort of men for such a move but he's probably brilliant compared with some others." Cox roundly condemned Monash, yet none of his own officers criticised him, either at the time or afterwards, while Lieutenant-Colonel Dare of the 14th Battalion wrote it was Monash who took control, sorted out the confusion and got things moving.[78]

Meanwhile, at the Nek a tragedy was being played out. With the New Zealanders expected to be advancing down the main range, Chauvel's and Hughes's LH brigades launched their assaults at 4:30 a.m. Those at the Nek and Quinn's Post were swept away in the first five to ten yards. Only at Pope's Hill was the 1st LH Regiment able to get into the Turkish trenches on Dead Man's Ridge, before being driven out two hours later, sustaining 154 casualties out of the

75 Ibid.; O.E. Burton, *The Auckland Regiment* (Auckland; Whitcomb and Tombs Ltd, 1922) pp. 50-60; Pugsley, *Gallipoli*, pp. 284-286; Richard Stowers, *Bloody Gallipoli: The New Zealanders' Story* (Auckland: David Bateman Ltd, 2005), pp. 158-159.
76 Bean, Vol. II, p. 588; Pedersen, *Monash*, p. 101.
77 Ibid., pp. 589-594; Ibid., pp. 100-102.
78 James, *Gallipoli*, p. 272; Pedersen, *Monash*, pp. 103-106; AWM38 7953/27 Part 3: Dare, Appendix in Letter Bean to Brig.-Gen. Edmonds dated 17 June 1931.

200 men who attacked.[79] While Chauvel cancelled the assault at Quinn's after the first line was shot to pieces, at the Nek it was persisted with despite calls by Lieutenant-Colonel Noel Brazier of the 10th LH Regiment to have the attack abandoned. Hughes was not at his headquarters; nor did Lieutenant-Colonel John Antill, the brigade major, know his whereabouts. In an acrimonious exchange Antill told Brazier to "Push on." After the first line of the 10th LH suffered the same fate, Brazier again sought to stop the carnage, searching the trenches until he eventually found Hughes in a forward sap observing what had occurred. There Hughes simply told him to go via Bully Beef Sap, a senseless instruction as it led into Monash Valley.[80] Meanwhile the second line of the 10th LH had gone forward with the same disastrous result.

Throughout the action Hughes exerted neither command nor control over his brigade, despite witnessing the futility of the initial attacks. In reality he abrogated his responsibility. By absenting himself from his command post without indicating where he would be, Hughes left control of the operation to his brigade major. When eventually located he offered no practical advice or sought to halt what was clearly a futile venture, simply observing the destruction of two of his regiments. It was a significant self-imposed failure of command and control on his part, and when evacuated in September, he was replaced by Antill.

Execution – 8 August 1915

Godley determined to renew the offensive on Sari Bair at dawn on the 8th. Monash's brigade would cross over to Abdul Rahman Bair and advance on Hill 971; 29th Indian Brigade, reinforced by the British 39th Infantry Brigade, would push for Hill Q; and the NZ Infantry Brigade, reinforced by two British battalions, would assault Chunuk Bair.

In an extraordinary decision, rather than control the advance himself Monash placed Lieutenant-Colonel Harold Pope of the 16th Battalion in charge of the operation, while he elected to remain at his headquarters in Australia Valley, and maintain contact via telephone. In effect, Pope controlled the brigade operation as well as commanding his own battalion but was given neither the staff nor the communications to do so. Why Monash did this is not known but, in doing so he abrogated control of his brigade's lengthy advance and seizure of Hill 971 to a subordinate. If they got into difficulties at any point, Monash, being too far from the scene of action, would have little or no ability to either command, or control the fighting.

Moving at 3:00 a.m. the Australians slipped over Damakjelik Bair into Kiaijik Dere, and up onto Yauan Tepe believing it to be Abdul Rahman Bair. Swinging right they advanced, but as dawn broke Ottoman machine guns engaged the head of the column, inflicting heavy casualties and forcing the survivors to ground. Monash was powerless to influence events; the telephone cable linking him with Pope was cut by shellfire. When it was eventually repaired at 7:00 a.m.,

79 AWM4 10/1/13 Part 1: 1st LH Brigade, War Diary, 7 August 1915; AWM4 10/3/7: 3rd LH Brigade War Diary, 7 August 1915; AWM4 10/6/4: 1st LH Regiment, War Diary, 7 August 1915; AWM 10/7/6: 2nd Light Horse Regiment, War Diary, 7 August 1915; AWM4 10/13/4: 8th LH Regiment, War Diary, 7 August 1915; AWM4 10/15/4: 10th LH Regiment, War Diary, 7 August 1915; Bean, Vol. II, pp. 612-631.

80 AWM38 3DRL 7953/27 Part 3: 'Letter Brazier to Bean dated 13 April 1931'; Bean, Vol. II, pp. 617-619.

Pope recommended withdrawal, advising Monash that his own casualties and the extent of the Ottoman opposition precluded any chance of reaching Hill 971. Monash referred the decision to Cox, who concurred. An orderly retirement was impossible, argument ensued among the forward commanders, and Monash lost control of the situation completely. Eventually the survivors trickled back. The entire action was a fiasco, lowering the morale of the decimated 4th Australian Infantry Brigade, and Monash's reputation. His attempt to command events from a rear headquarters via telephone failed miserably. It proved to be his worst performance of the war and reflected poorly on him.[81]

Johnston gave the task of taking Chunuk Bair to Malone, and under the cover of darkness, supported by a bombardment and Wallingford's machine guns, the Wellingtons found the position unoccupied. Following on behind in the early morning light, however, the 7th Gloucester and 8th Welsh regiments suffered heavily from Ottoman rifle and machine gun fire from their right flank along the main range to Battleship Hill, highlighting the difficulty of moving up Rhododendron Ridge in daylight.[82] Counter-attacking, the Ottomans annihilated the forward line of the Wellingtons, leaving the reserve line holding a shallow trench further down the slope. At 9:00 a.m. Johnston reinforced them, but it took most of the day as groups of eight to ten men rushed forward under a heavy fire. Malone continued to control the bitter fighting that ensued throughout the day, in tenuous contact with his brigade commander by a telephone cable that was regularly cut.[83] Johnston could do little to influence events and became an observer of the desperate fight for the height. Going forward would not have helped the situation as he could exert no more influence than Malone, and he would have lost control over the remainder of his brigade.

The final attempt – 9 August 1915

Abandoning any idea of taking Hill 971, Godley ordered another attempt to capture Hill Q and regain the crest of Chunuk Bair. Zero Hour was set at 5:15 a.m. on 9 August, 45 minutes after dawn. 29th Indian and 39th infantry brigades were to renew their assault on Hill Q from the west, while a composite brigade of four British battalions under Brigadier-General Anthony Baldwin (38th Infantry Brigade) was to make the main assault through Chunuk Bair north to Hill Q. The intention was that during the night Johnston would reinforce those clinging to the seaward slope of the Chunuk Bair, extend their hold to the crest, and lengthen it south towards Battleship Hill. At Zero Hour, Baldwin's force was to advance up Rhododendron Ridge and, passing through the New Zealanders, would turn left and assault along the range to Hill Q.[84]

81 Bean, Vol II, pp. 655-663; Pedersen, *Monash*, pp. 108-112.

82 AWM4 35/20/5: Wellington Battalion War Diary, 8 August 1915; W.H. Cunningham, C.A.L. Treadwell, & S.H. Hanna, *The Wellington Regiment (NZEF) 1914-1919* (Wellington: Ferguson & Osborn Limited, 1928), pp. 68-70; Pugsley, *Gallipoli*, pp. 287-288; Broadbent, *Gallipoli: The Turkish Defence,* p. 290; Stowers, *Bloody Gallipoli,* pp. 166-168.

83 Bean, Vol. II, pp. 666-667, p. 676. Pugsley, *Gallipoli,* pp. 287-304; Stowers, *Bloody Gallipoli*, pp. 167-168, pp. 174-177.

84 There are no extant orders for this attack, but Bean gives this as the intention, and in both the revised orders on 8 August, and the post action report Baldwin's objective is given as 'the position known as Q.' Bean, Vol. II, p. 687; AWM4 1/53/5 Part 3, Appendix 81: 'NZ and A Division Order No. 13

1. Europe and the Mediterranean 1914.

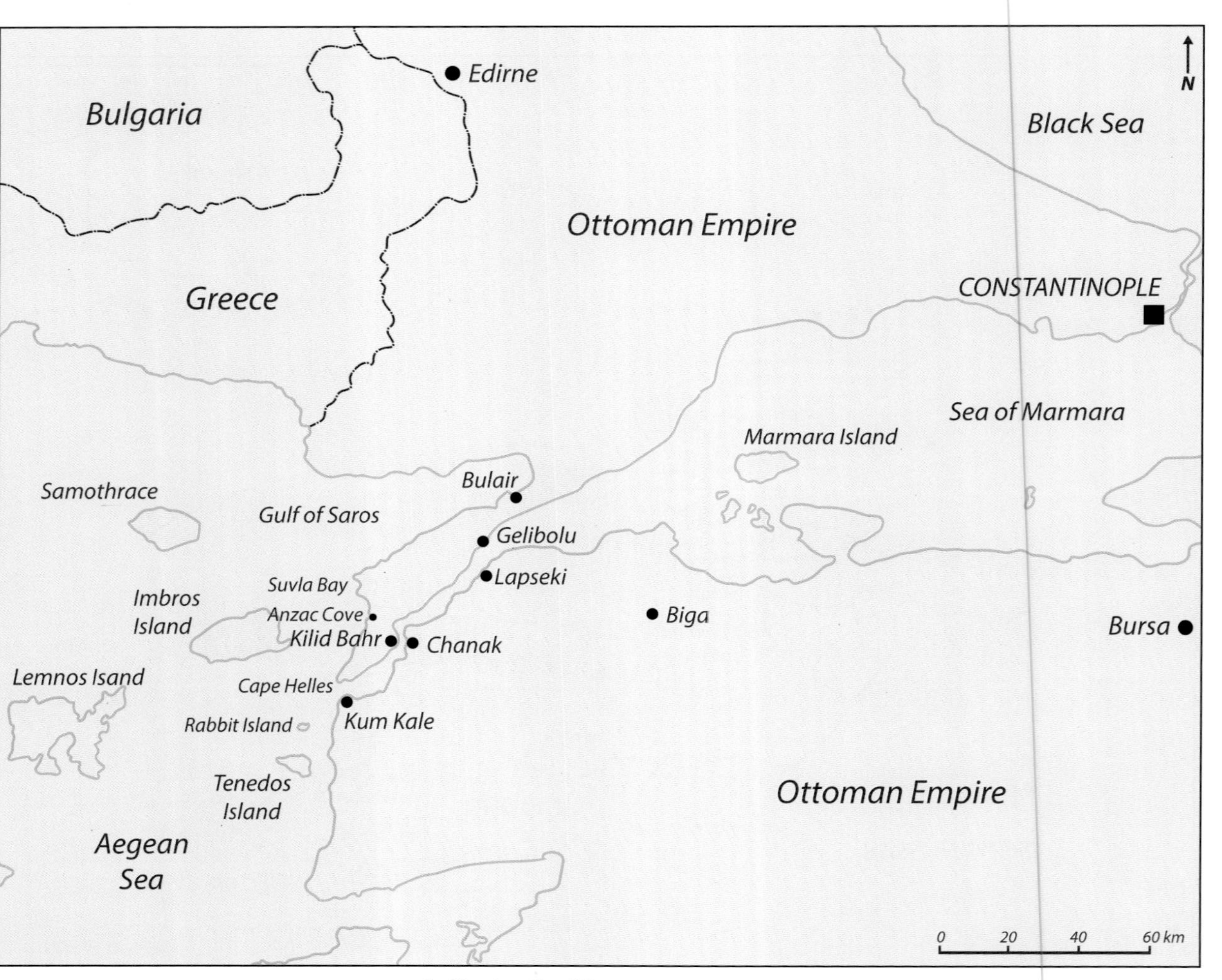

2. Dardanelles: The strategic context.

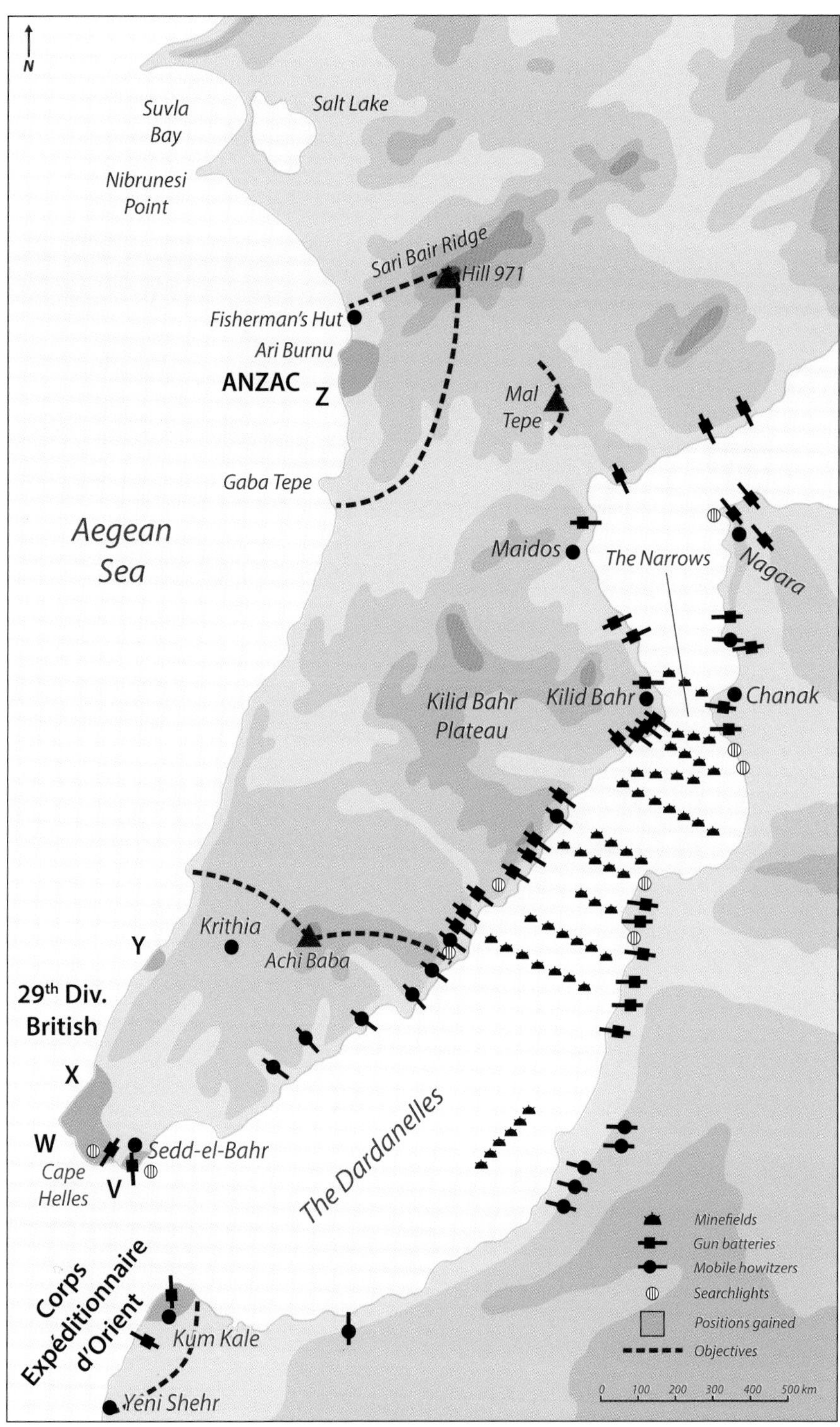
N
Suvla
Bay
Salt Lake
Nibrunesi
Point
Sari Bair Ridge
Hill 971
Fisherman's Hut
Ari Burnu
ANZAC
Z
Mal
Tepe
Gaba Tepe
Aegean
Sea
Maidos
The Narrows
Nagara
Kilid Bahr
Plateau
Kilid Bahr
Chanak
Krithia
Y
Achi Baba
29th Div.
British
X
W
Sedd-el-Bahr
Cape
Helles
V
The Dardanelles
Corps
Expéditionnaire
d'Orient
Kum Kale
Yeni Shehr
Minefields
Gun batteries
Mobile howitzers
Searchlights
Positions gained
Objectives
0 100 200 300 400 500 km

3. Gallipoli Peninsula.

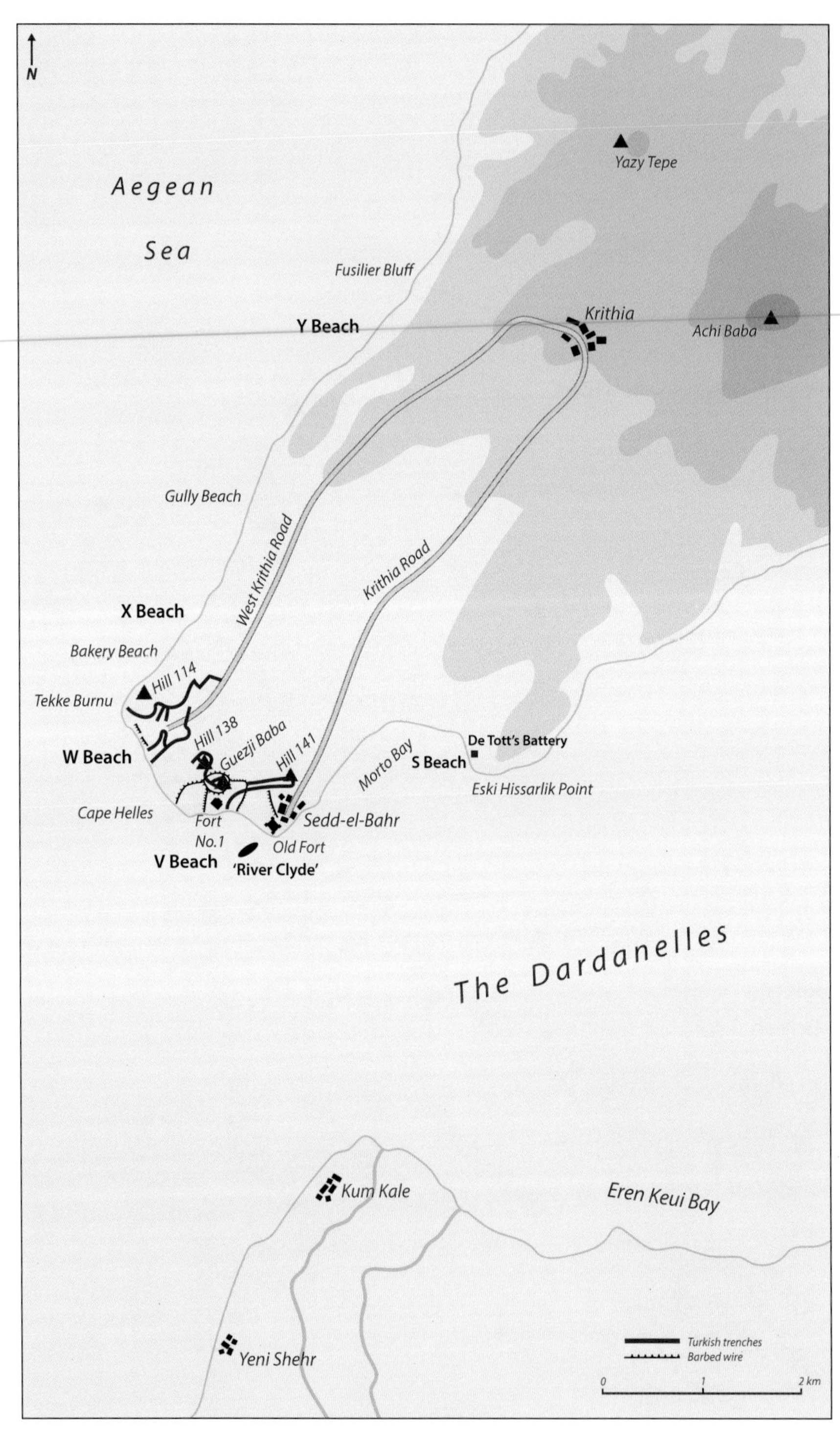

4. Cape Helles.

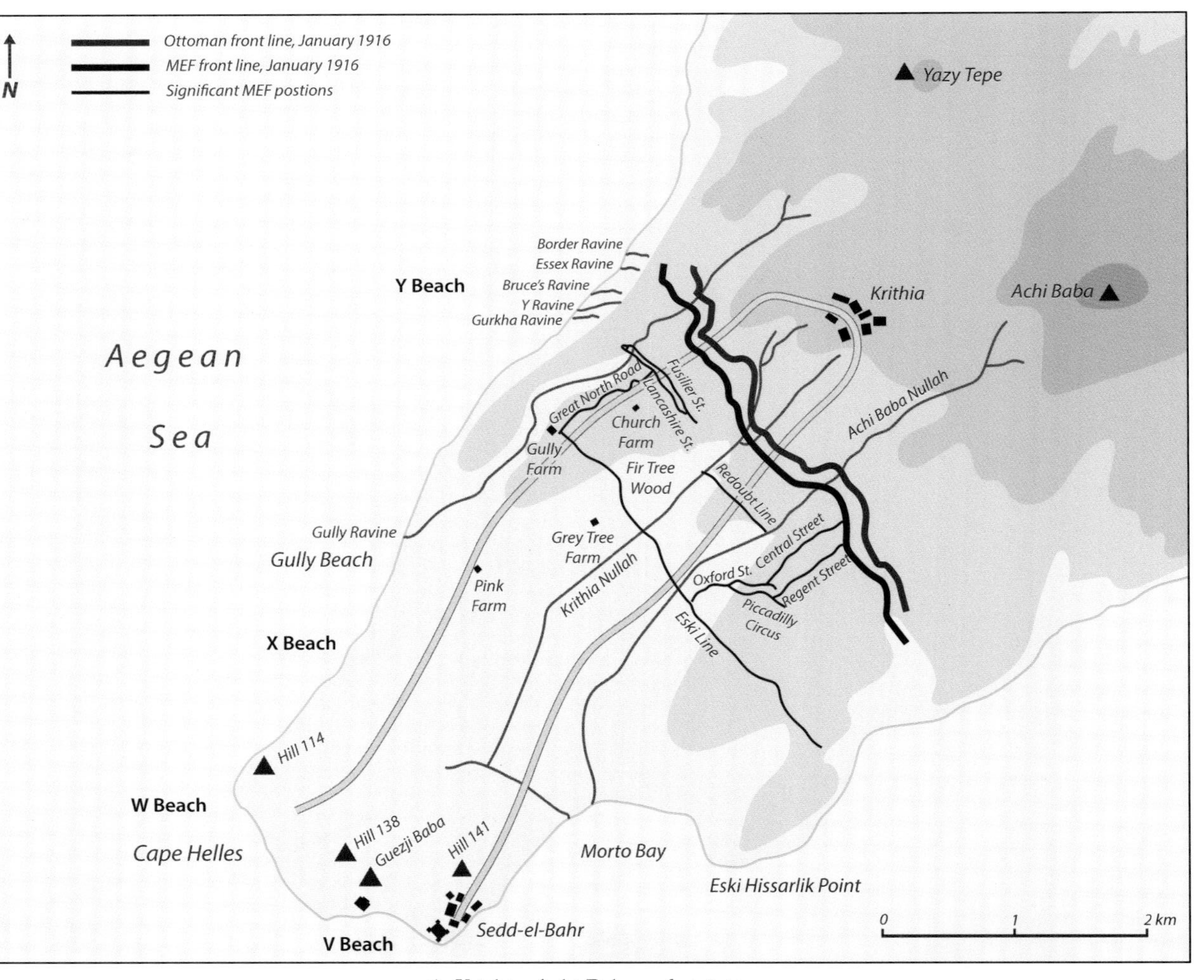

5. Krithia, Achi Baba and vicinity.

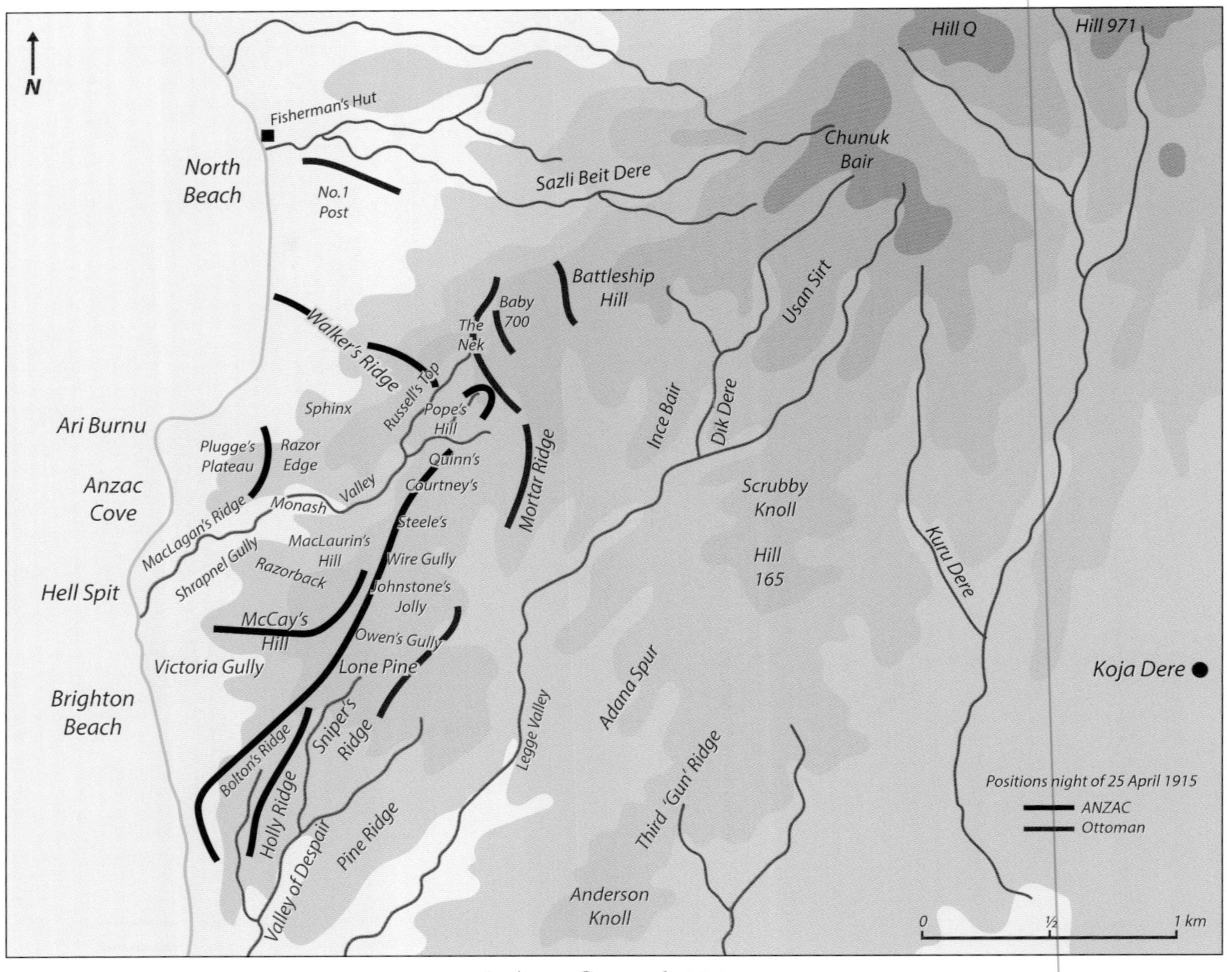

6. Anzac Cove and vicinity.

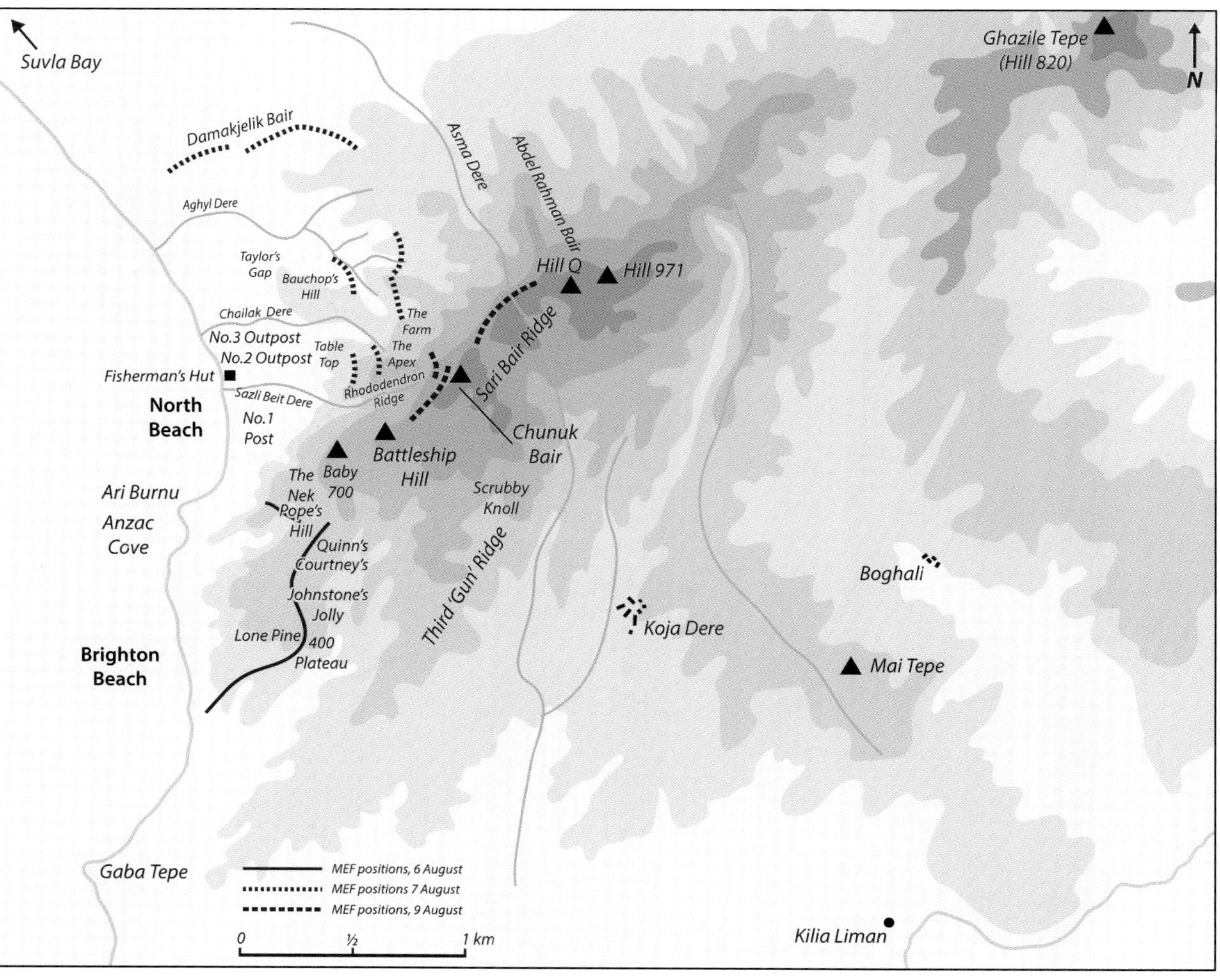

7. Sari Bair and vicinity.

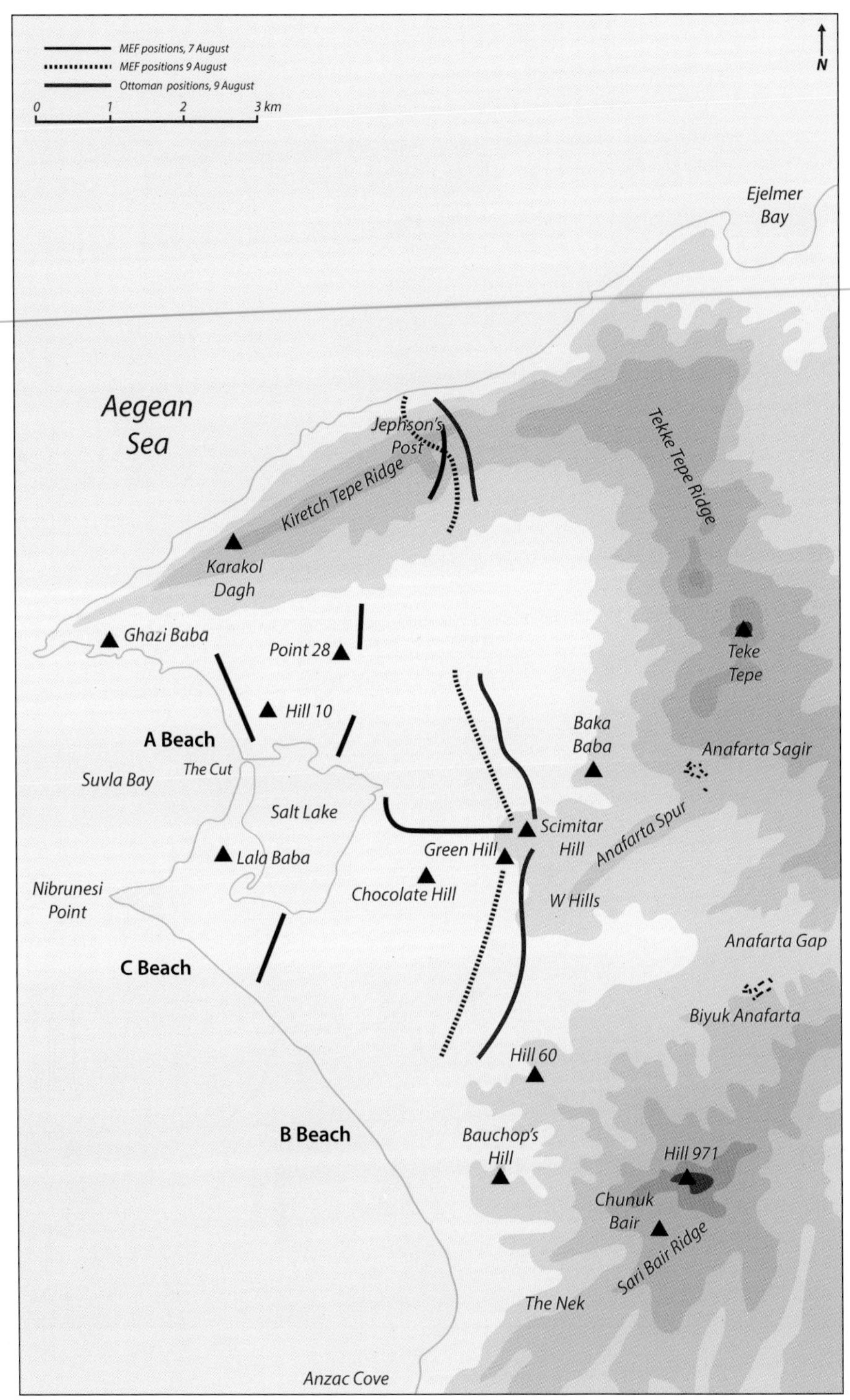

8. Suvla Bay and vicinity.

Godley called a conference at Johnston's headquarters to discuss how the task might be achieved, but he never turned up. Consequently, Johnston chaired the meeting during which he advised against taking the direct route up Rhododendron Ridge. Instead he recommended that, under the cover of darkness, Baldwin go over the steep sided Cheshire Ridge, drop into Aghyl Dere, and form up for the assault near the Farm, a small plateau 300 metres directly below Chunuk Bair. Temperley argued for the route up Rhododendron Ridge as intended, but Johnston rejected his views. After seeing the proposed route for himself, tortuous though it was, Baldwin accepted Johnston's advice.

Although he has been universally criticised for suggesting the change,[85] Johnston had good reason to advise against the direct route, and Baldwin had agreed with him. Given the results so far there was no guarantee the New Zealanders could secure Chunuk Bair. With Zero Hour 45 minutes after dawn and the heavy casualties incurred along Rhododendron Ridge on the previous two days, Baldwin's force, had they taken that route, would have suffered severely from Ottoman fire on the right flank, and certainly from Battleship Hill, before reaching Chunuk Bair. This would likely have thrown the attack into confusion. At least Johnston was no longer prepared to see more men slaughtered in an attempt to reach the feature along a narrow ridge that was swept by fire. The other option would have been to bring Zero Hour forward to allow the Baldwin to reach Chunuk Bair under the cover of darkness, but this was not contemplated, probably due to the rawness of his New Army battalions and a complicated passage of lines in darkness, especially in what turned out to be a desperate situation on Chunuk Bair.

Taking the roundabout route, Baldwin was short of the Farm at Zero Hour, and the preparatory bombardment had ceased well before his assault began. Met by a storm of fire his troops retired to the lip of the plateau. Meanwhile, fighting off a serious counter-attack the New Zealanders barely managed to maintain their tenuous hold on Chunuk Bair, where control of the fighting devolved on Johnston's subordinates. Back at The Apex which was as far forward as he could have been expected to establish his headquarters, Johnston could do nothing to influence the situation, reflecting the changing circumstances under which brigade commanders operated. All this was for naught. Mounting a three divisional attack at dawn the next day, successive waves of Ottoman infantry swept two recently arrived and inexperienced British battalions off Chunuk Bair, and cannoned into Baldwin's men at the Farm, killing over 1,000 of them including Baldwin himself. The August offensive was over.

Reflections on the August Offensive

The offensive indicated changes in the way in which brigades were tasked, and the extent to which brigade commanders were able to exert control once their units were committed to battle.

dated 8 August 1915, NZ and A Division General Staff War Diary. AWM41/53/5 Part 2, Appendix 79: 'Report of the Operations against the SARI BAIR position 6th-10th August of the Force under the Command of Major-General Sir A.J. Godley KCMG, CB Commanding New Zealand and Australian Division, 16 August 1915.

85 Bean, Vol. II, pp. 688-690; Aspinall-Oglander, *Military Operations Gallipoli*, Vol. II, *May 1915 to the Evacuation*, (London: Naval and Military Press reprint of 1932 edition), p. 217; Pugsley, *Gallipoli*, pp. 303-304; James, *Gallipoli*, pp. 288.

Initial planning was extensive, and orders were detailed, thorough, and prescriptive as to how the brigade task was to be carried out, detailing routes, timetables, fire support, communications and administrative requirements. Once battle was joined on the heights, however, with the demands to seek an early resolution planning and orders reverted to the old style with minimal preparation.

In the old Anzac bridgehead, the specific points to be captured within the enemy's trench systems were detailed, and the brigade commander's main contribution was detailing troops to task and briefing subordinates, ensuring they had time for reconnaissance and understood exactly what their objectives were. Although each of the brigade commanders established their headquarters close behind their attacking units, once those units were committed there was little they could do to influence events by personal intervention. Their functions were limited to organising reinforcements, reliefs, supplies and support to retain the gains won as Smyth and Johnston had done, or calling off futile attacks as Chauvel had.

In reality, it was obvious that the former notion of brigade commanders attacking with their troops only led to the unnecessary loss of experienced commanders. Control of the fighting itself was increasingly being devolved to battalion commanders and their subordinates. The brigade commander's contribution to the battle was best served through detailed coordination, issuing of clear orders and thorough briefings of subordinates, the provision of effective fire and administrative support, ensuring the operations they controlled gave their troops the best chance of success with minimal casualties and intervening when a crisis occurred. At No 2 Outpost Russell's close reconnaissance of the ground and detailed briefings set the foundation for the success. In the tangled ground and darkness, and with dispersed objectives he could do little to influence events as they unfolded – control of the fighting lay with his regimental and squadron commanders.

In the assault columns, while the commanders accompanied their brigades their ability to influence events once battle commenced was limited, largely by circumstance for Johnston, and a poor choice of exercising control by Monash. Perched at The Apex, Johnston could do little to control the fighting on Chunuk Bair, other than comply with his divisional commander's orders and move reinforcements forward. Temperely thought that while Johnston was "a capable tactician with a good eye for country" his "loyalty to the views of his superiors in the field was complete and unswerving whatever his personal opinions might be" and that he erred on the side of recklessness and was unable to weigh the situation calmly.[86] While he could be criticised for succumbing to Godley's order on 7 August, on the other hand the need to take Chunuk Bair early was essential if the offensive was to have any chance of success. His recommendation to divert Baldwin's force for the attack on the 9th was laudable in an effort to stem further bloodshed and chaos, but in the time available and with the route recommended it proved fatal. At Taylor's Gap Monash asserted firm control and got things moving, but his decision not to press on during the morning of 7 August is questionable, though the condition of his men obviously affected him. Deciding not to accompany the advance on the 8th, devolving control to a subordinate, and attempting to command a long and difficult assault from a headquarters too far back resulted in him completely losing control during the subsequent fighting, and contributed to the disintegration of his brigade.

86 Pugsley, *Gallipoli*, p. 279.

Hill 60 and beyond

The final offensive action at Anzac occurred at Hill 60 during the last week of August. Rather than the detailed planning preceding the August offensive, it was another rushed affair during which Russell worked under the direction of Cox. This was a brigade level operation in which both had control over events. With less than 24 hours' notice it was inadequately planned and supported. One British battalion, one Gurkha, two of Russell's regiments, and 500 men of Monash's depleted brigade were tasked to make the attack.[87] An inadequate fire plan failed to silence machine-guns firing down Kaiajik Dere, which annihilated the Australians and inflicted heavy casualties amongst Russell's troopers further down the valley.

With his troopers clinging to a small lodgment in the first Ottoman trench, at 11:45 p.m. Russell strongly urged another attack be mounted that night to reinforce the gains made. Rushed forward from Anzac, the raw, newly arrived 18th Australian Battalion reached the area at dawn and was thrown into the assault with little idea of their task, and no support, losing 50 percent casualties in seizing another small lodgment.[88] Although Russell's urging for a night attack was laudable, the time allotted to prepare for it was woefully inadequate, compounding the previous lack of preparation. It was another example of an ill-prepared assault reminiscent of Second Krithia. When a further effort was made on the afternoon of 27 August, Russell protested, requesting it be undertaken under the cover of darkness. Cox refused and again the attack failed to achieve its goal. Finally, on the night 28/29 August, a last effort secured most of the position except the crest, justifying Russell's view of conducting night attacks. However, the whole affair was under resourced, inadequately planned, and given insufficient fire support. It seemed that the lessons of the previous months had been forgotten.

Conclusion

For the Australians and New Zealanders, the campaign brought home the harsh reality of warfare compared to part-time soldiering at home. For the brigade commanders it had been a trying experience, and other than Walker and Smyth, it was one for which they had been unprepared or trained. Although Regular soldiers, Johnston, Sinclair-MacLagan, and Chauvel had no experience of commanding and controlling troops at even battalion or regimental level when appointed to command brigades. Those Australians who had previously held brigade command in the Militia and CF were largely self-taught, lacked any experience in controlling them, and had largely exercised a supervisory training and administrative function. Yet despite these disadvantages most adapted well in a vastly new environment. Sinclair-MacLagan's inexperience was evident at the landing, and his precipitous actions decided the fate of the operation in the first hour. Nonetheless, he performed satisfactorily in the defence that followed, growing in competence as the campaign progressed. Similarly inexperienced, McCay acquiesced in having

87 AWM4 1/53/5 Part 1: NZ&A Division General Staff War Diary, 20 August 1915; AWM4 35/1/4 Part 2: 'Operation Order No. 4 by Brig-General A.H. Russell Commanding NZ Mtd Rifle Bde dated 21 August' and 'NZMR Brigade Summary of Operations 21 August 1915', NZMR Brigade War Diary.

88 Bean, Vol. II, pp. 739-742; Pugsley, *Gallipoli*, pp. 323-324; Vennell, *The Forgotten General*, p. 81.

his brigade diverted as it came ashore, and lost control of it through vague orders. Despite agreeing to a rushed attack at Second Krithia, however, he displayed great gallantry in leading it, kept control of his battalions during the advance, and ensured the ground won was secured on both flanks.

While schooled in a doctrine of manoeuvre and quick attacks with brief orders, when faced with the realities of modern weapons this approach was found wanting, leading to an unnecessary loss of life for little gain. Some like Walker, Russell, and Monash made attempts to adopt a more measured approach, but under the pressure of time or their superiors' demands others too readily agreed in executing them. Yet in these circumstances their superiors had not served them well, insisting on impossible tasks at short notice with inadequate planning and fire support. As the campaign progressed it was becoming obvious the brigade commander's contribution to success lay in detailed planning, preparation, the coordination of effective support, together with clear orders and briefings rather than leading their troops into action, and very early Monash exhibited a preference for this.

Confronted by trench warfare, a commander's function widened with greater responsibilities for the coordination of the defensive sectors and cooperating closely with supporting engineers and artillery. In this environment Walker and Symth performed well, exerting firm control over the operations they undertook – the former demonstrating an aversion for futile operations and the moral courage to stand up to his superiors in averting them. So had Russell and he finished the campaign with a reputation as a strong commander with a firm control of his brigade's activities. Chauvel demonstrated an ability to swiftly take control of a critical situation, exercise firm leadership, and a readiness to call off an action early when the futility of it was evident. Monash's performance was mixed. Employing his engineer's training his planning, preparation, orders and briefings were thorough, and he took control of and sorted out a confused situation during the night march on 6/7 August. In abrogating responsibility for controlling his brigade during the advance on 8 August, however, he faltered at a critical time when combat leadership was needed most. Hughes simply proved unsuitable, abrogating his responsibilities and failing to take control when his regiments were being destroyed.

Of those who made the adjustments, several went onto higher command. Six became divisional commanders. Walker led the 1st Australian Division until June 1918, proving to be one of the best divisional commanders in the AIF, and Smyth commanded the 2nd Australian Division competently between December 1916 and May 1918. McCay as GOC 5th Australian Division gained notoriety after the Battle of Fromelles and was involved in another disastrous attack on the Somme in November 1916, after which his command was terminated. Holmes led the 4th Australian Division from January 1917 until he was killed near Messines the following July, after which Sinclair-MacLagan assumed command of it until the Armistice. Russell was promoted major-general in late November 1915, taking command of the NZ&A Division, after which he was appointed GOC of the newly raised NZ Division in March 1916, leading it with distinction until the end of the war. Two rose even higher. Chauvel temporarily commanded the 1st Australian Division from November 1915, after Walker was wounded, until March 1916 when he assumed command of the ANZAC Mounted Division. Elevated to command the Desert Column in July 1917, later renamed the Desert Mounted Corps, he was the first Australian to achieve corps command. In June 1916 Monash was given the newly raised 3rd Australian Division then assembling in England. Taking it to France in November, he performed well, and took command of the Australian Corps from Birdwood in May 1918, earning high praise for his performance during the last five months of the war.

The brigade commanders played an important role on Gallipoli, being the conduits who translated their superior's plans and orders into action and, through their subordinate units, executed those plans at the point of battle. With modern warfare forcing most formation commanders to command further from the front, the brigade commander's role changed from accompanying his units into battle and directly influencing its outcome. The experience at Gallipoli showed this was becoming a thing of the past. Instead, in the static phase of trench warfare they become more involved in the planning and preparation, the coordination of support and administration, thoroughly briefing subordinates to ensure everyone knew what was required to achieve the task and controlling the battle from a location further to the rear. For the ANZAC brigade commanders, the campaign provided the education and experience at brigade level that was missing in pre-war part-time soldiering.

13

Fighting at Anzac: A New Zealand Perspective

Christopher Pugsley

This chapter examines the performance of the New Zealand Expeditionary Force (NZEF) in the Gallipoli campaign. It examines how a hastily raised volunteer force drawn from an embryo Territorial Force with a stiffening of professional officers, warrant officers and non-commissioned officers adapted to the pragmatic realities of the Gallipoli campaign. On mobilisation of the NZEF in 1914 great attention was paid to the principles laid down in the various British Army training manuals that had been introduced after the South African War and also to lessons promulgated from British Expeditionary Force (BEF) experience on the Western Front. However, the peninsula terrain, particularly at Anzac, set its own rules, and tactical procedures had to adapt accordingly.

In the period from 1902 to 1914 the British Army underwent major organisational and doctrinal changes which codified doctrine and assessed the impact of technological change on its fighting organisations. An Imperial General Staff was established, and *Field Service Regulations* introduced to establish a commonality of organisation and doctrine throughout the military forces of the British Empire.

In 1908 Colonel E.M. Lloyd in his *A Review of the History of the Infantry,* succinctly summarised the issues facing armies in the first decade of the twentieth century.[1] He concluded that Infantry was emphatically the predominant partner but, as a Russian officer commenting on his army's infantry performance in the Russo-Japanese War, now had to adapt "To fight individually whilst co-operating for a common objective." This required the "substitution of 'Infantry Training' for 'Infantry Drill'" – the evolution of small group tactics within an infantry company and also for companies within a battalion.[2] All arms cooperation was a corollary to this development. Within the artillery the Russo-Japanese War saw the increasing use of field artillery in the indirect fire role and the increasing use of shrapnel against infantry at ranges under 4,000 yards.

The importance of machine guns in defence and in holding ground won was also recognised: "Attached to advanced guards, they [the machine guns] helped them hold ground that they had seized till other troops could come up …" Lloyd's study emphasised the power of the defensive

1 E.M. Lloyd, *A Review of the History of Infantry* (London: Longmans, Green & Co.1908), pp. 286-290.
2 Ibid., pp. 282.

and the difficulties of offensive operations particularly by day. "It was found that frontal attacks even by troops ready to give their lives without counting the cost, seldom succeeded ... Ground must be gained as far as possible by night, trenches must be made for cover." Any attack had to be developed over two or three days with the best option being to achieve an outflanking manoeuvre. Advance in daylight under fire could only be made by creeping in open order or by rushes by groups, who dug themselves in as soon as they halted, and were taught to dig lying down. Any attempt at a bayonet charge over open ground proved futile. There was no "decisive range" as the regulations had assumed: "Sometimes the two adversaries remain lying face to face at only fifteen or twenty paces from each other until some gallant men bound from the ranks with a shout and hurl themselves upon the enemy's trenches."[3]

These issues were addressed in part by the reforms initiated in the British Army, but the spectrum of imperial commitments saw *Field Service Regulations* and the resulting corps doctrinal pamphlets place emphasis on principles but made little attempt to formulate tactical procedures at regimental level. Its interpretation remained the training responsibility of battalion and regimental commanders. The adoption of the four double-strength company as the standard organisation for an infantry battalion in the British Army in 1913-14 meant that there was little practical training carried out on platoon tactics within the company structure. As a result, tactical procedures at regimental and formation level were in a state of flux when the Empire found itself at war in August 1914.[4]

The NZEF commanded by Major-General Sir Alexander Godley consisted of a divisional headquarters and two brigades: New Zealand Infantry Brigade and the New Zealand Mounted Rifles Brigade supported by a New Zealand Field Artillery Brigade with other supporting arms and services. In Egypt it was grouped into a combined New Zealand and Australian (NZ&A) Division that included the 4th Australian Infantry Brigade and the Australian Light Horse Brigade. In Egypt and at Gallipoli it formed part of Lieutenant-General Sir William Birdwood's Australian and New Zealand Army Corps (ANZAC).

The two infantry brigades of this formation with supporting arms were involved in the Gallipoli landings on 25 April 1915 but as infantry casualties reached critical proportions, they were joined by the New Zealand Mounted Rifles Brigade and the 1st Australian Light Horse Brigade serving in the infantry role on 12 May 1915.[5]

Raising the NZEF

Godley was the architect of the New Zealand Territorial Force in the period from 1911-1914. Service in the Territorial Force was compulsory, but overseas service was voluntary. The Territorial Force was structured to provide an expeditionary force in the event of war. All planning and training in New Zealand was driven by Godley to this end with brigade-level camps being conducted in 1912-1913 so that commanders and staff understood how formations would operate.

3 Ibid., pp. 286-90.
4 General Staff, War Office, *Infantry Training (4 – Company Organization) 1914* (London: HMSO, 1914).
5 ANZ: NZ&A Division, Division Headquarters War Diary, 12 May 1915, New Zealand Archives.

Major-General Alexander Godley.

Godley's forte proved to be administration and training. In training the Territorial Force Godley recruited the best warrant officers available from those on secondment to the New Zealand Defence Force but he also reached out to the Musketry School at Hythe and enticed members of the warrant officer staff to join the New Zealand Defence Forces with the promise of regular commissions in the New Zealand Staff Corps. It gave New Zealand a highly professional core of professional instructors who proved invaluable to the NZEF. These instructors, including Captains P.B. Henderson, J.M. Rose and J.A. Wallingford, were attached to the military districts where they concentrated on improving musketry skills and training the respective machine gun sections including the training of machine gun officers for each battalion and mounted rifles regiment.

Godley was equally innovative in structuring the NZEF. Each Mounted Rifles regiment was equipped with two Maxim guns but on mobilisation Godley directed that each of the four infantry battalions be equipped with four Maxim guns: double that laid down in the establishment tables for an infantry battalion. This gave the infantry brigade 16 machine guns. This too was invaluable on Gallipoli.[6]

The composition of the NZEF reflected the reality that the Territorial Force was still a year short of its planned completion date with many serving Territorials below enlistment age. On mobilisation of the 8,417 Main Body of the NZEF that sailed on 15 October 1914, 4,076 were currently serving in the New Zealand Military Forces. This included 3,602 Territorial Soldiers as well as British officers and Warrant Officers on loan and officers and permanent staff of the NZ Military Forces. In addition, 2,849 had some previous military training, leaving 925 with no previous military service.[7]

The greatest concern facing the staff in the weeks before deployment was the deficiencies in musketry training. Captain John Rose, NZSC who ran the musketry training for the Wellington section of the Main Body at Awapuni Camp in Palmerston North made this assessment. "The stamp of men is decidedly good: strong, hardy, resourceful fellows but it will take a long time to train them up to the necessary standard."[8] On sailing despite herculean efforts by the training staff, 721 of the Force were qualified as Marksmen, 2,415 were qualified, 765 were not qualified, 2,042 had not completed the musketry course and 1,043 were not classified: over 60 percent of the force were below the minimum shooting standard.[9]

This was made good in Egypt. Henderson became the machine gun officer for the New Zealand Mounted Rifles Brigade, Wallingford the machine gun officer for the New Zealand

6 New Zealand Defence Force, Special General Order, New Zealand Expeditionary Force (1914), 24 August 1914, pp. 1-2, 13 September 1914, Captain J.M. Rose, NZSC, Diaries 1914-16, Rose family.
7 Christopher Pugsley, *Gallipoli: The New Zealand Story* (Auckland: Oratia Books, 2016), p. 367.
8 Rose Diaries, 15 August 1914, Rose Diaries.
9 Pugsley, *Gallipoli*, p. 367.

Infantry Brigade and in the weeks immediately before sailing for the Dardanelles, Rose became the machine gun officer for 4th Australian Brigade. Each produced superb machine gun teams in addition to improving the musketry skills in their formations. Their professional understanding of the role of snipers and the brigading and employment of machine guns by Rose and Wallingford was critical to the securing of the Anzac perimeter in the initial days ashore. The New Zealand Mounted Rifles Brigade showed the same skills in shooting and use of its machine guns when they were deployed to Anzac from 12 May 1915.

The mobilisation of the NZEF for war and the commitment of a New Zealand Force to seize German Samoa and the preparation and sailing of the Main Body of the NZEF was Godley's achievement. Captain John Rose's professional assessment was shared by many of Godley's subordinates: "Can't help thinking what a mess we would have been in were it not for the Compulsory Training Scheme. The old volunteer system would have collapsed under the strain. There would have been no proper equipment etc. and it would have been utterly impossible to have attempted to send away a mixed division. As it is a large number of the men are quite raw and will require a good firm handling before they are fit."[10]

Godley's selection of commanders on the outbreak of the war was also finely judged. He had already assessed who would be his brigade commanders. Colonel Francis Earl Johnston, a 42-year-old, New Zealand-born, British Regular Officer commanded the infantry brigade. A Sword of Honour winner from the Royal Military College Sandhurst, with operational service in the Sudan and South Africa, and as son of the Speaker of the New Zealand Legislative Council, Johnston, had impeccable credentials.[11]

The 47-year old Colonel Andrew Russell was also an individual who Godley held in high regard. New Zealand-born, Harrow and Sandhurst educated, with five years Regular service in India and Burma, Russell was a sheep-farmer in the Hawkes Bay and active in the Territorial Force. Godley had unsuccessfully tried to entice him to join the New Zealand Staff Corps (NZSC) as a regular officer and regarded him in this light in appointing him to command the New Zealand Mounted Rifles Brigade.[12] Godley's instinct was to pick professional soldiers for the key brigade command positions, and Russell, the exception to this rule, was seen by Godley as someone who showed all of the attributes of a professional soldier suited to higher command. He proved this on Gallipoli, commanding the NZ &A Division at the end of the campaign and was the logical choice to command the New Zealand Division on its formation in February 1916.

The New Zealand Field Artillery (NZFA) Brigade was commanded by Lieutenant-Colonel George Napier Johnston of the Royal Garrison Artillery (RGA). Canadian-born and commissioned through the Royal Military College, Kingston, Canada and the Royal Military Academy, Woolwich, Johnston had a long working association with New Zealand. He had been a very effective Artillery Staff Officer in New Zealand in 1904-1907 and returned in 1911 as Director

10 Captain J. Rose Diaries 1914-16, Rose Family, 14 August 1914.

11 Ian McGibbon, (ed.), *The Oxford Companion to New Zealand Military History* (Auckland: OUP, 2000).

12 Jock Vennell, *The Forgotten General: New Zealand's World War I Commander, Major-General Sir Andrew Russell* (Auckland: Allen & Unwin, 2011). Chris Pugsley, 'Russell, Andrew Hamilton' from the *Dictionary of New Zealand Biography*, Te Ara: The Encyclopedia of New Zealand, updated 28 Jan. 2014 <http://www.TeAra.govt.nz/en/biographies/3r34/russell-andrew-hamilton> (Accessed 29 September 2017).

of Artillery during which New Zealand acquired the latest field artillery with 18-pounder field guns and 4.5-inch howitzers. On declaration of war and the decision to expand the artillery commitment of the NZEF from one to four batteries, Johnston oversaw this expansion as both Commander Royal Artillery (CRA) and Brigade Commander of the NZFA Brigade.[13] An austere, reserved demanding professional "Blinky" Johnston set the standards for New Zealand Field Artillery and continued as Commander Divisional Artillery (CDA) for the duration of the war.

Godley selected those he considered the best available commanding officers to command the infantry battalions and mounted rifles regiments. He sought younger men but showed that talent rather than age was an important criterion by his selection of the 56-year old, Lieutenant-Colonel W.G. Malone to command the Wellington Infantry Battalion. He was similarly careful in his selection of regular staff drawn from British officers on loan or members of the NZSC with warrant officers and senior NCOs drawn from the New Zealand Permanent Staff (NZPS). Both he and James Allen the Minister of Defence were conscious of the need to train the reinforcement drafts that would sustain the NZEF and ensured that capable professional officers, warrant officers and non-commissioned staff remained in training posts in New Zealand. Despite the high casualties among the Regular cadre on Gallipoli, Allen rejected most of Godley's requests to release training staff to the front to the long-term benefit of the reinforcement drafts.

Godley took the New Zealand Expeditionary Force (NZEF) to war in October 1914 in the expectation that it would join with the Australian Imperial Force (AIF). Initial discussions in 1912 suggested that the New Zealand Infantry Brigade would form one of the brigades in an Australian division. The Main Body of the NZEF provided a divisional headquarters and two brigades: one infantry brigade of four battalions and a mounted rifles brigade of three regiments. It was assumed that one of these was likely to serve in a different division depending on whether Godley's headquarters assumed control of infantry or mounted rifles/Yeomanry/Light Horse formations. However on the outbreak of war Australia mobilised a complete division of three infantry brigades and so in Egypt the NZEF joined with Colonel John Monash's 4th Australian Brigade and Colonel Harry Chauvel's 1st Light Horse Brigade to form the polyglot NZ&A Division, a curious mix of Mounted Rifles, Light Horse and the two infantry brigades and only one brigade of field artillery: the New Zealand Field Artillery (NZFA) Brigade consisting of three four-gun 18 pounder batteries and one four-gun battery of 4.5-inch howitzers: the only howitzer battery in Lieutenant-General Sir William Birdwood's ANZAC.

In Egypt, Godley was determined to have the NZEF ready for war as quickly as possible. He was pleased with the calibre of the men but recognised that enthusiasm alone was no substitute for training. His major concern was the calibre of his officers. "There is no doubt that, as I am always saying, the Officers are in many ways our weak spot, but they are improving enormously here and, I believe, by the time we get to France, will be fairly efficient."[14]

Godley embarked on a rigorous training regime that continued the ambitious training programme he set for the New Zealand Territorial Force. He demanded perfection. His impassive demeanour masked his feelings and neither his officers nor men saw how much he

13 'Unbroken War Record,' *Evening Post*, Wellington, 19 June 1920, p. 6.
14 ANZ: Godley to Allen, 26 December 1914, Godley Correspondence, New Zealand Archive.

appreciated the efforts they made. Brigade and Divisional training continued at pace with a brief interlude on the Suez Canal when elements of the New Zealand Infantry Brigade helped repel the bold but fruitless attempt by an Ottoman force to a crossing. By now Godley judged that the NZEF was fit and ready for combat, Godley confirmed this in his letter to Allen of 13 March 1915. "I really think that this division has now reached the stage at which only bullets can make it much better. The man are very hard and fit and well. The officers have undoubtedly begun to know their job, and realise their responsibilities, and I shall be quite happy to take the field with the force as it stands."[15]

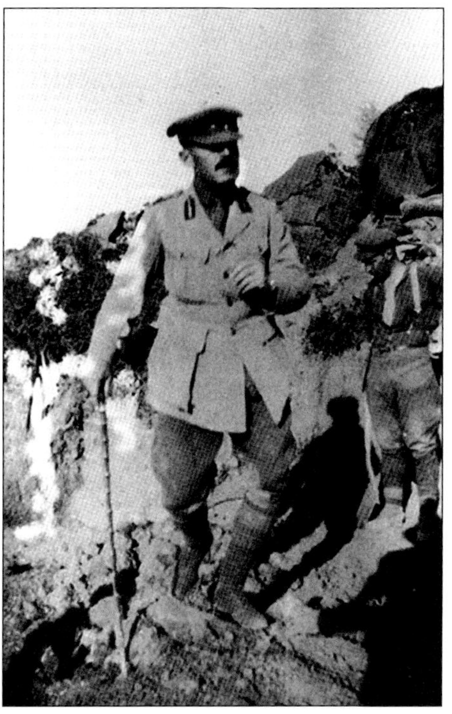

Brigadier-General Andrew Russell.

Gaining a Foothold: 25 April 1915

Birdwood's ANZAC landing north of the Gaba Tepe peninsula spearheaded by Major-General W.T. Bridges' 1st Australian Division dissolved into chaos ashore on the 25 April 1915. Ottoman counterattacks on the extreme left and right of the extended Australian line threatened disaster. The New Zealand battalions of the Infantry Brigade were thrown in piecemeal as they came ashore throughout the day to bolster the Australian line on the left flank. The brigade commander, Brigadier-General F.E. Johnston had gone sick with measles at Lemnos on 24 April 1915 and Birdwood's Brigadier-General, General Staff, Harold "Hooky" Walker was appointed to command the brigade as it came ashore. Walker used what staff he had to grasp control of the situation. One of these was the New Zealand Infantry Brigade machine gun officer, Captain Jesse Wallingford, NZSC.

Prior to the landing on 25 April, Godley and Wallingford had discussed the role of the Brigade's 16 machine guns. "Gen. Godley had arranged with me on the day previous to take charge of all the guns and that he relied on me to cover the landing, and if not successful to fight while the men got off even if the guns were sacrificed. I assured him that my guns would fight it out and that we would do the job alright."[16] Circumstance saw the New Zealand machine guns committed piecemeal with their battalions and in Wallingford's words "had a walloping and my best machine gun section [Auckland] smashed."[17] Wallingford was grimly aware that the infantry commanding officers did not have his knowledge and tended to commit the guns too far forward to support their attacks. This happened on 25 April, resulting in heavy casualties in the Auckland and Canterbury machine gun sections. What is interesting is the foresight

15 ANZ: Godley to Allen, 13 March 1915, Godley Correspondence, New Zealand Archives.
16 Captain Jesse Wallingford, NZSC, Diary, [Reflections on 25 April 1915], Wallingford Family.
17 Wallingford Diary, 26 April 1915.

Godley displayed in anticipating brigading the guns under Wallingford's control so that they could cover the force if it had to withdraw. The brigading of machine guns in the defence of the Anzac perimeter becomes a feature of their use in the campaign, and it is obvious that Godley appreciated the importance of centralised control: something that he is not normally given credit for. As Lloyd identified in his review of infantry in South Africa and the Far East, it was holding ground won that was the problem. This was certainly the case at Anzac from the very first hours ashore in the broken ground encompassing two ridges and the gullies between that became the Anzac bridgehead on the Gallipoli Peninsula.

Circumstance pushed Godley's NZ&A Division to the northern flank of the Anzac perimeter which was divided into four sections. Sections 1 and 2 were held by the 1st Australian Division and No. 3 and 4 by the NZ &A Division. No.3 Section covered from Courtney's to Quinn's Post and Pope's Hill. No. 4 Section included Russell's Top, Walker's Ridge and the outposts along the coast in the area of Fisherman's Hut. The line was consolidated in late April with Monash's 4th Australian Brigade holding No.3 Sector and the New Zealand Infantry Brigade, No.4 Sector.

War is Personalities

War is a personality business and whether citizen soldier or regular, pragmatic professionalism by individual officers, non-commissioned officers and soldiers forged the key that made the difference. Holding on at Anzac in late April 1915 was determined by a handful of men. Disaster threatened with heavy losses to battalion officers and NCOs, with frightened soldiers potentially overwhelmed by the realities of establishing a trench line sometimes only metres apart and overlooked by their enemy. In sniping and in digging-in the Ottomans had mastery over the ANZAC. Lieutenant-Colonel D. Macbean Stewart of the Canterbury Infantry Battalion was killed in the battle for Baby 700 on 25 April, his successor was badly wounded on 1 May. Plugge of the Auckland Battalion was slightly wounded on 25 April but remained on duty. Within days of the landing the New Zealand infantry companies were at half-strength and had lost most of their officers and non-commissioned officers. In these situations, leadership became the critical factor.

Within the NZEF a number of individuals stand out. Lieutenant-Colonel Malone of the Wellington Infantry Battalion consolidated the New Zealand line on Walker's Ridge and Russell's Top in late April. He imposed order and discipline to ensure that trenches were dug and defended. His actions embodied his favourite aphorism: "The art of warfare is the cultivation of domestic virtues." He applied this in those first crisis days on Walker's Ridge and Russell's Top and again in June when the New Zealand Infantry Brigade replaced the 4th Australian Brigade in No. 3 Sector with the Wellington initially occupying Courtney's Post and then because of the critical situation, taking over Quinn's Post.[18]

18 Jock Vennell, *Man of Iron: The Extraordinary Story of New Zealand WW1 Hero Lieutenant-Colonel William Malone* (Auckland: Allen & Unwin, 2015); Chris Pugsley, 'Malone, William George', first published in the *Dictionary of New Zealand Biography*, Te Ara: The Encyclopedia of New Zealand <https://teara.govt.nz/en/biographies/3m40/malone-william-george> (Accessed 29 September 2017).

At Quinn's Post, a tiny gully no more than two tennis courts in size and with a five-metre deep ring of ground protecting the depression, the trenches at their closest point were less than five metres apart. If discussed dispassionately as part of a tactical exercise Quinn's Post would be judged by Directing Staff as tactically untenable but it was held because of the interlocking arcs of fire from New Zealand and Australian machine guns sited on Russell's Top, Pope's Hill and Courtney's Post which provided an impenetrable belt of lead when the Very pistol lights requesting immediate fire was triggered. The defence of Anzac provided a masterclass in the use of machine guns in the defence and credit for this is due to Godley's foresight and the skills on the ground of the men he selected: Captains John Rose and Jesse Wallingford.

Machine Guns Dominate Ground

On 27 April the New Zealand Infantry Brigade focus was on the left flank on First Ridge where the spur of Walker's Ridge climbed to Russell's Top which linked at the saddle known as The Nek to the Ottoman strongpoint on Baby 700. This was the northern perimeter of the Anzac line. The fight to secure this flank involved the 16th Australian Battalion and New Zealanders of Malone's Wellington Battalion as Ottoman forces attempt to drive Anzacs off the ridge with potentially disastrous consequences to the beachhead. Wallingford became a key presence in consolidating the position. He employed one of the Wellington machine guns to secure the line, threatening to shoot any man who retired and for the first week ashore had little or no respite. "Getting played out; haven't had a night sleep since landing. Guns constantly being shot through, but we still continue."[19] Each of Wallingford's gun teams employed periscopes, the value of which Wallingford anticipated and had them manufactured in Egypt. They proved invaluable at Anzac because of the close proximity between the trench lines and the ever-present danger from snipers. These first difficult days proved to Wallingford that the New Zealand infantryman showed his potential. "These N.Z. boys will do me, they can fight as good as any of the old army, so I feel very comfortable."[20]

Wallingford wrote to his former Chief Instructor at the Musketry School in Hythe on the lessons drawn from using machine guns at Gallipoli. Their value and comparative scarcity made it vital that they be brigaded and used as one combined unit of 16 guns rather than dissipated under the control of individual commanding officers. It confirmed that "M. Guns ought to be one unit." Wallingford used them aggressively but commented that Commanding officers "want to use them constantly for any little thing." There were heavy losses among the trained men of the machine gun sections that could not be immediately replaced: "One M.G. Officer left, most of the Serg[eants] gone. This is due to the guns being pushed forward by regiments and company commanders. Since guns were brigaded the men are more pleased, do everything in their power [to hold the position]."[21] The losses and lack of trained reinforcements saw Wallingford recommend the establishment of a machine gun corps to ensure that lessons were learnt and that a regular supply of trained men guaranteed. Wallingford anticipated many of the changes initiated in 1916-18.

19 Wallingford Diary, 1 May 1915.
20 Ibid., Reflections.
21 Ibid., 3 May 1915.

Captain John Rose's diary entries echoed Wallingford's remarks. The 4th Australian Brigade held Pope's Hill, Quinn's and Courtney's Post at the head of Monash Gully, the critical positions whose defence was essential to the security of the Anzac position. If any of these posts should fall, then Anzac was untenable. Rose, like Wallingford, went wherever the situation was critical. By the end of April, he believed. "We have got a grip now and with a fair share of luck we should be hard to shift."[22]

Rose's diary records the fighting as being machine gun against machine gun, sniper against sniper to wrest fire ascendancy along the front line. Despite being wounded he and many of his Australian machine gunners stayed at their posts. On 8 May Rose noted that four of 4th Australian brigades eight guns were riddled with rifle and shrapnel fire and were out of action. "My losses [in the machine gun sections] since the fighting started are: Killed 10; wounded 27 & myself = 28; missing 1."[23]

The need to engage Ottoman machine gun positions as soon as they were located, demanded an immediate response. Both Rose and Wallingford were ceaselessly looking for alternate positions for their guns. "We have to be constantly shifting them as the Enemy locate our guns and then pour in Rifle fire or shell them and smash them up. We have such a small range of ground to put our Gun[s] on that it is very difficult to find alternative positions for them."[24]

The major Ottoman assault was defeated on 19 May, but there were continual attempts to break the Anzac line. At the beginning of June, the now exhausted 4th Australian Brigade was relieved by the New Zealand Infantry Brigade that had been in reserve on fatigue duties since returning from Helles. Rose remained as machine gun officer for No. 3 Section with Wallingford responsible for No. 4 Section encompassing Russell's Top and Walker's Ridge.

It is instructive to see the allocation of machine guns in No. 3 Section in July 1915 at the head of Monash Gully. The interlocking arcs of the guns from Pope's Hill and Courtney's Post cover Quinn's Post which is limited to two guns, both of which are in a ready reaction role to open fire only in the event of an attack. The support coming from 11 guns positioned on both flanks with a further three guns in reserve in the event of casualties and a further four guns in the inner lines at the head of the Gully in the event of a breakthrough shows how machine guns provide the backbone of the defence into which is coordinated, rifles, grenades, mortars, and artillery:

Courtney's Post		*Pope's Post*	
13th Battalion AIF	2 guns	2nd ALH	2 guns
14th Battalion AIF	2 guns	3rd ALH	2 guns
Otago Battalion	2 guns	Reserve 1st ALH 2 guns	
Auckland Battalion	1 gun		
Reserve Auckland Battalion	1 gun		
		Inner Defences	
Quinn's Post		15th Battalion AIF	2 guns
Wellington Battalion	2 guns	Canterbury Battalion	2 guns[25]

22 Rose Diaries 1914-16, 29 April 1915.
23 Ibid., 8 May 1915.
24 Ibid., 16 May 1915.
25 ANZ: Machine Guns in No. 3 Section of the NZ&A Division, Appendix No. 93 A, 4 July 1915, Wellington Infantry Battalion War Diary, July 1915, New Zealand Archive.

Quinn's Post designed by Lieutenant-Colonel Malone. The skyline on the left was held by Ottoman forces. The frontline was 10-15 metres beyond the crest on the right. The wooden chute was devised for mining operation earth removal; battalion cook houses are at bottom right.

Machine Guns in the Attack

Command ineptitude meant that the power displayed by Wallingford and Rose's defensive machine gun deployment was not given the same opportunities in the attack. This was seen in the first divisional attack mounted by the NZ&A Division on the night 2/3 May. It was the division's first coordinated attack and in addition to all available artillery which was very limited, Wallingford placed 10 machine guns in support of the attack. Despite this support it was a failure. Faulty planning and poor time and space appreciations by Johnston the New Zealand Brigade commander and by Lieutenant-Colonel Moore, the British regular officer commanding the Otago Infantry Battalion saw the New Zealand attack collapse against a strongly defended Ottoman position. The Otagos were an hour late in reaching the start line on Pope's Hill and were committed piecemeal as each platoon clambered up the hill, leading to heavy casualties. Even though it was a night attack, the operation confirmed the difficulties of any attack succeeding if launched against an expectant enemy in dug in positions which in this case consisted of a series of trenches in rows on rising ground, each providing massed rifle and machine gun fire against the ANZAC attack. This failure was repeated in the attacks at Helles by the New Zealand Infantry Brigade in the morning 8 May and then again in the same afternoon by the attacks by the New Zealand Infantry Brigade and the 2nd Australian Brigade in the Second Battle of Krithia, each without coordinated machine gun support.

Despite flashes of brilliance and obdurate courage displayed by both New Zealand brigades in the night assault on Chunuk Bair as part of the August offensive, the opportunities to provide meaningful machine gun support to the Auckland Infantry Battalion attack on the morning 7 August 1915 was ignored by Brigadier-General Johnston's inability to anticipate and structure support for the daylight attack, despite Wallingford's entreaties. A similar lack of forethought is evident again with the New Zealand Brigade attack on 8 August, only Malone's initiative and obduracy in defence of the high ground rescues the lack of planning and coordination by Johnston and his staff. Major Cunningham the surviving senior officer in the Wellington Infantry Battalion summed up the failures within the NZ &A Divisional command structure in particular the command failure within the New Zealand Infantry Brigade. Wallingford recorded. "Cunningham tells me that everything was slipshod – no meeting of commanders and talk over the situation. Very few bombs, no staff officer accompanied them. No set plan to work on etc etc. He states that with a proper force of machine guns and a Head Commander the whole of Chunuk Bair could have been swept clean."[26]

Wallingford agreed with this assessment. He later demonstrated the power of the New Zealand machine guns in the Ottoman counterattack on the 10 August that swept two British battalions off Chunuk Bair. Wallingford observed:

> More guns join in at this point and the next line gets scattered – line after line comes on to the zone of death. It cannot be called anything else, with my ten guns playing on to it (there are four 300 yards behind us). At about the fourth line, and every line after, they all go down – some in their tracks others on to their knees and others get thru but guns follow them, and they are no more. Poor beggars and gallant soldiers. No officers to lead them they are just simply forced forward. At last all is over. Individuals can be seen crashing back all that day, but we leave the poor beggars alone. The whole business seems a long time – I reckon we were killing for 30 minutes – but I don't think it could have taken more than 10 to 15 minutes. If they had got through (past our guns) they would have swept our thin line away and then God help the new Kitchener Boys ... What a good job it is that I am constantly "biting" about oil, water and cleanliness of guns – if some of the guns had jammed, it would have been all up. When in command, attend to small details and don't trust essentials to the juniors. If I had trusted my subalterns, even the best, I would have run out of oil and water many a time.[27]

Sniping at Anzac

The musketry training that was the focus of Wallingford, Henderson and Rose's efforts in New Zealand and Egypt proved its worth at Anzac.The Ottoman soldiers proved to be excellent snipers and it was a battle to gain ascendancy. Both Rose and Wallingford were key factors in meeting this challenge. Wallingford picked his subordinates for their skill and initiative, regardless of rank. Privates Arthur Fish, a self-employed bushman and Colin Warden, an

26 Wallingford letter to son, 5 September 1915.
27 Ibid.

Australian who was regarded as one of the finest scouts and shots in the NZEF, both members of the Auckland Infantry Battalion, were in this category and worked with Wallingford both as snipers and in directing machine gun fire.[28]

The Royal Marine Light Infantry Brigade replaced the New Zealand Infantry Brigade when it was sent to reinforce the Helles front on 5-6 May. Wallingford found that many of the Marines had no musketry training and could not load their rifles. He sought out the best shots of the 180 New Zealand soldiers who had just landed as reinforcements from the transports. Wallingford picked the best fifty shots out of the 180 and used them to stiffen the RMLI line on Walker's Ridge and the Outposts. Wallingford divided them "into two watches and placing them just wherever I pleased." He responded to where "casualties occurred most frequently I simply moved the snipers from place to place as wanted. By this means I am sure that the enemy thought that they had a picked body of marksmen in front of them – well so they had ... twenty-five New Zealand boys who were picked because they had done a little rabbit shooting or had chased a stag or had become marksmen in their musketry course."[29]

Rose adopted a similar approach in the 4th Australian Brigade: "I got up to Courtenay's Post and saw the enemy looking out of a new trench at the top of the Gully between 'Pope's Hill' and the New Zealander's position [forward]. They had an excellent chance of shooting straight down the [Monash] Gully and were making the most of their time. I got a couple of machine guns going at it and then got 9 expert shots to take them on. It took us about three hours to obtain fire superiority over them and then I divided the Turk's trench into three sectors, giving one to each man. 2 hours on and 4 hours off. My face is all swollen on the right and my right shoulder sore with the amount of hard shooting I had to do – to keep the beggars heads down."[30]

The replacement of the exhausted 4th Australian Brigade by the New Zealand Infantry Brigade saw a coordinated response to eliminate snipers at the head of Monash Gully. Rose reported. "The Wellington Regiment was in our trenches and they had the Turk beaten from the start. Our men broke their box loopholes and ripped their sandbags with their fire; the Turk meanwhile firing wildly by poking rifles in the air: two cases were throwing rifles up over the parapet firing sling uppermost."[31] On 11 June the Wellington Battalion War Diary observed: "The valley has been free from snipers for 2 days owing to the good work done by Lieut. Grace and the Brigade snipers. We have easily the upper hand of the Turks and have their fire completely down."[32]

Engineers in Defence

From the beginning connecting the ragged line of coffin trenches that was the front line was organised by sappers of the No.1 Company New Zealand Engineers (NZE), four officers and

28 12/735, Private Arthur Gordon Fish, Auckland Infantry Battalion, DOW France, 1 February 1918. (R21002969). 12/1114 Private Colin Airlie Warden, Auckland Infantry Battalion, KIA Gallipoli 8 August 1915, Walden Point, north of Anzac, although misspelt, is named after Warden.

29 Wallingford Diary, 3 May 1915.

30 Rose Diaries, 23 May 1915.

31 Ibid., 14 June 1915.

32 ANZ: WA 73/1: Narrative history, Wellington Battalion War Diary, New Zealand Archive.

141 men landed in the evening of 25 April.[33] Consisting of a headquarters section and four field sections, the available engineers faced overwhelming challenges. The sections were committed to digging in the howitzers, building roads and tracks up onto the higher ground and then laying out, linking and developing the firing line. The sections worked all along the front line to both of Godley's infantry brigades.[34] Many of the sappers were experienced engineers who enlisted in London. Among them was Sapper Charles Wallace Saunders, a certified maritime, electric and civil engineer, who prior to enlistment was Superintendent Engineer of the Twickenham and Teddington Electric Light Power Station in London.[35] His leadership saw him promoted from sapper to Corporal to Sergeant and then commissioned in the field on 16 June 1915 in the space of just over eight weeks.[36] On 1 June 1915 Saunders was awarded the Distinguished Conduct Medal for his work in consolidating the front line in late April.

On 27 April Saunders was on First Ridge as part of the No.4 Field Section supporting Wallingford. Despite his lack of rank Saunders took the initiative and organised his section of engineers to support the digging of the front trench line at the top of Walker's Ridge. His diary entries encapsulate the work of the field engineers in those first days ashore:

> After seeing the trenches well started and after putting a gang on to deepen the old original one, I took a couple boxes of ammunition back into the firing line, and was out there all night, alternately digging myself in and firing; we kept firing fairly rapidly to make it appear we were in big numbers and I think the Turks were afraid to come at us again as they had had a bad spin in their first attack on us. Their dead were lying everywhere and so were a lot of our own boys. The Turks lost their opportunity that night as we ourselves in and, although we didn't have a continuous fire trench, the holes we dug were fairly close together. On our left flank we turned the firing line round to the left and dug a fairly good trench facing north thus making our flank fairly secure.[37]

The job continued for the next few days, exhausted men getting a few minutes sleep whenever possible:

> With daylight [28 April 1915], we sappers had to do a bit of scouting and find out the breaks in the firing line and sap through and join up. It was a very risky game … and this will be realized when I say that, as a shovel went up in the air to throw dirt out, it was pierced with a Turkish bullet. This was general all along the line. I got men (sappers in pairs) in the end of each bit of trench, gave them their directions and they sapped towards another pair who were sapping towards them, from another part. One place where there was a big break (four men had been in the firing line digging themselves in and all four of them had been shot. 3 of them lay in the slight trough they had scratched out before being

33 ANZ: 1st Field Company, New Zealand Field Engineers War Diary, 25 April 1915, New Zealand Archives.
34 Ibid., April 1915.
35 Second Lieutenant Charles Wallace Saunders, DCM, NZE, Diary August 1914-August 1915, facsimile in author's possession.
36 Ibid., August 1914-August 1915, 16 June 1915.
37 Ibid., 27 April 1915.

> shot and the 4th lay about 3 y[ar]ds behind his trough, probably where he had thrown himself when hit) I had to put one of my men in the empty one. He was a towny of mine and I was sure I was sending him to death and so was he, but it was his turn. What a storm of bullets round us as we wriggled our way up to the spot; he got in and I came away. All day going alright and correcting a direction here and there. As I left one trench, I would have to jump out as quickly as I could, run like mad to another, if near enough and simply just dive into it; to dwell for a second was disastrous; or, if it was some distance, to throw myself flat behind some bush, get more breath and a little more courage, them off again, zig zag fashion. The number of times I did this during the day, it was simply miraculous I wasn't hit … Again, we were sapping communication trenches from the firing line back to the original first trench by the cliff, which became our reserve trench. We had several communications throughout the length of firing line to do, so we were working very hard. All ammunition, food, water, etc, had to be carried across the open from reserve trench to fire trench, through this atmosphere of lead.[38]

By 3 May the line on Walker's Ridge and Russell's Top was secure. "Got the communication trenches through and we now have a position, consolidated, that the Turk's will never drive us out of. We feel quite secure but, on the other hand, the Turks have a very strong position slightly above us and we have not enough men by half to shift them. I am sure they have two armies, one for fighting and one for digging, as their fire is ever so much heavier than ours and also, for every shovel full of earth that we pitched up, they pitched up three."[39]

The development of the trench systems moved underground with listening galleries being dug in under Quinn's Post to detect Ottoman mining on 9 May.[40] Ottoman mines were blown at Quinn's Post on 27-28 May as part of an attempt to seize the outpost. This was defeated but major mining work drawing experienced men from all units became an integral part of the Anzac defence system.[41]

This too was characterised by engineers of comparatively junior rank taking responsibility. Corporal Alexander Abbey, DCM, ran the mining operations under Quinn's Post. He and Saunders worked as a team, Saunders above ground, Abbey below. On 13 June Saunders wrote: "A[bbey] is at it again – mined the Turks and got them badly. Gee!!! He is doing fine work and even as a Corporal takes complete charge, with Capts and Lieuts galore asking him this and that. What he says, goes, and the miners themselves go to no one but him. He is more fit to be in charge of this most difficult mining operation, difficult by reason of the absolutely amateurish way in which it has been handled the last month – than anyone we have here and the men know it."[42]

The Ottomans were equipped with a German-designed cricket ball-shaped blast grenade whilst British Forces were not issued with grenades. Engineers manufactured a range of grenades, the most common of which were the "jam tin bombs" which were reused food tins packed with glass and shrapnel fragments with a detonator and fuze lit by match. The Headquarters section of 1st Field Company NZE set up a factory on the beach to provide the infantry with this weapon.

38 Ibid., 28 April 1915.
39 Ibid., 3 May 1915.
40 ANZ: 1st Field Company, NZE War Diary, 9 May 1915, New Zealand Archive.
41 Ibid., 27-30 May 1915.
42 2nd Lt. C.W. Saunders, DCM, NZE, Diary August 1914-August 1915, 13 June 1915.

At the same time periscopes were manufactured and an Australian non-commissioned officer designed a periscope rifle attachment which allowed rifles to be fired over the trench parapets without exposing the firer. The 1st Field Company NZE diary entry for 1 June 1915 details the ongoing engineer commitment. "No. 1,2,3 &4 section doing Engineering work in No.3 Section Defences (POPE'S, COURTENAY'S [sic] and QUINN'S – Improving and repairing fire and communication trenches, building bomb proof covers (QUINN'S), loopholes, machine guns, emplacements, mining, improving tracks, etc."[43]

On 13 May New Zealand Mounted Rifles Brigade and 1st Australian Light Horse Brigade arrived to reinforce Anzac and replace the Royal Marine Light Infantry Brigade in No. 3 and 4 Section. The new arrivals worked under engineer supervision to improve trenches in No. 4 Section. Corporal Saunders was in charge coordinating three 4-hour shifts of 80 men: "There were all ranks digging, Lieuts, Capts, Majors, and even Colonels taking a turn at the pick and shovel and encouraging the men, how they worked and I was kept busy all night answering questions and showing them what I wanted done. It was 'Corporal' here 'Corporal' there from all ranks."[44] Defending Anzac was vital work but an inordinate strain on the few engineers available: "I feel very stale and done in but I suppose one must keep going … Disgrace to have so few engineers."[45]

Infantry in the Trenches

It is sometimes forgotten that effective war fighting is all about procedures and routine. What made the difference with the NZEF at Anzac was the institution of effective procedures and discipline in running the routine of the defence. Malone of the Wellington Battalion was a master at this and set the standard for the rest of the brigade. He instituted order and discipline first at Courtney's Post and then at Quinn's Post and became Post Commander until withdrawn on 5 August for the August offensive. This saw his battalion take Chunuk Bair on 8 August, the day he met death with the majority of his battalion. The Wellington Battalion history states:

> From the 9th June on until 5th August Quinn's Post was held by the Wellington and Canterbury Battalions alternately the reliefs lasting 8 days. Half a Battalion held the front line and supports, in the post itself, the other half being in immediate reserve in a gully close by. The Companies in the front line were relieved every 24 hours. The other Battalions were in section reserve in Canterbury Gully, lower down Monash Valley. Colonel Malone commanded Quinn's Post nearly the whole time, and Major Cunningham, and, when he went away sick on 18th July, Major Cox commanded the Battalion. A tremendous amount of work was done in improving the defences of the Post and reorganising it, the fatigues entailed being mainly found by the Battalions in reserve. Men of the working parties were worked in 4 hour shifts day and night. Saps were dug, terraces made, and under the supervision of the engineers, a complete system

43 ANZ: 1st Field Company, NZE War Diary 1 June 1915, New Zealand Archive.
44 2nd Lt. C.W. Saunders, DCM, NZE, Diary August 1914-August 1915, 16 May 1915.
45 Ibid., 22 May 1915.

New Zealander operating a periscope rifle frame: Designed by Lance Corporal William Beech AIF, the upper mirror was so fixed as to be aligned with rifle sights. The consequent image reflected into the lower mirror defined the target. This makeshift device was often employed with observer and sniper working in unison.

> of mines dug. By the use of periscopes and periscope rifles – coupled with the work of the section snipers – the Turks were compelled to remain very quiet in the trenches during daylight. At first their bombs caused casualties – for the two lines of trenches were very few yards apart in places, but here, too, our men soon learned to throw two for one and obtained complete mastery.[46]

Cleanliness and sanitation were Malone's priority. The relevant war diary notes that men are "suffering from the colic, flies are very numerous no doubt this is caused by the amount of rubbish that has been allowed to accumulate by the other troops occupying the position. Sanitary conditions are good and the Reinforcements that have arrived seem to have no lectures on training in sanitation!!!" Malone was conscious of the strain that the conditions are having on his men: "Dysentery and colds are very prevalent amongst the troops."[47] This becomes a standard entry as is the constant struggle to improve the sanitation of the post. "Latrines. It seems to be useless stating in orders about covering up excreta, this is not being carried out and evidently no notice is being taken of it." Nevertheless, he directs each battalion in residence to continue to do battle with obdurate soldiery on health and hygiene.[48] He is fighting the steady attrition of the resident battalions in the heat of a Turkish summer with no-man's land crammed with decomposing dead, and a lack of fresh food in the soldier's diet.

46 ANZ: WA 73/1: Narrative history, Wellington Battalion War Diary, New Zealand Archive.
47 ANZ: Wellington Battalion War Diary, 19 June 1915, New Zealand Archive.
48 ANZ: Routine Orders, Appendix 6, Wellington Battalion War Diary, 17 June 1915, New Zealand Archive.

Routine was everything and Malone's procedures for Quinn's Post were adopted throughout the brigade:

To: Standing Orders for Coys in trenches

1. State of Readiness. Troops will enter the trenches in musketry order and mess tins and overcoats in carriers ruck sack will be stored with Coy QMS [Quartermaster Sergeant]. While in trenches they will wear web equipment less the haversack water bottle and great coat, which will be stored handy and clear of the floor of the trench.
   Nothing will be permitted which will interfere with free passage.
2. Bayonets will be fixed by night and day.
3. Troops in support trenches may rest but never take off their equipment. The firing line will always remain in the alert, supports will stand to arms at 3 a.m. and remained until orders are issued to the company by O/C Post [Malone]
4. Observation, at least one observer per section by day, at night two per section; a section being the command of 1 Non-Commissioned Officer or equivalent. A regular system of observers through section comders [sic] and platoon comders [sic] must be carried out. Company comders will place in trench a card showing the section of trench and No [number] of men who occupy it. Officers on duty in the trench will visit every portion of their line once every hour; by day the number of men in fire trench may be reduced to 36 for each Company; the remainder to rest in support trenches.
5. Reliefs: Coys will be relieved in rotation every 48 hours; reliefs will be carried out commencing 2 p.m. daily. [This became every 24 hours at Quinn's Post]
   The relieved Coy will stand by in support until the relieving Coy is in position and will then move to bivouac vacated by the other Company. Care must be taken that the fire trench is always properly manned while the relief is in progress.
6. Sanitation. All tins and refuse must be collected and put in to rubbish sacks of which there must be at least two in each Company trenches.
   Empty cartridge cases will be collected and placed in boxes or heaps in niches and the floors of trenches swept and ready for inspection at all hours. Rubbish bags will be emptied twice daily by Quarter Masters fatigue.
   Urine tins, two per Company will be placed in convenient positions for night use only.
7. All live ammunition at present in trenches will be examined. Dirty and rusty clips will be placed aside and returned to post Hqrs by 9 a.m. daily.
8. Tools will be collected and returned when not in use to post Hqrs – where they may be obtained on requisition by O/C Coy.
9. Reserve Company's will stand to arms at 3.30 a.m. daily and remain alert until orders from O/C Post. They will remain in bivouacs and Coy Comdrs will ensure they have maximum amount of rest.
10. Coy Comdrs [sic] will not any dangerous places in the trenches or in their opinion anything requiring to be done and will submit report to O/C Post.

Effective procedures underpin an army's operational effectiveness and despite the conditions the New Zealand Infantry and the New Zealand Mounted Rifles brigades adopted routines that became the bedrock of their performance for the rest of the war.

New Zealand Field Artillery at Anzac

The terrain at Anzac was an artilleryman's nightmare. New Zealand had the only 4.5-inch howitzer battery ashore at Anzac and the howitzer shell fired at dawn from Anzac Cove on 26 April 1915 was the first live round its gunners had fired. Naval gunfire support could not provide the close protection infantry demanded and the immediate support to the infantry were the mountain guns of 26 Indian Mountain Battery. The trajectory limitations of the 18-pounder field gun meant that at Anzac, positions had to be established in the direct fire role on exposed plateaus within 400-600 metres of the front line. After much reconnaissance Johnston sited two of his batteries, gun by gun as he found positions. Major Symons' No. 1 Battery was established on Russell's Top and Major Sykes No. 2 Battery on Plugge's Plateau with strictly limited arcs of fire. Both batteries were dug in on an exposed plateau under enemy observation with no alternative positions. Their role was to respond to any Ottoman attack on Quinn's Post and the area of the 400 Plateau known as Lone Pine. The 4th Howitzer Battery was split into two sections each of two howitzers providing indirect fire along the Anzac front. Godley wrote to Allen: "Our howitzers really have been the saving of the situation, few in number as they are, and I only wish to goodness we had more of them; the eighteen pounders are of practically little use, and we have only landed two batteries of them, while the third has gone to the 29th Division at Cape Helles."[49]

Colonel Johnston the CRA had no doubts about the difficulties facing his gunners. "The Plugges Plateau position was eminently one of those which would – in peace time – have been considered impossible, but which had to be occupied because all positions were 'impossible'."[50] Both batteries had very difficult targets to engage but showed their accuracy in the Ottoman attack on 19 May. Johnston wrote in his diary:

> From 12 o'clock onwards they delivered powerful assaults principally against Quinn's and Courtney's Posts but were driven back, the artillery (2nd Battery) powerfully assisting our infantry. They continued pressing, but towards dawn things became quieter, although a general artillery bombardment was ordered in anticipation of attack. All infantry officers loud in their praises of the artillery support. The 2nd Battery fired over 400 rounds over Quinn's Post. All good bursts and no prematures. The infantry say the shells passed just over their heads into the Turks 40 yards beyond.[51]

The gunners were as critical as the machine guns to sustaining the Anzac line on Second Ridge, however howitzer ammunition was limited to five rounds per day and it was only with the build-up of supplies for the August offensive could Johnston report on 31 July that: "We now have a fair amount of ammunition for the first time since landing."[52]

The August offensive saw the bulk of the New Zealand Field Artillery support the Australian feint at Lone Pine and Quinn's Post. They were their only available fields of fire. One section

49 ANZ: Godley to Allen, 6 May 1915, Godley Correspondence, New Zealand Archive.
50 ANZ: Headquarters New Zealand & Australian Division; New Zealand Division Artillery War Diary, Narrative, 14 August 1914-20; December 1915 (R23523687), New Zealand Archive.
51 Ibid.
52 Ibid.

of 4th Howitzer Battery supported the New Zealand assault on Chunuk Bair. It was never enough. Johnston reported. "Both attacks very nearly succeeded, but there was not sufficient artillery support. The ships' guns did not do much damage. They did their best, but there were only two destroyers. The N.Z. Howitzers fired over 1200 rounds in 28 hours."[53]

The New Zealand howitzers were critical in their support to the New Zealand defence of the seaward slopes of Chunuk Bair but the impact of howitzer fire on a narrow ridge saw this shell-fire cause considerable New Zealand casualties as atmospheric conditions altered the trajectory of the shells at first and last light. Malone was killed by this fire late on 8 August and there were heavy casualties in the Wellington Mounted Rifles and Otago Infantry Battalion on the morning of 9 August. This was the acceptable reality of the only available artillery support.

Consumed by Fire

The NZEF was consumed in the Gallipoli campaign and many of the lessons hard won at Anzac had to be relearned on the Western Front. The actual fighting strength of the New Zealand units on Gallipoli is difficult to establish. By examining the war diaries, it is possible to arrive at an approximate figure. First ashore on 25-26 April was the Infantry Brigade, (strength 4,055), then in May the Mounted Rifles Brigade (1,541),[54] followed in June by the Otago Mounted Rifles (540)[55] and in early July by the Maori Contingent (479). Add to that NZ Field Artillery that grew to six batteries (435),[56] Field Engineers and Signallers (582) Ordnance and Army Service Corps (467) and the NZ Field Ambulances with dentists attached (475),[57] amounting to 8,574 New Zealanders in the NZ&A Division.

Recent research estimates a figure of 16,000-17,000 New Zealanders who landed on Gallipoli.[58] This amounts to 100 percent reinforcements over and above the actual strength of the Force. Stower's research gives us a casualty figure of 2,779 deaths and 5,212 wounded.[59] (This includes multiple incidents of wounding and/or death to the one person). This total for battle casualties is 7,991 which is almost equivalent to the fighting strength of the New Zealand units ashore. It does not include those evacuated with sickness and disease. It is sobering to think that despite the 8,500-strong NZEF component receiving some 8,500 reinforcements,

53 Ibid.
54 ANZ: Godley to Allen, 29 May 1915, Godley Papers 1915, R24048325, New Zealand Archive.
55 ANZ: OMR War Diary, 1 June 1915, R23515973, New Zealand Archive.
56 The four 18-pdr batteries operated at a reduced battery strength of 70, as they had no horse teams ashore. This was instead of the normal strength of 146 all ranks. The two howitzer batteries operated on a reduced strength of 98, each battery having 16 horses ashore, p. 6, ANZ: HQ NZ Divisional Artillery War Diary, Narrative summary of New Zealand artillery operations on Gallipoli, 25 April-10 August 1915, R23523629, New Zealand Archive.
57 Extrapolated from Unit War Diaries and strengths detailed in Tables II and III, Chief of General Staff, Headquarters, NZ Military Forces, *New Zealand Expeditionary Force: Its Provision and Maintenance* (Wellington: Government Printer, 1919). pp. 13-14.
58 Richard Stowers, *Bloody Gallipoli* (Auckland: David Bateman, 2005), pp. 260-262; David Green, 'How Many New Zealanders Served on Gallipoli' <http://ww100.govt.nz/how-many-new-zealanders-served-on-gallipoli> 'Enumerating New Zealand Expeditionary Force Service on Gallipoli. Interim Report for the Gallipoli Service Working Party, 25 February 2016, NZDF 1325/1, 24 February 1916.
59 Stowers, *Bloody Gallipoli*, pp. 260-262.

battle casualties and sickness and disease meant that it was just over half-strength at the time of the December evacuation: a raw casualty rate of 150 percent.[60]

These figures were known at the time and were discussed in the correspondence between Major-General Sir Alexander Godley commanding the NZEF and James Allen, New Zealand Minister of Defence. They explain Allen's reluctance to raise a 20,000-strong New Zealand Division in Egypt in January 1916 which together with the 1,764 men of the NZ Mounted Rifles Brigade totalled 21,809 personnel in the fighting formations not counting training and support units. At the Gallipoli attrition rates, Allen did not believe he could provide the necessary reinforcements to sustain the New Zealand Division in France. He reluctantly faced a fait accompli when Australia determined to raise a force of five infantry divisions and had no choice but to accept the raising of a New Zealand Division.

The New Zealand performance at Anzac was underpinned by a handful of individuals who made a critical difference in moments of crisis. Some survived the campaign. Andrew Russell commanded the NZ &A Division at the end of the Gallipoli campaign and proved an outstanding commander of the New Zealand Division on the Western Front. He was ably supported by Brigadier-General G.N. Johnston as Commander Divisional Artillery. However, others such as Lieutenant-General Sir Alexander Godley who commanded ANZAC on Birdwood's assumption of MEF command, and Brigadier-General F.E. Johnston showed their limitations. Leadership is more than individual bravery, both were brave men who frequented the front line, but they lacked the tactical skills commensurate with their rank. Godley's achievement was the creation and training of the NZEF but his limitations as a commander are evident in his conduct of the NZ & A Division in the August offensive in 1915. Brigadier-General G.N. Johnston reflected on this in Egypt shortly after returning from Gallipoli in January 1916:

> In the afternoon read some of Ian Hamilton's recent despatches mostly highly coloured and inaccurate. What a journalist the man would have made, has all the qualifications, highly coloured stuff, interesting, imaginative, compelling, as he saw practically nothing, any more than most of the other senior generals, he hasn't done badly, but how well he has dressed up our report. The N.Z. and A., which under Godley's directions had already been wonderfully exaggerated, the fact of the matter is that Godley handled the battle in the most amateurish way, he has no idea of country and although an excellent organiser and administrator is an exceedingly poor fighting general and poured in regiments to reinforce in driblets over country he knew nothing about and didn't attempt to have reconnoitred as he should have. The whole battle was badly managed by him and Shaw [GOC, 13th (Western) Division, A Kitchener New Army Division]. British Generals have, like politicians, been made in many cases by self-advertisement and push and often are not much good. All of us the N.Z. and A. Staff are agreed about Godley's conduct of the battle. However, the truth seldom or never comes out.[61]

60 Not all figures are available. A survey of unit war diaries reveals: Wellington Infantry Battalion 423 out of 1000; Canterbury Infantry Battalion 539; Wellington Mounted Rifles 337 out of 540; Otago Mounted Rifles 322.

61 IWM 01/12/1: Lieut. Col G.N. Johnston Diary, CRA, NZ&A Division Expeditionary Force, 22 January 1916.

14

Bright's Disease and "Blooding the Pups": The Hunter-Weston – Egerton Feud, June-July 1915

David Raw

On 6 May 1917, the Army Council issued instructions that there should be a compulsory medical examinations of all officers prior to active service posting:

> 736. Medical examination of Officers prior to proceeding overseas: In future when an officer is placed under orders to proceed overseas, he will be medically examined as to his fitness for the particular service on which he is proceeding. This medical examination will be held as near the date of embarkation as practicable, and no officer will be allowed to proceed overseas unless certified by a military medical officer to be physically fit.[1]

Compulsory medical examinations for other ranks had always been the norm. Why it took almost three years after British entry into the war to make the same requirement for commissioned officers is surprising. There had indeed been cases of pre-existing medical unfitness amongst officers over the previous three years, the most well-known being that of Lieutenant-General Sir James Grierson (1859-1914) whose obesity and consequent ill-health resulted in a fatal heart attack whilst enroute to assume II Corps command.[2]

Obviously, compulsory medical examinations were not in force during the Gallipoli campaign. This chapter seeks to examine how the health of two senior officers may have influenced two well-known episodes of the campaign and how it led to a life-long feud between Major-General Granville George Algernon Egerton CB (1859-1951), commanding 52nd Lowland Territorial Division, and Lieutenant-General Sir Aylmer Gould Hunter-Weston KCB, DSO, GStJ, (1864-1940) commanding VIII Corps at Gallipoli, and after a period of ill health, again on the Western Front. It will also consider the impact it had on relations between Egerton and MEF Commander-in-Chief General Sir Ian Hamilton.

1 TNA WO 293/6: Army Council Instructions, 6th May 1917. I am grateful to Dr J.M. Bourne for sharing this information.
2 Tim Travers, *The Killing Ground: The British Army, the Western Front & the Emergence of Modern War 1900-1914* (London: Allen & Unwin, 1987), p.14.

The fifty-four-year-old Egerton was appointed General Officer Commanding (GOC) of the Lowland Territorial Division in March 1914. He was extremely well-connected as the great grandson of the first Duke of Sutherland, and son of the Honourable Arthur Frederick Egerton, a colonel of the Grenadier Guards. His paternal grandfather, the Earl of Ellesmere, was Secretary of State for War in Wellington's Government, two uncles were members of Parliament, another an admiral. The Sutherlands were the largest landowners in Scotland. The first Duke's role in the Highland clearances had made the family unpopular but Granville Egerton was of a more liberal disposition.

Egerton was a prolific writer. His large collection of private papers, diaries, journals, photographs and newspaper cuttings are held in the National Library of Scotland, the Imperial War Museum and the National Archive at Kew and go back to his earliest days with the army in 1879. They not only provide a detailed account of events but are extremely frank about his personal feelings, opinions and health. They also provide a vivid picture of the events and of the personality of the man himself. He was also a published author on military matters.[3]

Major-General Granville Egerton.

Unlike Hamilton's *Gallipoli Diary*, Egerton's short diary, and a more detailed type-written daily diary (sent weekly by King's Messenger from the Dardanelles to his mother, Lady Helen Gascoigne in Bournemouth), are contemporary documents written at the time. Hamilton's published "Diary" is best described as post hoc self-justification written later with an eye to his post-war reputation even though it purports to have been written at the time. Hamilton's publication mentions Egerton only twice even though for almost three months he was one of Hamilton's divisional generals.[4] The near silence indicates the bad feeling between them. For his part, Egerton also kept a journal. It is frank and forceful, recording conversations with contemporaries including Kitchener, Henry de Beauvoir De Lisle, John Spencer Ewart, Hamilton, Hunter-Weston, Archibald Paris and Frederick Stopford.

In June 1915, Egerton was described by fellow Scot, the celebrated author Compton Mackenzie, as "a man of much charm and a fine courtliness."[5] A close reading of his papers reveals a man of wide cultivated tastes with an interest in fine arts, literature, the theatre and botanical gardening. The diaries, prior to and during the war, reveal many acts of personal kindness and concern by a man with humane and liberal inclinations, the earliest being, as a

3 TNA CAB 45/249: War Diary of Major-General G.G.A. Egerton, June-September 1915; IWM: 13802 Papers of Major-General G.G.A. Egerton and NLS: Acc. 1656 and Acc. 1669 Major-General G.G.A. Egerton papers, diaries and Gallipoli campaign journal.

4 Ian Hamilton, *Gallipoli Diary*, Vols. 1 & 2 (London: Edward Arnold, 1920). See also Jenny Macleod, *Reconsidering Gallipoli* (Manchester: Manchester University Press, 2004) for the contemporaneous authenticity of Hamilton's "diary".

5 Compton Mackenzie, *Gallipoli Memories* (London: Cassell & Company, 1929).

20-year-old subaltern in Afghanistan, a personal protest to his colonel on the imposition of public flogging:

> At Sherpur cantonments, Afghanistan, my diary tells me that I saw a British soldier flogged on parade on April 14th, July 6th and July 23rd, 1880 – in each case 25 lashes – for drunkenness on guard, drunk and assaulting a sentry, and sleeping on sentry. I was a very young officer then, but I can remember to this day my feeling of disgust, and of astonishment that a country could expect self-respecting men to enlist voluntarily in an army which permitted such a punishment. These, thank God, were probably the last instances of flogging in the British Army.[6]

On assuming command of the Lowland Territorials – later 52nd (Lowland) Division – Egerton had had a long and successful army career spanning 35 years.

After Charterhouse, where he was captain of cricket, he entered Sandhurst at the age of 16. He joined the 72nd (Duke of Albany's Own Highlanders) Regiment of Foot as a 19-year old subaltern in November 1879. Under the Childers reforms, the 72nd was amalgamated with the 78th Highlanders to become the 1st Battalion Seaforth Highlanders in 1881. He did not attend Staff College. Egerton's photographic portrait in full Seaforth Highlanders uniform in the Royal Collection gives an indication of his society connections.[7]

In 1880, shortly after the flogging incident, he was severely wounded in the chest during the capture of the Asmoi Heights and was fortunate to survive after transportation to safety in Lord Roberts' well-known march from Kabul to Kandahar. His future Commander-in-Chief of the Mediterranean Expeditionary Force, Ian Hamilton, was also on the march with the Gordon Highlanders. Egerton's courage earned a Mention in Despatches and on recovery, and, despite his flogging protest, an early appointment battalion adjutant.[8]

Egerton used his convalescence to write and publish a detailed account of the march. Over the years he produced several publications – including an account of the Sudan campaign in 1898, a rifle marksmanship manual in 1905, and a detailed study of Lieutenant-General Sir John Moore's Corunna campaign in 1904. Indeed, Moore, a fellow Scot with a humanitarian approach, was a particular hero of Egerton.[9]

Whilst stationed in Egypt, Egerton formed a life-long friendship with General Sir John Spencer Ewart of the Cameron Highlanders. They dined together regularly in London and Edinburgh. Their conversations and opinions, particularly following retirement, are meticulously recorded in Egerton's journals They provide an interesting commentary on senior military figures such as Kitchener, French and Hamilton.[10] Ewart had a distinguished career, taking on the post of Director of Military Operations (DMO) at the War Office, Adjutant-General to the forces and ADC to King George V, although he subsequently resigned in March 1914 over the Curragh incident. Egerton, like Ewart, deeply disapproved about Curragh. Following

6 NLS Acc. 1669: Egerton papers, 1880 journal and diary.

7 Ibid.

8 *London Gazette*, 4 May 1880.

9 Colonel G.G.A. Egerton. *Some Notes and Remarks on Moore's Corunna Campaign* (Aldershot: Army Printing Office, 1905).

10 NLS Acc. 1669: Egerton papers.

the resignation, Asquith compensated Ewart by appointing him General Officer Commanding Scottish Command much to Egerton's delight after his recent appointment to as commander of the Lowland Territorial Division.

Early in his career, Egerton became an expert shot. After six years as Seaforth, he transferred for two years to be an instructor at the School of Musketry, Hythe. Whilst there he helped develop skill in rapid rifle fire which was a feature of the BEF from Mons to Ypres in 1914. Egerton took part in the International Occupation of Crete (1897) and the Sudan Campaign (1898). His courage and ability in the battles of Atbara and Khartoum were recognised by a third Mention in Despatches followed by promotion to brevet lieutenant-colonel.[11]

In 1903 Egerton was selected for promotion to command 1st Yorkshire Regiment based in Richmond Castle, North Yorkshire. His four years with this battalion was determined to be successful and led to further promotion. It was in this capacity as battalion commander that he again demonstrated a progressive liberal touch:

> No C.O. was more popular or progressive and the improvement of messing and barrack conditions was his special hobby. Two of his novel innovations were much discussed. He held an informal weekly "Pow Wow" with privates when all grievances and matters of regimental interest were talked over, and he upset long established custom by inviting privates to submit applications in writing when they desired promotion.[12]

After four years there was a further prestigious promotion in 1907 when he returned to Hythe, this time as commander. The term "Hythe trained" was widely recognised and was "synonymous with military excellence." Egerton wrote the standard manual on rifle marksmanship and introduced the principle of cascading skills to be shared by the graduates on return to their units. The close-knit nature of the pre-war army is illustrated by the fact that Egerton succeeded Charles Monro at Hythe. Monro had succeeded Hamilton at Hythe and replaced Hamilton at Gallipoli in October 1915.

In 1909 Egerton was promoted brigadier-general in command of the Malta Brigade. Having served with Hamilton in Afghanistan in 1880, he came into contact with him again in October 1910 when the latter was appointed General Officer Commanding the Mediterranean and Inspector General of Overseas Forces. The Malta Brigade was part of Hamilton's command. They were to clash, and Hamilton never forgot the dispute. Egerton went on the serve four years in Malta. At the official level he was well regarded. In 1910 the Governor General and Commander-in-Chief, General Sir Leslie Rundle observed:

> The [Malta] Brigade is not only the finest in the Army, but best trained. Would go anywhere with him – No task too great.[13]

In 1912 Hamilton submitted a confidential report to the War Office on Egerton with his usual felicitous pen: "Brigadier-Gen Egerton possesses unusual ability. He is a good disciplinarian

11 *London Gazette*, 24 May 1898.
12 *The People*, August 1909, newspaper clipping in Egerton Journal.
13 LHCMA: Hamilton Papers, Rundle 5/2/6 Malta Confidential Reports, Officers 1910.

and Administrator", but there was a note of caution, "Of his calmness and quickness in field emergencies, I have no good opportunity of judging."[14]

Hamilton's guarded comments give early indication of difficulties in their relationship. Notes in Egerton's 1912 diary detail an exchange of letters with Hamilton on the rank and file being compelled to make a contribution to officers' leaving gifts. Egerton thought they should not and clashed with Hamilton who believed otherwise.[15] Echoing the challenge to his colonel in 1880, Egerton took the matter direct to Haldane, the Secretary of State for War, whom he knew socially. Haldane confirmed Egerton's view and Hamilton appeared to accept the outcome with good grace but did not forget.

When, in May 1915, Kitchener decided to send the 52nd (Lowland) Division as reinforcements for Gallipoli, Hamilton indirectly tried to resist Egerton as its commander cabling Kitchener on 12 May:

> Many thanks for your promise of the Lowland Division which will be a most welcome reinforcement. Please take stock of Egerton. In peacetime he is an excellent commander and a strict disciplinarian, but at Malta I found him to be highly strung and apt to be excitable under stress. Calm imperturbability is above all things required in these operations by the commander. Rundle knows Egerton well.[16]

Hamilton's request was couched in indirect fashion. Rundle, Governor of Malta during Egerton's period there, wrote, as previously noted, a glowing report, and was now employed at the War Office. Kitchener demurred at Hamilton's subtle hint and responded, "Rundle thinks Egerton ought to do well. I have seen him and also think so. He will therefore go with his division." One wonders why if Hamilton had serious doubts he failed to press his argument. This episode says much of Hamilton's deference to Kitchener. Later, with Kitchener safely dead, Hamilton's disingenuous evidence to the Dardanelles Commission implied that Kitchener never asked for Rundle's opinion directly.[17]

Two events in Malta during 1912 may explain Hamilton's wariness. In March of that year, King George V and Queen Mary stayed at the Governor's Palace on returning from the Delhi Durbar. Egerton subsequently recorded his disgust at the King's behaviour in not thanking the servants and failing to arrange a tip or gift for them, making an adverse comparison with King Edward and predicting the monarchy would not last for fifty years. He expressed similar views after a Royal visit to Glasgow to inspect the 52nd Division in 1914. His diary for 1917, remarking on a review of H.G. Wells' *The Future of the Monarchy*, observed: "We are fed up with Kings, Princes and Emperors."[18]

There is also evidence of Egerton's low opinion of the most prominent political participant in the Dardanelles saga well before 1914. On 31 May 1912, Prime Minister Asquith, accompanied by the First Lord of the Admiralty Winston Churchill, arrived in Malta on the Admiralty yacht

14 Ibid.
15 NLS Acc. 1669: Endnotes, Egerton papers.
16 LHCMA: Hamilton papers 8/2/27, 12 May 1915.
17 Ibid., 8/2/27. Kitchener to Hamilton, 13 May 1915. 17/4/1/43 evidence to Dardanelles Commission.
18 NLS Acc. 1669: Egerton Diary, notes written during late March 1912.

Enchantress. Egerton, responsible for arranging an inspection parade of Malta Brigade and the Royal Navy personnel remarked on the eve of the event:

> Dined on the *Enchantress.* Sat opposite Asquith the Prime Minister and next to Miss Asquith – very clever. At the last-minute Winston proposed to change the arrangements for the parade tomorrow, interfering little ass. Beatty (Mediterranean Fleet) and Ruck Keen (*Enchantress*) furious. Order, counter-order, disorder.[19]

Three years later, Egerton used much stronger invective than "interfering little ass" when referring to Churchill and his responsibility for the Dardanelles.

Egerton was promoted to major-general after his four years in Malta and returned home. After a four month break he took command of the Lowland Territorial Division in March 1914. The division's chaplain, the Reverend Robert Hunter-Smith, gives a vivid picture of him immediately after the outbreak of war in August 1914:

> He talks forever, but I must say, to great purpose and is an expert with his pen. An appeal to the Division, when on home service, to volunteer for foreign service, was one of the wisest and most potent political appeals I ever saw. He is a first-rate lecturer. Most of his language is of a very sulphuric order. Excitable and impatient, he keeps his staff, and the Brigade staffs under him constantly on the jump.[20]

Egerton was indeed forthright and outspoken and, as Hamilton observed, on occasion, "excitable and highly strung" but there may have been a reason. Had WO 293/6 been in force in May 1915, it is highly likely Egerton would not have taken 52nd Division to the Dardanelles. Suffering from Bright's Disease, his fiery entries for early 1914 reveal the frequency and the impact of the illness:

> 20 January Bad dose of Bright's
> 22 January Dose of Bright's but not so bad as yesterday
> 23 January Dined with Charles Monro
> 24 January Dined with Ewart. Had a very bad night. God knows why.
> 18 February A wretched day for me with Bright's. Worst three nights on record.
> 24 February A poor night with B's.
> 10 March Lunch at Travellers (Club). Snow in p.m. A poor p.m. followed by dreadful night – worst in weeks. I am getting very low.
> 11 March Had a very good night.
> 17 March Dined at Travellers. Had an indigestible night.
> 20 March To Scotland 12 Midnight. Slept well. New sleeping car.
> 21 March Central Hotel Glasgow. Took over the Lowland Division Territorials from General Spens. Edinburgh for weekend.

19 Ibid., 31 May 1912.
20 IWM 96/38/1: Rev. Robert Hunter-Smith, 'Incidents and impressions'.

Bright's disease is the historical classification of kidney disease. It would now be described as acute or chronic nephritis characterised by oedema, an abnormal accumulation of fluid in the interstitium, located beneath the skin and in body cavities which cause severe pain and the presence of albumin in the urine. It is frequently accompanied by high blood pressure (hypertension). Common symptoms are decreased urine output, blood in the urine, enlarged veins and a distended abdomen from fluid build-up. It involves chronic inflammation of the kidneys resulting in acute stomach pains, vomiting, diarrhoea and pain in passing water. It can only be imagined what impact the conditions and summer heat would have in the Dardanelles.[21]

It is not known when Egerton caught nephritis. The most likely cause was a waterborne infection in Malta where it was first diagnosed. It can be intermittent with periods of remission, but from Egerton's diary it was frequent in 1914 and 1915. The side effects match descriptions of outbursts of anger and excitability. Certainly, before and during the Gallipoli campaign Egerton was often unwell. The weather, physical demands of the peninsulas and prevailing insanitary conditions compounded his problems. Nephritis led to outbursts of anger which, however justified, exacerbated his poor relationship with his corps commander and commander-in-chief.[22]

The 52nd Division was dispatched as reinforcement for the newly formed VIII Corps (commanded by Lieutenant-General Hunter-Weston) at Cape Helles, disembarking over a period of four weeks in June. Five days after landing, on 28 June, a part of the Division (156th Brigade) was involved in a fierce engagement at Gully Ravine and suffered severe casualties. The other brigades (155th and 157th) took part in the Battle of Achi Baba Nullah on 12-13 July, again with severe casualties. One battalion (1/6th Highland Light Infantry) was involved in a failed attack at the Vineyard on 15-16 August resulting in a court of enquiry. Egerton recorded his command's experience in his post-war journal:

> I landed at Cape Helles Gallipoli Peninsula in Command of the 52nd Lowland Division on June 21st and left it on September 16th, 1915. I landed a weak Division of 10,900 men and within three weeks had lost 4,800 killed and wounded, and about 1,000 sick – of the officers over 70% were hors de combat during this short period.[23]

Elaine McFarland, in a recent biography of Hunter-Weston, claims Egerton is, "uncritically portrayed as a caring officer damned by Hunter-Weston for protesting at the handling of his men".[24] However, McFarland makes no mention of his illness despite quoting from his diaries. Conversely, Michael Hickey concludes:

> It is hard not to feel sorry for Egerton. He had brought an excellent division to Gallipoli to see it butchered by what he considered to be inept handling by Hunter-Weston, and,

21 J.S. Cameron, 'Bright's Disease Today', *British Medical Journal*, No. 4 (5832), 14 October 1974, pp. 87-90.
22 NLS Acc. 1669: Egerton diaries, November 1915.
23 NLS Acc. 1669: Egerton journal, Summary in 1931.
24 Elaine McFarland, *"A Slashing Man of Action": The Life of Lieutenant-General Sir Aylmer Hunter-Weston MP* (Oxford: Peter Lang, 2014), p. 196.

> briefly, de Lisle. Devoted as he was to his men, he now felt hard done by and blamed the Commander-in-Chief.[25]

Hickey devotes an entire chapter to, "The Destruction Of the 52nd Division."[26] Close examination of Egerton's papers raises questions over the veracity of Hamilton and Hunter-Weston and confirm a view expressed by Jenny Macleod that, "Hamilton gilded the pill not only in commanding his subordinates (and) corresponding with his superiors."[27]

Egerton's liberal inclinations and a willingness to speak his mind, compounded by his state of health led to clashes with both Hunter-Weston and Hamilton. There is a sharp contrast between Hamilton and Egerton's views on the nature of the ordinary soldier. According to Hamilton, a reluctance to be vaccinated by some Territorials demonstrated they were "just sufficiently advanced in education … to be especially susceptible to the bigotry of cranks and faddists." To Egerton, "the present-day man in the ranks is no unreasoning fool and doesn't like being written down to." Evidence of several deaths from vaccination supports Egerton's view.[28]

Egerton suffered from Bright's intermittently throughout the Gallipoli campaign, although he showed determination and effort in coping with the physical demands of command (more so than Douglas of the 42nd East Lancashire Division). However, his state of health had a sapping effect on his energy and morale and it clearly affected relations with Hamilton and Hunter-Weston.

In March 1914, Egerton had not been the only officer interested in the command of the Lowland Division. Brigadier Aylmer Hunter-Weston, 27th Laird of Hunterston on the Ayrshire coast had been Chief Staff Officer in Scottish Command between 1908 and 1911. He was a Royal Engineer and a Staff College graduate, subsequently becoming Assistant Director of Military Training and then brigadier in command of 11th Infantry Brigade at Colchester. The two men had known of each other as fellow Scots but belonged to different levels of the Scottish aristocratic social strata. Hunter-Weston was five years younger and at the outbreak of war Egerton was more senior as a major-general. It appears Hunter-Weston had coveted the post going to Egerton in March 1914. In a somewhat preening letter as "a bigger boss" Hunter-Weston wrote to his wife in June 1915:

> Curious that the Lowland Division, as to which we spoke of as a pleasant command (HQ of Division in Glasgow) should actually come under my command as one of my three Divisions. Of course, a Corps Commander has many more troops under him and is a bigger boss than the Commander-in-Chief in Scotland![29]

Egerton faced other problems which went beyond his personal health, stretched his patience and did nothing for his peace of mind. They illustrate a lack of coherence and organisation in the War Office under Kitchener.

Prior to embarking for overseas service, 52nd Division had seven artillery batteries including a howitzer battery, three engineer field companies, a signal company and three field ambulance

25 Michael Hickey, *Gallipoli* (London: John Murray, 2000).
26 Ibid.
27 Macleod, *Reconsidering Gallipoli*, p. 195.
28 Peter Dennis, *The Territorial Army 1906-1940* (Woodbridge: Boydell Press, 1987), p. 13.
29 BL 48362: Hunter-Weston papers, letter to wife, 10 June 1915.

units. Each brigade, on Egerton's initiative, formed a trench mortar battery in May and June 1915 prior to embarkation for Gallipoli.[30]

The post-war 52nd Division historian, Lieutenant-Colonel R.R. Thompson MC, who served with the 1/5th Argyll and Sutherland Highlanders at Gallipoli observed:

> By way of armaments the three RFA brigades each had three four-gun batteries and were armed with the 15-pounder converted gun. The fourth howitzer battalion had two four-gun batteries armed with the 5-inch howitzer. The infantry battalions were armed with the long charger loading Lee-Enfield rifle and with two machine guns to each battalion.[31]

However, it will be shown that Egerton was surprised to be told by Kitchener that the Division would not need to take its artillery with them. He also faced problems with equipment and training the division. Much of the existing equipment was either unsuitable or of poor quality. Much energy was expended, not all successfully, to rectify this. Four battalions of 155th Brigade had four different types of web equipment.[32] The 1/5th Kings Own Scottish Borders had leather bandoliers reported as "unserviceable" before Egerton's arrival.[33] He also discovered that plans to mobilise the 1/5th Royal Scots Fusiliers were delayed by five weeks because there was an insufficient supply of boots.[34] The Division faced serious problems with obsolete rifles. They were replaced shortly before embarkation, but it reduced the possibility of shooting practice. Thus in his diary, Egerton expressed his impatience with what he took to be Kitchener's decision to give precedence to raising and equipping the "New Armies." "War Office delays are driving me crazy."[35]

Under Hamilton's overall command, the MEF had landed on the peninsula on 25 April, 1915. On the same day, unaware of events, and in an attempt to sort out incompetence at the War Office, Egerton took the overnight train to demand a meeting with Kitchener. The only outcome was a telegram to his hotel warning that the Western Front was not to be their destination, but it was not revealed where:

> Sunday 25 April Grosvenor Hotel. I received telegram warning us not to go to France.
> Monday 26 April Hung about town waiting for orders. Down to WO.
> Tuesday 27 April to War Office after lunch. Tried to see Lord K but not admitted. 11.45 p.m. train back to Scotland.[36]

On 7 May the Division was warned for early embarkation to Gallipoli. Egerton was summoned to see Kitchener, Secretary of State for War, in the War Office on 11 May. The outcome

30 A. F. Becke, *Order of Battle of Divisions Part 2A: The Territorial Mounted Divisions and the First Line Territorial Force Divisions (42-56)* (London: HMSO, 1936), pp. 112-113.
31 R.R. Thompson, *The Fifty-Second (Lowland) Division 1914-1918* (Glasgow: Maclehose Jackson & Co., 1923), pp. 4-5.
32 K.W. Mitchinson, *The Territorial Force at War 1914-1916* (Basingstoke: Palgrave Macmillan, 2014), pp. 23-24.
33 TNA WO 95/4320: 1/4th Royal Scots Fusiliers War Diary, 6 August 1914.
34 Ibid., 155th Brigade War Diary, May 1915.
35 NLS Acc. 1669: Egerton diary, 20 August 1914.
36 Ibid., 25-27 April 1915.

regarding 52nd Division's artillery is highly significant and revealing. The meeting came three days before the famous *The Times* leader:

NEED FOR SHELLS

BRITISH ATTACKS CHECKED

Limited munitions supply was the cause. What became known as "The Great Shell Scandal" led to the formation of the Asquith Coalition Government. The outcome of the meeting with Kitchener was to have devastating consequences for 52nd Division at Gully Ravine on 28 June and Achi Baba Nullah on 12-13 July. Egerton recorded a fateful meeting with the Secretary of State for War on the same day as the controversial headline:

> K asked me what my Division was like and I told him the truth, always I suppose a foolish thing to do, and said some of my battalions were better than others, and that my three best battalions had already been filched away to France. I asked him, "What about my artillery, was I to take all of it, particularly the heavy battery of 4.7' guns?" He said, "I think we have plenty of guns out there – I would not take all of it." I replied I should like to take my 5' Howitzer Brigade of two batteries, and he said, "Oh, yes, take them and mind you take plenty of shell." I said, I can only take the regulation allowance – and he again said, "take plenty of shell" – as if I had only to go round to the Artillery stores and order "100 dozen 5' Lydite [sic] and put it on account please. How about the heavies", he went on, "I don't think they would be much use there, I tell you what, we'll ask Hamilton." He pulled out a piece of paper and he and I roughed out a cable to Sir Ian on the subject. I thought to myself – well if you as Secretary of State go into all these details of General Staff work the WO must be a funny place. Lord K. showed me a large-scale map of the Gallipoli Peninsula and described what had taken place and how far we had got – which as everyone knows was a damned little way. I remarked, "Then we haven't got to Achi Baba?", and he replied, "No, we haven't, and that's why I'm sending you out" I immediately went off and saw General Sclater, the Adj't General and recounted the conversation. Sclater turned to me and said, "Now Egerton you have some idea of what we have to put up with in this house."[37]

The 52nd Division disembarked at Gallipoli over a period of three weeks in June and July 1915 without most of its artillery. Despite Kitchener's assurances they discovered there were not "plenty of guns" and certainly not "plenty of shells." The meeting demonstrates Kitchener's faults. Peter Simkins has observed:

> The multitude of issues facing Kitchener daily, and the crushing weight of responsibility he bore, progressively wore him down, diminishing his standing in the Cabinet and rendering him increasingly vulnerable to the interference of amateur strategists such as Churchill and Lloyd George – whose opportunistic schemes sucked the British Army into costly

37 NLS Acc. 1669: Egerton papers, Minutes of meeting with Lord Kitchener, 11 May 1915.

> or unrewarding operations on Gallipoli and in Salonika. (He) exacerbated his own problems by his secretiveness, distrust of politicians, reluctance to delegate, and neglect of the General Staff.[38]

The fate of 52nd Division could be said to be a product of the dysfunctional relationship between Kitchener and Hamilton.

The haste with which 52nd Division departed affected outcomes on the peninsula and did nothing to improve Egerton's state of mind. Some troops embarked attired in khaki serge uniforms unsuitable for the Mediterranean service and obsolete rifles. Embarkation originated from three different ports – Liverpool, Devonport, and Plymouth – over a period of three weeks, prior to arrival at three different ports en-route to Gallipoli over the period of one month.[39] This spread the risk of submarine attack, but it did not allow for effective coordinated preliminary planning. Egerton was due to sail from Liverpool on the *Acquitania* on 20 May, but the vessel ran aground. A half-battalion of the 1/7th Royal Scots was due to sail with him. He sailed on the *Empress of Britain* four days late having had to deal with the aftermath of a tragedy. The delayed half battalion was virtually destroyed in what is still the worst railway disaster in British history.[40]

At 6:49 a.m. on Saturday 22 May 1915, a Liverpool bound troop train carrying the half battalion (498 all ranks) collided with a local passenger train at Quintinshill near Gretna. A northbound night sleeper to Glasgow then ploughed into both trains. Only 64 men survived physically unscathed; 216 died and 218 were badly injured or burned. Only 83 of the fatalities were subsequently identified. For his part, Egerton was extremely shaken and distressed:

> I have had a nerve-wracking 36 hours, caused by this appalling tragedy to one of my troop trains. I was had up in the middle of the night at 2 a.m. this morning, to be informed of the full extent of the disaster – Over 200 men killed and well over another 200 wounded. The survivors 58 in number with the Colonel (Peebles), the Adjutant and two others came in at 3 a.m. and I saw and spoke to them this forenoon – there were many of them without coats or hats and have lost all arms and equipment and I am glad to say WO have agreed to my not taking them on. The Col. Adjt and 2 officers will of course come on with the 1/2 Bn safe, though the Adjt is still half dazed. The troop train had collided with the local train, but was going quite slow and standing on the up line when bang into it went the express at 60 mph. And simply cut it to bits. The Colonel tells me he saw the side of his carriage absolutely reduced to splinters and how he emerged he does not know. The 3 engines were piled up in one heap and in one minute the whole 3 trains were blazing. The officers in the front carriage were never seen or heard of, they were under the engines – He says there must be a number of victims in the Express, for he saw them, and he saw three obvious officers taken for dead out of the sleeper in their pyjamas – (How many times have I been in that sleeper, the conductor was killed). He tells me several amputations were performed to rescue men

38 Peter Simkins, 'Kitchener's War: British Strategy from 1914 to 1916' (book review), *The Journal of British History*, Vol. 7, No. 1, January 2006, pp. 253-254.
39 Thompson, *The Fifty Second Lowland Division, 1914-1918*, p. 11.
40 NLS: Lt. Col. E. Druitt, 'Accident at Quintinshill', 22 May 1915. Report, Board of Trade, 17 June 1915.

> pinned down. It was the most ghastly scene the mind of man can imagine – He has over 200 men missing from his battalion, but he has only identified 70 odd bodies. Most of the rest are no doubt in ashes – I talked to Ewart over the phone this morning. He only arrived on the scene at 3 p.m.. Stayed there some time and then went on to Carlisle, getting back to Edinburgh at 3 a.m. today. Edinburgh is a city in mourning as all the men come from there. Some of the (survivors) were evidently quite knocked out, and so were the officers. I cannot write anymore.[41]

Tragedy aside, Egerton knew he was taking an inexperienced division to a war in a hot climate unsuitable for his health problems. The division was not fully equipped, clothed or trained and without its artillery. This, and the appalling Gretna disaster, did nothing for his peace of mind.

"Nobody's Children": Gully Ravine, 28 June 1915

Egerton's awkward early morning arrival on the peninsula was humorously recollected by Compton Mackenzie:

> There was a good deal of stamping and saluting to which I could not respond with any bravura owing to my being barefooted and in pyjamas. However, I told them that battle was about to begin presently and that if they cared to come up to General Hunter-Weston's observation post after they had some breakfast I thought they might enjoy it.[42]

The GOC 52nd Division's diaries record a marked improvement in his health in the early part of 1915, but it was short lived. He was to suffer poor health throughout his time on the peninsula, between June and September. He made valiant efforts to continue a gruelling series of trench visits with Walshe, (his Chief of Staff) and Laverton (ADC) but Egerton's health, according to his diary, affected his morale and relations with his superiors:

24 May	Bad aching face from an abscess.
29 June	Pretty seedy today. Diarrhoea.
30 June	C.L. [ADC Laverton] pretty seedy today. What a dog's life.
2 July	Rather seedy still
20 July	Got my first anti-cholera inoculation.
28 July	Diarrhoea is increasing. I fear cholera. [in reference to division].
31 July	What a life.
2 August	Nerves and Bright's.
4 August	Received a very unpleasant report [by Douglas-acting GOC VIII Corps].
5 August	Passed a sleepless night. Sent in letter asking to be relieved of command of 52nd Division.

41 IWM 13802: Egerton Papers, letter to mother, 24 May 1915.

42 Mackenzie, *Gallipoli Memories*, p. 165. The imminent "battle" was a French attack on 21 June. See Simon House's chapter in this volume.

6 August	News from GHQ. I am to remain in command of 52 Div. AND WHY NOT ?
17 August	all advanced trenches from 9 a.m. to 5 p.m. Nearly dead when I got back.
18 August	Pretty seedy today and threatening of Diarrhoea.
19 August	Dr McIntosh gave me castor oil and I went nowhere.
21 August	Seedy all day
22 August	Went nowhere all day. Inside pretty queer again
23 August	Very bad early morning.
2 September	Up to front trenches at Vineyard. Glad to get back 1.30. GOD WHAT A LIFE.
5 September	Not feeling well. Got worse later. Indigestion and stomach out of order.
6 September	Not very well and went nowhere.
7 September	Better.
12 September	To Brigade HQ's (and trenches). Pretty tired. Very filthy dusty day.[43]

In a pre-antibiotic world the castor oil treatment on 19 August dehydrated him further. It may have cleared his system in the short term, but it would exacerbate his fatigue. Hunter-Weston was given similar castor oil treatment and his subsequent dehydration may have accelerated his collapse leading to his evacuation with sunstroke on 16 July.[44]

A side effect of Bright's is hypertension. It exacerbated Egerton's outbursts of anger and compounded difficult relations with Hamilton and Hunter-Weston both of whom were under pressure to achieve results, especially Hamilton who was incapable of pressing Kitchener for adequate support. Instead the MEF C-in-C maintained a constant stream of optimistic reports as if seeking the Secretary of State for War's approval.

Egerton and his staff had landed in the dark at one in the morning of 21 June disembarking through the beached SS *River Clyde* at Cape Helles. They had travelled via Gibralter, Malta, Alexandria and Mudros – where Egerton had found Hamilton "very civil." His first impressions of Hunter-Weston were also favourable, but this rapidly changed:

> I dossed down on the sand and slept very indifferently till 5 a.m. when I wandered to General Hunter-Weston's Headquarters on the top of the cliff. He has a wonderful underground labyrinth of small rooms dug out and connected by passages. The rooms are roofed over. He was a real Good Samaritan and gave me his own bed to sleep on till 12, and a wash and a shave. I felt however very seedy and full of indigestion. What a rotten game it is![45]

It became apparent that for the most part Egerton was not fully allowed to act as divisional commander and was in effect commander in name only. This state of affairs began in the first engagement involving a portion of 52nd Division at Gully Ravine on 28 June.

43 NLS Acc. 1669: Egerton short diary.
44 McFarland, *"A Slashing Man of Action"*, pp. 208-09.
45 TNA CAB 45/249: Egerton, long diary, letter to mother.

SS *River Clyde*: The path to shore, Sedd-el-Bahr fortress in the distance. (*The Sphere*, 25 September 1915)

Egerton's first days were spent familiarising himself with the trench system in Helles. He also began a long series of daily diary letters to his mother that were sent by King's Messenger. Despite his questionable health he demonstrated energy and initiative:

> Wednesday 23 June Visited nearly whole of trenches occupied by 42 Div. Long tiring walk of seven to eight miles in very hot sun and pretty dangerous.
> Thursday 24 June visited whole of 29 Divn trenches with De Lisle part of the way within 40 yards of Turks. Several shrapnel shells on way, lots of bullets.
> Friday 25 June visited Naval Division trenches with Walshe and Tollemache, and very nearly got killed at Backhouse Post by shrapnel – not a shell.[46]

The nature of their duties in Scotland meant that the division had had little training in trench warfare. Egerton was disturbed by what he found, and his own health concerns made him aware of the dangers of the insanitary conditions:

> In places we were only 30-40 yards from the Turks; in others 200 yards. Very narrow – very deep – very smelly and damnably hot. We must have an epidemic. We are simply screaming for it. Every condition is present that is favourable for producing one. The main trenches when we reached them were narrow, stinking and blazing hot; no shade anywhere. Every drop of water, ammunition and tools have to be carried up for about one and a half miles.[47]

46 Ibid.
47 TNA CAB 45/429: Egerton long diary, 21 June 1915.

He was further disturbed after meeting the French *Corps Expeditionnaire d'Orient* commander, Henri Gouraud; the meeting shook his confidence about the future outcome of the campaign:

> He did not like having to lend us some of his Seventy-fives; and yet Lord K. when I saw him before leaving, said he "had enough artillery on the Peninsula", and would leave therefore two Brigades of mine at home. I don't believe they grasp this affair one bit at home. If it does not come off it means in my humble opinion the end of Imperial Great Britain. If Churchill is responsible for this expedition as arranged he has much to answer for.[48]

General Henri Gouraud.

When Egerton first arrived, he had no division to command. The 157th Brigade failed to arrive until 3 July after a collision at sea and 156th Brigade was at half battalion strength after the Gretna tragedy. Egerton's gratitude to Hunter-Weston as a "Good Samaritan" soon evaporated after Gully Ravine on 28 June. A hand-written notation in Egerton's 1932 long diary stated, "God, what we suffered from that man!"[49]

Hamilton's first day objective on 25 April was to capture Achi Baba, a prominent hill giving the Turks a commanding view of the peninsula. By the time Egerton arrived three failed attempts (all with heavy casualties) had been made by Hunter-Weston then commanding 29th Division. The former was subsequently promoted to command the newly-formed VIII Corps after reinforcements began to arrive.

Hunter-Weston informed Egerton that 156th Brigade (which was not yet acclimatized), was to be attached to Major-General de Lisle of 29th Division in an attack on the left of the British line at what was known as Gully Ravine. The detached brigade was to be on the east of the Gully and 29th Division on the west adjacent to the sea. Egerton, observing from the corps observation post, took no part in planning or command which was entirely under the aegis of de Lisle and Hunter-Weston. The outcome was disastrous.

The inexperienced 156th Brigade went to its baptism of fire in a blazing sun after only five days on the peninsula wearing unsuitable serge uniforms. They had spent those five days under continual shell fire suffering thirty casualties including a battalion Colonel. As Egerton observed them moving up he wrote, "a lot of poor chaps are going to be killed, I fear."[50] The brigade faced real difficulties. A company commander in the 1/7th Scottish Rifles observed:

> The inexperience of all ranks in their first battle was naturally great and no adequate orders or instructions regarding our part in the battle were, so far as my knowledge goes, ever

48 Ibid.
49 Ibid., hand-written note added after the war.
50 Ibid., 28 June 1915.

issued to officers as a whole, and if they were, they were certainly not conveyed to Platoon Commanders.[51]

Apart from the inadequacy of Hunter-Weston and de Lisle's orders, Egerton, already deprived of his own artillery after the meeting with Kitchener, feared a lack of artillery support. There was in fact no proper artillery support. Hunter-Weston and his artillery commander, Simpson-Baikie, had focused all of their land-based artillery on 29th Division's front. According to Simpson-Baikie: "I understood success was more important there than on our right flank."[52] There was added irony. The one organic 52nd Division howitzer battery available was used for the left assault.[53] This artillery deficiency was compounded by the inability of three supporting Royal Navy vessels to reach the Turkish trenches attacked by 156th Brigade with their guns.

The 156th Brigade seized all its objectives – trenches H.11, H.12, H.12a and H.12b – but at terrible cost, including a brigadier and three colonels. The survivors were led out in darkness by the Brigade Major Eric Girdwood (a future Sandhurst Commandant) who Egerton described as "one of the very best."

Egerton employed a controversial word in his diary, "the *remnants* (my emphasis) of the Brigade crept into their dug outs at 2 a.m." The use of "remnants" as a describer was to have repercussions, as did a Hunter-Weston visit to what was left of the brigade on 30 June. Egerton, his Bright's disease rekindled by nervous tension and "living on Horlicks tablets", was furious to learn from Girdwood that Hunter-Weston had said, "he was glad to have blooded the pups" – Egerton diary comment, "What a dog's life." He demonstrated his inherent compassionate nature on 2 July, "I had to arrange today to fire off home one of my senior T.F. officers who failed on the 28th June. We are letting him down as easily as possible."[54]

On 3 July, Egerton recorded details of 156th Brigade losses: "I got the full lists of the casualties in my 156th Brigade today and it is a sad one. I can see a field of khaki out of reach lying in the heat of the sun beyond the trenches."

	Killed		**Wounded**		**Total**	
	Officers	**Men**	**Officers**	**Men**	**Officers**	**Men**
1/4th R.Scots	14	202	8	143	22	345
1/7th R.Scots	8	141	3	69	11	210
1/7th S. Rifles	9	175	5	93	14	268
1/8th S. Rifles	13	334	11	114	24	448
Total	44	852	27	419	71	1,271[55]

On 4 July, Hamilton visited 52nd Division. An angry Egerton conducted the formal introductions. Hamilton recalled the occasion in *Gallipoli Diary*:

51 TNA CAB 45/245: C.M. Weir to C.F. Aspinall-Oglander, 30 April 1929.
52 Brigadier-General Sir H. Simpson-Baikie statement, Hamilton, *Gallipoli Diary*, Vol. 2 (London: Edward Arnold, 1920), Appendix I.
53 Thompson, *The Fifty Second Lowland Division*, p. 51.
54 TNA CAB 45/249: Egerton, long diary, 30 June 1915.
55 Ibid., 30 June 1915, 3 July 1915.

> I went off with Hunter-Weston and Staffs to see General Egerton of the Lowland Division. Egerton introduced me to Colonel Mudge, A.A.G., Major Maclean, D.A.A.G (an old friend), Captain Tollemache, G.S.O.3, and to his A.D.C., Lieutenant Laverton. We then went on and saw the 156th Brigade. I passed the time of day to a lot of the Officers and men. Among those whose names I remember were Colonel Palin, acting Brigadier; Captain Girdwood, Brigade Major; Captain Law, Staff Captain; Colonel Peebles, 7th Royal Scots; Captain Sinclair, 4th Royal Scots; Lieutenant McClay, 8th Scottish Rifles. The last officer was one of the very few – I am not sure they did not say the only one – of his Battalion who went into the assault and returned untouched. The whole Brigade had attacked H12 on the 28th ult. and lost a number of good men. The rank and file seemed very nice lads but – there was no mistaking it –they have been given a bad shake and many of them were down on their luck. As we came to each Battalion Headquarters we were told, these are the remnants of the ****! whatever the unit was. Three times was this remark repeated but the fourth time I had to express my firm opinion that in no case was the use of the word "remnant", as applied to a fighting unit "in being" an expression which authority should employ in the presence of the men. Re-embarked in HMS Basilisk and got back to Imbros fairly late.[56]

The MEF commander's insouciance and insensitivity is marked in his description of his arrival at Helles on the morning of the same visit:

> The Turks, inconsiderate as usual, were shelling as we got ashore. Every living soul had gone to ground. Strolled up the deserted road with an air of careless indifference, hopped casually over a huge splosh of fresh blood, and crossed to Hunter-Weston's Headquarters. Had I only been me simple self, I would have out-stripped the hare for swiftness, as it was, I, as C-in-C, had to play up for the dug-outs.[57]

For his part, Egerton was in no mood for "careless indifference". A bitter hand-written note in his long diary observed:

> The 156 Bde was very cruelly treated in the battle of 28th June. They were given no Artillery preparation or support of any kind. Every gun was allotted to the 29 Division. They were lent to the 29 Divn for the day. They were no-body's children. When the casualty lists were analysed, the losses of 156 Bde, surpassed those of the entire 29 Division. Hamilton in his "Gallipoli Diary" permitted himself to allude to the shocking losses of the 156 Bde in the following facetious terms – "It is regrettable that my young fellow-countrymen of the 156 Bde, caught hold of the red –hot end of the poker". Very funny Sir Ian Hamilton, thank you.[58]

56 Hamilton, *Gallipoli Diary,* Vol. I, p. 371.
57 Ibid.
58 TNA CAB 45/249: Egerton, hand-written notes added to long diary in 1932.

Hamilton did not forget Egerton's angry words, nor did Hunter-Weston. Significantly, Egerton's name appeared only twice in the 736 pages of Hamilton's published two-volume diary. Thus it appears that both men contrived to undermine Egerton's position.

Indeed, Jenny Macleod has written of, "Hamilton's various attempts to manipulate perceptions" of the campaign in *Gallipoli Diary*. Moreover, in "General Sir Ian Hamilton and the Dardanelles Commission", she highlights his "clandestine attempts to influence the verdict of this, the first official assessment of his defeat at Gallipoli."[59] Egerton's remarks on Hamilton's veracity confirm Macleod's view, "I do not think Ian Hamilton wicked not to speak the truth, but he was always, long before Gallipoli, constitutionally unable to do so."[60]

Achi Baba Nullah, 12-13 July 1915

On 10 July, Egerton wrote:

> Now I have been ordered to attack the Turkish trenches in front of me with my Division, and an awkward job it is going to be. The plan has been formed by Headquarters, and I have little to say to it except as regards detail.[61]

His command HQ was at Backhouse Post. The attack was to take place along the Krithia Spur towards the Vineyard by 155th Brigade and 157th Brigade, the weakened 156th Brigade remaining in reserve, linking up with the French on the immediate right. The objective was to draw Turkish forces away from the projected Suvla landings. It was the sixth (and final) attempt by Hunter-Weston to secure the Achi-Baba eminence. As with the five previous attempts, it failed.

Paradoxically, during the previous March, well before the 25 April landing, Hunter-Weston had expressed personal reservations about the impending campaign to Hamilton in a carefully considered operational assessment:

> I was of the opinion therefore that it was very unlikely that we should be able to effect a landing, and that, even if we did effect a landing, we should be seriously delayed by the Turkish entrenchments and involved in a war of trenches, in which, as we had insufficient numbers of men and an altogether inadequate supply both of howitzers and of ammunition, the Turks would be likely to hang us up for a very long time. I brought to notice the other points mentioned in my appreciation and emphasised the fact that ships' guns with flat trajectory and projectiles designed to pierce armour and fight a vertical target, were ill-adapted for engaging enemy howitzers and guns in concealed positions behind hills. There appears to be every prospect of getting tied up on an extended line across the Peninsula, in front of the Turkish Kilid Bahr plateau trenches – a second Crimea … We shall have a most

59 Macleod, *Reconsidering Gallipoli*, p. 202 and Jenny Macleod, 'General Sir Ian Hamilton and the Dardanelles Commission', *War in History*, Vol. 8, October 2001, p. 418.
60 NLS Acc. 1656: Egerton papers, 'Some Remarks on the Gallipoli Campaign'.
61 BL 48364: Hunter-Weston papers, 28 March 1915.

> precarious and insufficient landing place and shall be entirely cut off if stormy weather intervenes.[62]

Lieutenant-General Sir Aylmer Hunter-Weston.

It is difficult to disagree with these conclusions given the early warning by the failed naval attempt to force the narrows during February-March 1915. Thus Hunter-Weston discovered VIII Corps in the predicted circumstances. His response was an early "bite and hold" campaign of attrition, the consequences thereof related by Hunter-Weston to Major-General Paris (GOC Royal Naval Division): "Casualties? What do I care for casualties?"[63]

With self-deceptive optimism, Hunter-Weston mounted repeated attacks, all with heavy casualties. Hamilton's hands-off method of command combined with his deference to Kitchener and with the same self-deceiving optimism, permitted a commander whom he referred to as "this slashing man of action" to continue despite mounting casualties. Moreover, the prevailing shortage of artillery ammunition also contributed to the snail-like progress. According to Tim Travers:

> From 1 June to the last attacks on 12/13 July, the troops advanced 500 yards and suffered 17,000 casualties. Yet Hamilton and Hunter-Weston believed that great successes were being achieved.[64]

Hunter-Weston compounded this by denying his division commanders practical operational autonomy. According to Egerton:

> The most detailed orders for the battle of July 12th were issued verbatim by Hunter-Weston, commander of the Corps aided by his GSO1, Street, the first a sapper the latter a gunner. They were absurdly voluminous orders, in fact they were silly and ludicrous, anyone who doubts this assertion can turn them up and see – just the sort of rubbish that the "Scientific Corps" would issue. The Div'l Commander had simply to adopt them word for word. Tom Snow tells me that some of Hunter-Weston's orders in later periods of the war in France were of the same type, & that H.W. was the laughing stock of his Army accordingly.[65]
>
> I have to prepare and write orders for the attack in question [,] but I find after consultation with other G.O.C.s that all orders are practically issued by the Corps Commander

62 Ibid.
63 Mackenzie, *Gallipoli Memories*, p. 152.
64 Tim Travers, 'Command and Leadership Styles in the British Army: the 1915 Gallipoli Model', *Journal of Contemporary History*, No. 29 (1994), pp. 414-415.
65 TNA CAB 45/249: Egerton long diary, hand-written notes added in 1932. Brigadier-General Rees (94th Brigade, 31st Division) made the same complaint in June 1916.

> who runs, or tries to run, all the different Divisions himself. You are sent long lists of "suggestions" for orders, but if you do not incorporate every one of these, then your orders come back not approved. It would be far better if the 8th Corps would issue the orders in detail and get done with it at once.[66]

Following the unfortunate Gully Ravine experience, Hunter-Weston proposed two separate advances, each to benefit in turn from the maximum concentration of available artillery support. Egerton subsequently observed:

> These were entirely devised and directed by the 8th Corps. If, as I assert, the conception of the battle was wrong, the tactics of the action were far worse. The division of the attack of two Brigades on a narrow front into two phases, no less than nine hours apart, was positively wicked. The left, 157th Brigade, had been cooped up in narrow trenches for close on twenty-four hours, exposed to the heat of a tropical sun since daybreak, and under continuous shell and rifle fire during the whole of that time. This was their initiation into their first fight in war.[67]

The 155th Brigade attack on the right took place at 7:35 a.m.; 157th Brigade on the left followed at 4:50 p.m. The 156th Brigade, "owing to their losses on 28th June and subsequent active trench warfare consisted only of two weak amalgamated battalions" were in reserve next the Royal Naval Division and French forces.[68]

On 11 July, Egerton received a personal message from Hunter-Weston addressed to 52nd Division:

> GOC 8th Corps does not anticipate that there will be many Turks alive in the trenches when you enter them. If every man goes straight for the part of the enemy's line which is the object of his unit, the capture of the trenches is assured.[69]

The VIII Corps commander's over-confident message bears remarkable similarities to the official message communicated to 16th West Yorkshire (1st Bradford Pals) Regiment on the eve of the opening of the Somme offensive: "He told us not to worry because not even a rat would be left alive in the German trenches after our bombardment."[70] Hunter-Weston had no doubts he had given "an inspiriting [sic] address, with most excellent results. I was given the power to strike the right note and to enthuse the men."[71] Private George Morgan of the Bradford Pals was less impressed, "[He] led us to believe it was just going to be a tea party. Some bloody tea party."[72] Egerton witnessed the resultant shambles of from Backhouse Post which was situated near an

66 TNA CAB 45/249: Egerton, long diary, 9 July 1915.
67 Ibid., hand-written note dated 1932 attached to long diary.
68 Ibid., long diary, 9 July 1915.
69 Ibid.
70 Private George Morgan, (16/1205) 16th West Yorkshire Regiment, taped interview transcript (1976) in David Raw, *The Bradford Pals* (Barnsley: Pen & Sword, 2005), p. 171.
71 BL 48353: Hunter-Weston papers, Letter to Lady Hunter-Weston, 30 June 1915.
72 Morgan, op. cit., p.172.

advanced dressing station. Private James Barnet of the 2nd Lowland Field Ambulance recalled "an unforgettable baptism of active service" stretchering back the wounded from Backhouse Post. "It was ceaseless work for almost three days of utter weariness."[73]

The battle raged for three days. It was believed the 155th and 157th brigades would be facing a labyrinth of three lines of trenches fronted by thick barbed wire that the artillery failed to cut. VIII Corps employed aircraft to photograph the Turkish lines, but the outcome resulted in confusion. What appeared to be a third trench objective turned out to be a ditch incapable of capture or defence. Hunter-Weston's decision to forbid officers to carry maps beyond the front line also caused confusion. One resolute party of KOSB went past the ditch and pressed on up the Achi Baba slopes before vanishing. They were never seen or heard from again.

Every objective was captured by 52nd Division, but not before counter attacks and consequent "panic" caused by Hunter-Weston's flawed orders led to confusion over whether to retire or dig in. The "panic" ended within the hour with assistance from the Royal Naval Division.[74] Major C.S. Black of the 1/6th Highland Light Infantry recalled:

> The 12th July had been awful but the days that followed were hideous. On Gallipoli there were no reserves. The troops that stormed and carried a position had to consolidate and hold on the captured ground for days or it might be weeks afterwards. And what ground it was to hold on to during those sweltering July days! All around in the open lay our own dead, whom no one could approach to bury by day or by night, for to climb out of the trench even in the dark was to court disaster. The trenches themselves were littered with the Turkish victims of our shell-fire, in places piled on top of one another to the depth of several feet. The stench was indescribable. In one communication trench that had to be used for days until another could be cut, it was necessary to crawl on hands and knees for many yards over the reeking bodies in order to keep within shelter of the parapet. The heat was stifling both day and night; water was almost unobtainable. Turkish snipers could fire direct on to the floor of some of the trenches. It was hell![75]

Egerton recorded the casualty figures and a subsequent disturbing incident with Hunter-Weston.

52nd Division losses 12-14 July

	Killed	**Wounded**	**Missing**	**Total**
Officers	32	49	17	98
Other ranks	1,331	1,132	1,326	2,789
	1,363	1,181	1,343	2,887[76]

> I fought this battle till 5 p.m. Tuesday when that mountebank of a General of ours H-W said I was physically done and sent me on board the hosp. ship for 2 night's rest. I got

73 Private James Barnet, 52nd Lowland Field Ambulance, RAMC, 52nd Division, Manuscript, Liddle Collection, Brotherton Library, University of Leeds.
74 Egerton papers, Letter to Aspinall Oglander, 15 December 1929.
75 C.S. Black, *The Book of the Sixth Highland Light Infantry* (Commemorative booklet, 1919).
76 TNA CAB 45/429: Egerton Long Diary, 16 July 1915.

> no rest (having to change ships in the middle of the night) not reaching the ship until 2.30 a.m. and leaving it next afternoon at 4 p.m. Returned to my Divn that evening. H-W is an oily humbug and I think has got a down on me. He may be a great soldier (but) the men call him "The Murderer."[77]

This was not the first time Hunter-Weston had dispatched an officer to convalesce on a hospital ship, but not one of Egerton's seniority. Hunter-Weston waited almost 24 hours to inform Hamilton of the incident and report inconsistencies:

> Yesterday afternoon I visited General Egerton and found him very exhausted after two day's fighting. He had not been able to sleep. I did not think him fit enough to do justice to his command in another night's continuous fighting. As General Shaw was available on the Peninsula, learning the ground in anticipation of the arrival of his Division, I put General Shaw into temporary command of the 52nd Division; I brought General Egerton into my Headquarters, gave him some dinner which he was too exhausted to eat much of, and sent him onto a Hospital Ship to get a couple of nights' complete rest. I visited General Egerton on this Hospital Ship about midnight and found that he was much better. The Medical Officer in charge of the Hospital Ship said that there was nothing wrong with him except exhaustion and that he would be all right again after a couple of nights' rest. He will therefore return to his Division tomorrow.[78]

Hunter-Weston's claim to have visited Egerton at Backhouse Post is false. In fact, the 52nd Division commander was required to visit him:

> At 5.30 I was sent for to Headquarters which entailed a two-and a-half mile walk in a burning sun and was covered by self and A.D.C. in thirty-five minutes. There, to my horror and annoyance, General Hunter-Weston insisted on my going on board ship for rest as he said the battle was over and I was done.[79]

It appears odd to require a 56-year-old old major-general to abandon his post and trek over two miles in heat and shell fire before informing him he is exhausted and in need of rest. This raises questions about Hunter-Weston's motives and veracity. Indeed, there are major contradictions in the statements that "the battle was over" and anticipation of "another night's continuous fighting." Egerton may well have been exhausted. Perhaps Hunter-Weston's ADC (Carter), present at Backhouse Post during the attack, telephoned VIII Corps HQ to warn about perceived – as reported by the Royal Naval Division – 52nd Division panic thus causing an over-reaction on the corps commander's part. Moreover, Egerton returned to his command in under 24 hours, so the claim of "two nights rest" is also untrue. These puzzling contradictions, the probable result of harsh words about attack "remnants" and "blooding the pups" point to a concerted attempt by Hunter-Weston to discredit Egerton and protect his own reputation.

77 BL 48364: Hunter-Weston papers, July 1915.
78 LHCMA: Hamilton papers, Hunter-Weston to Hamilton, 14/7/1915, 7/2/5.
79 TNA CAB 45/249: Egerton, long diary, 15 July 1915.

On reflection, Hamilton appears to have been happy to comply although his initial response was critical:

> I should have been informed of these grave matters instantly and by a priority cable, which ordinarily takes about a quarter of an hour to come across. Supposing fighting to be in progress, it is clear that a General Commanding-in-Chief must know of casualties amongst the officers commanding his Divisions with an absolute minimum of delay. The orders I might approve for a force commanded by Egerton would not necessarily be those I should approve for a force commanded by Shaw. But I need not labour the point. It is self evident. Finally, you should not have replaced him in his command without any reference to higher authority. In taking such action you seem to have exceeded your powers. But this is a small matter compared with the fact that you have thereby rendered it more difficult to put things square for the future. Every officer and man knows that something was wrong. The matter cannot rest there. Will you then please at once send in an official account of this matter to the Deputy Adjutant General? There is no way out of it.[80]

Hunter-Weston forwarded an emollient reply the following day, but again repeated the aforementioned inaccuracies:

> You are quite right. I was remiss in omitting to inform you at once by wire that Major-General Egerton was tired and that I had given him two nights' rest. My only excuse is that my mind was so concentrated on the difficult military problem that had to be dealt with, that this report which did not affect the operations, escaped my attention. The more so that I found when I visited him at midnight, that his exhaustion was nothing serious and that he would be quite fit for duty again in a couple of days. I was very busy next day, and it was not till the evening that I remembered my omission and wrote to report to you. I am very sorry. But I know that you who have both experience and sympathy will understand. General Egerton was not relieved of his command by me but finding him exhausted after the hard work of the fight on the top of several days' stomach trouble I thought it best that he should take a short rest.[81]

After three nights in the front line, 52nd Division – three battalions exclusive – was relieved late on the evening of 15 July. Egerton visited them the following morning. That same day, Hamilton, in a correspondence to Hunter-Weston, revealed his attitude towards Egerton. Macleod has tellingly recorded Hamilton's adroit correspondence with Churchill and others in preparation for the Dardanelles Commission.[82] The MEF C-in-C's letter is of the same ilk. The underlined passages sanctioned the undermining of Egerton in a vinegar in the syrup note of "friendly feelings." Indeed, it is a devastating ex post facto indictment of Egerton. Obviously, to be "a friend" of Hamilton was of dubious benefit:

80 LHCMA: Hamilton papers, Hamilton to Hunter-Weston, 15/7/1915, 7/2/5.
81 Ibid., Hunter-Weston to Hamilton, 16/7/1915. 7/2/5.
82 Jenny Macleod, 'General Sir Ian Hamilton and the Dardanelles Commission', *War in History*, Vol. 8, October 2001.

> Thank you very much for your typed letter of 16th in answer to mine about the two night's rest you gave to a General Officer. I quite sympathise with all your difficulties, and any reference I make now is only with a view to coming to an understanding with you how best we may mutually help the show along. When my own fellow countrymen, i.e. Lowlanders, are in question, I feel sometimes that I am vouchsafed (through) instincts. As you know, I twice saw the men of the Lowland Division and, seeing them, I felt so to say in my bones that they were just on the turn, i.e. they might develop into a very fine and reliable formation, or that they might buckle up and become useless. The decisive factor in such a case is always the personality and character of the Commander. I know that Commander well. I looked at him, spoke to him and came to the firm conclusion that there was not a grain of generous inspiration in the whole of the man from the top of his head to the sole of his foot. Plenty of ability, competent at his job, an excellent disciplinarian, and knowing the routine of military business from A to Z, he is no leader of men and has not a capacity for arousing enthusiasm. Now just think of it. It was not affection, but rather respect and fear on which the man's powered rested. But who will respect or fear a soldier regarding whom exaggerated stories will pass round that after two days' fighting he left his division to go on board ship, and that somebody else acted in his place. In the interests of the State, I must say it seems to me it would have been better for him, and better for us, had he remained on board his ship. Remember, personally speaking, I regard the man we are speaking of with very friendly feelings. He has dined, lunched etc. etc. etc. In my house I am sure a hundred times or more. I like him, and my wife and all her people like him very much also. But what is the use of all this if he is unable to lead his men victoriously against the Turk. However, there it is. If I am wrong, I thank God for it.[83]

Perhaps "remnants" and the pre-war clash in Malta had re-surfaced in Hamilton's mind. Having the power to dismiss Egerton, one can only speculate why he failed to do so. Perhaps he harboured hopes that Hunter-Weston would do it thereby avoiding consequent personal odium.

Hunter-Weston collapsed in a fit of ill-health shortly after receipt of Hamilton's correspondence. Evacuated to a hospital ship, Egerton remarked:

> Saturday 17 July. The funny things is that H.W. whilst going round my lines this morning fell suddenly ill himself and has taken himself off for two days' rest. He really was bad today. I wasn't. A very hot day, an alarming shortage of water reported.[84]

Hunter-Weston never returned to the peninsula although, with the absence of WO 293/6, he resumed command of a re-constituted VIII Corps in France by spring 1916.

In assessing Egerton's leadership and command performance, it is interesting to compare Rundle's aforementioned report on describing the future 52nd Division commander as "a leader of men ... The Brigade is not only the finest in the Army, but best trained. Would go anywhere with him. No task too great" with Hamilton's comment, "not a grain of generous inspiration in the whole of the man from the top of his head to the sole of his foot."

83 LHCMA: Hamilton Papers 7/2/5: Letter to Hunter-Weston, 16 July 1915.
84 TNA CAB 45/429: Egerton, long diary, 17 July 1915.

As an individual, there are numerous recorded acts of kindness by Egerton to his staff and men. As Compton Mackenzie later observed, he was a man of "fine courtliness and charm." This is confirmed by diary entries that reveal an abiding personal disposition towards intellect, culture, and liberalism. Conversely, Egerton was a straight-talking Regular soldier unafraid to stand up to his superiors as demonstrated by his open doubts – relayed by de Lisle to Hamilton – about the on-going Gallipoli campaign.[85]

Egerton soldiered on for six more weeks despite recurring sickness and failing health. Apart from one failed minor assault by 1/6th HLI on 16 August 52nd Division took no part in offensive operations until the following winter. Displaying his personal qualities of decency and humour – recognisable to anyone with a knowledge of Glasgow – one of Egerton's final Gallipoli diary entries records a risky excursion to the forward area:

> September 12 1915. I went up the nullah to the Eski line; from there up No 7 Sap They begged me not to go up No. 8 Sap because the enemy had shelled the working parties there last night and this morning, and six men had been wounded. I privately thought the nullah and No. 7 were likely to be just as unsafe but complied. From No 7 I turned along the Redoubt line and made a thorough inspection of it. They were quite cheerful, pleased with their mail and their small parcels which most of them had received. Two fellows were trying to brew Oxo, from a box labelled, "Oxo in the trenches", with some patent burning substance sent with it. Poor chaps, they looked so very haggard and worn and tired. Nothing but the ground and that of the hardest, and one blanket to sleep on. Every other man with or having lately had diarrhoea. I told them we were all pretty well fed up, but we had got to stick it. My favourite Battalion is the 8th Scottish Rifles, what is left of them; recruited from the lowest slums of Glasgow, many of them awful little ruffians, just "Glasgow Keellies", but cheery game fellows. Some of them looked very young and very tired. It is much colder, and rain is gathering all round. I dread it more than I can say and its effect on the health of the troops with no cover. Today I have two officers and 390 men sick here, and seventy officers and 1750 men sick away from here. Mudros, or Imbros, or Alexandria – God knows where. Pretty tired. Very filthy dusty day.[86]

Hamilton achieved his desired goal by convincing Kitchener to replace Egerton with the able Major-General Herbert Lawrence on 15 September:

> Long morning in the trenches – had not suffered much from 2 a.m. Conference at 4.30 a Corps Hqrs. Whilst we were there a Taube dropped a bomb 50 yards off us. At 9.30 tonight received a great shock in the receipt of the following telegram: "Appointment approved, Major-General G. Egerton C.B. appointed to be base commander Alexandria, and to report I.G.C. Mudros, for orders." At first I was furious. I am very grieved at parting with the Lowland Division that I know so well, but one has to obey orders. I know that a great many of them will be very sorry. Deeply grieved at leaving Division which I handed over to Lawrence – Joey Davies came to see me in the morning & say goodbye.[87]

85 LHCMA: Hamilton Papers: de Lisle to Hamilton, 17 July 1915.
86 TNA CAB 45/429: Egerton, long diary, 17 August 1915.
87 Ibid., 12 September 1915.

The MEF C-in-C lasted just four more weeks, his next and only campaign was to protect his reputation by defending himself against the Dardanelles Commission and writing the post hoc justification *Gallipoli Diaries;* he never held an important military appointment again.

Recollecting his harsh and disheartening Gallipoli experience, Egerton later observed:

> I think it was probably high time that I left the Peninsula. I was greatly run down and had lost two stone, and on arrival at Alexandria had to undergo a painful operation for fissure. I doubt if I should have lasted another three weeks at Helles. Writing as I do 17 years later one can recognize what a ghastly awful mess we made of the whole business.[88]

Shortly after arrival at Alexandria, Egerton collapsed and underwent an operation for a fissure (torn bowel). His diary entry for 21 October observed: "Operated on at 9.30 by Captain Boyd assisted by Lieutenant Green. HELL."[89] On making a full recovery in December 1915, Egerton assumed command of convalescing British troops in Sicily, a post he retained until the Gallipoli evacuation. Subsequently appointed Inspector of Home Forces infantry, Egerton made a full recovery from Bright's disease and lived to the ripe old age of 91. His intense animosity towards Hamilton and Hunter-Weston continued for the remainder of his life and was shared by a close circle of friends including Ewart and Lieutenant-General Sir Frederick Stopford. The unfortunate events and subsequent feud may have never occurred had compulsory senior officer medical examinations been a matter of course in 1914.

88 Ibid.: Egerton hand-written 1932 notes in rear of long diary.
89 NLS Acc. 1669: Egerton papers, short diary, 21 October 1915.

15

The Valour of Ignorance: The Experience of the 53rd and 54th Territorial Divisions at Suvla Bay

Tom Williams

The MEF was, throughout the early stages of the Gallipoli campaign, a composite of Regular Army, Territorial Force (TF), New Army, Royal Naval and ANZAC divisions. The "immortal" 29th Division was the only Regular formation, although it contained a single Territorial battalion (1/5th Royal Scots) that served from 25 April until withdrawn in a reduced manpower state on 18 October 1915. The 42nd (East Lancashire) Division was the first Territorial formation sent overseas, embarking for Egypt on 10 September 1914 and landing at Cape Helles on 6 May 1915. The Scottish Territorials of 52nd (Lowland) Division, having left their component artillery in Egypt, disembarked at Helles on 6 June 1915.

From the very beginning, the Gallipoli campaign was predominantly fought by inexperienced troops who, apart from the Regulars of 29th Division and Royal Marines, had only minimum training and little or no experience of war. With the decision to launch the August offensive, Kitchener agreed to the 10th, 11th and 13th (New Army) divisions for projected operations. In a later decision by the War Council (Dardanelles Committee), two additional divisions were despatched to act as a reserve and provide replacement drafts for the MEF's Territorial infantry.[1] These formations were the 53rd (Welsh) Division and 54th (East Anglia) Division. Both have received a certain amount of criticism for subsequent performance at Suvla Bay. Was this negative assessment, levelled by Regular and New Army officers, justified or was it a persistent manifestation of contemporary bias against TF formations?

The reasons for the failure of the Suvla Bay landings are discussed elsewhere in this volume.[2] The war on the Western Front had consumed most of the Regular Army and drawn on available reserves including TF units deemed complete and efficient enough to be despatched to the continent from September 1914. The first four complete Territorial divisions arrived in France during March-April 1915, and the first two divisions of Kitchener's First Army were ready for overseas service in May 1915. The three remaining New Army Divisions were made available for the Suvla Bay. Field Marshal Lord Kitchener and General Sir Ian Hamilton were prepared

1 TNA CAB 22/2: 'Minutes of the War Council: Dardanelles Committee and War Committee, June-July 1915'.
2 See Jeff Cleverly's chapter in this volume.

to deploy untried New Army troops in a nocturnal landing against a defended enemy shore. Conversely, on the Western Front in April 1915, Field Marshal Sir John French (C-in-C BEF) wanted to avoid, if possible, sending New Army divisions into the murderous Second Battle of Ypres (22 April-25 May) as their first taste of combat.[3]

The New Army divisions disembarked on the islands of Imbros and Lemnos at the beginning of July 1915. There was little time to finalise training or regain fitness levels after weeks at sea. For some units there was an opportunity to practice night landings from transport ships and lighters. With such large numbers of men crowded on to the islands and only rudimentary sanitary facilities, diarrhoea and enteric outbreaks became common prior to embarkation for the Gallipoli peninsula. The Territorial divisions did not begin to arrive until 53rd Division landed during the period 28 July–7 August 1915. The 54th Division arrived during 6–9 August 1915. In some cases, the troops did not have the opportunity to disembark from transports. Thus there was no time for region acclimatisation or landing practices.

On reviewing veteran correspondent compilations for the Gallipoli campaign official history, a number of queried veteran participants were somewhat dismissive about the military performance of TF officers and men, some correspondents suggesting that New Army formations/ units performed better. Considering that Territorial and New Army divisions had followed roughly the same training regimen since September 1914 and had access to the same limited facilities and instructors, there should have been little if any difference in their overall efficiency. There is much evidence of pre-war Regular prejudice of towards the TF, the New Army, more often than not, adopting the same attitude. Indeed, many went so far as to view themselves as part of a "New Regular Army". This preconception remained evident more than a decade after the Armistice. Nevertheless, the majority of Territorials did have one advantage in that many had some degree of pre-war training under the same officers and were now on active service together. The majority would have been known to each other prior to the war and were often from the same district which greatly encouraged *esprit de corps.*

The relevant volume of Official History is recognised as a seminal source for the Suvla Bay operations.[4] It was during the routine compilation of sources for this monograph that author Brigadier-General Aspinall-Oglander sought personal accounts and comments from officers involved as a means of verifying existing chapter drafts prior to publication. Therefore, the accounts and opinions expressed benefit from a great deal of hindsight. Amongst the brigade and regimental level officers there is an almost universal support for troops under their command accompanied by a significant level of criticism of the high command and subordinate staff. However, the entrenched opinions of some Regular officers can be discerned within the commentary made by one attached to a Territorial unit. At the time of the Suvla landing, Major The Hon. H. C. O'C Prettie, later Lord Donally, a staff officer with 162nd Brigade (54th Division), observed in 1931: "The three regular adjutants ran the brigade. Of course, Terrier COs were not taken seriously."[5] Such antipathy was not universal, but pre-war prejudice may have influenced Regular and New Army officer perspectives on perceived Territorial performance at Suvla Bay which appears to have lasted well into the inter-war years.

3 Sir James Edmonds, *Official History of the Great War: Military Operations France and Belgium 1915*, Vol. I (London: Macmillan, 1927), p. 211.
4 C.F. Aspinall-Oglander, *Military Operations Gallipoli*, Vol. II (London: Heinemann, 1932), p. 314.
5 TNA CAB 45/241: Author letter to Historical Section re. Gallipoli.

Territorial Force Origins

The TF was a mass civilian volunteer organisation that was able to provide around 250,000 officers and men for immediate use by the British Army in August 1914. Its efficiency has been questioned from inception.[6] The primary criticism was that it would never reach the standard of Regular Army training or achieve the necessary proficiency and skills to counter a hostile invasion or raid. In the eyes of the general public, the TF would never be anything other than "Saturday night soldiers". This contemporary criticism was unjust; it was never intended to be capable of meeting a trained army on equal terms or to achieve the levels of efficiency found in the Regular Army in peacetime. Instead, it was to be retained in partially-trained readiness, the TF's primary training to occur only when war broke out. Secretary of State for War Richard Haldane and his military advisors were fully aware of volunteer limitations, and therefore, from the outset there was no plan to establish a partially trained force capable of engaging enemy troops on anything approaching equal terms. Therefore, the essential part of TF training would take place for six months following mobilisation. It was during this period that any deficiencies would be resolved.

The TF's primary role was home defence. Individual soldiers had the option to volunteer for overseas "Imperial Service". Haldane anticipated that if the TF was mobilised for war, by the end of six months' training they would volunteer en-masse to expand and support the Regular Army. His aim was to establish a peace-time force of 250,000 men which in time of war, would expand to 300,000.[7] The TF was therefore to be mobilised, not for immediate fighting, but for war training on as close a pattern to that of Regular forces. Their primary role was home defence against enemy coastal raids whilst providing a modicum of support and expansion of the Regular Army.

Kitchener's instinctive dislike and distrust of "volunteers" and therefore the TF, was exemplified by his refusal to use the well-founded and structured Territorial County Associations to recruit the first 100,000 volunteers he called for in August 1914. Moreover, the Secretary of State for War viewed TF duties as home defence only with little or no obligation for overseas service. Throughout the early months of the war, Kitchener was preoccupied with the defence of Great Britain against a possible German invasion. Thus the TF was assigned home front "war duties": defending railways, ports and vital installations. It was only after the threat of invasion had diminished (late 1914) that the Territorials were permitted to proceed with war training.

It was one of Kitchener's arguments that he did not want the home defence function of the TF disrupted by county associations having to cope with raising and training volunteers who had responded to his plea for recruits. For his part, Kitchener preferred to ignore this army of "Town Hall clerks" in order to establish a New Army based on attaching new-raised "Service battalions" to regiments of the Regular Army. Thus he entirely disregarded the established plans of his predecessor Lord Haldane and the Asquith government.[8]

6 K.W. Mitchinson, *England's Last Hope: The Territorial Force, 1908-1914* (Basingstoke: Palgrave, 2008), p. 1.
7 *Parliamentary Debates*, 4th Series., Vol. 169 (25 February 1907), cols. 1279-1345.
8 P. Simkins, *Kitchener's Army: The Raising of the New Armies 1914-1916*, (Barnsley: Pen & Sword, 2007), pp. 40-46; K.W. Mitchinson, *England's Last Hope*, pp. 1-6; I.F.W. Beckett & K. Simpson, *A Nation in Arms* (Barnsley: Pen & Sword, 2004), pp.128-152.

The Secretary of State for War also felt he could not call upon the Territorials to supply replacements and reinforcements for the Regular Army as only seven percent of the TF had taken on Imperial Service obligation by July 1914. However, by 25 August, Kitchener was advised that over 70 Territorial battalions had volunteered for service abroad. Once entire units had volunteered, and a second line Home Service battalion had been established complete with officers and other ranks obtaining an acceptable standard of training equal to that of an Imperial Service unit, they would also be considered for overseas service.[9] During September and October 1914, three Territorial divisions were sent abroad to relieve Regular garrisons. Thus the TF was temporarily disorganised, and its training delayed by the frequent station changes and the reorganisation into Home Service and Foreign Service units. Training personnel had to be identified and distributed between both categories, as many of the instructors were re-assigned to the New Armies. Kitchener's need to despatch individual TF battalions to France in the early months of the war resulted in 48 Territorial infantry battalions embarking by February 1915. This timely use of available manpower did, however, delay the assembly of TF brigades and divisions into homogeneous formations prior to spring 1915.

Kitchener and the Territorials

When the Dardanelles Committee met on 7 June 1915, its members were confronted by the decision to either continue or abandon the on-going Gallipoli campaign. They were confronted by three alternatives:

1. Abandon the operation and withdraw from the peninsula.
2. Dispatch large numbers of reinforcements in order to obtain a conclusion.
3. To press forward gradually without any significant increase in strength.

Secretary of State for War Lord Kitchener had originally been in favour of option three, as it would distract Turkish forces from Egypt, Mesopotamia and the Caucasus. More importantly, it would prevent a blow to British Imperial prestige. However, the Secretary of State for War, along with the other committee members, was persuaded by Churchill to favour option two – a vigorous renewal of Gallipoli offensive operations.

The committee, having obtained clear guidance, agreed to send out the three remaining divisions of the First New Army. They did so in the hope of putting an end to an enterprise that was draining manpower and material resources. Moreover, it was also determined, Gallipoli was the "only theatre with the prospect of an early important success."[10] When the committee met again on 5 July 1915, Kitchener had begun preparations for the embarkation of a fourth division to leave for the Dardanelles on 13 July. He also sought a free hand to dispatch a fifth division to Egypt as an immediate reinforcement reserve for the previously deployed Territorial formations. It was also

9 TNA WO 32/5266: 'EMPLOYMENT OF MILITARY FORCES: Defence Schemes (Code 53 (D)): Memorandum by Chief of Imperial General Staff on Home Defence and forces necessary to resist invasion. Procedure for reorganising Territorial Force for Foreign Service and Home Defence, with plan'.

10 Aspinall-Oglander, *Military Operations Gallipoli*, Vol. II, pp. 56-60

agreed that should a fifth division be sent, it must was made clear that this formation was intended to be a font for drafts and not, as Hamilton had hoped, for the extension of operations to the Asiatic shore. Kitchener's ready compromise was for this division to be utilised as a general MEF reserve. The despatch of the two Territorial divisions without artillery would make no material difference to arrangements on the Western Front, as available troops could be drawn from the Home Forces.[11]

During their period of wartime training, Territorial divisions destined for Gallipoli had a number of their original battalions removed from their strength and sent to France. The 53rd Division had a total of nine battalions exchanged before embarking for the Mediterranean, including the entire 160th (Welsh Border) Brigade, which was subsequently replaced by four composite battalions from the Home Counties Division. The 54th Division had three of its original battalions exchanged and one battalion, attached in February 1915, was reassigned prior to embarkation. In contrast, the three New Army divisions assigned to the Suvla Bay operations had just one infantry battalion per brigade re-assigned as divisional pioneers. Intended as adjuncts to the Suvla Bay operations, the Territorial divisions experienced changes to brigade structure and the removal of component artillery units. Thus their intended role as a draft reserve meant these incomplete formations were never to be part of the initial assault force.

Prejudice

A good deal of academic and popular interest has been focused over the last few decades on the New Armies and therefore, the Territorial's contribution has received little attention. The prejudices and criticisms of the TF prior to 1914 have been well documented by historians such as Beckett, Simpson, Mitchinson and Simkins.[12] This bias appears to have continued throughout the war and into the inter-war period.

Within the plethora of CAB 45 correspondences are scathing comments concerning the TF military performance at Suvla Bay. These perspectives no doubt originated with the controversial claim – as stated in the Official History – by Lieutenant-General Sir Frederick Stopford (GOC IX Corps) that the assault on Scimitar Hill (10 August 1915) failed due to 53rd Division's inexperience and lack of training.[13] Moreover, such criticisms were preceded and reinforced by the publication of General Hamilton's *Gallipoli Diary* in 1920. In an 11 August 1915 letter to the MEF C-in-C from Stopford lamented the failure of 53rd Division and, by inference, the proficiency of 54th Division:

> [N]o attacking spirit at all. They did not come under heavy shell fire nor was the rifle fire very severe, but they not only showed no dash in attack but went back at slight provocation and went back a long way. Lots of the men lay down behind cover, etc. they went on when called upon to do so by Staff and other officers, but they seemed lost and under no

11 TNA CAB 22/2: 'Minutes of the War Council, Dardanelles Committee and War Committee, June–July 1915'.

12 Simkins, *Kitchener's Army: The Raising of the New Armies 1914-1916*; Mitchinson, *England's Last Hope;* Beckett & Simpson, *A Nation in Arms.*

13 Aspinall-Oglander, *Military Operations Gallipoli*, Vol. II, p. 314.

leadership – in fact, they showed that they are not fit to put in the field without the help of Regulars.

Stopford had evidently changed his mind, for two days previously, on 9 August 1915, he assured Hamilton "that given water, guns and ammunition he had no doubt about being able to secure the hills" with Territorial formations. However, on 11 August he observed: "I am sure they [Territorials] would not secure the hills with any number of guns, water and ammunition assuming ordinary opposition, as the attacking spirit was absent, owing to the want of leadership by the officers."[14] Later that same day Stopford disparagingly described his Territorial divisions as "sucked oranges".[15]

Stopford's published remarks were no doubt influenced by an incident, to be described below, in which a battalion withdrew, but one wonders if he formed this opinion of the 53rd Division's performance entirely on this incident? Stopford did not witness the incident, so no doubt he relied upon reports from subordinates. The incident was raised again by several CAB 45 correspondents, some of whom were not directly involved in the action. By evaluating Territorial performance issues and accusations, this chapter hopes to establish whether these opinions are well-founded or a consequence of prevailing institutional prejudices.

53rd (Welsh) Division Training

Following mobilisation of 53rd Division, the battalions were distributed in camps at Church Stretton, Oswestry, Conway and Shrewsbury. Training during August 1914 was rudimentary concentrating on recruit, company and battalion training. At the end of August 1914, the division concentrated near Northampton.

The systems for individual and collective training in the pre-war TF were based on the then current Infantry Training manuals. The 1914 Infantry Training manual, published for the Regular Army on 10 August 1914, was followed by Army Order AO 324, of 21 August 1914; this brought the First New Army into existence and introduced a syllabus of training for the New Armies.[16]

On 1 September 1914, 'Training of the Territorial Force' instructions were issued. This provided a training program for both TF categories; for those units that had taken the obligation to serve abroad and for the Home Defence units. The syllabus covered the training of both recruits and the "trained" soldiers of the Yeomanry, Artillery, Engineers, Signal Units and Infantry. The training of the New Army and TF were practically identical.[17]

For the first time there was now a defined period of intense continuous training for the Territorial Infantry. The recruits' training, including a musketry course, was to be completed within three months. Trained men, those who had qualified in a recruit's musketry course, had to then repeat specific sections of the recruit's course, in addition to 20 hours of company, and

14 General Sir Ian Hamilton, *Gallipoli Diary*, Vol. II (London: Edward Arnold,1920), pp. 90-91
15 Aspinall-Oglander, *Military Operations Gallipoli*, Vol. II, p. 314
16 Simkins, *Kitchener's Army*, p. 296.
17 'Army Orders dated 1 September 1914. 9/Gen. No. 4118, Training of the Territorial Force', pp. 11-13.

16 hours of battalion training within the first month. This was then followed by a further two weeks each of company training, battalion training and finally, two weeks of brigade training.

The intensity of training for 53rd Division increased during September 1914, consisting mostly of company and battalion training interspersed with route marches, night operations and musketry. 200 new recruits of the North Wales Infantry Brigade attended a musketry course on 23 September.[18] The month of October continued in the same manner but now included brigade tactical training and brigade attacks. Musketry courses were held at the end of the month including the new musketry course for Trained Soldiers. Within the Administrative Report for October 1914, as included within the divisional war diary, were the following comments about training:

> Training: It is almost impossible to carry out company training as it should be done owing to the lack of knowledge and experience of officers. Officers learn nothing at the depots, and the whole system of training officers appears to be wrong.
>
> Discipline: The same remarks apply as above. Officers as a rule have no idea of discipline or enforcing it.[19]

The first week of November was spent on musketry near Northampton before the division moved to Ipswich where they practiced entrenching. They moved back to Northampton on 13 November and resumed company and battalion training until 9 January 1915 when the division moved to Cambridge. This was accompanied by increased physical training with continued, platoon, company and battalion training and musketry courses.

This pattern of training was interrupted in some battalions when a draft of 810 men was sent out to the four battalions already serving in France. Recruit training began again on 17 February 1915 as replacements for these men were brought in from the second line battalions. There was now a constant supply of drafts to the units serving in France until the following April.

Throughout March and April 1915, recruit training ran alongside battalion training, including night operations and route marching. In mid-April the divisional GSO1 was replaced and the Divisional Commander Royal Artillery left to join one of the Kitchener Divisions. By the time the division was re-organised on 17 April 1915 it had lost six of its best trained infantry battalions. The divisional history later erroneously described the loss of the battalions: "At the outbreak of the war the Welsh Division was ready and was promptly raided by the War Office as though it had been a casual pool of battalions for reinforcement."[20] Unfortunately supplying reinforcements to the regular army was one of the original roles assigned to the TF.

Orders to re-construct the division resulted in 1/1st Hereford Regiment transferring to the North Wales Infantry Brigade, whilst the 1/4th and 1/5th Welsh Regiment were re-assigned to the Cheshire Infantry Brigade. On 24 April 1915 the following battalions joined the Welsh Border Infantry Brigade:

18 TNA WO 95/4323: 1/5th Royal Welsh Fusiliers War Diary.
19 Ibid.
20 C.H. Dudley-Ward. *History of the 53rd (Welsh) Division (TF) 1914-1918* (Uckfield: Naval & Military Press 2009 reprint of 1927 edition), p.12.

1/5th Welsh Regiment officers prior to embarkation. (Private collection)

- 2/4th Queens, a composite battalion of the Queens Royal West Surrey Regiment made up of one company from each of the four second line battalions
- 4th Royal Sussex Regiment
- 2/4th Royal West Kent Regiment, a composite battalion made up of from the East and West Kent second line battalions
- 2/10th Middlesex Regiment, a composite battalion made up of two second line battalions (8th and 9th)

The division was renumbered the 53rd Division on 13 May 1915; component brigades were subsequently renumbered thus:

North Wales Brigade	158th Infantry Brigade
Cheshire Brigade	159th Infantry Brigade
Welsh Border Brigade	160th Infantry Brigade

By mid-June the recently appointed GSO1 left the division. On 2 July the division received orders to prepare for Mediterranean service. The following day orders were received for each man to fire 25 rounds Mk VII ammunition (practices 3, 4, 5, 6, and 7 of the General Musketry course). The 53rd Division, less its artillery and supply train, then proceeded to Keyham Dockyard, Devonport for embarkation to the Mediterranean on eight transports.

54th (East Anglia) Division Training

The 54th Division has no surviving war diary. There are, however, two component battalions with records that provide some organisational and training details prior to embarkation. Within the 1/4th Essex Regiment war diary are notes of the period from mobilisation to early November 1914 at which time the unit was split into Home Service and Foreign Service battalions.[21] Following mobilisation, 54th Division moved to war stations near Brentwood, Essex and 10 days later moved to brigade concentration areas near Chelmsford, Bury St. Edmunds and Norwich. During the first weeks of the war, it was employed on coastal defence duties. During this time, the 1st Hertfordshire Regiment was re-assigned to France on 6 November 1914. It was closely followed by 4th Suffolk Regiment on 9 November. The latter battalion was eventually replaced by the 1/8th Hampshire Regiment which joined the division in April 1915. The Hampshire's war diary contains a seven-page account of the battalion's personnel issues, problematic training and subsequent participation in the Suvla Bay operations during 12-15 August 1915. This stark narrative document – apparently written by an officer with previous military experience, chronicles the unit's unpreparedness for active service.[22]

Apart from one platoon, the 1/8th Hampshire Regiment was comprised of Isle of White men. The CO was an ex-militia man who had served as a regular officer. The second in command had served with 21st Lancers at Omdurman and had experienced additional active service but was too old to adapt to modern soldiering. The Regular adjutant was withdrawn shortly after the declaration of war, and without him there was no one capable of providing an instructional syllabus that would produce an efficient fighting unit. His replacement was a solicitor by profession who had seen previous service as a volunteer in South Africa. Other than this exception, no other officers had military experience. Meanwhile, the first eight months of the war were spent garrisoning the obsolete eastern forts on the Isle of White. Company training was seldom carried out whilst battalion training proved impossible given the circumstances. In April 1915, the 1/8th Hampshire Regiment replaced 1/4th Suffolk Regiment. Assigned to 163rd Brigade, its GOC, Brigadier-General C.M. Brunker, was a man of "considerable age" (b. 1858) and service who had been invalided home from France in 1914. As a leader, his advocacy of out of date Victorian military ideas inspired little confidence before the aging brigadier was invalided home on 15 August 1915.

On leaving the Isle of White, the 1/8th Hampshires spent three months training at Bury St Edmunds and Watford. From a purely military perspective, the anonymous author claimed that subsequent training was worse than useless. The dearth of available training grounds often resulted in company commanders resorting to route marches as a means of occupying their underemployed men. A lack of suitable shelter meant that in wet weather no lectures or instruction could be delivered. Moreover, none of the weapons or related methodology introduced since 1914 had been taught the first encounters with hand grenades occurring on the Gallipoli Peninsula. The battalion had been issued with the obsolete long-barrelled CLLE (Charge Loading Lee Enfield MK I*) rifle accompanied by poor quality P14 leather

21 TNA WO 95/4325: 1/4th Essex Regiment War Diary.
22 Ibid., 1/8th Hampshire Regiment War Diary

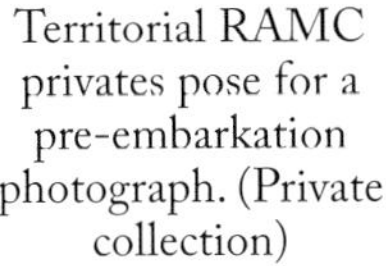

Territorial RAMC privates pose for a pre-embarkation photograph. (Private collection)

equipment. First ball ammunition prior to active service was during a rapid one-day course on an eight-target range. As it turned out, a number of men inevitably missed this pre-embarkation opportunity. The anonymous 1/8th Hampshire account is atypical of the composition and training of the majority of the TF battalions during 1914-15. It does, however, demonstrate the difficulties encountered by the loss of senior staff officers and Regular adjutants. The TF and New Army experienced identical problems caused by the shortages of experienced officers and NCO's, accommodation, training facilities and weapons and equipment. In contrast, if 1/4th Essex Regiment is more representative of 54th Division as a whole, the battalion immediately settled into a programme of intensive training with route marches, company drill, musketry and night work. This progressive regimen suggests the unit was following the recently distributed programme for "Training of the Territorial Force" (1 September 1914). Meantime, the component 1st Cambridgeshire Regiment left for France in February 1915. Thus three of 54th Division's trained battalions had been re-deployed as reinforcements for the Regular Army.[23]

The 54th Division entrained for the St. Albans and Watford areas in May 1915, and on 8 July orders were received for MEF service. Embarking from Devonport and Liverpool during 14-19 July, its component artillery and supply trains were left behind. First transports arrived at Lemnos on 6 August, the entire formation landing at Suvla Bay on 10 August. Unfortunate transfers of Regular staff officers, many of whom were sent to France, had the effect of reducing overall formation cohesion and efficiency. Subsequent performance was also affected by transfer to the Western Front of competent battalions along with additional drafts of trained men.

23 Ibid., 1/4th Essex Regiment War Diary.

Suvla Bay

Elements of the 53rd Division (GOC Major-General J.E. Lindley) arrived at Lemnos and Imbros from 28 July to 6 August 1915. Ordered to Suvla Bay on 8 August, it subsequently embarked with one RE field company minus stores and one field ambulance; there would be no accompanying artillery. Moreover, the divisional signal section did not arrive until 13 August. At 7.00 p.m. on 8 August, 53rd Division headquarters and the 1/4th Cheshire Regiment landed on "C" Beach. Lindley's division was immediately ordered (8.30 p.m.) to dispatch two brigades, less one battalion assigned beach duties, to 11th (Northern) Division under the command of Major-General F. Hammersley.[24] The intention of IX Corps GOC Lieutenant-General Stopford was that Hammersley should deploy 53rd Division in such a way that by evening it could be re-assembled as a corps reserve under Lindley. However, as only one battalion had landed, 53rd Division was unable to comply. Units continued to land throughout the night and morning of 9 August. This piecemeal deployment had obviously been anticipated before they landed.

Stopford's plan of operations for 9 August, with some modifications by Hamilton and further elaborations by Hammersley, contained no reference to 53rd Division or its assigned operational role. Without foreknowledge of brigade and battalion landing schedules, it would have been impossible to delegate tasks, hence units would have to be despatched as soon as they were landed and available. Deployment of battalions in ones and twos to critical points in this manner removed them from divisional/brigade structures and reduced efficiency. Thus, battalion and company commanders with no previous war experience were effectively left to their own devices.

Between midnight and 2:00 a.m. on 8/9 August, 2/4th Queens and 1/4th Royal Sussex of 160th Brigade, 53rd Division, landed on "C" Beach. At approximately 6:30 a.m., they were ordered to a line running southwest from Chocolate Hill in order to construct a trench there. At this time, the 11th Division was deployed at two points; the 32nd Brigade was engaged in an assault on Teke Tepe Ridge, and 33rd Brigade was encountering difficulties in attacks against Scimitar Hill and the W Hills.

Having spent the previous three weeks at sea, 53rd Division immediately sent two battalions into the battle. For their part, Lindley, his staff officers and regimental officers had not seen a map or been given the opportunity to reconnoitre the ground; assigned objectives and the existing frontline was completely unknown to them. The division's first action involved two battalions (2/4th Queens and 1/4th Royal Sussex) of 160th Brigade. Ordered to assist 33rd Brigade at Chocolate Hill, the Queens moved off the beach to Yilghin Burnu at 6:30 a.m. Coming under effective enemy artillery and rifle fire as they crossed the open ground south of the Salt Lake, on reaching the hill, the battalion was directed about the north slope to support hard-pressed forward units. On arrival, the Queens were instructed to dig in and consolidate the position, but on no account to go "off into the blue."[25] The 2/4th Queens moved off, but with no maps available the battalion CO, Colonel Watney, sought advice from the CO 6th Royal Dublin Fusiliers (30th Brigade, 10th (Irish) Division) which was then in reserve. Directed to an old Turkish trench and instructed to hold it, but with no maps, difficult terrain and vague orders, the situation was one of general confusion.

24 Nigel Steel & Peter Hart, *Defeat at Gallipoli* (London: Macmillan, 1994), p. 141.
25 Dudley-Ward, *History of the 53rd (Welsh) Division*, p. 29.

At 9:00 a.m. on 9 August, the 1/4th Cheshire and 1/5th Welsh were ordered to report to Brigadier-General W.H. Sitwell (GOC 34th Brigade) at Hill 10. Soon after at 9:30 a.m., 1/4th Royal Sussex was ordered forward to support 2/4th Queens at Chocolate Hill. The remaining battalions of 159th Brigade (1/7th Cheshire and 1/5th Welsh Regiment) were also instructed to report to Sitwell. Having disembarked on the night of 6/7 August, their New Army counterparts had discovered that unless astride an easily recognisable feature, they had little idea of where they were. The newly arrived units of 53rd Division also had little to no idea of where they were at.

At 11:00 a.m., 1/4th Royal Sussex was ordered to go forward and support 33rd Brigade at Chocolate Hill. Arriving at 1:00 p.m., the battalion was directed by Brigadier-General R.P. Maxwell (GOC 33rd Brigade) to push on to Scimitar Hill from the west.[26] The Royal Sussex went forward without maps and with only the vaguest orders to "restore the line". As no one knew where the line was, they were instructed to go in the direction of a rising column of smoke from burning scrub where they would find 2/4th Queens. The battalion took up position to the left of the 2/4th Queens in an abandoned Turkish trench about 1,000 yards west of Scimitar Hill, with the 6th Lincolnshire Regiment on the right. In the absence of written orders, it was difficult for both battalions to discern what was expected of them. Advancing up Scimitar Hill, the weight of enemy fire made the hilltop untenable and those reaching the crest were forced to withdraw on encountering hostile shellfire and inaccurate British naval gunfire.

Turkish resistance proving too strong, the 1/4th Royal Sussex and 2/4th Queens withdrew back to the jumping-off line. This unsuccessful attack by five battalions resulted in over 1,500 casualties. Brigadier-General Maxwell was somewhat unfair about the TF performance during the assault: "[N]either of these two battalions, as far as I can see, accomplished anything and did not appear able to go on after a few rounds of shrapnel and remained in the low ground northwest of Yilghin Burnu, and took little or no part in the operation."[27]

Two additional battalions were withdrawn from the 53rd Division to support 34th Brigade, 11th Division at Anafarta Sagir. At 8:30 a.m. on 9 August, the 1/5th Welsh received verbal orders to report to Brigadier-General Sitwell – "somewhere over there in the bush", and with no further orders or explanations the battalion were directed across the Salt Lake towards Anafarta Sagir.[28] The 1/4th Cheshire received the same order at 9:00 a.m. and were similarly directed. Facing a deluge of enemy rifle whilst traversing the open Suvla plain, the attackers – having had no sleep for 48 hours – struggled forward in the searing heat. The 1/5th Welsh took up positions near Anafarta Ova; the 1/4th Cheshire supporting 32nd Brigade's assault on Anafarta Sagir. The attack progressed slowly as the already exhausted men advanced over the rough scrub covered ground devoid of available cover. By noon, heavy rifle, machine gun and shellfire brought the attack to a halt. This rushed and disorganised assault by exhausted men lacking in food and water was doomed from the start. By 5:00 p.m., the operation had failed, 32nd Brigade retiring through the 1/4th Cheshire, which was later re-organised in partially constructed trenches to the north of Sulajik; 1/5th Welsh bivouacked for the night north of Sulajik near Anafarta Ova. At 10:55 a.m. that day, the two remaining battalions of 159th Brigade (1/7th Cheshire and 1/4th Welsh) were similarly directed to report to Sitwell; "somewhere in the bush"

26 Aspinall-Oglander, *Military Operations Gallipoli*, Vol. II, p. 292.
27 Dudley-Ward. *History of the 53rd (Welsh) Division*, p. 31.
28 Aspinall-Oglander, *Military Operations Gallipoli*, Vol. II, p. 290.

and eventually they too were ordered to support 32nd Brigade approximately 1,000 yards west of Scimitar Hill. Arriving there at dusk, 1/7th Cheshire was directed to the right and left flanks in order to connect the right of 34th Brigade; 1/4th Welsh remained in reserve.

At 6:35 p.m. on 9 August, Lindley instructed the 1/1st Herefords to proceed to the right flank of 9th Sherwood Foresters (33rd Brigade), which had been forced back with heavy losses to the line Kazlar Chair and Hetman Chair. There had been an attempt to link Suvla Bay with the now enlarged Anzac sector that extended to Damakjelik Bair. The Sherwood Foresters had encountered a strong force of Turks in an area that had been free of enemy the day before. Although a line had been established, no contact had been made with British troops on Damakjelik Bair. Lieutenant-Colonel Drage (CO 1/1st Herefords) knew nothing about the position of other British units, enemy positions or indeed anything about the ANZAC force. He only had a vague idea of the whereabouts of Sherwood Foresters, but no idea of current operations.

As the 1/1st Herefords departed from Lala Baba, they came under artillery fire which accompanied them as they crossed more than a mile of rough scrub. The battalion eventually made contact with the Sherwood Foresters who were considerably further east than anticipated. Advancing across a dried water course at Azmak Dere, the battalion pressed on to a low scrub covered hill. With no knowledge of enemy positions and only a vague idea of of the troops on the left flank, it was estimated that they were more than 1,000 yards ahead of anticipated British positions. Drage then made the decision to withdraw to Azmak Dere. Here at least was some cover behind the two-foot banks of the dried-up water course which also provided an open field of fire. As the companies retired, a divisional staff officer arrived on horseback with instructions that were typical of the Suvla Bay operations. Ordered to return to Lala Baba, the battalion duly withdrew, only to be informed on arrival to report back to the 9th Sherwood Foresters at dawn the following morning.[29]

At the close of their first day on active service, Major-General Lindley was in the extraordinary and confusing situation of having his entire division scattered about Suvla Bay. Divisional Headquarters was situated at Lala Baba. Of 158th Brigade, the 1/1st Herefords were in action near Hetman Chair and the remaining three Royal Welsh Fusilier battalions were bivouacked due west of Lala Baba. The 159th Brigade was inextricably mixed with 32nd Brigade to the north of Sulajik, but their exact position remained unknown to brigade staff. The 2/4th Queens and 1/4th Royal Sussex of 160th Brigade were in positions between Chocolate Hill and Sulajik, the 2/10th Middlesex assigned to beach duties whilst the 2/4th Royal West Kent remained off shore in transports.

On 9 August orders were received (7:50 p.m.) from IX Corps for 53rd Division to advance just south of the W Hills at Ismail Oglu Tepe Ridge. Thereafter, the assault was to continue eastward towards Anafarta Sagir. The 158th and 159th brigades were to carry out the attack supported by the artillery of 11th Division; naval gunfire would provide flank protection. The infantry of both 10th and 11th Divisions would stand fast in their present positions. Zero hour would be at 6:00 a.m. on 10 August.

Lindley was now confronted with the difficult task of trying to collect his scattered battalions. The best part of two brigades were subsequently concentrated close the positions held by 32nd Brigade near Sulajik. From here 159th Brigade would lead the assault to capture Scimitar

29 Dudley-Ward, *History of the 53rd (Welsh) Division*, p. 34.

Teeming with invasion craft: Suvla Bay as seen from Lala Baba.

Hill. The 158th Brigade, with 2/10th Middlesex attached in place of 1/1st Herefords still in support of 9th Sherwood Foresters, was to follow through and attack the Anafarta Spur. The Official History, commenting on the scheme's prospects, later observed: "From the moment of inception the odds were heavily against the success of this attack. Lindley had only just arrived from England and had no knowledge of the ground over which his troops were to attack."[30]

The 159th Brigade staff spent a sleepless night vainly trying to locate 1/4th Cheshire and 1/5th Welsh. Divisional arrangements for the supply of such basics as ammunition, rations and water had yet to be organised. Signals would be almost no-existent, the divisional signal section lacking the necessary equipment to carry out its duties. Moving off without maps or the any idea of the terrain ahead, the unfortunate 158th Brigade advanced. The 159th Brigade set off at 6:00 a.m. from the rear of 32nd Brigade trenches situated north of Sulajik with two companies of 1/7th Cheshire leading supported by elements of 1/5th Welsh and 1/4th Welsh. The supporting artillery opened fire on the line of the first objective. At first the advance was unopposed as the attackers traversed the flat, scrub covered landscape. Some of the troops intended for the attack had, however, remained in 32nd Brigade trenches.

After advancing about 1,000 yards, the dense undergrowth forced the attackers into small groups that became mixed with other units prior to becoming easily discernible targets for Turkish rifle fire. All communication and cohesion lost, the ad hoc attack stalled.[31] At approximately 8:45 a.m., a field message stating that the Turks were counter-attacking from the direction

30 Aspinall-Oglander, *Military Operations Gallipoli*, Vol. II, p. 300.
31 TNA WO 95/4322: 53rd Division War Diary and correspondence between Brig-Gen. F.C. Lloyd and official historian Aspinall-Oglander.

British infantry advance across the Salt Lake, August 1915.

of Baka Baba was sent back. In response, a portion of 32nd Brigade was rushed forward only to be met by men of 1/4th Welsh falling back. This retirement was eventually halted before resumption of the advance, but subsequent losses amongst officers and NCO's resulted in small groups pressing on before, casualties mounting, the attackers withdrew to the jumping-off line.

The 158th Brigade left Lala Baba at 5:00 a.m. and, on advancing across the Salt Lake, came under heavy shrapnel fire resulting in several casualties. There was no time for reconnaissance of brigade objective routes. As the 158th Brigade reached the edge of the Salt Lake, they came under increasing hostile shrapnel and rifle fire from hills to the south-east. This forced them to advance south of the intended objective line that would have led through the 159th Brigade positions. Shrapnel fire increased on the approaching the slopes of Scimitar Hill. They now came across disparate groups of men from 32nd and 34th and 159th brigades milling about in a confused body of intermingled of units.

Leading off for 158th Brigade, the 1/5th Royal Welsh Fusiliers passed through elements of 159th Brigade and advanced to within 200 yards of the Turkish positions before coming under effective enemy fire at 11.30 a.m. Thus stalled, the line was reinforced with new arrivals and one company of 1/6th Royal Welsh Fusiliers. By this time, 1/5th Royal Fusiliers CO Lieutenant-Colonel Phillips, and Lieutenant-Colonel James of 1/6th Royal Welsh Fusiliers had also arrived.[32] Phillips then sent a message to the 1/6th Royal Welsh Fusiliers: "Bring all the men you can find to where I am, 200 yards in advance of 159th Brigade trenches. We can rush the hill they are shelling as soon as they stop."[33] Thick scrub and narrow paths prevented a broad charge on Scimitar Hill where a platoon of 1/6th Royal Welsh Fusiliers had managed to reach the summit in small isolated groups. Enfiladed by enemy machine gun and shrapnel, they were unable to hold. Phillips was killed whilst leading the men he had trained in peacetime.

By noon, brigade and battalion disorganisation accompanied by heavy shelling and increased Turkish pressure on the left flank, brought the attack to a standstill. On the right, hard-pressed units began to fall back in a general withdrawal to the 159th Brigade line. The attack had failed with heavy casualties amongst officers and NCOs, the survivors suffering from the heat and lack of food and water. Orders for a renewal of the attack were issued by Stopford at 1:00 p.m. The assault was scheduled occur at 5:00 p.m. Having recovered and reorganised, the enemy were now much stronger than they had been that morning. Pressing forward at the designated

32 TNA WO 95/4323: 1/5th Royal Welsh Fusiliers War Diary.
33 TNA WO 95/4322: 53rd Division War Diary, Correspondence between Brig-Gen. F.C. Lloyd and official historian Aspinall-Oglander, *Military Operations Gallipoli*, Vol. II, p. 301.

zero hour, the attack progressed just 200-300 yards before it was brought to a halt. The 1/5th Royal Welsh Fusiliers and the battalion on its left advanced but, units on the right that had not received the order, failed to move forward simultaneously.[34]

The 2/10th Middlesex, now detached from 160th Brigade, acted as reserve to 158th Brigade throughout the 10 August operations. The battalion CO was at brigade headquarters to receive orders for the afternoon attack when he requested a delay until 5:30 p.m. in order to allow him time to return to his battalion. The request granted, he returned to his command at 4:15 p.m. before being informed that "some Staff Officer" had instructed two companies to "push forward the attack", after which they moved forward. Passing through the current frontline, they advanced some 500 yards through the scrub. Unfortunately, no attempt was made to provide immediate support and, with flanks exposed and the enemy advancing, the survivors were forced to retire.[35]

Prior to this attack, IX Corps had issued (4:50 p.m.) a crucial message: "If the attack is held up, don't press it to such an extent as it will prevent you reorganising and consolidating the position gained before nightfall." By 9:05 p.m., the 158th and 159th brigades received further instructions to entrench territory gained. So ended the operations that left 53rd Division's battalions scattered and disorganised.[36]

The 11 August was a day of reorganisation for 158th and 159th brigades which re-deployed to take over a line situated on the Kavak Tepe and Tekke Tepe slopes just south of Sulajik. With component units spread out across the Suvla plain, this proved a difficult task, and it was not until approximately 1:00 p.m. that the renewed assault started. The 158th Brigade was tasked with improving the line on the left of 11th Division. For its part, 159th Brigade would link-up with 10th Division on the left. However, strong elements of the enemy were encountered instead of the Irish formation's flank. This caused 159th Brigade to establish a northern facing flank that could not extend beyond Anafarta Ova. This consequent weakness in the British defence line needed to be addressed prior to further offensive action.

The 54th Division (GOC Major-General F.S. Inglefield) began to disembark during the afternoon of 10 August. By nightfall it had landed seven battalions. Hamilton was anxious the division should not enter the fray piecemeal. His intention was to use it for an assault on Tekke Tepe. Air reconnaissance had shown the Tekke Tepe Ridge was not entrenched or held in strength. Turkish reserves, however, were nearby or not too far distant.

Hamilton was adamant that the attack on Tekke Tepe must proceed. Refusing to accept Stopford's lack of confidence in his Territorial divisions, he insisted that the heights overlooking the Suvla plain must be occupied. However, the GOC IX Corps claimed that as no preparations had been made, any advance would have to be delayed for 24 hours. Hamilton accepted this, but insisted that 54th Division, supported by 10th and 11th divisions, must assault the Tekke Tepe Ridge at dawn on 13 August.

The 24-hour respite allowed time for reorganisation, but the constant movements and enemy sniping afforded little rest for hard-pressed and exhausted units. The intermixing of divisions also caused difficulties with the supply of rations, water and ammunition. By the evening of 12 August, the 1/1st Herefords had returned and later, during the night of 12/13 August, the

34 TNA WO 95/4323: 1/5th Royal Welsh Fusiliers War Diary

35 Ibid., 'Account of Suvla Bay, 8-10 August 1915', 2/10th Middlesex Regiment War Diary.

36 Aspinall-Oglander, *Military Operations Gallipoli*, Vol. II, p. 302.

2/4th Queens and 1/4th Sussex (160th Brigade) had also returned. The units of 158th and 159th Brigades were by now exhausted.

Stopford's plan for the Tekke Tepe assault was for 54th Division to advance during the afternoon of 12 August in order to reduce the lengthy night march required before storming the crest at dawn; 53rd Division was to push the line forward into the foothills at the same time. However, by this time 53rd Division was in no fit state to push the line forward. Major-General Inglefield offered to dispatch 163rd Brigade to carry out this task, the 159th Brigade to consolidate the line and thus secure the ground for 54th Division to pass through after an unopposed night march prior to assaulting the ridge at dawn on 13 August. Across no man's land, Turkish numbers increased in the hills surrounding the Suvla Plain, from positions to the north on Kidney Hill, and in the foothills east of Sulajik. Ensconced in these positions by dawn, they could bring enfilade fire to bear on the next British attempt to advance.

The offensive, supported by artillery and naval gunfire, was timed to start at 4:00 p.m. on 12 August. The gunners had been given no specific targets and were unaware of the position of the British frontline. Orders were vague and many of the maps supplied were of another area. The infantry assault started late at 4:45 p.m. with 1/5th Suffolk on the left, 1/8th Hampshire in the centre and 1/5th Norfolk on the right. Following on the left flank was 1/4th Norfolk. The terrain was a combination of thick scrub with areas of cultivated fields, ditches and trees. After advancing approximately one-half mile, enfilade fire from Kidney Hill on the left, and also from the right flank was inflicting casualties. By the time the attackers had covered 1,000 yards, losses became so heavy that units became disorganised and the pace slowed. On the right, the 1/5th Norfolks pressed forward unsupported, fifteen officers and 250 men were never seen again. Thereafter, the attackers began to fall back to their jumping-off positions. By dusk, the advance had been brought to a halt, the 159th Brigade having suffered some 200 casualties. By nightfall only 800 men could be collected to form a defensive line along a cart track to the north, the position remaining out of touch with the open left flank of 53rd Division.

During the night of 12/13 August, Hamilton, unaware of the failure of 163rd Brigade, was now considering a renewed attack on the W Hills and Anafarta Spur with 11th and 54th divisions. Early on the 13 August, Stopford contacted MEF HQ to inform them that "The troops had done well against strong opposition in 'difficult country.'"[37] It would take time to withdraw to a new line and the GOC IX Corps doubted if 54th Division would be ready to attack the Anafarta Spur until the morning of 15 August.

Shortly thereafter, Stopford received a message from 53rd Division GOC Major-General Lindley to the effect that the intermittent Turkish shelling was causing difficulties for one of his brigades, it was also "so exhausted that it was finding it very hard to hold on". A simultaneous report from 11th Division advised that a brigade of 53rd Division appeared "very shaky". Stopford notified MEF HQ that a critical situation was developing in the centre of the line where the Turks were inclined to be aggressive and the 53rd Division had been reported as exhausted and incapable of defence. The GOC IX Corps had only 54th Division available to replace 53rd Division, "which are only a danger and may bolt at any minute". The alarmist tone of these messages was unwarranted. The Turks did not attack; the 53rd Division did not vacate

37 Ibid., p. 319

its line; and, as Lindley subsequently reported, he had made a "personal tour of his front and found his men in much better shape."[38]

Stopford met with Hamilton that afternoon and insisted that 53rd Division was finished and 54th Division was incapable of attack. Time was required before another assault could be launched with any chance of success. Hamilton thought the criticism of the Territorials was unduly severe. In most units, officers and men would fight well if properly handled. Indeed, most were "losing heart from ignorance of the situation and lack of intelligent orders".[39] After considering various options, Hamilton decided not to call on IX Corps for further offensive efforts. Instead, it was to consolidate and make the line impregnable before endeavouring to push forward as far as possible.

Disregarding the order for consolidation, Stopford instructed Major-General Sir B.T. Mahon (GOC 10th Division) to push forward along the Kiretch Tepe Ridge on 14 August. The objective was to capture a Turkish strongpoint situated on the summit. This position and the adjacent defences on Kidney Hill threatened the left flank of any succeeding advance across Suvla plain.

The 10th Division was holding a line astride the Kiretch Tepe Ridge at Jephson's Post, with 30th Brigade astride the northern slope and 31st Brigade situated on the southern slope. Brigadier-General F.F. Hill (GOC 31st Brigade) was delegated to command the forthcoming attack. Immediate support would be provided by 162nd Brigade, which was still at "A" Beach. Orders were issued at 8:40 a.m. on 15 August. The infantry advance began at 1:00 p.m., but orders arrived too late for Hill to distribute further details to battalion officers before their units set off.

The 31st Brigade was to advance along the southern slope as far as a position 400 yards short of Kidney Hill, whilst 30th Brigade, traversing the northern slope, was to capture the aforementioned strong point prior to pressing on to Kidney Hill; 162nd Brigade would be in position to support on the right flank. The Kiretch Tepe Ridge had been reinforced by the Turks and, although the artillery and naval bombardments were having the desired effect, overall progress was slow. At approximately 6:00 p.m., a vigorous effort was made, after which the strongpoint was overrun and consolidated.

Advancing along the southern slope, the 31st Brigade advance commenced at 1:15 p.m. Good progress was made but, wholly unsupported, it came under heavy fire before coming to a halt. The three battalions of 162nd Brigade arrived at the right flank of 10th Division at 1:00 p.m. Tasked as a flank guard, there had been no time for reconnaissance over the difficult ground. Moreover, there was no indication of the whereabouts of the enemy positions. Pressing forward some 400 yards, the leading battalion, 1/5th Bedfords, came under heavy machine gun and rifle fire. On manoeuvring to the left, the battalion began to lose cohesion and progress slowed amongst the many gullies thereabout. Small parties from 1/10th and 1/11th London Regiment were then sent forward to reinforce the advance.

The 54th Division had suffered crippling losses before a last effort by weak parties from all three assault battalions advanced as far as the southwest shoulder of Kidney Hill. Here they remained unsupported whilst the remainder of 162nd Brigade withdrew to a line that extended the frontage of 31st Brigade.

38 Ibid., p. 319.
39 Ibid., p. 320.

By the morning of 16 August 30th Brigade was still in possession of positions gained on the ridge crest and the northern slope. It was shortly after 4:00 a.m. that the Turks launched a fierce counter-attack with bombers to the fore. British casualties mounted; by 9:00 a.m. units were in desperate need of reinforcements. Facing continued enemy counter-thrusts without reinforcements and short of bombs, 30th Brigade's position was desperate. At 7:00 p.m. Hill ordered a general withdrawal to the old frontline. With a casualty rate of over 2,000 killed, wounded and missing, the three-brigade assault had produced no territorial gain. Thus it was evident that without additional reinforcements and increased artillery support, the chances of operational success had vanished during what was the last offensive involving the two Territorial divisions.[40]

Commentary Correspondence

Captain Atkins of 1/8th Northumberland Fusiliers, 34th Brigade, 11th Division, described an incident in which Territorial Force troops were accused of throwing their arms away. Writing to the official historian, Atkins recounted the actions of his battalion following the Suvla landing. By 11 August, "our division has lost about 60% of its men and nearly all its officers." He continues with an accusation that a brigade of 53rd Division had precipitously fled:

> The 53rd and 54th Divisions (Terriers) landed two days after us and I hope they are better than when I saw them. The Welsh Brigade ran away, throwing their rifles and equipment down. They were held up by two of our Coys (Passy's and Tyrrells) they were both hit that morning – the 10th we were flank guard to the 53rd Div. that morning.[41]

The first query addresses to which brigade is Captain Atkins referring? The 158th Brigade – formerly the North Wales Brigade – and the 160th – Welsh Border Brigade were both present on the morning of 10 August during the attack on Scimitar Hill. By noon, 159th Brigade was estimated to be in a line "almost" at the first objective, but 158th Brigade was too far to the right and, not as intended, behind 159th Brigade. Therefore, it did not pass through the latter as planned. The right of 159th Brigade had been forced to retire by a strong enemy counterattack which brought 158th Brigade under direct shrapnel and rifle fire whilst traversing the Salt Lake. Most of this fire came from the direction of Green Hill which was situated just east of Chocolate Hill. This had the effect of drawing 158th Brigade to the right. Eventually the entire brigade found itself to the right of the intended line of advance. Some 159th Brigade units began falling back on to lines occupied by elements of 11th Division. This resulted in a paralysing mix-up of the assaulting brigades.[42]

The 1/7th Royal Welch Fusiliers war diary, of which 158th Brigade made reference to the withdrawal, stated:

> In the early afternoon heavy casualties were experienced when my men were first coming up to the leading trenches owing to the retirement from them of troops of another brigade,

40 Ibid., p.324.
41 TNA CAB 45/241: Letter correspondence to Historical Section re. Gallipoli.
42 Dudley-Ward, *History of the 53rd (Welsh) Division,* p.40.

who carried my men with them for a short distance. This retirement was checked, and the advance resumed.[43]

Other participating unit war diaries unsurprisingly make no mention of a disorderly retirement. The diary of Captain Atkins' battalion, 1/8th Northumberland Fusiliers, contains only the single line entry: "Battalion remained in firing line and consolidated position."[44]

More light is thrown on this stage of the attack by Major Arthur Crookenden, Brigade Major of 159th Brigade, a Regular army officer and Staff College graduate. Writing to the Historical Section he chronicled how 159th Brigade advanced with the 1/7th Cheshire Regiment in the van and the 1/4th Welsh Regiment in immediate reserve. On reaching the line of trenches held by 32nd and 34th brigades, the now inextricably mixed attackers could push on no further. Crookenden admitted that the 11th Division men looked "utterly cooked". It was here, about noon, when he observed that "the 1/4th Welsh of 159th Brigade, bolted from the positions in the rear of the trenches, but the 1/7th Cheshires did not – they were safe in the trench anyhow." The retreating battalion was subsequently brought to a halt by a divisional staff officer brandishing a revolver.[45]

The 1/5th Royal Welsh Fusiliers (158th Brigade), having passed through the lines of 159th Brigade, reached a point about 200 yards from Scimitar Hill. The leading units were held up here but reinforced by successive lines and one company of 1/6th Royal Welsh Fusiliers. The commanding officers of 1/5th and 1/6th Royal Welsh Fusiliers were together at this point as they prepared for the final assault, but the density of the scrub prevented any chance of an organised push, the attackers forced to negotiate goat tracks and water courses in single file. Soon the leading troops were reduced to small parties of 1/6th Royal Welsh Fusiliers and both battalion commanders. Reaching the crest of Scimitar Hill as the enemy withdrew, the attackers came under enfilade shrapnel and machine-gun fire before falling back to the line held by 159th Brigade.[46]

It was around this time that other units on immediate right of 1/5th Royal Welsh Fusiliers were observed falling back. The 1/7th Royal Welsh Fusiliers, which had sustained heavy losses on approaching the firing line, also began to retire. A 1/5th Royal Welsh Fusilier officer was dispatched to discover what was happening. He returned with the information that a retirement had been ordered, by whom it was not known. In all probability it was the 1/7th Royal Welsh Fusiliers that drew the advanced line back with them. The precipitous retreat was eventually halted, and the advance resumed.[47]

Lieutenant-Colonel Jelf Reveley, officer commanding 1/7th Royal Welsh Fusiliers, was one of the few pre-war TF commanding officers considered sufficiently efficient for active service battalion command. Writing to official historian Aspinall-Oglander in February 1931, he raised a number of interesting and pertinent points. Revely recollected that prior to the second attack at 5:00 p.m. on 10 August 1915, he attempted to organise his men whilst discovering disparate parties of 10th and 11th division men sheltering beneath banks and inside ditches. "These men

43 TNA WO 95/4323: 1/7th Royal Welsh Fusiliers War Diary, Appendix III.
44 TNA WO 95/4299: 1/8th Northumberland Fusiliers War Diary.
45 TNA CAB 45/241: Letter correspondence to Historical Section re. Gallipoli.
46 TNA WO 95/4323: 1/5th Royal Welsh Fusiliers War Diary.
47 C.H. Dudley-Ward, *Records of the Welch Fusiliers*, Vol. IV (London: Forster Groom, 1929), p. 38.

proved quite incapable of further advance and could not be carried on when the time came."[48] As an illustration of the prevalent attitudes towards the TF, he also recounted a visit by Captain Hardy, ADC to Major-General Lindley, after the battalion eventually came out of the line on the night of 13/14 August 1915. Hardy enquired how it was that so many rifles belonging to 1/7th Royal Welsh Fusiliers had been found lying about. Had the men cast them away? Reveley, on turning the men out, discovered his command armed with standard issue Lee Enfield No. 1 MKIII short rifles as substitutes for the obsolete CLLE MKI* long rifles they had embarked with. Indeed, many of the latter were so antiquated that the barrels had been worn smooth by decades of use. Reveley's pre-embarkation attempts to replace these weapons with the current service rifle came to naught as they were "only Territorials".[49]

As per standard publication procedure, the relevant Official History chapter draft was circulated to officers involved in the Suvla landing. Major John Duncan (GSO 2, 11th Division) strongly objected to the harsh judgement on 53rd Division's performance: "The most serious aspect of the day's fighting was the proof it had given of the unreliability of one of Sir Hamilton's five reinforcing divisions." The comment appears to have been removed from the final published version.[50] Colonel F.D. Watney, officer commanding 2/4th Royal West Surrey Regiment, 160th Brigade, 53rd Division, also responded by commenting on the fighting during 9-10 August 1915:

> 1. Most unjustly much of the blame for the failure of the Suvla landing has been laid on the two Territorial divisions, the 53rd and 54th, when as a matter of fact, the element of surprise had disappeared and the fight for the hills had been fought and lost before a single man of either of those divisions had set foot on the peninsular [sic].
> 2. I have never met Brigadier-General Maxwell, nor have I ever seen his official reports but from what I have been told he was disappointed because the 2/4th Queens and the 1/4th Sussex could not, late in the day, do what three battalions of his brigade, plus two battalions had failed to do in the early morning and apparently reported that the Queens and Sussex did nothing at all. Colonel Broadrich of the Borders (who was killed on 21 August) told me that if the Queens had not arrived when they did the line would have been driven into the sea. This statement was confirmed by several senior officers present.[51]

A portion of a report by Maxwell was reproduced in the post-war 53rd Division history:

> Neither of these battalions as far as I can see, accomplished anything, and did not appear able to go on after a few rounds of shrapnel, and remained in the low ground northwest of the word Burnu. [A contemporary map this places them over 1000 yards west of Scimitar Hill].[52]

48 TNA WO 95/4323: 1/5th Royal Welsh Fusiliers War Diary.
49 Ibid.
50 TNA WO 95/4297: Letter to Aspinall-Oglander, 15 February 1931, 11th Division War Diary.
51 TNA WO 95/4323: 2/4th Royal West Surrey Regiment War Diary.
52 Dudley-Ward, *History of the 53rd (Welsh) Division*, p. 30.

In an earlier account, compiled from notes and original orders on 3 October 1915, Colonel Watney described the actions of 2/4th Queens – temporarily attached to Maxwell's 33rd Brigade – on 9 August. As 2/4th Queens reached the summit of Scimitar Hill, the battalion came under severe enemy fire in addition to friendly fire from British batteries supporting the assault. A short retirement followed before the crest was occupied again. Heavy losses and raging scrub fires forced the attackers to withdraw a second time. By noon they had occupied some old Turkish trenches 1,000 yards northwest of Scimitar Hill. These defences were improved, the 2/4th Queens remaining there until relieved at 9:00 p.m. on 12 August. Battalion casualties amounted to eight officers and 250 men from a combined strength of 700.[53]

The same early Official History draft engendered a response fron Major C. Jarrett of 2/10th Middlesex Regiment, 160th Brigade, 53rd Division:

> I think it hardly fair to say that all units of this (53rd) Division were unreliable. Had the 2/10 Middlesex been supported it is probable even at that juncture the line might have gained considerable ground and probably occupied Scimitar Hill which would have formed a "jumping off" place for the advance to have continued the next day.[54]

This was the battalion sent forward by "some staff officer".

The 53rd Division commenced the assault from scattered positions more often than not unknown to their commanders. The situation was not helped by the lack of communications or inherent fatigue from earlier fighting. With no maps or prior reconnaissance, little water and suffering from a lack of acclimatisation, it was far from an easy introduction to the Suvla sector.

The 54th Division's reputation also underwent similar condemnation when another senior officer, Brigadier-General L. L. Nicol commander of 30th Brigade, 10th Division, recollected:

> Late on the morning of 16 August, I received a long called for reinforcement of 2 Territorial battalions – one of which was a Hants battalion and the other I forget. I received a message at the same time that these battalions were not to be used in the front line. [sic] This message was lost, and I was consequently not able to produce it, presumably it was from their Divisional commander. As reinforcements they were useless to me.[55]

The two Territorial battalions referred to were 1/8th Hampshire Regiment and 1/5th Suffolk Regiment both of 163rd Brigade, 54th Division.

The 15 August plan was for 10th Division to advance along the Kiretch Tepe Ridge bordering the north of Suvla Plain with 31st Brigade pushing forward along the southern slopes as far as a small knoll denoted as Kidney Hill. Support on the immediate right would be provided by 162nd Brigade. At 5:40 a.m. a message was sent to IX Corps stating that the first line was undergoing heavy attacks, the battalions of 31st Brigade were "being knocked about"; demands for reinforcements were urgently requested. This was followed at 9:03 a.m. by a message stating that although not being so severely pressed, the troops were reaching the limit of endurance and

53 TNA WO 95/4323: 2/4 Battalion Queens Royal West Surrey Regiment (July-December 1915), 160th Brigade War Diary.
54 Ibid., 2/10th Middlesex Regiment War Diary.
55 TNA CAB 45/241: Letter correspondence to Historical Section re. Gallipoli.

British dead near Scimitar Hill.

if they were to hold on throughout the day, two battalions were required as reinforcements. This message from 7th Royal Munster Fusiliers was repeated at 3:15 p.m. It stated that the men were "utterly done up. I do not consider this line can be held unless two fresh battalions are sent up." Nicol, on returning to 30th Brigade HQ at 7:20 p.m., ordered the brigade to hold on: "Hants and Suffolks have arrived here and are now being put into second line." Late that evening a situation report was dispatched to IX Corps: "2 battalions in reserve. 4th Norfolks have arrived. 54th Div. bombs arrived."[56] An eyewitness of 1/8th Hampshire battalion reported that as 162nd Brigade advanced across a mile of open ground under heavy shrapnel fire, elements of 1/8th Hampshires observed a company in front refuse to advance under sustained hostile fire. They were ordered back to the beachhead whilst the remainder of the battalion halted on the ridge.[57] Thus both reinforcing battalions, less this one company, reached the objective before settling into the reserve line. Having disembarked the day before, these battalions could hardly have anticipated their deployment to the firing line. Moreover, their war diaries record only receipt of orders to proceed in support of 10th Division to the north side of Kiretch Tepe. Arriving at this position on the evening of 16 August, they remained in support until 54th Division's relief of the frontline on 17 August.

The most virulent attack on the Territorial divisions came from Major Boyd Shannon of the 6th Yorkshire Regiment. Commissioned as a subaltern in the 2nd Volunteer Battalion of the South Staffordshire Regiment in 1895, Boyd Shannon transferred to the Reserve with 4th Yorkshire Regiment in 1908. The 6th Yorkshire Regiment, 32nd Brigade, 11th Division, was a New Army battalion that landed at Suvla on the night 6/7 August 1915. The following passages

56 TNA WO 95/4276: Part III, Gallipoli 1 June to 30 September 1915, XI Corps War Diary.
57 T. Travers, *Gallipoli 1915* (Stroud: Tempus, 2004), p. 217.

from a 1921 correspondence with official naval historian Sir Julian Corbett was inserted into the 6th Yorkshire Regiment War Diary:

> Dear Sir,
> I enclose the narrative of the operations of the night of landings 6th Aug 1915, Suvla Bay. The matter contained was official but abridged naturally in my report when I commanded the 6th Bn of the Yorkshire Regt (Green Howards). Brig Gen Haggard 32nd Bde. 11th Div. being severely wounded the following day seems to have resulted in the information not being dealt with at the time. It is in my opinion, of some historical interest, as it was the first occasion [sic] in which a unit of the New Regular Army was employed in an offensive operation. From my own knowledge it does not seem to be sufficiently put forward that the difficulties met with were owing to the very heavy loss in Officers, especially senior Officers in the initial fighting who could not be replaced. The 11th Div. and the two Brigades of the 10th Div. at Suvla were available for attack and took positions with heavy loss in Officers and NCOs. The two Territorial Divs. 53rd and 54th were not, as Divisions "Troupes d'assault". This meant in first few days, original troops landed 11th & 10th Divs doing double duty. I know a number of Officers were sick, Gallipoli dysentery, or fever and went on duty, of themselves, to land for attack. More than two years later I acted as officer in charge of training Kantara, Egypt. I found the Territorial divisions (from Gallipoli) still hopelessly untrained and reported this officially to GHQ/EE Forces. This must have greatly affected offensive operations in Egypt. The New Regular Divisions were effectively retrained six months after leaving Gallipoli. The 13th showed it in Mespot [sic]. The 11th on the Somme in France. Had the 53rd and 54th been of equal fighting value at Suvla it would have had a tremendous effect on that operation. The final attack in that action the 20th Aug failed owing to loss of direction. The 6th Bn YORKS was the directing unit. They lost direction thro' all the Officers becoming casualties in the first few hundred yards. The ground to be covered was some 1,000 yards. Only one was heard of again. Capt. A.C.T. WHITE who was wounded (VC at operations in Somme 1916) As the senior officer of my battalion I went to a lot of trouble in obtaining all information from survivors, the officers killed or died of wounds in my unit were a score. The attack here was a justification of Lord Kitchener's policy in forming a New Regular Army. It was superior to the Territorial in general as shock troops.[58]

Boyd Shannon was wounded and evacuated by 6:00 a.m. on 7 August 1915, two days prior to 53rd Division's landing. The 6th Yorkshire Regiment had arrived at Lemnos on 10 July 1915, before transfer to Imbros on 20 July. Over the succeeding two weeks, the battalion practiced night landings and attacks. Conversely, Territorials – by the very nature of their training – had never been intended as vaunted *Troupes d'assault.*

58 TNA WO 95/4299: 6th Yorkshire Regiment War Diary.

Military Performance: Were the Territorials really that poor?

There is little doubt that the Territorial divisions that landed at Suvla Bay were unprepared and ill-equipped for the task at hand. After a lengthy and gruelling voyage, they were sent into combat without necessary training. In theory, these formations should have had a proficiency advantage vis-à-vis New Army divisions. Indeed, during the annual training camps 1908-13, Territorial units had participated in field exercises at battalion, brigade and, on occasions, division level. Having been instructed by Regular adjutants and training staff and, for the most part, under the command of their own battalion and company officers, many adjutants had been recalled for service in France.

Among the many participant observations forwarded to the Historical Section, there was a fair amount of support for the Territorials, the major criticism being levelled at senior commanders. For example, Lieutenant-Colonel F.D. Watney, commander of 2/4th Royal West Surrey (The Queen's) Regiment, remarked on 21 January 1923:

> [S]o much has been written about the 9th August, principally by those who either were not present at all or too far away from the frontline to appreciate the position. Most unjustly much of the blame of the failure of the Suvla landing has been laid on the two Territorial divisions, the 53rd and 54th, when as a matter of fact, the element of surprise had disappeared and the fight for the hills had been fought and lost before a single man of either of those divisions had set foot on the peninsula. I had no orders before landing and no map and no effort had been made to acquaint Commanding Officers as to what had happened on the 7th and 8th.[59]

Major Cyril Jarrett of 2/10th Middlesex Regiment, writing about the Scimitar Hill assault (10 August 1915) on 26 January 1931 observed that orders were extremely sketchy and objectives vague. He attributed the subsequent failure to four key factors:

> 1. Bad staff work. The battalion might have been guided over the Salt Lake under cover of dark and laid up in the foothills and officers might have had the opportunity of reconnoitring the ground and forming up immediately in rear of the front on which the attack was to be carried out. What actually happened was that as soon as battalions left the cover of Lala Baba they came under shell fire and to fresh troops this in itself was demoralising.
> 2. Condition of men. Before embarkation the division was undoubtedly in hard condition. The transports were crowded, and the voyage out took about fourteen days. This during the hottest time of the year. The only time the men were ashore was for one march Alexandria. By the time they landed they were soft and out of condition and many suffering from something like dysentery.
> 3. Lack of water. As far as I am aware no water was procurable after landing until after the 10th.
> 4. Fatigue caused by unaccustomed heat.[60]

59 TNA WO 95/4323: 2/4th Royal West Surrey Regiment War Diary.
60 Ibid., 2/10th Middlesex Regiment War Diary.

Captain Frank Mills, subsequent CO of 1/6th Royal Welsh Fusiliers, emphasised that the Official History draft did not make enough of the terrible experiences endured. His comments collectively amplified the difficulties encountered:

> I do not think you are justified in blaming the troops. The higher command are the ones to blame, the troops were splendid. The whole operation seemed and still seems like a very bad nightmare, situation unknown, also the country, maps were only issued at the last moment, and they were very incomplete, and orders practically nil. I venture to say, that with very few exceptions, not an officer nor man had ever seen a shot fired in anger up to this time. The want of success in this campaign was due, in the first place to giving away to the enemy, the intention, and then attacking with insufficient troops. Had the whole number of troops landed during the first week, been available when the first attack was launched, and had there been sufficient artillery support, I am sure the line would have been pushed forward to the required positions, water of course being a vital factor. It always appeared to me in the early days that no one really knew what was required of the troops.[61]

Thus it appears that Mills remained unaware of the Territorial role as a general reserve to exploit gains made by New Army divisions. Indeed, the 54th Division was intended as a draft pool for replacement of casualties and represented the last available reserve only to be deployed on receipt of MEF GHQ sanction.[62]

Captain A. Crookenden, a former 159th Brigade staff officer with 18 years of military service, echoed previous comments about the failure to provide clear orders: "Here are some remarks on your excellent summary." This complimentary opening is followed by a statement of pent-up resentment retained over many years:

> You haven't quite caught the awful atmosphere. No one at Suvla seemed to care a solitary damn. One's first day in action, terribly keen to get the best out of the Terriers one has been training, ready and anxious to prove their metal, confident that they had been well taught, keyed up to concert pitch, one was absolutely amazed, baffled and finally enraged by this sort of tepid blanket of "Fanny Annie" which hit one at every turn. It spread to the ranks like a fog and very rapidly. What killed us was the complete absence of orders and enthusiasm. The more serious aspect of the day's fighting was, not the unreliability of the 11th Division, poor devils, but the absolutely incomprehensible stupidity, not merely of Generals, but of their trained staffs. Has a Staff Officer fulfilled his duty if he watches his General do nothing? Can he not issue orders himself and tell the man what he has done or what to do? – I think so. As much as the Generals I blame the G.1's. Fancy a P.S.C. officer putting his name to an order "The left flank of the attack will be protected by naval guns of H.M.S. Pinafore." What confidence in the Staff can troops have who get an order like that – H.M.S. Pinafore lying out in the bay umpteen miles from your left flank? You do not know where your left flank is, it is lost in the bush; yet H.M.S. Pinafore can protect it. Fancy a S.C. graduate acquiescing in his chief issuing an order that the "53rd Div. can

61 Ibid., 1/6th Royal Welsh Fusiliers War Diary.
62 Aspinall-Oglander, *Military Operations Gallipoli*, Vol. II, p. 313.

> be used in such a way that it would be possible to reassemble them in the evening. One wonders why they did not add 'in time for tea.'"[63]

It was not just Territorial officers that voiced sentiments of what had gone wrong. Lieutenant-Colonel Neill Malcolm, an 11th Division staff officer, observed:

> The simple fact is that neither the commander nor the troops were equal to the task which they were called upon to perform. This statement is true of other divisions as it is of the 11th. Such troops require leaders with exceptional power of infusing fire and vigour into every undertaking. These leaders unfortunately we did not possess. The system of selection at the War office – i.e. in the Military Secretary's department – was undoubtedly a contributory cause. We did not make the best use of available material. Age and length of service seemed to be almost the only – certainly the principal – qualifications to be considered. These "Dug-out" officers were not well equipped to inspire the enthusiastic undergraduates or the young business men – engineers, etc. – who had come from all quarters of the globe. It was experience not training that was lacking.[64]

The theme of inexperience and poor quality of officers was also highlighted by 31st Brigade commander Brigadier-General Sir Felix Hill:

> Nearly all the officers except the actual staffs had no previous military experience beyond that obtained in officers training corps etc. – of the Captains a few were posted from the Indian Army, others from the R, of officers and Special Reserve. Many had not been employed for years. The NCO's were all from the retired ranks and Army Reserve and of these there were few, others had to be trained with the men ... The units were mostly trained in trench warfare ... It is to be wondered at that movements were slow, and officers and men inclined to hesitate – it was all so new, nearly everyone so inexperienced in open warfare.[65]

One of the so-called "Dug-out" officers referred to by Malcolm was Lieutenant-Colonel J.G. King-King D.S.O., who had had been recalled from the official Roll of Officers in August 1914. Acting as G.S.O.1 10th Division, an old school approach to military matters is evident, but his overall conclusions are nonetheless accurate:

> I think it should be more definitely stated that the Herefordshire Division in no way represented the Herefordshire division proper, since all its best units had been taken away intact, and replaced by any 2nd line people without any military training whatever to speak of. Summing up, I attribute the failure – and it only just failed in spite of all:
>
> a) Faulty appointments of certain commanders.
> b) Giving the entire responsibility of the attack to the one least qualified by reason of health etc. to bear it.

63 TNA CAB 45/241: Letter correspondence to Historical Section re. Gallipoli.
64 TNA CAB 45/258: Letter correspondence to Historical Section re. Gallipoli.
65 TNA CAB 45/241: Letter correspondence to Historical Section re. Gallipoli.

c) Inefficiency in acquainting those with their job who had to do it.
d) Main attack directed correctly on paper but not adhered to.
e) Breaking up divisions and brigades of unseasoned troops.[66]

Major John Duncan, G.S.O.2 11th Division, strongly objected to Aspinall-Oglander's debatable remarks concerning 53rd Division's performance:

> [T]he hopeless failure of the 53rd Div. was not altogether its own fault, but was in my opinion, more due to the manner in which it was thrown into the attack. You bring out the way it was handicapped on pp. 19 and 29, but you might have added that that it had no signal company and could not take forward its machine guns for lack of transport. I believe it had no maps, but of this I am not sure. It had 6 battalions in the frontline mixed up with rather demoralised troops, it had been taken straight off the transports in which it had arrived from England, the orders were very hastily written, there was no previous reconnaissance and no means of preliminary deployment facing its objectives before moving to the attack. I do not think that any except the most experienced troops could have succeeded in such circumstances. The 53rd Div. broke badly, certain of its units entirely lost their morale, but I have always felt that this was not so much due to faulty personnel and lack of training as to the hopeless way in which it was committed to the attack.[67]

It was Lieutenant-Colonel Reveley, commander of 1/7th Royal Welsh Fusiliers, who effectively summarised the overall Territorial experience at Suvla:

> As one of the few pre-war TF commanding officers who were considered sufficiently efficient to command their own units overseas, I would like to state that the 158th Brigade had since august 1914 received a training conducive to the successful carrying through of the operations required at Suvla Bay. We were not, however, prepared for the disorganisation so obvious on all sides, for orders based on a misconception of the conditions prevailing, or for dependence on maps discovered to be quite inaccurate when compared with the terrain encountered. The men had not set foot on land since July 15th. In the evening the battalion lay under the east slopes of Lala Baba and were warned for an attack the next morning. The orders were that the brigade would pass through a definite line already held N. of Sulajik and carry on the attack to the ridge from there. These orders were issued in a great hurry and the brigade moved off without the Coy. Commanders having time to let their subordinates know what was impending. In conclusion I would submit that, that if the original landing had been entrusted to Territorial troops, trained for years past in field operations, the surprise attack would have been successful. A heavy price indeed has been paid for notorious prejudice against the TF.

Attached to Reveley's correspondence is a letter of reply from Aspinall-Oglander (23 February 1931) in which the latter sympathises with the problems encountered by the newly-arrived Territorial formations:

66 TNA CAB 45/243: Letter correspondence to Historical Section re. Gallipoli.
67 TNA WO 95/4297: Letter correspondence with Historical Section, 15 February 1931, 11th Division War Diary.

> I do indeed realise what a poor chance you and your fellows were given when you first landed in Gallipoli, and how extremely difficult it must have been for you – pitch-forked like that into the middle of operations without any proper orders or any knowledge of the situation in front, or what was expected of you. I tried to bring some of these points out in my first draft – for I was quite determined that the troops should bear none of the blame which ought to be carried by the staff.[68]

This statement is of great interest when one considers Aspinall-Oglander, as Hamilton's chief operations officer, was responsible for planning much of the Suvla Bay operations. Since then, a number of authors have accused Aspinall-Oglander of producing a biased account that obscured criticism of MEF GHQ whilst condemning subordinates.[69] Therefore, once again it must be noted that a battalion commander was generally unaware of the overall operational plan or the anticipated role of the Territorial divisions. For his part, Reveley remained conscious of the persistent, albeit somewhat latent, prejudice against the TF which no doubt coloured the views of some of the previously consulted Regular and New Army officers.

The subject of poor command and control consequent of egregious staff work had been raised by a number of the consulted official history correspondents. Moreover, the topic had also been discussed in a series of annual reports by the Inspector-General of Home Forces during 1909-1913. General C.W. Douglas, commenting upon the "Command" section in his 1913 report, observed:

> Unfavourable comments were made by my predecessor in every report from 1909 to 1911 and by myself last year on the capacity for leadership and the exercise of command shown by higher Commanders of the Army. These failings are still far from being remedied … The work of Brigade-Majors and other junior staff officers in the field has been slipshod and showing evidence of insufficient practice in the writing of orders etc., particularly when pressed for time … The fact is that the spread of military education is such that officers of the Army demand capable commanders and instructors, and the supply at present is not equal to the demand.[70]

These Regular Army shortcomings had been repeatedly identified during peacetime. Therefore, the inadequacies of command and control exhibited at Suvla Bay had been previously identified, but not acted upon during the previous five years before the First World War.

Conclusion

Documentary evidence suggests that the pre-war prejudice against the Territorial Force continued throughout war and well into the interwar period. Such attitudes only distracted from the real issues surrounding the failure of the Suvla Bay operations. The only major

68 TNA WO 95/4323: 1/6th Royal Welsh Fusiliers War Diary.
69 R. Crawley, *Climax at Gallipoli, The Failure of the August Offensive* (Norman, Oklahoma: University of Oklahoma Press, 2014) and Travers, *Gallipoli 1915*.
70 TNA WO 27/508: 'Report by the Inspector-General of the Home Forces, 1913', pp. 4-5.

difference between Territorial and the New Army formations/units was that a large proportion of the former were pre-war part-time soldiers mostly led by their original officers. As with the Kitchener armies, the Territorial ranks were also swelled by the same eager rush of volunteers during the first months of the war. Thus the manpower source was almost identical for both Territorial and New Army units, all of which followed an almost identical training syllabus and suffered shortages of equipment, stores and accommodation.

It was during the first six months of the conflict that the Territorials endured the unforeseen effects of a prolonged continental war. The TF was originally intended to provide a Home Defence force, and to act as a reserve for the Regular army. This was then complicated by the introduction of war duties that included the guarding of ports, railways, coastal areas and other vital installations that prevented them from concentrating on vital training. It was during this period that the TF fortunes and planned deployment began to go wrong. Kitchener's concerns for invasion security required two Regular divisions and the use of the TF for home defence. As the anticipated threat diminished and the demand grew for reinforcements on the Western Front, the secretary of state for war had little option but to send Territorial battalions piecemeal to the front. The structure and cohesion of TF brigades and divisions was thus disrupted from September 1914.

The 53rd Division began to send their best trained battalions to France in November 1914, and by April 1915 the entire 160th Brigade had embarked for the front. They were replaced by composite battalions from the Home Counties Division. Its component RE Field Companies dispatched to France and were replaced by second line units. The division's proficiency was also influenced by changes of divisional, staff officers, adjutants and artillery commanders during the nine months following August 1914. Likewise, 54th Division began sending battalions to the Western Front the following November. There are insufficient records to confirm if the same happened to 54th Division. Some of its battalions had only been attached to the divisions for three months before receipt of orders to prepare for Mediterranean service.

As plans for the Suvla landings were being drawn up, Kitchener and the Dardanelles Committee, no doubt conscious of the demands of the Western Front, subsequently agreed (5 July 1915) to dispatch three New Army divisions, but it remained undecided if a fourth division should be sent as well. Shortly afterwards, the Secretary of State for War asked the committee to allow him a free hand in arranging for the dispatch of a fifth division to Egypt as a general reserve for the MEF. Allocated to the forthcoming Suvla operation, the fourth and fifth divisions would be dispatched without component artillery. Meeting again on 24 July, the committee resolved to send further reinforcements from the Home Defence force as soon as possible. These consisted of two detached Territorial divisions. One would be utilised as "a general reserve for the supply of drafts or for such purposes as may be required. They were to go without artillery".[71] The lack of supporting artillery and supply trains limited their performance in operational terms. Moreover, the TF divisions were never intended to take part in large scale operations. Indeed, Hamilton had no definite intentions for this reserve; they were not committed to his plans but were to be used as a situational reaction force.[72] Nevertheless, 53rd Division was deployed (night of 8/9 August) almost immediately after landing. During

71 TNA CAB 22/2: 'War Council: Dardanelles Committee and War Committee minutes of meetings 5 July and 24 July 1915'.

72 Hamilton to Kitchener telegram, 29 June 1915 cited in Crawley, *Climax at Gallipoli*, p. 55.

the morning of 9 August, two of its brigades, less one battalion detached for beach duties, were attached to the 11th Division for operations directed by Major-General Hammersley. Lacking artillery, stores and sufficient signal and medical support, each infantryman carried two hundred rounds of ammunition and two days iron rations.

The 54th Division landed on 11 August. Similarly, it lacked artillery, signal and medical support, ammunition stores or mule transport. Its arrival came as a complete surprise to Stopford who later observed:

> I had no idea it was intended to employ the 54th Territorial Division at Suvla bay until I received information on 11th that it was arriving and was beginning to disembark at "A" Beach, and I received instructions not to employ it without direct orders from the G.O.C in C.[73]

Stopford, in the same account, was of the opinion that once exploitation of the initial landings had failed to get through on 7 and 8 August, there was little chance of progressing with raw troops and inadequate artillery. Therefore, the battle for the surrounding hills had been fought and lost before the Territorials had set foot at Suvla Bay.

For their part, the New Army troops at least had the opportunity to acclimatise and, in some instances, train at Mudros and Lemnos. They did, however, suffer from poor sanitary arrangements resulting in enteric outbreaks. The Territorials, disembarking direct from transports after weeks at sea, had no time to acclimatise before going into action. Not a man had heard a shot fired in anger and there was no time for a gradual frontline introduction/acclimatisation. Conversely, formations/units sent to France were gradually introduced to frontline conditions whereas at Suvla IX Corps' green New Army and TF divisions were thrust into one of the largest amphibious assaults of the First World War.

The inexperienced Territorial troops were also hindered by vague and hurried orders, dearth of maps or issued cartographic renderings that bore little relation to local topography. In addition, the 1917 Dardanelles Commission report concluded that 11th Division HQ, under which a large proportion of 53rd Division served, issued ambiguous and confusing orders. Moreover, when Major-General H. de B. de Lisle assumed command of IX Corps from Stopford (16 August), he found that much of the staff work had not been up to army standards.[74]

In addition to facing a tenacious enemy, the 53rd and 54th divisions endured heat, thirst and consequent exhaustion. There were, as implemented in France later that year, no Regular troops to "stiffen" the Territorials and Stopford later speculated that had he been provided with just one brigade of seasoned infantry supported by adequate artillery, IX Corps would have seized the high ground.[75] Artillery support was badly lacking at Suvla. During the early landings, only one battery of 59th Brigade R.F.A. and two Highland Mountain batteries were available, the remainder of the brigade, less horse transport, landed on 9 August. The 58th Brigade and 15th Heavy Battery R.G.A. joined IX Corps from Anzac on 12 and 13 August respectively. During

73 TNA WO 138/40: 'Lieutenant-General Stopford's statement on operations of IX Army Corps, 6-15 August 1915'.

74 Steel & Hart, *Defeat at Gallipoli*, pp. 159, 294.

75 TNA WO 138/40: Lieutenant-General Stopford's statement on operations of IX Army Corps at Suvla Bay 6-15 August 1915.

the first two days of operations, only 8 guns supported the on-going offensive. Hesitant to order an immediate assault, Stopford and Brigadier-General H.L. Reed VC (BGGS XI Corps) were imbued with the idea that advances, as in France, could not be made until the full force of available artillery was disembarked and deployed.[76] By the time the Territorials landed, there were still only 24 guns facing 54 Turkish guns.[77] With its flat trajectory, naval gunfire had little effect. Edmonds subsequently observed that large numbers of inexperienced troops, Territorials inclusive, required a greater proportion of artillery support than seasoned troops.[78] For their part, the MEF and IX Corps staffs completely disregarded or at least failed to recognise the fact that they were dealing with inexperienced and relatively undisciplined troops. This was compounded by vague orders and ignorance of the overall plan at brigade and battalion level. This resulted in a feeling of hopelessness – "a whole flock of more than willing sheep without a shepherd."[79]

The Territorial divisions at Suvla Bay performed no better and certainly no worse than New Army formations. Comprised of relatively untried troops led by older officers also unprepared for modern war, this was the price paid for the massive army expansion from August 1914 which resulted in commanders obtaining positions of responsibility for which they had no recent experience or training.[80] As Tim Travers asserts, the Suvla Bay operation was beyond the capabilities of everyone involved from Hamilton and Stopford to subordinate commanders at division, brigade and battalion level.[81] Lieutenant-Colonel W.J.K. Rettie, commander of 59th Brigade Royal Field Artillery, summed it up when he observed in July 1931: "If we had had the infantry Brigadiers of 1918 or the infantry of 1914, I think there would have been a different tale to tell."[82] This statement more than adequately summarised command and control weaknesses and faults. However, it is evident that a few officers with no knowledge of the general plan or situation retained a pre-conceived notion that the Territorials had somehow been inferior.

76 T. Travers, 'Command and Leadership Styles in the British Army: The 1915 Gallipoli Model', *Journal of Contemporary History*, Vol. 29, 1994, pp. 403-442.
77 Crawley, *Climax at Gallipoli*, p. 74.
78 Edmonds, *Military Operations France and Belgium 1915*, Vol. I, p. 211.
79 TNA WO 95/4323: 1/4th Royal Sussex War Diary, Letter from Lt. Col. J.M. Hulton to Historical Section.
80 Gary Sheffield, *The Somme* (London: Cassell, 2004), p. 25.
81 Travers, 'Command and Leadership Styles in the British Army, pp. 403-442.
82 TNA CAB45/244: Letter correspondence to Historical Section re. Gallipoli.

16

"These Brave Irishmen": Lieutenant-General Bryan Mahon and 10th (Irish) Division at Gallipoli

Brian Curragh

> *Suvla – [A] name which has brought sorrow to many homes, and which will be perpetually associated with failure, but there are many glorious memories associated with it.*[1]

When Major Bryan Cooper's *The Tenth (Irish) Division in Gallipoli* was published in 1918, the great and the good were foremost in their praise of, what has been to date, the only approximation to a divisional history the formation ever received. Former Prime Minister Herbert Asquith found it "a moving and inspiring record of which Irishmen everywhere may well be proud" while Foreign Secretary Arthur Balfour observed that "neither in bravery nor endurance have the 10th Division in the Gallipoli campaign been surpassed by any of their brothers-in-arms who have been fighting in Europe and Asia for the cause of civilisation and freedom." More interestingly, two political heavyweights – both very much involved in the debate on the future governance of Ireland – also contributed. Sir Edward Carson, then First Lord of the Admiralty but better known for his role in promoting the Ulster Unionist cause, submitted a brief paragraph which included his feeling that "I think it particularly apt that the history of the actions of these brave Irishmen in the campaign should be recorded by a gallant Irish officer." Carson's contribution was dwarfed however by the two and a half page foreword composed by John Redmond, leader of the moderate Irish Parliamentary Party, which concluded:

> The men who had differed in religion and politics, and their whole outlook on life, became brothers in the 10th Division. Unionist and Nationalist, Catholic and Protestant … lived and fought and died side by side, like brothers. They combined for a common purpose: to fight the good fight for liberty and civilisation, and, in a special way, for the future liberty and honour of their own country.[2]

1 Bryan Cooper, *The Tenth Irish Division in Gallipoli* (London: Herbert Jenkins, 1918), p. 76.
2 Ibid., pp. vii-xiii.

Clearly both sides of the political debate saw merit in promoting the unique nature of the 10th Division. By the time the volume was published, however, the Irish political landscape had been "changed utterly" by the Easter Rising in April 1916 and the subsequent executions of the principal rebellion leadership.[3] General public perceptions of the future political direction of Ireland had polarised between the north and the south and, as far as the south was concerned, the military achievements of 10th Division vanished into the "Great Oblivion" or national amnesia into which Irish military involvement in the Great War was now cast. This political myopia – perhaps best illustrated in the words of the post-Easter Rising song "Foggy Dew" which includes the line "Twas better to die 'neath an Irish sky than at Suvla or Sedd-el-Bahr" – has had the effect of throwing a curtain over the military actions of the 10th Division on the peninsula and, in particular, on the personal behaviour, during the height of the action, of its GOC Lieutenant-General Sir Bryan Mahon KCB, KCVO, PC, DSO.

This cultural shroud meant that 10th Division received relatively poor treatment in written histories of its activities. Immediately following its time on Gallipoli, three volumes of personal reminiscences were published in 1916 – Henry Hanna's *The Pals At Suvla: D Company, the 7th Royal Dublin Fusiliers*, an engaging account of the "the toffs amongst the toughs" of Dublin society and effectively a "Pals" battalion in all but name only; John Hargrave's, *At Suvla Bay*, a personal account of the author's service as a member of 32nd Field Ambulance and Juvenis, *At Suvla Bay and After*. Juvenis was the pseudonym of Ormiston Galloway Edgar McWilliam, a young officer serving with the Royal Inniskilling Fusiliers, who four years earlier had been nearing the end of his time at Charterhouse. He was subsequently killed in 1942 as a 49-year-old flight lieutenant with 226 Squadron RAF Volunteer Reserve. It was not until the end of the war that the first divisional monograph, Bryan Ricco Cooper's *The Tenth (Irish) Division in Gallipoli*, was released for public consumption. Five decades later, Hargrave revisited the campaign with *The Suvla Bay Landings* (1964).[4] Despite numerous books (Timothy Bowman, Richard Grayson, John Horne, Keith Jeffery et al) on Ireland and the Irish in the Great War published during the period 2000-09, only two authors (Philip Orr and Stephen Sanford) have examined 10th Division's historical record. Orr's *Field of Bones: An Irish Division at Gallipoli* (2006) is oral history in content. This was followed by Sandford's *Neither Unionist nor Nationalist: The 10th (Irish) Division in the Great War* (2015). Whilst the latter work did cover the division's activities, a considerable element of the research focused on statistical analysis and a comparative study of division morale.[5] In all of the above works, for a variety of reasons including, unsurprisingly, personal loyalty and allegiances, Lieutenant-General Bryan Mahon's role as division commander received scant detailed coverage.

3 William Butler Yeats, *Easter 1916* (1921).

4 Cooper, *The Tenth Irish Division in Gallipoli*; Henry Hanna, *The Pals at Suvla: D Company, the 7th Royal Dublin Fusiliers* (Dublin: Ponsonby, 1916); John Hargrave, *At Suvla Bay* (London: Constable, 1916); John Hargrave, *The Suvla Bay Landing* (London: MacDonald, 1964) and Juvenis, *At Suvla Bay and After* (London: Hodder & Stoughton, 1916).

5 Timothy Bowman, *Irish Regiments in the Great War: Discipline and Morale* (Manchester: Manchester University Press, 2003); Richard Grayson, *Belfast Boys: How Unionists and Nationalists Fought and Died Together in the First World War* (London: Continuum, 2009); Keith Jeffery, *Ireland and the Great War* (Cambridge: Cambridge University Press, 2000); Philip Orr, *Field of Bones: An Irish Division at Gallipoli* (Dublin: Lilliput Press, 2006) and Stephen Sandford, *Neither Unionist Nor Nationalist: The 10th (Irish) Division in the Great War* (Sallins: Irish Academic Press, 2015).

Before Gallipoli

Mahon joined the 8th (King's Royal Irish) Hussars as a newly commissioned subaltern in 1883. His subsequent military credentials were established during his involvement in the Mahdist War (1881-99) when he was mentioned in despatches for his role in the final defeat of the Khalifa:

> Brevet Lieutenant-Colonel Mahon (8th Hussars) acted as Assistant Adjutant-General and was also in charge of the Intelligence Department. I cannot speak in sufficiently strong terms of the excellence of the services performed by this officer. I invariably placed him in general command of all the mounted troops; his personal disregard for danger, intrepid scouting, and careful handling of men, all fit him for high command; his bold and successful seizure of the position in front of Fedil's camp, and his conduct of the fight before I came up, show him to be possessed of exceptional qualities as a commander, and I have the greatest pleasure in recommending this valuable officer to your favourable consideration.[6]

Lieutenant-General Sir Bryan Mahon.

During the South African War (1899-1902), Mahon led the flying column that lifted the Siege of Mafeking on 17 May 1900. In his report to the Secretary of State for War, Field Marshal Lord Roberts not only attached Mahon's own account of the action, but also singled him out for specific praise: "The operation entrusted to Brigadier-General Mahon was conducted by him with conspicuous ability and energy, and I would draw special attention to the skill which he displayed in evading the enemy, who had arranged to dispute his advance along the main road, by deflecting his line of march to the West. Credit is also due to Brigadier-General Mahon for the dispositions which resulted in the defeat of the Boers on 13 and 16 May and opened the way into Mafeking."[7] Mahon was awarded the Companion of the Order of the Bath for his efforts. Interestingly, the other officer in receipt of Roberts' particular attention was Lieutenant-Colonel Herbert Plumer of the York & Lancaster Regiment who commanded 1st Brigade of Mahon's force, in the relief on Mafeking. Mahon, in a report dated 23 May 1900, mentioned "for the favourable consideration of the Commander in Chief", Plumer's military performance as follows: "This officer handled his brigade in a masterly way, and turned the Boers out of several positions. His brigade had a lot of fighting on the front and right flank."[8]

6 *London Gazette*, 30 January 1900, pp. 599-600.
7 The National Archives (TNA hereafter) WO 32/7989: Roberts to Secretary of State for War, 9 July 1900.
8 TNA WO 32/7989: Roberts to Secretary of State for War, 9 July 1900.

The contrast between Mahon, the relief column commander and his subordinate Plumer, both in terms of upbringing, education and subsequent military careers, is striking. Plumer, an Eton and Sandhurst graduate, was born in Kensington and commissioned six years before Mahon. Lacking Plumer's illustrious educational antecedents, Mahon hailed from rural Galway. Despite a five-year age difference, he received a brevet lieutenant-colonelcy one year after and a brevet full colonelcy eight months before Plumer. Here their career paths parted, Mahon taking up assignments with the Egyptian and Indian armies. Plumer was appointed GOC 4th Brigade and 10th Brigade in 1902 and 1904 respectively and by August 1914 was GOC Northern Command. Subsequent wartime appointments as GOC V Corps and GOC Second Army during 1915 were followed by elevation to Field Marshal in 1919. Conversely, Mahon was relegated to sideshow commands at Gallipoli, Salonika and Egypt prior to appointments as GOC Ireland and then Governor General of Lille. The early promise demonstrated in the Sudan and South Africa did not materialise into the army career Mahon expected.

Mahon's command at Gallipoli, the 10th (Irish) Division, had its origins in the Army recruiting district that covered Ireland as opposed to the 16th (Irish) and 36th (Ulster) Divisions, which were primarily raised from Nationalist and Unionist unofficial militias respectively. The three component brigades of 10th Division reflected local geographic ties: 29th Brigade included regiments from all four provinces of Ireland whilst 30th Brigade was comprised of units from southern Ireland and 31st Brigade with recruits from Ulster. That said, with recruitment proving slow particularly in the southern provinces, a decision, taken by Secretary of State for War Lord Kitchener in September 1914, to transfer drafts from Great Britain was a means of diluting the "Irishness" of the division. Cooper attempted to demonstrate that 90 percent of the officers and 70 percent of other ranks were in fact of Irish origin; Sandford has questioned this assertion.

The 10th Division spent the first nine months of war training in Ireland, principally at the Curragh before decamping at the end of April to concentrate in the Basingstoke area where a further two months refining the lessons learned readied them for active service. During this period the division was inspected by both King George V and Field Marshal Lord Kitchener who "expressed himself as highly satisfied with all he saw of the 10th Division".[9] Following the decision to renew the stalled Gallipoli campaign, the division's next stop was to be the Dardanelles.

Embarking during the first week of July, the bulk of 10th Division sailed via Malta and Alexandria for Mudros, with the Division HQ and certain other units sailing direct from Liverpool. On arrival at Mudros, the assigned billeting area was found to be insufficient to handle three divisions with the result that one and a half of 10th Division's brigades were diverted to Mitylene on the Greek island of Lesbos. The division spent the remainder of July spread across the two islands, its men becoming acquainted with the four "Gallipoli plagues" – dust, flies, thirst and enteritis – that were to feature heavily during two subsequent months on the peninsula. This splitting of the division's component units over two islands, one hundred miles apart by sea was a recurring complaint by Mahon as the summer progressed. Indeed, the circumstances did little to promote formation cohesion. His unhappiness increased at the start

9 10th Division Order No. 34, 1 June 1915, quoted in Cooper, p. 32

of the August offensive when 29th Brigade was detached to serve under Birdwood's command at Anzac. The remaining two brigades went on to serve with Stopford's IX Corps at Suvla Bay.

The 10th Division did have some experienced officers, but this experience had all been some time ago. As Cooper observed: "The General commanding the 10th Division had seen the last warriors of Mahdism lying dead on their sheepskins around the corpse of their Khalifa in 1898. One Brigadier witnessed the downfall of Cetewayo at Ulundi in 1879; another marched with the Guards Brigade to Tel-el-Kebir in 1882; whilst the third had played his part in the desperate fighting outside Suakim in 1884."[10]

The concept of the August landings at Suvla Bay, insofar as it involved IX Corps, was passed on to Stopford on the 22 and 29 July. "The general plan is, while holding as many as possible of the enemy in the southern theatre, to throw the weight of our attack on the Turkish forces opposite the Australian and NZ Corps. The front and right of these forces will be attacked and crushed and the remnants driven towards Kilid Bahr. It will then be our object to seize a position across the Peninsula from Kaba Tepe to Maidos with a protected line of supply from Suvla Bay." Specifically, "your primary objective will be to secure Suvla Bay as a base for all the forces operating in the northern zone."[11] Securing the bay was contingent on taking the high ground to the north, east and south – "It would also appear almost certain that until these hills are in your possession, it will be impossible to land either troops or stores in the neighbourhood of Suvla Bay by day." Stopford passed on these instructions via 'IX Corps Operation Order No.1' on 3 August with the comment, "These orders are absolutely secret. The contents are not to be divulged to any officer or other ranks until the latest moment at which it is necessary for the performance of his duty".[12] This extreme secrecy was to seriously compromise the operation, as officers below division level subsequently landed with little concept of their role or the state of the enemy. For his part, Mahon viewed Stopford's operational plan as "far too intricate and complicated to have a reasonable chance of success" and, after visiting the Anzac sector, remarked: "I came to the conclusion that the ground was even more difficult than what I had thought the previous day from reading it on the map, and the chances of success even more remote."[13]

Hamilton issued a stirring call to his troops on the night of the landing: "Soldiers of the old army and the new. Some of you have already won imperishable renown at our first landing or have since built up our foothold upon the peninsula, yard by yard, with deeds of heroism and endurance. Others have arrived just in time to take part in our next great fight against Germany and Turkey, the would-be oppressors of the rest of the human race." He also specifically addressed the men of the New Army: "As to you, soldiers of the new formations, you are privileged indeed to have the chance vouchsafed you of playing a decisive part in events which may herald the birth of a new and happier world. You stand for the great cause of freedom. In the hour of trial, remember this and the faith that is in you will bring you victoriously through."[14]

Superficially, the semi-circular Suvla Bay should have provided the perfect opportunity to establish the supply base required. Sheltered to the north by Suvla Point and to the south by Nibrunesi

10 Cooper, p. 47.
11 TNA WO 95/4264: Synopsis of Instructions given to GOC IX Corps, 22 and 29 July 1915.
12 TNA WO 95/4294: Attachment to Operation Order No. 1, 3 August 1915.
13 TNA CAB 19/30: Mahon's witness statement to the Dardanelles Commission.
14 TNA WO 95/4284: Hamilton, Special Order, 5 August 1915.

Point, the inland topography consisted of four miles of flat plain extending to the range of hills to the north and south of Tekke Tepe. A natural bowl was formed by the 600-foot-high Kiretch Tepe Sirt (ridge) to the north and the Sari Bair heights to the south. The only obvious complication being the one-mile wide expanse of "white sticky mud" that was the Salt Lake. Securing the lightly defended heights should have been a relatively straightforward operation. Unfortunately, the combination of the inability on the part of British commanders to advance combined with the scrub-covered terrain opposite provided sufficient scope for the Turkish defenders to carry out an effective harrying defence that ensured IX Corps' plans went awry.

Exactly one year after Great Britain's declaration of war, the first steps that ensured 10th Division would not fight as a unified division occurred when its component 29th Brigade was ordered to Anzac to participate in the Sari Bair assault. Its subsequent attempts to hold Rhododendron Ridge, situated on the western slopes of Chunuk Bair, with the 10th Hampshire Regiment resulted in crippling casualties. Indeed, by 10 August, the battalion had sustained 136 fatalities. Cooper later observed that it "had gone into action on the morning of the 9th, with a strength of approximately twenty officers and over 700 men, had at noon on the 10th one combatant officer (Captain Hellyer) and not more than 200 men fit for duty."[15] The other significant 29th Brigade action concerned the attack on Kaba Kuyu Wells (28 August) during which 10th Hampshires lost a further 124 men killed in what was subsequently described as the "last great show" of the August campaign. According to Cooper, this was "a hand-to-hand struggle with the old enemy of Christendom … in the last of the crusades"; an emphasis that is echoed a century later by non-secular elements of the Erdoğan government.[16] Cooper's description appears apropos when one considers that some Turkish troops were heard "shrieking at the top of their voices and calling on Allah" – although this so confused one Connaught Ranger who was certain that the regiment had no-one called Allen present in their trenches![17]

Confusion surrounded 10th Division's Suvla operations from the outset. The original intention was to land its two remaining brigades at A beach but following an early morning conference (7 August) with Commodore Edward Unwin, Stopford subsequently decided on a landing at C Beach with orders for Brigadier-General F.F. Hill (GOC 31st Brigade) to subordinate his command to Major-General Hammersley (GOC 11th Division) until Mahon had landed. Hammersley, on hearing of this, wanted Hill to move along the Kiretch Tepe Ridge. He also recommended that landing within the bay would save the division from a two-mile march inland. Unfortunately, 31st Brigade were already underway and disembarked at C Beach. Meanwhile, Mahon disembarked with his staff at Suvla Bay's northern extremity. This placed the GOC 10th Division at the western end of the Kiretch Tepe Ridge with three battalions, a pioneer battalion and three RE field companies – a fraction of his command.

Unable to brief his brigade commanders in advance, Mahon was further frustrated by poor communications on the day of the landing: "I had not been able to communicate with General Hill at Mitylene or send him orders. I applied to go and visit him but could not get a boat. I tried to send him orders through HMS *Aragon* but they never reached him" with the result that when

15 Cooper, p. 69.
16 Ibid., p. 107.
17 Ibid., p. 113.

5th Royal Irish Fusiliers tows on the way to C Beach. (Royal Irish Fusiliers collection).

"Hill arrived at Suvla on the morning of the landing he had no orders until he reported himself to Sir F. Stopford, and got them from him."[18]

Following on from Stopford's instruction with regard to absolute secrecy, Hill's first intimation that his brigade would land at Suvla was related by Captain Grant of HMS *Canopus*: "[W]ith the exception of 5 maps of the Peninsular [sic], and an unusual telegram from 10th Division – 'When you move bring Canvas Buckets' – the news communicated to me by Captain Grant was the first and only intimation I received of the intended move and destination of the troops under my command – no orders or instructions of any kind." Hill was then verbally briefed by Stopford on the morning of 7 August – he was to report to Hammersley but the GOC IX Corps was unable to inform him where 11th Division's HQ was situated. By 7:30 a.m. on 7 August, Hill was at Lala Baba searching for Hammersley and his staff.[19]

At 8:00 a.m., Hammersley ordered 31st Brigade to protect the left flank of 32nd and 34th Brigades during the forthcoming assault on Chocolate Hill "by advancing south-east from Hill 10 with the right of its line directed on Ismail Oglu Tepe" (W Hills) but, having just landed, it would take approximately three hours to get into position. This circumstance effectively delayed the assault until late morning at the earliest. It was at this point that Hammersley's HQ was struck by Turkish shellfire. Following this, the first order was cancelled and replaced (8:35 a.m.) by an instruction for the 31st to assault the W Hills rather than provide flank protection. Hill, having arrived at Hammersley's HQ ten minutes afterwards, was verbally ordered to attack Chocolate Hill whilst 11th Division's component 32nd Brigade (GOC Brigadier-General Haggard) advanced on the W Hills. Confusion continued when (9:05 a.m.) the third written order of the morning instructed Haggard to employ his reserve rather than the entire brigade.[20]

18 TNA CAB 19/30: Mahon's witness statement to the Dardanelles Commission.
19 TNA CAB 45/242: Hill report.
20 C.F. Aspinall-Oglander, *Military Operations Gallipoli*, Vol. II (Nashville, Tennessee: Battery Press 1992 reprint of 1932 edition) (*OH* hereafter), pp. 251-3.

Chocolate Hill in British hands.

By 10:30 a.m., Hill had ordered the 6th Inniskilling Fusiliers, 5th Royal Irish Fusiliers and 7th Royal Dublin Fusiliers to attack Chocolate Hill and Green Hill by marching via the the Salt Lake's northern shore. With confusion between Haggard and Brigadier-General W.H. Sitwell (GOC 34th Brigade) over boundaries and written contradictory orders, it was evident that Hill's troops could expect no support from either and, at midday, the GOC 31st Brigade ordered his three battalions to halt and await further orders. By early afternoon, they had taken up a line running from the north-eastern corner of the Salt Lake where they came under hostile fire from Tekke Tepe Ridge and Baka Baba. Hill was about to dispatch 6th Royal Irish Fusiliers as support when the operation was suspended for a second time in order revise the assault plan. Zero hour now rescheduled for 5:30 p.m., the reinforced attackers were to focus on securing Chocolate Hill. Nonetheless, both Hill and Sitwell ignored the decision to halt as by this time their battalions had closed with the enemy. Further progress was, however, limited due to continuing enemy fire. The sun was setting when, with the support of 32nd and 34th brigades, the Irish battalions finally reached the foot of Chocolate Hill. By 7:00 p.m., the defenders' fire lessened following a hasty retreat to the Anafarta Spur, after which Green Hill and the eastern end of Chocolate Hill fell into British hands by nightfall. Hill later observed: "My 31st Brigade … [was] in a position to advance to the attack soon after landing on the morning of the 7th August, but owing to the hesitation, confusion & delay, I met with in the XIth Division, the orders & counter-orders re the move forward towards Chocolate Hill was very seriously delayed, & the attack on Ismail Oglu Tepe did not materialise at all … my troops were the only ones which made any concerted movement towards the Corps objectives … I can confidently assert that but for the Irish Troops attached to XIth Division even Chocolate Hill would not have been captured on 7th August." Hill's final observation was made in bitter response to the poor coverage his troops had received in Hamilton's subsequent official despatch of 26 August 1915.[21]

Delays had also occurred inside Suvla Bay where 6th Royal Munster Fusiliers (RMF) of 30th Brigade finally went ashore (11:30 a.m.) after a three-hour period of confusion whilst awaiting

21 TNA CAB 45/242: Hill to Aspinall-Oglander, 16 July 1928.

receipt of "special orders".[22] Casualties sustained by Turkish beach mines also contributed to the prevailing sense of turmoil. As a result, the next battalion to disembark, 7th RMF, were directed to a nearby cove at 1:00 p.m. With the sun now overhead, the two RMF battalions moved off in the direction of Kiretch Tepe to offer support to the 11th Manchesters. This advance was brought to a halt by hostile fire approximately 800 yards west of the ridge summit. Later that evening, the third battalion, 5th Royal Inniskilling Fusiliers, relieved the Manchesters.

By the close of 7 August, the Suvla landing had achieved few of its designated objectives, the invaders suffering casualties in killed, wounded and missing that approached the total number of Turkish defenders present that day. The British *Official History* (OH) was scathing in its criticism: "Sitting about near the open beach, or advancing slowly in the full light of day, they had offered an unrivalled target to the Turkish snipers. Throughout the day the British troops had scarcely used their rifles; the guns ashore had done little firing; and the naval guns … had done no damage at all."[23] The volume's author, former MEF GHQ staff officer C.F. Aspinall-Oglander, did not solely direct this criticism towards those that had congregated on the beach: "[L]ooking at it in retrospect, it is perhaps difficult to understand why, upon receipt of this message [from Stopford], which disclosed the slow progress of the IX Corps, Sir Ian Hamilton did not at once proceed to Suvla. Had he done so, and insisted upon an immediate advance, the duration of the World War might have been very considerably shortened."[24] Thus it was that Stopford's off-shore inactivity combined with Hamilton's remoteness on Imbros conspired to create a command vacuum that doomed the August operation to failure. Taking advantage of prevailing enemy indolence, the Turks despatched powerful reinforcements from Bulair.

Mahon can have derived little pleasure from the landing. As Cooper later observed: "[N]othing remained of the Division which he had raised and trained for nearly a year, but the three battalions which he had brought with him and the 5th Royal Inniskilling Fusiliers, which had not begun to disembark. It was an extraordinary position for an officer who was a Lieutenant-General of three years' standing and had commanded a division for more than six years, to find himself entering into an action with only four battalions under his command."[25] Conversely, Stopford's mistaken belief in the apparent success his corps had achieved was clear: "The Lieutenant-General commanding the Corps is extremely gratified with the report he has received from the GOCs 10th and 11th Divs. respecting the gallant conduct yesterday of the troops under their command. He heartily congratulates the Corps on the landing which was so successfully carried out in the face of <u>strenuous</u> opposition by day and by night … He feels confident that the troops animated with such a fine spirit will prove equal to any call that may be made upon them."[26] The gap between perception and reality was steadily widening. Nevertheless, in chronicling the situation as 8 August dawned, subsequent campaign official historian Aspinall-Oglander had not entirely given up on military success: "[T]he door to victory was still ajar for the IX Corps to enter … Victory was still beckoning. But no more time could be wasted. By the morning of the 9th at the latest the door would be bolted and barred."[27] Hammersley, initially enthusiastic to advance, succumbed to the

22 *OH*, p. 260.
23 Ibid., p. 261.
24 Ibid., p. 264.
25 Cooper, p. 140.
26 TNA WO 95/4294: IX Corps Order, 8 August 1915 (My emphasis).
27 *OH*, pp. 267.

inertia already present in Sitwell and Hill, whilst Mahon reported that he could not advance on Kiretch Tepe "without the help of artillery".[28] This opinion was not based on any firm communication from Brigadier-General L.L. Nicol (GOC 30th Brigade) who reported that his front was clear and he was preparing a support line. Stopford, on receipt of Nicol's report, concluded that his best course of action was to consolidate positions currently held – the door to success was slowly swinging shut. Thereafter, units began to dig in even though Suvla plain and Tekke Tepe were, with only three companies of defenders ensconced on Kiretch Tepe, largely devoid of Turkish troops. Thus the elaborate defences that only existed in Stopford's fertile imagination, stunted operational tempo which, in turn, ensured that future success evaporated.

Meanwhile, at 10th Division's Headquarters, Mahon – a divisional commander with just three battalions under his command – found himself rendered powerless to act as news arrived of trickling Turkish reinforcements along with a disconcerting report that 11th Manchesters had withdrawn following receipt of a direct order from Sitwell. With all fronts stagnating, Hamilton was slowly concluding that matters were not proceeding according to plan. In need of a reliable eyewitness, he dispatched Colonel Aspinall, accompanied by Lieutenant-Colonel Maurice Hankey, Secretary of the Committee of Imperial Defence, as a means of obtaining an accurate report on the current situation.[29] Disembarking at noon, they discovered what the OH described as a "holiday appearance … The whole bay was at peace, and its shores fringed with bathers."[30] Aspinall met Hammersley who informed him that he had no orders to advance. Taken aback by this revelation, he promptly made his way to Stopford's HQ vessel, *Jonquil*. The GOC IX Corps was in good spirits, believing that the men had "done splendidly". He had no intention of making a further advance until the men were rested and re-supplied. Aspinall, wiring Hamilton shortly afterward, observed: "No rifle fire, no artillery fire and, apparently no Turks. IX Corps resting. Feel confident that golden opportunities are being lost and look upon the situation as serious."[31]

Finally spurred into action, Stopford went ashore and approved Hammersley's plan to advance on 9 August only to find on returning to the *Jonquil* that Hamilton had already ordered both divisions to advance. The 11th Division was to cover the right flank whilst 10th Division, comprised of five battalions only, were to seize the Kiretch Tepe Ridge, which was held by one battalion of Turkish *Gendarmerie*. At 6:30 p.m., Hamilton arrived on board *Jonquil* to review the situation with Stopford. Following this, he proceeded to the peninsula to meet with Hammersley *sans* Stopford who had a painful knee. The two had an involved discussion that resulted in Hammersley being ordered to send the 32nd Brigade immediately to seize Tekke Tepe so that any further advance on 9 August had additional support. With delays and consequent confusion continuing, it would not to be until the early hours of 9 August that 32nd Brigade advanced only to find that Turkish reinforcements were on Tekke Tepe – Aspinall's "door to victory" had been shut. Coincidently, at the same time, a perception of similar inactivity on the Turkish side had lead *Generalleutnan*t Otto Liman von Sanders to appoint Mustafa Kemal as overall commander of the Suvla front.

28 Ibid., pp. 270.
29 Colonel Aspinall would later restyle himself as "C.F. Aspinall-Oglander" as part of a post-war marital arrangement.
30 *OH*, pp. 276.
31 Ibid., pp. 276.

On 9 August, Mahon made his way to 30th Brigade headquarters, arriving there at 6:00 a.m., the same time that the HMS *Foxhound*, an offshore destroyer, was instructed to commence the bombardment of Kiretch Tepe's highest point. Although rations and water had yet to arrive on shore, Mahon ordered the attack to commence at 7:30 a.m. Two companies of the Royal Inniskilling Fusiliers, tasked with the assault, moved along the northern seaward side of the ridge with the 6th RMF deployed along the spine and 7th RMF, flanked by 5th Dorsetshire Regiment, on the south landward side.

Whilst the Inniskillings made good progress on the side of the ridge shelled by HMS *Foxhound*, the 6th RMF encountered resistance from an enemy strongpoint on the ridge itself. With few Turkish troops on Kidney Hill, the advance on the southern slopes was more affected by fatigue and thirst with exhausted men subsequently falling back to their jumping-off point. At approximately 2:00 p.m., 6th RMF, under the command of Major J.N. Jephson captured a post at the south-western end of the highest point, the position being thereafter known as 'Jephson's Post', but this was the limit of the advance that day. Not all those involved felt the action was meaningful – Captain Victor Scott of 5th Royal Inniskilling Fusiliers believed they were "just taking back the bit of land some silly ass had ordered to be returned to the Turk" – a reference to the initial decision to establish a line 900 yards behind where the Manchesters were holding prior to withdrawal.[32] Nicol felt the reasons for failure were clear: "I cannot emphasise too strongly that I consider the want of water and the want of proper orders to me, entailing hurried and make-shift orders on my part, together with my reinforcing battalions and battery having received orders from, goodness knows where, were the chief causes of failure on the 9th."[33]

Mahon, observing the assault from brigade headquarters, encountered Hamilton on one of the latter's increasingly frequent visits to the front. The latter noted that the GOC 10th Division seemed reluctant to lose "men in making frontal attacks" and was focused on the flanks.[34] The day ended with Hamilton again attempting to encourage Stopford to act – "every day's delay in its [Tekke Tepe] capture will enormously multiply your casualties".[35] Hamilton remained positive, but the OH was rather more critical: "There can be little doubt that Sir Ian Hamilton was underestimating the difficulties that now confronted him, and in particular the really serious condition of the IX Corps. At this moment, a miasma of defeat was rising from the Suvla plain, and all ranks of the corps were rapidly becoming infected."[36] Three more days passed while Hamilton debated with Stopford the need to use the recently-arrived 54th (East Anglia) Division to take Tekke Tepe, the latter's apprehension delaying the assault. The lack of any significant progress was ably summed up in Hamilton's cable to Kitchener on the evening of 12 August. It included the following deliberate understatement: "This morning, the 10th Division captured a trench."[37]

On the afternoon of 12 August, 163rd Brigade (54th Division) advanced across the Suvla plain, only to falter before retiring to their jumping-off positions under heavy flanking fire from Kidney Hill. With the failure of this attack and the increasingly uncertain state of 53rd (Welsh)

32 TNA WO 95/4296: 31st Infantry Brigade: 5th Battalion Royal Inniskilling Fusiliers Aug. – Sept. 1915.
33 Ibid., Note from Nicol to Aspinall-Oglander, 21 January 1931.
34 *OH*, p. 296
35 Ibid., p. 298
36 Ibid., p. 313
37 Ibid., p. 317

Division, Hamilton journeyed to Suvla again on 13 August where, on meeting with Stopford, he agreed IX Corps should consolidate the line rather than risk further assaults. Puzzlingly, Stopford interpreted Hamilton's order as inspiration to ask Mahon to press along Kiretch Tepe Ridge to occupy Kidney Hill. The attack commenced at 1:00 p.m. on 15 August, but now instead of facing three companies of enemy *Gendarmerie*, Hill's brigade was tasked with seizing a line defended by the *19th* and *2/127th* regiments. Progress was slow until 6:00 p.m. when Nicol ordered a renewal of the stalled assault with the RMF storming the line with fixed bayonets. The result of this was the seizure of the ridge's highest point. Nevertheless, progress on the landward side of the ridge was disappointing. Although the Inniskillings, supported by 162nd Brigade (54th Division) managed to reach the edge of Kidney Hill where they hung on throughout the evening before being forced back to the jumping-off line. This left the extremely awkward situation where units holding the high point were entirely unsupported on the right flank. Unsurprisingly, they came under Turkish attack at 4:00 a.m. on 16 August, the hard-pressed defenders resorting to throwing rocks and stones, in addition to their small supply of bombs, to hold the enemy at bay. By 9:00 a.m. the situation was almost untenable despite Nicol's unsuccessful appeal for reinforcements. With casualties mounting, he ordered a retreat to the original front line which was carried out before dawn. The offensive was over with Hamilton remaining completely unaware of what had occurred.

Hamilton subsequently shared his growing doubts with Kitchener during the early hours of 14 August: "The result of my visit to the 9th Corps … has bitterly disappointed me. There is nothing for it but to allow them time to rest and reorganise, unless I force Stopford and his divisional Generals to undertake a general action for which, in their present frame of mind, they have no heart. In fact, they are not fit for it … These favourable conditions were not taken advantage of, the swift advance was not delivered, and therefore the mischief is done."[38] Kitchener responded to this criticism of his previously appointed commanders the following day: "If you deem it necessary to replace Stopford, Mahon and Hammersley, have you any competent generals to take their places? … This is a young man's war and we must have commanding officers who will take full advantage of opportunities … If, therefore, any generals fail, do not hesitate to act promptly".[39] Hamilton, not having intended to place Mahon in the same category as Stopford and Hammersley, informed Kitchener that he wished to retain the GOC 10th Division. Thus on the evening of 15 August, Stopford was relieved of his command with Lieutenant-General Hon. Sir Julian Byng being appointed as his successor. While Byng embarked from France, Hamilton instructed Major-General Sir Henry de Beauvoir de Lisle (GOC 29th Division) to embark from Helles to take temporary command of IX Corps.

With the decision to replace Stopford, matters came to a head on 15 August when MEF Chief of the General Staff Major-General W.P. Braithwaite sent the following signal to Mahon: "Lord Kitchener has appointed de Lisle to command 9th Corps with rank of Lieut. General as it is essential commander should have intimate experience of this type of warfare and of local conditions. Although de Lisle is junior to you, Sir Ian hopes you will waive your seniority and continue to command 10th Division at any rate during the present phase of operations. Please acknowledge." Mahon duly replied at 11:45 a.m.: "In reply to your B.234. I respectfully

38 TNA WO 95/4264: Hamilton to Kitchener, 14 August 1915.
39 *OH*, p. 326

decline to waive my seniority and to serve under the officer you name. Please let me know the command of Division should be handed over by me, I suggest Brig. Gen. F.F. Hill. [Sic]" The CGS responded at 3:10 p.m. that same day: "Brig. General Hill will assume temporarily command of 10th Division vice Lt. General Mahon who is relieved at his own request. General Mahon will proceed [to] MUDROS to await orders."[40] Despite this, and in case there was any doubt as to the esteem in which Hamilton held Mahon, the former wrote (16 August) to the Secretary of the War Office that "there has never been any question affecting Lieutenant-General Mahon's efficiency as a Divisional Commander; indeed, the only time I had mentioned his name to you has been in terms of commendation."[41] Moreover, by his own account, Stopford later observed that Hamilton had "made it practically impossible for Lieutenant-General Sir B Mahon to remain, to serve under a junior officer … I consider Lieutenant-General Sir B Mahon quite the most capable of the Divisional Generals who were serving under my command and I have every confidence in him."[42] To his credit, de Lisle was also well aware of the difficult situation he was stepping into: "Being the most junior of all the Division Commanders in the Force, I had to feel flattered, but I was not elated as I realised all it meant. I realised the cause of failure before I was told, nor could I blame the local commanders. My arrival at the H.Q. of the IX Corps was one of the most trying events of my career, and I knew that the difficulties of the situation would increase."[43]

At 9:00 a.m. on 16 August, 10th Division's war diary noted, "Lt. Gen. Sir Bryan Mahon relinquished command of the Div. which was temporarily assumed by Brig. Gen. F Hill, Cmdg 31 Inf Brig … GOC and GSO1 to conference at 9th Corps HQ."[44] The divisional AA&QMG war diary contains details of Mahon's parting message to the troops:

> I cannot express to all ranks of the 10th (Irish) Division the regret with which I give up command of you and thank you all for the gallant service you have done. Since the Division landed you have been fighting day and night and no men could have done better than you have done. Your losses have been heavy, but nothing has shaken your morale or courage. Ireland can well be proud of you. It is the saddest day of my life leaving you all and if I thought it was to your advantage I would not do so but you are better off without me and I feel certain you will serve my successor with equal loyalty and devotion – you cannot excel it. Farewell & good luck to you all.

The diary also notes that the message was received with "bitter regret of all ranks who loved and trusted him."[45]

Nicol's comments (1931) to the Official Historian shed further light on the GOC 10th Division's abrupt departure:

40 TNA WO 138/63: General Sir Bryan T. Mahon correspondence.
41 Ibid., Letter from Hamilton to War Office, 16 August 1915.
42 TNA WO 95/4264: Stopford memorandum, 18 August 1915.
43 Liddell Hart Centre for Military Archives: GB0099 De Lisle, Gen. Sir (Henry De) Beauvoir (1864-1955), 'My Narrative of the Great German War' by Lt-Gen Sir Beauvoir de Lisle, (27 July 1919), pp. 87-90. My thanks to Rhys Crawley for bringing this source to my attention.
44 TNA WO 95/4294: War Diary, 16 August 1915.
45 Ibid., AA&QMG War Diary, 16 August 1915.

> General Mahon, in his note of farewell, says he believed it better for the 10th Division for him to leave. Gen. de Lisle, I believe, owed him a grudge and Gen. Mahon knew his man and expected that grudge to be repaid on him and probably on his division. My experience proved that he was right. I knew what to expect from Gen. de Lisle after the events of the 16th, from what I had heard of him, but I did not expect that my brigade would be victimised too, for the responsibility was mine alone; but General Mahon was right. Every one of my recommendations for recognition in the brigade was quashed and not one soul was mentioned.[46]

The GOC 30th Brigade went on to quote a note Mahon had sent him: "My dear Nicol, Just a line to wish you farewell and to thank you for all you have done for me and the 10th Division. No one could have led a brigade in more gallant manner. I cannot say how sorry I am to leave you all, but I honestly believe you are all better off without me."[47] Meanwhile, the action continued on Kiretch Tepe Sirt following Mahon's departure when Private Albert Wilkin of 7th Royal Dublin Fusiliers earned a posthumous mention in despatches for his role during a fierce Turkish bombing attack: "Turkish bombs were caught and thrown back again. One private (Wilkin by name) caught four but [the] fifth unfortunately blew him to pieces."[48]

One of de Lisle's first orders was to make clear that "the protection of SUVLA BAY cannot be assured until the high ground running South from AJA LINAN to KAVAK TEPE, the roadways running through ANAFARTA SAGIR, and the ridge running SW from ANAFARTA SAGIR are denied to the enemy."[49] In reality, there was little further movement or action thereafter. Mahon was to return to command 10th Division on 23 August, although there is little comment in the relevant war diaries. However, Orlo Williams, Hamilton's cipher officer (GSO3), rather tartly observed that "Mahon, having eaten humble pie, is returning to command 10th Division."[50]

It was during late September that Deputy CIGS Lieutenant-General A.J. Murray composed an appreciation of the Suvla operations that was not wholly supportive of Hamilton's narrative: "Stopford's Corps at Suvla had landed most successfully but owing to lack of energy and determination on the part of the leaders, and perhaps, partly to the inexperience of the troops, had failed to take advantage of the opportunities". In response to the MEF C-in-C's statement that the task facing Stopford was "comparatively easy", Murray opined that Hamilton had underestimated landing difficulties, inadequacies in artillery, shortage of water and the strength and resolve of the enemy: "I incline to the belief that the whole series of tasks as planned for the IX Corps was somewhat of a risky business and not a thoroughly sound practical operation of war."[51]

Contemporaneously, following the signing of a convention between Germany, Austria-Hungary and Bulgaria, the latter nation mobilised its armed forces which prompted Greece

46 TNA WO 95/4296: Note from Nicol to Aspinall-Oglander, 21 January 1931.
47 Ibid., Mahon to Nicol, 16 August 1915
48 Ibid., Captain R G Kelly comments to Aspinall-Oglander, 11 May 1931.
49 TNA WO 95/4294: IX Corps Operation order No. 5, 19 August 1915.
50 Imperial War Museum: Documents: 14119 Private papers of Dr. O C Williams. My thanks again to Rhys Crawley for highlighting this reference.
51 TNA WO 95/4264: Murray to CIGS, 21 September 1915.

Stalemate at Suvla: Royal Munster Fusilier barricade erected in gully, September 1915. (Private collection)

and Serbia to call on the Allies for support pledged by past treaty obligations. Kitchener's initial reaction was to inform Hamilton that he must lose two divisions for the occupation of Salonika, this reduction in available manpower to be addressed by withdrawal from Suvla Bay. Hamilton strongly objected and convinced Kitchener to sanction the withdrawal of one formation only. Thus ended 10th Division's participation in the Gallipoli campaign. Its brigades began to embark for Mudros on 29 September. The departure was received with some regret: "[S]omehow one was not as glad to be leaving Gallipoli as one had anticipated … we were leaving the Peninsula again, our work unfinished and the Turks still in possession of the Narrows. Nor was it possible to help thinking of the friends lying in narrow graves on the scrub-covered hillside or covered by the debris of filled-in trenches, whom we seemed to be abandoning."[52]

Aftermath

Whilst giving evidence to the Dardanelles Commission, Mahon was supportive of his former superior:

> I can only say that General Stopford's orders were to me always to push on as far as possible, and he always impressed on me the importance of getting forward before the enemy were reinforced. He never gave me an order or made a suggestion that delayed me one minute or hampered me in any way, and I also think that no men under the circumstances could have

52 Cooper, p. 131.

> advanced further or done better than the men under my command. The strength of the enemy, the amount of their resistance and the strength of their positions were very much under-estimated by General Headquarters.

He went on to justify the extent of the limited advance made during the first two days, remarking that "the line held on the second day with two divisions less one brigade has never been advanced, although eventually – 21 August – five divisions with a considerable proportion of artillery tried to advance, and failed."[53] Unsurprisingly, Mahon made no reference to his resignation. More than twelve years later, as the Official History was in the process of compilation, former officers of the 5th Royal Inniskilling Fusiliers remained bitter, Lieutenant-Colonel. J.A. Armstrong stating in no uncertain terms: "I knew before I'd been there 24 hours that the whole show was a "wash-out". No orders, no scheme, nothing told us as to what we were expected to do on landing – or anything." Captain Victor Scott congratulated Aspinall-Oglander: "Thank goodness you've got the pluck to forget his [Hamilton] reports and to strike out on your own. The result is excellent." He also observed that "throughout my period on the Peninsula, everyone on Kiretch Tepe thought we had practically no Turks in front of us and we were all keen to advance and grousing because we were doing nothing, both officers and men." This was echoed by Captain Terence Verschoyle: "Occasionally we moved forward a few hundred yards, and occasionally retired a few, both apparently quite aimlessly; it had been only too obvious since the morning of the 8th that something was very much amiss in high places."[54]

Brigadier-General Hill began his Official History correspondence in 1926. Twenty-one letters followed over the succeeding six years. His view was made clear in an early correspondence: "Ian Hamilton's Despatches on the subject were inaccurate and misleading – when they were published, I at once wrote to him pointing out this out, also to Braithwaite, Stopford & Hammersley ... but I got little or no satisfaction from any of them".[55] His view of the failures was equally uncompromising:

> I do not think there can be any doubt, that the Scheme of Operations set to this 1&2/3 Divisions of the New Army – which had under a year's training – was a very ambitious one. In spite of this, however, it is difficult to understand or explain, the complete lack of movement of the troops of the XIth Division ... this made failure certain ... the reasons which militated against success – reasons more adverse and powerful than any Turkish opposition encountered ... the unusual nature of the mission & surroundings, which these New Army troops were called upon to deal with, did not militate in favour of rapidity. Heavily loaded, with extra ammunition, extra rations, entrenching tools, only a limited supply of water, and coming under fire for the first time from the moment of landing, in an unknown & difficult country, at the hottest season of the year, was a high trial.[56]

Hill had also taken offence that his brigade had not played its part sufficiently:

53 See TNA CAB 19/30: 'Dardanelles Commission Witnesses M-R'. This file contains Mahon's witness statement to the commission.
54 TNA WO 95/4296: 31st Infantry Brigade: 5 Battalion Royal Inniskilling Fusiliers Aug-Sep 1915.
55 TNA CAB 45/242: Hill to Aspinall-Oglander, 16 July 1928.
56 Ibid., Hill to Aspinall-Oglander, 13 March 1930.

> Regarding your PS: I absolutely and most emphatically deny that I told Hammersley or suggested to him, or any of his staff, that my troops were in any respect unfit to undertake whatever work he wishes to give them, nor did I make any such suggestion to Stopford, who told me what I was to do should I not find Hammersley. Such a statement or suggestion would have been untrue & most unfair to the troops under my command & quite unworthy of a British commander – I can only say that your informants are LIARS. There seems no doubt, Aspinall, that there are some people connected with those days, who are out to cover up their own failures & shortcomings by efforts to fog the issue, or to deprecate & disparage the work of those who loyally tried to do their best – may God frustrate such knavish tricks.[57]

However, he was not to totally convince Aspinall-Oglander that his view was the correct one: "the fact that I haven't been able to convince you as to the justice of my claims, is a real disappointment to me – I have tried to give you full reasons to account for the slowness of my attack, which I still think were warranted under the circumstances existing but their parrot-like repetition do not seem to have made any impression on the armour in which you have been clothed by the XIth Division! ... I cannot forget or excuse to my own satisfaction, the memory of the many unnecessary difficulties, unconnected with any Turkish opposition, which my troops were put up against during that day – which cramped their style – or the black draught of Ian Hamilton's Despatch.[58]

Continuing the correspondence well into 1931, Hill regretfully noted: "Nearly all the officers except the actual staffs had no previous military experience beyond that obtained in Officers Training Corps; of the captains, a few were posted from the Indian Army, others from R[eserve] of Officers & Special Res[erve] – many had not been employed for years. The NCO's were all from the Retired Ranks & Army Res[erve] ... I have often thought that had I under the circumstances, disregarded the normal system of attack & sent them off hell for leather, like a mob after a pickpocket, that we should have captured Chocolate Hill in a few hours."[59]

As for Lieutenant-General Bryan Mahon, he was to accompany 10th Division to Salonika where he spent eight months prior to being "suddenly ordered to hand over my command to another officer, I was given no reason nor have I ever been told the reason since; as far as I know there was nothing wrong and up to the time I left I had had letters from Lord Kitchener saying he was quite satisfied with how things were going at Salonika & with my work." Clearly somewhat perplexed, he was posted to Egypt for a short period prior to being invalided home to spend five months convalescing. Later, at Lloyd George's request, Mahon was promoted Commander in Chief of British Forces in Ireland. Having returned to his roots, Mahon was to work once more with Sir John French (Lord Lieutenant of Ireland) regarding the possibility of introducing conscription throughout the island. This posting lasted until May 1918 when he was placed on half-pay. After this, there was clearly some confusion as to where Mahon expected to go next. To this end, his personal file contains a long-running correspondence with French, Secretary of State for War Lord Alfred Milner and the War Office as to whether the former had promised him "the next Lieutenant-General's command which fell vacant" in

57 Ibid., Hill to Aspinall-Oglander, 18 March 1930.
58 Ibid., Hill to Aspinall-Oglander, 4 May 1930.
59 Ibid., Hill to Aspinall-Oglander, 5 March 1931.

addition to his right to receive full pay based on his Lieutenant-General's rank. While Milner remained unclear on what precisely had been promised, French was equally certain that such a promise had been made with the acquiescence of Milner, Chief of the Imperial General Staff General Sir Henry Wilson and Lloyd George. The intended position was the Western District Command. By September 1922, the matter had been passed on to the Army Council which rejected Mahon's claims, albeit with a degree of regret, in January 1923. Disappointed, Mahon appealed directly to King George V. The matter was further complicated by the fact that there were at least three other general officers who, having also reverted to a lower rank, were requesting pay and rewards equivalent to previously held rank.[60] Concerned by precedent, the War Office unsuccessfully appealed to the Admiralty and Air Ministry to make exceptions in these four cases, after which no similar cases would be raised. The Chancellor of the Exchequer ultimately rejected the matter in December 1924; the decision being communicated to Mahon in February 1925. Nevertheless. the matter appears to have remained unresolved by the time of Mahon's death in September 1930.[61]

Mahon set down his version of Gallipoli in a hand-written account five months after the Armistice. It is unclear as to whom this was addressed. Curiously, following his refusal to waive seniority, the narrative begins with his 1914 offer to do precisely that: "I asked him [Kitchener] if I might revert from Lieut. General to Major General as I knew my rank & seniority would be a disadvantage to me as regards active service, but he said it was impossible." Seeking then to explain what had changed in August 1915, he continued: "When at Suvla Bay, Genl [sic] Sir I Hamilton asked me if I would object to serve under Major Genl [sic] de Lisle. I said I did object; not because I objected to serve under a junior but I objected to serve under that particular officer. I had been serving under a junior (Major General) all the time I was in Ireland; and immediately after the above incident served under a junior (Sir Julian Byng) and raised no objection."

Mahon's problem was apparently not with the procedural waiving of seniority but clearly with his relationship with de Lisle himself. By 1919, he was still clearly sensitive as to how he was regarded:

> I was the youngest Lieut. General in the Army when I was promoted. I presume I was promoted by selection & merit; it certainly was not by interest as I never asked anyone to help me. I believe I have never had an adverse report from any of the many generals I have served under, at least I have never seen one … Every Lieut. General with one exception that has been promoted during the war was junior to me; this I only state as a fact and do not in any way consider it a grievance.

Mahon also pondered the reason for the treatment he received:

> In the spring of 1914, at the time of the Curragh Incident, I wrote to the Mil. Secretary and said that if troops were sent to coerce Ulster, I would resign my commission; at that time a good many senior officers said they were going to do the same thing.

60 The other generals involved were Major-General Sir J. Adye; Major-General G.G.A. Egerton and Lieutenant-General E.A.H. Alderson.

61 TNA WO 138/63: Correspondence from 1922/4.

He concludes his account of his military service as follows: "I do consider I have been unfairly treated and at the present, consider myself in disgrace & under a cloud & think it is hard that after 36 years' service in the Army, I should end my life under a cloud; if there is any reason for this I ought to be told & given a chance of defending myself."[62]

Five days after composing this account (12 April 1919), Mahon appealed directly to Lloyd George:

> My dear Prime Minister, my appointment in France has come to an end … I would very much like to continue serving His Majesty as a soldier or under the Foreign or Colonial Office … I would be very grateful if you would make a note of my name as an applicant for employment and hope you will forgive me for troubling you as I know how very precious your time is.

He then offers his views as to the current political conditions in Ireland: "I am afraid I do not see any improvement in the state of this Country [sic] since I left it, there is no doubt it is in a very unsettled state and people are very nervous. But as to any armed rising or rebellion, there is not any chance of that occurring."[63]

By late May, matters had not progressed to Mahon's satisfaction. He next wrote to the Secretary of the War Office to request either gainful employment or, if none was forthcoming, for his pension to be activated. Unfortunately, this resulted in official confirmation that his only option was half-pay. With no other alternative, Mahon finally took steps in August 1921 to bring his military career to an end by writing a short note to the Military Secretary: "Sir, I have the honour to request that you will forward this, my application to retire from His Majesty's service. I have the honour to be your humble servant, Bryan Mahon, General."[64] Mahon had served the British Crown from 27 January 1883 to his retirement on 31 August 1921 – a military career that lasted 38 years, seven months and five days.

Following a short spell as a Privy Councillor in the Southern Ireland Senate, Mahon was appointed to the Irish Senate by W.T. Cosgrave, President of the Executive Council of the Irish Free State, and sworn in on 11 December 1922 – a position he was to hold until his death.[65] The act of joining the Senate was a courageous one, as twelve days earlier, Liam Lynch, Chief of Staff of the Republican forces, had ordered "that the houses of all senators should be burnt". The threat came true for Mahon on the morning of Friday 16 February 1923, when seven armed men arrived in a stolen motor lorry at Mullaboden House, his wife's family home in County Kildare with seventy cans of petrol. The house's occupants being absent, five servants in the house were ordered to pile the furniture at the centre of each room. Having soaked the piles in petrol and smashed the windows, the house was set alight while one of the arsonists donned Mahon's uniform whilst playing records on a gramophone. The men then departed, taking with them the uniform, gramophone, a typewriter and a pair of field glasses. By the time the mili-

62 TNA WO 138/63: Mahon's account dated 7 April 1919.
63 Ibid., Mahon letter to DLG dated 12 April 1919.
64 Ibid., Mahon letter to Military Secretary, 12 August 1921; *London Gazette* (Supplement) No. 32441. p. 6912, 30 August 1921.
65 *Tithe an Oireachtais Houses of Oireachtais* <http://www.oireachtas.ie/membershist/default.asp?housetype=1&HouseNum=1928&MemberID=1516&ConstID=215> (Accessed 9 November 2015).

tary fire brigade – situated in nearby Curragh Camp – arrived, "the residence was … a mass of roaring flames, absolutely beyond hope of extinguishing."[66]

Mahon died seven years later on 24 September 1930. With Ireland having been divided into north and south by that time, funeral attendance by men in British military uniform was a sensitive subject. Thus only four officers attended in mufti together with Brigadier-General the Rt. Hon. the Earl of Meath representing the Army Council. Nevertheless, illustrating the ambivalent attitude towards the war in some quarters, the funeral was also attended by half of the Irish Cabinet. Mahon's *Irish Times* obituary unsurprisingly focused on his military service and concluded with his role as GOC Ireland. His controversial Gallipoli experience received no mention at all.[67]

Conclusion

Unlike Western Front veterans who could easily return to former battlefields, the majority of 10th Division veterans left Gallipoli in late September 1915 never, regretfully, to return – "when one thinks of Gallipoli one thinks first of graves". Cooper summed up the feelings of many: "[N]ot a man came back from the Peninsula without leaving some friend behind there, and it is bitter to think that the last resting-place of those we loved is in the hands of our enemy."[68] The division did have a certain uniqueness – it was the first to be primarily composed of Irish regiments fighting under one flag; the political significance was not lost on Cooper, its unofficial historian: "Ireland is a land of long and bitter memories, and these memories make it extremely difficult for Irishmen to unite for any common purpose. Many … would have prophesied that the attempt to create an Irish Division composed of men of every class, creed, and political opinion would be foredoomed to failure. And yet it succeeded … the bond of common service and common sacrifice proved so strong and enduring that Catholic and Protestant, Unionist and Nationalist, lived and fought and died side by side like brothers." Cooper optimistically concluded "it is only to be hoped that the willingness to forget old wrongs and injustices, and to combine for a common purpose, that existed in the 10th Division, may be a good augury for the future." Despite the price paid by the men involved – "officers and men did all that was required of them. They died" – events in Dublin seven months later proved this optimism to be sadly misplaced.[69] Cooper's final wish that "Ireland will not easily forget the deeds of the 10th Division" was also to take a century to be recognised. For their part, returning veterans were faced by a politically-driven "great oblivion", their service rejected by the Nationalist and Republican groups in post-war Ireland.

Nonetheless, Lieutenant-Colonel M.J.W. Pike, CO 5th Royal Irish Fusiliers, optimistically reflected on Irish involvement in the Gallipoli campaign:

66 *Kildare Observer*, 17 February 1923 <http://www.kildare.ie/ehistory/index.php/the-burning-of-mulloboden-house/> (Accessed 3 December 2015).

67 *The Irish Times*, 4th October 1930 quoted in Ronan McGreevy (ed.), *"Twas Better to Die" The Irish Times and Gallipoli 1915-2015* (Dublin: Irish Times LTD, 2015), p. 99.

68 Cooper, p. 133.

69 Ibid., pp. 137-138.

> All those who fought in the abandoned Gallipoli Peninsular [sic] have left behind them many dear friends and comrades, in common with all other present survivors who have been engaged in this world conflict no matter where serving but perhaps we may be pardoned if, in our memories of the past, the many gallant deeds and loyal services done by our comrades in the Peninsular appear at first sight to such as were engaged there to have been of little or no avail and hardly to have been appreciated in the way they should have been. The description of these operations as "a legitimate war game" has not been considered by those engaged in them as a satisfactory explanation of their origin but it is now realised that the work done there, far from being of little use had indeed a far reaching and important effect on events as a whole, so let it rest at that.[70]

Whether events on Gallipoli are still seen to have had "a far reaching and important effect on events" is somewhat doubtful.

Mahon resigned his Gallipoli command on Sunday, 15 August; on that day, the two brigades under his direct command sustained 234 deaths, the worst day for fatalities 10th Division experienced during the campaign. The following day was little better, with a further 160 fatal casualties – the second highest daily loss experienced. That the GOC 10th Division, officially citing problems with seniority with respect to de Lisle but privately admitting to a personal grudge between the two men, chose this period to relinquish his post appears, on reflection, to be a serious dereliction of duty and a betrayal of trust with subordinates. It was, however, an act that neither superiors or those under his command held against him.

With Mahon, having departed the peninsula, now absent from his narrative, Cooper movingly described the situation on top of Kiretch Tepe Sirt:

> [T]he faces of the dead comrades, lying at their sides, stiffened and grew rigid, and the flies gathered in clouds to feast on their blood, while from the ridge in front came the groans of the wounded, whom it was impossible to succour … the unceasing noise of the burning grenades, the smell of death, the sight of suffering, wore their nerves to tatters, but worst of all was the feeling that they were helpless, unable to strike a blow to ward off death and revenge their comrades … everywhere the few remaining officers moved about among their men, calming the over-eager, encouraging the weary, giving an example of calmness and leadership, of which the land that bore them may well be proud.

By dusk on 15 August 1915, 10th Division was "shattered, the work of a year had been destroyed in a week, and nothing material had been gained."[71] No doubt wanting to avoid controversy, Cooper remained silent about Mahon's eight-day absence.

70 Bertrand Patenaude, *A Wealth of Ideas: Revelations from the Hoover Institution Archives* (Stanford: Stanford University Press, 2006), p. 25.

71 Cooper, pp. 100-02.

17

"Just taking back the bit of land some silly ass had ordered to be returned to the Turk":[1] Irish Regiments and the Gallipoli Landings, April–August 1915

Gavin Hughes

> *The military student of the future will, I hope and believe, realize the significance of the stroke whereby we are hourly forcing a great Empire to commit hara-kiri upon these barren, worthless cliffs – whereby we keep pressing a dagger exactly over the black heart of the Ottoman Raj.*[2]

So wrote the Corfu-born Scot, and GOC Mediterranean Expeditionary Force, General Sir Ian Hamilton, on 27 June 1915. Indeed, the irony of his comments does not go unrecognised by the "military student of the future". It is, perhaps, truly tragic that the "great Empires" of which he wrote, committing ritual suicide on the "worthless cliffs" of Gallipoli, was not the Ottoman Raj but the British one. As an integral part of this imperial military machine, drawn into a campaign which is so often dismissed as a "side-show", were the Irish regiments of the British Army.

As the Irish military experience of the Dardanelles campaign is a vast, complicated and intriguing subject, it would be unwise to attempt a comprehensive analysis here. Indeed, it would be equally ill-advised to attempt an account of the fifteen Irish infantry battalions (plus one garrison battalion) at Gallipoli, although service details of these are provided in the appendix. Instead, the purpose of this short, but rather eclectic, chapter is to primarily focus on the experiences of Irish infantry battalions in the landings at Gallipoli on 25 April and 6/7 August 1915. Its aim is to critically examine the shared military experience of the two Regular Irish battalions at V Beach and Sedd-el-Bahr, and balance this with the situation presented to volunteer Irish battalions at "A-West" Beach at Suvla Bay (and the initial phase of Kiretch Tepe Sirt). It is hoped that, consequently, the unique fighting conditions on the peninsula and the success of these operations will be gauged from the perspective of both Irish "Regular" and "Volunteer" soldiers. At the same time, the modern legacy and historiography of the Irish commitment to the Dardanelles will be explored, as will a brief consideration of associated controversies regarding national identity, senior officer losses and relevant casualty rates. All of

1 The National Archives, (TNA): WO 95/4296: Letter, Captain V.H. Scott, 5th R. Inn. F., 29 Jan. 1931.
2 I. Hamilton, *Gallipoli Diary*, 27 June 1915, Vol. I (Edward Arnold, London:1920), p. 252.

these areas will hopefully go a small way to contribute a little more to our understanding of how Irish infantry battalions were deployed and fought on the peninsula.

Historiography, Commemoration and Public Memory of the Irish at Gallipoli

In 1914-15, the unionist and nationalist communities in Ireland had both initially enlisted in the British Army to respectively (and paradoxically) halt Home Rule and to accelerate it. Equally, both communities seem to have hoped that their mutual contribution to a greater war, albeit for divergent motives, would persuade each other of the merit of their wider political arguments at home. Ironically, however, it was to be exactly those political events at home which made this greater war – and particularly Irish involvement in the Dardanelles – increasingly irrelevant. Following 1916, with the Easter Rising and Somme battles (and, certainly, after the partition of Ireland), the already stark divisions between the two communities on the island became evermore evident. Consequently, Ireland has had a fractured and damaged experience of remembering – and coming to terms with – its military role in the Great War. In his opening preface to the history of the 10th (Irish) Division in Gallipoli, Major Bryan Cooper wryly commented that it was "by no means easy for an Irishman to be impartial, but I have done my best."[3] Indeed, in the years since the Dardanelles campaign, it seems as if impartiality towards Irish involvement in the Great War can be a constantly shifting prize.

Irish nationalism's relationship with the Great War was (and to a certain degree remains) problematic. In Southern Ireland, as the new Irish Free State emerged into Eire and the Republic of Ireland, any pro-British sympathies were, understandably, treated with suspicion or hostility. In the wake of the creation of this emergent State, those Irish men and women who had served in the British army were seemingly cast aside or, worse still, relegated to the role of unionist puppets or dupes. Those Irish nationalists who had fought in British ranks found themselves in an awkward state of limbo; disconnected from and, in their minds, robbed of, their Irish military identity. As this military orphan-culture grew, it fell (a little uncomfortably at times, it must be said)[4] to Northern Irish unionism to officially keep the memory of all Irish soldiers who served in the Great War. Even at this, the role of the 36th (Ulster) Division was, equally understandably, given prominence. Yet, in all of these clashing re-imaginations of the period, somehow the 10th (Irish) Division, with its first rush of recruits drawn from both communities and containing men of all loyalties and none, has been left behind.[5]

Until fairly recently, the most familiar work to anyone interested on the subject was, indeed, that by Major Bryan Cooper, focusing solely on the 10th Division's role at Gallipoli. It remains a seminal work and, although some of its narrative has been questioned, it remains a volume

3 B. Cooper, Preface, *The Tenth (Irish) Division in Gallipoli* (London: Herbert Jenkins, 1918), p. 17.

4 At the unveiling of the Belfast Cenotaph on 11 November 1929, 16th (Irish) Division veterans were not invited to the official first ceremony; the 16th Division's Ex-Servicemen Association laid a wreath but only after proceedings were over. By contrast, in 1930, they were not only invited but near the top of the wreath-laying parties. See K. Jeffery, *Ireland and the Great War* (Cambridge: Cambridge University Press, 2000), p. 132 and C. Switzer, *Unionists and Great War Commemoration in the North of Ireland 1914-1939* (Dublin: Irish Academic Press, 2007), pp. 50-53.

5 The Ulster Volunteer Force and Irish National Volunteers were unionist and nationalist paramilitary 'armies' created in 1912 and 1913 respectively, because of the Third Home Rule Crisis.

with a strong thread of integrity. Major Cooper, of Markree Castle, Co. Sligo, had been born in Simla and was an artillery man by previous service but, by September 1914, had found himself serving with the 5th Connaught Rangers. As such, he soldiered in Gallipoli and Macedonia and, in 1918, published the first instrumental history of the 10th (Irish) Division's service in the Dardanelles. It was "rediscovered" in the 1990s and its presence on bookshelves both filled a void and emphasised the need for more work on the division and the Irish experience in the Mediterranean. By 2000, the noted Northern Irish historian, Professor Keith Jeffery, echoing the famous comments of F.X. Martin, lamented that "of all the amnesiac aspects of Ireland's engagement with the First World War, the history of the 10th (Irish) Division is the most profoundly forgotten."[6] It is an area which, despite steady subsequent scholarship, remains resolutely remote in the popular Irish imagination. However, since 2003, many excellent articles and chapters have been written on aspects of the Irish contribution in the Mediterranean, Macedonia, Balkans and Palestine. Perhaps unsurprisingly, most of these deal with elements of the Dardanelles campaign. There was an understandable surge in public interest during 2015 with the centenary commemorations of the Dardanelles campaign, public broadcaster coverage from both BBC and RTE, and the successful "Century Ireland" online exhibition on Gallipoli. Such events were mirrored by numerous conferences and media articles although, it is interesting to note that, by the time of the Suvla Bay anniversary in August, it seemed as if much attention had already begun to peter out. Largely, like history repeating itself, in favour of the impending centenary of the 1916 Easter Rising. Indeed, it is interesting to note that to date, only one history (by Dr. Stephen Sandford) has significantly attempted to academically analyse the 10th (Irish) Division's war experiences from 1914-1918. Yet another valuable recent major addition to the subject area, *Gallipoli* by Peter FitzSimons, whilst exploring the campaign in admirable detail (over 823 pages) somehow still manages to air-brush the volunteer Irish military contribution out of the Dardanelles.[7]

Composition of the Regular and Volunteer Irish Battalions at Gallipoli

One potential explanation may lie in the continually perplexing issue regarding the Irish battalions of the British Army and their perceived – and received – ambiguity in national identity. In short, were the Irish regiments "Irish" (however this may be defined)? The answer is closely

6 Jeffery, *Ireland*, p. 38; F. X. Martin, '1916: Myth, Fact and Mystery', *Studia Hibernia*, 7 (1967), pp. 7-124.

7 For example, see H. Hanna, *The 'Pals' at Suvla Bay* (Dublin: Ponsonby, 1916); Cooper, *The Tenth Irish Division in Gallipoli* (London: Herbert Jenkins, 1918); P. Orr, 'The Road to Belgrade; the Experiences of 10th (Irish) Division in the Balkans' in A. Gregory & S. Pašeta, *Ireland and the Great War: A War to Unite Us All?* (Manchester: Manchester University Press: 2002), pp. 177-189; G. Morgan, 'The Dublin Pals' in S. Alyn Stacey (ed.), *Essays on Heroism in Sport in Ireland and France* (Queenstown: Edwin Mellen Press, 2003), G. Hughes, *The Hounds of Ulster: Northern Irish Regiments in the Great War* (Oxford: Peter Lang, 2012), K. Myers, 'Gallipoli' in *Ireland's Great War* (Dublin: Lilliput, 2014), pp. 97-113, G. Hughes, 'The Gamble at Gallipoli' in *Fighting Irish: The Irish Regiments in the Great War* (Oxford: Peter Lang, 2015), pp. 72-90, P. Lecane, *Beneath a Turkish Sky* (London: History Press, 2015), G. Hughes & D. Truesdale, *Never Retire: the 6th Royal Irish Rifles at Gallipoli* (Solihull: Helion, forthcoming) and S. Sandford, *Neither Unionist nor Nationalist* (Sallins: Irish Academic Press, 2015).

associated with the frequently varied regional, and wider-national, recruitment within Irish units. As with other British battalions in regiments of territorial designation, manpower was drawn from areas within and without the normal recruitment centres. For example, as Regular battalions, the 1st Royal Dublin Fusiliers (RDF) and 1st Royal Munster Fusiliers (RMF) were engaged on Imperial Service in India and Burma respectively when the war was declared, but many of their personnel were still drawn from traditional Irish recruiting grounds.

However, their officer class was a slightly different matter and displayed the wider typical British Army experience. One observation of the 1st RMF has been its lack of an Irish officer base yet, upon further scrutiny, their pattern is far more revealing, with the majority of officers born in India or the Dominions, then England and Ireland. Equally, regarding NCOs, there is a strong case to be made for the large number of RMF campaign veterans who hailed from Ireland. For example, Company Quartermaster Sergeant Thomas Walsh came from Lisnabrin, Curraglass, near Tallow in Co. Cork. He was a Irish Regular soldier who had enlisted on 19 May 1897, had fought in South Africa (where, as a corporal, he was awarded the DCM), the North West Frontier and had been promoted to sergeant by 1902.[8] For the rest of the battalion, place of birth statistics (taken during the census at their last posting in 1911 at Rangoon) are extremely interesting and may give a good indication of their wartime composition. In this, they overwhelmingly suggest that rank and file were drawn from Ireland, the largest other national identity being English; there is then a huge drop in numbers with soldiers born in either Wales or India registering significantly.[9]

Whilst there has already been considerable research on the men who made up the 10th (Irish) Division, a brief consideration of some of the battalions directly referred to may be helpful. In particular, there appears to be a disconnect between John Redmond's form of Irish nationalist identity and the make-up of the 10th Division, with severe incongruities to this perspective within its battalions. Intriguingly, John Redmond's introductory comments in Cooper's work (perhaps a little awkwardly sandwiched between those of Herbert Asquith, Arthur Balfour, Edward Carson and Bryan Mahon) reveal a far-deeper agenda. He referred to the contribution of all sections of Irish society who had "combined for a common purpose …", although Redmond clearly considered this purpose as being two-fold; to defend "liberty and civilisation …" but also the "future liberty and honour of their own country".[10] It is this exact point that drives at the heart of the composition of the volunteer Irish battalions. For Redmond, desperate to reinforce the image of the 10th (Irish) Division as a largely nationalist, or at least "semi-culturally united" formation, maintained blunt – and slightly misleading – comparisons between it and those "Irish Divisions and Brigades … not in the service of England [sic]." These formations were, by their very nature, comprised of military émigrés distinctly hostile to Britain and, usually, created to fight the Empire in some shape or form (the case of the American Civil War being a debateable exception). This was clearly not the case with 10th (Irish) Division.

8 *London Gazette* 7 May 1901, *London Gazette,* 10 Sept 1901, TNA WO 100: Campaign Medal and Award Rolls 1793-1949, South Africa Medal & Clasp, 1899-1902, Piece: 347; India, 1909-1912, Piece: 397.

9 The 1st RMF, 1911 Census (Rangoon), suggests some 616 Privates were born in Ireland, as opposed to 193 in England; six were born in Wales, five in India and three in Scotland.

10 J. Redmond, 'Introduction', Cooper, *The Tenth Irish Division*, p. 13.

1st Royal Munster Fusiliers parade at Avonmouth following arrival from Rangoon, January 1915. (Private collection)

Furthermore, Redmond maintained that the composition of the 10th (Irish) was of "all creeds and classes … Irishmen of all political opinions were united in the Division." To this sentiment of "all political opinions" should perhaps have been added (most importantly) *"and none"*. For many of the first recruits to the division seem to have been the genuinely eager volunteers to Kitchener's First New Army and the recruits from either the UVF or INV felt urgently compelled to enlist.[11] As such, they clearly believed that their political standpoint was not as important as the need to be in khaki. Whether this need was driven by patriotism or adventurism is, naturally, debateable and it certainly does not mean that they left their politics at the door of the recruitment office. Which is why, in part, Redmond's suggested image of the 10th (Irish) Division is uncomfortable. He stated that, as an "independent" Irish division, its formation marked "a turning point in the history of the relations between Ireland and the Empire." This may have been simple wishful thinking. It may also comfortably "iron out" any discomforting differences in cultural allegiances. John Redmond's vision for the 10th (Irish) Division was determined by his own political imperatives and desires to forge a post-war "one-identity" Ireland. As such, he saw the 10th Division's experience at Gallipoli as vital to demonstrating how all sections of Irish society had "combined for a common purpose."

However, Redmond also deliberately obscured the many varied reasons *why* Irish and Ulster men volunteered, especially as he considered this "common purpose" as being not only the fight for "liberty and civilisation" but also the struggle for the "future liberty and honour of their own country". Whilst this may have been the case for some in its ranks, and probably for those supportive Irish Parliamentary Party observers, it was also a politically disingenuous view of the division's composition. The problem remained that the two politically divergent

11 Ulster Volunteer Force, Irish (National) Volunteers; until the split in the latter organisation in late 1914, it had been known as the Irish Volunteers. The rump of the organisation kept the original name and became increasingly revolutionary in its political aspirations, culminating in the Easter Rising of 1916.

communities had two varying images what "their own country..." should ultimately look like. One intriguing letter published in the *Belfast Newsletter* during late December 1915 hints at the internal political and cultural frictions within the 10th Division. It does not suggest that there was any blatant sectarianism within the division but, rather, that its political identity had been "hi-jacked" by those "outside" the division. One anonymous 9th Royal Inniskilling Fusilier officer (signing himself simply as "Tyrone Officer"), like many, had initially served in those Inniskilling battalions of the Tenth. He vociferously complained that unionists in this Irish division were often overlooked, largely "because Sir Edward Carson declines to go on the platform with Mr. Redmond so that the latter can say all are united on the question of Home Rule [yet] we have the fact blazoned forth in the Press to cover up the opposition of a large section of Nationalists to recruiting."[12]

It could be argued that Redmond was attempting to simply draw all dysfunctional strands of Irish society together for the British war effort and, in this, they did indeed come together successfully within the ranks of the 10th Division. Just as some within unionism perhaps felt that nationalist volunteers had begun to embrace Empire "loyalism", certain nationalists believed that unionist volunteers now saw themselves "growing into" an exclusively Irish identity. In this, they were in part correct; unionists in 1915 certainly saw themselves as Irish – but also as intrinsically British, an element of their identity they had no wish to diminish or whittle away.[13] For example, the personal cultural identity of one 17-year-old recruit, William Verschoyle Gray, was clearly part of a wider British pluralism; he was Welsh-born but brought up and resident in Dublin, with an Irish father and grandparents. He lived on Susanville Road, Drumcondra, Dublin and, like many of the young volunteers to his battalion (7th Royal Dublin Fusiliers), was a Protestant (Church of Ireland) from a modest middle-class background. Yet, even this background was not straight-forward for, as he wrote home to his mother, he clearly revelled in his newfound "Irishness" and what this meant to him; "Get dad to tell grannie that I am very proud to be Irish now when I see the way that Irishmen made a big charge and captured a position, singing 'Derry's Walls.'"[14] The irony here is quite provocative, as "Derry's Walls" (traditionally sung to the tune of "God Bless the Prince of Wales") is one of Irish (Ulster) unionism's most distinctive songs, rivalled only perhaps by "The Sash".

Given the nature of this unit, such unionist sentiments are perhaps unsurprising. In fact, several points immediately demonstrate the unique position of Gray's particularly notable volunteer battalion, the 7th Royal Dublin Fusiliers (the "Dublin Pals"). It had an incredibly high percentage of Protestant volunteers (around 70 percent)[15] and the overwhelming majority of the battalion were drawn from clerical, professional or student walks of life. Yet, what began life as a "Pal's" formation ('D' Company) soon appears to have developed into the nucleus of the entire battalion, to such an extent that the "Dublin Pals" became synonymous terminology for both in the public imagination. One of the senior battalion officers was the Yorkshire-born Charles Henry Tippet, who had served with the Royal Dublin Fusiliers in the Boer War and, pre-1914, had a prominent

12 *Belfast Newsletter*, 31 December 1915.

13 For example, Major Bryan Cooper, Unionist and Protestant historian of the 10th (Irish) Division elected to remain in the Irish Free State post-partition and stood as Dublin County TD; yet, upon his death in 1930, his coffin was draped with the Irish Tricolour and Union Flag.

14 W.V. Gray, *Kildare Observer*, 6 November 1915.

15 Sandford, *Neither Unionist*, p. 42.

role in Conservative politics in Suffolk where he lived with his family. By September 1914, he was deemed an "Hon. Lieutenant-Colonel" and had volunteered to serve with his old regiment; he was subsequently posted to the 7th Battalion and joined them in Dublin as a temporary major.[16]

However, this battalion's character appears to sharply contrast with other battalions from the 10th (Irish) Division, although it must be stressed that every battalion had distinct regional variations in composition. If this notion is taken further, it is interesting to note that the 5th Connaught Rangers had, perhaps, the highest cultural, religious and political composition of any unit in the 10th Division, standing at almost 90 percent Catholic volunteers. A very high percentage of Catholics also served in the 6th Leinsters (85 percent) and the pioneer battalion, 5th Royal Irish Regiment (75 percent). Such statistics would indeed appear to confirm Redmond and the Irish Parliamentary Party's rather bold public pronouncements. However, throughout the division, recruitment patterns were not so-clear cut. For example, the 6th Royal Irish Rifles (drawn mostly from Belfast and counties Antrim and Down) was also a "Protestant" battalion (again approx. 70-72 percent) but had very few farm labourers and a higher number of skilled men in its ranks than the divisional norm. Indeed, even within the 7th Dublin Fusiliers, there were difficulties in making sweeping generalisations. For, although its recruits were largely "well-to-do", one company was filled by a sizable contingent of Dublin dockers who, as one of their officers recalled, were "Larkinites" recruited straight off the city's quay-fronts; drawn by "the prospect of good food and pay, which were welcome to them after months of semi-starvation during the great strike of 1913 and 1914."[17] Equally, the above figures only refer to specifically Irish or Ulster volunteers; religious information for recruits from Great Britain is harder to define. Consequently, the religious content – and certainly the political/cultural identity – of the division becomes blurred and slightly obfuscated. For example, On 2 August, Hamilton made an inspection of 30th Brigade, visiting the HMTs *Alaudia*, *Andania*, *Canada* and *Novian* (where its troops were still ashore). Upon seeing them there, he noted that it seemed like most of the 5th Irish Fusiliers and 5th Inniskillings were about only 40 percent Irishmen, with "the rest being either North of England miners or from Somerset."[18] Yet, it is the active *Irish* battalion participation at Gallipoli that concerns us most here and, in this, the compared and shared experiences of the landings can be directly informative.

The Regular Military Experience: V Beach and Sedd-el-Bahr 25-26 April 1915

One of the most synonymous events associated with the Irish military experience of Gallipoli was the initial landings on V Beach and associated loss of the 1st Battalions of the Royal Dublin and Royal Munster Fusiliers. With a total strength on paper of 2,057 men, it was to become a highly visible illustration of the Irish regimental contribution to the entire British war effort. While these troops were on their way to the peninsula, a momentous naval engagement was fought on 18 March. The British naval commander, Vice-Admiral Sir John de Robeck, (the

16 *Suffolk and Essex Free Press*, 2 September 1914.
17 Many of these men followed the Trade Union leader, Jim Larkin, and had been involved in the 'Dublin Lockout'. H. de Montmorency, *Sword and Stirrup: Memories of an Adventurous Life* (London: G. Bell, 1936), p. 245.
18 Hamilton, *Gallipoli Diary*, Vol. 2, p. 45.

second son of John, fourth Baron de Robeck, of Gowran Grange, Naas, Co. Kildare), tried to bludgeon a way through the Dardanelles Straits with eighteen battleships. As they neared the Narrows, six vessels were struck by Turkish guns and floating mines; it convinced de Robeck that the Narrows could not be successfully entered without serious military involvement.

Unfortunately, by the time the troop element of this rather "cobbled together" amphibious operation landed on the beaches, all chance of surprise had disappeared. In its place, the Turks had strengthened their coastal defences and refortified those beaches where landings could be affected. In addition to this, the peninsula's natural terrain lent itself to the defensive, with innate topographical barriers and bluffs becoming easily defendable high ground. The potential for an undemanding establishment on the five beaches at Cape Helles was as deceptive as it was overwhelmingly complicated in practice. The chosen landing places were all very different in physical geography and in the extent of the Turkish defences. Added to this variable, nearly every attacking unit had to be transported to their designated beaches in different ways, either carried in packed lighters or small boats (which were lowered from the sides of the battleships/transports) and then either rowed or towed ashore. Other infantry companies were placed in specifically converted transports (known as "beetles") which were an experimental form of landing craft. At three of the beaches (X, Y and S) battalions were able to wade ashore, climb up the steep cliff-faces and then entrench with comparative ease. For example, on the morning of 25 April, Lieutenant-Colonel F.G. Jones and his 1st Royal Inniskilling Fusiliers landed at X Beach at 9:00 a.m. (supporting the leading battalions in 87th Brigade, 2nd Royal Fusiliers and 1st Border Regiment). The 1st "Skins" then calmly crossed the 200 yards of beach and then scrambled up the forty-feet high bluff before they "dug in" or, more accurately, "scraped in" and awaited the orders to push inland.[19]

EElsewhere, as dawn broke, the ANZAC landed at what became known as Anzac Cove. Although they gained a determined foothold, the Turks were able to quickly mobilise in the area and gallantly defended the dominant spine of Sari Bair Ridge and Chunuk Bair mount. Their control of this vital high ground effectively stopped any further ANZAC advance and, arguably, stalled the success of the entire operation. Ironically, the diversionary assaults at Kum Kale were a complete success, with the French succeeding in taking the position and capturing nearly 600 Turkish prisoners. However, at V Beach and W Beach (Lancashire Landing), events turned catastrophic.

The Landings at V Beach: an assessment of the Irish Regimental contribution, 25-26 April 1915

The day before the landings, Brigadier-General Steuart W. Hare, addressed his 86 "Fusilier" Brigade at Mudros; half of which was to be sent to W Beach (Lancashire Fusiliers and Royal Fusiliers) and half to V Beach (the Royal Dublin and Royal Munster Fusiliers). In his pre-battle speech, Hare exhorted his men by urging them to emulate their regimental ancestors in campaigns past, knowing very well that their "task will be no easy one. Let us carry it through

19 They left Mudros harbour aboard the RMS *Andania* the previous evening, with a fighting strength of 26 officers and 929 other ranks. TNA WO 95/4311: War Diary, 1st Royal Inniskilling Fusiliers War Diary.

in a way worthy of the traditions of the distinguished regiments of which the Fusilier Brigade is composed."[20] At 5:00 a.m., the naval bombardment would begin, followed by the actual landings; by 8:00 a.m. it was estimated that the ground above V Beach and Sedd-el-Bahr would be secured; by midday, that Krithia would be captured and, by nightfall, the hill of Achi Baba captured. It was to be a truly combined operation between the Army and Royal Navy, with an audacious plan (often referred to as the "Trojan Horse" of Gallipoli) formulated by Commander Unwin.[21] It was intended that just over 2,000 troops would be landed from the former collier ship SS *River Clyde* which would be deliberately run aground.[22] Hatchways (effectively "sally-ports") had been duly cut in the ship's reinforced armour-plated sides and the men inside (led by Lieutenant-Colonel Henry Tizard's 1st RMF) were to use these to run onto a series of lighters, lashed together, to form a bridge to the beach. Half an hour earlier – and pivotal to the assault's timetable – the 1st RDF, under Lieutenant-Colonel Richard Rooth, were to be landed ashore by picket-boat, rowed by Royal Navy crew. The RMF were placed in close support with orders to assist the inland push supported by 1st Hampshires. On paper, the plan seemed credible enough. However, the stark fact remains that the landings for the 1st RDF and 1st RMF became a murderous killing ground.

In hindsight, the reason why seems stark. The Turks may have been outnumbered but they still completely dominated the high ground (including the old fort at Sedd-el-Bahr) which overlooked the beachheads. Furthermore, the beaches at V and W provided virtually no cover whatsoever for any attacking troops and every possible advantage to the defenders. To make matters worse, intelligence of the terrain was fragmentary. As the Munster Captain, Guy Geddes, wryly recollected, the maps issued to them were "indifferent and painted but a poor picture of the topographical features that we found later." It is ironic that some of the best maps of the V Beach objectives were, in fact, done post-landings by officers who survived the event.[23] In the rather oddly detached comments by Sir Ian Hamilton (in his First Gallipoli Despatch), the success or otherwise of the landings seemed to depend on simply "having a go" at the enemy and seeing what happened:

> What seemed to be gun emplacements and infantry redoubts could also be made out through a telescope, but of the full extent of these defences and of the forces available to man them there was no possibility of judging except *by practical test.* [my emphasis][24]

20 O. Crighton, *With the Twenty-Ninth Division in Gallipoli* (London: Longmans, Green & Co., 1916), p. 46.
21 At 51, Commander Edward Unwin was made captain of the *River Clyde* during the landings, despite his age for active service; his indomitable spirit that day was to win him the Victoria Cross.
22 The following units were aboard the *River Clyde*: No. 1 Hold (upper deck): three companies, RMF; No.1 Hold (lower deck): one company, RMF, one company, RDF; No. 2 Hold: two companies Hampshire Regt. and one company, West Riding Field Engineers; No. 3 and No. 4 Holds: two sub-divisions Field Ambulance (stretcher-bearers), one platoon 'Anson' Battalion, RND and one signal section. TNA WO 95/4310: Report, Captain G.W. Geddes, 'X' Company, 1st RMF,
23 See also the excellent "V-beach from a sketch by Captain Geddes" in C.F. Aspinall-Oglander, *Military Operations Gallipoli*, Vol. I (London: Heinmann, 1929), p. 230, and sketch map drawn by Lieutenant G. Nightingale in his military diary, TNA PRO 30/71/5: Nightingale Papers.
24 I. Hamiliton, 'Despatch of General Sir Ian Hamilton, Commander in Chief of the Mediterranean Expeditionary Force', *London Gazette*, 6 July 1915.

The obvious naivety of Hamilton's observations almost demonstrates a cavalier disregard for the military consequences. Without darkness, or any element of surprise, there could only be one logical outcome to such a "practical test", as the Lancashires and "Dubsters" were to bitterly discover.

Blue Jackets and Blood Red Sea …

To support the amphibious landings at V Beach (Ertuğrul Bay), as elsewhere at Cape Helles, the naval bombardment of the Turkish defences began at 5.00 a.m. and continued until 6.30 a.m., when the *River Clyde* was due to beach. Shortly after the barrage started, the first wave of three companies of Dublin Fusiliers and a platoon from the Royal Naval Division (Anson Battalion) got into six tows of boats and made their way towards V Beach and a small makeshift harbour ("Camber") to its right. As they neared the shore in their boats, one Dublin officer watched the British shells as they fell on their targets, sending "many of the Turks running for their lives."[25] However, due to the fluctuations in current and drift, the tows began to have difficulty heading for the shore. This problem was then exacerbated by the large bulk of the *River Clyde* attempting to deliver the second wave of troops "behind time" as arranged; but it was moving at a faster rate than the RDF's transports. As the *River Clyde* beached at 6:25 a.m. (rather undramatically as it transpired),[26] the RN detail-parties, assisted by a number of Munster Fusiliers, including 30-year-old Lance-Corporal Henry Quenault (from Jersey), began to quickly lash the lighters together into a make-shift pontoon. By this time, the steam pinnaces had already set their tow-boats adrift and the RN crews had rowed furiously towards the beach to land the three attacking companies of the RDF.[27] As Hamilton rather wistfully commented, up to "the very last moment it appeared as if the landing was to be unopposed. But the moment the first boat touched bottom the storm broke."[28] It was at this point, when the RDF were within 20 yards or so of the shore, that the Turkish defenders opened fire with everything they had. Some 300 rifles and four machine-guns of the *26th Infantry Regiment* had a clear line of sight to their targets;[29] the RDF, caught in their boats; the RMF, about to file out down the gangplanks of the *River Clyde*.

One Dublin Fusilier, William Harris, recalled that the boats beached about 20-30 yards from the shore, forcing everyone to swim in their kit; but "whichever way you swam that day you faced death."[30] Lieutenant-Colonel Tizard (commanding 1st Royal Munster Fusiliers) believed that of those 240 or so RDF in the tows, no more than forty reached the shoreline unscathed.[31] Within the opening minutes of the assault, hundreds appeared to be killed or wounded. Although small

25 S.P. Kerr, *What the Irish Regiments Have Done*, (London: Unwin, 1916), pp. 138-39.
26 TNA WO 95/4310: Report, Captain G.W. Geddes, 'X' Company, 1st RMF; Geddes observed that the *River Clyde* came to rest at 06.30 hrs with 'not a jar.'
27 Some sources recall four tow-boats, others six, which may be from some confusion regarding the inclusion of the steam pinnaces. Aboard one of these tows was the platoon from Anson Battalion, Royal Naval Division.
28 Hamilton, 'Despatch', *London Gazette*, 6 July 1915.
29 Whilst the use of machine-guns (Maxims) by the Turkish is still a matter of debate (especially when applied to other beaches, such as Anzac), many accounts of V Beach suggest the *26th Infantry Regiment* did use them. See TNA WO 95/4310: War Diaries for 86th Brigade HQ War Diary, 25 April 1915.
30 *Leinster Leader*, 7 August 1915.
31 TNA WO 95/4310: Report, Lieutenant-Colonel Tizard, 1st RMF.

pockets of men clawed their way onto the beach, it appears that many of the Dublin Fusilier casualties were hit whilst still in their boats or as they tried to wade ashore. One Dublin officer recounted that his boat was rapidly filled with dead, as Turkish shells burst above them and then a hidden machine-gun (posted at the foot of the cliff) easily ripped through them at about "10 yards" range. The effect was immediate. The officer was knocked to the bottom of the boat and began to drown in the putrid liquid there. Men fell on top of him and he yelled at them to help him – but those around him were already dead or dying. Instead of heading for the shore, the boat headed back to its nearby mine-sweeper, the casualties removed and more RDF sent in to the attack. In the anonymous officer's words, he "was simply saturated all over with blood, and I could feel the hot blood all over me … the boat was awful to look at, full of blood and water."[32] As an example of the casualty rate on these piquet-boats, one contained thirty-three Dublin Fusiliers, of which only six survived relatively unscathed; the RDF's second-in-command, Major Edwyn Fetherstonhaugh, was just one of those mortally wounded in the congested boats.[33]

By most accounts, it seems that the majority of men were killed or fatally wounded during this initial phase, but some were undoubtedly drowned in the water by the weight of their packs.[34] There was even some suggestion that men were burnt alive when their boats caught fire.[35] Certainly, one Dublin Fusilier officer, Lieutenant Cuthbert William Maffet, recollected some form of incendiary shells targeting the row-boats and that many dying men "to add to their death agonies were burnt as well."[36] Although Lieutenant Maffet made it to shore and the cover of a sandbank, this was not before he had been grazed in the head by a machine-gun bullet; his back pack had been peppered by the same. He was not alone, as another Dublin officer, finding his backpack gouged by a fragment of shell, turned himself around in the boat and effectively tried to use his pack as a shield. Although his pack had saved his life, he saw "the poor fellow next to me with the top of his head taken off by the same piece of shrapnel."[37] Lieutenant-Colonel Richard Rooth was also killed on his way to the beach and was estimated that, out of 700 RDF, only 300 made it ashore. Their chaplain, Father William Finn, seems to have also made it to the beach before similarly being killed. He was the first member of the Royal Army Chaplain's Department (of any denomination) to be killed in action during the war.[38] One Turkish officer, Mahmut Sabri, from the 3rd battalion of the *26th Regiment*, later recalled that it was impossible for his men to fire and not hit a target. Indeed, "in many cases one bullet accounted for several of the enemy."[39] Those RDF who managed to struggle to the

32 Kerr, *What the Irish Regiments*, pp. 138-39.

33 TNA WO 95/4310: War Diary, 1st Royal Dublin Fusiliers War Diary, 25 April 1915, H.C. Wylly, *Neill's Blue Caps*, Vol. 2 (Aldershot: Gale & Polden, 1925), pp. 30-32.

34 TNA WO 95/4310: Report, Captain G.W. Geddes, 1st RMF: "There is no doubt that men were drowned owing chiefly, I think, to the great weight they were carrying – a full pack, 250 rounds of ammunition, and 3 days rations – I know I felt it. All the Officers were dressed and equipped like the men."

35 Some sources note that Turkish "pom-pom" guns fired a form of incendiary charge, although this still remains a point of controversy.

36 H.C. Wylly, *Neill's Blue Caps* (Aldershot: Gale & Polden, 1923), pp. 30-32.

37 Kerr, *What the Irish Regiments*, pp. 138-39.

38 M. McDonagh, *Irish at the Front*, pp. 109-10, Crighton, *With the Twenty-Ninth*, p. 67. See also Linda Parker's chapter in this volume.

39 M. Sabri, *Seddülbahir'in Ilk Şanlı Müdafaası: 26 Alay III Tabur'un Muharebsi (The First Glorious Defence of Seddülbahir: Battle of the 3rd Battalion, 26th Regiment)* (Konya: Yeni Anadolu Matbaası,1933), p. 4,

shallows, then soon discovered that the Turks had placed wire entanglements in the water. One Dublin-born Sergeant, Christopher Cooney, successfully got ashore and, despite being in full view of the Turks, continued to conspicuously rally the RDF forward, assisting his men and coolly organising them in the chaos of the landings.[40]

It is also of note that at least some determined effort at providing cover for the RDF and RMF was made by the unorthodox use of the eleven machine-guns of the Royal Naval Armoured Car Division, led by Lieutenant-Commander Josiah Wedgewood, which were mounted on the *River Clyde's* forecastle.[41] This must have had some small impact on the morale of Irish troops but, in reality, the enormity of the devastation around them seems to have been overpowering.[42] All of these events, if must be stressed, occurred within a savagely short space of time. It is hard to envisage the intensity of this fire, but it poured down upon the Dublin's unprotected boats and also swept across the decks and gangplanks of the *River Clyde*. The soldiers and sailors constructing the assault pontoon here came under direct fire from the Turks on the heights and were picked off by snipers. Somehow, the working parties succeeded in their task and the attackers charged out of the hatchways. As 'X' and 'Z' companies of the 1st RMF spilled out of the *River Clyde*, they were also struck down by a murderous hail of bullets and shrapnel. Captain Eric Henderson, 'X' Company Commander, was one of the first Munster officers to fall – badly wounded – whilst cheering his men on and Captain R. R. G. Kane took charge, before he too was wounded. By the time the second waves had made their way out of the ship, the fragile lighter-bridge broke away in the current; those men who were not drowned were cut down as they struggled to get ashore in their kit. At this point, Commander Unwin led a determined party of sailors who dived into the sea to try and secure the lighters, all the time under "murderous" Turkish fire. They did this for over an hour, physically holding the lighters together whilst under shell, rifle and machine-gun fire.[43]

It is believed that, of the first waves of some 200 RMF out of the *River Clyde*, over 149 were killed, wounded or knocked out of action. RDF Captain David French made it to V Beach but had been wounded in the arm; he was 50 yards or so from the *River Clyde* and could see the RMF from his position. He watched as the last platoons of the RMF 'X' Company charged out behind their commander, Captain Guy Geddes, a Boer War veteran. French counted 42 men following behind him, all of whom were hit. As French noted, despite his own regiment's

transl. in P. FitzSimons, *Gallipoli* (London: Bantam Press, 2015), p. 278. Sabri's comment may add weight to the theory that the Turks did not have as many machine-guns as the British believed.

40 R.W. Walker and C. Buckland (eds.), *Citations of the Distinguished Conduct Medal, 1914-1920* (Uckfield: Naval & Military Press: 2007), p. 1268; War Office, *Soldiers Died in the Great War, Vol. 66, Pt. 73, The Royal Dublin Fusiliers* (London: HMSO, 1921); The Committee of the Irish National War Memorial, *Ireland's Memorial Records 1914-1918*, (Dublin: Maunsel & Roberts, 1923); F. Deegan, Vol. 2, p. 291; W.T. Covill, Vol. 2, p. 179; *War Dead of the British Commonwealth Skew Bridge Cemetery, V Beach Cemetery, Helles, Gallipoli* (London: Maidenhead 1982 reprint of 1925 edition), pp. 21-30.

41 Lieutenant-Commander J.C. Wedgewood was awarded the DSO for commanding the machine-gun section "which rendered invaluable service on the 'River Clyde' and has shown exceptional courage and devotion to duty on several subsequent occasions." *London Gazette*, 8 November 1915.

42 In his report, Lieutenant-Colonel Tizard expressively noted that the shelling from *HMS Albion* and Wedgewood's machine-guns aboard the *River Clyde* "did no material good."

43 This Royal Navy party was awarded Victoria Crosses for their gallantry at V Beach; Commander Edward Unwin, Able-Seamen William Charles Williams (killed in action), George McKenzie Samson; Midshipmen George Leslie Drewry and Wilfred Malleson. *London Gazette*, 16 August 1915.

desperate efforts to get ashore, he saw the RMF as "a real brave lot. After a few minutes it became harder for them to get ashore." For his part, Captain Geddes soon discovered that he was alone on the lighter-bridge and shouted at those behind to come on. He later recollected that, by the time they made it ashore, 70 percent of 'X' Company had been lost, with "2nd Lieut's Watts and Perkins wounded and my CQM Sgt killed."[44] Privates Timothy Buckley (from Macroom, Co. Cork), James Fitzgerald (hailing from Blarney, Co. Cork) and another anonymous Fusilier found themselves lying flat on the lighter-bridge, as the bullets and shrapnel flew around them. Like so many recollections, Buckley recalled talking to the lad on his left and watched as "a lump of lead entered his temple." Not long afterwards, he turned to Fitzgerald and saw him mortally wounded and, within minutes, he too "was soon over the border."[45] To many aboard the *River Clyde* the cries from the wounded and dying were too much to bear without action. Sub-Lieutenant Tisdall from Anson Battalion RND, dived into the water and, pushing a boat ahead of him, tried to rescue as many Dublins and Munsters as he could. After the second (or third) trip, he was physically exhausted and was aided variously by Chief Petty Officer William Perring, Leading Seamen James Malia, Fred Curtis and James Parkinson.[46]

Inside the *River Clyde*, the remainder of the battalions of Hampshires, RMF and Lieutenant Henry O'Hara's 'W' Company of the RDF were completely pinned down; unable to exit the ship's hull and caught "like rats in a trap."[47] Only one RDF platoon attempted the journey, led by Sergeant C. McCann who simply said that as they "filed out of the old Clyde and down the gangway … Turkish machine-gunners picked them off. After ten minutes, the platoon had reached the dead on the two barges and … scrambled ashore."[48] A mere hour or so into the landings, Lieutenant-Colonel Tizard already knew that the RMF's part in the assault on V Beach, as originally planned, was over. In his words, it would have been "impossible to carry out the original scheme as to move out in any formation for the attack on to the objectives given to me meant certain death."[49] Indeed, fewer than 200 RMF had managed to lodge themselves on the enemy's shoreline.[50] Many of these were huddled together by a crowded sandbank or stuck behind shallow knolls and dunes, waiting for a chance to get into more substantial cover. For those who had somehow made it to shelter, without reinforcement, the prospect of holding this tragically small gain seemed faint. A detachment of men under veteran Munster Sergeant Patrick Ryan,[51] had taken cover behind a sand ledge, as a small group of mixed troops, led by Captain Geddes dashed

44 Imperial War Museum (IWM): 1964-05-86: Account, Captain D. French, 1st RDF; TNA WO 95/4310: Report, Captain G.W. Geddes; Geddes records 48 men.

45 McDonagh, *Irish at the Front*, p. 64.

46 Tisdall was posthumously awarded the Victoria Cross; Perring, Malia and Parkinson were awarded the Conspicuous Gallantry Medal. *London Gazette*, 31 March 1916. Leading Seaman Fred Curtis, from Liverpool, was to be killed at the start of June, aged thirty-five. His body was never recovered.

47 TNA WO 95/4310: Report, Captain G.W. Geddes.

48 Wylly, *Neill's Blue Caps*, p. 33.

49 TNA WO 95/4310: Report, Lieutenant-Col. Tizard, 1st RMF.

50 IWM: interview 4103: W. Flynn, 1st Royal Munster Fusiliers, 1964; S. McCance, *The History of the Royal Munster Fusiliers*, Vol. 2 (Aldershot: Gale & Polden: 1927), pp. 47-9.

51 Although difficult to ascertain such claims, it is traditionally held that Lance Sergeant Patrick Ryan (No. 8512) was the first Munster Fusilier to get onto V Beach; he had enlisted on 23 February 1907 and was finally discharged from the Army on 14 December 1916 due to wounds. See TNA WO 329/2817: Service Medal and Award Rolls, 1914-1915 Star, RMF, WO329–A0001-0300: Service Medal and Award Rolls, Silver War Badge, (Infantry, Cork).

up to them. Private William Flynn recalled that his small band of RDFs and RMFs then tried to work their way around to a safe position by the undercliff, in order to secure their right flank.[52] As they did so, Geddes was hit in the shoulder, two more fusiliers were killed and one wounded.[53] However, they actually forced their way into Sedd-el-Bahr fort (albeit briefly) before having to retreat from there to a nearby position, where they dug themselves in. The wounded Captain Guy Geddes managed to semaphore Lieutenant-Colonel Tizard, still aboard the *River Clyde,* to say that he "had no men left. He told me to go for my objective Fort No.1 but it could not be done." Shortly afterwards, Captain Thomas Singleton Tomlinson, with only three men left, managed to join their position; it was still not yet 9:00 a.m.[54]

In an attempt to relieve the pressure on these beleaguered knots of men, Lieutenant-Colonel Tizard ordered another tentative expedition onto the beach. Subsequently, half of 'Y' Company, led by the veteran Major Charles Harry Brownlow Jarrett, were sent to try and work their way slowly ashore and bolster the forces there. Major Jarrett was a man with a traditional British military background; he had been born in Calcutta in 1875 and was the eldest son of Colonel Charles Sullivan Jarrett. Accordingly, he and his brother both served in the Army, with Charles commissioned into the Royal Munster Fusiliers in 1894 and serving with them throughout the Boer War.[55] His half-company again came under direct fire from the Turkish defenders, with many more men hit, one of whom was 23-year-old Private Martin O'Malley from St. John's in Limerick, who may have given a false age upon enlistment.[56] In fact, as 'Y' Company staggered through the maelstrom, down the gangplank and onto the lighters, they found them now crowded with dead. Trying to make it across the lighters became even more difficult and Major Jarrett shouted to Lieutenant Guy Nightingale and his men to go back, as there was "no more room on them." Nightingale was another professional soldier, born in Darjeeling in 1890 and subsequently schooled in England. Like many of his class and generation, he left Rugby for a career in the Army, being commissioned into the 1st Royal Munster Fusiliers in 1910. Now, he was witnessing a scene of carnage which would not be repeated in his soldiering career. Nightingale wrote a few days later that he could not judge "how many were killed or drowned, but the place was a regular death trap." He returned through the hatchway and relayed Jarrett's instruction to Colonel Tizard not to send any more men ashore. Meanwhile, Major Jarrett somehow made it to the beach and got his surviving party from 'Y' Company under cover; from the *River Clyde*, Nightingale saw them on the shore, "all crouching under a bank about 10 feet high."[57]

Indeed, by just after 9:00 a.m., both Tizard and Lieutenant-Colonel Carrington Smith (in overall command and himself a former Royal Munster Fusilier) decided to pause the landing

52 TNA WO 95/4310: 1st RMF War Diary, 25 April 1915; IWM, Flynn, 1st RMF, (1964); McCance, *The History of the Royal Munster Fusiliers*, Vol. 2, pp. 47-49.

53 Guy Geddes coolly recorded later that he was "plugged" through the shoulder but that the bullet went straight through his back, so he continued his advance.

54 TNA WO 95/4310: Report, Captain G.W. Geddes.

55 His younger brother, Captain Alymer Vivian Jarrett, DSO, 2nd Yorkshire and Lancashire Regt., had been Mentioned in Despatches (*London Gazette*, 22 June 1915) and was officially awarded the DSO (*London Gazette*, 23 June 1915) a day later. However, Captain Jarrett had already died of his wounds near Vlamertinghe (Ypres) on 22 June 1915.

56 According to the census records for 1901, Martin was born in 1897; he had an older brother John, however, was born c. 1893. The details on the 1901 census could, indeed, be incorrect.

57 TNA PRO/30/71: Letter, Lieutenant G.W. Nightingale, 1st RMF, 1 May 1915.

View from the bow of the SS *River Clyde*, 25 April 1915. A cluster of 1st Royal Dublin Fusiliers and 1st Royal Munster Fusiliers survivors, having sought cover beneath an embankment, can be discerned in the centre distance. (Stephen Chambers)

operation. For the next few hours around 1,000 men were still inside the hull of the *River Clyde*. One of these was Captain Harry Stuart Wilson (the 1st Royal Munster Fusiliers' adjutant), from Marchdyke Chandler's Ford, Southampton. Wilson was another veteran of many British Imperial campaigns and had been commissioned into the King's African Rifles and fought in Jubaland 1907-09, before becoming Captain Commanding the Camel Corps in Somaliland 1908-10. After this date he transferred to the Royal Munster Fusiliers in Burma and was appointed Adjutant in 1914.[58] Like many aboard the *River Clyde*, he knew that they were trapped:

> [I]f the Turks had possessed any field artillery capable of being brought to bear on the Clyde's un-armoured hull, the troops inside would have been annihilated.[59]

This fact had not gone unnoticed by Hamilton, aboard the *Queen Elizabeth* who, somewhat blithely, recorded that "most fortunately" the collier was built to give "fairly efficient protection to the men who were still on board, and, so long as they made no attempt to land, they suffered comparatively little loss."[60] Certainly, Lieutenant O'Hara's 'W' Company was the only

58 Captain Harry Wilson was effective battalion CO following the landings at V Beach and briefly, whilst in Egypt, before the battalion was sent to the 16th (Irish) Division. He was killed in action, 9 September 1916 on the Somme. Rather sadly, his parents, Sir David Wilson, K.C.M.G., V.D., and Lady Wilson, of Clovelly Cottage, Ryden's Avenue, Walton-on-Thames noted, on his CWGC register memorial that he was also a "Sportsman and Artist". Wilson's body was never recovered and he is commemorated on the Thiepval Memorial to the Missing.

59 TNA WO 95/4310: Report, Captain and Adjutant H. S. Wilson, 1st RMF.

60 Hamilton, 'Despatch', *London Gazette*, 6 July 1915.

RDF unit intact, as it had been confined with the *River Clyde,* unable to get off. This seems to have largely saved them from the fate of their comrades.[61] Unfortunately, both Captain Wilson and Major Monck-Mason, the Munster's second-in-command, were wounded aboard the *River Clyde* and subsequently put out of action. By 09:30 a.m. or thereabouts, it was estimated that half of the original force had been similarly neutralised.

Many witness accounts note that the water by V Beach had turned red with blood; so many, in fact, that it becomes more than poetic exaggeration. Although the narrative of the veteran war correspondent, Henry Nevinson, perhaps over-dramatically, recorded that the "ripple of tormented sea broke red against the sand", it was a highly accurate description.[62] Commander Charles R. Samson, No. 3 Squadron Royal Naval Air Service (RNAS), was engaged in aerial reconnaissance during the landings and reported that he could see the water around V Beach a "strange colour" for about 50 yards out to sea. Upon closer investigation, he realised to his horror that it was "absolutely red with blood."[63] Captain Geddes, not prone to romanticism in his account of the landings, flatly stated that the "dead and wounded lay at the waters edge tinted crimson from their blood." His CO, Lieutenant-Colonel Tizard equally recalled that the water was "red with blood ..."[64] whilst Captain Wilson observed it "was deep red for 50 yards out to sea." [65] Indeed, the scene of devastation at V Beach is hard to readily imagine. The scattered corpses of Dublin and Munster Fusiliers lay thick on the snared or drifting tow-boats, lighters and shoreline, or floating in the shallows. For the Turks, the beach became an equally repellent sight, as Mahmut Sabri of the *26th Regiment* commented, it was simply "packed with enemy corpses like fish piled on top of each other."[66]

Indeed, of the Dublin Fusiliers already lying dead on the shoreline, or floating in the shallows, were 40-year-old Private Stephen Byrne, from Drogheda, Co. Louth, 22-year-old Charles Garvey from Portadown, Co. Armagh and 25-year-old Corporal (Acting Lance Sergeant) John Henry Beer, from Clapham, London. Amongst the Munster dead on the barges and beach, was Private Adolphus Francis Reuben, who was born in Mandalay and had lived and enlisted in Rangoon – where the 1st Battalion was stationed in 1914. Also included in the list of dead were many valued NCOs and warrant officers, including 35-year-old Company Quartermaster Sergeant Charles Cant from Bolton and Company Sergeant Major David Danagher, aged 37, from St. John's, Limerick. Like CQMS Walsh, Danagher was an Irish Regular who had soldiered in South Africa and along the North West Frontier.[67] The sudden loss of such experienced officers and NCOs could not be easily replaced, certainly not in the heat of a battle.

61 Wylly, *Neill's Blue Caps*, p. 32.
62 H.W. Nevinson, *The Dardanelles Campaign* (London: Nesbitt, 1918) p. 98.
63 A. Moorhead, *Gallipoli* (London: Hamish Hamilton, 1956), p. 143.
64 TNA WO 95/4310: Report, Lieutenant-Colonel Tizard, 1st RMF.
65 Ibid., Report Captain and Adjutant H. S. Wilson, 1st RMF.
66 Sabri, *Seddülbahir'in Ilk Şanlı Müdafaası*, p. 4.
67 *London Gazette* 7 May 1901; *London Gazette,* 10 Sept 1901; TNA WO 100: Campaign Medal and Award Rolls 1793-1949, South Africa Medal & Clasp, 1899-1902, Piece: 347; India, 1909-12, Piece: 397; National Archives of Ireland, 1901.

"Oh Lord, I am done for now": Assessing Senior Officer Casualties at V Beach

Meanwhile, the commander of 29th Division, Major-General Hunter-Weston, appears to have been absorbed by the slaughter happening on W Beach (Lancashire Landing) and unaware of the fate of his troops on V Beach. In the fighting there, the "Fusilier Brigade" had lost its commanding officer, Brigadier-General Steuart Welwood Hare, a former King's Royal Rifle Corps officer. Having first sought permission from Hunter-Weston, both Brigadier-General Hare and his Brigade-Major, Cork-born Major Thomas Frankland (Royal Dublin Fusiliers) had accompanied the first tows of the Lancashire Fusiliers into W Beach. However, it was during the following push towards X Beach, where Hare was badly wounded in the leg and forced to relinquish command.[68] The original plan had dictated that 88th Brigade would support the landings on V Beach but, incredibly, Hunter-Weston instead diverted its advance battalion, 1st Essex Regiment, to W Beach. However, the remaining battalions in 88th Brigade (the remaining Hampshires inclusive) were still heading towards the *River Clyde*, intent on making their way to shore. As Hamilton noted in his Despatch, the "covering force detailed for this beach was then to follow in tows from the attendant battleships."[69] At the head of this supporting force, the commander of 88th Brigade made his way to the besieged collier.

According to Captain Wilson, at around 10:00 a.m., 53-year-old Brigadier-General Henry Napier, arrived on the *River Clyde* with his 36-year-old Brigade-Major, Captain John Costeker from South Kensington, and a party of 4th Worcestershire Regiment. Like Hare, and seemingly in contrast perhaps to other senior commanders, Napier (a former Cheshire Regiment and Royal Irish Rifleman), was determined to see for himself what was happening. Typically, soon after his arrival, a direct (and rather detached) order from Hunter-Weston at 29th Division HQ came through to immediately push on with the assault, no matter what. Lieutenant-Colonel Tizard had little option but to send more men onto the beach. A company from the Hampshires, led by Major Arthur T. Beckwith, were sent forward and, entirely as expected, were targeted by sustained Turkish fire.[70] It seems as if fifteen men managed to get down the gangway when the barges again dislocated in the current and began to drift. At this point, Brigadier-General Napier and Captain Costeker "apparently not knowing the reason, dashed down the gangway ..."[71] which is the only account to openly detail events aboard the *River Clyde* before he was killed. Upon being bluntly told by Carrington-Smith that any such venture would be "impossible" and that he would not be able to get ashore, Napier apparently simply replied that he was going to give it a "damned good try."[72]

He and Costeker did indeed give it a "damn good try". The accounts of their deaths vary and several versions of Costeker's and Napier's last moments exist. In fact, the official war diary for 88th Brigade seems vague – and possibly even a little at odds – on the details of what may have happened. It records that Brigade HQ had been on *River Clyde* on 24 April and that at

68 Thirty-five-year old Major Thomas Hugh Colville Frankland, formerly adjutant with the 1st RDF in India, was subsequently killed later that day.
69 Hamilton, 'Despatch', *London Gazette*, 6 July 1915.
70 Lieutenant-Colonel Arthur Thackeray Beckwith, CMG, DSO, took over command of the 2nd Hampshires and ended up as brigadier-general commanding 153rd Brigade, 51st Division.
71 TNA WO 95/4310: Report, Captain and Adjutant H. S. Wilson, 1st RMF.
72 IWM: interview, R.B. Gillett, 1965.

8:30 a.m. the next morning it – and "500 Worcesters" transferred to a "mine-sweeper" and steamed to 500 yards off the shore, when the parties were transferred to boats and "rowed ashore". It then reports that at "10:30 a.m. As we neared the shore we came under heavy rifle fire; both Brigadier-General Napier and his Brigade-Major, Major Costeker were killed before landing."[73] Similarly, Private Ben Ward, 4th Worcesters, wrote an account (in June 1915 whilst convalescing in hospital) and reported that the brigadier-general was hit on his way to the *River Clyde* by massed Turkish fire that "dropped" around his boat.[74] Although two days later, Captain Gillam, 29th Divisional Supply Train, heard that Brigadier-General Napier had indeed been shot aboard one of the pinnaces, again on his way to, not from, the *River Clyde*. The confusion is understandable, certainly given the circumstances and, either way, Gillam also heard that Napier had died from a "machine gun bullet in the stomach."[75]

According to the recollections of Major George Davidson, RAMC, working aboard the *River Clyde*, the general was killed "on a barge attached to us."[76] Equally, the official Despatch from Sir Ian Hamilton recorded that, as they approached the shoreline, the barges containing men from the Hampshires (and Brigadier-General Napier and Captain Costeker) began to again drift dangerously away in the deeper water. All of this was under the sustained hail of Turkish fire from above and the men in the fragile boats were forced to lie down. According to Hamilton's official Despatch, this was the point that "General Napier and Captain Costeker were killed."[77] Before he died, the brigadier-general told Staff Captain Sinclair-Thompson to tell Lieutenant-Colonel Carrington Smith that he was now in command of the brigade. Shortly after this, he apparently apologised for "groaning" and died.[78] Gillam also recounted that he had been told that Costeker's last words were, "Oh, Lord! I am done for now ...", which, if not allegorical, might tend to suggest a mortal wound rather than an instantaneously fatal one.

Captain Wilson's account (presumably eye-witness, as he seems to have been on the deck of the *River Clyde* at the time) recalls that when Napier and Costeker got onto the shifting barge pontoon, they both lay flat as it was coming under very heavy Turkish fire. Then Captain Costeker dashed to the end of the barge (presumably to see what could be done) and returned to lie down beside Napier. At this, Turkish snipers picked both him and the brigadier-general off, killing them – not necessarily instantly.[79] Lieutenant Nightingale was watching from the deck of the *River Clyde* and saw him "hit in the stomach ..." on the barge lying between the collier and the shore. Nightingale thought he had tried to get some water but was again fired at whenever he moved; although he couldn't be certain that he hadn't been hit again, he knew that he died soon afterwards. All Nightingale was certain of was that, when he went ashore a few hours later, he passed the general's body, "turned him over and he was quite dead."[80] Irrespective of the

73 TNA WO 95/4312: War Diary, 88th Brigade War Diary, 29th Division, 25 April 1915.
74 'Hand-written Account', Pte. Ben Ward, 'My Tales of the Dardanelles (April-June 1915)' <http://www.worcestershireregiment.com/wr.php?main=inc/gallipoli_Ben_Ward> (Accessed 10 March 2016).
75 J. Gillam, *Gallipoli Diary* (Stevenage:The Strong Oak Press, 1989), pp. 46-47.
76 G. Davidson, *The Incomparable 29th and the 'River Clyde'* (Aberdeen: James Gordon Bisset, 1919), p. 45.
77 Hamilton, 'Despatch', *London Gazette*, 6 July 1915.
78 Gillam, *Gallipoli Diary*, pp. 46-47.
79 TNA WO 95/4310: Report, Captain and Adjutant H. S. Wilson, 1st RMF.
80 TNA PRO/30/71: Letter, Lieutenant G.W. Nightingale, 1st RMF, 1 May 1915.

details, shortly after the deaths of the brigadier-general and his brigade-major (at approximately 10:15 a.m.), attempts to land troops were again paused, this time for several hours.

Deadlock at Sedd-el-Bahr

Brigade command now fell to the Quebec-born (and former Royal Dublin Fusilier) Lieutenant-Colonel Herbert Carrington Smith of the 2nd Hampshires. However, around 10:20 a.m., when he was on the lower bridge of the *River Clyde*, he too was killed by a Turkish sniper. Lieutenant-Colonel Tizard found himself in immediate overall control of what was now a very depleted force, with Major Hutchinson in command of the battalion.[81] At 10:21 a.m., Hamilton sent Hunter-Weston an unusually direct order to send no more men ashore on V Beach. By now, it seems as if he was becoming exasperated by the lack of progress with the need for 29th Division to exploit the gain on Y Beach and support the men stuck on V Beach. Hamilton was well-aware of the situation there since 8:30 a.m. and had sent Hunter-Weston a message at 9:21 a.m. "suggesting" he divert the main part of 88th Brigade from V Beach to Y Beach, in an effort to outflank the Turks. No reply was received from Hunter-Weston, who was firmly ensconced within HMS *Euryalus* and conducting the operations on W Beach from there. Hamilton again sent the major-general a message (at 10:21 a.m.), this time demanding that he send a reply. This came at 10:35 a.m., rejecting the proposed move to Y Beach and insisting that W Beach must be reinforced. According to Hamilton, the outflanking manoeuvre was officially discounted as it "would have involved considerable delay owing to the distance …" and W Beach was "where the Lancashire Fusiliers had already effected a landing."

Yet a landing had indeed been achieved, somehow, at V Beach. It is thought that, since operations began at 6:30 a.m., some 1,000 men had left the *River Clyde* but half had been killed or wounded before they got up the beach. Captain Geddes, wounded and tired, was ensconced in makeshift cover and intent of trying to secure the beachhead's unprotected flanks whenever the opportunity arose. Further behind him, Major Jarret and his men were still stuck on the beach not far from a "spit of rock", unable to advance. Hamilton simply recorded that one Dublin Fusilier half-company, which had scrambled ashore at Camber, just east of Sedd-el-Bahr village, was pinned down and that "by mid-day had only twenty-five men left."[82] Any movement on the beach was a potential target and many men were stuck behind whatever cover they could find. Others simply lay on the beach and dared not move a muscle. As such, in the afternoon, Tizard could see troops (possibly from the Worcesters) at the cliffs to the left of the beach and sent a pressing appeal to Hunter-Weston for reinforcements to try and outflank the Turkish defences. Like so many appeals from other senior commanders to divisional HQ, this request was met with complete silence. At around 2:00 p.m., Lieutenant-Colonel Tizard finally ordered Lieutenant Nightingale to collect as many men as he could and "join the force on the shore", in another effort to support the beach. Nightingale's men met up with Jarrett, where he seems to have been surprised to see a "lot

81 TNA WO 95/4310: Report, Lieutenant-Colonel H.E. Tizard, 1st RMF. Tizard was effectively *de facto* brigade commander. He had only one platoon of 'Y' Company RMF, 'W' Company RMF, four machine-guns, one and a half-companies of 2nd Hampshires, 'W' Company Dublin Fusiliers, one platoon Anson Battalion RND, one platoon Worcester Regt and the West Riding Field Coy RE.

82 Hamilton, 'Despatch', *London Gazette*, 6 July 1915.

of men" but, tellingly, "very few not hit."[83] It was to be the last daylight attempt. For the remainder of the day, the men on the beach did their best to survive. One account, from Private William Harris, noted how he and three others (including his officer) were the only survivors ashore from his RDF platoon; they lay on the beach "for 13 hours and I saw some of my brave friends, the RMF, alongside me blown to pieces – heads, arms and everything off."[84] Captain French, also stranded on V Beach with "only about 20 men" recalled that the Turks kept firing all night as a steady drizzle descended. The dead lay all around their position and they could hear the wounded "groaning on all sides …"[85] Captain Wilson noted that the Turkish picked off any wounded (or otherwise) that tried to move, reporting that despite the danger, "several were brought back to the ship by officers and men who showed the most utter disregard for their personal safety …" [86] As dusk fell, Lieutenant-Colonel Tizard finally begin to send the pitiful remainder of the men aboard the *River Clyde* ashore (from approximately 7:30 p.m. to 12:30 a.m.); this was done "without too much loss."[87] Captain Geddes' party was joined, around 8:30 p.m., by the survivors of W, Y and Z companies led by Major Jarret and Lieutenants Russell, Lee and Nightingale. After a brief discussion, Jarret and Geddes decided to establish an outpost line and post sentries accordingly. During this operation, Lieutenants Russell and Lee were wounded and, as Major Jarret was touring the line, he was shot through the throat and died "very soon after."[88]

Perhaps the most pointless, frustrating fact of the bloody V Beach lodgment was that, as soon as darkness fell, the remaining troops within the *River Clyde* were able to disembark without significant loss. When they finally made it down the gangplanks later that evening, they saw the assault barges choked with casualties and, in one eye-witness' haunting words, the "pier formed by dead men."[89] As it was now pitch-black, the Hampshires made it ashore without a "shot being fired as they were unobserved." Captain Guy Geddes was finally relieved by the advance company from the Hampshires, under Majors Beckwith and Williams, some thirteen hours after he had been wounded through the shoulder. He was brought back to the *River Clyde* to have his wounds dressed before being taken onto a trawler, along with Captain Henderson, to be evacuated by the *Alaunia*.[90] In the early hours of the 26 April (around 2:30 a.m.), Lieutenant-Colonel Tizard received a message saying that Sedd-el-Bahr fort had been entered and, having cleared the walls of Turkish snipers, was finally secured.[91] Soon afterwards, it would seem that the Turks began to set some of the buildings in Sedd-el-Bahr village alight and this, no doubt, could also be seen by Tizard on the *River Clyde*. By now, the men ashore were all mixed up from their different companies/regiments and, mostly, without officers or senior NCOs. The battle for the nearby

83 TNA PRO/30/71: Letter, Lieutenant G.W. Nightingale, 1st RMF, 1 May 1915.
84 *Leinster Leader*, 7 August 1915; No. 5723 Pte. W.Harris had enlisted on the 10 August 1914 and was honourably discharged on 4 May 1917; the cause of his discharge is recorded as "mental".
85 IWM 1964-05-86: Account, Captain D. French, 1st RDF.
86 TNA WO 95/4310: Report, Captain and Adjutant H. S. Wilson, 1st RMF.
87 Ibid., Report, Lieutenant-Colonel H.E. Tizard, 1st RMF.
88 Ibid., Report, Captain G.W. Geddes, 1st RMF and TNA PRO/30/71: Letter, Lieutenant G.W. Nightingale, 1st RMF, 1 May 1915.
89 IWM interview, 1965, R.B. Gillett.
90 TNA WO 329/2952: Service Medal and Award Rolls, 1914-1920, RMF (Officers); Captain Guy Geddes survived the war during which he earned the DSO and was "Mentioned in Despatches", (*London Gazette*, 5 November 1915), leaving the RMF with the rank of Lieutenant-Colonel.
91 TNA WO 95/4310: Report, Lieutenant-Colonel H.E. Tizard, 1st RMF.

village, Hill 141 and the dogged push inland was to continue all that day, led by an officer from Sir Ian Hamilton's own staff, Lieutenant-Colonel Doughty-Wylie. Lieutenant-Colonel Tizard, perhaps controversially, stayed aboard the *River Clyde*, until both positions had been captured, later that afternoon. From this point onwards, due to their massive casualties, the RMF and RDF effectively fought as a single composite battalion, known simply as the "Dubsters". Of extreme interest is that, in the aftermath of V Beach, certain unusual events occurred regarding RMF's command. Lieutenant-Colonel Henry Tizard, effectively an "acting" – certainly *de facto* – commander of 86th Brigade, was summoned by Major-General Hunter-Weston and relieved of his command on 30 April. He was sent home, whereupon he took command of a non-effective training battalion (10th East Lancashires) based in Wareham; he never saw active service again.

The Volunteer Military Experience: Suvla Bay, 6-7 August 1915

Given the events at V Beach, a most interesting comparative analysis can be made between the Regular experiences and the "New Army" experiences of landing at A (West) and C beaches. Indeed, it appears the 10th (Irish) Division's Gallipoli experience was, like that of the 29th Division, a catalogue of incompetence and ultimately fruitless battles. In fact, by the time the 10th (Irish) Division had left Ireland, in May 1915, it was already quite clear in official quarters that the Gallipoli venture was failing. In an attempt to break the stalemate, Sir Ian Hamilton's force was further bolstered by three "New Army" divisions, which were to be employed on 6 August against Suvla, a deep crescent-shaped bay to the north of Anzac Cove. Based on a plan by Lieutenant-General Sir William Birdwood to outflank the Turks at Anzac, the landings were to be Hamilton's final gamble to shift the odds in his favour. Five divisions, under the newly appointed IX Corps Commander, the Anglo-Irish Lieutenant-General, Sir Frederick Stopford,[92] had the objective of pushing inland from Suvla, taking the heights and establishing contact with Anzac. However, Stopford apparently chose to "improve" upon Birdwood's relatively straight-forward aim by establishing the northern beachhead (A) and Hamilton, with typical deference, acquiesced.

The topography of Suvla was also an operational nightmare. The landing zones for the northern part of the operation (A Beach) had not been sufficiently charted and the Royal Navy raised immediate concerns to this effect. These appear to have been disregarded and were to have subsequent implications for the command and control of the 10th (Irish) Division. Above A Beach was the northern coastal high ground of Kiretch Tepe Sirt, which clung to the sea but, below this large ridge was another height (Tekke Tepe), four miles inland, with a series of southern hills (Chocolate, Green and Scimitar). Immediately beyond the southern landing beaches (B and C) was a low-hill called Lala Baba and a Salt Lake, which led directly onto a plain (Anafarta) which was hemmed in by dominating ridges to the north and south. Each of these prominences was, in turn, overlooked by the Sari Bair Ridge, the Gallipoli Peninsula's spine, which joined Suvla to Anzac. This feature was dominated by Rhododendron Spur, Hill 60, Chunuk Bair and

92 The appointment of the 61-year-old Stopford by the 62-year-old Hamilton remains extremely controversial; Kitchener's preferred candidate seems to have been Lieutenant-General Mahon, one of the most senior lieutenant-generals. His active divisional command, however, resulted in pertinent army protocol issues. See Brian Curragh's chapter in this volume.

Koja Chemen Tepe. The plan was now to land Lieutenant-General Sir Bryan Mahon's 10th (Irish) Division and Major-General Frederick Hammersley's 11th (Northern) Division at Suvla and launch a sudden massed infantry assault to seize the high ground of Kiretch Tepe Sirt. The intention was to capture this position as quickly as possible and then push on to take the vulnerable Turkish ammunition depot at Ak Bashi. This, in turn, would open up the possibility (as per Lieutenant-General Birdwood's original plan) to put pressure on Sari Bair and Koja Chemen Tepe. To cover the landings at Suvla Bay, diversionary assaults were made at Cape Helles and Anzac, whilst artillery support was to come from the Royal Navy. Indeed, the fleet of "beetles" was to be controlled by Commander Unwin based on his previous V Beach experience.

Yet, due to breath-taking mismanagement, the actual lodgement at Suvla was squandered, botched and the advance there paused, allowing the Turks enough time to prepare their defence. It was not aided by Stopford's lack of direction to his subordinates nor his general ineffectiveness for command (he was aboard the yacht *Jonquil* for much of the early operations). The three 11th Division brigades all landed according to time-table, consolidated the beaches, captured Lala Baba, with the 11th Manchesters ousting the Turks from Karakol Dagh and forcing them to fall back onto Kiretch Tepe Sirt. However, the landing at A Beach had already been fairly disastrous, with transports unable to get to the beach and men having to wade ashore with the water up to their necks. The scene was set, in the early hours of 7 August, for the massed Irish battalions to sweep on to the next phase of the attack on the other flank. However, instead of engaging the entire 10th Division against Kiretch Tepe, 29th Brigade had been rapidly redeployed to Lieutenant-General Birdwood's Australian and New Zealand Corps (ANZAC). As such, this brigade (comprising 6th Leinsters, 6th Royal Irish Rifles, 5th Connaught Rangers and 10th Hampshire Regiment) landed at Z Beach – Anzac Cove – on 6 August. Whilst Lone Pine was captured in the initial assault, the attack on Sari Bair Ridge stalled and 29th Brigade were flung into the battle there.

Meanwhile, Mahon and the 30th and 31st (Ulster) brigades – under Brigadier-Generals L. Nicol and F. Hill respectively – were due to continue the landings at Suvla as planned and were to be put ashore at A Beach. None of these senior officers had apparently received written orders from Stopford or Hamilton. Yet, at the last minute, the landing here was diverted, as many of the preceding transports had become snagged on unseen rocks. In the confusion, Brigadier-General Felix Hill was summoned at dawn to the *Jonquil* to get confirmation of his orders. It was subsequently decided to redeploy the leading five Irish battalions (6th Inniskillings, 5th and 6th Royal Irish Fusiliers, 6th and 7th RDF). Stopford was apparently "surprised to hear the G.O.C. [Hill] had rec'd no operation orders …" and, accordingly, told him to land his battalions at C Beach and find Major-General Hammersley. Perhaps, most interestingly, was Stopford's initial direct order to Hill, that IX Corps' objective was to "secure Suvla Bay as a base of operations … [and] … deny the enemy the heights which connect Anafarta Sagir and Eljelmer Bay." Whilst this order does refer to both Tekke Tepe and Kiretch Tepe (which overlooked Eljelmer Bay) there was no mention of the need to rapidly seize these heights by nightfall, as Hamilton wished. Hill was also told by Stopford that they faced some 30,000 Turks to the north, of which 12,000 were against the Australians; the remainder were reported holding Chocolate Hill, Anafarta village and the ridge beyond Scimitar Hill.[93] Brigadier-General Hill found himself in

93 TNA WO 95/4296: 31st Inf Bde. HQ War Diary, 7 August 1915.

effective command of the Irish troops ashore at C Beach, with little idea of what was expected of them.

Consequently, 31st Brigade landed, under accurate Turkish artillery fire, just south of Nibrunesi Point and miles away from their original objective. Recalling this landing at C Beach, John Hargrave, a RAMC sergeant from Westmoreland with 32nd Field Ambulance (10th Division), caustically noted that Hill's 6,000 men were landed "below Nibrunesi Point – on the wrong side of the bay. This was fatal."[94] It certainly dealt a further severe blow to the cohesion of the 10th Division's command and fighting structure as, unable to land effectively at A Beach, Lieutenant-General Mahon was impeded from getting ashore. As such, Mahon, with the accompanying troops of 5th Royal Irish Regiment (divisional pioneers) and 6th and 7th Royal Munster Fusiliers, became disconnected from the remainder of the division. Indeed, as the Royal RMF approached in their troopship, HMT *Rowan*, it "narrowly missed being hit by shell fire and was obliged to shift station …"[95] The split in 10th Division forces had serious implications for the operation against Kiretch Tepe Sirt.

As 31st Brigade disembarked, the Turkish guns (reported to be on Chocolate Hill) had the range of the transport lighters and rained shrapnel down upon the disembarking troops. Additionally, a German aeroplane was able to fly above the landings and "dropped three bombs but with little effect."[96] By 8:00 a.m., the 6th and 7th RDF were disembarked at C Beach but had also come under "accurate shrapnel fire", with one 7th RDF lighter sustaining 16 casualties (including 2nd Lieutenant C. D. Harvey, wounded) before it reached the shore.[97] Despite this, the casualties taken by the battalions on C Beach were relatively light but, as Hill discovered upon landing at 6:30 a.m., whilst the Turks were being slowly pushed back across the Anafarta plain they still held all the dominating high ground. Consequently, Hill and the Irish battalions came under the direct orders of Hammersley's 11th Division and were sent against the heights of Chocolate and Green Hills. By the time the Dublin Fusiliers got ashore, as Private William Gray recollected, the wounded from the leading waves were already making their way back. He and his friends scrambled into cover "under the edge of a bank on the shore" and, upon advancing onto the flat ground before them,[98] were instantly hit by Turkish fire. As shells began to burst above their heads, the order to "drop" was given and two of Gray's friends were wounded by shrapnel. In his words, the 7th Dublin Fusiliers' experience of the Suvla landing was "like that all the rest of the day, dodging and rushing and struggling through the sand."[99] However, as the events surrounding this engagement are well recounted, it is perhaps more useful to concentrate on the position before Mahon's depleted force and the role of the RMF and Inniskillings.[100]

94 J. Hargrave, *At Suvla Bay: Being the Notes and Sketches of Scenes, Characters and Adventures Of The Dardanelles Campaign* (London: Constable, 1916) and J. Hargrave, *The Suvla Bay Landing* (London: MacDonald, 1964), p. 198.
95 TNA WO 95/4296: War Diary, 7th RMF War Diary, 7 August 1915.
96 Ibid., 5th R. Inn. F. War Diary, 15-16 August 1915.
97 Ibid., 6th RDF and 7th RDF war diaries, 7 August 1915.
98 This was Salt Lake and the Anafarta plain.
99 W.V. Gray, *Kildare Observer*, 6 November 1915.
100 TNA WO 95/4296: 31st Inf Bde. HQ War Diary, 12 August 1915.The casualties from 7-11 August for Hill's force (including the 6th and 7th RDF and excluding the 5th Inniskillings) stood at 56 officers and 1337 men.

Landing at "A West" and the fight for Jephson's Post, 7-9 August 1915

The lack of intelligence and poor communication between command and troops on the ground was also to become a regular feature in the Irish Gallipoli experience. The error in 31st Brigade's landing was compounded when Mahon arrived on the *Jonquil*, some time after Hill, and Stopford commanded him to land his men nearer the original objective. With typically frustrating mismanagement, shortly after Hill's battalions had landed, another landing beach had been discovered, nearer to Kiretch Tepe Sirt, and hurriedly re-named "A West". However, this beach was also difficult to land the transports on, with many boats unable to get anywhere near the shore. Despite this, Mahon and his force accordingly made their way there.

Brigadier-General Nicol, with the two battalions of Royal RMF and the divisional pioneers (5th Royal Irish Regt.) were landed by late mid-morning, but their lodgement was not an easy one. Some of the lighters transporting the 6th RMF had already run aground in the rocky shallows, forcing the men to wade waist-high towards shore. When they got there, they found the shore booby-trapped with landmines, which caused a number of casualties. The Munster battalions were given a simple objective to head for Kiretch Tepe; the "horizon hills" that lay at right-angles to the Anafarta plain.[101] At around 11:30 a.m., 30th Brigade received a "verbal report from scout officer 6 R. M. Fus. that 11/Manchester Regt. was advancing along ridges"[102] and they too continued to advance up along the western slopes of Kiretch Tepe Sirt. Ten minutes later, the 7th RMF began to disembark from HMT *Rowan* and, by 2:00 p.m., the 6th RMF had passed through the Manchesters until they were stopped by concealed Turkish trenches to their front. Behind these troops, Lieutenant-General Mahon and his staff had also established GHQ ashore at "A West", with their force now bolstered by the unexpected arrival of the 5th Inniskillings. They had tried in vain to land at C Beach but intense shelling had forced their transports to withdraw. Instead, in contrast to Hill's 31st Brigade, they had also been hurriedly diverted to "A West" and, confusingly, temporarily attached to 30th Brigade. Three 5th Inniskilling officers in particular (Verschoyle, Scott and Armstrong), have left very vivid recollections of their experiences from "A West" to Kiretch Tepe. As Captain Terrence Verschoyle of the 5th "Skins" noted, by the time their battalion had reached the shore of "'A West', chaos had already set in … lighters got stuck on rocks that nobody had realised existed … [but we could see] odd troops moving through the scrub further inland."[103] One contemporary criticism of the inland advance focused on how these men had gone forward in tight drill formation, attracting unnecessary casualties. However, certainly regarding the 10th Division, this does not seem to have been the case at all. Many observers overtly declared otherwise. Captain V.H. Scott could see "A West" Beach very clearly from his ship and was "prepared to swear they [the troops ashore] were extended and, what is more, we were never taught to advance any other way."[104]

As the 7th RMF advanced, working their way up the eastern slopes of Kiretch Tepe Sirt, on their senior battalion's right flank, they famously encountered the "fly-infested corpses" of the 11th Manchesters, until they too made contact with what remained of this battalion.[105] It

101 Ibid., Letter, Lieutenant-Colonel G. Drage, 7th RMF, 1 Feb. 1931.
102 Ibid., 30th Brigade HQ War Diary, 7 August 1915.
103 IWM: interview 8185: T.T.H. Verschoyle, 5th R. Inn. F., 1984.
104 TNA WO 95/4296: Letter, Captain V.H. Scott, 5th R.Inn.F., 29 Jan. 1931.
105 Ibid., 6th RMF and 7th RMF war diaries, 7 August 1915; Cooper, *The Tenth*, p. 86.

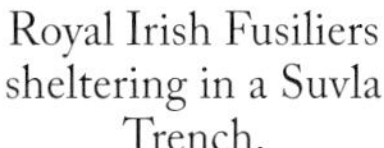
Royal Irish Fusiliers sheltering in a Suvla Trench.

was then a matter of trying to consolidate their position and continue the advance, as a thunderstorm erupted, soaking many to the skin.[106] Lieutenant-Colonel Gore then ordered Major Hendricks to send reinforcements to the 6th RMF, and Major Drage's 'C' Company went forward. The tactical difficulties for both battalions were significant; the topography was virtually unknown to the attacker whilst familiar to the defenders who, as they withdrew, naturally positioned snipers in the scrub and gullies to delay the British advance. As the 7th RMF moved upwards, the Turkish snipers picked them off at will. One of those killed was Captain Robert Hornidge Cullinan (from Ennis, Co. Clare), a Barrister-at-Law in peacetime, who led the forward waves of 'C' Company. They had reached a clearing in the scrub when he was hit by snipers and, despite men rushing to his aid under fire, he was discovered "riddled with five or six bullets and dead."[107] The progress increasingly ground to a halt, with the Turks still holding the dominating heights. Directly ahead, they held a rocky mound on top of the crest, from which "a good many bullets were fired at long range",[108] pinning any advance down. Yet, the 6th and 7th RMF still made a spirited attack against these Turkish defences, losing many men in the process but getting to within 100 yards of the Turkish line.

Interestingly, like many accounts, Lieutenant Verschoyle, of the Inniskillings, recalled that his battalion came under fire but had difficulty actually seeing any of the enemy, noting that "fire was intense throughout most of the advance and not a Turk could be seen anywhere."[109]

106 *De Ruvigny's Roll of Honour 1914-24* (Uckfield: Naval & Military Press, n.d.).
107 Ibid., p. 102.
108 TNA WO 95/4296: 7th RMF War Diary, 7 August 1915.
109 Ibid., Letter, Captain T. Verschoyle, 5th R.Inn.F., Jan. 1931.

At around 10:00 p.m., the 5th Inniskillings arrived in support to relieve the Manchesters, who had already sustained between 250-300 casualties, including 15 officers. [110] Equivalent casualty figures for the 7th RMF stood at five men missing, two officers and 58 men wounded, with two officers and nine men killed. Of the latter were 35-year-old Private George Ball (born in Pentre and from Swansea in Glamorgan) and Captain Robert Cullinan. As the light failed, Lieutenant Ernest Harper, from Mullaghadun (outside Dungannon, Co. Tyrone), went out to examine Captain Cullinan's body and retrieve his personal effects. Having done this, he then gathered a number of men and succeeded in bringing back the mortally wounded 2nd Lieutenant Francis Evans Bennett, who had been shot through the chest. By dusk, the Munster battalions had dug in, waiting to renew the assault at first light. However, no renewed assault was forthcoming.

In fact, for all day on the 8 August, absolute lethargy reigned.[111] Instead of continuing to drive the Turks back and pushing to control the dominating features ahead, all military progress paused. Into this military vacuum, the Turks gathered their resources and consolidated their positions, whilst the British forces appeared to do very little indeed. The 6th RMF spent the day improving their trench line whilst the 7th RMF, in Major G. Drage's account, "did little but reorganise and rest."[112] In fact, it seems as if several forward platoons were told to pull back from their positions in order to "straighten the line" and one of these was led by Lieutenants Good and Harper. The men were apparently unwilling to leave but Lieutenant Harper, in full view of the enemy, "urged them" to do so and ensured that every man got away safely. Later that evening, he again volunteered to lead a stretcher-party to bring in wounded men from the scrubland; despite getting lost in the darkness. However, for most of the day, the troops laid low and prepared for an attack; some were even seen strolling about and, in some cases, men at Anzac could see them infamously "brewing up" on the neighbouring beach. Such inactivity became a focal point for Peter Weir's film *Gallipoli*, although here the resentment is clearly aimed at the "Motherland" and the perceived lack of fighting spirit shown by British troops/commanders. The imperfections of this portrayal aside, as Professor Keith Jeffery wryly commented, it "may not have suited Peter Weir's dramatic requirements, nor one supposes any political subtext, for the radio operator to say "the British *and Irish* are sitting on the beach drinking cups of tea."[113] Nevertheless, the perception held by many troops on the ground, Anzac or otherwise, was that they would have to pay in blood for the hiatus in operations. The inaction was tortuous. It was clear that a determined – and continuing – push on Kiretch Tepe Sirt would not meet with as much opposition as might happen if the delay continued. Captain Scott recalled that "everyone on Kiretch Tepe thought we had practically no Turks in front of us and we were all keen to advance and grousing because we were doing nothing, both officers and men."[114] Another Inniskilling officer, Captain J. Armstrong, writing in 1931, could barely restrain his obvious frustration:

110 Ibid., 30th Brigade HQ War Diary, 7 August 1915.
111 Unfortunately, Bryan Cooper appears to have been in error when stating the first attack began on 8 August; *The Tenth Irish Division*, p. 86.
112 TNA WO 95/4296: Letter, Lieutenant-Colonel G. Drage, 7th RMF, 1 Feb. 1931.
113 K. Jeffery, *Ireland*, p. 38.
114 TNA WO 95/4296: Letter, Captain V.H. Scott, 5th R.Inn.F., 29 Jan. 1931.

> I knew before I'd been there 24 hours that the whole show was a "washout". No orders, no scheme, nothing told us as to what we were expected to do on landing – or anything. However, enough said.[115]

In order to discover the delay, a Royal Munster Fusilier Staff Officer, Colonel Cecil Aspinall (later Brigadier-General Aspinall-Oglander) had been dispatched by Hamilton to see Stopford aboard the *Jonquil*. Here, the inactivity in command frustrated him beyond measure. He consequently quickly left Stopford and sent two curt telegrams to Hamilton to this effect. Without any action from Sir Ian, Apsinall went directly to see him too. By then, in Hamilton's words, Aspinall was in a "fever" and told him quite bluntly that "our chances were being thrown away with both hands …"[116] As a result, Hamilton went immediately by motor boat to see what Stopford was doing – and found him in high spirits, insisting that "everything was quite all right and going well. Mahon with some of his troops was pressing back the Turks along Kiretch Tepe Sirt."[117] Indeed, largely due to their efforts here on the 7 August, A West was no longer being subject to Turkish fire. However, according to Hamilton's version of events, Stopford was still disinclined to push home the advantage his men had made at Kiretch Tepe and Hill 10, due to their tiredness and a lack of water and artillery. There followed a somewhat sharp exchange between Stopford and Hamilton; the latter supposedly pushing for an immediate advance to take the heights, the former reiterating how tired and unready the men were for such an exercise. Despite this, apparently on his own initiative, at around 8:00 p.m., Mahon issued orders for a general assault on Kiretch Tepe to be renewed, with the 5th Dorsets and 9th Lancashire Fusiliers now being attached to the brigade. Amazingly, these two battalions (along with a mountain battery) "without any orders from 30th Bde, having apparently received instructions from *some other source*" commenced a preliminary assault at 6:00 a.m. on 9 August.[118]

Finally, at 7:30 a.m., Nicol's brigade attacked the Turkish entrenchments, with the 7th RMF on the right (in contact with the 5th Dorsets on Anafarta plain), the 6th RMF in the centre and the 5th "Skins" on the right, with their backs to the sea. From this direction, HMS *Beagle* and HMS *Foxhound* provided an artillery bombardment in support of the attack, although due to the nature of the ground, this was fairly ineffective on the right flank. Additionally, the difficulty of the ground on the upward slopes caused the continuity of the assaulting battalions, advancing in extended line, to fragment. By the morning of 9 August it appeared that Turkish opposition had still not fully materialised, although Major Drage of 7th RMF considered that this began to strengthen as the day wore on. As the 7th RMF advanced across the undulating scrub, he saw figures, in what he believed were "British khaki", moving across behind them. It was only when the 7th RMF began to take casualties from the rear that they realised they had been outflanked. The extended assault line stopped and started, as the snipers in the rear were dealt with, but it became a very fragmented advance. It was here that Lieutenant Ernest Harper, ("one of the best and most honest officers in the battalion"), was shot through the back of the head. His loss was said to have had a profound effect on the battalion. Harper's reputation amongst the 7th RMF was already very well-established but he seems to have especially

115 Ibid., Letter, Lieutenant-Colonel Armstong, 5th R.Inn. F., Jan. 1931.
116 Hamilton, *Gallipoli Diary*, Vol. 2, p. 61.
117 Ibid.
118 TNA WO 95/4296: 30th Brigade HQ War Diary, 8 August 1915.

Jephson's Post after consolidation, autumn 1915.

distinguished himself in the events of 7-9 August; Major Drage wrote that he "should have got the VC if he'd pulled through."[119]

In addition to the Turkish snipers, the lie of the ground had also channeled the 5th Dorsets across the path of the 7th RMF, which had diverted both battalions' attacking fronts. The 7th RMF found themselves attacking along a line facing Kidney and Beacon Hills but, due to the determined resistance against them, three companies were ordered to pull back to the original British front line. Only 'C' Company remained in the forward position, which they held throughout the night. However, in the centre and the left, the 6th RMF and 5th Inniskillings were able to keep unit cohesion as they advance up the scrub, with 'A' Company, led by Major John N. Jephson, heading directly for the dominating mound ahead of them. They stormed and captured the summit of this mound (it was subsequently named "Jephson's Post" in his honour) and cleared it of the enemy. This was as far as the RMF and "Skins" could go; their advance was stopped in its tracks by the Turkish trench line proper across Kiretch Tepe. At around 4:00 p.m., they again dug in and made this the British front line – in practical terms, a further advance of only 800 yards or so. Indeed, the fierce resistance now coming from the Turkish defenders suggested to some that the opposition on the ridge may not be simply comprised of the 350-strong field force of local Gendarmes that Mahon had been assured were there.[120] The 6th Munster's casualty list for the day's action stood at 127 killed, wounded or missing and it reflected the varied character of men in the 10th Irish Division. Among those killed in the desperate fighting was Patrick Cullinane, from St. Finbar's, Cork, Acting-Sergeant Andrew

119 *De Ruvigny's Roll of Honour*, p. 106.

120 For example, Staff Captain Herbert Goodland (30th Brigade) recalled seeing two Turkish corpses on the slopes wearing Regular army uniforms; quoted in C.E.W. Bean, *The Official History of Australia in the War of 1914-1918. The Story of Anzac: From 4 May 1915 to the Evacuation*, Vol. II (Sydney: Angus & Robertson, 1924), pp. 711-712.

Joyce, from St. Michael's, Limerick and 21-year-old Lieutenant Spencer Robert Valentine Travers. Lieutenant Travers had been born in Stillorgan (Co. Dublin) and was a former pupil of Bromsgrove Grammar School; his father was Judge's Registrar, Queen's Bench Division (Probate), Dublin.[121]

However, the battle for dominance of Kiretch Tepe Sirt only increased in desperation. On 12 August, the 5th Royal Inniskilling Fusiliers were finally reunited with 31st Brigade, which had moved up for another massed attack on Kiretch Tepe on 15-16 August. It left hundreds dead and wounded in two days' fierce combat. By the end of September, however, the 10th (Irish) Division was withdrawn from Gallipoli completely; to fight in a new and even-more forgotten campaign – Macedonia (Salonika). Events for all the Irish battalions concerned on the peninsula were moving on.

Casualties, Reputations and Burials

As such, it is perhaps fitting to conclude this chapter with an appraisal of these operations in practical military achievement and in manpower cost. For the Irish regiments, the price was as heavy as those to other contingents, if not actually slightly more so. Yet, the public recognition for their achievements was soon to be smothered by the events in Dublin and on the Somme during 1916.

From an Irish regimental perspective, the landings on V Beach were not only costly in human terms, but were presented to the public back in Ireland, arguably justifiably, as an incredible feat of arms. The massacre and subsequent formation of the "Dubsters" is well-known but it is generally assumed that these deaths gained little militarily. Of course, it is hard to measure these gains unemotionally, yet the RDF, RMF (and Hampshires) managed to secure the beachhead, drive the Turks from the dominating heights and hold this until French reinforcements arrived. In the bluntly honest assessment of the *Irish Times*, it was a "marvel that even so many men were able to effect a landing against almost insuperable barriers and the point-blank fire of the securely entrenched Turkish troops."[122] Indeed, the real nature of the casualty rates only trickled back to Great Britain and Ireland in drips and drops. As Lieutenant Guy Nightingale commented in a letter written a fortnight or so after V Beach, "they are breaking the casualties gently to you at home … they'll try and make out its been nothing at all out here, just a scrap with the Turks whereas its been hell and frightfully mismanaged."[123]

At V Beach, out of nearly a thousand men, the 1st RMF sustained around 600 casualties including 17 officers. One of these was Dublin-born Captain Eric Lockhart Hume Henderson, mentioned in Despatches for his gallantry on 25 April; due to the severity of his wounds he was evacuated to The Deaconess Hospital, Alexandria, but died there on 20 May 1915.[124] Indeed,

121 TNA WO 95/4296: 6th RMF and 7th RMF war diaries, 7-8 August 1915; A. Joyce, *Irish Memorial Records*, Vol. 4, p. 294

122 *Irish Times*, 25 December 1915.

123 TNA PRO/30/71: Letter, Lieutenant G.W. Nightingale, 1st RMF, 14 May 1915.

124 Captain Henderson was buried in the nearby Chatby Military Memorial Cemetery, Alexandria. Major C.H.B. Jarrett was buried at 'Lancashire Landing' Cemetery. Captain John Henry Dives Costeker, DSO, Royal Warwickshire Regt. was buried at V Beach Cemetery, Helles. Officially,

at their first roll call following the landings, the Munster's strength stood at only five officers and 372 men. Similarly, the 1st RDF were just under a thousand strong before the landings and, by their end, had only one officer unwounded and 374 men remaining.[125] Major Davidson, RAMC, noted very sadly that most of his friends had been officers in the Dublin Fusiliers and that, following the landings, only "three of these left out of twenty-seven." As his duties took him ashore to recover the dying and dead, in the village of Sedd-el-Bahr, he discovered the body of another Dublin officer whom he had got to know well on the *Ausonia*, Lieutenant Bernard, who was found "all huddled up among long weeds and nettles."[126]

On 27 April, Captain John Gillam, Army Service Corps, 29th Divisional Supply Train, was ordered to establish a forward depot to support the tenuous front line along the beachheads. As part of this operation, it was decided to salvage all the equipment and weapons from V Beach and make this the main centre of logistics, so Captain Gillam was sent there with a small fatigue party. However, upon arrival, they saw around 200 corpses, all neatly laid out for "burial" along the shoreline, lying "in all postures, their faces blackened, swollen, and distorted by the sun. The bodies of seven officers lie in a row in front by themselves." Among these dead officers lay a Major's body, with red tabs on his collar and a khaki handkerchief covering his face. When Colonel Gostling (88th Field Ambulance) lightly lifted the handkerchief, Gillam recognised the body as Captain Costeker, whom he had known well, having worked in the brigade-major's office for two months when in England. In Gillam's words, he was "looking forward to working with him in Gallipoli. It was cruel luck." Gillam noted that he had been carrying a cigarette-case in his breast pocket and a number of letters, one of which was from his wife. Captain Costeker had been shot through the heart and also noted how the captain's body had been hit, probably post-mortem, by a bullet which had "torn the toes of his left foot away."[127]

Of extreme interest is that Gillam did not note seeing Brigadier-General Napier's body among these recovered corpses, only two days after the landings. Other "notable" casualties, dead or dying, had already been recovered if possible during or just after the fighting and the apparent "disappearance" of Napier's remains from the official records may confirm an immediate burial sometime around the 25 April (and equally immediate loss of the plot in the confusion) or the loss of the body in the intervening period. This, for Gallipoli, would not have been unusual. For example, Sub-Lieutenant Arthur Walderne St Clair Tisdall (Anson Battalion, Royal Naval Division) was killed in action during the Second Battle of Krithia by a sniper on 6 May 1915. It happened in full view of his men, who duly buried him, within 24 hours, at the spot where he had been killed. However, his body was never officially recovered, and his name is also on the memorial to the missing at Cape Helles. In this, the place of the brigadier-general's death is, perhaps key. If, as most sources suggest, Napier was killed on a barge or the lighter-bridge – alongside Costeker – then it may be reasonably expected that his body would be recovered as Costeker's was. It may also be likely that, somehow, the brigadier-general's body found itself in the shallows and, as Lieutenant Maffet of the RDF noted regarding their own dead that

Brigadier-General Henry Edward Napier was listed as having died of wounds on 27 April but, by all accounts he seems to have been killed on the 25 April. He has no-known grave and is commemorated on Panel 16 of the Helles Memorial.

125 TNA WO 95/4310: 1st RMF and 1st RDF war diaries.

126 Davidson, *The Incomparable 29th*, p. 47.

127 Gillam, *Gallipoli Diary*, pp. 46-47.

"bodies drifted out to sea or lay immersed a few feet from shore."[128] Under these circumstances, it would be easy to see how Napier's body might not be easily recovered. However, it seems as if the brigadier-general's body was, in fact, actually retrieved from the lighter barge. Major George Davidson, RAMC, working with the wounded and dying noted that on 26 April they had the "naval funeral of Brigadier-General Napier and Colonel Smith-Carrington [sic]" who were buried along with an undisclosed number of men. Major Davidson received blunt orders that "all bodies to be got rid of before we advanced. A warship pinnace was signalled for and all were taken out to sea." The only person allowed to be present in the pinnace was apparently a Catholic chaplain.[129] For those recovered bodies on land, like Cosketer's, burial on V Beach was required. In early June 1915, Lieutenant Nightingale saw this embryonic cemetery in its earliest form and wryly noted the changes since the April landings. Although it was now being used by the French as a landing depot:

> [There was] a great round patch of cornfields and poppies in the middle, surrounded by barbed wire – the grave of 430 RDF and RMF and 14 officers of these two regiments who were killed in the landing at V Beach.[130]

From Cape Helles to Suvla, Gallipoli has been variously seen as bold strike for a quick way to end the war, or a disastrous and unnecessary military abattoir. In the words of Sir Ian Hamilton, as "often happens in war, the actual course of events did not quite correspond with the intentions of the Commander."[131] It is perhaps a shamefully light-hearted statement, especially given the attendant casualty rates for Cape Helles, Anzac and Suvla Bay. The blunt cost of the entire operation stood at almost 200,000 British Imperial casualties, wounded, killed or missing. However, to the Irish regiments, the casualties of V Beach, Anzac and Suvla cast a very long shadow. As Lieutenant-Colonel Greer of the Royal Irish Fusiliers bitterly commented, the failure of the Suvla landings was entirely due to high command's incompetent leadership. He later said simply that "no-one knew where they were or what they had to do" – it seemed to sum up the entire venture.[132] Neither was it an empty statement when A.J. Smithers famously observed that Gallipoli witnessed the "most abject collection of general officers ever congregated on one spot."[133] However, perhaps the most appropriate last words, expressed in a direct Ulster style, should go to Captain Scott of the Inniskillings. To him, the entire frustrating campaign appeared to boil down to "just taking back the bit of land some silly ass had ordered to be returned to the Turk."[134]

128 Wylly, *Neill's Blue Caps*, p. 30.
129 Davidson, *The Incomparable 29th*, p. 45.
130 TNA PRO/30/71: Letter, Lieutenant G.W. Nightingale, 1st RMF, 1 June 1915.
131 Hamilton, 'Despatch', *London Gazette*, 6 July 1915.
132 Public Record Office of Northern Ireland, D/3574/E6/6b: Papers, Lieutenant-Colonel F.A. Greer, 6th RIF.
133 A.J. Smithers, *Sir John Monash* (London: Leo Cooper, 1972), p. 122.
134 TNA WO 95/4296: Letter, Captain V.H. Scott, 5th R. Inn. F., 29 Jan. 1931.

Appendix

Irish Infantry Battalions in the Dardanelles, April 1915–January 1916

(With dates of service and commanding officers)

Royal Irish Regiment

5th Battalion (10th Div., 29th Bde.): Landed Suvla, 7 August; disembarked 29/30 September. Commanding Officers: Lieutenant-Colonel Bernard A. W. P. H. Granard (Forbes) 19/08/1914 – 14/01/1916.

1st Garrison Battalion: Posted to Lemnos, Mudros and Suvla, mainly on guard details for Ottoman PoWs, road/dugout construction and fatigue duties; landed on Lemnos, 24 September; disembarked 1 December. Commanding Officer: Colonel Richard Charles Clement Cox 02/08/1915 – 17/05/1916.

Royal Inniskilling Fusiliers

1st Battalion (29th Div., 86th Bde.): Landed A Beach, 25 April; disembarked 9 January 1916. Commanding Officers: Lieutenant-Colonel Francis G. Jones 04/08/1914 – 02/05/1915 KIA; Major Stafford J. Somerville 02/05/1915 – 06/05/1915; Lieutenant-Colonel Edward J. Buckley 06/05/1915 – 20/08/1915; Captain. William Pike 20/08/1915 – 21/08/1915 KIA; Lieutenant-Colonel Robert C. Pierce 10/09/1915 – 01/07/1916 KIA.

5th Battalion (10th Div., 31st Bde.): Landed Suvla Bay, 7 August; disembarked 1 October. Commanding Officers: Lieutenant-Colonel Arthur S. Vanrenen 03/03/1915 – 15/08/1915 KIA; Captain. George C. Adams 15/08/1915 – 22/08/1915; Major James A. Armstrong 22/08/1915 – 01/09/1915; Lieutenant. A P Lindsay 01/09/1915 – 14/09/1915; Major George C. Adams 14/09/1915 – 30/11/1916.

6th Battalion (10th Div., 31st Bde.): Landed Suvla Bay, 7 August; disembarked 30 September. Commanding Officers: Lieutenant-Colonel Harold M. Cliffe 11/03/1915 – 07/08/1915 (Wounded); Lieutenant-Colonel William P. B. Frazer 07/08/1915 – 08/01/1916.

Royal Irish Rifles

6th Battalion (10th Div., 29th Bde.): Landed Anzac, 5 August; disembarked 29 September. Commanding Officers: Lieutenant-Colonel Edward Chaloner Bradford 19/08/1914 – 07/08/1915 (Wounded); Captain. Richard de Ras Rose 08/08/1915 – 03/10/1915; Captain. Robert Otway Mansergh 03/10/1915 – 28/11/1915; Lieutenant-Colonel Cecil Morgan Ley Becher 28/11/1915 – 03/08/1916.

Royal Irish Fusiliers

5th Battalion (10th Div., 31st Bde.): Landed Suvla Bay, 7 August; disembarked 30 September. Commanding Officers: Lieutenant-Colonel Markham J. W. Pike 18/01/1915 – 02/12/1915; Lieutenant-Colonel Michael J. Furnell 03/12/1915 – 05/11/1916.

6th Battalion (10th Div., 31st Bde.): Landed Suvla Bay, 7 August; disembarked 30 September. Commanding Officers: Lieutenant-Colonel Frederick A. Greer 19/08/1914 – 09/08/1915 (Wounded); Major Herbert J. Thompson 09/08/1915 – 17/08/1915 (Wounded); Captain. George C. Adams 17/08/1915 – 14/09/1915; Major John S. Crothers 14/09/1915 – 26/01/1916.

Connaught Rangers

5th Battalion (10th Div., 29th Bde.): Landed Anzac, 6 August; disembarked 29/30 September. Commanding Officer: Lieutenant-Colonel Henry F. N. Jourdain 19/08/1914 – 08/02/1916.

Leinster Regiment (Prince of Wales' Royal Canadians)

6th Battalion (10th Div., 29th Bde.): Landed Anzac, 5 August; disembarked 29 September. Commanding Officers: Lieutenant-Colonel John Craske 19/08/1914 – 10/08/1915 (Wounded); Lieutenant-Colonel Robert G. T. Currey 10/08/1915 – 28/09/1915 (Invalided Home); Lieutenant-Colonel Julian C. Colquhoun 29/09/1915 – 24/08/1916 (Wounded).

Royal Munster Fusiliers

1st Battalion (29th Div., 86th Bde.): Landed V Beach, 25 April; disembarked 2 January 1916. Commanding Officers: Lieutenant-Colonel Henry E. Tizard 04/08/1914 – 30/04/1915 (Replaced); Major William A. Hutchinson 30/04/1915 – 19/05/1915; Lieutenant-Colonel Guy W. Geddes 19/05/1915 – 02/12/1915 (Invalided Home); Lieutenant-Colonel Harry S. Wilson 02/12/1915 to 19/04/1916.

6th Battalion (10th Div., 30th Bde.): Landed Suvla Bay, 7 August; disembarked 1 October. Commanding Officer: Lieutenant-Colonel V. T. Worship 19/08/1914 – 03/11/1916.

7th Battalion (10th Div., 30th Bde.): Landed Suvla Bay, 7 August; disembarked 1 October. Commanding Officers: Lieutenant-Colonel Herbert Gore 10/03/1915 – 17/09/1915; Major Henry Aplin 17/09/1915 – 21/11/1915; Lieutenant-Colonel Godfrey Drage 21/11/1915 – 03/11/1916.

Royal Dublin Fusiliers

1st Battalion (29th Div., 86th Bde.): Landed V Beach, 25 April; disembarked 2 January 1916. Commanding Officers: Lieutenant-Colonel Richard A. Rooth, KIA 24/04/1915; Lieutenant Henry D. O'Hara 28/04/1915-15/05/1915; Captain. Cecil B. J. Riccard 15/05/1915 – 25/07/1915; Lieutenant-Colonel Thomas R. R. Ward 25/07/1915 – 30/08/1915; Lieutenant-Colonel James W. O'Dowda 30/08/1915 – 19/11/1915; Captain. Hugh F. De Wolf 19/11/1915 – 22/12/1915; Lieutenant-Colonel Herbert Nelson 22/12/1915 – 29/09/1917.

6th Battalion (10th Div., 30th Bde.): Landed Suvla Bay, 7 August; disembarked 30 September. Commanding Officer: Lieutenant-Colonel Patrick G. A. Cox 29/09/1914 – 16/09/1917.

7th Battalion (10th Div., 30th Bde.): Landed Suvla Bay, 7 August; disembarked 30 September. Commanding Officers: Lieutenant-Colonel Geoffrey Downing 19/08/1914 – 15/08/1915 (Wounded); Major Malcolm P.E. Lonsdale 15/08/1915 – 18/08/1915 (Invalided Home); Major Charles B. R. Hoey 18/08/1915 – 20/02/1916.

18

A New Army Battalion at Gallipoli: The 7th Battalion The Prince of Wales's (North Staffordshire) Regiment[1]

J.M. Bourne

Accounts of the Gallipoli campaign at the operational and tactical levels have focused on the role of ANZAC troops and British Regulars. This is understandable. These formations and units were the spearhead of the bloody and confused MEF landings, they were most often trusted with breaking the stalemate that ensued and they were still there at the last. This has rather obscured the fact that Gallipoli saw the debut of the New Armies, otherwise the focus of so much British writing about the war. Three New Army divisions took part in the campaign, the 10th (Irish), 11th (Northern) and 13th (Western). Only one of these has an inter-war published history and only the 11th subsequently served on the Western Front.[2] None of the divisions arrived in theatre until July/August 1915 and the 10th Division left in October to go to Macedonia (Salonika), where it remained for the rest of the war. The absence of a published divisional history, inter-war or modern, is perhaps most regrettable in the case of the 13th Division, which later became the only British division to serve in the Mesopotamia campaign, whose political effects remain with us to this day.

The 7th Battalion North Staffordshire Regiment was part of 13th Division. The battalion has a slim published history written by its last adjutant, Captain Lionel Missen.[3] Missen did not take

1 I should like to thank the following friends, colleagues and former students who gave generously of their time and expertise in helping me research this chapter and to make sense of what I found: Chris Baker; Nick Beeching; Dr Derek Clayton; Dr Trevor Harvey; Dr Alison Hine; Dr Michael LoCicero; Justin Nash; Dr Geoffrey Noon; Ian Rose; Mick Rowson; Professor Gary Sheffield; Professor Peter Simkins; William Spencer; Dr Mike Taylor; Bill Thompson; and Andrew Thornton.

2 Major Bryan Cooper, *The Tenth (Irish) Division in Gallipoli* (London: Herbert Jenkins, 1918). The 10th is also the only division to attract modern scholarly attention, see Stephen Sandford, *Neither Unionist nor Nationalist: The 10th (Irish) Division in the Great War* (Sallins, Co. Kildare: Irish Academic Press, [2015]).

3 L.R. Missen MC, *The History of the 7th (Ser.) Bn. Prince of Wales's (North Staffordshire Regiment) 1914-1919* (Cambridge: W. Heffer & Sons Ltd., 1920). Temporary Lieutenant (Acting Captain) Leslie Robert Missen CMG MC (1893-1983) was born at Chesterton in Cambridgeshire in 1893, the son of Robert Symonds Missen (1871-1915), a millers', corn and coal merchants' traveller. He was commissioned in the 10th (Reserve) Battalion of the North Staffordshire Regiment with effect from 22 July 1915. After the war he pursued a career in educational administration, rising to become the

part in the Gallipoli campaign and his history deals with events from the arrival of the battalion at Tidworth on Salisbury Plain to the withdrawal from the Gallipoli Peninsula in a brisk eleven pages. These pages are not error free. The battalion war diary is often fragmentary and sketchy, a state of affairs that owed much to the casualties suffered by its adjutants and is entirely missing for November 1915.[4] Why therefore choose this battalion for particular attention? The answer lies in family history. It was my grandfather's battalion. 14755 Private Jesse Sheldon volunteered at Burslem town hall on 29 August 1914. He was a thirty-four-year old miner with a wife and five children, the youngest of whom was only six weeks' old. He was originally posted to the 10th (Reserve) Battalion of the North Staffordshire Regiment, serving on Guernsey and with the Tyne Garrison. He was not posted to the 7th Battalion until September 1915 in the aftermath of the August offensives. He later deployed with the battalion to Egypt and then Mesopotamia. He was wounded in the failed attempts to relieve Kut-al-Armara in April 1916[5] and invalided to India, then to home, on medical grounds, in 1918.[6] He was discharged from the army at Whittington Barracks, Lichfield, as unfit for further military service on 19 October and dropped dead ten days later. It remains for others to determine whether the experience of the 7th North Staffords was typical of New Army units in the Gallipoli campaign, but there seems little doubt that my grandfather was entirely typical of the kind of men who volunteered for the North Staffords in August 1914 and of the experience of so many of them who served in the Balkans and middle east.

"K1"

Four hundred and four New Army infantry battalions saw active service during the Great War. Eighty of these battalions belonged to the First New Army or "K1". Thirty-nine of them served in the Gallipoli campaign.[7] As a group, "K1" battalions have never attracted the same scrutiny as the Regular, Pals or Territorial battalions. This chapter is a small step towards remedying the neglect.

Field-Marshal Earl Kitchener, the newly-appointed Secretary of State for War, appealed for 500,000 recruits for the army on 7 August 1914. Responsibility for raising these troops fell upon the existing Regular Army recruiting organisation, run by the War Office. The United Kingdom was divided into eight military commands: Northern; Southern; Eastern; Western; Irish; Scottish; Aldershot; and London District. All but the last two were ordered to raise another line battalion, to be numbered sequentially after existing units. In the case of the North Staffordshire Regiment, with its two Regular, two Reserve and two Territorial battalions, this

Chief Education Officer of East Suffolk County Council. He was made CMG in 1956 for his work as a Member of the Colonial Office Advisory Committee on Education in the Colonies. He died at Aldeburgh in Suffolk on 27 August 1983. For his service file, see TNA WO339/35329.

4 TNA WO 95/4302. For the brigade war diary, see TNA WO 95/4302 and for the divisional war diary TNA WO 95/4300.

5 The attempts to relieve Kut were among the costliest actions of the war for North Staffordshire, though lacking the dramatic focus on one deadly day as with 13 October 1915 and 1 July 1916.

6 Ancestry: British Army Pensions Records, 1914-20, file of Jesse Sheldon.

7 The three New Army divisions, unlike the divisions that landed earlier in the campaign, were allocated pioneer battalions, giving them thirteen battalions each.

became the 7th Battalion. It came into official existence on 29 August 1914 at Whittington Barracks, Lichfield.[8]

Much of our knowledge and apparent understanding of "K1" battalions remains beholden to Ian Hay's famous account of his own experiences as a Kitchener volunteer in the 10th Battalion Argyll and Sutherland Highlanders, thinly disguised in his best-selling *The First Hundred Thousand* as the Bruce and Wallace Highlanders.[9] Hay's portrayal captured the public imagination and left a permanent impression on British perceptions of the period of voluntary recruiting. Hay's battalion was full of men who had chosen to respond to a national emergency, but who were entirely without military experience and who would never have joined the army but for the peculiar circumstances of 1914. The situation in 7th North Staffords was very different.

Gentlemen and Officers

Battalion building began at the top. Major T.A. Andrus, OC Depot of the North Staffordshire Regiment, was appointed Commanding Officer. This was the pattern in other K1 battalions as well.[10] Andrus was 42 when the war broke out.[11] He was four years younger than the commanding officers of the North Staffordshire Regiment's two Regular battalions, so may still have harboured battalion command ambitions himself. His marriage in 1913 would have been an asset.[12] The war was to have a dramatic impact on his military career and his life. Andrus took the battalion to war, was wounded on 9 August 1915, returned to command the 7th in Mesopotamia in April 1916 before being promoted GOC 39th Brigade on 8 August 1916. He held this post until the end of hostilities. In the space of two years he went from an ageing major, to a youngish temporary lieutenant-colonel to a young brigadier. He seems to have been a dedicated and competent officer in the best Regular regimental tradition.

He was not alone in being a Regular. The battalion also had a Regular adjutant, Captain H.P.L. Heyworth,[13] a Regular 2i/c, Major F.H. Walker,[14] and two Regular company commanders,

8 Whittington Barracks was the depot of both the North Staffordshire and South Staffordshire Regiments and the headquarters of No. 6 Recruiting District, Northern Command. (Staffordshire was one of only five English counties to have more than one Regular infantry regiment of the line: the others were Kent, Lancashire, Surrey and Yorkshire).

9 Ian Hay, *The First Hundred Thousand: Being the Unofficial Chronicle of a Unit of "K (1)"* (Edinburgh & London: William Blackwood, 1915). "Ian Hay" was the pen name of John Hay Beith (1876-1952), soldier, writer and propagandist.

10 Peter E. Hodgkinson, *British Infantry Battalion Commanders in the First World War* (Farnham: Ashgate, 2015), pp. 28-9.

11 Lieutenant-Colonel (later Brigadier-General) Thomas Alchin Andrus CMG (1872-1959), son of a Kent landowner; GOC 39 Brigade, 8 August 1916-23 January 1919.

12 The mantra of the Regular army was "subalterns should not marry, captains may, majors should and colonels must".

13 Captain Heyworth Potter Lawrence Heyworth (1877-1915), Reserve of Officers, North Staffordshire Regiment. He retired on half-pay on 21 September 1913 after 13 years with the regiment. He was killed by a shell at Rest Gully on 8 August 1915, aged 37.

14 Major (later Lieutenant-Colonel) Frank Hercules Walker (1870-1916), Major Reserve of Officers, North Staffordshire Regiment. He was killed in action on 7 January 1916 while commanding the 7th Battalion.

Captain W.A.S. Edwards[15] and Captain E.D.D. Henderson.[16] This was a level of Regular officer provision that would be unknown among K2, K3 and K4 battalions.

Besides the Regulars, a further nineteen officers landed on the Gallipoli Peninsula with the battalion in July 1915. All of them were civilians when the war broke out. They included two university students,[17] two law students,[18] three schoolmasters,[19] a bank clerk,[20] a manufacturer[21] and a barrister.[22] Eleven were definitely public schoolboys, nine went to Oxford or Cambridge universities and one to London University. Family backgrounds were solidly upper middle-class, including commerce, manufacturing, the church, the law and medicine. These men would seem more compatible with the pages of *The First Hundred Thousand*, but this is a little misleading. As a group they were not entirely without previous military knowledge or experience. Several of them had been in their school or university OTCs, while Captain Clifford Grail had founded the Ravensbourne School Cadet

Major (later Brigadier-General) T.A. Andrus.

15 Captain William Augustus Spencer Edwards (1874-1916), killed in action 30 April 1916.
16 Captain (later Lieutenant-Colonel) Edward Elers Delavel Henderson VC (1878-1917). He was originally commissioned in the British West India Regiment. Awarded a posthumous Victoria Cross for actions on the west bank of the River Hai in Mesopotamia on 25 January 1917, while commanding 9th Battalion Royal Warwickshire Regiment.
17 Lieutenant Aubrey de Selincourt (1894-1962) was a Classics Scholar at University College, Oxford. His father owned the Swan & Edgar department store in London. De Selincourt was hospitalised with jaundice at Gallipoli. He later transferred to the RFC. He was shot down on 28 May 1917, Werner Voss's 31st victory. He spent the rest of the war as a POW. He was later renowned as a classicist and translator. A.A. Milne was his brother-in-law. Lieutenant Laurance Alfred Pinsent (1894-1915) was a law student at Trinity College, Oxford. He died of his wounds on 15 August 1915 after being shot in the head by a sniper at Walker's Ridge (Dead Man's Gully). Pinsent belonged to a well-known Birmingham legal family. The Olympic rower, Sir Matthew Pinsent, is his great nephew.
18 2nd Lieutenant Gerald Colpoys English (1889-1972), Malvern and Brasenose College, Oxford. English was severely wounded at Sanniyat on 9 April 1916, but survived the war, which he ended as a Lieutenant in the Labour Corps. 2nd Lieutenant George Doughty Wheway (1893-1983). Wheway belonged to the great Black Country manufacturers of harnesses, Job Wheway & Sons, though was never involved in the business himself. He lost his right eye following a gunshot wound on 17 July 1915.
19 Captain Clifford George Grail, Captain William Bass Hamlyn and Captain John Yate Robinson. Grail was the first officer in the battalion to be killed (on 23 July 1915).
20 2nd Lieutenant Gavin Campbell Arbuthnot.
21 Captain Raymond Linay Armes (1879-1916), coir and matting manufacturer. Armes suffered a bad case of sunstroke on 1 August 1915 and was evacuated to England on 20 August. He was killed in action at Kut on 9 April 1916.
22 Captain Bernard Kedington Rodwell Wilkinson (1872-1918). Wilkinson came from a rich and successful legal family. His father left more than £233,000 at his death in 1903 and Wilkinson, himself, £30,000. Wilkinson was invalided back to England on 21 December 1917. He committed suicide on 24 January 1918 in a Chelsea nursing home by shooting himself in the head. His service file gives a graphic and chilling account of this event, see TNA WO339/21334.

Corps.[23] Nor were they all callow youths. There were three twenty-year olds and two twenty-one-year olds, but Raymond Armes was 36, Gerald English 26, Clifford Grail 24, William Hamlyn and William Ratcliffe 30, John Robinson 29 and Bernard Wilkinson 42.

The battalion's officers felt the full fury of the Gallipoli campaign. Andrus was wounded, his successor Frank Walker killed. The battalion's first adjutant was killed and his successor severely and cruelly wounded.[24] Three more officers died of wounds,[25] twelve were wounded and two were invalided home sick. When Andrus returned to the battalion in Mesopotamia in April 1916 he sought in vain to discover from his fellow officers what had happened after he had been wounded on 9 August 1915.[26] Some of their replacements were cut from the same cloth, but there were also indicators of change. The new officers included three working-class rankers,[27] three "colonials",[28] a racehorse trainer[29] and a Jew.[30] Most exotic of all, perhaps, was Lieutenant Paul Sherek, the Berlin-born son of a theatrical agent, who had joined the Westminster Dragoons under age and

23 The Ravensbourne School War Memorial Library is dedicated to him.

24 Captain John Yate Robinson MC (1885-1916) succeeded Captain Heyworth as Adjutant in August 1915. Robinson was an outstanding sportsman, who captained Oxford at hockey and won an Olympic gold medal for hockey in 1908. Robinson was the son of a clergyman, Rev. E.C. Robinson, Vicar of Malvern. He was educated at Radley College and Merton College, Oxford, and was a schoolmaster at Broadstairs in Kent when the war broke out. He was paralysed by a shell splinter in his spine on 5 April 1916 in the attempts to relieve Kut. He died on 23 August 1916 at St Mary's Hospital, Roehampton. His last days were not pleasant and his personal file makes for uncomfortable reading. See TNA WO339/12040.

25 One of them was Lieutenant Gavin Campbell Arbuthnot (1893-1915). Arbuthnot was seen to have been wounded on 8 August 1915 and there were reports of his being evacuated from the beach, but he has no known grave. His father, Rev. William Arbuthnot, Vicar of Lea Marston in Warwickshire, refused to believe that his son was dead. His attempts to discover what happened to his son and the army bureaucracy's humane response make piteous reading, the feelings of loss and bewilderment still raw even after the passage of time. See TNA WO339/17760.

26 Andrus commented drily to the Official Historian, Cecil Faber Aspinall-Oglander, on 25 January 1931 that when he returned to the battalion in April 1916 he found "fresh officers". A copy of the letter is in the battalion war diary.

27 2nd Lieutenant James Duguid, killed in action near Kut, 9 April 1916; 2nd Lieutenant Percy Maddock; 2nd Lieutenant (later Captain) George Salt (1889-1977), a railway goods' clerk in Derby. Salt was the son of an aspirational working-class family from the Potteries. He suffered trench feet at Gallipoli, but recovered to command 'C' Coy., 7th North Staffords, twice being wounded. On 18 July 1917 he was appointed to a permanent commission in the Indian Army. Several other men from middle-class backgrounds were also commissioned from the ranks.

28 Acting Captain Basil Elmo Atkins (1892-1917) was a Canadian Rhodes Scholar at Hertford College, Oxford. He was wounded right at the end of the Gallipoli campaign but recovered to command 'B' Company, 7th North Staffords in Mesopotamia. He was wounded four times before being killed at Kut on 25 February 1917. He seems to have been an outstanding officer, a true warrior. Captain Albert Haynes was commissioned from the ranks of the Australian 2nd Light Horse Brigade, with which he was Equestrian Sergeant Major. He died on 20 July 1917. 2nd Lieutenant Augustine Conway Marlowe was a British-born auditor with the Canadian Pacific Railway. He enlisted with the 2nd Canadian Contingent and went abroad with the 17th Battalion CEF before being commissioned in the North Staffordshire Regiment.

29 Lieutenant Francis Vickerman Priestly (1872-1945) subsequently commanded 39th Brigade Supply & Transport Company.

30 The Jewish officer was Lieutenant James Albert Marks (1893-1917), the son of a Newcastle-on-Tyne jeweller. He was killed in action on 25 January 1917 at the recapture of Kut, having previously been wounded there in the unsuccessful attempts to relieve the Kut garrison in April 1916.

was commissioned in the North Staffordshire Regiment on 11 September 1915, aged only 17.[31] When subsequent losses suffered by the battalion's original tranche of officers in other theatres are considered the casualty rate was enormous. Only a handful made it through the war unscathed.

Men of Gallipoli

A contemporary list of the men of the 7th North Staffords who served on Gallipoli does not seem to have been kept and if it was has not survived. Fortunately, the North Staffordshire Regiment organised its Medal Rolls by theatre of war. The 7th Battalion was the only North Staffords battalion to serve in "Theatre 2(B) Balkans" so any man listed in that theatre with a 1914-15 Star must have served on the peninsula.[32] Two thousand and seventy-nine men have been identified in this way.[33] This extraordinary number, an entire battalion's worth of "turn-over", is a testimony to the level of sickness during the campaign. The battalion's total fatalities came to 240, 134 (55.8 percent) of whom were killed in action, 63 (26.25 percent) of whom died of wounds, and 43 (17.91 percent) of whom died from illness or injury.[34] These figures do not confirm the view expressed by a sergeant of the Newfoundland Regiment that "bullets did not take a big toll. It was death from germs".[35] Death was principally from enemy action, but the figures fail to reflect the impact of sickness levels, owing to diarrhoea, dysentery and malaria in the summer months and trench foot, frostbite, hypothermia, exposure and exhaustion in the autumn and winter months.[36] Difficulties in burying the dead in the rocky ground, the lack of clean water for drinking and washing, extremes of heat and cold, and the omnipresence of flies made for a challenging medical environment.[37] Sickness lowered morale, degraded military

31 Sherek later transferred to the RAF and was killed on 1 October 1918 flying a DH4 with 57 Squadron. He was still only 20.

32 The 1914-15 Star was awarded to officers and men who served in a theatre of war between 5 August 1914 and 31 December 1915. A few men in the 7th North Staffords held the 1914 Star, having previously served with the BEF before transfer.

33 This total includes a few men who were identified from other sources (mainly local newspapers) as having served with the battalion in the Gallipoli campaign but whose names do not appear on the 1914-15 Star Medal Roll. These men's names are generally to be found in other battalions of the regiment, in the Machine Gun Corps or the Labour Corps. There are doubtless more men who have not been identified. The identified total, despite being large, is therefore a *minimum* figure.

34 A further 390 of the men who served at Gallipoli were later killed or died of wounds or died of sickness in Mesopotamia, a further 102 in France & Belgium and a further 11 in other theatres, making a total, including Gallipoli, of 773 fatalities, 37.18 percent of the 2,079 men who served on the peninsula. The true texture of the battalion's war may be appreciated from the burial places of those who served with it at Gallipoli: at sea; in Britain; in France and Belgium; in Malta; in Egypt; in Turkey; in Greece; in India; in Mesopotamia (Iraq); in Persia (Iran); in Azerbaijan; and in Georgia.

35 Quoted in Yvonne McEwen, *The Company of Nurses: The History of the British Army Nursing Service in the Great War* (Edinburgh: Edinburgh University Press, 2014), p. 103.

36 The battalion also suffered from malaria during its later deployments in Mesopotamia and south Russia. There were enough men with long term medical problems for a Tropical Diseases Clinic to be set up in Glebe Street, Stoke, after the war.

37 For a pithy account of the medical problems posed on Gallipoli, see Peter Hart, "Hell at Helles: Sweating in the Trenches, Summer 1915", *Stand To! The Journal of the Western Front Association* (Special Edition, September 2015), pp. 18-22.

efficiency and led to a very high incidence of medical evacuations. The lack of in-theatre hospital beds often made it easier to return soldiers direct to Britain.[38] Soldiers from the 7th North Staffords who were evacuated home rarely returned to the battalion after recovery and therefore constituted a permanent loss.

The patchy survival of soldiers' service files has made it impossible to obtain a biography for each of the 2,079 men who served with the battalion at Gallipoli.[39] A significant proportion of full and partial biographies have, however, been constructed from other sources, including Medal Index Cards, pension files, the registers of soldiers' effects, the 1911 census, the Commonwealth War Graves Debt of Honour Register, *Soldiers Died in the Great War*, local newspapers and miscellaneous on-line genealogical and war memorial websites. These sources make it possible in many cases to identify a man's date of birth, place of birth, place of residence, place of enlistment, date of enlistment, age, marital status, religious denomination, employment and, in some cases, height, weight, chest size and identifying marks, such as scars and tattoos. Many of the conclusions drawn from the biographies of men who have been identified have been confirmed by Ian Rose's research on the 7th North Staffords' sister battalion, the 9th Royal Warwicks.[40] These conclusions do not conform to the picture presented by Ian Hay or to the statistical evidence of voluntary recruitment nationally.

One thing we know about *all* the men who served with the 7th North Staffords is their names. Soldiers' names have attracted little, if any, attention, but names are central to identity and to the individual's sense of belonging. Neil Burdess has argued that "Even in the late 1700s, the names William, John and Thomas accounted for over half of all male baptisms ... However, from the nineteenth century onwards, there was a constant decline in the importance of the most popular names".[41] Burdess, and others, attribute this change to the impact of industrialisation. In a quintessentially industrialised part of England, like north Staffordshire, the change was far from dramatic. Thirty-one percent of the men in the battalion were named William, John or George. If the fourth most popular name, Thomas, is added, the percentage rises to 38.

38 Major-General Sir W.G. Macpherson & Major T.J. Mitchell, *Medical Services General History: Vol IV: Medical Services During the Operations on the Gallipoli Peninsula; in Macedonia; in Mesopotamia and North-West Persia; in East Africa; in the Aden Protectorate, and in North Russia. Ambulance Transport during the War* (London: HMSO, 1924; Uckfield: Naval & Military Press, 2009); the excellent Lieutenant-Colonel A.D. Carbery, *The New Zealand Medical Services in the Great War 1914-1918: Based on Official Documents* (Auckland: Whitcombe & Tombs 1924); Uckfield: Naval & Military Press, 2004); and Phylomena Badsey's contribution to this volume.

39 Soldiers' service files suffered extreme damage in the first German night raid on London on 7/8 September 1940. The survival rate of service files for men in the 7th North Staffordswas 37.5 percent, for men who were commissioned (8), 35 percent for men who died, 39.56 percent for men who were killed in action, 43.3 percent for men who died of wounds, 4.5 percent for men who were discharged on medical grounds, and an astonishing 0.01 percent for men who survived the war and were discharged to the Class Z Reserve in 1918 and therefore still considered fit for military service. The overall survival rate of service files for the battalion was 16.56 percent, much lower than the 30-40 percent survival rate for service files often quoted.

40 Ian Rose, 'Rushing to the Colours: The 9th (Service) Battalion of the Royal Warwickshire Regiment and Voluntary Recruitment in Warwickshire 1914-1916', Unpublished MA Dissertation, University of Wolverhampton (2016).

41 Neil Burdess, *Hello my name is: The Remarkable Story of Personal Names* (Dingwall: Sandstone Press, 2016), pp. 98, 99.

Forty-four percent of the men were called William, John, George, Thomas or James. The wider predominance of other traditional names, such as Albert, Arthur, Edward and Joseph, is also apparent, with a significant tail of Biblical names such as Elijah, Enoch, Ephraim, Jeremiah and Job, in a part of the country where Protestant non-conformity was strong. The modern trend for names that express a unique individuality was alien. Names were not designed to express individuality, but to honour family tradition. These were men who were located in the past as well as the present, who knew who they were, where they came from and what they owed to family and community.

Although the 7th North Staffords were not as focused in their recruitment as a Pals battalion or a Territorial unit, they were very much local to the north of the county, men from the Staffordshire Potteries, Biddulph, Burton-on-Trent, Leek, Newcastle-under-Lyme, Uttoxeter, and from the area's plethora of mining and industrial villages –Audley, Bignall End, Brindley Ford, Brown Edge, Chesterton, Goldenhill, Knutton, Leycett, Milton, Norton, Packmoor, Red Street, Smallthorne and Talke. The men of the battalion were overwhelmingly born in the county and resident in it at the time of their enlistment. Very few men who lived south of Stone joined the battalion and genuine outsiders were few and far between.[42] They were the products of tight-knit communities, which were sometimes narrow in outlook and hostile to "foreigners", but in the major urban centres at least were exposed to a vivid working-class culture of pubs, clubs, sports teams, "the fancy", church and chapel, drunkenness and sobriety, hedonism and respectability, social conservatism and (often) political radicalism.[43]

Adrian Gregory has pointed out that, contrary to contemporary propaganda, "[the volunteer army of 1914-15] was not a cross section of Britain. It included more clerks than miners and railwaymen combined".[44] This was not true of the 7th North Staffords, where clerks are very hard to find.[45] Although the battalion did not reflect the general pattern of voluntary recruitment, it certainly reflected the area from which it came. It was a battalion of potters, miners (coal and ironstone), iron and steel workers, silk weavers, brewers, brick makers, gas workers and general labourers. In whatever industry the men worked, they were overwhelmingly

42 The most exotic recruit to the battalion was 17101 Private Joseph Aloysius Travers. Travers's real name was Joseph O'Donnell. He was a native of Co. Donegal. At the time the war broke out he was a teamster in New York City. He joined the North Staffords in Liverpool on 10 March 1915 and was posted to the 7th Battalion in August. He served with the battalion to the very end, on the Black Sea, and was discharged on 23 September 1919. He then returned to New York and resumed his life as a teamster! See Ancestry: British Army Pensions Records, 1914-20, file of Joseph A. Travers.

43 For a discussion of this, see J.M. Bourne, 'Burslem and its Roll of Honour, 1914-1918', *Midland History*, 39 (2) (Autumn 2014), pp. 202-18.

44 Adrian Gregory, *The Last Great War: British Society and the First World War* (Cambridge: Cambridge University Press, 2008), p. 81.

45 Some of the few were 10995 Private Wilfred Barks, a book-keeper's clerk in a Leek silk factory. He died of wounds on 9 August 1915; 10483 Private Frank Hanson Moorcroft, a clerk in a Burton-on-Trent wine merchant's. He survived the war; 10059 CSM Charles William Hughes, a clerk at the brewer's Bass, Ratcliff &Gretton. He died of wounds on 8 August 1915; and 8716 Sergeant Percy Maddock, who was later commissioned (see TNA WO339/43116). The battalion could, however, boast an actor and a professional cricketer. The actor was 16964 Lance Corporal Ernest Alfred Fosse. He was one of the few not born in the county. He died in 1963, aged 80. The professional cricketer was 9485 Sergeant Richard Henry Simms. At 6' 2", he was the tallest man in the battalion. He was discharged on medical grounds on 2 December 1915.

unskilled.[46] As Adrian Gregory has also pointed out, far from being men who would not have contemplated joining the army in peacetime, they were exactly the sort of men (unskilled urban workers) who did join the pre-war Regular army and, in some cases, had. There is little evidence, however, to suggest that these early volunteers for the 7th North Staffords were propelled into the army by the same forces of poverty and unemployment that had been the Regular army's most reliable recruiters in the past. In so far as it is possible to tell, the majority of men were in employment when they joined up and quite a high proportion were married men with families.[47] It should also be stressed that this was an overwhelmingly working-class battalion and a battalion of *employees*. The self-employed working-class were conspicuous only by their absence, as were the lower middle-class "shopocracy". Many of the men were employed in physically demanding and dangerous industries where team-working was the norm and group loyalty and solidarity was at a premium. These existential realities were not so dissimilar from life in the army and the business of war.[48]

Although the 7th North Staffords was a "K1" battalion, it does not mean that all the men who served with it joined in August 1914. The lowest service number of men in the battalion was that of 4560 Sergeant John Drew. He was one of 506 men with a four-digit service number. These men were largely Reservists or Special Reservists.[49] Although they were called to the colours on the outbreak of war, most did not deploy with the 7th North Staffords in June 1915. Seven hundred and three men who landed with the battalion at Cape Helles on 13 July 1915 have been identified.[50] Of these "originals" only 60 (8.54 percent) had four-digit numbers. The largest group were men with service numbers 10000-10999, who constituted 341 "originals" (48.57 percent). These men enlisted in August 1914. Together with the ex-Regulars and Special Reservists, these early joiners represented more than half the battalion that landed on 13 July. A further 89 men (12.67 percent) enlisted in late August and September 1914. The third biggest group, however, consisted of 68 men (9.68 percent of the "originals") with service numbers between 15000 and 15999 who mainly enlisted in October and November 1914. There were also a significant number of men, including my grandfather, who enlisted in August and September 1914, but who were not posted to the battalion until later in the campaign, mainly in September 1915, after the August offensives.

46 The unskilled workers also included a number of agricultural labourers from the area's farming heartlands, round Uttoxeter.

47 For the relationship between voluntary recruitment and employment, see P. E. Dewey's brilliant article, 'Military Recruiting and the British Labour Force during the First World War, *Historical Journal*, 27 (1) (1984), pp. 199-223.

48 For this, see J.M. Bourne, 'The British Working Man in Arms', in Hugh Cecil & Peter H. Liddle, (eds.), *Facing Armageddon: The First World War Experienced* (Barnsley: Pen & Sword, 1996, 2003), pp. 336-52.

49 Special Reservists enlisted for 6 years with the option to extend for another 4. They received 6 months' training and then returned to their jobs, with the obligation to attend 4 weeks' training a year. The Special Reserve seems to have been particularly attractive to unskilled labourers as a way of supplementing often uncertain incomes.

50 These men were identified from their Medal Index Cards, which show their entry into a theatre of war as 2 July 1915. This date was before the battalion actually landed and appears to refer to the establishment of 13th Division HQ at Mudros Bay. TNA WO 95/4300: War Diary of 13th Division, 2 July 1915.

Two other aspects of the battalion's Other Ranks are worthy of comment. The first is their age. Much ink has been spilled over the years on the subject of under-age soldiers. The battalion certainly had one, 14229 Private Alfred Norman Walters, son of the Urban District Rate Collector for Smallthorne. Walters enlisted on 19 August 1914, giving his age as 19, when he was actually only 16. He was posted to the 7th Battalion in September 1915 but was invalided back to Britain with ulcerated legs. In April 1916 his father sought to prevent Walters from "going again into the firing line until such time as he shall attain the age of 19 years". Alfred Walters Sr. received a brusque dismissal from the i/c Infantry Records No. 6 District at Lichfield, restating the official army point of view. Even so, the parental intervention may have had some effect. Jr. was not posted to the BEF until 2 March 1917, by which time he was 19. He was reported "missing" on 21 March 1918 and was later considered to have died on that day, aged 20, official age 23.[51] Doubtless there were other under-age soldiers who have not been identified, but the striking thing about the battalion is not how young its soldiers were but how old.

Reliable information on soldiers' ages is hard to come by and even when available somewhat dubious. The following "hard" looking statistics must be taken as indicative rather than definitive. The age of soldiers in the 7th North Staffords on recall (for those with pre-war service) or on enlistment (for those who joined after the outbreak of war) has been located for only a fifth of the men. The average age of this group was 27 years 3 months. The optimum age for infantrymen is generally considered to be between 21 and 28. The average age of the men in the 7th North Staffords, however, disguises the proportion (36 percent) who were aged 30 or over. This was partly a consequence of the number of Reservists, Special Reservists and time-expired Regulars who filled its ranks.[52] It also owed something to the (irrational) voluntary recruitment system. Recruiters during 1914-15, especially in 1915 when the flow of recruits began to dry up, had every incentive to take men for their regiments, regardless of the bigger picture. Take, for example, the case of 17069 Private Samuel Charles Woodward. He enlisted at Burton-on-Trent on 8 March 1915, aged almost 36. He had a wife and three children. His occupation was "engine driver". It is difficult to believe that under conscription a 36-year old engine driver would have been taken for the infantry. He would either have been retained at home or posted to the Railway Operating Department of the Royal Engineers. These plausible explanations aside, however, it remains something of a mystery why so many older men joined the battalion.

The "elderly" nature of the battalion's soldiers also gives rise to a second aspect that is worthy of comment, their health and especially their physique. Did the large number of older soldiers contribute to the battalion's high turnover from sickness? To answer this would require much more research, but a provisional answer might be "perhaps". The question of physique, however, may be much more authoritatively dealt with. The physique of British soldiers at Gallipoli often attracted unfavourable contemporary comment, especially from dominion observers.[53] The

51 Ancestry: British Army Service Records, 1914-20, file of Alfred Norman Walters.

52 For example, 16748 Private George Thomas Heath, a time-expired Regular, volunteered on 26 January 1915, aged 39 years 9 months. He was a pottery warehouseman from Newcastle-under-Lyme with a wife and two children. He died of dysentery on 8 November 1915.

53 For example, see Jock Vennell, *The Forgotten General: New Zealand's World War I Commander, Major-General Sir Andrew Russell* (Auckland: Allen & Unwin, 2014), Kindle edition location 1649-54. Vennell describes Russell's appointment as "advisor to the British Territorial regiments on Gallipoli,

Australian official historian, C.E.W. Bean, was convinced that the industrial revolution had ruined the health and "character" of the British urban working class; it was the dominion troops who had the stature, individuality and physical strength of "true Britons".[54] The soldiers of the 7th North Staffords were smaller and lighter than adult males nowadays, but they were almost certainly stronger. The average height of men in the 7th was about 5' 6". The average height of British males now is 5' 9". This is not a huge increase over a century of improved health, nutrition and housing. The big difference is in comparative weights. The average British male now weighs 13.16 stones.[55] It is unusual to find a soldier in the 7th who weighed more than 10½ stones.[56] In boxing terms, their median weight was somewhere between lightweight (9st 9lbs) and welterweight (10st 7lbs). And like boxers they were "wiry strong", with whipcord bodies honed by years of hard physical labour; by no stretch of the imagination could they be characterised as physically weak.[57]

In Harm's Way

The 7th North Staffords' fate was sealed on 17 May 1915. The military situation on the peninsula was causing grave concern in London and on 14 May, as its last act, the War Council asked Sir Ian Hamilton, the Commander-in-Chief, to state what level of reinforcement he would need in order to bring the campaign to a successful conclusion. Hamilton had been most reluctant to ask for reinforcements. His reply was extraordinarily opaque. In Robin Prior's words "On the one hand, [Hamilton] thought lack of space and water would not allow him to absorb any reinforcements at all. On the other hand, two additional divisions and a Balkan ally to distract elements of the Turkish army might allow him to get forward. Failing an ally, he asked for four divisions – provided he could manage a further 1,000 yards at Helles to shelter the new arrivals from shellfire".[58] Given this astonishing dithering and the political upheaval at home occasioned by the resignation of Admiral Fisher, the removal of Churchill from office as First Sea Lord, the shell crisis in France and the formation of a coalition government, this was – perhaps – an opportune moment to terminate the campaign. The opportunity was not taken. Instead, the Dardanelles Committee, as the War Council was now called, decided that Hamilton would be reinforced immediately with three New Army divisions, including the 13th.

a role that only reinforced his poor impression of the troops of Kitchener's Army. He found them not only difficult to motivate but lacking in physique and fighting spirit".

54 Bean's romanticised view of Australian soldiers has been comprehensively demolished by Australian historians. See, for example, Dale Blair, *Dinkum Diggers: An Australian Battalion at War* (Carlton South Victoria: Melbourne University Press, 2001). This was the 1st Australian Battalion that fought at Gallipoli.

55 Office for National Statistics, quoted by BBC News, 13 October 2010 <http://www.bbc.co.uk/news/uk-11534042>

56 The heaviest soldier I have found was 15601 Private Robert Davies, who weighed 168lbs (12st or super-middleweight). He was killed in action at Cape Helles on 7 January 1916, aged 29. At 5' 11.5" he was perhaps uncomfortably tall for a miner.

57 My grandfather had the typical build of a coal miner. He was 5' 7.5" and weighed 138 lbs (9st 12 lbs).

58 Robin Prior, *Gallipoli: The End of the Myth* (New Haven & London: Yale University Press, 2009), p. 161.

The first thing the 7th North Staffords knew of these developments was when "a large consignment of Wolseley sun helmets" arrived at Blackdown and "the officers were ordered to obtain khaki drill clothing and sun goggles".[59] Nothing was recorded of how news that the battalion was to deploy to the eastern Mediterranean was received. A considerable proportion of the battalion had volunteered in August 1914. Whatever their motives for joining up, they were certainly volunteering for a war against Germany. At that time Britain was not at war with the Ottoman Empire. Was the news received with disappointment or relief? If it was the latter, the feeling was to be short-lived.

The battalion went to war as part of the 39th Brigade, 13th Division. Its sister battalions were the 9th Royal Warwicks, the 7th Glosters and the 9th Worcesters. 39th Brigade was commanded by Brigadier-General W. de S. Cayley.[60] Cayley had what is known as a "good war", succeeding to the command of 13th Division in Mesopotamia in July 1916 and to the command of III Tigris Corps in May 1918. The division was commanded by Major-General F.C. Shaw.[61] Shaw had served with the BEF in France as GOC 9th Brigade but was invalided home after being wounded by a shell that struck his headquarters in an estaminet east of Hooge on 12 November 1914. After recovering, he was given the rather plum command of GOC 29th Division but was transferred to the 13th Division in March 1915 for reasons that are not apparent. His experience of the Gallipoli campaign would have been very different had he remained in command of 29th Division. His command of 13th Division was to prove something of a disappointment through no real fault of his own. The campaign presented few, if any, opportunities to command his division as a complete formation in meaningful operations. The Order of Battle of Divisions lists only two engagements for 13th Division under Shaw's command: "6-10 August Battle of Sari Bair [Godley's Force]; 7 August Russell's Top (8/Ches and 8/R.W.F.)." The division was mainly used a reserve to fill in piecemeal when necessity arose. The sense that Shaw was a "nearly man" pursued him through the rest of his career, not least in his supercession as GOC Ireland in 1920.[62] He never held a combat command after August 1915.

59 Missen, *The History of the 7th (Ser.) Bn. Prince of Wales's (North Staffordshire Regiment)*, p. 2.
60 Brigadier-General (later Major-General Sir) Walter de Sausmarez Cayley (1864-1952), West Yorkshire Regiment; GOC 39th Brigade (28 August 1914-10 July 1916); GOC 13th (Western) Division (10 July 1916-20 May 1918); GOC III Tigris Corps (20 May-29 June 1918). His brother Douglas commanded 4th Worcesters and then 88th Brigade, 29th Division, in the Gallipoli campaign and the 29th Division itself on the Western Front in 1918.
61 Major-General (later Lieutenant-General Sir) Frederick Charles Shaw (1861-1942), Sherwood Foresters; GOC 9th Brigade, 3rd Division (Mobilisation-12 November 1914), GOC 29th Division (18 January-10 March 1915); GOC 13th (Western) Division (15 March-22 August 1915); MGGS Home Forces (19 December 1915-12 May 1918); GOC-in-C Forces in Ireland (13 May 1918-20). Shaw was close to Sir John French and his post-Gallipoli career trailed in French's wake.
62 See Michael Hopkinson, *The Irish War of Independence* (Dublin: Gill & Macmillan, 2002). Kindle edition location 1299.

First Impressions

The battalion sailed from Avonmouth on 26 June 1915[63] in SS *Ivernia*, a former Cunard Line vessel specialising in the trans-Atlantic emigrant trade and therefore capable of accommodating large numbers.[64] The account of the voyage in the battalion history is inaccurate.[65] The battalion war diary provides no account of the voyage at all other than noting the date of leaving Avonmouth. It begins with the battalion's arrival at Mudros on the island of Lemnos, Advanced Base of the Mediterranean Expeditionary Force [MEF], on 12 July, where three officers and 150 men were left behind to act as "first reinforcements".[66] The rest of the battalion sailed directly to Cape Helles, landing at V Beach at 10:00 p.m. on 13 July.[67] They immediately came under enemy fire, "two men being wounded by shrapnel *on the beach* [my emphasis]".[68] The battalion then marched to Gully Beach, where they bivouacked, this camp also being shelled in the evening, though without casualties. Protection was extemporised in the "many gullies and nullahs running down to the beach".[69]

SS *Ivernia.*

63 In surviving soldiers' service files 26 June 1915 was the date on which they were considered to have left Home Forces and joined the Mediterranean Expeditionary Force [MEF]. According to Missen, *The History of the 7th (Ser.) Bn. Prince of Wales's (North Staffordshire Regiment)*, p. 3, the battalion "sailed 1100 strong with 28 officers".

64 SS *Ivernia* could accommodate almost 2,000 passengers, and rather more soldiers. She was torpedoed and sunk by *UB-47* on 1 January 1917 off Cape Matapan in Greece while transporting 2,400 troops from Marseilles to Alexandria.

65 Missen has the battalion passing Gibraltar a day *before* it left Avonmouth.

66 TNA WO 95/4302: War Diary of the 7th North Staffords, 12 July 1915. According to the battalion history, all regimental transport had been left behind during a stop at Alexandria "as it could not be landed on the Peninsula", Missen, *The History of the 7th (Ser.) Bn. Prince of Wales's (North Staffordshire Regiment)*, p. 3.

67 TNA WO 95/4302: War Diary of the 7th North Staffords, 13 July 1915.

68 Ibid.

69 Missen, *The History of the 7th (Ser.) Bn. Prince of Wales's (North Staffordshire Regiment)*, p. 4.

If this had been a new battalion arriving on the Western Front it would have been given time to adjust to the realities of trench warfare in a "quiet sector", but there were no quiet sectors or safe rest areas on Gallipoli. At this time, wherever they were posted, British troops were liable to come under shell fire. The battalion's vulnerability was increased when they entered the forward trenches on 15 July, taking over positions vacated by 28th Division. The 7th North Staffords spent a fortnight holding these trenches. It was a costly time. Captain Grail and nineteen other ranks were killed and three officers, including two other company commanders,[70] and thirty-nine men wounded.[71] This introduction to Gallipoli ended on 30 July, when the battalion returned to Mudros.

This initial experience encapsulated the whole problem of the Gallipoli campaign. Even after the best part of three months' fighting the Allied position still had no depth. The enemy still held the high ground. Artillery resources, the key to break-in, break-through and manoeuvre on Great War battlefields, were still feeble and overly-dependent on often spectacular but equally often ineffective naval gunfire. It would take a major effort to break the stalemate. This came in August and would involve the 7th North Staffords.

Assault on Sari Bair

General Hamilton was expected to do something with the reinforcements he had been sent. As usual, he dithered. Lieutenant-General Birdwood, the GOC ANZAC, emerged as the chief mover in planning the next step, but the closer the adopted plan came to execution the less likely it appeared capable of bringing the campaign to a successful conclusion.[72] Another step forward is all it was likely to achieve. Even so, as the experience of the 7th North Staffords shows, the plan remained too ambitious and beyond the capabilities even of brave and determined troops.

Simply put, the plan involved three elements, of which the key one was the capture of the Sari Bair Ridge. This would be assisted by a diversionary attack at Cape Helles, to be carried out by the Regular 29th Division. This ended disastrously. On the left (northern) flank of the attack on the Sari Bair Ridge there would be a new landing at Suvla Bay. This would be carried out by two of the New Army divisions, the 10th and 11th, formed into a new IX Corps under the rather elderly and ineffective General Sir Frederick Stopford.[73] This landing has been mired in controversy and recrimination ever since. The ANZAC assault on Sari Bair would be reinforced by the 13th Division and would constitute the division's and the battalion's most important contribution to offensive operations in the Gallipoli campaign.

70 Captain Edwards and Captain Henderson.

71 6.66 percent of the battalion's total fatalities on Gallipoli were incurred on 23 July 1915 and 8.95 percent of those killed in action.

72 Prior, *Gallipoli*, p. 164. Birdwood's original plan was to push a division across the peninsula after the capture of the Sari Bair Ridge, thus isolating the Turkish positions at Helles and making possible the capture of the forts at the Narrows. This was delusional and was abandoned once Birdwood realised how difficult an operation the capture of the Ridge would be.

73 Stopford was 61 and in poor health. He had spent most of his career as a staff officer and he began the war as Lieutenant of the Tower of London. His appointment seems another extraordinary moment in an extraordinary campaign.

The 7th Battalion's part in the August offensives did not begin well.[74] The battalion embarked for transport back to the peninsula on 3 August. It disembarked at Anzac at 2:00 a.m. on 4 August. As in July, the battalion came under enemy fire as soon as it reached the beaches. It then marched to the inappropriately-named Rest Camp Gully, where it remained overnight in reserve. On 6 August the Australians launched an attack against the Turkish position at Lone Pine. This was the signal for the Turks to shell Rest Camp Gully, killing the 7th Battalion's Regular Adjutant, Captain Heyworth, a grievous loss at the outset of a challenging endeavour.

Once the Turks had been pinned by the attack at Lone Pine there would be an attempt to outflank them to the north by occupying the "whole crest of the Sari Bair ridge from Koja Chemen Tepe (Hill 971) to Battleship Hill".[75] This country was extremely difficult, a maze of "wild and tortuous spurs" and steep, rugged gullies thick with "dense prickly scrub".[76] There were also a series of ravines and it was up the Aghyl Dere ravine that the 7th North Staffords would enter the battle. Anzac was such a cramped position that it was very difficult to deploy large numbers of troops. This led to the attacking troops being arranged in *ad hoc* columns under extemporised command arrangements.

The constricted nature of the ground was immediately apparent to Colonel Andrus when he undertook a reconnaissance with Brigadier-General Cayley on 7 August. "I fully agreed with [Cayley's] opinion that the eastern area of Rhododenron spur was far too narrow for the deployment of the 39th Brigade as well as the battalions of the New Zealand brigade already on the spur," recalled Colonel Andrus. "During this period my battalion had with other battalions of the 39th Brigade moved towards Chailak Dere. It was late that evening when we reassembled in the Aghyl Dere." The scene was set.

The 39th Brigade remained in reserve until 7 August, when Brigadier-General Cox, commanding the "Left Assaulting Column",[77] succeeded in persuading Major-General Godley (GOC New Zealand and Australian Division) to release them to his command. Cox believed this was necessary because the failure of the "Right Assaulting Column", under Brigadier-General Johnston, to capture Chunuk Bair had jeopardised the whole plan of operations. Cayley received his orders at 11:00 a.m. on 7 August. The brigade was also "Balkanised" and split into columns. Andrus took command of No. 2 Column, which consisted of the 7th North Staffords and the 9th Worcesters. Andrus was ordered to join up with the 1/6th Gurkhas "and the three battalions to be in a position to assault the crest of the spur leading to Hill Q after the cessation of the artillery bombardment at 4:15 a.m." On joining up with the Gurkhas Andrus was to come

74 This account is based on the battalion history, the war diaries of the 7th Battalion and 39th Brigade and on a considered analysis written by Colonel Andrus in December 1930 after being sent a draft for comment of Vol. II of the British official history of the campaign by its author, Brigadier-General Cecil Aspinall-Oglander. A copy of the letter may be found in the battalion war diary.

75 C.F. Aspinall-Oglander, *Military Operations Gallipoli*, Vol. II (London: William Heinemann, 1932; London & Nashville, Tennessee.: The Imperial War Museum Department of Printed Books in association with The Battery Press, Nashville, 1992), p. 182.

76 Rhododendron Spur, Damakjelik Spur and Abdul Rahman Spur.

77 Brigadier-General (later General Sir) Herbert Vaughan Cox (1860-1923), Indian Army. The Column consisted of Cox's 29th Indian Brigade, 4th Australian Brigade (Brigadier-General J. Monash), 21st (Kohat) Indian Mountain Battery (less one section) and No. 2 Field Company New Zealand Engineers. Cox arrived at Anzac only five days before taking command of the Column. He later commanded 4th Australian Division on the Western Front.

under the orders of the Lieutenant-Colonel commanding "that battalion, if he was my senior in rank – otherwise I was to command the column!"

The task facing the 7th North Staffords was formidable. Andrus was at pains to explain the events fully to Aspinall-Oglander. "I would like, in detail, to describe the conditions of a night march up the higher portion of the Aghyl Dere, which possibly corresponds with the difficulties of many of the other columns moving by night through … narrow [,] twisting, rocky [,] dried-up water courses, because it accounted for much of the lack of success of the morning of the 8th," he wrote. The 7th North Staffords and 9th Worcesters had "through misunderstanding" moved some way from the Aghyl Dere and it took some time to collect and organise them. "The men were very tired and very thirsty – the orders had to be explained to officers and Senior NCOs when dusk was already closing on the scene." The first part of the approach was not too difficult. Men could move two abreast, but further up the defile narrowed and became strewn with large boulders, which "were very smooth and slippery giving no foothold for men in heavy marching boots". The men had gone two nights without sleep and had had a long tiring day even before the approach march began. It was extremely hot, and thirst became a major problem. "As the night wore on, the column got more and more strung out and it became essential to halt and close up by companies." Dawn had broken before contact was made with the 1/6th Gurkhas, who had already advanced. Andrus sent his leading company to join them.

Although No. 2 Column had failed to arrive on time, Andrus was still hopeful that it might be possible to get at least one of the battalions into action, especially as the Column had barely come under fire from the Turkish positions on the high ground. "Within a few minutes, however, the whole scene changed. Heavy Turkish rifle fire was put on to the Knoll and on to the Dere above it. It became impossible to move the rear companies any further up the Dere." Andrus lost touch with the company he had sent forward to reinforce the Gurkhas and he did not discover how they had fared until he received Aspinall-Oglander's draft account of the attack in 1930. "The rear companies of the battalion below me were under fire from both sides of the Dere and were returning the fire from what cover they could get in the Nullah itself. Thus ended the attempt of the No. 2 Column." And, in many respects, thus ended the 7th North Staffords' part in offensive operations on the Gallipoli Peninsula, although fighting continued until 11 August and the battalion held its position until relieved on 30 August.[78] By then the 13th Division was under new management.

In his post-war reflection, Andrus identified three major issues that compromised any real prospect of success. The first was "that the whole operation required Divisions trained in *Hill warfare*, and that, with the exception of the Gurkhas, we hadn't any units trained in it." The second was the impact of "exceptional thirst". "The 39th Infantry Brigade served for nearly 3 years in Mesopotamia, after the evacuation of Gallipoli, and fought in excessive heat at times, but personally I have never felt it more than I did on the 8th August 1915." The third was the

78 The cost was heavy. One officer (Lieutenant Pinsent) was killed and ten officers, including Colonel Andrus, were wounded; 266 other ranks were killed, wounded or missing. 11.25 percent of the battalion's total fatalities on Gallipoli and 18.65 percent of those killed in action were incurred on 8 August 1915.

lack of "really good maps", a point emphasised also by the official historian.[79] These are damning observations.

"Nothing very special going on"[80]

The eventual failure of the August offensives saw the campaign enter what Michael LoCicero has called elsewhere in this volume a "post-strategic phase". Given that the whole purpose of the campaign was to achieve wide-ranging strategic (even geo-political) effects, this is a polite way of saying that the campaign had become moribund and without purpose. This was not lost on the men of the 7th North Staffords.

On 22 August Major-General Shaw shared the fate of so many of his men when he was invalided home with dysentery. His replacement was Major-General Stanley Maude.[81] Maude, like his predecessor, had been wounded while serving with the BEF in France. This was his first (and only) divisional command. Maude seemed satisfied with his inheritance, though as someone who had served in the BEF he immediately commented on the fact that the division was without its "Artillery, Train and Div[isiona]l Squadron".[82] Had he wished to make personnel changes in the division this would have been the time, but he did not.[83] Some changes had already been made for him. Brigadier-General A.H. Baldwin (GOC 38 Brigade) had been killed on 10 August and was replaced by Brigadier-General J.W. O'Dowda. Andrus was evacuated after his wounding and Maude came to regard the 7th Battalion's new CO, Frank Walker, as "one of our best commanding officers".[84] He also came to have a high regard for Cayley.

Lieutenant-Colonel F.H. Walker. (Missen, *The History of the 7th (Ser.) Bn. Prince of Wales's (North Staffordshire Regiment) 1914-1919*)

79 Aspinall-Oglander, *Military Operations Gallipoli*, Vol. II, p. 182. Aspinall-Oglander described the available maps, with admirable understatement, as "inadequate".

80 Andrew Syk, (ed.), *The Military Papers of Lieutenant-General Frederick Stanley Maude, 1914-1917* (Stroud: The History Press for the Army Records Society, 2012), p. 93.

81 Major-General (later Lieutenant-General Sir) (Frederick) Stanley Maude ("Systematic Joe") (1864-1917), Coldstream Guards; GSO1 DMT War Office (February-August 1914); GOC 14 Brigade, 5th Division (23 October 1914-12 April 1915); GOC 13th (Western) Division (23 August 1915-10 July 1916); GOC Tigris Corps (July-August 1916); GOC Mesopotamia Expeditionary Force (August 1916-death). He died of cholera in Baghdad on 18 November 1917 apparently after drinking infected milk at a performance of *Hamlet* in Arabic. He was one of the outstanding British military commanders of the war.

82 Syk, (ed.), *Military Papers … of Stanley Maude*, p. 92.

83 Ibid., pp. 92, 95. Maude's opinion was that he had "a very nice and I should say capable Staff". He soon became less enamoured of two of his brigadiers but was clear that Cayley was "good".

84 Ibid., p. 115.

Maude was less pleased, however, with the military situation he inherited. At the outset of his command he was firmly of the view that the campaign not only should be continued but could also be brought to a successful conclusion, provided there were no more "half measures".[85] The next few weeks were to prove a disappointment to him. He felt that "everyone had gone to sleep and the lethargy and drift is too sad to contemplate".[86] He was later to admit that when evacuation finally came "we ought to have gone at least 4 months ago".[87]

What Maude and the 7th North Staffords actually endured was described by the battalion historian as "a long round of solid trench warfare, during which time the principal occupations were digging forward, wiring, and patrol work".[88] The latter activity was insisted upon by Maude. "Am busy trying to stimulate offensive spirit but it is uphill work in sedentary warfare," he confided to his diary at the beginning of October. "Still we can do something in the way of patrolling and the 39th Infantry Bde have started well, two young officers having already distinguished themselves."[89] The 7th Battalion's war diary is not exactly replete with accounts of aggressive patrolling, but it was noted that "Captain C.V. Cole with two N.C.O.s, Sergeant Wilcox and Corporal Evans of 'A' Coy reconnoitred almost up to the enemy's trenches & brought back valuable information".[90]

This period of trench stalemate was exceptionally demanding and worse than "trench warfare" on the Western Front. In France and Belgium the trenches eventually evolved into what Rob Thompson has called "trench city", with fire, support, reserve and communication trenches, dugouts, traverses, fire-steps, duckboards, sandbags, organised systems of relief and rotation that minimised the time individual soldiers spent in the very front line, safe rest areas where soldiers could bathe and obtain clean uniforms, in-theatre training facilities, high quality medical treatment and casualty evacuation, decent and plentiful (if dull) food, specialist equipment, massive artillery support.[91] The trenches on Gallipoli, in contrast, never amounted to more than "trench shanty town" in positions with no depth, overlooked by the enemy, with no safe rest areas, poor food, patchy casualty provision, lack of supporting artillery, rarely far from the unburied dead and the flies they attracted, a veritable "gigantic morgue and open latrine".[92]

85 Ibid., p. 97: "If we only had a Wolseley now, a scientific soldier and a man of vigour to grip hold of the situation and hit hard."
86 Ibid., p. 95
87 Ibid., p. 118
88 Missen, *The History of the 7th (Ser.) Bn. Prince of Wales's (North Staffordshire Regiment,* p. 7. The battalion received drafts of 500 men and six officers betweeen 4 and 15 September. Maude regarded these men as only "partially trained" and lacking in "offensive spirit". See Syk (ed.), *Military Papers … of Stanley Maude*, p. 96.
89 Syk, (ed.), *Military Papers … of Stanley Maude*, p. 95.
90 TNA WO 95/4302: War Diary of the 7th North Staffords, 7 October 1915. For the development of trench warfare at Gallipoli, see Gary Sheffield, 'Shaping British and Anzac Soldiers' Experience of Gallipoli: Environmental and Medical Factors, and the Development of Trench Warfare', *British Journal for Military History*, Vol. 4, Issue No. 1 (November 2017). Sheffield points out that the Turkish trenches were so close as to prohibit patrolling. There is no evidence that the 7th North Staffords took part in two other trench warfare activities noted by Sheffield, "raiding" and "minor enterprises".
91 Author discussion with First World War logistics historian Rob Thompson.
92 Lieutenant-Colonel R.R. Thompson, *The Fifty-Second Lowland Division 1914-1918* (Glasgow: Maclehose & Jackson, 1923), p. 147.

The most noticeable feature of the 7th North Staffords' and the 39th Brigade's war diaries in September and October is the mounting sickness rates. The 7th's war diarist kept a careful note of the battalion's effective strength throughout October, including a daily casualty report in which sickness was the main feature: 7 men sick on 2 October, 2 sick on 4 October, 2 on 5 October, 5 on 6 October, 6 on 9 October, 5 on 8 October, 5 on 9 October, 6 on 10 October, 9 on 11 October, 4 on 12 October, 7 on 13 October, 7 on 14 October, 9 on 15 October, 14 on 16 October, 6 on 17 October, 8 on 18 October, 2 on 19 October, 7 on 20 October, 10 on 21 October, 8 on 22 October, 8 on 23 October, 6 on 24 October, 12 on 25 October, 7 on 26 October, 11 on 27 October, 9 on 28 October, 14 on 29 October, 5 on 30 October, 8 on 31 October. During the same period only seven men were killed as a result of enemy action. During this month the battalion never had more than 17 officers at any one time and generally somewhere between 650 and 800 men. A heavy burden fell on those who remained relatively healthy, just constant stress and no prospect of relief other than by succumbing to sickness themselves. And then came November.

There is no battalion war diary for November 1915. On 26 November the peninsula was hit by a ferocious storm, which was not forecast by British meteorologists. Maude described the thunderstorm as the worst he had ever seen. "Rain terrific and torrents soon running down all gullies. Pitch black and we had difficulty in getting home being fully wet to the skin. Men had a terrible night with everything flooded."[93] In the 7th Battalion trenches water "poured down from the higher ground occupied by the Turks".[94] "Many men drowned in their dug-outs, caught without any chance of escape; others were killed by collapsing trench walls and dug-out roofs; while others were carried away by the rush of water, and were battered to death against the sides of traverses and trenches. Those who escaped were left destitute in a waterlogged morass."[95] And this on top of three months of unrelenting labour, stress and deteriorating health and physical conditioning.

The flood was followed two days later by a "violent blizzard" and plummeting temperatures. Maude described the plight of the troops as "miserable". He went forward to visit 39th Brigade. "Saw three Commanding Officers and Cayley and they are all doing splendidly."[96] The trenches were "waist high in mud and water in some places". The freezing weather added a new dimension to the suffering of the troops who had "few shelters and are far from adequate with regard to warm clothing."[97] Sickness levels rocketed, especially from exposure and frostbite: 1,600 men went sick following the storm. The 39th Brigade was especially badly affected and was only some 1,500 men strong. The 7th Battalion's historian claims that 8,000 men were evacuated from the 13th Divisional area during the first three days after the storm. The battalion spent December endeavouring to restore the trench system by clearing the trenches of mud and water and building breastworks "all along the line in case of a second flood".[98] It soon became clear, however, that relief was at hand.

93 Syk, (ed.), *Military Papers … of Stanley Maude*, p, 99.
94 Missen, *The History of the 7th (Ser.) Bn. Prince of Wales's (North Staffordshire Regiment*, p. 8.
95 Ibid.
96 Ibid.
97 Ibid. Maude expressed his dissatisfaction with the state of affairs, complaining in his diary of "the want of decision by which we did not either decide to get on or get out of here months ago. Secondly the total lack of provision of winter clothing for the troops in adequate quantities and the absence of material for making shelters. It is too lamentable and has cost many valuable lives that might have been saved." These were lessons well learned by Maude when he came to command in Mesopotamia.
98 Missen, *The History of the 7th (Ser.) Bn. Prince of Wales's (North Staffordshire Regiment*, p. 8.

The Bitter End

Whatever the "ifs", "buts" and "maybes" of the Gallipoli campaign there has been near universal agreement that the eventual withdrawal of the expeditionary force from the peninsula was a triumph. There was an element of relief in the triumphalism because many contemporaries feared that the withdrawal would be bloody and catastrophic. As far as the 7th North Staffords are concerned, however, the word triumph is entirely inappropriate. Far from rescuing the battalion from an increasingly pointless and uncomfortable existence, it inaugurated the worst single day of the campaign and one of the worst days it endured during the whole war.

The failure of the August offensives finally forced the government's hand. The Commander-in-Chief of the Mediterranean Expeditionary Force, General Sir Ian Hamilton, was recalled on 16 October. His replacement, General Sir Charles Monro, landed on the Gallipoli Peninsula on 27 October. He had received an extensive briefing before leaving, including four meetings with Kitchener. Kitchener told Monro that he wanted an "honest" answer about staying or leaving, but there is little doubt that the honest answer Monro returned was not the one Kitchener wanted to hear.[99] Churchill was to blight Monro's reputation with the withering phrase "he came, he saw, he capitulated". This is unfair on Monro for many reasons, not least because his was only a recommendation. Kitchener was shocked by Monro's report, writing to Lieutenant-General Birdwood (GOC ANZAC) that he regarded "evacuation as a frightful disaster to be avoided at all costs", but after visiting the theatre himself in November he agreed to the evacuation of Suvla and Anzac. The cabinet approved the withdrawal on 7 December.

Kitchener's decision did not imply acquiescence in Monro's damning assessment of the campaign, however. Kitchener was influenced by recent events that led him to believe that Suvla and Anzac were now particularly untenable. Bulgaria entered the war on the side of the Central Powers in October. This sounded the death knell for Serbia, which was now attacked on two fronts. The Serbian army was forced into a cruel retreat over the mountains of Albania before finding sanctuary on Corfu. The Allies declared war on Bulgaria and opened yet another front in Salonika, which immediately took the 10th (Irish) Division from the peninsula. The removal of Serbia from the war allowed Ottoman forces on Gallipoli to be reinforced with powerful Austrian 240mm mortars and 150mm howitzers. The Germans also sent a delegation of staff officers and engineers from the Western Front to advise the Turks how to make maximum use of their new resources. With winter setting in and the British trenches still recovering from the November storm, which had destroyed trenches and landing piers and severely reduced fighting efficiency through frostbite and hypothermia, there was no prospect of further advances at Suvla and Anzac and every prospect of rising casualties from Turkish artillery, to which the British could make no effective response.[100] Kitchener was still determined to hang on to Helles, but the withdrawal from Suvla and Anzac allowed Turkish concentration against the tip of the peninsula and ensured that Helles, too, would have to be evacuated.

When orders for evacuation came the 7th North Staffords were still at Suvla Bay. The events of the autumn had severely depleted the battalion and it received a draft of six officers and 300

99 See J.M. Bourne, 'Charles Monro' in Ian F.W. Beckett & Steven Corvi (eds.), *Haig's Generals* (Barnsley: Pen & Sword Military, 2006), pp. 127-29.

100 See Edward J. Erickson, *Gallipoli: The Ottoman Campaign* (Barnsley: Pen & Sword Military, 2010; 2015), pp. 178-79.

men on 2 December. This did not seem to handicap arrangements for the evacuation. Planning for the withdrawal demonstrated all the professionalism and attention to detail that would later characterise General Maude's conduct of operations in Mesopotamia. Maude himself considered the evacuation a "masterpiece".[101]

The first part of December was taken up in repairing damage suffered by the trenches during the great storm. The weather was also extremely cold and frost bite became a major problem. 2nd Lieutenant Alexander Norman Tod, who was on attachment to the 7th North Staffords from the 5th Wiltshires, was one of those affected by frostbite. This was so severe that he had to have his right leg and part of his left foot amputated. The army's position on frostbite was almost to regard it as a self-inflicted wound. When challenged about the circumstances of his having incurred the condition, Tod replied that he was unaware he had it until he was taken aboard the hospital ship, adding that "no precautions were ordered, no gum boots were issued and what little [whale] oil there was went to keep the men's feet in good condition".[102]

It was decided that all men who were not fit to "do hard work in the trenches" should be sent away. The "hard work" was principally confined to erecting new wire where the flood had breached the trenches. Three lines were constructed, and nightly patrols made to ensure that the Turks had not cut them. Gaps were left so that engineers could pass through to lay mines. The gaps were closed-up by the RE on the night of 18 December once the mines had been made active. All stores not considered indispensable were taken down to the Brigade dump each night between 8 and 18 December. Each man was allocated 220 rounds of small arms ammunition. Firing was discouraged, and periods of silence observed every night "from 1:00 a.m. onwards". Everything that could be of value to the enemy was either destroyed or buried. The numbers holding the trenches were gradually thinned out until there was only a rear party consisting of fifty all ranks from each battalion in 39th Brigade and one machine gun. "The whole line was held from 23.00 [on 18 December 1915] until 1:30 a.m. by only 100 men. Fires were kept burning, occasional shots were fired from each bay, and the communications [trenches] not to be used were blocked. At 1:30 a.m. the last party left the trenches."[103] The battalion arrived safely on Imbros on 20 December 1915.[104]

This ought to have been the end of the affair for the 7th North Staffords, but it was not. Along with other units of 39th Brigade they were destined to be evacuated twice. No decision had yet been taken about the evacuation of Helles.[105] Major-General Maude was informed on Boxing Day that he and 39th Brigade were to go to Helles on 27 December. He was not amused: "Why they mention the 39th by name I cannot think. Bad staff work," Maude wrote in his diary: "It is the last Brigade I should send, first because it only arrived [at Mudros] the day before yesterday and secondly because it has scarcely recovered from the blizzard and the Gloucesters

101 Syk, (ed.), *Military Papers … of Stanley Maude*, p. 64.
102 TNA WO 330/1554. Tod added that "Beyond the fact that my own feet got exceedingly cold, I did not think there was anything wrong until Dec. 3rd, 1915 when I was unable to walk anymore, and my feet began to go black". Tod, despite his amputations, saw out the war in uniform on the staff of Southern Command in England.
103 TNA WO 95/4302:. War Diary of the 7th North Staffords, 19 December 1915.
104 On arrival at Imbros the battalion found no accommodation and had to bivouac. It was later moved into better accommodation at Mudros.
105 The decision was taken by the Dardanelles Committee on 23 December 1915.

especially."[106] There is no evidence that he pressed his concerns with higher authority. If he did they had no effect. Subsequent events suggest that the troops shared their commander's dismay and had had enough.

There is evidence that the accumulated effect of disease, appalling weather and a sense that there would be no victorious conclusion to the campaign had taken its toll on morale. Eleven members of the 7th North Staffords were tried on capital charges between 8 October and 7 December.[107] The charge in ten of the eleven cases was "sleeping at post".[108] All the men were found guilty and sentenced to death, which was commuted in all cases to terms of penal servitude. In practice, the men remained with the battalion. The ten men thus charged were 8085 Private William Hickton, 16827 Private Charles Ellis, Private T. Goodfellow, 10356 Private Daniel Hackney, 10592 Private Voisey John Trivett, 13052 Private Edgar Birch, Private A. Payne, 16625 Private J. Thickett and 15079 Private William Finney.[109]

But the most striking evidence that higher authority thought morale was becoming a problem was the execution of Sergeant John Robins, 5th Battalion Wiltshire Regiment, 40th Brigade, on 2 January 1916.[110] The execution took place on the beach at Cape Helles. The offence for which Robins was tried on 8 December actually took place on 10 August. The charge was "wilfully disobeying an order given by a superior officer in the execution of his duty". The delay between the act, the trial and the execution strongly suggest that Robins was conveniently available for an exemplary display of military authority. If his execution was to "encourage the others", however, it appears not to have had the desired effect on the 7th North Staffords.

On 7 January 1916 the 7th North Staffords were holding Fusilier Bluff at Cape Helles. By then the men were well aware that their re-evacuation was only days away.[111] At 11:15 a.m. the Turks began a "violent bombardment" of the battalion's lines. There is no evidence that the Turks were aware that another evacuation was in the offing. The bombardment searched

106 Syk, (ed.), *Military Papers … of Stanley Maude*, p. 108. Maude was scathing in his diary about the landing arrangements and the state of the trenches at Helles for what he described as "this ill-considered move of my division".

107 See Gerard Oram, *Death Sentences Passed by Military Courts of the British Army 1914-1924* (London: Francis Boutle, 1998), pp. 29-30.

108 9789 Private Henry Tagg was charged with desertion. He was two days off his 46th birthday when he volunteered on 7 September 1914. A former Regular with the Royal Warwickshire Regiment, he later served in France and Belgium with the 9th North Staffords, a Pioneer battalion, and with the Labour Corps. He was discharged on 23 December 1918 aged 50!

109 Hickton's low service number suggests pre-war military service, but his service file has not survived. His sentence of five years' penal servitude was suspended on 19 October 1915 and remitted on 11 February 1918. He died in Persia on 29 September 1918. Ellis was a post-August offensive reinforcement. He was killed in action on 26 January 1917. Hackney and Trivett were "originals" who landed with the battalion in July 1915. Hackney survived the war. Trivett died of wounds on 5 November 1915. There is no mention of his offence either on his Medal Roll Index Card or the Medal Roll itself. Birch had been on the peninsula since the end of August 1915, though he had volunteered a year earlier. He was killed in action on 14 September 1918. Finney was also an "original". His sentence of five years' penal servitude was suspended on 6 November 1915. He survived the war. Neither Goodfellow nor Payne appears on the Medal Index Cards or on the Medal Roll for the North Staffordshire Regiment.

110 For Robins's case, see Julian Putkowski & Julian Sykes, *Shot at Dawn: Executions in World War One by Authority of the British Army Act* (London: Leo Cooper, 1989), p. 58

111 This is clear from the battalion war diary.

the "firing line, supports and communications [trenches]" with "large H.E. and high velocity shrapnel". The bombardment continued until 3:45 p.m., when "it increased in intensity and was accompanied by rifle fire and bombing". The war diary continues:

> Their bombing was very violent, our supply of bombs ran short, and it was almost impossible to get supplies along the Mule Track. All the telephone lines were broken by the bombardment, and messages had to be sent by hand to the Brigade, and to the Companies.

The Turks launched an infantry attack at 4:15 p.m., but this was beaten off and the Turkish officers were unable to prevail upon their men to repeat it. Firing died away about 5:00 p.m.

The costs of this attack were severe. Colonel Walker was killed. According to the war diary, his death took place "in the firing line at the start of the attack". It is at least possible that the CO was aware of men leaving their posts and had gone forward to assess the situation for himself. Besides Walker, 44 men were also killed, and three officers and 106 other ranks wounded.[112] None of the men killed in the attack, including Colonel Walker, has a known grave, a testimony perhaps to the ferocity of the Turkish bombardment or more sadly to the impending withdrawal, which meant that the dead were left behind.

Despite this debacle, the evacuation proceeded on the night of 8/9 January 1916. The 7th North Staffords ended the Gallipoli campaign where they had begun it. It was not quite the end, however. In Egypt in January and February 1916 13625 Private Albert Brown, 8251 Private Richard Davis, 14648 Private Frank Dutton, 8280 Private Thomas Whittle, 16404 Private Richard Ernest Elson, Private J. Jones, 17145 Private Leonard Richard Sillitoe and 14305 Private Woodfine Smith were charged with cowardice.[113] It seems that they abandoned their posts during the Turkish attack of 7 January and took shelter on the beach. None of the men was actually executed. Brown survived the war and was discharged on 29 November 1919. Davis's charge was suspended on 14 February 1916. He died in Mesopotamia on 14 September 1917. Dutton had been on the peninsula since October 1915. His sentence was suspended on 14 February 1916. He was killed in action on 9 April 1916 at Kut. Whittle had been on the peninsula only since November. He survived the war. Elson had been on the peninsula since October. His sentence was suspended on 14 February 1916. He was killed in action on 18 April 1916 at Kut. Sillitoe had been in theatre since October. He was discharged as unfit for further military service on 16 January 1917. Smith's sentence was eventually remitted. He survived the war and was discharged in June 1919. There is no reference to these trials and convictions in the divisional, brigade and battalion war diaries or in the battalion history.[114]

112 12.08 percent of fatalities suffered by the 7th Battalion during the Gallipoli campaign were incurred on 7 January 1916 and 21.64 percent of those killed in action.

113 Oram, *Death Sentences*, pp. 29-30.

114 There were no more capital convictions in 13th Division after July 1916. Sergeant Robins was the only member of the division whose death sentence was carried out.

Conclusion

By the time the 7th Battalion North Staffordshire Regiment landed on the Gallipoli Peninsula the unit was less than a year old. As Allan Mallinson has written, "a year was hardly time in which to train an individual soldier, let alone battalions, brigades and divisions".[115] The battalion had no time to acclimatise to the theatre. It had no special training for fighting in mountainous terrain and there was to be neither time nor space for "in-theatre training". It had no special equipment. And, like all other units on the peninsula, it was under-gunned. It faced a determined enemy defending their own soil, entrenched on higher ground and with an easier supply line. They also faced a series of intractable problems to do with terrain, logistics, relief, casualty evacuation, rest, protection from the elements, food and health. During the First World War many armies discovered to their cost that what was strategically desirable was often not operationally possible. This problem was confronted in extreme conditions at Gallipoli, where even tactical success was very difficult to achieve and rarely at acceptable cost. There is nothing in the experience of the 7th North Staffords to suggest that the Gallipoli campaign could ever have achieved the ambitious strategic and geo-political aims it was set and which it so signally failed to deliver.

115 *The Times*, 19 September 2015. Brigadier Mallinson was remarking specifically about Loos.

Part III

Support, Enablers and Constraints

19

"All this seemed full of promise": British Air Power and the Gallipoli campaign

Ross Mahoney

> *The Gallipoli adventure has a unique place in the history of war. For the first time a campaign was conducted by combined forces on, under, and over the sea, and on and over the land.*
>
> H.A. Jones[1]

> *[W]hen in future years the story of Helles and Anzac and Suvla is weighed, it will, I think, appear that had the necessary air service been built up from the beginning and sustained, the Army and Navy could have forced the Straits and taken Constantinople.*
>
> Major-General Sir Frederick Sykes[2]

"All this seemed full of promise."[3] This view, proferred by the first Royal Air Force (RAF) official historian, Sir Walter Raleigh, succinctly sums up the conclusions presented by his successor H.A. Jones, and Major-General Sir Frederick Sykes who, from August 1915 to the end of the campaign, commanded air assets at Gallipoli. Raleigh's hyperbolic statement related to the early use and testing of torpedoes during 1914-15 while referencing their use at Gallipoli. However, it could also be used as a metaphor for the failure of the Gallipoli campaign more broadly as well as more specifically the challenges that faced the Royal Naval Air Service (RNAS) throughout the campaign. Nevertheless, as Jones reflected in volume two of the RAF's official history, *The War in the Air*, this was the first time that all three services of the British military had been used together to seek a strategic aim.[4] The challenges that confronted the RNAS became evident when, in July 1915, Sykes delivered a damning report into the state of air assets at Gallipoli. Sykes, a British Army officer, was given command of the RNAS at Gallipoli and slowly delivered key changes in the provision of air support during the disastrous campaign in the Dardanelles, though problems persisted. Nevertheless, air power played an important role

1 H.A. Jones, *The War in the Air: Being the Story of the Part Played in the Great War by the Royal Air Force*, Vol. II (Oxford: The Clarendon Press, 1928), p. 75. Hereafter, cited as Jones, *OH*, Vol. II.
2 Frederick Sykes, *Aviation in Peace and War* (London: Edward Arnold & Company, 1922), p. 49.
3 Walter Raleigh, *The War in the Air: Being the Story of the Part Played in the Great War by the Royal Air Force*, Vol. I (Oxford, The Clarendon Press, 1922), p. 467.
4 Jones, *OH*, Vol. II, p. 75.

during the Gallipoli campaign, and it is the purpose of this chapter to consider some of the challenges and successes regarding the use of British military aviation in support of operations in the Dardanelles.

Writing the History of British Air Power at Gallipoli

Before examining the use of British air power at Gallipoli, it is appropriate to consider what has been written on the subject. In his preface to volume one of the British Army's official history of the Gallipoli campaign, published in 1929, Brigadier-General Cecil Aspinall-Oglander remarked that:

> In the original scheme for the official war histories it was decided that the operations in Gallipoli and the Dardanelles should be dealt with in two distinct compartments, the naval historian telling the story of the fleet's efforts, and the military historian that of the campaign on land.[5]

Aspinall-Oglander's remark is interesting for several reasons. First, it highlights the procedure that underpinned the writing of the official histories and the demarcation of responsibilities between the senior services for recording the history of the Gallipoli campaign. Second, and most importantly for this study, the preface suggests that Jones' work was not consulted in the production of the Aspinall-Oglander's volumes. It certainly does not appear in his bibliography (yet Sir Julian Corbett's relevant *Naval Operations* volumes and the Australian official history by Charles Bean, are listed).[6] We know that Aspinall-Oglander was aware of Jones' work, as it is clear that they knew each other and that the latter was not uncritical of the former's work.[7] We also know that volume two of *The War in the Air* dedicated 77 pages to the Gallipoli campaign.[8]

Jones' analysis was undoubtedly supported by a sizable narrative produced by the Air Historical Branch (AHB) because the Branch gathered "materials and [wrote] short accounts of operations" to support the official historian.[9] The AHB had been formed in July 1918 as the Air History Section of the Historical Section of the Committee of Imperial Defence (CID) and control transferred to the Air Ministry in 1920. Before becoming the official historian, Jones

5 C.F. Aspinall-Oglander, *Military Operations Gallipoli*, Vol. I (London: Heinemann, 1929), p. v. Hereafter cited as Aspinall-Oglander, *OH*, Vol. I.

6 While Aspinall-Oglander might not have been able to use volume two of *The War in the Air* (1928), to inform his first volume (published in 1929), it certainly could have been used for volume two. For examples of Corbett's and Bean's works see C.F. Aspinall-Oglander, *Military Operations Gallipoli*, Vol. II (London: Heinemann, 1932), p. 497. Hereafter, cited as Aspinall-Oglander, *OH*, Vol. II.

7 Royal Air Force Museum (RAFM), London, UK: X003-8803: H.A. Jones to Group Captain A.A. Walser, 2 November 1932.

8 Jones, *OH*, Vol. II, pp. 1-77.

9 Air Historical Branch (AHB), Ministry of Defence, UK: *The Dardanelles Campaign, 1914-1916: A Narrative prepared by the Air Historical Section*. Hereafter cited as *Narrative*. A copy of this document can be found at The National Archives (TNA), Kew, UK: AIR 1/681/21/13/2209. The author is grateful to Stuart Hadaway of the AHB for providing a copy of the version held by the Branch. John J. Abbatiello, *Anti-Submarine Warfare in World War I: British Naval Aviation and the First World War* (Abingdon: Routledge, 2006), pp. 137-8.

had joined the AHB in 1918 and served as its director between 1920 and 1923. By 1920, the role of the AHB was laid down, and one of the Branch's key responsibilities was the "supply of historical information and material, as required by the [...] official historians."[10] Given that the role of the AHB included the provision of material to the official historians the omission of Jones' volume from Aspinall-Oglander's volumes is perhaps even more curious, in that as well as covering aspects related to naval operations, the latter also noted the use of air power in both his volumes. Additionally, Aspinall-Oglander had served at Gallipoli on the General Staff of the Mediterranean Expeditionary Force (MEF) and would have been aware of the work of the RNAS.

Similarly, more recent contributions to the Gallipoli historiography have tended to overlook Jones' contribution to the field. For example, Jenny Macleod, in her otherwise excellent *Reconsidering Gallipoli*, did not discuss Jones when examining the influence of the official histories in shaping the early narratives surrounding our understanding of the campaign.[11] This is, perhaps, indicative of the land-centric focus of much of the writing about Gallipoli. Nevertheless, Jones' contribution remains relevant and the starting point for any analysis on the use of air power at Gallipoli. While at times he strained verity, Jones, for example, drew out the importance of control of the air during the campaign and stated:

> The Dardanelles formed a section over a vast front, every stretch of which cried out for the new air weapon. That enough material was found to ensure continuous air superiority over the peninsula was, perhaps, even more that might have been hoped.[12]

Given the status of what had, or had not been written in the various official histories, an important question remains concerning what has been written since volume two of *The War in the Air*. The reality is that little has been written on air power at Gallipoli despite the fact that the campaign "has been a beguiling and fruitful subject for historians."[13]

Building on the land-centric focus of the historiography, another issue in the literature is the link between the Gallipoli campaign and the birth of Australian national identity.[14] Here it is possible to suggest that one potential reason for the lack of focus on air power might well be that only one Australian, Captain A.H. Keith-Joppe has been readily identified as flying during the campaign.[15] The challenge here is one of identifying individual Australians who

10 Denis C. Bateman, 'The Record Holders,' *Air Clues*, 32:6 (1978), p. 211.
11 Jenny Macleod, *Reconsidering Gallipoli* (Manchester: Manchester University Press, 2004), pp. 57-102.
12 Jones, *OH*, Vol. II, p. 76.
13 Macleod, *Reconsidering Gallipoli*, p. 4.
14 On the challenges of viewing Australia's military past before 1915, see Craig Wilcox, 'Australian military history doesn't begin on Gallipoli,' in Craig Stockings (ed.), *Anzac's Dirty Dozen: 12 Myths of Australian Military History* (Sydney: New South Publishing, 2012), pp. 11-34. On issues surrounding Gallipoli and Australian national identity, with reference to Anzac Day, see Tom Frame (ed.), *Anzac Day: Then & Now* (Sydney: New South Publishing, 2016). Also, see Michael J.K. Walsh and Andrekos Varnava (eds.), *Australia and the Great War: Identity, Memory and Mythology* (Melbourne: Melbourne University Press, 2016).
15 Charles Samson, *Fights and Flights* (London: Ernest Benn, 1930), p. 225. A recent online article has identified another two Australians as flying during the campaign. These were Charles Miles and Shirley Goodwin. See Bernie Freyberg, 'Gunners over Gallipoli', *Aegean Air War, 1915-1918* <http://aegeanairwar.com/articles/gunners-over-gallipoli> It should, however, be noted that only

flew at Gallipoli in contrast to discrete Australian units that served during the campaign. Even the example of Keith-Joppe causes potential confusion as Air Commodore Charles Samson, who commanded No. 3 Squadron RNAS (later No. 3 Wing RNAS) at Gallipoli described him in 1930 as "Captain Jopp"; however, a roll of officers serving with the RNAS that was prepared for Lieutenant-General Sir Aylmer Hunter-Weston in 1927, shows him as Keith-Joppe.[16] Moreover, given the imperial composition of Britain's air arms at this time, and that the Australian Flying Corps did not serve at Gallipoli, it remains challenging to identify nationalities in a period when such concepts were fluidic within the British Empire. For example, Flight Sub-Lieutenant Cecil Horace Brinsmead, who died on 11 January 1916 at Gallipoli, was Australian by birth but served in the Royal Navy (his service record does not note his place of birth).[17]

Wing Commander Charles Samson.

The only book-length study of air power at Gallipoli is Hugh Dolan's competent 2013 *Gallipoli Air War*. However, this book is problematic, in part because there is no referencing to support the assertions made. For example, Dolan suggested that Jones relied on the Samson's "personal narrative" as found within the pages of the 'Mitchell Report' of 1919, which was eventually published in 1921.[18] The committee that produced the 'Mitchell Report' was established to

Goodwin appears on the officer roll of those who served at Gallipoli that was produced by the AHB, see TNA AIR 1/675/21/13/1563: Roll of Officers, Royal Naval Air Service, together with Officers, Warrant Officers, Midshipmen of the Royal Navy, RNR, RNVR, Royal Marines and Army, attached to the RNAS for Operations at the Dardanelles. However, as noted at the time, the list "may not be complete". See TNA AIR 1/675/21/13/1563: J. Morris, Director, Air Historical Branch to T.R. Barber, 4 March 1927.

16 Ibid. Hunter-Weston was trying to locate officers who had served during Gallipoli campaign, see TNA AIR 1/675/21/13/1563: Lieutenant-General Sir Aylmer Hunter-Weston to Air Vice-Marshal Sir Philip Game, Air Member for Personnel, 24 February 1927.

17 Royal Aero Club Aviator's Certificate Record Card for Flight Sub-Lieutenant Cecil Horace Brinsmead. Brinsmead died along with his observer, Lieutenant N.H. Boles of the Dorset Regiment, see Jones, *OH*, Vol. II, p. 75. At least one Canadian, Flight Sub-Lieutenant H.S. Kerby, served at Gallipoli, see TNA AIR 1/2386/228/11/10: War Experience of Flight Lieutenant H.S. Kerby, 19 August 1922. Kerby joined the RAF post-First World War and rose to the rank of Air Vice-Marshal. Adam Claasen has recently identified one New Zealander, William Angus, as flying as an observer at Gallipoli. Angus transferred to the RNAS as a mechanic and occasionally flew, see Adam Claasen, *Fearless: The Extraordinary Untold Story of New Zealand's Great War Airmen* (Auckland: Massey University Press, 2017), pp. 81-2. TNA AIR 76/55/75: Service Record for Flight Sub-Lieutenant Cecil Horace Brinsmead; TNA ADM 273/29/398: Service Record for Flight Sub-Lieutenant Cecil Horace Brinsmead.

18 Hugh Dolan, *Gallipoli Air War: The Unknown Story of the Fight for the Skies over Gallipoli* (Sydney: Macmillan, 2013), pp. 373-4; Australian War Memorial (AWM), Canberra: AWM 124, 3/48: 'Report of the Committee Appointed to Investigate the Attacks Delivered on and the Enemy Defences of the Dardanelles Straits' 1919. Hereafter cited as the 'Mitchell Report'.

consider lessons learnt from the Gallipoli campaign, and Arthur Marder described it as "highly significant," but he also noted that "the essential facts are lost in a mass of verbiage and a faulty layout."[19] In 1919, as a Group Captain, Samson was appointed as the RAF's representative to the committee, and there is evidence that he shared his original typewritten notes with the AHB as early as 1920.[20] However, Samson's work that supported the production of the 'Mitchell Report' was not a "personal narrative" as Dolan inferred. Samson's contribution was that of an experienced officer who had been appointed to a committee created to examine the lessons learnt from the Gallipoli campaign. Of all the RNAS or Royal Flying Corps (RFC) officers who served at Gallipoli, Samson arguably had the most experience of the campaign, thus making his appointment entirely appropriate and he was directed to produce relevant aspects of the report.[21] Moreover, Jones' chapter was almost certainly based, in part, on the narrative mentioned above, which while drawing heavily on the 'Mitchell Report' as a source of official rather than anecdotal evidence also included references from Sykes' report of July 1915.[22]

A key reason for relying heavily on the 'Mitchell Report' was because while many documents, such as Sykes' report, have been preserved, a number were apparently destroyed by Samson. As Jones reflected in a 1932 letter to Group Captain A.A. Walser concerning the problem of missing records:

> I tackled Samson on this point and he told me that he took a sheaf of records to Gallipoli when he went out with the Mitchell Committee, and that after he made his contribution to the Report, he burnt the records as being of no further use.[23]

In 1932, Walser was serving on the directing staff of the RAF Staff College at Andover, but in 1915, as an RFC captain attached to the RNAS, he served at Gallipoli. Walser also produced a reflection of his time at Gallipoli while a student at Andover in 1923 and 1924.[24] This wanton destruction of the historical record also built on the fact that during the Gallipoli campaign "nearly all of 3rd Wing's records" were destroyed in a fire on 4 November 1915.[25] A final problem with Dolan's work are some of the sources used, or at least quoted in the bibliography. It would appear that despite using material held by the RAF Museum, Dolan did not consult Sykes' papers at Hendon nor the latter's autobiography. Similarly, Dolan did not make use of Eric Ash's

19 The 'Mitchell Report', p. xiv; Ian Speller, 'In the Shadow of Gallipoli? Amphibious Warfare in the Inter-War Period,' in Jenny McLeod (ed.), *Gallipoli: Making History* (London: Frank Cass, 2004), pp. 140-41; Arthur Marder, 'The Dardanelles Revisited: Further Thoughts on the Naval Prelude,' in Marder, *From the Dardanelles to Oran: Studies of the Royal Navy in War and Peace, 1915-1940* (Annapolis, MD: Naval Institute Press, 2015 [1974]), p. 1, fn. 1.

20 Imperial War Museum (IWM), London, UK: 72/113/3/41: Personal Papers of Air Commodore Charles Samson, Note from the Air Historical Branch to Group Captain Charles Samson, 19 July 1920.

21 IWM 72/113/3/41: Samson Papers, Detailed Arrangement of Report and Allocation of Chapters to Members of the Committee, 10 July 1919.

22 AHB: *Narrative*, preface.

23 RAFM: X003-8803: H.A. Jones to Group Captain A.A. Walser, 22 November 1932.

24 A.A. Walser, 'Memories of Gallipoli 1915,' in AP1097: *A Selection of Lectures and Essays from the Work of Officers attending the Second Course at the Royal Air Force Staff College, 1923-1924* (London: Air Ministry, 1924).

25 RAFM: MFC77/13/30: Personal Papers of Major-General Sir Frederick Sykes, Wing Captain F.H. Sykes to the Director of Air Services, Admiralty, 24 January 1916.

biography of Sykes, which would have at least abrogated against the issue of not consulting the latter's papers.[26] Ash's chapter on Gallipoli remains a vital contribution to our understanding on the role of air power during the campaign and draws heavily on Sykes' papers. Despite these criticisms, at least Dolan has attempted to recount the role of air power during the Gallipoli campaign as little has been written on the subject. Other key contributions come from the Australian historian Christopher Clark and passages and mentions in various works, such as R.D. Layman's *Naval Aviation in the First World War* and Peter Liddle's *Men of Gallipoli*.[27]

Understanding the role of air power at Gallipoli is also further complicated by the fact that little is known in the English literature about the role of the Ottoman aviation squadrons during the campaign. In English, the key sources on Ottoman aerial activities remain the 'Mitchell Report' and the reports of Major Erich Serno published in *Cross & Cockade* in 1970.[28] While little information is available, what is known is that Ottoman aviation suffered similar problems to the RNAS at Gallipoli concerning the lack of airframes.[29] It was only towards the end of the campaign that Ottoman strength increased. As such, the picture of the air campaign is unbalanced. This is made more difficult by the absence of work on the deployment of a French squadron, 98T, into the theatre during the Gallipoli campaign.[30] However, Wing Commander Geoffrey Bromet, who served at Gallipoli as a flight lieutenant in the RNAS, reflected in his 1923 RAF Staff College essay on how well-equipped this unit was compared to Samson's.[31] This unit operated from Tenedos, and the lack of work on its operations mirrors patterns in the broader writing on Gallipoli that largely ignores the French experience. This failure is something that given the scope of this chapter, this work does not rectify. Nevertheless, given many of the problems noted above, perhaps the time has come for a closer examination of the Gallipoli campaign from an aerial perspective.

Strategy and planning

While planning for Gallipoli is considered elsewhere in this volume, it is worth reflecting that the process that led to the campaign provides essential context for the deployment of the RNAS into the theatre to support the expanding effort to force the Dardanelles. Assaulting the

26 Eric Ash, *Sir Frederick Sykes and the Air Revolution, 1912-1918* (London: Frank Cass, 1999), pp. 75-91.
27 Chris Clark, 'Naval Aviation at Gallipoli', in David Stevens and John Reeve (eds.), *Sea Power Ashore and in the Air* (Sydney: Halstead Press, 2007), pp. 77-89; R.D Layman, *Naval Aviation in the First World War: Its Impact and Influence* (London: Chatham Publishing, 1996); Peter Liddle, *Men of Gallipoli: The Dardanelles and Gallipoli Experience August 1914 to January 1916* (Newton Abbott: David & Charles Publishers, 1988), pp. 237-49; Keith Issacs, 'Wings Over Gallipoli', *Defence Force Journal*, 81 (1990), pp. 5-18.
28 Erich Serno (trans. Brian Flanagan), 'The History History of the Ottoman Air Force in the Great War: The Reports of Major Erich Serno', Part 1 & 2, *Cross & Cockade Journal*, 11:2 (1970), pp. 98-144.
29 Aspinall-Oglander, *OH*, Vol. I, p. 139.
30 A key exception to this is the description provided in René Martel, *French Strategic and Tactical Bombing Forces of World War I*, translated by Allen Suddaby, edited by Steven Suddaby (Lanham, Maryland: The Scarecrow Press, 2007), pp. 417-30. Martel's work originally appeared in 1939 as *L'aviation française de bombardement (des origines au 11 novembre 1918)* (Paris: P. Hartmann, 1939).
31 TNA AIR 1/2387/228/11/30: War Experience by Wing Commander Geoffrey Bromet, 1923, p. 20.

Dardanelles and the associated Straits as a means of taking Istanbul in the case of war with the Ottoman Empire had long been considered a method to achieve a strategic end.[32] In 1906, the CID, as part of a wider assessment into the defence of Egypt, considered the challenge of taking the Dardanelles by combined operation.[33] The conclusions of the CID made clear that any combined attack against Gallipoli should not be conducted if other means existed to coerce the Ottoman Empire. Given this conclusion it is perhaps unsurprising that thinking about taking the Straits remained moot; however, the signing of a defensive pact between Germany and the Ottoman Empire on 2 August 1914 and the subsequent entry of the latter into the First World War in November 1914, shifted British strategic thinking.

Two key challenges emerged for British planners at this point. First, the Ottoman entry into the war threatened Britain's vital sea lines of communication to India and the defence of Egypt. Second, and the area that has received the most attention from historians, was the emerging strategic debate over a Western versus an Eastern strategy concerning the prosecution of the war. The First Lord of the Admiralty, Winston Churchill, has become indelibly linked to the idea of an Eastern strategy and the view that attacking Germany's allies, such as the Ottomans, would bring the war to a close more quickly than an approach focused on the Western Front in France. However, as Christopher Bell has suggested, it is "difficult to sustain" Churchill's image as a committed "Easterner."[34] Nevertheless, on 25 November 1914, Churchill suggested that the best means to defend Egypt would be to attack the Asiatic coast of the Ottoman empire.[35] Then, in January 1915, the British War Council accepted this as part of planning to reduce the strain on the Russian Empire. From this point on planning moved from a "demonstration" by the Royal Navy towards preparations for an attempt to force the Dardanelles by naval action alone.[36] Nevertheless, on 16 February 1915, three days before the first bombardment of the forts at the entrance to the Dardanelles, it had been concluded that troops should be provided to support the operation.[37]

Of course, as history records, the subsequent bombardment of the forts did not go to plan. The initial bombardment of Ottoman positions on 19 February 1915 was unsuccessful, and a major attack on 18 March 1915 was nothing short of catastrophic with a third of the British and French fleet lost or damaged. These losses led the naval commander, Vice-Admiral John de Robeck, to withdrawal his ships. The failure to force the Straits, unfortunately, resulted in mission creep with little attendant consideration of the strategic goals sought from the campaign. The appointment of General Sir Ian Hamilton was an essential step towards the deployment of a force that eventually

32 Rhys Crawley, *Climax at Gallipoli: The Failure of the August Offensive* (Norman, OK: University of Oklahoma Press, 2014), p. 3.

33 The Liddell Hart Centre for Military Archives (LHCMA), King's College London: 7/4/1: Personal Papers of General Sir Ian Hamilton, Memorandum by the General Staff Upon the Possibility of a Joint Naval and Military Attack upon the Dardanelles, 20 December 1906; Arthur Marder, *From the Dreadnought to Scapa Flow: Vol. II: To the Eve of Jutland 1914-1916* (Barnsley: Seaforth Publishing, 2013 [1965]), pp. 199-200; Yigal Sheffy, *British Military Intelligence in the Palestine Campaign, 1914-1918* (London: Routledge, 2013 [1998]), p. 23.

34 Christopher M. Bell, *Churchill and Sea Power* (Oxford: Oxford University Press, 2013), p. 61.

35 Jones, *OH*, Vol. II, p. 5.

36 Ibid.

37 Bell, *Churchill and Sea Power*, p. 67.

totalled 12 divisions by the start of the August offensive.[38] Ultimately, the Gallipoli campaign was a failure due to a lack of strategic direction, poor intelligence and mitigating challenges such as a long line of communication, geography, and an underestimation of the enemy.

Despite these strategic challenges, from an air power perspective, as Clark has noted: "[W]hat makes the Gallipoli air campaign so notable is that British planners expected so much from the Navy's air arm less than six months after the start of World War I."[39] This expectation is, perhaps, not as surprising as it might appear at first sight. The Royal Navy had a history of being technologically innovative and the desire to use RNAS aircraft in support of an offensive, as afforded by the opportunity at Gallipoli, is not so strange.[40] Also, in the years leading up the First World War, both the British Army and Royal Navy had, despite challenges, become increasingly interested in the development of air power and its potential use in war.[41] Thus the deployment of the seaplane carrier HMS *Ark Royal*, commanded by Commander Robert Clark-Hall, to support the initial naval phase should be seen in this light. As early as mid-January 1915, *Ark Royal* and its attendant seaplanes were to be committed to the fleet destined for the Dardanelles and its pilots and observers were to be attached to the British Army in France for training in "observing artillery fire."[42] *Ark Royal*, described in 1923 by Bromet, who served onboard her in 1915, as "an extraordinarily efficient carrier," had been commissioned in 1914 as the first ship to be designed as a seaplane carrier.[43] The issue of observation, however, was to be a perennial problem for the RNAS throughout the Gallipoli campaign. For example, when discussions emerged in late-February and early-March 1915 concerning the deployment of Samson's squadron into the theatre after the initial failure to force the Straits, Colonel William Sefton Brancker, then acting Director of Military Aeronautics at the War Office, noted that "3 or 4" regular British Army officers should be attached to help with "observation."[44]

Air power, both in support of naval and land forces, was one of the means by which Allied strategic ends could be enabled. There were, however, as this chapter discusses, problems, for example, in the form of technology and the uncoordinated character of the RNAS at this point of the war. Another problem not often reflected on, but one linked to the nascent character of aviation technology in this period, was the impact of weather and climatic conditions in the conduct of efficient air operations. For example, on 9 March 1915, in his report to the Admiralty, Clark-Hall noted that on days when flights did not occur, there had "usually been

38 For the most recent analysis of the problems associated with the August offensive, see Crawley, *Climax at Gallipoli*, passim.
39 Clark, 'Naval Aviation at Gallipoli', p. 77.
40 In this chapter the term aircraft is used as an umbrella terms for heavier-than-air craft. When referring specifically to seaplanes or aeroplanes those terms are used.
41 For example, on the challenge of doctrinal development of the RFC and RNAS before the First World War, see James Pugh, 'Oil and Water: A Comparison of Military and Naval Aviation Doctrine in Britain, 1912-1914' in Michael LoCicero, Ross Mahoney and Stuart Mitchell (eds.), *A Military Transformed?: Adaptation and Innovation in the British Military, 1792-1945* (Solihull: Helion & Company, 2014), pp. 124-38.
42 Stephen Roskill (ed.), *Documents Relating to the Naval Air Service: Vol. I: 1908-1918* (London: Spottiswoode for The Navy Records Society, 1969), p. 193; Christopher Bell, *Churchill and the Dardanelles* (Oxford: Oxford University Press, 2017), pp. 93-4.
43 TNA AIR 1/2387/228/11/30: War Experience, p. 6
44 LHCMA: Hamilton Papers, 7/1/3: Letter from W.S. Brancker to Hamilton, 1 March 1915; 'Mitchell Report', p. 518.

HMS *Ark Royal.*

a gale blowing of force from 8 to 10" or the sea had been too "rough for seaplanes to get off."[45] Despite challenges, as mission creep set in, air power became increasingly important for planners because, primarily, aviation assets, both heavier and lighter-than-air, provided the ways in which to support operations by delivering intelligence to planners as well as attacking targets, such as enemy logistical networks. The increasing importance of air power is evident from the support given to Sykes after his report into the state of aviation assets at Gallipoli and the subsequent relative growth of forces deployed. Also, when Colonel Maurice Hankey, the Secretary of the CID, reported on on the situation at Gallipoli to the British Government in late-August 1915, he noted that it was too early to report on the effect of air power due to Sykes' recent appointment to solve the problems the latter had identified. Despite this, on a positive note, Hankey also reflected that "every confidence is felt in the future."[46] However, Hankey also repeated many of the challenges that Sykes outlined in his report as discussed below and which would continue to be a limiting factor on air operations in the theatre. Over the course of the campaign, in-theatre aviation assets grew from the six seaplanes and two aeroplanes onboard *Ark Royal* to two aeroplane wings, No. 2 and No. 3, one seaplane squadron consisting of *Ark Royal* and HMS *Ben-My-Chree*, two kite balloon sections on HMS *Manica* and HMS *Hector*, and one SS airship section, with one airship in August 1915.[47]

Command challenges

Perhaps the critical challenge that emerged during the Gallipoli campaign was that of command and control of air assets in theatre. This challenge was one of conflicting personalities and service

45 TNA AIR 1/2099/207/20/7: Commanding Officer, HMS *Ark Royal*, to the Director, Air Department, 9 March 1915.
46 LHCMA: Hamilton Papers, 7/4/33: The Dardanelles: Memorandum on the Situation, 30 August 1915, p. 13.
47 'Mitchell Report', p. 519.

backgrounds that generated friction and has focused on the two principal protagonists: Samson, an RNAS officer, and Sykes, an RFC officer. Both had developed well-deserved reputations since the formation of the "joint" RFC in 1912. Samson was considered a brave and courageous officer, and while this was fine for leading from the front, his ability to manage and administer the requirements of air power in theatre led much to be desired. Even Stephen Roskill admitted that Samson's "idiosyncratic methods did not always endear him to those in authority."[48] No. 3 Squadron deployed to the Dardanelles during March 1915, though it is evident from a letter from Brancker to Hamilton on 1 March 1915 that had resources been available then the preference would have been for an RFC unit.[49] This was because Brancker had concerns about the ability of the RNAS to provide the necessary situational awareness required for the planned land phase of the Gallipoli campaign. However, the Secretary of State for War, Lord Kitchener, decided that the "air requirements of the army must be met by" the RNAS.[50] Also, given the geography of the air campaign with assets operating from island bases and flying over water, it is questionable whether the deployment of RFC units would have been effective. In highlighting contemporary views of Samson's abilities, it is worth reflecting that in the same letter to Hamilton, Brancker also quipped that Samson would "probably bring his own newspaper correspondent with him."[51] Nevertheless, despite such concerns, as Bell noted, the deployment of Samson's squadron illustrated a growing awareness of the increasing importance of air power to the campaign.[52] However, as Ash later observed concerning Samson:

> [He] was a courageous flyer, but well-known for his occasional lack of tact and unco-operative attitude. When visitors, regardless of rank, would walk across the airfield at 3rd Wing to reach his office, he would yell at them with a megaphone: "Get off my bloody aerodrome!"[53]

This attitude was hardly the professional officer needed to command air power in what rapidly became a complex combined operation. Furthermore, Samson's reputation as a problematic staff officer never appears to have improved.[54]

After the challenges encountered during the landings of 25 April 1915 and subsequent operations, it became apparent that it was necessary to examine the RNAS' requirements in the theatre to support operations at Gallipoli. At this point, the Admiralty sought the support of the War Office, which led to Colonel Sykes' appointment to produce a report on the RNAS at Gallipoli. While spotting and reconnaissance were conducted with vigour up to this point, there were challenges, such as inexperienced crews, poor techniques and wireless matters. As such, on 25 May 1915, the Admiralty requested Sykes' services, and by 24 June 1915, he was at

48 Roskill (ed.), *Documents Relating to the Naval Air Service*, p. 205, fn. 1.
49 LHCMA: Hamilton Papers, 7/1/3: Letter from W.S. Brancker to Hamilton, 1 March 1915.
50 Aspinall-Oglander, *OH*, Vol. I, p. 139; LHCMA: Hamilton Papers, 7/1/3: Letter from W.S. Brancker to Hamilton, 1 March 1915.
51 LHCMA: Hamilton Papers, 7/1/3: Letter from W.S. Brancker to Hamilton, 1 March 1915.
52 Bell, *Churchill and the Dardanelles*, p. 128.
53 Ash, *Sir Frederick Sykes*, p. 76.
54 TNA AIR 2/300: Minute from the Chief of the Air Staff to the Secretary of State for Air, 28 July 1927.

Gallipoli.[55] At this time, Sykes was, arguably, the RFC's leading airman, though he was a difficult officer with whom to work. Sykes spent a fortnight inspecting operations at Gallipoli and compiling his report, which included participating in a kite balloon operation flown off *Manica* that was supporting an attack on Chanak. Sykes later described this experience:

> One of the most wonderful sights I have ever seen was the observer's basket of the kite-balloon let up from s.s. "Manica" in June 1915. We were spotting for the guns of H.M.S. "Lord Nelson" bombarding Chanak. The sky and sea were a marvellous blue and visibility excellent, the peninsula, where steady firing was going on all the time, lay below us, the Straits, with their ships and boats, the Asiatic shore gradually disappearing in a golden haze, the Gulf of Xeros, the Marmora, and behind one the islands of the Aegean affording a perfect background. No one who was at the Dardanelles, however vivid the horrors and the heat and dust and flies, will forget the beauty of the scene, especially at sunset, and it was seen at its best from the basket of a kite-balloon.[56]

Importantly, in compiling his report, Sykes sought views from many sources including commanders on the ground.[57]

While Sykes' report was an essential point in the development of air power at Gallipoli, it is worth considering that the decision to send him to the Mediterranean is shrouded in a discussion over his removal from France in 1915. Andrew Boyle, in his 1962 biography of Marshal of the Royal Air Force Lord Trenchard, suggested that Major-General Sir David Henderson, the General Officer Commanding of the RFC, fired Sykes.[58] Given the animosity that existed at the time and subsequently between Trenchard and Sykes, this interpretation needs to be treated with caution. Still, while Sykes' personality is probably best described as prickly, and would continue to generate challenges during his career, it is clear that when the opportunity arose to use his abilities elsewhere, Henderson did not object. Nonetheless, Sykes had developed a good reputation and the request to examine the problems at Gallipoli came from the Admiralty.[59] As Ash has reflected, Skyes' so-called "exile" was not a "demotion but a promotion."[60] Yet, by the end of the Gallipoli campaign, Sykes' appointment had, in a relative sense, led him to be demoted in comparison to his peers, notably Trenchard, who had become a brigadier-general and commanded the RFC in France. As Sykes reflected in a letter to Churchill in November 1915, "[A]ll the Wing Commanders in France who were under me are now Brigadier-Generals

55 RAFM: Sykes Papers, MFC77/13/26: Admiralty to the Secretary, War Office, 25 May 1915; Sykes, *From Many Angles*, p. 162.
56 Sykes, *Aviation in Peace and War*, p. 73.
57 Sykes, *From Many Angles*, p. 162.
58 Andrew Boyle, *Trenchard: Man of Vision* (London: Collins, 1962), p. 139. Little has been written about Henderson; however, for an examination of his role in 1914 and early-1915, see James Pugh, 'David Henderson and Command of the Royal Flying Corps', in Spencer Jones (ed.), *Stemming the Tide: Officers and Leadership in the British Expeditionary Force, 1914* (Solihull: Helion & Company, 2013), pp. 263-90.
59 RAFM: Sykes Papers, MFC77/13/26: Admiralty to the Secretary, War Office, 25 May 1915.
60 Ash, *Sir Frederick Sykes*, p. 67.

(they were junior to me [...] and have been put over my head for some unknown reason)."[61] Sykes' letter, written to someone who had recently fallen from power due to his association with the Gallipoli campaign, is interesting because while it concerned the requirements needed to conduct operations in the most efficient means possible, it is also clear that Sykes did not want RFC units to be deployed into the theatre for both personal and practical reasons. At this point of the Gallipoli campaign, some consideration was being given to reinforcing the RNAS with RFC units. At a practical level, Sykes felt that this would upset the coordination that was slowly evolving at Gallipoli while at a personal level he was concerned with his standing as commander of the air assets in theatre, though he did reflect that this might be considered petty.[62] Concerning this latter point, it is worth highlighting that Sykes did not quote this section of his letter to Churchill in his 1942 autobiography.[63]

Sykes' report was wide-ranging, and he made several recommendations to improve the situation. The principal recommendation was one of centralisation in key areas. First, Sykes argued for the centralised control of air units under one officer who would co-ordinate operations with the vice-admiral of the Eastern Mediterranean Squadron (EMS) and the General Officer Commanding-in-Chief of the MEF.[64] This arrangement would then allow that officer to task units appropriately (similar to the modern idea of centralised control and decentralised execution). Sykes did not simply assume that this was the right recommendation but provided alternative schemes for commanding air assets.[65] However, based on previous experience, Sykes concluded that centralisation was best for several reasons including the efficient utilisation of both personnel and equipment that were his other key concerns. Sykes' further recommendations focussed on the broader theme of centralisation and the challenge of logistics (discussed below). Nevertheless, while Sykes' report made efficient and fruitful suggestions about how to improve the situation at Gallipoli, he may have also created the situation that generated tension between himself and Samson. Despite noting Samson's "assistance", Sykes also suggested that if the contents of his report were approved and to be implemented, then he was the person to do it.[66] Sykes wrote that "it will I think be advisable that I should initiate the arrangements under the instructions of the G.O.C-in-C and Vice Admiral."[67] Sykes, having returned to Britain, was appointed to command the RNAS on 24 July and returned to Gallipoli.

While Sykes' argument made sense given his experience, it created tension between those officers responsible for implementing the changes laid out in the report. Additionally, as Ash has suggested, Sykes' report sought to apply a "Western Front" model into a complex theatre where relationships had to be managed between both the British Army and Royal Navy.[68] The

61 RAFM: Sykes Papers, MFC77/13/45: Wing Captain F.H. Sykes to Winston Churchill, 4 November 1915, p. 8.
62 Ibid.; Ash, *Sir Frederick Sykes*, pp. 83-4.
63 Sykes, *From Many Angles*, pp. 178-80.
64 RAFM: Sykes Papers, MFC77/13/28: Report on RNAS Units and the Aerial Requirements of the Naval and Military Force at the Dardanelles by Colonel F.H. Sykes, 9 July 1915, pp. 5-6. Hereafter, cited as *The Sykes Report*.
65 Ibid., pp. 6-7.
66 RAFM: Sykes Papers, MFC77/13/28: Covering letter from Colonel Sykes to the Secretary, the Admiralty, 9 July 1915.
67 Ibid.
68 Ash, *Sir Frederick Sykes*, pp. 77-8.

Admiralty tried to manage this tension by appointing Sykes to a temporary commission as a colonel in the Royal Marines.[69] However, this appears to have created further tension even though Samson recorded in 1930 that:

> [C]olonel Sykes and his staff didn't worry me at all, but left me to go on in my own routine as usual, the only thing being that we had to send in reports to him as well as to the usual people; in fact, as far as my wing was concerned they might have not been there at all.[70]

Interestingly, Samson's reflection supports the argument that while Sykes centralised aspects of command and control, he left his subordinates to execute the air campaign. Additionally, in 1928, Rear-Admiral Murray Sueter, who at the time of Gallipoli, as a commodore, was director of the Royal Navy's Air Department, praised Sykes for his "valuable help" in the Dardanelles and that he had "felt with [Sykes] and Samson's good efforts everything would go well, and it did."[71]

Despite these post-facto reflections, these sources need to be treated with care as it is evident the views presented by Samson are not wholly accurate. While Sykes might have left Samson to get on with his "routine as usual," in August 1915, de Robeck wrote to the Admiralty describing an "unfortunate publication of the air department."[72] He was referring to letters from Samson that criticised Sykes. While these letters predated the Gallipoli campaign, de Robeck was clearly concerned about the relationship between the two. Indeed, in July 1915 Sueter recognised the need to manage relations between Sykes and Samson.[73] Lieutenant-Colonel L.H. Strain, who, as a lieutenant in the Royal Naval Volunteer Reserve served as Sykes' head of operations and intelligence, later reflected on Sykes' appointment:

> There could have been no more ill-conceived appointment. Samson, who was senior to Sykes, had stated some time before that he thought nothing of Sykes and would refuse to work with, much less under, him, and this letter had, for some unknown reason, been published by the Admiralty.[74]

Strain argued that "all distrusted Sykes' ability to command."[75] This is a serious criticism and indictment of Sykes' abilities and highlights his character faults, which may have already caused

69 RAFM: Sykes Papers, MFC77/13/26: Admiralty to Colonel Sykes, 24 July 1915.
70 Samson, *Fights and Flights*, p. 265.
71 Murray F. Sueter, *Airmen or Noahs: Fair Play for our Airmen: The Great "Neon" Air Myth Exposed* (London: Sir Isaac Pitman & Sons 1928), p. 47.
72 TNA AIR 1/361/15/228/17: Extract from a semi-official letter to the First Sea Lord from Vice Admiral de Robeck, 25 August 1915.
73 Ash, *Sir Frederick Sykes*, p. 80.
74 RAFM: Personal Papers of Lieutenant-Colonel L.H. Strain, AC75/33/3/2: Typed Reminiscence (n.d.), pp. 74-5. Strain's reminiscence, in effect an unpublished memoir, has no date; however, given several indications within the text, it is likely that it can be dated to 1940. Specifically, when describing operations on 18 March, Strain reflected "[A]s I write, it is twenty-five years to a day since the attack." See Typed Reminiscence, p. 47. This unpublished memoir was based on an inconsistent diary of the period. See RAFM: Strain Papers, AC75/33/3/3: Diary of Lieutenant-Colonel L.H. Strain, 1915.
75 RAFM: Strain Papers, AC75/33/3/2: Typed Reminiscence, p. 75.

him problems in his relationship with senior RFC officers, including Trenchard. Sykes may have been an intelligent and able staff officer, but it is clear that tact and temperament were not in his repertoire and made it difficult for him to lead as he took on increasingly more senior roles as the war progressed. While de Robeck hoped that Sykes and Samson would "work together," by late-September, the Director of Air Services at the Admiralty, Rear-Admiral C.L. Vaughan-Lee, recommended that Samson be posted back to Britain (though this took time due to the increase in strength in theatre and lack of officers with necessary experience).[76] On the issue of relations between Sykes and Samson, Strain recollected that:

> It was a strained atmosphere until I had a heart to heart talk with Samson who was too keen on getting our job done to nurse his resentment at the expense of the Service.[77]

Furthermore, it is evident from Sykes' autobiography that he was at least tangentially aware that Samson was "extremely hurt" by the "unpleasant task" of taking over command, and he noted that he was "grateful" to him for his support.[78] Finally, it would appear, for at least pragmatic reasons, Sykes was not happy when he received news that Samson was to be posted back to Britain.[79]

On arrival at Gallipoli in August 1915, Sykes outlined his plan for the reorganisation of the RNAS in the theatre that, while facing numerous ongoing challenges, began the process of developing some cohesion to the work of the RNAS in supporting both the EMS and MEF. Sykes' views were accepted by de Robeck, to whom he reported, and on 26 August 1915, the latter outlined the reorganisation of RNAS units.[80] The eventual deployment of No. 2 Wing RNAS increased assets in theatre, and Sykes took on the role of the key air commander and advisor on operations in theatre. This appointment rationalised and improved the control of air assets; however, while the situation slowly improved it is worth reflecting that while Sykes reported to de Robeck, this did not see him separated from the MEF's command and control arrangments. It is evident that there was a line of responsibility to Hamilton and his commanders – the RNAS was, in part, in the theatre to provide support to their operations. Furthermore, personal contacts and socialisation were maintained between Hamilton and Samson and latterly Sykes.[81] For example both Samson and Hamilton visited W Beach at Cape Helles shotly after the landings.[82] Indeed, it was just after the landings that Samson began the process of selecting a suitable site for what became the advanced landing ground at Cape Helles whose "usefulness [...] outweighed its disadvantages."[83] Key amongst the disadvantages was its proximity to Ottoman artillery which led to the loss of at least four aircraft.

76 TNA AIR 1/361/15/228/17: Minute by the Director of Air Services, 27 September 1915; AIR 1/361/15/228/17: Minute by the Director of Air Services, 3 November 1915.
77 RAFM: Strain Papers, AC75/33/3/2: Typed Reminiscence, p. 75.
78 Sykes, *From Many Angles*, p. 170.
79 RAFM: Sykes Papers, MFC77/13/35: Wing Captain F.H. Sykes to Vice-Admiral Commanding EMS, 13 December 1915.
80 RAFM: Sykes Papers, MFC77/13/33: Vice-Admiral Commanding EMS to Wing Captain F.H. Sykes, 21 August 1915; and Eastern Mediterranean Squadron Confidential Memoranda No. 6 – Reorganisation of RNAS Units, 26 August 1915.
81 For example, see LHCMA: Hamilton Papers, 7/4/9: Diary Entries, 15 April, and 20 September 1915.
82 LHCMA: Hamilton Papers 7/4/9: Diary Entry, 30 April 1915.
83 Samson, *Fights and Flights*, p. 238; 'Mitchell Report', p. 512.

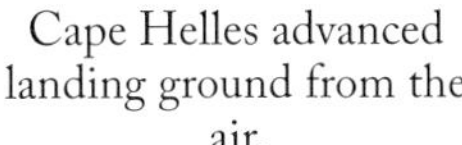
Cape Helles advanced landing ground from the air.

One of the first improvements to emerge from Sykes' report was the move and concentration of units from Tenedos to Imbros Island. Eventually, another airfield was built at Imbros for No. 2 Wing, though it took a while for this unit to get fit for purpose. The concentration of assets allowed for better communication with GHQ MEF and improved co-operation between the services, which had been indifferent at best. Sykes also created a staff to support the increasingly complex air situation; however, even here challenges exist relating to our understanding of the personalities at play. For example, in his autobiography, Sykes recollected that he appointed Major P.R.C. Groves as his head of operations.[84] However, Strain, in his reminiscences, recalled being put in charge of "operations and intelligence" by Sykes when the latter arrived in August 1915.[85] Why Sykes failed to note this is perhaps down to issues of personality and that Strain got on with Samson. Additionally, Strain's appointment was clearly temporary while Sykes organised his staff and brought in those officers he wanted.[86] That Strain was in charge of both operations and intelligence supports this view as Sykes recollected placing 'E.A.O.A. Jamieson and O.W. Raikes' in charge of the latter in his autobiography.[87]

Despite personality challenges, Sykes continued to assess his capabilities, and by autumn, had concluded that his two key roles were to provide better situational awareness to land and

84 Sykes, *From Many Angles*, p. 171.
85 RAFM: Strain Papers, AC75/33/3/2: Typed Reminiscence, p. 75
86 Ibid., p. 80.
87 Sykes, *From Many Angles*, p. 171.

naval forces as well as attacking Ottoman logistics in an attempt to cut off supplies.[88] This did not, however, stop Sykes from seeking to expand his force. On 21 October 1915, for instance, Sykes argued for expanding the RNAS in theatre.[89] His reasoning comprised of two factors. First, air assets at Gallipoli were inadequate for his current priorities – providing support to the MEF and the EMS. Second, Sykes took his argument for expansion further by looking towards the future and recognising that the control of the air could only maintained if the forces deployed were strengthened. Sykes recognised that it was unlikely that the enemy would not seek to reinforce their own air arm and noted that the time was coming where an Ottoman "aerial offensive" was probable. To combat this, and to carry out a "strong aerial offensive" (that included bombing), Sykes' forces would require reinforcement and expansion to ensure continued "command of the air."[90]

Sykes' desire to expand his force should also be understood within the context of the expanding war of 1915. While at a strategic level, it might be wrong to label Sykes an "easterner," he believed that if enough resources were provided, then the Gallipoli campaign had a chance to succeed and that the RNAS could have had a greater impact on the course of the campaign.[91] In this respect, in 1942, Sykes described Gallipoli as "the most tragic episode of the Great War."[92] On 15 October 1915, Sykes, writing to de Robeck, grasped that the potential entry of Bulgaria into the war would change the character of operations in the Eastern Mediterranean. It was at this point that Sykes argued for the centralised control of air assets in the region not just at Gallipoli.[93] This argument built on those of his July 1915 report. Sykes believed that the campaign would continue through 1916 and began to develop views about how the RNAS might bomb Constantinople.[94] Interestingly, when Samson advocated similar plans in September, de Robeck vetoed them on the grounds that valued aircrews may be lost, but mostly because he did not believe the operation would have the strategic effect it sought to achieve.[95]

The view that the Gallipoli campaign might have succeeded was shared by Sykes' head of operations, Groves, who in 1934 described the initial attack as an "admirable strategy."[96] While Groves did not specifically reference air power at Gallipoli, it is evident that he viewed the use of aviation as Britain's key means of military power. The emergence of air power in the early years of the twentieth century presented a challenge to Britain's so-called traditional "way in warfare." Indeed, even by the time of the Gallipoli campaign there were those who viewed air power as

88 Ash, *Sir Frederick Sykes*, p. 81.
89 RAFM: Sykes Papers, MFC77/13/34: Memorandum by Wing Captain Sykes to Vice-Admiral Commanding EMS, 21 October 1915.
90 Ibid., p. 8.
91 On British strategic debates, see David French, *British Strategy and War Aims, 1914-1916* (Abingdon: Routledge, 2014 [1986]). For a brief and useful introduction to the so-called "side-shows", see Gary Sheffield, *Forgotten Victory – The First World War: Myths and Realities* (London: Review, 2002 [2001]), pp. 94-7.
92 Sykes, *From Many Angles,* p. 186.
93 RAFM: Sykes Papers, MFC77/13/31: Wing Captain, RNAS to Vice-Admiral, EMS, 15 October 1915; Sykes, *From Many Angles*, p. 178.
94 RAFM: Sykes Papers, MFC77/13/45: Wing Captain F.H. Sykes to Winston Churchill, 4 November 1915, p. 6.
95 RAFM: Sykes Papers, MFC77/13/31: Vice-Admiral Eastern Mediterranean Squadron to Wing Commander, No. 3 Wing, 18 September 1915.
96 P. R.C. Groves, *Behind the Smoke Screen* (London: Faber & Faber, 1934), p. 262.

potentially having strategic effect and influencing the outcome of war either independent of, or at least as equals with the other services. In 1914, for example, Colonel George Aston, a Royal Marine officer who specialised in combined operations, reflected that the impact of air power might be such that it would no longer suffice to study "strategy from the 'amphibious' point of view."[97]

Given the context of drifting opinions over the continuation of the Gallipoli campaign, Sykes' ideas, while illustrating a degree of strategic thinking, also showed that his "visionary" views could, at times, be out of place to the reality of the situation. Nonetheless, it is evident from both Sykes' memoranda, and the views of the Air Department of the Admiralty, that while air power could, and did, have a tactical effect, it was only by providing a broad strategic picture that assets could be effectively employed at key points in support of operations. Despite these views and as discussed in further detail below, the key challenge for Sykes was the battle for resources with the Admiralty who, despite providing resources, did not reinforce Sykes to the level he ultimately wanted: on 20 October, for example, the total force at Gallipoli totalled 69 aircraft of all types, though serviceability meant that only a proportion of this strength was ever available at one time; by the time of the evacuation only 15 pilots, 12 observers and 17 aeroplanes were "fit to fly."[98]

Air power roles

As Clark wrote, "it is amazing how many of the roles for which air power was employed were actually performed by the machines available to the RNAS contingent at the Dardanelles [...]"[99] In a modern sense, the RNAS conducted three roles readily identifiable in modern capstone air power doctrine: control of the air, attack, and intelligence and situational awareness. More specifically, operations conducted over Gallipoli covered reconnaissance and observation, aerial photography, anti-shipping strikes, anti-submarine patrols, bombing and interdiction, and air superiority operations.

The need for air superiority has been little discussed, in part, because of what little has been written in English on the Ottoman aviation squadrons during the First World War. In the early phase of the Gallipoli campaign Ottoman operations were limited due to a lack of airframes with only "two or three aeroplanes and one seaplane available."[100] Also, from January 1915, the Ottoman squadrons were in the process of being reformed by the Germans. The German officer, Erich Serno, who was loaned to them as Inspector of Air Services, took a hands-on approach to his new command and in March 1915 conducted the first Ottoman reconnaissance of the Anglo-French fleet attempting to force the Dardanelles.[101] These factors initially limited the

97 George Aston, *Sea, Land and Air Strategy: A Comparison* (Boston: Little Brown, 1914), p. 264. On Aston, see Jim Beach, 'The British Army, the Royal Navy, and the "big work" of Sir George Aston, 1904-1914', *Journal of Strategic Studies*, 29:1 (2006), pp. 145-68.

98 RAFM: Sykes Papers, MFC77/13/48: Major-General Sir F.H. Sykes to General Sir Ian Hamilton, 22 November 1919.

99 Clark, 'Naval Aviation at Gallipoli,' p. 80.

100 AWM, AWM 124, 'Mitchell Report', p. 513.

101 Edward J. Erickson, *Ordered to Die: A History of the Ottoman Army in the First World War* (Westport: Connecticut: Greenwood Press, 2001), p. 228; Serno, 'The Reports of Major Erich Serno,' p. 106;

impact of Ottoman air power on the campaign though this began to change towards the end of 1915.

Although it was recognised in 1915 that control of the air was necessary over the battlespace, how to achieve this state was much more challenging. In 1915, air-to-air combat was in its infancy. However, Sykes recognised the importance of competing for control of the air and linked the need for an increasing number of aeroplanes to the need to be able to "retain complete command of the air" in the case of potential enemy air action.[102] Given the numbers of Ottoman aeroplanes in theatre, opportunities for air-to-air combat were limited as well as being affected by the state of aircraft development. For example, in one of the rare air-to-air engagements of the campaign, on 22 June 1915, Flight Commander C.H. Collet and his observer, Major R.E.T. Hogg, an RFC officer, shot down an Ottoman aeroplane near Achi Baba. It took 20 minutes to bring the aeroplane down using a rifle. To ensure the aeroplane was destroyed, Collett and Hogg returned later to bomb it, though it had been moved. Eventually, the Ottoman aeroplane was located by French aeroplanes and destroyed by French artillery.[103]

Hogg reported on this action in one of several reports he wrote to the War Office during his service at Gallipoli. While Hogg's motivation for writing them is unclear, they nonetheless illustrate a willingness to share knowledge between theatres.[104] Hogg's reports dealt with a range of issues ranging from his involvement in operations to general observations on matters such as co-operation with ships. Through the Directorate of Military Aeronautics, copies of the reports made their way to various units of the RFC including the recently formed Fourth and Fifth Wings, the Administrative Wing, and the Central Flying School.[105] Copies were also sent to the Admiralty and most significantly, to the RFC in France.[106] There is also evidence that they were further distributed to squadron level, at least in Britain.[107] This all suggests that even in 1915, the British Army and its constituent arms, in this case the RFC, through officers attached to the RNAS, shared knowledge concerning the challenges that they confronted on

James Streckfuss, *Eyes All Over the Sky: Aerial Reconnaissance in the First World War* (Oxford: Casemate Publishers, 2016), p. 63.

102 RAFM: Sykes Papers, MFC77/13/34: Memorandum by Wing Captain, RNAS, to Vice-Admiral, Eastern Mediterranean Squadron, 21 October 1915, p. 8.

103 TNA AIR 1/2119/207/72/2: Notes (third) by Major R.E.T. Hogg, C.I.E, Central India Horse, attached to the R.F.C as Observer on aeroplane work carried out in conjunction with operations on the Gallipoli Peninsula and Asiatic Mainland, 25 June 1915, p. 3; Jones, *OH*, Vol. II, p. 55.

104 For the original copies of Hogg's reports, see TNA AIR 1/137/15/40/273: Notes on Aeroplane Work Carried out in Connection with the Operations on the Gallipoli Peninsula and Asiatic Mainland, 9 May to 19 July 1915.

105 TNA AIR 1/137/15/40/273: Captain, General Staff for Deputy Director of Military Aeronautics to the Officer Commanding, Administrative Wing, RFC, 11 July 1915; Captain, General Staff for Deputy Director of Military Aeronautics to the Commandant, Central Flying School, 19 July 1915; Captain, General Staff for Deputy Director of Military Aeronautics to the Officer Commanding, 4th Wing, RFC, 19 July 1915; Captain, General Staff for Deputy Director of Military Aeronautics to the Officer Commanding, 5th Wing, RFC, 19 July 1915.

106 TNA AIR 1/137/15/40/273: Captain, General Staff for Deputy Director of Military Aeronautics to the Director, Air Department, Admiralty, 19 July 1915; Captain, General Staff for Deputy Director of Military Aeronautics to the General Officer Commanding, RFC in the Field, 19 July 1915.

107 TNA AIR 1/2119/207/72/2: Adjutant, Administrative Wing, RFC, to Captain F.L. Cogan, No. 2 Reserve Aeroplane Squadron, 24 July 1915

Extemporised Ottoman anti-aircraft guns.

various fronts. It is hard to assess from the archival record what further impact these reports had beyond being shared between units.[108]

As well as air-to-air action, the Ottomans also used counter-air operations and sought to attack Allied air assets at their source. For example, on 28 March 1915, *Ark Royal* was attacked by Ottoman aeroplanes in an attempt to limit her operations, though little damage was done to the ship.[109] Additionally, to counter the lack of aeroplanes in theatre, the Ottomans sought to battle for control of the air through the use of ground-based air defences (GBAD). As the 'Mitchell Report' reflected, "[T]he Turks very early realised that anti-aircraft guns were a necessity to force our aeroplanes to keep at high-altitude and to protect their bases."[110] This latter point is important because as well as the fleeting opportunities for aerial combat, the Allied air arms at Gallipoli also undertook a counter-air campaign to maintain control of the air. For example, on 5 July 1915, 10 British and French aeroplanes attacked Chanak and essentially wiped out the 1st Aviation Squadron, though the Germans continually reinforced it with new aeroplanes and pilots.[111] As well as having to deal with the threat of enemy GBAD, Allied air assets also contended with the threat of being shot at by friendly troops. This was not an

108 On issues related to inter-theatre learning in the British Army during the First World War, see Aimée Fox-Godden, 'Beyond the Western Front: The Practice of Inter-Theatre Learning in the British Army during the First World War,' *War in History*, 23:2 (2016), pp. 190-209.

109 TNA AIR 1/2387/228/11/30: War Experience; TNA AIR 1/2099/207/20/7: HMS *Ark Royal* – Report of Operations No. 11, 28 March 1915.

110 'Mitchell Report', p. 502.

111 Clark, 'Naval Aviation at Gallipoli', p. 87.

unheard of experience in the early days of the First World War as many troops were unused to operating in conjunction with aircraft. The situation was made more complicated as the RNAS provided support for land forces at Gallipoli, and before the landings of 25 April 1915, the MEF issued orders clarifying the rules of engagement to ground troops operating against enemy aeroplanes.[112]

The Allies generally maintained control of the air throughout, although it became increasingly difficult to maintain air superiority against the Ottomans towards the end of the campaign. Indeed, Commodore Roger Keyes blamed Sykes for what he perceived as the loss of air superiority by the RNAS.[113] Nevertheless, given the role played by the RNAS in supporting the withdrawal from Gallipoli, the air arm continued to combat for control of the air. Any view that the RNAS lost control of the air probably emerges from the loss of several aeroplanes in January 1916 due to enemy air action; however, this needs to be understood within context.[114] First, RNAS strength had been drawn down and second, as noted below, the quality of new aircrew was not as good as those they replaced. Finally, at this time, the Ottomans had transferred several Fokker Eindecker's from Macedonia, which, as with the so-called "Fokker Scourge" on the Western Front, provided them with a qualitative edge.[115] Moreover, two of the previoulsy mentioned aeroplanes were brought down over enemy lines, which illustrates the offensive character of Sykes' battle for control of the air. It also shows that assessments simply based on statistics, rather than operational effect, is unhelpful. What is clear is that Sykes' ongoing demands for greater resources was driven by an appreciation of his enemies' reinforcement by the Germans.[116] This awareness shaped Sykes' use of air assets during the final weeks of the campaign, which enabled the RNAS, with varying degrees of success, to conduct operations in support of land and naval forces. By the time of the evacuation, it is clear that control of the air had taken over as the key role of air assets in theatre – and they were ultimately successful in keeping Ottoman air assets away during this phase.[117]

In preparation for the evacuation from Suvla and Anzac, Sykes shaped his effort to battle for control of the air by concentrating all his assets to provide a "continuous hostile aircraft patrol."[118] To support this Sykes maintained what today would be referred to as a quick reaction alert force in the form of "one scout [standing] ready to move on short notice" from the

112 LHCMA: Hamilton Papers, 7/5/5: Force Order No. 4, Issued by the Chief of the General Staff, Mediterranean Expeditionary Force, 22 April 1915.
113 Ash, *Sir Frederick Sykes*, p. 80.
114 'Mitchell Report' records two aircraft lost to enemy aircraft while Jones noted four losses between 6 and 12 January. One of these aircraft, piloted by Flight Commander H.A. Busk was lost to unknown causes while Flight Sub-Lieutenant S.A. Black was lost in an accident at Imbros. 'Mitchell Report', p. 521; Jones, *OH*, Vol. II, p. 75.
115 Clark, 'Naval Aviation at Gallipoli', p. 88.
116 RAFM: Sykes Papers, MFC77/13/29: Wing Captain F.H. Sykes to Vice-Admiral Commanding EMS, 27 December 1915.
117 This was a view shared by both the British Army and the Royal Navy, see RAFM: Sykes Papers, MFC77/13/43: Appendix F to Memorandum No. 229A – General Orders for the Final Stage of the Evacuation of the Army from Suvla and Anzac, 12 December 1915; RAFM: Sykes Papers, MFC77/13/43: Lieutenant-Colonel, General Staff, Dardanelles Army to Officer Commanding, RNAS, 12 December 1915.
118 RAFM: Sykes Papers, MFC77/13/43: Preliminary Instructions to Units of the RNAS with regards to the evacuation of Anzac and Suvla, 14 December 1915.

aerodromes.[119] This force would respond to intelligence related to incoming hostile aeroplanes. Ash suggested that a compromise was reached by 16 December because Sykes "disagreed with the orders" of 12 December.[120] However, both the EMS and MEF orders were necessarily brief and Sykes, acting in his capacity as an air component commander, developed a fuller plan on 12 December, which, through negotiation, on 16 December was accepted.[121] Indeed, while there was compromise over key issues such as an aircraft on standby, the tenor of Sykes' 12 December instruction remained. In his autobiography, Sykes himself did not suggest that he either "disagreed" or reached a compromise on the appropriate use of air assets during the withdrawal.[122] Moreover, Aspinall-Oglander noted that Sykes was given leave to develop "[S]pecial arrangements" for operations, thus highlighting the increasing trust placed in Sykes by both naval and land commanders.[123] As well as providing control of the air during the evacuation period, Sykes also detailed his force to provide situational awareness for the withdrawal and bombing operations. The latter were to be undertaken with care to avoid hitting hospitals or areas designated by "red Crescent flags."[124]

The most important role for aircraft during the First World War was reconnaissance in varying guises, and this was the case at Gallipoli. The 'Mitchell Report' devoted an entire chapter to the subject of "Observation by Aircraft and Balloons."[125] The need to provide intelligence and situational awareness to naval and land forces had become clear before the outbreak of the war and was reinforced by early operations in France in 1914.[126] Operations ranged from tactical reconnaissance and artillery observation to mapping and strategic operations. As Sykes reflected in the covering letter to his 9 July 1915 report, "[T]he necessity for aerial reconnaissance is very real and urgent."[127] Also, support for artillery – the key killer on the battlefield – was vital during the war. Similarly, spotting for naval gunfire was also critical but problematic, and the decision to deploy *Ark Royal* in February 1915 stemmed from a desire to support the ships forcing the straits. As soon as *Ark Royal* arrived in theatre, she launched seaplanes to conduct reconnaissance of Forts Nos. 1 to 6 (with some success).[128] Two days later, during the bombardment of 19 February, *Ark Royal* again supported operations with her seaplanes. During the afternoon, two seaplanes tried to spot for HMS *Inflexible* over Helles; however, it is here where a key technical problem occurred that often plagued reconnaissance at this point of the war.[129] Wireless was, as with aircraft, a technology that was in its infancy. In theory it provided

119 Ibid.
120 Ash, *Sir Frederick Sykes*, p. 85.
121 RAFM: Sykes Papers, MFC77/13/43: Preliminary Instructions for Units of the RNAS, 12 December 1915.
122 Sykes, *From Many Angles*, pp. 182-3.
123 Aspinall-Oglander, *OH*, Vol. II, p. 350.
124 RAFM: Sykes Papers, MFC77/13/43: Preliminary Instructions to Units of the RNAS with regards to the evacuation of Anzac and Suvla, 14 December 1915.
125 'Mitchell Report', pp. 500-21.
126 On pre-First World War British Army manoeuvres, see Andrew Whitmarsh, 'British Army Manoeuvres and the Development of Military Aviation, 1910–1913,' *War in History*, 14:3 (2007), pp. 325-46. For an interesting look at Hamilton's views of military aviation pre-First World War, see LHCMA: Hamilton Papers, 4/2/7: Letter from Hamilton to the Chief of the General Staff, 2 January 1909.
127 RAFM: Sykes Papers, MFC77/13/28: Colonel Sykes to the Secretary of the Admiralty, 9 July 1915.
128 TNA AIR 1/2099/207/20/7: HMS *Ark Royal:* Report of Operations No. 1, 17 February 1915.
129 Ibid., Report of Operations No. 2, 19 February 1915.

a means to communicate information to ships. However, on this occasion, the problem was that the transmitters either jammed or short-circuited meaning that the seaplane sent up to spot for *Inflexible* was unable to transmit information. Additionally, another problem was that few ships had experience of this form of communication, which hampered operations as well as co-operation with aircraft. For example, again on 19 February 1915, when a seaplane was sent up to spot for HMS *Cornwallis*, the ship was ordered to cease fire before the aircraft was in position.[130]

The technical problems presented by *Ark Royal's* seaplanes did not go unnoticed in the 'Mitchell Report', though it suggested that given these difficulties, the relative performance achieved was "more creditable than would at first appear."[131] Bell has argued that the problem of air support for the fleet was "a constant hindrance," though given that ad-hoc on the spot adaptations were developed to cope with problems related to spotting for naval guns, it is clear that the truth lies somewhere in between.[132] Interestingly, the 'Mitchell Report' argued that had aeroplanes been used in February and March 1915 then better results might have been achieved.[133] Given the challenge of operating aeroplanes in 1915, it is arguable whether even the Sopwith Tabloid's deployed on *Ark Royal* would have achieved any more effect than the seaplanes. More specifically, the challenges encountered highlights the poor planning undertaken for Gallipoli with a key issue being one of a lack of trained observers as well as cultural issues discussed below.[134] The former point remained a key weakness for the RNAS, and even when No. 3 Squadron deployed to the Dardanelles to support land operations, the British Army provided observers to support operations. Despite challenges, the orders issued for the landings on 25 April 1915 made clear that the RNAS was to be used to provide situational awareness for operations.[135] Importantly, at this time, it also became apparent that the mere appearance of aircraft over Ottoman positions could reduce their fire. This was well-received by pilots and observers who, despite the challenges they faced, wanted to be of "some real value" to ground troops.[136] As well as aeroplanes and seaplanes, kite balloons were also deployed to support operations in the form of No. 1 Kite Balloon Section deployed on *Manica*; the latter was eventually reinforced with the deployment of *Hector* and in turn HMS *Canning* arrived to replace *Manica*.[137]

As well as providing spotting for ships, air power was also used to provide situational awareness for anti-submarine operations in the Dardanelles. By Autumn 1915, a Submarine Scout (SS) airship had been deployed to Gallipoli for anti-submarine operations. The flight initially operated out of Kephalo and between 13 September and 22 October 1915 a total of 46 flights were undertaken. While it is unclear whether any submarines were spotted, the 'Mitchell

130 Ibid.; Marder, 'Dardanelles Revisited', p. 10.
131 'Mitchell Report', p. 30.
132 Bell, *Churchill and the Dardanelles*, p. 121.
133 'Mitchell Report', p. 31, 49; TNA AIR 1/2099/207/20/7: Commanding Officer, HMS *Ark Royal*, to the Director, Air Department, 9 March 1915; Marder, 'Dardanelles Revisited', p. 8.
134 'Mitchell Report', p. 30-1.
135 LHCMA: Hamilton Papers, 7/4/18: Confidential Memorandum No. 49L: Orders for Combined Operations, 12 April 1915, p. 3.
136 TNA AIR 1/2387/228/11/30: War Experience, p. 18.
137 Jones, *OH*, Vol. II, p. 33-6, 58, 63. On the experience of the kite balloon section and ships, see Ian Burns, 'Kite Balloons at Sea: Gallipoli and Salonika, 1915-1916', *Cross & Cockade International*, 46:1 (2015), pp. 22-38.

Report' reflected that it felt enemy operations were restricted due to the presence of airships.[138] Nevertheless, their deployment created some consternation because, on 16 September, the sheds at Kephalo were attacked by Ottoman aeroplanes.[139] It is evident that airships became a high-value target, and while the lack of firm statistics make a judgement call on their effectiveness at Gallipoli difficult, evidence from the maritime war around Britain suggests that SS airships produced a scarecrow effect against enemy submarines and formed one element that reduced the latter's effectiveness.

Intelligence in support of operations at sea also came in other forms, for example, to help hinder Ottoman anti-submarine actions. Allied submarines were used to great effect, in conjunction with aircraft, to interdict troop movement. To limit this, the Ottomans deployed anti-submarine nets. This was not an unknown problem. Indeed, Captain H. Fyler of the battleship HMS *Agamemnon* convened a committee in September 1915 to examine the question of how to destroy nets to stop them impeding Allied submarine operations. As well as officers from Royal Navy ships, Squadron Commander Cecil L'Estrange Malone, commander of *Ben-My-Chree*, was also interviewed concerning the nets. Malone provided valuable intelligence, and several proposals were put forward about how to deal with them. One, and that which was favoured was an idea to drown the "bouys supporting the nets by means of charges" dropped from aircraft.[140] After a period of discussion and experimentation, by December, methods were tried, and while many charges either sunk under the nets or failed to explode, the attempts at least illustrate an effort to utilise air power to solve a problem that posed a challenge for submarine operations.[141]

Overland, reconnaissance and spotting were of paramount importance. No. 3 Squadron performed 203 spotting, 71 photographic and 291 bombing or reconnaissance flights from 9 May 1915 to the start of the August Offensive.[142] However, while reconnaissance through photo intelligence or observation was necessary for the planning of operations, it was limited by technical, atmospheric and cultural limitations. Despite these challenges, a critical problem that faced planners during the Gallipoli campaign was the provision of accurate and high-quality maps, and this was one area where air power played a role.[143] To help solve the problem of mapping, the Director-General, Survey of Egypt, E.M. Dowson, made use of aircraft to undertake survey work and as his report reflected, this was conducted "quite independent of any work that had been done elsewhere."[144] However, there were still challenges with the quality of images obtained with cameras. For example, of the 1,500 exposures taken by No. 2 Wing from 28 August to 19 November 1915, 160 were failures with a further 120 lost due to inci-

138 'Mitchell Report', pp. 512-3.

139 RAFM: Sykes Papers, MFC77/13/44: Flight Commander E.H. Sparling, Commanding Officer Airship Expeditionary Force, to Wing Captain F.H. Sykes, 23 September 1915, p. 5.

140 RAFM: Sykes Papers, MFC77/13/40: Captain H. Fyler to Vice-Admiral Commanding EMS, 5 September 1915.

141 Ibid., Report from Wing Captain F.H. Sykes, 8 December 1916; Report from Squadron Commander, HMS *Ark Royal* to Wing Captain F.H. Sykes, 19 December 1915; Sykes, *From Many Angles*, pp, 177-8.

142 The Mitchell Report, p. 245.

143 On the issue of mapping during the Dardanelles campaign, see Peter Chasseaud & Peter Doyle, *Grasping Gallipoli: Terrain, Maps and Failure at the Dardanelles, 1915* (Stroud: Spellmount, 2005).

144 TNA AIR 1/2284/209/75/10: Notes on Mapping from Aeroplane Photographs in the Gallipoli Peninsula by E.M. Dowson, Director-General Survey of Egypt (n.d.) (1915), p. 1.

dents involving aircraft.[145] Nevertheless, it should be reflected that even on the Western Front, where air units were better resourced, it was only in March 1915 that planners for the Battle of Neuve Chapelle were able to map the battlefield. Similar successes in mapping trench systems at Gallipoli occurred at the Third Battle of Krithia in June 1915 and the Australian attack at Lone Pine during the August offensive, and in Sykes's opinion, the use of air power did improve the quality of the Gallipoli maps.[146]

Mapping was not the only area where evidence exists of local solutions to local problems. Concerning artillery observation, as the campaign progressed, the use of aeroplanes became critical to the support of artillery fire on the ground.[147] However, means were sought as to how best direct fire and as Walser reflected, "we gradually evolved a kind of grid system similar to the one used by the French artillery, which gave good results."[148] The clock code, which had been introduced in France during 1915, only reached the Gallipoli theatre towards the end of the campaign (the 'Mitchell Report' suggested that it became standard from July).[149] This illustrates two salient points. First, it took time for developments to be shared amongst theatres and second, so-called sideshows were not incapable of developing solutions to local challenges. This learning on the job was not limited to the support of land forces. As Strain reflected on the challenge of developing a code for naval gunfire spotting, "[F]or the type of warfare we were engaged in there was no experience to guide us" which led to local solutions being developed.[150] This "on the job" problem solving is supported by Bromet's recollection that there was no "official form" used for flying orders and reconnaissance reports and that the ones used were developed locally on board *Ark Royal*.[151]

As the Gallipoli campaign progressed so too did procedures for how to request aerial reconnaissance. A distinction was drawn between pre-planned operations and those of an "emergency nature."[152] Such distinctions were important for operations as it allowed for the increasingly efficient use of overstretched resources during the latter part of the campaign. Methods of collection, through the use of daily and flying reports, were outlined for the collation, dissemination and sharing of intelligence.[153] The development of these methods is significant as it illustrates that in 1915, the air arms and the British military more broadly came to terms with the impact of air power on the complex character of modern war and the need to regulate and formalise operational methods. Also, it is clear that in developing a standardised reporting system for intelligence, Sykes drew on his experience in France, thus further highlighting the transfer of knowledge between theatres.[154] Similar ideas existed for photography and the use of wireless

145 RAFM: Sykes Papers, MFC77/13/42: Report on the Photographic Work carried out between the 28th August and the 19th November 1915 by No. 2 Wing RNAS, 5 December 1915, p. 1.
146 Aspinall-Oglander, *OH*, Vol. II, p. 44, fn. 4; Clark, 'Naval Aviation at Gallipoli', p. 82; Sykes, *Aviation in Peace and War*, p. 48.
147 Aspinall-Oglander, *OH*, Vol. II, pp. 393-4.
148 Walser, 'Memories of Gallipoli', p. 4.
149 'Mitchell Report', p. 507.
150 RAFM: Strain Papers, AC75/33/3/2: Reminiscence, p. 38.
151 TNA AIR 1/2387/228/11/30: War Experience, p. 9. Bromet gave an example of this form in an appendix to his Staff College essay.
152 RAFM: Sykes Papers, MFC77/13/33: Instructions Laid Down by RNAS Eastern Mediterranean Squadron, Issued to the all units, 1 November 1915, Section I: Intelligence.
153 Ibid.
154 Ash, *Sir Frederick Sykes*, p. 81.

and, for example, with regards to the former, it was noted that one advantage of instituting a "definitive system" was to "expedite the work of the Survey Office."[155]

One issue, nevertheless, that frustrated the effective use of situational awareness provided by air power was the attitude of some British Army and Royal Navy officers. For example, Brigadier-General Hamilton Reed, Chief of Staff for IX Corps, was sceptical about reports generated from air power sources.[156] This attitude needs to be understood within the context of what was possible at the time. For example, Squadron Leader Keith Park, who had served at Gallipoli in a New Zealand artillery battery, later reflected in an essay at the RAF Staff College that a common complaint was that aeroplanes often returned to base too early to be useful.[157] This was reinforced by a general ignorance as to what role the RNAS were playing in the campaign.[158] Despite this, it is evident that the RNAS took British Army officers up in aeroplanes to try and solve this cultural bias while educating ground troops about the challenge of providing situational awareness.[159] Furthermore, at least one RNAS officer was attached at Helles and lived with "corps artillery staff," in an attempt to improve relations and understanding between these key combat arms.[160] Much of this scepticism stemmed from challenges encountered on the Western Front and from some pre-war attitudes to air power but was not limited to officers of the British Army. Despite building *Ark Royal* and showing interest in air power, reflections suggest that the Royal Navy struggled to adapt to how to best use aviation to spot for guns.[161] Despite this cultural challenge, through the experience of working with air assets, and the role of officers such as Sykes, Samson and Clark-Hall, the recognised importance of air power as a key component in conducting the campaign improved over the course of operations.

Some of the sorties classified as reconnaissance flights also included bombing operations. Early on, however, this had as much to do with maintaining the aerodynamic stability of the seaplanes as it did with attacking targets.[162] Nevertheless, as the Gallipoli campaign developed, bombing became an important aspect of operations primarily because the Ottoman lines of communication became important targets. This consideration became of further importance when Bulgaria entered the war in October 1915.[163] In November 1915 there were a series of attacks against the Constantinople to Berlin railway line crossing over the Maritza River.[164] While the damage was slight, the attacks led the Ottomans to deploy GBAD to defend the area from further attacks. Sykes also noted the personal danger inherent in attacking these targets when he wrote of Flight Commander J.R.W. Piggot's attack on 13 November 1915:

155 RAFM: Sykes Papers, MFC77/13/33: Instructions Laid Down by RNAS Eastern Mediterranean Squadron, Issued to the all units, 1 November 1915, Section II – Photography.
156 Crawley, *Climax at Gallipoli*, p. 18.
157 Keith Park, 'Experiences in the War, 1914-1918: An Essay' in AP956: *A Selection of Lectures and Essays from the Work of Officers attending the First Course at the Royal Air Force Staff College, 1922-1923* (London: Air Ministry, 1923), p. 93.
158 Ibid.
159 TNA AIR 1/2387/228/11/30: War Experience, p. 18.
160 'Mitchell Report', p. 507.
161 TNA AIR 1/2387/228/11/30: War Experience, p. 9.
162 Ibid., pp. 8-9.
163 Aspinall-Oglander, *OH*, Vol. II, p. 378.
164 The Mitchell Report, p. 206.

> The flight was probably the longest night flight undertaken during this war and I think constitutes a record night flight. The attendant risks were much enhanced by the fact that none of it was over territory held by our own troops, a large proportion of it was an oversea flight, and the bridge was known to be well guarded.[165]

Similarly, the Ferejik railway junction was attacked throughout November and December, with buildings and rolling stock damaged. It was during the attack on 19 November 1915 that Squadron Commander Richard Bell-Davies received his Victoria Cross for saving Flight Sub-Lieutenant G.F. Smylie whose aeroplane had been brought down after the raid. Bell-Davies' VC citation described the action in the following terms:

> On the 19th November, these two officers carried out an air attack on Ferrijik Junction. Flight Sub-Lieutenant Smylie's machine was received by very heavy fire and brought down. The pilot planed down over the station, releasing all his bombs except one, which failed to drop, simultaneously at the station from a very low altitude. Thence he continued his descent into the marsh. On alighting he saw the one unexploded bomb, and set fire to his machine, knowing that the bomb would ensure its destruction. He then proceeded towards Turkish territory. At this moment he perceived Squadron-Commander Davies descending, and fearing that he would come down near the burning machine and thus risk destruction from the bomb, Flight Sub-Lieutenant Smylie ran back and from a short distance exploded the bomb by means of a pistol bullet. Squadron-Commander Davies descended at a safe distance from the burning machine, took up Sub-Lieutenant Smylie, in spite of the near approach of a party of the enemy, and returned to the aerodrome, a feat of airmanship that can seldom have been equalled for skill and gallantry.[166]

Compared to this citation, Davies' report on the action was succinct and to the point: "Returning saw H. 5 burning in marshes. Picked up Pilot."[167]

As well as the use of air power for interdiction, as already noted, plans were mooted to use bombing more strategically. Indeed, the attack on 17 May 1915 using the Breguet flown by Flight Commander Reginald Marix, with Samson as a passenger, was designed to test this aeroplanes' capability. As Samson reflected in 1930, "our principal objective with this aeroplane was an attack on Constantinople."[168] Carrying one 100lb and fourteen 20lb bombs, Marix attacked Ak Bashi Liman after noticing some activity, and the attack led to a break in activity. Samson had "great expectations" for "Reggie Marix's Breguet", although as noted below, this aeroplane was replete with logistic headaches.[169] As the Gallipoli campaign progressed, plans

165 RAFM: Sykes Papers, MFC77/13/39: Wing Captain F.H. Sykes to Vice-Admiral Commanding EMS, 14 November 1915.

166 *Supplement to The London Gazette*, 1 January 1916, p. 86.

167 RAFM: DC74/21: Flying Report by Squadron Commander R.B. Davies, 19 November 1915. Bell-Davies provided a longer recollection of this action in his memoirs, see Vice-Admiral Richard Bell-Davies VC, *Sailor in the Air: The Memoirs of Vice-Admiral Richard Bell-Davies VC, CB, DSO, and AFC* (London: Peter Davies, 1967), pp. 134-5.

168 Samson, *Fights and Flights*, p. 241.

169 Ibid., p. 215.

were put forward to use bombing against strategic targets. However, due to a lack of resources and the changes in the character of the Gallipoli campaign, these ideas came to nothing.

Returning to the use of air power at the operational level, the subject of interdiction against lines of communication was subsequently deemed of such significance that the 'Mitchell Report' devoted a chapter to the topic. The 'Mitchell Report' codified aircraft operations against lines of communication as those targeting railways, roads, landing places, store depots, maritime communications, road transport and camps. Concerning attacks on road transport from Ak Bashi Liman to the front, it was reported by an Ottoman officer, Major Mouzafa Bey that:

> Owing to aeroplane bombing, transport columns were split up into sections of five carts or 20 pack animals marching at intervals of a mile apart, with orders to halt and take cover whenever an aeroplane was sighted. As far as possible, convoys were marched at night.[170]

Nevertheless, while bombing affected Ottoman operations, bombs were not dropped in a large enough quantities, nor was the concentration of aircraft sufficient to achieve a decisive effect. With specific reference to operations on Ottoman landing places, such as Ak Bashi Liman, The 'Mitchell Report' argued that while aircraft were useful in attacking lines of communication, the lack of numbers in the theatre meant that operations were undertaken "spasmodically," thus limiting their overall effect.[171] Overall, during the Gallipoli campaign, 1,150 bombs, or nearly 27 tons, were used against Ottoman targets.[172]

Aircraft were also used in anti-surface warfare against Ottoman ships. Indeed, Gallipoli was notable for a first; the "sinking" of a ship by a torpedo. This was undertaken by Flight Commander Charles Edmonds on 12 August 1915 against an Ottoman supply vessel in the Sea of Marmara. Flying a Short 184 seaplane at the height of 15 feet, Edmonds launched a 14-inch torpedo from a range of 300 yards. As Edmonds reported: "[L]ooking back I observed the track of the torpedo which struck the ship abreast the mainmast the starboard side. The explosion sent a column of water and large fragments of the ship as high as her masthead."[173] Unfortunately, this ship had already been disabled by a submarine several days before, and Edmonds was but finishing off the job.[174] In his report, Edmonds had noted that the ship was lying close to land and that it could not sink due to being in the shallow water.[175] Nevertheless, on 17 August 1915, Edmonds attacked another ship in Ak Bashi Liman, which limped back to Constantinople.[176] There is some controversy over whether Edmonds attacked an Ottoman hospital ship, although Edmonds' report of the action noted their presence and it is therefore improbable that he attacked them.[177] While not generally successful, bombing and torpedo attacks illustrate the challenges inherent in the early use of an immature technology. Overall, and despite challenges,

170 'Mitchell Report', p. 208.
171 Ibid., p. 207.
172 Ibid., p. 521.
173 RAFM: Personal Papers of Air Vice-Marshal Charles Edmonds, MFC76/19/3: Report of Flight, 12 August 1915.
174 Jones, *OH*, Vol. II, p. 64.
175 RAFM: Edmonds Papers, MFC76/19/3: Report of Flight, 12 August 1915.
176 Ibid., 17 August 1915.
177 Ibid; Clark, 'Naval Aviation at Gallipoli', p. 83.

in a limited sense, the RNAS illustrated effectiveness in one of their key roles, and increasingly, in a supporting manner, began to deny the use of the sea to their opponents.

Logistics and equipment challenges

A key challenge identified in Sykes' 9 July 1915 report, and something he continued to strive to improve, was the logistic state of the RNAS at Gallipoli. He clearly viewed the issues of concentration, centralised control, and logistics as inherently linked.[178] As Peter Dye has recently argued, the "development and effective employment of the air weapon [...] required a radical and unprecedented change in the way national resources were employed [...] to achieve tactical and operational advantage."[179] Sykes recognised this argument: "[T]he efficiency of an Air Service is peculiarly dependent upon an adequate system of supply and facilities for quick repair."[180]

A key challenge of the Gallipoli campaign was that the EMS, the MEF, and of course RNAS assets, operated at the end of a long line of logistics that ultimately stretched back to Britain.[181] Sykes knew this and suggested solutions that might ease some of these challenges.[182] Amongst the challenges identified included the problem of shipping supplies from Mudros to Imbros after they arrived in the theatre. One solution included the provision of a hulk to be based at Mudros to store supplies and trawler to move them to Imbros, though these were never supplied and neither was a parent ship to help with engine maintenance.[183]

The logistic challenges were not helped by several factors, such as the wide variety of aeroplanes that No. 3 Squadron had when it deployed in late March 1915. It consisted of 18 airframes of six different types: eight Henri Farmans, two BE2cs, two BE2s, two Sopwith Tabloids, one Breguet, and three Maurice Farmans.[184] The reason for such a wide variety of aeroplanes stemmed from the character of units at this point in the war. Nonetheless, such a large number of diverse types of aeroplanes not only caused supply problems but also further negated any "operational advantage" Samson's unit might have initially delivered at Gallipoli by reducing No. 3 Squadron's combat power. The squadron's arrival caused resentment from the crews on board *Ark Royal* who felt that the "Air Department were only too ready to provide a squadron of

178 RAFM: Sykes Papers, MFC77/13/28: *The Sykes Report*, p. 4.
179 Peter Dye, *The Bridge to Airpower: Logistics Support for Royal Flying Corps Operations on the Western Front, 1914-18* (Annapolis, MD: Naval Institute Press, 2015), p. 19.
180 RAFM: Sykes Papers, MFC77/13/36: Wing Captain F.H. Sykes to Vice-Admiral Commanding EMS, 28 October 1915.
181 For the broader challenges of logistics during the Gallipoli campaign, see Rhys Crawley, 'Supplying the Offensive: The Role of Allied Logistics' in Ashley Ekins (ed.), *Gallipoli: A Ridge Too Far* (Wollombi: Exisle Publishing, 2013), pp. 254-71.
182 RAFM: Sykes Papers, MFC77/13/36: Suggested Scheme for the Improvement of Supply and Repair Facilities for the RNAS EMS, 28 October 1915. For de Robeck's reply, see (in the same series) Vice-Admiral de Robeck to Wing Captain F.H. Sykes, 7 November 1915.
183 Ibid., Wing Captain F.H. Sykes to Vice-Admiral Commanding EMS, 5 December 1915; RAFM: Sykes Papers, MFC77/13/46: Memorandum on a Resume of Operations and Recommendations Made, January 1916, p. 2.
184 Jones, *OH*, Vol. II, p. 24.

BE2.

Sopwith Tabloid.

aeroplanes and give them all their wants."[185] No. 3 Squadron's state, however, was not as good as *Ark Royal's* crew perceived, and it was made more challenging due to the lack of experience in conducting expeditionary operations using air assets.[186]

Each aeroplane also generated unique challenges. For example, due to the limited vision offered by the aeroplane's design, the Tabloids were relegated to aerial fighting.[187] Operational difficulties were made more challenging by the BE2cs, which often could not take passengers high enough for spotting while the Breguet was an experimental type that should never have been deployed.[188] Indeed, Bell-Davies described it as "horrible [and] blundering."[189] Another commented that little was known of it before the campaign except that "the French government,

185 TNA AIR 1/2387/228/11/30: War Experience, p. 12.
186 RAFM: Sykes Papers, MFC 77/13/28: *The Sykes Report*, p. 4.
187 'Mitchell Report', p. 518.
188 Ibid.
189 Bell-Davies, *Sailor in the Air*, pp. 117-8.

for some reason, do not like it."[190] Rather than increase the combat power of the RNAS, this aeroplane merely added to the logistic burden. Due to its size, for instance, special arrangements had to be made to transport it to the Dardanelles, and then it only conducted three successful flights.[191] It was eventually crated up, though, it appears to have remained on the strength of No. 2 Wing.[192] The amateurish attitude towards logistics illustrated by the RNAS is best summed up by Samson's desire to ensure that his horse, which he captured from the Germans in 1914, made it to the Dardanelles – in the end, the horse collapsed "in his box helplessly seasick."[193]

For his part, Sykes saw the difficulties this was creating and asked for 36 aeroplanes of two types and engines (as well as sufficient spares to maintain this strength) to rationalise logistical problems.[194] Specifically, more Henri Farmans and BE2s were sought in addition to SS airships and "standard RFC cameras and material."[195] Reducing the types of aircraft would allow the RNAS to increase its combat power through improved serviceability and availability of airframes. Simply put, more aircraft in the air meant the more efficient use of assets to support operational objectives. However, challenges with the numbers of types of airframes in the theatre were never significantly resolved, and when No. 2 Wing deployed to Gallipoli, it too brought with it additional types of aeroplanes.[196] Nevertheless, Sykes and his commanders regularly tried to be constructive in their criticism by sharing knowledge on problems as well as local developments about the use of weapons.[197] For example, the RNAS were to be provided with several of the new CFS Bombsights for experimentation, but they never arrived.[198]

An important aspect of the proposed concentration of air assets was the recommendation to locate units at Kephalo on Imbros Island.[199] The initial airfield at Tenedos Island for No. 3 Squadron had been selected in March 1915.[200] The move to Imbros was designed to improve cooperation with the fleet and the troops at Gallipoli. It also had advantages over Tenedos: there was greater potential for stores and repair facilities, and was closer to the peninsula, thus reducing travel time and increasing the time and range available to conduct operations.[201] Given Sykes' desire for concentration, it is ironic that after the deployment of the SS airship section to

190 RAFM: Sykes Papers, MFC77/13/37, Wing Commander E.L. Gerrard to Wing Captain F.H. Sykes, 10 October 1915.
191 Bell-Davies, *Sailor in the Air*, pp. 118-19; 'Mitchell Report', p. 518.
192 RAFM: Sykes Papers, MFC77/13/37: Wing Captain F.H. Sykes to Wing Commander C.L. Samson and Wing Commander E.L. Gerrard, 9 October 1915.
193 Bell-Davies, *Sailor in the Air*, p. 119.
194 RAFM: Sykes Papers, MFC77/13/28: Telegram from the Vice Admiral Eastern Mediterranean Squadron to the Admiralty, 9 July 1915.
195 Ibid.
196 'Mitchell Report', p. 519.
197 RAFM: Sykes Papers, MFC77/13/37: Wing Captain F.H. Sykes to Vice-Admiral Commanding EMS, 14 September 1915; Wing Captain F.H. Sykes to Vice-Admiral Commanding EMS, 9 December 1915; Wing Captain F.H. Sykes to Director of Air Services, Admiralty, 28 December 1915.
198 RAFM: Sykes Papers, MFC77/13/30: Air Department, Admiralty to Wing Captain Sykes, 5 December 1915; Report by Wing Commander Samson to Wing Captain Sykes, 29 December 1915. On the development of the CFS Bombsight, see Neville Jones, *The Origins of Strategic Bombing: A Study of the Development of British Air Strategic Thought and Practice up to 1918* (London: William Kimber, 1973), pp. 69-76.
199 RAFM: Sykes Papers, MFC 77/13/28: *The Sykes Report*, p. 5.
200 The Mitchell Report, p. 511.
201 Ibid., p. 512.

the Dardanelles, the use of Kephalo for the lighter-than-air craft was deemed unsuitable. One key reason for this was the distance between Kephalo and Ottoman bases and the attendant threat of air attack as had been experienced on 16 September.[202] Shortening the distance to the front had been one of Sykes' arguments for moving to Kephalo, but given that there was only one airship, the need to protect this high-value target took precedence to other considerations, and eventually it moved to Mudros.[203]

Centralisation may have eased supply issues, but it did not solve the problems discussed above. Indeed, as serviceability rates show, these problems persisted throughout the campaign. The average serviceability rate between 22 October 1915 and 14 January 1916 was 56 percent with a low mark of 42 percent during the week beginning 24 December.[204] The high mark for serviceability came on the week beginning of 14 January 1916 with 65 percent of aircraft available for operations, though by this time there were only 23 aeroplanes at Gallipoli (by comparison, at the same time, serviceability on the RFC on the Western Front stood at 82 percent).[205] Problems of serviceability also affected the kite balloons: continuous use led to perennial gas leakages, for example.[206]

By the end of the campaign, and aware that the RNAS might be called on to support other endeavours, such as Salonika, Sykes wrote to de Robeck noting that the lack of reinforcements meant that the assets available were "inadequate" to deal with future operations.[207] Sykes reinforced this when, in 1916, he wrote that he felt the Admiralty did not do enough to support his operations by providing him with necessary supplies or facilities (such as a depot ship), which might have increased serviceability.[208] Despite his protestations, it does appear that the Admiralty was trying to meet Sykes' demands.[209]

Personnel problems

As well as dealing with the problem of equipment and logistics, the Gallipoli campaign brought with it attendant issues in managing personnel. The critical problem for Sykes was one of a lack of trained personnel and replacements. As already noted, one critical area of concern was the lack of well-trained observers, which was never fully rectified.[210] The lack of reinforcements led

202 RAFM: Sykes Papers, MFC77/13/44: Flight Commander E.H. Sparling, Commanding Officer Airship Expeditionary Force, to Wing Captain F.H. Sykes, 23 September 1915, p. 16.
203 'Mitchell Report', p. 513.
204 Figures derived from RAFM: Sykes Papers, MFC77/13/48: Statement attached to a letter from Major-General Sir F.H. Sykes to General Sir Ian Hamilton, 22 November 1919.
205 Dye, *The Bridge to Airpower*, p. 169.
206 RAFM: Sykes Papers, MFC77/13/30: Report from Commanding Officer, No. 3 Kite Balloon Section to the Commanding Officer, HMS *Hector*, 16 December 1915.
207 RAFM: Sykes Papers, MFC77/13/29: Wing Captain F.H. Sykes to Vice-Admiral Commanding EMS, 27 December 1915.
208 RAFM: Sykes Papers, MFC77/13/46: Memorandum on a Resume of Operations and Recommendations Made, January 1916, pp. 1-2.
209 TNA AIR 1/654/17/122/503: Enclosure D: Arrangements Made to Reinforce RNAS at Gallipoli, 20 November 1915.
210 RAFM: Sykes Papers, MFC77/13/35: Wing Captain F.H. Sykes to Vice-Admiral, HMS *Triad*, 7 September 1915, p. 1.

RNAS aviators at Tenedos. (*Illustrated War News*, 23 June 1915)

to a local adaptation whereby Sykes sought to recruit people from the EMS and MEF and train them "on the spot."[211] He also highlighted that one of the problems in getting observers was their status within the RNAS and the challenge of promotion, and suggested ways in which the RNAS could make their role more rewarding.[212] That Sykes, while dealing with operational challenges, was able to produce such forward-leaning recommendations highlights his thinking, though whether it helped at the time is open to question. These personnel problems were not limited to pilots and observers but extended to other trades. Sykes also needed "Good fitters and carpenters [and] photographers" to help support the expansion of his force.[213]

The problem of training affected the quality of pilots sent out to Gallipoli as reliefs. As Walser noted in 1923: "[m]any of the pilots that came out to us were not sufficiently trained and some of them had only done about ten hours solo on any type of machine."[214] Samson's contemporary view reinforces Walser's recollection. For example, the former noted to Sykes on 2 December 1915: "[P]ilots are sent out to my Wing insufficiently trained. A large number of them having only done less than 15 hours in the air before leaving England."[215]

While there were local challenges, both Samson's and Walser's views illustrate the state of training more generally in 1915. Indeed, when more experienced officers, such as Flight Commander Charles Collett, died during operations, they were increasingly replaced by those coming out of a training pipeline struggling to cope with demand. Deaths of close friends, such

211 RAFM: Sykes Papers, MFC77/13/46: Memorandum on a Resume of Operations and Recommendations Made, January 1916, p. 2.
212 RAFM: Sykes Papers, MFC77/13/35: Memorandum on the Status and Training of Observers of the RNAS by Wing Captain F.H. Sykes, 30 November 1915. On issues surrounding observers and navigators in the RFC, RNAS and RAF, see C.G. Jefford, *Observers and Navigators: And Other Non-Pilot Aircrew in the RFC, RNAS and RAF*, Updated and Expanded Edition (London: Grub Street, 2014).
213 RAFM: Sykes Papers, MFC77/13/28: Telegram from the Vice Admiral Eastern Mediterranean Squadron to the Admiralty, 9 July 1915.
214 Walser, 'Memories of Gallipoli', p. 6.
215 RAFM: Sykes Papers, MFC77/13/35: Wing Commander Samson to Wing Captain F.H. Sykes, 2 December 1915, p. 1.

as Collet, hit fellow personnel hard. Samson buried both Collet and "Garwood".[216] Samson, however, continued to report on the problems caused by insufficient training. On 2 December 1915 he reflected that he had had "three aeroplanes smashed" by inexperienced pilots.[217] Samson went as far as to describe two recently posted-in Flight Sub-Lieutenants, C.W. Jamieson and W.E. Gardner, as "totally unfit at present for employment."[218] As a unit commander dealing with both the operational efficiency of his wing and the welfare of his personnel, Samson's key concern was the safety of his people and the effect that untrained pilots would have on No. 3 Wing's combat power. At No. 2 Wing, Gerrard shared Samson's views and further illustrated concern for his personnel by suggesting that where possible, pilots should be rotated back to Britain due to the impact of active service on their effectiveness.[219] Samson suggested that new pilots should not be posted to active units until they had "30 to 40 hours" experience (a situation that would not be achieved until much later in the First World War).[220] Later that month, Samson voiced his frustration that despite his reports over the "last 3½ months" the situation had not improved.[221] His proposed solution, thus maintaining the effectiveness of the RNAS, was to merge Nos. 2 and 3 Wings and that he, alongside several officers, should be sent back to Britain to "rebuild the Wing."[222]

Throughout 1915, Sykes had argued for a more extensive complement of personnel to support ongoing and future operations. As well as the operational losses that affected his frontline personnel strength, by late-1915, Sykes' stretched force began to lose experienced officers to Britain. Specifically, this took the form of an Admiralty request on 25 October 1915 to send Samson, Davies, one flight commander and three flight lieutenants back to Britain to support the formation of new squadrons.[223] As already reflected, there were personality issues between Sykes and Samson that contributed to this posting. However, Sykes recognised Samson's abilities as a wing commander and sought to keep him in the post for as long as possible, on the grounds that his knowledge and expertise could be transferred to new and inexperienced officers.[224] Sykes suggested that Gerrard from No. 2 Wing be transferred back to Britain instead of Samson.[225] Despite this, at a practical level, Sykes suggested that if "a Wing Commander" had to be transferred then Davies should remain at Gallipoli and be promoted to maintain expertise at No. 3 Wing.[226] Despite making a valid case, the situation ultimately came to a head in December 1915 when Samson and Davies departed Gallipoli. This led to a 21-year-old flight

216 Samson, *Fight and Flights*, p. 262, 272; LHCMA: Hamilton Papers, 7/4/9: diary entry, 20 August 1915.
217 RAFM: Sykes Papers, MFC77/13/35: Wing Commander Samson to Wing Captain F.H. Sykes, 2 December 1915.
218 Ibid., p. 1.
219 RAFM: Sykes Papers, MFC77/13/33: Wing Commander E.L. Gerrard to Wing Captain F.H. Sykes, 1 November 1915; Wing Commander E.L. Gerrard to Wing Captain F.H. Sykes, 23 December 1915.
220 RAFM: Sykes Papers, MFC77/13/35: Wing Commander Samson to Wing Captain F.H. Sykes, 2 December 1915, p. 1.
221 RAFM: Sykes Papers, MFC77/13/36: Wing Command C.R. Samson to Wing Captain Sykes, 22 December 1915, p. 1.
222 Ibid., p. 2.
223 RAFM: Sykes Papers, MFC77/13/35: Admiralty Letter, 25 October 1915.
224 Ibid.,
225 Ibid., p. 2.
226 Ibid., pp. 2-3.

commander being the most senior officer at No. 3 Wing.[227] Sykes in turn appointed Squadron Commander H. Fawcett from No. 2 Wing to command No. 3 Wing, thus denuding this unit one of its dwindling numbers of senior officers.[228] However, much of this ongoing discussion needs to be understood within the context of the shift towards Salonika and the closing down of the front at the Dardanelles. As such, it is understandable, though frustrating for Sykes, that the Admiralty would seek to shift experienced personnel to other postings.

Another factor affecting personnel at Gallipoli was the impact of local conditions. For example, Sykes later reflected that the "trying conditions [placed] great strain [...] on individual pilots owing to the shortage of personnel and a considerable amount of sickness."[229] He had made similar statements during the campaign, noting the need for extra personnel because of sickness, that the individual workload on personnel in the Dardanelles was greater than that in France, and that the self-contained character of units required an increase in establishments.[230] While not suffering the same level of privations as those serving in the trenches, the harsh conditions of the Eastern Mediterranean affected personnel who suffered high sickness rates.

Conclusion

On 9 January 1916, Sykes submitted to de Robeck plans for how the RNAS might be used after the MEF's evacuation. As well as distributing many of the functions established under the headquarters he had set up in August 1915, contained within this plan was the recommendation that Sykes himself was no longer required and he requested to be sent back to Britain "either with a view to further service [...] or my return to the Army."[231] The Admiralty subsequently notified de Robeck that Sykes should go back to Britain to "terminate" his work with the RNAS.[232] Vice-Admiral de Robeck noted that, despite many of the challenges reflected in this chapter, Sykes had provide much "valuable service" and that he should be confirmed in the rank of Colonel "by Brevet."[233] Sykes' commission with the RNAS was terminated on 14 March 1916.[234]

By the end of the Gallipoli campaign, air power had played a major role in supporting operations as an enabler. The RNAS provided intelligence and situational awareness to both the Royal Navy and the British Army, and supported operations on land and sea. Importantly, the

227 RAFM: Sykes Papers, MFC77/13/29: Wing Captain F.H. Sykes to Vice-Admiral Commanding EMS, 27 December 1915.
228 Ibid.
229 RAFM: Sykes Papers, MFC77/13/48: Major-General Sir Frederick Sykes to General Sir Ian Hamilton, 22 November 1919.
230 RAFM: Sykes Papers, MFC77/13/34: Wing Captain F.H. Sykes to Vice-Admiral EMS, 2 November 1915.
231 RAFM: Sykes Papers, MFC77/13/33: Wing Captain F.H. Sykes to Vice-Admiral Commanding EMS, 9 January 1916.
232 Ibid., Admiralty to Vice-Admiral Commanding EMS, 18 January 1916.
233 Sykes, *From Many Angles*, p. 184.
234 RAFM: Sykes Papers, MFC77/13/47: Secretary to the Admiralty to Wing Captain F.H. Sykes, 13 March 1916.

RNAS – in the battle for control of the air – had also conducted a variety of offensive operations both against land and maritime targets and had illustrated what was possible using concentrated air power. However, it would be wrong to suggest, as Sykes did, that had enough resources been available then greater strategic effect might have been achieved. This was an overestimation of air power's capabilities in 1915. Simply put, while ideas existed, the technology, even if the resources had been abundant, did not. Yet, the argument that air power could have done more to change the course of the Gallipoli campaign was not unique to Sykes. For example, Bromet, in 1923, argued that had more aircraft been provided to the naval phase of the campaign then more effect could have been achieved. In short, Bromet inferred that had Samson's squadron been deployed in February 1915 then perhaps there would have been no need for the subsequent landing operations and ultimately futile land campaign.[235] Such is a teleological argument based on perceived capabilities that did not exist in 1915.

It remains difficult to quantify the impact of air power at Gallipoli; however, several key examples illustrate its importance. First, for instance, towards the end of the campaign, on 5 December 1915, Lieutenant-Colonel Aspinall wrote to Sykes noting that: "[P]hotographs taken by the Air Service have proved of such value that an increased distribution is desirable in order that subordinate Commanders may be supplied with sets covering their immediate front."[236] This at least illustrates that by the end of the Gallipoli campaign senior officers recognised the importance of air power as an enabler. Moreover, Hamilton's third dispatch of 11 December 1915 praised the work of the RNAS, though the view from the soldier on the ground, as illustrated by Park's recollections, was not always so positive.[237]

Second, the 'Mitchell Report', as a critical example of organisational learning after the First World War, included many references to air power as well as dedicating two chapters on the subject. Furthermore, the evidence deployed in the 'Mitchell Report', some of which came from Ottoman sources, supports the view that air power had some impact on the enemy. Finally, the report deduced lessons in line with the experience gained, notably issues surrounding the concentration of air effort, the challenge of battling for control of the air and the importance of an "Air Force commander" to centralise control.[238] These would be key ideas for the RAF during inter-war years in its discussion with its sister services over combined operations and the development of the *Manual of Combined Operations*. Finally, the RAF itself did not ignore Gallipoli or its lessons. While Bromet may have overplayed the potential of air power, Gallipoli remained a critical topic of discussion when considering combined operations at the RAF Staff College. Finally, the three service staff colleges regularly came together to examine the challenges of combined operations and discussions regularly centred around Gallipoli as a key historical example, though whether the right lessons were learnt remains open to question.

235 TNA AIR 1/2387/228/11/30: War Experience, p. 12.
236 RAFM: Sykes Papers, MFC77/13/42: Lieutenant-Colonel C.F. Aspinall, General Staff to Officer Commanding, Royal Naval Air Service, 5 December 1915.
237 'Dispatch of Sir Ian Hamilton, 11th December 1915', in Cmd. 371, *The Final Report of the Dardanelles Commission: Part II: Conduction of Operations with Appendix of Document and Maps* (1919), p. 139-40; Park, 'Experiences in the War', pp. 92-3.
238 'Mitchell Report', pp. 397-98.

20

Care-giving and Naval Nurses at Gallipoli[1]

Phylomena Badsey

> *As usual, with the start of all British expeditions, the medical arrangements were totally inadequate to meet the requirements of the hour.*[2]

The most difficult and demanding nursing/care-giving service during the First World War was carried out on hospital ships which evacuated sick and wounded from the Gallipoli Peninsula. This work was performed throughout the whole of the campaign prior to intensification during the period December 1915–January 1916.

The principal role of all the hospital ships, operating in the English Channel between France and Great Britain's south coast, was that of sea-going ambulance i.e., to safely transport patients for further treatment. In so doing they were following the well-established medical "chain of evacuation" first developed and employed by the Royal Army Medical Corps (RAMC) during the Second Anglo-Boer War (1899–1902). The two most important professional nursing figures to emerge out of that conflict, Dame Ethel Hope Becher (1867–1948) and Dame Maud McCarthy (1859–1949), both served as "Specially Appointed Nurses" – by the Princess of Wales – with the British Army Nursing Reserve. Their individual nursing and administrative skills were honed by the challenging conditions. In 1910, Becher became Matron-in-Chief of the Queen Alexandra's Imperial Military Nursing Service (QAIMNS) and remained at this War Office post until 1919. In 1914, McCarthy was the Principal Matron at the War Office and became Matron-in-Chief for the British Expeditionary Force in France and Flanders, serving on the Western Front for the duration of the conflict. Their combined knowledge and experience of military nursing and culture was vital in the training and application of procedures and practices employed by all nurses and care-givers during the First World War; their combined influence was considerable, and their experience greatly valued.[3]

1 A version of this chapter was pressented at the Gallipoli Conference, Princess Royal Gallery, Portsmouth, 22 October 2016.
2 Ellis Ashmead-Bartlett, *The Uncensored Dardanelles* (London: Hutchinson & Co, 1920), p. 48.
3 Yvonne McEwen, *In the Company of Nurses: The History of the British Army Nursing Service in the Great War* (Edinburgh: Edinburgh University Press, 2014), pp. 41-42. See also Erica Nadin-Snelling, *Matron at War: The Story of Katy Beaufoy (1869-1918)* (Warwickshire: Brewin Books, 2014), p. 8.

The magnitude of the task of treating the Gallipoli campaign sick and wounded requires the reader to be well-grounded in the medical care and evacuation practices of the time. These patients, whether sick or wounded, would not usually be in "trench condition," except, for example, during a "heavy push" such as the opening of the Somme offensive in July 1916. For the wounded this was of particular medical importance for trench condition meant wearing the original uniform a Tommy had been injured or gassed. Thus a wounded man was a source of infection to other patients and medical personnel. Moreover, the uniform could also be permeated with lice, blood, mud and gas. Indeed, accounts exist of nurses – always in close contact with solider-patients – being overcome by the effects of phosgene, chlorine and mustard gas contaminated uniforms.[4]

If a solider-patient was still in trench condition, then a full medical assessment and examination could not take place, so blood loss and additional internal injuries, including "traumatic shock" may not have been identified. The "golden hour" – the first 60 minutes following a traumatic injury – is the most important for successful emergency treatment.[5] In the First World War military context, this meant applying field dressings, reassurance, warmth and safety, whilst requesting medical assistance usually in the form of the RAMC-trained stretcher-bearers (many of whom, as civilians, had also undergone formal Red Cross training), which, on the Western Front, ideally operated in teams of between three to six men. If employed at collecting or relay posts, they were expected to "carry" an individual for up to four miles before passing them on to the next bearer team.[6]

First there would be the regimental aid post for primary assessment and treatment; limited facilities meant that solider-patients could not remain there for more than a few hours. Medical officers were highly skilled in triage and the stabilisation of patients for medical evacuation, if needed, down the line to an advanced dressing station. Here patients could remain for up to one week to be treated prior to return to active duty or transport by a motorised field ambulance to the well-staffed (trained professional nurses inclusive) and equipped Casualty Clearing Station (CCS) usually located six miles behind the lines. Complex surgical operations were performed in these locations, which in addition to appropriate facilities also had a secure fresh water supply and good communication links via road or rail networks. The sick and wounded could remain at a CCS for up to four weeks before – if return to assigned unit was not an option – prior to movement to stationary or general hospitals in the base area. Long-term treatment could also be

4 This was a serious problem on river hospital barges. Gas, as a chemical irritant was first used by the Germans on the Western Front at Neuve Chapelle, France in October 1914, while the Germans first used poisoned gas (chlorine) at the Second Battle of Ypres on 22 April 1915. While gas was not employed by either side at Gallipoli, reports exist "that German gas warfare experts had arrive in Constantinople." This development was taken seriously by the British military and medical authorities with 60,000 gas helmets being dispatched but no plans were made for the British to employ gas at Gallipoli. John Lee, *A Soldier's Life: General Sir Ian Hamilton 1853-1947* (London: Macmillan, 2000), p. 192.

5 Since from the time of Homer and Hippocrates it was known in military medical circles that the sooner the patient received treatment, however basic, the greater their chance of survival and recovery. See McEwen, *In the Company of Nurses*, pp. 12-13. In modern terms this treatment is given within an hour of the injury.

6 Ian R. Whitehead, *Doctors in the Great War* (Barnsley: Pen & Sword, 2013), pp. 126-50; McEwen, *In the Company of Nurses*, pp. 50-58.

provided, sometimes for months, with solider-patients subsequently returned to active service. Patients with "Blighty" wounds or medical conditions requiring specialist treatment, long-term convalescence were transported by hospital ships for treatment in Great Britain or Ireland.[7]

It must be emphasised that *all* patients awaiting to board the hospital ships had already received considerable medical attention – washing and meals inclusive – and had been assessed as stable and fit to travel. Acute medical or surgical crisis did of course occur but the journey – usually at night – was short and in such a case the patients' first destination would be a well-equipped and staffed hospital. It does need to be noted that hospital ships, in effect were always in considerable danger, for example HMHS *Lanfranc* was torpedoed, without warning, and sunk by a German U-boat on 17 April 1917. Forty lives were lost, including 18 German prisoners of war. HMAT *Warilda*, was sunk on 3 August 1918 with the loss of 125 lives.[8]

The medical "chain of evacuation" for the sick and wounded British, ANZAC and in particular Indian troops at Gallipoli, was a "shambles". The journey, for staff and patients alike, was long and dangerous for everyone concerned. Only the most basic medical facilities were physically located on the Gallipoli Peninsula itself: regimental aid posts, advanced dressing stations and limited CCS with no facilities to treat long-term sick and wounded patients. For their part, hospital ships acted as floating CCS, but there were not enough of them.[9] Throughout the Gallipoli campaign, the main medical facilities were in Alexandria, Lemnos and Malta. For the majority of sick and wounded Indian troops, Alexandria and Lemnos were a staging post prior to embarkation to Bombay for long-term treatment at institutions such as Lady Harding's War Hospital.[10] Some Indian sick and wounded did find themselves in Great Britain by bureaucratic accident or because the nature of their wounds required specialist treatment.[11]

However, the "shambles" did function from day one of the campaign because due to the care and dedication of medical professionals and those supporting them in a near impossible situation. With great skill, they saved many lives by doing what they could with the resources available.

At Gallipoli, the stretcher-bearers and walking wounded utilised communication trenches to reach the regimental aid posts in the rear of the front line, but up-coming re-enforcements had priority, so the injured had to wait – sometimes for hours – before receiving medical attention. Later in the campaign separate medical evacuation trenches were dug in parallel with communication trenches. The system was limited but even these could be overwhelmed with wounded.

7 Whitehead, *Doctors in the Great War*, pp. 181-217.

8 Emily Mayhew, *Wounded: The Long Journey Home from the Great War* (London: Vintage Books, 2014); Iain Gordon, *Lifeline: A British Causality Clearing Station on the Western Front, 1918* (Stroud: The History Press, 2013). For details of HMHS *Lanfranc* see <http://forgottenwrecks.maritimearchaeologytrust.org/forgottenwrecks/casestudywrecks/hmhs-lanfranc; for HMAT *Warilda* see https://www.awm.gov.au/articles/blog/ss-warilda-troopship-hospital-ship-ambulance-transport-wreck>

9 For a detailed and accessible account of CCS work on the Western Front, which was replicated on the formal hospital ships serving Gallipoli, I recommend Thomas Scotland and Steven Heys (eds.), *War Surgery 1914-18* (Solihull: Helion & Company, 2014), which describes the operations and medical treatments being routinely carried out.

10 Peter Stanley, *Die in Battle, Not in Despair: The Indians on Gallipoli 1915* (Solihull: Helion & Company, 2015), p. 168.

11 Ibid, p. 234.

Motor ambulances load disembarked wounded at Alexandria pier during the Gallipoli campaign.

Captain George Pirie, RAMC wrote (20 May 1915) of his experience at a regimental aid post located in an old farm house with an enclosed yard and deep well, which provided a good supply of clean water – a rare luxury – near V Beach:

> It is more or less in ruins and I sleep in the corner of the yard on a stretcher with a waterproof sheet stretched over me to keep off the dew. The bullets whizz like a bee over our heads and strike the far wall of the yard, but I am quite safe. We can also hear the Turkish shells whistling past over us and our batteries around us likewise make a nasty noise.[12]

If necessary the wounded would next be moved, perhaps by ambulance wagon drawn by horses or mules – often Indian troops were the muleteers – to an advanced dressing station. But primary efforts were in the form of stretcher-bearers mainly responsible for the transport of the sick and wounded. This was a dangerous and physically demanding task; "stretcher-bearer hand" was the most common injury they suffered. Leather gloves, if available, afforded little protection and would soon became contaminated with blood and other bodily fluids. In wet and muddy conditions gloves could also cause hands to slip and lose control of wooden stretcher poles. Moreover, hands, with or without gloves, soon become callused, blistered, and cut, not to mention painful bruising.[13]

12 Michael Lucas (ed.), *Frontline Medic: Gallipoli, Somme, Ypres. The Diary of Captain George Pirie, R.A.M.C. 1914-17* (Solihull: Helion & Company, 2014), p. 48.
13 John Wells, 'A Burden to Bear: The Mental and Physical Demands on WW1 Stretcher Bearers', Waterford Institute of Technology conference, 'World War 1: Caring in Conflict', 10 April 2017.

All RAMC trained stretcher-bearers at Gallipoli took on an enhanced medical role, which drained the emotional and spiritual resources of the individuals concerned. In modern terms, they acted as "first responders and paramedics". Their patients had a multi-complex set of medical issues; not just traumatic wound injuries but long-term debilitating medical conditions such as trench fever. Moreover, patients had to be prevented from going into shock and developing the most serious consequences of dehydration.

From the deck of the SS *Aragon,* which was acting as a hospital ship, Captain Pirie watched the naval bombardment and landings on the Gallipoli Peninsula on 25 April 1915. Within minutes, three boatloads of wounded were visible: "We could see the troops being landed all day long and advancing on to the top of the cliff and lying in captured trenches and men cutting the barbed wire. We could also see the stretcher-bearers at work."[14] Following consolidation of the landing beaches, advanced dressing stations were usually situated on the beach in a canvas tent in a "sheltered" part of the front line, perhaps behind a sand-dune but still within range of enemy shelling and small-arms fire. Further selection and treatment of the wounded subsequently took place, with the most seriously injured being transferred to fixed CCSs, which provided advanced medical treatment. These, given the cramped Gallipoli rear areas, were located nearby. With limited equipment and medical supplies, no nurses, and often only one medical officer and several medical orderlies, medical procedures and complex surgical operations did take place. Mobile field ambulance units also carried out surgical procedures, often in dug-outs or other temporary accommodation; thus they provided additional support to overtaxed CCSs. It was impossible to keep either sick and wounded for any length of time at CCSs, so those that could be treated were returned, almost at once, to the firing line.[15] Only the most serious cases were evacuated, not least because the process was long and exposed the patient to further danger and risk of injury. General Sir Ian Hamilton (GOC MEF) cared deeply for the sick and wounded. In a letter to his wife Jean, Lady Hamilton, on 3 June 1915 he observed: "The guns are making a great noise as I write but it is nothing serious. Tomorrow we expect a big battle. How I wish we could have them without casualties. I hate to think of the number we shall have ..."[16] This in part reflected the reality of a struggling complex medical organisation. Indeed, from the start the number of wounded nearly overwhelmed the medical facilities, including the "chain of evacuation," during the April landings. According to the British official history:

> Fifteen thousand men were ashore; a comparatively favourable beach had been secured; the troops were in occupation of a position which, except at one point, where a dangerous gap existed, was practicable for defence; and, finally, they had succeeded in beating off a series of counter-attacks. The casualties, which amounted to two thousand, were undeniably heavy; yet they were no larger than might have been suffered by 3rd Infantry Brigade in the first hour had its landings been strenuously opposed.[17]

14 Lucas (ed.), *Frontline Medic*, p. 43.
15 Robin Prior, *Gallipoli: The End of a Myth* (London: Yale University Press, 2009); and Stanley, *Die in Battle.*
16 Celia Lee, *Jean, Lady Hamilton, 1861-1941: A Soldier's Wife* (London: Celia Lee, 2001), p. 128.
17 C.F. Aspinall-Oglander, *Military Operations Gallipoli*, Vol. I (Nashville, Tennessee: Battery Press 1992 reprint of 1929 edition), p. 196.

John Lee, Hamilton's biographer, writes: "Nobody at the time had any idea how many casualties would occur during an amphibious assault. The only modern study of medical arrangements available to them were those implemented during the Battle of Mons in August 1914."[18]

It does need to be stressed that even if all requested medical supplies, equipment and staff were made available on the peninsula, this would have reduced the Western Front of medical supplies, facilities and personnel. It was, therefore, impossible to provide the MEF with appropriate medical care and treatment. Evacuation by formal hospital ship or so-called "black ships" (see below), was the only option for both the military authorities concerned. Hamilton stressed this state of affairs to the War Office: "I am aware that it is not usual to make extensive preparations for a specified battle, but the circumstances here are altogether exceptional, as the only means of removing men from shell fire is to place them on board ship."[19]

The greatest numbers of Gallipoli casualties resulted from disease and sickness; this is not surprising given the climate, with extremes of heat and cold, which caused sunstroke, hypothermia and frostbite causalities.[20] MEF soldiers never had time to properly acclimatise to local conditions and uniforms, in particular winter issue, were quite inadequate for the task of protecting troops from the bitter cold encountered during the final months of the campaign. Living conditions – in dugout, under canvas, within trenches or at rest in ad hoc camps – afforded little protection, making sleep difficult and, in winter, trench systems flooded, which caused trench foot. Diet, primarily consisting of hard-tack biscuits and bully beef was monotonous; fresh fruit and vegetables were rare. For the Indian troops, the majority Gurkhas or Sikhs, were provided with ration alternatives such as rice, lentils and chickpeas with extra flour issued to make chapattis and curries. On rare occasions, fresh goat and sheep meat, sourced from local herds were issued.[21] Nonetheless, calories, vitamins and minerals needed to sustain hard manual labour and fight off infection were lacking in issue rations.[22] Fresh bread was of poor quality but made more appealing with tinned plum and apple jam; tea remained a constant source of comfort. The lacklustre diet also produced stomach problems whilst hard-tack biscuits broke teeth and caused other dental related issues. Fresh water sources were scarce and often contaminated – all drinking water was rationed and very little was available for any other purpose, personal hygiene inclusive. To this end, troops were expected to use sea water for all washing and bathing, which often resulted in skin irritations and delayed the healing of scrapes and cuts. The majority of available drinking water was shipped in by sea to be stored in large tanks situated at beachheads where it was filtered and distributed in empty petrol tins. Sea water was also treated by a desalination process, which involved boiling, the condensed vapour stored in water distillation towers where further purification processes occurred. Strong measures were taken to protect water resources and care taken to prevent dehydration the symptoms thereof including dizziness, low blood pressure and rapid heart rate which could lead to confusion and shock with internal organs failing if not treated. Despite extreme thirst, many men refused to drink

18 John Lee, *A Solder's Life*, p. 154.
19 Ibid., p. 196.
20 Prior, *Gallipoli*, pp. 224-26.
21 Stanley, *Die in Battle*, pp. 109-13, 248-49, 268.
22 Alison Wishart, '"As fit as fiddles" and "as weak as kittens": The importance of food, water and diet to the Anzac campaign at Gallipoli', *First World War Studies*,7:2 (2016), pp. 131-64.

Walking-wounded embarking from Suvla.

the desalinized product because the local sea water was often contaminated with the bloated corpses/carcasses of men and animals, thus almost constant thirst was a feature of the Gallipoli campaign. Conversely, the Ottoman defenders enjoyed access to fresh water via deep wells.[23]

The endemic flies and other pests were also a constant source of infection. Given the troops' impaired immune system, any cut or graze could become septic and insect bites rapidly transformed into sores. While rest camps were established on the islands of Lemnos and Imbros, the amenities at both were inadequate for the needs of the exhausted men. They were, nevertheless, better than the so-called rest areas on the peninsula, which were always within range of enemy batteries.[24]

Even fit healthy young men will physically deteriorate without suitable diet, plenty of fresh water and opportunities for rest and recuperation. If not provided, they become susceptible to a wide range of diseases and infections. Dysentery was a major health risk at Gallipoli. Over 80 percent were infected with the disease which is caused by endemic bacteria penetrating intestine/bowel linings. This produced swelling and ulcerations that prevented fluids from being absorbed. Other symptoms are severe diarrhoea, liquid in form, composed of blood and pus. Enteric Fever (Typhoid), also caused by bacteria-based symptoms, can be mild and present as diarrhoea or constipation. However, usually within a week or months' time, further symptoms (loss of appetite, headaches, general aches and pains, including abdominal pain, lethargy and in the later stages a high fever, bleeding and perforation of the intestines) can also develop. In severe cases, patients become delirious, one out of three patients infected expiring. Vaccinations were available but did not always take. Malaria was also a particular risk at Cape Helles and Suvla Bay, symptoms including shaking chills, high fever followed by profuse sweating with

23 Kevin Fewster (ed.), *Bean's Gallipoli: The Diaries of Australia's Official War Correspondent* (Crow's Nest: Allen & Unwin, 2007), pp. 60, 104-05, 123, 240; Nigel Steel & Peter Hart, *Defeat at Gallipoli* (London: Papermac, 1994), pp. 122, 259.

24 Aspinall-Oglander, *Military Operations Gallipoli*, Vol. I, pp. 77, 99.

accompanying headache and nausea, vomiting and diarrhoea, which resulted in the patient becoming anaemic and more susceptible to other infections. Due to its relapsing symptomatic nature, Malaria could take years to develop into its most chronic and debilitating form, which over time destroys the patient's health and contributed to early death.[25]

Last, but not least was Trench Fever. The result of body lice infestation, it has a two-week incubation period. Thereafter, a man so affected can develop sudden high fever, severe headaches, resulting in a debilitating "relapsing fever". Symptoms include pain during eye movement, dizziness, muscle soreness, increased shin sensitivity to the touch and occasional rashes. An effective drug treatment was available at the time but, with consequent side effects to liver and kidneys, patients remained in need of rudimentary tender loving care (TLC), with plenty of rest, cleanliness of surroundings and a good diet. With application of this regimen, a patient could recover in four to six weeks' time. Nevertheless, Trench Fever had long-term after effects – fatigue, anxiety, headaches, heart palpitations and high blood pressure. At Gallipoli, issue uniforms did undergo a form of treatment to remove mature adult lice and eggs using improvised disinfectants. Thus clothing was soaked in "Serbian Barrels" but the process proved ineffective due to wood and hot water shortages in addition to a dearth of active disinfectant ingredients required to eliminate bacteria and other microorganisms ingrained within fabric and garment seams.[26]

A common sight on the peninsula were queues outside the medical officer's tent as part of the morning "sick parade" during which routine medical assessment and basic treatments were carried out but, given prevailing conditions and circumstances, treatment was very limited indeed. Only during May and mid-August 1915 due to fierce fighting, did traumatic wound injuries become the primary cause of MEF casualties. The Ottoman artillery, skilled and well-practiced, inflicted shrapnel and HE injuries whilst offensive and active trench warfare resulted in a plethora of serious injuries. Constant sniping was an ever-present danger, bullets causing shattered bones and soft tissue damage. Journalist Ellis Ashmead-Bartlett recalled a common sight: "Endless processions of wounded, covered with dirt, congealed blood, half-dead with thirst, worn out with fatigue, and tormented with flies, were carried down to the beaches."[27]

Only the most severe cases of the sick and wounded reached CCSs from which they were subsequently evacuated. Those most fortunate were dispatched to hospital ships; those less so were directed to troop ships employed as medical transports ill-equipped to transport or treat the sick and wounded. Unflatteringly known as "black ships" because, unlike the officially designated hospital ships, they did not bear internationally recognised Red Cross emblems.[28] There are indications that the Germans believed British military authorities were abusing, in contravention of the Convention, the Red Cross symbol by evacuating able-bodied men on

25 T.J. Mitchell, *Medical Services: Casualties and Medical Statistics of the Great War* (Uckfield: Naval & Military Press reprint of 1931 edition), p. 199; Steel & Hart, *Defeat at Gallipoli*, pp. 315-20.

26 Steel & Hart, *Defeat at Gallipoli*, pp. 310-11, 381.

27 Ellis Ashmead-Bartlett, *The Uncensored Dardanelles* (London: Hutchinson & Co, 1920), p. 154.

28 The Red Cross emblem has no religious connotations, being the inversion of the national flag of Switzerland and marking the historic connection between Switzerland and the original Geneva Convention of 1864, which sought to protect injured war victims and those authorised to care for them. Internationally recognised as the generic symbol for medical services, the Red Cross emblem (employed since 1876), has no connection with the International Red Cross or Red Crescent.

Nr. 3
Berlin, den 16. Januar 1916
LXIX. Jahrgang
Kladderadatsch
Die Kreuzritter von Gallipoli
Die Rückzugsoperationen werden durch die praktische Benutzung des Roten Kreuzes
„einen unvergänglichen Platz in der englischen Geschichte einnehmen"!

German cartoon claiming British misuse of the internationally recognised protective symbol: "The crusaders of Gallipoli. Through the practical application of the Red Cross the withdrawal 'occupied an incomparable place in English history.'" (*Kladderadatsch*, 16 January 1916)

hospital ships. This was, of course, untrue but clearly demonstrates the enemy's willingness to propagandize MEF difficulties when evacuating sick and wounded.[29]

Conditions on black ships were overcrowded and horrendous. Patients remained unwashed and in "trench condition", throughout the voyage. Accommodation was found on or below deck, but food, fresh drinking water and bed linens were often lacking, as were basic sanitary arrangements, the latter of particular concern when treating dysentery cases. Moreover, soldier-patients often acted as medical orderlies to those in worse condition. The on-board mortality rate was very high, the medical staff – if they existed at all – usually consisting of a small team of four or five doctors and orderlies assisted by a few trained nurses. They did sterling work, but it amounted to the most urgent cases receiving basic first aid treatment. For example, one officer recalled: "On one ship, the only man with any knowledge of medicine was the veterinary officer who, assisted

29 British Red Cross <https://www.redcross.org.uk/about-us/what-we-do/protecting-people-in-armed-conflict/the-emblem##>

by clerks and grooms of the waiting Echelon B, saved dozens of lives by prompt and careful action."[30]

The majority of black ships sailed to Alexandria, the primary Mediterranean theatre hospital base, a journey of approximately three to four days. At one point during the campaign, medical facilities there were overwhelmed. As Dr Yvonne McEwen subsequently observed:

> Due to the shortage of hospital accommodation the casualties languished on the decks and passageways of the transporter, awaiting medical and nursing intervention. For six days their wound dressings remained unchanged and many of the wounded still had on their original field dressing. The situation arose because there were no nurses on the transporter and only three doctors and four orderlies, overworked and exhausted.[31]

In such instances, unloaded vessels sailed on to Great Britain or Ireland, the latter destination ships docking at the east coast ports of Belfast, Dublin, Cork and Waterford.[32] The deplorable conditions ensured some soldier-patients died enroute, whilst the medical condition of others deteriorated until treatment following disembarkation.

Back in Alexandria, offers of qualified medical help were not always accepted by the military medical authorities. In July 1915 a "lady doctor," Miss R.E. Glanville, offered her professional services and was rejected. The cable read: "Do not want lady doctors number doctors in Egypt ample."[33] Despite this, in addition to the aforementioned examples, the medical facilities at Alexandria were rapidly expanded and all suitable buildings converted into "temporary hospitals". The professional medical staff, which included Indian Army medical units – famed for the consideration and skill with which they cared for their patients – was increased the doctors and surgeons were already familiar with many of the diseases and broader medical conditions from which the sick and wounded from Gallipoli were suffering.[34] Professional nurses – all women – from the Australian Army Nursing Service (AANS) arrived, serving in Egypt and on Lemnos, but a few, discerning urgent requirements, also served aboard the black ships. The local British expatriate community of Egypt also provided practical assistance for Alexandria temporary hospitals, wives and daughters becoming Voluntary Aid Detachment (VAD) nurses whose Egyptian servants also found themselves employed in improvised hospitals as support staff. A large sum of money was also raised to equip and furnish the "temporary hospitals". This reflected generous community and financial support to the wounded and sick so common in Great Britain from August 1914 onwards.[35]

Hospital ships or medical transport were dispatched on the basis of which vessels filled-up first. Lighters and steam pinnaces, which ordinarily brought in supplies to beachfront piers, embarked wounded directly after unloading. This usually took place at sun-down. The walking sick and wounded made their own way to the piers; others were carried by stretcher-bearers from CCSs that doubled as "clearing stations". The embarkation process to evacuate sick and

30 McEwen, *In the Company of Nurses*, p. 96.
31 Ibid., p. 99.
32 Ibid., pp. 98-104; Mitchell, *Medical Services*, pp. 198-207.
33 Stanley, *Die in Battle*, p. 234.
34 Ibid., pp. 143-46.
35 McEwen, *In the Company of Nurses*, p. 99.

wounded during heavy fighting, bad weather or prioritization of incoming supplies over the outgoing wounded could last for days and is a tribute to the work carried out by non-combatant elements throughout the Gallipoli campaign. As Ashmead-Bartlett later observed:

> Day after day, night after night, the officers and men of the Royal Army Service Corps, the Army Ordnance Department, the Army Medical Corps, and the hundreds engaged in clerical work, toiled and sweated in the great heat, amidst storms of sand, tormented by millions of flies and ever opposed to the nerve-racking shell fire. The officers and men of the naval beach parties, and all those engaged in the handling of tugs and lighters worked without cessation, fully exposed on the improvised quays. During this time an incalculable quantity of stores, munitions, and ammunition passed through their hands, and it was only their unselfish and devoted labours, under unparalleled conditions, which made it possible for us to maintain this large army in the field.[36]

It was not uncommon for wounded to receive further injuries from stray bullets or shrapnel whilst awaiting evacuation. All were transferred to lighters – small flat-bottomed boats which could take 12 stretcher-cases per trip but were unstable in rough seas. Both walking wounded and stretcher-cases, together with supporting care-givers, continued to be regarded as legitimate targets, though it was apparent this was a medical evacuation and not troop deployment. Coming alongside hospital or black ships anchored offshore, rope ladders and walk-ways were utilised by the wounded able to do so, whilst stretcher-cases were hoisted aboard by derricks.[37]

Designated hospital ships, such as HMHS *Aquitania*, were requisitioned passenger liners fitted out and equipped for medical service. They could accommodate on average between 400 and 2,000 patients, some of which would be treated in ship hammocks. On the smaller vessels, the medical staff consisted of four doctors, six trained nurses and six to eight orderlies. The larger hospital ships, for example, HMHS *Britannic* which could accommodate 2,000 patients, had a prescribed RAMC staff of 1,066. Experience on these vessels was in stark contrast to black ships and similar craft. Australian Lieutenant Hugo Throssell VC wrote of his experience of medical evacuation:

> Dr Bently came and had a look at me and packed me straight off to hospital on the ship. I cannot describe the luxury of a bath and clean pyjamas, clean sheets and a comfortable bunk. I slept for hours and woke up with the beautiful face of one of those grand Red Cross Nurses bending over me.[38]

From there, Throssell was sent to hospitals on Lemnos, Malta, Gibraltar and finally Wandsworth, London. But he appears to have been in error, for no Red Cross trained VAD served aboard hospital ships. Rather, Gallipoli assigned vessels were staffed by members of Queen Alexandra's

36 Ashmead-Bartlett, *The Uncensored Dardanelles*, pp. 171–72.
37 Lucas (ed.), *Frontline Medic*, pp. 42-46.
38 Malcolm Higham and John Sweetman, 'Lieutenant Hugo Throssell VC: 10th Australian Light Horse, AIF', *Sabretache*, Special Issue (2015), pp. 17–18.

QARNNS sisters pose with Royal Navy, Royal Marine personnel and civilians at the entrance of the Royal Marine Infirmary, Deal 1913. (Private collection)

Royal Naval Nursing Service (QARNNS) and QAIMNS.[39] British military nurses were attired in a very distinctive grey serge (washable dress), veil and a short shoulder cloak known as a "tippet" on which were piping, badges or other insignia. Both QARNNS and QAIMNS were founded in 1902 to be followed by the Territorial Force Nursing Service founded 1908, which consisted of civilian nurses who could be mobilised in time of war. They wore dresses of grey/blue material with a cape edged in scarlet and a veil. Working alongside QARNNS these British military nursing services had their individual entry and service requirements but all were professional, trained nurses who provided medical care throughout 1914-18. Throssell's confusion might have arisen of the Red Cross insignia, a recognised symbol of the medical profession, worn on the naval nurse rank badge.[40]

Assigned to hospital ships, nurses from the various services would employ their wide-ranging clinical training for the benefit of wounded charges, something readily acknowledged by the doctors on-board. Indeed, sisters triaged patients and, in a life and death decision-making process, establish the order by which causalities were treated, the most seriously wounded, requiring long and complex operations. In a war zone, sometimes under fire, the triaging of patients certainly saves lives but is a difficult undertaking for those responsible. Under these trying circumstances, it also meant that those deemed capable of recovery took priority over

39 QARNNS nurses followed in a long and distinguished Royal Navy traditionfrom 1884 onwards. Sisters nursed at the Royal Naval hospitals at Haslar and Plymouth and, from 1897, on-board ships. Though small by other service standards, there were 81nurses in the regular service and 200 in the reserve by 1919. During 1914-18 they served on nine hospital ships and at 15 naval hospitals.

40 *The British Red Cross* <http://www.redcross.org.uk/en/About-us/Who-we-are/History-and-origin/Beginning-of-the-Movement>

those mortally wounded, so contemporary nursing practices of "sitting with the dying" seldom occurred. Sister Anna Cameron, a 36-year old QAIMNS serving aboard HMHS *Delta* observed: "[T]he memory of some things which have often had to be left undone in the stress of War nursing stabs and stabs in the quiet days."[41]

The triage process having taken place, soldier-patients were stabilised and made comfortable prior to surgery or other treatments. Sister Cameron's vessel was staffed and equipped to take 536 patients.[42] Nevertheless, during one trip from Gallipoli to a British seaport, HMHS *Delta* carried 1,240 sick and wounded all of whom required intensive nursing services.[43] In her letters home Cameron remarked – somewhat breathlessly at first – how she was when within range of enemy shellfire:

> Shells from the Turks were actually dropping round our ship. We were actually in the firing line. We saw one ship hit. Her aft torn away. We weren't a bit nervous. It all seemed so matter of fact somehow, but the awful noise of the guns was trying.[44]

Observing the fighting on land through borrowed field glasses, she claimed to have witnessed "R.A.M.C men being shot as they tried to rescue the wounded, and a padre killed by a sniper fire as he ministered to casualties on the beach.[45] Cameron also recorded "the hopelessness of struggling against heavy odds and unable to relieve suffering adequately tries me so dreadfully. The other sisters keep calmer inside – I can't. If only I could."[46] She also wrote of the new medical responsibilities assigned by doctors. They were no longer to simply follow a doctor's orders, but practice diagnosis, deciding on treatment and dispensing drugs when necessary. It must be remembered that these were professional, trained nurses with years of clinical experience, much of it gained in military hospitals. Thus it is more than likely that similar practices were applied on other hospital ships. Further to this, one doctor instructed Cameron to "give morphia at my own discretion and to do as I like. Oh dear that few hours. I had scares."[47] This was an unprecedented level of trust between doctor to a nurse; nursing as a distinct profession did not yet exist at the time, but this ad hoc arrangement demonstrates both the professionalism of the nursing staff and the often-desperate situations in which medical staff found themselves throughout the Gallipoli campaign. On board HMHS *Delta,* nursing focus was on clinical assessment, triage and stabilisation of patients awaiting treatment – patient ablutions and change of clothes could wait. As Dr Yvonne McEwen observed:

> The policy makes sense; nurses learned very quickly that mud and dirt were less life-threatening than haemorrhage, shook, undressed wounds, uncontrolled pain, and physical and mental exhaustion.[48]

41 Vivien Newman, *We Also Served: The Forgotten Women of the First World War* (Barnsley: Pen & Sword, 2014), p. 40.
42 The official medical complement of HMHS *Delta* was six medical officers, 12 nursing sisters, 45 additional support staff i.e., medical orderlies and stretcher-bearers.
43 Newman, *We also served*, p. 40.
44 Ibid., p. 39.
45 McEwen, *In the Company of Nurses*, p. 95.
46 Newman, *We also served*, p. 40.
47 McEwen, *In the Company of Nurses*, p. 97.
48 Ibid., p. 98.

On 8 May 1915 Cameron observed:

> We had taken in 400 horribly wounded men straight from the field. Some were shot further in the boats which took them to us. The gangway ran with blood. Some of the poor fellows hadn't got one dressing on. One needed all one's common sense and courage. We 3 sisters had 200 of the wounded and only 6 orderlies at that time, so many were needed for stretcher bearers. We had to recognise the seriousness of a case at once and decide at lightning speed which to leave and which to do first. They came pouring in – and oh the wild rushes stopping haemorrhage, treating shock and collapse. The orderlies were good but untrained, and no good for emergencies. The doctors were operating as hard as they could tear, only 4 of them you see, and many lives were saved. By 3 a.m. all went to bed quite dead beat except one sister and myself.[49]

QARNNS Sister Eveline Campbell wrote of her hospital ship experience on 7 August 1915, just as the casualties from the August offensive started coming in:

> Worked to get place ready for wounded which arrived in p.m. 1380 of them, mostly stretcher cases & very bad. Some brought on dead. Had 20 deaths during voyage. Saw aeroplane very close to us, one French one, also submarines & T.B.Ds [torpedo boat destroyers]. Heard firing all day. Could see smoke distinctly – We spent all afternoon & night dressing wounds. We left 8 p.m. Men in every comer of the ship. Wards frightfully hot. A good many Australians amongst men. M.Os [medical officers] operated nearly all night.[50]

Naval terms might have been employed but the same procedures were applied on the Western Front. Ideally, all solider-patients were washed, their clothes, dressings and bandages changed in a long and painful process. For some, this could occur three or four times a day and last up to 30 minutes. Diet and hydration was in itself a basic form of medical treatment. Ensuring that a soldier-patient could sleep undisturbed was also part of nursing care, which included the "cold sponging" procedure. Routine nursing care comprised of the taking of pulses/temperatures, and drug dispensing. Meals were served according to diet sheets. Bed pans were in constant demand and soiled bed linens changed whenever necessary. Surgical patients required constant monitoring. While most urgent cases would have undergone on-board procedures, many operations were carried out at land-based CCSs beforehand. These patients required the most intensive round the clock care which focused on stabilization due to haemorrhage and infection risks.[51]

The unfortunate result of shrapnel and bullets, soldier-patients frequently suffered from double trauma injuries in addition to dysentery and malaria. Fresh water was always limited, the wounded suffering from heat and lack of ventilation encountered whilst recuperating in on-board sick bays. The atmosphere below deck often reeked of bodily odours and infection combined with carbolic soap, iodine and "Edinburgh University Solution of Line" (Eusol), a powerful antiseptic formula. Medical staff encountered cramped and stuffy shipboard working

49 Newman, *We Also Served*, p. 39.
50 Imperial War Museum (IWM): Document No. 947, Miss E. Campbell Papers, diary.
51 For a clear and detailed analysis of nursing procedures and practices see Mayhew, *Wounded*.

conditions where hygiene standards for sterile operating theatres and epidemic prevention had to be carefully maintained whilst constantly moving up and down with sea swell.

Having been assessed by the medical staff of formal hospital ships, patients expected to recover within three weeks were dispatched to tented hospital camps on Lemnos, a journey of four hours. The most serious cases, often requiring surgery, were dispatched to Alexandria, a journey of up to four days. By the end of the Gallipoli campaign, 36,000 hospital beds were available, many in requisitioned buildings such as hotels. Malta could be reached in six days. These sailing times are approximate and in bad weather could take longer. Sea sickness another problem shipboard medical staff had to deal with.[52]

The deep harbour of Mudros, on Lemnos Island, and surrounding area had been, from February 1915, a hospital stores depot. By May it had a bed capacity of 18,000 but it was not an ideal location for development and expansion of a medical establishment that served British, ANZAC and Indian sick and wounded. With a limited fresh water supply, Lemnos was lacking recuperation and convalescence facilities. Medical staff support facilities, accommodation and sanitation arrangements inclusive, were also poor.[53] Appearances could be deceiving. Awed by the picturesque Mediterranean vista, Eveline Campbell observed:

> Arrived at Mudros Bay at 1 p.m. Beautiful entrance. Many battleships & cruisers. "Lord Nelson" & "King George" among them. The twin ship to the [RMS] "Lusitania", [RMS] "Mauretania" also [RMS] "Aquitania" biggest boats afloat. Four hospital ships counting our own in harbor.[54]

Having been successfully treated, patients were returned to active service as soon as possible. For its part, Malta was at the centre of medical provision for the sick and wounded of the Gallipoli campaign. The first patient arrived on 4 May 1915. By the time of the evacuation some 57,900 men had been treated there. At its peak in January 1916, Malta had 334 medical officers and 913 nurses employed in 27 hospitals established in fixed and tented locations; on average 2,000 sick and wounded patients were treated per week.[55]

Hospital and black vessels were vulnerable to enemy action. Ship crews, as Campbell made clear, were aware of this danger. On 15 August 1915 she remarked in her diary:

> Expect to sail at 6 p.m. – Word came that troopship had been sunk on way from Alex[andria] to Mudros. 1100 troops on board – it was torpedoed. No other particulars. Very comfortable on this boat. She is a P & O & very cool cabins. Heard that nearly 1000 perished on "Royal Edward". Slept nearly all day.[56]

And the next day:

52 *Military Hospitals: Malta During the Great War* <http://maltaramc.com/articles/contents/greatwar.html>
53 Mudros Bay was a small Greek port on the island of Lemnos in the Mediterranean Sea. It became a vital staging post for British hospital ships evacuating sick and wounded from the peninsula.
54 IWM: Document No. 947, Miss E. Campbell Papers, diary.
55 *Military Hospitals: Malta During the Great War* <http://maltaramc.com/articles/contents/greatwar.html>
56 IWM: Document No. 947, Miss E. Campbell Papers, diary.

> Passed Rhodes Is[land]. To have a memorial service for those on board Royal Edward – Ship stopped at the spot where the disaster occurred & the burial service was read. Very impressive. Dead March was played. We saw a great deal of wreckage as we passed the region.[57]

With the failure of the August offensive, the Gallipoli campaign reached a military stalemate, resulting in the Suvla and Anzac sectors being evacuated in December 1915, and the abandonment of Cape Helles in January 1916. In terms of the care and evacuation of the sick and wounded, care-givers on the Gallipoli Peninsula and the wider theatre of operations performed to the professional standards given the trying circumstances. This extended beyond the stretcher-bearers to include all who provided practical help, support and comfort to the sick and wounded.

Throughout this chapter the term "soldier-patient" has been stressed because medical evacuation as experienced at Gallipoli *vis-à-vis* other fronts proved impossible given the nature of the campaign. ANZAC force documents and letters often comment on the contemporary cultural phenomena of "mateship" culture that developed during the campaign and its subsequent importance in the creation of an Australian sense of identity. I suggest that an element of this also took place within the MEF's British formations/units. More importantly, nursing and care-giving at Gallipoli provided a successful working model for the military hierarchy to emulate, enhance and develop for the high-risk MEF evacuation during December 1915–January 1916. According to an official account of the MEF withdrawal:

> The hospital tents were standing as usual; and a few as were the men in front, they were busy keeping the usual bivouac fires burning and giving the last touches to the devices by which the final retirement was to be masked and a possible advance of the enemy checked.[58]

Hamilton biographer John Lee marvelled at the evacuation's success:

> Despite the sad need to slaughter all the animals ashore and the destruction of vast supplies and stores, not one man was lost in the process. The deception plans and stealth of the whole proceedings remain among the greatest achievements in military history. It had all been planned and executed by those same staff officers who had been, and were still being, reviled and despised by journalists and politicians at home.[59]

QARNNS and Reserve personnel are an under-researched topic, their contribution little known outside a specialist area. University of Edinburgh academic Yvonne McEwen has done much to correct this with her seminal *In the Company of Nurses* (2014). For her part, Sue Light has done excellent work in uncovering the nursing services lost records. Housed at the National Archives (Kew), they are very scant indeed, providing little more than name and base service record that require further linking with official records and/or private papers and diaries. In order to determine and understand context together with individual, not just with regard to professional

57 Ibid.

58 Julian Corbett, *Naval Operations: History of the Great War Based on Official Documents*, Vol. 3 (Uckfield: Naval & Military Press reprint of 1923 edition), p. 239.

59 John Lee, *A Solder's life*, p. 225.

nursing but also as a woman from a particular cultural, political and social background, it is important that these nurses' collective and individual contribution is not lost. Adhering to the highest professional standards, naval nurses were disciplined with a strong sense of duty. Thus there was some reluctance to record details of their working lives in personal diaries. The few letters that exist have, following contemporary conventions of taste and tone, been self-censored. Of those examined, none commented upon individual colleagues nor patients or criticised the conduct of the war. Whilst I am most grateful for the few that do exist, they are general and unassuming in tone, often discussing the weather and off-duty activities. Such understatement conveys a false impression of the writer's work on formal hospital ships, if one is lacking the necessary historical and, to a lesser extent, medical background. To quote once again the diary of Miss Eveline Campbell:

> Very hot morning. We were to have gone for a sail at 9 a.m. but no wind, played bridge instead. Went over to "Tunisian" for lunch – Got home at 7.30. Played bridge & ate chocs.[60]

When first researching this chapter, I encountered an on-line collection of photographs from a nursing sister's private album. Taken on-board, a requisitioned passenger liner making its way to the Gallipoli Peninsula. Although difficult to discern, it appears the subjects are QARNNS or reserve personnel. They are depicted strolling about decks unconcerned and conversing with ship officers in a decorous manner, as one would expect of the best traditions of the service. I do not begrudge these ladies these fleeting days of enjoyment on the high seas, but nor do I welcome a perception that this was some sort of pleasure cruise given their vital contributions to the Gallipoli campaign and subsequent nursing service throughout the First World War.

60 IWM: Document no. 947, Miss E. Campbell Papers, diary.

21

"Each read each other's soul": British and ANZAC Chaplains at Gallipoli

Linda Parker

Father William Finn, the Roman Catholic padre attached to 1st Royal Dublin Fusiliers, perished during the legendary amphibious assault on V Beach (25 April 1915). Ignoring a direct order to absent himself from the battalion as it approached the shore under fierce Ottoman machine-gun fire, the steadfast chaplain was struck by a hail of bullets. Seriously wounded, Finn carried on comforting the wounded until his death. He was the first British Roman Catholic padre to die in action during the First World War. His fatal decision to flout official orders is one that was emulated by many other chaplains when confronting the unique, as opposed to the Western Front, difficulties and dangers experienced throughout the Gallipoli campaign.

The British Army Chaplains Department had, during 1914-15, previously dealt with multiple recruitment and deployment problems with regard to its perceived role in a global conflict. The outbreak of war in August 1914 resulted in a certain amount of rapid decision making on the part of the Anglican Church hierarchy. Archbishop Davidson unequivocally observed to diocesan bishops that: "The position of an active combatant in our army is incompatible with one who has sought and received holy orders."[1] Therefore, clergy desiring involvement had to resign their post prior to enlistment as combatants. Some 730 priests subsequently served in the British and Imperial armies of whom 535 were combatants.[2] Others applied to the Army Chaplains' Department for a commission as a "Temporary Chaplain to the Forces". The situation was complicated by the fact it was difficult to obtain accurate numbers of how many chaplains would be required from the War Office. Many priests applied for immediate appointment as chaplains, with varied responses. The Revd E.J. Kennedy who had volunteered at the outset, was informed that he was not wanted at that time, but several days later he was called up with "alarming suddenness" and joined the 7th Division which was embarking for France.[3] Christopher Chavasse, the Bishop of Liverpool's son, was immediately accepted and departed for France on 20 August 1914. Curates had to wait until they were released by incumbents. This

1 J.R. Moorman, *B.K. Cunningham: A Memoir* (London: SCM Press, 1947), p. 72.
2 Email correspondence from Charles Beresford, 23rd July 2016. See Charles Beresford, *The Christian Soldier: The life of Col. Bernard William Vann, VC, MC and Bar, Croix de Guerre avec Palmes* (Solihull: Helion & Company, 2016).
3 E.J. Kennedy, *With the Immortal Seventh Division* (London: Hodder & Stoughton, 1915), p. 7.

was the case for the celebrated Phillip "Tubby" Clayton who did not enlist until early 1915. For their part, incumbents had to manage a suitable parish prior to enlistment.

The needs of nonconformist recruits for the expanded Kitchener's Army resulted in the rationalisation of chaplain enlistments from various nonconformist denominations. The Wesleyan Methodists and Scottish Presbyterian churches maintained an independent relationship with the Army Chaplains' Department. However, Congregationalists, Baptists, United Methodists and Primitive Methodists formed a "United Board"[4] in January 1915. Henceforth, all men attesting to these denominations were placed under the aegis of minsters represented by the board. Further to this, Army Instruction No. 231 of 25 April 1915 stated that each infantry and cavalry division would have one Church of England chaplain, one Roman Catholic chaplain and one Nonconformist minister. The latter appointment was to be Presbyterian if the brigade hailed from Scotland or Northern Ireland, but otherwise could be Wesleyan, Methodist or any other United Board denomination.[5]

At the start of the war there was a flood of eager volunteer priests from all sections of the Roman Catholic Church. As with the Anglican experience, there were long delays between volunteering and subsequent appointments. The initial shortage of Roman Catholic priests was addressed by parliamentary campaign and contemporary religious press despite the fact that the number of Roman Catholic volunteers was of greater proportion than other denominations.[6]

By early 1915, the temporary chaplains were experiencing nascent development of trench warfare on the Western Front whilst simultaneously trying to identify their role within the expanding BEF. Their mobilisation had been somewhat chaotic, with no provisions for postings, rations or transport. Roger Lloyd, commenting on the chaplain's task, observed: "He could indeed become necessary, but he must create that necessity himself."[7] Were they to be the purveyors of "Holy Grocery",[8] expending their energies on provision of material comforts and troop recreation, or were the spiritual needs of all ranks to be their primary role? When behind the lines, was the chaplain's place to administer services at base camp and hospitals? If attached to a field ambulance, was he to provide spiritual succour and medical assistance? In addition, were chaplains meant to be in the frontline? From the outset, the respective army headquarters developed a general policy of forbidding chaplains to enter the frontline because it was believed they would serve no useful purpose there. These orders were often disregarded, especially by Roman Catholic chaplains who carried on with the theological imperative of administering the sacraments of Holy Communion or last rites to the dying. This led to a contentious perception, highlighted in the post-war publications of Siegfried Sassoon, Robert Graves and Guy Chapman among others, that Roman Catholic padres were fearless and of more use at the front than their other denomination contemporaries.[9]

4 TNA WO/298. Detailed arrangements were announced in War Office Instruction 125.

5 TNA WO/293 cited by P. Howson, *Muddling Through: The Organisation of British Army Chaplaincy in World War One* (Solihull: Helion & Company, 2013), p. 84.

6 Tom Johnstone & James Hagerty, *The Cross on the Sword: Catholic Chaplains in the Forces* (London: Geoffrey Chapman, 1996), Chapter 7.

7 Roger Lloyd, *The Church of England 1900-1965* (London: SCM Press, 1966), p. 215.

8 A phrase coined by the Revd Neville Talbot, senior chaplain, describing the work of chaplains in providing material comforts to servicemen.

9 For example, see Robert Graves, *Goodbye to All That* (London: Jonathan Cape, 1929), p. 158.

There was, however, a great deal of high level opposition to the army orders from the Anglican and Reformed churches in addition to the chaplains themselves. Senior chaplain Neville Talbot was extremely outspoken with regard to official proscription and utilised his connections as the son of Bishop Edward Talbot as a means of expressing dissatisfaction. The Revd Edmund Kennedy, who embarked for France at the beginning of the war, observed: "The question is often asked should a chaplain be under fire? It is impossible to avoid if he is serving troops under fire, and he must take his chance like everyone else."[10] For example, the Revd Maurice Peel was badly wounded going forward with his battalion during the First Battle of Ypres (19 October–30 November 1914). Nevertheless, BEF chaplains were still officially forbidden to enter the frontline as late as autumn 1915.

The Gallipoli campaign commenced after the Army Chaplains' Department had a certain amount experience of a chaplain's role in battle. Unlike the situation on the Western Front, where Anglicans were under the sole control of Bishop Gwynne and those of all other denominations under Chaplain General Dr Simms, the principal Mediterranean/Middle East chaplain was the Revd A.W. Horden. The Gallipoli landings put a huge strain on Horden's command, chaplains being required for troop and hospital ship, base camps, as well as on the peninsula. William Ewing remarked, "[M]uch of the comfort and consequent efficiency of the chaplains was due to the Revd A.V.C. Horden, principal chaplain and his assistant the Revd A.C.E. Jarvis ... his administration was broad in outlook generous in spirit."[11] Ewing met Horden in Alexandria. The latter was a high church Anglican and a regular chaplain: "His ideals of religious and military duty combined with a wide experience and a generally broad outlook. These made him an ideal administrator of the various denominations of the chaplains' department in the MEF ... He was the friend and helper of all."[12]

The Australian Army Chaplains' Department has been formed as early as 1913. Each denomination (Anglican, Presbyterian, Roman Catholic and Methodist) had an appointed Chaplain General and one senior chaplain per state. The six senior denominational chaplains forwarded the names of suitable chaplains to a military board, so the AIF, as in Great Britain, had little input with regard to the selection process. The four chaplain ranks, 1st to 4th class, corresponded with the British military ranks of colonel, major, captain and lieutenant.

At the outbreak of war, it was decided that chaplains from each denomination in Australia would be allocated on the basis of the 1911 census. Anglican chaplains maintained throughout the war that more Anglican soldiers had enlisted than the census suggested; therefore, Anglican chaplains were underrepresented in the forces. Chaplains who were engaged on a "voyage only" contract would embark with the troops to their destination prior to hospital ship service on the return voyage whereas chaplains between 30 and 40 years of age remained on "continuous" contract. According to the Australian War Memorial,[13] chaplains were overwhelmingly of British origin. They received little training but experienced a long sea journey to settle into their new role. H. S. Gullet aptly described the inherent difficulties: "The chaplain was to be a

10 M.F. Snape, *The Royal Army Chaplains' Department 1796-1957: Clergy Under Fire* (Woodbridge: Boydell Press, 2008), p. 218.

11 William Ewing, *From Gallipoli to Baghdad* (London: Hodder & Stoughton, 1917), p. 59.

12 Ibid.

13 Australian War Memorial, Introductory article about First World War chaplains <https://www.awm.gov.au/collection>

man's man and a soldier of Christian character. Were they to be religious guides only, mainly welfare officers, counsellors, fighters or loafers. It was up to the individual chaplain to find out."[14] Michael McKernan, in his study of the AIF chaplaincy, observed with regard to the average Australian serviceman's antipathy to religion: "Many officers and men ... merely tolerated the chaplains, looking at their appointment as an example of the Australian habit of paying lip service to religion."[15] For their part, military chaplains had accompanied the New Zealand contingent in the South African War and, on the outbreak of war in 1914, were prepared to embark with the NZEF in October 1914.

British, Australian and New Zealand Chaplains: Background and Training

Researching the backgrounds of the Anglican clergy, Edward Madigan examined a sampling of 32 chaplains recorded in Bishop Gwynne's surviving 'Army Book'.[16] In it he also found that 411 were Oxbridge educated, a further 62 having attended Trinity College Dublin. Thus the majority were from what Madigan refers to as an "atmosphere of exclusive privilege."[17] However, many had taken advantage of the opportunity to work at East End university settlements or served as curates in tough working class parishes.[18] These experiences would have provided the opportunity to expand their social horizons. Other pre-war experiences (prison chaplaincies, school and missionary work) also contributed to the generally broadened milieu which proved useful during active service. Thus it is evident that the majority of Church of England chaplains had a variety of pre-war experience whether or not they had been the recipients of a privileged education.[19] Their military training, however, remained woefully inadequate. Indeed, much of it was left to the newly-arrived chaplain's own initiative.

Some of the British Church of England chaplains who left written accounts of Gallipoli service belonged to clergy with similar background to that described by Madigan. John William Charles Wand had obtained First Class Honours at St Edmund Hall Oxford in 1907. Following curacies at Benwell and Lancaster, Wand become Vicar of Old Sarum in 1914. Enlisting at the outbreak of war, he disembarked at Gallipoli in July 1915. Arthur Groom Parham was Precentor of Christ Church Cathedral Oxford where he was appointed chaplain in August 1914 prior to joining the South Midland Mounted Brigade of 2nd Mounted Division (TF). Oswin Creighton, son of a prominent clerical family, graduated from Keble College Oxford and trained at Farnham Hostel and, although very much a part of the English ecclesiastical establishment,

14 See Michael McKernan, *Padre: Australian Chaplains in Gallipoli and France* (Sydney: Allen Unwin, 1986), p. xiii.
15 Ibid., p. xi.
16 CMS Archives, University of Birmingham XACC/18Z/1, Army Book. Contains press cutting about chaplains that Gwynne had collected and comments on individual chaplains.
17 Edward Madigan, *Faith Under Fire: Anglican Army Chaplains and the Great War* (Basingstoke: Palgrave Macmillan, 2011), pp. 67-68.
18 For example, The Revd P. B. Clayton, TCF 1915-1919, had worked weekly at Oxford and Bermondsey mission as had the Revd Neville Talbot TCF 1914-1917. The Revd F. R. Barry, TCF 1914-1919, had been employed at Oxford House, Bethnal Green.
19 L. Parker, *Shellshocked Prophets: Former Anglican Army Chaplains in Interwar Britain* (Solihull: Helion & Company, 2015), pp. 29-30.

had experience of a Nottingdale, London slum curacy in addition to missionary work in Canada prior to appointment to 29th Division. Keith Best also hailed from a clerical family. Educated at Lancing and Queen's College Cambridge, he trained for the priesthood at Egerton Hall, Manchester prior to taking up the curacy of Lytham St Anne's in 1911. In August 1914, he was assigned to the 1st/3rd East Lancashire Brigade, Royal Field Artillery, 42nd (East Lancashire) Division.

Roman Catholic Father William Finn hailed from Hulland and was educated at Ushaw College, County Durham, the premier Roman Catholic seminary of North England. Serving as curate to St Mary's Cathedral Durham and chaplain to Houghton Hall, he was subsequently assigned to 29th Division. Father H. C. Day, prior to enlistment, was officiating at Holy Name Parish in central Manchester. This Jesuit was so keen to enlist that he approached the Lord Mayor of Manchester for assistance with immediate assignment to a battalion bound for overseas service. Assigned to 2nd Midland Mounted Brigade, his brother Arthur Day was attached to the Sherwood Rangers Yeomanry. Other Catholic Chaplains included Father T.A. Harker, chaplain to 1st Royal Munster Fusiliers, and Father Francis Charles Devas, who entered the Jesuit order at 18. Amongst the Nonconformist padres were several from Scotland. The Revd Hunter Smith was a minister to the Crieff United Free Church from 1909. William Ewing having previously served as a minster to the Edinburgh United Free Church was attached to the 1/4th Royal Scots TF.

Anglican Chaplain Walter Dexter.

As in Great Britain, there were initially more Australian applicants than available vacancies, such was the prevailing enthusiasm. Many were middle aged, but these volunteers were usually assigned to troop ships, the maximum age to accompany troops in battle being between 30 and 40.[20] William McKenzie was the only Salvation Army chaplain appointment. Walter Ernest Dexter, a popular ANZAC personality was an Anglican padre. One of 12 chaplains whose official appointment dated from 8 September 1914, previous service during the South African War as well as that of a merchant seaman provided Dexter with valuable life experience to draw on. Wesleyan Senior Methodist Minister James Green had also experienced service as a chaplain in South Africa. In addition to his senior clerical status, he was also correspondent for *The Sydney Morning Herald*. Educated at the University of Edinburgh, Presbyterian padre Andrew Gillison had held postings in Scotland and the United States before immigrating to Brisbane in 1903. This was followed by part-time chaplaincy service to the Victoria Scottish regiment from 1909. Presbyterian Ernest Merrington was an academic who had studied at Edinburgh and Harvard prior to becoming minister to St Andrew's Brisbane in 1910. The

20 Australian War Memorial, Introductory article on chaplains in the First World War.

senior Anglican chaplain to the AIF was Albert Edward Talbot, Dean of Sydney. Keith Best, on encountering him during the voyage to Gallipoli, observed:

> He has very broad views – says we fall behind the RCs every time, e.g. services and discipline. Considers that HC should be taught as essential – the service of absolution and forgiveness of sin. Teach congregation to put on hold certain non-essentials e.g. virgin birth, bodily resurrection of Jesus, etc. Teach modern critical view of inspiration of the bible. He would run a parish mainly for men ... He would take matins and HC and football in the afternoon, leave Sunday school to lay people and evensong to curate. He was a great scholar-double first in theology.[21]

New Zealand Chaplain Patrick Dore.

The NZEF embarked from New Zealand in October 1914. Among its numbers were William Grant, who was to dic at Gallipoli, and Father Patrick Dore. Posted to the Wellington Rifles, Grant originally hailed from Scotland, but was educated in New Zealand before, aged 20, Presbyterian ordainment there in 1890. Dore, a native of Southern Ireland, had ministered in Kaikoura and Foxton prior to embarkation with the Auckland Mounted Rifles and subsequent death in action. Revd Henare Wepiha Te Wainohu was a Maori Chaplain. Educated at Te Aute College, he joined the Maori contingent as a reinforcement prior to landing at Gallipoli July 1915. A sermon preached by Te Wainohu prior to embarkation was widely quoted at the time. In it he encouraged the troops to fearlessly uphold the Maori warrior tradition.[22] Grant's farewell address expressed unequivocal support for the war effort: "This is not a time for words, It is a time for deeds ... from north and south and from east and west ... our sons are marching or sailing to the help of the old motherland and our defend our possessions and liberties."[23]

Gallipoli Landings

The initial Gallipoli landings occurred at two locations, Cape Helles and Ari Burnu (subsequently designated Anzac Cove). These were selected by MEF GOC General Sir Ian Hamilton

21 Imperial War Museum (IWM) 10297: Revd J. K. Best Papers.

22 Dictionary of New Zealand Biography, *Te Ara: Encyclopaedia of New Zealand*, updated 4-Mar-2014 <http://www.TeAra.govt.nz/en/biographies/3t23/te-wainohu-henare-wepiha>

23 Address quoted but not referenced by Chaplain First Class Lance Lukin in R. Lang & J. Betham Lang, *Chaplains of Anzac: New Zealand's Fallen Chaplains of the Great War* (Wellington: Lang Book Publishing LTD, 2015), p. ix.

as the first phase of a scheme to conquer the entire peninsula. The Cape Helles landings at the peninsula's southern tip took place at five locations (Y, X, W, V and S Beaches), the invasion force consisting of 35,000 men of 29th Division.

At V Beach on 25th April, the S.S. *River Clyde*, employed as a "Trojan Horse" conveyance, contained 1st Hampshire Regiment and 1st Royal Munster Fusiliers. The plan was to ground the vessel in order to allow the troops to disembark. However, it did not reach the shore and the troops had to scramble ashore across lighters or wade in. Father Finn, chaplain to the 1st Royal Dublin Fusiliers in the process of being towed ashore in row boats, refused to remain on the *River Clyde* despite orders to remain aboard. Subsequent reports and eyewitness accounts conflict with regard to Finn's fate. For example, Peter Howson, in his study of chaplain casualties notes that the war diary of 1st Royal Dublin Fusiliers War Diary is missing from the National Archives. Moreover, no mention of Finn is made in the 86th Brigade or 86th Field ambulance war diaries.[24] A report from an Egypt-based *Reuters* correspondent had Finn leaving the *River Clyde* almost immediately before scrambling from lighters to beach: "He stepped off the gangway and immediately received a bullet through his chest. Undeterred, Finn received bullets in the thigh and leg. Riddled with bullets by the time he set foot on the beach, he carried on. Whilst in the act of attending to the spiritual needs of one of his fallen men that Finn's head was shattered by shrapnel."[25]

The preceding account is similar to one by landing eyewitness Revd H.C. Foster who observed the scene from a minesweeper: "Many of the gallant Dubliners fell into the water and when father Finn saw this he jumped in and tried his utmost to rescue them. He succeeded in rescuing several men but suddenly bullets entered his body and he fell just at the water's edge. It was seen at once that his condition was serious, and he was carried by some of the men to whom he ministered so faithfully into a place under cover. He only lived a few minutes and his servant knelt at his side. His last words are said to have been 'are our lads winning?' and then amidst the thunder of guns on sea and land he passed."[26] A later report from The Revd T.A. Harker, who buried Finn that evening, provided a different version of events: "Father Finn was in one of the boats and out of 45 in his boat 40 never reached the shore. He was shot in the boat and four more times as he reached the shore and tried to crawl to shelter. He died after two hours of agony. I buried him myself."[27] Howson points out that it has been important to try and ascertain the course of events.[28] Conversely, Harker had no doubt that whatever the actual sequence of events, now lost to the fog of war, that Finn's actions were not exaggerated: "Good zealous priest that he was, he needs no lies to endear his memory among the Dublins."[29] Oswin Creighton wrote about Finn's relationship with the battalion: "The men never forgot him and were never tired of speaking of him. I think they felt his death almost more than anything that happened at that terrible landing."[30]

24 Peter Howson, *Muddling Through: The Organisation of British Army Chaplains in World War I* (Solihull: Helion & Company, 2013), p. 164.
25 Ibid., pp. 163-164.
26 *The Tablet*, 5 July1915.
27 Ibid., 31 July 1915.
28 Howson, *Muddling Through*, p. 165.
29 Johnstone & Hegerty, *Sword on the Cross*, p. 116.
30 O. Creighton, *With the Twenty Ninth Division in Gallipoli* (London: Longmans, Green & Co., 1916) p. 117.

Meanwhile, Creighton had a different experience on 25 April. Instructed by the principal chaplain on the correct place for junior chaplain's during the impending amphibious assault, "His orders [the principal chaplain] are that chaplains are in no case to go in front of the advanced dressing station. He says that they are always anxious to get up to the front where they can only be of use at one point in the line, and meanwhile men are being brought into the clearing station from all along the line." Nevertheless, Creighton harboured his own reservations: "Of course this means that I shall be presumably be pretty safe. But I am very much wondering whether I shall be able to watch the others go off and stay behind."[31] However, it appears he condoned this order prior to the landing:

> The chaplain is a non-combatant and surely it must be wrong for him to go out on the attack, much though he may hate not to share the danger of his men to the full. His work come after the attack and perhaps most of all when the men come away tired and worn out for a rest or when they are spending those continuous days of wearisome strain in the trenches. And not least of all is the fact that he is the best channel of communication between the men and home. Very often one is asked to promise to write if anything happens and the little personal letters the chaplain can write home are most welcome and the knowledge that all that can be done by decent burial has been done.[32]

On 20 April, a chaplain's conference was convened on one of the invasion vessels: "We discussed all sorts of things, where to go and what to do and how to work together. We are not to advance beyond the first dressing station." Following the landings, Horden, the principal chaplain, realised that conditions rendered previous instructions redundant. As Creighton subsequently observed, "[L]ater the principal chaplain laid it down quite clearly that while under normal circumstances the above rule is the best to follow, each chaplain must use his own discretion and be where he feels he can be of the greatest use to the men."[33]

Creighton later transferred to another ship carrying the 86th Field Ambulance, to which he had been assigned for the landings. Prevailing confidence can be discerned in unit orders which stated that the field ambulance was not to land until a five-mile advance inland had been achieved and no wounded were to be evacuated during the first 48 hours. Anxiously awaiting news of the X, Y and V beach landings, Creighton remarked: "I ought to have been there, at least on the beach, seeing the poor wounded fellows and burying the dead, there seems to have been no chaplain with them. But what can I do? I am ordered to be with my field ambulance." He later learned that two chaplains, in addition to Finn, had disembarked by the end of the first day to provide succour at the disembarked field ambulance.

Creighton did not disembark on the peninsula until 2 May 1915. Once there, he made contact with "Senior Chaplain H—" who explained the general situation. Creighton's subsequent attempt to reach the frontline to take services was foiled by the heavy fighting. Shown around the beachhead, he also met another chaplain "K----" who had already been ashore for several days. Here he heard about Finn: "It seemed to me that Father Finn was an instance of

31 Ibid., p. 32.
32 Ibid., pp. 32-33.
33 Ibid., p. 22.

the extraordinary hold a chaplain and perhaps especially a RC can have on the affections of his men, if he absolutely becomes one of them and shares their danger."[34]

The 86th Field Ambulance having finally disembarked, Creighton, after assisting Harker with funeral services, carried on work with his assigned unit. On 6 May, he noted that 86th Brigade's line infantry regiments were in the frontline. Meanwhile, at the dressing stations, it was "very difficult to know what to do … Either the wounded were able to hobble off the CCS or they were so bad they were given morphia. So I went back to the camp to see the wounded as they came in. I went to the CCS and chatted as far as possible to the ones I saw; however, it was impossible to make things any better."[35]

Keith Best landed on 6 May, the first day of the Second Battle of Krithia. Hall, his senior chaplain, assigned him to the 126th (East Lancashire) Brigade RAMC, then disembarking on the peninsula. Appalled by the lack of medical officers and stretcher-bearers, he seems to have adjusted to prevailing conditions more easily than Creighton. By 9 May, the day after landing, Best had collected the many unburied corpses lying about before burying them in a newly-created cemetery. On Sunday 8 May he observed: "As usual a day of blood. Went up the nullah. Stray bullets spattering the sand. Streams of New Zealand wounded coming down at the top of the gully we formed a cemetery and buried a number of poor fellows … No one scoffs at religion now."[36] By 11 May, Best had arranged to attach himself to 126th Brigade Headquarters. The contrast between his early experiences and those of Creighton demonstrate the need for chaplains to seek out a useful role during the confusing aftermath of the landings.

Meanwhile, the ANZAC landing was taking place at Ari Burnu. Father Fahey, attached to the 11th Battalion AIF, reached Imbros approximately 15 miles from the landing beach at 9:00 p.m. on 24 April. Following an evening meal, 11th Battalion embarked on destroyers which were to convey its companies and platoons to shore by row boats. Fahey, speaking plainly to his spiritual charges, observed prior to departure: "I put the position plainly and forcibly before the Catholic soldiers. I insisted on their going to confession … so that when they went into action I had no anxiety as far as their spiritual welfare was concerned."[37] Despite this reassurance, he decided to ignore orders to remain offshore. In a piece published by *The Catholic Press*, Fahey confirmed how he flagrantly "disregarded orders and sneaked off with the men, and it was fortunate for many a dying man that I was ashore that morning … Had I known the inferno I was rushing into I believe I should have remained behind." His subsequent experience was graphically described as follows:

> The destroyer next to us began to man her boats, and suddenly inferno broke loose from the shore. Such a fearful hail of bullets from rifle, machine-gun, and shrapnel as passes all imagination! It was appalling. There was no cover. We were packed so closely together that one bullet would wound or kill three men, and we could not hit back, for the enemy was invisible. The bullets were dancing off the funnels and upper parts of the destroyers. The order was given us to man the boats, and we tumbled in as fast as possible, and pushed off for the shore. It was only 300 yards away, but to me it seemed miles, and to have taken

34 Ibid., p. 67.
35 Ibid., p. 79.
36 IWM 10297: Diary of the Revd J.K. Best, p. 10.
37 McKernan, *Padre*, p. 47.

> hours to reach. There was dreadful slaughter in the boats … I could then see only what was happening in my own. It was horrible. I never expected to reach the shore alive. There was only one anxiety amongst the men – to reach the shore and rush the Turks with the bayonet. After what seemed like endless hours the boat touched bottom about 20 yards from the beach. As I jumped up to get out a bullet went through the sleeve of my jacket and caught the lad behind me. A shrapnel [sic] splashed a man's brains over me. Another caught the gunwale of the boat between my knees as I was getting out, and nearly blinded me with splinters. I was pushed from behind and fell into about four feet of water. I went promptly to the bottom, and, being loaded with a pack, three days' rations, a water bottle, and an overcoat, I found the utmost difficulty in rising; I almost thought I had been shot. I never realised till then how difficult it is to walk quickly through water dressed. I got on the beach exhausted and had to lie down amongst the falling bullets to get my breath. I had made up my mind by this time that I had but a poor chance of getting through the morning alive. Anyhow, I picked up a flat stone, and held it in front of my head, and it was fortunate I did so, because a bullet that would have brained me glanced harmlessly off it. I moved forward then to where the tide had made a little bank along the shore. All the soldiers carry a small entrenching tool but being a non-combatant, I had none. I tore up the sand with my bare fingers and made a little shelter in front of me. I never felt so small in my life. I felt as if I could squeeze myself into a thimble. I must also admit that I felt a little cowardly, but it was only for a few minutes. The lad on my left, not feeling safe, raised himself a little, and began to dig with his entrenching tool. He was shot through the heart. The man on the other side of me got a bullet in the thigh and was in great pain. I pulled him towards me, and lying flat as I was, cut his trousers open, and put on a dressing. Every soldier carries a little bottle of iodine, and a field dressing, which can be applied in a few minutes … I remained on the beach all day and all night as all the wounded were collected in a certain place to be removed to the hospital ship.[38]

Three weeks later, Fahey was still in the same set of clothing and had only washed twice.[39] His first weeks at Anzac consisted of administering confession and daily frontline visits "in case anyone should want to see me."[40] Walter Dexter, regardless of strident efforts to do so, was denied the opportunity to accompany his men. Assigned to a hospital ship as the first casualties were brought on board, he recorded that the approximately 700 casualties were treated by just two doctors and a few orderlies. "O God, the cruelty of war", he later remarked with regard to this sad state of affairs.[41]

Sixty-year-old Methodist, the Revd John Luxford was one of six chaplains who landed with the NZEF. Three days earlier he had written: "I shall be glad to get to the real work".[42] On 26 April he observed: "Helped our wounded this morning. With Father McMenamin, I buried nine poor fellows. We had to shelter for an hour. The guns were booming. Then as we read the

38 *The Catholic Press* (Sydney), 28 October 1915, p. 7 and Fahey to *Advocate*, 31 July 1915 quoted in McKernan, *Padre*, p. 50.
39 *The Catholic Press* (Sydney), 28th October 1915, p. 7.
40 Ibid.
41 Walter Dexter diary quoted in McKernan, *Padre*, p. 60.
42 Allan Davidson, 'Centenary Reflections on Gallipoli', *Tui Motu Interislands*, December 2015.

service we had to kneel down in the dug grave. It was terrible. Six were buried in one grave and three in another. Buried nine more men … four from boats where they had been killed in trying to land under fire."[43]

Services

To take services was one of the military chaplain's primary tasks. Conditions on the peninsula often rendered this problematic. Once landed, he had to organise services as soon as possible. It has already been demonstrated how, given the confined space available just beyond the beachheads, service provision was particularly difficult at Gallipoli. The extent of the Chaplain Department's collective success remained dependent on individual circumstances, physical location and the willingness of commanding officers to grant unit attendance.

Jesuit Father Francis Devas recollected how services were established in the immediate aftermath of the landings: "On the southern end of the peninsula of Gallipoli, for some weeks now, Mass has been said nearly every day by the small band of Catholic Chaplains. The altars are constructed variously – of ammunition boxes, a board on trestles, a packing case, a shelf cut in the wall of a cliff. The place is sometimes picturesque, more often merely inconvenient, the men being huddled together behind some screen, so that the existence of a shell-worthy group may not be revealed to the enemy."[44]

Keith Best, having landed during the Second Battle for Krithia, spent most of his time with burials. By 21 May, the necessary means to conduct services had been gathered together: "I managed to borrow vessels from another padre, my altar was a pair of biscuit boxes, my vestment a khaki shirt, dirty greasy tunic and riding breeches. We fixed it for 6 a.m., hoping to anticipate the usual morning hymn of hate … unfortunately, they rose early … To my surprise, regardless of shrapnel about 100 men were present. Never shall I forget my first service under fire. We all felt that that God's good providence watched over us and nobody was hit."[45] Two days later, on Whit Sunday, Best organised a service with the 1/4th East Lancashire Regiment: "About 200 men present and a dozen officers lying in dugouts. I spoke of the love and joy which accompanies true repentance." The service came under shell fire: "I had not the courage to get down or take cover for fear of appearing a coward, so I got reputation for courage when my action was really due to fear of public opinion."[46]

For his part, Oswin Creighton found services difficult to arrange in the days following the landing. On 9 May he observed: "It was impossible to hold services. The camp was busy full of wounded and my regiments were up the firing line. There was a mass of wounded everywhere. The only services possible were several small services with the less serious cases." On 16 May he remarked it was "unwise to have a service in the opens when they [shells] were dropping around." He seems surprised when the senior chaplain H— held a service regardless of the shell fire. On Whit Sunday the service was "a fiasco" as it had been poorly publicised, but by Trinity Sunday (30 May) he managed a 7:00 a.m. celebration with 30 in attendance and a service on "Divisional

43 John Luxford diary quoted in Davidson.
44 October 1915 letter reproduced in *Patheos,* No. CXCII, January 1916, pp. 323-326.
45 IWM 10297: Revd K.J. Best Papers, Correspondence with Father 21 May 1915.
46 Ibid., 23 May 1915 diary entry.

Hill" followed by a communion service. Creighton appears to have been aware of his timidity in taking service under fire. This is demonstrated by a rather patronising description of fellow chaplain: "AB is one of the cheeriest people I know. He runs about everywhere and holds endless services and is always being nearly blown up with the men ... But nothing worries him at all."[47]

Father Fahey, the first chaplain to land at Anzac, commented on his general experience up to the fifth Sunday ashore: "I have not said Mass during that time, as my vestments have not yet come from the troopship, and even if they had, it would not be advisable to gather men together in close formation, as a shrapnel shell might exterminate the whole lot."[48] Walter Dexter arrived at Anzac in time for the costly Ottoman offensive of 18 May: "[N]o part of the place was safer than anywhere else." On Sunday 22 May he held a Holy Communion celebration: "Officers and men attended, and one feels that the beautiful service drew them nearer to God than they had been before bullets were whistling over our heads all the time ... At 10.00 a.m. I held a voluntary service for 2nd brigade and most of the men attended who could. The men dispersed and got around the humpies ready to dive out of sight. I stood on a box on the lower slope and spoke up to the men."[49]

Presbyterian chaplain William Ewing was stationed at Big Gull in order to conduct a variety of services. "War brings a fairly complete if temporary abolition of the Sabbath." Voluntary service, however, appeared to be popular with the rank and file: "In the bright sunny Sunday mornings of early summer we had excellent congregations and, in the evening, when hymn singing of their own choosing was a prominent feature, very large companies assembled."[50] Holy Communion was observed every Sunday so that those who wished to partake could do so before returning to the frontline. Close proximity to the line ensured that rear area services were subject to the same dangers as those held in the forward trenches. Indeed, Ewing recalled a Christmas Day 1915 incident during which three men were killed by shell bursting on to his tent entrance.[51] Hunter Smith observed: "Church parades in the day are rare, mostly services and prayers with small groups." Nevertheless, on one occasion after nightfall: "The men gathered in the trenches leaning on the parapets with the officers grouped around me. I took a central position and conducted public worship."[52]

The Revd Parham, in the immediate aftermath of the fight for Chocolate Hill, conducted "Holy Communion somewhere in the trenches" each morning. These services were held with an ammunition box as altar: "While the congregation consisted of some thirty men who under fire knelt down in the mud and received the sacrament."[53] The Revd Dennis Jones recollected hospital services held as often as possible in addition to those "held amongst regiments or units placed in out of the way positions, such as artillery posts." Moreover, "The trenches in which my brigade were [sic] stationed were situated on the extreme left on a steep hill. I paid constant visits to the lines each day as a rule. We came under fire from snipers as we walked in the open to the various headquarters, but although we had near shaves I escaped injury."[54]

47 Creighton, *With the 29th Division,* p. 115.
48 *The Catholic Press*, 28th October 1915, p. 7.
49 Walter Dexter diary quoted in McKernan, *Padre*, p. 81.
50 Ewing, *From Gallipoli to Baghdad*, p. 69.
51 Ibid, p. 170.
52 IWM 5606: Revd H. Smith, Appendix to my record of service in Gallipoli, p. 14.
53 *The Reading Mercury*, 14th June 1916.
54 Dennis Jones, *Diary of a Padre at Suvla Bay* (Manchester: The Faith Press, 1916).

Inter-Denominationalism

The situation on the Gallipoli Peninsula was conducive to close relations between chaplain and military congregation. This resulted from the frequency of funerals that brought both together. Thus a system was worked whereby each chaplain, regardless of denomination, took turns officiating at evening's burial parties.

Ewing shared a tent with Roman Catholic Father Legros. They got on well, the former recollecting a "Good friendship … With the growth of mutual understanding we became true and fast friends … Roman Catholics of course were unable to take part in any united service. A regulation that surely cannot be justified to reason shut the Church of England chaplains out of the goodly fellowship of united church parades; but many of them valued highly the privilege of sharing in the joint voluntary service held whenever possible in the evening."[55]

An example of this kind of denominational tension was the impossibility of conducting public beach prayers where wounded lay on stretchers by the hundreds or in hospitals wards because, as Ewing's companion observed, "My men would not like hearing your prayers nor yours mine." Ewing, having buried many Roman Catholics, observed: "yet I am informed that such a burial is no proper burial but such as a layman might perform." He also observed that Nonconformists were always anxious to participate in united services. Indeed, they were amongst the most constant of communion attendees. For their part, impromptu evening services were attended by Roman Catholics. Ewing concluded: "I am glad to say that all along our area the church was conspicuous by its services and was always ready to administer to members of any other denomination under the sun."[56]

Methodist minister James Green shared a communion with Anglican Dean Talbot, a remarkable event considering that the communion service was reckoned to be a mark of denominational membership. It also demonstrates the diversity of opinion and consequent resistance within the Church of England. Talbot hailed from Sydney, the most unequivocal evangelical diocese within the Anglican Communion. Of this ceremony, Green observed: "The kneeling men in the twilight, the boom of the guns, the ranks of men marching through the gap up to the trenches and the rest of the worshipers still singing softly, was deeply impressive and will be a sacred memory to me as the sight and occasion were a blessing to us all."[57] Walter Dexter, writing during a lull in the vicious fighting at Lone Pine, reflected on the denominational issue with regard to a chaplain's work: "[T]he problem of the union of churches is solved, and more than anyone has anticipated, for the Roman church is in the union as well."[58] Patrick Dore of the Auckland Mounted Rifles observed: "[D]evotional distinctions carried little weight … especially in those days of grim realities." The chaplain, he concluded, "was the friend and counsellor of everyone."[59] Ewing, however, was aggrieved by signs that the religious divide had not been entirely eradicated: "As never before perhaps, the various denominations are brought in closer touch with one another. But also one realises more than ever the sad fact of the division

55 Ewing, *Gallipoli to Baghdad*, p. 59.
56 Ibid.
57 *The Methodist*, 14 August 1915.
58 *Church of England Messenger*, 28 January 1916.
59 C.G. Nichol, *The Story of Two Campaigns: Official War History of the Auckland Mounted Rifles Regiment. 1914-1919* (Auckland: Wilson & Horton, 1921), p. 47.

of Christendom. At the very time when religion should speak with an authoritative tongue we find faction. It must be great hindrance to the men who are looking for spiritual guidance and support."[60] This interdenominational optimism was not embraced by all. For example, Horden received reports from disgruntled New Zealand padres that Major-General Alexander Godley had ordered them to "Attend and help conduct interdenominational services." In response, one Australian padre resigned his commission, a resignation that the GOC New Zealand & Australian Division refused to accept.[61]

Chaplains in Action

As we have seen, most chaplains were attached to field ambulances and dressing stations. Unlike the Western Front, there was no guarantee that these postings were beyond the line of fire, so whether in hospital tents, dressing stations or visiting the frontline trenches, chaplains shared the myriad dangers and deprivations experienced by officers and men. Principal Chaplain Horden eventually rescinded the order banning chaplains from the frontline. Keith Best remarked on 22 June that a senior chaplain observed that his subordinates were now independent and should proceed at their own discretion: "He approves of going into the firing line when it seems advisable."[62] Horden, during a short fact-finding excursion to Gallipoli in June, saw for himself the proximity to danger that his charges faced: "The difficulties are very great as no part of the peninsula is free from shell fire." Having spent a certain amount of time conducting formal interviews, he recorded: "Working with dispositions of chaplains and their tasks."[63]

In the days following the Anzac landing, a small number of chaplains who managed to come ashore kept busy by assisting with the succour of accumulated wounded on the beachhead. According to Ernest Merrington: "Work among the wounded and in the trenches, the care and burial of the numbers of the dead had required so much attention from the chaplains that these had represented the utmost that could be attempted."[64] Andrew Gillison disembarked, following days of shipboard duty during which he assisted the wounded and officiated over burials at sea at Anzac on 26 April. Now on land, he reported to the assigned battalion HQ prior to assignment to its component field dressing station. As Anglican chaplains, Gillison and F.W. Wray experienced heavy enemy fire from the top of a gully: "Such a storm of lead I had of course never before seen and could not have imagined tearing up the ground and littering it with fragments of undergrowth and mangled men."[65] Wray, as described by Chaplain Merrington, arrived at Anzac at the beginning of May: "The padre himself was moving about in full view of the enemy and was a very conspicuous figure, as he wore a cover of maroon coloured rubber suspended from his cap over the back of his neck." Wray, notebook in hand, was jotting down the names of the dead lying about the road edge. Merrington, well-aware of the obvious target

60 Ewing, *Gallipoli to Baghdad*, p. 58.
61 TNA WO/95/2023: Principal Chaplain A.W. Horden Diary, 5 November 1915.
62 IWM 10297: Revd J.K. Best Papers, Diary entry, 22 June 1915, p. 18.
63 TNA WO/95/2023: Diary of A.W.Hordon, 17 June 1915.
64 E.M. Merrington, Diary, Australian War Memorial 3DRL/0373, cited by McKernan, *Padre*, p. 73.
65 AWM 3DRL/6277: Andrew Gillison, Diary, cited in McKernan, *Padre*, p. 67.

presented when wearing the distinctive officer's Service Dress uniform, decided to attire himself in the tunic of a "light horse trooper, with bandolier and slouch hat, but no rifle."[66]

Known as "Fighting Mac" or "Anzac Mac", Salvation Army chaplain William McKenzie entered the firing line immediately after landing at Anzac on 9 May; he went almost immediately to the firing line. One of his first tasks the recovery of a fallen colonel's body from No Man's Land. Quartered with a nearby dressing station, he officiated over hurried burials, often under fire, whilst befriending the living: "I spent a considerable time among the boys in the trenches and had a good time with them."[67] Dexter, his time aboard hospital ship having come to an end, was reunited with 5th Battalion on 17 May.

The large-scale Ottoman assault of 19 May was repulsed with heavy losses. Reflecting on the carnage, Merrington observed how the padre had, by overseeing removal and burial of the dead, transformed into an "auditor of war". ANZAC chaplains Wray, Gillison and Green met with Brigadier-General John Monash (GOC 4th Australian Brigade) to organise arrangements for corpses to be transported by mule carts to a new cemetery in Shrapnel Valley. On 24 May the famous truce was arranged to clear the decomposing dead from No Man's Land. Dexter was an eyewitness to the grim clearance:

> Things are very quiet this morning ... At 8.30 the armistice began for the purpose of burying the dead. The smell is something awful ... it is only by identification discs that the corpses are known. It was arranged that a central line between the trenches be fixed. Each on their own half of ground could take their dead away and also rifles and ammunition ... The ground was simply covered between the trenches at various points and after the day's work of burying estimates of 1,000 Turks killed have been made. Among this awful mass of dead Turks were some of our boys who had been killed on the first and second day's fight and have lain there since ... The bodies were horrible to look at being black and swelled up.[68]

Dexter went on to experience several close calls including being grazed by a bullet in mid-September: "This is my sixth hit, I must be pretty thick skinned, a little iodine soon put things right.[69] For his gallantry at Gallipoli, Dexter was awarded a DSO.

Catholic Padre James McMenamin, at Anzac since 25 April, saw much of the worst fighting at Walker's Ridge and the Daisy Patch prior to evacuation with influenza in late July. Chaplain William Grant of the Wellington Rifles landed at Anzac on 12 May. On 23 August he participated in the costly, but ultimately unsuccessful general assault on Hill 60 where he was killed whilst tending to a wounded friend and foe six days later. The author of the post-war Wellington Rifles history tellingly summed up the circumstances related to this forlorn attack: "We are most assuredly in the valley of the shadow of death."[70] On 22 August, Andrew Gillison, accompanied by former stretcher-bearer and former Methodist minister R.H. Pittendrigh, entered No Man's

66 AWM 3DRL/0373: E.M. Merrington, Diary, cited in McKernan, *Padre*, p. 67.
67 McKernan, *Padre* p. 77.
68 Walter Dexter cited in Jonathan King, *Gallipoli Diaries: The Anzacs Own Story Day by Day* (East Roseville: Kangaroo Press, 2003), p. 73.
69 Ibid.
70 Major A.H. Wilkie, *Official History of the Wellington Mounted Rifles Regiment 1914-1919* (Wellington New Zealand: Whitcomb and Tombs Ltd: 1924), pp. 66-67.

Land to rescue a wounded man. Both were hit by enemy fire but managed to return, Gillison expiring from his wound hours later; Pittendrigh was evacuated. New Zealand Padre Patrick Dore was severely injured on 24 August and would have died if he had not been carried by a Trooper Foley and several stretcher bearers despite "the system which required the wounded to go from one party to another." Dore, on making a full recovery, subsequently served on the Western Front where he died of wounds in July 1918.[71]

Roman Catholic Padre H.C. Day landed at Suvla Bay on 18 August. Assigned to participate in IX Corps' impending general assault of 21 August, the 2nd Mounted Division, to which he was attached, moved inland to take up assigned jumping-off positions. At Lala Baba, Day learned of plans to cross the barren Anafarta Plain: "[E]very yard of which the enemy guns had most accurately ranged … Any attempt to cross that plain was could only be made at the cost of terrible sacrifice of human life … but apparently it was unavoidable."[72] Between dawn and zero-hour, Day claimed to have visited all Roman Catholics within proximity: "They welcomed the opportunity of making their confessions before entering into the maelstrom of war." Accompanying the attackers, he noted "shells were bursting just ahead … We had to set our teeth and go forward." The advancing battalions were scattered by shrapnel fire that burst all around: "Through this corridor of fire the division walked steadily forward … In less than half an hour we had lost 25% of our force … I cannot recall any example of collective coolness comparable to the silent passing of the yeomanry through that first ordeal of battle."[73] Day reached Chocolate Hill at about 5.00 p.m. and was instrumental in identifying a track through the raging bushfire before assisting at the recently established Chocolate Hill dressing station. Over 1,000 wounded were attended to there, Day providing last rites to moribund cases.[74] For his part in the 2nd Mounted Division assault, Anglican Chaplain Arthur Parham also risked life and limb to retrieve the wounded from bush fires. Thereafter, he organised volunteer stretcher bearers and, according to a Reading newspaper, was "chiefly instrumental in evacuating the wounded from Chocolate Hill."[75] Remaining under fire for the next two weeks, he went on to attend the wounded, direct burials and celebrate Holy Communion services. Parham was awarded the Military Cross for these collective acts of gallantry.

Roman Catholic Chaplain Father H.C. Day.

71 Nichol, *The Story of Two Campaigns*, p. 84 cited in Lang & Betham Lang, *Chaplains of Anzac*, p. 49.
72 H.C. Day, *A Cavalry Chaplain* (London: Heath Cranton Ltd, 1922), p. 127.
73 Ibid., p. 132.
74 Ibid.
75 *The Reading Mercury*, 19 June 1916.

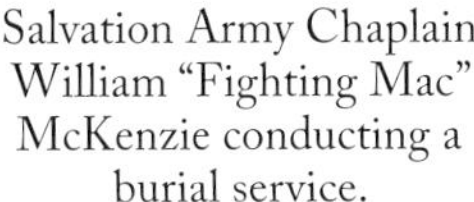
Salvation Army Chaplain William "Fighting Mac" McKenzie conducting a burial service.

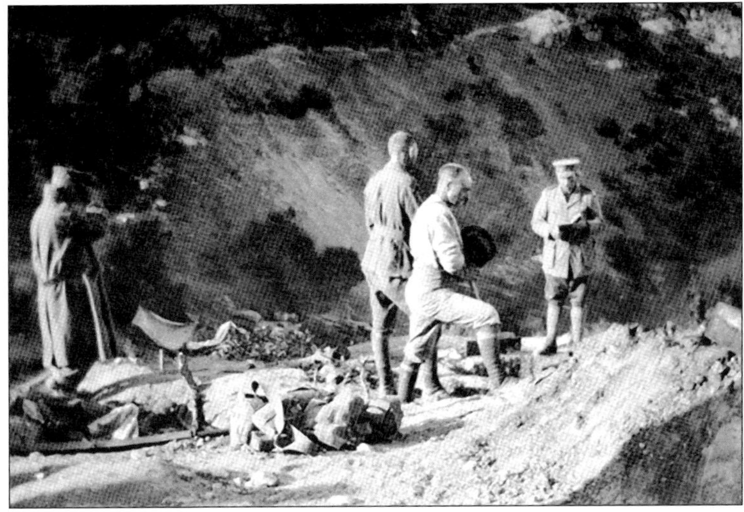

Funeral services were necessary for religious and sanitary reasons. Considerable effort was made to identify the dead prior to the provision of Christian burial. Over time, disparate gravesites were arranged into cemeteries, but many bodies remained unidentified. McKenzie, commenting on the human cost of the Lone Pine assault, observed: "The sight afterwards in the trenches was beyond conception, the piles of dead and dying were appalling and the number of wounded was being continually increased as the Turks were being constantly reinforced ... My experiences of getting the wounded out of the trenches, over the dead and wounded, underneath the dead was sickening ... When this was done I buried in all some 450 men killed in this charge. These burials covered a period of three weeks when the smell of the bodies after the first few days was overpowering and frequently I had to leave the graves to retch from the effects of the smells."[76]

Reactions

Chaplains had varied reactions to the Gallipoli campaign experience. Many had enlisted in a spirit of patriotism and optimism. James Green, in a letter composed prior to embarkation to Gallipoli, observed: "I think we are all proud to be here and personally I look upon my present ministry as a great privilege as well as a great responsibility."[77] Keith Best remarked in September 1914: "Much to my surprise and delight I received a telegram from the bishop saying he had sent my name up an army chaplaincy."[78] Although William Grant welcomed the world-wide conflict, he was also well aware of the gravity: "War at any time is horrible and this war upon which we have entered is the most terrible war in all the ages."[79] Dexter, having

76 McKernan, *Padre*, p, 117.
77 James Green to AIF Chaplain General, *Methodist*, 3 July 1915.
78 IWM 10297: Revd K.J. Best Papers, Best correspondence with father, 9 September 1914.
79 Lang & Betham Lang, *Chaplains of Anzac*, p. ix.

determined to get fit prior to embarkation, stated: "I have laid it down that I must get as hard as iron, so that whatever comes I will be ready." Best, uncertain of what the future held, prepared for the daunting prospect of preaching to fighting men: "I am afraid I shall not be much hand at addressing the Tommies."[80] Indeed, his earliest sermons grappled with the "difference between patriotic feelings and patriotism."[81]

Consequent exhaustion and disillusionment amongst MEF chaplains resulted from stress and strain engendered by the peculiar circumstances of a campaign whereby MEF combatants, due to close proximity of teeming beachheads to the firing line, were never far from death or wounding. Father Fahey, one of the first chaplains to land, observed: "I feel that I have done more work during these four weeks than during all the years I have been a priest. I have seen some wonderful manifestations of divine mercy during those weeks. I shall never volunteer again in any capacity, for I have seen enough of it. It is not so much personal fear that would deter me, as the awful sights and nerve-shaking ordeals of fire one has to go through.[82] This statement was later tempered by the observation that "In spite of the inconvenience and horrors of war I am glad I came and I shall never regret being associated with such splendid men."[83] Keith Best, appalled by the lack of medical organisation, expressed disgust at perceived incompetence that contributed to unnecessary deaths. He was also unreservedly critical of senior officers and employed tactics.[84]

Despite the awful conditions and difficulty in performing assigned tasks, most chaplains retained a firm sense of faith and justice for the cause. As H.C. Day subsequently observed:

> What did I think of war? In a week it had robbed me of two friends and countless companions. Was it still fine, or was it mean, murderous and dastardly? Hs I changed my mind. No, from the outset I gauged the calamity and counted the cost ...Courage counts, character and conduct live. In this sense war is fine – splendid in life, most splendid of all, as I saw it in the grandeur of that last sacrifice.[85]

Conversely, Ernest Merrington, writing in early October 1915, remarked: "My health is beginning to fail under the strain of the campaign", whilst McKenzie "had to force himself to continue" following the ghastly Lone Pine attack. The situation was made worse when Horden ordered that "no more chaplains be posted to the peninsula at that moment due to the smallness of the area."[86] By September, the situation had changed with many succumbing to dysentery. Of this, the chaplain general remarked: "It is very difficult to keep a full supply of chaplains with the various units."[87]

80 IWM 10297: Revd K.J. Best Papers, Best correspondence with Father, 9 September 1914.
81 Ibid., 16 September 1914.
82 *The Catholic Press* (Sydney), 28 October 1915, p. 7.
83 *Kalgoorlie Western Argus*, 10 August 1915.
84 IWM 10297: Revnd J.K. Best Papers, *ex post facto* diary entry.
85 Day, *Cavalry Chaplain*, pp. 154-155.
86 TNA WO 95/2023: Principal Chaplain The Revd A.W. Horden War Diary, 27 June 1915.
87 Ibid., 29 September 1915.

Army and Religion

MEF chaplains, having grown close to officers and men, remarked on their congregation's attitudes towards religion. Maitland Woods observed: "Their attitude to us of the clergy is, so far as I see it, quite changed."[88] He also commented on the Bible's popularity: "It is wonderful the way the men read their testaments"[89] In another correspondence he discussed the shortage of bibles: "We want bibles very badly. There seem to be none on the peninsula. Most of the men who first came here have testaments which they prize very highly, and I gave out 24 prayer books after an open-air service. I could have given away a 100 or so. The men who got them were simply delighted."[90] This is echoed by Australian war correspondent Charles Bean: "I have found one or two officers starting to read the bible and one told me he had found it extraordinarily interesting "[91] A subaltern also remarked: "[H]ave been spending this couple of hours reading passages from my bible and a feeling of calm reassurance and confidence comes over me."[92] James McMenamin's experience was similar to that of other chaplains in that "there was a decided quickening of religious sensibilities of the men while under fire and they showed an eagerness for spiritual consolation rare in their own countries.[93] Francis Devas was impressed with the quality of Roman Catholic devotion: "For these men love Jesus Christ, the hours spent on the hillside in the growing darkness of the previous evening, waiting their turn for confession, proved it to their confessor."[94] Ewing commented on the intimacy gained from a gruelling active service existence under constant shellfire: "[T]he sharing of the perils and appalling conditions in dimly lit dug outs, led to heart to heart talks and prayers seemed to lend a new worth to life."[95] Arthur Parham thought otherwise: "Of the number men in Army who professed allegiance the church, he believed that at least 50 percent were only attached to it by the most slender ties and that an exceedingly small number only grasped the real meaning of the Churchmanship."[96]

Officers and other ranks have left far less evidence of their personal thoughts on religion and chaplains than the chaplains, who were, as a general rule, conscientious diarists and correspondents. The fact that the former expressed little on the topics should not be construed as indifference. Rather, it appears military chaplains had more cause to reflect on religiosity than those they ministrated to. That said, layman that did express their thoughts were mostly positive with regard to religious belief and chaplains. For example, Alan Treloar remarked: "This morning I went to divine service at 9.30. I have attended some strange services since I left Australia, but this one was the strangest of all. We met down in a gully below our HQ and there in the shelter of the cliffs we worshipped our God." Atop the cliff was a Maori working

88 State Library of Queensland OM74-101, letter from Maitland Woods to John Garland, Archbishop of Brisbane, 23 November 1915.
89 Ibid.
90 Ibid., 4 December 1915.
91 Charles Bean, diary entry for 10 July 1915, quoted in Jonathan King, *Gallipoli Diaries: The Anzacs Own Story Day by Day* (East Roseville: Kangaroo Press, 2003), p. 117.
92 AWM 1DRL/0185: Diary of Lieutenant W.M. Cameron, 9th Light Horse Regiment.
93 *New Zealand Herald* Vol. LII, 1 November 1915.
94 *Patheos Letters and Notices* No. CXCII (January 1916), pp. 323-326.
95 Ewing, *Gallipoli to Baghdad*, p. 183.
96 *The Daily Gazette for Middlesbrough*, 14 June 1916.

party, Treloar remarking that the service was punctuated by the noise of these men dragging iron water tanks about: "It was to this accompaniment that we sung hymns. For the sermon we 'disposed ourselves comfortably', to use the words of the chaplain. The text was Revelations 21: 5: 'And he that sat upon the throne said, behold I make all things new.' The address was helpful and altogether I felt that it was good that I had been there."[97]

Such criticism as existed focused on the lack of services; Petty Officer Bert Webster complaining that "Sunday being just like any other day, we have not had the opportunity of attending a church service since we landed here."[98] On 11 October, Australian Private Caddy wrote: "Yesterday we had church service, it seems so peculiar, at times you could not hear the parson for the noise."[99] That prevailing conditions often prevented Sunday services was acknowledged by Captain Bill Knox: "They do have church services at all times, but so far I have not been able to go as one had one's job to do first."[100]

Conclusion

A chaplain's role at Gallipoli represented a relatively unknown consequence of total war in the twentieth century. As the revolution in military technology and consequent dominance of defensive warfare resulted in an uneven learning process with regard to operations and tactics during 1914-18, so it was that the attitudes and actions of the chaplains were also affected. Their collective experience was a multifaceted role involving pastoral, medical and social aspects influenced by a necessity to be with their men whether in the frontline, base or hospital environment as a means of providing succour and religious services whenever possible. Precise figures for the number of chaplains that served during the Gallipoli campaign are hard to establish. Chaplains' Department official records, although incomplete, show that at least 55 were present on the peninsula during the period 25 April 1915 – 9 January 1916. Furthermore, Michael McKernan notes that ANZAC chaplains were not organised until later in the war but estimates approximately 30 Australian chaplains took part.[101] It is also known that of the 13 New Zealand Chaplains who left New Zealand in September 1914, six landed at Anzac.[102]

Past First World War chaplain literature, particularly that of Anglican chaplains, has been one of criticism, by such well-known contemporary observers as Graves and Sassoon, but also from recent historians such as Stephen Louden[103] and Albert Marrin[104] who have disparaged the "Holy Grocery" and morale boosting aspects of military chaplains. Alan Wilkinson and Gordon Zahn have explored role conflict and chaplains, the latter remarking that "by his very presence the pastor in uniform represents a symbol of legitimacy ... if it were not permissible for

97 King, *Gallipoli Diaries*, p. 122,
98 Ibid., p. 197.
99 Ibid., p. 204.
100 Ibid., p. 182.
101 Michael McKernan to Linda Parker email correspondence, 18 July 2015.
102 Allan Davidson, 'Centenary Reflections on Gallipoli', *Tui Motu*, December 2015.
103 Stephen Louden, *Chaplains in Conflict* (London: Avon Books, 1996).
104 Albert Marrin, *The Last Crusade: The Church of England in the First World War* (Durham, North Carolina: Duke University Press: 1974).

believers to take part in the war, would the priest be there?"[105] At variance with this perspective are the works of Michael Snape, Edward Madigan and Linda Parker[106] who have defended chaplains in studies which examine ministerial roles and effectiveness. More recent studies have considered question of morale, Andrew Totten going so far to suggest that "If the cause or simply the conduct of the fighting soldier were justified, why would the maintenance of his morale not be a proper object for concern?."[107] He also defines the difference between morale – the psychosocial state – and the moral – ethical state. Soldiers require an easing of conscience and moral sensibility. Maintenance of good morals was, as much as promotion of moral and ethical values, a vital part of a chaplain's portfolio: "The challenge ethically is to generate morale that is grounded on civilised behaviour."[108] Having demonstrated how MEF chaplains were present in a soldier's life throughout the campaign it can be concluded that the former was an important aspect in the maintenance of morale in the truest sense of the word.

Much of the criticism levelled at the time and since then was/is inapplicable to Gallipoli. Complaints about the dearth of chaplains and the early disorganisation of the Army Chaplains' Department does not appear to have been a problem on the peninsula. Despite sickness amongst chaplains, principal chaplain Horden appears to have worked hard to bring about a balance in MEF requirements for a steady supply of personnel. This increased presence, combined with assignment to the constricted peninsula battlezone, increased chaplain initiative and flexibility. For some, however, it was never apparent what their role should be. Chaplain personal accounts often speak of meetings with other denomination chaplains with regard to joint services, funeral arrangements and other related tasks. Thus it appears, with some exceptions that the diverse Christian padres worked well together for the greater good.

"Holy Grocery" criticism was less prominent at Gallipoli, although some chaplains recall procurement and distribution of home comforts and large quantities of sweets and cigarettes. Circumstances at Gallipoli did not allow for a regular establishment/organisation of canteens, entertainment or sports. Indeed, chaplain accounts are, more often than not, primarily concerned with avoiding shell fire in order to take services.

With no safe place at or beyond the landing beaches, criticisms of MEF chaplains not sharing the dangers experienced by their spiritual charges are less relevant. As previously discussed, padres were prevented from participating in the initial landings on the grounds of taking up limited space in the assault boats. This order was ignored by two Roman Catholic chaplains, one of whom subsequently perished. Indeed, Father Finn's decision to accompany the 1st Royal Dublin Fusiliers landing force prefigures the actions of D-Day invasion chaplains 29 years later. Horden, recognising the need to rescind an order that seriously challenged a military chaplain's remit, subsequently encouraged subordinates to proceed as they thought best.

105 G. Zahn, *Chaplains in the R.A.F.: A Study in Role Tension* (Manchester: Manchester University Press, 1969), p. 112.

106 M.F. Snape, *The Royal Army Chaplains' Department 1796-1957: Clergy Under Fire* (Woodbridge: Boydell Press, 2008); Edward Madigan, *Faith Under Fire: Anglican Army Chaplains and the Great War* (Basingstoke: Palgrave Macmillan, 2011); L. Parker, *The Whole Armour of God: Anglican Army Chaplains in the Great War* (Solihull: Helion & Company, 2009).

107 Andrew Totten, 'Moral Soldiering and Soldiers Morale' in Andrew Todd (ed.) *Military Chaplaincy in Contention* (Farnham: Ashgate, 2013), p. 21.

108 Ibid., p. 31.

Despite the dreadful conditions and enormous casualties, MEF chaplains retained a "just war" perspective that promoted spiritual comfort and cheerful endurance. Church parades, the cause of much resentment in France, were seldom organised on the peninsula. This provided padres with greater scope to convene informal voluntary services that appear to have been popular and well-attended. Thus a variety of circumstances peculiar to the Gallipoli campaign conspired to allow for increased engagement with spiritual charges, something their clerical counterparts on the Western Front found difficult to emulate throughout 1915. Subsequent service in other theatres provided MEF veteran chaplain with the opportunity to serve as valuable role models to less experienced contemporaries. As Michael McKernan, in a poignant observation that equally applies to BEF padres, observed: "Chaplains, now, were on an equal footing with all – there were no distinctions or props to rescue a man from the steady gaze of his fellows. At Gallipoli, each read the other's soul."[109]

109 McKernan, *Padre*, p. 40.

22

"We'd climb up the side of a signboard an' trust to the stick o' the paint"[1] – The Gallipoli Experience of 1/4th Highland Mountain Brigade, Royal Garrison Artillery

Rob Langham

The establishment of the Territorial Force (TF) as part of the Haldane Reforms of 1908 saw the birth – or re-birth of pre-existing Volunteer formations/units – of formations/units some of which would experience active service for the first time at Gallipoli. Amongst their number was the 1/4th Highland Mountain Brigade, Royal Garrison Artillery (1/4th HMB RGA). Consisting of the Argyll Mountain Battery, Bute Mountain Battery and Ross & Cromarty Mountain Battery (often referred to as "Ross Mountain Battery"), the brigade was a component part of the Highland Division – 51st (Highland) Division from 12 May 1915. TF RGA batteries were, as with most RGA units, normally equipped with heavy guns. For inland-based batteries, this would most likely be 4.7-inch guns mounted on wheeled carriages or, for those stationed in vital seaport areas, coastal guns such as those belonging to the Durham RGA Battery. Action for this unit came early when its 6-inch guns engaged German warships during the infamous East Coast bombardment of Hartlepool in December 1914. Uniquely amongst RGA TF units, the three RGA batteries of Argyll, Bute and Ross were all equipped with 10-pdr mountain guns usually supplied to equivalent Indian Army units. Moreover, the locally bred native Highland ponies – a small but tough breed – proved as ideal as their Indian counterparts for the transportation of disassembled mountain guns, ammunition and equipment.[2]

The 10-pdr mountain gun was a direct descendant of the Victorian era "Screw Gun"' celebrated by Rudyard Kipling in a poem (published 1890) that would become the unofficial mountain gunner/Royal Artillery anthem. The 10-pdr and its earlier brethren were known as "Screw Guns" as they were designed to be disassembled – the barrel unscrewing into two portions – to be transported by pack animal, usually by mule transport. Introduced in 1901, it was not much different in appearance than the 2.5-inch RML (Rifled Muzzle Loader) it replaced aside from the latter's breech loading design slightly larger 2.75-inch calibre. Although a breech loader, there was no recoil buffer or recuperator. This was checked by wooden scotches inserted behind

1 Rudyard Kipling, 'Screw-Guns' in *Barrack Room Ballads and Other Verses* (London: Methuen & Co., 1915).
2 M. Morrison, 'Highland Mountain Gunners at Gallipoli', *The Gallipolian*, No. 113, 2007.

10-pdr mountain battery during a pre-war exercise. (Author)

the wheels, but this did not prevent violent bucking and re-laying repetition. Ammunition was separately loaded – the 10-pdr shell with fuse was inserted, followed by a bagged charge. A friction tube inserted into the breech ignited the six-inch long, fourteen-dram bagged charge of cordite that was discharged by lanyard. Specifically designed as an anti-personnel weapon, the ammunition of choice was shrapnel, maximum range with a percussion fuse approximately 6,000 yards or 3,700 yards with a timed fuse, muzzle velocity being 1,289 feet per second. The 10-pdr was a designated "gun" as opposed to a howitzer, so it did not have a box or split trail, the short stubby carriage providing a maximum elevation of 25 degrees and a maximum depression of minus-15 degrees.[3]

There were several types of 10-pdr projectiles: shrapnel, consisting of lead balls encased in resin which, upon fuse ignition, would shift the plate at the bottom of the shell to expel hundreds of lead ball projectiles over a wide trajectory. For short range anti-personnel fire, there was case-shot similar to that employed by Napoleonic era cannon and carronades that muzzle discharged cased shrapnel balls. This would only have been employed in extremely desperate situations with the enemy at very close range. Component smoke shells consisted of a phosphorous/high explosive mixture. The high explosive shell consisted of gunpowder ignited by direct-action fuse. Magnesium star shells operated on the same principle as shrapnel shells, the slow-burn magnesium drifting in the night sky to illuminate the battlefield.[4]

The 10-pdr was designed to be disassembled into four pieces – the fore barrel; rear barrel and breech; wheels and axle and carriage – for transport. In addition to four pack animals (horses or mules) others were employed to transport ammunition, spare parts and other miscellaneous issue equipment. The prescribed gun detachment consisted of nine men, pack animal drivers exclusive. According to C. S. Mackenzie:

3 I.V. Hogg & L.F. Thurston, *British Artillery Weapons and Ammunition, 1914-1918* (London: Ian Allan, 1972), p. 41.
4 War Office, *Handbook for 10-pr Jointed B.L. Gun, Mule Equipment* (London: HMSO, 1902).

> Each Mountain Battery would normally in peacetime have possessed six commissioned officers – the Battery Commander (usually a Major of considerable experience and physical toughness) supported by his second-in-command, the Battery Captain, and four subalterns as the Section and Half-Section Commanders. These artillery sections were of course very much larger than infantry sections and each was required to be able to operate independently of the Battery proper for long periods. Each section operated two guns, one gun therefore representing a half section or detachment. Under the commissioned officers came the Battery Sergeant Major (who was the kingpin of the whole outfit) assisted by the Battery Quartermaster Sergeant, eight sergeants, one Farrier sergeant, eight corporals, eight bombardiers and lance bombardiers, four Gunners No 1, four Drivers No 1, six batmen and one Battery Clerk. Then came the rank and file numbering over two hundred in all when at full strength. Of these about thirty may have been signallers and surveyors; some sixty-four would have been "Gun Numbers" in the gun team, and perhaps one hundred were pony and mule "gunners as drivers". These were divided between the sections. Various specialists; farriers, blacksmiths, shoeing-smiths, saddlers, carpenters, tailors (sometimes), cooks, and trumpeters comprised the balance.[5]

TF artillery units attended annual summer camps lasting for two weeks duration. At the outbreak of war, the Argyll and Ross Mountain batteries had attended one more annual camp than the Bute Mountain Battery thus the Bute Mountain Battery was junior. It was not long after the 1914 annual camp that war was declared, and the opportunity to volunteer for overseas service presented itself. The experiences of the Argyll Mountain Battery at Campbelltown – which sponsored the battery right section – on mobilisation would have been similar to that of other TF units:

> By 10 a.m. soldiers' pay books (Army Book 64), Identity Discs (one grey and one brown) all with Regimental numbers and names on them, and Jack Knives (including tin opener – forget not that), had been served out. By 11 o'clock officers and policemen in motor cars were scouring town and country for riding horses and pack ponies. Drivers who could ride were sent to Southend, Ballochantee and Tayinloan, where the commandeered animals were to be concentrated. Shopkeepers and merchants, on contracts arranged some years before, delivered men's and horses' rations in time to be served out for a mid-day meal. You queued up at the Harness Room, received one pound of meat (including bones) and one pound of bread, were told that this was to do to you till next afternoon, and you were to find salt and pepper by yourselves. You discovered that your mother or your wife was to get one shilling per night to billet you, and that she was to provide a fire to cook the rations. A few of the older women had done this service for the old Argyll and Bute Militia. During that afternoon and evening and all next day the horses kept arriving and were pegged out, watered and fed on "Stewart's Green". Some had cost sixty pounds, the lowest eighteen. The "Vet" of that day was the valuator and satisfied everybody by being liberal. Farmers everywhere were not quite so pleased with their bargains, a few weeks later, when the value

5 C.S. Mackenzie, *The Last Warrior Band: The Lewis Connection – Gallipoli 1915-16* (Private publication), p. 585.

> of horse flesh went up fifty percent, but new prices for cattle, sheep, grain, butter and cheese compensated them for being caught on the hop. Next day harness had to be fitted and new holes punched to fit all sizes and shapes of ponies. The risks were many. How was one to know that one animal it and another kicked if you went near it? We saw one N.C.O. with the outline of a horse's muddy shoe on his chest. He had been near enough its hind end to get marked, but not quite close enough to have his chest smashed in. Some of the men knew one end of a horse from the other and that was about all.[6]

Of the Highland ponies available in the Campbelltown area, only 14 had been employed by the Argyll Mountain Battery on a regular basis. This left the unit with the unenviable task of familiarising its four-legged new recruits with harnesses and pack loads. The right section was subsequently joined by the left section (hailing from Oban and Tobermory) thus bringing together the entire battery. Making their journey separately, the three batteries of the 1/4th HMB entrained for Inverness and then to Bedford, arriving at the latter destination on 14 August. Subsequent training as a unit in 51st (Highland) Division took place until spring 1915.

Formed from overseas garrisons during January-March 1915, the 29th Division was earmarked for the forthcoming Gallipoli landings. Its component artillery, consisting of one horse and two field artillery brigades, had no RGA units. This was amended with the addition of 90th Heavy Battery (four 60-pdr guns), 14th Siege Battery (four 6-inch 30 cwt howitzers) and 1/4th HMB, Bute Mountain Battery exclusive, on 10 March. The Bute Battery remained at Bedford with recruits from the other two batteries deemed too young or otherwise unfit for service. Some Bute personnel filled vacancies created by those left behind to accompany 29th Division. They also provided reinforcements to the peninsula. With two batteries designated for active service, the 1/4th HMB was divided into two component parts – 1/4th Highland Mountain Battery (assigned to 29th Division) and 2/4th Highland Mountain Battery (to remain at Bedford). Those off to war did not have long to prepare before entraining for Avonmouth. Embarking for the Mediterranean on 16 March, conditions aboard the transport ship were particularly unpleasant, especially for animals housed in poor ventilation below deck. Disembarking at Alexandria on 1 April, the 1/4th HMB paraded with 29th Division for the first time. Embarking on HMT *Mercian* on 9 April, battery guns were mounted on deck as an anti-submarine foil. Disaster during a subsequent encounter with a Turkish torpedo boat (17 April) was narrowly avoided when two 18-pdrs stationed on the upper deck failed to engage due to crew unreadiness. Fortunately, the three discharged torpedoes missed, however, three men drowned during *Mercian*'s temporary abandonment. Arriving at Mudros, 1/4th HMB disembarked with the horses and guns to temporarily occupy positions prior to leaving for Gallipoli on 24 April.[7]

Lying off W Beach until after the costly amphibious landing, two sections – one each from Argyll and Ross batteries – disembarked first, horses and disassembled guns heading for shore in horse barges. Taking position above the now secure beachhead, the gunners dug in for the night as a measure against counter-attack. That the 1/4th HMB was the first British artillery unit ashore is irrefutable, although the Indian mountain gunners, also equipped with 10-pdrs

6 RSM J.H. Mackenzie, *Crowded Hours of Argyll and Ross Batteries RGA (TF)* (Campbelltown: Reprinted from the Campbelltown Courier, 1936), pp. 8-9.

7 1/4th HMB War diary transcript in possession of M. Morrison.

at Anzac Cove, were justified in claiming to be the first artillery unit to have disembarked on the Gallipoli Peninsula. Having prepared fixed positions, the HMB guns were soon in action – Bombardier Nelson, who would later earn a DCM, of Ross Mountain Battery firing the first round together with 460th Howitzer Battery Royal Field Artillery (RFA) – in support of infantry advancing inland to link up with V Beach. Priority was the transport of guns and ammunition to assigned positions. Following this, horses were employed to carry supplies for the infantry and other units on shore. Owing to the prevailing dearth of horses and mules, the movement of water, ammunition and stores inland became the immediate task of the HMB's plucky Highland ponies. Under the aegis of Major Allen of Ross Mountain Battery, supply convoys were rapidly organised and sent forward.[8]

Mobile mountain guns proved their worth in the days following the Helles landings, the 1/4th HMB contributing its firepower as part of 20 guns supporting three infantry brigades during the First Battle of Krithia (28 April 1915). Perhaps the smallest gun available on the peninsula, the 10-pdr provided welcome support to the meagre MEF artillery bombardments of this time. It was during this first major MEF land offensive that the section of the Argyll Mountain Battery provided close support for 87th Brigade's assault on trench 176H. Furthermore, the Ross Mountain Battery section aided the French, north-east of Sedd-el-Bahr, prior to returning the British sector two days afterwards. The horse transport role continued until 29 April by which time other units landed, drivers returning to the battery. The remaining sections of component HMB batteries landed at Helles on the evening of 28 April. Ammunition scarcity was already an issue less than a week after the landing, the importance of economising stressed to units concerned. By late April, it was organised into "Left Group (Group III)" commanded by Lieutenant-Colonel Wynter.[9]

The Ross Mountain Battery was heavily engaged on 1 May when No. 3 Gun breech was blown out. For the Second Battle of Krithia (6-8 May 1915) batteries were divided into four groups, a composite mountain battery formed and detached from 1/4th HMB despite remaining in Group III.[10] This first of several amalgamations following personnel and material losses, resulted in unit re-designation as "Highland Mountain Battery" or "The Highland Battery".

Batteries replenished by nightfall of 8 May, it was discovered there were no 10-pdr ammunition reserves at the beachheads, despite 1,040 available in offshore ship hulls.[11] The 10-pdr gun's utility was aptly demonstrated in what was to become a commonplace role as the campaign went on when, on 13 May, a gun commanded by Lieutenant Wallace was brought near the frontline to engage a troublesome enemy machine-gun opposite Gurkha-held trenches which was duly knocked out.[12] Whilst deployed in this forward support role, Wallace's gun was replaced with a reserve gun so as not to deplete already limited artillery assets. The new role did not go unnoticed by the high command. Indeed, recognition of 10-pdr efficacy was demonstrated when

8 Lieutenant-Colonel R.M. Johnson, CMG, DSO, *29th Divisional Artillery War Record and Honours Book 1915-1918* (London: Royal Artillery Institution Printing House, 1921), pp. 164-165.
9 Ibid.
10 Ibid., p. 167.
11 Martin Farndale, *History of the Royal Regiment of Artillery: The Forgotten Fronts and the Home Base* (London: The Royal Artillery Institution, 1988), p. 25.
12 Johnson, *29th Divisional Artillery War Record and Honours Book 1915-1918*, p.168.

Mountain battery changing positions, Helles summer 1915. (C.S. Mackenzie)

Royal Navy 12-pdrs – a similar but slightly larger design employed by naval landing parties – were dispatched the following June for forward work use by the Royal Horse Artillery (RHA) and RFA. Moreover, unlike the 10-pdrs, not to mention every other British artillery piece ashore, 12-pdr ammunition stocks were plentiful.[13]

At approximately 11:15 p.m. on the night of 16 May, the Turks stormed the British left flank at Helles. Defended by the 1st Royal Inniskillings Fusiliers and 14th King George's Own Ferozepore Sikhs, the 10th Battery RFA and HMB responded with fire, during which four men of the former battalion were injured in an unfortunate "friendly fire" incident. At 8:00 a.m. the following day, both batteries engaged two enemy guns at square 176 H5 (map reference). The dearth of shells meant further application of conservation measures, and on 22 May MEF Headquarters ordered a daily rationing of four rounds per gun for 10-pdrs; double that for 60-pdrs, 4.5-inch howitzers and 6-inch howitzers.[14] Carrying on with the counter-battery role, 10-pdrs engaged enemy batteries at Square 176 M4 and 176 H5 respectively. On 26 May, seven direct hits on a Turkish howitzer situated opposite 1st Lancashire Fusiliers, frontline witnesses reporting direct hits. It was during this time, the first HMB reinforcements, consisting of one officer and 34 other ranks, reported for duty. Meantime, the period of counter-battery work continued for Group III, 97th Battery RFA participating in aeroplane co-operation whilst the Highland Mountain Battery engaged Turkish mountain guns.[15]

Throughout the Third Battle of Krithia (4 June 1915), the HMB fired an impressive 1,156 shrapnel rounds,[16] the second highest number of projectiles discharged by the 21 batteries (Naval 12-pdrs inclusive) available for the four-hour preliminary bombardment on a three-mile

13 Ibid., pp. 168-169.
14 Ibid., p. 168.
15 C.S. Mackenzie, *Gael Force on Gallipoli: Some experiences of the Ross Mountain Battery (and others) in the 4th Highland Mountain Brigade RGA* (Stornoway: Shore Print, 2015), pp. 302-303.
16 Johnson, *29th Divisional Artillery War Record and Honours Book 1915-1918*, p. 170.

Contemporary illustration of Bombardier Nelson earning the DCM, 9 August 1915.

front. Disappointing in its results, the first bombardment was followed by a second on a front of 500 yards which, reinforced by naval gunfire, proved more effective.

A heart-warming episode occurred during June when, at the Gully Beach horse lines, a foal was born to a HMB pony despite all animals supposedly having been neutered prior to military service. The new-born was christened "Lady Gallipoli", but responded to "Lady" or "Polly" and men were given leave to visit the now designated battery mascot. An order from a Lieutenant Brownlees, on detachment to the HMB from the Army Veterinary Corps, to euthanize Lady Gallipoli went unheeded after the unfortunate Brownlees was killed by a shell.[17]

Now divided into two batteries, the HMB fired 680 shrapnel projectiles in support of the Battle of Gully Ravine (28 June-2 July 1915) despite reduction from full-strength complement of eight guns to six.[18] Second Lieutenant Mackenzie was killed early on whilst his gun operated in the forward trenches, Sergeant Bell taking charge and earning a DCM for the effort. It was during a Turkish counter-bombardment that 97th Battery RFA was shelled in enfilade from the Asiatic shore. One projectile struck No 3 gun; another an 18-pdr, killing and wounding the crew; a third struck a General Service wagon loaded with shells before setting it ablaze. Observing this, HMB subaltern Macdonald rushed forward to remove the ammunition under

17 Morrison, 'Highland Mountain Gunners at Gallipoli'.
18 Johnson, *29th Divisional Artillery War Record and Honours Book 1915-1918*, p.171.

continuous hostile shellfire. Rodger, Subaltern McLaughlan and others were awarded the MM. Courageous incidents such as this were depicted by popular illustrators of the day.[19]

Subsequently based on both sides of Gully Ravine, headquarters at Pink Farm, the HMB shifted position twice, remaining in its final location throughout the remainder of June and July. Shifting its guns forward in ones or twos, the policy of deployment at the sharp end was carried out whenever and wherever necessary. In addition to these exciting forays whereby machine-guns and snipers were engaged with a few rounds prior to gun withdrawal, 70 rounds per night were fired into the enemy line opposite. Ammunition now available in sufficient quantities, the HMB provided vital sector fire support whilst sustaining (12 July) several fatalities.[20] Recalling the events of that dreadful day, Gunner Cunningham of Argyll Mountain Battery observed:

> We started firing again, but all at once our gun-pit parapet was blown up and all of us buried in amongst the sand bags and earth. When we had extricated ourselves, it was found that the only serious damage was one man wounded. Three times our gun-pit parapet was blown away in this manner, the Turks having evidently got our range. Altogether that day we had four men killed and six wounded. On the 13th we had this state of recurrent upheaval even worse, but I am glad to state that there were no casualties.[21]

No. 1 Gunner Sergeant Matheson was subsequently awarded a DCM for maintaining fire throughout the enemy bombardment. This affair is illustrative of the extreme vulnerability of batteries deployed in teeming rear areas where there was little available shelter and too many tempting targets for alert Turkish gunners. Far from home, the men of 1/4th HMB also suffered from the inherent miseries of Mediterranean climate extremes, fly swarms, disease and poor diet often associated with the Gallipoli campaign.[22]

The collective number of rounds fired by 29th Division batteries during July amounted to 37,740.[23] A second 1/4th HMB MC was awarded to Captain Burney during this time

> This officer was in command of the Highland Mountain Battery (organised from the Ross and Argyll Mountain Batteries) in the Gallipoli operations. He was indefatigable in reconnoitring forward positions for his guns, close to the frontline trenches, placing his guns in them and superintending their fire. It is due to his initiative, resource and personal example that this Territorial battery has done such excellent work. During the first two months this battery had 3 officers killed and 4 wounded and 54 NCO's and men were killed and wounded. It never had a day's rest and yet its morale remained as good as ever, greatly due to Captain Burney's example.[24]

Withdrawn at the end of July, the HMB embarked for Imbros on the night of 3/4 August for an all too brief rest prior to the Suvla Bay landings. New drafts as well as new guns – obtained

19 Ibid., pp. 39, 46.
20 Ibid., p. 173.
21 Morrison, 'Highland Mountain Gunners at Gallipoli'.
22 Johnson, *29th Divisional Artillery War Record and Honours Book 1915-1918,* p. 38.
23 Ibid., p. 174.
24 Ibid., p. 5.

A "Beetle" landing craft bow ramp is lowered at Suvla Bay.

from the hull of a steamer recently arrived from India – that were more than likely intended for equivalent Indian batteries at Anzac.

It was during its time at Lemnos that 1/4th HMB was featured in the national press:

HIGHLAND MOUNTAIN ARTILLERY

GRAND WORK AT THE DARDANELLES

ALWAYS IN THE FRONT TRENCHES[25]

> Ever since they landed at the Dardanelles the Highland Mountain Battery, which includes the Argyll and Bute Artillery, has earned high praise for its good work. In every account of the artillery operations received the fine performances of the battery are noted with admiration, and the performances of the battery are noted with admiration, and the undermentioned official acknowledgments have been forwarded by an Argyllshire officer. After the battle the end of June General Simpson Baikie wrote as follows to Captain Burned. Adjutant. 1/4th Highland Mountain Brigade, R.G.A.:

25 *Daily Record*, 4 August 1915.

Highland Mountain Battery gunners.

> "I am just sending these few lines to tell you how sorry I am to hear of the losses sustained by your battery in yesterday's action. I am particularly sorry to hear of the death of Lieutenant Mackenzie and of Captain Todd's very bad wound. (Captain Todd, who was the burgh surveyor of Lochgilphead, has since died from the wound). We all realise that your battery is always up in the front trenches and in the very thick of the fight, and I assure you that the very hard work of your officers and men is much appreciated, and that we Regulars are proud to have such gallant fellows as yours fighting alongside us."[26]

On the night of 6/7 August one section from each of the two HMB batteries embarked from Imbros for Suvla Bay. Attached to 11th (Northern) Division, the HMB gunners came ashore in a novel type of amphibious armoured landing craft, the 105-foot X-Lighter which was unofficially christened "Black Beetle" owing to its general appearance.[27]

The early success of the Suvla landings was squandered due to operational/tactical command and control failures.[28] Indeed, an incident involving 1/4th HMB sums up the consequent confusion. Moving inland on the night of 7/8 August, the battery marched to the sheltering slope of a nearby hillock to await sunrise. Assuming they were in secured territory, gunfire had been discerned to the battery's left; nothing had occurred to the front. Settling into position, an unexpected rifle fusillade, a bullet of which fatally struck a highland pony employed in milk delivery

26 *Daily Record*, 4 August 1915.
27 Mackenzie, *Gael Force on Gallipoli*, pp. 372-373.
28 See Jeff Cleverly, Brian Curragh and Tom Williams' chapters in this volume.

before the war, forced the nonplussed gunners to seek cover. Shortly after this, an unidentified officer mounted on a large black stallion galloped up and, informing all within reach that the battery was a mile and a half in front of the infantry, ordered them to retire. Withdrawing to safety, the HMB spent 8 August identifying suitable gun positions about Kiretch Tepe Ridge. Organisation and a semblance of battery routine were established during the following days as communication wires were run to 11th Division Headquarters and remaining battery sections disembarked.[29]

The Ross Mountain Battery was part of the land-based artillery support for 11th Division's advance to the W Hills on 9 August. Two of its 10-pdrs were out of action; this left two along with eight 18-pdrs and Royal Navy gunfire to carry out the preparatory bombardment. Brigadier-General Sitwell (GOC 34th Brigade) remarked: "The Mountain Gun Battery had two guns put out of action very soon, but the other two supported me well particularly shelling Hill 70 with the greatest accuracy whenever the Turks got on it, and assisted us splendidly when the scrub fire drove us back"[30] Some miles to the north, the Argyll Mountain Battery's four 10-pdrs were of little assistance to 10th (Irish) Division, the advance of which was hampered by water shortages. Further fire support was provided for 10th Division's advance astride Kiretch Tepe on 13 August. Initially successful, this second assault was foiled by fierce Turkish counter-attacks that forced the attackers back to jumping-off positions. Bombardier Nelson was awarded the DCM for his actions on 9 August:

> For having conspicuous bravery on August 9th. All the other gun numbers having been wounded, he was left alone to work his gun under the accurate fire of the enemy's guns at close range. With the greatest courage and devotion to duty he kept up his fire single-handed and rendered inestimable service at a critical period.[31]

The ambitious but ultimately unsuccessful IX Corps general attack of 21 August saw four HMB guns together with (12) 4.5-inch howitzers, (12) 5-inch howitzers, (32) 18-pdrs, (7) 60-pdrs and offshore naval guns participate in the preliminary bombardment. Impressive in scale when compared with previous MEF bombardments, it was still not enough. Moreover, available shell stocks were at worryingly low reserve levels, particularly in case of counter-attacks. The guns available had their faults too. For example, 5-inch howitzers of the type employed at Omdurman in 1898 were highly inaccurate whilst the modern 60-pdrs suffered from spring defects that plagued RGA batteries throughout the campaign. For their part, RFA, RHA, RGA and 1/4th HMB's considerable efforts in support of this offensive were not enough to make up for deficiencies in equipment and ammunition.[32]

The failure of the 21 August offensive resulted in stalemate at Suvla for the remainder of the campaign. From 22 August, guns were rationed to just two rounds per day. With battery horse lines and ammunition stores within range of hostiles guns, no such rationing appeared to effect

29 Mackenzie, *Crowded Hours*, pp. 35-37.
30 34th Brigade, 11th Division War Diary quoted in Morrison, 'Highland Mountain Gunners at Gallipoli'.
31 Johnson, *29th Divisional Artillery War Record and Honours Book 1915-1918*, p. 41.
32 Farndale, *History of the Royal Regiment of Artillery*, pp. 52-53.

Turkish projectile stocks. Subsequent enemy bombardments inflicted severe losses on men and transport animals, a single shell killing 113 horses and mules on 29 August.[33]

Frustrated by the continued deployment of obsolete guns, Brigadier-General R.W. Fuller was uncomplimentary about the 10-pdr's operational capabilities: "This gun is notoriously out of date, practically worn out; its shrapnel shell is unsatisfactory, due to its not opening out properly. It has for years been contemplated in India to replace this gun." By this time, there had been 8,125 10-pdr shells expended at Helles; 19,265 at Anzac and 1,702 at Suvla. Deployed at Anzac, the Indian Mountain Brigade had been in continuous action since the April landings. Only six of its original 18 guns had been replaced by worn-out pieces from India. Moreover, despite delivery of four similarly worn Indian guns delivered to 1/4th HMB prior to the Suvla landings, the battery arsenal had been reduced to four operable pieces by the following September.[34]

The 10-pdrs effectiveness against enemy trenches and machine gun posts had also been recognised in Fuller's report. This was not always the case, Corporal Mackenzie of Argyll Mountain Battery remarking that accuracy "depended on which side of the muzzle was last touched by the shell."[35] Wholly ineffective against trenchworks, the 10-pdr shrapnel shell was useless against enemy parapets and mined dugouts. A steady supply of high explosive (HE) shells was required. Unfortunately, the War Office denied the consequent request for 50 percent HE projectiles due to stock shortages. Fuller's report concluded by listing the 10-pdrs shortcomings:

> To recapitulate:
> The stock of 10-pdr B.L. guns is exhausted, and the equipment worn out
> They are of obsolete pattern
> The shrapnel shell is not fully effective
> They are not quick firers
> A sufficiency of common shell is not forthcoming
>
> It is now a question as to whether it is worth while trying to keep these Mountain Batteries in action, as further casualties in equipment occur.
>
> I suggest that pressing representations be made to War Office for a Q.F. equipment with a high percentage (50%) of common and High Explosive shell, or failing rearmament, India be asked to send either a British mountain, or Indian Mountain Brigade, with the very best guns available.

As no new guns were dispatched from Great Britain or India, Fuller's concerns appear to have produced no satisfactory response from the authorities. Manpower reinforcements did arrive however, replacements from Bedford disembarking at Suvla on 16 September. One of these was the author's Great-Grandfather, 392 John McLean of Argyll Mountain Battery.[36]

Mountain guns were low on the artillery priority list. Nonetheless, despite the pressing need for heavy guns as well as the ubiquitous 18-pdr field gun and 4.5-inch howitzer, there was a recently manufactured mountain gun available to the RFA arsenal. Approved for service in

33 Ibid., p. 53.
34 TNA WO 95/4334: 1st Australian Division War Diary, July-December 1915.
35 Mackenzie, *Crowded Hours of Argyll and Ross Batteries RGA (TF)*, p. 31.
36 Mackenzie, *Gael Force on Gallipoli*, p. 579.

1911 and issued in 1914, the 2.75-inch was, for all practical purposes, an improvement on the 10-pdr design rather than a newly designed weapon. Best suited for employment in mountainous terrain, it has a split or box trail and cranked axle for increased elevation. Although the 10-pdr barrel was maintained as a component part, a recuperator beneath the barrel acted as a recoil compensator despite the sharp kick when discharged. Nevertheless, it was a welcome improvement to the previous design. Although entering production prior to Gallipoli, there is no evidence of subsequent employment there.[37]

With the campaign now deadlocked in the immediate aftermath of the August offensive, fighting devolved into routine trench warfare at Helles, Anzac and Suvla. Establishing themselves on the Kiretch Tepe Ridge, Argyll Mountain Battery gunners laboured with pick and shovel to dig battery pits and makeshift shelters out of the slate-like ground. Excavating two feet down whilst stacking stones two feet high, roofing dugouts with issue ground sheets, blankets and accumulated branches, the position was to be 1/4th HMB's home for almost four months. Although rustic in appearance, this elevated trench and dugout complex was uncomfortably hot until winter when its occupants suffered from extremes of cold. Situated thus, the desire for necessities and additional comforts were manifested in scrounging expeditions to obtain corrugated iron sheets for the sergeant major's leaky billet roof or bringing off cunning ploys such as substituting sugar sacks for barley behind the back of an easily distracted New Army captain.[38] One useful acquisition was a gramophone which was duly hauled to a remote gun position lest it be overheard by its previous owners. Another more questionable trophy was a pet monkey purloined from a Welsh unit that dispatched a party to reclaim the lost mascot. Fresh meat, a welcome change from the monotonous diet of bully beef, cheese, jam and biscuits, was also covertly obtained:

> For four days the Gunners were supplied with a fresh leg of mutton each day. Inquiry revealed that some Australians who were repairing boats on the beach, had taken a boat one night and visited Samothrace Island, returning next morning with 25 sheep, which they penned in a barbed wire enclosure meant for Turkish prisoners, and placed an armed sentry over them. That sentry had to be kept amused; a few cigarettes had to be expended, and wire cutters brought into play next night, but our "reivers" got four of the sheep.[39]

Thus by dint of a few extra in-theatre months, the HMB gunners were proper "Old Sweats" when compared with their New Army contemporaries.

With the end of the campaign in sight, spare personnel and disabled guns were withdrawn. This left two guns of Argyll Mountain Battery on the northern side of Kiretch Tepe, one of which was positioned as far north as possible without toppling over the cliff; the other gun was situated close to the main supply track. Fired at fixed times over a two-week period, battery silence was maintained after nightfall on select dates. This clever ruse, a necessary preliminary to IX Corps' impending evacuation on the night of the 19/20 December 1915, was designed to take advantage of consequent Turkish assumptions about anticipated British fire schedules. And so it was that the northern gun was clandestinely withdrawn whilst the other remained in

37 I.V. Hogg, *Allied Artillery of World War One* (Crowood: Marlborough, 2004), p. 35.
38 Mackenzie, *Crowded Hours of Argyll and Ross Batteries RGA (TF)*, p. 41.
39 Ibid., pp. 42-43.

position until the infantry in front abandoned their trenches and marched to the rear. Its crew alert to possible enemy interference, the second gun was then withdrawn without incident. Arriving at the crowded beachfront, slabs of gun cotton to be employed should the 10-pdrs have to be abandoned were dispensed with as, duly loaded on to a lighter, they were towed off by a naval pinnace prior to unceremonious tipping into the murky Aegean depths where they presumably still lie.[40]

The traumatic trials and tribulations of the Highland mountain gunners at Gallipoli were just the beginning of the survivors' war. Disembarking at Alexandria on 26 December, 1/4th HMB concentrated at Ismalia where it was re-equipped with the 2.75-inch mountain gun. Dispatched to Salonika where it was joined (November 1916) by the Bute Battery, the brigade proved its worth in the mountainous terrain of the Macedonian front. Plans to re-equip with the 18-pdr field gun came to naught, its mountain gun complement being retained throughout the campaign. As for the gunners, service in distant theatres ensured there was no home leave until the close of hostilities with Bulgaria (29 September 1918). It was not until 1919 that surviving brigade members returned home. Mountain battery lineage was carried on by the Territorial Army after the war. Of longer duration, the comradeship of HMB's Gallipoli veterans was maintained for decades to come.[41]

40 Ibid., p. 46.
41 C.S. Mackenzie, *Gael Force on Gallipoli*, pp. 205-206.

23

Gallipoli: A Mining Overview

Ritchie Wood & John Dixon

On the declaration of war in summer 1914, senior commanders of the opposing Allied and Central Powers armies envisaged a war of movement as a means of exploiting rapid battle-field developments. There were few who thought that the few short months of open warfare on the Western Front would transform into strategic deadlock from the English Channel to the Swiss frontier. By autumn 1914 the French and Germans resorted to the age-old method of military mining. The British Army was not unfamiliar with the techniques thereof and as recently as June 1913 had carried out field mining exercises. Nevertheless, with the coming of European war, it had not been anticipated that such methods would be required against a sophisticated enemy. Therefore, from January 1915, ad hoc brigade mining sections were organised to commence underground work that ultimately culminated in the capture of Messines Ridge. This much-lauded success of June 1917 required a great deal of previous foresight and labour by officers and men alike not least that of the celebrated Major John Norton Griffiths (1871-1930), who had been instrumental in organising Royal Engineer Tunnelling Companies tasked with burrowing beneath German lines as a means of detonating explosive charges.[1] By the time the Gallipoli landings had occurred in April 1915, the first of the new companies (171st Tunnelling Company) had successfully exploded a series of mines beneath Hill 60 on the southern flank of the Ypres Salient. Whilst the mining in France and Belgium was, over time, carried out with effect by specialist companies, the same cannot be said of the similar operations during the ill-fated Gallipoli campaign.

The geological difficulties faced by Gallipoli miners differed from those encountered on the Western Front. For example, BEF miners had to contend with Flanders clays, running sands and high-water tables resulting in the need for extensive timbering essential to wet workings. Later mining in the French downlands required different techniques as the hard chalk was difficult to excavate though water was seldom encountered. The Gallipoli Peninsula, forming

1 Twenty-one RE tunnelling companies, which absorbed the previously established mining sections, were operational by the end of 1915. See Sir J.E. Edmonds, *Military Operations France and Belgium 1916*, Vol. II (London: Macmillan, 1932), p. 73.

as it does part of the Tertiary Thrace Basin,[2] has a sequence of sedimentary rock, mainly sandstone and limestone inter-bedded with sands and clays. In some parts these beds are overlain by Quaternary alluvial material, usually confined to existing river and stream beds that contain rich sand and clay layers associated with pebbles and boulder layers.[3] Perhaps the greatest difference was the absence of water. The Tertiary limestones are aquifers but usually far below ground level and out of the reach of boring equipment technology of the time. Some water was present in the alluvial material but in general terms this presented no problem since these areas were not in close proximity to mining areas. However, some wells originated in the alluvial material.[4]

Based on geology and geomorphology, the Gallipoli Peninsula is divided into a number of "Terrains", two of which are of particular relevance.[5] The first is known as "Plateau Terrain", the flat-topped escarpments trending NE–SW which at Anzac are deeply dissected by arid river valleys. Water is only found in deep limestone aquifers in the peninsula plateau regions. The softer rocks of the plateau are readily excavated, and this is of significance when considering mining at Anzac. The second terrain of importance is "Limestone Cliff Terrain". This resulted from the inter-layering of limestones and softer, often sandy, rocks. It is prevalent in the southern part of the peninsula and to the north and south of Anzac Cove where steep cliffs confined the beachhead thereby diverting attacks along the dissected hinterland Plateau Terrain. Both terrains dominate Anzac and Helles, whilst Suvla is dominated by a "Coastal Plain Terrain" and "Linear Ridge Terrain" which defines the Antafarta Ridge and the Karakol Ridge (Kirtech Tepe Sirt).[6] These features played no important part in the mining operations discussed in this chapter. In terms of ground conditions for military engineering work:

> The softer sedimentary rocks of the plateau tops provide suitable ground conditions for trench, dugout and tunnel construction, especially where, as at Sari Bair, there are hard bands that could be, and were, used to give support to the roofs of offensive tunnels later in the campaign.[7]

However, the same could not be said for areas dominated by limestone where heavy equipment and explosives were necessary. Moreover, these areas tended to the establishment of more permanent defensive works. This immediately suggests that mining activity at Helles was always going to be difficult unless mine works were shallow and essentially excavated through superficial materials.[8]

The Gallipoli campaign planners prepared for a short campaign that would result in seizure of the Ottoman capital. There had been no consideration of the need for siege techniques and, given subsequent logistical support, it was deemed unnecessary to provide the MEF with additional

2 M. Cemel Goncuoglu. 'Introduction to the Geology of Turkey: Geodynamic Evolution of the Pre-Alpine and Alpine Terranes' (MTA 2010). <https://www.researchgate.net/publication/293958942_Introduction_to_the_Geology_of_Turkey_Geodynamic_Evolution_of_the_Pre-Alpine_and_Alpine_Terrains>
3 E. Jordan, 'Geology and Warfare' (n.d.) <www.geo.tu-freiburg.de>
4 P. Chasseaud & P. Doyle, *Grasping Gallipoli* (Staplehurst: Spellmount, 2005).
5 Ibid., p. 8.
6 Ibid., p. 10.
7 Ibid.
8 Ibid., p. 11.

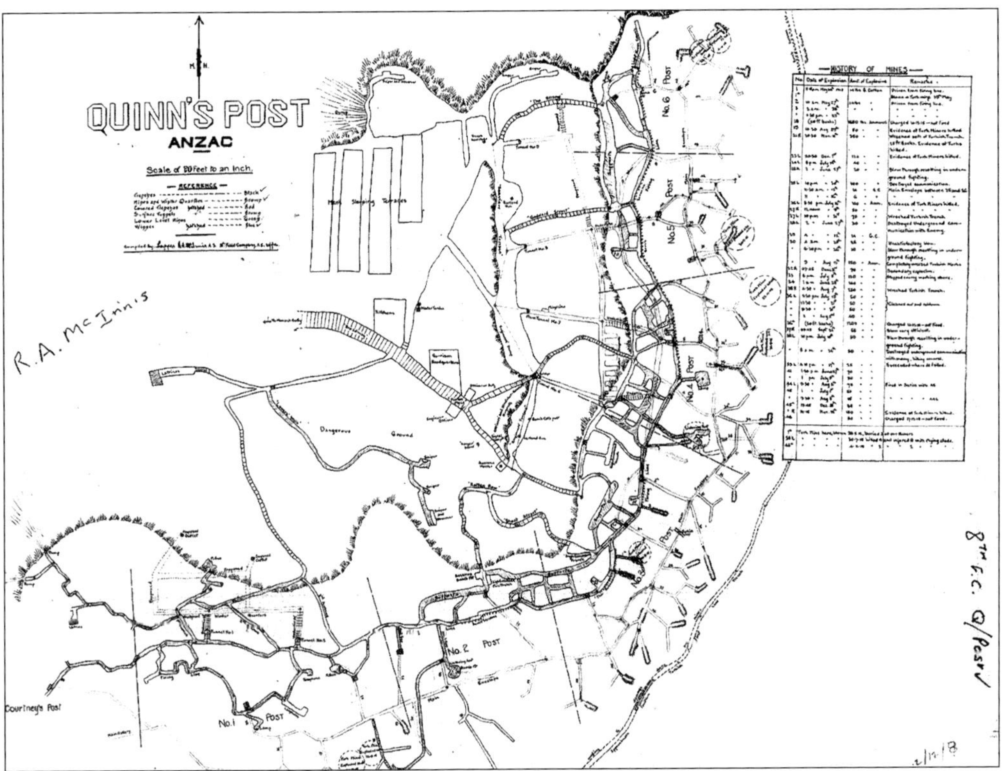

Map 23.1 McInnis rendering of Quinn's Post. (AWM RC00826).

engineering support beyond the established three field companies per division. This had not changed significantly by the time of the evacuation. Tasked with carrying out routine work such as water supply, road and shelter construction, this lack of foresight in the raising of specialist mining companies strained MEF field company efforts, supported by infantry labour, to the limit. As chronicled below, mining commenced within days of the landings both to provide shelter and as a means of confronting the enemy. There were no experts in military mining, but some infantry battalions had experienced miners within their ranks. This was particularly true of Australian units raised in mining areas such as Tasmania or Western Australia although the collective experience was not always relevant to prevailing conditions. Nevertheless, throughout the eight months of the campaign, offensive/defensive mining became a significant part of operations, as field companies took up the challenge from aggressive Turkish miners. Indeed, as the campaign progressed, mining efforts increased until, during latter operations, most offensive efforts occurred below ground.[9]

9 C.E.W Bean, *The Story of Anzac*, Vol. II (Sydney: Angus & Robertson, 1938), p. 255

Case Study: Quinn's Post

Quinn's Post was the key to the Anzac sector. Situated on a ridge crest, it was the most advanced ANZAC position, the garrison subject to almost unceasing artillery, rifle, sniper fire and bomb throwing. It is perhaps for this reason that it lent itself to the development of extensive fighting tunnels as a means of defending the post, the loss of which would threaten the whole of the tenuous frontline astride the second ridge.

The map drawn by Sapper R.A. McInnis, 5th Field Company, Australian Engineers, clearly indicates the vast tunnelling network at Quinn's Post (see Map 23.1). Given the garrison was precariously perched on the ridge and barely 50 yards away from the enemy trenches, infantry protection was of the utmost importance. Quinn's Post was divided into six sections. Established strongpoints were connected by a series of covered communication and support trenches affording protective access to the firing line. Underground the development of an "envelope" that literally "wrapped up" the entire Turkish frontline ensured that hostile mining operation would be confronted by underground galleries where assigned listeners detected enemy underground activity. Turkish mining thus identified, their efforts were parried by means of defensive underground mines known as camouflets which were designed to destroy enemy workings without breaking the surface. In addition, it was from these defensive galleries that offensive mines were extended beyond the envelope.[10]

The first indication that Quinn's Post's precarious position may well have been compromised by enemy mining occurred on 30 April 1915 when Captain Hugh Quinn, 15th Battalion AIF – whom the vital position was named after – reported that "the Turks were in a slight dip in front of them, well concealed. They appeared to be tunnelling, with a view to blowing up the post." Such was the defenders' unpreparedness that Quinn also observed: "I cannot get at them well but if I had a bomb or two it would probably shift them."[11] Three captured Turkish bombs were thrown but were reported as "unsuccessful". Retaliatory mining did not appear to be an alternative at the time. That same day, the Turks were observed advancing forward saps to such an extent that the post garrison were barely 50 yards distant from the enemy before hostile bombing intensified. Moreover, a mound of earth indicating a possible mine shaft was observed in the Turkish lines. Concerned about this possible threat, immediate defensive measures were undertaken.[12]

The arrival of the 1st Field Company New Zealand Engineers (1st FCNZ) on 4 May could not have been at more opportune time.[13] Equipped with explosives, engineering tools and other mining equipment, it was reinforced by No. 3 Field Company, Australian Engineers on temporary attachment. 2nd Lieutenant Farquhar, with portion of No. 3 Section, was allotted to Quinn's Post. Orders were received on 5 May from 1st Australian Division headquarters to drive three listening tunnels, 15 feet deep, from the rear slope in order to ascertain if the Turks were carrying out mining operations. Faced with a steep learning curve to gain immediate knowledge of the suitability or otherwise of local ground conditions, 1st FCNZ listeners prepared to remain in small "one man" tunnels for hours on end to differentiate between the somewhat delicate sound

10 AWM RC00828: Quinn's Post, Sapper R.A. McInnes, 8th Field Company (Australian Engineers).
11 C.E.W Bean, *The Story of Anzac*, Vol. I (Sydney: Angus & Robertson, 1924), p. 580.
12 Bean, *The Story of Anzac*, Vol. II, p. 98.
13 AWM: AWM4 35/10: 1st FCNZ, NZ&A Division.

of the Turks "picking" at a mine face as opposed to routine above ground battle noises. Such was their progress that by 9 May it was reported that no enemy mining sounds had been overheard. Major H.R. Carter, the then Quinn's Post commander, confidently reported that the mound over the supposed mine-shaft was more than likely a machine-gun post. This news did not in any way remove the fear that the Turks may well be mounting a surprise surface attack. Having no real idea of just what the enemy was planning, it was decided to carry out a bold reconnaissance on the night of 9/10 May. The result was a fierce but ultimately unsuccessful engagement that nevertheless determined the enemy was "definitely mining towards the Quinn's Post."[14]

As a precaution, the 1st FCNZ was ordered to advance five saps simultaneously from the firing line.[15] These saps served the purpose of listening and, if necessary, provided the means to prepare camouflets should Turkish mining be detected. Working conditions, to say the least, were unpleasant. The urgent need for advancement minimized sap dimensions. Subsequent candlelight excavations consumed available oxygen and, unaccompanied by forced ventilation, the available air quickly became fouled. For their part, miners recruited from 14th and 15th battalions and 1st Light Horse Brigade were set to work under the supervision of 10 sappers. Spoil disposal posed a problem. Carelessly discarded, it informed an observant enemy that mining operations were underway. At Quinn's Post, the solution was brilliant in its simplicity. A large tunnel was driven into the rear of the ridge crest after which subterranean galleries were extended from there. Accumulated spoil was then disposed unseen into nearby Monash Gully.[16]

The 15th Battalion, having been previously involved in the 9 May sortie, did not ignore the previously determined threat of Turkish mining. However, battalion officers and supporting engineers insisted there was no present danger. A contrary report of a hostile mine tunnel opposite the right confirmed their worst fears. The possible threat was passed on to the relieving 16th Battalion which included a large proportion of miners:

> [T]hose of the 15th from Mount Morgan, Charters Towers, and other fields in Queensland, and from the Tasmanian tin mines; those of the 16th from goldfields and other mines of Western and South Australia. With their special mining knowledge, they realised how easily and quickly the enemy could undermine Quinn's, driving from the farther side of the ridge deep tunnels by which he could presently blow the whole post into the air.[17]

The 15th Battalion decided to take their own precautions. On 17 May, a man known as "Ganger Slack"[18] was listening in a forward No. 3 sap. Certain he overheard enemy mining, this was confirmed by CSM T. Williams and company commander Lieutenant B. Sampson. Others listening at the same sap determined that "Jacko" i.e., the Turks, were "getting under us."[19] Subsequent reports received little official response. The 15th Battalion relieved 16th Battalion at Quinn's Post on 23 May. Ganger Slack, now convinced he could hear enemy picking not in one but three places, was ably assisted by a nearby engineers' gallery listener who estimated

14 Bean, *The Story of Anzac*, Vol. I, p. 116.
15 AWM: AWM4 35/10: 1st FCNZ, NZ&A Division, War Diary, May 1915.
16 Bean, *The Story of Anzac*, Vol. II, p. 204.
17 Ibid., p. 198.
18 Cpl. J. Slack, M.M. (No. 653). 15th Bn., Railway ganger: b. Wellington, N S.W., 1870.
19 Bean, *The Story of Anzac*, Vol. I, p. 200.

enemy mining activity at a distance of two feet.[20] Urgent action was subsequently sanctioned by higher headquarters. The sounds were estimated to be a few feet away and immediately below the listener's position. A light 32lb charge of gun-cotton was prepared by the 1st FCNZ. The "tamping" process, whereby sandbags were placed immediately behind the charge to ensure the explosion and accompanying gases rose upwards, was implemented and the defensive mine detonated at 5:30 p.m. Initially assumed to have destroyed the head of the enemy works the enemy was overheard within a few hours. This was the first indication of the Turkish miners' resourcefulness and determination to press on regardless of cost, something that did not bode well for the future maintenance of Quinn's Post. The NZ Engineer's post-war history later observed.

> [I]nsignificant charges used by us naturally appear to invite comment, but the difficulty was that we dared not use large charges even had they been available, for fear of threatening the stability of the position. All we had in mind was to forestall the Turk by blowing in his galleries or exploding his charges while he was still as far as possible from our trenches.[21]

With the aid of a "special mining party from the infantry" the struggle was taken to the Turks.[22] Mines were blown on the 26, 27 and 28 May in response to overheard enemy activity with perceived local advantage but Ganger Slack was not to be denied. Despite the action taken, he was convinced it was all too late. On the evening of 28 May Slack visited his company headquarters to inform the officers there that Quinn's Post would be destroyed in a matter of hours. There is no evidence of officer reaction to the "doomsday" statement but the seemingly dubious correction proved correct. That night, at 3:20 a.m., the garrison was awoken by a series of explosions that threatened to eradicate Quinn's Post in its entirety. The Turks succeeded in destroying one-half of the post prior to storming the ruins from which they were able to toss or roll bombs on to the Australian supports below. After a desperate struggle resulting in the death of Major Quinn amongst many others, the defenders managed to regain the lost trenches.[23] Had the enemy succeeded, neighbouring positions would have been exposed to enfilade fire. The 1st FCNZ war diary reported that day:

> During the night Turks blew up two mines at Quinn's Post damaging only parapets one place and a communication trench in the other. The mine heads which we previously blown in [sic] having evidently hampered the enemy and prevented them laying their main mines.[24]

Such understatement is difficult to comprehend given Quinn's Post's precarious position on the ridge and particularly when such a large explosion preceded the attack.[25] As a result, two mine craters, designated "A Crater" and "B Crater", were formed on the surface. Crater B had been

20 AWM: AWM4 35/10: 1st FCNA, NZ&A Division, War Diary, May 1915.
21 N. Annabell, *Official History of the NZ Engineers During the Great War 1914-1919* (Uckfield: Naval & Military Press reprint of 1927 edition), Chapter 2.
22 AWM: AWM4 35/10: 1st FCNA, NZ&A Division, War Diary, May 1915.
23 Bean, *The Story of Anzac*, Vol II, p. 206.
24 AWM: AWM4 35/10: 1st FCNA, NZ&A Division, War Diary, May 1915.
25 F. Waite, *The New Zealanders at Gallipoli* (Auckland: Whitcombe & Tombs, 1921), p. 29.

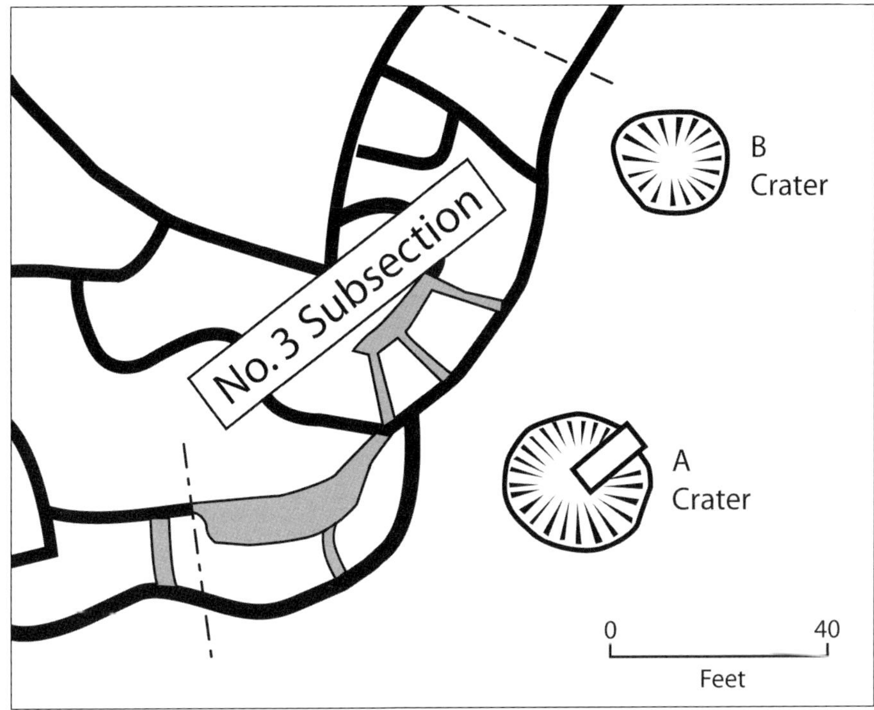

Sketch illustrating craters formed following the 29 May attack at Quinn's Post. The blockhouse was constructed in 'A' Crater. (Terence Powell)

captured during 29 May but Crater A remained in Turkish hands.[26] An attempt to secure Crater A by a sergeant and six men of the Canterbury Battalion failed as the party found themselves under heavy fire from loop-holes in what was perceived to be a strongly timbered rectangular blockhouse. With insufficient timber available to tunnel beneath the structure and the risk that charge laid directly against it could well damage part of Quinn's Post it was decided to seek volunteers to lay a charge on top of the troublesome structure.[27]

Two 1st FCNZ engineers, Lance Corporal Fear and Sapper Hodge, volunteered to carry out the demolition work.[28] At approximately 10:00 p.m., 1 June, they crawled over the trench parapet working their way slowly forward and, in the face of bullets and bombs, approached the blockhouse some 20 feet away. Having previously prepared a safety connection with electric exploder in the Australian trench opposite, they placed a 12lb gun cotton charge to be detonated by two timed fuses. Falling back to the frontline trench, the device exploded with a tremendous

26 Bean, *The Story of Anzac*, Vol. II, p. 223.
27 Ibid., p. 206.
28 Cpl. F.J.H. Fear, D.C.M.; N.Z. Engineers; cheese factory manager of Wellington, N.Z.; b. Kilbirnie, Wellington, 28 November 1887; KIA 20 September 1916.; Sapper E.A. Hodges, DCM N.Z. Engineers; motor mechanic, b. Northampton, 1888.

roar, the blockhouse and attendant garrison being destroyed. Unscathed, Fear and Hodges were awarded DCMs for their effort.[29]

Tunneller inexperience was oft-related in a comic-dramatic story of the "panicking miner". Enemy activity having been detected in a Quinn's Post tunnel on 2 June, its occupants were placed on full alert. On striking a soft spot with his pick, a miner was certain he had broken into a Turkish gallery. Unarmed, he rushed past equally panicked comrades. Lieutenant Hon. R. P. Butler, the engineer officer in charge, responded by entering the now vacated tunnel accompanied by an armed escort. Making their way along the tunnel, they found a lone listener calmly making his rounds. He reported the enemy was just a few feet away. A 100lbs charge was laid and fired after a somewhat anxious two hours. On re-entry, the investigating party were confronted by a burst of flame. Beating a hasty retreat, they heard a loud explosion from the Turkish workings, the enemy miners therein perhaps annoyed at losing the detonation race. Remarkably, there were no injuries but the need for a miner discipline code was deemed necessary. Moreover, there was a fierce determination that the shock and confusion of 29 May should not be repeated. It was not going to be enough to institute defensive measures. The necessity to adopt an offensive stance now part of the overall mining programme, the call went out for experienced officers and men. Two mining engineers and 100 miners from 2nd Australian Infantry Brigade and a similar number from 3rd Brigade were dispatched from Monash Valley.[30] Mining was now undertaken on a larger scale. Bean later observed: "[I]n the long run more was affected at Quinn's Post by entrenching than by all the bloody local assaults undertaken from that post."[31] Given the surface stalemate, it is not surprising that the General Staff should look to encourage offensive mining as a means of tackling the Turkish trenches.

The 1st FCNZ, now greatly strengthened by the presence of infantry miners, went on the offensive. Throughout June, it exploded ten mines on detecting enemy workings. On the 26th and 27th, Turkish mines were broken into. There was an exchange of gun fire before both parties were retired with no reported casualties. Throughout July and August work on an envelope extending from No.1 Post to No. 6 Post effectively ensured that enemy works would be confronted by a manned defensive gallery. This brought the opposing miners into close contact; whispers and banishment of noisome issue footwear were the orders of the day. An indication of just how much care had to be taken is related in an interesting albeit frightening anecdote. An ANZAC camouflet had developed a slight opening between the opposing tunnels. The enemy were overheard talking but suddenly all was quiet. Realising the light of their candle had alerted the enemy to their presence, they pretended to withdraw whilst, as quietly as possible the tunnel was charged and mine detonated.[32]

The 1st FCNZ was relieved in July by the 3rd Australian Field Company (3rd FC AE).[33] The latter's war diary entries for of July and August are unavailable but the McInnis map, "History of Mines" does record the mines detonated during those months. In July, no fewer than 12 mines are indicated as blown with accompanying notes asuch as "stopped enemy working above

29 H.L. Pritchard (ed.), *History of the Corps of Royal Engineers: Gallipoli, Macedonia, Egypt & Palestine*, Vol. VI (Chatham: Institution of Royal Engineers, 1952), p. 40.
30 Bean, *The Story of Anzac,* Vol. II, p. 233.
31 Ibid., p. 126.
32 Ibid., p. 280.
33 AWM: AWM4 14/22: 3rd Aust. FC.

... evidence of Turks killed" and "blew through resulting in underground fighting." There is, however, a sober note that on 30 July an explosion in No. 27A, No. 3 Post killed three miners and injured six others. During August, a further five mines were detonated. Accompanying notes indicate "wrecked Turkish trench ... completely wrecked Turkish works" and "evidence of Turk miners killed." Perusal of the McInnis map denotes two additional mines being blown on 23 and 24 July. From this evidence it can be determined that the underground battle continued with some intensity, the 3rd FC AE fully extended during a two months tour. Relieved by the 5th Field Company, Australian Engineers (5th FC Aust.) on 14 September, the latter remained at Quinn's Post until the evacuation in December.[34] The war of deep and shallow galleries continued apace throughout its time there:

> Where explosives were being handled, candles or torches with their glowing elements were banned, and men worked in the faint but safe glow of sheets of zinc coated with "Balmain's luminous paint." Inspired by the War Office manual, Charles Elsom ingeniously rigged up a series of reflectors using flattened biscuit tins to bring sunlight into the shallower galleries.[35]

The 5th FC AE's immediate task was to repair, enlarge, deepen and timber the main envelope and listening galleries which had long been targeted by Turkish artillery. Frustrated that work was held up due to the short supply of candles, the company's war diary for 31 October observed: "During the month half a dozen hurricane lamps were tried. It was found, however, that the lamp glasses would not stand the draught and were soon broken. Rough slush lamps were manufactured out of tobacco tins. These proved successful in short galleries and in the main envelope where ventilation was good. Candle consumption was also greatly reduced."[36]

Selection of suitable listeners was essential. The 5th FC AE was subsequently alarmed to receive reports of hostile mining opposite No. 1 Post (No. 18 gallery) extending through other galleries across the entire line right up to No. 6 Post (No. 45A gallery). On 21 September, listeners reported that the Turks were just four to five feet away from No. 37 gallery. A charge of 60lbs ammonal was quickly placed. The enemy was not overheard from this time and the charge remained unfired. This "wait and see" approach was in direct contrast to mining on the Western Front where enemy silence was an indicator of "blow before they blow". Despite no subsequent reference of the enemy being overheard at No. 18 listening gallery, No. 1 Post, the Turks detonated a mine there on 22 September. This resulted in some consternation given the fact that sounds were overheard in other galleries, not to mention the aforementioned unfired charge in No. 37 gallery. As a result, listeners were placed on full alert and new tunnels pushed out into unprotected areas. The 5th FC AE reluctance to mount underground offensives was demonstrated when a newly-constructed tunnel at the head of No. 18 gallery broke into an unguarded Turkish gallery. A charge of 350lbs ammonal was placed but left unfired as a "precautionary measure". Owing to continuous enemy activity being overheard in the surface

34 AWM: AWM4 14/27: 8th Aust. FC.
35 P. Stanley, *Quinn's Post: Anzac, Gallipoli* (Crows Nest: Allen & Unwin, 2005), p. 111.
36 AWM: AWM4 14/27/2 Part 1: 5th FC. Aust. Engineers, War Diary, 31 October 1915.

tunnel, orders were issued to construct an effective sandbag barrier – presumably with the 350lb charge remaining – left in situ until further notice.[37]

Given 1st FCNZ reluctance to employ large charges for fear of destabilizing the position, it is of note that such a large charge was laid. This can be defended by examination of how far the gallery had been extended from the main envelope. It also illustrates how mining operations had increased in intensity coupled with the need to "keep ahead of the game" as a means of avoiding serious repetition of the 29 May debacle. This was further illustrated by the first recorded damage from an enemy mine detonated on 4 November. At 5:20 p.m., the Turks fired a surface mine approximately 15 yards to the left of No. 6 Post. No damage was done to underground works, but such was the force of the explosion that men deemed safe beneath cover in the support trenches were injured when struck by large clods of earth breaking through the overhead shelter. The first recorded mine (11 November) detonated by 5th FCAE occurred when enemy activity was overheard approximately five feet away in gallery No. 21 of No. 2 Post. The laying of a 340lbs charge of ammonal was delayed due to the foulness of the air but was fired that evening. Utilised as a bombing post, the Turkish trench above was demolished by the blast.[38]

Whatever the situation above ground, the miners prepared for a long stay by constructing an underground magazine to accommodate five tons of ammonal. In addition, tunnels were driven to afford communications between existing tunnels and on-going repairs to envelope and existing galleries. Having blown their first offensive mine, additional charges were fired in galleries 21 (18 November), 32 (3 December), 25A (9 December) and 45A (13 December).[39]

The evacuation of Anzac imminent, two half-ton charges for galleries 18 at No. 1 Post and 36A respectively were prepared. Sergeant Evans and Sapper Johnson were to remain at Quinn's Post to detonate, but the mines were deemed unnecessary for no other reason than that they would alert the enemy to the withdrawal. Considering the size of previous explosions and consequent concerns about collapsing Quinn's Post, the effect of the charges can only be assumed.

Mining at Helles

Three RE field companies were attached to 29th Division, but there was little or no effort to commence mining operations during the immediate aftermath of the Helles landings. This may reflect to some extent the difference in the underlying geology, but also the fact that the subsequent inland fighting was rather more mobile to begin with than at Anzac. As other divisions disembarked at Helles, there was little or no coordination/cooperation of mining activities. However, it soon became clear that the Turks were employing defensive mines as a means of delaying MEF progress. Shallow listening galleries were established in a rather haphazard manner. Defensive counter-mining measures, employing small explosive charges, were only undertaken on Turkish mining being overheard in a particular sub-sector, that is the

37 AWM: AWM4 14/2: 8th FC Australian Engineers War Diary, 24 September 1915.
38 AWM: AWM4 14/27/3 Part 2: 8th FC Australian Engineers War Diary, 11 November 1915.
39 AWM: AWM4 14/27/4 Part 1: 5th FC Australian Engineers War Diary, 13 December 1915.

mining tended to be reactive and not pro-active. Assistance was at hand; Corporal J. Nixon,[40] an experienced Scottish miner, recalled how easy it was to know where the Turks were mining.[41] Discarding their newly dug earth behind the frontline, its contrasting colour when compared with the surrounding ground and the presence of steam rising from the damp earth was a clear indication of substantial excavations in progress.[42]

Experienced miners were few and far between and spread far too thin. Infantry working parties were supervised by experienced miners wherever possible. For example, an open sap was excavated down from the front of a trench until a sufficient depth of top cover was attained, after which a tunnel was driven forward. Difficulties occurred when working by candlelight which often meant maintenance of sight lines and straight tunnels were compromised.[43] Venting his frustration with the tendency of each shift having its own idea of constructing and maintaining a straight tunnel, Nixon remarked:

> Very few thought of hanging plumb lines after setting the course by compass, and in some instances where-plumb lines were hung, some miners were observed using only one line to try to drive, a straight course. When asked why they did not use the two plumb lines they would reply: "Oh, the string broke" or "the plumb-line fell down". The tunnels driven in this manner were all turns twists and bends."[44]

This could not continue, as the Turks were making slow but steady progress towards the British frontline. A decision was made to form a specialised unit designated "VIII Corps Mining Company" to operate under the control of Captain H.W. Laws, Royal Naval Division.

Despite rigorous research, no VIII Corps Mining Company war diaries/reports were discovered in the relevant archives. Fortunately, two of its miners provided excellent written accounts of their experiences.[45] In addition to the previously mentioned Corporal Nixon, there is Able Seaman Joseph Murray and his celebrated memoir *Gallipoli As I Saw It* (1965). Nixon and 15 others of 1/7th Highland Light Infantry volunteered for duty; Murray (Hood Battalion) had little option.[46] After spending a short period of time with the 29th Division engineers, he was informed on 20 August:

> Those of you mining chaps that are left are to be transferred to the newly formed Mining Company with headquarters at Pink Farm. You can report there tomorrow morning.[47]

From this time on there was an organised response to Turkish mining efforts. With high command sanction, parties consisting of an experienced miner accompanied by 20 infantrymen

40 Corporal (later Sergeant) J. Nixon served with 1/7th Highland Light Infantry (HLI) at Helles. His subsequent account was composed whilst residing in Beacon, Western Australia under the pseudonym H.L.I. Beacon.
41 H.L.I. Beacon, 'Mining on Gallipoli', *Western Mail* (Perth, WA), 8 July 1937.
42 Ibid.
43 Ibid.
44 Ibid.
45 Ibid. and J. Murray, *Gallipoli As I Saw It* (London: William Kimber, 1965), p. 110.
46 Murray, p. 110.
47 Ibid., p. 109.

Up-way passage to Quinn's Post. (AWM CO1135)

Quinn's Post at an early stage of development. (AWM AO2009)

were assigned to specific Helles sub-sectors. Incline shafts, four-foot high and two-feet-two inches in width were driven, approximately 20 yards apart, from the firing line to a depth of 28 feet.[48] On "T-ing" out at the tunnel heads, the galleries were joined to form an envelope as a manned barrier to Turkish encroachments. In the long term, all sub-sectors would, as at Quinn's Post, be joined-up as a means of providing a defensive envelope covering the entire line.

Throughout the following month a relentless battle ensued as both sides fought to gain superiority. For their part, the Turks were on the offensive with the detonation of six mines in September, the British retaliated with three mines. As a matter of course, on 10 September, British miners waited until the enemy was just three feet away before detonating the charge. The VIII Corps Mining Company maintained an offensive role during October and November but could claim nothing more than an honourable draw by the time of the evacuation.

It is worth mentioning that infantrymen, whenever possible, were permanently attached to the miners but not all were suited to the difficult work which had its own form of compensation since it was away from the Mediterranean sunshine. However, given the increased demand for surface duties, many had to "volunteer" for mining work whilst on rest. The transport of clay-filled sandbags along galleries and up steep inclines was laborious work in the hot and humid conditions during so-called rest periods. The situation did little to promote miner/infantry cooperation. The situation subsequently improved when trollies were made available. These were approximately two-feet long and one-foot in breadth with rubber-coated castor wheels to muffle subterranean activity.[49] There remained the difficult and often frustrating job of soil disposal. Situated near a gully, mining earth could be disposed of at once. If not, the earthen waste was piled into a trench until nightfall, after which it was removed by infantry working parties maintaining absolute silence.[50]

Further difficulties with regard to the miner/infantry relationship concerned the policy of the latter providing underground sentries. Making his subterranean rounds, Corporal Nixon, recalled discovering a sentry absent from his post. On being located, the missing man stated he was terrified to be down the mine. He was subsequently excused this duty. The posting of two sentries became the norm thereafter. As experienced as Nixon was, he later admitted to having been frightened when alone at the tunnel face where the thought of destruction at any moment or having to engage in an underground mêlée was always a clear and present danger.[51] For his part, Joseph Murray experienced the consequences of combat against a resolute and determined enemy. Whilst employed in a two-man tunnel drive, his comrade went outside to obtain timber at the same time as a surprise Turkish riposte from the trenches opposite. It was during subsequent fighting that an enemy bomb blew Murray's "pal to pieces." He had no option but to carry on until relief by the next two-man shift.[52]

Throughout the Helles tunnelling operations, the lives of those above or below ground remained dependent on listeners' detection abilities. In addition to the dire necessity of discerning hostile mining progress, it was also of crucial importance to determine – based on the accumulated evidence – the proximity thereof. Indeed, if the Turks appeared to down picks

48 Ibid., p. 111.
49 Beacon, 'Mining on Gallipoli'.
50 Ibid.
51 Ibid.
52 Murray, *Gallipoli As I Saw It*, p. 110.

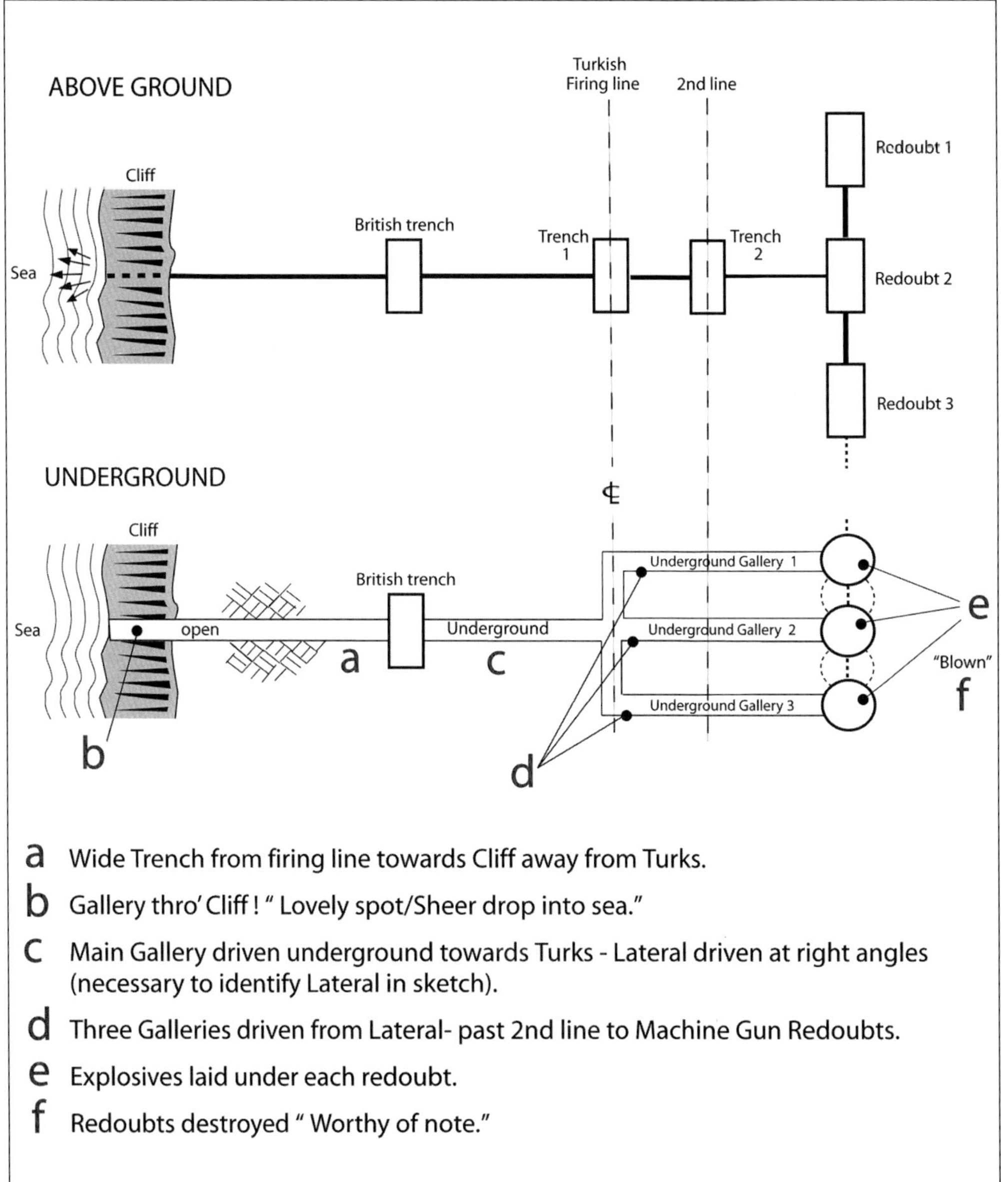
ABOVE GROUND
Turkish
Firing line
2nd line
Cliff
Sea
British trench
Trench
1
Trench
2
Redoubt 1
Redoubt 2
Redoubt 3
UNDERGROUND
Cliff
Sea
open
British trench
Underground
Underground Gallery 1
Underground Gallery 2
Underground Gallery 3
"Blown"
a
b
c
d
e
f
a Wide Trench from firing line towards Cliff away from Turks.
b Gallery thro' Cliff ! " Lovely spot/Sheer drop into sea."
c Main Gallery driven underground towards Turks - Lateral driven at right angles (necessary to identify Lateral in sketch).
d Three Galleries driven from Lateral- past 2nd line to Machine Gun Redoubts.
e Explosives laid under each redoubt.
f Redoubts destroyed " Worthy of note."

Tunnelling beneath Turkish lines. (Terrence Powell)

and shovels, there was a less than remote possibility of imminent mine detonation. If not ... why not? It was all too easy to prepare a counter-charge, but this risked the chance of betraying the position to the enemy. In much the same way as on the Western Front, the search for improvised listening devices was on-going. One crude method employed at Helles was to place a water bottle, tightly packed with earth and spout facing outwards, into a recess carved into the gallery face. The listener, placing his ear to the spout, would attempt to detect bottle vibrations as a possible indicator of enemy pick and shovel work. Another ad hoc overhearing apparatus was employment of a commonplace tin funnel with wide end sealed by soldered disc. An iron spike was then riveted to the disc centre. Hung from support beams or with an iron wall pin, the placement of one's ear to the funnel's narrow end was a general improvement when compared with the water bottle device. The funnel device was superseded by a stethoscope-like apparatus – earphones with cords extending from each earpiece connected to an iron spike inserted into gallery walls – employed as a suitable means of sound detection.[53]

A Brilliant Mining Offensive[54]

During September 1915 Fusilier Bluff was the scene of an VIII Corps Mining Company offensive original in conception and ultimately successful in outcome. Opposite the British line were three redoubts sited beyond the Turkish second line. Targeted for destruction by three simultaneous offensive mines, the primary difficulty was the disposal of soil obtained from three galleries extending approximately 30 feet towards the enemy line.[55]

The adopted spoil disposal method was to excavate a wide trench in the direction of the nearby cliff top – to all intents and purposes just one of many trenches then under construction – so accumulated spoil was more than likely to be determined as routine by alert Turkish observers. Thus carried out, a deep gallery was run beneath the trench, the accumulated spoil dumped into the latter. Extended through the cliff-side, the exit provided an unseen method of spoil disposal. The mining operation sanctioned, the charges were placed. As planned, the infantry opened rapid-fire with machine-guns and rifles. The Turkish garrisons, responding in kind, occupied their firing line prior to returning fire. Conscience of the above ground din, the miners exited the tunnels. Remaining in the immediate vicinity to witness the results of their labour, a tremendous explosion followed by black smoke and dust cloud shrouded the area as the Turkish redoubts were completely eradicated.[56]

Mine Ventilation

Mine ventilation was a particular problem on the Gallipoli Peninsula. Indeed, in one gallery the air was so foul that a "Heath Robinson" device was assembled that proved useful only in the shortest of tunnels. A long one-foot square tube was attached to the roof timbers running from

53 Becon, 'Mining on Gallipoli'.
54 Murray, *Gallipoli As I Saw It*, pp. 124-25.
55 Ibid., p. 124.
56 Ibid., pp. 124-25

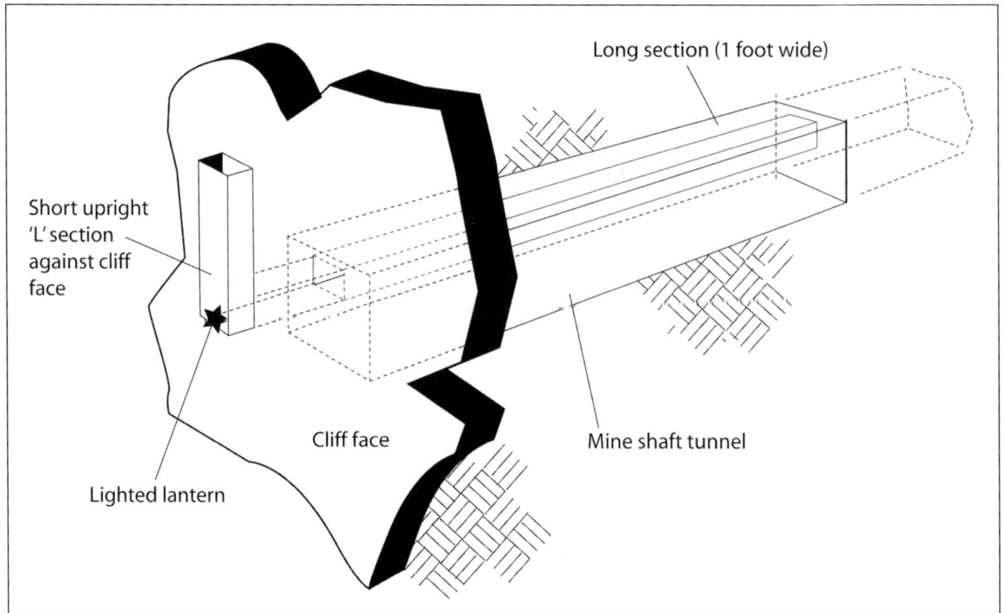

Tunnel ventilation. (Terence Powell)

gallery face to entrance. A similar shortened tube was inserted upright against the cliff-face and attached to the longer tube. A lighted lantern was then placed behind a trap door at the elbow joint of the L-shaped configuration. Heated air within the shorter tube caused the cold air in the long tube to flow towards the lantern thus allowing for a general circulation of fresh air at the tunnel face. This complex arrangement's obvious limitations were subsequently exposed but, given the circumstances, those concerned deserve credit whatever length of time was gained.[57]

A "blower fan" was duly produced. Feeding fresh air via a column of pipes to the face, a bicycle chain and sprocket affixed to the fan shaft was "pedalled" by an assigned infantryman. The rotating blades drove fresh air to the mine face as foul air was dispatched through a suspended tube extending as far as the mine entrance. Issue blankets, hung approximately eight feet from the mine face, ensured the miners could carry on in an enclosed fresh air environment.[58]

Boring Machine

Employment of boring machines for military mining met little success at Gallipoli or on the Western Front, so the VIII Corps Mining Company was delighted to receive one that worked. Instead of large diameter blades designed to cut full-sized tunnels, the new machine had a six-inch diameter cutting bit just six inches long. This was attached to a series of hollow drill lengths which, in turn, were attached to a hand-wheel similar to that found on a ship's bridge. To operate

57 Beacon, *Western Mail*, Perth, WA, 12 October 1939.
58 Murray, *Gallipoli As I Saw It*, pp.124-25.

required a simultaneous turn and push of the wheel as a means of driving the hollowed drill into the mine face. Having penetrated to maximum depth, the cutting bit would be withdrawn, and the hollow lengths emptied to determine the state of the ground ahead. The hole cleared, further drill extensions were added before the process was repeated; 100 feet was considered satisfactory progress. Several holes, if necessary, could be bored to allow ease of earth collapse. Routine operating procedure dictated that every 100 feet or less if necessary, a charge would be pushed into a hole and detonated, the remaining earth collapsing prior to removal. Care had to be taken of encountered ease during drilling, as this might indicate close proximity of a Turkish gallery face.[59]

Unfortunately, the boring machine's demise resulted in an error of judgement. Hearing of its success, other miners cajoled headquarters into allowing them to borrow it. Ignoring warnings to avoid drilling into a Turkish gallery, this occurred within a very short time. Enemy resistance to the drill prompted the miners to withdraw it prior to inserting gelignite, complete with primer and cable through the aperture following which they were only too willing to tie-off the cable to side timbers. The element of surprise gone, the machine was hurriedly withdrawn from service. Some days later, a Turkish prisoner informed his captors of the laughter and celebrations that took place in the Turkish gallery over the capture of "mighty" British machine.[60]

Tragedy

With the onset of autumn, the nights became cold and chilly, off-duty infantrymen seeking the warmth of the mining galleries only to be forced out to make way for fatigue parties or changing shifts. The proximate comfort was too hard to resist so many persisted only to lose life or limb when a Turkish charge closed the gallery. Two miners, some fatigue men and about a dozen infantry were buried under the debris. Rescue teams were greatly hampered by splintered roof timbers which meant the rescuers would need to insert supporting timber prior to moving forward. Six bodies were recovered before the rescue attempt was halted due to dangerous conditions. The recovered remains were buried at the foot of the cliff, a memorial cross erected for those whose remains were not recovered.[61]

Entombed

There were several reported cases of entombed miners, and such was the determination to survive that some clawed their way out, sometimes over a period of several days. On 15 September, Joseph Murray along with his mate Alec, were trapped at a depth of 28 feet in the aftermath of a Turkish explosion. Having managed to remove damaged timbers and fallen earth before reaching daylight, they found themselves on the enemy side of a crater. Despite this and the

59 Beacon, *Western Mail*, Perth, WA, 12 August 1939.
60 Beacon, 'Mining on Gallipoli'.
61 Beacon, *Western Mail, Perth*, WA, 29 July 1939.

desperate need for "a cup of tea", Murray and his companion risked shouting for help. To their relief, bayonets appeared on the British side followed by men of 42nd Division.[62]

Corporal Nixon related a similar tale of two miners, equipped with two candles and a full water bottle. Despite the candles and water running out, they managed to free themselves after three days. Emerging into no-man's land, they were fired on by an alert British sentry, without injury. Reduced to more of a croak than a shout and a tired hand wave, they were spotted by other sentries and rescued. The Turks were described as "sporty" for not firing at men and rescuers. Tragically, following a month's leave, one of the men was killed the first morning of his return to the trenches.[63]

Corporal Nixon's DCM

Corporal Nixon was awarded the DCM for a particular act of bravery. Alone in a mine gallery, he was adjusting a tamped charge when a seemingly disembodied enemy hand emerged from a hole in the gallery face. Fortunately, the primer and coiled cable were beyond the Turkish miner's grasp. Nixon, rushing out of the mine, shouted at the infantry to retire before re-entering the gallery. Uncoiling the cable, he made his way back but found the cable ten yards too short. Having no time to obtain and splice a substitute cable, he grabbed the firing battery located at the entrance, inserted the connection to the cable and, lying as flat as possible, detonated the charge. Fortunately, Nixon received nothing more than a good "scorching". Treated to a mug of rum by his officer which no doubt contributed to a somewhat "groggy" demeanour, he retired to his dugout. Questioned by Major-General W. Douglas (GOC 42nd Division) the following morning, he was subsequently awarded the DCM.[64]

Mining at Hill 60

The August offensive did not bring about the hoped-for success to bring the campaign to a satisfactory end. All along the front from Anzac to Suvla, the MEF had encountered a resilient Turkish defence resulting in heavy casualties. The final attack took place at Hill 60, situated at the western extremity of Anzac, on 21 August. Unfortunately, all that was gained was tenuous overland communications with the Suvla sector. By 28 August most of the Hill 60 trench network was in ANZAC hands.[65] However, the hill crest remained in Turkish hands. Thus the newly-won ground, although secure, was overlooked by the enemy. Unwilling to launch further above ground attacks, further ANZAC efforts went underground.[66]

The tunnelling that followed the battle for Hill 60 is not well-documented, so it remains unclear when the underground offensive commenced, or which unit started it. It is known that

62 Murray, *Gallipoli As I Saw It*, pp. 114-19.
63 Beacon, 'Mining on Gallipoli'.
64 Ibid.
65 C.F. Aspinall-Oglander, *Military Operations Gallipoli*, Vol. II (London: Heinemann, 1932), p. 355, fn.
66 It is known that the Australians, more than likely 10th LH, commenced mining activity at Hill 60. This work was subsequently taken over by British sappers following LH relief.

several tunnels were started by the recently disembarked Welsh Horse during October. This unit of part-time cavalrymen had been attached to 54th Division for pioneer work – not an obvious choice. Nevertheless, the dismounted regiment made every effort to carry out the task at hand.[67] A published account suggests that the regiment fired a mine shortly after taking up position at Hill 60,[68] according to available war diaries and regimental histories, this was in error. However, a map prepared by Second Lieutenant Hancock of the 1/4th Northamptonshire Regiment suggest that mining, originating from a shaft at the north-western end of a support trench known as "Pitt Street", had commenced as early as September.[69] Furthermore, the battalion war diary indicates that a mining party of 24 men relieved the Australian miners of their duties there[70] on 1 October.[71] The enemy exploded a mine on the day the Welsh Horse arrived. No damage was done.[72] For their part, the 1/4th Northamptons continued to participate in mining operations until the second half of October. It is not known whether they operated independent or in unison with their Welsh Horse counterparts.

Lieutenant-General Sir William Birdwood (GOC ANZAC), during an inspection of the Hill 60 sector shortly after the Welsh Horse takeover, came upon a worried Major-General F.S. Inglefield (GOC 54th Division) who reported receipt of a message from the Welsh Horse miners to the effect that they were in anticipation that a Turkish mine would be blown shortly:

> I told him "Rot. There's nothing in it." Inglefield was rather hurt, telling me that the Welsh Horse was full of expert miners who were not likely to have made a mistake. I told him he might withdraw men from the parapets, but that strong posts were to be maintained at the two main salients. I then went up there to look into things for myself, and when I asked the officer about the Turkish mine he looked rather sheepish. He then acknowledged that two squads of his own miners, working in separate galleries, had mistaken the sound of each other's picks for a Turkish mine.[73]

Australian newspapers took a keen interest in all things relating to their overseas force, and the actions at Hill 60 were no different. Indeed, several antipodean newspapers carried stories which included a questionable account of the Turks accidentally detonating a mine beneath their own lines. However, the same report tells of an exploded mine which entombed five British miners for no less than three days. It is not known to what unit they belonged, but the tale aptly demonstrates the myriad perils of military mining at this time. According to the report, the miners dug themselves out of their tomb and "were little the worse for the ordeal."[74]

It was not until 15 November that the Welsh Horse was in position to detonate five mines prepared following a month of underground labour. The 1/5th Suffolk Regiment was holding the line at Hill 60 at this time:

67 R. Westlake, *British Regiments at Gallipoli* (Barnsley: Pen & Sword, 1996) p. 282.
68 N. Steel, *Gallipoli* (Barnsley: Pen & Sword, 1999), p. 205.
69 Ibid., p. 206.
70 There is no indication of which Australian unit was relieved of mining duty during this time.
71 Westlake, *British Regiments at Gallipoli*, p. 176.
72 Ibid.
73 W.R. Birdwood, *Khaki and Gown: An Autobiography* (London: Ward & Lock, 1941) p. 277.
74 *The Northern Miner*, 22 October 1915. Several other periodicals such as the *Crookwell Gazette* and *Brisbane Courier* also printed the same tale.

> [T]he following evening mines were exploded, the Turks being subjected at the same time to heavy artillery and machine gun fire. An immense fountain of earth shot up into the air in front of the battalion, working parties immediately sapping forward and establishing bombing posts near the edge of the crater which however, they had been ordered not to occupy.[75]

The Turkish trenches were destroyed and falling debris caused casualties to British troops holding the line there. The resultant explosion, in addition to inflicting friendly casualties caused by falling debris, created a substantial crater and "two mounds of earth which proved rather disadvantageous from our point of view."[76] The line did not advance. As a result, the Turks occupied the crater lip improving their already dominant position slightly. The 163rd Brigade War Diary considered the result "disappointing." It appears that only one crater resulted from the blowing of five mines. This suggests five small charges inserted into small powder chambers very close together.[77]

By this time, it was also clear that Turkish counter-mining was underway, the Welsh Horse miners ascertaining tell-tale sounds of enemy progress. The 1/5th Suffolks also reported overhearing the enemy but "the gallant Welsh Horse were hard at work … Have you heard them tamping?" became a popular phrase amongst the Hill 60 garrison.[78] Unfortunately for the Welsh Horse, the Turks prepared a mine first and on 20 November detonated a substantial charge that collapsed their now elaborate workings and entombed nine men. Of this party, only one, Lieutenant W.L. Renwick, was unearthed alive. Major-General Alexander Godley (GOC NZ & Australian Division) and Brigadier-General C. Brudenell White (ANZAC chief of staff) had visited Hill 60 that day. The latter observed: "Cold Day with Generals Godley and Inglefield making a careful inspection of Hill 60 this morning. Turks exploded a mine there not long after we left." Perhaps, in view of the vital withdrawal staff work White was to undertake in the coming weeks, it was more than just a lucky escape. Following this episode, there appears to be no record of mines detonated by the Welsh Horse or any other British unit at Hill 60. The Turks, however, detonated a mine (24 November) near a barricade situated at "Beech Lane" that inflicted some loss to 1/7th Essex Regiment.[79] The Welsh Horse sustained five casualties, none of which were fatal, as a result of a hostile mine detonated near "Ivy Lane" on 19 December.[80] It was the last act for the Welsh Horse miners. That same day, they were ordered to man the Hill 60 garrison whilst the evacuation was under way before they in turn departed.

75 C.C.R. Murphy, *The History of the Suffolk Regiment 1914-1927* (Uckfield: Naval & Military Press reprint of 1928 edition), p. 108.
76 B. Owen, *Roscomyl and the Welsh Horse* (Caernarfon, Gwynedd: Palace Books, 1990), p. 30.
77 Ibid.
78 Murphy, *The History of the Suffolk Regiment 1914-1927,* p. 108.
79 Westlake, *British Regiments at Gallipoli*, p 168.
80 Owen, *Roscomyl and the Welsh Horse*, p. 30.

Mining in other sectors

Mining was not confined to the aforementioned Anzac and Helles sub-sectors, underground operations also occurring at Russell's Top, Pope's Hill, Courtney's Post, Steele's Post, The Pimple, Johnston's Jolly, Lone Pine and Krithia Nullah.[81] An Australian engineer subsequently obsereved that it was possible to walk a mile and a half underground though he is unclear in which direction.[82] Whilst this may be difficult to verify today, it is known that most of the Gallipoli mining operations adhered to the pattern developed at Quinn's Post. To avoid repetition, the following sub-sector activities are briefly recounted below.

Russell's Top

There were three mining systems in operation at Russell's Top. The 5th FC AE ran both the low level and high level systems by extending tunnels. The third system was something of an anomaly. Low level as per a divisional scheme under the direct supervision of Captain H. F. Arnall of Truro, Cornwall, the idea for this subterranean work, subsequently known as "Arnall's Folly", was to tunnel below Turkish lines at the Nek and destroy the objective of the tragic light horse assault of 7 August. At Arnall's disposal were skilled miners recruited from the infantry, thus there was no reason why he could oversee an efficient underground operation. However, managing three mining system presented problems of divided command. This in turn required the mutual co-ordination between associated engineering and infantry units, something that proved difficult to sustain. Indeed, a 5th FC report (17 October) observed: "Found that O.C. No. 1 Post had connected all the ends of Engineering T-heads together without any authority and generally messed up the whole system." This suggests that the Russell's Top mining endeavours were complicated enough for one section of the 5th FC to impinge adversely upon that of another section. For its part, brigade headquarters was less than pleased. An order that engineering workings were not to be interfered with without previous consultation with senior officers soon followed. The effect this had on the working relationship between division, brigade, and engineers is not recorded but it could only have been a distraction from the enemy opposite.[83]

A recently arrived boring machine was called upon as a means of identifying enemy workings. Driving on a 1 in 4 downward grade (decline), initial progress on 21 October was satisfactory and 35 feet obtained in 50 minutes. High hopes for a significant advance in local mining techniques were dashed when the device stalled at 38 feet due to jammed cutting blades. Partially withdrawn and blades cleared of earth, it stalled at the same distance a second time. Reluctantly dismantled and turned over to Arnall, no documentation of further employment has come to light. It is relevant that those involved described the soil where the machine stalled as "toughish" clay. On the Western Front, a similar machine was employed with identical results during

81 See Michael LoCicero's chapter in this volume for Krithia Nullah mining operations of November-December 1915.

82 R. East, (ed.), *The Gallipoli Diary of Sergeant Lawrence of the Australian Engineers – 1st A.I.F. 1915* (Melbourne: Melbourne University Press, 1981).

83 AWM: AWM4 14/27/2 Part 1: 8th FC Australian Engineers, War Diary, 18 November 1915.

excavations of the so-called Flanders "blue clay". Whilst ground conditions were different at Anzac, it is certain that contemporary boring machines were of little use in clay soils.[84]

Mining continued unabated throughout the remaining months of the Gallipoli campaign. A 29 October 5th FCAE war diary entry records 15 sappers, 26 infantry miners and 56 infantrymen labouring on eight mine faces. The Turks were also active during this period. On 18 November they blew in the head of an Anzac gallery, killing two miners and wounding three others. Bodies hastily recovered, a sandbag barricade was constructed opposite the breach.[85]

The Russell's Top works were often the scene of unexpected breakthroughs into hostile galleries, savage underground engagements ensuing as a result. A detonation on 9 November blew a hole into a Turkish gallery, the enemy immediately opening small arms fire. Crawling forward through dust and debris, Lieutenant F.T. Small approached the breach with an explosive charge in hand. Patiently awaiting a lull in the enemy's response, he lit the fuse, pushed the charge through the aperture before hastily retiring. The shattering discharge enlarged the hole, but it was not what had been hoped for, so the steadfast subaltern repeated the dangerous exercise. All was quiet following the resultant explosion, after which a sandbag barricade was constructed. The Turks, on opening a rapid fire over the barricade the following day, propelled Captain (later Major) R.V. Cutler to crawl over the obstruction, remove several topside sandbags and insert an explosive charge despite sustained enemy rifle and revolver fire. Lighting the fuse, Cutler shoved the smoking charge into the Turkish gallery before withdrawing. The Turks, retiring from the gallery, remained quiet. Some days afterwards, Cutler and Small, no doubt bolstered by previous combats, responded to yet another episode of small arms fire pouring over tunnel barricades now separated by 20 feet. Crawling over heaps of debris to within seven feet of the Turkish barricade, they tossed stones and flashed a pocket torch whilst carefully inserting a left-hand charge. The consequent explosion had the desired effect. To put this remarkable feat into context, the galleries would have been approximately four to five feet in height and two to three feet in width, barely wide enough for two men to work side by side. Poorly ventilated, available oxygen was hot, humid and fouled. Access was problematic without the added difficulty of carrying and igniting an explosive charge in complete darkness; it is left to the imagination the effect of a stray bullet on a detonator primer. All too often such active valour, not to mention the commonplace variety indicative of the active service experience, resulted in fatalities. For example, on 11 November Lance Corporal J. Moy was clearing out accumulated debris from a gallery open to the surface as the Turks actively tossed bombs at the exposed gap. Four hours into this relatively routine task, a grenade entered the breached gallery to fatally injure Moy.[86]

Courtney's Post

Heroic actions were not confined to Quinn's Post. Following an eruption at nearby Courtney's Post, a hole appeared between the New Zealand and Turkish galleries. Sergeant H.W. Newman,

84 For example, see Beacon and relevant war diaries.
85 AWM: AWM4 14/27/2 Part 1: 8th FC Australian Engineers, War Diary, 18 November 1915.
86 Ibid., 11 November 1915.

A tunnel believed to have been excavated by the Australians near Johnston's Jolly. This is associated with a still discernible crater situated to the east. Note the condition of the roof which appears to be jointed sandstone. (John Dixon)

Remains of a mine entrance situated to the west of the Apex on the eastern edge of Rhododendron Spur. Note the rather loose and pebbly material in the tunnel roof and the fact that it is now almost filled-in with the same aggregate spoil. (John Dixon)

1st FC NZ silently widened the consequent hole until he was able to enter the enemy tunnel.[87] Disregarding proximate voices, he carried out a thorough reconnaissance of the hostile work. Returning to retrieve an explosive charge, Newman attempted to place it before alert enemy miners advanced on the opening. Holding off his would-be assailants with small arms fire, Newman's comrades frantically sealed the hole after which a hastily placed charge destroyed the Turkish gallery head.[88]

Mine Gas

Mine gas resulting from camouflet discharge was a danger throughout the peninsula. Designed to detonate without forming a crater, a detonated camouflet could discharge deadly carbon monoxide gas, a colourless, odourless, tasteless and non-irritating presence with a tendency to hang about undetected. With an in-air concentration of less than one and a half percent, the respiratory system is compromised with death following in less than three minutes. The threat was first encountered on the Western Front when two sappers of 171st Tunnelling Company were, in direct disobedience of orders, asphyxiated on entering a shaft immediately after a mine explosion. Strict measures were introduced to avoid a repeat of this tragedy although this was not universal throughout the BEF until autumn of 1915.[89] Moreover, forced ventilation devices to expel gas, rescue training and issue of "PROTO" self-contained breathing apparatuses was made available throughout designated underground mining after June 1915.[90] There is no evidence of similar safety procedures being implemented on the peninsula and rescue equipment was not issued during the campaign. It can be argued that such measures were unnecessary when comparing peninsula mining efforts with those of France and Belgium. Nevertheless, incidents of gas poisoning at Gallipoli suggest similar measures should have been put into effect. The following case studies are illustrative of this.

Lone Pine

As a necessary preliminary to 1st Australian Division's Lone Pine assault,[91] a mine was detonated in Gallery B37 by 2nd FC AE on 6 August. No fewer than 30 of the 36 men present experienced debilitating gas effects. Such was the shallow depth of mines that a small party of sappers were able to break "air holes" into a neighbouring gallery as a means of providing "natural" ventilation. Nonetheless, three hours lapsed before a "decent" air passage was identified. This form of ventilation is at best less than adequate given dependency on surface wind conditions particularly in the hot humid summer atmosphere. As deeper mines became the sector norm, even this form of ventilation was easily available. This circumstance should have suggested the

87 AWM: AWM4 35/10: 1st FCNZ, NZ&A Division, War Diary.
88 Annabell, *Official History of the NZ Engineers during the Great War 1914-1919*, p. 30.
89 Anon., *The Work of the Royal Engineers in the European War 1914-19: Military Mining* (Uckfield: Naval & Military Press reprint of 1921 edition), p. 59, fn.
90 Ibid.
91 See Aspinall-Oglander, *Military Operations Gallipoli*, Vol. II, pp. 178-81.

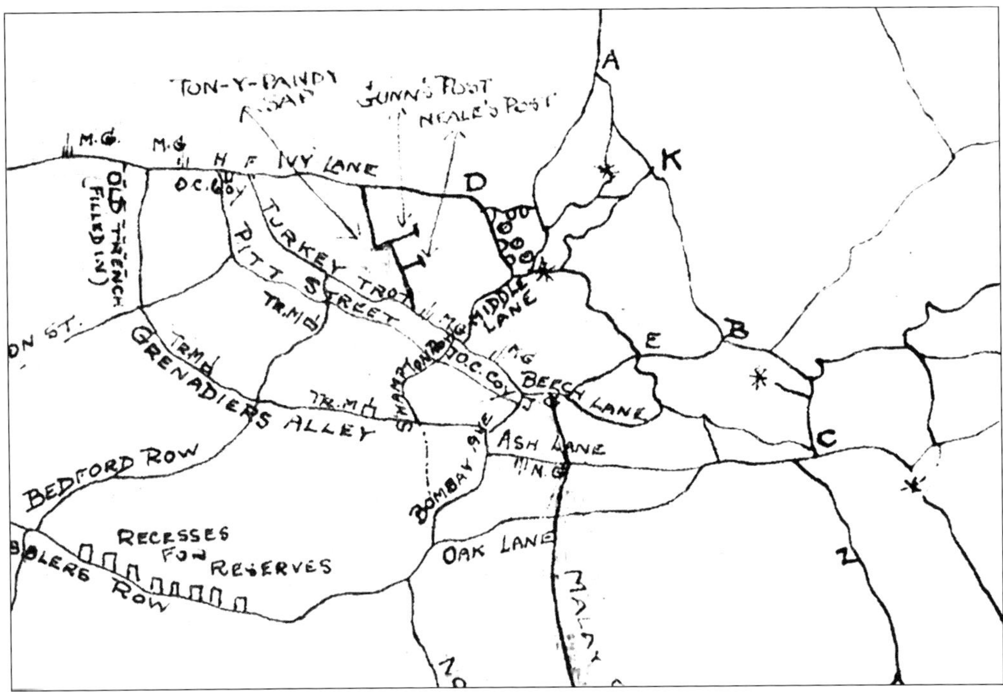

Map 23.2 Contemporary map denoting a section of the Hill 60 trench system (15 November 1915). The Welsh Horse detonated mines beneath the Turkish frontline between points D to E on 20 December; a third mine was detonated near Ivy Lane. (TNA WO 95/4325: 163rd Brigade War Diary)

need for forced ventilation and issue of PROTO rescue sets familiar to experienced miners of the day.[92]

Russell's Top

On the night of 30 September, Lieutenant E.J. Howells (5th FCAE) was, following an explosion, overcome by gas in the main Russell's Top gallery. Responding to the disaster, Corporal J.H. Precious entered the gallery. Immediately affected by the gas, he rushed back to raise the alarm before re-entering to assist the injured officer. Having gathered up the fallen Howells, Precious proceeded half-way down a 19-foot winze before collapsing. Suffering from severe gas poisoning, Precious was the awarded the DCM for his selfless act of bravery.[93]

92 Bean, *The Story of Anzac*, Vol II, p. 500.
93 AWM: AWM4 14/27: 8th FC Australian Engineers, War Diary.

Johnston's Jolly

At Johnston's Jolly on 29 October, a mine blown at a depth of 35 feet in C3 Tunnel resulted in no discernible above-ground rupture. Fifteen minutes later, Lieutenant Frederick Bowra (4th FC AE) re-entered the gallery to ensure it was safe for his men enter. Despite a gas presence warning – the candle Bowra was carrying caused a minor residual carbon monoxide explosion – he descended into the shaft by rope ladder only to be asphyxiated. When he did not return, Lieutenant E.T. Bazeley (22nd Battalion AIF), who had previously warned Bowra of the danger, climbed down the same ladder accompanied by Sapper F. Currington. Observing the collapsed Bowra, the would-be rescuers were overcome, Bazely managing to ascend the ladder whilst the unfortunate Currington plummeted to the bottom. Summoned from 4th FC headquarters, Lieutenant C.H.W. Thom entered the mineshaft where he was also overcome. Gazing into the darkened depths, sappers and infantry were well-aware of the high gas concentrations. Nevertheless, Corporals J.A. Park, C.F. Mills, and W. Bowden, accompanied by Privates W.B.S. Good and G. Stelling, vainly attempted to rescue the trapped officers and men.[94] Lieutenants Thom and Bowra, Sapper Currington and Privates Good and Stelling all perished. Those standing outside the shaft – Lieutenant-Colonel G.C.E. Elliot (CRE 1st Australian Division), Major Newcombe and 12 others – were "seriously gassed".[95]

In the above three cases, there is no mention of rescue procedures being in place, no record of forced ventilation or availability of PROTO set rescue teams. Indeed, given the number of men involved, headquarters officers inclusive, the participants appear to have been in complete ignorance of the carbon monoxide threat though this seems unlikely given the presence of experienced miners. Whatever the circumstances, a saving rather than preserving lives organisational approach contributed to the tragic Johnston's Jolly incident.

Listeners

Underground listener provision proved to be a challenging problem throughout the Gallipoli campaign. It was simply a case of a trial and error selection process. As some infantrymen were found to be well-suited and keen to take advantage of the comparative safety provided by subterranean duty, the casting for volunteers extended beyond those with previous mining experience. Always ready to confound their alert adversaries, the Turks readily employed subterfuge to confuse even the most experienced of listeners. This was illustrated by an incident at Lone Pine on 29 June when two listeners, remaining at posts whilst their mates retired for a much-needed tea-break, took no notice of overheard hostile activity based on the previously determined belief that the enemy had yet to charge the mine opposite. The unanticipated detonation of two mines proved fatal to Sappers Weekes and Rogasch, unfortunate victims of an enemy ploy whereby a deliberate "picking" noise masked placement of the explosive charge. This raised the stakes considerably, but no repeat of this clever Turkish ruse is on record.[96]

94 Bean, *The Story of Anzac*, Vol. II, p. 823, fn.
95 AWM: 1DRL/0278: Personal Diary of Lieutenant William Gordon Farquhar (8th FCAE); AWM4 14/23: 4th FC Australian Engineers, War Diary.
96 Bean, *The Story of Anzac*, Vol. II, p. 278.

Turkish Miners

Accounts of the Turkish mining efforts are rare in the available historiography. Nevertheless, it is clear the enemy high command recognised offensive mining as a means to breaking the stalemate. Having, as we have seen, commenced mining at Quinn's Post in early May, it was the apparent sounds of their labours that encouraged Australian miners to respond in kind. Indeed, in an early counter-mining operation on 25 May, Australian miners succeeded in destroying a section of an encroaching Turkish mine gallery, burying alive the hostile miners in the process.[97]

Turkish mining techniques differed from that of their MEF opponents. Whereas the latter tended to excavate flat-roofed tunnels, the former took advantage of frequent bands of slab-like limestone to form a stabilized roof.[98] This approach undoubtedly increased the amount of labour required and it remains unclear why this was done beyond the speculation that certain rock types may have contributed to structural stability. Also, in contrast to their subterranean opponents, it is believed that the Turks formed specialist mining units as opposed to reliance on engineers supported by infantry labourers.[99]

Regarding the adversary's tunnels unexpectedly intersecting during counter-mining operations, the Turks met with some measure of success most notably at Quinn's Post on 29 May when, on following up a successful mine explosion with and infantry assault, they gained a foothold, albeit temporarily, in the Australian lines. Such successes proved short-lived, the determination of MEF miners proving too much to counter in the end. For example, at Quinn's Post subsequent Australian aggression took the fight to their stalwart opponents. This ultimately led to sector-wide ascendency as complex galleries and fighting tunnels provided the means to intercept and destroy enemy works more or less at will. Nevertheless, as the campaign came to an end, the Turkish miners carried on, their last recorded mine detonation at Hill 60 on 19 December. The general effect of the underground war on the "other side of the wire" was ably summarised by a German participant who subsequently observed: "It was as if one was sitting on a volcano … Whole areas were turned into a crater desert."[100] The scale of mining operation during the Gallipoli campaign is seldom appreciated.

Evacuation

The withdrawal from Anzac and Suvla scheduled for the night of 19/20 December 1915, arrangements were made for mining to continue up to the last day. Although by this time deep mines had been driven beneath many of most important positions in Turkish possession, Godley and White were loath to sanction discharge due to the belief that the enemy would be alerted to the impeding withdrawal. Further to this, Birdwood ordered all mines along the centre of the Anzac front to be charged and ready for firing in case of emergency. Godley, on the other hand, ruled that on sanction by a senior officer, the mines must not be fired unless a hostile attack was imminent. Scheduled to be detonated as a means of preventing the enemy from following up

97 Fewster, Basarin & Basarin, *Gallipoli: The Turkish Story* (Crows Nest: Allen & Unwin, 2003), p. 86.
98 Fewster, et al, p. 87.
99 Ibid., Edward J. Erickson, *Gallipoli: The Ottoman Campaign* (Barnsley: Pen & Sword, 2015), p. 178.
100 Fewster, et al, p. 87.

the retirement, the mines at the Nek (Table 1) were the sole exception. Discretion was therefore delegated to the rear-guard commander should this be necessary.[101]

Table 1

Location	**Gallery**	**Charge**
Russell's Top	L 11	¾ ton
	L 8	¾ ton
	Arnall's	2 tons
Pope's Hill	8	¼ ton
Quinn's Post	18	½ ton
	36 A	½ ton
Courtney's Post	D 25 B	1 ton
	D9 A4	¼ ton
	D 26 E	¼ ton
	D 3	2 tons
Opposite Johnston's Jolly	C 7	2 tons
	C 38	3 tons
	C 2	1 ton
	C 5	¼ ton
Lone Pine	Two mines	¼ ton each

Most of these mines were deep, the average charge far heavier than that previously adopted at Anzac. At the more distant positions, The Apex, Ryrie's Post and Hill 60, the evacuation was to be at least three-quarters of an hour before those in the centre where the mines were not charged.[102]

The most dramatic moment during the Anzac evacuation was the firing of three mines. One, under the supervision of Captain Arnall, was 50 feet below ground and charged with two tons of ammonal. The remaining two, 30 feet below ground, were charged with three-quarter tons each. Detonated at 3:30 a.m. on 20 December, a tremendous but fruitless din of hostile enemy machine-gun and rifle fire was directed on to the now empty Australian trenches. According to one Turkish eyewitness:

> The order was given to keep a very good watch. But the first real sign of evacuation was the blowing of mines at Jessaret Tepe (Nek). They killed about seventy men. "Why did you blow them up?" I fancied there was a hint of reproach in Zeki Bey's voice as he said this. I think he meant: "You had completely succeeded in your objective – we had come to the end of a long and honourable campaign. Was it necessary to kill these." I too had wondered as to that but the decision whether to fire the mines had been left in the discretion of an officer who, I suspected, must have felt like a child with a huge firework. It was almost inevitable

101 Bean, *The Story of Anzac*, Vol. II, pp. 878-79.
102 Ibid., p. 879.

that these mines should be fired; from a purely military point of view there was no reason to hesitate.[103]

Conclusion

Conceived by Whitehall to achieve a rapid strategic outcome, the Gallipoli campaign's unanticipated deadlock resulted in an ad hoc military mining effort that was reactive in the first instance, and of little tactical value to the subsequent battles/engagements that determined ultimate defeat and withdrawal from the peninsula. Whilst outlying positions such as Quinn's Post and Russell's Top were amongst the first to occupy the collective mining skills of Dominion engineers and infantry, the application of underground warfare techniques developed apace at Helles and, following the failure of the August offensive, Suvla. However, defensive mining schemes had to be organised before the offensive could be taken to the enemy. Defence security having been obtained in a given sector, tactical schemes whereby local mining efforts were incorporated into defensive/offensive schemes were duly, if not always efficiently, implemented. For example, the discharge of two mines at Helles on 19 December as a means of providing ground cover for a 42nd Division assault. The subsequent operation failed to achieve all of its objectives when, despite careful preparations, one of the mines failed to form a crater. Nevertheless, tactical advantage was almost always obtained whenever and wherever close co-operation between miners and infantry was achieved.

Gallipoli mining operations were never on the scale of equivalent Western Front efforts. Moreover, its application to thwart Turkish underground machinations whilst simultaneously providing shelter, digging wells, etc., contributed to what must be deemed an overall success. Mining on the peninsula was far more extensive than realised. Applied mining schemes such as those implemented at Quinn's Post and Fusilier Bluff, resulted in the development of complex subterranean systems. Tunnel construction, considered counter-productive by some contemporaries, occupying much of a field company's labour. Nevertheless, it remains debatable whether or not the MEF's underground efforts provided an important tactical advantage, although overall dominance was eventually achieved to the cost of its erstwhile Turkish adversaries. That said, there is no question that the doleful campaign's outcome was inevitable with or without the consequent mining effort.

103 Bean, *Gallipoli Mission* (Canberra: Australian War Memorial, 1948), p. 250.

24

Terrain and the Gallipoli Landings, 1915

Peter Doyle

This chapter examines the impact of terrain on the outcome of the Gallipoli landings. The landings of 25 April 1915 were made at Cape Helles and Anzac Cove, with objectives to take the heights and dominate the Dardanelles shore, neutralising the Ottoman defences. Analysis demonstrates that these landing places were disadvantaged by terrain. The Helles sector is characterised by steep, deeply incised slopes and narrow beaches that were easy to defend with adequate preparation. The Anzac sector, characterised by its "badland" topography, was found to be deeply gullied and difficult to traverse, hampering both attack and supply. Though General Sir Ian Hamilton had expected to plant "two feet" on the peninsula, hoping in the absence of adequate preparation to carry the heights and overcome inertia from "friction", terrain and a determined defence by the Ottomans put paid to this, and the campaign was therefore doomed from its opening days. The trench warfare characteristic of both sectors later in the campaign was challenging, with cramped, closely confined trenches and dugouts in the loose soils of Anzac being particularly challenging, with inadequate water supply. This chapter examines aspects of: (1) pre-campaign terrain evaluation; (2) siting of defensive positions according to terrain; (3) terrain multiplication of defensive firepower; (4) trench warfare on the peninsula; (5) transport routes; and (6) groundwater supplies.

The Gallipoli campaign ranks as one of the most controversial of the First World War, a costly gamble intended to knock Turkey out of the war and to command the main ice-free supply line to Russia through to the Black Sea ports. The land-based Gallipoli campaign evolved from a plan to "force" a way through the narrow Dardanelles using ships alone, knocking out the fortresses commanding the straits, and ultimately threatening Constantinople – with the belief that this alone would be sufficient to drive Turkey from the conflict. A combination of factors led to the failure of this plan, most particularly the difficulty of naval artillery fire against land targets, the presence of mobile batteries on both the European and Asian shores and ineffective minesweeping by the Allies. This caused an escalation of the conflict, and a commitment to deploy troops in an invasion of the Gallipoli Peninsula, intended to neutralise the coastal batteries and minefields. This deployment was to support the naval operation, but increasingly, this aspect of the campaign became forgotten as it was prolonged, with the Navy never again making an attempt to force the Dardanelles.

The distinguished war correspondent, H.W. Nevinson, attended the Gallipoli campaign as he had done the Greco-Turkish War of 1897. Writing in 1918, he reviewed the what-ifs of the campaign, which emphasised what could have been gained from the enterprise:

> The occupation of Constantinople would have paralysed Turkey as an ally of the Central Powers; it would have blocked their path to the Middle East, and averted danger from Egypt, the Persian Gulf, and India; it would have released the Russian forces in the Caucasus for action elsewhere; it would have secured the neutrality, if not the active co-operation of the Balkan States, and especially of Bulgaria…by securing Bulgaria's friendship, it would have delivered Roumania from similar apprehensions along the Danube and in the Dobrudja; it would have confirmed the influence of Venizelos in Greece and saved King Constantine from military, financial and domestic temptations to Germanise; above all it would thus have secured Russia's left flank …[1]

With the failure of the campaign, it is difficult to assess whether these claims might have been reasonable. But it is clear that with so much at stake, the campaign has been dissected endlessly, with an impressive body of research examining every last aspect of its planning, development and execution.

In early January 1915, the Secretary of State for War, Field Marshal Lord Kitchener, had himself indicated that the Dardanelles were probably the best place to stage a "demonstration" in support of Russian allies; though pledging no military support, he had engaged in discussion with the First Lord of the Admiralty, Winston Churchill, regarding the use of ships alone (Map 24.1).[2]

In his version of events published in the 1915 volume of *The World Crisis*, Winston Churchill made no bones of his enthusiasm for the naval campaign, with or without military support:

> We had undertaken to begin a serious bombardment of the Dardanelles forts, and to attempt, *without the aid of an army*, by a new and piecemeal reduction, to fight our way slowly into the Marmora …We had undertaken this operation, not because we thought it was the ideal method of attack, but because *we were told that no military force was available* [italics for emphasis].[3]

Absent from this account is the reliance on an offer from the Greeks on 27 August 1914 to engage the Ottomans in military action, providing military resources that would commit sufficient troops to take the peninsula – thereby assisting the passage of ships through the Dardanelles straits.[4] The Greek plan was initially to land 60,000 men at Gaba Tepe, and two battalions on the Asiatic shore at Kum Kale, in order to neutralise the gun batteries there, followed by operations to land troops at Bulair, Alexandretta and the Gulf of Adramyti intended to support and hold the beachheads.[5] The Greek offer very soon evaporated with growing tensions in the Balkans, and the passage of the ships as a military force alone was set. Yet the likelihood of naval action alone bringing about the required results were very slim indeed, and Lord Kitchener's opposition to sending troops to the theatre to support them evaporated.

1 H.W. Nevinson, *The Dardanelles Campaign* (London: Nisbet, 1918), pp. vii–viii.

2 C.F. Aspinall-Oglander, *Military Operations, Gallipoli*, Vol. I (London: Heinemann, 1929), pp. 52-53.

3 Winston Churchill, *The World Crisis: 1915* (London: Thonton Butterworth, 1923) pp. 166-67.

4 Aspinall-Oglander, 1929, *op. cit.*, pp. 39-44; P. Chasseaud & P. Doyle, *Grasping Gallipoli: Terrain Intelligence, Maps and Failure at the Dardanelles, 1915* (Staplehurst: Spellmount, 2005), pp. 26–28.

5 Aspinall-Oglander, 1929, *op. cit.*, p. 43.

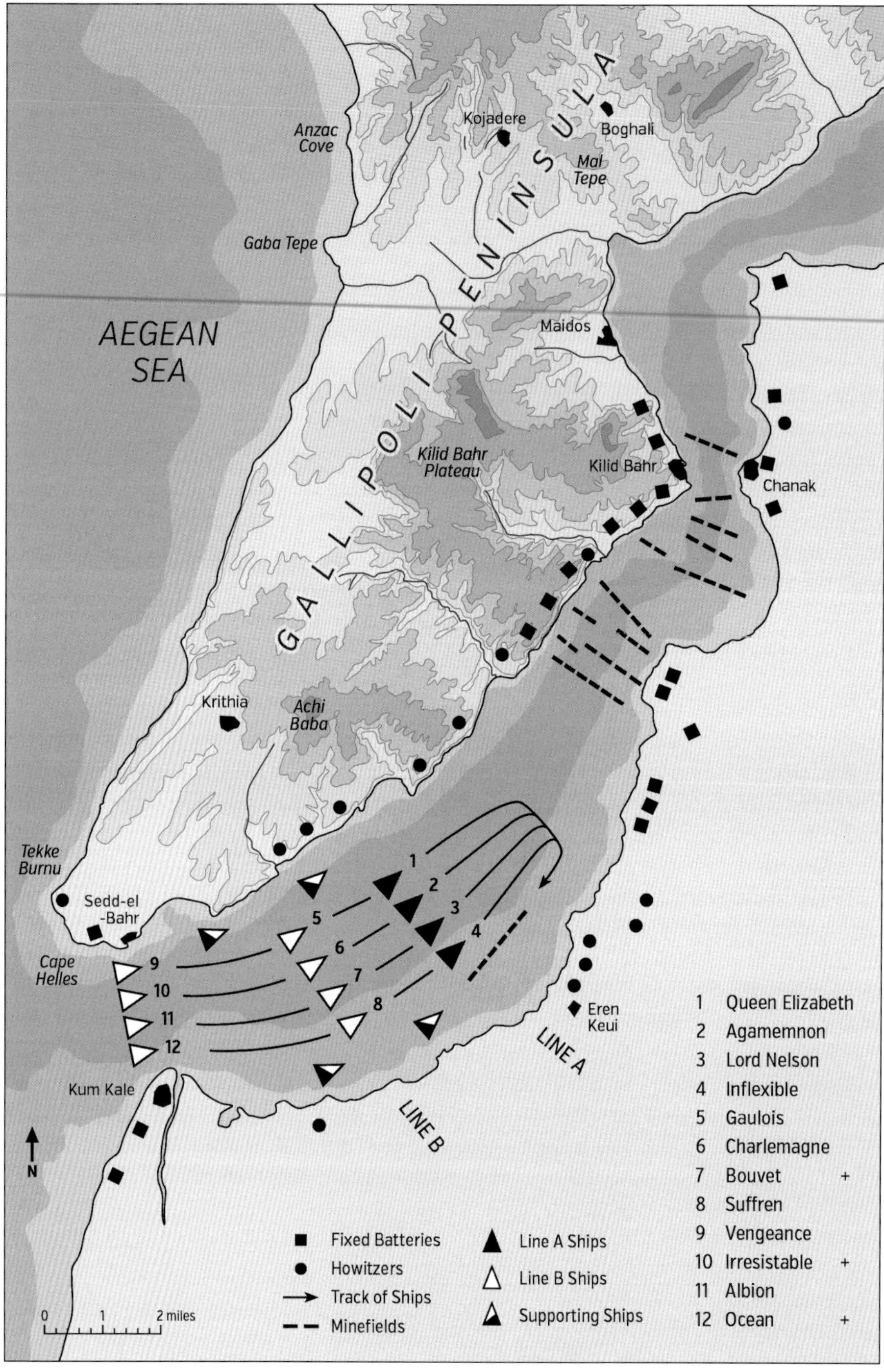

Map 24.1 The defences of the Dardanelles and the outcome of the naval attack on 18 March 1915. (Author)

Once the naval bombardment of the outer defences had commenced, and it became clear that, despite initial claims to the contrary, there was no chance that the attack would be called off if it achieved naught. As early as 24 February 1915 the War Council recognised that commitment to the Dardanelles was now make-or-break:

> If a success at the Dardanelles could win the Balkans to the entente, a failure must have the opposite effect. The opening of the bombardment had attracted such world-wide attention that, for the sake of prestige, the enterprise must be carried through, no matter what the cost.[6]

Already, at a meeting of the War Council on 19 February – the day of the opening naval bombardment – Lord Kitchener had accepted this view and had committed his last division of regular troops, the 29th, together with the Australian and New Zealand Army Corps to supporting the campaign.[7] From this point onwards a greater consideration of the challenges set by the geography of the Dardanelles straits and the Gallipoli Peninsula was required. General Sir Ian Hamilton, one of Britain's most senior soldiers, was selected to command the expedition by Kitchener on 12 March 1915. The outcome of the meeting between the two men is controversial, as it has helped define the conception of the campaign as hastily conceived and poorly executed – and thereby open to severe criticism. Hamilton himself suggested in his post-war memoir *Gallipoli Diary*, that his appointment with Kitchener was matter-of-fact, supported by the minimum of information and a peremptory treatment:

> Opening the door I bade him [Kitchener] good morning and walked up to his desk where he went on writing like a graven image. After a moment, he looked up and said in a matter-of-fact tone, "We are sending a military force to support the Fleet now at the Dardanelles, and you are to have Command".[8]

Hamilton's account continues with the story of a briefing by Major-General Sir Charles Callwell, Director of Military Operations, who used a map (unspecified, but most likely to be the 1908 one-inch map of the peninsula and the Dardanelles discussed below) to illustrate the original plan to attack the peninsula that had been worked out by the Greeks. Callwell knew all too well the issues presented – he had been instrumental in developing a report on the defences some nine years before, in 1906. This report was not alone. There had been other appreciations constructed by both Military and Naval Intelligence, that were both available for view and known to the very general who was explaining the plan to Hamilton on that fateful afternoon – Callwell.[9]

Recent research[10] casts doubt on the long-held view that the Allied general staff had a poor understanding the nature of the terrain that they were expected to fight on, with inadequate and poorly-surveyed maps, and little aerial reconnaissance, with a mythology developed that

6 Ibid., p. 75.
7 Ibid., p. 71.
8 Ian Hamilton, *Gallipoli Diary,* Vol. I (London: Edward Arnold, 1920), p. 2.
9 Presented in detail in Chasseaud and Doyle, *op. cit.* See Table 1 for summary of available documents.
10 This is the main thesis of Chasseaud & Doyle, 2005, *op. cit.*

much of the information was "gathered from guidebooks bought in the shops of Egyptian city of Alexandria".[11] This has always appeared in stark contrast to the extensive understanding and wise use of terrain by the Turkish troops, which led ultimately to their victory in the campaign, and the withdrawal of Allied troops. It has been said that terrain either dictates or influences battle – in this case, it is the former that is writ large, leading one Australian historian to comment that: "At virtually every stage of the campaign the advantages and limitations imposed by terrain dominated the battlefield and largely determined the outcome."[12]

Appreciation of terrain, and the capability of exploiting it in the face of uncertain odds forms part of the concept of warfare as developed by the Prussian theorist Carl von Clausewitz (1780–1831), and in particular the concept of "friction", originally defined by him as "the effects of reality on ideas and intentions in war".[13] "Friction" can be identified as a widespread phenomenon, a concept that invests most military campaigns throughout history. As theorist Barry Watts has identified

> The diverse difficulties and impediments to the effective use of military force that those possessing military experience instinctively associate with this phrase are generally acknowledged to have played significant roles in most, if not all, the wars that have taken place since Clausewitz's time.[14]

Onc of the most significant components of what has become known as "General friction" relates to the balance between intelligence and uncertainty in prosecuting a campaign, as well as the danger and exertion experienced by troops on the ground. With greater uncertainly comes greater danger; as troops are affected by these conditions, so increasing friction creates a lag that prevents the plan from being enacted to its fullest degree. With this in mind, the idea that "friction" impeding the success of a campaign could be overcome by the momentum of a force of arms at Gallipoli, with men jumping from open boats, on a hostile shore, without adequate artillery, and facing the uncertainty of the unknown terrain, seems a little fanciful.

In preparing to both prosecute landings on, and defend the terrain of, the Gallipoli Peninsula, both sides were also aware that there were a limited number of locations, determined largely by the disposition of major terrain elements, where a landing could be successfully executed. The 29th Division was the last of the British regular army divisions to be deployed, and was sent with much reluctance by the Secretary of State for War, Lord Kitchener, to the Dardanelles. It was to be the spearhead of the campaign, sent with intention to the most heavily defended part of the southern peninsula, while the more inexperienced ANZAC was sent to the topographically

11 A. Moorehead, *Gallipoli* (London: Hamish Hamilton, 1956), p. 117.

12 A. Elkins, 'A Ridge Too Far: Military Objectives and the Dominance of Terrain in the Gallipoli Campaign' in K. Celik, & C. Koc (eds.) *The Gallipoli Campaign: International Perspectives 85 Years On.* (Cannakale: Cannakale: Onsekiz Mart University, 2001), pp. 5-34.

13 Carl von Clausewitz, *On War.* The concept of "Clausewitzian friction" in warfare is exhaustively discussed in B.D. Watts, *Clausewitzian Friction and Future War: Revised Edition, McNair Paper 68* (Washington, DC: National Defense University, 2004).

14 Watts, *op. cit.*, pp. 1-2.

challenging, but less well defended area that has since become known as Anzac. This chapter follows on from previous works on the campaign from a terrain perspective.[15]

Terrain intelligence 1914

Exhaustive discussion of the terrain intelligence resources available to Hamilton and his staff may be consulted in Chasseaud & Doyle.[16] Much of the controversy relates to the resources made available to Hamilton at or close to his briefing by Kitchener and Callwell on 12 March 1915. The material provided to Hamilton, according to the *Official History*, was slight:

> The catalogue was not a long one. Three intelligence officers, who had left England a few days before, would, it was hoped, be able to furnish him with news of the enemy; but, for the moment, his store of knowledge consisted of Lord Kitchener's instructions, a handbook of the Turkish army, dated 1912, a pre-war report on the Dardanelles defences, and a map which subsequently proved to be inaccurate.[17]

Hamilton himself had claimed in his *Gallipoli Diary,* that he had been underserved by the General Staff:

> Ten long years of General Staff ... where are your well-thought-out schemes for an amphibious attack on Constantinople? Not a sign! Braithwaite [Hamilton's Chief of Staff] set to work in the Intelligence Branch at once. But beyond the ordinary text books those pigeon holes were drawn blank. The Dardanelles and Bosphorous might be on the moon for all the military information I have to go upon. One text book and one book of traveller's tales don't take long to master ... There is no sense trying to make plans unless there is some sort of material, political, naval, military or geographical, to work upon.[18]

As discussed above, Chasseaud & Doyle have detailed the actual terrain intelligence resources available to Hamilton and his staff.[19] In summary, it has been established that, at the time of his briefing there was more to be seen than has been claimed. In handbooks alone, there were at

15 P. Doyle, & M.R. Bennett, 'Military Geography: The influence of terrain on the outcome of the Gallipoli Campaign 1915', *Geographical Journal*, 165, 12-36; P. Doyle, 'Terrain and the Gallipoli Campaign 1915' in Celik, & Koc (eds.) *The Gallipoli Campaign*, 46-69; P. Doyle & M.R. Bennett, 'Terrain and the Gallipoli Campaign 1915'; P. Doyle & M.R. Bennett (eds.) *Fields of Battle, Terrain in Military History* (Dordrecht: Kluwer, 2002), pp. 149-169; P. Doyle, '"Six VCs before breakfast": Terrain and the Gallipoli landings, 1915' in C.P. Nathanail, R.J. Abrahart, R.J. & R.P. Bradshaw, (eds.), *Military Geography and Geology, History and Technology* (Nottingham: Land Quality Press, 2008).

16 Chasseaud & Doyle, 2005, *op. cit.*, p. 54.

17 Aspinall-Oglander, 1929, *op. cit.*, p. 90.

18 Hamilton, 1920, *op. cit.*, pp. 13-14; Jenny Macleod has dissected Hamilton's published work and recognizes it as post-factual recollection intended to boost aspects of the author and subordinates' conduct. See J. Macleod, *Reconsidering Gallipoli* (Manchester: Manchester University Press, 2004).

19 Chasseaud & Doyle, 2005, *op. cit.*, pp. 54, 78, Table I.

least eleven individual major pieces of work that provided accurate assessments of the status of the Dardanelles defences, and the nature of any potential landing beaches (Table 1). These were available for consultation, and with Callwell surely aware of them (having materially contributed to the development of one of them), Hamilton was overstating his case when he said "There is no sense trying to make plans unless there is some sort of material, political, naval, military or geographical, to work upon."[20] Callwell himself took the view that:

> [T]he information contained in the secret official publications which the Mediterranean Expeditionary Force took out with it was by no means to be despised. All but one of the landing places actually utlised on the famous 25th April were, I think, designated in these booklets...A great deal of the information proved to be perfectly correct, and a good deal more of it might have proved to be correct had the Expeditionary Force ever penetrated into the interior of the Peninsula to test it.[21]

Table 1: Summary of Intelligence handbooks available in 1914

1905 (Confidential)	*Military Report on Eastern Turkey in Europe*
1906	Extracts from *Military Reports on Western Turkey in Europe*
1908 (NID 838)	*Turkey Coast Defences* (with charts, maps, plans & photos)
1909 (Secret)	*Report on the Defences of Constantinople* (Including the Gallipoli Peninsula; with a separate folder of plates, maps, plans, panoramas and photos)
1909 (Confidential)	*Military Report on Eastern Turkey in Europe and the Ismid Peninsula*, 2nd Edition (With separate folder of plates, maps, plans and photos)
1909 (Secret)	*Report on Certain Landing Places in Turkey in Europe*
1912	*Handbook of the Turkish Army*
1913	*Manual of Combined Naval and Military Operations*
1913	*Military Report on Western Anatolia*
1913	*Military Report on Asia Minor*
1913	*Handbook on Western Turkey in Europe*

The greatest ire has been poured on to the quality of the one-inch scale 1908 *Map of the Peninsula of Gallipoli and the Asiatic Shore of the Dardanelles* (GSGS 2285). The value of this map – based on French surveys in the mid-nineteenth century – on the ground has been much discussed;[22] and the absence of "any maps at all" was referred to in evidence presented to the

20 Hamilton, 1920, *op. cit.*, p. 14.

21 C.E. Callwell, *Experiences of a Dug-Out* (London: Constable, 1920), p. 98.

22 Aspinall-Oglander, 1929, *op. cit.*, p. 90 famously refers to it as "a map that subsequently proved to be inadequate." Elkins, *A Ridge Too Far* (Wollombi; Exsile e-book with no pagination, 2012) comments on the value of the maps available for accurate artillery fire, and for detailed operations on the ground. These claims are unrealistic. The simple fact was that no detailed survey *was possible* of a hostile shore, and that the map used was arguably sufficient for planning, though not actual field operations.

Dardanelles Commission.[23] The fact was that this was the only map available; there were no detailed national surveys of the ground then available from which to construct a map in a hostile country – indeed, there were few large-scale maps available to the opposing sides on the Western Front in 1914–15. There was no chance of making a map based on aerial photography; this would take photogrammetric techniques that were not available at the time. Once in theatre, naval aviators used aerial photography and plotting techniques to produce plans and diagrams showing the development of Ottoman preparations; these attempts to gather aerial intelligence have been scorned by some authors.[24] Nevertheless, arguably, they provided valuable information within the technical constraints of the day.

Notwithstanding overinflated claims to the paucity of information and the inaccuracy (or non-availability) of maps, it is clear that an amphibious undertaking requires the maximum amount of detailed planning based on the greatest degree of information. Without this, "Clausewitzian friction" would play its part in dictating the outcome of the campaign.

Gallipoli and the Dardanelles

To appreciate the Allies' difficulties, we must consider briefly the topography of the Straits. Their northern shore is formed by the peninsula of Gallipoli, a tongue of land some fifty miles long, which varies in width from two or three miles. The country is a mass of rocky ridges rising to a height of over 700 feet from the sea. The hills are so steep and sharply cut that to reach their tops in many places is a matter of sheer climbing. There is little cultivation, few villages, and no properly engineered roads.[25]

The terrain characteristics of the Gallipoli Peninsula and their broader influence on the defeat of the Allied troops, has been the discussed in a wider context in a number of sources.[26] The peninsula forms part of the Alpine Pontide range, which has a strong east-west structural grain, and comprises ancient crystalline massifs developed in Anatolia, and folded younger rocks in Thrace and basement margins of Anatolia.[27] The most dominant feature is the North Anatolian Fault zone, separating the European and Anatolian tectonic plates, which runs under the Sea of Marmara and crosses the peninsula to the Gulf of Saros, forming the northern, rifted and strongly rectilinear margins of the peninsula and separating it from the rest of Thrace. During the last twenty million years (in the Neogene), movement of the fault developed a sedimentary basin which produced the Sea of Marmara, with a maximum depth of 1,000 metres, and led

23 Chasseaud & Doyle, *op. cit.*, p. xiv.

24 Elkins 2012, *op. cit.* "No *significant* ground reconnaissance had been carried out on the peninsula prior to the landings in April, but British officers had conducted *sporadic* visual reconnaissance of the peninsula from destroyers and aeroplanes [my italics]." This was 1915; the shores were hostile; techniques available were few.

25 John Buchan, *Nelson's History of the War*, Vol. VI (London: Thomas Nelson & Sons, 1917), p. 156. Though Buchan's work is generally considered to be "propagandist", his descriptions of the issues at stake in the Dardanelles are insightful.

26 Doyle & Bennett, 1999, 2002; Doyle 2001; Elkins 2001, 2012, *op. cit.*

27 Z. Ternek, C. Erentöz, H.N. Pamir and B. Akyürek, *1:500 000 Ölçekli Türkiye Jeoloji Haritasi. Explanatory Text of the Geological Map of Turkey. Istanbul* (Ankara: Maden Tetkik ve Arama Genel Müdürlügü Vayinlarindan, 1987).

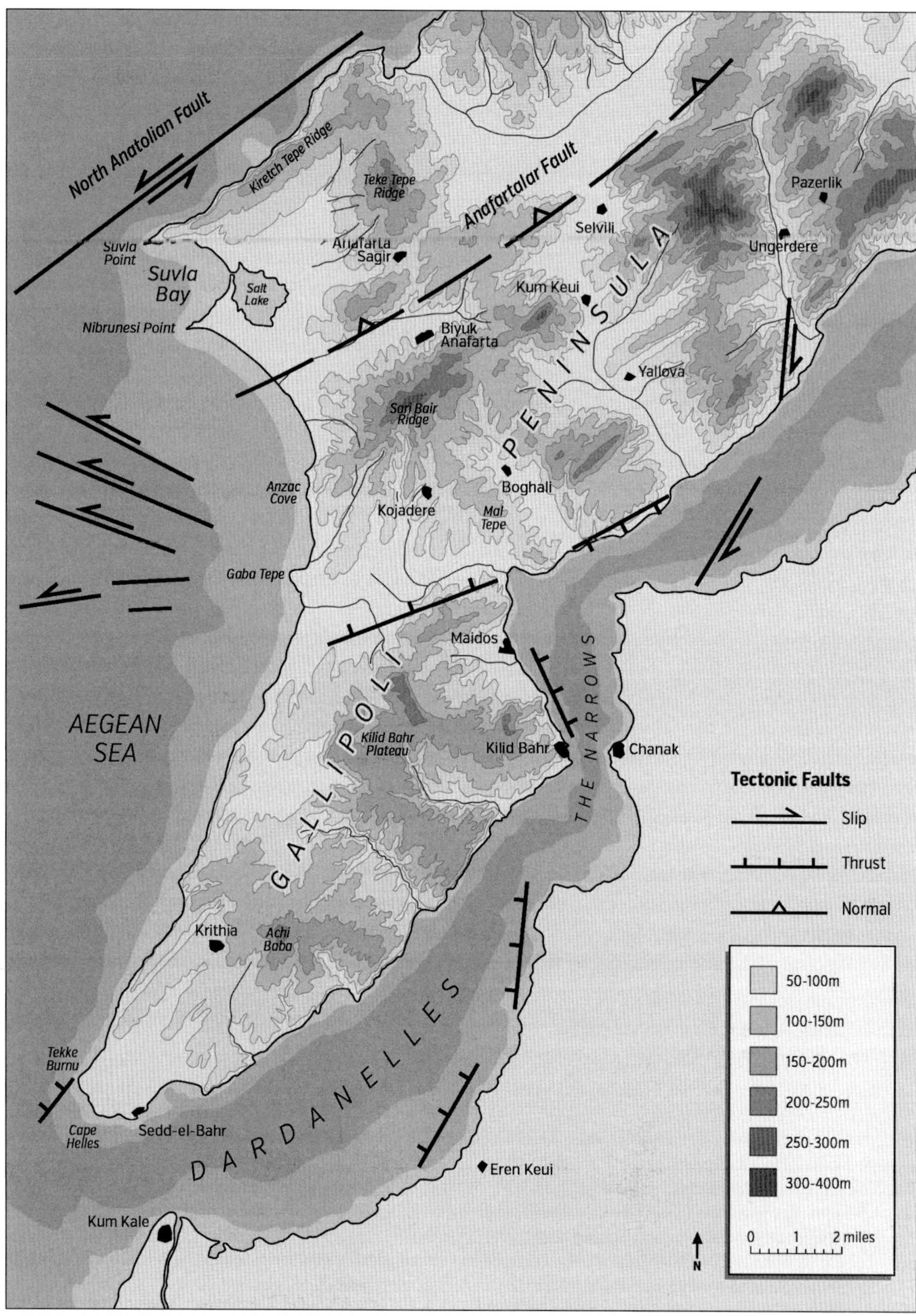

Map 24.2 The main tectonic faults (left) of Gallipoli and the Dardanelles. (Author)

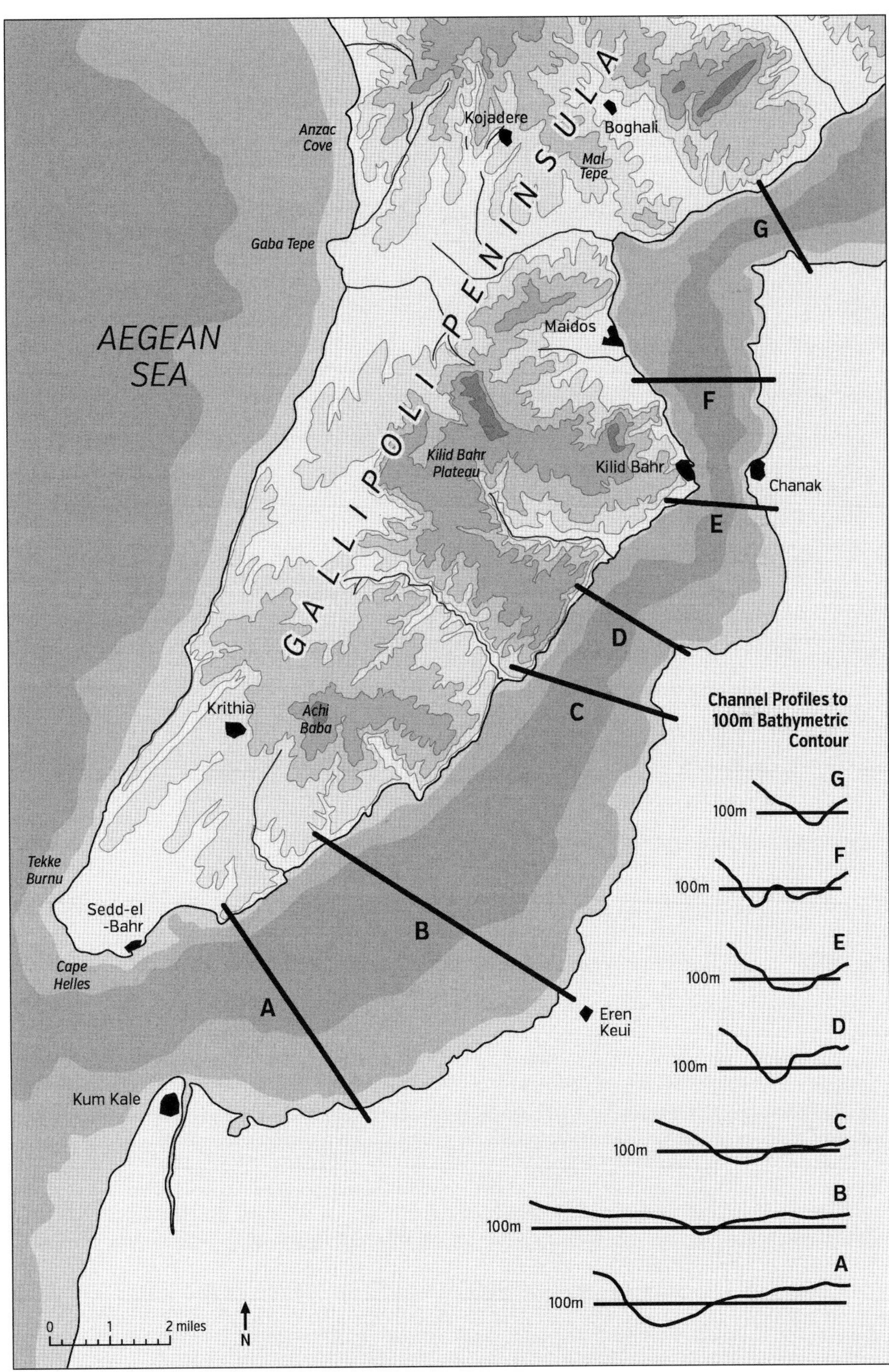

Map 24.3 The channel (right) of the Dardanelles showing the importance of fault systems in creating it. (Author)

to the deposition of the thick sediments on either side of the Dardanelles. These are associated with soft, crumbly yet nevertheless resistant cliff lines. This fault zone has predominantly lateral ("strike-slip") movement, and is complex, as other branches of it form the Dardanelles and the Sea of Marmara, again creating the strongly offset coastlines that are characteristic of the Dardanelles (Maps 24.2 & 24.3).

These faults were material in affecting the shape and form of not only the peninsula itself, but also the channel of the Dardanelles. The constant lateral movement of the North Anatolian Fault system has strongly influenced the shape of the coasts and its tearing action has led to tectonic faults in which the movement of the individual fractured blocks has been vertical, creating a deep and steep channel form in places. This has created the cliff lines at its narrowest point – so commented upon by contemporary geographers.[28] These so-called "normal" faults define the Dardanelles in both the peninsula and the Asiatic shores.[29] This characteristic has not only helped define the channel, it also assisted the funnelling of the downstream flow of the prevailing current, which meant that all ships moving up-stream had to do so in the face of a strong downstream flow – a current that was likely as not to bring with it any mines laid by the defenders.[30] Fortunately for the attackers, the strong current was no match for modern naval engines.

The faults also help create the cross-peninsula defile from Gaba Tepe to Maidos that was such a feature of invasion planning, and of defence. This is the result of a fracture that cuts the peninsula at the point opposite the Narrows. In addition, cutting through the peninsula is a major and active tectonic feature, the Anafartalar Fault, which forms the boundary of the upland block of the Sari Bair range. South of this fault, the Gallipoli Peninsula is therefore mostly composed of younger sedimentary rocks that have been subject to tectonic disturbance during the last twenty or so million years. This fault is active, associated with the North Anatolian Fault System, which every now and again results in a major earthquake. Regular movement of the Anafartalar Fault means that the Sari Bair range is subject to periodic uplift, in turn creating erosion and coarse sedimentary flow that produces a mixture of coarse sandstones and clays that provide a unique substrate – one that is intensely weathered, gullied and rilled.[31]

The relief of the southern part of the Gallipoli Peninsula is nevertheless relatively subdued, the dominant topographic elements being a series of ridges in the north and two northeast-southwest

28 "The cliffs, formed of clayey or sandy marls, are not indeed precipitous; but they are steep enough to form insurmountable obstacles to landing except at comparatively few points." W. Leaf, 'The Military Geography of the Troad'. *Geographical Journal,* 67 (1916), p. 402.

29 The evolution of the Dardanelles, its faults and its sedimentary rocks have the discussed in detail in the geological paper by C. Yalitarak, *et al*, 'Origin of the strait of Canakkale (Dardanelles): regional tectonics and the Mediterranean-Marmara incursion', *Marine Geology,* 164 (2000), pp. 139-56. The influence of these structures on defining the shores of the Dardanelles was well known to geographers of the day as described by D.G. Hogarth, 'Geography of the War Theatre in the Near East', *Geographical Journal,* 65, 1915, pp. 457-51 and W. Leaf, 'The Military Geography of the Troad', *Geographical Journal,* 67 (1916), pp. 401-21.

30 Commented upon by the geographer D.G. Hogarth in April 1915 (Hogarth, *op. cit.,* p. 461). Hogarth would serve with Naval Intelligence later in 1915.

31 Discussed in P. Doyle, '"An unfortunate Accident of geography": Badlands and the ANZAC Sector, Gallipoli, April–September 1915' in E. MacDonald & T. Bullard (eds.) *Military Geoscience and Warfare* (London: Springer, 2016).

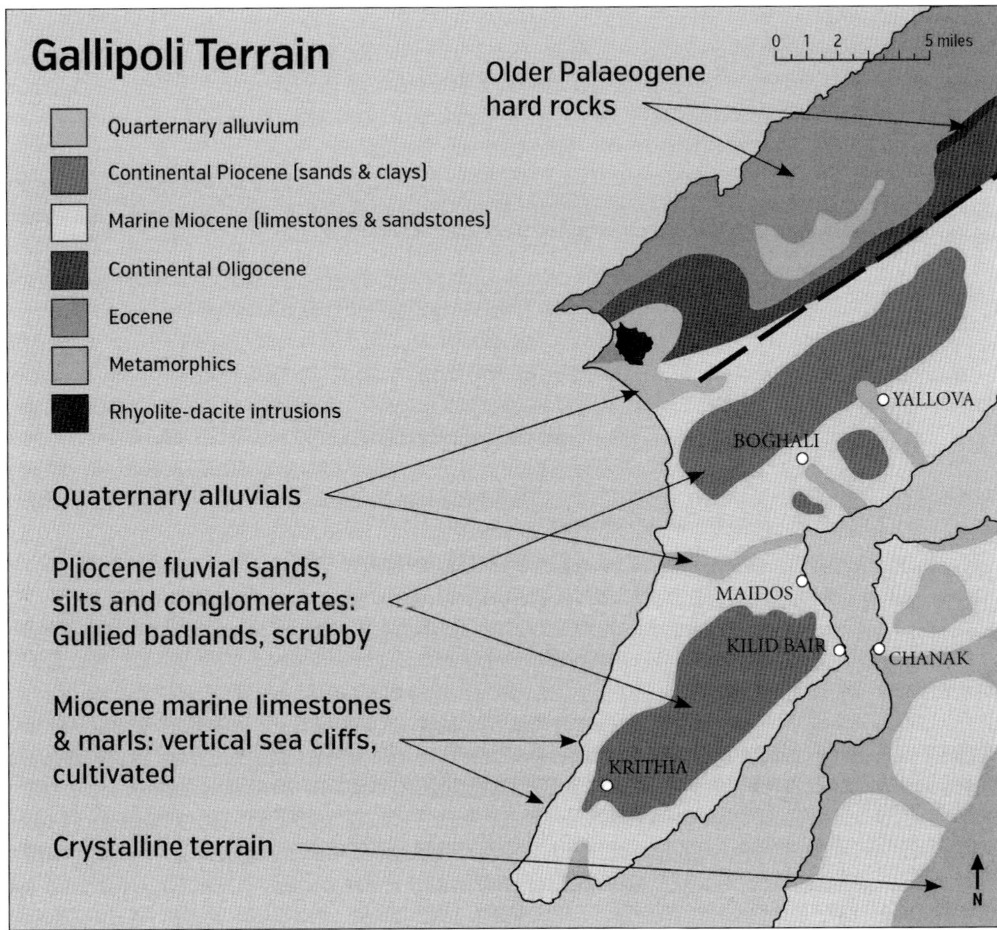

Map 24.4 Geological map of the Gallipoli Peninsula denoting main terrain features. (Author)

trending plateaux in the south. Doyle and Bennett[32] subdivided the topography of the peninsula into "land systems" or zones of similar features as a means of identifying its dominant terrain features, recognising: northeast-southwest trending plateaux of mostly Pliocene continental sediments; Miocene coastal cliffs and dissected limestone topography; low-lying alluvium-filled valley floors; low lying coastal plain; and east-west trending linear ridge systems (Map 24.4).

The northern ridges forming the Aegean margin of the peninsula – Kiretch Tepe Ridge and Karakol Dagh – are formed from folded sandstones and limestones. This contrasts with the southern plateaux, which are formed from younger sedimentary rocks. The margins of the plateaux are heavily dissected, forming a complex network of sharp-crested interfluves. In most cases the slopes are heavily vegetated with low scrub. The exception is the northern margin of

32 Doyle & Bennett, 1998, 2002, *op. cit.*

the Sari Bair plateau, which is marked by a fault line scarp of the Anafartalar fault. Beneath the steep upper face of the scarp the slopes are heavily gullied and are barren of vegetation, forming classic "badland" topography typical of arid zones with high degrees of weathering and erosion.[33] In the south-eastern part of the peninsula, the slopes of the Kilid Bahr Massif are strongly gullied, in some cases forming deep ravines. These ravines exploit the structural grain of the peninsula, to give a parallel-alignment to the drainage, dividing it into recognisable spurs and ravines. In his *Despatches* General Sir Ian Hamilton rightly described the dominant features of the Gallipoli landscape as "three formidable fortresses", fortresses that would need breaking down in order to achieve the primary objectives.[34]

The majority of rivers within the southern Gallipoli Peninsula are seasonal, and most valleys are dry for much of the year (Map 24.5). Exceptions occur in the northern part of the study area, on the margins of the Suvla Plain, where there are some perennial streams. All the major strata have potential as aquifers. However, it is clear from studies of the southern margin of the Dardanelles that the main aquifer potential lies with the limestones and alluvial deposits.[35] For the most part, these aquifers were exploited with wells on the Dardanelles coastal region of the peninsula and were therefore more likely to remain in Ottoman hands.

The Landing Beaches

This combination of simple geology and dominant relief creates the limited choice available to the attackers, and reduced the need to defend some of the most hostile parts of the peninsula. The choice of beaches available to the commander of the Allied forces, General Sir Ian Hamilton included: (1) in the northern part of the peninsula near Bulair, the narrowest part of the isthmus connecting Gallipoli with the rest of Thrace; (2) either side of the promontory known as Gaba Tepe, in a depression separating the two main massifs of the southern peninsula; (3) at the narrow beaches of Cape Helles, threatening the southern slopes of the Kilid Bahr Plateau; (4) on the Aegean coast of Anatolia – known in contemporary accounts as the Asiatic shore – notably at Kum Kale at the entrance to the Dardanelles, and at Besika Bay; and (5) at Suvla Bay, a wide expanse of beach with an open plain beyond, interrupted by a salt lake, and surrounded, in the distance, by an amphitheatre of hills. The pros and cons of these options have been discussed by numerous authors, even before the war was at an end.[36]

Hamilton rejected both Bulair and the Asiatic shore as main landing sites. Bulair was ruled out because: (1) defensive positions were known to be strong here, having been first developed by the British themselves during the Crimean War, and had a consequent concentration of enemy troops; (2) that the topography of Bulair would cause a bottleneck of British troops landing

33 Doyle, 2016, *op. cit.*

34 Ian Hamilton, *General Sir Ian Hamilton's Despatches from the Dardanelles* (London: George Newnes, 1917), pp. 18-19.

35 Doyle 2016, *op. cit.* See also A. Beeby Thomson, *Emergency Water Supplies* (London: Crosby Lockwood & Sons, 1917). Thomson, a civilian, was contracted to provide geological advice to the MEF.

36 For example, see Hogarth, 1915, *op. cit.*; J. Masefield, *Gallipoli* (London: Heinemann, 1916), pp. 3-35; Leaf 1916, *op. cit.*; Hamilton, *Ian Hamilton's Despatches from the Dardanelles, op.cit.;* Nevinson, 1918, *op. cit.,* pp. 74–80.

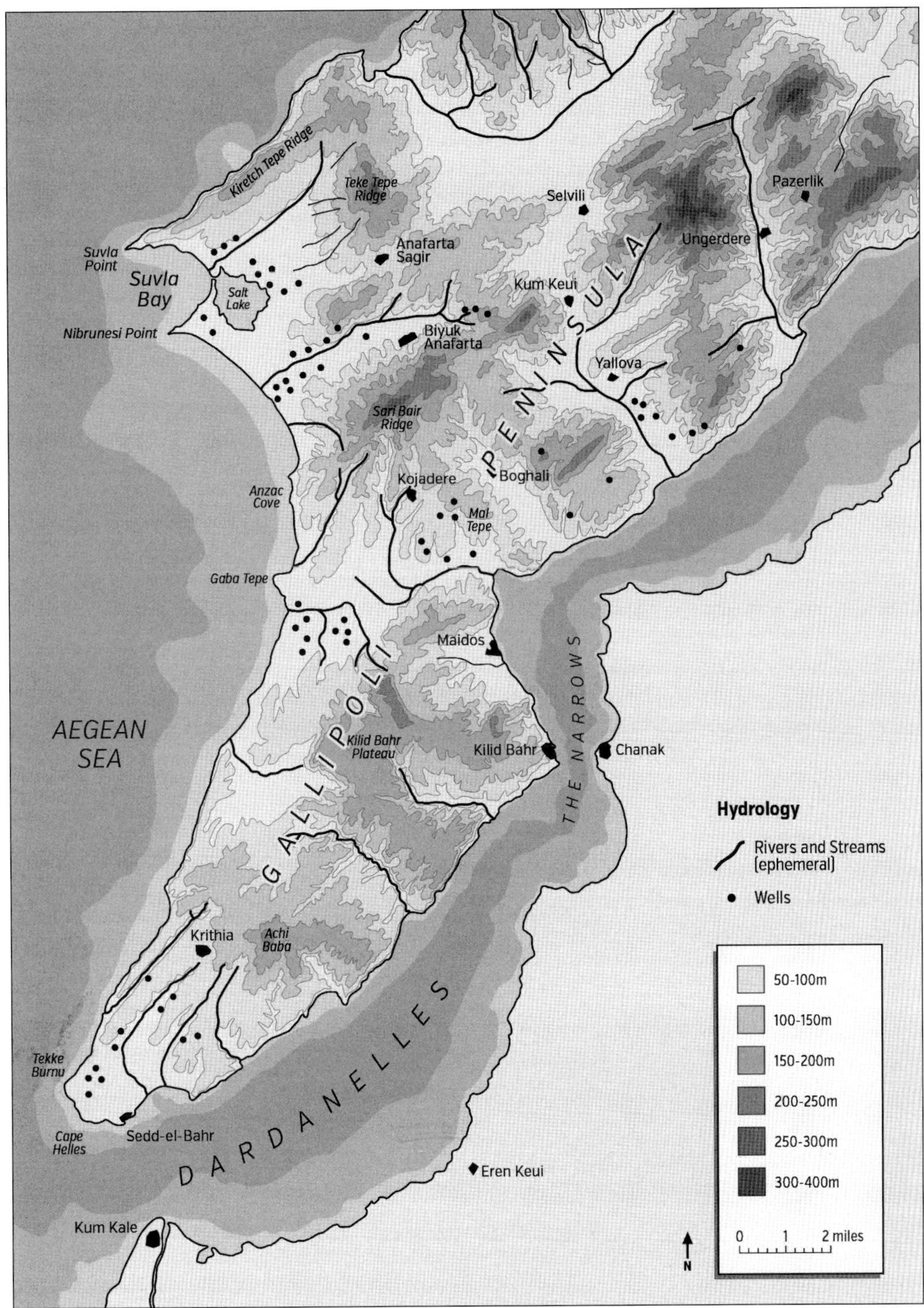

Map 24.5 Hydrology of the Gallipoli Peninsula, showing ephemeral streams and well-heads. (Author)

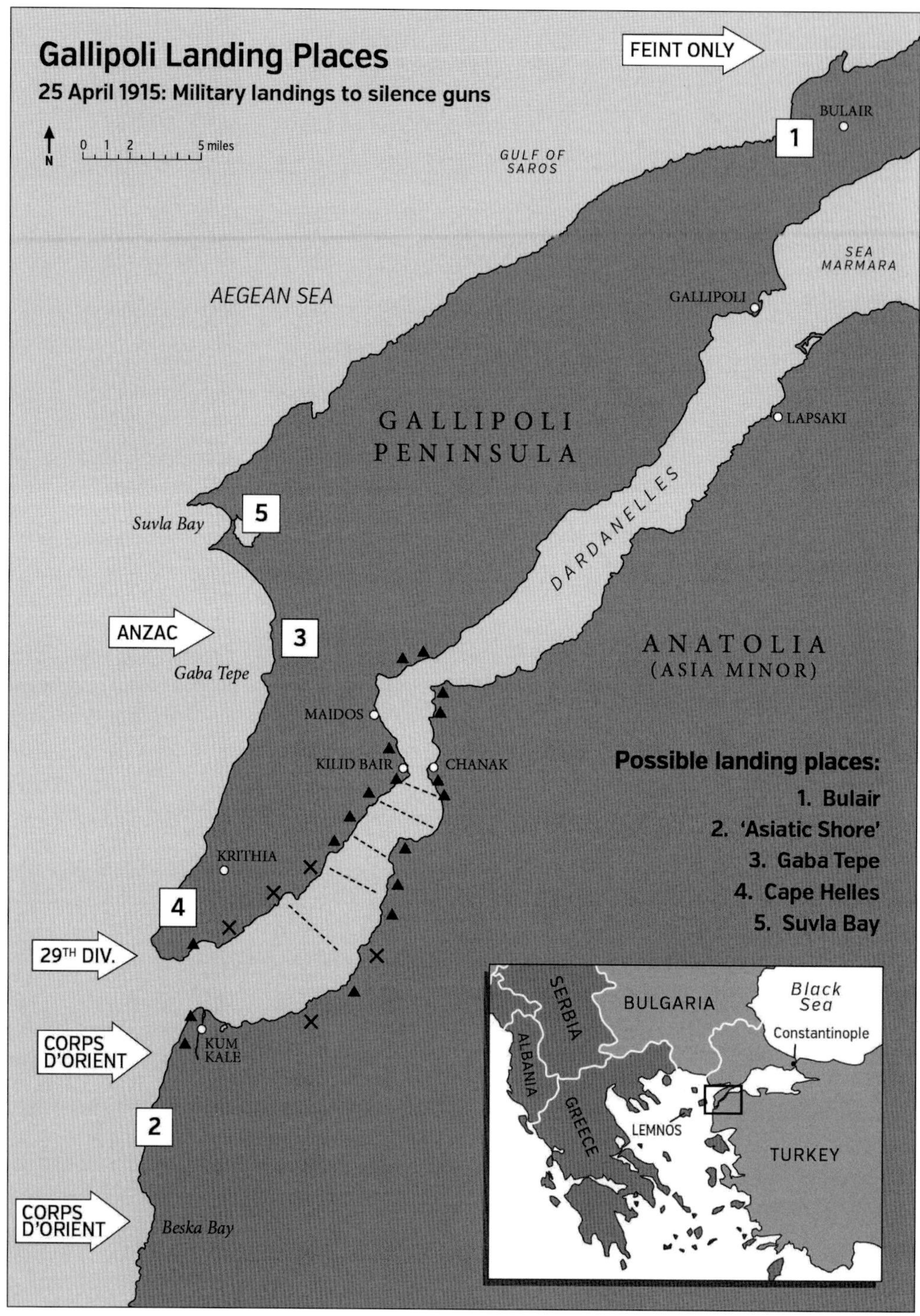

Map 24.6 Gallipoli landing beaches, 25 April 1915. (Author)

from the Gulf of Saros and overlooked by high ground both to the northeast and to the southwest. He also rejected a massed landing on the Asiatic shore at Kum Kale and Besika Bay on two grounds: (1) that supply would be difficult, and opposition would be strong, as troops could be easily derived from the Anatolian heartland and central Thrace; and (2) that the heights of the Gallipoli Peninsula commanded the Dardanelles, and therefore a landing there would not effectively achieve the main strategic objectives. The classical scholar Walter Leaf, writing in 1916, held this firm view while discussing the geographical area of "The Troad", the Asiatic shore of the Dardanelles:

> [T]his rhombohedral land-mass could hardly be better designed as a defence to cover the passage of the Hellespont. It is a well-defined district which can easily be made impassable for any force advancing from the land side with the object of occupying the Asiatic Shore of the Dardanelles.[37]

Instead, a concentration of effort was to be made in the southwestern part of the peninsula – seemingly against contemporary geographical advice. The archaeologist D.G. Hogarth was well acquainted with the region and was Keeper of the Ashmolean Museum. Speaking at the Royal Geographical Society on 26 April 1915, the day after the landings, Hogarth advised:

> All the western end of the Gallipoli peninsula, indeed, is of broken hilly character, which combines with lack of water and consequent lack of population and roads to render it an unfavourable area for military operations. No general if he had the choice, would land a considerable force upon it at any spot below the Narrows.[38]

Hogarth would be recruited to Naval intelligence and would serve in the Middle East later in 1915.

The landings in the southern part of the peninsula were intended to capture the Kilid Bahr Plateau which overlooked the main fort of the same name, and the narrows of the Dardanelles. In so doing this would achieve the main objective of the landing, the support of naval operations. Suvla Bay was ruled out as it was too far away from the Kilid Bahr Plateau to be of value, and because there was little reliable information about its terrain characteristics – though, as pointed out by the correspondent H.W. Nevinson "from Suvla Point to Gaba Tepe it would certainly have been possible to put the whole united force ashore, and, to judge from subsequent events, this might have been the wisest course."[39] The main landings were therefore to be made at the southern end of the peninsula at Cape Helles, and on the west coast at Gaba Tepe (Map 24.7).

For his part, the German commander of the Ottoman 5th Army, General Liman von Sanders, considered the most likely landing places to be Bulair and Besika Bay; the former because of its strategic position in controlling the neck of the peninsula, the latter because of the possibility provided by its relatively wide beaches.[40] It was for this reason that he created heavily fortified

37 W. Leaf, 1916, *op. cit.*, p. 401.
38 Hogarth, 1915, *op. cit.*, p. 461.
39 Nevinson, 1918, *op. cit.*, p. 77.
40 Otto Liman von Sanders, *Five Years in Turkey* (Nashville, Tennessee: Battery Press reprint of 1927 edition), pp. 59-60.

positions in these areas. The Ottoman commander also realised the threat from attacks at Gaba Tepe and Cape Helles; the former because of the fault-bound defile that crossed the peninsula between the Sari Bair and Kilid Bahr plateaux, threatening Maidos, the latter because of the long slope up from the beaches to the peak of Achi Baba which could easily be threatened by naval gunfire. Both of these areas were therefore protected by extensive trenches and barbed wire entanglements, in the month preceding the Allied landings in 1915.

Hamilton decided that there were to be three main landing areas, and two feints, all to be attacked on 23 April, although this was delayed by weather conditions to 25 April. The feints at Bulair and at Besika Bay (on the Asiatic shore) were intended to draw Turkish troops away from the main landing areas, and to keep open an element of surprise as to where the main landings were going to take place. The three main landings were at the southern end of the peninsula, near Gaba Tepe and at Cape Helles, and on the Asiatic shore at Kum Kale.

The landings north of Gaba Tepe at Z beach were to be made by the men of the Australian and New Zealand Army Corps (ANZAC, commonly referred to as "Anzacs"). They were to be landed from towed open boats which were commanded by junior naval officers who had orders to stay in set positions as they approached the shore. In his Despatches, General Sir Ian Hamilton wrote "the actual point of embarkation was rather more than a mile north of that which I had selected",[41] while the British official historian identified that the landings were intended to be on the beach south of Anzac Cove and Ari Burnu;[42] recent research by Robin Prior suggests that plans were never that specific; somewhere north of Gaba Tepe was all that was required.[43] Whether by accident or design, the landings were affected in front of the confused coastal cliffs of the Sari Bair range, reaching the sea at the place now known as Anzac Cove. Here the Ottoman defenders depended upon the hostility of the terrain to magnify the defence of a relatively small number of men with small arms. As evens unfolded, this was effective – allowing them to reinforce more vulnerable points on the coast.

The Cape Helles landings were made by the men of the British 29th Division at five beaches, code lettered, from west to east: Y, X, W, V, S. The landings at S and Y beaches were virtually unopposed, but due to poor communications, the tactical advantages of the situation were not exploited. The landings at V and W, and to a lesser extent at X, met fierce opposition from the Turks in their well-prepared positions, as discussed below. In all the landings, terrain was to be as important to the defender as it was the attacker.

X, W and V Beaches

Cape Helles represents the most southerly part of the Gallipoli Peninsula, facing the Aegean Sea, and as such, it has for centuries been well fortified, particularly as it is at the entrance to the Dardanelles itself. This was seen as one of the most important parts of the coast of the peninsula to defend, and one of the most important areas to land. From the Aegean Coast at Cape Helles north-eastwards to the prominence of Achi Baba (more properly the hill of Alci

41 Hamilton, 1917, *op. cit.*, p. 42.

42 Aspinall-Oglander, 1929, *op. cit.*, p. 169–175

43 R. Prior, *Gallipoli: The End of the Myth* (Hartford, Connecticut: Yale University Press, 2009), pp. 111–12

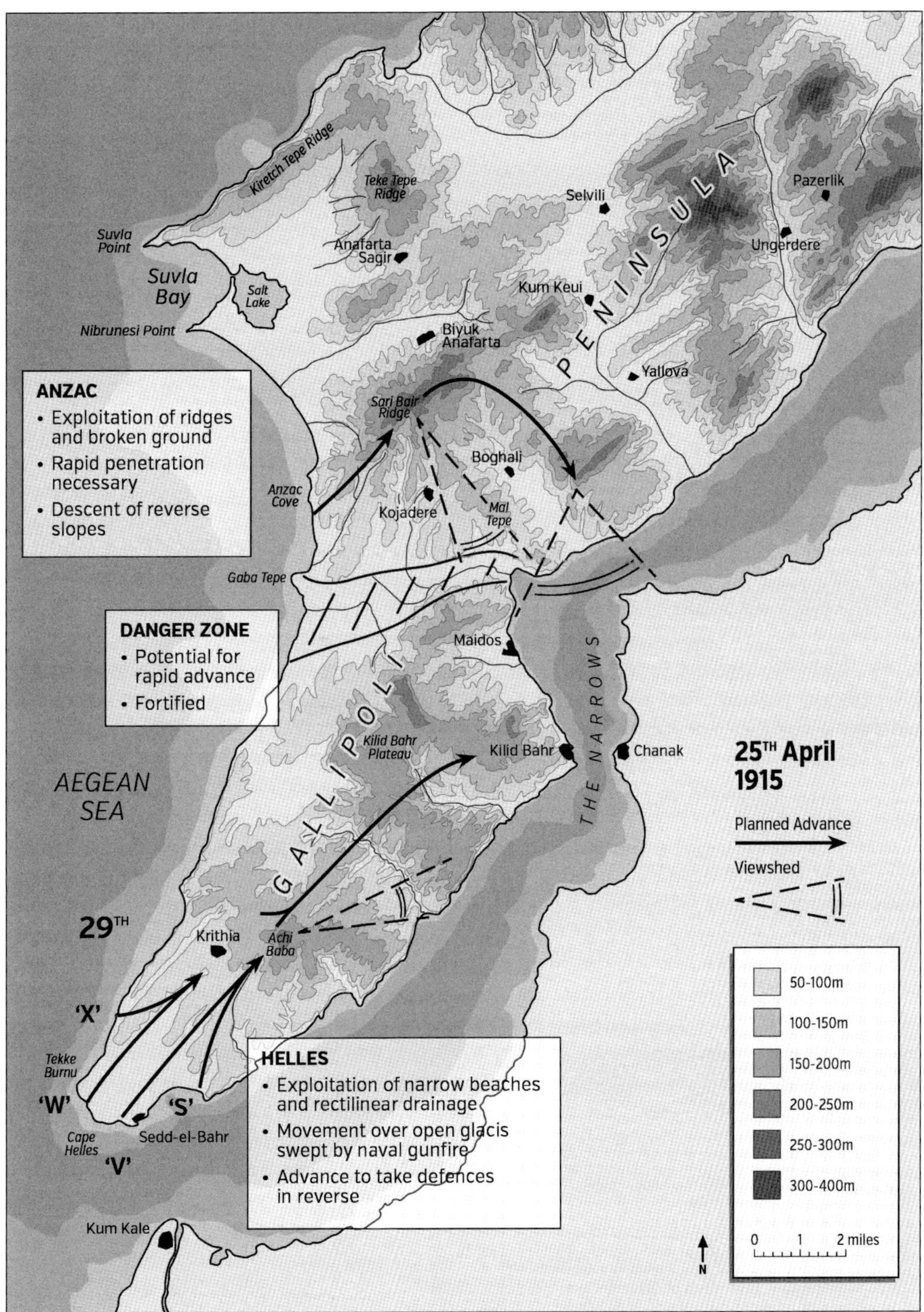
Kiretch Tepe Ridge
Teke Tepe Ridge
Suvla Point
Suvla Bay
Salt Lake
Anafarta Sagir
Nibrunesi Point
Selvili
Pazerlik
Ungerdere
Kum Keui
PENINSULA
Biyuk Anafarta
Yallova
ANZAC
• Exploitation of ridges and broken ground
• Rapid penetration necessary
• Descent of reverse slopes
Sari Bair Ridge
Boghali
Anzac Cove
Kojadere
Mal Tepe
Gaba Tepe
DANGER ZONE
• Potential for rapid advance
• Fortified
Maidos
THE NARROWS
GALLIPOLI
Kilid Bahr Plateau
Kilid Bahr
Chanak
AEGEAN SEA
25TH April 1915
Planned Advance
Viewshed
29TH
Krithia
Achi Baba
'X'
Tekke Burnu
'W'
'S'
Cape Helles
'V'
Sedd-el-Bahr
HELLES
• Exploitation of narrow beaches and rectilinear drainage
• Movement over open glacis swept by naval gunfire
• Advance to take defences in reverse
50-100m
100-150m
150-200m
200-250m
250-300m
300-400m
Kum Kale
N
0 1 2 miles

Map 24.7 Landing beaches, intended objectives and potential Narrows viewsheds. (Author)

Tepe) the Helles sector is deceptively open, with relatively low gradients which in effect create an open glacis over which the low-trajectory naval gunfire can traverse. This glacis leads directly up-slope to the summit of Achi Baba, a flat-topped hill that was hoped would dominate the Dardanelles, and the fort of Kilid Bahr below. While possession of this hill gave the Ottomans the capability of commanding the terrain south-westwards towards the landing beaches, post-war exploration of the hill by Allied officers revealed that the hill gave little or no view of the Narrows below.[44]

Towards the coast, and forming the cliffs surrounding this part of the peninsula, are hard, well-bedded limestones overlain by sands and marl sediments that form the plateaux. The slopes are well-cultivated, then as now, with none of the dense scrub that characterises the Anzac battlefield farther north – except were there are uncultivated valleys, the "nullahs" or "deres" in the language of the day. The strong structural control of the form of the peninsula is well demonstrated at Helles, where the Aegean and Dardanelles coastlines are rectilinear. These match the pattern of drainage inshore, with a series of northeast-southwest trending valleys and ravines paralleling the coasts, presumably exploiting fractures and faults related to the North Anatolian Fault system. These valleys are steep and ravine-like, dissecting the southwestward facing slopes of the Helles "glacis", separated by broad interfluves. This pattern relates to the northeast-southwest structural grain, which is also enhanced by a series of broad flexures, the valleys exploiting faults that run along the axial traces of the folds. Together the structural "grain" of this part of the peninsula creates a framework within which the opposing sides were operating, the Ottoman troops using the terrain to their advantage, the British, the reverse.

Of the landing beaches, X is on the Aegean coast of the Gallipoli Peninsula. It is not served by a valley or "nullah" but is in a small sheltered cove with prominent cliffs and a narrow beach, the cliffs comprising two units of strata, a lower one of coarse limestones, overlain with softer sediments above. W Beach (Tekkekoyu), is a narrow beach that feeds into a ravine to the north-east. The beach has an initial steep (c. 30 degree) narrow swash zone before grading to a low gradient sand beach behind it. The beach is constrained by vertical cliffs of limestones to the northwest (Tekke Burnu, with Hill 114 above it) and southeast, with the beach area similarly constrained to the rear by the wall of the same rocks, the back wall of which is formed by an outcrop pattern that shows the rocks have been folded, helping to define the bay and beach. The infill of this arcing valley form is predominantly that of alluvial debris and a line of narrow dunes to the rear of the beach.

V Beach (Ertugrul Koyu) is a broader beach area, with what was described in many contemporary accounts as "ampitheatral" in form. The beach is bounded to the north west by the same line of steep cliffs that forms the southeast boundary of W Beach, here developed as a fort as part of the Dardanelles defences (Ertugrul Fort or Fort No. 1 to the Allies). Three small knolls exist in the hinterland, Hill 138 (Aytepe) to the north, between W and V beaches, Guezi Baba, east of Fort No 1, and Hill 141 (Harabkale, later named Doughty Wylie Hill by the British) at the rear of the beach area, above the village of Sedd-el-Bahr. The southwestern margin of the beach is picked out by the Sedd-el-Bahr fort, below the village itself. A "rocky spit" picks out the outcrop of another rock flexure within the bay, with cliffs themselves developed father to the southwest within Morto Bay itself. The beach is narrow, with a low angle and

44 Discussed in some depth in Elkins, 2012.

less well-developed swash zone than is encountered at W Beach. The amphitheatre is filled in part by alluvial fans, and these are dissected by the sea to form what was described as an "earth bank". No distinct sand dunes are developed here.

Ottoman Preparations for Defence: Vantage

The Ottoman preparations for defence were thorough, and consisted of three major components: (1) infantry fire trenches; (2) strongpoints; (3) barbed-wire obstacles; and, more controversially, (4) machine gun positions. The intention of the defenders was to give maximum vantage, with observation of potential attacks from the sea, and in creating a strong defensive position with maximum opportunity to use the terrain to good effect, multiplying the fire-power of the defending forces. These defences were picked out during aerial reconnaissance flights over the peninsula by the British Royal Naval Air Service (RNAS), who used 1:40,000 and one-inch base maps.[45] Reconnaissance took the form of annotated overlays which showed the build-up and improvement of defensive positions during the period between the cessation of the naval battle on 18 March, and the landings on 25 April.[46]

According to a contemporary account written by Colonel Mahmut, commander of the *3rd Battalion* of the Ottoman *26th Regiment*[47] the defences along 5 km of coastline "consisted of trenches for riflemen", with those in the west (at W Beach), being "weak because the ground consisted of sand". In front of the fire trenches along this stretch of coast were "two or three rows of barbed wire obstacles" that were apparently incomplete. The *3rd Battalion* comprised 1,100 men, with 100 unarmed, along with divisional engineers and "four small 37.5 mm guns", all of which at least were later to be put out of action during the landings. In his official history of the campaign, Aspinall-Oglander noted that the Ottomans had a company of *3rd/26th Regiment* in defence at V and W beaches, with a much smaller number of men at X Beach.[48]

A map – "Plan of S.W. End of Gallipoli Peninsula" (Map 24.8) – prepared ten days after the landing by Commander H. Douglas and Lieutenant T.C. Nicholas, a geologist serving as "maps officer" with General Sir Ian Hamilton's staff, picked out the defences prepared, and indicated the prominence of the trench systems described by Colonel Mahmut.[49] These effectively contour the slopes, and provide an excellent enfilade field of fire for the Turkish riflemen, covering the coves and steep valley coastal cliff areas of V and W beach. As indicated by near-contemporary published accounts,[50] this represents "textbook" defensive positioning, the attacker drawn into a field of fire from which he cannot escape, the creation of a "kill zone", the intention being to drive the attacker back into the sea, a stated aim of the Normandy "Atlantic Wall" defences utilised in 1944.

45 Chasseaud & Doyle, 2005, *op. cit.*
46 The value of these has been called into question by Elkins 2012, *op. cit.*; there was little else that could have been done with the prevailing technology of the day.
47 Imperial War Museum (IWM) DPB 116.17 K34980.
48 Aspinall-Oglander, 1929, *op. cit.*, p. 159.
49 The National Archives (Kew), ADM 137/787.
50 The paper by H.A.S. Pressey, 'Notes on Trench Warfare', *Royal Engineers Journal*, Vol. 29, 1919 concentrates on the siting of trenches relative to terrain and topography; these "textbook" principles are fully demonstrated by Ottoman trenches situated at the southern extremity of Helles.

Map 24.8 "Plan of S.W. End of Gallipoli Peninsula" showing defences. (Author)

Douglas' and Nicholas' map also picks out hills as fortified redoubts, strongholds no doubt intended to hold up any advance. These two elements of the Turkish defences are supported by extensive barbed wire entanglements, which by all accounts, Turkish inclusive, were exceptionally heavy, placed in two belts at V Beach at least, and extending into the sea, with torpedo heads used as landmines.[51] In many ways, the siting of trenches and defensive positions to command routes of the beaches – "draws" in 1944 – resembles the position faced by the Americans at Omaha Beach during the Normandy invasion on 6 June 1944.[52]

The Question of Machine Guns

There is a question mark over the use of machine guns at the landing beaches, the use of which would have inevitably increased the fire capability of the Turkish defenders. In Colonel Mahmut's contemporary account, there is no mention of machine guns, quite the reverse: "our force had been reduced to 800 and which had no support from any weapons, except the rifles in their hands". This view that the defending Turks had no machine guns is supported by Turkish historian Kenan Celik in his study of Turkish sources,[53] although, apparently the presence of pom-pom type Nordenfeld guns is admitted.[54]

According to Aspinall-Oglander, four "old pattern maxim guns" were installed at Sedd-el-Bahr and V Beach,[55] although the question of machine guns at W Beach was a moot point. In a manuscript account of the landing from the beached *River Clyde*, Captain G.W. Geddes of the 1st Royal Munster Fusiliers noted: "I estimated the strength of the Turks at 400 to 500, with 1 Pom-Pom and 6 machine guns. *They had* machine guns [original emphasis]".[56] Geddes was aboard the ship and was wounded getting ashore, and was therefore in a good position to comment, and his use of emphasis suggesting his strength of feeling on this issue. A footnote added to a version of the manuscript in The National Archives in London comments that machine gun belts were found at V Beach, giving extra credence to the assertion.

In other contemporary manuscript accounts Captain Guy P. Dawnay, observing from offshore, noted on 29 April that at V Beach "the tows going in [with boats carrying the landing forces] were met by a terrific fire from rifles, machine guns and pom-poms",[57] while Commander I.W. Gibson, Captain of HMS *Albion* off V Beach, noted on 26 April that: "When the boats got close to shore a terrific fire [of] rifle and maxim [guns] I think opened on them".[58] At W Beach, Captain (subsequently Commodore) Phillimore, beach master at Helles, noted that "The beach was covered with barbed wire, the cliffs were lined with trenches at the top and had maxims, in sand caves, half way up".[59] The map prepared in May 1915 by Douglas and Nicholas also picks

51 Aspinall-Oglander, 1929, *op. cit.*, p. 225; Sanders, 1927, *op. cit.*, p. 62.
52 See, for example map GSGS 4490: "Omaha Beach – East, 1944". The planning for the Normandy Landings was, unsurprisingly, influenced by the failure of the Gallipoli campaign.
53 Kenan Celik, correspondence with author.
54 One, captured beyond X Beach, is housed in the Royal Fusiliers Regimental Museum, London.
55 Aspinall-Oglander, 1929, *op. cit.*, p. 159
56 Copies in the IWM Department of Documents (DD) and TNA, Kew.
57 IWM: D.D. Dawney Papers 69/21/1.
58 IWM: D.D. Gibson papers.
59 IWM: D.D. Phillimore Papers.

out the position of machine guns, sited in enfilading positions on both V and W beaches. These and other accounts suggest, that at V Beach at least, machine guns were deployed as part of the defences. As depicted in the map by Douglas and Nicholas, these were sited for maximum effect, sweeping across the open field creating a "kill zone" – similar again to that experienced by a different 29th Division, American this time, that landed at Omaha Beach, Normandy, some 29 years later.

The landings

The British 29th Division was to land at the Helles from open boats, each taking between 32-42 men in full equipment towed by naval picket boats, and at W Beach, from the converted merchant ship, the *River Clyde*. Only the *River Clyde* was armed and armoured. The main landings were at the toe of the peninsula, at X, W and V beaches, with flanking landings farther to the northwest at Y Beach, on the Aegean Coast, and S Beach, just into the Dardanelles. Much has been made of lost opportunity at Y and S beaches, where opposition was slight, and where successful landings were followed by inactivity,[60] but further discussion of them is beyond the scope of this paper.

X Beach

X Beach looked unpromising, and like other locations on the Aegean coast, particularly Y Beach farther up it, was relatively undefended, with twelve men occupying the trenches, and no barbed wire defences. The cliffs are steep, but not vertical, and about 15 metres high, the beach itself being narrow and around 200 metres long. The Turkish trenches were conspicuous, on a forward slope, and were as such targeted by the guns of the ships HMS *Swiftsure* and HMS *Implacable*, who remained close inshore, allowing the Royal Fusiliers to storm the cliffs.[61] Inshore, however, was Hill 114 situated between X and W beaches, and this was more resolutely held by the defending Turks. As commented upon by Callwell,[62] the Turkish defences were poor here as the possibility of getting more than just men ashore was limited – the cliffs precluding the landing of artillery pieces and other heavy equipment.

W Beach

As described above, W Beach presented a difficult proposition for the attackers. It was heavily defended, in the words of General Sir Ian Hamilton: "Much time and ingenuity had been employed by the Turks in turning this landing-place into a death trap".[63] As at X Beach, naval bombardment was a feature of the landing process, but here the inability of HMS *Euryalus* to

60 See comments in C.E. Callwell, *The Dardanelles* (London: Constable, 1924); Aspinall-Oglander, 1929, *op. cit.*; Robert Rhodes James, *Gallipoli* (London: Batsford, 1965).
61 Callwell, 1924, *op. cit.*, p. 66-7; Aspinall-Oglander, 1929, *op. cit.*, p. 224-25)
62 Ibid., p. 68.
63 Hamilton, 1917, *op. cit.,* p. 36.

stand in close to the beach meant that the opening naval bombardment was to have a lesser affect, with the barbed wire entanglements, which were comprehensive and which extended down to the water level, were intact. Ian Hamilton was to comment in his despatches that: "So strong were the defences of W beach that the Turks may well have considered them impregnable".[64]

As the boats approached the beach, one veered off to the rocky headland of Tekke Burnu, while the others headed straight for the steep swash zone. Up until this point, the men approaching the beach were greeted with silence, and there was a general feeling that the opening bombardment had done its job. As described by Major-General Callwell: "All this time the Turks were obstinately holding their fire. Only at the moment when the leading boats touched the beach did a murderous, converging fusillade from rifles, machine-guns and pompoms suddenly meet the assailants as these made their way to land. The losses were extremely heavy as the men struggled out of the boats. Many were shot in the water, others were hit before they tried to disembark, some were drowned."[65] It was for bravery in the face of this that six Victoria Crosses were awarded to the battalion for their actions in landing "before breakfast" on 25 April 1915.

Examination of the ground explains the difficulty of the landing, executed as it was from open boats. The fire discipline of the Turks meant that the men of the Lancashire Fusiliers were caught between the boats and the barbed wire before they were able to open fire. An excellent opportunity for defence was provided by the arcuate form of the beach, which created a perfect enfilading field of fire. Superb vantage provided by the cliff line positions meant that on the open beach there was not one piece of dead ground, and no cover – at least before the line of low dunes to the rear of the beach is reached. As such, losses were high as the attackers valiantly struggled with the barbed wire entanglements. The attackers were able, however, to overcome the defence, again a function of the natural disposition of the Miocene outcrop. The men that had landed under the cliffs at Tekke Burnu – the western beach cliffs – were able to scale these steep, but benched cliffs, the benching a function of softer marl units between the harder limestone levels. According to Callwell, they were able to dispose of the machine gun crews they found there, and relieve pressure on the beach, as well as enfilading the Turkish trenches.[66] This afforded an opportunity for the main body of the battalion, who had by now cut lanes through the wire to shelter in the lee of the cliffs, while another party of Fusiliers scaled the steep cliffs to the east.[67] Together with reinforcements from other regiments, this opportunity meant that the Turkish defenders were driven back from Hill 114 at Tekke Burnu, allowing them to link with the attackers from X Beach, while Hill 138 between V and W beaches was put under increased pressure.

V Beach

A larger beach than either X or W, V beach is described in all accounts as a "natural amphitheatre". As Captain Geddes, a company commander with the Royal Munster Fusiliers landing from the *River Clyde* was to report a few days after the landing:

64 Ibid., p. 37.
65 Callwell, 1924, *op. cit.*, p. 71.
66 Ibid., p. 71.
67 Aspinall-Oglander, 1929, *op. cit.*, p. 228.

> V Beach formed an Amphitheatre about 300 yards in diameter with Sedd-el-Bahr fort on the right and on the left high cliffs surmounted with Fort No. 1 [Map 25.10]. In no instance was the range greater than 300 yards. There were two lines of trenches in front of each barb [sic] wire fence, the most fearsome I saw on any front.[68]

These defences were to be assaulted by men of the Royal Dublin Fusiliers, the Royal Munster Fusiliers and the Hampshire Regiment, in two ways, from open boats towed to the western extremity of the beach, and in the converted collier SS *River Clyde*, which was to beach adjacent to the "rocky spit" – a natural reef formed by the outcrop of the dipping Miocene limestones. Doors ("sally ports") had been cut in the bows of the ship and gangplanks fitted, enabling the men to disembark from the ship, hopefully using the "spit" to wade ashore. A contingency was the possibility of towing lighters into position to provide a continuation of the gangways to the beach.

In common with the actions at the other beaches under consideration, the fortifications observed by the RNAS reconnaissance flights prior to the landings were bombarded by the navy, in this case the guns of HMS *Albion* and HMS *Queen Elizabeth*. As before, the defending Turks remained silent, until about 6:00 a.m., when the open boats landed at the western end of the beach. Again, as at V Beach, the Turkish defenders displayed excellent fire discipline, opening fire as the boats approached the beach. The result was aptly described by Callwell:

> Only a few of the [Royal Dublin] Fusiliers succeeded in attaining cover … The majority were either shot down in the water or else as they reached the beach, or they were placed *hors de combat* while still in the boats… Within a few minutes, this portion of the attack had been to all intents and purposes defeated, the troops detailed for the operation were almost wiped out of existence, and the few survivors were cowering at the water's edge under the inadequate protection of the lip scooped by the waves.[69]

This "lip" or "earth bank" is an important part of the story of the landing at W Beach. It represents a truncated low angle fan of alluvial fill that abuts the beach; the beach here is narrow and without dunes. As described above, the swash zone is less steep than at V Beach, and the survivors climbing ashore would have found the opportunity for cover provided by this roughly one-metre soft cliff inviting. Remarkable photographs of the landings, now in the Imperial War Museum, show the men hunkered down sheltering from the fire, which, as at W Beach was received from the arcuate pattern of fire trenches surrounding the beach. Maintenance of fire discipline by the defenders meant that there was little opportunity for escape from the hail of fire, and the cliffs to the west, beneath Fort No. 1, are that much more steep and formidable than those at V Beach.

The story of the beaching the *River Clyde* is every bit as remarkable at the other aspects of the landings, the brain child of Commander Unwin, a naval officer who was to win the Victoria Cross in trying to secure the lighters from the ship to the "rock spit". As described by Hamilton himself in his *Despatches*:

68 IWM: DD, G. Geddes papers.
69 Callwell, 1924, *op. cit.*, p. 80.

> Now came the moment for the *River Clyde* to pour forth her living freight; but grievous delay was caused here by the difficulty of placing the lighters in position between the ship and the shore. A strong current hindered the work and the enemy's fire was so intense that almost every man engaged upon it was immediately shot.[70]

The concentration of effort to a narrow set of gangplanks and the precarious nature of the lighter link to the "rock spit" provided the perfect target for the Turkish defenders: a concentration of men bunched together with no effective escape from the concerted Turkish fire.

Some men did get ashore, heading again to the safety of the low "earth bank". Covering fire from machine guns mounted on board the *River Clyde* was an important factor: "in preventing the enemy from delivering a counterattack upon the troops who were crouching at the water's edge, shielded by the low escarpment, and who would have found it hard to beat off a determined onset."[71] And so the attackers remained throughout the rest of the day, the fire from the Turkish trenches continuing until they were low on ammunition.[72] At this point, at around 8:00 p.m., the remainder of the men were able to emerge from the beached ship and take cover in the lee of the ruined fort of Sedd-el-Bahr, where they remained until the morning. Under the inspiring leadership of Lieutenant-Colonel Doughty-Wylie, one of General Hamilton's staff officers, survivors sheltering beneath the fort were able to gain a foothold in the village, finally taking Hill 141 at the rear of Sedd-el-Bahı by 2:00 p.m. Doughty Wylie was killed in the attack – and was awarded the Victoria Cross posthumously for his gallantry. The Hill he stormed was named Doughty Wylie Hill for the remainder of the campaign, and his grave may still be found there today.

The open, bowl-like amphitheatre of V Beach created by the flexed structure of the folded limestones, meant that the opportunities for vantage were almost as perfect for the Turkish defenders here as they were at W beach. The chance of nature provided by the "rocky spit" (the exposed flexed limestone), the "earth bank" (the seaward truncated alluvial fan) and the limestone blocks of the fort of Sedd-el-Bahr itself materially assisted the attackers, who had otherwise found themselves drawn into an almost perfect killing zone of enfilading fire provided by the defenders.

Z Beach

The Australian and New Zealand Army Corps (ANZAC) were to be landed at the beach (Z Beach) north of Gaba Tepe, facing the formidable, dissected landscape of the Sari Bair range. The range terminated to the northwest, its steep face created by the active Anafartarlar Fault, associated with the North Anatolian Fault system.[73] The underlying rocks were easily eroded from fluvial action and intermittent rainfall over centuries producing a rugged landscape. The vegetation consists of a low, unforgiving scrub; with rough and easily disturbed soils, resulting in little flat ground. This confusion was described by General Hamilton himself:

70 Hamilton, 1917, *op. cit.*, p. 31.
71 Callwell, 1924, *op. cit.*, p. 81.
72 IWM: Department of Printed Books: Colonel Mahmut manuscript.
73 Yalitarak, *et al.*, 2000, *op. cit.*

> [I]nland lie in a tangled knot the under-features of Sari Bair, separated by deep ravines, which take a most confusing diversity of direction. Sharp spurs, covered with dense scrub, and falling away in many places in precipitous sandy cliffs, radiate from the principal mass of the mountain, from which they run northwest, west, southwest, and south to the coast.[74]

Behind Z Beach (soon to be dubbed Brighton Beach after its namesake in Melbourne, Australia), three parallel spurs or ridges (identified as first, second and third) seemed to provide the best means of assaulting the peak in the initial stages of the operation. These spurs are a function of the continued uplift of the active Anafartalar fault, and the North Anatolian Fault system, and mirror the "structural grain" of the peninsula. To the south, at Gaba Tepe, the whole block is interrupted by the fault trending across the peninsula, as discussed above. Uplift along the fault systems exposed the Sari Bair range to intense run off and erosion, creating deep, steep-sided, southwest-northeast trending valleys that are exploiting fractures in the bedrock, leaving the three spurs. With increased uplift the arid soils are subjected to erosion that sculpted the complex terrain that was so different from that seen in the Helles Sector. Unlike at Helles, here, ground water supply is extremely limited and this added to the aridity and friable nature of the ground. In addition, the westward face of Sari Bair is therefore subject to intense erosion, with run-off to the sea between Ari Burnu and Gaba Tepe

If the ANZAC could get ashore in this inhospitable place, it was intended they could clamber up the slopes that led to Second Ridge, which would aid them as a transport route; in moving through the scrub along the ridge, where they would be in a position to "take the high ground" and dominate the ridge top, leading to the high point. From here there would be views across Suvla Bay and its plain to the northwest, and back down to the southeast in the direction of Helles. It was hoped that there would be the chance to observe the Narrows, though, as at Achi Baba, in reality this was limited.[75]

Z Beach (defined approximately as between Gaba Tepe and Fisherman's Hut/Ari Burnu)[76] was to be assaulted by the ANZAC at one hour before dawn, in an effort to maximise surprise, and to try and reach the first positions before daybreak. Three battalions of the Australian 3rd Brigade (together with supporting troops) would lead the assault landing from seven destroyers, which were to approach close in to the beach. The plan dictated that the main force would land from transports. With the three ridges leading to the summit of the Sari Bair range as the target, and Second Ridge just behind the beach, the 3rd Brigade was ordered to advance over its slopes, with the intention of gaining – and holding Third Ridge. Following on closely, the Australian 2nd Brigade, would then be in a position to advance up the ridge, taking the nearest summits, Chunuk Bair at the flat plateau top joined by the three ridges, and "Scrubby Knoll" a prominent feature on Third Ridge. The main force would then arrive to press on to a hill known as Mal Tepe, on the Dardanelles side of the peninsula – which, it was hoped, would serve as a strong point that would help secure the Dardanelles defences. As with Achi Baba, the actual view, observed post-war, would be disappointing.[77] In taking the ridge tops, the ANZAC hoped

74 Hamilton, 1917, *op. cit.*, pp. 42-43.
75 Elkins, 2013, *op. cit.*
76 Prior, *op. cit.*, pp. 111-112.
77 Elkins, 2013, *op. cit.*

to be able to deny them to the enemy – and ultimately link up with the British advancing from Cape Helles to conquer the northern shore of the Dardanelles and silence the guns.

The Landing

As discussed above, the intended landing place for the ANZAC troops has been subject to some debate. Though there is evidence to suggest that the actual landing places were anywhere between the heavily defended and wired position at Gaba Tepe and the Fisherman's Hut that marked the northwards extent of the Sari Bair ridges,[78] it has long been held that the eventual landings in Anzac Cove were by chance, a factor of the northwards drift of the boats.

Gaining the shore at about 4:30 a.m., the Australians struggled up the shingle beach in their combat equipment. The water was deeper than expected as the soldiers leaped out of the boats; several must have been dragged under. Ahead of them were unfamiliar slopes that would lead up to the top of Sari Bair. The tortuous ground of the heavily gullied slopes was a considerable obstacle, a factor described in some detail by the British official historian:

> Even in the time of peace the precipitous ridges and tortuous ravines which formed the first Australian and New Zealand battlefield are an arduous climb for an active and unarmed man, while the steep, scrub-covered gullies are so confusing that it is easy to lose one's way. To preserve the cohesion of an attack across such country, immediately after an opposed landing in the dark, and without previous reconnaissance, would be an impossible task for the best-trained troops in the world.[79]

Small arms fire was directed at them by the Ottoman defenders. It was heaviest at the northern part – the promontory known as Ari Burnu, and close to the small ramshackle building known as Fisherman's Hut. But this was not the only resistance facing the Australians. In front of them were the first slopes that they knew would lead up to the top of the Sari Bair range; expecting them to be part of Second Ridge, the landing had placed them in front of the steep slopes of the First, and the deep gully – Shrapnel Gully – that separated the two ridges. The Australian battalions struggled to the top of a slope vegetated with thick scrub that was later to be called Plugge's Plateau – a small flat-topped extension of what was actually the First Ridge. They were unable to push on – confronting them was a bald, narrow ridge that the forces of nature had eroded from both sides – the Razor Edge. This was to be impassable; north of this feature was a forbidding bowl of bare earth that sat at the foot of what the soldiers (in memory of their time in Egypt), would later call "The Sphinx". This steep-sided cliff, part of Walker's Ridge that had been created by the erosion of a particularly hard band of cemented conglomerate that was resistant to weathering. This was in contrast to most of the Sari Bair Range, made up of fine sedimentary rocks that were easily eroded by both wind and water action, creating a myriad of gullies, sharp spurs and innumerable dead-ends. Devoid of much water, these soils promoted the growth of stunted bushes and shrubs. The Razor's Edge came as a complete surprise to the

78 Prior, *op. cit.*, pp. 111-112.
79 Aspinall-Oglander, 1929, *op. cit.*, p. 175.

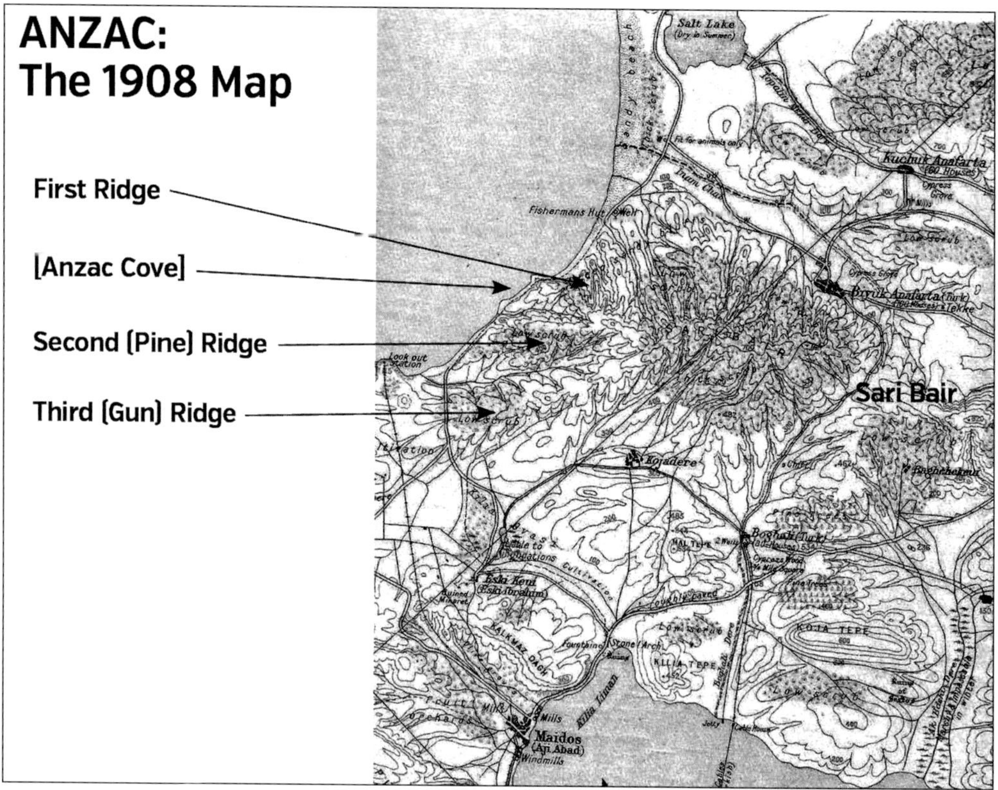

Map 24.9 The 1908 One-inch map depicting continuity of all three ridges. (Author)

Australians. The 1908 vintage map (Map 25.9) supplied to the troops indicated a continuous ridge that could be easily traversed. This was not to be the case, and as discussed above, became a major point of contention in post-war discussions of terrain intelligence failure, starting with the British Official History.[80]

For the men landing north of Ari Burnu, not only would the harsh terrain of the Sphinx and Walker's Ridge be in their way, so would the fire of the defending Ottomans at Fisherman's Hut. The next wave of men came ashore from the boats also released by the seven destroyers standing off the coast. Now daylight, the boats were more spread out, delivering men onto a beach that was in the order of 1,500 yards wide, part of them to the north of Ari Burnu, the remainder to the south. By 4:45 a.m., some 4,000 men of the ANZAC covering force were released into the confusing and inhospitable badlands landscape of the sector – much easier to defend than attack. Under attack from the defenders in the north, and facing uncertain terrain in front of them, it was difficult to know in what direction they should press ahead. Led by officers as unsure of the terrain as their men, the ANZAC troops scrambled through the

80 Aspinall-Oglander, 1929 *op. cit.*; C.E.W. Bean, *The Story of Anzac*, Vol. II (Sydney: Angus & Robertson, 1924), p. 164; Elkins, 2012, *op. cit.*

unforgiving terrain towards their target, Hill 971 and "Baby 700" at the junction of the three main ridges.

The remainder of the Australian troops began landing from the transports at 5:30 a.m., the press of men adding to the confusion of those already onshore. As they advanced farther up the coast past Ari Burnu and Walker's Ridge, and close to the "Fisherman's Hut", the ANZAC troops were once more engaged by the Ottoman defenders – at a high cost to the attackers. Men from the second wave were pressed into the attack. The commander of the covering force was aware that he had to press on from the beaches to capture the Third Ridge, hold it and force his troops on to the high ground. Yet with passing time, the cohesion of his fighting units was breaking down, and it was difficult to identify just who was where, with small groups of men engaged in their own battles with the landscape. It was more realistic to try and concentrate on Second Ridge, securing its length from close to Hell Spit, at the southern end of Anzac Cove, upwards from the beach until the ridge coalesced with the great mass of summit of the Sari Bair range. Though some scouts had reached Scrubby Knoll at around 9:00 a.m., briefly viewing the Narrows in the distance, they soon had to withdraw. No other ANZAC troops would stand on the knoll during the war.

With Third Ridge seemingly out of his grasp, the ANZAC commander directed his forces to form strong posts along the edge of the Second Ridge, posts that would hold throughout the campaign (soon to become named after their commanders – "Courtney's", "Steele's" and "Quinn's"). Baby 700 sat at the junction of Second Ridge with the main mass of the mountain. It would also have to be held. Not for the last time, the deep, scrub-filled gully that divided the First from the Second Ridges, Shrapnel Gully, leading to Monash Valley, would serve as a route towards the apex of the ANZAC line. The line would also have to hold across the broader expanse of the 400 Plateau, a wider area on Second Ridge covered in dense scrub.

On Second Ridge, a flat plateau that was the scene of fierce fighting within the scrub vegetation in the first hours of the campaign, still presented difficulties. Attack and counterattack followed each other over possession of Baby 700. Holding out until 4:00 p.m., the ANZAC line finally broke, the hill lost, when the Ottomans made a concerted effort to drive them from it. With the benefit of artillery support (naval gunfire in this opening part of the campaign), the ANZAC line melted away, its survivors streaming back over the narrow saddle of land that connected First Ridge with the plateau top. Lieutenant-General Birdwood, commanding the ANZAC, observed the loss of cohesion first hand:

> The first brilliant advance was now checked, for the Turks had been able to bring up guns and there was a constant hail of shrapnel all afternoon. In the scrub it was impossible to keep men together, and many stragglers found their way down gullies to the beach.[81]

Both defenders and attackers were in a perilous state as night descended. The line was held in an arc rising from the beach along Second Ridge (leading to 400 Plateau) through the isolated posts (Steele's, Courtney's and Quinn's) to the head of Monash Gully (Map 24.10); from there it descended down to the sea on the other side of the Sphinx, along Walker's Ridge. The front line formed an arc of rilled and gullied ground, just less than one and a half miles in length,

81 William Birdwood, *Khaki and Gown* (London: Ward, Lock & Co., 1941), p. 260.

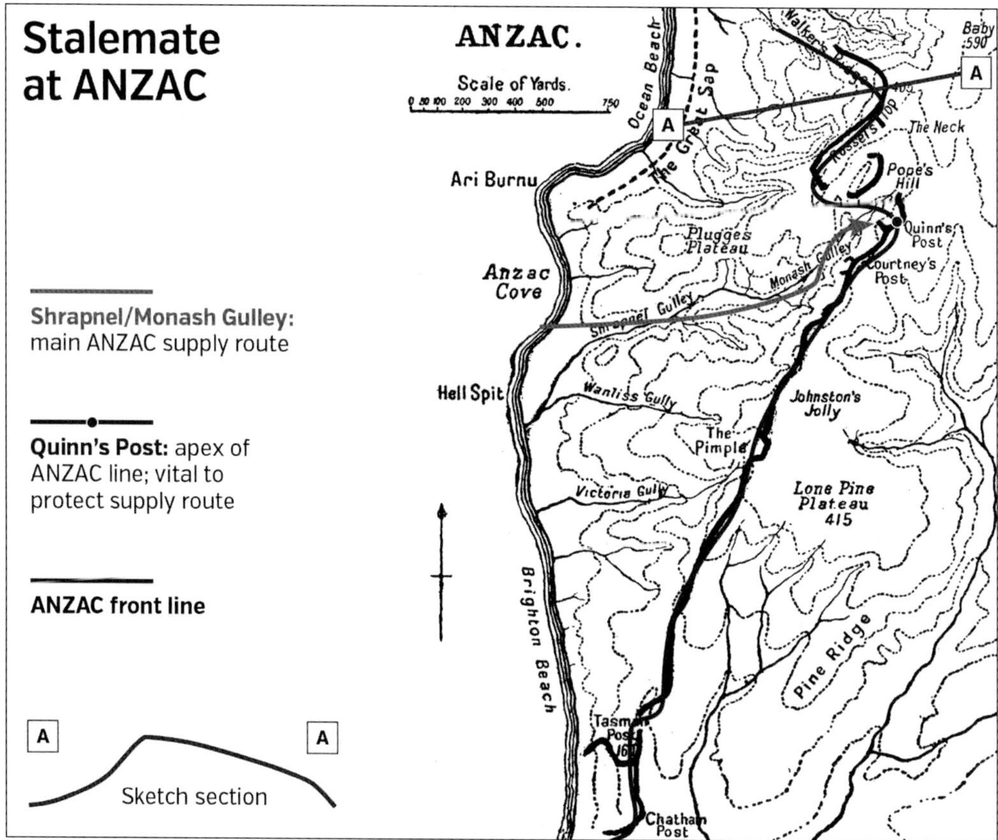

Map 24.10 Anzac trench lines secured at the ridge margin, Quinn's Post at the apex. (Author)

and its greatest penetration amounting to no more than a mile. Having landed and dug-in, the ANZAC was now ordered to await events and hold the line. Hamilton's communication to Birdwood, who had countenanced re-embarkation, was recounted in *Gallipoli Diary*:

> Your news is serious. But there is nothing for it but to dig yourselves right in and stick it out…Make a personal appeal to your men and Godley's [commander of the New Zealand and Australian Division] to make a supreme effort to hold their ground. Ian Hamilton.
>
> P.S. You have got through the difficult business, now you have only to dig, dig, dig, until you are safe. Ian H.[82]

82 Hamilton 1920, *op. cit.*, p. 144

Postscript and Commentary

Hamilton's plan required force of action that would overcome two of the main enemies to effective campaigns, the lack of effective intelligence, and inertia from combat shock – two of the main contributory factors[83] to "Clausewitzian friction":

> Altogether the result of this and other reconnaissances was to convince me that nothing but a thorough and systematic scheme for flinging the whole of the troops under my command very rapidly ashore could be expected to meet with success ...[84]
>
> There will be and can be no reconnaissance, no half measures, no tentatives ... No; we've got to take a good run at the Peninsula and jump plump on – both feet together. At a given moment we must plunge and stake everything on the one hazard.[85]

General Sir Ian Hamilton's words underline the fact that it was essential to pile men ashore, supported only by the artillery that could be provided by the navy standing off the cost of the peninsula. The Commander in Chief had placed his hopes in the experience of the regular troops of the 29th Division, who were expected to carry the intelligently defended shores of Cape Helles, and at the ANZAC bravura, with the inexperienced troops forcing their way to the heights of the topographically complex battleground that faced them north of Gaba Tepe.

In landing on a defended shore, the Allies in 1915 had hoped to take the defenders by force of arms and had hoped to drive the enemy before them in order to open up the Turkish coastal defences to attack, thereby letting the fleet thorough to threaten Constantinople, modern Istanbul. What would happen then is open to question, but hopes were high that the Turks would capitulate. What they found was somewhat different. At Helles, a well motivated, well trained and well led defence force occupying well sited and carefully planned "textbook" trenches, redoubts and barbed wire fortifications. It is axiomatic these days that landing on a defended shore the attackers need to land in force and greatly outnumber the defender; there needs to be adequate room to land troops, to manoeuvre and to bring up reserves.

In choosing his landing beaches, Hamilton was constrained by nature. The natural landing sites of Bulair and Gaba Tepe were also the best defended. Suvla Bay, the only area available to land large numbers of troops, was too far from the main objective, the coast of the Dardanelles. Instead, Hamilton decided to send his best trained troops to crack the toughest nut: a series of narrow and unpromising beaches, onto which he would have to cram six battalions landing from open boats or in a hastily improvised "landing craft infantry" in the form of the modified SS *River Clyde.* Little was left in reserve.

The gamble was costly, and the defenders were ready. The terrain of the southern peninsula, forged by the North Anatolian Fault system which created its strongly rectilinear drainage system, created narrow slot-like beaches and steep cliffs of limestone. The structure of these cliffs is of gentle flexures with fold axes paralleling the faults. Gently plunging rock flexures create open beaches, the outcrop of the coastal limestones typically arcing in "V" pattern, creating a perfect arc to create enfilade fields of fire. The defenders fortified the natural advantages of this

83 Watts, 2004, *op. cit.*, p. 17
84 Hamilton, 1917, *op. cit.*, p. 20
85 Hamilton, 1920, *op. cit.*, p. 96

outcrop pattern, using strong points behind the trench systems, and extensive belts of barbed wire to trap the attackers on open beaches. Machine guns or not, this trap was completed by the careful fire discipline of the Turks, who were silent until the first wave of attackers had leapt from their open boats onto an open beach. Once ashore they were trapped between the wire and the sea, a perfect "kill zone", and casualties were high. Exploitation of what "dead ground" was available, by experienced troops, was the factor that finally allowed the 29th Division ashore, at V and W beaches. Such is the quirk of fate that one metre of unpromising cliff – that of a truncated alluvial fan – was to be a deciding factor in allowing sufficient men ashore to storm the weakening defences at V Beach.

At Anzac Cove, the peculiar conditions of the still-active fault zone meant that the uplift of the soft, dry and friable strata that composed the Sari Bair range was a continuous process, a process that created a unique set of conditions and forced a heavily eroded, gullied and eroded landscape. The "structural grain" of the peninsula was such that three ridges paralleled the main faults, leading up to the summit of Sari Bair. These were accompanied by equally deep ravines either side, in turn gullied and cut through to create a complex and tortuous terrain. Whether or not the men landed "at the wrong location" – and there is evidence both ways – what faced Anzac was a difficult terrain that promoted confusion and required the discipline of experience to overcome. As the inevitable confusion, "the fog of war", set in so the grinding of friction meant, as at Helles later in the morning, the "two-footed jump" of Hamilton's men was restricted to the very margins of the peninsula. His gamble, the opportunity to escape the increasing inertia of friction and thereby carry the enemy, was lost. With the Ottomans skilfully defending the vulnerable points at Helles, using the natural characteristics of the ground to best advantage, the Allies were held and forced to re-gear for incremental attrition, for "bite and hold" tactics that would be costly, and require greater investment in supply lines, in men and materiel, in artillery and, significantly, in water supplies. These were hard to come by.

After 25 April, the "Battle of the Beaches", static trench positions similar to those of the Western Front developed. Soon after the landing at Cape Helles, the British overcame, with terrible losses, the Turkish positions located on the surrounding cliffs. Their final objective of this first phase was the summit of Achi Baba, the high point of the Kilid Bahr Plateau at 218 metres, which should have commanded the village of Kilid Bahr itself, one of the main fortresses of the Dardanelles. In fact, the view from Achi Baba is disappointing, with Commodore Roger Keyes, Chief of Staff to the admiral commanding the British Fleet, later commenting that it was: "an unpleasant shock to us to find that the forts we had hoped to destroy, with the assistance of observation from Alcitepe [Achi Baba] were not even visible from that gigantic fraud".[86]

Although it became an obsession of the Allied General Staff, Achi Baba was never captured. Instead, a series of bloody, set piece, frontal-assault battles for the village of Krithia and Achi Baba beyond ensued through the summer months, aided by inadequate land-based artillery and often ineffective naval gunfire over the supposedly inviting open glacis provided by the terrain at Helles. Stalemate was achieved some 50 metres in front of Krithia and remained there until the final Allied withdrawal from the peninsula in January 1916. As one participant, Joseph Murray was to comment in May 1915:

86 Keyes, reported in Elkins, 2001, *op. cit.*, p. 11.

> It appears that our tactics of advancing and digging in and then moving forward again, groping for the Turk's positions and losing quite a lot of men in doing so, does not achieve the desired result. We seem to be committed to trench warfare and all our ideals of capturing Achi Baba in a single day would have to be forgotten for the time being.[87]

Trench warfare in the Anzac sector was grim. Making the best of it, the Australians and New Zealanders fell into a routine that would ensure their part of the line was protected from Ottoman attacks. Everywhere in the frontline the conditions were poor. The relatively soft sediments enabled the relatively rapid development of rudimentary trench systems, although this was hampered in the opening hours of the campaign by an absence of adequate construction tools, and by the degree of root penetration. By the end of the campaign, the trench systems were complex with a parallel underground system of tunnels and saps, and with terraces cut in the reverse slope to provide rudimentary dwelling areas. At the apex of the line was Quinn's Post, at the head of the main supply gully; tightly held by the Anzacs in the face of repeated attacks, it represents the endurance of the occupiers in the face of severe and significant terrain issues, and a determined enemy.[88]

With the establishment of trench warfare conditions on the night of 25/26 April 1915, the campaign was stalled, effectively doomed. To come were attritional battles and a new offensive phase in August. These would come to naught. Hamilton's gamble had not paid off. Though there was undoubtedly more terrain intelligence than he alluded to in his personal accounts of the campaign, the planning was inadequate – even discounting the benefit of hindsight and the study of later campaigns. The Ottomans were a determined enemy, well led, motivated. The terrain of the peninsula, so beguiling for visitors, was deadly. At Helles, the peculiarities of the ground meant that the Ottoman defence was magnified, the effect of firepower enhanced. At Anzac, with minimal defenders, terrain did its job. Contributing to the confusion, adding to the tension felt by the attacking troops, the tortuous ground meant that the ANZAC troops were not only fighting a human enemy, they were fighting the terrain. There was no escape from the effects of friction.

The lessons of vantage, of force of arms and of specialist training are clear from this campaign. They were to influence British planning at least for the Normandy invasion. Terrain intelligence gathering was of paramount importance prior to the landings, and included considerations of going surfaces and vantage, and was to influence the selection of the beaches themselves.[89] The hurried preparations for the Gallipoli landings, the lack of a truly combined operations command, and the poor communications were lessons taken on board for the planning of the biggest amphibious landings in history. Although there are direct parallels between Gallipoli and Omaha Beach, where brave men alone struggled against the force of arms in well prepared, and terrain-advantaged positions, overall the Gallipoli campaign served as a lesson of what could go wrong. In this aspect at least, the Gallipoli campaign served a useful purpose, and the sacrifices of the men of the 29th Divisions in both World Wars, were not in vain.

87 Murray, *Gallipoli*, p. 74.

88 See discussion in Stanley, *Quinn's Post*.

89 See, for example, discussion in E.P.F. Rose & B.C. Pareyn, 'British applications of military geology for "Operation Overlord" and the Battle of Normandy, France, 1944' in J.R. Underwood & P. L. Guth (eds.) *Military Geology in War and Peace* (Boulder, Colorado: Geological Society of America, 1995), pp. 55-66; S. Badsey, 'Terrain as a factor in the Battle of Normandy, 1944' in Doyle & Bennett (eds.) *Fields of Battle*, pp. 265-66.

25

Guests of the Sultan: MEF Prisoners of War

Stephen Chambers

The history of the British prisoners of war in Turkey has faithfully reflected the peculiarities of the Turkish character. Some of these, at any rate to the distant spectator, are sufficiently picturesque; others are due to the mere dead-weight of Asiatic indifference and inertia; others again are actively and resolutely barbarous. It has thus happened that at the same moment there have been prisoners treated with almost theatrical politeness and consideration, prisoners left to starve and die through simple neglect and incompetence, and prisoners driven and tormented like beasts. The violent inconsistencies make it very difficult to give a coherent and general account of the experience of our men.[1]

During the First World War there were internationally accepted procedures, enshrined in both domestic military and international law, for the treatment of prisoners. Thus the Geneva Conventions of 1864 and 1906 respectively, stipulated that wounded men in enemy hands must be provided with proper medical care. Moreover, the Hague Conventions of 1899 and 1907 outlined a series of protocols that became the standard for the humane treatment of prisoners. Despite the fact that there were numerous no quarter acts amongst other atrocities[2] committed on the far-flung battlefields of 1914-18, the abuse and/or murder of prisoners of war (POWs) was more the exception than the rule throughout the Gallipoli campaign.

One of the worst First World War captivity death rates occurred during the Mesopotamian campaign, a consequence of the surrender of the Kut-al-Amara garrison after a lengthy siege (December 1915–April 1916). The majority of the Anglo-Indian captives – approximately 10,000 officers and men – subsequently experienced a horrific 1,000-mile desert "death march". The majority, already weakened by the effects of a long siege, harsh climate, food shortages and physical abuse, died by the hundreds enroute to prison camps. A post-war British Government report, *Treatment of British Prisoners of War in Turkey,* determined that 16,583 British, Indian and Dominion servicemen were "missing, believed captured" on the combined Turkish fronts

1 British Library (BL) IOR/L/MIL/7/18737: *Treatment of British Prisoners of War in Turkey* (London: HMSO, 1918).

2 Siegfried Sassoon, *Atrocities* (1917) in which the soldier-poet relates what a British serviceman told him about butchering prisoners.

Types of MEF prisoners: Indian, French, Australian and African.

during 1914-18.[3] Of that number, 3,290 were known to have perished with an additional 2,222 untraceable and presumed dead. These figures primarily relate to the Kut garrison. The number of known Gallipoli captives amounted to 512 officers and men.[4] Of this number, 142 are known to have perished in Turkish captivity, a staggering 28 percent of those captured at Gallipoli.[5] This was a result of the campaign's length and nature of the fighting during which the capture of individuals or small parties of men was a common occurrence.

At Gallipoli, captivity was considered a risky affair to be avoided if at all possible. Tales of German and Turkish atrocities, many unfounded, painted a lurid and sensationalist picture of violence and torture by "German Hun" and "Unspeakable Turk". The latter sobriquet was reinforced by the gruesome fate of Royal Marine Sergeant Ernest Turnbull who was found mutilated and dead during a February 1915 shore raid on the Dardanelles forts.[6] Similarly,

3 BL IOR/L/MIL/7/18737: *Treatment of British Prisoners of War in Turkey.*

4 Prisoners of War Australians Captured in Turkey – 1917 (NAA MP1565/4) and Australian Red Cross Society Wounded and Missing Enquiry Bureau Files, 1914-18 War and HQ RAF, List of British Prisoners of War in Turkey, 21-22 February 1916 (TNA AIR/1/892/204/5/697).

5 Patrick Gariepy, *British and Dominion Servicemen Captured at Gallipoli who Died in Captivity* (Eugene, Oregon: Privately published, 1999). This figure does not include those from the French *Corps Expeditionnaire d'Orient* who died in captivity.

6 On 26 February 1915, Midshipman Peverill William-Powlett of HMS *Vengeance* noted in his diary that during the RMLI raid on No.6 Fort they had "Only one was killed and three wounded. The one killed I am afraid was mutilated – the Turks venting their whole wrath on him. His head was smashed in, four bullet holes in his face, one in his wrist, one in [the] shoulder and one in the knee –

two unsubstantiated accounts of the Helles landings perpetuated the widespread torture and mutilation myth. The first concerned the discovery of a British corpse bound with barbed wire floating in the open sea. The second claimed that Irishmen taken prisoner at V Beach were found murdered and mutilated.[7]

Early Capture: "I immediately threw up my hands"

The first Entente servicemen to be taken captive were the crew of French submarine *Saphir*, when on 15 January 1915 it accidentally grounded whilst attempting to force the Dardanelles. It is believed that she managed to pass ten lines of mines and then either hit a mine or was hit by a Turkish shore battery before grounding. Her crew scuttled the boat leaving 14 who were killed or drowned and the remaining 13 were captured. This was one of four French submarines lost during the campaign. Three months later on 17 April 1915, the British submarine *E15* ran aground in the Dardanelles whilst attempting a similar passage into the Sea of Marmara. Unfortunately, having dived too deep, *E15* was overtaken by a strong current prior to running aground near Kephez Point and directly under the guns of the Dardanos Battery. Seven crewmen, including their commander Lieutenant Theodore Brodie, were killed and the remaining 25 officers and men captured. On the night of 25 April, Australian submarine *AE2* became the first Entente submarine to successfully pass through the Dardanelles. Spending the next four days marauding about the Sea of Marmara, her luck ran out when spotted by a Turkish torpedo boat. Damaged and scuttled, the entire crew, including her commander Lieutenant Commander Henry Hugh Stoker, were captured.

The first MEF prisoners captured on land were two French officers and 19 men deceived into captivity during a white-flag incident at Kum Kale on 25 April. Several Australians and at least one New Zealander[8] were captured at Anzac that same day, although their numbers may have been greater; no official record exists to collaborate this. No British prisoners were officially recorded that day. Had this been the case, they would have died before leaving the peninsula.[9] Many of those captured on land had advanced too far. In at least two recorded cases near the end of the campaign, men were captured after venturing the wrong way down trenches[10] that were

this was an explosive bullet that had blown his knee cap off. Both his legs were broken, and a bayonet wound in his abdomen."

7 Patrick Gariepy, *Gardens of Hell: Battles of the Gallipoli Campaign* (Lincoln, Nebraska: Potomac Books, 2014), pp. 14-15.

8 Pte. Thomas Burgess, Auckland Battalion, was wounded and captured on 25 April 1915, but died of the combined effects of wounds, typhus and appendicitis at Gulkhane Hospital, Constantinople on 25 September 1915.

9 Twenty-five POWs died when a British shell hit and destroyed a hospital in Maidos on 29 April. In a letter that Sergeant Alfred Rawlings, 2nd Bn, AIF, sent to his mother (published in the Melbourne *Argus*, 14 June 1918) he mentions "Kelly of the RDF" being"'one of the lucky ones" having escaped the shelling. It is probable that other wounded British soldiers like Private J Kelly, 1st Royal Dublin Fusiliers, were captured on, or just after, 25 April 1915.

10 D. Ogilvie, *The Fife and Forfar Yeomanry and 14th (F. & F. Yeo.) Battn.* (Whitefish, Montana: Kessinger Publishing reprint of 1921 edition). Shoeing Corporal W. Pearson, Fire & Forfar Yeomanry, was captured on 29 November 1915 whilst in the line at Highland Barricade in Azmak Dere, Suvla. He was carrying water when he mistakenly wandered into the Turkish lines and

half-occupied by the enemy. There were many such trenches at Gallipoli, where friend and foe were separated by a barricade or "bomb block."

It was during the Anzac landing that more than the "official" four Australian soldiers Charles Bean subsequently recorded were captured.[11] Unfortunately, some of their names have been lost to time. One known captive remains a mystery to this day. Private Edgar 'Rolun' Adams, 8th Battalion AIF, an 18-year old engineer and surveyor from Koorlong, Victoria, enlisted with his brother Frederick, a fruit grower, in September 1914. Born in Yorkshire, Fred immigrated to Australia with his family aged two. Both siblings joined up on the outbreak of war. Landing at Anzac on the morning of 25 April, Fred was killed and Edgar reported missing.[12] He was last seen that afternoon when the battalion was forced to retire in the face of strong enemy resistance. The fighting was heavy, and it was normal for a man to disappear amongst the thick scrub, broken ground and resultant confusion. In fact, no one realized that he was missing until the first roll call was taken days later. Even then, it was considered possible that he had been cut off and was either "out there" alone or fighting with another battalion. Subsequently denoted as missing, those failing to turn up within a week were assumed to have been either killed or captured. In Edgar Adams' case, the mystery deepened when a bottle washed ashore near Montaza, Alexandria. It contained a note that read: "Am prisoner about 2 miles from where we landed between the dry lake and the other. E.R.C. Adams, 8 AIF."[13]

The International Red Cross Society in Switzerland immediately initiated enquiries through the Ottoman Red Crescent, but the latter, although good about reporting Entente captives, responded that it had no knowledge of him. On 11 November 1915, Sergeant David Muir, 8th Battalion AIF, made the following statement from No.3 Australian General Hospital at West Mudros:

> I have received letters from Adams' people and as a matter of fact wrote to them only yesterday and gave them all the information I have been able to obtain, which is that Adams was missed between 3 and 4 o'clock on the 25th April during the retirement at Anzac and has not been heard of since. My own opinion is that he was killed as the casualties were very heavy indeed on that day. His brother was shot through the head on the Tuesday night about 12 o'clock within a few feet of me and was buried on the Wednesday morning.[14]

Weeks dragged into months and years, and still nothing was learned of Edgar's fate. To make matters worse for his family news that his older brother, Fred, reached home that he had been killed the same day that Edgar disappeared.

captured. Unfortunately, Privates R. McGregor and T. Moffat of the same regiment repeated this the following day. McGregor and Moffat survived captivity, Pearson died in captivity on 25 May 1916.

11 The four men were Captain Ronald McDonald, Lieutenant William Elston, Private Reginald Lushington and Bugler Frederick Ashton

12 Pte. Fred Adam was killed on 25 April 1915. In Ron Austin's battalion history *Cobbers in Khaki* (Rosebud: Slouch Hat Publications, 1997), veteran Bill Groves of C Company remembers Fred: "The shooting started, and we got caught in the crossfire … [the battalion was then given orders to dig in] I was on the shovel and a fellow named Fred Adams was on the pick. He got shot through the forehead and he died instantly."

13 National Archives of Australia (NAA) B2455: ADAMS, E.R.C.

14 Ibid.

Fellow Victorian, Private Fred Symonds, 5th Battalion AIF, remarked on 20 May 1915:

> Heard the other day that Fred and Rolun Adams, of Mildura, whom I know well, were killed and missing respectively since the first Sunday, so looks like both dead. Terribly hard for their parents, as they are the only two boys in the family. I feel set up over it, as they were such decent chaps.[15]

By 1918, the case was finally settled by a court of enquiry held in London that ruled that Edgar was captured and died in enemy hands. Edgar was an extraordinary case, at least in terms of a message in a bottle. If he was held as a prisoner he did not appear on any of the POW lists provided by authorities, although we know today that these lists were inaccurate.

Lance Corporal Vivian Cyril Brooke, 12th Battalion AIF, is another interesting case and a known 25 April captive. Brooke, a 27-year-old bank clerk from New Town, Tasmania was a well-known amateur athlete, footballer and cricketer. He enlisted on 20 August 1914 and landed with the battalion amongst the initial waves of the covering force. Private Trevor Young, a fellow athlete and also from New Town, of the same battalion reported that Brooke was last seen in the vicinity of White's Gully on the first day of the landing.[16] The Turks were counter attacking in that area and a withdrawal was decided upon, but Brooke refused to retire. He was evidently wounded in this action and was taken prisoner, later transported to the nearby town of Maidos (Eceabat).

This was confirmed by Sergeant Alfred John Rawlings, 2nd Battalion AIF, who was also taken prisoner during the first day of the landing.[17] He was in the same Maidos hospital with Brooke and told the Red Cross in 1919 that Brooke's arm was torn off when a shell hit the building. Brooke was not the only casualty. During the same naval bombardment on 29 April some "twenty-five wounded British became victims of the conflagration, which spread with irresistible force."[18] Brooke was rescued and operated on by the Turkish doctors at Chanak (Çannakale) and "I saw him about two hours after he had been wounded and was with him until he died at Biga where we both had been taken in bullock wagons. He was barely conscious most of the time and was buried in the Christian cemetery at Biga."[19]

One of the four officially named prisoners was Bugler Frederick Ashton, 11th Battalion AIF, who was captured while tending the wounded on a hill named Baby 700. The hill had changed hands up to five times during the first day of the landing before, under immense pressure, the Australians yielded the ground. During that afternoon Ashton was in the process of bandaging a wounded New Zealander soldier when the poor fellow was hit again. Ashton wrote in his report after the war: "He was in terrible agony and asked me to finish him off. I told him to lie still while I went and sought a stretcher-bearer. But when I looked around me I could see no sign

15 Private Fred Symonds diary was sent home and published in the *Inglewood Advertiser* (September 1915).

16 Trevor Young, later Lance Sergeant, was killed with 12th Bn, AIF, on the Western Front in 1917.

17 Rawlings was awarded the Meritorious Service Medal in 1920 "in recognition of devotion to duty and valuable services rendered whilst prisoner of war." Rawlings returned to Australia in 1919.

18 Otto Liman von Sanders, *Five Years in Turkey* (Uckfield: Naval & Military Press reprint of 1927 edition), p. 72.

19 Biga is about 90 kilometres northeast of Çannakale.

of our former firing-line, nor could I see anyone – they seemed to have vanished completely". Ashton still looking for a stretcher-bearer became disoriented and instead of descending into Monash Valley, found himself in Turkish held Mule Valley by mistake. Here he found a wounded Australian who had been shot through the hip. Ashton wrote:

> I helped him down the gully till he could go no further, while I went on to see if I could find a stretcher. I heard a shout, and on looking up, saw about 8 or 10 Turks covering me with their rifles. At the same time bullets were coming from the rear on the right. I immediately threw up my hands and the Turks immediately came forward and knocked me on the head with their rifle-butts, dazing me.[20]

Ashton was interrogated there, and later in what appeared to be a Turkish Headquarters. He stated:

> I was taken into a tent and interrogated in Turkish by some officers, who gave the job up as hopeless, and sent for another officer who could speak about four words of English. They produced a big map of Egypt, the Suez Canal, and the Dardanelles, and made me try to understand that they wished me to tell them how long it had taken me to come from Egypt; and also, whether I had been to Cairo, Lemnos, Mudros etc. Amongst my papers was a money order from Australia drawn on the Post Office at Cairo, and when they saw that, they knew I had been evading the truth. So they ceased questioning me, giving the job up as hopeless. One of the officers signed to me to follow him and I went into his tent, where he provided me with a two-course meal, after which I was sent into his orderly's tent, and was given an old Turkish overcoat to sleep under. After I had been asleep some hours, I was woken up and taken out of the tent and found three more Australians standing outside.[21]

The three Australians were Captain Ronald McDonald, Lieutenant William Elston and Private Reginald Lushington, all from 16th Battalion AIF. Ashton continued:

> In the morning we were marched to another Turkish Headquarters, where we were given some boiled eggs and bread for breakfast, and from there to a seaport. After the examination we were taken to an empty house and placed in a small room, where we were given a meal and then taken to another room furnished with two beds. At this place we received exactly the same treatment as the officers, our Battalion colour patches having apparently misled the Turks as to our rank.[22]

McDonald, Elston and Lushington, the latter a Hindustani and Tamil speaker, had all been captured in what was an embarrassing misunderstanding in the "fog of war". By the evening of 25 April there was much confusion, not only on how the battle was going, but also where the ANZAC and Turkish positions were. When 3rd (Australian) Brigade was pushed back with heavy losses, gaps had appeared in the line. In the failing light, Lieutenant-Colonel Harold

20 NAA B2455: ASHTON, F.
21 Ibid.
22 Ibid.

Pope, commanding officer 16th Battalion AIF, positioned his battalion on a spur that would later bear his name towards the top end of Monash Valley. Pope was made aware by a sergeant of that brigade that 'Indian' troops were fighting on the left. The message "Don't fire, the Indians are on our left" was duly passed down the line. Pope sent Lieutenant Elston, supported by Private Lushington, forward through the thick scrub to make contact with this left flank. Pope and Captain McDonald heard them talking to the "Indians" who apparently asked for a senior officer. McDonald went forward but was stopped by a figure with a rifle. McDonald said "I'm an English sahib. I want burra sahib" (literally meaning "big man" or officer in charge). Pope heard these voices and as he moved towards McDonald, something made him suspicious. Shot at, Pope only escaped capture by plunging himself down a 30-foot steep slope back into Monash Valley. They were not "Indians" but Turks. McDonald, Elston and Lushington were surrounded and all made prisoner, but luckily not Pope. If it was not unlucky enough for these three men to fall into the hands of the Turks, what made it worse was McDonald was carrying the battalion orders and maps.[23] This was not a good start for 16th Battalion AIF.

"They are surrendering, take them"

In the heat of battle there is often a fine line between the period when the killing ceases and a surrendering enemy is captured. Private Alexander Nixon, 1/4th KOSB, was wounded in the assault on trench E12 near Achi Baba Nullah, Helles, and was "bayonetted six times in the back whilst lying there". Only to be saved by a "Turk officer, at the point of his revolver, ordered the Turks to release me."[24] Others disappeared without a trace, and a number were witnessed to have been killed after surrendering. At Suvla, on 9 August 1915 the 6th East Yorkshire Regiment, CO Lieutenant-Colonel Henry Moore, led the 32nd Brigade advance up the slopes of Tekke Tepe. Cut off, unsupported and outnumbered, the forward elements of the battalion, mainly D Company, found themselves surrounded by Turks.[25] Captain Derrick Elliot wrote of the incident:

> It was impossible to advance further; the enemy was in large numbers round by the east of the hill. I waited for reinforcements. We were now about thirty strong and under heavy rifle fire. Lieutenant-Colonel Moore, Lieutenant Still and Major Brunner RE came up about fifteen minutes later with some more men and I reported to Colonel Moore that the enemy was above us in very superior numbers and, after considering, he ordered us to retire with the remnants. I took charge of a small party to cover the retirement where necessary. When nearly at the bottom of the hill we were surrounded, and Colonel Moore ordered us to surrender. When we had surrendered Colonel Moore made an attempt to sit on the bank of the ravine and was bayoneted through the back; he died about ten minutes later.[26]

23 Reginald Lushington, *A Prisoner of the Turks, 1915-1918* (London: Simpkin, Marshall, Hamilton, Kent & Co., Ltd., 1923), pp. 2-3.

24 *The Glasgow Herald* (7 August 1915), and *The Scotsman* (10 August 1915).

25 Stephen Chambers, *Suvla: August Offensive* (Barnsley: Pen & Swords, 2011) pp. 80-83.

26 TNA CAB 45/242: Statement made to War Office by Captain R.D. Elliott.

Lieutenant John Still, 6th East Yorks observed:

> Of those taken with me, one was not molested; one was fired at from five yards' distance, missed and quietly captured; one was beaten and fired at. Thank God the man who fired at him hit the man who was beating him and broke his wrist. The fourth, my Colonel, was bayoneted. Then, for the moment, their fury ceased. He did not seem to suffer any pain at all, only to be intensely thirsty. He drank the whole of the contents of my water bottle as well as his own. They even allowed me to carry him on my back; and on my back the Colonel died. May he rest in peace! He was a brave man, and a good friend to me.[27]

The Turkish counter attack on 9 August was a decisive move in stopping the half-hearted British advance at Suvla, even catching some British units by complete surprise. Turkish officer Ismail Hakki Sunata, *2/35th Infantry Regiment*, wrote how his men soon overran the British forward elements:

> Lieutenant Cerkez Fehmi was shouting "They are surrendering, take them". Five or ten soldiers had got there ahead of me and were bayoneting them when I shouted to stop them. These British are either really stupid or unprepared. In a strange country, in a streambed, they had sat down to have breakfast. Jam, biscuits, sugar, chocolate, butter, cheese, forks and napkins. The napkins are pure cotton. They had been surprised at breakfast. They could not escape. Or did not. Several of them are dying. How terrible. I did not think of killing and dying any more. We have to take them prisoner. I sent the three survivors back with two of my soldiers with a note saying 'Prisoners'.[28]

A similar incident occurred a few days later on 12 August 1915 at Suvla during the advance of 163rd Brigade, 54th (East Anglian) Division, in the area of Kuchuk Anafarta Ova. One battalion, 1/5th Norfolk Regiment, had advanced so far that they ended up separated from the remainder of the brigade. Unsupported, a Turkish counter attack quickly overwhelmed these men causing heavy casualties. An eye witness stated seeing Captain Arthur Pattrick and Sergeant Ernest Beart from that battalion disarmed and marched into captivity.[29] Neither man was seen again; they do not appear on any prisoner of war lists. Were these prisoners killed by the Turks or maybe a British shell? Several men from this battalion made captive and survived to tell the tale; Captain Cedric Coxon and Bugler Donald Swan were both wounded near a cluster of stone buildings and, whilst trying to make their way back to the British lines, were captured. In total the Turks captured at least two officers and 31 other ranks during 163rd Brigade's assault. Two officers and 15 other ranks were from the 1/5th Norfolks; eight of these were to die in captivity, whilst 13 other ranks were from the 1/8th Hants and three were from the 1/5th Suffolks.[30]

27 John Still, *A Prisoner in Turkey* (London: John Lane, 1920), p. 30.
28 Ismail Hakki Sunata, *From Gallipoli to the Caucasus* (Gelibolu'danKafkaslara) (Istanbul: Turkiye Is Bankasi, 2003).
29 The witness was Private Alfred Pearson, Lynn Company, 1/5th Norfolks. See Nigel McCrery, *The Vanished Battalion* (London: Simon & Schuster, 1992), p. 74.
30 Ibid.

On 8 August 1915 a tragic episode in Australian military history occurred when a demoralised 4th Australian Brigade failed in their assault on Hill 971. There were "agonising scenes during the retreat, with the uncharacteristic abandonment by Australian soldiers of their dead and injured comrades"[31] Officers and men from 14th Battalion AIF were amongst those left in advanced positions without realising a withdrawal had happened. The battalion's historian described the incident:

> Prior to the retirement, a small handful of C Company had forced its way into the Turkish position and after a vigorous struggle, been cut off and destroyed. Opposite our left flank were three small outlying ridges held by the Turks in front of their main position on the Abdel Rahman Bair. Lieut. Warren. O.C. of C Company – a man of keen and resolute character – promptly determined to attack them, but falling mortally wounded, ordered Lieut. Luscombe to push on. The Turks retreated behind the second ridge as Luscombe advanced with about a dozen men, reinforced a few minutes later by Lieut. Curlewis with several more men. Curlewis was soon mortally wounded by machine gun fire. Reinforcements were badly wanted, and a 15th Battalion man volunteered to carry back a message requesting them but was killed by shrapnel while crossing the ridge enroute. The Turks now counter-attacked. The handful of Australians built a barricade of ammunition boxes, and fought desperately until several had been killed, when the thirteen survivors (only two of whom were unwounded) surrendered. Sgt. Neyland, Cpl. Kerr, and Pte. Masterton did excellent work under very trying conditions. This little body of brave men is believed to have made the furthest advance in the ranks of the 4th Brigade that day.[32]

One of their numbers, Lance Corporal George Kerr, recounted the moment of capture:

> Several were wounded, myself amongst them, and when one of the wounded men asked the officer [Lieutenant Leslie Luscombe] if he did not think it would be better to sling it in, the officer replied, "The word to surrender will never come from me". I think they told him that he had better sling it in, as we had done all we could do and were nearly all wounded. Even then, he hesitated and after a little consideration, pulled his cap off his head (for what reason I do not know) and threw his revolver away and put up his hands.[33]

Australian Official Historian Charles Bean wrote that "on other occasions, very few of the wounded left in Turkish hands survived. Some were shot or bayoneted." Lieutenant Luscombe's party was slightly luckier and he and several of his men were captured.[34]

The Turks were often in no mood to take prisoners. Private Patrick O'Connor, a 23-year old farmer from Brunswick, Victoria serving with 14th Battalion AIF, was hit in the foot during the assault and became isolated. He wrote of his first face-to-face encounters with the Turks that day:

31 Peter Pederson, *Monash as Military Commander* (Melbourne: Melbourne University Press, 1985), p. 112.
32 Newton Wanliss, *The History of the Fourteenth Battalion, A.I.F.* (Melbourne, 1929), pp. 62-3.
33 AWM PRO 953: Diary transcript kept by George Kerr (27 April 1916).
34 C.E.W. Bean, *The Story of Anzac*, Vol. II (Sydney: Angus & Roberstson, 1938), p. 663.

Shortly afterwards I saw a Turk coming towards me through the bushes at my rear. I closed my eyes and pretended to be asleep. The Turk touched me with his foot. Then he unbuttoned my tunic and saw a money belt that I was wearing. Apparently, he was unable to see how it unbuckled for he seized hold of it and bumped me up and down by it until it snapped. The process gave me intense pain. The Turk took the belt away with him, gaining thereby about £8/=, and left me. Another marauding Turk came along shortly and went through my pockets. He got a few cards and letters, but missed my watch, which I had strapped into a Havelock tobacco tin. As soon as I was wounded I had worked off my equipment, hiding the water bottle in a bush within easy reach of me. This second Turk emptied the beef and bully beef out of my haversack but did not take them away. Then he left me. A third Turk came along. He was luckier than his predecessor for he found my watch and also robbed me of a ring I was wearing. I had not been able to "gammon sleep" all the time. Seeing that I was awake and conscious, he signed to me to come along with him. I signed back that I couldn't walk & that I wanted a stretcher. I was sparring for a time, thinking that the longer I could keep him the better chance I should have of being picked up by some of our own fellows. However, he, too, eventually went away and never came back. Within 10 minutes another Turk came along. On his way to me he had to pass a number of other Australian wounded. I saw the brute draw a bayonet from the scabbard of a wounded Australian and then thrust it into the wounded man's stomach. I yelled out at him. I could stand it no longer. He heard me all right. I cursed him in good Australian. I could no longer play dumb. When he came towards me I at first pretended to be asleep. But he soon made it clear that he had heard me speak. He picked up a 4-pound lump of rock that lay nearby and, holding it in his hand, began to pound my head with it. When I raised my hands to fend the blows off my head he transferred his attentions to my body, about the ribs. Eventually he battered me till I lost consciousness. When I came to there was a party of four or five Turks nearby. They were talking loudly and rapidly, and it was their voices that had wakened me. They signed to me to follow them, but when they found that I was helpless they seized hold of my hands and began hauling me down low towards a gully nearby. My idea is that they intended down there to "do me in" properly and then strip me. But an officer suddenly appeared, accompanied by a Turkish orderly, the latter carrying a rifle. I think the officer was a German; he certainly was not a Turk. As soon as they saw the officer they dropped me and started to run away. But when the officer called them they came back again, the Turkish orderly covering them with his rifle. At the officer's orders the Turks packed me up and carried me to him. He did not speak English, but I heard him say "hospital." I was handed into the care of the armed orderly. He also ordered me to walk. I worked myself along for about 10 yards, backwards, using my hands. So far the fire had been so intense that I had not been able to sit up and apply my field dressing. When I had scrambled along, in the fashion indicated, for about 10 yards, I signed to the orderly that I could go no further. He cocked his rifle and put the muzzle to my ear. But I spied a dug-out in the side of the hill and eventually managed to scramble my way into it. When I got there the orderly apparently wished me to go further. He prodded me with the rifle and again threatened me with it. But when he saw that I was "clean done in" he left me.[35]

35 AWM AWM30 B1.27: Repatriation Statement – Private P. O'Connor; NAA B2455: O'CONNOR PATRICK, pp. 24-26.

The man whom O'Connor had seen bayoneted in the stomach was Private Brendan Calcutt of D Company, a member of the 6th Reinforcements who had only arrived at Anzac before the attack. On 18 December 1916 he died of septicaemia in Hadji-Kiri camp.[36]

Of the others, Kerr, who had been wounded in the left thigh and right arm, was threatened with execution for holding himself with his right hand while urinating. This, he realised, was a violation of Islamic custom, so he quickly changed hands and thus saved his life. Luscombe, who was unconscious after a bullet grazed the side of his head, had his boots stolen off his feet, but a Turkish officer ordered the thief to put them back on their owner. Others were stripped of their personal possessions and sometimes articles of uniform. Most sustained beatings with fists or rifle butts. When the violence ended they were marched to the rear, where the wounded were treated.

Rifleman Joseph Stallard, 1/8th Hants (Princess Beatrice's Isle of Wight Rifles) was born and bred on the Isle of Wight. A pre-war Territorial, he was unmarried and apprenticed as a coppersmith to Messrs. W. White and Sons of Cowes. On 12 August 1915 he was wounded and captured during the assault across the Kuchak Anafarta Ova, Suvla, along with several other Hants and men from 1/5th Norfolks and 1/4th Suffolks. Private Daniel Creedon, an Australian, recorded the moment this group arrived:

> We got out of bed and discovered that there were twenty-eight in all and had been captured at Anafarta where a new landing had been made. They told us that some of them had been treated well when they had been captured but there were others who had been very badly treated. They told us that thousands of our men who had been wounded had been bayoneted by the Turks. One of them told me that he had been captured with about fifteen others and when the Turks had got them together they had lined them up and fired point blank at them from about thirty yards, killing one man and wounding another, the one they wounded was bayoneted by one of the Turks. One of the number [Stallard] who came to hospital died a few days after from neglect I think.[37]

Stallard died of his wounds in Tasch Kishla (Taşkışla) Hospital, Constantinople on 25 August 1915, aged 19 years. In the *Isle of Wight County Press* (16 October 1915) Rifleman Stallard's death was reported and last letter to his mother, written from captivity on 22 August 1915, was published:

> Just a line to let you know I am in hospital in Constantinople. I was wounded in the back and was picked up by the Turks and taken to a dressing-station. It has been a bit bad and at present I cannot sit up and write, so Alec Mabb [Corporal Mabb, 1/8th Hants] is doing it for me. The people here are very good and the doctors A1, so I expect it will soon be all right. I hope you will not upset yourself now that you know where I am, and that I am in good hands.[38]

36 One of his brothers, Lance Corporal Gerald Calcutt, 7th Battalion AIF, was killed in action at Anzac on 4 May 1915.

37 AWM RCDIG1062409: Pte. Daniel Creedon diary (unpublished).

38 *Isle of Wight County Press* (16 October 1915).

The Turks were by no means alone in their reluctance to take prisoners. Lieutenant Frank Yeo, No. 4 Squadron, RNAS Armoured Car Detachment, wrote the following in a letter home during the Battle of Gully Ravine (28 June–5 July 1915). The correspondence is dated 28 June:

> Have just been up to our front trench, the sights are too ghastly for words, our men have done wonders. The Turks have left everything behind them, rifles, ammunition, water bottles, etc. The place is covered with dead and wounded. I found a Turkish officer shamming he was hurt. I felt inclined to shoot him before he shot some of our men, the Tommies were furious. I had an awful job to save his life, eventually I ordered two Tommies to take him to the Base.[39]

Chief Petty Officer Gerald Sharkey, in the same RNAS squadron as Yeo, recalled his attitude to the taking of prisoners in his diary:

> 28 April: The Turks are doing a lot of dirty work such as killing our wounded & cutting up our dead, but we can play the same game, & by orders – no prisoners are to be taken.
> 1 May: No quarter is shown here either as the Turks from the start did dirty work & the Australians & Marines are paying them back in their own coin. Strict orders have been issued that no prisoners are to be taken so everybody is shot. At the top of the Gully on the road down to the beach stands a Sgt Major who examines all stretchers as the wounded are being carried down & if the being be a German or a Turk the order rings out "Drop it & stand clear!" Immediately there is a sharp report & the wounded man is a dead one.
> 22 May: The Turks made a desperate attack but were driven back leaving 500 dead & wounded in front of our position, also a few prisoners who never reached the beach.
> 3 June: Up to the present my unit has not taken a single prisoner which is something to boast about. We up our minds on that point after the horrible sights we saw when we first landed. I shall remind them once again tomorrow. One has only to think what these Huns did to the Belgians & I say that when you catch one, kill him slowly, but make sure that you are doing away with him. I can give hundreds of examples of their dirty ways.[40]

Few diarists were as open as Sharkey in describing the treatment of Turkish prisoners, but he was certainly not alone. Men on both sides were driven to near-madness by the sights they had witnessed and saw nothing at all wrong with taking out their frustrations on the enemy.

Captain Hicks, 10th Hants, wrote of the events on 9 August in and around The Farm, a plateau close to Chunuk Bair. He witnessed two New Zealanders bringing in four snipers they had just captured. The snipers were led off to be shot: "the Turks caught us by the hand and begged for mercy. But we weren't feeling very merciful to snipers just then."[41]

39 Frank Yeo, 'Letters from Frank', *The Gallipolian* (No. 57, 1988), p. 18.
40 IWM: Documents 2791, G.V. Sharkey.
41 TNA: CAB 45/254, Captain F. M. Hicks, 10th Battalion, Hampshire Regiment, diary, 8-10 August 1915.

Interrogation: "I will tell you everything"

Those that survived the initial capture were then questioned by Turkish or German officers, either in English or French. Many of the original interrogation reports survive in the Turkish Military archives and can make interesting reading. One report on Private John Regan, 5th Connaught Rangers, who was taken prisoner at Hill 60 on 21 August states: "He does not know anything as he is an illiterate person. Even his speech is incomprehensible."[42] It makes you think whether a strong Irish accent proved a challenge too much. Another soldier, Private James, 32nd Field Ambulance, captured on Kiretch Tepe has in his report "He is trying to confuse us by not telling anything."[43] According to Article 9 of the Hague Convention (1907) every "prisoner of war is bound to give, if he is questioned on the subject, his true name and rank, and if he infringes this rule, he is liable to have the advantages given to prisoners of his class curtailed."

Lieutenant Leslie Luscombe, who was Patrick O'Connor's platoon officer, was interrogated by none other than General Liman von Sanders. He wrote:

> As required by the terms of the Geneva Convention I answered questions concerning my name, rank and regiment without hesitation. I then politely refused to answer any further questions. After further attempts by the interpreter to obtain more information from me, I was agreeably surprised to find that General von Sanders respected my refusal to answer further questions. He ordered the Turkish interpreter to desist from asking further questions and I was taken back to the tent which I had just left. Subsequent contact with other German officers during my sojourn in the land of the Turks confirmed my impression that they looked on their Turkish allies as an uncivilized race of people and they wished to show the British officers that they, the Germans, were truly civilized.[44]

Interestingly, one of Sanders' staff officers, a German naval officer, told Lieutenant John Still, that they found it almost impossible to get the Turks to take prisoners, or having taken them, to keep them alive.[45] Still experienced this firsthand!

Prisoners were routinely questioned by their captors, but these interrogations seem generally to have produced little in the way of intelligence for their captors. When the campaign ended with the final evacuation in January 1916 most interrogations decreased or stopped. The naval campaign continued in that region and a particular interest in Entente submarines prompted impromptu questioning:

> Some of us were taken out one by one to be interviewed by an officer who spoke English for information regarding our movements while in the Sea of Marmora and questions about the boat, but he didn't learn anything good for him. So about 10 of us were interviewed out

42 Dr Ög Alb Ahmet Tetik(Ed), *Prisoners of War at the Canakkale Battles: Testimonies and Letters,* Vols. I & II (Ankara: Genelkurmay, Basimevi, 2009).

43 Ibid.

44 Leslie Luscombe, *The Story of Harold Earl: Australian* (Brisbane: W. R. Smith & Paterson, 1970).

45 Still, *A Prisoner in Turkey.*

> of the crew but we were not allowed back into the same room. As each man finished he was marched into another room and we were not allowed to see or speak to the remainder.[46]

Some officers, unlike Luscombe, said rather more than they should have done. Second Lieutenant Stanley Jordan, 9th Battalion AIF, a 21-year old British born accountant from Lismore, NSW, was commissioned from the rank of sergeant in the field at Gallipoli. He was captured on 28 June during the assault on Sniper's Ridge, in an attack that was supposed to draw off Turkish reinforcements from the Battle of Gully Ravine at Helles. One man captured with Jordan was Private David Creedon, 9th Battalion AIF. Creedon refers to him as 'Lieut. J' so was hesitant to mention his full name for reasons that will become clear:

> When we arrived at the dressing station I saw two more prisoners from our platoon (G. King and J. O'Callaghan) also the platoon commander (Lieut. J.) very soon after another was brought in (C. Matthews). King and O'Callaghan were wounded in the legs, the officer had a slight flesh-wound in the forearm. Matthews had a nasty wound in the upper part of the right arm. All our wounds were dressed, and we were given plenty of cigarettes and a cup of coffee each. Matthews, King and O'Callaghan were captured with Lieut. J. They told me that they got to the bottom of the ridge – there were five of them together at the time – here O'Callaghan was wounded. They considered it was useless to stop there so they worked back a bit and discovered a fairly safe position. Here they dug-in themselves with O'Callaghan. When they had got themselves dug-in Lieut. J. came running down the hill without equipment or rifle. They thought he was badly wounded, so they dug him in – after they had dug him in, he drank all the water they had. When they were finished digging in Lieut. J. sent one of the number for reinforcements – he knew then he was cut off – after this one of them proposed to open fire on the enemy, but the Lieut. (a British officer) gave them orders not to fire as they might draw fire on him. He then gave them orders to go down further to open fire. The place he sent them to was a ploughed field without a vestige of cover; they were four of them against a couple of hundred Turks. They had not gone very far when one of the number was killed (O'Sullivan) and another wounded (King). The remaining two helped the wounded one back to where they were before. One of these (Lee) he sent for reinforcements and wanted the other (Matthews) to go back and keep up fire but seemed to think better of it and after some time sent him also for reinforcements. Lee had gone about ten yards when he was hit in the abdomen; Matthews went about the same distance when he was hit. After our wounds had been attended to we were placed on mules and sent to a General. On arriving here, we were taken into the General's dug-out and were again given cigarettes. The only one who was questioned here was the Officer. The questions that I remember which were asked him were these: Q. Where do you get your water from? A. We get some from the boats and some from the gullies. Q. How many men are there? A. About twenty thousand. Q. Are all your trenches covered? A. Some are covered, and some are open. Q. What time do the men have their breakfast? A. Between six and seven o'clock. Q. There is a gun somewhere near your trenches on the right? A. There is one

46 National Library of Australia (NLA) 6540844: Diary of Able Seaman Albert Edward Knaggs, Royal Australian Navy, May 1915.

9th Battalion AIF prisoners captured near Sniper's Ridge, 28 June 1915 (L to R): Second Lieutenant Stanley Jordan, Private William Allen and Private Daniel Creedon who died (February 1917) in captivity; Jordan and Allen were repatriated after the Armistice. (Başar Eryöner)

> on the trenches and one – but C. Matthews interrupted and said they were everywhere. Lieut. J. got nettled at this and said that he was giving the information and did not want assistance. However, Lieut. J. then turned to the interpreter and said, "I will tell you everything after." No more questions were asked after this. But Lieut. J. started craving to the Turks for mercy saying, "Will you give me mercy and good treatment for myself and my men and I will tell you everything" – this was after they (the Turks) had told us they were sending us to Hospital.[47]

Although this may seem like a reward for his "cooperation", officers did on the whole live through captivity in fair comfort. Jordan, promoted to lieutenant in 1917, was repatriated in November 1918 and arrived in Alexandria five days before the Armistice was signed. Whether or not he was punished for so freely offering up information to the enemy is not known; Creedon did not survive the war, dying of typhus in captivity on 27 December 1917. It is likely that Jordan's conduct was never reported, his service record does not mention it.

47 AWM RCDIG1062409: Pte. Daniel Creedon diary (unpublished).

Constantinople Journey

Those who recovered from the initial shock of capture and interrogation had a long journey ahead of them, and this was rarely without danger. Private O'Connor recounted his experience:

> While we were at this dressing station our shrapnel opened up and poor Woods received another wound in the arm, making four. At about 5 o'clock in the morning Turkish Red Crescent carts came for the wounded. Each ambulance cart carried four stretcher cases and in them we were taken a journey of some 10 miles to another dressing station. Here there were two German doctors and we were put to bed on pallets of clean straw. The German doctor gave us tea; in fact, they were good to our wounded in every way. But we only remained at this dressing station for about an hour. Then we were carried about a quarter of a mile on stretchers and placed on other carts. These were Turkish transport carts – wide at the top and narrowing at the floor. They were jolty and uncomfortable and riding in them under our circumstances was something to remember. They were also short in the body, these transport carts; the tail-board appeared to be too close up, and we could not stretch our bodies. I had to hold up my wounded leg the best way I could. Then the Turks in charge were very bad drivers. They loafed along over the smooth patches of road and trotted over the bumpy patches. Moreover, the surly driver refused to allow us to do what we could to make ourselves comfortable. At about 2 o'clock in the morning two of us were capsized out of our cart into the middle of the road. The cumbrous cart had lurched and thrown us out. We narrowly escaped being run over by the carts that were following up, but the drivers managed to pull up in time. My comrade in misfortune had been shot through the stomach and we both fairly screamed with pain. Our sorry plight seemed to highly edify & amuse the Turks. They gathered around and laughed heartily at us. We were too badly done up to properly curse them. The Turks heaved us back into the cart and we journeyed on without mishap until about 8 a.m. I can't say precisely where we were, but I was on the coast. Alongside a pier there lay a small steamer, probably a pleasure launch before the war. She was flying a hospital flag, but I rather fancy that she had been carrying stores also.[48]

The Turks had constructed piers along the Dardanelles, and places like Maidos and Akbash which were close to the battle areas were used to evacuate the wounded. Maidos, a town on the eastern coast of the peninsula, was an Entente target because of its function as a communication hub in the area. For his part, O'Connor was:

> [H]auled out of the transport cart and dumped into what appeared to be a convalescent camp for sick & wounded Turks. Here we were given yet another exhibition of Turkish hospitality and true Oriental courtesy. Whenever the opportunity presented – and those were pretty frequent – these Turkish convalescent patients spat upon us and kicked our wounded. They gave us a very rough time of it, but we stood it as long as we could. Then we formed ourselves into a ring, placing the more badly wounded of our chaps in the centre where they could not be so readily molested by the Turks. I did see a Turkish officer

48 AWM AWM30 B1.27: Repatriation Statement – Private P. O'Connor.

> there, but he was 200 yards away. The Turks would not give me a stretcher and I endeavoured to crawl along the pier to the little steamer, on my stomach. I suffered fearful agony! Eventually, I waylaid a couple of orderlies who were returning with an empty stretcher and persuaded them to put me onboard. The little steamer almost immediately pulled out from the pier. The reason was soon clear. Our aeroplanes were bombing a village near by and had started a fire there. The authorities were evidently afraid that the Turks might take panic and rush the steamer. So they pulled her out from the pier. There were still two of our wounded comrades left on the pier and when the vessel pulled out I thought that was the last we should see of them. But, to our great surprise, later on that evening they were brought alongside in a rowing boat and taken aboard.[49]

From places like Maidos, injured and uninjured alike were carried by steamer to Constantinople. Private Robert Long, 32nd Field Ambulance, RAMC, who was captured on Kiretch Tepe,[50] wrote of the journey:

> We marched all that night and next morning came to a camp where we were questioned. Set off again that night and reached another camp where we stayed three days along with three Greeks out of the French Foreign Legion. On the third night we marched to the beach somewhere in the Narrows and went aboard an old steamer which had been torpedoed but not bad enough to sink. We found thirteen other prisoners there. Next morning an aeroplane came along and dropped bombs on the beach. The previous day she had dropped one on the deck over our cabin, but it failed to go off. We had to sleep on the floor of the cabin which was full of flies. On the second day the boat started but when the water got rough she started to sink, and she had to put in opposite the town of Gallipoli. Nothing but bread and water all this time. Stayed there three days while they were making a patch to put over the torpedo hole. While there a submarine popped up and fired a torpedo at us which missed by about three feet. Turks very much afraid of aeroplanes and submarines. Patch turned out a failure and were taken across to Gallipoli in a destroyer. Walked four days and four nights on bread and water to a railway station somewhere near Adrianople. None of us had boots on, all had been stolen by the Turks. Terrible suffering on the march, sun very hot. All hands bad with dysentery. Got the toothache lying on the hard ground. Very cold at nights. Got to the station anyhow and had two days travelling in the train to Constantinople.[51]

49 Ibid.

50 This is described by Sergeant John Hargrave, 32nd Field Ambulance, RAMC, in his wartime memoir *At Suvla Bay* (London: Constable, 1916). On 17 August 1915 several men from a stretcher party were captured after they had set off to look for wounded soldiers following an earlier attack between Green Knoll and The Pimple. Apart from Private Long, three other men from the same unit were captured: Private Valentine Flood, Private George Keeping and Private Alexander James. All three would die in captivity.

51 Diary of Private Robert Thomas Long, 32nd Field Ambulance, RAMC, 19 February 1916 (Tauranga City Libraries Staff, licensed under a Creative Commons Attribution-Non-commercial 3.0 New Zealand License <http://tauranga.kete.net.nz/remembering_war/topics/show/2604-the-pow-diary-of-robert-long-1894-1961>.

Upon reaching Constantinople, the wounded were immediately sent to hospitals manned by Turkish and German physicians. Private Patrick O'Connor described the treatment afforded them was generally good:

> I was kept in Harbia Hospital for 11 days, when I was taken to Tash Kishla Hospital in Taxim, a suburb of Constantinople. At the hospital at Harbia, a Turkish doctor who saw my wounded leg had said that it would have to be amputated. But the same afternoon a German doctor who saw the leg said that there would be no need to have the leg taken off. I asked the friendly German sister to have my leg examined by the principal doctor at the hospital – the "Pascha Doctor" he was called. She'd so arranged it and the "Pascha Doctor" proved to be a really good man. I told him that if my leg had to be amputated I was content to let it be so but that I did not want to be practiced on or experimented upon. He replied that it would be a shame to take my leg off. It might take some little time, but the leg could be saved. Furthermore, he asked me if I fancied any special diet. When I mentioned a cutlet and eggs he instructed the Sister to let me have them. I got them all right. This "Pascha Doctor" was a Turk – but a rare one. Thereafter the treatment extended to us at Harbia was very good.[52]

The Turks largely respected the Geneva Conventions, treating prisoners of war in front line casualty clearing stations and the home front hospitals. Corporal George Oliver, 1/8th Hants who was captured with Stallard at Suvla, had been wounded in the leg and was treated in the Marine Hospital, Constantinople:

> I am writing these few lines to let you know I am still alive and kicking, although my kicks are rather limited, as I am in a Turkish hospital with one wound in the leg, but don't worry. I am getting on first rate. The people are awfully kind here. The doctor, one of the nurses, and one of the men speak English, so we can have a talk to them. We get plenty of smokes but please send something to eat, and put it in a box that will not break ... There are 14 English, and they [sic] are all a jolly lot of Turks to look after us. An officer brought us in some sweets and the doctor brought some flowers. They have decorated us all with them because it is Sunday, and there was plenty of fun. I went to see the pictures here the other night. We have just had the band under our window, and it was a treat...My word, I won't half make a raid on the pastry shops when I get home; there will be no holding me![53]

Private James Barrett, 1/8th West Ridings, was wounded and captured on 12 August 1915 not far from Stallard and Oliver. He died of wounds at Tasch Kishla Hospital in Constantinople, Turkey, on 19 February 1916. News appeared in a Keighley newspaper under the heading IN THE HANDS OF THE TURK – KEIGHLEY MAN IN CONSTANTINOPLE – American Red Cross Doing Good Work – LETTER FROM NURSING SISTER. An American Red Cross Society sister named Martha H. Peet who was caring for Barrett observed:

52 AWM AWM30 B1.27: Repatriation Statement – Private P. O'Connor.
53 *Isle of Wight County Press* (11 September 1915).

> Dear Madam, I am writing to give you news of your son Mr. Barrett, who is now ill in the Turkish Hospital in this city. About three weeks ago he was brought with a number of English soldiers in the Pash Krishla [sic] Hospital in which the American Red Cross has 550 beds. Mr. Barrett is not on one of our wards, but he is allowed to have one of our nurses, as the Turkish nurses cannot speak English. He was not very seriously wounded, but he was suffering from a very serious attack of dysentery which has greatly weakened him. I regret to be obliged to tell you that the doctor considers his recovery somewhat doubtful, although he says he has a chance … He is in the care of one of our best nurses, who is much interested in the case, and is doing everything possible for his comfort and welfare.

Sister Peet's letter managed to reach Barrett's family to at least inform them that he was alive. Sadly, Barrett never really recovered and died from dysentery at the same hospital five months later. Many others received no letters at home and their deaths, unless noted in personal diaries, mainly went unrecorded.

Not every facility provided the same quality of care. O'Connor describes transfer from Harbia, after a fortnight, to Tasch Kishla Hospital in Constantinople where conditions were worse and the unfamiliar Turkish food a shock:

> In the morning, for breakfast, we were given a basin of wheat boiled in water, precisely the same as you would feed fowls on. At 9 o'clock that morning I was carried on a stretcher to a dressing room. Here the bandages on my wounds were unrolled & my wounds examined. A chloroform "bag" was thrust over my nose and when I recovered consciousness my leg had been amputated. A chap named Callaghan, or O'Callaghan,[54] from Brisbane was close by when I came to. At my request he lifted up the bed clothes, and we found that my leg was gone! When I left Harbia Hospital my leg was real well. The German sister was looking after it splendidly, assisted by an Armenian doctor who also spoke English. It was about noon when I recovered from the influence of the chloroform. Almost immediately a meal was placed in front of me. It was steamed wheat with some dirty molten fat on top of it. And that was just after my leg had been amputated. Needless to say, I didn't touch that "meal." Altogether I had a rotten experience there at Tash Kisschler [sic].[55]

O'Connor also refers to Private Joseph Kelly, 15th Battalion AIF, and Private John Hennessy, 14th Battalion AIF, dying there. Both Kelly and Hennessy had been wounded and captured with Luscombe's group on 8 August 1915. Kelly had become "delirious and died on the mattress" next to him, and "for a full fortnight [Hennessy's] wounds were left untended and undressed. To make matters worse the poor beggar was suffering from diarrhea [sic] and his wounds became fearfully foul on that account." According to O'Connor, Kelly and Hennessy "had been getting along splendidly in Harbia."The conditions here most probably hastened their deaths.[56]

54 The man who was with O'Connor when he discovered that his leg was missing was Private John O'Callaghan, 9th Battalion AIF, captured on 28 June 1915 with Jordan, Creedon and others. He was wounded in the right thigh and knee and although his wounds healed he died of typhoid in captivity on 21 January 1917.

55 AWM AWM30 B1.27: Repatriation Statement – Private P. O'Connor.

56 Ibid.

British and Dominion POWs, Kiangri Camp, October 1915: "The grub was very much improved, and we were quite satisfied with Kiangri." (Author)

For the uninjured, conditions elsewhere in Constantinople were also poor where military barracks and civilian prisons were utlised. While no evidence exists of any individual mistreatment, many were publicly marched through the streets of the Ottoman capital before being sent into the bleak, vermin-ridden cells of the city's main prison:

> When we reached there we were marched to a large prison in a kind of park. We were put in a big room, with a wooden partition down one side in the cracks of which were millions of bugs. Next morning, we were served out with a loaf of decent bread. About ten o'clock a dish of boiled wheat was brought in and we yaffled that. Then we were all brought out to be questioned again. When we returned to the room we found it full up of other prisoners about 60 altogether. In the evening a dish of haricot beans and soup was brought in. Not too bad. We stayed in this prison about two weeks. ... Everyone in the room was infested with lice, two "chats" or searches we had every day and we caught more in the evening than we did in the morning it was marvellous where they came from. There was no such thing as sleep there. It was very cold at night and we had nothing to cover us at all and as soon as darkness fell the bugs advanced to the attack. I was covered with itchy lumps soon and they all broke out and festered afterwards. My hands and neck were covered with them. I shall never forget that time in the prison as long as I live. It was torture.[57]

57 Ibid.

Entente prisoners who were used to a diet rich in meat were unimpressed by the monotonous issue of bread and boiled wheat soups, "we are treated well but OH! the grub. They do not have food like we have in England, it is nearly all slops."[58] Those who did not have adequate clothing were issued with Turkish Army issue trousers and greatcoats. Soon all old uniforms were collected, and the men dressed similarly in an odd mixture of Turkish greatcoats, civilian suits and slippers.

Before long, those prisoners healthy enough to move were sent by train or on foot to camps in the interior. One of these was at Afion Kara Hissar in Asia Minor, which was the largest prisoner of war camp and served as a distribution centre to the network of other camps across the Ottoman Empire. Situated at the junction of the Constantinople, Baghdad and Smyrna (Izmir) railway at an altitude of 3,000 feet and 200 miles from the sea, it was a secure and comparatively healthy spot, the summers pleasantly cool with severe winters. An inhospitable place, its name translates to "black opium fortress" after the towering rock situated behind and the drug trade that once flourished there.

Private Robert Long was dispatched to Kiangri by forced march, a journey that commenced on 14 October 1915:

> I have read a lot about long marches and suffering on the march but the march to Kanguari [sic] beats all I ever heard of. It was over a hundred kilometres to Kanguari and we had to walk this on bread and water carrying our four loaves on our backs. Nearly all the prisoners there, about 150, were suffering from the effects of wounds, nearly all were without footwear except the rubbishy slippers supplied in the hospitals. I had a pair of Turks boots about four sizes too large turned up in the front like the hoofs of a mountain ass. I had to sling them away the first day and put on a pair of slippers that a sailor of *E7* [British submarine] gave me. His name by the way was Reid[59] and he came from Belfast. We got on all right during the day but when night fell nearly everyone was beaten and there was scores of laggards trailing on behind. It was pitiful to see chums trying to help one another along. About half a dozen collapsed and were put on arabas or carts. They wouldn't take some of them on and they had to be carried by their comrades. The Sergeant whom we had appointed leader over us was a brick. His name was Babister[60] of the Berkshire Yeomanry and I shall never forget how he behaved on that march. I think I can see him now, carrying a man on his back or trying to get one on an araba. There was no such thing as selfishness about him, he was a gentleman right through. About twelve o'clock we came to a village and we were distributed amongst the huts, crammed in like sardines. We were glad to get a rest anyhow and though none of us could lie down we managed to sleep a little sitting. We were roused up early next morning and had our breakfast of dry bread and then off again,

58 Quote from letter written by Lance Corporal Frank Fox, 1/5th Norfolks, to his parents on 8 October 1915.Fox was captured during the assault across the Kuchuk Anafarta Ova on 12 August 1915 and reported missing on 28 August. He died in captivity at Angora Hospital on 4 April 1917.

59 Able Seaman William Reid was taken prisoner on 5 September 1915 when HM Submarine *E7* was scuttled off Nagara, after the vessel was brought to the surface by depth charges dropped from a row boat by *Kapitänleutnant* Heimburg, commander of U-boat *UB-14* and his cook. *E7* had previously been trapped in an anti-submarine net. Reid died in Angora on 12 January 1916.

60 Sergeant William Babister, 1/1st Berkshire Yeomanry, was captured at Scimitar Hill on 21 August 1915.

> stiff and footsore. I needn't dwell on the sufferings of that march any longer, each day was worse than the previous one and the last day was the worst of all. The worst torture you can give a man I am sure is to compel him to walk round and round a ploughed field for four days in the middle of summer, with nothing but sour stale bread to eat, water to drink and no boots on his feet. Let him walk from sunrise until midnight and on the fourth day he will be a changed man.[61]

Long reached Kiangri on 17 October.

The Turks were not set up for handling and housing prisoners at the start of the war, and thus no provision was made for accommodation, feeding and clothing the captives. The British Foreign Office requested an investigation into the food and clothing given to the prisoners of war, which was conducted by Hoffman Philip, US *Chargé d'Affaires* at Constantinople. Enver Pasha, Turkish Minister of War observed that POWs were treated no better and no worse than the average Turkish soldier,[62] even so, this was a marked contrast to what the prisoners had been used to in their armies.

The majority of the POW camps in Turkey were located in remote locations in Anatolia; these often consisted of town buildings that were turned into improvised prisoner of war camps. The Turks initially ignored requests for inspection visits and they did not pass on any information as to the welfare of the prisoners. Eventually they divulged the camp locations that allowed neutral parties like the Red Cross and the American and Dutch embassies to make inspections on behalf of the British government. This was also at a time that the Turks had prevented the sending or receiving of letters for several months, and then only allowed them to send four lines a week. The restriction was said by the Turks to be in retaliation for restrictions imposed on Turkish prisoners by the British; the British Foreign Office said it was the other way around. Reprisals often ended amicably.

Camp Life: "A veritable hell"

The POWs main saviour was the American Ambassador to Turkey, 59-year old Henry Morgenthau. Morgenthau provided the British and Dominion prisoners with clothing, food, toilet articles and money, and most importantly he gave them hope. During an inspection of Belemedik in September 1917 the prisoners were reported as:

> [W]ell supplied with clothing (save for few minor necessities), they had what food was obtainable in the region, enjoyed freedom of movement and for the most part were in good health. Several who were in a disabled condition because of a former wound requested to be exchanged. Up to the end of May a large number of the original British (and French) prisoners from the Dardanelles remained at Belemedik preferring to work rather than risk bad treatment in the camps at Afion.[63]

61 *Tauranga Memories: The POW Diary of Robert Long (1894-1961)* <http://tauranga.kete.net.nz/remembering_war/topics/show/2604-the-pow-diary-of-robert-long-1894-1961>.
62 NAA A11803 1914/89/364: Hoffman Philip, Report Prisoners of War (12 June 1916).
63 NAA A2939 SC311: *Report Prisoners of War – Agreements with Turkey* (1917).

Food and clothing, supplemented by the American and Dutch embassies in Constantinople, was sent by relatives and friends in England, and distributed by the Ottoman Red Crescent.[64] Even though the United States was neutral in 1915, and would remain so for another two years, Morgenthau was a friendly face in the crowd who acknowledged their plight and did everything in his power to help them. It was never enough, but it was something and considering the little bit the Turks provided, it was something substantial: "The American Ambassador came one day and gave us all ten shillings each. Anyone could live well for three weeks on ten shillings in Turkey."[65]

Officers were luckier; the conditions were far better, they were not required to work, and they were paid a salary whilst in captivity. In addition, money could also be drawn by cheque against their British and India banks. These were accepted in payment for goods by local tradesmen, or at least before restrictions were imposed.[66] Officially the camp commandant would send the cheques off to either the American or Dutch embassies, however:

> [A] large number of cheques were cashed surreptitiously, particularly after the Turks tried to limit the amount held by Prisoners. Such cheques had of course to be held over till the end of the War … Unfortunately, it cannot be accepted as certain that all cheques will be good. There was naturally a marked absence of cheque books and it is very probable that many irregularities will be found to have taken place in the odd pieces of plain paper on which the bulk of the cheques were drawn, and which were accepted in full faith.[67]

Unlike prison camps elsewhere in the world, those in Turkey were so remote that no walls or barbed wire were required. The Turks knew that escape was nearly impossible, and this was relayed to their captives. Thus an honour system was employed. Officers were generally allowed to visit the nearby town whenever they wished. Other ranks were also allowed, but usually under guard and only when they were not required to work, maybe once per week. In addition to giving the men an occasional change of scenery, these trips also allowed them the chance to buy food, tobacco and alcohol from local merchants. Other ranks were not allowed to purchase the latter, but they did and often with predictable consequences:

> One of the woodcutting gang named Morrison and I went and got some "koniak" last Sunday evening. Three bottles we got, and we drank two coming home. I had the other one in my pocket. We came home and had our tea. The sailors had got some drink too and two or three of them started fighting. There was a dickens of a row. One of them struck one of the old "posthas [Turkish guards]" but he was given half a note to hold his tongue about it. Then the sailor guards came up at the double with the commander at the head. He got one of the sailors who had been fighting smacked his face and run him off to "clink". Then all the English prisoners were lined up, a roll-call taken and then came an examination which made me feel goosey. Everyone's breath was smelt by one of the guards. He came up the line smelling away and lo and behold he passed me: The next one to be yanked out was

64 NAA A11803 1917/89/377: *Report Prisoners of War* (1917).
65 *Tauranga Memories.*
66 TNA FO 383/462: Prisoners of War Interview Reports 1914-1918.
67 NAA A2939 SC311: Report Prisoners of War – Agreements with Turkey (1917).

> Morrison: Such a joke. I did laugh at him. After blowing and snorting in the commander's face for a few minutes he came to the conclusion he was sober, and he got off. It was very lucky for me I was not taken out and searched as I still had the bottle in my pocket. Three of the sailors were locked up. Things are getting a bit too hot here now. Two more sailors were locked up on Wednesday. They got koniak and were caught by the guards. They swam across a river and pelted the guards with stones. They were collared and knocked about a bit by the guards.[68]

Two of those thrown into Belemedik Camp jail for drunkenness were Privates James McSherry and John Regan,[69] 5th Connaught Rangers who were captured at Hill 60 on 21 August 1915.

As the number of Entente prisoners held by the Turks increased, captive other ranks were set to work. One of the major projects they were employed on was the construction of tunnels through the Taurus Mountains to accommodate the Berlin to Baghdad Railway. This new single-gauge rail line would allow the Germans a contiguous communications link with the Turks which would help supply goods and munitions overland and would allow the Turks to transport oil from their Middle Eastern territories to their allies in the west. The main construction camp for the project was at Belemedik, located nine hundred kilometres southeast of Constantinople. Compared to some of the other camps, such as Kiangri and Afion Kara Hissar, the camp itself was still somewhat unpleasant, but more livable. The buildings lined the sides of the railroad tracks and the unpleasantness was due, in large part, to the nature of the work.

Private Reginald Lushington, 16th Battalion AIF, recorded his initial impressions of Belemedik:

> We were being sent to work on the Baghdad Railway, and Belemidik [sic] itself was the last big engineering works before the line entered the Taurus Mountains. Here at Belemidik was the headquarters of a number of German, Austrian and Swiss engineers who had been entrusted with the huge task of tunnelling the Taurus Mountains; large machinery and workshops had been erected, and the town of Belemidik in this remote and savage part of Turkey was swarming with workmen of every nationality.
>
> As the train entered slowly into this hive of work, many feelings of misgiving arose in the breasts of our men as we saw gangs of Turks and Gypsies working by "flares" along the line sawing wood and carrying rails. It was remarked by many, "If the blankety blanks think we are going to work like that they will be jolly well mistaken." Anyhow we hoped for more considerate treatment from the Germans, who were running the show, than we had had from the Turks.[70]

The project was planned and supervised by a German firm called the Baghdad Railway Construction Company. The work carried out on the tunnels was terribly dangerous and the men who worked on them were assigned their duties; they did not volunteer, but they were paid. Workers were paid nine piastres per day for their efforts; carpenters were paid 12; and skilled

68 *Tauranga Memories*.
69 Regan died of disease on 26 January 1917.
70 Reginald Lushington, *A Prisoner With the Turks 1915-1918* (London: Simpkin, Marshall, Hamilton, Kent & Co., Ltd., 1923), p. 35.

workers, employed in the machine shops and doing clerical work, earned 18. The few employed on the woodcutting detail and duties in the camp received only four:

> Prisoners formed into camps were stationed along the line, old "Blue Bottle" had charge of one at Hatchkeri [Hadjihiri], about 10 miles from Belemedik, parties of British prisoners who were working in the tunnels lived near their work. The line emerged from the tunnel, travelled a few yards in the open, and then disappeared.A tremendous project this of making a tunnel through these mountains, as solid rock had to be blasted, and only pick, hammer and drill could be used.[71]

Many men suffered emotional breakdowns and physical injuries working in the tunnels. Some also lost their lives in accidents that might have been prevented had experienced workers been employed on the project, and rudimentary safety measures taken. One particular accident occurred when Private Leonard New, 15th Battalion AIF, who was captured during the assault on Hill 971 on 8 August 1915, was killed in his bed when a log smashed through his barracks roof. After his repatriation Private Walter Williams described the incident:

> On the morning of May 7 1916, 2186 Private L.G. New, 15th Battalion, and myself were asleep in the Turkish house which was our quarters, when a number of our men started a few logs down the hill (which was high and steep). One big log weighing about a ton struck a rock in its descent, leapt into the air and came down on through the roof of the house. It crashed into New and completely smashed the left side of him, whilst I was struck on the head and rendered unconscious. New died within 20 minutes and we buried him next day.[72]

New, aged 22 when he died, immigrated to Australia from Beckenham, Kent at the age of 16 "for the benefit of his health."[73]

There is no evidence of systematic abuse in the Ottoman prisoner of war system. Men were not routinely tortured or intentionally starved, nor were they deprived of the Red Cross parcels or money sent them by the American and Dutch ambassadors. That is not to say, however, that the Turks were not capable of cruelty. They certainly were, but it was employed on an individual basis and usually in response to a serious transgression such as escape or assaulting a guard:

> Yesterday being St Patrick's Day, we took the day off. We didn't take any booze though. Three of the Connaughts [Connaught Rangers] came down from the tunnel and got drunk in the town. They got into contact with the guards of course and there was a row. While the guards were knocking one of them about, the other two made a run for it towards our camp. One of them was stopped by "postha" and was going quietly with him but one of the sailor guards came up and took a running kick at his stomach. The other prisoner got into the marquee, but he was seen and hauled out. The commander came running up and struck him in the face and then those two men got the most terrible treatment. They were surrounded by guards each one eager to get a blow at them. Those that had rifles clubbed

71 Ibid., p. 36.
72 NAA B2455: WILLIAM, WALTER W.
73 AWM AWM30 B1.32: Repatriation Statement: Private W. Williams (11 December 1918).

> them and struck as hard as they could. Those that had no rifles tore up paling posts and branches off trees. They were beaten black and blue. It was inhuman savagery. All the prisoners were out looking on of course and roars of rage could be heard on all sides. Everyone was strung to the highest pitch of excitement. It only wanted someone to say "Go!" and we would have been at the guards' throats like a pack of wolves. Thank God there was no-one to say the word though. We could have finished the guards of course but the next day we would pay for it with our lives.[74]

At least one camp commandant was known for his brutality. He was Major Mazlum Bey, commandant of Afion Kara Hissar. Lushington encountered him for the first time in September 1916:

> Afion at the end of September 1916, was a veritable hell. The Turkish commander, by name Maslum Bey, had made some of the lives of the prisoners a ghastly nightmare by his acts of cruelty and beastliness. Whether this man suffered the extreme penalty of the law for inhuman conduct towards captives I don't know; but if ever a man deserved the death penalty for downright murder, then Maslum Bey is that man. His atrocities were the flogging of prisoners, in many cases the bastinado; leaving parties of Kut-el-Amara [sic] men who were dying out in the courtyard and making no effort to alleviate their misery; arming his sentries and permitting them to hit prisoners with a raw hide whip; ransacking and stealing prisoners' parcels and selling the contents to merchants in the town, and other inhuman acts which are too bad to write about. The Armenian graveyard at Afion contains dozens of bodies of men who died under his neglect and ill treatment.[75]

An officer who was planning to escape was called before the commandant shortly before the attempt was carried out. He described him as follows:

> At the eleventh hour our plans were given away, and late one night I was called before the commandant of the camp. He was a foul beast, half Arab and half Turk, with the vices of both. He was a short sturdy man with a coarse, evil face, named Mazlum Bey. He had committed terrible bestialities, beaten men to death, stolen our food, and done unnameable offences by force on our soldiers imprisoned elsewhere in the town. When angered he became a wild raging madman capable of any atrocity. I lied to him freely and he believed not a word because he had expected such lies and I and my four companions were shut into two rooms and isolated from the rest of the camp until we should give our parole.[76]

74 *Tauranga Memories.*

75 Lushington, *A Prisoner With the Turks 1915-1918*, p. 63.

76 Harold Armstrong, *Turkey in Travail* (London: John Lane, 1925), p. 54. Captain Armstrong, 67th Punjabis (Indian Army), was captured at Kut-al-Amara in Mesopotamia when the town surrendered to the Turks after a long siege on 29 April 1916. He was held in the camp with officers who had been captured at Gallipoli, and after the war he would be one of the officers chosen to prosecute Mazlum Bey for his crimes.

Lieutenant John Still, 6th East Yorks had nothing but hate for Mazlum Bey and throughout his memoir, he was specific in his reason:

> There was a Russian named Constantine B., who had become estranged from the other Russians for a fault of his own. He was afterwards forgiven, and taken back, so it would not become me to say anything about it. For the time, however, he lived separately in a small house with a Russian anarchist and a Russo-Armenian thief, and the three of them were outlaws. Also, they hated each other, and used to quarrel. One of their quarrels became acute enough to attract the attention of the Turkish Commandant, the infamous Maslum Bey, who visited their house to make inquiries, and there lost his temper and struck Constantine B. Constantine was not really a bad fellow. He had done one bad thing, but he was out of place in that house. He was a man of about thirty, tall, well built, with very fair hair. A brave man, and quick-tempered. He put up his arm to protect himself, and he was lost. The Commandant accused him of trying to reach for his, the Turk's, sword, and had him arrested. Constantine B. was taken away from the officers' camp to the church where were some British soldiers; in the little courtyard where we used to box he was stripped and tied head downwards with his feet in the air. The Commandant stood by while Constantine was beaten upon the soles of the feet with raw hide whips until he fainted. An hour later he was beaten again until he lost consciousness once more. As they grew tired the Commandant called new hands to beat him; every Turk there had a turn at beating him. And, when he could feel no more, Maslum Bey kicked and struck him all over, everywhere on his body, and spat upon him. Then he was taken into a dungeon and thrown upon a heap of quicklime where his face got burnt. Maslum's cup was not yet full. Constantine recovered in time, though he is lame. Maslum went on to his worst offence. He had flogged our men and the Russians. He had imprisoned British officers in filthy holes, for little or no cause. He had lied, and swindled, and stolen, and grown rich. He now proceeded to overstep even the line which a Turkish officer draws. All through the writing of this book there has loomed ahead of me the grave difficulty of dealing with Maslum Bey's greatest offence. It ought to be recorded, but I loathe doing it. Let those who can read between the lines. Some of the British soldiers were very young, fair-haired Saxon boys from Wessex. They had seen a vast deal of cruelty, and they knew how easy it was for Maslum Bey to flog them, even to kill them, or to send them to places where they would almost certainly die. Four of these became the victims of the abominable wickedness of Maslum. Under the shadow of a raw hide whip, in the hands of Turkish noncommissioned officers, they were his victims.[77]

Private William Surgenor of Wellington Battalion NZEF was one of 25 New Zealanders captured at Gallipoli, and one of 21 captured at Chunuk Bair on 8 August 1915. After the war he recorded the following about his experiences in captivity. The crimes to which he made reference were among those for which Mazlum Bey was held accountable:

> At Afion Camp the Turks took young fellows by force away to the officers' quarters. The chaps had no option. They would come back looking horribly ashamed and would talk to no

77 Still, *A Prisoner in Turkey*, pp. 199-201.

> one. At last one of them made a clean breast of it. It was reported to the Swiss Commission. I don't know what the result was. On one occasion two Turks tried to get me away but I knocked them out. The Commandant was the worst of all at it.[78]

In the end, Still managed to pass a coded message out of camp to report Mazlum Bey:

> All these offences of Maslum Bey, from the tragedy of Constantine downwards, were duly reported to England by code. The very names of the offences were squeezed into that code. I had the pleasure of sending the messages myself, and the framing of them. They got home safely, and our Government acted at once. In the end we got rid of Maslum Bey. He was court-martialled by a commission of utterly corrupt Turkish officers. The British soldiers bravely told their stories. I say bravely, for their lives hung by a hair. A British officer who knew Turkish equally bravely conducted the prosecution for our side; and his life hung by a hair too. But we got rid of Maslum Bey. He was given five and a-half months' simple imprisonment. Not six months, for that would have involved loss of rank. His judges did not think he had deserved to lose rank. That is why I watch the papers to see if Maslum Bey has been hanged.[79]

Unfortunately, Mazlum Bey was not held accountable for his crimes. In 1921 he, along with 49 other "war criminals"[80] who had been held by the British in Malta, were traded for 50 British soldiers held captive by Turkish nationalists. Despite the damning personal accounts published in this chapter it is uncertain at this stage what other evidence the British authorities had to prosecute Mazlum Bey.

Repatriation: "Freedom! Freedom!"

In the camps, officers were kept separate from the other ranks in different buildings. The conditions for officers were also better, including food and activities. Officers were given more opportunities to venture out of the camps unguarded and, since they tended to receive more money from home, they were able to supplement their rations on a much more regular basis. They were also exempt from work thanks to an amendment added to the 1907 Hague Convention. Other

78 New Zealand National Archives (NZNA) R24428210: Statement of William Surgenor (13 December 1918).

79 Still, *A Prisoner in Turkey*, pp. 201-202.

80 Sixty Turkish subjects were arrested and sent to Malta on the instruction of the British High Commissioner in Constantinople. According to H. E. Keeling's post-war memoir *Adventures in Turkey and Russia* (London: John Murray, 1924), p. 232. "The charges against them included murder, the manslaughter of hundreds (collectively thousands) by neglect, merciless flogging, gross cruelty of various kinds, unnatural offence against our men, wholesale theft of their property." The British waited for the peace Treaty of Sévresto be signed, and even when it was in 1920, it was never ratified, and the 60 men remained in Malta. Mustafa Kemal in the meantime became the dominant nationalist authoritarian in the region and captured 30 British officers and men. The British government quickly agreed to an unconditional exchange for prisoners confined in Malta. No trial ever took place.

Captured crewmen of British Submarine *E15*. They are attired in Turkish issue overcoats and slippers due to a dearth of surviving uniforms. (Başar Eryöner)

rank captives, in contrast, were usually forced to work, though a pitiful payment was made. Always with their men in mind, officers such as Commander Henry Stoker and Lieutenant Leslie Luscombe managed to anonymously send money to the other ranks. Second Lieutenant Jordan wrote home to his mother on 15 July 1915 to remark of the good treatment:

> I am quite well, and my arm is almost better. I am with a lot of other officers. There are some from the submarine E15 and also some from the Australian submarine AE2. We also have French and Russians here with us and we form a lively entente. I am learning Turkish and French languages; a submarine officer teaches me Turkish, and a French officer teaches me French. I am living really well, but it is a lazy life. I study most of the day and play bridge or chess at night. It was hard luck being captured within seven weeks of getting a commission, as it did not give me a chance, but I did my bit and now am tied up till the end of the war. The Turkish officials are exceedingly kind and courteous. For most of the time I was at their headquarters, and in Constantinople I was treated more like a guest than a prisoner.[81]

But the "guest" experience did not extend to the officers all of the time. Henry Stoker and Sub-Lieutenant Geoffrey Fitzgerald of the submarine *E15* were imprisoned as a reprisal by Enver Pasha for alleged maltreatment of Turkish prisoners held in Egypt. After 32 days detention of

81 AWM 1DRL/0428: ARC Wounded and Missing Bureau Case File of Stanley Rupert Jordan, Jordan correspondence to Mother, 15 July 1915.

which 25 were in solitary confinement in a dark, damp dungeon under the Turkish War Office in Constantinople, they were released. Proof had reached Enver Pasha that there was no such maltreatment of Turks by the British, and with the intervention of the American Ambassador, Mr Henry Morganthau, the two emaciated men were given five full days in a luxury hotel in Constantinople. When the time came to return to their prison camp, the young men declared that they would be glad to spend another month in dungeons if they could have a corresponding period of freedom in the city when liberated.[82]

The American Ambassador, with support from the Vatican, can also be credited with the release of Fitzgerald, a Roman Catholic. Fitzgerald was repatriated on parole as an apology for the reprisal and, in January 1916, returned to Great Britain to marry his sweetheart. Fitzgerald, Morgenthau had been told, was engaged to marry the daughter of the British ambassador to the Vatican. He was not, but the mistake was not learned of until Fitzgerald had returned home. For his release Fitzgerald had to give his word to Enver Pasha as an officer and gentlemen that he would not take up service connected with the operations of war pending the duration of hostilities between Britain and Turkey. He kept his promise.[83]

Stoker had no romantic attachments back home that would have justified a similar plea, but soon, with two other officers escaped from Afion Kara Hissar on 23 March 1916. They covered most of the rugged 130 miles to the Mediterranean coast where, starving and exhausted, they sought shelter from a shepherd. This they got, but the shepherd's report of the incident led to their capture. Imprisonment followed for months as the Turkish court deliberated the sentence. Fearing execution having been so long in prison, they received an absurd sentence of 25 days imprisonment for Stoker, and 20 days each for the other two. The officers burst into laughter, joined apparently by the court officials when they realised the effect of their decision. Pursuant to his duty to escape, the determined Stoker organised a further attempt after receipt of secret maps, section by section, in a series of postcards from an officer who had already escaped to freedom. But this escape attempt also failed.[84]

The chief preoccupations of all prisoners would seem to be the same the world over: Food, boredom, women and homesickness. Men captured at Gallipoli certainly suffered from all of these, but it was only the latter that they were not able to find a temporary solution to. Food, especially, was a major preoccupation. Turkish rations were poor and there was never enough to satisfy the men's hunger. However, thanks to the money they earned and received from the American and Dutch ambassadors, they were able to supplement their own rations. And even though they were separated from the officers, the latter did find ways to get money to them.

In an effort to make that money go farther, prisoners established groups of fellow captives in the same barracks that they termed "messes" or "firms", and each had an appointed head. Kerr was the head of his mess and it was his responsibility to take the pooled money, go to town and purchase whatever he could to supplement the Turkish rations. During their trips

82 Henry Morgenthau, *Ambassador Morgenthau's Story* (New York: Doubleday, Page & Co., 1918), p. 259.

83 Ibid., p. 260. Article 12 (Hague Convention, 1907) stated that "prisoners of war liberated on parole and recaptured [would] forfeit their right to be treated as prisoners of war and can be brought before the courts."

84 TNA: ADM 137/2077: Report by Lieutenant Commander Stoker, 9 January 1919 and Arthur W. Jose, *The Royal Australian Navy 1914-18* (Sydney: Angus & Robertson, 1938), pp. 241-248.

to town, the prisoners could purchase bread, fruit, vegetables and sometimes alcohol (wine, cognac, vermouth and Turkish *raki*). They could even obtain meat and poultry:

> We started buying eggs and chickens. They were very cheap. Eggs 8 a piastre, Fowls 2 piastre each (4d). Cheap, isn't it? On Dec. 11th we had fried eggs for breakfast. Fleet went to town and bought a kerosene tin to act as pot. When we examined it we found it was leaking and had to buy another. We all liked Fleet, he was such a hard case. He did the butchering for the cookhouse. We had two Angora goats every day in the "carrawana" but amongst such a crowd it was little enough. The grub was very much improved, and we were quite satisfied with Kanguari.[85] Tea is 9/-[shillings] a lb., and butter 2/6 [2 shillings 6 pence]. Sugar is about 5/-. Everything else is fairly cheap. Oh, for a cup of tea with milk and sugar in it and a slice of white bread with butter that doesn't kill at a hundred yards spread on it! A tin of condensed milk costs 2/6 in town.[86]

Some men were able to satisfy their lust for women while in captivity. While they were certainly in the minority, the fact that some were able to carry out such liaisons speaks to the fact that captivity in some Turkish camps was anything but rigid:

> There is a woman in the town who does it. There are several for that matter. A woman named Mme. Sophia and her daughter are not very sensitive about taking money, only the daughter wants too much. Johnny was with Mme. Sophia for a dollar yesterday, but he tells me he was with a girl of about 19. That would be her daughter who would want more than that. Perhaps Johnny's imagination has helped him a little. A man will always make out that his girl, or the like, is a lot better than she is. In reference to the forgoing, I must say that we never expected to get so much liquor in the town, nor did we ever dream that any of us would be able to sleep with a woman.[87]

Homesickness was the one aspect of captivity that the prisoners had the least control over. They could send and receive mail but that did little to make up for their loss of freedom. Escape attempts were common, successful attempts less so, particularly because of the location of the camps in relation to the nearest Entente troops, and the terrain the men had to cover to make it to the coast where they then had to locate a boat. Still, a great many men tried and nearly all were caught, including Stoker, who tried twice. A stay in a primitive, vermin-infested prison cell awaited those who were captured, and they were usually forced to spend their time there with Turkish deserters and criminals from throughout the Ottoman Empire. Lushington described his time in one after his unsuccessful attempt at escape:

> Back to prison again, in a building which held no Britishers. The place was crowded with a seething mass of conscripts of all nationalities. The door would be flung open and a new crowd would come pouring in. Many were brought up to the door roped together, clothed

85 *Tauranga Memories*.
86 Ibid. Passage written whilst at Belemedik, 26 March 1916.
87 Greg Kerr, *The Lost Anzacs: The Story of Two Brothers* (Melbourne: Oxford University Press, 1997), p. 171 and AWM PR00953: George Kerr diary (6 March 1916).

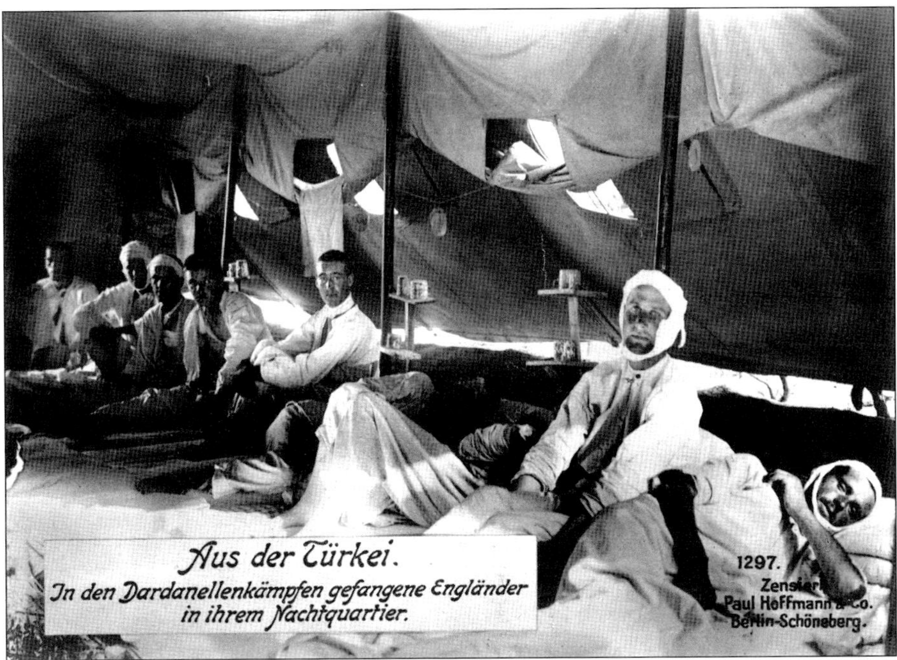

Wounded British prisoners recuperate in a tented hospital. (Başar Eryöner)

> in disreputable ragged garments, driven like sheep and herded like sheep. They had lost all vestige of pride of race, and if they were given a chance they would bolt to the fastnesses of the neighbouring hills and become brigands. In my present position I was lucky enough to get near one of the barred windows and wedged tight round me were the heterogeneous crowd. The place was always in a roar of voices speaking all languages, and general fight would take place around the Karawana dishes. These men were desperately hungry, their faces showed it, and they behaved like wild animals. Sleeping in my clothes and boots, and with my money in my shirt which I never showed, I was left unmolested; if I had discarded my boots in the night or showed I had a cent about my person I should have been robbed; and no appeals of mine to the Turkish guards at the door would have been of any avail.[88]

Generally, the only means of escape that a man had was the grave. Of over 500 that were captured at Gallipoli, 137 British and Dominion prisoners died from disease or wounds. One was killed by accident and another four died after their release from captivity. The main cause of death in prisoner of war camps was typhus; a result of poor conditions with lack of hygiene and sanitation. Typhoid, malaria, dysentery and influenza were also common killers.[89]

88 Lushington, *A Prisoner With the Turks 1915-1918*, pp. 60-1.
89 NAA MP1565/4: Prisoners of War Australians Captured in Turkey – 1917; TNA AIR 1/892/204/5/697: HQ RAF, List of British Prisoners of War in Turkey, 21-22 February 1916 and Patrick Gariepy, *British and Dominion Servicemen Captured at Gallipoli Who Died in Captivity* (Eugene, Oregon: Private publication, 1999).

The Turks appear to have largely respected the Geneva Conventions in terms of prisoner treatment in casualty clearing stations and home front hospitals. Nevertheless, their prisoner of war camps were lacking in supplies and proper medical care. It was not until after arrival of the Kut captives that the British prisoners were granted the privilege of having their own medical officers treat them. Captain Cedric 'Bill' Coxon, 1/5th Norfolks, who was wounded and captured at Suvla, studied medicine before the war and while in captivity obtained medical books through the British Red Cross. He continued his medical studies and acted as unofficial medical officer of his prison camp. In John Still's *Prisoner of War*, he wrote: "Our Stalwart Bill, the medical student of the party, a splendid person, was better than all the Turkish doctors. Much do we all owe to Bill and none more than I do, for he nursed me through several bad illnesses, although as he frankly confessed he hadn't done fevers."[90] That said, a lack of medicine and poor hospital conditions ensured that, regardless of the skill of the doctors, men would continue to die. Private William Allen, 9th Battalion AIF, who was captured with Jordan and Creedon on 28 June 1915, died in 1917 following a lengthy bought of malaria and dysentery.[91]

Incapacitated prisoners with serious wounds or ailments could be repatriated in a prisoner exchange. One such soldier was Private David Melling, 1/8th Lancashire Fusiliers who suffered a bullet wound in the head that nearly missed his brain, but blinded him in both eyes, during the Battle of Krithia Vineyard (7 August 1915). Nothing could be done for him at the hospital in Constantinople, where the American Ambassador, Henry Morgenthau, noticed him while visiting the facility. The ambassador successfully negotiated his release, the first British prisoner to be released by the Turks. After his return to England, he was one of the first to join St Dunstan's, the national charity established in 1915 to care and retrain men blinded during the war.[92]

Conditions slowly improved as the war progress; Enver Pasha personally sent "a case of bacon during the lean winter of 1917-18" while the notoriously violent Commandant Mazlum would allow the prisoners "to wander about at will after a show at the theatre."[93] Colonel Zia Bey, the official Turkish camp inspector, also helped improve camp conditions by refining administrative practices and dismissing poor camp commandants. In early 1918 a number of British and Dominion prisoners, considered unfit for further service, were repatriated.[94] One of these men was Private Patrick O'Connor, 14th Battalion AIF, who on 27 November 1917 left hospital in Constantinople for England. The journey would carry them to the Austro-Hungarian prisoner of war camp at Mauthausen, where after a stay of several weeks, they went on to Switzerland, which was neutral, then on to France, from whence they would depart for England. During the trip they were effusively welcomed as returning heroes:

> On January 10, 1918, we left Mauthausen for Switzerland, arriving at St. Margaretine near morning. The Swiss people made a tremendous fuss of us. Swiss sisters greeted us with shouts of "Freedom! Freedom!" As soon as we arrived in Switzerland they gave us

90 Still, *A Prisoner in Turkey.*
91 Gariepy, *British and Dominion Servicemen Captured at Gallipoli Who Died in Captivity.*
92 *Blind Veterans UK* <https://www.blindveterans.org.uk/about-us/our-history/>.
93 IWM 07/14/1: J. G.Stilwell, From the Tigris to the Mediterranean in 34 Months.
94 NAA A2939 SC311: Report Prisoners of War: Agreements with Turkey (1917).

> cigarettes and cards and chocolates. They had had the cigarettes with them all along but are not allowed to distribute them in Austrian territory. Our journey across Switzerland was "one long birthday." Even the children climbed up to the windows or were lifted up by their elders that they might bombard us with flowers. They fairly flooded us with coffee. At one station, when we declined more coffee, saying that we couldn't drink more, as we had had enough already, they called out, "Then wash yourselves in it!" We crossed straight through Switzerland to France, crossing the French frontier at Bellegarde. Then we were met by a brass band and a guard of honor. There was a great crowd and we were given a tremendous reception. The band played the British National Anthem and Marseillaise. Tables were spread with champagne. At Lyons, where we spent the night in hospital, we were given another immense demonstration. We were treated to a splendid dinner and to a concert in the officers' rooms ... that evening the RAMC lads gave us a splendid concert and we were issued with clean underclothes and treated to a warm bath. We reached Southampton Docks at about 10 o'clock on the morning of January 18, 1918. We had a big welcome at Southampton and another when the train reached London.[95]

Those left behind would be released after the Armistice on 30 October 1918 and would all be home by early 1919. However, their homecomings would not be as glorious as that received by O'Connor. As prisoners, they would not return home with their battalions and so would not be accorded the parades that their comrades were. Nevertheless, their people were glad to have them home and they did all they could to show it.

Conclusion

In general the "Gallipoli" prisoners of war were treated according to the Geneva and Hague conventions. There was no regular abuse and men like Mazlum Bey were the exception, rather than the rule. Nevertheless, there was suffering, but this was more from neglect and inefficiency than deliberate ill-treatment. Food was poor, medical care sometimes primitive, and all experienced a casual brutality. Wounded died not only of their injuries, but also from neglect. All were susceptible to disease, extremes of climate and the emotional trauma of captivity.

In comparison to other combatant nations, the Turks were no worse; they employed forced labour to build the railway in the Taurus Mountains; the Germans forced POWs to labour within close proximity of the frontline, as did the French who also dispatched captives to North Africa where malaria was rife and treatment harsh. And is any of this worse than conditions suffered by captives in Russian hands? Often referred to as "Dante's hell in Russia", the strategically vital Murmansk railway was constructed with forced POW labour, an estimated 25,000 perishing out of 70,000. The sub-zero temperatures, lack of shelter, food, medical treatment and a severe Typhus outbreak was the primary cause of prisoner fatality in Russia, the epidemic alone caused up to 17,000 deaths.[96]

95 AWM AWM30 B1.27: Repatriation Statement – Private P. O'Connor.

96 Reinhard Nachtigal: *Seuchenuntermilitärischer Aufsicht in Rußland* (Jahrbücherfür Geschichte Osteuropas 48-2000), p. 386.

The experience of Turkish captivity has been a subject virtually ignored by historians and if examined, the ordeal is often viewed through a prejudicial Western lens. Most Gallipoli POWs did return home, even though the mortality and sickness rate was high, it was comparable to other nations. More research needs to be carried out on this subject as well as compiling an accurate list MEF POWs. After all this time we still do not know the total number captured, and probably never will as so many names went unrecorded or records lost. Hopefully this "coherent and general account of the experience" of the 512 officers and men currently known to have been captured during the Gallipoli campaign will give the "distant spectator" an insight into what it was like to be a "guest of the Sultan".

Index

PEOPLE

PLACES

FORMATIONS/UNITS

Armies

Corps

Divisions

Brigades